Y0-ABF-163

THE PAPERS OF

THOMAS JEFFERSON

BARBARA B. OBERG
GENERAL EDITOR

THE PAPERS OF

Thomas Jefferson

Volume 41

11 July to 15 November 1803

BARBARA B. OBERG, EDITOR

JAMES P. MCCLURE AND ELAINE WEBER PASCU,
SENIOR ASSOCIATE EDITORS

TOM DOWNEY AND MARTHA J. KING,
ASSOCIATE EDITORS

W. BLAND WHITLEY, ASSISTANT EDITOR

LINDA MONACO, EDITORIAL ASSISTANT

JOHN E. LITTLE, RESEARCH ASSOCIATE

PRINCETON AND OXFORD

PRINCETON UNIVERSITY PRESS

2014

Published by Princeton University Press, 41 William Street,
Princeton, New Jersey 08540

In The United Kingdom:
Princeton University Press, 6 Oxford Street,
Woodstock, Oxfordshire OX20 1TW

ISBN 978-0-691-16420-5

Library of Congress Number: 50-7486

This book has been composed in Monticello

Princeton University Press books are printed on acid-free paper and meet the guidelines for permanence and durability of the Committee on Production Guidelines for Book Longevity of the Council on Library Resources

Printed in the United States of America

DEDICATED TO THE MEMORY OF

ADOLPH S. OCHS

PUBLISHER OF THE NEW YORK TIMES

1896-1935

WHO BY THE EXAMPLE OF A RESPONSIBLE

PRESS ENLARGED AND FORTIFIED

THE JEFFERSONIAN CONCEPT

OF A FREE PRESS

ADVISORY COMMITTEE

CONSULTANTS

SUPPORTERS

THIS EDITION was made possible by an initial grant of $200,000 from The New York Times Company to Princeton University. Contributions from many foundations and individuals have sustained the endeavor since then. Among these are the Ford Foundation, the Lyn and Norman Lear Foundation, the Lucius N. Littauer Foundation, the Charlotte Palmer Phillips Foundation, the L. J. Skaggs and Mary C. Skaggs Foundation, the John Ben Snow Memorial Trust, Time, Inc., Robert C. Baron, B. Batmanghelidj, David K. E. Bruce, and James Russell Wiggins. In recent years generous ongoing support has come from The New York Times Company Foundation, the Dyson Foundation, the National Trust for the Humanities, the Florence Gould Foundation, the "Cinco Hermanos Fund," the Andrew W. Mellon Foundation, the Pew Charitable Trusts, and the Packard Humanities Institute (through Founding Fathers Papers, Inc.). Benefactions from a greatly expanded roster of dedicated individuals have underwritten this volume and those still to come: Sara and James Adler, Helen and Peter Bing, Diane and John Cooke, Judy and Carl Ferenbach III, Mary-Love and William Harman, Frederick P. and Mary Buford Hitz, Governor Thomas H. Kean, Ruth and Sidney Lapidus, Lisa and Willem Mesdag, Tim and Lisa Robertson, Ann and Andrew C. Rose, Sara Lee and Axel Schupf, the Sulzberger family through the Hillandale Foundation, Richard W. Thaler, Tad and Sue Thompson, The Wendt Family Charitable Foundation, and Susan and John O. Wynne. For their vision and extraordinary efforts to provide for the future of this edition, we owe special thanks to John S. Dyson, Governor Kean, H. L. Lenfest and the Lenfest Foundation, Rebecca Rimel and the Pew Charitable Trusts, and Jack Rosenthal. In partnership with these individuals and foundations, both the National Historical Publications and Records Commission and the National Endowment for the Humanities have been crucial to the editing and publication of *The Papers of Thomas Jefferson*. For their unprecedented generous support we are also indebted to the Princeton University History Department and Christopher L. Eisgruber, president of the university.

FOREWORD

THE ACQUISITION of Louisiana dominated Thomas Jefferson's executive responsibilities and public life for the four months covered by this volume. Although news of France's stunning offer to sell the Louisiana Territory to the United States had arrived indirectly in early July, formal notification did not come until the 14th, when Jefferson received the treaty and accompanying papers. The official news brought forth great rejoicing, and he received letters expressing optimism for the future of the country and congratulations for what he had achieved: "Let the Land rejoice, for you have bought Louisiana for a Song. never was a happier moment Seized, for concluding so Glorious a Negotiation," wrote Horatio Gates. John Page referred to the "brilliancy" of Jefferson's negotiations. That a transaction of such magnitude could take place "without a Convulsion, without spilling one drop of blood" was an achievement without parallel in the history of any other nation. Republicans were jubilant over the success of the negotiations, but it was not only members of Jefferson's own political party who commented on the president's expansion of the country's borders. In New England, where the news broke even before it reached Washington, some Federalists were "vexed, disappointed, mortified, enraged," as Attorney General Levi Lincoln reported. Many other Federalists, however, were pleased with the bargain and willing to give Jefferson credit. This sudden growth in the size of the country would enhance its stature in the eyes of the world and strengthen its place in international politics. The expansion of the country also brought Jefferson a steady stream of applications for office.

Jefferson promptly summoned his cabinet to consider significant issues that the treaty raised. On 16 July, Jefferson, James Madison, Henry Dearborn, Albert Gallatin, and Robert Smith met, and Jefferson laid out two important questions that confronted them. Should both houses of Congress be convened to consider the treaty, or only the Senate? Should the treaty itself be made public, or only its substance? They were unanimous in recommending that the entire Congress should meet on 17 October, three weeks earlier than scheduled, and that punctual attendance should be encouraged. They also decided that only the substance of the treaty should be made public and that the House would not receive it until ratified by the Senate. The terms of the treaty stipulated that it was to be ratified by the American government within six months of its signing in Paris, that is, by 30 October. The United States could not dally, lest Napoleon Bonaparte have second thoughts about the magnitude of his offer and declare it void. In addition to summoning Congress early, Jefferson instructed Smith to have a public armed vessel ready to transport the treaty by 31 October.

Earlier in July, Jefferson drafted a series of questions about the new territory and its people so that he could provide Congress with information and also satisfy his own hunger for knowledge. The precise boundaries of the new territory were not even known. He sent his queries to William C. C. Claiborne, Daniel Clark, and William Dunbar and began to receive their replies. Dunbar responded that he had begun his own investigation of the geography and population of the region even before hearing from Jefferson. Clark said that he would send information as he acquired it and that he was forwarding to the secretary of state as accurate a map as he could find. Claiborne sent a lengthy letter answering Jefferson's queries one by one and offered the discouraging information that there really were no accurate maps to be obtained. The information the administration acquired on Louisiana, particularly from Clark, informed a printed report sent to Congress on 14 November. During his regular summer sojourn at Monticello, Jefferson turned to his own collection of books and maps for answers. His research proved to his satisfaction that United States territory extended certainly as far east as the Perdido River and, arguably, as far west as the Rio Grande.

Although not mentioned in his notes of the cabinet's discussions, the thorny issue of whether the government had the constitutional authority to acquire and incorporate territory into the existing nation was in the background. Jefferson expressed his private opinion that an amendment seemed necessary. The Constitution, he wrote, had not given the government the power to hold foreign territory, "still less of incorporating it into the union." He would have to put the treaty in front of "the nation" and seek an addition to the Constitution. After receiving warnings from Robert Livingston and James Monroe that France was reconsidering its offer, Jefferson came to think differently. To several friends he expressed his revised opinion on the need for a constitutional amendment, and to Madison he observed that "the less we say about constitutional difficulties respecting Louisiana the better." He wrote to James Madison, Thomas Paine, and John Breckinridge that whatever was required should be done "sub silentio" and with "as little debate as possible." On 20 October, after only three days of debate, the Senate approved the ratification by a vote of 24 to 7. Samuel A. Otis, secretary of the Senate, delivered the resolution approving the treaty and conventions to the President's House late in the afternoon of that day.

FOREWORD

Even before the expansion of the nation's boundaries by the Louisiana Purchase, Jefferson had asked Meriwether Lewis, his secretary, to lead an exploratory trip to the west. Lewis asked William Clark to join him on the journey, and on 24 July, Clark wrote Jefferson that he would accept the invitation. Dearborn thought Clark's participation would greatly add to the chances of success for the expedition. Preparations for the journey were now underway, although proceeding more slowly than Lewis had hoped. In July, he wrote from Pittsburgh that the boat builder was behind schedule. On 8 September, he reported from Wheeling, in western Virginia, 100 miles from Pittsburgh by river, that the level of the Ohio—as low as had ever been known, according to the oldest settler in the area—made for slow going. At some points he had to hire horses or oxen from neighboring farmers to drag the boat over the obstructions in the river. Five days later he had gone another 100 miles and was at Marietta, Ohio, and three weeks later at Cincinnati, where he paused to give the men a rest. He also wrote Jefferson that he needed more vaccine and that he would be visiting the Big Bone Lick, where he would see specimens of the bones of mammoths and attempt to forward to Jefferson two huge molar teeth and an enormous tusk.

In early October, Jefferson began to compose his third annual message to Congress. As he had done previously, he prepared a draft and circulated it to the attorney general and, with the exception of Robert Smith, who was detained in Baltimore because of illness in his family and the subsequent death of his daughter, his heads of departments. As before, Jefferson drew upon their advice, but did not always follow it. He did accept the recommendation of Madison and Gallatin that he not send the treaty and conventions to the House of Representatives until after ratification by the Senate. The message concluded with a lengthy paragraph on the renewal of war between England and France. As he had done at other times when the most powerful nations in Europe were at war, Jefferson urged that the United States cultivate the friendship of both, follow the path of "industry, peace, & happiness," and look upon "the bloody Arena" with commiseration.

While Jefferson and members of the cabinet assumed that the acquisition would be peaceful, they acknowledged that Spain might refuse to give up the territory. This threat hung over Jefferson throughout the summer and fall. The minutes of the 16 July cabinet meeting anticipated that possibility and proposed that if Spain stood in the way of America's right to the territory, two or more companies of troops should be transferred from Fort Adams in Mississippi Territory to New Orleans to "get the Spanish troops off as soon as possible." In addition, Claiborne should be prepared to take possession and act as governor and intendant under Spanish law. In early September, Gallatin urged that the administration have "everything in readiness" to take New Orleans whether Spain was willing to give it up or not. At the end of October, Jefferson drafted thorough notes on the preparations that should be made for taking over New Orleans. He laid out in detail two courses of action, using "force or no force," depending on what the Spanish did. Under each heading he described precisely what steps should be taken. If force was not required, inhabitants, and "officers particularly," should be treated with courtesy; the governor should be allowed to remain in his house; and Americans should be "particularly civil & accommodating" when taking possession of lands. If force was called for, 500 mounted militia should be sent to Natchez immediately and troops from Ohio, Tennessee, and Kentucky organized, all to be in the field by 10 December. In the midst of Jefferson's list of specific steps was the injunction to "treat the inhabitants as fellow citizens." All private property was to be regarded as sacred.

ACKNOWLEDGMENTS

MANY individuals have given the Editors the benefit of their aid in the preparation of this volume, and we offer them our thanks. Those who helped us use manuscript collections, answered research queries, assisted with translations, or advised in other ways are William C. Jordan, Princeton University; Valeria Escauriaza-Lopez Fadul for Spanish translations; Russell Hopley for Arabic translations; Neil Ann Stuckey Levine for German translations; in the libraries at Princeton, Karin A. Trainer, University Librarian, and Elizabeth Z. Bennett, Colleen M. Burlingham, Stephen Ferguson, Daniel J. Linke, Deborah T. Paparone, AnnaLee Pauls, Ben Primer, and Don C. Skemer; James H. Hutson, Barbara Bair, Julie Miller, and the staff at the Manuscript Division of the Library of Congress, especially Frederick J. Augustyn, Jennifer Brathovde, Jeffrey Flannery, Joseph Jackson, Patrick Kerwin, Bruce Kirby, and Lewis Wyman; Peter Drummey, Anna Clutterbuck-Cook, Elaine Heavey, and Laura Wulf of the Massachusetts Historical Society, especially Nancy Heywood for providing digital scans; Alan Degutis of the American Antiquarian Society; Francis P. O'Neill, Maryland Historical Society; Emily Guthrie, Winterthur Museum, Garden & Library; Robert C. Ritchie, Sara N. Ash Georgi, Juan Gomez, and Olga Tsapina at the Huntington Library; Anna Berkes, Endrina Tay, and Gaye Wilson of the Thomas Jefferson Foundation at Monticello; Nicole Bouché, Regina Rush, and the staff of Special Collections at the University of Virginia Library; Beatriz Hardy, Susan A. Riggs, and Ute Schechter, Swem Library, the College of William and Mary; Brent Tarter, Library of Virginia; Molly Kodner of the Missouri History Museum Library and Research Center; Martin Levitt, Roy Goodman, Charles B. Greifenstein, Earl E. Spamer, and Keith S. Thomson of the American Philosophical Society; the Gilder Lehrman Institute of American History and Jean W. Ashton and Edward O'Reilly of the New-York Historical Society; Wayne K. Bodle, History Department at Indiana University of Pennsylvania; Charles M. Harris of the Papers of William Thornton, and our fellow editors at the Thomas Jefferson Retirement Series at Monticello, the Adams Papers at the Massachusetts Historical Society, the Papers of George Washington and the Papers of James Madison at the University of Virginia, the James Monroe Papers at the University of Mary Washington, and the Papers of Benjamin Franklin at Yale University. For sharing her wisdom and knowledge about Monticello and its peoples, we are grateful to Lucia C. Stanton. For assistance with illustrations we are indebted to Alfred L.

Bush of Princeton, Bonnie Coles of the Library of Congress, and Jaclyn Penny of the American Antiquarian Society. Stephen Perkins, Helen Langone, Jason Bush, and Paul Hayslett of IDM provided essential technical support. We thank Gretchen Oberfranc and Alice Calaprice for careful reading and Jan Lilly for her unparalleled mastery of what a Jefferson volume must be. We appreciate especially the support and leadership of Peter J. Dougherty, Director of Princeton University Press. Others at the Press who never fail to give these volumes the benefit of their expertise are Adam Fortgang, Dimitri Karetnikov, Neil Litt, Elizabeth Litz, Linny Schenck, and Brigitta van Rheinberg.

For many years, Timothy Connelly of the National Archives has been our NHPRC program officer. We extend our heartfelt thanks for his commitment to documentary editions and his assistance to us in matters large and small.

EDITORIAL METHOD AND APPARATUS

1. RENDERING THE TEXT

Julian P. Boyd eloquently set forth a comprehensive editorial policy in Volume 1 of *The Papers of Thomas Jefferson*. Adopting what he described as a "middle course" for rendering eighteenth-century handwritten materials into print, Boyd set the standards for modern historical editing. His successors, Charles T. Cullen and John Catanzariti, reaffirmed Boyd's high standards. At the same time, they made changes in textual policy and editorial apparatus as they deemed appropriate. For Boyd's policy and subsequent modifications to it, readers are encouraged to consult Vol. 1:xxix-xxxviii; Vol. 22:vii-xi; and Vol. 24:vii-viii.

The revised, more literal textual method, which appeared for the first time in Volume 30, adheres to the following guidelines: Abbreviations will be retained as written. Where the meaning is sufficiently unclear to require editorial intervention, the expansion will be given in the explanatory annotation. Capitalization will follow the usage of the writer. Because the line between uppercase and lowercase letters can be a very fine and fluctuating one, when it is impossible to make an absolute determination of the author's intention, we will adopt modern usage. Jefferson rarely began his sentences with an uppercase letter, and we conform to his usage. Punctuation will be retained as written and double marks of punctuation, such as a period followed by a dash, will be allowed to stand. Misspellings or so-called slips of the pen will be allowed to stand or will be recorded in a subjoined textual note.

English translations or translation summaries will be supplied for foreign-language documents. In some instances, when documents are lengthy and not especially pertinent to Jefferson's concerns or if our edition's typography cannot adequately represent the script of a language, we will provide only a summary in English. In most cases we will print in full the text in its original language and also provide a full English translation. If a contemporary translation that Jefferson made or would have used is extant, we may print it in lieu of a modern translation. Our own translations are designed to provide a basic readable English text for the modern user rather than to preserve all aspects of the original diction and language.

2. *TEXTUAL DEVICES*

The following devices are employed throughout the work to clarify the presentation of the text.

[...]	Text missing and not conjecturable.
[ ]	Number or part of a number missing or illegible.
[roman]	Conjectural reading for missing or illegible matter. A question mark follows when the reading is doubtful.
[*italic*]	Editorial comment inserted in the text.
<*italic*>	Matter deleted in the MS but restored in our text.

3. *DESCRIPTIVE SYMBOLS*

The following symbols are employed throughout the work to describe the various kinds of manuscript originals. When a series of versions is recorded, the first to be recorded is the version used for the printed text.

Dft	draft (usually a composition or rough draft; later drafts, when identifiable as such, are designated "2d Dft," &c.)
Dupl	duplicate
MS	manuscript (arbitrarily applied to most documents other than letters)
N	note, notes (memoranda, fragments, &c.)
PoC	polygraph copy
PrC	press copy
RC	recipient's copy
SC	stylograph copy
Tripl	triplicate

All manuscripts of the above types are assumed to be in the hand of the author of the document to which the descriptive symbol pertains. If not, that fact is stated. On the other hand, the following types of manuscripts are assumed *not* to be in the hand of the author, and exceptions will be noted:

FC	file copy (applied to all contemporary copies retained by the author or his agents)
Lb	letterbook (ordinarily used with FC and Tr to denote texts copied into bound volumes)
Tr	transcript (applied to all contemporary and later copies except file copies; period of transcription, unless clear by implication, will be given when known)

4. LOCATION SYMBOLS

The locations of documents printed in this edition from originals in private hands and from printed sources are recorded in self-explanatory form in the descriptive note following each document. The locations of documents printed from originals held by public and private institutions in the United States are recorded by means of the symbols used in the National Union Catalog in the Library of Congress; an explanation of how these symbols are formed is given in Vol. 1:xl. The symbols DLC and MHi by themselves stand for the collections of Jefferson Papers proper in these repositories; when texts are drawn from other collections held by these two institutions, the names of those collections will be added. Location symbols for documents held by institutions outside the United States are given in a subjoined list.

CLU-C	University of California, Los Angeles, William Andrews Clark Memorial Library
CSmH	The Huntington Library, San Marino, California
CtY	Yale University, New Haven, Connecticut
DLC	Library of Congress
DeGH	Hagley Museum, Greenville, Delaware
MA	Amherst College, Massachusetts
MHi	Massachusetts Historical Society, Boston
MWA	American Antiquarian Society, Worcester, Massachusetts
MdAA	Hall of Records Commission, Annapolis, Maryland
MdHi	Maryland Historical Society, Baltimore
MeHi	Maine Historical Society, Portland
MiU-C	University of Michigan, William L. Clements Library
MoSHi	Missouri History Museum Library and Research Center, St. Louis
Ms-Ar	Mississippi Department of Archives and History, Jackson
NBuHi	Buffalo & Erie County Historical Society, Buffalo, New York
NHi	New-York Historical Society, New York City
NIC	Cornell University, Ithaca, New York
NN	New York Public Library
NNMus	Museum of the City of New York
NNPM	Pierpont Morgan Library, New York City
NcD	Duke University, Durham, North Carolina

NcU	University of North Carolina, Chapel Hill
NjP	Princeton University
PHi	Historical Society of Pennsylvania, Philadelphia
PPAmP	American Philosophical Society, Philadelphia
PU	University of Pennsylvania Library
PWacD	David Library of the American Revolution, Washington Crossing, Pennsylvania
ViU	University of Virginia, Charlottesville
ViW	College of William and Mary, Williamsburg, Virginia
ViWC	Colonial Williamsburg Foundation

5. *NATIONAL ARCHIVES DESIGNATIONS*

Documents in the National Archives have the location symbol DNA, with identifications of record groups and series as follows:

RG 11	General Records of the United States Government	
RG 42	Records of the Office of Public Buildings and Public Parks of the National Capital	
	LRDLS	Letters Received and Drafts of Letters Sent
RG 45	Naval Records Collection of the Office of Naval Records and Library	
	LSO	Letters Sent to Officers
	LSP	Letters Sent to the President
	MLS	Misc. Letters Sent
RG 46	Records of the United States Senate	
	EPEN	Executive Proceedings, Executive Nominations
	EPFR	Executive Proceedings, Foreign Relations
	EPIR	Executive Proceedings, Indian Relations
	LPPM	Legislative Proceedings, President's Messages
RG 56	General Records of the Department of the Treasury	
	PFLP	Papers Relating to the Financing of the Louisiana Purchase
RG 59	General Records of the Department of State	
	CD	Consular Dispatches
	DD	Diplomatic Dispatches

	GPR	General Pardon Records
	LAR	Letters of Application and Recommendation
	MLR	Misc. Letters Received
	MPTPC	Misc. Permanent and Temporary Presidential Commissions
	NL	Notes from Legations
	PTCC	Permanent and Temporary Consular Commissions
	RD	Resignations and Declinations
	TP	Territorial Papers
RG 75	Records of the Bureau of Indian Affairs	
	LSIA	Letters Sent by the Secretary of War Relating to Indian Affairs
RG 76	Records of Boundary and Claims Commissions and Arbitrations	
RG 84	Records of the Foreign Service Posts of the Department of State	
RG 107	Records of the Office of the Secretary of War	
	LRUS	Letters Received by the Secretary of War, Unregistered Series
	LSMA	Letters Sent by the Secretary of War Relating to Military Affairs
	LSP	Letters Sent to the President
	MLS	Misc. Letters Sent
	RLRMS	Register of Letters Received, Main Series
RG 233	Records of the United States House of Representatives	
	PM	President's Messages

6. *OTHER SYMBOLS AND ABBREVIATIONS*

The following symbols and abbreviations are commonly employed in the annotation throughout the work.

Second Series The topical series to be published as part of this edition, comprising those materials which are best suited to a topical rather than a chronological arrangement (see Vol. 1:xv-xvi)

TJ Thomas Jefferson

TJ Editorial Files Photoduplicates and other editorial materials in the office of The Papers of Thomas Jefferson, Princeton University Library

TJ Papers Jefferson Papers (applied to a collection of manuscripts when the precise location of an undated, misdated, or otherwise problematic document must be furnished, and always preceded by the symbol for the institutional repository; thus "DLC: TJ Papers, 4:628-9" represents a document in the Library of Congress, Jefferson Papers, volume 4, pages 628 and 629. Citations to volumes and folio numbers of the Jefferson Papers at the Library of Congress refer to the collection as it was arranged at the time the first microfilm edition was made in 1944-45. Access to the microfilm edition of the collection as it was rearranged under the Library's Presidential Papers Program is provided by the Index to the Thomas Jefferson Papers [Washington, D.C., 1976])

RG Record Group (used in designating the location of documents in the National Archives)

SJL Jefferson's "Summary Journal of Letters" written and received for the period 11 Nov. 1783 to 25 June 1826 (in DLC: TJ Papers). This register, kept in Jefferson's hand, has been checked against the TJ Editorial Files. It is to be assumed that all outgoing letters are recorded in SJL unless there is a note to the contrary. When the date of receipt of an incoming letter is recorded in SJL, it is incorporated in the notes. Information and discrepancies revealed in SJL but not found in the letter itself are also noted. Missing letters recorded in SJL are, where possible, accounted for in the notes to documents mentioning them or in related documents. A more detailed discussion of this register and its use in this edition appears in Vol. 6:vii-x

SJPL "Summary Journal of Public Letters," an incomplete list of letters and documents written by TJ from 16 Apr. 1784 to 31 Dec. 1793, with brief summaries, in an amanuensis's hand. This is supplemented by six pages in TJ's hand, compiled at a later date, listing private and confidential memorandums and notes as well as official reports and communications by and to him as Secretary of State, 11 Oct. 1789 to 31 Dec. 1793 (in DLC: TJ Papers, Epistolary Record, 514-59 and 209-11, respectively; see Vol. 22:ix-x). Since nearly all documents in the amanuensis's list are registered in SJL, while few in TJ's list are so recorded, it is to be assumed that all references to SJPL are to the list in TJ's hand unless there is a statement to the contrary

V Ecu

f Florin

£ Pound sterling or livre, depending upon context (in doubtful cases, a clarifying note will be given)
s Shilling or sou (also expressed as /)
d Penny or denier
₶ Livre Tournois
₰ Per (occasionally used for pro, pre)

7. SHORT TITLES

The following list includes short titles of works cited frequently in this edition. Since it is impossible to anticipate all the works to be cited in abbreviated form, the list is revised from volume to volume.

ANB John A. Garraty and Mark C. Carnes, eds., *American National Biography*, New York and Oxford, 1999, 24 vols.

Annals *Annals of the Congress of the United States: The Debates and Proceedings in the Congress of the United States ... Compiled from Authentic Materials*, Washington, D.C., Gales & Seaton, 1834-56, 42 vols. All editions are undependable and pagination varies from one printing to another. The first two volumes of the set cited here have "Compiled ... by Joseph Gales, Senior" on the title page and bear the caption "Gales & Seatons History" on verso and "of Debates in Congress" on recto pages. The remaining volumes bear the caption "History of Congress" on both recto and verso pages. Those using the first two volumes with the latter caption will need to employ the date of the debate or the indexes of debates and speakers.

APS American Philosophical Society

ASP *American State Papers: Documents, Legislative and Executive, of the Congress of the United States*, Washington, D.C., 1832-61, 38 vols.

Bear, *Family Letters* Edwin M. Betts and James A. Bear, Jr., eds., *Family Letters of Thomas Jefferson*, Columbia, Mo., 1966

Betts, *Farm Book* Edwin M. Betts, ed., *Thomas Jefferson's Farm Book*, Princeton, 1953

Betts, *Garden Book* Edwin M. Betts, ed., *Thomas Jefferson's Garden Book, 1766-1824*, Philadelphia, 1944

Biog. Dir. Cong. *Biographical Directory of the United States Congress, 1774-1989*, Washington, D.C., 1989

Brigham, *American Newspapers* Clarence S. Brigham, *History and Bibliography of American Newspapers, 1690-1820*, Worcester, Mass., 1947, 2 vols.

Bush, *Life Portraits* Alfred L. Bush, *The Life Portraits of Thomas Jefferson*, rev. ed., Charlottesville, 1987

DAB Allen Johnson and Dumas Malone, eds., *Dictionary of American Biography*, New York, 1928-36, 20 vols.

Dexter, *Yale* Franklin Bowditch Dexter, *Biographical Sketches of the Graduates of Yale College with Annals of the College History*, New York, 1885-1912, 6 vols.

DHSC Maeva Marcus and others, eds., *The Documentary History of the Supreme Court of the United States, 1789-1800*, New York, 1985-2007, 8 vols.

Dictionnaire *Dictionnaire de biographie française*, Paris, 1933- , 19 vols.

DNB H. C. G. Matthew and Brian Harrison, eds., *Oxford Dictionary of National Biography, In Association with The British Academy, From the Earliest Times to the Year 2000,* Oxford, 2004, 60 vols.

DSB Charles C. Gillispie, ed., *Dictionary of Scientific Biography*, New York, 1970-80, 16 vols.

DVB John T. Kneebone and others, eds., *Dictionary of Virginia Biography*, Richmond, 1998- , 3 vols.

EG Dickinson W. Adams and Ruth W. Lester, eds., *Jefferson's Extracts from the Gospels*, Princeton, 1983, *The Papers of Thomas Jefferson*, Second Series

Evans Charles Evans, Clifford K. Shipton, and Roger P. Bristol, comps., *American Bibliography: A Chronological Dictionary of All Books, Pamphlets and Periodical Publications Printed in the United States of America from … 1639 … to … 1820*, Chicago and Worcester, Mass., 1903-59, 14 vols.

Ford Paul Leicester Ford, ed., *The Writings of Thomas Jefferson*, Letterpress Edition, New York, 1892-99, 10 vols.

Gallatin, *Papers* Carl E. Prince and Helene E. Fineman, eds., *The Papers of Albert Gallatin*, microfilm edition in 46 reels, Philadelphia, 1969, and Supplement, Barbara B. Oberg, ed., reels 47-51, Wilmington, Del., 1985

HAW Henry A. Washington, ed., *The Writings of Thomas Jefferson*, New York, 1853-54, 9 vols.

Heitman, *Dictionary* Francis B. Heitman, comp., *Historical Register and Dictionary of the United States Army*, Washington, D.C., 1903, 2 vols.

Heitman, *Register* Francis B. Heitman, *Historical Register of Officers of the Continental Army during the War of the Revolution, April, 1775, to December, 1793*, new ed., Washington, D.C., 1914

Jackson, *Lewis and Clark* Donald Jackson, ed., *The Letters of the Lewis and Clark Expedition, with Related Documents, 1783-1854*, 2d ed., Urbana, Ill., 1978

JEP *Journal of the Executive Proceedings of the Senate of the United States ... to the Termination of the Nineteenth Congress*, Washington, D.C., 1828, 3 vols.

JHR *Journal of the House of Representatives of the United States*, Washington, D.C., 1826, 9 vols.

JS *Journal of the Senate of the United States*, Washington, D.C., 1820-21, 5 vols.

L & B Andrew A. Lipscomb and Albert E. Bergh, eds., *The Writings of Thomas Jefferson*, Washington, D.C., 1903-04, 20 vols.

LCB Douglas L. Wilson, ed., *Jefferson's Literary Commonplace Book*, Princeton, 1989, *The Papers of Thomas Jefferson*, Second Series

Latrobe, *Correspondence* John C. Van Horne and Lee W. Formwalt, eds., *The Correspondence and Miscellaneous Papers of Benjamin Henry Latrobe*, New Haven, 1984-88, 3 vols.

Leonard, *General Assembly* Cynthia Miller Leonard, comp., *The General Assembly of Virginia, July 30, 1619-January 11, 1978: A Bicentennial Register of Members*, Richmond, 1978

List of Patents *A List of Patents Granted by the United States from April 10, 1790, to December 31, 1836*, Washington, D.C., 1872

Madison, *Papers* William T. Hutchinson, Robert A. Rutland, J. C. A. Stagg, and others, eds., *The Papers of James Madison*, Chicago and Charlottesville, 1962- , 35 vols.

Sec. of State Ser., 1986- , 9 vols.

Pres. Ser., 1984- , 7 vols.

Ret. Ser., 2009- , 2 vols.

Malone, *Jefferson* Dumas Malone, *Jefferson and His Time*, Boston, 1948-81, 6 vols.

MB James A. Bear, Jr., and Lucia C. Stanton, eds., *Jefferson's Memorandum Books: Accounts, with Legal Records and Miscellany, 1767-1826*, Princeton, 1997, *The Papers of Thomas Jefferson*, Second Series

Miller, *Alexandria Artisans* T. Michael Miller, comp., *Artisans and Merchants of Alexandria, Virginia, 1780-1820*, Bowie, Md., 1991-92, 2 vols.

Miller, *Treaties* Hunter Miller, ed., *Treaties and Other International Acts of the United States of America*, Washington, D.C., 1931-48, 8 vols.

Moulton, *Journals of the Lewis & Clark Expedition* Gary E. Moulton, ed., *Journals of the Lewis & Clark Expedition*, Lincoln, Neb., 1983-2001, 13 vols.

NDBW Dudley W. Knox, ed., *Naval Documents Related to the United States Wars with the Barbary Powers*, Washington, D.C., 1939-44, 6 vols. and *Register of Officer Personnel and Ships' Data, 1801-1807*, Washington, D.C., 1945

NDQW Dudley W. Knox, ed., *Naval Documents Related to the Quasi-War between the United States and France, Naval Operations*, Washington, D.C., 1935-38, 7 vols. (cited by years)

Nichols, *Architectural Drawings* Frederick Doveton Nichols, *Thomas Jefferson's Architectural Drawings, Compiled and with Commentary and a Check List*, Charlottesville, 1978

Notes, ed. Peden *Thomas Jefferson, Notes on the State of Virginia*, ed. William Peden, Chapel Hill, 1955

OED J. A. Simpson and E. S. C. Weiner, eds., *The Oxford English Dictionary*, Oxford, 1989, 20 vols.

Parry, *Consolidated Treaty Series* Clive Parry, ed., *The Consolidated Treaty Series*, Dobbs Ferry, N.Y., 1969-81, 231 vols.

Peale, *Papers* Lillian B. Miller and others, eds., *The Selected Papers of Charles Willson Peale and His Family*, New Haven, 1983-2000, 5 vols. in 6

PMHB *Pennsylvania Magazine of History and Biography*, 1877-

Preston, *Catalogue* Daniel Preston, *A Comprehensive Catalogue of the Correspondence and Papers of James Monroe*, Westport, Conn., 2001, 2 vols.

PW Wilbur S. Howell, ed., *Jefferson's Parliamentary Writings*, Princeton, 1988, *The Papers of Thomas Jefferson*, Second Series

RCHS *Records of the Columbia Historical Society*, 1895-1989

RS J. Jefferson Looney and others, eds., *The Papers of Thomas Jefferson: Retirement Series*, Princeton, 2004- , 10 vols.

S.C. Biographical Directory, House of Representatives J. S. R. Faunt, Walter B. Edgar, N. Louise Bailey, and others, eds., *Biographical Directory of the South Carolina House of Representatives*, Columbia, S.C., 1974-92, 5 vols.

Shaw-Shoemaker Ralph R. Shaw and Richard H. Shoemaker, comps., *American Bibliography: A Preliminary Checklist for 1801-1819*, New York, 1958-63, 22 vols.

Sowerby E. Millicent Sowerby, comp., *Catalogue of the Library of Thomas Jefferson*, Washington, D.C., 1952-59, 5 vols.

Stanton, *Free Some Day* Lucia Stanton, *Free Some Day: The African-American Families of Monticello*, Charlottesville, 2000

Stets, *Postmasters* Robert J. Stets, *Postmasters & Postoffices of the United States 1782-1811*, Lake Oswego, Ore., 1994

Syrett, *Hamilton* Harold C. Syrett and others, eds., *The Papers of Alexander Hamilton*, New York, 1961-87, 27 vols.

Terr. Papers Clarence E. Carter and John Porter Bloom, eds., *The Territorial Papers of the United States*, Washington, D.C., 1934-75, 28 vols.

TJR Thomas Jefferson Randolph, ed., *Memoir, Correspondence, and Miscellanies, from the Papers of Thomas Jefferson*, Charlottesville, 1829, 4 vols.

Tulard, *Dictionnaire Napoléon* Jean Tulard, *Dictionnaire Napoléon*, Paris, 1987

U.S. Statutes at Large Richard Peters, ed., *The Public Statutes at Large of the United States ... 1789 to March 3, 1845*, Boston, 1855-56, 8 vols.

VMHB *Virginia Magazine of History and Biography*, 1893-

Washington, *Papers* W. W. Abbot, Dorothy Twohig, Philander D. Chase, Theodore J. Crackel, Edward C. Lengel, and others, eds., *The Papers of George Washington*, Charlottesville, 1983- , 59 vols.

Confed. Ser., 1992-97, 6 vols.

Pres. Ser., 1987- , 17 vols.

Ret. Ser., 1998-99, 4 vols.

Rev. War Ser., 1985- , 22 vols.

WMQ *William and Mary Quarterly*, 1892-

Woods, *Albemarle* Edgar Woods, *Albemarle County in Virginia*, Charlottesville, 1901

CONTENTS

CONTENTS

APPENDICES

ILLUSTRATIONS

Following page 394

HISTORY OF LOUISIANA BY LE PAGE DU PRATZ

Antoine Simon Le Page du Pratz went to Louisiana in 1718 at the age of 23. He remained there for 16 years, living first in the vicinity of Natchez and afterward across the Mississippi River from New Orleans. After returning to France, he wrote a description of the colony that appeared as a three-volume *Histoire de la Louisiane*. First published in Paris in 1758, the book became an influential source of information. Jefferson owned a two-volume English translation published in London in 1763. He cited the work several times in his compilation of information about the extent and boundaries of Louisiana (see the editorial note and group of documents at 7 Sep.). Horatio Gates, as he mentioned in a letter to Jefferson in October 1803, owned a one-volume edition, and because Le Page du Pratz's work was "a very scarce Book in America," Gates loaned his copy to Albert Gallatin. The copy illustrated here, of a translation printed in London in 1774, belonged to the Philadelphia physician, natural scientist, and professor of medicine Benjamin Smith Barton, whose signature appears above the title. As indicated by a note that Meriwether Lewis wrote in the book, Barton loaned him the volume in June 1803. Lewis took it "to the Pacific Ocean through the interior of the Continent of North America" and returned it to its owner in 1807. Barton died in 1815; in the margin of the title page, dated July 1820, is the signature of John Vaughan, who, like Barton, was an officer of the American Philosophical Society. The volume is in octavo format, its pages approximately 8$\frac{1}{4}$ inches tall (Shannon Lee Dawdy, "Enlightenment from the Ground: Le Page du Pratz's *Histoire de la Louisiane*," *French Colonial History*, 3 [2003], 17-34; Patricia Galloway, "Rhetoric of Difference: Le Page du Pratz on African Slave Management in Eighteenth-Century Louisiana," same, 1-15; Carolyn Gilman, *Lewis and Clark: Across the Divide* [Washington, D.C., 2003], 22-3, 354; Sowerby, No. 4068; Gates to TJ, 23 Oct.).

Courtesy of the Library Company of Philadelphia.

BOAT FOR THE WESTERN EXPEDITION

To transport equipment and supplies up the Missouri River, Meriwether Lewis desired a keelboat that his men could pole, tow, or row upstream against the current. He encountered delays in the construction of the boat in Pittsburgh, but finally set off with it down the Ohio River on 30 Aug. 1803. In its design, the craft resembled galleys used by the Spanish in the Mississippi Valley. It originally had two masts for sails to provide additional motive power. Lewis later referred to it as the "barge." Illustrated here is a detail from a page of William Clark's notes made in January 1804, while the party was in winter camp on the Mississippi River. Clark was making calculations for building storage lockers for the boat, and his diagrams, depicting the boat from above and from the side, provide the only contemporary depiction of the 55-foot-long vessel. The expedition used the boat as far up the Missouri River as Fort Mandan. There in April 1805, unable to take the boat any farther upstream, Lewis and Clark sent it back down the Missouri with some of their men carrying dispatches and natural history specimens, including a magpie and a prairie dog. In Clark's original diagrams, the boat is about 6 inches long (Jackson, *Lewis and Clark*, 1:231-42; 2:534; Moulton, *Journals of the Lewis & Clark Expedition*, 2:65, 66n, 161-3, 164n; Carolyn Gilman, *Lewis and Clark: Across the Divide* [Washington, D.C., 2003], 85; New Haven *Connecticut Herald*, 23 July 1805; Vol. 40:246-7, 249-50n, 445; Lewis to TJ, 15, 22 July, 8, 13 Sep. 1803).

Courtesy of the Yale Collection of Western Americana, Beinecke Rare Book and Manuscript Library.

WILLIAM CLARK

"I will chearfully, and with great pleasure Join My friend Capt Lewis in this Vast enterprise," William Clark wrote to the president in July 1803, in response to the invitation from Meriwether Lewis to become co-leader of the expedition to the Pacific. Clark and those who knew him considered this portrait to be the best likeness of his features. Attributed to various artists, including Chester Harding and Gilbert Stuart, the unsigned painting, as suggested by an entry in the inventory of Clark's estate, was probably the work of John Wesley Jarvis. Born in England in 1780, Jarvis emigrated to the United States with his family when he was a child. He began his career as an apprentice to Edward Savage. The portrait, which is in oil on canvas, 29¾ inches tall by 25⅛ inches wide, may date from around 1810 (Carolyn Gilman, *Lewis and Clark: Across the Divide* [Washington, D.C., 2003], 72, 358; Harold E. Dickson, *John Wesley Jarvis, American Painter, 1780-1840: With a Checklist of His Works* [New York, 1949], 347; George C. Groce and David H. Wallace, *The New-York Historical Society's Dictionary of Artists in America, 1564-1860* [New Haven, 1957], 346; Clark to TJ, 24 July).

Courtesy of the Missouri History Museum, St. Louis.

SEA LETTER

The purpose of a sea letter or ship passport, Jefferson wrote in December 1802, was "to ascertain our flag"—that is, to certify that a vessel was owned by Americans. "Sea letters are never given out but in time of war," Jefferson affirmed, and at that time, with the Amiens peace still in place, he refused to bend to merchants' wishes for documents to protect their ships. In May 1803, however, even though they did not yet know for certain that Great Britain and France were once again at war, he and the cabinet agreed to begin issuing sea letters. One reason for his earlier reluctance, as he wrote in December, was that the issuing of sea letters was "very troublesome, and extremely burthensome to the Post office." He made this declaration from experience: as secretary of state in 1793, he had written a detailed opinion on the issuance of ship passports for President Washington and the cabinet, and then arranged for the printing of 800 blank sea letters, all of them requiring his and President Washington's signatures and the seal of the United States before being distributed by the Treasury Department. Now, a decade later, Jefferson would again have to put his name to scores of blank sea letters. The secretary of the Treasury began sending the signed forms out in batches to collectors of customs in June. The one seen here, numbered 108, bears Jefferson's and James Madison's signatures and was issued by David Gelston, the collector at New York City, on 11 June 1804, for the schooner *Little Tom*, which had a burden of 89 tons and carried a crew of seven. The document is $11\frac{1}{4}$ inches wide and $17\frac{1}{2}$ inches high. Addressed below the seal "To all Persons whom these may concern," the document declared that the vessel belonged to one or more citizens of the United States and asked that it be allowed to pass "without any hindrance, seizure or molestation." The top edge of the paper is indented, meaning that a clerk cut it in a wavy line that matched a duplicate to be retained at the custom house to prove, if necessary, the authenticity of the certificate. Another form had attestations regarding the ship's ownership (Vol. 25:645-8; Vol. 27:402; Vol. 39:113, 119-20, 217; Vol. 40:331; papers for ship *May Flower*, 8 Sep. 1803, in DNA: RG 76, French Spoliations).

This example of a sea letter is from the collection of Franklin Delano Roosevelt, who was an avid collector of historical manuscripts, especially relating to naval subjects and the Hudson Valley. Among the experts on historical documents that Roosevelt and his staff consulted about his manuscripts collection and presidential archive was Julian Boyd, the first editor of *The Papers of Thomas Jefferson* (Roosevelt to Boyd, 1 Dec. 1938; Boyd to Roosevelt, 9 Dec. 1938; Roosevelt memorandum about planned library, n.d.; Boyd to Roosevelt, 7 Nov. 1942; Margaret Suckley to Boyd, 19 Sep. 1944; and Boyd to Suckley, 4 Oct. 1944, all in NjP: Julian P. Boyd Papers, box 25; *New York Times*, 11 Dec. 1938).

Courtesy of the Franklin D. Roosevelt Presidential Library and Museum, Hyde Park, New York.

MONTICELLO BY ROBERT MILLS

This drawing by Robert Mills, which architectural historians believe may date from 1803, is of the west front of Monticello but does not record the building as it actually appeared at that time. Mills may not have seen the house before 1807. Mills, who had spent some time studying architecture under James Hoban, was acquainted with Jefferson by 1802, and the president gave the young man access to his books. In addition, either as an exercise for the young man or in an effort to explore possibilities in his own building plans, Jefferson let Mills make drawings of Monticello and Shadwell. Mills's studies of Monticello were probably based on drawings and notes from Jefferson's papers rather than observation, for some features of Monticello seen in the drawing illustrated here were not yet in place, and Mills incorrectly rendered some details of the house. Mills did not sign this drawing, but it is similar in technique to one showing a proposed redesign of Monticello that he did sign. Jefferson, who earlier had written Mills a letter of introduction to Charles Bulfinch, recommended Mills for a place in the office of Benjamin Henry Latrobe. Latrobe, in a letter of 2 Oct. 1803 printed in this volume, commented about Mills's qualities as a beginning architect and his religious devotion. This drawing, in ink and wash on paper, $14\frac{1}{2}$ inches wide and $8\frac{1}{4}$ inches high, passed from Jefferson to his granddaughter Ellen Wayles Randolph, and then to her descendants (Susan R. Stein, *The Worlds of Thomas Jefferson at Monticello* [New York, 1993], 152-3, 447; ANB; John M. Bryan, *Robert Mills: America's First Architect* [New York, 2001], 20-6; Rhodri Windsor Liscombe, *Altogether American: Robert Mills, Architect and Engineer, 1781-1855* [New York, 1994], 10-16; Fiske Kimball, *Thomas Jefferson, Architect: Original Designs in the Collection of Thomas Jefferson Coolidge, Junior* [Boston, 1916], 68-9, 165-6, 180; Nichols, *Architectural Drawings*, 37; Vol. 38:4).

Courtesy of the Massachusetts Historical Society.

WILLIAM CHARLES COLES CLAIBORNE

Claiborne, born in 1775, passed the Virginia bar before he was 20 years old, became a judge of the Tennessee Supreme Court when he was 21, and won election to the U.S. House of Representatives before he attained the constitutionally mandated age of 25. He was governor of Mississippi Territory in 1803, when Jefferson and his advisers put him in charge of the transfer of civil administration of Louisiana to the authority of the United States. This small circular portrait, $2\frac{3}{16}$ inches in diameter, is a proof engraving retained by its creator, Charles Balthazar Julien Févret de Saint-Mémin. It depicts Claiborne in 1798. Someone with access to the artist's records wrote the identifying information above the engraving (ANB; Ellen G. Miles, *Saint-Mémin and the Neoclassical Profile Portrait in America* [Washington, D.C., 1994], 206-13, 270).

Courtesy of the National Portrait Gallery, Smithsonian Institution / Art Resource, NY.

VIEW OF NEW ORLEANS

John L. Boqueta made an opportunity of the change of ownership of Louisiana. He completed this painting of a view of New Orleans in November 1803, before the United States assumed authority. Yet he placed an American flag (with 18 stars and many stripes) in the scene and surmounted the image with an eagle holding a star-festooned streamer that foretold prosperity. Boqueta transformed the painting seen here into an aquatint engraving that he offered, along with a plan or map that showed the layout of the city, for sale by subscription by February 1804. Boqueta suggested to potential subscribers that the pair of images furnished "as accurate and complete a plan and view of Louisiana, and the city of New Orleans, &c as ever can be drawn." He dedicated the engravings to Jefferson, who, according to his catalogue of works of art, may have displayed the two prints in the dining room at Monticello.

In an advertisement for the engravings, Boqueta, who was perhaps from Saint-Domingue and whose name also appears as Boqueta de Woiseri and in several other variants, labeled himself a "Designer, Drawer, Geographer and Engineer" and stated that he had lived in New Orleans for "a number of years." He later published views of Philadelphia, New York, Baltimore, Boston, Richmond, and Charleston as aquatint engravings that could be sold separately or as a conjoined "View of the First Cities of the United States." He painted portraits and miniatures in oil and watercolors and did copper engraving. He later created and exhibited in Norfolk, Virginia, a "Grand Moving Panorama" that included, among other images, scenes from classical mythology, depictions of farming and daily life, a "*very feeling*" shipwreck episode, and George Washington "Passing in the Clouds in a Chariot, drawn by Four Horses, carrying the Great and Illustrious Hero to the Temple of Memory." Boqueta wrote to Jefferson from Philadelphia on 26 June and 4 Aug. 1804, but those letters, which are recorded in Jefferson's epistolary record as received on 5 July and 16 Aug., respectively, have not been found (Philadelphia *Aurora*, 23 Feb. 1804; Worcester *Massachusetts Spy*, 20 Nov. 1805; New York *Mercantile Advertiser*, 6 June 1810; *Richmond Commercial Compiler*, 31 July 1818; Norfolk *American Beacon*, 2 June, 22 Sep., 9 Nov. 1818; Susan R. Stein, *The Worlds of Thomas Jefferson at Monticello* [New York, 1993], 186, 449; Gail Feigenbaum, *Jefferson's America & Napoleon's France: An Exhibition for the Louisiana Purchase Bicentennial*, ed. by Victoria Cooke [New Orleans, 2003], 234-5; George C. Groce and David H. Wallace, *The New-York Historical Society's Dictionary of Artists in America, 1564-1860* [New Haven, 1957], 65; I. N. Phelps Stokes and Daniel C. Haskell, *American Historical Prints: Early Views of American Cities, Etc., From the Phelps Stokes and Other Collections* [New York, 1933], 53, pl. 40; I. N. Phelps Stokes, *The Iconography of Manhattan Island, 1498-1909*, 6 vols. [New York, 1915-28; repr. Union, N.J., 1998], 872-3).

This *View of New Orleans Taken from the Plantation of Marigny*, in oil on canvas, is 58½ inches high and 90½ inches wide (photography and imaging by Shelby Silvernell).

Courtesy of the Chicago History Museum.

NOTICE OF WASHINGTON JOCKEY CLUB RACES

On 9, 10, and 11 Nov. 1803, President Jefferson left his official responsibilities behind and spent at least part of each day at the horse races. He had attended the races hosted by the Washington Jockey Club the previous year also, when the heats were held on a course that straddled Pennsylvania Avenue just northwest of the President's House. In 1803, the meet was held at a new location a couple of miles north at present Columbia Road between 14th and 16th Streets, which then served as the racing venue for several years. In many years, senators and members of the House of Representatives would not yet have arrived in Washington when the racing meet took place in November. In 1803, however, Jefferson summoned Congress to convene at an early date to take up matters relating to Louisiana. When the days of the races arrived, both the Senate and the House found reasons to curtail their legislative business. For some members, especially northerners, the event provided their first exposure to the spectacle of horse racing as it was enjoyed by inhabitants of the southern and middle states. Fortunately, some of those northerners recorded elements of the experience in their letters and diaries. Senator John Quincy Adams attended the first day, recording only that "I have never seen regular horse races before." He declined to go on the second day, and, after finding almost no one around when he tried to make professional calls, spent the remainder of the day reading Plutarch. Representative Manasseh Cutler of Massachusetts captured more of the event, observing that the course was a one-mile circuit with a track 50 feet wide. A judges' booth stood on one side. In the center of the infield, the Jockey Club rented out booths that held tables for refreshments and supported rooftop platforms that served as viewing stands. Outside the track on the west side, well-to-do people, dressed in fine attire and attended by servants, arrayed their carriages. "These," Cutler noted in a letter, "if they were not all *Democrats*, I should call the *Noblesse*." Samuel L. Mitchill of New York described the scene to his wife as a "great and fashionable exhibition." Jefferson may have had a carriage in that area, for he paid a dollar for expenses at the races each day he attended, and according to the notice illustrated here, that was the cost of admission for a four-wheeled carriage. More vehicles and many people on horseback filled the space in the infield, the riders including women "in rich and elegant dress." Cutler noted that as races were in progress, "the whole ground within the circus was spread over with people on horseback" who rode "full speed" from spot to spot to see the action—"a striking part of the show." A notice by the Jockey Club admonished spectators to keep their horses and their dogs off the track. Cutler estimated attendance to be "between 3,000 and 4,000 people—black, and white, and yellow; of all conditions, from the President of the United States to the beggar in his rags; of all ages and of both sexes, for I should judge one-third were females." The winning horse on the first day, as President Jefferson was no doubt pleased to observe, was a bay colt named True Republican (Adams, diary 27 [1 Jan. 1803 to 4 Aug. 1809], 52, in MHi: Adams Family Papers; William Parker Cutler and Julia Perkins Cutler, eds., *Life, Journals and Correspondence of Rev. Manasseh Cutler, LL.D.,* 2 vols. [Cincinnati, 1888; repr. Athens, Ohio, 1987], 2:141-3; Samuel L. Mitchill to Catharine Mitchill, 8, 19 Nov. 1803, in NNMus; *Washington Federalist*, 24 Oct., 7, 18 Nov. 1803; Wilhelmus B. Bryan, *A History of the National Capital from Its Foundation through the Period of the Adoption of the Organic Act*, 2 vols. (New York, 1914-16), 1:609-11; JS, 3:309; MB, 2:1087, 1111).

The notice illustrated here is from the *Washington Federalist* of 24 Oct. 1803.

Courtesy of the American Antiquarian Society.

Volume 41

11 July to 15 November 1803

JEFFERSON CHRONOLOGY

1743 • 1826

1743	Born at Shadwell, 13 April (New Style).
1760	Entered the College of William and Mary.
1762	"quitted college."
1762-1767	Self-education and preparation for law.
1769-1774	Albemarle delegate to House of Burgesses.
1772	Married Martha Wayles Skelton, 1 Jan.
1775-1776	In Continental Congress.
1776	Drafted Declaration of Independence.
1776-1779	In Virginia House of Delegates.
1779	Submitted Bill for Establishing Religious Freedom.
1779-1781	Governor of Virginia.
1782	His wife died, 6 Sep.
1783-1784	In Continental Congress.
1784-1789	In France as Minister Plenipotentiary to negotiate commercial treaties and as Minister Plenipotentiary resident at Versailles.
1790-1793	Secretary of State of the United States.
1797-1801	Vice President of the United States.
1801-1809	President of the United States.
1814-1826	Established the University of Virginia.
1826	Died at Monticello, 4 July.

VOLUME 41

11 July to 15 November 1803

16 July	Issues proclamation to convene Congress on 17 Oct.
17 July	Receives address from Philadelphia ward committees protesting the paucity of Federalist removals.
19 July	Leaves Washington for Monticello, arriving 22 July.
20 July	É. I. du Pont de Nemours seeks government contract for new gunpowder mill near Wilmington, Delaware.
24 July	William Clark accepts invitation to join Meriwether Lewis on western expedition.
26 Aug.	Frigate *Philadelphia* captures Moroccan cruiser *Mirboka* and liberates American brig *Celia* near Spain.
31 Aug.	Meriwether Lewis commences journey down the Ohio River with equipment for western expedition.
20 Sep.	Renews lease of fields and slaves to John H. Craven.
22 Sep.	Leaves Monticello for Washington, arriving 25 Sep.
29 Sep.	Donates $100 for victims of yellow fever outbreak in Alexandria.
1 Oct.	Orders eight barrels of Newark cider from John Condit.
2 Oct.	Samuel Adams dies in Boston.
11 Oct.	Sultan of Morocco reaffirms peace with the United States.
17 Oct.	Sends third annual message to Congress.
19 Oct.	Arranges to send 40 Balsam poplars to Monticello.
21 Oct.	Proclaims ratification of the Louisiana treaty and conventions.
26 Oct.	Dines with Jerome Bonaparte at the President's House.
31 Oct.	Frigate *Philadelphia* and crew captured by Tripolitan gunboats in the Mediterranean.
2 Nov.	Mary Jefferson Randolph, TJ's granddaughter, born at Edgehill.
9-11 Nov.	Attends annual races of the Washington Jockey Club.

THE PAPERS OF
THOMAS JEFFERSON

From Albert Gallatin

DEAR SIR Monday [11 July 1803]

I enclose a letter from the Collector of Philada respecting a new modification of mr Bond's complaint

a letter from a gentleman in Providence respecting a New Bank

a letter from the Superint. of mil. stores

recommendations in favr. of Mr Nicholas & Mr Garrard which I had forgotten to enclose

a list of officers of the external revenues and some corrections of your own list

Be good enough to look at them & I will call tomorrow to explain some parts & to have some conversation on those several subjects as well as on Louisiana.

With respectful attachment Your obedt. Servt.

ALBERT GALLATIN

RC (DLC); partially dated; endorsed by TJ as received from the Treasury Department on 11 July and "Bond's complt. republican bank. Superintendt. mily. stores" and so recorded in SJL. Enclosures: (1) Peter Muhlenberg to Gallatin, Philadelphia, 8 July 1803, noting that Phineas Bond was giving "a different turn" to his concern over vessels clearing the port with articles of contraband on board; Bond now charges that two vessels, the schooners *Nancy* and *Adventure*, are owned by Frenchmen and armed as privateers; Muhlenberg assures Gallatin that the two vessels "are not own'd by Frenchmen, but by Citizens of the United States" and there is no evidence "the vessels were intended for Cruizers"; the *Nancy* cleared for Cap-Français, Saint-Domingue, on 5 July, with neither guns nor military stores on board; the *Adventure* cleared on 7 July, with a cargo of flour, soap, and nankeens, and armed with four mounted gun carriages and ammunition for defense of the vessel; the owner of the *Adventure* is French-born, but Alexander J. Dallas, the district attorney, reports that he is a naturalized U.S. citizen and "A Merchant of great respectability and generally esteem'd"; the owner produced his papers along with instructions to the captain to proceed to Jamaica in case of a blockade at Cap-Français (Tr in DNA: RG 59, NL). (2) Seth Wheaton and Henry Smith to Gallatin, Providence, Rhode Island, 1 July 1803, informing the Treasury secretary that Providence Republicans are considering the establishment of a bank "supported entirely by Individuals who are warmly attached to the present Administration"; the Providence Bank, where U.S. Treasury funds are now deposited, is controlled by Federalists, who favor others of their party and influence "the political conduct of their more dependant fellow citizens," indicating the need for another bank; assurances that Gallatin will transfer public deposits to the new bank "will greatly promote the undertaking," gratify the Republican "monied Interest" in Providence, and "advance the public wellfare" (RC in NHi: Gallatin Papers; endorsed: "Henry Smith on Establishing a Bank"). (3) List of Officers of the External Revenue, 4 Mch. 1801-16 June 1803, organized by states and territories with seven columns labeled "Districts," "Ports," "Offices," "Officers on the 4th of March 1801," "Remarks," "Successors," and "date of first Commission"; the "Offices" column includes that of collector, naval officer, and surveyor at the various ports, with many districts in Massachusetts having ports with collectors only and those in North Carolina with surveyors only; the "Remarks" column gives reasons for a new appointment, with comments including "dead," "misbehaviour," "resigned," "vacant," "abolished," and "erected" or "organized," with the date for newly established offices; there is no entry under "Remarks" for many changes in officers; the "Successors" column names TJ's appointees, including collectors at 35 out of a total of 90 ports, naval officers at 4 out of 13, and surveyors at 20 out of 65 (MS in DNA: RG 59, Appointment Papers; in a clerk's hand). (4) For Gallatin's corrections of a list by TJ, see Document VI of the group of documents on the party affiliation of federal officeholders, at 11 July. For other enclosures, see below.

BOND'S COMPLAINT: see Enclosure No. 1, above, and Enclosure No. 2, described at Gallatin to TJ, 12 July (second letter).

The Roger Williams Bank in PROVIDENCE received a charter from the Rhode Island General Assembly in late 1803. Seth Wheaton and Sylvanus Martin, bankruptcy commissioners at Providence, Jonathan Russell, collector at Bristol, Samuel Thurber, Jr., and Henry Smith were among the Republican directors of the NEW BANK. In the next three years, the Roger Williams Bank received over $500,000 in public deposits (*The Charter of the Roger Williams Bank, in Providence* [Providence, 1803; Shaw-Shoemaker, No. 4990], 12; ASP, *Finance*, 2:216-17; Vol. 33:187-8; Vol. 37:602-3).

SUPERINT. OF MIL. STORES: William Irvine (Vol. 38:93n). The correspondence has not been found.

TJ may have given Gallatin the recommendations he had received for Robert C. NICHOLAS and William GARRARD, as TJ and his secretary of the Treasury were deciding on the appointment of a commissioner to serve along with Ephraim Kirby in the district East of Pearl River (see TJ to Gallatin, [9 July 1803], second letter, and Gallatin to TJ, 9 July). Gallatin had evidently FORGOTTEN to return them in his letter of the 9th. For the recommendations, see John Brown to TJ, 5 Dec. 1802, and Wilson Cary Nicholas to TJ, 31 May 1803.

From Albert Gallatin

SIR, Treasury Department July 11th. 1803.

I had the honor, on the 5th. october 1802, to communicate the opinion of the Collector of Boston, that another mate should be added to the revenue cutter. Since which similar applications have been made from almost every collector who has a Cutter under his direction. Upon mature deliberation I think that the measure will be conducive to the safety of the revenue; and that it will be also proper to authorize an encrease in the crew, of two men or boys. It appears certain that the cutters cannot always man their boats for the purpose of boarding vessels, and leave a sufficient number of hands to manage the cutter; and the want of an additional mate, often prevents the master leaving an officer on board foreign vessels, even when suspicious circumstances recommend this cautionary measure. Some symptoms of an inclination to smuggle, have lately appeared, which, as they render it necessary for the cutters to be more at sea, than had been usual, induce me to submit, at present, this alteration in the establishment, to your decision.

I have the honor to be very respectfully Sir, your obed. Servt.

ALBERT GALLATIN

RC (DLC); in a clerk's hand, signed by Gallatin; at foot of text: "The President of the United States"; endorsed by TJ as received from the Treasury Department on 11 July and "revenue cutters" and so recorded in SJL.

Benjamin Lincoln's 1802 OPINION has not been found, but see Vol. 38:445-6.

Memorandum from Albert Gallatin, with Jefferson's Note

[ca. 11 July 1803]

Officers of the external revenue

The sea shore from St. Croix to St. Mary's, the northern frontier from Lake Champlain to Lake Superior both inclusive, the Mississippi, & the Ohio below the Pennsylvania line are divided into Districts. In each District there is one Port of entry; and in several districts, there are, besides the port of entry, one or more Ports of delivery only. Every port of entry is also a port of delivery. All goods imported in a district must be entered at the port of entry, whether they are intended to be landed there or at any port of delivery in the district; and goods must be landed at the port of entry or at one of the ports of delivery. For each District there is one Collector whose authority extends over the whole district & who must reside at the Port of entry. There are, at present   Districts & Collectors. In   of the districts there is a Naval Officer residing at the Port of entry. In   , including the   last mentioned, there is also for the Port of entry a Surveyor residing there. In the other districts the duties of Surveyor devolve on the Collector. There is a number of Districts having subordinate ports of delivery, where the powers of the officers residing at the port of entry extend in every instance over all the ports of delivery; but in several extensive Districts, although the powers of the Collector extend over the whole district, there is a Surveyor attached to each port of delivery. In every port, whether of entry or delivery, where there is a Surveyor, he receives also a commission of Inspector of the revenue for the port: that commission, in ports of entry where there is no Survey[or,] is given to the Collector.

[*Note by TJ*:]
duty of Collectors.
1799. Mar. 2. Surveyors
c. 128. § 21. Naval officers
Inspectors

MS (DLC: TJ Papers, 133:22992); in Gallatin's hand, with TJ's note in left margin; undated; frayed at margin; endorsed by TJ as received from the Treasury Department in July 1803 and "organization of [. . .]."

Gallatin may have sent TJ this memorandum on revenue DISTRICTS about the same time he enclosed the List of Officers of the External Revenue, 4 Mch. 1801-16 June 1803 (see Enclosure No. 3, described at Gallatin to TJ, [11 July 1803], first letter). The list included the COLLECTOR for each district and the NAVAL OFFICER and SURVEYOR, where applicable, all officers appointed by the president. Here Gallatin notes that if a surveyor is appointed, he receives the COMMISSION OF INSPECTOR as well. The collector receives the commission only if the district has no surveyor. In several instances, TJ had to issue separate commissions for inspector, because they were not included with the original appointment (see Vol. 37:324-5; Vol. 38:680, 682n; Vol. 39:130-3). In his note, TJ referred to the 2 Mch. 1799 "Act to regulate the collection of duties on imports and tonnage," which names the port of entry and ports of delivery for each collection district. For instance, the state of New Hampshire had one district, with Portsmouth being the sole port of entry and New Castle, Dover, and Exeter named ports of delivery. Section 21 of the act describes the duties of the revenue officers (U.S. Statutes at Large, 1:627, 642-4).

To Horatio Gates

DEAR GENERAL Washington July 11. 03.

I accept with pleasure, and with pleasure reciprocate your congratulations on the acquisition of Louisiana: for it is a subject of mutual congratulation as it interests every man of the nation. the territory acquired, as it includes all the waters of the Missouri & Missisipi, has more than doubled the area[1] of the US. and the new part is not inferior to the old in soil, climate, productions, & important communications. if our legislature dispose of it with the wisdom we have a right to expect, they may make it the means of tempting all our[2] Indians on the East side of the Missipi to remove to the West, and of condensing instead of scattering our population. I find our opposition is very willing to pluck feathers from Munroe, although not fond of sticking them into Livingston's coat. the truth is, both have a just portion of merit, & were it necessary or proper it could be shewn that each has rendered peculiar services, & of important value. these grumblers too are very uneasy lest the administration should share some little credit for the acquisition, the whole of which they ascribe to the accident of war. they would be cruelly mortified could they see our files from May 1801, the first organisation of the administration, but more especially from April 1802. they would see that, tho' we could not say when war would arise, yet we said with energy what would take place when it should arise. we did not, by our intrigues, produce the war: but we availed ourselves of it when it happened. the other party saw the case now existing on which our representations were predicated, and the wisdom of timely sacrifice. but when these people make the war give us every thing, they authorise us to ask what the war gave us in their day? they had a war. what did they make it bring us? instead of making our neutrality the grounds of gain to their country, they were for plunging into the war. and if they were now in place, they would now be at war against the Atheists & disorganisers of France. they were for making their country an appendage to England. we are friendly, cordially & conscientiously friendly to England. but we are not hostile to France. we will be rigorously just, and sincerely friendly to both. I do not believe we shall have as much to swallow from them as our predecessors had.

With respect to the territory acquired, I do not think it will be a separate government as you imagine. I presume the island of N. Orleans and the settled country on the opposite bank, will be annexed to the Missipi territory. we shall certainly endeavor to introduce the American laws there, & that cannot be done but by amalgamating the people with such a body of Americans as may take the lead in legislation & government. of course they will be under the Governor of Missisipi. the rest of the territory will probably be locked up from American settlement, and under the self[3] government of the native occupants.

You know that every sentence from me is put on the rack by our opponents to be tortured into something they can make use of. no caution therefore I am sure is necessary against letting my letter go out of your own hands. I am always happy to hear from you, and to know that you preserve your health. present me respectfully to mrs Gates, and accept yourself my affectionate salutations and assurances of great respect & esteem. TH: JEFFERSON

RC (NN); at foot of first page: "General Gates." PrC (DLC); with Gates's name at foot of first page overwritten in ink.

[1] Word interlined in place of "compass."
[2] Word interlined in place of "the."
[3] Word interlined.

From Benjamin Hawkins

Creek agency 11 July 1803

I had the pleasure to receive your favour by Mr. Hill at a time when my mind was greatly agitated with the state of affairs in my agency. The opposition with us joined by the Simanolie seemed determined to usurp the direction of affairs, to place a chief of their own choice over the nation, and to disturb the peace of the agency. In their progress, meeting but little opposition publicly, they believed that to be true which they wished to be true, organized their body, formed an imaginary union of the four nations under one leader, and began to fulminate edicts of death against their opponents. The plan to counteract them was devised in november, steadily persued and executed with dignity, at the time, when the opposition had brought their plan, to that awful crisis, which crowns with success or annihilates both project and projectors. And we have been so singularly fortunate hitherto as to do this without bloodshed.

Occupied as I have been I have had but little time to devote to my friends or to that crisis in our affairs which threatened the dissolution of our government. I was surprised at what I heared, but never dispaired, as I firmly believed the elective system had the proper corrective and would place us right and keep us so. The bitterness with which the Federal sect tincture every thing opposed to their hopes and persuits shews their disappointment and their deadly hatred to those who administer the government. Possessing, and avowing this hatred, they must have expected to be placed in a situation to contemplate on their own conduct and contrast it with that of their successors. As the change has taken place, and peace economy and a government bottomed on popular election is the order of the day, there is no doubt the United States will be consolidated in their antient principles.

It has afforded me and those with whom I am placed much satisfaction to understand from yourself your personal dispositions and opinions respecting the Indians, we feel ourselves worthy of the trust confided to us and shall act accordingly. The business of hunting has already as you suggest become insufficient to furnish cloathing and subsistence to the Creeks. Stock raising, agriculture and household manufactures are essential to their preservation and must be resorted to. I have encouraged them by all the means in my power as well private as public. They begin to be the general theme of conversation, have taken deep root and success finally is no longer doubtful. I intend next year to introduce letters. By turning their minds to things useful, and by teaching them to rely upon their own exertions and resources for support, they will become honest and peaceable neighbours, they will first seek the necessaries, then the Luxuries of life, and in this way they can and will spare their superfluous land.

The idea of incorporating them with us is not a novel one. It was first suggested in a conference of the commissioners of the United States appointed to treat with the southern Indians at Keowee in the year 1785. It was carried so far then by some of the commissions as to admit them into Congress as a state. but instead of this it was provided in the treaty with the Cherokees that they might send a deputy of their choice to Congress. The Creeks are less mixed with white people than any other indians and adhere rigidly to their antient customs in most things. They are excessively jealous and the women have invariably the habit of governing absolutely in all cases when connected with a white man. The husband is a tenant at will only so far as the occupancy of the *premises* of the woman but permanently bound in his property if he has children. Towards a white man a woman can commit no crime, if she is adulterous, it is a subject of laughter whereas if her husband was red she would forfeit her ears. Men of spirit fly from this; tame and base ones submit, and such people have given[1] a taint to the opinion formed of us by the red people. I witnessed myself the degradation of the white man, and the rude insatiable conduct of their wives and families in several instances. I came in favour of the idea of forming amorous connexions with the women, had it in contemplation to set the example myself and order all my assistants to follow; commenced it with the Blacksmiths, was myself at the expense of an experiment under my own eye, and in my own yard, and found it would not do. The wife and family first took directions of the provisions, then the house and pay and finally the absolute government of every thing at the agency whether connected with the Smith or not. The Smiths and their wives parted, and I published an order against such connexion in future, and prohibited all amorous intercourse between red and white people at the agency. My young men were permitted to go to town after girls, and to have white girls, who, if they were clean neat and usefully instructive to the indian women were permited to reside at the agency and to be at my table. Indian women were invited to dine at the agency, treated with the most friendly attention, and on the footing of daughters of the house. This banished jealousy and gives a considerable degree of influence over them and their connexions. A perseverance in this line has brought the Indian women to reflect on and form proper ideas on the subject. They have recently made propositions to me to submit themselves and children to be governed by white men if I will rescind the order; I have some young girls of good families raised under my own roof to usefulness, with whom I shall begin the experiment a new, with the smiths and strikers in the public service, or such young men as I can get to marry them, and settle out on farms at such places as I shall direct.

If we succeed in bringing the Indian mind to accommodate Georgia to Ocmulgee we shall have gained much as that boundary will satisfy Georgia for the present and may remain for ten or twenty years, which will give the time as well as the means to perfect our plan of civilization. I need no stimulous from you on this head, and my journal to the proper officer will shew you the course I have pursued and am pursuing to attain it. The issue is doubtful.

The suspicions excited in Georgia are for local and private[2] purposes and by speculative characters. The plan has some affinity to assassination, as I reside 200 miles from the frontiers, they combined their measures so as to succeed before a scrutiny could be had. It was first tried with the grand jurys of some courts and failed, and then by the Legislature of which the members are already ashamed. I was apprised at the Treaty of F. Wilkinson of an attempt to oust the agent for Indian affairs, and witnessed myself, some of the cunning, and blunderbuss language, of the person sealing the office, but it excited in me contempt only towards those concerned, and I did not think it worth while to report it to the Secretary of War. In truth, I have been so much occupied with the divisions among the Indians, the projects of Bowles, the helpless situation of my neighbours of Spain, the plan of civilization and the diffusing generally a spirit of peace and good will to all men, that I have but little time to devote to myself.

Accept for your present and future prosperity the sincere wishes of My dear Sir, your friend and obedient Servant,

BENJAMIN HAWKINS

RC (DLC); at foot of first page: "Mr. Jefferson"; endorsed by TJ as received 10 Aug. and so recorded in SJL.

YOUR FAVOUR BY MR HILL: TJ to Hawkins, 18 Feb. 1803, which had been carried by Hawkins's assistant, William Hill (Vol. 39:334, 546-9).

THE OPPOSITION WITH US: Hawkins had come under increased pressure by both American and Spanish authorities to apprehend British adventurer William Augustus Bowles, the self-proclaimed "Director General of Muscogee," whose activities in East Florida were blamed for strengthening Creek resolve against further land cessions to the United States. Hawkins used a gathering of Creeks, Cherokees, Choctaws, and Chickasaws planned for May 1803 at the Hickory Grove (near present-day Montgomery, Alabama) to lure Bowles into United States territory, believing that Bowles would use the opportunity to reassert his influence among the southern Indians and have himself declared "a king of the four nations." Arriving at the council with a band of Seminole followers, Bowles was seized by a party of Upper Creeks, handcuffed, and carried away to be turned over to Spanish authorities in West Florida. He was eventually imprisoned at Havana, where he died in 1805 (Florette Henri, *The Southern Indians and Benjamin Hawkins, 1796-1816* [Norman, Okla., 1986], 233-8; J. Leitch Wright, Jr., *William Augustus Bowles: Director General of the Creek Nation* [Athens, Ga., 1967], 162-7, 171; Madison, *Papers, Sec. of State Ser.*, 5:14-15, 44, 49, 161-3; Vol. 32:52n; Vol. 36:154-7n; Vol. 37:8n).

THAT CRISIS IN OUR AFFAIRS: in his 18 Feb. letter, TJ remarked on Hawkins's long absence "from this part of the world" and the "great change in social intercourse" that had occurred in the interim. In particular, TJ emphasized the schism over the Jay Treaty that "went on widening and rankling till the years 98. 99. when a final dissolution of all bonds civil & social appeared imminent." Since then, however, the people had awakened from the "phrenzy," returned to their "sober & antient principles," and united overwhelmingly behind a sentiment of "peace, economy, and a government bottomed on popular election in it's legislative & Executive branches" (Vol. 39:546).

For the SUSPICIONS EXCITED IN GEORGIA that accused Hawkins of favoring Creek interests over those of the United States, see Vol. 39:518-23, 548.

[1] Word interlined.

[2] Preceding two words interlined.

To Meriwether Lewis

TH: JEFFERSON TO CAPT. LEWIS Washington July 11. 03

I inclose you your pocket book left here. if the dirk will appear passable by post, that shall also be sent, when recieved. your bridle, left by the inattention of Joseph in packing your saddle, is too bulky to go in that way. we have not recieved a word from Europe since you left us. be so good as to keep me always advised how to direct to you. accept my affectionate salutations & assurances of constant esteem.

PrC (DLC); endorsed by TJ in ink on verso.

JOSEPH: Joseph Dougherty.

Party Affiliation of Federal Officeholders

I. MEMORANDUM FROM HENRY DEARBORN, [CA. MAY 1803]

II. TABLE ON PARTY AFFILIATION OF FEDERAL OFFICEHOLDERS IN THE STATES, [BEFORE 11 JULY 1803]

III. TABLE OF FEDERAL OFFICEHOLDERS IN THE STATES, [CA. 11 JULY 1803]

IV. TABLE OF OFFICEHOLDERS IN THE GENERAL GOVERNMENT, [CA. 11 JULY 1803]

V. NOTES ON REPUBLICAN APPOINTMENTS, [CA. 11 JULY 1803]

VI. ALBERT GALLATIN'S COMMENTS, [CA. 11 JULY 1803]

EDITORIAL NOTE

Spurred by dissension in Republican ranks in Philadelphia over Federalists who remained in lucrative offices, Jefferson decided to study the party affiliation of those who had received presidential appointments. Writing Peter Freneau on 20 May, he reviewed his administration's patronage policy, noting that when he took office the Federalists "possessed all." By removing those Federalists who took "an active & bitter part against the order of things established by the public will" and through delinquencies, resignations, and deaths, Republicans now had "our full proportion of offices in all the states except Massachusetts." To support this assertion, Jefferson collected and evaluated evidence during the weeks before he left for Monticello. Writing William Duane on 24 July in response to the Address of the Philadelphia Ward Committees, the president contended that of the 316 offices "subject to appointment & removal by me 130. only are held by federalists." The documents printed below provide insight into how he arrived at those numbers. In Document III, Jefferson calculated that 158 officers, exactly half of his total, were Republicans.

Of the 316 offices, 109 were in the "general" government composed of the executive officers in Washington; holders of diplomatic and consular posts; officers of the U.S. Mint in Philadelphia; and officers of the territorial governments, including land office receivers and registers (see Document IV). The 207 federal offices held at the state level were the collectors, naval officers, and surveyors appointed by the president to collect external revenues; the marshals and district attorneys appointed as officers of the federal courts; and loan commissioners (see Document II). All of these appointments required Senate approval. Jefferson excluded judicial and military appointees from the count, arguing that they were not removable "but by established process." He excluded internal revenue officers because their offices were discontinued through repeal of the direct taxes. He left out postmasters because they were "solely within the gift & removal of the Post Mast. Genl. the President & Senate having nothing to do with them" (Vol. 40:466). Government clerks, who were appointed by the department heads and did not require Senate approval, were also excluded. With the passage of the April 1802 amendment of the Judiciary Act, the president became responsible for the naming of bankruptcy commissioners. Jefferson paid careful attention to these nominees and entered their names on several lists, including the chronological one he kept throughout his presidency (Vol. 37:697-711). The Senate did not confirm these appointments, however, and Jefferson, realizing the Bankruptcy Act would be repealed during the next session of Congress, did not include the bankruptcy commissioners in his study. The president was undecided over incorporating the officers of revenue cutters, perhaps because they were part of the custom house establishment. Their appointments did not require Senate confirmation and their names usually did not appear on his list. In the end, Jefferson excluded them in Document II, but not before he had entered them at several states in Document III, where he calculated the total number of officers.

The president received input from at least two members of his cabinet. Henry Dearborn's memorandum (Document I) provides the party affiliation of government clerks and of army, navy, and marine corps officers. If these categories had remained in Jefferson's calculations, Federalists would have outnumbered Republicans by more than two to one. On 11 July, Gallatin sent the president an updated list of the collectors, naval officers, and surveyors at each port, that is, all customs officers appointed by the president and confirmed by the Senate. The manuscript had separate columns for those selected after Jefferson took office and the reason for the change. The list included the latest nominations: Thomas Durfee, surveyor at Tiverton, Rhode Island; Charles Gibson, surveyor at Easton, Maryland; and Brian Hellen, collector at Beaufort, North Carolina. All of them had been appointed to newly created posts in June 1803 (see Enclosure No. 3, listed and described at Gallatin to TJ, [11 July], first letter). Assuming that only Federalists were appointed before 3 Mch. 1801 and only Republicans after that date, the schedule enabled the president to determine the affiliation of external revenue officers. Jefferson also turned to the roll of civil, military, and naval officers in the United States, which Gallatin compiled in 1801 and published in early 1802. The roll provided the names of all employees in charge of collecting the revenues, including weighers, gaugers, and masters and mates of the revenue cutters. The president sent the Treasury secretary at least one of his compilations, upon which Gallatin made extensive comments (see Document VI). Gallatin noted the names of several revenue officers who, although appointed during previous administrations, were Republican. Jefferson prepared his own list of Republicans in office, perhaps in response to Gallatin. Jefferson emended Document II to reflect Gallatin's comments.

Documents III, IV, and V are all on one, undated, sheet. It would be difficult to determine the state officeholders included in Document III, if it were not for Jefferson's data from Document II. There he noted the number of Republican, nonpartisan, and Federalist collectors, surveyors, naval officers, revenue cutter officers, marshals, U.S. attorneys, and loan commissioners by state. By adding the figures in the three columns for each state, he obtained the totals he needed for Document III. However, the results in Document II often vary with those in Document III. The decision to exclude officers of revenue cutters and other emendations Jefferson made to Document II are not reflected in Document III, the table that he used to derive his totals when he added the results from Document IV to it.

Jefferson singled out Massachusetts as the state where Republicans did not yet have a fair share of offices. Republicans in Rhode Island complained that

Federalists still controlled the lucrative offices in their state (Joseph Stanton and Samuel Potter to TJ, 14 Dec. 1803). Jefferson's emended table (Document II) supports the complaint. In New Hampshire, Vermont, New York, and the western states, Republicans held almost all of the offices. Pennsylvania was evenly divided. But in Maryland and the southern states, including Virginia, Federalists significantly outnumbered Republicans. Only Georgia was evenly divided. As Nathaniel Macon wrote Jefferson from North Carolina on 3 Sep., "during the present administration, not a single person has been dismissed from office in this state, although with one exception I believe they were all federal."

I. Memorandum from Henry Dearborn

[ca. May 1803]

	Republican.	Fedl.
Heads of Departments—including the Post M. G.	6.	0
secondery officers in the above Departments—	2	5
Clerks in said departmts.	19	77
Foreign Ministers	3	0
Judges	8	25
District Attorneys	17	2
Marshalls	16	3
Territorial Officers	4	6
Surveyors Genl.	1	1
Collectors of the customs	23	41
others officers in the customs who receive considerable pay	25	50
Loan officers	4	9
	128	219
Officers of the Army	38	140
Do—of the Navy	7	70
Marine Corps	0	29
	176[1]	458
Indian Agents	6	4

MS (DLC: TJ Papers, 235:42199); in Henry Dearborn's hand; undated, but see below.

The absence of a Federalist at Dearborn's entry for FOREIGN MINISTERS indicates that he compiled this list after Rufus King had officially left his position as U.S. minister to Great Britain in May 1803. In June, Monroe proceeded to London as the new U.S. minister, carrying a commission dated 18 Apr. (Vol. 39:66; Vol. 40:229-30).

SURVEYORS GENL.: on 7 Apr. 1803, TJ appointed Isaac Briggs to the newly established office of surveyor general of lands south of the state of Tennessee and, on 21 May, asked Jared Mansfield to replace Federalist Rufus Putnam as surveyor general of lands north and west of the Ohio River. Mansfield traveled to Washington in early June to converse with Albert Gallatin and obtain more information on the office, but it is not clear when Dearborn knew of the proposed change. At the time Dearborn prepared his list, the Republican Briggs had taken office and Putnam remained the surveyor general (Vol. 40:12, 410-12, 497, 717).

COLLECTORS OF THE CUSTOMS: not all are included in Dearborn's count of 64. Seventy-eight collectorships were listed in the 1802 roll of government officers. Using the up-to-date list of external revenue officers provided by Gallatin, TJ tabulated (Document II) 85 collectors—35 Republicans, 47 Federalists, and 3 who were neutral (ASP, *Miscellaneous*, 1:261-80; Enclosure No. 3, listed at Gallatin to TJ, [11 July 1803], first letter).

Although the president sent promotions for OFFICERS OF THE ARMY to the Senate for confirmation, he left the recommendations up to Dearborn and did not include the nominations in his chronological list (Vol. 40:717-18). Because of the established process for handling military promotions, the officers were overwhelmingly Federalist (Vol. 39:551-2, 614-15; TJ to William Duane, 24 July). TJ followed the same procedure with Robert Smith for NAVY and MARINE CORPS appointments (Vol. 39:600, 614-15; Vol. 40:10; Robert Smith to TJ, 27 Mch. 1804). Early in the process, TJ decided not to include military appointments in his tabulations.

[1]Thus in MS. The actual sum is "173."

II. Table on Party Affiliation of Federal Officeholders in the States

[before 11 July 1803]

	New Hampsh[1]			Massachu[2]			R. Island[3]			Connecticut[4]			Vermont[5]			New York[6]			New Jersey			Pennsylva			Delaware			Maryland[7]			Virginia[8]			N. Carola[9]			S. Carola			Georgia			Tennissee[10]			Kentucky			Ohio		
	r		f	r		f	r		f																																							
Collectors	1			10	1	12	1		2	2		2	1			3	1	1	3		2	1		1			1	2		8	5	1	8	2		4			3	2		3				1			1		
Naval Officers	1			1	1	1	1		1							1								1						1			1			1			1			1									
Surveyors	1			1	1	5	3		6	1		5				3			1					1				2		3	2		6	8		9	1					1									
<Mstr rev. cuttr.>	*<1*		*1*			*1*				*1*								*1*						*1*									*1*						*1>*												
<mates of do>	*<1*		*1*			*1*				*1*								*1*						*1*									*1*			*1*			*1>*												
District Atties	1			1		1	1			1			1			1			1			1			1			1		1	1					1			1	1			2				1		1		
Marshals	1					2			1	1			1			1			1			1			1			2			1				1		1			1				1		1			1		
Commrs. loans	1					1			1			1				1					1		1				1			1			1			1			1	1											

MS (DLC: TJ Papers, 133:22993); undated; entirely in TJ's hand; on a vertically lined, thin sheet of paper; three blank categories are not reproduced above; at some point, TJ canceled the categories for revenue cutter officers as indicated by the italicized text and numerals in angle brackets; other emendations made by TJ, sometimes in pencil, after receiving comments by Gallatin (see Document VI and notes below).

TJ evidently began this table early in his efforts to determine the number of Republicans and Federalists in public office, and he continued to update it. After entering categories for land surveyors and land office receivers and registers, he decided that those officers were connected with the territories and not the states; he canceled and transferred them to his tabulation of federal officers in the general government (see Document IV). They are not entered above. In the end, TJ also canceled the categories of masters and mates of revenue cutters, but not before he had made entries under the states and, subsequently, included some of the information in his tally of officeholders in Document III. The president appointed the officers on revenue cutters, but they did not require Senate confirmation and, therefore, did not meet all of TJ's requirements for inclusion.

Before TJ made the emendations as indicated in the notes below, he used this table to establish the total number of Republican, neutral, and Federalist officeholders by state in Document III. TJ updated the table, above, to its final form after receiving Gallatin's notes (Document VI), but he did not change the state tallies in Document III. This accounts for many of the discrepancies between the two documents. For instance, in Document III, TJ records that there are six Republicans and six Federalists in office in Rhode Island. In Document II, above, in response to Gallatin's comments, TJ emended the number of Federalist surveyors to six, increasing the Federalist total to 11. TJ included the revenue cutter officers at several states, indicating that he retained the entries for masters and mates until later in the process.

DISTRICT ATTIES: states were usually a single district for U.S. attorneys in 1803. In the table above, Massachusetts has two district attorneys because it included the District of Maine; Maryland has two because TJ decided to include the Potomac District under the state. At the time, Tennessee was divided into eastern and western districts. The same applied to marshals in the entries above (Vol. 33:671, 676; Vol. 37:608-9).

[1] At the New Hampshire entry, TJ added the "1" in pencil in the Republican column at "Mstr rev. cuttr." and the "1" at mates. In the Federalist column, he altered, perhaps in pencil, a "2" to "1" at master; the "1" in ink at mates is canceled with pencil strokes.

[2] At Massachusetts, TJ interlined "10" in place of an illegible number in the Republican column for collectors. In the Federalist column he altered the "11" to "12." At the district attorney entry, TJ may have altered a "2" in the Republican column to a "1" and added the "1" in the Federalist column after Gallatin noted that Silas Lee, U.S. attorney for the District of Maine, was a Federalist (see Document VI).

[3] At Rhode Island, TJ altered the number of surveyors in the Federalist column from an illegible numeral to "6."

[4] At Connecticut, TJ altered the number of surveyors in the Federalist column, probably from a "4" to a "5."

[5] At Vermont, TJ erased the number in the Federalist column at commissioner of loans.

[6] At New York, TJ altered the number of collectors in the Federalist column from an illegible number to "1." At the same time he may have added the "1" in the neutral column.

[7] At Maryland, TJ probably altered the political affiliation of the five surveyors, adding "2" to the Republican column and altering the "5" in the Federalist column to a "3." TJ evidently decided to add the U.S. attorney and marshal from the Potomac district to the Maryland tally, adding "1" to the Republican column for district attorney and altering the number of Republican marshals from "1" to "2."

[8] At Virginia, TJ altered the number of collectors from an illegible numeral to "5"

in the Republican column; added a "1," in pencil, in the neutral column; and altered the "6" to an "8" in the Federalist column.

[9] At North Carolina, TJ altered the number of surveyors in the Republican and Federalist columns by overwriting indecipherable numerals in ink.

[10] At marshals under this state, TJ partially erased the "2" in the Republican column and added a "1" in the neutral column. He forgot to enter a "1" over the erasure. In Documents III and VI, both TJ and Gallatin entered "4" Republicans at the tally of Tennessee officeholders.

III. Table of Federal Officeholders in the States

[ca. 11 July 1803]

	r	o	f		
N.H.	6		3		
Mas.	13	1	24		
R.I.	6		6		
Conn.	7		5		
Verm.	3		1		
N.Y.	10		5		
N.J.	6		3		
Pens.	3	1	5		
Del.	2		2		
Maryld.	4		13		
Virga	10	1	16		
N.C.	9	1	12		
S.C.	1		9		
Georg.	5		5		
Ten.	4				
Kenty.	2	1			
Ohio	2				
	93	5	109	=	207
Genl.[1]	65	21	23	=	109
	158	26	132		316

MS (DLC: TJ Papers, 234:41919); undated; entirely in TJ's hand; on same sheet as Documents IV and V.

This table is TJ's final tally of Republican and Federalist officeholders. He compiled the individual state totals using data from Document II before he emended that table. Thus, several state tallies, above, include officers of revenue cutters, a category TJ ultimately deleted. They do not reflect Gallatin's comments (see Document VI), which TJ incorporated through emendations to Document II. But Document III, above, is the one to which TJ added his totals for officers in the general government from Document IV to obtain his grand totals.

N.H.: all six federal officers in New Hampshire were Republican. They included the collector, naval officer, and surveyor at Portsmouth, and the U.S. marshal, U.S. attorney, and commissioner of loans. All appeared on the List of Appointments and Removals TJ prepared after 10 May 1803. Joseph Whipple, collector, and William Gardner, commissioner of loans, were two of the four TJ had restored to office (Vol. 33:670-2). The three officers TJ entered in the Federalist column were evidently those he associated with the revenue cutters (see Documents II and VI). For variances in TJ's totals for Massachusetts, which included the district of Maine, see same.

R.I.: Rhode Island had a total of 14 external revenue officers, including nine surveyors, six of whom were Federalists. For the six Republicans in TJ's tally, see Documents II and VI. Gallatin surmised that TJ overlooked five Federalist surveyors in his count.

In Document II, TJ calculated that there were seven Republican officers in Connecticut (CONN.), including the master and mate of the revenue cutter. Without them there were only five—Alexander Wolcott and Samuel Bishop, collectors, William Munson, surveyor, Pierpont Edwards, U.S. attorney, and Joseph Willcox, marshal (Vol. 33:331n, 669, 671, 672, 674n, 675, 678; Document V, below). In his comments, Gallatin indicated that there were five Federalist surveyors in the state. TJ evidently included only two in his tally, above, because two collectors and the loan commissioner were also Federalists (see Documents II and VI).

VERM: Documents II and VI indicate that Vermont had a total of three officeholders, all Republican. Here TJ included Nathaniel Brush as the Federalist commissioner of loans, perhaps following the 1802 roll of Federal officeholders, where he was identified as such. He was actually Vermont's supervisor of internal revenues, a position TJ did not include in his calculations (ASP, *Miscellaneous*, 1:281, 305).

TJ included the masters and mates of revenue cutters in his Federalist count for New York (N.Y.) and Pennsylvania (PENS.); see Document II. For Gallatin's argument that there was only one Federalist officeholder in New York, see Document VI. Gallatin and TJ agreed that Stephen Moylan, Pennsylvania's commissioner of loans, was associated with neither party (ASP, *Miscellaneous*, 1:305).

MARYLD: TJ made very few changes in Maryland's external revenue offices. He appointed two collectors—Alexander Scott at Nanjemoy and John Oakley at Georgetown—and named Charles Gibson surveyor at the newly erected district of Easton. Reuben Etting, marshal of the Maryland district, was definitely one of the four Republicans in TJ's count (Vol. 33:231n, 668, 670, 673, 675, 677; Vol. 36:335; Vol. 37:579n; Vol. 39:131, 314, 315n; Appendix I). For the Virginia (VIRGA) totals, see notes to Document VI.

N.C.: by the end of the process, TJ and Gallatin agreed that North Carolina had 10 Republican and 16 Federalist officers. U.S. Marshal John S. West, reappointed by TJ in 1802, was the neutral officer (Vol. 38:635-6; Vol. 39:127n; Documents II and VI). After consultation, TJ and Gallatin also agreed that there were two Republican officers in South Carolina (S.C.). Gallatin's comments (Document VI) indicate that Edward Weyman, surveyor at Charleston since 1793, was a Republican. In Document II, TJ identified the marshal, that is, Robert E. Cochran, as the other Republican (Vol. 33:514n; Vol. 38:515n).

TJ and Gallatin assigned Joseph Hamilton Daveiss, appointed U.S. attorney for the Kentucky (KENTY) district by Adams in December 1800 and usually identified as a Federalist, to the neutral or nonpartisan column. TJ removed him from office in 1807 (DAB; Madison, *Papers, Pres. Ser.*, 2:205; Vol. 32:562-3n; Vol. 38:666; TJ to Madison, 14 Mch. 1807).

GENL.: for TJ's totals of officers in the general government, see the next document.

[1]For the tallies here TJ first wrote "58," "20," and "16" for a total of "94," the results TJ entered from Document IV (see note 4) before he added several categories. TJ then overwrote the numbers to read as above, which reflects his final totals in Document IV. TJ also altered the grand totals from "151" to "158," "25" to "26," "125" to "132," and "301" to "316."

IV. Table of Officeholders in the General Government

[ca. 11 July 1803]

	r	o	f
heads of deptmts.	5		
Secondaries[1]	3	1	1
Purveyor	1		
Mint officers[2]	1		1
foreign ministrs.	3		
Secs. of legn	2		
Consuls	34	20	12
Govs. of territories	2.		
Secretaries do	1		1
Attornies	1		
Marshals	1		
Collectors[3]	4		1
Directrs. marine hosp.			
	<58	*20*	*16* >[4]
Survrs. Genl.	2		
Recievrs.	2		4
Registers	3		3
	65	21	23

MS (DLC: TJ Papers, 234:41919); undated; entirely in TJ's hand, made in several sittings; at the head of this table, TJ entered notes on which the first twelve entries, with several variations, are based (see notes below); on same sheet as Documents III and V.

HEADS OF DEPTMTS.: TJ included Attorney General Levi Lincoln. The SECONDARIES probably included Republicans Gideon Granger, postmaster general, Gabriel Duvall, comptroller, and Thomas T. Tucker, treasurer. Joseph Nourse, register of the Treasury, who began serving in the Treasury Department under the Confederation Congress, was considered nonpolitical or neutral. Richard Harrison, auditor, was probably the Federalist TJ had in mind. He was in charge of settling TJ's accounts as minister to France (Noble E. Cunningham, Jr., *The Process of Government under Jefferson* [Princeton, 1978], 103, 180-1, 328-30; ASP, *Miscellaneous*, 1:304; Vol. 24:169, 171-5; Vol. 33:62, 423n, 670).

Tench Coxe assumed the office of PURVEYOR of public supplies in place of Israel Whelen on 1 Aug. 1803 (TJ to Madison, 12 July).

MINT OFFICERS: TJ here included Federalist Elias Boudinot, director of the U.S. Mint, and Republican Benjamin Rush, treasurer (Vol. 33:423n; see note 2, below).

For a list of the 63 CONSULS and commercial agents in office in late 1801, see ASP, *Miscellaneous*, 1:307-8. TJ made several consular appointments to locations not on the 1801 list due to vacancies or new designations, including William Stewart to Smyrna, Marien Lamar to Madeira, and Levett Harris to St. Petersburg (Vol. 35:154; Vol. 37:205n, 348; Vol. 39:214).

SECRETARIES DO: in May 1800, John Adams appointed William Henry Harrison governor and John Gibson secretary of the newly established Indiana Territory. TJ included Harrison as one of the eight Republicans in office on 3 Mch. 1801. The Senate confirmed, on 3 Mch. 1803, TJ's appointment of Cato West in place of Federalist John Steele, who had continued as secretary of Mississippi Territory after William C. C. Claiborne became governor in May 1801 (*Terr. Papers*, 7:9-10, 13-17; Vol. 33:599n, 671; Vol. 37:3-5; Vol. 39:196n, 615; Document v, below).

ATTORNIES: TJ included his appointment of John Thomson Mason as U.S. attorney for the District of Columbia under the heading of general government. MARSHALS: Daniel Carroll Brent for the District of Columbia (Vol. 33:345, 380n, 671, 675).

At the head of the sheet, TJ noted that Indiana Territory had three Republican, one Federalist, and no neutral—"o"—COLLECTORS and that Mississippi had one Republican collector. TJ canceled Ohio with its one Republican collector and recorded the information under Ohio as a state (see Documents ii and iii). TJ considered Matthew Ernest, appointed collector at Detroit by John Adams in January 1800, a Federalist. Gallatin informed the president that David Duncan, whom TJ had appointed collector at Michilimackinac in 1801, was also a Federalist and that Daniel Bissell, assigned to Massac in 1802, was "unknown" or neutral, but TJ retained the designations above (JEP, 1:332, 333; Vol. 33:671; Vol. 38:21, 518, 682; Vol. 39:258n; Document vi, below).

Gallatin identifies the land office receivers (RECIEVRS) and REGISTERS, along with their party affiliations, in Document vi.

[1] In the draft list above this table, TJ clearly noted that there were "3" Republicans, "1" neutral, and "1" Federalist in this category. Here, however, he initially entered "0" in the neutral column. He later emended it to read "1," as above. He also emended the final total from "20" to "21."

[2] In the draft list, TJ entered: "Mint. Director f.1" and "Treasurer r.1."

[3] This is the final entry in TJ's draft list.

[4] Before TJ canceled these totals, he entered them under totals for the "Genl." government in Document iii, where he then had to alter them to reflect the totals from the added categories in this table and the emendation (see note 1).

V. Notes on Republican Appointments

[ca. 11 July 1803]

<*Offices expd & not renewed*		*6.*
restorations to office		*4.*
Atties & marshals on principle		*5.*
other officers.		*14*
removals for delinqs.		*23*
		52
vacancies	*12*	
deaths, resignns, promotions	*25*[1]	
offices expd & not renewed	*6*	
restorns to office	*4*	
removls. on principle participn	*19*	
removals for delinquency	*23*	
	52	
deaths resignns promns	*99*	
	151>	

Removals	to restore formr officers	4	
	on principle of particpn	19	
	for delinquency	23	46
Expired offices not renewed			6
deaths, resignns, promotions			98[2]
			<*151*>
republicans under formr admn.[3]			8
			158

Repub. found in office

Conn.	Wm. Munson
	Pierpoint Edwards
N.Y.	W. S. Smith
Del.	George Read
Virga	Laurence Muse
	Thos. Nelson
Pensva	Benj. Rush.
Indiana	W. H. Harrison.

MS (DLC: TJ Papers, 234:41919); undated; entirely in TJ's hand; the two canceled sets of notes appear to the right of TJ's final compilation; with the names of those Republicans found in office written on verso; on same sheet as Documents III and IV.

TJ consulted his List of Appointment and Removals "arranged in classes," which extended to 10 May 1803 (see Vol. 33:670-4), to compile the data, above, on Republican officeholders in both the state and general government. He used that document, printed as List 3 in Appendix I in Vol. 33 of this series, to obtain the figures for all of the final categories, above, except for those individuals "resigned, declined, promoted or dead," the first class under which 25 Republicans are named, as indicated in the first entry in the canceled text, above, for "deaths, resignns, promotions." Another 12 names appear on the 10 May list under "Vacancies left unfilled when I came into office." TJ had a category in that list, not included above, for "Midnight appointments," which TJ "considered as Null." There he named another 22 Republicans, for a total of 59 in the three categories (Vol. 33:670-2). According to the total in Document III, above, however, 158 Republicans were holding office. To obtain that number in the compilation, above, TJ had to increase significantly his total of deaths, resignations, and promotions to "99." He decreased that number to "98" after he added a new classification for those Republicans already in office (see notes 2 and 3, below).

TO RESTORE FORMR OFFICERS: according to TJ's 10 May list, four Republicans had been removed "on principles not justifiable" and were restored to office (Vol. 33:672).

ON PRINCIPLE OF PARTICPN: this combines categories six and seven from the 10 May list, that is, the 5 "Attornies & Marshals removed for high federalism" and the 14 other "removals on the principle of giving some participation in office to republicans," 19 in all. TJ handled these categories separately in his first set of canceled notes, above. The 23 removed for DELINQUENCY or misconduct are named in categories eight and nine. The six officers who did not have their commissions RENEWED made up the third group, which included Cato West, appointed secretary of Mississippi Territory in March 1803, upon the expiration of John Steele's term (same, 671-3).

REPUBLICANS UNDER FORMR ADMN: this category was not on TJ's May 1803 list, and, therefore, he identifies these Republican officeholders by name. Appointed by Washington in 1793, William MUNSON was the surveyor and revenue inspector at New Haven. Washington appointed PIERPOINT EDWARDS U.S. attorney for the District of Connecticut in September 1789 (JEP, 1:29-30, 129-30; Vol. 33:44-6). For the debate over Adams's appointment of his son-in-law William S. SMITH as surveyor and revenue inspector of the port of New York, see Vol. 32:351-2 and Vol. 39:490, 491n. At the same time Edwards received his appointment, George READ became U.S. district attorney for the state of Delaware. Washington appointed Lawrence MUSE collector and revenue inspector for the port of Tappahannock in 1794 and Thomas NELSON, U.S. attorney for the District of Virginia in 1796 (JEP, 1:29-30, 149, 205, 206). For other Republicans in office when TJ became president, see Document VI.

[1]TJ canceled this and the preceding entry before he canceled the whole section. At the same time he altered the total from "89" to "52" and added another line for deaths, resignations, and promotions, with a designation of "99."

[2]Altered from "99" (see note 3).

[3]After adding this category, TJ altered the "99" to "98," to give a new total of "158," the total number of Republicans in Document III.

VI. Albert Gallatin's Comments

[ca. 11 July 1803]

N. Hampshire— only one Master & one Mate revenue Cutter—Hopley Yeaton & Benj. Gunnison. appd. 31 Augt. 1802—both rep. — rep. 6.—. —.

Massachusset— Jonas Clarke collect. Kennebunk—fed. appd. only Inspector of revenue by Mr Jefferson

Fred. L. Delesdernier collect. Passamaquody rep. certainly
Melatiah Jordan Do. Frenchmen's bay do. says so
Asa Andrews Do. Ipswich do. or neut.
} —see page 52— 23 collectors in all & 7 surveyors old appointments

<*James Lovell Nav. Officer Boston*>
Ths. Melville Surv. Boston
} neutral } do.

} 13. 3. 21

Silas Lee dist. att. Maine fed. new appt.

10 coll.	1 coll.—	12 coll.
1 nav.	1 nav	1 nav.
1 Surv	1 surv	5 Surv.
1 D attor.	3	2 Mars.
13		1 Com
		21[1]

Rhode Island—	in all 9 Surveyors—3 rep. 6 fed. supposed		6.—.11
Connecticut—	in all 6 do 1— 5 do.		5.—. 7
	Mate rev. cutter—unknown		
New York—	only 5 Collectors—Niagara not organised Henry P. Dering Collect. of Sag harbour rep. in all—3 rep. 1 fed. 1. neut. (Wolsey) Caleb Brewster Mast. rev. cutter—rep. new appt.		10. 1. 1
Vermont—	No Commissioner of loans		3.—.—.
Pennsylva.—	Richd. Howard Mastr. rev. cutter rep. appd. 1802 Joseph Sawyer mate do. do. reappd. do.		3. 1. 3
		Delaware	2.—. 2
Maryld.—	in all 5 Surveyors of which 3 fed. & 2 rep. vizt. Gibson & Delozier of Baltimore		5.—.14
Virginia—	Isaac Smith Collect. of Cherry Stone *neut* & not rep. who is the other neutral?[2] Bright Mast. rev. cutter rep. } two cutters Ham do neut. } two cutters 2 Mates unknown } two cutters in all 12 Surveyors—say 2 rep. 10 fed		9. 2.18
		Kentucky	2. 1
N. Carolina—	in all 16[3] Surveyors 7 do. 9 do.		9. 1.16
Tenessee—	Hays Mars. W. Tenessee *neut.* a new appt. expected		4.—.—
S. Carolina	E. Weyman Surveyor *rep.*[4]	S. Car.	2.—. 6
Indiana—	D. Duncan collect. Michillimakinac—fed.	Geor.	5.—. 5
	Bissel do—Massac—unknown		3.—.— total
	officer of army	Ohio	87.9.104. 200

Secondaries—The Accountants of War & Navy dep. Omitted—both fed: perhaps Symons *neut.*

Mint officers—Coiner &a. appd. by President omitted—Voight rep.

Att. & Mars. Territories—Who?

	Steubenville–	Marietta–	Zaneville–	Chilicothe–	Cincinnati–	Natchez–	Mobile
Registers L. Offices–	Hoge– *fed–*	Woods *rep*	vacant	Jesse Spencer. *rep.*	Ludlow *fed*	Turner *rep*	vacant
Receivers do–	Biggs do–	Bacchus *neut*	do	S. Finley do.	J Findly do.	vacant	vacant

Total

2 fed. 3 rep. 2 vacant

2 do. 1 rep. 3 vacant —1 neut.

Superintendent Mil. Stores. W. Irvine—rep. omitted.

States—[5]	87.	9.	104
Territ. —.	3.	—	1
Collect. do.	2.	1.	1
Land	11.	1.	4
Mint	2.	—.	1
Purv. & Super. M.S.	2.	—.	—.
Departments	8.	1.	3
For. ministers & Sec.	5.		
Barbary	2.	—.	1
	122	—12	—115

MS (DLC); undated; entirely in Gallatin's hand. Enclosed in Gallatin to TJ, [11 July] (first letter).

N. HAMPSHIRE—ONLY ONE MASTER & ONE MATE: evidently Gallatin was commenting on Document II, above, or possibly a similar set of notes on which TJ had entered the number of masters and mates of revenue cutters. Before he altered Document II, TJ indicated that New Hampshire had two Federalist masters and a Federalist mate. While Gallatin commented on the revenue cutter appointments, he did not include them in his state totals. For the appointment of Hopley Yeaton and Benjamin Gunnison as officers of the new revenue cutter at Portsmouth, see Vol. 38:243n, 301n, 373, 425.

Adams appointed Jonas Clark (CLARKE) collector at Kennebunk in May 1800. In August 1801, Gallatin informed the president that for some reason Clark had not received a commission as inspector of the revenue. For the discussion of his appointment, where it became clear that Clark was a Federalist, see Vol. 35:54, 57n, 85, 108, 158. On his appointment list, TJ entered Clark as a nominee to fill a vacancy and, therefore, assumed that he was a Republican (Vol. 33:671, 677).

Early in his administration, Washington appointed Lewis F. DELESDERNIER, a Gallatin friend, collector at Passamaquoddy. In the 1802 roll of government officers, Delesdernier's information does not appear with the other 22 collectors at Massachusetts and Maine ports, but instead is entered at the end of the section on external revenues, that is, PAGE 52 of the publication ordered by the Senate (*Message from the President of United States, Transmitting a Roll of the Persons Having Office or Employment under the United States* [Washington, D.C., 1802; Sowerby, No. 4166], 12-21, 52; Washington, *Papers, Pres. Ser.*, 3:378; Raymond Walters, Jr., *Albert Gallatin: Jeffersonian Financier and Diplomat* [New York, 1957], 137). Washington nominated MELATIAH JORDAN, JAMES LOVELL, and Thomas Melvill (MELVILLE) at the same time he appointed Delesdernier (Washington, *Papers, Pres. Ser.*, 3:44-5, 378; Vol. 35:726n). In March 1803, TJ appointed Thomas Lovell, son of the Boston naval officer, commercial agent at La Rochelle, France (Vol. 39:283-5, 614, 615n).

For the appointment of SILAS LEE, a Federalist, see Vol. 33:219, 670; Vol. 34:131n; and Vol. 38:612, 613n.

RHODE ISLAND: the three Republican surveyors included John Cross, Jr., at Pawcatuck, and John Slocum, at Newport, both appointed in February 1802, and Thomas Durfee, appointed to the newly erected district at Tiverton after TJ compiled his May 1803 list of appointments. The other three Republican appointees in Rhode Island were Walter Nichols, naval officer at Newport, Jonathan Russell, collector at Bristol, and David Howell, U.S. district attorney (Vol. 33:187-8, 670-3, 675, 678, 679; Vol. 36:331, 332; Vol. 37:323, 324n; Gallatin to TJ, 11 June). 6 FED. SUPPOSED: in Document II, above, TJ altered the number of Federalist surveyors to agree with Gallatin's comment.

According to TJ's tally in Document II, CONNECTICUT had eight Federalist officeholders, not seven as indicated by Gallatin, who apparently forgot to include the commissioner of loans in his total. MATE REV. CUTTER—UNKNOWN: TJ had recently promoted George House, the Republican mate of the revenue cutter at New London, to master. Evidently the vacant office of mate had not been officially filled (Vol. 40:339, 344, 347, 718).

NEW YORK: Washington appointed Henry P. Dering in March 1792. The two other Republican collectors were David Gelston, at New York City, and Joel Burt, at Oswego. The Federalist collector was Henry Malcolm at Hudson. Gallatin considered Melancthon L. Woolsey (WOLSEY), appointed collector at the port on Lake Champlain in 1793, as neutral in politics (Washington, *Papers, Pres. Ser.*, 8:503-4n; 10:42-3; 12:247-8; Vol. 38:89n, 677n; Vol. 39:155n).

NO COMMISSIONER OF LOANS: see note at Document III, above.

For the appointment of Richard HOWARD and JOSEPH SAWYER to the Delaware River revenue cutter, see Vol. 37:325, 326n, 578.

MARYLD.: for TJ's appointment of Charles Gibson, see Document III, above. Washington appointed Daniel Delozier surveyor at the port of Baltimore in August 1793. Republican congressman Samuel Smith was among those who highly recommended him (Washington, *Papers, Pres. Ser.*, 13:382-3n).

TJ appointed ISAAC SMITH collector at Cherrystone in November 1801. He was highly recommended by Samuel Smith, who described him as "Invariably a Whig," but also a Federalist, in a county where almost all were Federalists, though "not of the Vicious kind" (Vol. 33:673, 677; Vol. 35:665, 674). Two revenue cutters were stationed at Norfolk. Francis BRIGHT served as master of the first and William HAM of the second (ASP, *Miscellaneous*, 1:274; Vol. 34:356-7, 527). IN ALL 12 SURVEYORS: TJ appointed two surveyors at Virginia ports, perhaps the two Gallatin designated as Republican. John Eason replaced Thomas Blow at Smithfield, and William White became the twelfth Virginia surveyor when he was appointed to the newly created district of East River in 1802. A new collector, Francis Armistead, was also appointed at East River. TJ appointed three other collectors—Thomas Archer, at Yorktown, John Shore, at Petersburg, and Mount Edward Chisman, at the port of Hampton—all assumed to be Republican. Gallatin calculated that there were 29 federal officeholders in Virginia while TJ had 27 (see Document III). Perhaps Gallatin included Federalists Charles Simms and Hugh West, collector and surveyor at Alexandria, respectively, while TJ included them in the District of Columbia under the general government. It is not clear whether Gallatin identified Lawrence Muse and Thomas Nelson as Republicans as TJ did (see Document V). TJ perhaps consulted an earlier list that did not include the recent appointments at East River. It is not certain how they arrived at their different totals (ASP, *Miscellaneous*, 1:274; Vol. 33:672-3; Vol. 38:6, 7n, 447n, 462, 568, 680, 682; Vol. 39:131; 1803 list of external revenue officers described as Enclosure No. 3 at Gallatin to TJ, [11 July], first letter).

NEW APPT. EXPECTED: for the Treasury secretary's efforts to replace Robert Hays, marshal of Tennessee's western district, see Gallatin to TJ, 18 Aug.

For testimony that Edward WEYMAN, appointed surveyor at Charleston by President Washington in 1793, was a Republican, see Vol. 33:514n. Gallatin interlined this entry and changed his tally for South Carolina and the total for the states to reflect one more Republican, indicating that he gained the information after he had completed his comments (see notes 4 and 5, below). The five custom officers in South Carolina retained their offices after TJ became president. TJ, however, did not include Weyman on his list of Republicans in office in March 1801 (see Document V, above). The second Republican in Gallatin's tally was probably Robert E. Cochran, who replaced Charles Burnham Cochran, his brother, as U.S. marshal in South Carolina in October 1802 (Vol. 38:515, 682). In Document II, above, TJ agreed with Gallatin and designated two Republicans in South Carolina, the surveyor and marshal. In Document III, however, TJ counted only one Republican officeholder. His total of ten officeholders, compared to Gallatin's eight, indicates that he included the master and mate of the revenue cutter at Charleston.

In his TOTAL of 200 state officeholders, Gallatin did not include those of New Jersey. He undoubtedly agreed with TJ's total of six Republicans and three Federalists and, therefore, made no observations. He did not comment on officeholders in Delaware, Kentucky, or Georgia, but he entered tallies for those states.

ACCOUNTANTS: William Simmons at the War Department and Thomas Turner at the Navy Department (ASP, *Miscellaneous*, 1:304; Noble E. Cunningham, Jr., *The Process of Government under Jefferson* [Princeton, 1978], 330).

In January 1793, Washington appointed Henry VOIGHT chief coiner in the U.S. Mint (JEP, 1:127). ATT. & MARS.: probably presidential appointments for the District of Columbia (see Document IV and the 1803 list of external revenue officers described as Enclosure No. 3 at Gallatin to TJ, [11 July], first letter).

LAND: under this total, it is not clear how Gallatin arrived at 11 Republicans. He identified four in the land offices, and both surveyors general were Republican (see Document IV). Perhaps Gallatin assumed the five vacancies would be filled with Republicans.

[1]Preceding tabulation from "10 coll." to "1 Com" (for commissioner of loans) was inserted by Gallatin to explain how he arrived at the the totals for Massachusetts. He circled the tabulation and connected it with the brace at the state's totals, "13. 3. 21." Gallatin forgot to add "1" district attorney at the Federalist column, which accounts for the discrepancy with Document II, where TJ accounts for 22 Federalists, excluding the two officers of the revenue cutter.

[2]Question interlined.

[3]The numbers "17" and "8" are inserted below "16" and "7," respectively.

[4]Entry interlined. At the same time, Gallatin altered the "1" to "2" in the Republican column and the "7" to "6" in the Federalist column at the tally for South Carolina. He also altered the totals for this section to agree with the change.

[5]Gallatin here altered "86" to "87" in the Republican column and "105" to "104" in the Federalist column to reflect the change at South Carolina (see note 4). He also altered the grand total, below, from "121" to "122" for the Republicans and "116" to "115" for the Federalists.

To William Thornton and Family

Monday July 11. 03.

Mr. Madison and his family take a family dinner with Th: Jefferson tomorrow (Tuesday). Will Doctr. Thornton and his family join us?

RC (DLC: William Thornton Papers); addressed: "Dr. Thornton."

To James Wallace

SIR Washington July 11. 03.

Your letter of May 19. was recieved in due time, and that of the 6th. inst. came to hand last night. the duties of my present office calling for the whole of my time, and even that being insufficient, and rendering it necessary to leave unacted on whatever will admit of it, the first of your favors remained unanswered. under these circumstances I am obliged to deny myself the gratification of indulging in speculations of the nature of those in your letters, and which, were I free, would be peculiarly agreeable to me. trusting that your candour and good sense will admit this apology as arising from the necessity of my situation, I tender you my salutations and best wishes.

Th: Jefferson

PrC (DLC); at foot of text: "Mr. James Wallace. N. York."

Wallace's lengthy letter of the 6th expanded on some of the ideas expressed in his earlier letter, which he characterized as an attempt "to give an Idea of the System of the Universe, from some expressions found in the 15th. Chapter of St Paul to the Corinthians." Pointing to Columbus's explorations and Newton's development of his theories of gravity and of light and color, Wallace praised their benefactors, without whom they would have lacked the resources to carry out their pursuits. Although Wallace was not assuming that his embryonic system was "entitled to any degree of merit" or support, he hoped that it would get a hearing from qualified judges. He had turned to TJ because he understood him to be less prejudiced in his cultivation of knowledge than professors at colleges and universities. Now "fully convinced of the truth of" his system, he saw it as a way of harmonizing "philosophy and revelation, Uniting, and declaring to man the Extent of the Creation." It was, Wallace argued, "from the motions observed in the System of the World we draw such undenible arguments of the existance of a Deity." Subsequent mechanical innovations and scientific discoveries would reveal the ways that light supplied the motive force for the universe and that it was "the cause of every active principle and property in matter, abstracted of divine influence." Although "these things requiring deep investigation cannot be settled in a hurry," Wallace intended to disprove through his theory of light some of Newton's conclusions regarding planetary motion. He did not want to imply that science should be yolked to a particular religious tenet, as in previous eras, "yet in our enquiries, where there is a manifest agreement between Nature and Revelation, it ought to be noticed." True philosophy and true religion were both founded in nature. In his closing paragraphs, Wallace hinted that he would benefit from TJ's help in securing a position at an institution "where my assistance might be useful—where I could pursue these Studies with advantage to the Subject, and help to diffuse the Knowledge of these Sciences among many of the youth of Columbia" (RC in DLC; at head of text: "To his Excellency, Thomas Jefferson President of the United States"; endorsed by TJ as received 10 July and so recorded in SJL).

From Caleb Bickham

District of Southwork 7. Mth. 12th. 1803

On the fall & Rising of the Tide in Every Creek River & Bay the one & same Cause so ordered & ordained by the Great Creator of all things both Land & Sea. And whereas many learned & wise men has made some steps towards finding out the cause why it should be so but have failed in their researches and left this Generation to wander farther in this great Secret without comeing to the true point & for

After ages to Ramble in the falling & raising of the Tide in Every Creek River & Bay

To Begin right in every thing we undertake is the surest way to End right. Therefore I begin at the falls of the river Delaware to shew the Beginning of the Ebb Tide & falling of the Waters which I think every Man of Common Reason will agree with the Author that the Land Springs Rains and melting of the Snows which flow from the Land into every River is the Beginning of the Ebb Tide which forceth its ways by degrees to the Sea this being the case I proceed to shew the beginning & cause of the flood Tide so leaving the Ebb Tide a little way from its beginning & passing over several Ebb & Flood Tides down to the Sea shore where the Great Mystery is hid the beginning & rising of the flood Tide & the cause thereof whose bounds is set by God Almighty to go so far & no further. now to make this more easy for Readers understanding in the first place to know that where two Body's that move & meet the Lightest Body must Give way to that which is more Weighty Just so it is with the Ebbs & Floods. I must confess that while I am penning these Lines I am at a Great Loss for words to Convey my true meaning but I pass on in hopes to Give more Light on this Undertaking & so begin with the Ebb Tide that Empty's itself out of the Delaware Bay in to the Sea now it is a point agreed on by most Men if not all that the Ebb Tide passes but a few Miles into the Sea however less or more it matters not it passes so far untill it can pass no further now here lies the Mystery it is true the Ebb in passing out is of greater Weight than the Shoal Waters along the Sea Shores therefore they give way & fall a few feet But when these small waters compared with the great & boundless Ocean they appear to be light almost Nothing at all so that the Weight of the Great & mighty Sea pressing on the Small Waters of the Bay that passeth out causes them to return into the Bay & River from whence they came & this is the Beginning of the Flood & the Wonderful Workings of God thus to Bring things to pass which he has Ordained it is Wonderful to behold the Change & Manner of this Great Weight of Water Working in the Sea in Raising the Flood I have a Machine forty feet Long will shew the Strivings of the two Waters the Flood & the Ebb by the machine when the Water is clear to the Bottom shews the Flood breaks in underneath the Ebb first in a Small flow at the Bottom of the Sea which increaseth forward with still greater power where it can be plainly seen the Water pass by each other for a Short Season at Length the Weighty waters of the Sea prevail as I said before & that is underneath which causes the Water to Rise & this is the rising of the Tide of Flood The Ebb Tide

I conceive passeth off[1] from the Top of the Water & this will account for the falling of the Water or Ebb Tide But to return again to the Tide of Flood that is running up the Bay where it continues running & rising untill it meets a more powerful & weightier Water than its Self & then[2] it must Give way back again & is called the Ebb Tide Just so is the Ebb Tide after it Passeth down a certain Distance it meets a Flood which brings a Weightyer Water with it & turns the Ebb Waters as before & so on I believe there never was or Ever will be a Flood turned or an Ebb Tide turned without a more Weightier bodys of Water to do it The Ebb is the Great & Mighty machine if I may so Name it that forceth the Flood to do his Work so Ordered in the Course of things was the Land Springs of Water to cease & flow no more in the River the Rains & Snows done away which no power can Effect but God Almighty for in him is all power then & not untill then the Bays & Rivers would become a dead sea Now what is Wrote in this Piece in Regard to the falling & rising of the Tides if any person is at a loss to Comprehend the true meaning of what the Author has set forth it would be well for him to suspend his Judgment[3] for a While untill he has it in his power to ask the Author some Questions on the point relating to the falling & rising of the Tide which he will be Ready & willing to answer any Question that may be proper on the Occasion for these things are true & must remain unchangeable only the Winds sometimes may alter the rising or falling of the Tide from one Hour to Three what lead me to look into this great secret at this time was This I was conveying water down in a machine for Quite another purpose which gave me a sight and understanding & cause of the falling and rising of the Water or Ebb & Flood Tides I believe it will be acknowledged by some that my remarks are reasonable On the falling and rising of Tides yet I go further & shew it by the machine to those that are desirous to see it after I had written these lines it was then to whom shall I dedicate them & I said in my Heart to thee the Chosen of the People I have taken this Freedom hoping thee will excuse me for it has arisen out of pure motives for thy approbation or otherwise these remarks has not gone out nor have been seen by any person neither shall they until thee shall say something on them I have no wish to give the trouble But only wish a few lines from thee at some leisure time directed to Caleb Bickham in the District of Southwark adjoyning the City of Philadelphia By Post. May the God of Peace grant thee tranquility and Length of days and give thee wisdom to do his will for he has set thee over a Great People to raise them up & save them from there Enemies & after a final close of thy days may God Allmighty grant thee a resting place among the Blessed is the sincere prayer of one of thy best Friends.—

CALEB BICKHAM

RC (DLC); at foot of text: "Thomas Jefferson Presidt. of the United States"; endorsed by TJ as received 21 Oct. and so recorded in SJL.

Caleb Bickham (ca. 1736-1811), a Philadelphia Quaker stave and lumber merchant, retired from the business at the beginning of April 1803. His interest in hydrography continued and resulted in the publication of *An Essay on the Falling and Rising of the Tides* printed by Daniel Humphreys in Philadelphia on 12 July 1805, with portions of the text drawn from this letter (Shaw-Shoemaker, No. 8033; *Gazette of the United States*, 9 Apr. 1803; Anna M. Watring, *Early Quaker Records of Philadelphia, Pennsylvania*, 2 vols. [Westminster, Md., 1998], 2:278).

[1] MS: "of."
[2] MS: "thon."
[3] MS: "Judgmet."

From Stephen Cathalan, Jr.

DEAR SIR Marseilles the 12th. July 1803

I had the honor of Paying my Respects on the 31st. May Last, in answer to your much respected favor of the 7th. Feby. Last; remitting you Bill of Lading & the Invoice of Sundries Shipped by your order & for your account on the american Brig fair american John Spear Master bound for Boston; hereunto Inclosed you will find a Bill of Lading for the Same, with another one for one chest Conting. 50 Bottles old hermitage White wine, which was shipped at Cette, on the american Ship Pyomingo Pascal Blagge Mastr. for new york to be Consigned unto the Collector of the Customs to be forwarded to you; I also remit you, here Inclosed The Invoice of the whole, amounting together to F885—which I charge on your Debit, & when convenient, you may Remit me on Paris;—I will not fail of Sending you the other articles you desire from me, when it will be the proper Season, too far advanced now; very happy I will be when you will procure me opportunities to be usefull to you, in any thing you will command me;

Mr. Monroe has favored me with a very friendly Letter, mentioning that tho' he is[1] not the Minister Resident, he will do Every thing in his Power, even near Mr. Livingston, to Cause my exequatur to be Granted;—I have Since Learned, that "it was to the Minister Resident to make the official Demand for Such exequaturs, & this Information I had from the chief in the office of the forreing Relations, which was the Cause that my exequatur had not been yet Granted, & my Memorials unanswered; that there was not any Doubt now, it would be, Since Two french natives had obtained their own, thro' their respective Embassadors;"—I have then, advised Mr. Livingston of what occurs, on the 22d. ulto., entreating him to make the official demand, by a note to the forreign Relation's Minister, (which he had never made by writing) begging to take in Consideration my Request, & your wishes for me;—& I doubt not that if he makes the demand it will be Granted, as Soon as this Minister & the 1st. Consuls, will be returned from their voyage in Paris;—

I have (entre nous) Some Reasons to apprehend that Mr. Livon. in Stead of having assisted me Since the Two French natives obtained their Exequatur, and having asked the Same for me, was protecting Some of his Friends, near you;

Messus. Cathn. & my Daughter, are at the Baths of *ax*, in the Pyrenean Mountains, my old Father & Mother Presents you their Best respects & wishes;

I have the honor to be with Great Respect Dear Sir Your most obedient humble & Devoted Servant

STEPHEN CATHALAN JUNR.

I am to the 21st July & I have received a Lettr: from Mr. Livingston, dated Paris the 12th. July Inst. mentioning me "I will make the application on the Subject you Require, when I See the Minister, he is now absent, & Should I write, the Business, will Probably be neglected till his return"

Then now at Last my affair is en bon train;

I have a young man in Philadelphia of 20 years of age under Care now of Mr. felix Imbert my Power of attorney who failed 10 months ago, whom I Sent in the year 1796, with the american Captives from algiers, & the young orleans there; almost the proceeds of my 12 Shares in the Bank of the U.S. have been employed for his maintainance, but it appears that now the Situation of Mr. Imbert, is the Cause he is himself in a poor Situation, & these dividens are not all applied to him!, I am writing to him (his name is *Julius olivier*,) & to Mr. Felix Imbert, & if necessary Shall transfer my Power of attorney, but I would wish he Should be acknowledged an american Citizen, & if Possible employed in Some line as Clarke in a Public office, meantime I could have him back as my chancelor &ca. I will take the liberty Probably to introduce him to you by a Letter;

here Inclosed one of his Letter; you would add and Confer a new favor, if you would extend your kind Protection over him;—as I have not any male child, and want in my old Days to be assisted, I hope he will, be able of Conducting in a few years my affairs, & to give him a Comerce, to encourage him.

Your most obedt. Servt. STEPN. CATHN JUNR.

I am writing to Jas. Madison Esqr. Secy. of State, on the affairs of this agency.

RC (DLC); below first signature: "The honble. Thos. Jefferson President of the United States of America"; endorsed by TJ as received 14 Oct. and so recorded in SJL. Enclosure: Julius Olivier to Cathalan, Philadelphia, 15 Mch. 1803; Olivier, being not yet 28 years old, must wait to become an American citizen; he is lacking many necessities, such as decent clothing, but Felix Imbert says that the allowance from Cathalan has been expended; Imbert "has Scarcely any money for himself Since the misfortune has happened to him"; "I am afraid," Olivier writes, "you dont think of me often, nevertheless it is my duty to look up to you as my preserver" (RC in MHi). Other enclosure not found. Enclosed in Cathalan to Madison, 13 July (Madison, *Papers*, *Sec. of State Ser.*, 5:173-4).

The merchant ship PYOMINGO arrived at New York by 11 Aug. (New York *Daily Advertiser*, 11 Aug.; David Gelston to TJ, 12 Aug.).

MR. LIVON.: Robert R. Livingston.

EN BON TRAIN: well underway.

Philadelphia merchant FELIX IMBERT had been in the import-export trade and speculated in land (Philadelphia *Dunlap's American Daily Advertiser*, 26 July 1794; *Philadelphia Gazette*, 9 Nov. 1798; *Aurora*, 12 Jan. 1805).

In 1796, several dozen AMERICAN CAPTIVES released by ALGIERS were taken to Marseilles, where Cathalan as U.S. consul provided them with aid until they could complete a quarantine and he could arrange passage for them to the United States. Most of them arrived in Philadelphia in February 1797. YOUNG ORLEANS: also in 1796, the Duchesse d'Orléans sent her son Louis Philippe to the United States for his safety. He remained until 1799 (Gary E. Wilson, "American Hostages in Moslem Nations, 1784-1796: The Public Response," *Journal of the Early Republic*, 2 [1982], 139-40; Vol. 29:312-13, 369).

[1]Word supplied by Editors.

To Henry Dearborn

TH:J. TO GENL. DEARBORNE. July 12. 03.

The dangers on the road to Natchez are really serious, & calling for attention. mere stationary posts, as proposed by Govr. Roan, appear to me inefficient. either a small body of cavalry, or mounted infantry, to be perpetually scouring the road and hovering about the caravans of passengers, as a marechaussée, seems worthy of consideration, as also the employing Indians in the same way, or offering rewards for apprehension & conviction of offenders.[1] altho' the running the Creek line would be a useless expence if we acquire adjacent territory, yet as that acquisition seems to be put off indefinitely, perhaps it may be our duty to have the line run.

RC (PHi: Daniel Parker Papers); endorsed by Dearborn. PrC (DLC); lacks final sentence. Recorded in SJL with notation "outrages on road to Natchez."

DANGERS ON THE ROAD TO NATCHEZ: on 11 July, the War Department received a letter from Governor Archibald Roane of Tennessee, dated Knoxville, 9 June, regarding "a robbery committed on the 10. May last" (DNA: RG 107, RLRMS). During that month, several persons traveling the road between Nashville and Natchez were assaulted and robbed, including a United States mail carrier and a man named Alexander Wilkins. Another traveler, Reuben White, was murdered. On 18 July, Dearborn issued a proclamation, "By order of the President of the United States," offering a reward of $400 for the apprehension of those involved in these crimes or any person committing like offenses on the road during the next year (FC in Lb in DNA: RG 107, MLS; *Federal Gazette and Baltimore Daily Advertiser*, 24 Sep. 1803). On the same date, he directed Thomas H. Cushing, the adjutant and inspector of the army, to station a detachment of troops on the Tennessee and Duck Rivers with orders to use every exertion "to apprehend any persons who have or shall be guilty of murdering, robbing or in any way annoying Post Riders or any other persons peacably travelling sd road" (*Terr. Papers*, 5:224-5). Dearborn wrote Roane, also on 18 July, informing him of these actions and assuring the governor that the president "is desirous of affording every aid in his power" to render the road "as safe & convenient as circumstances will permit." This included TJ's desire to establish inns on parts of the road through Indian territory, which would "afford great security as well as convenience to travellers." In the meantime, Dearborn advised those traveling the road with large sums of money to organize themselves into armed caravans, but anticipated that transporting money through the wilderness would become less frequent once New Orleans and its dependencies were in possession of the United States (FC in Lb in DNA: RG 107, MLS).

[1]PrC ends here.

To Albert Gallatin

TH: JEFFERSON TO MR GALLATIN July 12. 03.

The strengthening the revenue cutters by the addition of another mate & 2. hands is approved. while our cutters must be large enough to go safely to sea, and should be well manned for their size, we should avoid making them larger than *safety* will require; because many small vessels will watch the coast better than a few large ones. *resistance* will not be attempted probably. Genl. Muhlenberg's idea of forming the cutters into a line of communication seems to be a good one. I should suppose it well to partition the whole coast among them by certain limits.

It is difficult to see what mr Bond would be at. I suppose he aims at our citizen laws. there is a distinction which we ought to make ourselves, & with which the belligerent powers ought to be content. where, after the commencement of a war, a merchant of either[1] comes here & is naturalized, the purpose is probably fraudulent against the other, and intended to cloak their commerce under our flag. this we should honestly discountenance, & never reclaim their property when captured. but merchants from either, settled & made citizens before a war, are citizens to every purpose of commerce, & not to be distinguished in our proceedings from natives. every attempt of Gr. Brit. to enforce her principle of 'once a subject & always a subject' beyond the case of *her own subjects*, ought to be repelled. a copy of Genl. Muhlenburg's letter, stating the fact of citizenship accurately, ought to satisfy mr Bond, unless he can disprove the fact; or unless, admitting the fact, he at once attacks our principle. on that ground we will meet his government.

As to the patronage of the republican bank at Providence, I am decidedly in favor of making all the banks republican, by sharing deposits among them in proportion to the dispositions they shew. if the law now forbids it, we should not permit another session of Congress to pass without amending it. it is material to the safety of republicanism, to detach the mercantile interest from it's enemies, and incorporate them into the body of it's friends. a merchant is naturally a republican, and can be otherwise only from a vitiated state of things. affectionate salutations.

RC (NHi: Gallatin Papers); endorsed. PrC (DLC). Recorded in SJL with notation "revenue cutters. Bond. republicn. bank."

STRENGTHENING THE REVENUE CUTTERS: on 13 July, Gallatin sent a circular letter to Benjamin Lincoln, David Gelston, Peter Muhlenberg, and other collectors with revenue cutters, authorizing them "to employ two additional hands" and to "recommend a proper person as second mate." They were cautioned to hire the extra seamen only if they thought it "essential to the public Service" (see Gallatin, *Papers*, 8:534; 47:860). MUHLENBERG'S IDEA: in the closing sentences of his 8 July letter to Gallatin, the Philadelphia collector suggested forming a line of communication between the revenue cutters on the coast to enable them to keep "an eye on the different inlets between the Capes" where coasting vessels carried on "an unlawful traffic with Vessels from Foreign Ports." Muhlenberg concluded: "If this communication between the Cutters is found practicable, I have no doubt it will tend more to prevent an illicit trade, than any other precaution that can be taken" (see Enclosure No. 1, listed at Gallatin to TJ, 11 July, first letter).

Immediately after receiving the 7 July letter of complaint from Phineas BOND, Muhlenberg submitted it to Alexander J. Dallas. The district attorney agreed with Bond that vessels owned by French citizens and armed in Philadelphia after the rupture between Britain and France should not be permitted to leave the port. This did not apply, however, to an American citizen, who was naturalized "previously to the existing hostilities between those Nations." So far as respects our government, Dallas contended, the act of naturalization "forever closes the question of the place of nativity. Our Constitution and laws make no difference between an adopted, and a native, Citizen" (Tr in DNA: RG 59, NL). For the Bond letter, see Enclosure No. 2 at Gallatin to TJ, 12 July (second letter).

[1]Preceding two words interlined.

From Albert Gallatin, with Jefferson's Reply

Dear Sir   Tuesday [12 July 1803]

You will perceive by the enclosed that the port of Allburg, which Mr Bradley insisted upon so much that the commission in favr. of Mr Pennyman is given as Collector of that port, is an ideal town where vessels cannot come to & deliver their cargoes for want of a wharf, & where it would be most inconvenient to Secure duties as the Merchants do not live there. Indeed I think the commission not valid, & that his acts may hereafter be disputed. He should have been entitled "Collector of the district of Vermont"; and I would advise issuing a new one & revoking the order which makes Allburg the port of entry

Respectfully Your obedt. Servt.   Albert Gallatin

I enclose the draft of letter to Mr Heard

[*Reply by TJ*:]

I think full enquiry should be made not only as to the port of Alburg, but as to the best place for the final establishment of the Custom house, & this being done we may proceed with safety. important circumstances in the selection of a port are vicinity to the line, vicinity to the residence of merchants, deep water to the shore commanding a view of all the vessels which pass &c. the 2d. condn is the least essential. the 3d important, because I doubt our right to build wharves, & have no doubt of the inexpediency of entering into the exercise of it.

Th:J.
July 12. 03.

RC (DLC); partially dated; endorsed by TJ as received from the Treasury Department on 12 July and "Allburgh" and so recorded in SJL; with TJ's reply at foot of text; TJ wrote "copy" to the left of his initials, indicating that he sent a separate response to Gallatin and this was TJ's FC, but the letter was not recorded in SJL and has not been found. Enclosures not found.

For the recommendations by Stephen R. Bradley and others in favor of Jabez Penniman (pennyman), see Gallatin to TJ, 18 Jan. Penniman was confirmed by the Senate as "Collector and Inspector of Allburgh, on Lake Champlain." To the consternation of the British, Alburgh, a few miles from the Canadian border, had been designated the port of entry in 1791 when Vermont entered the union. A controversy erupted in 1792, when the British laid claim to jurisdiction over the town because of its proximity to the British post of Pointe-au-Fer. When David Russell, Penniman's predecessor, took office in early 1797, he was appointed "Collector of South Hero" in the district of vermont. The Treasury Department noted that the port of entry was changed from South Hero back to Alburgh when Penniman was appointed. Alburgh kept that designation for decades. When Samuel Buel succeeded Penniman in 1811, he was appointed "Collector of the district of Vermont, and Inspector of the Revenue for the port of Alburgh." In 1850 a bill was introduced to make Burlington the port of entry and delivery instead of Alburgh, but it did not pass (Washington, *Papers, Pres. Ser.*, 8:229-31; 10:457-8; *Spooner's Vermont Journal*, 18 Mch. 1811; JEP, 1:223, 441; 2:165; 9:152; JS, 41:279; "List of Officers of the External Revenue," 4 Mch. 1801-16 June 1803, in DNA: RG 59, Appointment Papers; Vol. 20:467; Vol. 24:160-2n; Vol. 39:437).

Gallatin had received a complaint that John HEARD, collector at Perth Amboy, was not paying "the proper monies in his hands" to the Treasury. Gallatin later noted that on 12 July 1803, he wrote Heard "that unless he made payment, his conduct would be reported to the President." On this date, Gallatin also wrote New Jersey senator-elect John Condit, requesting that he look into the situation at Perth Amboy and recommend a replacement if it became necessary. Condit noted that it would be difficult to find a candidate, explaining, "there is not I believe One Single Character living in that place that would accept & could do the Duties of the Office who is not a Violent and bitter Opposer of the present administration." Condit agreed to search for a suitable candidate, but he hoped Heard would "Comply with his Duty and Prevent the Necessity of a Change." During 1804, the collector was "more prompt and regular" in his payments, but in early 1806 he was removed for delinquency. It was found he owed the U.S. Treasury $3,549.30 (Gallatin, *Papers*, 8:547; 19:417; *Biog. Dir. Cong.*; Gallatin to TJ, 29 Jan. 1806).

From Albert Gallatin

Treasury Department
July 12th. 1803.

SIR,

I have the honor to enclose the copy of a letter from the Collector of Philadelphia, covering one from the British Consul in that City, and of the answer which I have prepared.

The orders issued from this Department on the 8th. of April 1797 and 21st. of March 1798 are also enclosed. Subsequent to these last, the law of the 25th. of June 1798 regulated the same subject, but expired in 1802. Whether it may be necessary to add any further instructions is respectfully submitted to the President.

I have the honor to be, very respectfully, Sir, Your most obed. Ser.

ALBERT GALLATIN

RC (DLC); in a clerk's hand, signed by Gallatin; at foot of text: "The President of the United States"; endorsed by TJ as received from the Treasury Department on 14 July and "Bond's complt." and so recorded in SJL. Enclosures: (1) Peter Muhlenberg to Gallatin, Philadelphia Custom House, 8 July 1803 (see Enclosure No. 1 described at Gallatin to TJ, 11 July, first letter). (2) Phineas Bond to Muhlenberg, Philadelphia, 7 July, questioning the neutrality of two vessels, the schooners *Nancy* and *Adventure*, by charging that they are "owned by French men, who upon the first Report of a Rupture between England & France armed their vessels" in violation of "that Neutrality, which I earnestly hope may subsist between Great Britain & the United States"; the character of one of the masters and "the Number of Guns, on board, and the quantity of Amunition they have provided, shew they have in View Purposes beyond the mere Defence of their Vessels, against the Barges of the Brigands, as was at first insinuated"; Bond wants the vessels detained "until You can obtain the Sense of Your Government"

(RC in DNA: RG 59, NL). (3) Circular to the Collectors of Customs, Treasury Department, 8 Apr. 1797, responding to the question of whether it is lawful to arm merchant vessels of the United States for protection while engaged in regular commerce; Treasury secretary Oliver Wolcott, Jr., advises that it is lawful for vessels engaged in the East Indies trade to be armed, but if vessels "destined for European West-India commerce" are armed, they are to be "restrained" until Congress ordains otherwise (Tr in same). (4) Circular to the Collectors of Customs, Treasury Department, 21 Mch. 1798, modifying the circular of 8 Apr. 1797, under the direction of the president of the United States, so as to no longer "restrain Vessels of the United States from sailing in an armed condition, when destined to be employed in a regular and lawful commerce"; collectors are to continue to seize and detain all vessels suspected of being employed "contrary to law" and to uphold the Act of 14 June 1797, "prohibiting for a limited time the exportation of arms and ammunition, and for encouraging the importation thereof" (same). For other enclosure, see below.

ANSWER WHICH I HAVE PREPARED: probably TJ made no changes to Gallatin's answer to the Philadelphia collector dated 12 July. The Treasury secretary assured Muhlenberg that the information provided in his letter of the 8th (see Enclosure No. 1, above) left "no doubt" that the vessels "had a right to proceed on their voyage." The expiration of the law of 25 June 1798 left it to the discretion of the collector to investigate and detain vessels suspected of disobeying neutrality laws. Gallatin also responded to Muhlenberg's remark that he had refused "to enter into further discussion" with Phineas Bond, the British consul, and had "referr'd him to the Secretary of the Treasury." Gallatin advised Muhlenberg that as a collector he should not "enter into discussions with the consuls of either of the Belligerent Powers." It was sufficient that he investigate the facts when a complaint was made and then decide in conformity with instructions from the Treasury Department and his own view of the subject. Gallatin encouraged Muhlenberg to communicate doubtful cases to his office, but warned that he should never refer a consul of a foreign nation to the Treasury Department. If the consul did not agree with the collector's decision, "let him apply" to his "Minister who may communicate with the Secretary of State, this being the only proper channel for every discussion of that Nature" (Tr in DNA: RG 59, NL; Gallatin, *Papers*, 8:531). Bond did inform Edward Thornton, the British chargé, of the case (see note to TJ to Madison, 16 Aug.).

LAW OF THE 25TH. OF JUNE 1798: Section 3 of the "Act to authorize the defence of the Merchant Vessels of the United States against French depredations" demanded that before the collector issued a clearance, the owner or master of an armed U.S. merchant vessel had to give a bond equal to twice the value of the vessel. The bond guaranteed that the ship would not "commit any depredation, outrage, unlawful assault, or unprovoked violence upon the high seas, against the vessel of any nation in amity with the United States." The ship was to return to the U.S. with the same guns, arms, and ammunition, or give an accounting of them. The guns were not to be "sold or disposed of in any foreign port" (U.S. Statutes at Large, 1:572-3).

Memorandum from Albert Gallatin

[on or after 12 July 1803]

Mr Mansfield misunderstood me on the subject of instruments. I requested him, as he went through Philada., to order them to be made, & to let me know the price, which I intended to remit to him. Salary cannot be advanced; it must be paid quarterly at the end of the quarter; the only exceptions are in case of officers going out of the United States, & that of the President who does not receive quarterly; and even in the last case no advance has ever been made during the *present* Presidency. If Mr M. had done what I requested, he would have met, however, with less embarrassment. The enclosed sketch of a letter I may send to him; but wish to know his direction & present office.

The date of his commission will not alter the time from which his salary must commence. That, in case of existing offices, always commences from the time only when the new officer takes possession of the papers &a. Till then the former officer's salary continues; and unless you should give special instructions to the contrary which must be officially communicated to the Auditor & Comptroller, they will certainly settle the accounts in conformity to the universally received practice— A. G.

MS (DLC: TJ Papers, 124:21447); entirely in Gallatin's hand; undated, but see below. Enclosure not found.

MANSFIELD MISUNDERSTOOD: see Jared Mansfield's letter to TJ of 7 July, which the president received this day and evidently forwarded to the Treasury secretary. Probably after TJ received this memorandum, he and Gallatin met and worked out a solution for Mansfield's predicament (TJ to Mansfield, 18 July 1803).

From Reuben Harvey

Pleasantfield near Cork
July 12th 1803

I made free to write thee a few lines the 3rd of last month from Kinsale on the matter of Men being pressed out of American Vessels that arrive & touch at Cork & in a few days after I received an answer from your Consul at London to my communications of the 27th & 28th May with his request that I would continue to acquaint him when fresh causes of complaint arose; The pressing your people having met no check from the Regulating Captain I wrote Earle St Vincent, first Lord of the Admiralty, a Letter the 27th ulto, of which I enclose thee a Copy & in course of post received a reply as follows— Lord St. Vincent presents his Compliments to Mr. Harvey and assures him that a particular order has been given with respect to Americans & that his Lordship will cause the Circumstance he Stated to have happened at Cork to be enquired into.—

Admiralty 2nd. July 1803—

Immediately after my receiving this Letter, I transmitted to Lord Gardner (who had then just arrived at Cove) Copys of my letter to the First Lord of Admiralty & his reply & I now enclose thee a Copy of Lord Gardner's Answer, the last lines of which are remarkable, he there Says "That he will pay due attention to all Such Seamen as can procure fair & clear documents of their being Citizens of America.—I shall not presume to Comment on what he reckons is to constitute an American Citizen, but refer that point to thee, observing however that if all the Crews of American Ships must be *Natives* of America to free them from the Press, your Commerce must Suffer extremely for I apprehend there are many thousands of Irish English & Scotch, settled & become Citizens of America,—The Bearer being on the point of Sailing, I conclude with Sincere Regard &c.

REUBEN HARVEY SENR.

RC (DLC); at head of text: "Thomas Jefferson Esqr. President of Congress"; endorsed by TJ as received 7 Sep. and so recorded in SJL. Enclosures: (1) Harvey to Earl St. Vincent, Pleasantfield near Cork, 27 June 1803; Harvey begins by stating that his character is known to their mutual friend, the Marquess of Landsdowne, that he corresponded with Colonel Isaac Barré during the American Revolution, and that he received the thanks of George Washington and Congress in 1783 for his efforts on behalf of American prisoners at Cork; Harvey proceeds to call St. Vincent's attention to the excesses of British press officers against American vessels at Cork, few of which escape without losing at least one or two, or as many as five, crew members; Harvey feels these actions are especially severe since these men carry no protections because they entertained no idea of war between Great Britain and France, and thus had no need for sea letters; Harvey believes that "limitted conduct" toward American vessels would benefit both America and Britain; Harvey's continued attachment to America animates him "to wish well to her Citizens & to hope that nothing should ever cause a misunderstanding between Great Britain & the United States," and he asks St. Vincent to order the regulating officer at Cork, Captain Chilcott, not to treat Americans harshly; Harvey adds that an American from Portland named Reuben Mitchell, who carried a protection, was nevertheless taken away and detained overnight, and was not liberated until his captain made oath that he was born in America; after visiting Chilcott, Harvey was told that the incident was caused by "some ill Language between American Seamen & the Press Gang" (Tr in same). (2) Lord Gardner to Harvey, *Dryad* in Cork Harbor, 9 July 1803, acknowledging the receipt of copies of Harvey's correspondence with Earl St. Vincent on the subject of American seamen "indiscriminately impressed" at Cork; Gardner replies that Harvey will always find him "exceedingly disposed" to keep up good relations between Great Britain and the United States, and that he would attend to "any well founded representations of any improper Conduct of those officers appointed at this Crisis to superintend the Impress Service, within the Limits of my Command, and that I Shall pay due Attention to all such Seamen as can produce fair & clear documents of their being Citizens of America" (Tr in same).

CONSUL AT LONDON: George W. Erving.

Admiral Alan GARDNER, first Baron Gardner, was the Royal Navy's commander of the Irish station (DNB).

Memorandum to James Madison

Commissions to be made out:

Thomas Rodney of Delaware to be judge of Missipi. vice S. Lewis

Thomas Rodney of Delaware } to be Commnrs. &c West of
Robert Williams of N. Carolina } Pearl river.

Ephraim Kerby of Connecticut } to be Commnrs. &c East of
Robert Carter Nicholas of Kentucky } Pearl river.

a blank commission for the Register East of Pearl river.

Tenche Coxe of Pensylvania to be Purveyor. his commission to bear date Aug. 1. 1803. on which day mr Wheelen has fixed his own resignation.

TH: JEFFERSON
July 12. 1803.

MS (PWacD: Feinstone Collection, on deposit PPAmP); entirely in TJ's hand; check marks later added in left column next to each entry in an unidentified hand; addressed: "The Secretary of State."

A commission appointing RODNEY and WILLIAMS to ascertain the rights of persons claiming lands in Adams County, Mississippi Territory, and another for Kirby (KERBY) and NICHOLAS to carry out the same duties in Washington County are dated 12 July (Lb in DNA: RG 59, MPTPC).

To John Armstrong

SIR Washington July 13. 1803.

Your favor of June 4. has been duly recieved. on recurring to the deed of Genl. Kosciuzko to Madame Felix I observe he guarantees to her 1st. the existence of the land, that is, that these lands were real, and not merely ideal, as many which had been sold in Europe. 2. the situation, to wit geographical situation. 3. title. 4. contents. 5. delivery of possession. the objections mentioned in mr Smith's letter are 1. that Made. Felix purchased this for 1st. rate land and thinks it only 2d. 2. the want of a spring noted in the plat. 3. the want of a run noted there also. with respect to the spring they appear & disappear so frequently as never to be deemed sufficient to invalidate a sale. and with respect to all the objections they are such as make no part of the guarantee, and you are sensible would not be thought in this country to affect the bargain. altho' the expence of resurveying the land by mrs Felix's order can[1] not legally be put on Genl. Kosciuzko, yet in the case of a stranger I would yield what a native would not expect. if you will be so good, or Colo. Worthington to whom perhaps it might be more convenient, as to pay mr Smith I will either pay the money here to order (as I did in the former occasion to mr McShane), or I will remit it in bank bills if they pass with you. I make no account of these things to Genl. Kosciuzko, as so small a trifle would not be worth the trouble it would cost. accept my salutations, and my thanks on his behalf which you are so kind as to take.

Th: Jefferson

PrC (MHi); at foot of text: "John Armstrong esq."; endorsed by TJ in ink on verso.

THE LAND: for Armstrong's involvement in the location and sale of Tadeusz Kosciuszko's military grant in Ohio to Louise Françoise Felix, see TJ to Armstrong, 21 Dec. 1802, and Armstrong to TJ, 4 June 1803.

FORMER OCCASION TO MR MCSHANE: see TJ to Barnabas McShane, 28 June 1803.

[1] Word interlined in place of "would."

To Pierre Jean Georges Cabanis

Dear Sir Washington July 13. 1803.

I lately recieved your friendly letter of 28. Vendem. an. 11. with the two volumes on the relations between the Physical & moral faculties of man. this has ever been a subject of great interest to the inquisitive mind, and it could not have got into better hands for discussion than yours. that thought may be a faculty of[1] our material organisation, has been believed in the gross: and tho' the modus agendi of nature in this as in most other cases, can never be[2] developed and demonstrated to beings limited as we are,[3] yet I feel confident you will have conducted us as far on the road as we can go, and have lodged us within reconnoitring distance of the citadel itself. while *here*, I have time to read nothing. but our annual recess for the months of August & September is now approaching, during which I shall be at Monticello, where I anticipate great satisfaction in the perusal of these volumes. It is with great satisfaction too I recollect the agreeable hours I have passed with yourself and M. de la Roche, at the house of our late excellent friend Madame Helvetius, & elsewhere: and I am happy to learn you continue your residence there. Auteuil always appeared to me a delicious village, & Madame Helvetius's the most delicious spot in it. in those days how sanguine we were! and how soon were the virtuous hopes and confidence of every good man blasted! how many excellent friends have we lost in your efforts towards self-government, et cui bono? but let us draw a veil over the dead, and hope the best for the living. if the heroe, who has saved you from a combination of enemies, shall also be the means of giving you as great a portion of liberty[4] as the opinions, habits, & character of the nation are prepared for, progressive preparation may fit you for progressive portions of that first of blessings, and you may in time attain what we erred in supposing could be hastily siesed & maintained, in the present state of political information among your citizens at large. in this way all may end well.

You are again at war I find. But we, I hope, shall be permitted to run the race of peace. your government has wisely removed what certainly endangered collisions between us.[5] I now see nothing which need ever interrupt the friendship between France and this country.[6] twenty years of peace, & the prosperity so visibly flowing from it, have but strengthened our[7] attachment to it[8] & the blessings it brings, and we do not despair of being always a peaceable nation. we think that peaceable means may be devised of keeping nations in the path of justice[9] towards us, by making justice their interest, and injuries to react on themselves. our distance enables us to pursue a course which the crowded situation of Europe renders perhaps impracticable there.

Be so good as to accept for yourself and M. de la Roche, my friendly salutations, and assurances of great consideration & respect.

TH: JEFFERSON

RC (PWacD: Feinstone Collection, on deposit PPAmP); at foot of first page: "M. Cabanis"; endorsed. PrC (DLC). Dft (DLC). Probably enclosed in TJ to Tobias Lear, 14 July.

With his LETTER of 28 Vendémiaire Year 11 (20 Oct. 1802), Cabanis sent TJ the TWO VOLUMES of his *Rapports du physique et du moral de l'homme* (Vol. 38:524-5).

[1] Here in Dft TJ canceled "matter."

[2] Here in draft TJ canceled "scrutinised."

[3] Preceding four words interlined in Dft in place of "with our faculties only."

[4] Word interlined in Dft in place of "self govmt."

[5] In Dft TJ first wrote "removed the only stumbling block between us."

[6] Here in Dft TJ canceled "we shall certainly cherish it with sincere" and "we rejoice <*under*> <*at our relief*> that we are relieved from the danger we apprehended from."

[7] Here in Dft TJ canceled "desires."

[8] Preceding two words interlined in Dft in place of "to peace & it's good."

[9] In Dft TJ first wrote "the blessings profusely flowing from it: and we do not despair of peaceable means of keeping nations in the path of justice" before altering the passage to read as above. Also in Dft he canceled "justice" and substituted "friendship."

From William C. C. Claiborne

DEAR SIR, Town of Washington July 13th. 1803.

I have been honored with the receipt of your Letter of the 24th. of May, and the Communication enclosed therein, I shall, with great pleasure, lay before the House of Representatives of this Territory, at their next meeting.—A free and innocent passage along the Waters running into the Bay of Mexico, will contribute greatly to the convenience and Interest of many of your fellow Citizens, and from the early and uniform attention of the Executive to this Object, we may reasonably count upon its ultimate attainment.

From the unsettled state of Europe, the restless and *successful* ambition of Bonaparte, the pride of England, and her well founded Jealousy of the Power of France, there seems to me, but little prospect of Peace. I find however, by the latest accounts, Negociations were yet depending, and the event of Peace or War involved in some uncertainty. From the aversion of France to immediate hostilities, it is possible Bonaparte may administer some Opiates to the British Lyon;—But the Concessions will probably, not proceed from honest sincerity, but rather from a temporising designing policy, which advises a short delay, in order that the meditated Blow, may hereafter be struck with greater force and more certainty of success.—Bonaparte appears to me, to have very little regard for the Rights and happiness of any People—War is his delight, and he will only be restrained from waging it, from an inability to meet the expences.—The times are certainly very favorable to Mr. Monroe's Mission. If there is War "our Neutrality will be cheaply purchased by a Cession of the Island of New-Orleans & the Floridas";—If there is Peace, Bonaparte will not be disposed to hazard an immediate Breach by refusing a just accommodation to the United States.—

The policy you propose to observe, in relation to the Indians, shall receive my most cordial support; our South Western Frontier is at present, the only vulnerable part of our Country, and the means you contemplate, will considerably encrease the security, and provide protection for all our possessions in this quarter. The Choctaws are well enclined to a sale of Lands, and I believe General Wilkinson will be enabled (without difficulty) to negociate for a purchase on the River you mention.—The Chickasaws have also (of late) manifested a wish, to sell some of their Lands, with a view to pay their debts, and have named their Claim to the Duck River Lands, as least useful to them. Mr. Mitchell the agent has heretofore been advised to encourage this Disposition, and he shall now be instructed to press the subject of a sale, and to point out the extension of our purchases on the Mississippi, as best suited to the convenience of both Parties. I cannot Speak with certainty, but I shall be much deceived, if it should *not* be in my power to induce the Chickasaws to consent to[1] the desired cession in a few Months.—I have understood that many Cherokees, Choctaws and Creeks have emigrated West of the Mississippi, and that many other's are expected to follow. The Game (in a great measure) seems to have retired from the Territory East of the great River, & hence their present Country, has ceased to be the object of Affection, unless to those of them, who instead of the Chase, now seek a livelihood by the Cultivation of the Soil.—The Chickasaws are few in number, and appear much attached to the Soil of their Ancestors; they are becoming Herdsmen and Planters, and indeed the arts of Civilization generally, are in a state of progression. The Choctaws continue a poor, humble and savage people;—Mr. Dinsmoor is making great exertions to better their Condition; some of the Natives are turning their attention to domestic pursuits, and a few have made considerable progress in aggriculture. I find that many of the Chiefs of this Nation are in possession of Medals and Commissions, which have been presented them by the present & former Governors of Louisiana, and which they hold in high estimation. I have myself supposed, that if the Governor of this Territory, was furnished with a few blank Commissions or Certificates, handsomely printed, and decorated with the Emblems of Peace and domestic happiness, and also a few Medals which he was authorised to confer on such Chickasaws and Choctaws who had made the greatest improvements in Aggriculture and domestic manufactories, it would excite a laudable Spirit of Emulation.—That a part of the Southern Indians, will in a few Years be civilized, I do verily believe, but their numbers will probably be small, for as Civilization advances, Emigration will encrease, and the Warrior and Hunter will withdraw from a Country, where the manly Amusement "the Chase," is not held in the first estimation.—The Choctaws are at present without a King; the last Monarch, "Francismechubbey," died a few years since, and no Character has yet been Selected as his Successor. It seems, that among the Choctaws, the King is elected, and serves during Life: The election too must be unanimous, and hence it is, that the Throne remains vacant, for I understand there are several petty Chieftains, who aspire at the Supreme authority, and each has his Supporters.—Several Individuals of the Nation, have expressed a wish, that I would nominate for them a King, and it is not improbable, but a similar request may be made by the Chiefs.—If so, I shall make for them a Selection, and altho' he will be a Shirtless, unletter'ed Savage King, yet I think it probable, that for real intrinsic Merit, few if any of the reigning Monarch's of Europe, will possess equal Claims.—There is no doubt with me, but a Road in a direct Line from Natchez to Knoxville, would save 200 Miles in the carriage of the Mail, and also prove a great convenience to Travellers.—The Road (at present used) by the way of the Chickasaws and Nashville, is a long circuitous Route, and the Traveller is exposed to innumerable difficulties and imminent Danger;—frequently suffering for provisions and Water, and often robbed by Indians, or some abandoned White-Men, who of late have committed several outrages. The present Road is therefore, very justly an object of fear. If the Indians could be prevail'd upon, to take White-men into partnership, and to establish Houses of entertainment every 12 or 13 Miles distant, the Traveller would feel much greater Comfort & Security: I am persuaded, that the Chickasaws and Choctaws might be brought into the measure: As for the Cherokees, I cannot say much in favour of their discretion or friendly disposition—Perhaps of late years, they may have become virtuous and well disposed, but when I lived in the neighbourhood of Knoxville, I thought them a very unworthy Tribe, seldom enclined to friendly Deeds, and only restrained thro' fear, from Acts of violence.

I greatly rejoice at the encrease of *Republicanism* in the Atlantic States; I believe it to be the surest guarantee of the Glory and happiness of my Country.—There was a time, when the principles of Republicanism were rarely seen in the measures of our Government, & yet many of the People, reposed entire Confidence in their Rulers;—But this time is now past, & its recollection will serve I trust, to keep alive a Spirit of Enquiry, always serviceable to virtuous Majistrates, and to prevent a return of that political Lethargy, which proved so favorable to Federalism, and the enemies of Republican freedom.—

It is with regret I acknowledge, that Monarchism, "which has been so falsely miscalled Federalism," has its admirers in this Territory—We have a formidable British party, not in point of numbers, but rendered so, by unanimity in their movements, the Activity and Cunning with which they circulate their wicked doctrines among the ignorant & credulous part of this Society, and the Calumnious Affrontery with which they assail the Reputation & Actions of those in authority who differ with them in political sentiment.—In a former Letter, I gave you a general description of the Characters which compose this *Faction*, & I will now add that of late *it* has acquired no additional strength.—The Emigrants (unless some disbanded officer or disappointed Partizan should form an exception) are Americans in feeling and sentiment, and encourages me to hope, that Federalism, will have ultimately & shortly to take its flight from this Territory.—

The paper enclosed you is an Account of the Celebration of the Anniversary of American Independence at this place. You will discover Sir, that the principles of *Seventy Six*, warm the Breasts of many of our Citizens, and I trust in God, that on the Banks of the Mississippi, many Patriots will be reared, who to their latest Breath, will cherish & support *these principles.*—The Select Party which is spoken of in the paper, consisted of the Ex-Judge (Mr. Lewis) a dismissed Atty. General for a District in this Territory, three of the late disbanded officers of the Army, and ten deluded young Men. From such a party, little else could be expected, but evident proofs of passion Imprudence and folly.—

Mr. Briggs has not yet reached Natchez; I shall welcome his arrival with friendly sincerity, & will with promptitude & pleasure render him all the Services in my power: He will be a great acquisition to this District, and I doubt not, but the appointments of Commissioners and Register will be confer'ed on Characters, whose Residence among us, will be highly useful:—I continue in the opinion, that a Selection of Commissioners & Register from some one of the U. States, will be the best for the general Interest, and I am certain, that decisions made by Men, who are no ways interested in the Land Claims, will be most satisfactory, & most correct.—

Louisiana remains under the Government of Spain; the French Prefect is yet in Orleans, but not in the exercise of any Authority. General Wilkinson has been detained at Fort Adams for some time past, by a severe indisposition, but his health is now so far reinstated, as to justify a Journey to Tombacbee (on the Indian Business) which he proposes undertaking in a few Days.—This Territory has for the last five Weeks been uncommonly sickly; a great Mortality has taken place in Natchez & its vicinity, but confined chiefly to Strangers.—Mrs. Claiborne has had a recent and severe Illness, but her Fevers have subsided, & the probability is, I shall have the happiness to see her (in a few Weeks, in good health.)[2]

About six Weeks ago, I procured a Box of sound *Paccans*, and anticipating that these delicious Nuts were among the few good things, which are not be met with in the Atlantic States, I forwarded *them* to you, by the Schooner Indiana, bound for *New-York*, to the care of a Mr. William Cumming of that *City*. I hope the Box will ultimately reach you, but it is probable, the Nuts may be injured by Age. I shall in future, with great pleasure, regularly transmit you a Barrel of them, every Autumn, and in return a small package of Garden Seeds, or Stones of such Fruit, as you may suppose will be suitable to this Climate, and you can conveniently procure, will be very acceptable.—

Believe me, you have my best Wishes for your happiness in public & private Life, and that I am with great Respect, your friend.

William C. C. Claiborne

RC (DLC); at foot of text: "Thomas Jefferson President of the U. States"; endorsed by TJ as received 17 Aug. and so recorded in SJL. Enclosure not found.

THE RIVER YOU MENTION: the Tombigbee River (see TJ to Claiborne, 24 May 1803).

FRANCISMECHUBBEY: that is, the prominent Choctaw chief Franchimastabé, who died in 1801. His reputation among Americans and Europeans led Winthrop Sargent to praise him as a "universal friend of the white people" (Greg O'Brien, *Choctaws in a Revolutionary Age* [Lincoln, Neb., 2002], 1-2).

[1] Preceding two words interlined in place of "make."

[2] Closing parenthesis supplied by Editors.

To Caesar A. Rodney

Dear Sir Washington July 13. 03.

Your favor of the 7th. is now before me. mr Mendenhall wrote to me in Feb. last, asking the communication of a paper against him which he understood had been delivered to me. I wrote him in answer Feb. 25. that I did not remember ever to have recieved such a paper: that tho' I might ascertain the fact by a recurrence to my files, yet it was unnecessary for another reason, which was, that as it was important to the public service that I should be the center of information, so to induce it freely to be given, I considered what I recieved as sacredly confidential, never to be given up. on the reciept of your letter of the 7th. I again reflected on the subject, & could not, nor can I now recollect such a paper. I have searched my files, carefully, over & over again, & under every head where I thought it could be placed. I cannot find such a one. still I have some recollection of the fact you remind me of, that after reading a paper to me, I asked you if you could leave it with me; but I do not recollect the nature of the paper. probably it has got misplaced, and that the constant recourse I have to my files may bring it under my eye, in which case I will return you a copy of it. your saying what the paper was, & that you delivered it to me, satisfies me of the fact, and I shall keep it in my mind whenever I may come across it. Capt Lewis left this on the 5th. on his journey up the Missisipi. I shall leave it on the 25th. to be absent during the months of August & September. I salute you with respect and sincere affection.

Th: Jefferson

RC (British Library); at foot of text: "Caesar A. Rodney esq." PrC (DLC).

MENDENHALL WROTE TO ME: see Thomas Mendenhall's letter to TJ of 12 Feb.

To James Taylor, Jr.

SIR Washington July 13. 03.

In a letter to Colo. Newton some time ago I informed him I should take two pipes of Madeira of the Brazil quality annually, that being about my annual consumption of that kind of wine. he mentioned in reply that they should be imported annually with his own, and what he ordered for a few particular friends, and that his correspondents had assured him these should be of superior quality. having recieved from you this spring two pipes, I shall not need a further supply till the next spring, so that; with my thanks for those offered in your favr. of the 7th. inst. I write the present that you may not miss the sale of them to any other applicant. respectful salutations.

TH: JEFFERSON

PrC (MHi); in ink at foot of text: "Mr. James Taylor"; endorsed by TJ in ink on verso.

TJ wrote Thomas NEWTON on 4 Mch., the day after receiving TWO PIPES of Madeira from Taylor (see also Vol. 39:556).

From George Divers

DR SIR Farmington 14th. July 1803

Soon after the Rect. of your favor of the 18th. May inclosing a drawing of an architrave frize & Cornice for my two fire places, I wrote you that the frize boards must be 5 f. 7 inches by $7\frac{1}{2}$ inches in place of 5 f 4 I. by 6 I. as soon as they are ready & the composition ornaments are done be so good as to direct them to be ship'd to the care of either Gibson & Jefferson or Picket Pollard & Johnston of Richmond, with a request that they will give me notice when they come to hand, my workmen have but very little to do & I fear will be waiting for the ornaments, If the man who did some plastering for you or any other good plasterer can be engaged to come out here from the City of Washington I shall be glad to employ one to plaster my two Room passage & Columns, perhaps you may also have a Room or two ready, I shall be ready by the middle or the last of august at farthest. I must ask the favor of you to engage a good hand to come out, and advise me by post, when he will be here or whether such a man can be engaged or not. with respect & esteem

I am Dr. Sir Yr. very Hble Servt George Divers

RC (MHi); endorsed by TJ as received 17 July and so recorded in SJL.

TJ's favor of 18 May has not been found. It was likely a response to Divers's letter of 9 May, recorded in SJL as received 11 May, but not found. A subsequent letter of 7 June from Divers to TJ, recorded in SJL as received 12 June, has also not been found.

In his financial memoranda, TJ recorded on 23 June paying George Andrews $49.69 "for ornaments for Geo. Divers" (MB, 2:1103).

To Tobias Lear

July 14. 03.

Th: Jefferson presents his friendly salutations to Colo. Lear, and prays him to give the best conveyance he can to the inclosed letter. he wishes a pleasant voyage & happy issue of his peacemaking mission: and the rather as the purchase of Louisiana will require the aid of all our resources to pay the interest of the additional debt without laying a new tax, and of course call for the adoption of every possible economy.

PrC (DLC); endorsed by TJ in ink on verso. Enclosure: probably TJ to Pierre Jean Georges Cabanis, 13 July.

peacemaking mission: TJ signed two commissions for Lear, one on 10 June as consul general for the city and kingdom of Algiers and another on 19 July as commissioner to negotiate a treaty of peace with Tripoli (both in DNA: RG 59, PTCC). In instructions for Lear dated 14 July, Madison explained that the consular position at Algiers was designated as consul general, and the consuls at Tunis and Tripoli made "subordinate" to it, to reflect the special relationship of the United States and Algiers relative to the other North African states. Madison informed Lear that the annuity to Algiers was the only payment required by "written obligation," but "usage, equally imperious," required a biennial present, which Richard O'Brien calculated to be $16,000, as well as gifts valued at about $20,000 on the introduction of a new consul. If Lear found that James L. Cathcart had not concluded a peace with Tripoli, Madison instructed, "the President has thought fit to entrust" those negotiations to Lear. The secretary of state also informed Lear that ships' passports for the Mediterranean had been counterfeited, prompting the U.S. government to issue a newly engraved form for ships' passes. In a postscript, Madison wrote that the "universal toleration in matters of religion established in most of our states, and the entire want of power respecting them in the general government, has, as we understand, induced the Barbary powers to view us more favorably than other Christian nations, who are exclusively so." The government recommended that Lear "avail us of this fact and opinion, as far as it can be used to lessen the unequal condition of the intercourse between us" (Madison, *Papers*, *Sec. of State Ser.*, 5:175-9).

From Robert Smith

navy Department
July 14—1803

SIR,

I enclose a blank warrant for your signature to be filled with the name of Joseph Nicholson as midshipman should you approve it—He is son of Capn. S. Nicholson of Boston, and is recommended by Commodore Preble—

I have the honor to be with much respect Sir yr. obt. Serv.

RT SMITH

RC (DLC); in a clerk's hand, signed by Smith; at foot of text: "The President"; endorsed by TJ as received from the Navy Department on 15 July and "Nicholson. midshipman." FC (Lb in DNA: RG 45, LSP).

Upon receiving his warrant, JOSEPH NICHOLSON was assigned to duty on the frigate *Constitution* (NDBW, *Register*, 40).

From Joseph Croswell

Plymouth, State of Massachusetts,
July 15th, 1803

SIR

I took the liberty to write You last Feby. but have reason to suppose the letter was not deliver'd at the post Office in Boston again I presume to enclose a production of mine, altho' fully convinc'd the minutest faults cannot escape your notice, if nothing else is meritorious, You will observe a tincture of Republicanism, particularly in the latter part of the Epilogue, . . . where my aim was to render Honor where I really thought it was due, but if I might presume to point out a passage to attract your notice, it would be to the last part of Govr. Carvers last Speech, William the Conqueror divided the Lands in England amongst his favorites & the consequence is, nearly all their Farmers are now abject tenants and their unequal modes of raising a Revenue operate substantially like a Poll tax, this is the very source that produces frequent Wars, Famines, Roberies & continual Executions in that Country, these thoughts have cast a gloom over my mind especially when I reflect that "like Causes will produce like effects" which induces me thus freely to usher them into your presence.—The writer of this is a Widower of 60 years of age, Son to a Minister of Boston some years since deceas'd who was well known to Govr Adams & many other Gentlemen now living there, as a zealous advocate for the Liberties of our Country, my inclination prompted me to imbibe his principles & to write frequently in the Boston papers, I was also an evidence against the Soldiers who were try'd for the Masacre in Boston in 1770, moving to this Town just before our revolutionary War commenc'd & finding it divided between Whigs & Tories, my exertions were of some weight to turn the scale & till this time have occasionally continued to publish political pieces in favour of Liberty, there is no other person in this Town that has publish'd any thing of that nature, I am sure I can clear the Warren family, for I must have known it if they had & I think I may include the County. When our British Treaty appear'd I was much alarm'd & was the first promoter of a Town meeting when We protested against it & publish'd our doings, in consequence of my exertions I have suffer'd more persecution than all the Republicans in this County together, from the federalists who predominate here, they took the advantage of my losing a Vessell by the Baratry of the Master & of some other misfortunes to plot my ruin; it would require a volume to relate all the fraudulent measures they pursur'd & other conduct shocking to humanity when I had a sick family & lost my Wife & a Daughter who participated in my persecution, they finally effected their purpose so far that I have been, unavoidably oblig'd to diminish my small property yearly in supporting my self & Children til it is nearly all expended.

Notwithstanding I have continued conscientiously inflexible in my principles, to the supprize of the Tories who have tamper'd with me in vain, the Warren family by their Riches & temporizing conduct were screen'd from the Storm & view'd my Ship wreck with complacency knowing that poverty in the judgment of an Ignorant world is an essential disqualification in a Candidate for any Office & that a rival to their Son would be put down by the Tories themselves—However near five Years ago, before it was generally known how much I had been reduced, many were determin'd to support me as a Candidate for a seat in Congress, my name was publish'd & circular letters were sent to many Towns in this district, recommending me, it was agreed that delegates from each town should meet at *Abington* previous to the choice. Genl Warren who is one of the most artfull politicians in this World, had the address to send two Men from this Town, one of them not remarkable for honesty & who was displeas'd with me for preventing his defrauding an Orphan as I was a Commissioner on settling the Estate, the other I plac'd some confidence in as he had sent several letters into the Country recommending me, but Genl Warren induc'd him to prove a traytor—their orders were to promote Mr Henry Warren if possible if not to set up a Man in a distant Town that was unknown & unfit—to depreciate my Abilities & to harp strongly on my poverty as a standing text, they had no orders to mention any kind of immorality as they were sure of not being credited—but with all their management, aided by Genl Warrens letters they could not set Mr H Warren up, for it appear'd evident to the meeting that he had acted the Federalist & then wore the black Cockade, it was expected they would nominate me but they would not break orders, consequently the meeting ended in confusion & the federal Candidate Mr Reed again obtaind his Election—At the last choice Genl Warren had influence enough to try his son Henry again, he had took out the Cockade & declar'd himself a Republican, but when it was recollected his being so lately a federalist his signing the Plymouth address to Mr Adams, approving of every part of his administration & promising support &c, also his celebrating all his birth days while in office, at one of which He & the whole Company at Boston appeard by agrement in new suits to do The more honor to their patrons, these things operated to his disadvantage with those who disaprove the conduct of the *Batt* in the *fable* and Mr Mitchell a moderate federalist easily obtain'd his Election. Genl Warren was anxious to obtain the post office for his Son James & imploy'd the beforemention'd Delegates to assure Mr Goodwin who is also a moderate Federalist & succeeded in the attempt, soon after their wishes were compleatly crown'd by Henry's being invested with the Custom house, Emediately the thin veil of Republicanism was thrown off, a Mr Crandon a Noted *Fed* who had threatned the Whigs with transportation was appointed Searcher & Gauger another Fed appointed to Measure Salt—my name was mention'd for one of those very small offices, but invain—

One of the sd Delegates that betray'd me was incouraged by them to set up for a seat in our State legislature, but as they Had no further service for him, they used their influence for a Mr Dunbar a federal Lawyer who was chosen—I have labour'd in the Republican vinyard most of my life & my reward has been, loss of property—This man that appears at the 11th hour has the fatted Calf!. The profits of the Custom house are suppos'd to net 2000 Doll ℔ ann—a sum enormous in this small Town, where living is cheap, one third would be esteem'd an ample compensation by Men equally Capable, if a port of Entry was Establish'd at *Duxborough*, which is 9 Miles north to include Marshfield 15 miles N also *Scituate* 21 Miles North it would reduce the profits of this office one third & afford a comfortable support for a Collector—

Sr. I should not wish to have this communication made known it might create animosity which never serves to elucidate facts, Every unbiased intelegent person here I believe would confirm every part of this naration to any private Gentleman that might enquire & would further add that the writer of this hath always preserv'd a character for strict integrity I hope Sr you will pardon this bold intrusion & as an incentive it is not probable I shall ever again trespass on your patience.

with real Esteem of your patriotism & abilities I am with due defference yr Humble Servt JOSEPH CROSWELL

PS having mention'd my writing in the Newspapers shall instance only two pieces out of many—1st an Ode on the 4th March 1801. in the Boston Chronicle & sung in this Town on sd day. begining—

Behold fair freedoms Banners rise
Adding new lustre to the skies
The Standard fix'd with care & toil
On Monticello's fruitfull soil—7 or 8 Verses

The other stiled "the Mammoth Cheese" wrote in Hudibrastic verse in the Chronicle of July 8, 1802. This was design'd to check the nonsense of the Federalists on this subject & to turn the ridicule upon themselves & I think it had that effect

Assist me Muse while I rehearse
A curious tale in humble verse
Built on such facts as Tories tell
In *Federalist* & *Centinel*—this is something lengthy & satirical

RC (DNA: RG 59, LAR); ellipses in original; addressed: "Thomas Jefferson Esq President of the United States at the City of Washington"; endorsed by TJ as received 22 July and "to office" and so recorded in SJL. Enclosure: Joseph Croswell, *A New World Planted; or, The Adventures of the Forefathers of New-England; Who Landed in Plymouth, December 22, 1620, An Historical Drama—in Five Acts* (Boston, 1802; Shaw-Shoemaker, No. 2102).

WRITE YOU LAST FEBY.: Croswell to TJ, 28 Feb. 1803 (Vol. 39:602-6).

POINT OUT A PASSAGE: in his final speech of Croswell's historical drama, Governor John Carver of Plymouth Colony expressed two requirements for the country's ongoing prosperity—equal taxation and the avoidance of monopolies of public lands (Croswell, *A New World Planted*, 43).

Croswell was part of an eleven-member committee at a Plymouth town meeting on 28 Oct. 1795 that expressed alarm at the "ruinous nature" of the Jay or BRITISH TREATY and recorded their "marked and decided reprobation" of it. Mathew Carey published a report of the proceedings (*The American Remembrancer; or, An Impartial Collection of Essays, Resolves, Speeches, etc. Relative, or Having Affinity, to the Treaty with Great Britain*, 3 vols. [Philadelphia, 1795-96], 2:283-4; Evans, No. 28389).

BARATRY OF THE MASTER: that is, "barratry." In marine law it is fraud or gross and criminal negligence on the part of the master or mariners of a ship to the prejudice of the owners (OED).

Residents of Plymouth, Kingston, and Duxbury agreed to a joint ADDRESS TO MR ADAMS in May 1798, to which Adams replied on 8 June 1798. Similar XYZ addresses were compiled as *A Selection of the Patriotic Addresses, to the President of the United States. Together with the President's Answers* and published in Boston in 1798 (Boston *Massachusetts Mercury*,

22 May 1798; Boston *Columbian Centinel*, 4 July 1798; Sowerby, No. 3525; Vol. 32:201-2n).

BATT IN THE FABLE: in the fable of the bat and the weasels, as popularized by La Fontaine, a bat saved itself from being eaten by weasels, once by claiming to be a bird and once by claiming to be a mouse (Jean de La Fontaine, *Fables: Psyché-oeuvres Diverses*, ed. Roger Delbiausse [Paris, 1947], 61).

OBTAIN THE POST OFFICE: James Warren, Jr., became postmaster at Plymouth in place of William Goodwin in February 1803 (Vol. 38:663n).

John D. DUNBAR was elected to represent Plymouth in the state legislature in 1803 (*Newburyport Herald*, 20 May 1803).

To Jones & Howell

GENTLEMEN Washington July 15. 1803.

Be pleased to forward for me without delay, to the care of Gibson & Jefferson of Richmond 2½ ~~Cwt~~ of iron in flat bars, of the toughest quality, and 5. ~~Cwt~~ of a harder quality in bars ¾ I. square. Accept my salutations & best wishes. TH: JEFFERSON

P.S. mr Barnes will remit you 309.42 D in the beginning of the ensuing month for the last supply of rod.

PrC (MHi); in ink at foot of text: "Jones & Howell"; endorsed by TJ in ink on verso. Recorded in SJL with notation "250. ℔ flat bars. 500. ℔ sq. do. ¾ I."

A letter of 2 May from Jones & Howell to TJ, recorded in SJL as received 4 May with the notation "309.42," has not been found.

To Ephraim Kirby

DEAR SIR Washington July 15. 03.

I yesterday signed a commission appointing you one of the Commissioners to recieve & determine the titles of lands held on the East side of Pearl river. the place of sessions will be Fort Stoddart. I am happy in having in that commission the name of a person already so well known to the public as to ensure their confidence. the other Commissioner will be mr Robert Carter Nicholas of Kentucky, son of the late George Nicholas of that state. I am desirous of appointing to the Register's office, some worthy inhabitant of that part of the country, but I have never been able to get a recommendation of any one. he should be of perfect integrity, good understanding, and, if a lawyer, so much the better. under these circumstances I have thought it best to ask you to take charge of a blank commission, to be filled up by yourself as soon after your arrival there, as you can acquire information of the best character. your own judgment will suggest to you the advantage of keeping it entirely secret that you have such a power, in order that you may obtain disinterested information. but I am obliged to impose on you another task, quite out of the line of your official duty, yet within that of a citizen of the US. we have had no means of acquiring any knolege of the number, nature & extent of our settlements West of Pearl river: yet it is extremely important we should recieve accurate information. I have therefore taken the liberty of stating some queries to which I will pray your attention, and that you will take all the pains you can to obtain for me full and faithful answers. I leave this place within a few days for Monticello to remain there through the months of August and September. I pray you to accept my friendly salutations & assurances of great esteem & respect.

Th: Jefferson

RC (NcD: Ephraim Kirby Papers); addressed: "Colo. Ephraim Kerby Litchfield Connecticut"; franked and postmarked; endorsed. PrC (DLC).

ENCLOSURE

Queries on Pearl River Settlements

Queries.

1. What are the settlements of citizens on the East side of Pearl River? stating their geographical position, extent & numbers.
2. are there good lands adjoining them to render them capable of enlargement
3. have they encroached on the Indians?
4. are the settlements in a course of enlargement by persons settling down on lands without title?
5. the general character of the inhabitants & from whence they are?
6. a special list by name of all such individuals worthy of appointment to such offices as may be necessary among them, and characters so particularised as that we may know for what each is fit.
7. a general account of the Spanish settlements in the adjacent country, stating all material circumstances relative to them, particularly their geographical position & numbers. those on the Chatahouchy, Excambia, Mobile & Pascagoula rivers especially.
8. their military posts, the position & strength of each, and especially on the Mobile.

PrC (DLC); undated.

To Meriwether Lewis

Dear Sir Washington July 15. 1803.

I dropped you a line on the 11th. inst. and last night recieved yours of the 8th. last night also we recieved the treaty from Paris ceding Louisiana according to the bounds to which France had a right. price $11\frac{1}{4}$ millions of Dollars besides paying certain debts of France to our citizens which will be from 1. to 4. millions. I recieved also from Mr. La Cepede at Paris, to whom I had mentioned your intended expedition a letter of which the following is an extract. 'Mr. Broughton, one of the companions of Captain Vancouver went up Columbia river 100. miles, in December 1792. he stopped at a point which he named Vancouver lat. 45.° 27.′ longitude 237.° 50.′ E. here the river Columbia is still a quarter of a mile wide & from 12. to 36. feet deep. it is far then to it's head. from this point Mount Hood is seen 20. leagues distant, which is probably a dependence of the Stony mountains, of which mr Fiedler saw the beginning about lat. 40.° and the source of the Missouri is probably in the Stony mountains. if your nation can establish an easy communication by rivers, canals, & short portages between N. York for example & the city [they were building] or [to be built] [for the badness of the writing makes it uncertain which is meant, but probably the last] at the mouth of the Columbia, what a route for the commerce of Europe, Asia, & America.' Accept my affectionate salutations.

Th: Jefferson

PrC (DLC); brackets in original; at foot of text: "Capt M. Lewis"; endorsed by TJ in ink on verso.

we recieved the treaty: George A. Hughes delivered the Louisiana treaty and conventions on 14 July (Madison, *Papers*, *Sec. of State Ser.*, 5:238; John Mitchell to TJ, 21 May).

recieved also: Lacépède's letter of 13 May, received by TJ on 14 July.

From Meriwether Lewis

Pittsburgh July 15th. 1803.
3. O'Clock P.M.

Dear Sir,

I arrived here at 2 O'Clock, and learning that the mail closed at 5 this evening hasten to make this communication, tho' it can only contain the mere information of my arrival. No occurrence has taken place on my journey heither sufficiently interesting to be worthy of relation: the weather has been warm and dry; the roads in consequence extreemly dusty, yet I feel myself much benefitted by the exercise the journey has given me, and can with pleasure anounce, so far and *all is well.*—

I have not yet seen Lieut. Hook nor made the enquiry relative to my boat, on the state of which, the time of my departure[1] from hence must materially depend: the Ohio is quite low, but not so much so as to obstruct my passage altogether.—

Your Obt. Humble Sert. MERIWETHER LEWIS.

RC (MHi); at foot of text: "Thos. Jefferson Presidt. U'States"; endorsed by TJ as received 25 July and so recorded in SJL.

SO FAR AND ALL IS WELL: in the spring when TJ developed a cipher for Lewis's use, he posited that the captain might someday write from the head of the Missouri, "all well, and the Indians so far, friendly" (Editorial Note and Document I of Cipher for Meriwether Lewis, printed above in this series at the end of April 1803).

Moses HOOK, a first lieutenant, commanded the army's garrison at Pittsburgh and also served as assistant military agent there. Dearborn had ordered Hook to assist Lewis, see that he and his men had enough provisions to reach the post at Massac, and provide them with 18 light axes (Jackson, *Lewis and Clark*, 1:101-2, 119-20; Heitman, *Dictionary*, 1:540).

[1] MS: "departue."

From John Minor

DEAR SIR Fredericksburg. July 15th 1803

Few things could have afforded me more genuine satisfaction than that which I feel at the proof contained in your Letter of the 9th. Inst, that I possess your good opinion and Confidence; I pray you to accept my sincere thanks.

It is true that Eighteen years of Laborious Practice in my Profession, has created in me a strong wish for retirement, provided I could retire with Enough to support my family and Educate my Children in the Stile I wish, and my wish would not be extravagant; your goodness has tendered me the wished for Boon, and yet I must decline the acceptance of it; Prudence bids me decline it. I think the Office will be of short duration, indeed I think that it ought to be for I cannot but consider the Territorial Government as an unnecessary burthen upon the United States, and upon their Government should I therefore relinquish my present practice, which is lucrative, and accept the appointment you are so good as to offer me, and the office should be abolished, it would cost me much time to regain my present position at the bar; whereas by continuing to pursue my practice, I think I shall be inabled, in a few Years, to retire to the Enjoyment of ease and Independence, if not Dignity.

Accept, Dear Sir, my assurance of High respect and affectionate regard JOHN MINOR

RC (DLC); endorsed by TJ as received 17 July and so recorded in SJL.

An extant letterpress copy of TJ's LETTER OF THE 9TH. INST. is badly damaged and largely illegible, rendering it unclear which office was being offered to Minor (PrC in DLC; at foot of text: "Colo. Minor"; endorsed by TJ in ink on verso).

To Thomas Mann Randolph

TH:J. TO TMR. Washington July 15. 03.

The arrival of the treaty of cession of Louisiana last night, and the short day given for ratification (Oct. 30.) will oblige me to call Congress about the middle of that month; & consequently to return here earlier than I had calculated; I shall therefore go home earlier. I think I shall be with you on Friday or Saturday next. my affectionate love to all of you.—the price of Louisiana 11,250,000. D. and from 2. to 4. millions more to be paid to our merchants.

RC (DLC); endorsed by Randolph as received 18 July. PrC (MHi); endorsed by TJ in ink on verso.

From Thomas F. Riddick

SIR Chillicothe Ohio July 15th 1803

I am a petitioner to you for the Office of Register Of the Land Office, to reside in Washington county Mississippi Territory. I have Written on to my friends Messrs. Gray & Newton Members of Congress, to Recommend me & expect ere this they have complied with my request

I am a Virginian born In the county of Nansemond And lately removed to this place you perhaps may know my family They with myself are friends of the present Administration and were Opposed to the latter

As to my moral charachter and capability To perform the duties of the Office as well as responsibility in point of property Sufficient testimonials of which my friends can produce to you

I am with due respect Sir Your Most Obt. Svt.

THOMAS F RIDDICK

RC (DNA: RG 59, LAR); at head of text: "The President of the United States"; endorsed by TJ as received 29 July and "to be Register of Missipi" and so recorded in SJL.

A native of Nansemond County, Virginia, Thomas F. Riddick (1781-1830) did not receive an appointment from TJ. He left Ohio shortly after writing the above letter and settled in St. Louis, where he went on to hold a number of public offices and become an influential business and civic leader (Frederic L. Billon, *Annals of St. Louis in Its Territorial Days from 1804 to 1821* [St. Louis, 1888], 188-9).

Letters recommending Riddick from Virginia Congressmen Edwin GRAY and Thomas NEWTON, Jr., have not been found. Riddick did secure a recommendation from Michael Baldwin, speaker of the Ohio House of Representatives, who wrote nearly identical letters to Albert Gallatin and Gideon Granger on 18 July. Deeming Riddick an "acquaintance of mine," Baldwin described him as a young man of integrity and ability, who had also served an accountant's apprenticeship. In his letter to Granger, however, Baldwin added that Riddick was "an uniform, genuine Republican" (both in DNA: RG 59, LAR, both endorsed by TJ; Donald J. Ratcliffe, *Party Spirit in a Frontier Republic: Democratic Politics in Ohio, 1793-1821* [Columbus, Ohio, 1998], 109). The latter recommendation may have been enclosed in an undated letter to TJ from Granger, recorded in SJL as received 1 Aug. 1803 with notation "Thos. F. Riddick Register E. of Pearl riv.," but not found.

To John Strode

Washington July 15. 1803.

Th: Jefferson presents his friendly salutations [to mr] Strode. the arrival of the treaty of cession of Louisiana, [rendering it] necessary to call Congress in October, he will leave this place earlier than he had intended. he will probably breakfast with [him] on Thursday or Friday morning next. he wishes him health.

PrC (DLC); torn; endorsed by TJ in ink on verso.

From Joshua Danforth

SIR, Pittsfield July 16th. 1803

Although I have not the honor of being personally acquainted with you, yet my veneration & esteem for you is great.—I feel grateful towards you because you have devoted a great portion of your useful life to the service of our Common Country for which you ought to receive the thanks of the American People.—

My principal object in making this Communication is to send you the last Pittsfield paper which contains the Toasts drank, on the fourth of July, by the Inhabitants of Lenox & Pittsfield.

There has been a republican paper established in this Town for almost three years.—It has in my Opinion, been well conducted.—I believe that the editor of the "Sun" at the request of Mr. Bidwell forwarded to you his paper for some months, but not knowing whether it was agreeable to you he discontinued it.—I wish you would become a Subscriber to this paper as it would encourage the printer—I think it is probable you have a great many applications of this kind, but I doubt whether many of them are entitled to as much Consideration as this.

A motion will be made at the next Session of the Legislature of Massachusetts to divide the State into districts, for the Choice of electors of President &c, but it is very uncertain whether it will suceed, if it should, Massachusetts will give eight or nine Votes to the republican Candidate for President.

I am personally acquainted with Judge Lincoln the Attorney Genl. & Mr. Granger P.M. Genl.—Please to enquire of them as to my Character.

With the most Sincere wishes for your happiness & prosperity I am with great respect Your friend JOSHUA DANFORTH

RC (DLC); endorsed by TJ as received 27 July and so recorded in SJL. Enclosure not found, but see below.

Joshua Danforth (1759-1837), a native of western Massachusetts, commenced service in the American Revolution as a 15-year-old clerk under his father's company. He became an officer and, in 1781, was promoted to paymaster with the rank of captain. After the war, he settled in Pittsfield and entered the mercantile business. From 1794 to 1823, he held a variety of state and national offices, including justice of the peace, postmaster, town clerk, treasurer, selectman, assessor, representative to the state legislature, and sessions court justice in Berkshire County. During the Madison administration, he received appointments as marshal and revenue collector for his district (David D. Field, *A History of the Town of Pittsfield in Berkshire County, Mass.* [Hartford, Mass., 1844], 63-5, 77; *Pittsfield Sun*, 2 Feb. 1837).

FOURTH OF JULY: Danforth probably enclosed a copy of the *Pittsfield Sun* of 11 July, which included accounts of the Independence Day festivities in Lenox. The celebration consisted of a procession, a reading of the Declaration of Independence at the courthouse, and a formal dinner followed by 17 toasts and cannon discharges. According to the same issue of the newspaper, the ladies of Pittsfield had their own independence celebration with 7 toasts and an elegant repast at sundown in the shade of a green bowery.

Phinehas Allen was the EDITOR of the *Sun*, the weekly Pittsfield newspaper established in 1800 and continued until after 1820. With the 23 May 1803 issue, the title changed to the *Pittsfield Sun* (Brigham, *American Newspapers*, 1:391).

Barnabas BIDWELL of Stockbridge was a Massachusetts state senator from 1801 to 1804 (*Biog. Dir. Cong.*).

From Henry Dearborn

SIR. War Department July 16th. 1803.

I have the honor to propose Docr. Calvin Taylor for a Surgeons Mate in the Army of the United States.

Accept Sir, the assurance &c.

FC (Lb in DNA: RG 107, LSP).

CALVIN TAYLOR of Vermont would be on the list of nominations and promotions TJ sent to the Senate on 18 Nov. 1803. He died in 1806 (JEP, 1:458; Heitman, *Dictionary*, 1:946).

To Mustafa Baba, Dey of Algiers

GREAT AND GOOD FRIEND,

Our Consul Mr OBrien has forwarded to me the letter you wrote me on the 17th of October last. I read in that the welcome assurances of your friendship and good will to the United States, and reciprocate them with sincerity, hoping that these sentiments will long subsist between us, and long preserve peace and intercourse[1] between our Nations.

Your interposition with the Bashaw of Tripoli on behalf of our prisoners is an acceptable[2] testimony of the earnestness of your friendship. I receive it as such and return you my sincere thanks for this good office.

The conduct of Mr Cathcart having ever been such as to give satisfaction to his government he was named to reside near you, because we believed he would use his best endeavours to cement the friendship so happily subsisting between us. But as he has had the misfortune to render himself unacceptable to you,[3] I have named Colonel Tobias Lear one of our most trustworthy and respectable citizens to reside near you, as our Consul General, and to do whatever may tend to strengthen and preserve peace and good understanding between us. I pray you to give entire credence to whatsoever he shall communicate to you on my part, and most of all when he shall assure you of my friendship and esteem.

I pray God, Great and Good friend to have you always in his holy keeping.

Done at the City of Washington, this Sixteenth day of July 1803.[4]

TH: JEFFERSON

FC (Lb in DNA: RG 59, Credences); in a clerk's hand; at head of text: "Thomas Jefferson, President of the United States of America, To the Most Excellent and Most Illustrious Mustapha Pacha, Dey of the City and Regency of Algiers"; below signature: "By the President" and "James Madison Secretary of State." FC (Lb in DNA: RG 59, PTCC). PrC (DLC); in TJ's hand, unsigned. Recorded in SJL under 17 July.

[1] PrC: "useful intercourse."

[2] PrC: "a solid and acceptable."

[3] Sentence continues in PrC: "it is reason sufficient with me to dispose otherwise of his services, and to depute another to you."

[4] PrC concludes: "&c."

Notes on a Cabinet Meeting

July 16. Present the 4. Secretaries.

The cession of Louisiana being to be ratified by the 30. Oct.[1] shall Congress be called, or only Senate, & when? answer unanimous Congress on the 17th of October.

a Proclamation to issue. a copy to be enclosed to every member in a letter from the Secretary of state, mentioning that the call 3. weeks earlier than they had fixed was rendd. necessary by the treaty, and urging a punctual attendance on the 1st. day.

the substance of the treaty to be made public, but not the treaty itself.

the Secretary of state to write to our Consul at N. Orleans, communicating the substance of the treaty, and calling his attention to the public property transferred to us,[2] & to archives, papers & documents relative to domain and sovereignty of Louisiana and it's dependencies.

if an order should come for immediate possession, direct Govr. Claiborne to go & take possn and act as Governor & Intendant under the Spanish laws, leaving every thing to go on as heretofore, only himself performg functions of Govr. and Intendt. but making no innovation, nor doing a single act which will bear postponing.

order down 2. or more companies from Ft. Adams, & get the Spanish troops off as soon as possible.

write to Livingston & Monroe, approving their having treated for Louisiana & the price given, and to say we know of no reason to doubt ratification of the whole. mr Gallatin disapproves of this last as committing ourselves or the Congress. all the other points unanimous.—

Edward Livingston to be removed from the office of Attorney for the US. in New York for malversation.

mr Madison not present at this last determination.

Monroe to be instructed to endeavor to purchase both Floridas if he can, West if he cannot East, at the prices before agreed on: but if neither can be procured, then to stipulate a plenary right to use all the rivers rising within our limits & passing through theirs. if he should not be gone to Madrid, leave it discretionary in him to go there, or to London, or to stay at Paris as circumstances shall appear to him to require. we are more indifferent about pressing[3] the purchase of the Floridas, because of the money we have to provide for Louisiana, & because we think they cannot fail to fall into our hands.

MS (DLC: TJ Papers, 131:22677); entirely in TJ's hand; follows, on same sheet, Notes on a Cabinet Meeting of 7 May.

RATIFIED BY THE 30. OCT.: the tenth and final article of the treaty for the cession of Louisiana to the United States required the exchange of ratifications within six months of the date the negotiators signed the treaty. Officially that was 30 Apr., although the papers were not actually signed on that day (Miller, *Treaties*, 2:505; Robert R. Livingston to TJ, 2 May).

For the PROCLAMATION and the circular letter to members of Congress from the secretary of state, see the next document.

SUBSTANCE OF THE TREATY TO BE MADE PUBLIC: 16 July was a Saturday. On Monday the 18th, the *National Intelligencer* printed the proclamation followed by a summary of the terms of the Louisiana cession. TJ drafted or approved the information in the summary, for in letters of the 17th, after the cabinet meeting and before the publication of the newspaper, he assured William C. C. Claiborne and William Dunbar that they could rely on the details they would see in the *Intelligencer*. The published statement shows evidence of hasty typesetting and perhaps of hurried writing, including the omission of the word "the" before "Executive," the probable deletion of "conventions" in the phrase "the Treaty and signed on April 30th," and a mistake in the year of the Convention of 1800: "Dispatches from the American ministers at Paris were received by Executive on Thursday evening. They were brought by Mr. Hughes of Baltimore, as confidential bearer, and contain the Treaty and signed on April 30th which conveys Louisiana to the United States. The extent of the territory ceded is defi[n]ed by a general reference to that in which Louisiana was ceded to France. The terms are, 1st. 11,250,000 dollars to be paid to France in six per cent stock, within three months after the exchange of ratifications and the delivery of possession. 2nd. An assumpsit of the debts due and captures provided for under the Convention of the Sept. 30th 1803, between the United States and the French Republic which are to be liquidated by Commissioners at Paris, and paid at the Treasury of the United States on debts from their Minister at Paris. The assumpsit is not to go beyond 3,750,000 dollars, and it is conjectured, that the amount of the debts and claims will fall short of that sum. 3d. French and Spanish vessels and merchandises directly from their own ports the merchandizes being of the respective countries are to pay, in the ports of the Ceded Territory, for a period of 12 years, no higher duties than are paid by American citizens, and this privilege is not to be extended during that period to any other foreign nation. After that period France and Spain are to enjoy within the ports of the ceded territory the privileges only of the most favored nation. The treaty is to be ratified, and the ratifications exchanged within six month from its date. This circumstance will require the convening of Congress a little earlier than the 1st Monday of November. It is understood that the ratification of the First Consul is on its way to the United States. Immediately after the ratifications of the treaty, possession is to be delivered. The inhabitants of Louisiana are to be incorporated with the U.S. as soon as can consistently with the constitution of the U.S. be effected; and in the mean time are to be secured i[n] their liberties prosperity and religion" (two typesetting errors corrected in brackets). Many newspapers republished the proclamation and summary (corrected to read "the Executive" and "the Treaty, signed on April 30th," and with the correct date for the Convention of 1800). In most cases the text ended with "possession is to be delivered," omitting the final sentence as the piece appeared in the *Intelligencer*. The provisions relating to customs duties were in the seventh and eighth articles of the treaty (Baltimore *Republican*, 20 July; *Poulson's American Daily Adver-*

tiser, 20 July; New York *Daily Advertiser*, 21 July; *Albany Gazette*, 25 July; Northampton, Mass., *Republican Spy*, 26 July; Miller, *Treaties*, 2:502-4).

WRITE TO OUR CONSUL: Madison wrote to Daniel Clark on 20 July, enclosing copies of Articles 2 through 6 of the treaty and probably enclosing a copy of the summary from the *National Intelligencer*. Madison called Clark's attention to Article 2, according to which the United States would take possession of PUBLIC PROPERTY in Louisiana, including vacant lands, public buildings, and fortifications, as well as the ARCHIVES of the province. For Madison's comments to Clark about the third and sixth articles of the treaty, see TJ to Madison, 17 July (Madison, *Papers*, *Sec. of State Ser.*, 5:202-3; Miller, *Treaties*, 2:500).

Article 4 of the treaty indicated that a French *commissaire* would receive the cession of Louisiana from Spanish officials—if that act had not already taken place—and transfer possession to an agent of the United States (same, 501). Madison wrote a brief communication to William C. C. CLAIBORNE on 20 July to cover the letter to Clark, which Madison left unsealed so that Claiborne could see its contents. Madison also enclosed a copy of the proclamation calling Congress into session and, probably from the *Intelligencer*, "a summary of the contents of the Treaty with France." Not until the end of October, after the Senate had ratified the treaty, did the secretary of state dispatch instructions to Claiborne for taking possession of Louisiana (Madison, *Papers*, *Sec. of State Ser.*, 5:202, 589-92).

ORDER DOWN 2. OR MORE COMPANIES: by the terms of the treaty's fifth article, the United States would take possession of all military posts in Louisiana as soon as both countries had ratified the cession. Fort ADAMS, located on the Mississippi River near the southern border of the United States, "we have been silently making a place d'armes," TJ reported to Horatio Gates in January 1803. On 18 July, Dearborn issued orders to halt construction of fortifications near the fort and to assemble materials for boats "sufficient for transporting four Companies down the River to New Orleans (say in November)." Dearborn also halted the army's preparations for a new post at the mouth of the Illinois River. The company of soldiers intended for that post would instead wait at Kaskaskia and be ready to replace the Spanish garrison at Ste. Genevieve (Miller, *Treaties*, 2:501-2; Dearborn to Decius Wadsworth, 18 July, to commanding officer at Fort Adams, 18 July, and to Amos Stoddard, 19 July, in DNA: RG 107, LSMA; TJ to Henri Peyroux de la Coudrèniere, 3 July; Vol. 39:401, 494n).

Writing to Robert R. Livingston and James MONROE jointly on 29 July, Madison conveyed the president's "entire approbation" of the agreement for the purchase of Louisiana. When the diplomats' instructions were drawn up, he explained, no one could have anticipated that any territory west of the Mississippi River would be subject to acquisition by the United States. He pointed out that the administration had only received Livingston's memorandum to the French government proposing a cession of land north of the Arkansas River several weeks after Monroe's departure for France, that such an arrangement would have left France in control of the west bank of the lower Mississippi, and that the French government had showed no interest in proposals from Livingston. What moved the French to sell any part of Louisiana, Madison declared, was the appearance of "a favorable crisis" through a combination of the revocation of the right of deposit at New Orleans, problems for France in Saint-Domingue, "the distress of the french finances," and the increase in friction between France and Great Britain. In the expectation that these circumstances would "open the eyes of France to her real interest, and her ears to the monitory truths which were conveyed to her thro' different channels"—a reference to TJ's communications with Pierre Samuel Du Pont de Nemours—the administration had sent Monroe to Paris and empowered him and Livingston to negotiate for New Orleans and the Floridas. That the envoys' "zealous exertions" resulted in the purchase of all of Louisiana was "just ground for mutual and general felicitation." Although the price of the sale would be considered "highly advantageous" in general, Madison noted that the financial terms "would have been more satisfactory if they had departed less from the plan prescribed" and the appropriated $2,000,000 had been used "to reduce the price or hasten the delivery of possession." Also, the terms for the payment by the United States of its citizens' claims were less favorable than what had been anticipated in the diplomats' instructions. All told, Madison confided, the "unexpected weight of the draught now to be made on the treasury will be sensibly felt by it and may possibly be inconvenient in relation to other important objects." Madison stated that the president had summoned Congress to meet "in order that the exchange of ratifications may be made within the time limitted," but he did not declare that there was NO REASON TO DOUBT ratification by the Senate (Madison, *Papers*, *Sec. of State Ser.*, 4:371; 5:238-9; Miller, *Treaties*, 2:518).

EDWARD LIVINGSTON had failed to turn over the proceeds of impost bonds or render a full account; see Gallatin to TJ, 16 June.

MONROE TO BE INSTRUCTED: understanding from George A. Hughes that Monroe had probably gone to Madrid, Madison in a letter of 29 July authorized the envoy to go ahead with a negotiation in Spain even though the purchase of Louisiana "has more than exhausted the funds" they had expected to use for the acquisition of the Floridas. Soon to be cut off from Spain's other possessions in North America, Florida would be expensive for the Spanish to maintain and impossible to defend, Madison asserted, and Monroe could prompt the Spanish government to consider the prospect that Britain might seize Florida and offer it to the United States "on some conditions or other." Although the problem of navigation of the Mississippi River was now solved and it seemed certain that Florida "must drop into our hand" eventually, Madison reported that the president would allow an expenditure of up to $2,250,000 for the acquisition of Florida to bring about "a peaceable and fair completion of a great object." Both the assumption by the United States of American claims against Spain and indemnification by Spain of damages caused by the revocation of the right of deposit at New Orleans were likely to be issues in the negotiation, Madison advised. If the Spanish would not part with all of Florida, Monroe should try to obtain West Florida, and if that failed he must attempt to get a guarantee of free passage on the rivers that ran from U.S. territory through West Florida to the Gulf of Mexico. Although it would "not be adviseable" to threaten war over access to the rivers, anything "short of that" would be appropriate, Madison indicated (Madison, *Papers*, *Sec. of State Ser.*, 5:240-3).

LEAVE IT DISCRETIONARY IN HIM: Madison sent his letter in duplicate, one copy going to Madrid, the other to Paris with instructions to forward it to London if necessary to catch up with Monroe. Whether a need to be at Paris or London would supersede Monroe's going to Spain for the Florida negotiation "must be left to your own decision," Madison wrote (same, 244). For the blank commissions and letters of credence that gave Monroe the choice of becoming U.S. minister to France or Great Britain, see Preparations to Negotiate an Alliance with Great Britain at 18 Apr.

[1] TJ first wrote an abbreviation for September before overwriting "Oct."

[2] Remainder of sentence interlined.

[3] Word interlined.

Proclamation to Convene Congress

By the
President of the United States
of America.
A PROCLAMATION.

WHEREAS great and weighty matters, claiming the consideration of the Congress of the United States, form an extraordinary occasion for convening them; I do by these presents appoint Monday the 17th day of October next for their meeting at the City of Washington, hereby requiring the respective Senators and Representatives, then and there to assemble in Congress, in order to receive such communications as may then be made to them, and to consult and determine on such measures, as, in their wisdom may be deemed meet for the welfare of the United States.

In Testimony Whereof, I have caused the Seal of the United States to be hereunto affixed, and signed the same with my hand.

Done at the City of Washington, the sixteenth day of July, in the year of our Lord, one thousand eight hundred and three; and L. S. in the twenty-eighth year of the Independence of the United States.

(Signed) TH: JEFFERSON.

By the President,
(Signed) JAMES MADISON, *Secretary of State.*

Broadside (DLC: Printed Ephemera Collection, Portfolio 227, Folder 3). Enclosed in James Madison to members of Congress, printed circular, 18 July, announcing the president's call for the meeting of the Senate and House of Representatives, which "is rendered necessary by conventions with the French Republic, involving a cession of Louisiana to the United States"; this matter "may require the presence of both Houses, and of which conventions the ratifications are to be exchanged within six months computed from the 30th of April last"; the necessity for prompt action, "with the very great importance of the subject to the interest of the United States, claim from every member the most punctual attendance"; the secretary of state is "charged by the President to urge these considerations on your patriotism, and your sense of duty" (Madison, *Papers*, *Sec. of State Ser.*, 5:192; a copy signed by Madison and addressed to John Breckinridge is in DLC: Breckinridge Family Papers).

EXTRAORDINARY OCCASION: according to Article 2, Section 3 of the Constitution, the president "may, on extraordinary occasions, convene both Houses, or either of them."

Address from the Philadelphia Ward Committees

SIR [before 17 July 1803]

In addressing you on a subject, highly interesting to the Citizens of Pennsylvania, and particularly to that portion of them which we immediately represent, we feel it incumbent on us to declare, that our confidence in you, testified on so many occasions has never abated.—

But when our opinions have been misrepresented; when the great body of the Republicans of Pennsylvania have been outrageously called "an interested minority" we have deemed it our duty to make our real sentiments known with that respectful deference due to the first magistrate of a free people.—

On the subject of removal from office the opinion of Pennsylvania has long been well known; the unanimous applause and confidence which have followed the measure of our State Executive, the conversion of his Libellers into eulogists, the result of every election in this State since his elevation to the Governmental chair; and particularly the late general Congressional election, speak a language too explicit to be mistaken; too solemn to be opposed by any private, partial, or insidious allegations.

The same intolerant spirit governs the federal officers in this section of the union, which has ever been characteristick of their party; their official influence is exerted to excite prejudices against the administration; their official expenditures to purchase proselytes to their cause. It is a fact deeply affecting that in Philadelphia, publick employment under the federal administration in all its grades, with scarcely an exception, is confined not to federalists merely but to Apostates, persecutors, and enemies of Representative Government.—

We believe we express the sentiments of the people of Pennsylvania, we know we speak those of our immediate constituents, and we have thought it proper to communicate them to you directly. Knowing that you act from the purest views, feeling the happy result of your wise administration, we wish not our prospects of progressive prosperity to be over clouded by a policy which may tend to paralize the efforts of the Friends of the administration.—

Three years have nearly passed away in unexampled efforts of conciliation, and we have witnessed as the consequence, increased audacity and the circulation of the most unfounded slanders and misrepresentations of the government, and those who administer it, while not a few who disseminate discontent are fostered by a too indulgent administration.—

We look, Sir, to an election fast approaching when our whole strength must of necessity be exerted. Our opponents have already commenced their operations, and are maturing their plans of hostility and intrigue. It behoves us therefore not to stand indifferent spectators. We pledge ourselves to be calm, firm, and collected, and we look up to you, Sir, for that aid which a good cause requires, to enable us to resist the combination of Mercantile & Banking influence, which cooperating with that of men in office, menaces us with an opposition which tho' formidable, is not such as to dismay if we continue united & receive that support from the General Government which it is in their power to afford, & which the people confidently hope for and expect.—

We address you, Sir, with the Independence & unreserve of Freemen, under a sincere conviction of the necessity of making you acquainted with the truth, believing, that a continuance of the power to do good must depend much on the removal from office of men, who abuse the power entrusted to them & pursue their incurable propensity to do mischief, assuring you at the same time of our belief that there would be no occasion for this procedure, if you had been faithfully and correctly informed of the sentiments of the people of Pennsylvania.—

We are with the truth and sincerity of Freemen your most affectionate friends & Fellow Citizens.—

Geo Bartram Secretary
& a Representative from Walnut Ward.

Lewis Rush Caspar Rehn Andrew Geyer Junior	Uper Delaware Ward
John Butler Robert Cochran Thomas T. Peters	Lower Delaware Ward
John Willis Sallows Shewell Joel Gibbs	High Street Ward
Thos. Armstrong Wm Duane Js. McGlathery	Chesnut Ward
James Ker Liberty Browne	Walnut Ward
Thos. Wright John Purdon	Dock Ward
Samuel Carver. James Carson John Douglass	Newmarket Ward

JOHN M SMITH JACOB MYNICK DANIEL CLAWGES	North-Mulberry Ward
JOHN BARKER LAMBERT SMYTH	South Mulberry Ward
ADAM HENCHMAN THOS. BRADLEY JOHN MEER	north Ward
JOHN L. LEIB PETER GRAVENSTINE JAMES GIRVAN	Middle Ward
JOSEPH SCOTT ANTHY CROTHERS PETER BOB	South Ward
ABM. SHOEMAKER JACOB MANSFIELD	Locust Ward
THOMAS TOMKINS PHILIP MASON WM. STEVENSON SENR *Chairman*:	Cedar Ward

RC (DLC); undated; in George Bartram's hand, signed by all; at head of text: "The Ward Committees of Philadelphia in General Committee assembled" and "To Thomas Jefferson President of the United States"; endorsed by TJ as received 17 July and so recorded in SJL.

TJ received this address reluctantly. He wrote Gallatin on 28 Mch.: "I hope those of Philadelphia will not address on the subject of removals. it would be a delicate operation indeed." Several of the signers above were leaders in the city government. George Bartram, a graduate of the University of Pennsylvania and a militia leader, was a member of the Philadelphia Select Council and in 1809 became its president. John L. Leib was clerk of the council. Caspar Rehn, Sallows Shewell, Robert Cochran, James McGlathery, John Purdon, Abraham Shoemaker, and Thomas Tomkins served a term or more on the city's common council between 1802 and 1805, with Joseph Scott as the clerk for several years; John Barker and John Douglass served as aldermen; James Ker as a city, and Samuel Carver and Thomas Bradley as the county, commissioner. In 1803, Barker was elected sheriff of Philadelphia, and in 1808 he became mayor. The signers were appointed at ward meetings to become part of the general committee to draw up the address to the president. For instance, Bartram, on 4 Apr., chaired the meeting of "democratic citizens" of Walnut Ward held at the house of James Ker. The meeting appointed Bartram, Ker, and Liberty Browne to the general committee to write the address (James Robinson, *The Philadelphia Directory, City and County Register, for 1802* [Philadelphia, 1802], [6]; Robinson, *The Philadelphia Directory, City and County Register, for 1803* [Philadelphia, 1803], Appendix, i; Robinson, *The Philadelphia Directory for 1804* [Philadelphia, 1804], 290; Robinson, *The Philadelphia Directory for 1805* [Philadelphia, 1805], liii; PMHB, 49 [1925], 91-2; 50 [1926], 86-7; Thomas Scharf and Thompson Westcott, *History of Philadelphia: 1609-1884*, 3 vols. [Philadelphia, 1884], 3:1708; *Aurora*, 12 Mch., 5 Apr., 13 Aug., 9, 30 Sep. 1803; *Philadelphia Repository, and Weekly Register*, 22 Oct. 1803). For an account of the ward meetings, see Gallatin to TJ, 21 Mch. William Duane publicized the ward meetings as they were held in the spring of 1803, but the address to the president did not appear in the *Aurora* at the time (Sanford W. Higginbotham, *The Keystone in the Democratic Arch: Pennsylvania Politics 1800-1816* [Harrisburg, 1952], 59).

INTERESTED MINORITY: the ward meetings passed a resolution expressing concern that some Republicans were misleading the president by noting that calls for the removal of Federalist officeholders in Philadelphia were "confined to a small minority of our fellow citizens, and more particularly to interested individuals." They were quoting from the draft of a letter that William Jones and other Pennsylvania congressmen had planned to send the president, assuring him of their undiminished confidence in his appointment policies (*Aurora*, 11, 17, 31 Mch., 2 Apr. 1803, 6 Aug. 1805).

Thomas McKean, the STATE EXECUTIVE, was noted for his aggressive removal of Federalists when he took office (Vol. 38:636, 639n; Vol. 39:77; Vol. 40:500). As a result of the LATE GENERAL CONGRESSIONAL ELECTION, Pennsylvania's entire delegation to the Eighth Congress was Republican, 18 representatives and 2 senators (Vol. 39:471-2).

To William C. C. Claiborne

DEAR SIR Washington July 17. 1803.

Before you recieve this you will have heard thro' the channel of the public papers of the cession of Louisiana by France to the US. the terms & extent of that cession, as stated in the National Intelligencer, are accurate. in order to obtain a ratification in time I have found it necessary to convene Congress on the 17th. of October. before that time it will be necessary for me to procure for them all the information necessary to enable them to take understandingly the best measures for incorporating that country with the Union, & for it's happy government. for this purpose I have sent a set of queries, of which the inclosed is a copy, to mr Daniel Clarke of New Orleans to obtain & forward answers before the meeting of Congress. my object in inclosing them to you, is to engage you to select such of them as may lay within the compass of your enquiry, and to obtain for me any information on them which you may be able to obtain. no doubt, many of them may be within the knowledge of some persons within your acquaintance, and statements on any parts of them will be acceptable. I consider the acquisition of this country as one of the most fortunate events which have taken place since the establishment of our independence, & the more fortunate as it has not been obtained by war & force, but by the lawful & voluntary cession of the proprietor, a title which nothing can hereafter bring into question. it secures to an incalculable distance of time the tranquility, security & prosperity of all the Western country. I set out on the 19th. for Monticello, to be here again on the 25th. of October. accept my friendly salutations, and assurances of great esteem & respect. TH: JEFFERSON

PrC (DLC); at foot of text: "Governr. Claiborne." Enclosure: see Queries on Louisiana, at 9 July 1803, Document IV.

For the terms of the Louisiana cession, AS STATED IN THE NATIONAL INTELLIGENCER, see Notes on a Cabinet Meeting, 16 July 1803.

To Daniel Clark

DEAR SIR Washington July 17. 03

You will be informed by a letter from the Secretary of state of the terms and the extent of the cession of Louisiana by France to the US. a cession which I hope will give as much satisfaction to the inhabitants of that province as it does to us. and the more as the title being lawfully acquired & with consent of the power conveying, can never be hereafter reclaimed under any pretence of force. in order to procure a ratification in good time I have found it necessary to convene Congress as early as the 17th. of October. it is essential that before that period we should deliver all the information respecting the province which may be necessary to enable Congress to make the best engagements for it's tranquility, security & government. it is only on the spot that this information can be obtained, & to obtain it there I am obliged to ask your agency. for this purpose I have prepared a set of queries, now inclosed, answers to which, in the most exact terms practicable, I am to ask you to procure. it is probable you may be able to answer some of them yourself; however it will doubtless be necessary for you to distribute them among the different persons best qualified to answer them respectively. as you will not have above 6. weeks from the reciept of them till they should be sent off, to be here by the meeting of Congress, it will be the more necessary to employ different persons on different parts of them. this is left to your own judgment, and your best exertions to obtain them in time are desired. you will be so good as to engage the persons who undertake them to compleat them in time, and to accept such recompense as you shall think reasonable, which shall be paid on your draft on the Secretary of state. we rely that the friendly dispositions of the Spanish government will give such access to the archives of the province as may facilitate information, equally desireable by Spain on parting with her antient subjects, as by us on recieving them. this favor therefore will, I doubt not, be granted on your respectful application. Accept my salutations and assurances of esteem & respect.

TH: JEFFERSON

PrC (DLC); a few words overwritten by TJ in ink; at foot of text: "Daniel Clarke esq." Enclosure: see Document IV in Queries on Louisiana, at 9 July.

For the letter to Clark from the SECRETARY OF STATE, see Notes on a Cabinet Meeting, 16 July, and TJ to Madison, 17 July.

To William Dunbar

DEAR SIR Washington July 17. 1803

Before you recieve this you will have heard thro' the channel of the public papers, of the cession of Louisiana by France to the US. the terms as stated in the National Intelligencer are accurate. that the treaty may be ratified in time I have found it necessary to convene Congress on the 17th. of October: and it is very important for the happiness of the country that they should possess all the information which can be obtained respecting it, that they may make the best arrangements practicable for it's good government. it is the more necessary because they will be obliged to ask from the people an amendment of the constitution authorising their recieving this province into the union, & providing for it's government; and the limitations of power which shall be given by that amendment will be unalterable but by the same authority. I have therefore sent some queries to mr Clarke of New Orleans, to be answered by such persons as he shall think best qualified, and to be returned to me before the meeting of Congress, and knowing that you have turned your attention to many of the subjects, I inclose you a copy of them, and ask the favor of you to give me what information you can in answer to such of them as you shall select as lying within the scope of your information. I am encouraged to propose this trouble to you by a thorough persuasion of your readiness & desire to serve the public cause by whatever shall be in your power: and by the belief that you are one of those who will sincerely rejoice at our success in relieving you by peaceable means from a powerful & enterprising neighbor & establishing on a permanent basis the tranquility, security and prosperity of that interesting country. I tender you my friendly salutations and assurances of my great esteem & respect. TH: JEFFERSON

July 18. P.S. Since writing the preceding your favor of June 10. has been recieved. the exchange of a peaceable for a warring neighbor at New Orleans was undoubtedly ground of just and great disquietude on our part: and the necessity of acquiring the country could not be unpercieved by any. the question which divided our legislature (but not the nation) was whether we should take it at once, & enter single-handed into war with the most powerful nation on earth, or place things on the best footing practicable for the present, and avail ourselves of the first war in Europe (which it was clear was at no great distance) to obtain the country as the price of our neutrality, or as a reprisal for wrongs which we were sure enough to recieve. the war happened somewhat sooner than was expected; but our measures were previously taken, and the thing took the best turn for both parties. those who were honest in their reasons for preferring immediate war, will in their candour, rejoice that their opinion was not followed. they may indeed still believe it was the best opinion according to probabilities. we however believed otherwise and they, I am sure, will now be glad that we did. the letter of yesterday will shew you my desire of recieving information from you, and I shall always be thankful for it. my wish is to hear every thing, compare all together, and to do what on the whole I conscientiously think for the best. I repeat my salutations & esteem.

PrC (DLC); at foot of first page: "William Dunbar esq."; postscript written on a separate sheet. Enclosure: see Document IV in Queries on Louisiana, at 9 July.

For the publication of the TERMS of the treaty in the *National Intelligencer*, see Notes on a Cabinet Meeting, 16 July.

To William Falconer

SIR Washington July 17. 1803.

An old man of the name of Duncan Brown, who exhibits respectable attestations of character, complains of a robbery committed on him in North Carolina by an inhabitant of S. Carolina. he has been very illy advised, for he says he was advised to come to me to have justice done him. he shews me your opinion, which I immediately informed him was exactly what he ought to have pursued and to have spared himself the terrible journey he has taken. but he insists on being right, and that he will not move unless I will write to you to have justice done him. finding it more practicable to comply with, than to correct his judgment, I do so, only praying that you will ascribe the liberty I take to the sollicitations of the old man, who seems to have interested your feelings as he is calculated to do those of every other. I pray you to accept this apology & my respectful salutations.

TH: JEFFERSON

PrC (DLC); in ink at foot of text: "Wm Falconer esq. S.C."

William Falconer (d. 1805), a Scottish-born attorney, settled in Chesterfield, South Carolina, sometime after 1785 and represented the district in the South Carolina House of Representatives from 1792 to 1805. He was a Federalist elector in the presidential election of 1800 and a member of the first board of directors for the University of South Carolina (*S.C.*

Biographical Directory, House of Representatives, 4:196-7; John Belton O'Neall, *Biographical Sketches of the Bench and Bar of South Carolina*, 2 vols. [Charleston, S.C., 1859], 2:343-4; Vol. 32:265).

Gallatin's Comments on Address from Philadelphia Ward Committees

[17-18 July 1803]

+ Lewis Rush—	carver, a respectable & firm republican—	not known personally
+ Sallows Shewell—	shop-keeper, a consistant republican, honest man, rather weak, candidate for office	known persony.
+ James Ker—	coachmaker, an old, warm, consistant republican, honest man—	do
+ John Barker—	I presume the General of Militia, same as Ker, but more intelligent & conspicuous—	do
John L. Leib—	lawyer, the Doctor's brother—	do. slightly
+ P. Gravenstine—	keeps a fruit shop, old republican—	not known persony
Joseph Scott—	the Geographer—warm, & I believe honest—a new man—	known person[ly]
W. Duane	——also new—	do.

The five marked + which are distinguished by the name of old republicans were active whigs during the war & republican ever since—Scott & Duane came since the war but uniform republicans since they came—Of Leib's former politics I know nothing; the family were I presume whigs; but it is only since the French revolution that the Doctr. was with us. Before that he wanted to support Fred. Muhlenberg for Govr. against Mifflin whom the repub. then[1] supported. That, however, might be merely personal. I do not know a single one amongst the other signers, but have heard the names of Geyer, Willis, Gibbs, Purdon, & Shoemaker. My not knowing them is no proof of their not being conspicuous in their respective spheres or wards. I never mixed with the people, & hardly any of the citizens in Philada.

As I will stay a few days in Philada., would it not be better, if you intend to answer, to wait until I have been there.

The assertion that public employment in Philada. under the fed. administration in all its grades is confined to federalist is singular.

The Marshal Smith,[2] Superintt. Irvine[3] of military stores, store keeper Leonard,[4] Supervisor, & Collector are republicans. They have in their hands the appointment of almost the whole subordinate offices. The naval officer, Surveyor, & Commissioner of Loans do not appoint a single subordinate officer. The clerk hire of the three together is only 4,696 dollars; of which 2,500 dollars are in the last office. The patronage of the two obnoxious officers is clerk hire to the annual amount of 2,196 dollars. The total amount of custom house expences in Philada. was for 1800—56,115 dollars; of which 9,847 was the compensation & patronage of M'pherson & Jackson; the whole remainder is Muhlenberg's, about 1500 dollars excepted which belong to the revenue cutter; and the officers of this are republicans.

MS (DLC: TJ Papers, 119:20589); entirely in Gallatin's hand; undated, but see below; frayed at margin.

After TJ received the address from the Philadelphia ward committees on 17 July, he immediately shared it with Gallatin. They conversed and the Treasury secretary drew up these observations before the president left for Monticello on the 19th (TJ to Gallatin, 25 July 1803). TJ relied heavily on Gallatin's last paragraph when he drafted a letter to William Duane on 24 July.

In 1811, LEWIS RUSH succeeded JOHN BARKER as commander of the Militia Legion of Philadelphia (PMHB, 49 [1925], 91-2).

I NEVER MIXED WITH THE PEOPLE: during the 1790s, Gallatin had divided his time between Philadelphia and his home in western Pennsylvania, first as a state legislator, briefly as a U.S. senator, and then as a congressman (ANB; *Biog. Dir. Cong.*).

STORE KEEPER LEONARD: probably William Linnard, the military agent at Philadelphia responsible for obtaining and transporting military stores (Vol. 37:194-5).

Tench Coxe became SUPERVISOR of the revenue after Peter Muhlenberg replaced Federalist George Latimer as COLLECTOR at Philadelphia in the summer of 1802 (Vol. 38:31-2; Vol. 40:636n).

NAVAL OFFICER, SURVEYOR, & COMMISSIONER OF LOANS: William McPherson, William Jackson, and Stephen Moylan, respectively. Moylan received a $1,500 salary and $289 in commissions. He was allowed five clerks, each with a $500 salary. The compensation and patronage figures cited by Gallatin conform exactly to those published in the 1802 roll of federal officers (see ASP, *Miscellaneous*, 1:271-2, 305; Vol. 36:568-71). The REVENUE CUTTER officers were Richard Howard and Joseph Sawyer (see Document VI in Party Affiliation of Federal Officeholders, printed at 11 July).

[1] MS: "than."

[2] Name interlined above "Marshal."

[3] Name interlined above "Superintt."

[4] Name interlined above "store keeper."

To James Madison

TH:J. TO J.M. July 17. 1803.

It was agreed yesterday

1. that a copy of the proclamation should be inclosed to each member in a letter from the Secy. of state, mentioning that the meeting of Congress had been necessarily anticipated three weeks, because the

ratificns of the treaty & conventions for the cession of Louisiana were to be exchanged on the 30th. day of October, & suggesting the importance of a punctual attendance on the 1st. day.

2. that the Secretary of State should write to Messrs. Livingston & Monroe, expressly approving their obtaining Louisiana, and sum agreed to be given for it.
3. that Monroe be instructed to endeavor to purchase both or either Florida at the prices before settled, or at any rate to establish a plenary right to the use of all rivers which rising within the Spanish territories, pass thro' ours. to observe at the same time that we are not now so anxious for the purchase of the Floridas, because of the large sum we have to provide for Louisiana, & because we believe they will fall into our hands in good time:[1] but still if to be obtained easily, we will purchase.
   he should know their pretensions & proofs of the boundaries of Louisiana.
   if not gone to Madrid, he must determine according to circumstances whether to go there, or to London, or to stay at Paris.

The Secretary of state to write to our Consul at N. Orleans communicating the substance of the treaty and calling his attention to the public property transferred to us, to wit public buildings &c archives &c and to give assurances that the rights of the inhabitants will be liberally protected.

RC (DLC: Madison Papers, Rives Collection); final paragraph added as postscript; addressed: "Mr. Madison"; endorsed by Madison.

For what was AGREED at the meeting of the heads of departments and actions that Madison took as a result, see Notes on a Cabinet Meeting, 16 July.

KNOW THEIR PRETENSIONS & PROOFS: in his letter of 29 July, Madison asked Monroe to collect "useful information and proofs" in Spain "of the first limits or of the want of fixed limits to western Louisiana" and information about "whether any and how much" of West Florida could be "fairly included in the Territory ceded to us by France." In his communication to Monroe and Robert R. Livingston jointly on that same day, Madison indicated that TJ wanted to know what understanding of the bounds of Louisiana had "prevailed in the negotiation," especially with regard to the Perdido River (Madison, *Papers*, *Sec. of State Ser.*, 5:239-40, 243).

RIGHTS OF THE INHABITANTS: Madison enclosed a copy of the third article of the treaty, the one relating to citizenship, with his letter to Daniel Clark on 20 July and authorized the consul to "give the most ample assurances that all the rights of the Inhabitants, provided for, will be faithfully maintained; and in general that their situation will experience every proper mark not only of justice but of affection & patronage. The provision contained in this Article was particularly enjoined in the instructions to our Ministers," Madison continued, "and there is every reason to believe that it formed a perfect coincidence in the wishes and purposes of the French Government." For the provision of the treaty relating to citizenship, see Vol. 40:684-5. In his letter to Clark, Madison also discussed the sixth article of the treaty, which obliged the United States to continue Spain's treaties with Native American tribes until the United States negotiated new agreements with them. Madison asked Clark to begin collecting information about the relationship between the Indians and the Spanish and about "any meliorations thereof, which the mutual consent of the United States and these Tribes may introduce. As far as there may be opportunities," Madison suggested, "it will be equally proper to prepare the Indians for the change which is to take place" (Madison, *Papers*, *Sec. of State Ser.*, 5:202-3; Miller, *Treaties*, 2:501-2).

[1] Preceding three words interlined.

From Charles Willson Peale

DEAR SIR Museum July 17th. 1803.

I have just received a letter from my Son Raphaelle at Norfolk, in which he says, a Doctr. Willson has promissed him "on his word of honour, that he will have conveyed to me a great many of the Bones of the Magalonic—Legs—feet—thighs—Vertebræ &c. he hopes the remainder may ere this have been dug from the Salt Petre cave, they are in colour and texture like those belonging to the A.P.S.—he expects the whole Skeleton, they are in Possession of one of his Tenants a labourer in the Cave."

Some individuals perhaps may hope to get money by this collection of Bones, which I suppose is the same that we have had in expectation from Green Bryer County. Altho.' so very interresting to me, yet from my Sons being from home, my situation at present is such that I cannot well leave the Museum or I should hasten to the Spot. However I hope from your interest, and what you wrote me in a former letter, that I shall have the pleasure of putting togather many of the Bones if not make a compleat Skeleton of this wonderful Animal.

I have also received a Letter from Rembrandt of 23d of April—He says "his Exhibition is nearly as productive as any in London, but not so much so as it ought to be when he pays the highest Rent in that City—requiring the Visits of 17 Persons to pay the daily expence of his Room. his Visitors are 30-40-60-80 & sometimes 100—the latter seldom. That in 2 or 3 weeks will determine whether he sells the Skeleton to some national Repository, or to Visit some few large Cities."

Mr. Hawkins is now on his passage to England—his engenious invention of the Physiognotrace has brought a great deal of company to my Museum—and my Son Raphaelle is making also some profit by it in Norfolk. Raphaelle says "I shall get here from every person a quarter of a Dollar if they even want bread—fashion leads fools—My guilotine will take off the heads of all Norfolk, tho' it does not decapitate."

I sent one of those Machines for Rembrandt to use. It is not only interresting but curious to know whether his success with it, will equal the *Run* in America.

I remember your approbation of Mr. Hawkin's improvement of the Forte Piano, I am apprehensive that some of his first Instruments having failed in strength of the frames, may have discreditted them with many. I have one that has a wrought Iron frame, which supports the Strings so well that it keeps in tune perfectly well. but on account of the inaccuracy of some of the work composing the dampers, the Powers of my Instrument is lost—altho' this moovement is one of his late improvements. Mr. Hawkins will in future get better workmen. Knowing his mecanical powers and his intended improvements on his first Claviol I expect he will have great success with that charming Instrument in Europe. I have in the Museum the first Organ he has made, except a very small one, and it is a good Instrument, sweet and powerful for its size. This will occasionally amuse the Visitors untill Mr. Hawkins can give me a complete finished Claviol.

I have undertaken to get manufactured his writing Machines—and knowing how important it is to have them perfect before they are brought into public view, I will not let them be sold before a number is compleated with all the improvements I can make on experience.

I am full as much empressed with the importance of this Invention as when I first wrote to you on this subject.

That you may long enjoy perfect health is the ardent wish of your friend C W PEALE

RC (DLC); at foot of text: "His Excellency Thomas Jefferson Esqr."; endorsed by TJ as received 22 July and so recorded in SJL. PoC (PPAmP: Peale-Sellers Papers).

Peale's son RAPHAELLE, who had been in Virginia since March making profiles with the Hawkins physiognotrace and painting miniature portraits, had written to his father on 30 June (Lillian B. Miller, "Father and Son: The Relationship of Charles Willson Peale and Raphaelle Peale," *American Art Journal*, 25 [1993], 17-18; Peale, *Papers*, v. 2, pt. 1:542).

IN EXPECTATION FROM GREEN BRYER COUNTY: Peale, with TJ's assistance, had for several months been attempting to obtain bones from a cave in Greenbrier County, Virginia. Peale thought from descriptions of the remains that they were probably of a megalonyx (Peale to TJ, 19 Apr.). The FORMER LETTER from TJ was of 3 Nov. 1802, in which he informed Peale that he was asking Michael Bowyer for information about the bones (Vol. 38:634-5).

REMBRANDT Peale wrote his letter of 23 Apr. to another relative with a request to pass it along to his father (Peale, *Papers*, v. 2, pt. 1:8n, 539-40, 541n).

John Isaac HAWKINS intended to organize the manufacture of some of his musical inventions in England (Vol. 40:476, 501).

GUILOTINE: that is, the physiognotrace, a device to "take" heads (profiles). For a diagram of the Hawkins physiognotrace, see Vol. 39:408-9. The elder Peale did not always respond favorably to Raphaelle's spontaneity and sense of humor (David C. Ward and Sidney Hart, "Subversion and Illusion in the Life and Art of Raphaelle Peale," *American Art*, 8 [1994], 105-7).

SENT ONE OF THOSE MACHINES FOR REMBRANDT: Hawkins completed improvements on his physiognotrace design during the spring, and when he departed for Britain, at Peale's request he took one of the devices for Peale's sons (Peale, *Papers*, v. 2, pt. 1:517, 518n; Peale to TJ, 2 June).

Initially intrigued by Hawkins's innovative design for a PIANO, TJ bought one for the house at Monticello but returned it when it failed to stay in tune. He meanwhile became interested in obtaining a CLAVIOL from Hawkins (Vol. 38:83-5, 130; Vol. 40:501).

Hawkins's WRITING machine was the polygraph. Peale FIRST WROTE to TJ about the device in January (Vol. 39:306-7).

Petition of Ambrose Vasse and Others

Alexandria 17th July 1803.

We the undersigned Inhabitants of the Town of Alexandria most respectfully beg leave to lay before the President of the United States the following statement & Petition.

in the month of March last a certain Samuel Miller was indicted & convicted of a burglary commited in the store of Ambrose Vasse, one of the undersigned Petitioners, and was, during the present session of the court, sentenced To be capitally Executed on the 20th of August next. The witnesses who proved the fact were the said Ambrose Vasse and his two sons, who inhabited the upper story of the house in which they kept their store, containing flour & groceries.—about 10 oclock in the Evening mr Vasse & his sons were alarmed by a noise in the store resembling the falling down of a Barrel of flour.—upon examination they found that an alley-door, leading into the store, had been opened by some device which left no marks of violence. Entering the store, accompanied by some of their neighbors, they found the prisoner lying down on the floor, between the Tiers of flour. after the minutest inspection, they found not a single article removed out of its place, but the flour &c exactly in the same situation as they had left it when they shut up their store in the Evening. upon referring to the Indictment it will be found that the prisoner is charged with only a simple Burglary, unaccompanied by any actual robbery or theft. it was proved on the Trial, by a certain Thomas Steel, that the prisoner had been drinking very freely, and had left his house at about nine oclock that Evening, very much intoxicated. it is therefore very probable that the noise, which first alarmed mr Vasse & his sons, was caused by the prisoner's falling with some force on the floor, when he attempted to lie down between the Tiers of flour;—for there appeared no reason whatever to suppose that the noise proceeded from the overthrow of a flour-barrel or any other article. a loaded pistol was found in his pocket, but he attempted not the least resistance.—

having no intention to mislead by any concealment or misrepresentation of circumstances that may Tend to a fair Estimate of the character & probable reform of this man, we cannot omit stating that there was but too much reason to suspect he had been connected, in some degree, with a combination of plunderers, who had contemplated very daring & Extensive depredations, by means of pick-locks, false keys, &c. as an implement of this nature was found in his pocket, and a number of others in situations calculated to exite strong suspicions against him.—

from the most impartial enquiries into his past life & conduct, it appears that he came to this Town late in the year 1800, or early in the year 1801, and engaged himself as a Journeyman with a mr John Harrison, a respectable boot & shoe manufacturer, since removed to the federal city. he remained in that employment for six or seven months, during which Time mr Harrison declares his character to have been not only unsuspected, but exemplary for sobriety, industry & honesty. after forming other engagements here of a similar nature, we are informed he began to indulge in many extravagances & irregularities; and there is reason to beleive that these dissipated courses brought him at length into the company & acquaintance of the persons forming the nefarious combination before mentioned. many of them are known to have been very artful & plausible men; and it is probable that the necessities, consequent from his idleness & dissipation, contributed to render him a more easy victim to their seductions.—he cannot therefore be considered among the number of those criminals, who have been irretrievably inured to guilt by long & inveterate habit; but rather as one who has been recently Initiated into crimes, by the combined influence of complexional vices & of wicked & dangerous associates.—his conduct, since his confinement in Jail, evinces a mind the most accessible to emotions of the deepest contrition, such as could scarcely be consistent with a state of depravation beyond the hopes of reform. he has been afflicted at various Times since his confinement with frightful convulsion fits, attended with such violent symptoms, as have nearly proved fatal. The physician who attended him is clearly of opinion that these fits were produced entirely by violent affections of the mind.—indeed his countenance & general appearance exhibit the injurious Effects of mental Torture, almost unexampled under similar circumstances. from the whole Tenor of his conduct, since his confinement, there seems to be no doubt of his being profoundly penetrated with the most unaffected repentance & sorrow, nor of The sincerity & ardor of his present resolutions for reform.— he is now in the flower of his age, and is possessed of uncommon intelligence for one of his opportunities, with a vivacity of mind that may, at first, have brought him into the way of criminal seduction, but may, now that it is chastised into humility, carry him more safely thro the world, and contribute to the felicity & usefulness of a reformed Life.—

We beg leave also to suggest that a capital execution for a simple Burglary, unaccompanied by actual robbery or theft, is unprecedented in our Jurisprudence; and that suspicions of other crimes, not Judicially ascertained, ought not to aggravate the offense, of which he is actually convicted, so far as to foreclose the claims to mercy admitted by the nature of the Latter.—in the present case there would be something shocking to the sense of moral Justice if this man should be executed. for altho most of his associates have been dispersed & variously punished, yet none have incurred a greater punishment than fining, whipping & imprisonment; and there are the strongest reasons to beleive that they far exceed the guilt of this man, in the extent & number of their crimes, and the injury to individuals, besides the presumptions that exist of this man's having been a deluded instrument in their hands.—

We therefore earnestly and respectfully pray the president of the United States to interpose, and prevent, by a pardon, the Execution of the above mentioned Samuel Miller. AMBROSE VASSE

MS (DNA: RG 59, GPR); in an unidentified hand, signed by Vasse and 51 others; at head of text: "To the President of the United States." Enclosed in Madison to TJ, 26 July 1803.

A native of France, Ambrose Vasse (d. 1831) emigrated to the United States at the close of the American Revolution, where he resided as a merchant in Philadelphia for many years. Falling victim to bankruptcy, he relocated to Alexandria around 1802 and resumed his mercantile endeavors. At the time of the above-mentioned burglary, Vasse occupied a store on King Street (*Alexandria Advertiser*, 6 Oct. 1802; *Gazette of the United States*, 28 Oct. 1802; *Alexandria Gazette*, 26 Oct. 1831; Miller, *Alexandria Artisans*, 2:205; Vol. 24:743n, 745-6; Vol. 35:65).

TJ signed a pardon for SAMUEL MILLER, dated 25 July 1803, "hereby remitting and releasing all pains and penalties by him incurred" by his burglary conviction (MS owned by C. Fred O'Conner, Jr., Arlington, Va., 1946, in a clerk's hand, signed by TJ and James Madison; FC in Lb in DNA: RG 59, GPR; enclosed in Madison to TJ, 26 July 1803). For the confused circumstances surrounding Miller's pardon and its date, see Madison to TJ, 26 July; Petition of Samuel Miller, with Recommendation of William Kilty and William Cranch, 28 July; TJ to Madison, 31 July; and TJ to Jacob Wagner, 11 Aug. It would later be discovered that Miller was actually an escaped convict named Smith, who had been found guilty of burglary in New York and sentenced to life imprisonment (see Petition of Jacob Hoffman and Others, 12 Nov. 1803).

From Caspar Wistar

Dr Sir Philada. July 17th. 1803—

I received the two french works which accompany this—viz A Plan of Public Education, & a Treatise on the Intellectual Operations, from Mr Livingston the Minister at Paris I am afraid that I have detained them too long & crave therefore that Indulgence you have ever extended

to your faithful friend C. Wistar Junr

RC (DLC); at foot of text: "His Excellency The President of the United States"; endorsed by TJ as received 22 July and so recorded in SJL.

The two french works have not been identified but were perhaps Pierre Laboulinière, *Essai d'un plan d'enseignement public* (Turin, 1802), and Octave Alexandre Fallette-Barol, *Éclaircissemens sur plusieurs points, concernans la théorie des opérations et facultés intellectuelles* (Turin, 1803).

To Benjamin Austin, Jr.

Sir Washington July 18. 1803.

This serves to acknolege the reciept of your favor of the 7th. inst. and the pleasure I derive from the expressions of approbation which it contains. we have lately recieved the treaty and conventions for the cession of Louisiana. 11¼ millions of Dollars to the government of France, the discharge of their debts to *our citizens* under the Convention of 1800. not to exceed 20. Millions of francs, the right to France & Spain to import for 12. years, into the ceded territories, their own productions & manufactures on paying the same duties only as citizens, & ever after on the footing of the most favored nation, with a saving of the rights of religion, & property to [the inhabitants][1], & of being ta[ken] into the Union on our general principles, constitute the conditions of the acquisition. they will of course require an amendment of the constitution adapted to the case, that will leave the inhabitants & territory for some time in a situation difficult to be defined. but the acquisition has decided the painful question whether we are to be a peaceable or a warring nation? Accept my salutations and assurances of great esteem & respect. Th: Jefferson

PrC (DLC); blurred; at foot of text: "Benjamin Austin esq."

[1] Preceding three words interlined.

To William C. C. Claiborne

Dear Sir Washington July 18. 03.

I wrote to you yesterday, and in the evening recieved your favor of June 23. as I am just now setting out to Monticello to pass two months there, I am not able to turn to your letters; but as far as my memory can be trusted I think I have not recieved the one in which you say you had applied for my approbation of your paying a visit to Tennisee. if I had, I should certainly have answered it without delay. the government and public property, archives &c. of Louisiana are to be delivered up to us immediately after the exchange of ratifications, which will be between the 17th. & 30th. of October. as this is an operation with the French Commissary and Spanish Governor & Intendant which will require to be conducted with skill & delicacy, I had had it in contemplation to get you to repair thither at the time to transact it, and to hold the place some little time until Congress shall direct what is to be done more particularly. this order can be directed to you at Nashville where it will probably arrive about the 10th. of November, and would require instantaneous departure. this allows not quite 4. months from this time for your journey to Nashville & any other place and to be back at Nashville. I state these facts relating to the public service that you may decide for yourself on your own movements, as I know of no others which ought to controul them. should it be inconvenient for you to undertake the occasional mission to New Orleans, be so good as to inform me immediately, that some other may be thought of. we have supposed that if we order three companies from Fort Adams they will be sufficient to take care of the fortifications &c. Accept my salutations and assurances of esteem & respect. Th: Jefferson

PrC (DLC); at foot of text: "Governor Claiborne."

From Robert Crew

Sir London 18 July 1803

A person here has lately obtained a patent for a Churn on a new construction & Mrs Crew's Dairymaid speaks highly in praise of one of them which she has used for some months, as saving much time & labour

These being objects which deserve much attention in every Country, but in America are particularly valuable, I am induced to take the liberty of begging your acceptance of one of the Churns, which I now send ℔ the Atalanta Capt. Tucker, for Baltimore, to the care of Mr. Andrew Buchanan of that place.

Should you find this an useful machine, you will, I have no doubt, permit some of your workmen to construct others from the pattern, for the public benefit.—

The iron pins in the bottom are intended to be let into holes in a bench or dresser, in order to keep the Churn steady when in use.

The holes in the top are found, necessary for letting off bad air from the Cream.

I am with the greatest respect Sir Your most Obed Serv

ROBT CREW

RC (DLC); endorsed by TJ as received 9 Oct. and so recorded in SJL.

Virginia native Robert Crew was a successful tobacco importer and mercantile agent in London as of 1790 (Vol. 18:309n).

LATELY OBTAINED A PATENT: while the British patent holder is unknown, American patents for a churning machine had been granted to Isaac Baker on 20 Feb. 1802 and to Joel Pierce on 10 April 1802. Nicholas King received one for a revolving churn on 10 Mch. 1808 (*List of Patents*, 26, 27, 63).

A letter of 8 Oct. 1803 from Maryland merchant ANDREW BUCHANAN to TJ, recorded in SJL as received from Baltimore on the 9th, has not been found. In his financial memorandum for 18 Oct., TJ recorded sending Buchanan, by way of Robert Smith, $3.45 "for freight of a box" that presumably contained the churn (MB, 2:1110).

From Henry Dearborn

SIR. War Department July 18th. 1803.

I have the honor to propose William L. Brent of Maryland, and Charles M. Taylor of Pensylvania for 2d. Lieuts. of Artillerists—and Jonathan Eastman of Vermont and Neal Duffee of New York for Ensigns in the 1st. Regt. of Infantry.

Accept Sir, the assurances &c.—

FC (Lb in DNA: RG 107, LSP).

William L. BRENT, Charles M. TAYLOR, Jonathan EASTMAN, and Neal DUFFEE would all be included on the list of nominations and promotions TJ sent to the Senate on 18 Nov. 1803 (JEP, 1:457).

From Henry Dearborn

SIR. War Department July 18th. 1803.

I have the honor to propose the following persons for promotion in the Army of the U. States, Vizt.,

Richard S. Blackburn Capt. of Artillerists to be Major in the same Corps, vice Jackson resigned 30th. April 1803—

John Saunders Lt. of Artillerist to be Captain vice Blackburn promoted. Howell Cobb Lt. of Artillerists to be Captain vice Izard resigned June the 1st. 1803. Horatio Stark 2d. Lt. in the 1st. Regt. of Infy. to be 1st. Lieut. vice Whipple promoted 11th. April 1803. Anthony Campbell Ens. in the 1st. Regt. Infy. to be 2d. Lt., vice Stark promoted.

George Salmon 1st. Lt. in the 2d. Regt. of Infy. to be Captain, vice Butler deceased 6th. May 1803.

William H. Woolridge 2d. Lt. in the 2d. Regt. to be 1st. Lt. vice Salmon promoted.—

William Simmons Ensign in the 2d. Regt. of Infy. to be 2d. Lt. vice Wilkinson promoted 15th. Jany. 1803.

Joseph Doyle Ensign in the 2d. Regt. of Infy to be 2d. Lt. vice Wooldridge promoted.

With high consideration &c.

FC (Lb in DNA: RG 107, LSP).

The above candidates for PROMOTION would all be included on the list of nominations and promotions TJ sent to the Senate on 18 Nov. 1803 (JEP, 1:457-8).

From Gabriel Duvall

SIR, Washington, 18 July 1803.

About three months ago, I received a letter from Mr. Storey, of Salem, declining the appointment of Naval Officer of that port. The letter was put into the hands of Mr. Gallatin, who informs me that he left it with you. Another person has since been appointed.

Mr. Storey, in his letter, requested information from me on some particular points, to which I wish to make a reply, but cannot do it for want of the letter. Mr. Gallatin has frequently promised to ask you for it, but has, as often, omitted it. If you can, when at leisure, lay your hand upon it, I will thank you for it.— I am, with great Respect and esteem, your obedt. Sert. G. DUVALL.

RC (DLC); endorsed by TJ and recorded in SJL as received 18 July.

Joseph Story's letter to the comptroller DECLINING THE APPOINTMENT has not been found, but on 19 Apr. Gallatin returned Story's commission to Madison, and by 10 May TJ had decided to appoint Samuel Ward to the office (Levi Lincoln to TJ, 24 Apr.; Memorandum to James Madison, 10 May).

From Horatio Gates

DEAR SIR New York 18th July, 1803.

Let the Land rejoice, for you have bought Louisiana for a Song. never was a happier moment Seized, for concluding so Glorious a Negotiation: I took the Liberty to write you about a Week ago; in that letter I introduced Colonel Wm: Smith to your Future Notice, when the necessary appointment of Officers for your new acquisition shall take place, though I mention'd him, & gave my Reasons for it, as a proper person for to take possession of New Orleans, & to Remain Military Commandant of that Town; I by no means thought of him as a Governour for the Territory of Louisiana: There is another Man, who is your Warm Friend, & whose abillities are unquestionable in the Execution of that high Office.

What disposition you intend to make with regard to this immense Territory I know not, but take it for granted, that you will give it in the first Instance a Colonial Government; like those of the upper Mississipi, & Indiana; in that Event, I would Suggest confidentially; the Name of my, & your firm Friend, General Armstrong: as the Governour of it;—not having seen him for some time, I cannot assert that this Arrangment, would comport with his own Views; but I am induced to think, it would; because when I did see him, he talked of making an Establishment in one of the Southern States, from a belief, that a Northern Climate was unfriendly to His Health.

Your highly esteemed Favour of the 11th:, has arrived in due course by the Post; you may rest satisfied I shall most rigidly obey your Injunction, my word is ingaged, & you may depend upon it.

when the Cession of Louisiana is Complete, and your Officers have taken possession of New Orleans; & the posts at present occupied by Spain, you will still direct Fort Adams to be the main Object; whence, or in the Vicinity, I would wish the Seat of Government to be Fixed; but as soon as you get Possession, direct a Fort, & Batteries, to be[1] Erected on the properest Ground upon the West side of the River, as nearly opposite to Fort Adams as possible; this will make a Cross Fire with that Fort, which with the constant Current runing down, will, with the Strength of the back Country, make those Works a Gilbraltar to an approaching Enemy—New Orleans may be left as a mere Entrepos for Trade; as Norfolk in your State is at this Time.—Your Idea of removing all the Indians on this, to the other side the Missisipi; is Excellent: it will in great Measure prevent all Future Animosity with Them, restrict our own People to the East side, & add very considerably to the Furr Trade down the River.—with the Sinc'rest Friendship, & Attachment,

I am your Faithfull, Obedient Servant, HORATIO GATES.

RC (DNA: RG 59, LAR); endorsed by TJ as received 22 July and so recorded in SJL.

See Gates to TJ, 7 July, for Gates's recommendation of William Stephens SMITH.

Gates praised John ARMSTRONG to TJ and Madison in February 1802 (Vol. 36:573-4).

[1] Word supplied.

To Jared Mansfield

SIR Washington July 18. 1803.

Since the reciept of your favor of the 7th. inst. I have had a full conversation with mr Gallatin, and find that the rigorous rules of the treasury oppose insurmountable obstacles to the wishes I entertained in your favor. he shews me that by their rules, the expences of your journey here cannot be repaid, your salary cannot begin till that of your predecessor ends, which will be on your recieving or demanding the papers of the office, and that no advance can be made under the head of salary. there is no doubt but that in 99. cases in 100. these rules are proper, and it is only to be regretted that the obligation to adhere to rule in all cases, disables us from doing what would be right in some. mr Gallatin thinks you mistook him in supposing he would not advance money for instruments. on the contrary he will answer your draught for that purpose for a sum to be in your hands on account, and it may be such a sum as will not only pay for the instruments but enable you to proceed on your journey with the surplus[1] of that money, to be[2] placed to your debit in your future account of salary. he said for instance that he should consider your draught for 800. D. on account of the purchase of instruments as a justifiable advance on his part. while this proves a desire to accomodate you as far as is practicable, it will suggest the propriety of considering it as mentioned for your own information only, as it might in uncandid hands be injuriously perverted. I set off tomorrow for Monticello to be here again on the 25th of September. I shall sign & leave your commission with mr Gallatin who will proceed in a few days to New York to make some stay there. Accept my friendly salutations & assurances of great esteem & respect. TH: JEFFERSON

RC (NjP: Andre De Coppet Collection); addressed: "Capt Jared Mansfield Westpoint N.Y."; franked and postmarked. PrC (DLC); endorsed by TJ in ink on verso.

Mansfield's FAVOR OF THE 7TH. INST. inquired about the reimbursement of expenses incurred relating to his recent appointment as surveyor general.

I SET OFF TOMORROW: TJ left Washington on 19 July and arrived at Monticello on the 22d. The journey included a visit to the springs in Louisa County, where he met Mary Jefferson Eppes and John Wayles Eppes. TJ's travel expenses totaled $14.67 (MB, 2:1105; TJ to John Strode, 9 July 1803; TJ to Richard Morris, 29 Aug. 1803).

[1] Word interlined.
[2] TJ here canceled "allowed."

To J. P. G. Muhlenberg

DEAR SIR Washington July 18. 1803.

This will be delivered to you by mr Barnes, who being personally unknown to you, has asked of me a letter of introduction, as he proposes before I return to the seat of government, to visit Philadelphia, with a view to his removal there. he has been so long an inhabitant of that place that he can hardly live elsewhere. as he has been the subject of two former letters, I will add only that he is one of those grateful & correct men for whom one never repents of having done any thing. Accept my friendly salutations and great esteem.

TH: JEFFERSON

RC (Colonial Society of Massachusetts, Boston, 1950); at foot of text: "Genl. Muhlenberg." PrC (DLC); endorsed by TJ in ink on verso. Recorded in SJL with notation "by mr Barnes."

TWO FORMER LETTERS: TJ to Muhlenberg, 10 Oct. 1802 and 30 June 1803.

From Charles Willson Peale

DEAR SIR Museum July 18th. 1803.

Yesterday General Proctor called on me with the enclosed Letter to make what use I pleased with it, only reserving him a copy, which I have done.

A knowledge of the upper part of the head, is indeed very desirable—The Cranium and Nasal bones particularly, as being wholly deficient in my Skeleton.

I marval what are the teeth which he says weighs 19 or 20 pounds, can they be grinders—The largest I have seen belongs to Doctr Wistar, its weight 10 pounds.

The ends of the toes is wanting in my Skeleton; in some few toes I have three Phalanges, generally two, but some with only one.—These being small bones, in consequence passed over, or not often sought for. However as opportunities occur I mean to collect what bones I can, at little expence, in hopes of making up the dificiencies of this skeleton, or at least to make immitations by the aid of the Chizel from those that may not fit from belonging to a larger or smaller animal.

I cannot with freedom give answers to the queries, as I shall be considered much interrested. The cost and labour in this article has been great to me, but I shall be repaid in the issue, I contrive to make one part pay for the other expences of the Museum, still encreasing the value & utility[1] of the collection.

I am Dear Sir with much esteem your friend C W Peale

RC (DLC); at foot of text: "His Excellency Thos. Jefferson Esqr."; endorsed by TJ as received 22 July and so recorded in SJL. PoC (PPAmP: Peale-Sellers Papers). Enclosure: William Goforth, Jr., at Cincinnati to Thomas Procter of Philadelphia, 18 June, reporting that he has "found the greatest part of the bones of the Mamouth and am pretty confident that I shall be shortly able to procure a complete Skeleton"; extracting the bones is costing him "great labour & considerable expence," and he asks if it will be worth his while, if he does have a full skeleton, to transport it across the mountains for exhibition, or if he does not recover a full skeleton, whether exhibiting the bones he now has in his possession would pay back his expenditures; and he asks if there is any prospect of disposing of the bones or a complete skeleton in the seaboard cities or in Europe; the bones in his possession are "the upper part of the head and the under Jaws of the large Animal I have a large number of teeth from 19 or 20 pounds weight down to 4 or 5. one thigh bone weighing 31 pounds some ribs intire some broken the whole of the back bones one horn weighing about 100 pounds about twenty one Inches in Circumference & one horn about 5 feet long weighing 21 pounds and one other about Seven feet long" (DLC).

Goforth excavated the mammoth BONES from Big Bone Lick in Kentucky; see Meriwether Lewis to TJ, 3 Oct.

[1]MS: "utily."

From Caspar Wistar

Dear Sir Philada. July 18, 1803.

I beg leave to trouble you with the inclosed for Captain Lewis, they do not include many points, because his instructions have really anticipated every thing which occurred to me, & of course admitted of no additions but in detail. I have also avoided several subjects which I expected would be fully detailed by Dr Barton, as being particularly within those departments of Science to which he has devoted himself.

If the expedition should go on without any change in the original plan, in consequence of the late happy events respecting Louisiana, might not Mr Lewis derive some benefit from Monsieur Pirroux or Pierous, a Gentleman who applied to you when Secretary of State respecting an emigration which he wished to effect from Philada to the Spanish Main. He had been Governor (under Spain) of a fort near the mouth of the Missouri & appeared to know more of the trade & navigation of that River than any person I have seen. He said (so long ago as 1792) that the Canada Traders supplied the Indians on the upper parts of the Missouri with goods. If you think it proper to write to him I believe the letter would be very useful to Mr Lewis. What is the real direction of the Missouri? 'till the publication of McKenzie's book I believed it to be nearly west, & if I am not mistaken M. Pirroux spoke of it in the same way for 2000 miles of its extent—but McKenzies account is Confirmed by the Gentleman who gave the account of the Wild Sheep, in his narrative he mentions the Missouri as existing no great distance from the Saskatchevine river. I shall write this day to Mr Peter Pond (who is mentioned by McKenzie) on the subject, he lives in Connecticut & I believe will give any information in his power without any particular explanation respecting the reason for asking it.

I cannot conclude this letter without offering you my most sincere & cordial Congratulations on the very happy acquisitions you have made for our Country on the Missisippi—Altho no one here appears to know the extent or the price of the cession, it is generally considered as the most important & beneficial transaction which has occurred since the declaration of Independence, & next to it, most like to influence or regulate the destinies of our Country—I believe that allmost all impartial people here, who take the pains to think for themselves, consider the British reasons for the war as very slight—

With the greatest respect I am your affectionate friend

C. Wistar Junr.

RC (DLC); at foot of text: "His Excellency The P. U.S."; endorsed by TJ as received 22 July and so recorded in SJL. Enclosure not found.

TJ forwarded Wistar's queries or suggestions to Meriwether LEWIS on 16 Nov. For Benjamin Rush's queries for Lewis regarding Native American societies, see Lewis to TJ, 29 May, and see Rush to TJ, 11 June, for Rush's directions to Lewis "for preserving his health" on the expedition. Although TJ had asked Benjamin Smith BARTON to designate topics "in the lines of botany, zoology, or of Indian history which you think most worthy of enquiry & observation," no questions or guidelines from Barton for Lewis have been found (Jackson, *Lewis and Clark*, 1:161n; Vol. 39:588-9).

MONSIEUR PIRROUX: see TJ to Henri Peyroux de la Coudrèniere, 3 July.

For Duncan McGillivray's account of the bighorn SHEEP, see Edward Savage to TJ, 10 Mch.

From 1765 to 1788, Connecticut native PETER POND engaged in fur-trading ventures that took him to the Great Lakes, the upper Mississippi Valley, and as far west and north as the Saskatchewan and Athabasca Rivers. As TJ knew, the reliability of information from Pond was disputed (DAB; Vol. 23:240, 243n, 259; Vol. 27:793).

From Henry Dearborn

SIR. War Department July 19th. 1803.

I have the honor to propose Reuben Chamberlin for an Ensign in the 2d. Regt. of Infantry in the service of the United States.—

Accept Sir, the assurances &c.

FC (Lb in DNA: RG 107, LSP).

Reuben CHAMBERLIN of New Hampshire would be included on the list of nominations and promotions TJ sent to the Senate on 18 Nov. 1803 (JEP, 1:458).

From Benjamin Galloway

Hagers Town Washington County Maryland
SIR, July 19th. 1803.

The General Assembly of Maryland at their last Session gave Entertainment to a Bill entitled An Act for the better Administration of Justice &c &c &c; which they ordered to be published for the Consideration of the People. The Object contemplated by that Bill (if accomplished) is so fundamentally contrariant to my Ideas of Propriety; and the Consequences which must necessarily flow from the Enaction of *that Bill* into *a Law*; present themselves to my Understanding in so formidable a Point of View; that I have determined to use my utmost Endeavours to convince the Voters of Washington County, that the Bill as published ought not to be *countenanced by them.* I am sorry Sir to inform you, that in this opinion, I now am; and shall be opposed by some of the most respectable, and influencial Characters (Republicans) of said County. *But* Sir, "*Nullius addictus jurare in verba Magistri*"; The *Salus Reipublicæ* in my Judgment *is endangered*; and a strong Sense of Duty to my Country, and *that alone*, influences my Conduct on the present Occasion. In Truth the Bill was introduced into the Legislature by Men whose Intentions I well know, to be pure: but the want of professional Knowledge and Experience relative to the judicial Department of Government, have unfortunately placed them in a Situation, approximating to a *Dilemma.* I trust that no Citizen who has been a Witness to; or who is accurately informed of the Line of Conduct which I have *steadily pursued, as a Politician through Life*; will be induced to suspect my *political* Integrity; *because I* happen to differ in opinion (as to a State Measure) with some few Men in whose Company I have *with great pleasure* travelled on the *Turnpike Road of Republicanism.* Unable to meet my objections to "the Bill" on the ground of *solid* Argument, an Attempt will be made to deceive the People of this County into a Beleif, that I have *deserted* from the *Standard* of *Republicanism*; and am consequently unworthy of popular Trust or Confidence: i. e. in so many words; You Benjamin Galloway are *not* a Republican; "Because *you will not unhesitatingly support the Bill alluded to*"—I view that Bill as a "rudis indigestaq moles; non bene junctarum, *Discordia* semina Rerum"—I may have formed an *erroneous* Judgment—But most unquestionably I have a Right to express my *opinion* on *any* public Measure; and *more especially so*, on a Bill published *by the Assembly* for the Consideration of *their Constituents* unless it was the Intention of the Patrons of the Bill (which many of them *now confess*, is not perfect) that it should be *supported* by *its Friends*; but not *opposed* by its *Enemies*—such *I cannot suppose* to have been *the Design* of *the Assembly*—

Having premised that an attempt will be made (indeed it is now making, with no *inconsiderable* Activity) to establish a Position, derogatory to my political Character; I shall consider it as a signal Favour conferred on *me* by *You Sir*; if you will furnish me with an *authenticated Copy*, of a Letter written by Benjamin Galloway to Thomas Jefferson Vice President of US City of Washington, (which I think was) dated Novr. 30, 1800 but which I well remember to have delivered to Col: Smilie Pennsilvania; and which on his Return from the Session, he assured me, He had delivered to the *Vice President.* If Sir you can without a Waste of Time (which I presume *is precious* at this *Crisis*) lay your Hands on *that Letter* (I am told, you have for many years been in the practice of preserving all Letters written to you on the Subject of Politicks) and will suffer Mr Lewis to copy *it*; transmit the Copy to me, *and to say*, "that it is a true Copy of a Letter from Benjamin Galloway of Washington County Maryland to Thomas Jefferson Vice President of US. dated Novr 30th, 1800; which Letter is *now* in the Possession of *Mr. Jefferson*"; you will Sir confer an especial Favour, which will ever be remembered and acknowledged by Me—

I am Sir with high Consideration, and great personal Regard yrs. &c &c. &c. BENJAMIN GALLOWAY

PS. If I can obtain a copy of the Letter above referred to, I shall consider myself as armed with *a Shield*, whose Powers are *amply sufficient* to *repel* every Attack, that now is making, or that may be made on my *political principles*. BG.

RC (DLC); endorsed by TJ as received 27 July and so recorded in SJL.

On 19 Apr., the Maryland Council ORDERED TO BE PUBLISHED in the *National Intelligencer* and seven newspapers in the state a legislative proposal "to alter, change and abolish such parts of the constitution and form of government as relates to the establishing a general court and court of appeals." The bill called for the state to be divided into five districts, with two persons of integrity and legal training residing within each division to be appointed district judges. They would be joined by "one person of integrity, experience and knowledge" from each county to be an "Associate Judge." Thus, each county court would include two district judges and one associate, the latter of whom was not required to have legal training (Baltimore *Federal Gazette*, 26 Apr. 1803).

BILL AS PUBLISHED OUGHT NOT TO BE COUNTENANCED: Galloway probably wrote a piece critical of the proposed legislation, signed "A Constituent." The writer argued that in cases where the two district judges disagreed, the decision would be made by the associate judge, who was "unlearned in the law." He compared the situation to that of entrusting a carpenter rather than a blacksmith to shoe a favorite riding horse (*Maryland Herald and Elizabeth-Town Weekly Advertiser*, 7 Sep.). In a published letter dated 12 Sep. 1803, Galloway challenged the Washington County assembly candidates to declare publicly in the press how they would vote on the bill, characterizing it as "the very worst" introduced into either house of the general assembly in 20 years. If it became law "the Peace, Happiness and valuable Interests of the People, public, & private" would be "*most injuriously affected.*" Galloway offered himself as a candidate, if those running did not openly oppose the legislation. When the assembly met in late 1803, support for the bill was reported to be evenly divided. After debate, the House of Delegates voted 38 to 34 against the measure (same, 14, 28 Sep. 1803, 4 Jan. 1804; *Bartgis's Republican Gazette*, 30 Dec. 1803; *Votes and Proceedings of the House of Delegates of the State of Maryland. November Session, One Thousand Eight Hundred and Three* [Annapolis, 1804], 58). Another judiciary act was proposed in 1804 and ratified in 1805. It called for the establishment of six districts with county courts composed of a chief judge and two associate judges, all with "sound legal knowledge" (Alfred S. Niles, *Maryland Constitutional Law* [Baltimore, 1915], 377-8).

NULLIUS ADDICTUS JURARE IN VERBA MAGISTRI: "I am not bound to swear as any master dictates" (Horace, *Epistles*, 1.1.14).

SALUS REIPUBLICÆ: "safety of the state."

INTENTIONS I WELL KNOW, TO BE PURE: when they brought their report and bill before the Maryland Senate on 3 Jan. 1803, the judiciary committee noted that they found the mode of administering justice in the state to be "frequently grievous and oppressive to the citizens," who had to travel great distances from their homes to attend the general courts. These inconveniences could amount "to a denial of justice." The judiciary bill was introduced to "bring justice as near as may be to every man's door" (*Votes and Proceedings of the Senate of the State of Maryland. November Session, One Thousand Eight Hundred and Two* [Annapolis, 1803], 48).

RUDIS INDIGESTAQ MOLES: in the first book of *Metamorphoses*, Ovid refers to the "rudis indigestaque moles," that is, "a rough unordered mass." Ovid continues one line later, NON BENE JUNCTARUM DISCORDIA SEMINA RERUM, that is, "the discordant seeds of unassembled things" (Ovid, *Metamorphoses*, 1.7, 9).

TJ could not provide an AUTHENTICATED COPY of the letter requested by Galloway. According to SJL, the only correspondence TJ received from the Hagerstown resident while vice president was that of October 1797. It is not clear what happened to the letter entrusted to John SMILIE, a congressman from Fayette County, Pennsylvania (*Biog. Dir. Cong.*; TJ to Galloway, 28 July, 14 Oct. 1803).

To Hammuda Pasha, Bey of Tunis

ILLUSTRIOUS FRIEND,

As we have desired Mr Lear who has lately been appointed our Consul General to the Kingdom of Algiers to attend to several of our special concerns in the Mediterranean we have among others charged him to present himself at your Court to arrange with you certain subjects which may more and more consolidate the peace and good intelligence which prevails between us. I therefore pray you to give him a kind reception and full credence to whatever he shall say to you on our behalf, especially when he shall assure you of the continuance of our friendship and good will.

Written at the City of Washington the Nineteenth day of July 1803.

TH: JEFFERSON

FC (Lb in DNA: RG 59, Credences); in a clerk's hand; at head of text: "Thomas Jefferson, President of the United States of America, To the Most Illustrious and Most Magnificent Prince the Bey of Tunis, the abode of happiness"; below signature: "By the President" and "James Madison Secretary of State." FC (Lb in DNA: RG 59, PTCC); dated 16 July. Tr (NHi: Gilder Lehrman Collection at the Gilder Lehrman Institute of American History); dated 19 July. Not recorded in SJL.

TO ARRANGE WITH YOU CERTAIN SUBJECTS: in April, Madison had asked James Cathcart to negotiate with Tunis a system of regular payments by the United States, preferably on a biennial schedule, to replace the uncertainty of unpredictable demands such as Hammuda's recent request for the gift of a warship. In his instructions to Tobias Lear on 14 July, Madison asked Lear to take over that negotiation. Madison still expected Cathcart to assume the regular consular duties at Tunis (Madison, *Papers*, *Sec. of State Ser.*, 5:178; TJ to Hammuda, 14 Apr.).

From Thomas Waterman

SIR, Philadelphia July 19th 1803.

The object of this letter is respectfully to solicit the appointment as one of the Commissioners of Bankruptcy, in & for the Pennsylvania district, in the place of Joseph Clay Esqre:, whose commission I presume will expire, on taking his seat in the house of Representatives, as member for this place.—

Should you be pleased, Sir, to confer on me the appointment, I shall assiduously endeavor to discharge my duty—with satisfaction to yourself & the public, & credit to myself.

The necessary support of a numerous & increasing family, demanding the utmost exertion of my time & talents, urges me to this Solicitation.—

I have the honor to be with the highest respect, Sir, Your most obedient & very humble Servant, THO: WATERMAN

RC (DNA: RG 59, LAR); at foot of text: "The President of the U. States"; endorsed by TJ as received 25 July and "to be commr. bkrptcy" and so recorded in SJL.

A former Treasury Department clerk, Waterman had returned to Philadelphia, where he was employed as an accountant. There would be only four bankruptcy commissioners in Philadelphia when JOSEPH CLAY resigned later in 1803. The vacancy caused by the death of John W. Vancleve in 1802 had not been filled (Vol. 33:343n; Vol. 38:93-4; Joseph Clay to TJ, 29 Mch. and 19 Oct. 1803).

From Joseph Yznardi, Sr.

SIR! Cadiz 19th. July 1803.

It certainly causes me great uneasiness that your Excellency had received none of my letters; as they returned your Excelly. my most gracious thanks for the many honours & favours confer'd on me by your Excelly. while at that side of the Water, & particularly those shew'd me the day after my arrival; The 20th. July of last Year I did myself the honour of renewing and acknowledging my great obligations, and offering your Excelly. at same time my best wishes & desires; under which respects I continued after my arrival from Madrid; and on the 9th. instant I had the honour of repeating to your Excellency my best services, and requesting of your goodness not to forget my great friendship; but happily I see by your most valued & esteemed favour of the 10th. May, that your Excelly. has not forgot me & that I am still in your esteem & favour, assuring your Excelly. that

I am quite happy and joyfull to be informed of your Excy. enjoying perfect health.—

The Wine that your Excellency is pleased to order, will by very first oppertunity for either of the Places mention'd, be sent in 2 or 3. half Butts as they are easier stowed on board; & which I hope will meet entire approbation; and that your Excellency will have no need of availing of any Person for further missions; as in case I should not survive your Excy. my Son Patrick (who is well acquainted with the many obligations I am under to your Excely.) will on all occations & with the greatest pleasure obey any orders or Commands from your Excelly, with as much eagerness as myself—Mean time that I put in execution the remittance, believe me with the highest regard & veneration—

Sir! Your most obedt. & most humble Servant—

JOSEF YZNARDY

RC (DLC); in a clerk's hand, signed by Yznardi; at foot of text: "To His Excellency Thomas Jefferson"; endorsed by TJ as received 25 Sep. and so recorded in SJL. Quadruplicate (same); in a clerk's hand, not signed, written at head of text of Yznardi to TJ, 22 Oct. 1803; with notation at head of text that the RC, a duplicate (not found), and a triplicate (not found) were all sent via New York.

20TH. JULY OF LAST YEAR: Yznardi arrived in Cadiz from the United States on 20 July 1802 and wrote to TJ on 12 Aug. (Vol. 38:205-8).

PLACES MENTION'D: New York and Richmond (TJ to Yznardi, 10 May).

From Peter Carr

DEAR SIR Carr's-brook. July 20th 1803.

We arrived here on the 14th, all well, and found the accomodations on the road by Stevensburg, much better than we expected. The hospitality and politeness of Strode induced us to stay a day with him, greatly to the advantage of ourselves and horses. From what I heard in that neighbourhood, you will find the Marquis's road, a difficult one for a carriage.

Since my arrival, I met accidentally in Charlottesville, Mr Daniel of Cumberland, to whom you talked of offering the place of Judge, in the District of Columbia. In the course of conversation I sounded him on the subject, and am inclined to think he would accept it. If he would, I am sure there is no man who would discharge its duties with more integrity and ability. Mr Madison is well acquainted with him, and I believe will add his sanction to this opinion. I heard yesterday from Edge-hill, and they were all well. Accept assurances of my sincere and affectionate attachment. P: CARR

RC (DNA: RG 59, LAR); endorsed by TJ as received 27 July and so recorded in SJL.

Carr here offered information on William DANIEL, a lawyer who represented Cumberland County in the Virginia General Assembly for a number of years and later served as a judge in the state's General Court (DVB, 3:694-5; Leonard, *General Assembly*, 211, 215, 219, 223, 227, 242, 246, 250, 254, 259, 265, 269). In a letter of 23 July, Daniel requested more information from Carr and explained that although it was "probable" that he would "accept an appointment" as circuit court JUDGE for the DISTRICT OF COLUMBIA, Carr should not assume Daniel "to be bound to accept or refuse by this note" (RC in DNA: RG 59, LAR; endorsed by TJ: "Daniel Wm. to P. Carr to be judge of Columbia").

For the impending court vacancy, see John Thomson Mason to TJ, 7 July 1803.

From Éleuthère Irénée du Pont de Nemours

Eleutherian mill near
Wilmington (Del.)
Juillet 20 1803.

MONSIEUR LE PRESIDENT,

Vous avez été prevenu par mon Pere que J'etais occupé d'etablir dans les Etats-Unis une grande manufacture de Poudre de guerre et de chasse. Cette fabrique construite sur le même plan que les plus belles d'Europe est maintenant prête à être mise en activité. l'avantage que J'ai eu d'être éleve du célebre Lavoisier lorsqu'il etait administrateur des Poudres et les bontés qu'il a eu pour moi, m'ont mis à portée de suivre dans cet établissement les meilleurs procédés connus, et d'y ajouter des perfections nouvelles,[1] qui j'espere mettrons l'amerique en etat de rivaliser teutes les autres puissances pour cette branche d'industrie.

Mr. Ed. Livingston que etait ici il y a quelques Jours pourra vous rendre compte du resultat des epreuves que j'ai faites en sa présence et de la grande superiorité de la poudre que j'ai déja fabriquée sur celles qui ont êté faites jusqu'à present dans ce pays.

Indépendement de l'avantage de donner aux Poudres communes et aux Poudres de guerre au moins un quart de plus de portée, Je pourrai par la perfection des machines que j'ai importées[2] procurer à l'amerique le commerce de la Poudre de premiere qualité et de celle de carabine que jusqu'à present elle avait été obligée de tirer de l'etranger. La Poudre de carabine étant la seule que l'on employe dans les contrées de l'ouest et pour le commerce des Indiens, les Etats-unis possederont ainsi une importante branche de commerce, qui le deviendra bientot davantage encore par l'acquisition des belles contrées que votre sagesse vient de conquerir.

Puis-je esperer, Monsieur le President, que la bienveillance que depuis longtems vous avez temoignée à mon Pere vous fera voir avec interet l'etablissement que nous venons de former et vous engagera à lui accorder des encouragemens aux quels une grande perfection introduite dans une des branches de l'industrie nationale semble lui donner des droits. ma manufacture d'aprés l'etendue de son plan—a besoin de grands travaux pour se consolider jusqu'a ce que ses relations commerciales aient put s'etablir. Le gouvernement a plusieurs moyens de m'accorder l'espece d'encouragement que je reclame; Soit par une fabrication de Poudres de guerre s'il se trouvait en avoir besoin; Soit par la remise à neuf de la grande quantité de Poudres qui se trouve avariées dans ses magazins et qui depuis longtems ne peuvent être d'aucun usage à moins d'etre reparées; Soit encore par le raffinage de son Salpêtre que je m'engage à rendre parfaitement pur et propre à etre employé à la fabrication de la Poudre au moment ou le gouvernement en aurait besoin.

D'après les ordres qui ont été donnés par le secretaire d'Etat de la guerre, j'ai deja reçu des magazins de Philadelphie deux echantillons de Salpêtre dont j'ai fait l'epreuve; mais le résultat de ces epreuves ayant donné à l'une des especes de Salpêtre 21 Livres de dechêt par quintal, tandis que l'autre n'a dechut que de 7, il ne serait pas possible que je pu faire au gouvernement aucune proposition équitable sur ce raffinage [à] moins de connaitre toutes les especes de Salpêtre qui sont dans ses magazins et de les avoir eprouvées chacune en particulier. Si ce moyen a votre approbation, Monsieur le President, veuillez donner les ordres pour que les echantillons de Salpêtre me soient remis, avec indication de la quantité de chacune des especes. ou si vous jugez pouvoir utiliser ma manufacture de quelque autre maniere et que vous veuillez bien me l'indiquer ma reconnaissance pour vos bontés égalera le profond respect avec lequel J'ai lhonneur d'être,

Monsieur le President, Votre très humble et très obeissant Serviteur, E. I. du Pont de Nemours.

EDITORS' TRANSLATION

Eleutherian Mill near
Wilmington (Del.)
20 July 1803

Mister President,

As you know from my father, I am creating a large gunpowder factory in the United States for war and hunting. Modeled after the finest European factories, it is about to open. I had the good fortune of studying with the famous Lavoisier when he was in charge of powder works. Thanks to his guidance, I have been able to incorporate the most advanced practices into my factory and to add some innovations which I hope will enable America to rival all other powers in this domain.

Mr. Ed. Livingston who was here a few days ago can tell you about the tests I performed in his presence and the vast superiority of my gunpowder over what has been produced in this country until now.

Given the high-quality machines I have imported from France, I can not only extend the range of gunpowder by at least twenty-five per cent, both for ordinary use and for war, but I can also help America create a market for superior gunpowder and rifle powder, which you have previously had to import from abroad. Since rifle powder is the only kind used in the western territories, for trade with the Indians, the United States will control an important market that will soon increase thanks to the valuable new territory you have so wisely purchased.

May I hope, Mister President, that the good will you have long shown toward my father will lead you to look favorably on the factory we have just built and inspire you to grant it the advantages that are warranted by the quality it will bring to a branch of national industry. Given the scope of the project, my factory needs significant support to get established, until business develops. The government has several ways of providing the help I am requesting: ordering war munitions, if you need them; having my factory restore the vast quantity of powder that has spoiled in warehouses and is useless without being refurbished; or having us refine your saltpeter to a guaranteed level of purity that will allow it to be transformed into gunpowder whenever the government might need it.

At the request of the secretary of state for war, the Philadelphia military stores sent me two samples of saltpeter which I tested. Since one sample produced 21 pounds of waste per hundredweight, and the other only 7 pounds, I cannot provide an accurate estimate for refining without knowing what kinds of saltpeter are in these stores and testing each one individually. If this procedure meets your approval, Mister President, could you please have the saltpeter samples sent to me with an indication of how much there is of each kind? If my factory can be useful in any other way, kindly let me know. My gratitude will match the deep respect with which I have the honor of being, Mister President,

Your very humble and very obedient servant,

E. I. du Pont de Nemours

RC (DeGH: Papers of E. I. du Pont); torn at seal; addressed: "to his Excellency Thomas Jefferson President of the United States Washington-City"; sealed with E. I. du Pont de Nemours monogram; franked; postmarked Wilmington, Delaware, 21 July; endorsed by TJ as received 25 July and so recorded in SJL.

FC (DeGH: P. S. du Pont Office Collection); in du Pont's hand. Enclosed in TJ to Dearborn, 29 July.

Éleuthère Irénée du Pont (1773-1834), a son of Pierre Samuel Du Pont de Nemours and his first wife, Nicole Charlotte Marie Louise Le Dée de Raucourt, oversaw the branch of the family's business that involved refinement of saltpeter and the manufacture of gunpowder. In his youth he attended the Collège Royal in his native France, then learned the techniques of gunpowder production from Antoine Lavoisier and worked for a while in the French government's powder works. With his father he ran a newspaper and printing establishment in Paris. In 1791, he married Sophie Madeleine Dalmas, a shopkeeper's daughter. After the extended family moved to the United States, arriving early in 1800, du Pont perceived an opportunity to market high-quality gunpowder. He and his brother Victor went back to France in 1801 to obtain financing, equipment, and skilled workers, and on his return to the United States he established a powder factory on the Brandywine River in Delaware. He became a naturalized citizen of the United States in Novermber 1804. Like his father, du Pont often added "de Nemours" to his name, but unlike his father he did not tend to capitalize the "du" of their surname. The name Éleuthère Irénée, from Greek words for liberty and peace, was the suggestion of a family friend, the political economist Anne Robert Jacques Turgot (ANB; Vol. 30:503n; Vol. 32:314, 315n; Vol. 36:132-3n; Vol. 37:321-2, 454, 456, 457-8n).

RAFFINAGE DE SON SALPÊTRE: while their gunpowder mill was under construction the du Ponts sought contracts with the U.S. government for the refinement of saltpeter (Vol. 34:617-20; Vol. 35:74; Vol. 38:227, 228).

LE SECRETAIRE D'ETAT DE LA GUERRE: on 28 July, Dearborn wrote to William Irvine, the superintendent of military stores at Philadelphia, requesting him to be prepared to give du Pont a sample of gunpowder, information about the government's method of determining strength of gunpowder, and a sample of saltpeter in need of purification. Dearborn also wanted Irvine to obtain from du Pont samples of the two highest grades of his powder, his price for each grade, and his terms for purifying saltpeter and refurbishing damaged gunpowder (Dearborn to Irvine, 28 July, in DNA: RG 107, MLS).

VOTRE APPROBATION: du Pont's brother Victor, writing from New York on 11 July, had urged him to approach the president about the company's gunpowder business. A detailed letter, Victor advised, would be more effective than a personal visit. He suggested making the proposal in English, to present the company as an American enterprise (Bessie Gardner Du Pont, trans. and ed., *Life of Eleuthère Irénée du Pont from Contemporary Correspondence*, 11 vols. [Newark, Del., 1923-26], 6:243).

[1] Remainder of sentence lacking in FC.
[2] FC: "importées de france."

From Henry Dearborn

SIR — Washington July 21st, 1803

I take the liberty of enclosing a letter from Mrs. Stuart, daughter to Blair McClennigan of Philadelphia, whether you will think it expedient to give him the appointment his daughter requests, or not, I cannot pretend to say, but if something could be done for him, I presume it would be pleasing to our friends.

with sentiments of the highest respect I am Sir Your Huml Servt

H. DEARBORN

RC (DNA: RG 59, LAR); at foot of text: "The President of the United States"; endorsed by TJ as received 25 July and "Mc.lanachan Blair to be Commr. bkrptcy" and so recorded in SJL. Enclosure: Deborah Stewart to Dearborn, Philadelphia, 16 July 1803, requesting that Dearborn intercede with the president to procure for her father, Blair McClenachan, the vacant office of commissioner of bankruptcy at Philadelphia; her father has obtained a certificate that extricates him from his financial embarrassments and he will now be able to "devote his whole time and attention to any employment that may be given to him"; Stewart realizes that there are many applicants and few offices, but she hopes her father's patriotism and perseverance in the principles that have brought the country to the "present happy situation" will ensure "that he will not be neglected" (RC in same; Vol. 36:307-8n).

Deborah Stewart (STUART) previously wrote TJ requesting a position for her oldest son, William Stewart. He was appointed consul at Smyrna in 1802 (Vol. 37:204-5). For McClenachan's recent applications to the president seeking a position in Philadelphia, see Vol. 39:84-5 and Vol. 40:681. TJ appointed McClenachan a bankruptcy commissioner for the district of Pennsylvania with a commission dated 14 Oct. 1803 (FC in Lb in DNA: RG 59, MPTPC; Vol. 37:709).

From Mann Page

DEAR SIR Mannsfield July 21. 1803.

The Cession of Louisiana having now taken place, & my Views leading me to a new Country where by Industry & Vigilance I may at the same Time serve my Country & aid my Fortunes, I beg leave to state that should any Situation arise wherein my sincere Exertions to serve the United States might avail, I offer myself a Candidate trusting to the Report of my Friends as a Passport. Should an event of such a Nature occur, any Communication from you will be thankfully recieved by

Sir yr. mst obdt. hbl. Servt. MANN PAGE

RC (DNA: RG 59, LAR); endorsed by TJ as received 29 July and "for office in Louisiana" and so recorded in SJL.

From Meriwether Lewis

DEAR SIR, Pittsburgh July 22nd. 1803.

Yours of the 11th. & 15th. Inst. were duly recieved, the former on the 18th. inst., the latter on this day. For my pocketbook I thank you: the dirk could not well come by post, nor is it of any moment to me, the knives that were made at Harper's ferry will answer my purposes equally as well and perhaps better; it can therefore be taken care of untill my return: the bridle is of no consequence at all. After the reciept of this letter I think it will be best to direct to me at Louisville Kentuckey.—

The person who contracted to build my boat engaged to have it in readiness by the 20th. inst.; in this however he has failed; he pleads his having been disappointed in procuring timber, but says he has now supplyed himself with the necessary materials, and that she shall be completed by the last of this month; however in this I am by no means sanguine, nor do I believe from the progress he makes that she will be ready before the 5th. of August; I visit him every day, and endeavour by every means in my power to hasten the completion of the work: I have prevailed on him to engage more hands, and he tells me that two others will join him in the morning, if so, he may probably finish the boat by the time he mentioned: I shall embark immediately the boat is in readiness, there being no other consideration which at this moment detains me.—

The Waggon from Harper's ferry arrived today, bringing every thing with which she was charged in good order.

The party of recruits that were ordered from Carlisle to this place with a view to descend the river with me, have arrived with the exception of one, who deserted on the march, his place however can be readily supplyed from the recruits at this place enlisted by Lieut. Hook.

The current of the Ohio is extreemly low and continues to decline, this may impede my progress but shall not prevent my proceeding, being determined to get forward though I should not be able to make a greater distance than a mile pr. day.—

I am with the most sincere regard Your Obt. Servt.

Meriwether Lewis.

RC (DLC); at foot of text: "Thomas Jefferson President. U.S." Recorded in SJL as received 1 Aug.

Dearborn had given orders for the recruiting officer at CARLISLE, Pennsylvania, to select eight "of the most faithful and sober" of the army's new enlistees, make one of them a lance corporal to lead the others on the journey, and send them west to Pittsburgh. They were to be under Lewis's command from Pittsburgh to Massac "or Kaskaskais if necessary" (Dearborn to Thomas H. Cushing, 16 June, in DNA: RG 107, LSMA).

Notes on Shipment

July 23. 1803. wrote to G. Jefferson to send

✓	the cask syrop punch	by waggons
	cask (15. galls.) Sperm. ceti oil	
✓	sheet iron	
✓	9. of 10 packages	
✓	No. 6.	by water.
✓	clock	
	fish	

12 gross (1728) inch wood screws, round heads

MS (MHi); entirely in TJ's hand.

In his letter of this day, TJ informed George JEFFERSON that several items he expected to find waiting for him at Monticello had yet to arrive. The president asked his cousin to have the syrup of punch, sheet iron, whale oil, and some packages shipped from Washington transported via wagon, while ensuring a river portage for a tenth package (the CLOCK) and for barrels of fish ordered for Sam Carr and himself. He also extended an invitation to Monticello (PrC in MHi; faint; at foot of text: "Mr. George Jefferson"; endorsed by TJ in ink on verso).

From John Vaughan

DR SIR   Philad: 23 July 1803

The two pamphlets from the Society of Arts &c were intended to be retained by you, as we are in possession of duplicates—I now return them & add a Second copy of the premiums, of which some were sent to be destributed—it may be in your power to Select some of the ideas most likely to be usefull & to put them in the way of more general Circulation—Being much indisposed at the time I receivd them from you, the sending them back has been delayed.—

I remain with respect D Sir Yours Sincerely JN VAUGHAN

RC (DLC); at foot of text: "Thomas Jefferson Pt. of US"; endorsed by TJ as received 27 July and so recorded in SJL.

SOCIETY OF ARTS &C: see Vaughan to TJ, 25 June, and TJ to Vaughan, 28 June.

From William Clark

SIR   ClarksVille 24th. July 1803

I had the honor of receiving thro' Captain M: Lewis an assureance of your Approbation & wish that I would Join him in a North Western enterprise. I will chearfully, and with great pleasure Join My friend Capt Lewis in this Vast enterprise, and shall arrange my business so as to be in readiness to leave this Soon after his arrival. May I request the favour of you to forward the inclosed letter to Capt Lewis, Should he not be with you.

I have the honor to be with great respect Your Mo: Ob and Sincear

WM. CLARK

RC (DLC); at foot of text: "Mr: Jefferson"; endorsed by TJ as received 6 Aug. Dft (MoSHi: William Clark Papers); subjoined to Dft of enclosure; undated and unsigned. Dft (same); also subjoined to Dft of enclosure; partial; unsigned.

William Clark (1770-1838), born in Caroline County, Virginia, moved to Kentucky with his family when he was 15 years old. He served in the militia on the frontier beginning in 1789 and became a lieutenant in the regular army three years later. He resigned that commission in July 1796 to manage his family's assets, which included land, slaves, and a mill, and to contend with the substantial debts of his older brother, George Rogers Clark. In 1802, William Clark sold the family's tobacco plantation in Kentucky and moved into a modest dwelling with his brother at Clarksville or Clark's Point, across the Ohio River from Louisville. He was acquainted with much of the frontier of the United States, having traveled for the army or on business trips to Vincennes, Kaskaskia, Spanish posts on the Mississippi River, Chickasaw territory, Ste. Genevieve, St. Louis, New Madrid, and New Orleans. He lacked formal education but read works of philosophy, literature, history, and science, and in his travels he had developed a skill of observing details that he recorded in notebooks and journals. TJ later appointed him Indian agent of Louisiana Territory and brigadier general of the territory's militia. In Madison's presidency he became governor of Missouri Territory. Clark married Julia (Judith) Hancock in 1808. Following her death in 1820, he married a widowed relative of hers, Harriet Kennerly Radford (ANB; Landon Y. Jones, *William Clark and the Shaping of the West* [New York, 2004], 50-2, 55-7, 66-7, 70-1, 89-110, 112, 142, 155, 262; William E. Foley, *Wilderness Journey: The Life of William Clark* [Columbia, Mo., 2004], 24, 41-2, 48, 52; Heitman, *Dictionary*, 1:306).

ASSUREANCE OF YOUR APPROBATION: Lewis had written to Clark on 19 June asking him to join the transcontinental expedition. The two of them had become acquainted at Fort Greenville in the Northwest Territory in 1795, when Lewis was an ensign in the army and Clark a lieutenant. In the fall of that year, General Anthony Wayne assigned Lewis to a rifle company commanded by Clark. Several months later Clark left the army, but he and Lewis maintained their acquaintance. Clark also traveled through Washington, meeting TJ there in 1801 (Jackson, *Lewis and Clark*, 1:57-60; 2:572; Foley, *Wilderness Journey*, 39-40; Jones, *William Clark*, 108, 113; Vol. 40:172).

ENCLOSURE

William Clark to Meriwether Lewis

DEAR LEWIS — ClarksVille July 18th. 1803

I received by yesterdays Mail, your letter of the 19th. ulto: The Contents of which I recived with much pleasure—The enterprise &a. is Such as I have long anticipated and am much pleased With—and as my Situation in life will admit of my absence the length of time necessary to accomplish Such an undertakeing I will chearfully join you in an 'official Charrector' as mentioned in your letter, and partake of the dangers, difficulties, and fatigues, and I anticipate the honors & rewards of the result of Such an enterprise, Should

we be successful in accomplishing it. This is an under takeing fraited with many difeculties, but My friend I do assure you that no man lives Whith Whome I would perfur to under take Such a Trip &c. as your Self, and I shall arrange My Matters as well as I can against your Arrival here.
It may be necessary that you inform the President of My acceding to the proposals, so that I may be furnishd with such Credentials as the nature of the Toure may require—Which I Suppose had best be fowarded to Louisville. The Objects of this Plan of Government, are Great and Worthey of that great Charecetor the Main-Spring of its Action—The Means with which we are furnished to carry it into effect, I think may be Sufficintly liberal—The plan of operation, as laid down by you (with a Small addition as to the out fit) I highly approve of.

I shall indeaver to engage (temporally) a few men, such as will best answer our purpose, holding out the Idea as stated in your letter—The subject of which has been Mentioned in Louisville several weeks agoe.

Pray write to me by every post after recving this letter, I shall be exceedingly anxious to here from you.

With every sincerity & frendship Wm. Clark

Dupl (DLC); Clark first wrote the date as 17 before altering it to 18; addressed: "Captain Meriwether Lewis"; at foot of text: "Capt. Merriwether Lewis at Washington City or on his way to Pitts burgh"; below signature, indicated by a pointing hand: "Note one letter fowarded to Pitts burgh." Dft (MoSHi: William Clark Papers); dated 17 July; at foot of text: "Cap. Merrweth Lewis Pitts burgh." RC, not found, acknowledged by Lewis as a letter of 19 July (see Jackson, *Lewis and Clark*, 1:115).

In his letter of 19 June, Lewis proposed that Clark could either take an OFFICIAL role in the expedition or could accompany Lewis "as a friend any part of the way up the Missouri." If there should be anything "in this enterprise," Lewis had written, "which would induce you to participate with me in it's fatiegues, it's dangers and it's honors, believe me there is no man on earth with whom I should feel equal pleasure in sharing them as with yourself" (same, 60).

CREDENTIALS: Lewis asserted that the president "has authorized me to say that in the event of your accepting this proposition he will grant you a Captain's commission which of course will intitle you to the pay and emoluments attached to that office and will equally with myself intitle you to such portion of land as was granted to officers of similar rank for their Revolutionary services; the commission with which he proposes to furnish you is not to be considered temporary but permanent if you wish it." In March 1804, Dearborn wrote Lewis to say that it would not be possible to give Clark a commission as captain of engineers as anticipated. Clark was instead made a lieutenant of artillery, but, Lewis assured him, his compensation "by G–d, shall be equal to my own" (same, 1:60, 172-3, 179; 2:572).

HOLDING OUT THE IDEA AS STATED IN YOUR LETTER: in discussions with any potential recruits for the journey, Lewis suggested "holding out the idea that the direction of this expedition is up the Mississippi to its source, and thence to the lake of the Woods." Lewis expected to reveal the "real design" before requiring anyone to commit to the enterprise (same, 1:58).

Clark wrote to Lewis again on the 24th. Lewis received both letters at Pittsburgh by 3 Aug. (same, 112-13, 115; Dft of letter of 24th in MoSHi: William Clark Papers).

To William Duane

Dear Sir Monticello July 24. 1803.

The address of the Ward committees of Philada on the subject of removals from office was recieved at Washington on the 17th. inst. I cannot answer it, because I have[1] given no answers to the many others I have recieved from other quarters. you are sensible what use an unfriendly party would make[2] of such answers by putting all their expressions to the torture: and altho' no person wishes more than I do to learn the opinions of respected *individuals*, because they enable me to examine, and often to correct my own, yet I am not satisfied that I ought to admit the addresses even of those bodies of men which are organised by the constitution (the houses of legislature for instance) to influence the appointment to office for which the constitution has chosen to rely on the independance and integrity of the Executive, controlled by the Senate, chosen both of them by the whole union. still less of those bodies whose organisation is unknown to the constitution. as revolutionary instruments (when nothing but revolution will cure the evils of the state) they are necessary and indispensable, and the right to use them is inalienable by the people; but to admit them as ordinary & habitual instruments, put in as a part of[3] the machinery of the constitution, would be to change that machinery by introducing moving powers foreign to it, and to an extent depending solely on local views,[4] & therefore incalculable. the opinions offered by *individuals*, are of right, & on a different ground; they are sanctioned by the constitution; which has also presented, when they chuse to act in bodies, the organisation, objects, & rights of those bodies. altho' this view of the subject forbids me, in my own judgment, to give answers to addresses of this kind, yet the one now under consideration is couched in terms so friendly and respectful,[5] and from persons, many of whom I know to have been firm patriots, some of them in revolutionary times and others in those of terror, & doubt not that all are of the same valuable character, that I cannot restrain the desire that they should individually[6] understand the reasons why no formal answer is given: that they should see it proceeds from my view of the constitution, and the judgment I form of my duties to it, and not from a want of respect & esteem for them or their opinions,[7] which given individually will ever be valued by me. I beg leave therefore to avail myself of my acquaintance with you, & of your friendly dispositions to communicate to them individually the considerations expressed in this letter, which is merely private and to yourself, and which I ask you not to put out of your own hands lest directly or by copy it should get into those of the common adversary, & become matter for those malignant perversions which no sentiments however just, no expressions however correct can escape.

It may perhaps at first view be thought that my answer to the Newhaven letter was not within my own rule. but that letter was expressed to be from the writers individually, & not as an organised body chosen to represent and express the public opinion. the occasion too which it furnished had for some time been wished for, of explaining to the republican part of the nation my sense of their just right to participation of office, and the proceedings adopted for attaining it after due enquiry into the general sentiment of the several states. the purpose there explained was to remove some[8] of the least deserving officers, but generally to prefer the milder[9] measure of waiting till accidental vacancies should furnish opportunity of giving to republicans[10] their *due proportion* of office. to this we have steadily adhered. many vacancies have been made by death & resignation, many by removal for malversation in office, and for open, active and virulent abuse of official influence, in opposition to the order of things established by the will of the nation. such removals continue to be made on sufficient proof. the places have been steadily filled with republican characters, until of 316 offices in all the US. subject to appointment & removal by me 130. only are held by federalists. I do not include in this estimate the Judiciary & military because not removeable but by established process, nor the officers of the internal revenue because discontinued by law, nor postmasters or any others not named by me. and this has been effected in little more than two years by means so moderate and just as cannot fail to be approved in future. whether a participation of office in proportion to numbers should be effected in each state separately or in the whole states taken together is difficult to decide, & has not yet been settled in my own mind. it is a question of vast complications. but suppose we were to apply the rule to Pensylvania distinctly from the Union. in the state of Pensylvania 8.[11] offices only are subject to my nomination and informal removal. of these, 5. are in the hands of republicans, 3. of federalists to wit.

Republican:		Federal
the Attorney	Dallas	Naval officer
Marshal	Smith	Surveyor
Collector	Muhlenberg	Commissr. of loans.
Purveyor	Coxe	
Superintdt. mily. stores	Irving	
Store-keeper	Leonard[12]	

in the hands of the former is the appointment of every subordinate officer, not a single one (but their clerks) being appointable by the latter. taking a view of this subject in the only year I can now come at, the clerk hire of the Naval officer & surveyor is only 2196 D. that of the Commr. of loans 2500 = 4696. the compensation of the Nav. off. & surveyor were 7651. D. in that year. the residue of custom house expences were 46,268. D constituting the compensation & patronage of the Collector, except about 1500. D. to the officers of the revenue cutter who are republican. the emoluments & patronage of the 5. other republican officers, I have no materials for estimating: but they are not small. considering numbers therefore as the ratio of participation, it stands at 5. to 3. but taking emolument & patronage as the measure, our actual share is much greater. I cannot therefore suppose that our friends had sufficiently examined the fact when they alledged that 'in Philadelphia public employment, under the general government, in all it's grades, with scarcely an exception, is confined not to federalists merely, but to apostates, persecutors, & enemies of representative government.'

I give full credit to the wisdom of the measures pursued by the Govr. of Pensylvania in removals from office. I have no doubt he followed the wish of the state, & *he* had no other to consult. but in the general government, each state is to be administered not on it's local principles, but on the principles of all the states formed into a general result. that I should administer the affairs of Massachusets & Connecticut, for example, on federal principles, could not be approved. I dare say too that the extensive removals from office in Pensylva may have contributed to the great conversion which has been manifested among it's citizens. but I respect them too much to believe it has been the exclusive or even the principal motive. I presume the sound measures of their government, & of the general one, have weighed more in their estimation and conversion, than the consideration of the particular agents employed.

I read with extreme gratification the approbation expressed of the general measures of the present administration. I verily believe our friends have not differed with us on a single *measure* of importance. it is only as to the distribution of office that some difference of opinion has appeared. but that difference will I think be lessened when facts & principles are more accurately scanned, and it's impression still more so when justice is done to motives, and to the duty of[13] pursuing that which, on mature consideration is deemed to be right.

I hope you will pardon the trouble which this communication proposes to give you, when you attend to the considerations urging it, and that you will accept my respectful salutations & assurances of great esteem.

Dft (DLC); includes emendations by TJ after he made PrC (see notes 1-6 and 11-12 below); at foot of first page: "Mr. Duane"; in right margin on last page perpendicular to text: "Ward Commees of Phila answer written but not sent." PrC (same); with emendations made by TJ before document was pressed noted below as appearing on both Dft and PrC. Enclosed in TJ to Albert Gallatin, 25 July.

ANSWER TO THE NEWHAVEN LETTER: see Vol. 34:554-8.

316 OFFICES IN ALL THE US.: for TJ's arrival at this number, see Party Affiliation of Federal Officeholders printed at 11 July 1803, especially Documents III and IV.

In "Fair Play," TJ considered whether participation of Republicans in office should be calculated in EACH STATE SEPARATELY OR IN THE WHOLE STATES TAKEN TOGETHER (see Vol. 40:464-9).

See Gallatin's Comments on the Address of the Philadelphia Ward Committees, printed at 17 July, for information on the compensation of the officers at Philadelphia, which he derived from the 1802 roll of federal officers. TJ also may have consulted the 1802 document.

[1] In Dft TJ first wrote "received many such from other quarters, & have made it a rule to give no answers" before later altering the remainder of the sentence to read as above.

[2] TJ first wrote "use would be made" before later altering the preceding text to read as above.

[3] Preceding six words later interlined in place of "to direct."

[4] Word later interlined in place of "combinations of individuals."

[5] Preceding four words later interlined in place of "of such acknoleged respect."

[6] TJ later canceled "be made to."

[7] Preceding three words interlined in place of "individually" in Dft and PrC.

[8] Word interlined in place of "a few" in Dft and PrC.

[9] TJ here canceled "mode of" in Dft and PrC.

[10] Word interlined in place of "them" in Dft and PrC.

[11] TJ later altered this numeral from "9" to "8" and later in the sentence he altered the "6" to "5." See also note 12.

[12] TJ canceled this entry probably after he received Gallatin's first letter of 11 Aug. on the 17th. At the same time, he altered the numerals cited in note 11, above.

[13] Here canceled in Dft and PrC: "following."

Petition of William Johnson and Others

TO THE PRESIDENT OF THE UNITED STATES

District of North Carolina
Sneydesborough 24th July 1803—

The Petition of the subscribers Humbly Sheweth that on or about the 16th June last a commission of Bankrutpcy was obtaind from his Honour Judge Potter of this district on the application of Farquhard Campbell against John & Farquhard Campbell late Merchts. of Tindalsville in this district. which was directed to the commissioners of Bankruptcy. who have been duly notified of the same but from the distance (being 170 miles.) and indisposition have declind the Excution of the commission We the Subscribers Creditors of the said John

& Farquarhard Campbell there fore pray your Excellency to appoint other commissioners to execute the said commission and your Petitioners will ever pray &.c.

WM JOHNSON FOR
JOHNSON LAWRENCE & CO.
HURBERT PEARSON
ISAAC LANIER
LANIER & DICKSON
RBT W HARRIS

RC (DNA: RG 59, LAR, 12:0632); in Johnson's hand and signed by him and Pearson, Lanier, and Harris.

Virginia-born William Johnson (1761-1840), a Revolutionary war veteran who moved to North Carolina in 1781, was one of the founders of Sneedsborough (Sneydesborough), chartered in 1795, in Anson County near the South Carolina border. He was a prominent landowner in the town and proprietor of the large gin and mill patronized by grain farmers from a fifty-mile radius. For several years he represented Anson County in the North Carolina House of Commons. Johnson, Hurbert Pearson, and Isaac Lanier served as trustees of the Sneedsborough Academy when it was chartered in 1800. Robert W. Harris was the town's postmaster in 1803 (Virgil D. White, *Genealogical Abstracts of Revolutionary War Pension Files*, 4 vols. [Waynesboro, Tenn., 1990-92], 2:1860; Mary L. Medley, *History of Anson County North Carolina, 1750-1976* [Wadesboro, N.C., 1976], 72-6, 81, 184; Jedidiah Morse, *The American Gazetteer*, 2d ed. [Charlestown, Mass., 1804]; Stets, *Postmasters*, 202; *Journal of the House of Commons of the State of North-Carolina* [Raleigh, 1807; Shaw-Shoemaker, No. 13257], 10; same, [Raleigh, 1808; Shaw-Shoemaker, No. 15778], 1; same, [Raleigh, 1810; Shaw-Shoemaker, No. 20927], 1).

It is not clear when or through whom TJ received this letter. It may have been among the papers regarding the John and FARQUHARD CAMPBELL bankruptcy case, which North Carolina congressman Samuel D. Purviance brought to Washington and sent to TJ on 24 Oct. (*Biog. Dir. Cong.*; Samuel D. Purviance to TJ, 24 Oct.; Nathaniel Macon to TJ, 17 Nov. 1803). On 14 and 18 Nov., TJ appointed additional bankruptcy commissioners for North Carolinan (list of commissions in Lb in DNA: RG 59, MPTPC; Vol. 37:710-11).

From William Roberts

Charlottesville 24 July 1803

William Roberts lately from Norfolk, taking an Excursion with his Sister Mrs. Taylor and presuming on the honour of having been introduced to Mr. Jefferson almost an age ago in London, by Hector St. John Author of "Letters by an American Farmer"; intended to take the liberty this morning of expressing the singular gratification he should derive from a view of the Residence of Mr Jefferson, and from an opportunity of renewing his respectful remembrance. They heedlessly passed the entrance and proceeded down the Mountain until fatigue rendered it too late to return, but with his permission, they will visit Monticello to morrow or the following morning.

RC (MHi); endorsed by TJ.

William Roberts, brother of merchant Edward Roberts of Norfolk, was an artist of Virginia landscapes, including the Natural Bridge and Harper's Ferry, as well as a view of the junction of the Potomac and Shenandoah Rivers. TJ eventually acquired two of his oil paintings as well as engravings from them made by Joseph Jeakes (Barbara C. Batson, "Virginia Landscapes by William Roberts," *Journal of Early Southern Decorative Arts*, 10 [1984], 35-48; Roberts to TJ, 18 July 1804, 26 Feb. 1808).

J. HECTOR ST. JOHN, also known as St. John de Crèvecoeur, wrote *Letters from an American Farmer*, first published in London in 1782. He corresponded frequently with TJ and may have facilitated an introduction to Roberts when TJ was in London from 11 March until 26 April 1786 (Sowerby, No. 4018; Vol. 6:509n; Vol. 8:421-2; Vol. 9:2).

From Thomas Bridges

July 25th 1803
King & Queen Jail

DEAR SIR

I have been highly pleased with the happy administriation of affairs, Since you filled the presidential Chair—and I have reason to think your appointment will be [renewed?] as the people are dayly more and more united to your conduct—the enemies of the present administriation, have urged many things against you with out effect as yet (and I hope and beleive, Sir, they will continue ineffectual) Among others, as yourself very well know, that you were a friend to the Illuminati Band of Conspirators against Religion and every Social Compact which tended to the happiness of mankind and all Government on your appointment would be lost—But, Sir, It is found not to be so in you nor is your friends any way inclined to favor anarchy—I am Sir about to State a convincing proof of this fact—I will inform you that I have a good living lying forty five miles below the Town of Fredericksburg—married an amiable woman of good connextion have been remark for the most of my life for honesty and probaty I have kept the best State of Society till now—but, Sir, I now Stand Charged with feloneously taking a horse from my neighbourhood (forty five miles from Fredericksburg) and publickly selling him by the Crier—the owner got his horse in a few days as all would know he must and prosecuted me in the County of King and Queen (where all are Democrats) and the County Court has sentenced me to further trial—you must see Sir I could not hope to escape if I stole this horse only so small a distance from Fredericksburg and publicly sold him there, and where I had been raised, and was well acquainted thro life till now and where I must have expected him to be adver[tised] remark Sir I am to be tried at the Court house of King & Queen on the fifth tenth of September and fear a penetentiary seasoning for the charge as now stated—all here are Democrats and who will after this prosecution say that Democrats are not the friends of order and good governance s[ure none]—who again will venture to say that there is a Democratic combination on the principles of illuminism in this part of Virginia and I hope sir as this is the first Charge of any the least theft against me that it will prove at least that I did not know how to make a thief—I hope Sir you will think of some way in which this prosecution may give as usefull evidence againts the principles of Illuminism prevailing among Democrats since from circumstances, I hope, It is evident a felony was not intended and if this use cannot be made of the prosecution I am afraid it will be punishment without any profit only that I hope it will prove that I did not know how to make a rogue and therefore must have always been an honest man—my hope is that the Benevolence of your heart will incline you to think of my State and in your wisdom devise some plan for the releif of my person and Charector and for this I pray you will condesend to write to one to whom you can extend compassion on a state of trial by means which you can adopt—to one who wishes your life and labours to be an immortal blessing to mankind and who is your humble admirer—

THOMAS BRIDGES

It is evident that I am particularly situated in this Charge—I will remark that on my trial Democrats & Aristocrats or the friends of the present and former administration were equally determined to support the dignity of the Commonwealth—and cannot be against Goverment as far as respects the rights of Citizens in the security of property—I hope dear Sir as I have now stated my case you will see I am not guilty of Felony and will write to me even in this Dungeon Spedily may I turn my eyes to a Seat of Mercy may I hope you will condesend to reply to one who has seen pleasant days—yes I think I may hope for a reply at least and hope it will not be delayed as my trial which will determine my fate will soon commence

I am Dear, Sir, your humble petitioner THOMAS BRIDGES

RC (DLC); several words illegible; addressed: "His Excellency Thomas Jefferson President of the united St. City of Washington" and "By post"; endorsed by TJ as received 1 Aug. and so recorded in SJL. Enclosure: "A view, of a Charge against Thomas Bridges—the former and present state of his Charecter compared with the former and present state of his mind—by a friend to publick & private Justice secured by the Compact of Society," undated, warning of the dangers of "forming positive Conclusions from things only apparent in their nature"; the author asks if a man living a just and upright life for 30 years may, in a few weeks' time, be charged with crimes when "discovery & detection was certain"; it is "as clear as a mathematical problem" that another has imposed on him or that he has lost his reason; Bridges was raised 16 miles from Fredericksburg, resided nearby until he was in his twenties, and maintained his acquaintance in the town; why would

Bridges steal a horse following the May races, knowing that persons from where the horse was stolen were in town, then take it no more than 45 miles from Fredericksburg, knowing that it would be advertised in town, and finally sell it by the town crier, "thus knowing that he could not avoid discovery & detection"; if Bridges stole this horse, it would give lie to the law of self-preservation, "since it is certain he had no concern or regard for his life" (MS in same, in Bridges's hand).

From Daniel D'Oyley

SIR Charleston 25th. July 1803

I request the honor of your accepting the inclosed address to our fellow Citizens. This would not have been presumed but among the observations made on it by our Federal paper the Courier too [...]ld a connection with my admiration of your Character and administration was made by comparison with what was said of your predecessors in office. it is impossible for me not to believe that there have been views and that there are now wishes to change the form of our happy Government wisely averted under Providence by Your care & conduct. South Carolina, from the great weight justly merited of her former leading men, has long been considered a doubtful State as to her political inclinations. but *those men* have lost their influence by deserting her interests; and thanks to almighty God She is rescued from their wiles and intrigues to restore themselves: and her political horizon is now enlightened by the splendid Blaze of Republicanism that those who look against it are dazzled into inanity & confusion.

With that respect which gives Value to Virtue I beg ever to be considered with the greatest truth and Sincerity Sir your most Obedt: hble: Servt: DANIEL D'OYLEY

RC (DLC); blurred; at foot of text: "The President of the United States"; endorsed by TJ as received 5 Aug. and so recorded in SJL. Enclosure: Daniel D'Oyley, *An Oration, Delivered in St. Michael's Church Before the Inhabitants of Charleston, South-Carolina, on the Fourth of July, 1803; In Commemoration of American Independence* (Charleston, S.C., [1803]; Shaw-Shoemaker, No. 4108).

To Albert Gallatin

DEAR SIR Monticello July 25. 1803.

We agreed that the address of the Ward committees ought not to be formally answered. but on further reflection I think it would be better to write a private letter to one of the members, in order that he may understand the true grounds on which the subject rests, & may state them informally to his colleagues. I think these grounds so solid that they cannot fail to remove this cause of division among our friends, & perhaps to cure the incipient schism. of the signers of the address I know only Duane & Scott sufficiently to address such a letter to them: and of these I am much more acquainted with the first than the last, & think him on that ground more entitled to this mark of confidence. some apprehensions may perhaps be entertained that if the schism goes on, he may be in a different section from us. if there be no danger in this, he is the one I should prefer. give me your opinion on it if you please, and consider and make any alterations in the letter you think best, and return it to me as soon as you can. I am strongly of opinion it will do good. Accept my affectionate salutations & assurances of respect. TH: JEFFERSON

RC (NHi: Gallatin Papers); at foot of text: "Albert Gallatin esq."; endorsed. PrC (DLC). Recorded in SJL with notation "Ward commees." Enclosure: TJ to William Duane, 24 July 1803.

The ADDRESS of the Philadelphia WARD COMMITTEES is printed at 17 July.

From Lacépède

le 6. thermidor, an 11.
[i.e. 25 July 1803]

MONSIEUR LE PRÉSIDENT

M. Livingston veut bien se charger de faire parvenir à votre excellence, mon histoire naturelle des poissons, dont le cinquième et dernier volume vient de paroître.

J'ai l'honneur de vous prier de vouloir bien l'agréer comme un hommage de mon tendre dévouement, de ma très haute considération, de mon admiration, et de mon respect.

B. G. É. L. LA CEPÈDE

EDITORS' TRANSLATION

6 Thermidor Year 11
[i.e. 25 July 1803]

MISTER PRESIDENT,

Mr. Livingston has kindly offered to send your excellency my natural history of fish, the fifth and final volume of which has just been published.

I have the honor of asking you to accept it as a sign of my fond devotion, high esteem, admiration, and respect. B. G. É. L. LA CEPÈDE

RC (DLC); English date supplied; endorsed by TJ as received from Paris 28 Sep. and so recorded in SJL.

The fifth volume completed Lacépède's *Histoire naturelle des poissons*, which was published in Paris from 1798 to 1803. TJ had John March bind his set of the volumes in October 1804 (Sowerby, No. 1050; statement of account with John March for 16 Apr. 1804 to 7 Mch. 1805, in MHi).

From Meriwether Lewis

Dear Sir, Pittsburgh July 26th. 1803.

I have recieved as yet no answer from Mr. Clark; in the event of Mr. Clark's declining to accompany me Lieut Hooke of this place has engaged to do so, if permitted; and I think from his disposition and qualifications that I might safely calculate on being as ably assisted by him in the execution of the objects of my mission, as I could wish, or would be, by any other officer in the Army. Lieut Hooke is about 26 years of age, endowed with a good constitution, possessing a sensible well informed mind, is industrious, prudent and persevering, and withall intrepid and enterprising: he has acted as Military Agent at this place for a few months past, and of course will have some public accounts to adjust, tho' he tells me that he can settle those accounts, deliver the public stores to the person who may be directed to take charge of them, and prepare to go with me, at any time, within the course of a day or two. Should I recieve no answer from Mr. Clark previous to my leaving this place, or he decline going with me, I would be much gratifyed with being authorized to take Lieut. Hooke with me, first directing him to settle his public accounts, and make such disposition of the publick stores as the Secretary of War may think proper to direct. There is a Capt. Reed of the Arty. here, who will probably not leave this place untill an answer can be recieved, or if he should, Majr. Craig of Pittsburgh would take charge of the stores untill an officer could be ordered on for that purpose.—

It is probable that you will have left Washington before this letter can reach that place, and if so, knowing the delay incident to a communication between yourself and the Secretary of War at such a distance, and conceiving that it would be necessary that he should decide whether from the nature of his arrangements Lieut. Hooke could leave his present station with propriety or not, or his place be supplyed without injury to the public service, I have thought it best to inclose this letter to him unsealed, with a request that should you be absent, he would read it and give me an answer on the subject of it as early as possible. It is most probable that I shall leave Pittsburgh before an answer can be returned to this letter, I take the liberty therefore to suggest, that the answer to me had better be inclosed to Lieut Hooke, unsealed, with instructions to him that in the event of my absence, he should read it, and govern himself accordingly.—If Lieut Hooke sets out twenty days after me, by taking the rout of Limestone, Louisville and Vincennes he will reach the mouth of the Missourie as early as I shall.

I am with the most sincere attatchment Your Obt. Servt.

MERIWETHER LEWIS.

RC (DLC); addressed: "The President of the U. States. City of Washington" with notation "Mail"; endorsed by TJ as a letter of 25 July received 5 Aug. and so recorded in SJL. Enclosed in Dearborn to TJ, 3 Aug.

AUTHORIZED: writing to Moses Hook on 3 Aug., Dearborn gave the lieutenant permission to accompany Lewis "on his tour to the Westward" provided Hook could get his accounts as assistant military agent in order for settlement. The secretary of war also wrote to James Read, a captain in the regiment of artillerists, asking him to take charge of the public property that was in Hook's care and to fill the position of assistant agent temporarily. By the time Dearborn made those authorizations Lewis had an affirmative answer from William Clark. Hook remained at his post in Pittsburgh (Dearborn to Hook, 3 Aug., and to Read, same, in DNA: RG 107, LSMA; Jackson, *Lewis and Clark*, 1:115, 119-20; Heitman, *Dictionary*, 1:819).

UNSEALED: see Dearborn to TJ, 3 Aug.

To William Maddox

SIR

Monticello July 26. 1803

On the 26th. of March I wrote you a letter informing you that after our settlement of Sep. 7. making a balance due you of 254–7–11 I had paid an order of your's in favor of John Craven for £16–8–9. that I went on remitting you money from time to time, and in taking an account at the last remittance, which was Feb. 8. 1803. I omitted to note this order of Craven's, and remitted 98. D. which made up the sum of the £254–7–11 exclusive of Craven's order, which escaped my eye in stating my paiments, so that I overpaid you £16–8–9. to this letter you have given me no answer. as I have not time to [multiply liberties?] on this subject, unless I recieve your answer and acknolegement of this debt before I leave this place, I shall be obliged to commit the matter to other hands to settle with you, which will involve you in useless expence. if you cannot immediately repay the money, I am in no [hurry] but send me your's and mr Moran's joint & several note for it. the matter admits no question. our account is settled & signed by you both and no credit in it for this £16–8–9 because it was not then paid. Price and Peyton [now?][1] Gibson &

Jefferson's books will prove I have paid you *through them* the whole balance settled between us, to wit £254–7–11 and Craven will prove I paid him the £16–8–9. Accept my [...] wishes

TH: JEFFERSON

PrC (MHi); faint; at foot of text: "Mr. William Maddox"; endorsed by TJ in ink on verso.

William Maddox was a stonemason who worked with Joseph Moran on Monticello's nailery and L-shaped dependency wings. He later did masonry work at TJ's mills at Shadwell and at the Monticello stable (MB, 2:1072n).

For the payment through JOHN CRAVEN FOR £16–8–9, equivalent to \$54.70½, see TJ to George Jefferson, 26 Mch.

On this day, TJ also wrote Joseph Moran, but the letter has not been found. Maddox responded to TJ in a letter of 6 Aug., recorded in SJL as received from Columbia, Virginia, on 12 Aug. but not found.

PRICE AND PEYTON: TJ recorded in his financial memoranda on 7 Sep. 1802, that as part of his settlement with Maddox and Moran he gave "my notes to Richard Price & John Peyton to pay each of them 50.D. in the 1st. week of Oct." (MB, 2:1080).

[1]Preceding four words interlined.

From James Madison

DEAR SIR Washington July 26. 1803

Having received some days ago, but not in time for the last mail, the enclosed petition, I have thought it proper to forward with it a pardon, that in case it should be extended to the party, delay might be avoided. I know nothing more of the convict or of the merits of the petition than are to be gathered from the petition itself and the letter from W. Jones. It is signed, I observe by respectable names of all parties. Mr. Wagner will open your answer and make the proper communication to Mr. W. Jones.

No foreign information has been recd. since your departure; nor is any thing further known with respect to Bernadotte or Merry.

I have sent for a pr. of horses, and expect them here in two or three days. I am hurrying my preparations to leave this place as soon as they arrive; but have found the winding up the essential business more tedious than I was fully aware. Several letters which go into cypher particularly one to Mr. Monroe on the subject of Spain have run into considerable length. Mr. Gallatin is still here, but considers every as his last. Mr. E. Livingston made a visit for two days, and returned, I believe without saying a word to any one on the subject which was supposed to cause the visit; nor do I believe that a word was said to him on it.

With respectful attachment I remain yrs. JAMES MADISON

I got Mr. Wagner to see Mr. Mason on the subject of the Pardon. Mr. Mason has promised to write to you

I inclose a supplemental communication from Mr. King, in several views important. also a letter resigning a Commission of Bankruptcy

RC (DLC); at foot of text: "The President of the U. States"; endorsed by TJ as received from the State Department on 29 July and "Samuel Miller. E. Livingston. King's lre" and so recorded in SJL. Enclosures: (1) Petition of Ambrose Vasse and Others to TJ, 17 July. (2) Pardon for Samuel Miller, 25 July (see Petition of Ambrose Vasse and Others to TJ, 17 July). (3) Rufus King to Madison, [ca. 20] July (see TJ to Madison, 31 July). (4) Richard Skinner to Madison, Manchester, Vermont, 15 July, submits his resignation as bankruptcy commissioner, noting that the state office he holds precludes him from keeping the federal appointment; he recommends Jonathan E. Robinson, an attorney at Bennington of "real merit" and the son of Vermont's chief justice, Jonathan Robinson, as his successor (RC in DNA: RG 59, LAR; endorsed by TJ: "Skinner Richd. to mr Madison resigns as Commr. bkrptcy"). (5) Israel Smith to Madison, Manchester, 15 July, supporting Skinner's recommendation of Jonathan E. Robinson as bankruptcy commissioner; Smith is personally acquainted with Robinson and believes he is "well qualified to fill the vacancy" (RC in same; endorsed by TJ: "Robinson Jonathan E. to be Commr. bkrptcy at Bennington Vermt. v. Richd. Skinner resd.").

W. JONES: Walter Jones, Jr., the former U.S. attorney for the Potomac District (Vol. 33:288n). Jones was among those who signed the 17 July petition from Ambrose Vasse and Others to TJ recommending clemency for Samuel Miller.

For Madison's instructions of 29 July to MONROE about acquisition of the Floridas, see Notes on a Cabinet Meeting, 16 July.

To John Page

MY DEAR SIR Monticello July 26. 1803.

In a former letter from Washington I expressed a wish that the salubrity of our climate here, and the wishes of antient friends might make it agreeable to mrs Page and yourself to come and pass some time during my stay here which will be to about the 20th. of September. from your answer I concieved hopes it would be so. I nourish them still with fondness, and anticipate the pleasure of sweetening the relaxation from business by antient recollections. I have to take a journey to some possessions about 90. miles from hence, which will occupy about ten days. the time of going is absolutely indifferent. I shall not go therefore till I hear from you, lest I might be absent when you should do me the favor asked; but will time my journey entirely to your convenience. Accept my affectionate salutations and assurances of constant and unalterable friendship & respect, & make my compliments acceptable to mrs Page. TH: JEFFERSON

RC (NN); addressed: "John Page esquire Governor of Virginia Richmond"; franked; postmarked Milton, 29 July. PrC (DLC); endorsed by TJ in ink on verso.

FORMER LETTER: TJ to Page, 18 Mch.

From James Currie

DEAR SIR, Richmond 27th. July 1803

I have received Your Letter of the 29th Ulto. covering your Bond and find upon Accurate examination of my Books and Papers that your Statement is Correct and perfectly agreeable to me—have therefore taken the liberty of inclosing to you your former Bond, the receipt taken from Pickett for Braxton and your Note of Fifty pounds, which I thought proper to return as the new Bond settles all matters between us—Altho' I have been Confined three weeks with a violent fit of the Gout and other Complaints I still promise myself the pleasure of visiting you at Monticello during your absence from the Seat of Government—Accept my most Sincere wishes for your health and Happiness and believe me always with the most sincere attachment—

Your very Respectfull & Most Hble Servt. JAMES CURRIE

RC (MHi); at foot of text: "Thomas Jefferson Esqr."; endorsed by TJ as received 29 July and so recorded in SJL.

TJ's LETTER OF THE 29TH of June was recorded in SJL but has not been found. In his financial memoranda, however, TJ recorded on 28 June: "Made a statement of my debt to Dr. Currie and inclosed him a new bond for £158–19 principal and int. at 6. pr. cent from 1797. May 1. till paid. The old bond to be cancelled" (MB, 2:1104). TJ's letter was in apparent response to a note of 24 June from Currie, recorded in SJL as received 29 June but not found. TJ owed Currie for medical services and issued an initial bond in September 1783 for £215–17–6, but did not close out his debt until June 1808, after Currie's death (MB, 2:1226; Vol. 6:340-1).

RECEIPT TAKEN FROM PICKETT: possibly the cancellation of a payment for Carter BRAXTON, which TJ had long ago asked Currie to take in. The transaction may have gone through Richmond merchant George Pickett (MB, 2:809; Vol. 18:488). NOTE OF FIFTY POUNDS: Currie may have meant a $50 payment for legal services that TJ had made on Currie's behalf (see Vol. 39:435).

From Albert Gallatin

DEAR SIR Washington 27 July 1803

I have not yet heard whether you have arrived safe at Monticello; and I write only to inform you that I leave this city to day for New York. I will stop in Philada. to treat with the Bank & will communicate the result.

Nothing has taken place, since you left this connected with the Treasury, except E. Livingston's journey here. He called on me at my house, said nothing of his defalcation & left the city two days after without calling at the office. This compels me to take the commission to N. York where I will fix the matter. I have written on the subject to De Witt Clinton.

With sincere attachment & respect Your obedt. Servt.

ALBERT GALLATIN

RC (DLC); at foot of text: "The President of the United States"; endorsed by TJ as received from the Treasury Department on 29 July and "E. Livingston" and so recorded in SJL.

For Edward LIVINGSTON's misappropriation of public funds, see Gallatin to TJ, 16 June. The Treasury secretary had solicited DeWitt CLINTON, senator of New York, to convince Livingston of the necessity of resigning and to provide recommendations for a successor to the district attorney's office (same; Gallatin to TJ, 2 July). On 27 July, Gallatin informed Clinton of Livingston's visit to Washington, writing, "He was here, saw me, & did not speak on the subject. I am afraid that he is not impressed with the absolute necessity of a successor being appointed." Gallatin noted that he would bring a commission for Nathan Sanford with him to New York in early August. If Livingston did not resign, he would be removed. "As you have spoken to him on the subject," Gallatin concluded, "I thought it right to let you know the precise state of things" (Gallatin, *Papers*, 8:566).

To Benjamin Galloway

DEAR SIR Monticello July 28. 1803.

Your favor of the 19th is dated on the day I left Washington and finds me here, where I propose to pass our annual recess during the sickly season. the letter of which you desire a copy is among my papers at Washington, locked up, and the key here so that no copy of it can be obtained till I return, the last week in September when, if not too late for your purpose it shall be attended to. I have examined my papers here and find among them only a complimentary note recieved in November 1797. Accept my respectful salutations

TH: JEFFERSON

PrC (MHi); at foot of text: "Benjamin Galloway esq"; endorsed by TJ in ink on verso.

Petition of Samuel Miller, with Recommendation of William Kilty and William Cranch

To the Honourable Court.

The Humble petition of Samuel Miller

Most Humbly Sheweth.

Your petitioner having received the Auful Sentence of Death pronounced upon him for the Crime which he has Been found Guilty of Labouring Under a Weighty Oppression of Both Body and mind while penitent and Humble makes use of this as his Last rescourse to the Honourable Court praying you in your Goodness to recommend him to Mercy

Your petitioner most Humbly prays you will take his Unhappy Case into your Humane Consideration that this is the first time he was Brought Before the Court of Justice and always Obtained an Honest Livelihood till this Unfortunate Period which is to Terminate his Existence upon a Fatal Tree and to be Cut off From the face of the Earth in the prime of Life in a most Horrid Manner, Could Your Eyes Behold the Secrets of his afflicted Heart for these Several Months past and the Horrors of Conscience that has filled his mind, and how Sincerely he has Repented for his past folly you would be Inclined to pity his Doleful Situation and Recommend him to Mercy that his Life may be Spared on any Condition for this his first Offence

Your Petitioner is fully Convinced of his past Misconduct and Humbly prays to God that you will be the means of having his days prolonged and not sent out of the World in such an Ignomineus way But be a Living Monument of Mercy whose future Conduct shall be Never to deviate from the paths of Virtue any-more

Your Petitioner in the Greatest Affliction Begs for Mercy to be Saved from that Untimely End a few days from hence, should the Disconsolate Object Obtain a small portion of your Clemency he will as in duty Bound Ever pray, these are the prayers of the Unhappy and Miserable Captive that lays at the point of Death, Craveing for Mercy Both from God and the Humanity of an Honourable Court, should he be an Object of Mercy it will Never be Blotted from the Memory of the Unfortunate and Unhappy SAMUEL MILLER

The Undersigned Judges of the Circuit Court of the District of Columbia, Respectfully State to the President of the United States, that they have Considered the above Petition of Samuel Miller, and feel disposed to Comply with it, as far as the Circumstances of his Case, and a Sense of their Publick duty will permit

Samuel Miller was Convicted in March last of the Crime of Burglary—The Evidence was, that he was found in the night time in the Store House of Ambrose Vasse in Alexandria, with a Loaded Pistol in his Pocket Some evidence was brought forward by the Prisoner tending to Prove that he was in a State of intoxication, And, on the part of the United States it was proved that Several false Keys of Various kinds and Sizes were found under the Steps of his House—And on the Whole there appeared to be no doubt of his Guilt.

Sentence was not passed until the Close of the last June Term and the twentieth of August next is the day fixed for the Execution

Under these Circumstances, the Judges Cannot Ground their recommendation on the Merits of the Petitioner or on any doubts as to his Guilt.—But they feel themselves Justified in expressing an opinion that the Punishment of death would be too Severe for the Crime which was Committed, And, Altho, in their Judicial Capacities they are bound to declare the Law, whatever it may be, they consider it Strictly Consistent with their duty to recommend to the President the exercise of that power of Mitigating the Severity of the Law which the Constitution Vests in him

It may be matter of regret that there is not a provision for Commuting the Punishment of death in such Cases for one more proportioned to the Offence, which might be inflicted without any doubt of its Justice or Humanity

But Altho in this Case, the Alternative must be, either an Execution of the Sentence or an entire pardon, and of course an exemption from any Punishment, except what may have arisen from the imprisonment of the Offender—They do, (for the reasons and on the Grounds which they have Stated,) Recommend to the President of the United States to Grant a Pardon to the Petitioner Samuel Miller in Such Manner as He may deem expedient, either immediate or after Such repreives as may be Judged Necessary

W KILTY
W. CRANCH.
July 28th 1803

MS (DNA: RG 59, GPR); petition undated, entirely in Miller's hand; recommendation in a clerk's hand, signed by Kilty and Cranch; addressed by Miller: "To the Honourable Court"; also addressed in a clerk's hand: "To The President of the United States"; endorsed by TJ as received 10 Aug. and "Miller Saml. petn." and so recorded in SJL.

To Caesar A. Rodney

Dear Sir Monticello July 28. 1803.

Your favor of the 22d. finds me here. I have carefully perused the copy of[1] the paper addressed to you from Wilmington in July 1801. signed by Messrs. Tilton and others and inclosed to me in your letter: and altho' I really believe that you presented such an one to me while at Washington, yet I have had so many proofs of the little confidence I ought to place in my memory, surcharged with so much matter daily passing thro' it, that I do not venture to affirm the fact. the original, if I possess it, has slipped out of it's place, which, notwithstanding my care in arranging my papers, I have found sometimes to happen by one paper's slipping into another while lying together on the table; in which case it is found only when I happen to have occasion to turn to the other. in this way the one you desire may still be found, but it is impossible to say when. I should presume however that my testimony could easily be supplied by the declaration of the signers that they addressed such an one to you, & of Govr. Hall who I believe generally called with you while at Washington & probably saw you deliver the paper to me. according to your request I return you your letter & the paper it enclosed. with my affectionate salutations.

Th: Jefferson

RC (William S. Potter, Wilmington, Delaware, 1962); at foot of text: "Caesar A. Rodney esq." PrC (DLC); endorsed by TJ in ink on verso. Enclosure: Rodney to TJ, 22 July, recorded in SJL as received at Monticello on the 27th, but not found. For the paper enclosed in it, see below.

The July 1801 paper signed by James and Nehemiah tilton and others has not been found. On 30 June 1801, James Tilton wrote TJ that he and others had prevailed upon Rodney "to make a visit to Washing: for the express purpose of representing the true interest of republicanism in Delaware" (Vol. 34:487-8, 612-13). For the controversy over the delivery of the paper, see Rodney to TJ, 7 July.

[1] Preceding three words interlined.

To Joshua Danforth

Sir Monticello July 29. 03

The Editor of the Pittsfield Sun did for a while [forward me] the newspaper as mentioned in your favor of the 16th inst. which I recieved [here] a day or two after my arrival from Washington. I had [found] [...] of the character you give [it]. what has discouraged me from taking distant papers is the difficulty of making paiments at a distance of so small amount as not to be the object of a bill of exchange. I know not who is the representative in Congress from the neighborhood of Pittsfield, but if paiment could be made to him or any [person] in Washington I should gladly be a subscriber to the paper. my rule is to pay for my newspapers about the New years day, all together, [as paiment] at different times, some might escape me. at the ensuing one therefore I should without fail make the paiment to any person indicated to me. it is matter of great satisfaction to me to receive assurances of the approbation you express of my conduct in the state of [...] which a [certain] description of editors & [...] advantage [...] & by which they are endeavoring to undo the freedom of the press [itself]. my fellow citizens can judge of me only by [...] I [...] only by the indulgence [...] and to the different views which honest men [...] of the [same] object. Accept my salutations and best wishes.

TH: JEFFERSON

PrC (DLC); faint; at foot of text: "Joshua Danforth esq. Pittsfield"; endorsed by TJ in ink on verso.

REPRESENTATIVE IN CONGRESS Tompson J. Skinner was a former Massachusetts state senator, congressman, and judge. He represented Berkshire County in the Fourth, Fifth, and Eighth Congresses (*Biog. Dir. Cong.*).

PAY FOR MY NEWSPAPERS: prior to becoming president, TJ typically renewed a few subscriptions for himself and son-in-law Thomas Mann Randolph at the start of each new year, but he followed this practice less frequently once he was in office (MB, 2:976, 996, 1012, 1034, 1062; Vol. 31:342; Vol. 32:376).

To Henry Dearborn

DEAR SIR — Monticello July 29. 03.

I inclose you a letter from E. I. Dupont who has established a gunpowder manufactory at Wilmington. if the public can with advantage avail themselves of his improvements in that art, it would be to encourage improvement in one of the most essential manufactures. I should be the more gratified by it as it would gratify his father who has been a faithful & useful friend to this country. during my ministry in Paris he was at the head of the bureau of commerce, and I was constantly indebted to his zealous exertions for all the ameliorations of our commerce with that country which were obtained. on the late occasion too of Louisiana tho' he does not bring himself into view, I am satisfied that his just views of the subject have enabled him to make those energetic representations to Talleyrand, Marbois & others about the Consul, which his intimacy with them favored, and must have sensibly favored the result obtained. Accept my affectionate salutations and assurances of sincere esteem & respect

TH: JEFFERSON

PrC (DLC); at foot of text: "The Secretary at War." Recorded in SJL as a letter to the War Department with notation "Dupont's powder." Enclosure: Éleuthère Irénée du Pont de Nemours to TJ, 20 July.

From William Thomas

Columbia County State of Georgia
the 29th 7th mo:th 1803

Dear and much much much and very much respected friend, I wrote thee two volumes Some good while ago, but Since thou 'wast our President: The one was wrote principally in Verse the other in prose, But whether thou receiv'd them yea or nay I cannot tell, But if thou did and wrote back I never receiv'd a line: But Nevertheless as I am Writing a letter to my Son Abishai I thought I would inform thee of those things: It may Seem Strange and it is Strange Indeed that a Correspondence of this kind Should be carried on from one Stranger to another: What may it be call'd Impertinence Intruder Interloper busy body &c: Well So they may, For I am Such a dupe that where ever I hear of good Charectors Just human and liberal I like to be in the midst Encourageing their persuits and perseverance therein—Now friend what was upon my mind when I took up my pen was what follows—A Stranger came to my Dwelling and lodg'd with me all night, He Said he was a Soldier under Cousin Anthony during the whole war (Waynes Mother and my Father were Sisters Children) He was at the batling and discomfitting the Indians in Georgia, Taking Stony point, Battle of Brandiwine and Germantown, Also at the lakes driving the Indians and British out of their Strong holds, untill they were willing to Compound and treat: Acceding to the United States large Strides of Land exceeding rich and Valuable, So be it I could not contradict him

But here comes the Scruple, That he knew my Son Abishai very well That he married the relict of one Huston who Was member of congress for the State of Virginia: rode in his coach & four horses, That Abishai's Wife's Fathers name was Baker Lord Mayor of the city of Philadelphia: I instantly put that tale to a period, by telling him that there was no Such Titles allow'd of in the United States as Lord: He was a little fallen but Soon recovered his tale of prodigies: The next was in respect to thy Self my friend. He Said he was very well Acquainted with the president knew him very well had been at his mansion house many times, that it was built on the top of a Cone or pyramid one hundred feet high from the level of the plain, That the house on the top of the cone was the grandest by appearance That ever he Saw, made of hewen stone delicately rang'd as true as a line, That the kitchen and every room in the house was supply'd with cool fresh water out of Leaden Aquaducts or pipes—That the road or street ran Circular round the cone or Sugarloaf up to his house—I Query'd where he brought those cool waters from, for the fountain must be higher than the rooms it Ascended and dessended into—he Said from a mountain four miles of in a leaden pipe or aquaduct three feet under gound—he Says his name John findley

If all those things are true it may be call'd Wonderful Curiosity: There may be some part true but I question the whole—I don't doubt the Elegancy of thy house, AND Should be very fond to See it nicely delineated in my possession: I esteem it would make a fine Show among our Cabins here in Georgia: though we have Some Elegant houses both in Country and City: My paper is run And I must be done.

from thy ever as yet well wisher Wm Thomas

Give my love to Thomas Paine although I lash'd him very Severe yet I love the Man: Yea even in Simile I set Sir Isaac Newton to break his head—If the President desires it I'le send him a Copy, if well and no Obstruction Intervenes

T'is five Weeks past Since a Small whiteish speck rose up close by the candle or apple of my eye, As the Speck grew the pain increast Twas almost Intolorable Tis at present very easy But So foggy I can hardly see to write

Should the President in the rout of his Perambulation's take a Notion to pay Georgia a visit: As I live 35 miles due west from Augusta it would be no Injurous out of thy way to call See me for I live adjacent to the former travelling road from Augusta to Washington Wilkes county. perhaps Abishai and his consort may Accompany Thee: Abishai has been here: He would be a fine guide: And I believe would find him to be a very agreeable companion

I may point out
But much I doubt
Whether T'will be the case
Whether or not
I've not forgot
An invite thee to ease Wm Thomas

RC (MHi); addressed: "Thomas Jefferson President United States Washington City" and "from William Thomas Columbia County Georgia"; franked; endorsed by TJ as received 29 Aug. and so recorded in SJL.

NEVER RECEIV'D A LINE: according to SJL, this is the first correspondence TJ had received from Thomas.

WAYNES MOTHER: Elizabeth Iddings Wayne (ANB, s.v. "Wayne, Anthony").

MY SON ABISHAI: Abishai Thomas was principal clerk of the Navy Department from July 1799 through March 1802. A compulsive gambler who was imprisoned for debt on at least one occasion, he never received a more lucrative federal appointment, nor did he realize financial advantage in his marriage in the summer or fall of 1800. By the end of 1803 or early 1804, he left Baltimore, where he had been living in poverty, and moved to Darien, Georgia, where other members of his family had settled (Christopher McKee, *A Gentlemanly and Honorable Profession: The Creation of the U.S. Naval Officer Corps, 1794-1815* [Annapolis, 1991], 15; Washington, *Papers, Pres. Ser.*, 6:182; Vol. 35:446).

George HUSTON from Rockingham County had been a delegate to the Virginia General Assembly intermittently from 1782 to 1802 (Leonard, *General Assembly*, 147, 225).

Hilary BAKER, the mayor of Philadelphia from 1796 to 1797, had five daughters (J. Thomas Scharf and Thompson Westcott, *History of Philadelphia, 1609-1884*, 3 vols. [Philadelphia, 1884], 2:1571; Thomas Sergeant and William Rawle, *Reports of Cases Adjudged in the Supreme Court of Pennsylvania*, 17 vols. [Philadelphia, 1818-29], 8:13-15).

To James Madison

DEAR SIR Monticello July 31. 03.

I return you the petition of Samuel Miller with the pardon signed. mr Kelty had spoke to me on this subject and told me that he and mr Craunch should join in a recommendation. I wish mr Wagner would obtain this before he delivers the pardon. I return also mr King's letter which has really important matter, especially what respects the Mare clausum, the abandonment of the colonial system, & emancipation of S. America. on the subject of our seamen as both parties were agreed against impresments at sea, and concealments in port, I suppose we may practise on those two articles as things understood, altho' no convention was signed. I see that the principle of free bottoms free goods must be left to make it's way by treaty with particular nations. Gr. Britain will never yield to it willingly and she cannot be forced.

I think I have recollected a Governor for Louisiana, as perfect in all points as we can expect. sound judgment, standing in society, knolege of the world, wealth, liberality, familiarity with the French language, & having a French wife. you will percieve I am describing Sumpter. I do not know a more proper character for the place. I wish we could find a diplomatist or two, equally eligible, for Europe. Accept my affectionate salutations. TH: JEFFERSON

RC (DLC: Madison Papers); at foot of text: "The Secretary of State." PrC (DLC). Recorded in SJL as a letter to the State Department with notation "S Miller. pardon. King's lre. T. Sumpter." Enclosures: see first three enclosures listed at Madison, 26 July.

JOIN IN A RECOMMENDATION: see Petition of Samuel Miller, with Recommendation of William Kilty and William Cranch to TJ, 28 July 1803.

Written at New York and received by Madison on 26 July, Rufus KING'S LETTER discussed "a few miscellaneous articles by way of supplement" to his final dispatch as minister to Great Britain. He reported that before his departure from England, knowing that war between Britain and France was imminent, he attempted to negotiate a convention to protect American sailors from impressment. With effort, King framed an agreement with the first lord of the Admiralty, Lord St. Vincent. It prohibited armed vessels of either nation from seizing persons from any ship belonging to the other country on the high seas. It also required each country to prevent its citizens or subjects "from clandestinely concealing, or carrying away" seamen from the territories or possessions of the other nation. The convention was intended to be in effect for five years. The night before King left London, however, St. Vincent decided that the terms must be altered to allow Britain full jurisdiction over seas "immemorially considered to be within the Dominion of Great Britain." Faced with this assertion of the principle of a closed sea—MARE CLAUSUM—King "concluded to abandon the negotiation rather than to acquiesce in the Doctrine it proposed to establish" (Madison, *Papers*, *Sec. of State Ser.*, 5:203-4).

The prime minister, Henry Addington, hinted to King that if the disruptions of the new war should result in independence for South America, the COLONIAL SYSTEM "must every where be abandoned." EMANCIPATION OF S. AMERICA: King reported that a British expedition to support rebellion in northern South America, "in readiness to set sail," had been forestalled by the signing of the Amiens peace and would be put back in motion if Spain entered the war. It was "the Opinion of the first men of the nation," King noted, "that the secondary Object of the present war, and one that must give England Courage as well as Resources to go on with the Struggle is the entire independence of South America" (same, 205).

FREE BOTTOMS FREE GOODS: King passed along an "annecdote" that the Prussian government had offered to protect Hanover and northern Germany from the French in exchange for British agreement to the maxim "That free ships should make free Goods." According to the British response, "no advantage nor Service, which could be named, would be sufficient" to make England agree to that assertion of neutrals' rights. Finally, King informed Madison that he had declined to accept presents that the crown customarily gave to departing ministers and to plenipotentiaries who had signed treaties or conventions (same, 204-6). The State Department, perhaps in the autumn after it was known in Washington that James Monroe had gone to London as King's successor, sent Monroe copies of much of the text of King's letter (same, 206n, 471, 504-5).

SUMPTER: that is, Thomas Sumter, Jr., who recently resigned his position as secretary of the U.S. legation in France (Vol. 33:624-5; Vol. 37:410-16).

From "A Patriot of Our Glorious Revolution"

GREAT SIR July 1803

The following is the substance of a letter written to you in Autumn 1802. The reason it was not sent, was because the author soon learned the falsehood of the report which was the exciting cause of its being written; & because of the extreme delicacy of presuming to interupt the Chief Magistrate with such ideas without being able to state particulars.

However, finding too much reason to fear the defection, or want of integrity, in the second in authority; learning the slender health of the third—& knowing the increasing phrenzy & desperation to which your enemies are driven (such as often prompts men to stick at nothing to remove a single obstacle) his feelings have finally prevailed with him to send it.

He wishes not to have too much tho't of it—but yet to have the following questions fairly considered & applyed to existing circumstances, viz.

What will not some persons do for the acquisition of power, consequence & confidence, when there is but one way to obtain the desired object; or, in other words, to have their will gratified in the defeat of others?

To those who suppose that modern federalism would have nothing to fear, could you be put out of the way before the next Presidential election there is but one way, & that lies through patriotic[1] blood, a way which tyrants always take, either directly or indirectly.

Again, whether some honest bigots to an oposite sentiment do not really believe, & daily practice, on the popish tenet, that the end sanctifies the means?

Now what more important end can such persons have than the establishment of what they suppose to be the foundation of all civil & religious order on earth, & saintship in heaven?

Can a zealous Mahomidan take the sword to bring men to the true faith—a Papist burn & torture them into it—a British Royalist pay for poisoning, scalping &c. to support the good cause of civil & religious despotism, & yet a modern federalist, who is virtually & substantially of the same kind of deluded, self deceived, beings with the former, nothing to bring about that conformity to their own sentiments on which they suppose the present & future salvation of men to depend?

The Letter.

Inestimable Chief.

When you consider how dear you are to every genuine patriot you will, it is hoped, forgive this intrusion, & believe the writer when he assures you, that on reading, in a public paper that you was seriously indesposed, his heart, as it were instinctively, accused him for not advertising you of the danger which he supposed you to be in of designs upon your life, from a certain quarter—& his consequent fears that you might be helped to a supernatural indisposition which—should it happen through your own neglect of caution, will never, he fears, be forgiven by your real friends, who prize your life & health above all price.

He is not at liberty to mention the names (nor his own, lest he might be chalanged on facts which he cannot substantiate) nor the abodes of men, who are both able & willing, & who have suggested their willingness, to give thousands to have you assassinated.

This he learned some time ago, but hesitated to communicate it, least it should appear too much like the visionary fears of a child.

But Sir, is it not your duty to be very cautiously guarded, although you might be fearless as to your mere personal safety?

Have not your friends a most invaluable property connected with your existance which, for their sakes, or that of the public good, ought not to be exposed?

Have not the enemies of rational liberty as much, or more, to fear from your inflexible integrity of principle, than ever they had from the martial prowess of Buonaparte?

And are men less passionate & revengeful for the overthrow of their darling cause & interest in one country than another?

That a certain doctor had been heard to say that he would lay you in a lasting sleep for a few dollars—that he should think—no harm of it & the like, is not thought to be very pertinent—But the foregoing hints are judged to be sufficient, from one who thinks he would shed his last drop of blood to defend you, so long as you continue true to your avowed principles—but who will never cease to excecrate you, should you be guilty of that dereliction to which men in power are always courted, & generally yield, sooner or later—

To this corruption & degeneracy he trusts however that all the wealth of America will not bribe you—nor all the flatteries, or threats, of the world ever draw or drive you.

From a patriot of our glorious
revolution, who yet retains the
just and animating principles of 1776.

To Thomas Jefferson, the real Friend o Man.
Let others give you a *higher* title, they cannot give you a *better* one.

RC (DLC); partially dated; addressed: "Thomas Jefferson, President of the United States of America, Washington City or Monticello"; franked; postmarked Newtown, N.J., 12 Aug.; endorsed by TJ as received from "Anon." on 22 Aug. and "danger of assassination" and so recorded in SJL.

SECOND IN AUTHORITY: Vice President Aaron Burr. According to rules for presidential succession established by law in

1792, THE THIRD in line as chief executive was the president pro tempore of the Senate. The Senate elected Stephen R. Bradley to this position on 2 Mch. 1803 and John Brown of Kentucky on 17 Oct. 1803 (*Biog. Dir. Cong.*; U.S. Statutes at Large, 1:239-41; JS, 3:281, 295).

[1]MS: "patrotic."

From John Dickinson

Wilmington the first of
the eighth Month 1803

MY DEAR FRIEND,

Gratitude, a Duty pleasing even to a deeply wounded Heart, prompts Me to present my Thanks as a Father, as a Relative, as a Citizen, for the faithful and well-directed Application of thy powers to produce Happiness, of which, by the Divine Blessing on thy Exertions, my Children, my Kindred, my Country, are likely to largely to participate.

May Providence grant success to all thy benevolent Plans, and may thy Administration diffuse an useful Light to this and to following Ages.

I hope, that I may soon have occasion to congratulate thee on the Completion of thy Views respecting Territory, by the Addition of the Floridas to the Lands lately ceded.

In one of my Maps, the River Mexicani is laid down as the Western Boundary of the lower part of Louisiana next to the Gulf of Mexico, from the Head of which River the Boundary slants off greatly to the Westward, and seems to approach within three or four hundred Miles of the Spanish settlements of Santa Fee and the Mines of Saint Barbe on the River Del Nort or Rio Bravo.

Would not a slip from this upper part of Louisiana, be of Importance to the Spaniards by extending their Frontier? And would it not be advantageous to Us, to grant it to them in Exchange for the Floridas? And might not thus a Line admitting of no future Controversy be established?

Forgive Me for mentioning these Things, as in all probability the Documents in thy possession far exceed any I have. Thy indulgent Kindness persuades Me, that I shall be excused, as I firmly trust, that thou art convinced, I am thy truely affectionate Friend

JOHN DICKINSON

RC (DLC); endorsed by TJ as received 8 Aug. and so recorded in SJL.

RIVER MEXICANI: the Neches or the Sabine; see TJ to Thomas Mann Randolph, 5 July.

The province of Santa Bárbara, where the Spanish first opened MINES in the 1560s, was not on the Rio Grande but south of it, on branches of a tributary, the Conchos (John L. Kessell, *Spain in the Southwest: A Narrative History of Colo-*

nial New Mexico, Arizona, Texas, and California [Norman, Okla., 2002], 66, 86-7; Chantal Cramaussel, *Poblar la Frontera: La Provincia de Santa Bárbara en Nueva Vizcaya durante los Siglos XVI y XVII* [Zamora, Mex., 2006], 12-13).

From Lorcus Gibbs

THOMAS JEFFERSON, MooresTown New Jersey
RESPECTED FRIEND, 1 of 8 Mo. 1803

As thou art a statesman in power, and therefore capable of doing much good in the world, I shall trust to thy liberallity to excuse me in this plain address; since it is meant respectfully to call thy benevolent regard to a subject, wherein an obscure individual can only *wish*, what it is in the power of the *government alone* to perform. I have frequently heard thou hast liberated thy Blacks, or such of them as were willing to leave thee; and that thou standest friendly disposed toward that people. I have therefore beleived it right for me, thus in honest simplicity, to communciate a few hints concerning them; whilst I trust that the liberality of thy sentiments will redound to thy lasting memory; it being "righteousness" that "exalteth" an individual, as well as a "nation"; whilst "sin is a reproach to any people."

It having pleased the Creator of the world, to make of one flesh all the children of men, it becomes us then to feel for and assist each other, as children of one common Father; however different their lot as to rank, or colour.

It were but an uncomfortable prospect to the friend of human kind, to see one of the first of the civilized nations, subjecting to an Egyptian servitude, a people distinguished but for their ignorance, barbarity and weakness. Their brotherly sympathy should rather be called forth, and the kind hand of help extended. But to behold prejudice rankling into hatred, for the sole difference of colour would be still more strange and lamentable. Of the enlightened and human part of our fellow citizens, we may hope better things; and that we may not have to say in the name of injured African "look not upon me because I am black, because the sun hath shined upon me."

I am not, by any means, wishing to advocate an indiscriminate emancipation of all our blacks. The evils of a measure it is apprehended would surpass even those of their present slavery. My concern is more for the well being of such as have already been liberated; believing that whatever benefit is confered on a part of this people, must eventually redound to the general interest of their race. Indeed, in ruminating on the distressed condition of many of these freed men, the thought has mournfully occured to my mind, what shall become of this people in generations to come? and wherewithal shall atonement be made?

For though not in all instances, yet in many, the injustice of their bondage is flagrant, and crying to Heaven.

Nay, it is the humane spirit of philanthropy that the gospel inspires, must save from the uplifted arm of Justice.

In a religious view the state of this people has appeared similar to that of Israel in the wilderness. Though freed in especial manner, by the outstretched arm of the Almighty, with signs and miracles, wrought by the hand of his servant Moses, not only to awaken Egypt to a sense of their wrong, but Israel to obeisance, they nevertheless soon forgot his wondrous works, and abused their privileges; insomuch that they wer obliged to the observance of a law suited to their low and servile state, destitute as they had been, of many advantages during their state of oppression. Nay, so depraved were they still as to provoke the Most High to their destruction in the wilderness. Yet Moses, who was learned in all the wisdom of the Egyptians, was instrumental to lead them forward in this journey; the second generation being to possess the land. So that the friend of humanity has room to hope for the generations to come. For these I have faith, that light will arise; and that they will gradually become civilized, and attain unto the dignified rank of man; of man at once virtuous and independent;—save of Heaven only. Even *our* ancesters have once groaned beneath barbarism and vassalage.

Yet can we expect that the poor blacks will emerge without that aid from us, which retributive justice but demands? Some of us feel it a sacred duty to maintain a faithful guardianship over this degraded, helpless, and despised people; and regard the wounds of a tender-hearted conscience, in doing for them as we would wish should be done for us.

Please to be informed then, that it is the sentiment of many, having the cause of humanity at heart, that government might very consistently provide an asylum, for such of the Blacks, as are lawfully free, in some parts of the Western States. This, it is conceived, would be no great sacrifice since the acquisition of Louisiana; and it is thought must be popular with the thinking part of our nation. To designate the spot, is not for us. The climate is congenial with the race, and the proper population of these wilds must be desirable. I would wish therefore that a destrict might be allotted to such free Blacks, or people of colour, as might choose to emigrate thither, and improve the soil, no expences to accrue to them, save the fees of location. This is a policy for settlement, which the British in Canada, and the Spaniards in Louisana have resorted to, and which is therefore not unprecedented.

It is known that the agricultural employ is of all others most favourable to virtue and happiness. These Blacks therefore might in time learn to taste the sweets of industry and interest; and progressing in civilization make in time good citizens. We have some among us who have manifested tokens of improvement that deserve to be encouraged.

It is thought that an offer of government to this effect would be efficaceously patronised by many among us by way of subscription and donation. The society of Friends *it is thought*, would be particularly engaged to labour for their good, temporally as well as spiritually.

A hint of thy approbation of these proposals it is left at thy discretion to give; wishing the things to rest and weigh in thy mind, as wisdom may direct.

From thy friend and well wisher, LORCUS GIBBS

RC (DLC); addressed: "Thomas Jefferson President of U.S.A. Washing. City"; endorsed by TJ as received 28 Jan. 1804 and so recorded in SJL.

Lorcus Gibbs may have been the same individual who was identified as Lucas Gibbs in a testimonial to a patent windmill operated in Moorestown, New Jersey, and in a journal kept by a Society of Friends minister (*Aurora*, 7 June 1799; John Comly and Isaac Comly, eds., *Friends' Miscellany: Containing Journals of the Lives, Religious Exercises, and Labours in the Work of the Ministry, of Joshua Evans and John Hunt, Late of New Jersey* [Philadelphia, 1837], 304).

From Gideon Granger

DEAR SIR General Post Office August 1st 1803

Upon looking over some private letters which were carefully laid aside when I went to Connecticut in the Spring I found the enclosed which ought to have been returned to you immediately. On Thursday I expect to depart for New-England—With great Esteem and Respect Yours sincerely GIDN GRANGER

RC (DLC); at foot of text: "President of the United States Monticello Va."; endorsed by TJ as received 3 Aug. and so recorded in SJL. Enclosure not identified.

From John Vaughan

DEAR SIR Philad. 1 Augt 1803

M Dufief having applied to me to assist him in procuring D Priestlys Harmony for you, I took considerable pains to get it, without Success. As I thought it probable Mr Priestly might have a Copy, I requested him to Spare it, I inadvertently mentioned your name, & have received a Copy not from him, but from Dr Priestly, who requests you will favor him by the acceptance of it—Mr Dufief being out of Town, I wish to know whether any person here has directions how to forward such objects to you, Should I in the interim meet with a Safe opportunity to Washington, I shall Send it forward

I remain with respect Dr Sir Your obt Serv JN VAUGHAN

RC (DLC); at foot of text: "Thomas Jefferson Presidt. of US. Washington"; endorsed by TJ as received 5 Aug. and so recorded in SJL; below the endorsement TJ made notations "June 25," "July 23," and "Aug 1," which were all dates of letters from Vaughan.

PRIESTLYS HARMONY: see TJ to Nicolas Gouin Dufief, 9 Apr., for TJ's desire to obtain Joseph Priestley's *Harmony of the Evangelists* in Greek and English.

MR PRIESTLY: Joseph Priestley, Jr.

From George Hunter

SIR Philada. Augt. 2nd. 1803

If the Government of the United States has a desire to explore the new acquisition of Territory called Louisiana, In order to procure general & necessary information preveous to a Treaty to fix Boundaries between us & the Dominions of Spain.

To ascertain[1] the situation of, & circumstances relative to, those large bodies of good Land which shall appear best calculated to reimburse the purchase money of the Province, if not to discharge the Whole National Debt.

To have an accurate account of such of those natural Treasures, of Nitre, Sea Salt, Sulphur, Coal & other Minerals, Iron, Copper, Lead & other Metals as are already discovered & unapropriated, in order to their being disposed of to the best advantage for the general good.

And is inclined to accept my services to accomplish those & other objects the Government may have in veiw in that Country.

I will with pleasure make a tender of my best endeavours to execute such orders as I may receive, which from having some knowlege of the Customs & Languages of the French & Spaniards, of Chemistry

& Mineralogy, & not unused to travelling by Land & Sea, particularly in the Western Country, I flatter myself I can perform to the satisfaction of the Government.

I am with great respect & esteem, your Excellys. most obt. Servt.

George Hunter

RC (DNA: RG 59, LAR); at foot of text: "Thomas Jefferson President of the United States"; endorsed by TJ as received 17 Aug. and "to explore Louisiana" and so recorded in SJL. Enclosed in Gallatin to TJ, 11 Aug. 1803 (first letter).

A native of Scotland, George Hunter (1755-1823) came to America with his family in 1774, settling in Philadelphia and finding work as a druggist. After service in the American Revolution as an apothecary and surgeon, Hunter established his own business as a druggist and, later, a chemist. In 1796 and 1802, he made journeys to the west, visiting Kentucky, the Illinois country, and St. Louis. Hunter's reputation as a chemist and mineralogist grew as he secured a contract to purify saltpeter for the War Department in 1803 as well as a patent for improving the production of sea salt. The following year, TJ named him to join William Dunbar in an expedition to explore the Red and Arkansas Rivers. In practical knowledge of chemistry, TJ explained to Dunbar, "he has probably no equal in the US." Circumstances limited Dunbar and Hunter to a brief exploration of the Ouachita River from October 1804 to January 1805, but their findings provided the first published accounts of American explorations in the newly acquired Louisiana territory. Returning to Philadelphia in early 1805, Hunter declined further western ventures and refocused his attention on saltpeter contracts for the War and Navy Departments. In 1815, he removed to New Orleans, where he continued his various business enterprises until his death (John Francis McDermott, ed., "The Western Journals of Dr. George Hunter, 1796-1805," APS, *Transactions*, new ser., 53, pt. 4 [1963], 5-19, 123-4; Trey Berry, "The Expedition of William Dunbar and George Hunter Along the Ouachita River, 1804-1805," *Arkansas Historical Quarterly*, 62 [2003], 386-403; *List of Patents*, 33; Vol. 38:592, 593n; Éleuthère Irénée du Pont de Nemours to TJ, 22 Feb. 1804; TJ to William Dunbar, 15 Apr. 1804; TJ to Constantine S. Rafinesque, 15 Dec. 1804; Robert Smith to TJ, 22 Feb. 1809).

[1]MS: "a certain."

From John Page

My dear Sir Richmond August 2d. 1803

Your favor of the 26th. ultimo came to hand yesterday. Mrs. Page & myself are infinitely obliged to you for it, & will certainly tell you so viva Voce as soon as you shall have returned from the Journey you mention.

Within a Week after your return we hope to be with you. When you have finished your Business, I shall more freely indulge in the delightful Relaxation which you propose.

One line from you mentioning the day of your return to Monticello, will be answered by me fixing the day of my expected happiness in your company.

Late as it is, for I have been prevented from writing til late indeed, I can not conclude without congratulating you on the success & Brilliancy of your Negociations in France.

Accept my best Wishes, & Assureances of the highest respect & Esteem. JOHN PAGE

RC (DLC); endorsed by TJ as received 6 Aug. and so recorded in SJL.

From Thomas Paine

DEAR SIR Bordenton on the Delaware Augt. 2. 1803

I enclose a letter for Mr. Breckenridge, but as I know not his residence in Kentucky, I will be obliged to you fill up the direction and forward it to him after putting a Wafer in it. I send it to you open as it relates to the order of the day, Louisania.

I know not what are your Ideas as to the mode of beginning Government in the ceded country; but as we have thought alike on several subjects I make you a present of mine.

I take it for granted that the present inhabitants know little or nothing of election and representation as constituting a Government. They are therefore not in an immediate condition to exercise those powers, and besides this they are perhaps too much under the influence of their priests to be sufficiently free.

I should suppose that a *Government provisoire* formed by Congress for three, five, or seven years would be the best mode of beginning. In the Meantime they may be initiated into the practice by electing their Municipal government, and after some experience they will be en train to elect their state Government.

I think it would be not only be good policy but right to say that the people shall have the right of electing their Church Ministers, otherwise their Ministers will hold by authority from the Pope. I do not make it a compulsive article but to put it in their power to use it when they please. It will serve to hold the priests in a stile of good behavoir, and also to give the people an Idea of elective rights. Any thing, they say, will do to learn upon, and therefore they may as well begin upon priests.

The present prevailing language is french and spanish but it will be necessary to establish schools to teach english as the laws ought to be in the language of the Union.

As soon as you have formed any plan for settling the Lands I shall be glad to know it. My motive for this is, because there are thousands and tens of thousands in England and Ireland and also in Scotland, who are friends of mine by principle, and who would gladly change their present country and condition. Many among them, for I have friends in all ranks of life in those Countries, are capable of becoming Monied purchasers to any amount.

If you can give me any hints respecting Louisania: the quantity in Square Miles, the population, and amount of the present Revenue I will find an opportunity of making some use of it. When the formalities of the Cession are compleated the next thing will be to take possession and I think it would be very consistent for the president of the United States to do this in person.

What is Dayton gone to New Orleans for? Is he there as an Agent for the British as Blount was said to be?

As there will be but little time from the 17 October to the completion of the six Months it will require dispatch to be strictly in form. I know not your Manner of communicating with Congress, but as both houses have already acted upon the business I think it would be right to send a Copy of the Cession to each of them. This is not done in the case of Treaty; but as the instrument of the Cession is not of the Nature of a Treaty, because it does not connect us with a foreign Government which Treaties always do, the communication of it to Congress should keep clear of all the formalities of a Treaty. The federal Papers appear disposed to throw some stumbling block in the way and I see none they can lay hold of but that of construing it into a Treaty and rejecting it by a Minority.

Report says that Mr Monroe is gone to Madrid to Negociate for the Floridas. If it be so and is not a secret I should be glad to know it.

Yours in friendship THOMAS PAINE

I will be obliged to you to let your servant take the enclosed to Mr Coltman.

RC (DLC); at foot of text: "Thomas Jefferson President of the United States"; endorsed by TJ as received 8 Aug. and so recorded in SJL. Enclosure: Thomas Paine to John Breckinridge, Bordentown, 2 Aug.; offering advice on the impending congressional session called to finalize the acquisition of Louisiana, Paine notes that the "faction of the Feds who last Winter were for going to war to obtain possession of that country and who attached so much importance to it that no expense or risk ought to be spared to obtain it, have now altered their tone and say it is not worth having"; he worries that the cession will be deemed a treaty even though it does not entail "reciprocal consequences" and therefore "is not a Treaty in the constitutional meaning of the word subject to be rejected by a minority in the senate"; he thinks it possible that the Federalists will insist on taking up the matter as a treaty, thereby enabling the minority to block ratification; he urges also that the cession be accepted "in toto," as adding conditions or terms would "hazard the whole"; he praises the purchase amount and expresses some desire to go to New Orleans to help the inhabitants acclimate to representative government; he believes that the province should adopt the religious policy of France, where "no ceremonial of religion can appear on the streets or highways"—Anglo-Americans "will not move out of the road for a little wooden Jesus stuck on a stick and carried in procession nor kneel in the dirt to a wooden Virgin Mary"; as the United States are to absorb Louisiana's inhabitants as equal citizens, Louisianans should be treated as "a part of the national sovereignty," not provincial subjects (Philip S. Foner, ed., *The Complete Writings of Thomas Paine*, 2 vols. [New York, 1945], 2:1442-6). Other enclosure not found, but see below.

FORWARD IT TO HIM: see TJ to John Breckinridge, 12 Aug.

New Jersey senator Jonathan DAYTON, who had financial interests in the West, spent about six weeks in New Orleans, beginning in late May (New York *American Citizen*, 29 July 1803; William Bache to TJ, 1 June).

MR COLTMAN: possibly William Coltman, a longtime resident of the District of Columbia (Georgetown *Centinel of Liberty, and George-Town and Washington Advertiser*, 1 Nov. 1799; *National Intelligencer*, 1 Apr. 1833; Allen C. Clark, "The Mayoralty of Robert Brent," RCHS, 33-34 [1932], 289).

From Henry Dearborn

SIR Washington August 3d. 1803

I have the honour of enclosing a letter from Capn. Lewis which came open to me, I have given permission to Lt. Hook to accompany Capt. Lewis.

with respectfull concideration I am Sir Your Huml Servt,

H. DEARBORN

P.S. Your letter relative to Mr. Dupont has been duly recd. & attended to.

RC (DLC); at foot of text: "The President of the United States"; endorsed by TJ as received from the War Department on 5 Aug. and "Dupont.—M. Lewis" and so recorded in SJL. Enclosure: Meriwether Lewis to TJ, 26 July.

PERMISSION: see Lewis to TJ, 26 July.
DULY RECD.: TJ to Dearborn, 29 July.

From George Jefferson

DEAR SIR Richmond 3d. Augt. 1803.

I had previous to the receipt of your favor of the 23d. forwarded all the articles therein mentioned except the fish, which have not yet arrived.—the cask of oil which you say is missing was forwarded the 6th. of June by Mr. Higganbothams Harry, for which I inclose you his receipt.—the oil you will observe is not particularly specified, the rect. being for 6 barrels & one box; I therefore likewise inclose you a copy of the bill of loading recd. from Mr. Barnes, which you will find is for the same number of packages. I discover from our books that

you are charged on the 6th. of June with frt. toll &c on 7 packages *from George Town*—it follows therefore that the Cask of oil must be one of the six mentioned in Harry's receipt.—I always forward a copy of the receipt, or a list of the articles, by the boatman.—Mr. H. ought therefore to have observed that there was one package missing if they did not correspond with the receipt. it will probably I think be found in his WHouse. the wood. screws shall be sent by the first opportunity.—Pickett & Co. on shipping your Tobacco, found as I apprehended, that some of it was wet—it was not however materially injured except about 100. ℔ which they had cut off, and for which I gave them credit.—they were well pleased with the few Hhds. they saw, except that it was not so well assorted as it should have been—some Tobacco having been put in which should have been left out.—As there is now so great a difference made on account of the quality of Tobo. and of the manner of its being handled, and which I have no doubt will continue to be the case—I think you will certainly find it to be your interest to instruct your Overseer to be very particular with it.—I would have all the prime put together, and the inferior I would have stemmed—the extra price *generally* allowed for the latter, would make good the loss in weight by stemming, and would likewise pay for the labour; besides the advantage of making the rest more valuable. if this is done, and care is taken not to prize it when *too high in case*, it will certainly I think be found to answer well.—I would then, instead of having it inspected in Lynchburg, send it immediately here, so that the purchasers might see it, or the quality might be made known by the inspectors, if they did not.—
This plan might perhaps be objected to by an Overseer,[1] or at least not engaged in with willingness—as I know they are not generally fond of extra trouble; if however he has certain wages, he has no right to object to any plan you may propose: if on the contrary he is allowed a part of the crop, he ought not to object, as he will unquestionably[2] find his interest in it.

I fear that I cannot have the pleasure of seeing you this summer; my travelling plans being much deranged, and which I expect will continue to be the case for a year or two at least.

I am Dear Sir Your Very humble [servt.]

Geo. Jefferson

The fish I find arrived some days since in my absence. G. J.

RC (MHi); torn; addressed: "Thomas Jefferson esquire Monticello"; franked and postmarked; endorsed by TJ as received 6 Aug. and so recorded in SJL.

HARRY was a boatman apparently in the employ of David Higginbotham and was likely enslaved. A boatman of the same name, who was owned by Thomas Mann

Randolph, handled river shipments for TJ in later years (MB, 2:1265, 1317, 1355; RS, 3:512, 612-13; 4:99).

[1] Words from this point through dash interlined.

[2] MS: "unquestionally."

From Tobias Lear

SIR, Boston August 3rd: 1803

I have been duly favor'd with your friendly note of the 14th of July, and shall not fail to give its enclosure to most direct and ready conveyance I can.—The flattering marks of confidence which you have been pleased to repose in me, and the satisfactory arrangements which have been made on my present mission, are highly appreciated by me: And I trust, that, actuated by a proper sense of the situation in which I am placed, and an earnest wish to promote the best interests, & preserve the honor of our Nation, I shall not fail to use my best exertions for a happy & satisfactory termination of my Mission

Accept the assurances of true respect, and the Sincere wishes for your health & happiness which are offered by Your obliged & Obedt. Servt TOBIAS LEAR

RC (DLC); at foot of text: "The President of the United States"; endorsed by TJ as received 10 Aug. and so recorded in SJL.

From Thomas Blount

SIR Tarborough 4th August 1803

My friend Mr John G. L. Schenck—a respectable merchant of this place, a good Citizen, & a great admirer of your character and Administration—is about to travel for health and pleasure to the Sulphur & sweet Springs in Virginia—and as Monticello lies directly in his Route, and he feels the desire common to all Republicans to be personally known to you, I respectfully beg leave to introduce him to you, and to assure you that he is not unworthy the honor of your acquaintance—

I am, with the greatest Respect, Your obedient, humble Servant

THO. BLOUNT

RC (MHi); at foot of text: "The President of the United States"; endorsed by TJ as received 15 Aug. and "by mr Schenk" and so recorded in SJL.

Thomas Blount (1759-1812), a landowner and merchant from Craven County, served as a lieutenant in the North Carolina Continental line during the American Revolution and later as a major general in the state militia. Although captured and taken to England as a prisoner during the war, he joined his brothers William and John Gray in establishing a lucrative post-war mercantile business in North Carolina, with its Tarboro branch under his control. Blount was a trustee of the state university, a commissioner in the plan for the city of Raleigh, a state legislator in 1788, and a Republican member of Congress from 1793 to 1799, 1805 to 1809, and 1811 until his death (*Biog. Dir. Cong.*; Alice Barnwell Keith and others, eds., *John Gray Blount Papers*, 4 vols. [Raleigh, N.C., 1952-82], 1:xxv-xxvi; 4:124n; William S. Powell, ed., *Dictionary of North Carolina Biography*, 6 vols. [Chapel Hill, 1979-96], 1:182-3).

A native of Russia, JOHN G. L. SCHENCK, settled in Tarboro, where he had many business connections with the Blount family. In 1795 he traveled to Philadelphia intending to act as their commercial agent but eventually returned to Tarboro, where he died from tuberculosis in 1806 (*Blount Papers*, 2:209).

From Samuel Broome

Greenfield Hill Connecticut
Augt 4th. 1803

SIR

I am on my way to the City of Washington where I hope to find your Excellency in the enjoyment of perfect health. I took the freedom Sometime since to Address a line to your Excellency, respecting any Vacant office in this State, which I might be capable of discharging. A Vacency I believe will Shortly take place, if your Excellency will be pleased to Suspend, an Appointment to Said office, if such should happen until I appear with credencials, you will Oblige your Sincere friend and well Wisher SAMUEL BROOME

RC (DNA: RG 59, LAR); at foot of text: "His Excellency The President of the United States of America"; endorsed by TJ as received 10 Aug. and so recorded in SJL with notation "off."

ADDRESS A LINE TO YOUR EXCELLENCY: for Broome's earlier solicitations for an appointment, see Vol. 33:570-2 and Vol. 35:142-3.

From John Milledge

Executive department Georgia
Louisville 5th. August 1803

SIR

On the 19th. of May last I did myself the honor to address a letter to the Secretary at War in consequence of an Act passed by the Legislature of this State on the 27th. of November 1802, requiring me to appoint three persons as Commissioners to repair to the Creek nation and make demand, in conformity to existing treaties, of all prisoners, negroes and property detained from the Citizens of Georgia by the Indians—and requested him to have the goodness to lay the same before you as early as possible—to which I have received an answer under date of the 13th. Ulto.

Feeling the character of the State, over which I have the honor to preside, in some measure implicated by that part of the Secretary's letter, of which the inclosed is an extract, I am persuaded you will readily excuse me for adopting the measure of bringing this business immediately before you—hardly supposing that it can be presumed, that the Legislature would take a step in any transaction without conceiving it had a right to do so; or, that the claims of the Citizens of Georgia have been otherwise adjusted.

The time allowed the Indians for the delivery of the property, agreeably to the treaty of Colerain, was 'till the 1st. of January following the date of that treaty, which took place on the 29th. of June 1796. Since that period accounts, to an immense amount, have been rendered to the Executive of this State, by her Citizens, on Oath, of property (especially negroes) which had been taken from them both before & since the War, and otherwise improperly detained, and which they have not had restored to them at this day.

The 7th. Article expressly says that "the Governor of Georgia may impower three persons to repair to the said nation in order to claim and receive such prisoners, negroes and property, under the direction of the President of the United States," and has limited no time for the right to be exercised in.

The State not having been heretofore, on the subject of Indian Treaties, treated, as she conceived, with that respect the right she possessed as a member of the Union entitled her to, might be one reason, why this transaction has been suffered to remain for such a length of time neglected.

It is not the Citizens of Georgia alone that have claims on the Indians for negroes taken by them, or fugitives from their owners, but of South Carolina, who are frequently making application for passports to go into the nation in pursuit of their property.

Trusting that you will see the justice and propriety of the measure taken by the state in behalf of her unfortunate Citizens, in requesting me to appoint persons to claim their property in the possession of the Creek Indians, and that such directions will be given as you may deem proper for their guidance, while in the discharge of their duty,

I have the honor to be with the highest consideration & respect yr mo Obt. hble Serv. JNO. MILLEDGE

RC (DLC); in a clerk's hand, signed by Milledge; at foot of text: "Thomas Jefferson President of the United States"; endorsed by TJ as received 29 Aug. and so recorded in SJL. Enclosure: Extract of a letter from Henry Dearborn to Milledge, dated War Department, 13 July 1803, written in response to Milledge's letter of 19 May; Dearborn informs the governor that "the President doubts whether at this distant period it would be proper for him to take any measures relative to commissioners" and asks "why the business has been so long defered unless the object had been either abandoned or otherwise adjusted" (Tr in same; in an unidentified hand).

On 27 Nov. 1802, the Georgia LEGISLATURE passed "An Act Pointing out a mode for adjusting the Claims of the Citizens of this State, against the Creek Nation," which sought to secure the return of property taken from Georgians by the Creek Indians. Section 5 of the act directed the governor to "appoint three persons to repair to the Creek Nation, and make demand of all prisoners, negroes, and property in conformity to existing treaties" (*Acts of the General Assembly of the State of Georgia; Passed at the Sessions of June and November, 1802* [Louisville, Ga., 1803], 39-42).

For Georgia's dissatisfaction with the 1796 TREATY OF COLERAIN between the United States and Creeks, see Vol. 39:519-20, 522n.

From Joseph Prentis

DEAR SIR 5 Au. 1803.

My friend Dr Madison will probably visit you on his Journey to the upper Country; this presents me with a conveyance which I have embraced, solely to give you my assurances, that your requisition some time since, was most literally [com]plied with, in a few moments after the communication came to Hand. with Sentiments of unfeigned Esteem I am Yr Frd. JP.

RC (MHi); torn at seal; addressed: "Thomas Jefferson Esqr Monticello" and "Dr Madisons attention"; endorsed by TJ as received from Joseph Prentis on 19 Aug. and so recorded in SJL.

YOUR REQUISITION: perhaps Prentis is referring to TJ's request in his letter of 6 May, the last recorded in SJL to Prentis, in which TJ urged his friend to "burn now this letter." TJ expressed the wish that all correspondence "written on the subject"—that is the Walker affair—would be destroyed.

From Benjamin Rush

DEAR SIR, Philadelphia, August 5th 1803.

I return you herewith Sir John Sinclair's pamphlet upon Old Age with many thanks. I have read it with pleasure, and subscribe to the truth of most of his opinions. They accord with opinions which I published many years ago in the 2nd Volume of my Medical Inquiries and Observations.

I have just finished reading Col: now Sir Robt Wilson's account of the British Campaign in Egypt. It is well written, and is a very popular work in our City, chiefly from its containing the history of the cruelties exercised by Bonaparte's[1] in that country. Its merit to me consists much more in the facts he has related respecting the plague. The annexed extract from one of our news papers contains the substance of them. They will be followed Sir Robert says, by several valuable publications by Medical men in which the non-importation, noncontagion, and domestic origin of the plague will be fully and clearly proved. I wish this subject occupied more of the attention of the legislators of all countries. The laws which are now in force in every part of the world to prevent the importation of malignant fevers are absurd, expensive, vexatious and oppressive to a great degree. Posterity will view them in the same light that we now view horse-shoes at the doors of Farmers houses to defend them from Witches. We originally imported our opinions of the contagious nature of the plague from the ignorant and degraded inhabitants of Egypt. It is high time to reject them from countries where free inquiry is tollerated upon all subjects connected with the interests and happiness of nations. There is more hope upon this subject from *laws* than upon many others. A thousand considerations oppose the extinction of Wars, which cannot operate upon the extermination of pestilential diseases. There is no moral evil in them, and of course no obstacles to their destruction, but what arise from ignorance and prejudice. It would seem as if a certain portion of superstition belonged necessarily to the human mind, and that that part of it which had been banished from Religion, had taken sanctuary in Medicine, hence thousands of the Citizens of the United States who would be ashamed to exclaim "Great is Diana of Ephesus" now openly and zealously cry out "Great are the quarantines of all our States."

From Dear Sir with great respect Your sincere old friend of 1775

BENJN RUSH.

P.S. Had not Bonaparte been a believer in the contagion of the plague, he would not have added to his other crimes—the destruction of 580 of his soldiers who were confined with the plague, lest they should infect his whole army. There is no calculating the amount of the cruelty, and misery which have issued from a belief in that most absurd doctrine. It is just now beginning to produce distress of every kind in the City of New York. Our Citizens instead of offering its inhabitants an asylum have this day interdicted all intercourse with them by land and water.

Tr (PU); typescript; verso of last page has a transcription in an unidentified hand of an endorsement probably made by Richard Rush on the RC, which has not been found, reading in part "My father to Mr Jefferson August 5. 1803" (see L. H. Butterfield, ed., *Letters of Benjamin Rush*, 2 vols. [Princeton, 1951], 2:873n). Dft

(PHi: Thomas Biddle Family Papers); undated, unsigned, and not addressed; lacks postscript; contains an additional paragraph (see below). Recorded in SJL as received 12 Aug.

For the PAMPHLET by Sir John Sinclair, see TJ to Rush, 24 June.

Beginning in 1789, Rush published groups of his essays in volumes titled MEDICAL INQUIRIES AND OBSERVATIONS. The second volume of the series included "An Account of the State of the Body and Mind in Old Age; with Observations on its Diseases, and their Remedies." Sinclair reprinted Rush's paper in a compendium published in Edinburgh in 1807 (Benjamin Rush, *Medical Inquiries and Observations*, 2 [1793], 293-321; Butterfield, ed., *Letters of Benjamin Rush*, 2:873n).

The Philadelphia bookseller John Conrad was preparing an edition of Robert Thomas WILSON'S *History of the British Expedition to Egypt*, a work first published in London in 1802. The author, a British army officer, had been in Egypt for several months in 1801 with the expeditionary force that ousted the French from the region. The day before Rush wrote the letter printed above, *Poulson's American Daily Advertiser* published an EXTRACT from Wilson's book that described two instances of barbarity that were, according to Wilson, the result of orders from Bonaparte. One of the incidents was the execution by French troops of several thousand Ottoman Empire soldiers who had surrendered after a siege at Jaffa in Palestine in March 1799. The other event was the administration of lethal doses of opium in the form of laudanum to French soldiers who were ill with the plague. In the draft of his letter to TJ, Rush mentioned the incidents and declared of Bonaparte: "Both these Outrages upon humanity were perpetrated with circumstances of levity, and Apathy that mark a mind from which the World in its present state, has every thing to fear, and Nothing to hope." Bonaparte denied Wilson's version of the events and lodged an official protest with the British government (*Poulson's American Daily Advertiser*, 4, 5 Aug.; Robert Thomas Wilson, *History of the British Expedition to Egypt* [Philadelphia, 1803], 87-94; Paul Strathern, *Napoleon in Egypt* [New York, 2008], 323-8; Robert Solé, *Bonaparte à la conquête de l'Égypte* [Paris, 2006], 163-5; DNB).

DOMESTIC ORIGIN OF THE PLAGUE: in a discussion of "Diseases of Egypt," Wilson declared "that the plague is local, occasioned by a corrupted state of atmosphere, and never introduced by contagion." He gave anecdotal information to support the assertion and cited forthcoming or proposed works by European and British doctors who had been with the armies in Egypt or had other experience in the region (Wilson, *History of the British Expedition to Egypt*, 303-17).

In a final paragraph of his draft that he omitted from the letter as he sent it to TJ, Rush wrote of IGNORANCE AND PREJUDICE: "It is from a long & painful familiarity with the ignorance and errors which prevail upon the causes, & means of preventing plagues and yellow fevers that I have been led to despair of the melioration of the moral and political condition of man by the efforts of human Reason. If the causes of disease & death when Obtruded annually upon his senses of sight and smelling, by putrefying masses of matter, are sought for in the timbers of a ship, in a hogshead of rum, or in a loaf sugar,—how is it possible to awaken his Attention, or to direct his zeal to obviate the less perceptible causes of political misery?"

SINCERE OLD FRIEND OF 1775: in his draft, Rush expanded on his reference to the American Revolution. He wrote: "When I compare our citizens, with what they were in 1774. 1775. & 1776 I feel disposed to consider all the wise, and patriotic events of those years as miraculous. Human reason seems to have had nothing to do with them. Public men in those days acted like the twelve Apostles, under a divine and unerring impulse. That impulse has ceased, and hence the revival of *exploded*, and the promulgation of *new* Opinions equally absurd & destructive in thier nature and tendency,—hence the distracted Councils, and malignant party Spirit which prevail in every part of our Country. They are all the results of imperfect Reason.

May Heaven avert thier baneful influence upon our Government and people!—But Whither have I rambled?—My business is only to feel pulses—and inspect foul tongues. In every Obliquity in which the perverted passions and reason shall drive our citizens, I will continue to love them, and whatever effect they may Ultimately have in changing or Destroying our excellent form of Government; I shall always believe that a Republic is the best of all governments, and that it is the most conformable to all the moral & religious Obligations of Man."

DESTRUCTION OF 580 OF HIS SOLDIERS: describing the second instance of cruelty by the French in the Egyptian campaigns, Wilson claimed that Bonaparte, driven by a fear of "the danger of contagion" and ignoring the pleas of his chief medical officer, forced the killing by opiates of 580 plague-infected French soldiers as the army withdrew from the failed expedition into Palestine and Syria. Although Wilson's figure was too high, several dozen French soldiers in the hospital at Jaffa, including some who did not have the plague but were severely wounded, likely did receive large doses of laudanum because the army either could not or would not evacuate them. Bonaparte may have been more concerned about potential effects of the plague on morale and order among his troops than about contagion (Wilson, *History of the British Expedition to Egypt*, 91-2; *Poulson's American Daily Advertiser*, 4 Aug.; Strathern, *Napoleon in Egypt*, 329-32, 375-8; Solé, *Bonaparte à la conquête de l'Égypte*, 166-7, 181-2; Darcy Grimaldo Grigsby, "Rumor, Contagion, and Colonization in Gros's *Plague-Stricken of Jaffa* [1804]," *Representations*, 51 [1995], 7-9, 14, 26-33; Juan Cole, *Napoleon's Egypt: Invading the Middle East* [New York, 2007], 235-7).

OUR CITIZENS: a Pennsylvania statute of April 1803 created the Philadelphia Board of Health, which had five members, all appointed by the governor. Each received $400 compensation per year, and no more than two of the group could be physicians. A section of the April law empowered the board "to prohibit and to prevent all communication" BY LAND AND WATER with any "port or place within the United States or on the continent of America" where there was contagious disease. On 4 Aug., following the arrival of unsubstantiated reports of a yellow fever outbreak in New York City, a member of the board introduced a resolution to cut off connections between the cities. The board decided to wait for more information, but the following day a letter by "A Citizen," reluctantly published by William Duane in the *Aurora*, declared that "if our board will not use that vigilance which they ought, to preserve the city in health, by every means in their power, it is for us citizens to stir them up, and put them in mind of their duty." By an order dated 9 Aug., the Board of Health put vessels arriving from New York under quarantine, required any persons coming from that city to be in good health and to prove on oath that they had left there at least 15 days previously, and prohibited bringing into Philadelphia "goods, wares, merchandize, cloathing, or baggage" from New York that were "capable of retaining infection." Along with its decree, the board published the section of the statute that enabled it to cut off communication with other locales and a section that imposed a $500 fine for obstructing the board and a fine of $200 and a prison sentence of up to three years of hard labor for "any mariner, or other person" who, after the expiration of the quarantine, "shall commit any violence on the person of a member of the board of health, or any of the officers attached to the same, for any thing done in the execution of his duty." The board published the order in newspapers and issued 200 handbills. On 11 Aug., the Boston Board of Health also put ships arriving at that port from New York under quarantine. In September, the Philadelphia board announced the appearance of "a disease of a malignant aspect" in a portion of the city near the waterfront and prohibited ships from mooring at the adjacent wharves. The board removed its restrictions on contact between Philadelphia and New York City on 31 Oct. (*An Act for Establishing an Health Office, and to Secure the City and Port of Philadelphia from the Introduction of Pestilential and Contagious Diseases* [Philadelphia, 1803], 3-4, 23-5; *Aurora*,

5, 10 Aug.; *Gazette of the United States*, 6 Aug.; New York *Daily Advertiser*, 11 Aug.; *Poulson's American Daily Advertiser*, 13 Sep., 1 Nov.).

[1]Thus in Tr.

From David Jackson, Jr.

Honored Sir Philada: Aug. 6th 1803

I enclose you for your perusal, & satisfaction, the printed Extracts of the Genl. Assembly of the Presbyterian Church held in this City in May last; in the which you will observe the united testimony of said Church of the state of religion in their communion; this result is highly gratifying to the friends of piety in our connection, two thirds of whom are supporters of your administration—in this City, the Democratic Republican interest is supported by the Presbyterians,[1] Baptists, & Germans, and generally opposed by the Episcopalians, Friends & Methodists; the last mentioned denomination, are fast embracing republicanism—The great Head of the Church has seen proper greatly to succeed a preached gospel under your administration, and to dissipate the fallacy of those fears, which many entertained, upon your accession to the Presidential Chair— With Sentiments of the highest esteem permit me to subscribe myself

Your frend & supporter— David Jackson

RC (DLC); addressed: "Thomas Jefferson Esqr"; endorsed by TJ as received 10 Aug. and so recorded in SJL. Enclosure: *Extracts from the Minutes of the General Assembly of the Presbyterian Church in the United States of America* (Philadelphia, 1803; Sowerby, No. 1670).

David Jackson, Jr., was an active member of Philadelphia's First Presbyterian Church on Market Street and served as secretary-treasurer and trustee of its corporation (Donald Roth Kocher, *The Mother of Us All: First Presbyterian Church in Philadelphia* [Woodbine, N.J., 1998], 53; *Gazette of the United States*, 19 June 1799; *Poulson's American Daily Advertiser*, 24 Mch. 1801, 11 July 1808; Vol. 38:103-4n).

[1]MS: "Presbyterans."

From Étienne Lemaire

Monsieur De Washington Sity du 6 aout 1803

Je prend la liberté de vous adresser la presente pour avoir Lhonneur de vous Saluer, je soite de tou mon cœur que monsieur Jouisse une parfaite Sentez de même que vôttre repectable famille mes Sivilités Sil vous plai, monsieur je vous prie Engrâce de vouloir Bien Macorder une petit apsence de trois Semainnes, pour me reffaire la Sentez. Je vien encorre de faire une maladit qu'il m'aprise le landemain que monsieur est party, Sai une fievre interne, [et], n'a pas Eté aûsi Serieuse que l'anné passée Cependant je asé Souffaire E dant Se moment Ci je ne Sui pas Encorre Retabli. je vous Supli, monsieur Si Cela est possible vous mobligeré infinement. Sependent Si liavoit la moindre obgeption, je resterest; je vous prie m'onsieur êttre tranqu'il Sur les Soin de Vottre m'aison, de même que vos interest, Sa Sera la même chôsse que Si ji Étoit, d'alieur Je remettré les Clé les plus Esenciel, a monsieur Barnes. D'augherty vôttre Cochez a Eté aûsi indispossez, presentement il va Beaucoup Mieux toute la famille Ce porte Bien, ainsi que Vôttre oiseau, qui est toujour Charmant—

Monsieur Je fini avecque le plus Sincere atachement possible. Je Sui Vôttre humble Etres obeisant Serviteur, E. Lemaire

honnoré moy monsieur de votre reponse Sil vous plai

EDITORS' TRANSLATION

Sir, From Washington City, 6 Aug. 1803

I take the liberty of sending you this letter so that I may have the honor of greeting you. I hope with all my heart that you are in perfect health. My best regards to your distinguished family. I ask you, Sir, to grant me a short absence of three weeks to recover my health. I was taken ill with an internal fever the day after you left. It was not as serious as last year, but I suffered a great deal and am still not fully recovered. I beg you, Sir, if this is possible, I would be infinitely obliged. If you have the slightest objection, however, I will stay. I beg you, Sir, not to worry about the care of your house and your interests. Everything would be just as if I were here, since I would entrust the most essential keys to Mr. Barnes.

Your coachman Dougherty has also been ill but he is much better now. All the family here is well, as is your bird which continues to be charming.

I conclude, Sir, with the sincerest possible attachment. I am your humble and very obedient servant. E. Lemaire

Please honor me, Sir, with a reply.

RC (MHi); endorsed by TJ as received 10 Aug. and so recorded in SJL.

vôttre oiseau: on 31 May, TJ had given Joseph Dougherty an order on John Barnes for $10 to purchase the president a mockingbird and cage. Mockingbirds and other songbirds were sold in cities in markets, privately by individuals, and in a few cases in shops. In France, TJ had extolled the singing of the mockingbird—a native bird of Virginia—as superior to the music of the European nightingale. "Learn all the children to venerate it as a superior being in the form of a bird," he wrote to his daughter Martha about mockingbirds in 1793, "or as a being which will haunt them if any harm is done to itself or it's eggs." His financial records note the purchase of another mockingbird for $15 in November 1803. Margaret Bayard Smith recalled that TJ would open the cage to let his favorite mockingbird fly and hop around freely as he worked. The bird would perch on the president's shoulder and take food from his lips (MB, 2:1101, 1112; *Poulson's American Daily Advertiser*, 23 July 1801; New York *Morning Chronicle*, 14 July 1803; New York *Daily Advertiser*, 21 Aug. 1805; Boston *Columbian Centinel*, 23 July 1808; Margaret Bayard Smith, *The First Forty Years of Washington Society*, ed. Gaillard Hunt [New York, 1906], 385; Katherine C. Grier, *Pets in America: A History* [Orlando, 2006], 27, 59-64, 362; *Notes*, ed. Peden, 68; Vol. 8:241; Vol. 11:372; Vol. 26:88, 250).

From Richard W. Meade

SIR Philadelphia August 6. 1803.

I had the honor of addressing you, some time ago on the subject of the Spanish claims, & sollicited the appointment as Commissioner under the treaty about to be entered into with Spain for the settlement of the same.

The non ratification of the Treaty on the part of Spain, having precluded all possibility of redress for the present, & Finding myself owing a very large sum sunk in South America, & to the present unsettled state of mercantile affairs, compelled to seek some employment by which I can support a numerous family—& Being warmly sollicited by my friends, (a number of whom, are deeply interested in the claims on the French Republic,) to apply for the Appointment as Commissioner for the settlement of the same agreable to the Treaty lately entered into by our Minister's Plenipotentiary at Paris.

I take the liberty of addressing your Excellency on the subject, solliciting the appointment as Commissioner or Agent for the liquidation of the claims of our Citizens on the French Republic. With Respect to my Character, Integrity & Capacity for the office I beg leave to refer to His Excellency The Governor of this State, with whom I have the honor of being personally acquainted & who has given me the strongest assurances of his friendship & Protection.

I Beg leave to add, that a Residence of 18 months in France & near four years in the French West Indies, where the major part of the claims have originated has given me a pretty correct knowledge of the nature of them.

Under these Circumstances Should Your Excellency think it proper to confer the appointment on me, I shall retain a due sense of the obligation & Remain

With due Respect & Consideration Your Excellency's Most obt. hum Servt. R W MEADE

RC (DNA: RG 59, LAR); at head of text: "His Excellency Thomas Jefferson Esqr. President of the United States"; endorsed by TJ as received 12 Aug. and "to be Commr. to France" and so recorded in SJL.

HONOR OF ADDRESSING YOU: see Meade to TJ, 8 Dec. 1802. NON RATIFICATION OF THE TREATY: the Senate delayed ratification until January 1804; Spain did not ratify the Convention of 1802 until 1818 (Vol. 39:316-17). Later in 1803, Philadelphia merchants enlisted Meade as their agent to proceed to Spain to seek redress for American ships and property detained and confiscated at Spanish ports in South America, especially Buenos Aires (Madison, *Papers, Sec. of State Ser.*, 6:62-3; Vol. 38:220, 221n; Vol. 39:122-3n).

For the appointment of commissioners to oversee the LIQUIDATION OF THE CLAIMS of American merchants against France, see Fulwar Skipwith to TJ, 7 Aug.

GOVERNOR OF THIS STATE: Thomas McKean.

From John F. Mercer

SIR, Annapolis In Council August 6. 1803

I have the honor to inclose to you open for your perusal a letter which this Executive have addressed to William Pinkney Esquire, on the subject of the Bank Stock extending the powers formerly committed to him but confined to the case of Russell's Representatives to other claimants &c.

It will be necessary that this should receive your approbation, to give it a sanction under the Resolutions of the Assembly—if you approve thereof, you will be pleased to direct that our Letter should be forwarded to Mr. Pinkney, with such intimations from yourself as you shall deem necessary.

With assurances of high & respectful Consideration I have the honor to be Your obed Servant. JOHN F: MERCER

RC (DLC); in a clerk's hand, signed by Mercer; endorsed by TJ as received 12 Aug. and so recorded in SJL. FC (MdAA: Letterbooks of Governor and Council); at foot of text: "The President of the United States." Dft (MdAA: Executive Papers). Enclosure not found, but see below.

SUBJECT OF THE BANK STOCK: for Maryland's efforts to gain control over its funds invested in Bank of England stock, see Vol. 23:589, 609n; Vol. 37:547-8; Vol. 40:377-9. William Pinkney was acting as the state's agent in the negotiations, replacing Rufus King. In an attempt to expedite the ongoing settlement negotiations, on 5 Aug. the Maryland Council authorized Pinkney to relinquish up to £10,000 sterling from the bank stock to any person on condition that the remainder of the stock in trust be paid immediately to the state. The order, however, added a proviso that it must first be approved by the president of the United States. Writing Pinkney on 6 Aug., Mercer enclosed additional information on the bank case and urged him not to grant any part of the funds to individuals in England "except what is absolutely necessary to insure that Maryland may collect the rest" (Morris L. Radoff, *Calendar of Maryland State Papers, No. 2, The Bank Stock Papers* [Annapolis, 1947], 31-2; Jacob M. Price, "The Maryland Bank Stock Case: British-American Financial and Political Relations Before and After the American Revolution," in Aubrey C. Land, Lois Green Carr, and Edward C. Papenfuse, eds., *Law, Society, and Politics in Early Maryland* [Baltimore, 1977], 27-8).

RUSSELL'S REPRESENTATIVES: London merchant James Russell had been one of the trustees of the bank stock fund prior to the American Revolution. In 1781, after Russell and his fellow London trustees refused to pay bills drawn on the fund by Maryland, the state confiscated Russell's extensive property holdings in Baltimore County. The two sides subsequently spent years wrangling in British courts over the return of the bank stock trust to Maryland and compensation for Russell and his heirs (Price, "Maryland Bank Stock Case," 7-18).

From Francis W. Thomas

Williamsport Maryland
August 6. 1803

DEAR SIR

Had not an occasion offer'd wherein you will have it in your power to exercise the Philantrophy—I conceive you possess—tis certain you would never have been troubled with a line from an unfortunate man—who thus Boldly solicits the Illustrious President—for a Pardon—

I am perfectly concious of my Incapability [in] making a Sufficient Appollogy for this Singular—Liberty—yet with confidence I rely on your superior Talents and Generosity

Viz

In the year 1797—I left the U.S. in confind circumstances—at the age of Seventeen—In the course of a 2 years I accumulated a hansome Fortune—embarkd for the U.S. was taken by His Britainic majestys Frigate Arab, Commandd by Thos. B. Cabel—by this Catastrophe, I was left destitute of the means of subsistance—I was set ashore in Jamaca—from thence I came to Philadelphia—at the time the United States Frigate was recruiting—this was the truley deplorable situation in which I was placed—when I volunterily enterd as a seaman—I remaind on Board two months and Ill assure you Sir I found British tyranny Prevaild on board a Republican Ship—I allude to the Inferior Officers—

I acknowledge Sir, I left the Frigate in a Clandestine Manner, not alltogether on account of Bad Discipline—But Sir my principal Reason for so doing—common decency forbids my mentioning it—I offer neither as an excuse for my conduct—I was young and Intractable and now[1] repent for my past Reprehensible conduct—and if Sir through your goodness I am entitled to enjoy the Blessings of Liberty—under the present administration—you will confer new Life to an unhappy man—Ive respectable Connections and sooner than be tried by a Court Martial—Id put a period to my existance—No Power on earth shall ever Bring me to Trial—I arrived here last month from E Florida and I am confident there are a few Midshipman Possessd with the

Pompossity of a Mandarian—who Intend to Signalize themselves by makeing an excursion in this quarter—I wish to Become a usefull Member of Society. I shall endeavour to cultivate Peace and harmony with all rational Animals

tho I am Stigmatized with the Appelation of a deserter—if I am taken it must be man—yet I Flatter myself—through your Sympathic disposition—the threatening Storm may Blow over—My Brother in law not being at home has Induced me to take this liberty—or through his Influence, I Immagine you would be Solicited by—men of Popularity—on his return Its Possible an acquaintance of yours may Intercede in my behalf—I think it proper to observe that the money I recd. was returned by my Security.

With well wishes for your health and Prosperity—I am your most obet. Sert

Francis W. Thomas
Will. Port
Washington County

N B

if it is convenient I should[2] be happy to hear from your excellency next mail—and be at once assured of my Fate—I lament that my youthful conduct should be the means of exileing me to a foreign country—yet Ill hope for the best

yours F. Thomas

RC (DLC); torn; addressed: "The Hon Thomas Jefferson President of the U.S" with "Milton" interlined in another hand in place of "City Washington"; postmarked 8 Aug.; endorsed by TJ as received 15 Aug. and so recorded in SJL.

Francis W. Thomas served as an ordinary seaman on the frigate *United States* during the closing months of the Quasi-War with France (NDQW, Dec. 1800-Dec. 1801, 62).

THOS. B. CABEL: that is, Thomas Bladen Capel, commander of the British frigate *Arab* from 1799 to 1800 in the West Indies, who went on to a distinguished career in the Royal Navy (DNB).

For a solicitation by Thomas's BROTHER IN LAW on his behalf, see Thomas Kennedy to TJ, 26 Aug. 1803.

[1] Word interlined.
[2] MS: "hould."

From John A. Hanna

Sir Harrisburg Aug: 7th 1803

Presuming that from the cession of Louisiana to the US: a number of offices will be in the gift of the Executive I take the liberty to mention my name—My Family is large and my means small when compared with the manner in which they have been educated—I was brought up to the Law, and would have practised still, had not imperious, (and I may say Republican)[1] necessity forced me to stand a Candidate for the Legislature—I will be at Washington in due time when I will have the honer of communicating more freely with the President

I am Sir with great Respect your Obedt Servant

JOHN A HANNA

RC (DNA: RG 59, LAR); endorsed by TJ as received 17 Aug. and "office" and so recorded in SJL.

Born in Flemington, New Jersey, John Andre Hanna (1761 or 1762-1805) was the son of Mary McCrea and John Hanna, a Presbyterian clergyman. The younger Hanna graduated from the College of New Jersey at Princeton in 1782. Three years later he began practicing law in Dauphin County, Pennsylvania, and married Mary Read Harris, of the founding family of Harrisburg. In 1787, Hanna served as a delegate to the state convention considering the new federal Constitution. He voted against ratification and was one of the 21 members of the dissenting minority who signed the address to the public setting forth objections to the document. He was secretary of the 1788 Harrisburg convention of Antifederalists who proposed amendments to the Constitution. Hanna represented Dauphin County in the state senate from 1792 to 1794. A general in the militia, he led troops to quell the Whiskey Insurrection in western Pennsylvania. Elected to Congress as a Jeffersonian Republican in 1796, Hanna continued to serve as a Pennsylvania congressman until his death (*Biog. Dir. Cong.*; Richard A. Harrison, *Princetonians, 1776-1783: A Biographical Dictionary* [Princeton, 1981], 363-6; *Journal of the Senate of the Commonwealth of Pennsylvania. Commencing on Tuesday, the Fourth Day of December, in the Year of Our Lord One Thousand Seven Hundred and Ninety-Two* [Philadelphia, 1793], 4-5, 70-2; *Journal of the Senate of the Commonwealth of Pennsylvania. Commencing on Tuesday, the Third Day of December, in the Year of Our Lord One Thousand Seven Hundred and Ninety-Three* [Philadelphia, 1794], 4, 248).

[1]Closing parenthesis supplied by Editors.

From Andrew Jackson

Hunters Hill near Nashville
August 7th. 1803

SIR

The late arrest of Colonel Thomas Butler, added to the novelty of the order upon which it is founded, has occasioned a number of the good citizens of this District to solicit me to state to you the real Charector and Conduct of the Colo. during his command within this State—This application Combined with a real desire of my own, that you should be acquainted with his Charector and conduct, and the sentiments of the citizens with reguard to him under his present circumstances, Induces me to write you—

Shortly after Colo. Butler reached this state the removal of Judge Campbell from off the Indian land and his arrest by Military Authority, occasioned a great noise and the circumstance was Notified to the then delegation in congress, by letter from Judge Campbell, which was laid before the then President—Soon after an Explanation Took place between the Colo and Judge, friendship was restored and the thing ended without enquiry Whether in making the arrest the Military had kept within the orders furnished them by the Government—Leaving this Solitary act out of View, as far as I have seen heard or been informed, the people of this State has always found in him the citizen and soldier, by his conduct as an officer, by his strict probity and honesty, he has endeared himself to the Citizens—in Short Sir his removal for the disobedience of such an order, would raise unpleasant sensations in the minds of the citizens—It is thought by many that the renewal of the order was bottomed on a plan to drive the Colo. out of the service—It is stated that his well known attachment to his hair, which he had wore both as an ornament and for health untill it had grew gray in the service of his country were such, that nothing but death itself could seperate them from him—It is also thought that such an order approches too near to the despotism of a Suarrow, and better calculated for the dark regions of the east, than for enlightened America—Should it be decided that the hair is a part of uniform and subject to the order of the commander in chief it may be extended to the nose eye or Ear, they are all equally the gift of nature—all equally recognised by any written rule we have for the government of the army—The feelings of the Militia are alive upon the occasion—when called into the field, they well know they are subject to the same orders and liable to the same pains for disobedience—and it will open[1] a door (which ought to be kept shut) thro' which the greatest tyranny may be exercised by the commander in chief—by which he may deprive his country in the most Perilous situation, of the service of its most valuable officers—When he may think they have become too honest—too œconomical too independant to be subserviant to his views—

To conclude I will Just remark, that the novelty of the order, and if countenanced its consequences—its renewal at the time it was—the uniform upright conduct of the Colonel during his command in this state—his hospitality and polite attention to the Citizens and those passing through the state all combind to encreas our wishes for his honourable acquittal and safe return—And we hope in the golden moment of American prosperity, when all the western Hemisphere rejoices in the Joyfull news of the Cession of Louisiana—an event which places the peace happiness and liberty of our country on a permanent basis, an event which generations yet unborn in each revolving year will hail the day and with it the causes that gave it birth, such

Joy as this we hope will not be interrupted, by the scene of an aged and meritorious officer, being brought before a court martial, for the disobedience of an order, which went to deprive him of the gift of nature, which has grew gray in the service of his country and which was worn by him for ornament and health—Accept Sir of the unanimous Congratulations of the Citizens of Mero, on the Joyfull event of the cession of Louisiana and New Orleans, every face wears a smile, and every heart leaps with Joy—

With sentiments of Esteem and reguard I am Dr. Sir yr, mo, ob, serv,

ANDREW JACKSON

RC (DLC); addressed: "Thomas Jefferson President of the United States of America City of Washington"; franked; postmarked Hendersonville; endorsed by TJ as received 24 Aug. and so recorded in SJL.

In late May 1803, James Wilkinson ordered the court-martial of COLONEL THOMAS BUTLER, commander of the Second Regiment of Infantry, for his refusal to obey an 1801 regulation requiring all soldiers, without exception, to crop their hair. He was also charged with disobeying an 1802 order to assume command at Fort Adams in the Mississippi Territory. The ensuing trial, held in November and December 1803 at Frederick, Maryland, acquitted Butler of the second charge, but found him guilty of disobeying the order to cut his hair. Despite the verdict, the colonel continued to defy the regulation, resulting in more than a year of acrimony between Butler, Wilkinson, and their respective supporters, with Jackson serving as an ardent ally of Butler throughout the contest. A second court-martial, held in July 1805, found Butler guilty of disobeying orders and mutinous conduct and suspended him from command without pay and emoluments for a year. Before the sentence could be carried out, however, Butler succumbed to yellow fever, presumably with his tresses intact (Donald R. Hickey, "The United States Army Versus Long Hair: The Trials of Colonel Thomas Butler, 1801-1805," PMHB, 101 (1977), 462-74; Harold D. Moser and others, eds., *The Papers of Andrew Jackson*, 9 vols. [Knoxville, 1980-], 1:353-4, 2:32-3, 64-5).

In early February 1798, Butler had ordered the arrest of Judge David CAMPBELL for intruding on Indian lands in Tennessee. Writing John Adams on 5 Mch., the state's delegation in Congress, which included Jackson, Joseph Anderson, and William C. C. Claiborne, protested the arrest as a violation of state sovereignty and civil rights and asked that Butler be removed from command (Moser, *Papers of Andrew Jackson*, 1:176, 185-6).

SUARROW: Russian general Alexander Suvorov, who gained infamy among Republicans for his role in suppressing the Polish insurrection of 1794, especially the massacre of thousands of defenders and inhabitants of the Warsaw suburb of Praga (Piotr S. Wandycz, *The United States and Poland* [Cambridge, Mass., 1980], 56; Miecislaus Haiman, *Kosciuszko: Leader and Exile* [New York, 1977], 26).

[1]Jackson first wrote "it opens" and then altered the text to read as above.

From Fulwar Skipwith

Dear Sir Paris. 7 August 1803.

I was favored about the middle of June with your letter of the 4th. May, with a remittence, in a bill on Messrs. Dupont de Nemours pere et fils & Co., for 2100 francs, to be invested in Wines, principally of the non-mosseux Champagne. Your predilection in favor the Wines raised formerly by Mr. Dorsay induced me to address myself to his family, he though living being ruined & insane. By his Daughter I was informed of his Estate having been divided and sold in small parcels, but that the most precious portion, for the excellence of its Wines, now belonged to a Mr. Biston. I wrote to Mr. Biston, and he sent me a few Bottles of his Wine of 1798 and 1800. The last has with my palate a most decided preference. I have therefore ordered the 400 Bottles you desire, of that Vintage to be put up with great care and forwarded so as to be at Havre by the 1st. of Septr.—The extraordinary heat of the Summer here, Reaumurs Thyrmometre having been for the last fortnight at from 24 to 29 degrees in the shade of a northern exposition, determined me not to put your Wine sooner in motion. There are at Havre three American Vessels that will sail in all september for the Chesepeak & the Delaware, by one of them I shall send you a 100 Bottles each of Chambertin & Monrachet of a remarkable good quality. If these as well as the Wine non-mosseux should please you, I hope to have again the satisfaction of receiving your orders for a fresh supply.

Mr. Livingston left us a fortnight ago on an excurtion to Switzerland, & has charged me to correspond, when occasion requires, with this Government, and to forward with Mr. Marbois the execution of the late Convention respecting claims. His absence from Paris he fixed before his departure to six weeks. In the mean time no inconvenience has resulted from it. His indeavors with this Government to obtain a reasonable modification of their Arreté of the 1st. messidor concerning Neutral Vessels entering the ports of France, have proved ineffectual, nor do I expect, by what I am told at the Department of foreign Affairs that a change of that Arrete will be adopted untill some time of experience shall demonstrate how prejudiceable it is to the true interests of France herself. The American Board has been organized since five Weeks, and is now seriously engaged in the investigation and final liquidations of our Countrymens claims. It has become my duty to prepare & report on them for the Board, and I am happy to add that I have every prospect of being aided by Mr. Marbois, & Mr. Dufermon (the Counsellor of State now at the head of the french

Council of Liquidation) in detecting & causing to be rejected some millions of fraudulent claims, which through the intrigues of some Individuals here, had been formerly liquidated as American claims.

I pray you, Sir, to accept assurances of my constant attatchment & wishes for the preservation of your health.

FULWAR SKIPWITH

This Government has lately granted an Exequateur to Mr. Cathalan to exercise his functions of Commercial Agent.

Our former Consul at Dunkerque Francis Coffyn has been promised by Mr. Talleyrand a similar favor, should you think proper to name him for that Port. No foreigner I can assure you is better qualified for this office than Mr. Coffyn, & unless a suitable American should present himself, who would preside at Dunkerque, I am of opinion that you would render service to the United States by appointing that Gentleman.

RC (DLC); endorsed by TJ as received 4 Nov. and so recorded in SJL.

REAUMURS THYRMOMETRE: derived from the temperature scale developed by French scientist René-Antoine Ferchault de Réaumur, these thermometers assumed 80 degrees as the boiling point of water and zero degrees as the freezing point. They were widely used in France (DSB, 11:330-1; Maurice Daumas, *Scientific Instruments of the Seventeenth and Eighteenth Centuries*, trans. Mary Holbrook [New York, 1972], 211-12).

Robert R. LIVINGSTON was on a trip to Lyons and Switzerland, where he viewed glaciers. He was back in Paris by early September (Madison, *Papers*, *Sec. of State Ser.*, 5:380; George Dangerfield, *Chancellor Robert R. Livingston of New York, 1746-1813* [New York, 1960], 381).

The second CONVENTION negotiated by Livingston and Monroe as part of the purchase of Louisiana required the United States to pay up to approximately $3,750,000 in principal and interest for claims of American citizens against France. The payments were for restitution of certain categories of losses due to embargoes and ship captures, and only claims filed on appeal with the French government prior to the Convention of 1800 would qualify. The convention for resolution of the claims empowered Livingston and Monroe to appoint three individuals to examine the claims in Paris and determine which ones met the criteria for settlement. Under Article 10 of the convention, the U.S. commercial agent at Paris—that is, Skipwith, who was himself a claimant and represented other claimants—would have the power to examine the records and refer cases to the commissioners. The convention must be ratified within six months of the date it was signed, which officially was 30 Apr., and all decisions respecting the claims were to be completed within a year after the exchange of ratifications (Miller, *Treaties*, 2:516-28; John Bassett Moore, ed., *International Adjudications, Modern Series, Volume V: Spanish Spoliations, 1795; French Indemnity, 1803; French Indemnity, 1831* [New York, 1933], 149-52; Livingston to TJ, 2 May).

ARRETÉ OF THE 1ST. MESSIDOR: the French government's decree of 20 June barred the importation of merchandise and commodities from Britain and its colonies. In addition, a neutral vessel arriving in a French port must have a certificate from the French commissary for commercial relations in the port of departure that attested, among other things, that the cargo contained nothing of British, or British colonial, origin. If a ship arrived without the certificate or entered a port other than the one named in the certificate, the vessel would have to take away French-made goods equal in value to the cargo it had brought in. Livingston protested the order and attempted to persuade the French government that it would harm French commerce. In response, the French modified the *arrêté* in October. Among other changes, the revisions stated that there would be no interference with the importation of goods that were not from Britain or its colonies (Jean B. Duvergier and others, eds., *Collection Complète des Lois, Décrets, Ordonnances, Réglemens, avis du Conseil-d'État,* 108 vols. [Paris, 1834–1908], 14:187; Madison, *Papers*, *Sec. of State Ser.*, 5:119, 122n, 380, 568n).

AMERICAN BOARD: on 18 May, Monroe and Livingston provisionally appointed John Mercer, Isaac Cox Barnet, and William Maclure as the three claims commissioners, subject to approval by the president. Mercer, who had traveled to France with Monroe, resided in Monroe's household in Paris and had acted as Monroe's unofficial secretary and assistant during the Louisiana negotiations. Barnet, the U.S. commercial agent at Antwerp, left a deputy in charge of that office and traveled to Paris to serve on the board. Maclure had been in Europe since 1799, studying geology, soils, and agriculture. On 18 June, Livingston and Monroe signed a commission for Skipwith as the board's agent under the provisions of Article 10 of the convention. Mercer and Barnet began to hold meetings on 5 July, with Nathaniel Cutting, a native of Massachusetts who had lived in France for several years, as their secretary. Maclure, who was in England when the other commissioners began their work, joined the meetings on 1 Sep. (Moore, *International Adjudications, Modern Series, Volume V*, 214-17; Madison, *Papers*, *Sec. of State Ser.*, 5:5, 70, 94, 165n, 296-7; Vol. 30:498-501; Vol. 32:184n, 194; Vol. 34:503-4; Vol. 35:706-8; Vol. 38:60n).

MR. DUFERMON: Jacques Defermon, who headed the commission on finances of the *Conseil d'État*, reviewed claims that Skipwith thought should not be paid under the terms of the convention (Tulard, *Dictionnaire Napoléon*, 582; Madison, *Papers*, *Sec. of State Ser.*, 5:342, 408).

For a number of years beginning in the American Revolution, FRANCIS COFFYN had taken care of U.S. commercial affairs at Dunkirk. TJ named Charles D. Coxe as commercial agent there in 1801 in place of a late-term appointment by John Adams. Coxe declined to serve, however, and later in 1803, TJ appointed Coffyn to the post (Vol. 27:9; Vol. 33:677; Vol. 36:333; TJ to the Senate, 9 Dec. 1803).

On 20 May, before he received the commission as the board's agent, Skipwith wrote to Madison lamenting his lack of compensation for duties he had performed in Paris, his "sacrifice of property" in the public service, and the high cost of living in the city. Livingston, however, still expected him to handle most complaints by Americans to the French government. Monroe had assured him that the administration would find him a position "susceptible of a reasonable compensation." Skipwith asked that Madison and the president consider him for one of the several positions that would be necessary in Louisiana. At Skipwith's request, Monroe in a letter to Madison on 16 May recommended that Skipwith be made collector of customs at New Orleans. Madison passed Skipwith's letter along to TJ (Skipwith to Madison, 20 May, in DNA: RG 59, LAR, endorsed by Jacob Wagner as received 17 Aug. and endorsed by TJ: "Skipwith Fulwar. for appointmt New Orleans. his lre to mr Madison"; Madison, *Papers*, *Sec. of State Ser.*, 5:6, 21-2).

To Henry Dearborn

DEAR SIR Monticello Aug. 8. 1803.

It is suggested to me (indirectly from the person himself) that Jerome Bonaparte is at Baltimore under the name of Monsr. Dalbarton, with a son of Rewbell, and that they mean to ask a passage to France in one of our frigates. if this be the fact, he will have satisfied thereof the minister of his nation, thro' whom we shall be apprised of it, and relieved from all trouble in deciding on it. this may yet be done, perhaps just as a frigate is ready to sail, and accompanied with a request of a passage in her, when no time will be left for consultation. our duty to our constituents would require us to lose no occasion of conferring personal obligation on the first Consul of France, and of procuring by just attentions the advantages of his good will to them. the same duties require us equally to give no just offense to the other belligerent party, and that we should not expose our flag to the humiliation of having a frigate searched by superior force,[1] the search proved rightful by it's result, & ourselves placed in the wrong. we should therefore be prepared with an answer, yea or nay, should the application be made in proper form; for which reason I ask the favor of yourself, as I do of the other gentlemen of the administration, to advise me as to the answer to be given. I presume there is little time left for my recieving it.

I inclose you an address from Kaskaskia. I presume our late acquisition will have given them more confidence in their safety. Accept my affectionate saluations & assurances of constant esteem.

TH: JEFFERSON

RC (NN: Lee Kohns Memorial Collection); addressed: "Genl. Henry Dearborne Secretary at War Washington." PrC (DLC). Recorded in SJL as a letter to the War Department about Jerome Bonaparte and with notation "address from Kaskaskia." Enclosure: Address from citizens of Randolph County, Indiana Territory, at Kaskaskia, undated, recorded in SJL as received 29 July, but not found.

SUGGESTED TO ME: see TJ to Madison, 8 Aug.

Serving as a naval officer in the West Indies, 18-year-old JEROME BONAPARTE had contracted yellow fever and was under orders to return to France to recuperate. Expecting interception by the British if he tried to sail directly from Martinique, he traveled to the United States with the intention of continuing on to France from an American port. With him were Pierre Meyronnet, another officer of the French navy; Alexander Lecamus, Bonaparte's secretary; and Jean Jacques Reubell, son of Jean François Reubell, one of the original members of the French Directory. Bonaparte traveled up Chesapeake Bay from Norfolk and on 22 July arrived in Washington, where he stayed for two days and conferred with Louis André Pichon before going to Baltimore. Meyronnet arranged for a merchant vessel to take them to France, but Bonaparte decided to remain in Baltimore and let Meyronnet sail without him. The young officer then pressed Pichon to obtain passage for him on a U.S. frigate (Glenn J. Lamar, *Jérôme Bonaparte: The War Years, 1800-1815* [Westport, Conn., 2000], 6-10; Edouard Dentu, ed., *Mémoires et correspondance du roi Jérôme et de la reine Catherine*, 7 vols. [Paris, 1861-66], 1:128-37; Tulard, *Dictionnaire Napoléon*, 969, 1455-6).

UNDER THE NAME OF MONSR. DALBARTON: the attempt to disguise the young Bonaparte's identity could have only limited effect. A brief, unconfirmed newspaper story, which first appeared on 23 July and received wide circulation thereafter, reported his arrival in the United States. Later in August a report circulated that he and an accompanying entourage of gentlemen and ladies received a 21-gun salute during a public visit to a Spanish corvette at Baltimore (Baltimore *Federal Gazette*, 23 July; New York *Commercial Advertiser*, 27 July; Boston *Columbian Centinel*, 30 July; New York *Daily Advertiser*, 30 Aug.; Salem, Mass., *Salem Register*, 1 Sep.).

[1]Word written over partially erased "power"; compare TJ to Gallatin, TJ to Madison, and TJ to Smith of this date, below.

To Albert Gallatin

Dear Sir Monticello Aug. 8. 03

It is suggested to me (indirectly from the person himself) that Jerome Bonaparte is at Baltimore under the name of Monsr. Dalbarton, with a son of Rewbell, and that they mean to ask a passage to France in one of our frigates. if this be the fact, he will have satisfied thereof the minister of his nation, thro' whom we shall be apprised of it, & relieved from all trouble in deciding on it. this may yet be done, perhaps just as a frigate is ready to sail, and accompanied with a request of a passage in her, when no time will be left for consultation. our duty to our constituents would require us to lose no occasion of conferring personal obligation on the first Consul of France, and of procuring by just attentions the advantages of his good will to them. the same duties require us equally to give no just offence to the other belligerent power, and that we should not expose our flag to the humiliation of having a frigate searched by superior power, the search proved rightful by it's result, and ourselves placed in the wrong. we should therefore be prepared with an answer, yea, or nay, should the application be made in proper form; for which reason I ask the favor of yourself, as I do of the other gentlemen of the administration, to advise me as to the answer to be given. I presume there is little time left for my recieving it. Accept my affectionate salutations & assurances of constant esteem. Th: Jefferson

RC (NHi: Gallatin Papers); addressed: "Albert Gallatin Secretary of the Treasury now at New York"; franked; postmarked Milton; endorsed. PrC (DLC). Recorded in SJL, along with letters to the State, War, and Navy Departments, with notation "Jerome Bonaparte."

From Ephraim Kirby

Litchfield, Connecticut
August 8th. 1803

Sir

Having been absent from home about two weeks, the letter which you did me the honor to write on the 15th. ulto., and the blank Commission which followed by the next Mail did not reach me until this day. The Secretary of State has conveyed the Commission which was filled for myself.—

The confidence which you have been pleased to repose in me, meets my grateful acknowledgement, and so far as a faithful exertion of my talents extend, it shall be justifyed.

It will be useful and convenient that I should be at the place of meeting some short time before the Commissioners come together.—For this purpose I have determined to commence my journey at the close of the present month, and to pursue it leisurely across the country to Pittsburgh, and from thence through Kentucky and Tennessee.

I am with great respect Sir Your most obedt. Servt

Ephm Kirby

RC (DLC); at foot of text: "The President of the U. States"; endorsed by TJ as received 17 Aug. and so recorded in SJL.

Madison conveyed the commission to Kirby in a letter dated 16 July (Madison, *Papers, Sec. of State Ser.*, 5:190).

place of meeting: Fort Stoddart (TJ to Kirby, 15 July).

From William Lee

American Consulate Bordeaux
Aug. 8. 1803

Sir

The feeble state of my health will but just permit me to acknowledge the rect. of the letter you did me the honor to write me under date of the 14 June enclosing a bill on V Dupont de Nemours & Co. Being at this moment on my departure for the waters of the Pyrenees to avoid the distressing heat of this month I have taken the liberty to hand your order to my worthy and respectable partner Mr. Perrot to whom I have given a very particular charge respecting the wines and I feel persuaded he will do his best endeavours to meet your approbation.

It would have given me peculiar to have fulfilled this order myself but such Sir has been my weak state for six weeks past that it is with difficulty I have been able to get through the duties of my office.—

With great respect I have the honor to remain your obedient servant. WILLIAM LEE

RC (MHi); at head of text: "*duplicate*"; endorsed by TJ as received 2 Oct. and so recorded in SJL.

To James Madison

DEAR SIR Monticello Aug. 8. 03.

If M. Dalbarton be really Jerome Bonaparte, he will have satisfied thereof the minister of his nation, thro' whom we shall be apprised of the fact, and relieved from all trouble in deciding on it. this may yet be done, perhaps just as a frigate is ready to sail, and accompanied with a request of a passage in her; when no time will be left for consultation. our duty to our constituents would require us to lose no occasion of conferring obligation on the first Consul of France personally, and of procuring by just attentions the advantages of his good will to them. the same duties require us equally to give no just offence to the other belligerent party, & that we should not expose our flag to the humiliation of having a frigate searched by superior power, the search proved rightful by it's result, and ourselves placed in the wrong. we should therefore be prepared with an answer, yea or nay, should the application be made in proper form, for which reason I ask the favor of yourself, as well as of the other gentlemen of the administration, to advise me as to the answer to be given. I presume there is little time left for it.

I return you mr Dawson's letter of July 29. 1803.[1] mr Pichon's papers in the case of Cloupet await the information you expect from the Collector of Norfolk. Accept my affectionate salutations and unvarying esteem & attachment TH: JEFFERSON

RC (DLC: Madison Papers); at foot of text: "The Secretary of State." PrC (DLC). Recorded in SJL as a letter to the State Department about Jerome Bonaparte. Enclosure: John Dawson to Madison, 29 July, written at Baltimore, reporting that earlier in the day he had met a "Mr. Dalbart" who is staying with Joshua Barney; Barney informed Dawson that the traveler is actually Jerome Bonaparte, in the United States on his way back to France with his secretary and Jean Jacques Reubell; Barney also informed Dawson that the British naval captain John Murray, who has been refused permission to travel on a United States frigate, is aware of Bonaparte's identity and knows that the young French officer hopes to sail on an American warship; Murray intends to give the Royal Navy "every information respecting Bounaparte" and says "that every exertion will be made to capture him" (Madison, *Papers*, *Sec. of State Ser.*, 5:247).

Madison probably wrote to TJ about CLOUPET, the master of a French merchant vessel, on 29 July. According to SJL, TJ received a communication of that date from the State Department on 1 Aug. about "Pichon on importn negroes." The letter of 29 July has not been found, but it likely accompanied one from Louis André Pichon to Madison of 26 July. In it, the French diplomat asked for the president's assistance in Cloupet's case. The sea captain had made a stop at Norfolk on a voyage from Port-au-Prince to Martinique. Authorities in the port put under arrest three black servants who were accompanying passengers on Cloupet's ship. The three men were released from imprisonment on the condition that they leave Virginia, but despite Cloupet's assurances that there had been no intention to bring the men into the state, the collector of customs levied a fine of $3,000 on the captain. In addition to asking for the president's intervention in the case, Pichon requested that U.S. officials take a lenient approach toward the many inhabitants of French colonies, especially Saint-Domingue, who might seek refuge in the United States without knowing that the law prohibited them from bringing their servants with them (same, 232-3). A letter of 31 July from the State Department, recorded in SJL as received 3 Aug. and pertaining to something from Pichon, also has not been found.

INFORMATION YOU EXPECT: see TJ to Madison, 29 Aug.

[1]Date interlined. TJ did not make the change on the PrC.

To Robert Smith

DEAR SIR Monticello Aug. 8. 1803.

It is suggested to me (indirectly from the person himself) that Jerome Bonaparte is at Baltimore, under the name of Monsr. Dalbarton, with a son of Rewbell, [&] that they mean to ask a passage to France in one of our frigates. if this be the fact, he will have satisfied thereof the minister of his nation, thro' whom we shall be apprised of it, & relieved from all trouble in deciding on it. this may yet be done, perhaps just as a frigate is ready to sail, & accompanied with a request of a passage in her, when no time will be left for consultation. our duty to our constituents would require us to lose no occasion of conferring personal obligation on the first Consul of France, & of procuring, by just attentions, the advantages of his good will to them. the same duties require us equally to give no just offense to the other belligerent power, and that we should not expose our flag to the humiliation of having a frigate searched by superior force, the search proved rightful by its result, & ourselves placed in the wrong. we should therefore be prepared with an answer, yea or nay, should the application be made in proper form, for which reason I ask the favor of yourself, as I do of the other gentlemen of the administration, to advise me as to the answer to be given. I presume there is little time left for my receiving it.

What is the present prospect of the departure of our [frigates and] remaining small vessels? Accept my affectionate saluations & assurances of constant esteem. TH: JEFFERSON

PrC (DLC); faint; at foot of text: "The Secretary of the Navy." Recorded in SJL as a letter to the Navy Department about Jerome Bonaparte.

From Samuel Broome

Greenfield Hill Connecticut Augt. 9th. 1803.

I did myself the Honor to address a line lately to your Excellency, Since the date thereof, the Office of Collector has become Vacant by the death of Samuel Bishop Esqr. My friends advise me to apply for said office, once more. your Excellency may recollect, you was then adresed upon the Subject,[1] by my son in Law, Joseph Fay Esqr. of New york, as also by myself, I again take that freedom, in the hope that I may be thought Suitable to discharge the trust, which should I be so fortunate as to be appointed, it shall be guaranteed in the most ample manner.

I believe your excellency will be Written to, in my behalf, those letters, I should bring with me, but if I pass through New york, I cannot through Philadelphia, as I am informed, the Communication betwixt said Cities is suspended. I expect to leave home tomorrow for the City of Washington, where I hope I shall meet your Excellency in the enjoyment of health, and disposed (if I am thought worthy) to add to the favors Confer'd on me some years since in Paris.—It not being proper to pass through New york may Occasion a delay of some days.

I am with Sincere regard, your Excellincys Most Obedient Servant

SAMUEL BROOME

RC (DNA: RG 59, LAR); at foot of text: "His Excellency the President of the United States"; endorsed by TJ as received 17 Aug. and "to be Collectr. New Haven vice Saml. Bishop decd" and so recorded in SJL.

ADDRESS A LINE LATELY: Broome to TJ, 4 Aug.

JOSEPH FAY had written TJ on 11 Apr. 1801, soliciting an appointment for Broome and enclosing a letter from Broome to TJ of 8 Apr. (Vol. 33:570-2). Fay would be among the victims of the yellow fever outbreak in NEW YORK, dying on 26 Oct. 1803 (New York *Evening Post*, 26 Oct. 1803). For the restricted COMMUNICATION between New York and Philadelphia due to the disease, see Benjamin Rush to TJ, 5 Aug. 1803.

Broome first made TJ's acquaintance in PARIS in 1789 and received a passport from him in July of the same year (Vol. 14:560; Vol. 15:92, 486; Vol. 33:572n).

[1] MS: "Susject."

From J. P. P. Derieux

Monsieur New-york ce 9: Augt. 1803.

Mr. Monroe ayant eu la bonté depuis le 1er. Mai der de voulloir bien m'appointer pour vous apporter ses Dépêches, j'ai L'honneur de vous informer que je viens ce jour de débarquer a New-york, d'ou suivant ses ordres je dois me rendre a Washington-City dans la plus grand diligence; mais comme il m'a très particulierement recommandé de ne les remettre qu'a vous ou Mr. Madison, et quon vient de me dire que n'y vous n'y lui n'y êtes actuellement, voudrés vous bien my honorer de vos ordres pour m'indiquer a qui je dois les délivrer. Je vais partir cet aprés midi par le courier de la Malle et serai dans peu de jours a Washington, dont je ne partirai qu'aprés avoir recu L'honneur de votre reponse, n'ayant de plus grand empressement que de suivre exactement les instructions de Mr. Monroe qui a bien voulu mettre confiance dans mon exactitude, et me faire esperer que le Gouvernement m'en accorderoit quelque gratiffication en outre du remboursement qui me seroit fait a mon arrivée, a Washington, de mes dépenses a Paris et fraix de Voyages depuis le 1er. mai qu'il m'a employé jusqu'au moment ou j'aurois eu rempli la mission importante dont il me Chargeoit.

D'aprés l'interet que Mr. Monroe a eu la bonté de montrer sur mon grand désappointement dans la Succession de Mde. Bellanger, dont je prends la liberté de vous communiquer cy joint ce qui m'en est révenu, j'ai lieu de croire que cette malheureuse circonstance pour moi, Lui a eté d'un grand encouragement, pour le faire m'employer auprés du Gouvt. de préferance a toutte autre personne, et cela me seroit, Monsieur, un dedomagement bien sensible, si je puis obtenir de vos bontés que vous veuilliés bien me faire la grace de seconder ses bonnes intentions, en m'accordant quelque Gratiffication qui seroit ma principalle ressource pour former L'etablissement durable auquel j'espére depuis tant d'années pour ma malheureuse famille; car la révolution ayant ruinés Ceux de mes parents qui auroient pû m'ètre de quelque utilité, je n'en ay pu obtenir que de trés foibles secours, si ce n'est en promesses pour Lavenir aussitot que leure fortunne se sera rétablie. Je les ay tous quittés trés disposés en ma faveur, et les ay informé de ce que je devois en Virginie, et particulierement a vous, Monsieur, dont j'ose encore supplier les bontés indulgentes pour ce nouveau retard, et je ne puis qu'esperer vu leurs bonnes dispositions, que j'en obtienne avant Longtems les moyens de faire honneur a mes engagements, et pouvoir donner un Etablissement honnête a chacun de mes enfants.

Recevés je vous prie, Monsieur, la nouvelle assurance des sentiments du plus profond respect et reconnaissance avec les quels j'ai L'honneur d'être Monsieur Votre trés humble & trés obt Servteur.

P. DeRieux
poste restante a Washington-City

P.S. Voullés vous bien permettre Monsieur que Monsieur et Madame Randolph ainsi que Monsieur et Madame Epse trouvent ici L'assurance de mon plus profond respect; et excuser la grande precipitation de ma Lettre que je vous ecris trés a La hate et a Bord du Batiment qui est encore sous voile et au moment de mouiller.

M'ayant procuré L'attestation que je prends La Liberté de vous communiquer, afin de pouvoir Justiffier a mes Crs L'impossibilité ou je me trouve aussi malheureusement de pouvoir encore les satisfaire, je vous serai trés obligé, Monsieur de voulloir bien me faire la grace de me la renvoyer.

EDITORS' TRANSLATION

Sir, New York, 9 Aug. 1803

Since Mr. Monroe was good enough to designate me, as of the first of May last, to transmit his messages to you, I have the honor of informing you that I have just arrived in New York. As he requested, I will proceed in all haste to Washington City. But since he specifically asked me to entrust them only to you or Mr. Madison, and I have been told that neither of you is currently there, could you please do me the honor of informing me to whom I should deliver them? I am leaving this afternoon by the mail coach and will be in Washington in a few days. I will not leave there until I have had the honor of your response, since I most earnestly seek to carry out Mr. Monroe's instructions to the letter, in keeping with his generous trust in my reliability. It is my hope that the government will accord me some recompense on my arrival in Washington, in addition to reimbursing my expenses in Paris and my travel expenses from the first of May until the time I complete this important mission.

I take the liberty of enclosing a document concerning Madame Bellanger. Judging from Mr. Monroe's sympathy with my great disappointment about her inheritance, which is an unfortunate circumstance for me, I have been led to believe that he will give me priority for a government appointment. It would be a great help if you could second his good intentions by giving me some compensation. This would be my principal means of establishing the solid foundation I have long sought for my unfortunate family. The relatives who could have helped me lost everything in the Revolution, and could provide only modest support, except for promises for some future time when their fortune is restored. All of them were well disposed in my favor when I left and when I informed them of my debts in Virginia, and especially to you, Sir, whose indulgent goodness I once again dare implore for this latest delay. Given their favorable disposition, I can only hope that I will soon be in a position to honor my commitments and provide a suitable foundation for each of my children.

I beg you, Sir, to accept this renewed assurance of my most profound respect and gratitude, with which I have the honor of being your very humble and obedient servant.
P. DeRieux
general delivery, Washington City

P.S. Please convey my deep respect to Mr. and Mrs. Randolph and Mr. and Mrs. Eppes, and forgive the haste of this letter, which I am writing quickly on board the ship which is still under sail and about to dock.

I would be grateful, Sir, if you could return the attestation that I take the liberty of communicating to you. I obtained it to certify to my creditors the unfortunate fact that I am currently unable to repay my debts to them.

RC (DLC: Madison Papers); endorsed by TJ as received 17 Aug. and so recorded in SJL. Enclosed in TJ to Madison, 18 Aug. Enclosure: attestation by Fulwar Skipwith, not found (see Derieux to TJ, 29 Aug.).

On 17 Aug., Derieux delivered the second official set of the treaty and conventions for the purchase of Louisiana to Jacob Wagner at the State Department along with dispatches from James MONROE and Robert R. Livingston. George A. Hughes had delivered the first set of the purchase documents a month earlier (Madison, *Papers*, *Sec. of State Ser.*, 5:320; John Mitchell to TJ, 21 May).

MON GRAND DÉSAPPOINTEMENT: Derieux had hoped to obtain an inheritance from the estate of his aunt, Madame Plumard de BELLANGER. Wagner reported to Madison that Derieux had expected to receive "more than 100,000 livres and has returned with only about 700" (Madison, *Papers*, *Sec. of State Ser.*, 5:320; Vol. 38:535-7; Vol. 39:68-9).

To John Dickinson

Dear Sir
Monticello Aug. 9. 1803.

Your friendly favor of the 1st. inst. is recieved with that welcome which always accompanies the approbation of the wise & good. the acquisition of New Orleans would of itself have been a great thing, as it would have ensured to our Western brethren the means of exporting their produce: but that of Louisiana is inappreciable, because, giving us the sole dominion of the Missisipi, it excludes those bickerings with foreign powers, which we know of a certainty would have put us at war with France immediately: and it secures to us the course of a peaceable nation.

The *unquestioned* bounds of Louisiana are the Iberville & Missisipi on the East, the Mexicana, or the high lands East of it, on the West; then from the head of the Mexicana gaining the high lands which include the waters of the Missisipi, and following those highlands round the head springs of the western waters of the Missisipi to it's source where we join the English, or perhaps to the lake of the Woods. this may be considered as[1] a triangle, one leg of which is of the length of the Missouri, the other of the Missisipi, and the hypothenuse running from the source of the Missouri to the Mouth of Missisipi. I should be averse to exchanging any part of this for the Floridas, because it would let Spain into the Missipi on the principle of natural right we have always urged & are now urging to her, that a nation inhabiting the upper part of a stream has a right of innocent passage down that stream to the ocean; and because the Floridas will fall to us peaceably the first war Spain is engaged in. we have some pretensions to extend the Western boundary of Louisiana[2] to the Rio Norte, or Bravo; and still stronger the Eastern boundary to the Rio perdido, between the rivers Mobile & Pensacola. these last are so strong that France had not relinquished them & our negociators expressly declared we should claim them. by properly availing ourselves of these, with offers of a price, & our peace, we shall get the Floridas in good time and in the mean while we shall enter on the exercise of the right of passing down all the rivers which, rising in our territory, run thro' the Floridas. Spain will not oppose it by force. There is a difficulty in this acquisition which presents a handle to the malcontents among us, tho' they have not yet discovered it. our confederation is certainly confined to the limits established by the revolution. the general government has no powers but such as the constitution has given it; and it has not given it a power of holding foreign territory, & still less of incorporating it into the Union. an amendment of the constitution seems necessary for this. in the mean time we must ratify & pay our money, as we have treated, for a thing beyond the constitution, and rely on the nation to sanction an act done for it's great good, without it's previous authority. with respect to the disposal of the country, we must take the island of New Orleans and West side of the river as high up as Point coupée, containing nearly the whole inhabitants, say about 50,000, and erect it into a state, or annex it to the Missisipi territory; and shut up all the rest from settlement for a long time to come, endeavoring to exchange some of the country there unoccupied by Indians, for the lands held by the Indians on this side the Missisipi, who will be glad to cede us their country here for an equivalent there: and we may sell out their lands here & pay the whole debt contracted before it becomes due. the impost which will be paid by the inhabitants ceded will pay half the interest of the price we give: so that we really add only half the price to our debt. I have indulged myself in these details, because, the subject being new, it is advantageous to interchange ideas on it, and to get our notions all corrected before we are obliged to act on them. in this view I recieve

& shall recieve with pleasure any thing which may occur to you. Accept my affectionate salutations & assurances of my constant & great esteem & respect.

TH: JEFFERSON

RC (PHi); addressed: "John Dickinson esquire Wilmington Del."; franked; postmarked Milton, 10 Aug. PrC (DLC).

[1] MS: "a."
[2] Preceding two words interlined.

From James Mease

SIR Philadelphia Aug. 9. 1803.

Your esteemed favour, accompanying the German pamphlet by Angermann, on the preservation of Timber, came to hand in due time. I am highly indebted to you for the consideration, and interest which you take in the work which I am preparing for press, and I only regret that the merits of Angermann's tract did not render it more worthy of the trouble it has occasioned you. I do not understand German, but my friend Dr Seybert of this City is master of that language, and without any possible exception, the best chemist in America theoretical and practical. He was polite enough to read the work, by Angermann, and to give me his opinion of it, which amounted to this, that as not a single prooff was adduced in support of the efficacy of the preservative compositions recommended, and as some of the articles decomposed others and left one alone to act on the wood, he did not think the use of all the articles necessary. The active ingredient appeared to be common salt! the efficacy of which is well known. But in my opinion the best remedy to preserve timber is to use it after being *well seasoned*, and to provide for the due ventilation of it, when necessarily exposed to moisture.—I shall touch on this subject under the article "House." In the second vol: under the article "Dry rot" some remarks are made by Dr Willich, and also under the head "Timber."—

I have lately been reading your description of the mould board of a plough, and prevailed upon an ingenious pattern maker to attend to the explanation of the various parts of the model blocks, in the possession of the Phil: Soc: he understood them perfectly, and has agreed with me to make one, but I wish if possible to[1] have the plates Cast in order that they may be generally used, and their merits fairly ascertained. In reading your explanation something occurred which required still further explanation from you, and I shall esteem myself much indebted to you, for the necessary illustration.—you say p 319. "In practice I have found some other modifications of it advantageous."—again p 320 "But now satisfied, that for a furrow of nine by six inches, the dimensions I have stated are the best, I propose to have the mould board made of Cast iron."— Permit me to ask, what are the circumstances, requiring the "modifications" and by what rule can we ascertain the proper thickness of the mould plate when Cast?—Have any been cast which meet your full approbation, and can I obtain one?—As I deem the most[2] proper form of a plough of infinite Consequence, I am exceedingly anxious to see an experiment tried with[3] one having a plate of your particular form, and also to gratify myself by introducing your pattern into Pennsya; for, from all the inquiries I have made, I cannot learn that a single mould board has been made agreeably to the plan you recommend. Our Philosophers here are not farmers, and our farmers never heard of your mould board. Thus it is, that this seperation of science from practice, proves so injurious to the progress of improvement. I offered to make an attempt to unite both, but was prevented, and by those who ought to have encouraged my zeal.—

The patent mould plate of Mr Smith of Bucks County, has attained great Credit in that part of the Country, on account of the ease with which it works; I have seen the plough made under his direction, but not at work. When I get one of your construction I am determined to try it along side of Smith's, and to procure the English[4] contrivance of a screw or spring steel yard, fixed so as to tell the precise force with which both ploughs[5] draw.—

I am the more anxious respecting the detail of the principles, and of the precise[6] dimensions of your plate, because I am desirous to mention it in my work, and I should be very happy in recommending it from my own experience to our farmers.—

Wishing you all health and happiness I remain yours Sincerely

JAMES MEASE

RC (DLC); at foot of text: "The President of the U States"; endorsed by TJ as received 15 Aug. and so recorded in SJL.

YOUR ESTEEMED FAVOUR: TJ to Mease, 28 June.

WORK WHICH I AM PREPARING FOR PRESS: Mease was preparing an American edition of Anthony F. M. Willich's five-volume, *Domestic Encyclopædia; or, A Dictionary of Facts, and Useful Knowledge* (Vol. 39:128).

Chemist and mineralogist Adam SEYBERT was also a secretary of the American Philosophical Society (DAB).

For TJ's DESCRIPTION of his moldboard plow, see Vol. 30:197-209.

Robert SMITH of Bucks County, Pennsylvania, received a patent for a plow moldboard on 19 May 1800. TJ learned of his work earlier that same year. Describing the device in the *Domestic Encyclopædia*, Mease called it "a cast mould-board plate, constructed upon mathematical principles, which is much approved of" (*List of Patents*, 22; *Domestic Encyclopædia*, 4:292; Vol. 31:456-7).

[1] Mease here canceled "make."

[2] Word interlined.

[3] Mease here canceled "your."

[4] Word interlined.

[5] Mease here canceled "move."

[6] Mease here canceled "mode of."

From John Smith

Baton Rouge 50 Leagues
Above New Orleans—
August the 9th 1803

Sir

The fluctuating state of the Commerce, and Government of this Country, has till now prevented the adjustment of my business, but I flatter myself that in two or three weeks, I shall set out from this place for the City Washington.

It is with great pleasure—that I see announced in the papers Officially, the Cession of Louisiana to the United States; and also the Island of New Orleans. I conceive this to be the most valuable acquisition that could be made to the Western Country. It will secure to them the permanent & exclusive right, to the navigation of the Missisippi under the patronage of the general Government, It will tend to conciliate their affections, and confirm their hopes and confidence in the benign intentions of the present administration—It will add to the vigour and springs of Commerce, as well as to the agriculture of this province, Indeed Sir, it will be a very pleasing negociation to thousands in this Country; and I am very sorry that the Floridies are not included.

I often regretted, that in our late treaty with Spain[1] we had not negociated for The Floridies, and Island of New Orleans. But, we are better able to pay a valuable consideration for it now. The advantage of this Cession to our generation will be small and inconsiderable, compared with what it will be in future. It will effectually prevent all cause of discontent, obviate every doubt, and definitively settle all matters in controversy both as it may respect the boundary of our Government, and the Commerce of the Western Country. I have not yet heard the terms of the Cession. But, I am sure we had much better pay a large sum in a fair purchase, then in a long & bloody war. By it I have no doubt but we shall save much. We probably will save much of our Treasure, much public Credit, and the Blood & morals of thousands of our Citizens.

I have the honour to be Sir with consideration & respect your most obedient Servant

John Smith of
the State of Ohio

RC (DLC); addressed: "The President of the United States City Washington"; franked; postmarked Natchez, 12 Aug.; endorsed by TJ as received 7 Sep. and so recorded in SJL.

[1]Preceding two words interlined.

From George Jefferson

DEAR SIR Richmond 10th. Augt. 1803.

I am very sorry that I was so remiss, as to delay looking out for the wood screws until I had an opportunity of sending them; as I ought to have foreseen there was a *possibility* at least; of my not being able to procure such as you required and so it has turned out—there are none at all in the whole City with round heads[1] except some few of brass, and they are much too large. I found some few of the size you want with *flat* heads, at different places, but the quantity could not be half made up, even if they would answer.

I suppose from their scarcity, there are but few used here, as there are not more than a groce or two of a size in any one Store.

I forwarded the day before yesterday by Higganbotham's boat 13 barrels of the fish—I do not know how many of them are S. Carr's, so that I shall have to charge the expence on the whole to you.

I am Dear Sir Yr Very humble servt. GEO. JEFFERSON

RC (MHi); at foot of text: "Thos. Jefferson esqr."; endorsed by TJ as received 12 Aug. and so recorded in SJL.

For the order of WOOD SCREWS, see TJ to George Jefferson, 23 July.

[1]Preceding three words interlined.

From Thomas Newton

SIR Norfolk Aug 10—1803

Agreeable to your desire I wrote for two pipes best wine for you & one for myself which I am in hopes agreeable to my freinds promise will be of far superior quality to any we have yet had. we have nothing new here no late arivals. the Brittish Creuze of our Coasts impress men & have as I have heard taken some Spanish vessels laden with flour from Baltimore to Havanna. wishing you health & happiness I am with the greatest respect

Yr obt Servt THOS NEWTON

Mr Lindsay will inform you that we are fast increasing & expect the port will be valuable if the Brittish will do as they ought—

RC (DLC); endorsed by TJ as received 23 Aug. and so recorded in SJL.

MR LINDSAY: possibly Adam Lindsay, previously a Norfolk merchant with whom TJ corresponded but who had since settled in the District of Columbia (Vol. 36:216-17n).

To Thomas Paine

Dear Sir Monticello Aug. 10. 1803.

Your favor of the 2d. came to hand on the 8th. I shall willingly communicate to you all I know on the subject of Louisania. it is new, and therefore profitable to interchange ideas on it, that we may form correct opinions before we are to act on them.

The unquestioned extent of Louisania on the sea is from the Iberville to the Mexicana river, or perhaps the high lands dividing that from the Missisipi. it's original boundary however as determined by occupation of the French was Eastwardly to the river Perdido (between Mobile & Pensacola) & Westward to the Rio Norte or Bravo. the former was founded on the establishment of the French at Mobile and isle Dauphine[1] which they maintained from 1699. till they gave up the country in 1762. the latter on the original establishment made by La Sale on the West side of the bay of St. Louis or St. Bernard. how far subsequent operations have narrowed this extent on the ocean we are now to discuss with Spain. the boundary of the country inland is by the highlands including all the waters of the Missisipi, & of course of the Missouri. the advantage of this boundary is that it places the Misipi on the footing of the Potomak or Delaware, entirely an internal river, [one] which no foreign nation can enter but with leave. not a foot of it's water should ever be given up because it would, on our principle [defeat] a right to navigate the whole river, for we have always maintained, and now maintain as to Florida that a nation inhabiting a stream in it's upper parts has a right to an innocent passage through it to and from the Ocean. the unquestioned extent of Louisania may be called a triangle where one of it's legs extending from the head of the Misipi to that of the Missouri, the other from the head to the mouth of the Misipi, & the hypothenuse from the mouth of the Misipi to the head of the Missouri. it is larger than all the US: and what is called the Western valley of the Misipi has always been said to surpass in fertility the Eastern valley, that is to say Kentucky, Tennissee, & the Misipi. territory.

It's population is said to be of about 60,000. persons, French, Spaniards, Germans, British and Americans. the great body of these are in the island of New Orleans & on the West side of the river from Point Coupée downwards. above this are a few scattering posts only, to wit, one a little way up the Missouri, St. Louis at the mouth [of] that river, Ste. Genevieve opposite the Illinois, New Madrid opposite Ohio, and one other down the Missouri opposite the Chickasaws bluffs or not far distant. these settlements consist barely of inhabitants enough to raise provisions for the small garrisons kept there. the country below Point Coupée must doubtless be formed into a government either by itself or joined with the Misipi. territory. I imagine the best footing to put it's religion on is to leave it free as in the other territorial governments, liable only to voluntary contributions. this is tantamount to an [election?] of ministers, & better as even a majority cannot force the will of a minority. the rest of the country from Point Coupee upwards should be shut up against new settlements for a long time, only allowing us to give unoccupied portions of it to the Indians on this side the Mispi. in exchange for their present country, so that we should be able to fill up the Eastern valley, instead of depopulating it for the Western. this would be a better field for the emigrants you mention to enter on, than the Western. When we shall be full on this side we may cross the river & begin to settle it's Western margin, & extend back by regular compact progressions as numbers increase. it would be very wrong to think of giving up any of the Western valley for [the Floridas], except from the Mexicana to the Rio Norte, because we have now a good claim on Florida[2] as far as the Perdido, which [is at Mobile a] most valuable [port?], & because we shall get the whole peaceably the first war Spain is engaged in. We shall undoubtedly lay the cession before both houses, because both have important functions to exercise on it. the Representatives are to decide on the paiment of the money. besides this I believe we must lay it before *the nation* & ask an additional article to the Constitution that has made no provision for holding foreign territory, & still less for incorporating foreign countries into our union. yet we have stipulated that the Louisanians shall come into our union. in thus making this stipulation the Executive has done an act beyond the constitution, and in ratifying it & paying for the country the legislature will do the same. we must throw ourselves for this on our country, saying that we have not hesitated to do for them what we were sure they would have done for themselves, by securing a great good in the only [...] in which it would ever have been in their power: by asking them their confirmation after the act, for which they would have given previous authority had it been foreseen; acknoleging at the same time that we cannot have bound them, that they are free to reject it, and to disavow us, restoring every thing to it's former state. but I trust we shall meet their approbation, and not their disavowal.

You ask whether Monroe is gone to Spain? I think it rather probable, according to our previous arrangements, & on the newspaper information that he is gone; for we have no letter from him since the one accompanying the treaty, in which he says nothing of going. your letter to mr Breckenridge shall be immediately forwarded to Kentucky, & that to Coltman sent back to Washington.

Accept my respectful salutations & best wishes for your health & happiness. TH: JEFFERSON

PrC (DLC); faint; at foot of first page: "Thomas Paine esq."

TJ's discussion of Louisiana reflected the prevailing, limited geographical and historical knowledge of North America, as well as confusion resulting from the competing territorial claims of the European powers. The IBERVILLE River, or Bayou Manchac, a waterway connecting the Mississippi River on the west and the Amite River to the east below the site of Baton Rouge, formed part of a horizontal boundary between Louisiana and Spanish West Florida, extending through Lakes Maurepas and Ponchartrain. In implying that the Iberville helped define Louisiana's coastal boundary, TJ was probably just phrasing the matter imprecisely. During his final voyage, Robert Cavelier de La Salle (LA SALE) established a fort at what in present-day Texas is known as Matagorda Bay. Accounts consulted by TJ, a journal of the La Salle expedition written by Henri Joutel (Sowerby, Nos. 4073, 4074) and Antoine-Simon Le Page du Pratz's *History of Louisiana, or of the Western Parts of Virginia and Carolina* (Sowerby, No. 4068), labeled the bay ST. LOUIS and ST. BERNARD, respectively. The first settlement TJ mentioned was presumably St. Charles, which was UP THE MISSOURI River from St. Louis. After the Pinckney Treaty of 1795, the Spanish disbanded Fort San Fernando de las Barrancas, their outpost on the last of the four Chickasaw BLUFFS (the site of Memphis, Tennessee), which TJ mistakenly placed down the Missouri rather than the Mississippi. To maintain watch over the area, they left a small garrison across the river, Campo del Esperanza, and began issuing land grants there. This encampment, however, hardly constituted a village. A more substantial community to the south, Arkansas Post, contained perhaps 450 inhabitants at the time of the purchase (Henri Joutel, *Journal historique du dernier voyage que feu M. de la Sale fit dans le Golfe de Mexique, pour trouver l'embouchure, & le cours de la Riviere Missicipi, nommée à present la Riviere de Saint Loüis, qui traverse la Louisiane* [Paris, 1713], 112; Antoine-Simon Le Page du Pratz, *The History of Louisiana, or of the Western Parts of Virginia and Carolina: Containing a Description of the Countries That Lye on Both Sides of the River Missisipi: With an Account of the Settlements, Inhabitants, Soil, Climate, and Products*, 2 vols. [London, 1763], 2:6, 216; William E. Foley and others, *A History of Missouri*, 6 vols. [Columbia, Mo., 1971-2004], 1:48-9; Morris S. Arnold, *Colonial Arkansas, 1686-1804: A Social and Cultural History* [Fayetteville, Ark., 1991], 20-3; Vol. 40:234-5, 660-2; The Boundaries of Louisiana, printed at 7 Sep., Document I).

[1] Preceding three words interlined.
[2] Preceding two words interlined.

To Isaac Briggs

Dear Sir Monticello Aug. 11. 1803.

Mr. Fitch proposes to set out from hence for the Missisipi about the 1st. of October, and to go by Knoxville & Nashville along the post road. as there is still time enough to recieve an answer from you by post before his departure, the object of this letter is merely to ask if you have any thing to advise him of before his journey which may be useful to him either on the road or preparatory to it: as also to direct him to what place he must go to find you. you will have learned by the public papers the cession of Louisiana to us for the sum of 15. millions of dollars. Congress will probably authorise us to explore the principal streams of the Missisipi & Missouri, and to settle with accuracy given points in the high lands inclosing the waters of those rivers, which high lands constitute the exterior boundary of the acquisition, terminating at the head spring of the Missisipi or more probably at the lake of the woods. Accept my friendly salutations & best wishes for your health & happiness. Th: Jefferson

PrC (DLC); at foot of text: "Mr. Isaac Briggs"; endorsed by TJ in ink on verso.

MR. FITCH: that is, Gideon Fitz, a surveyor and protégé of TJ's who sought employment with Briggs in the Mississippi Territory (Vol. 40:118-20, 299-300, 404).

From Albert Gallatin

Dear Sir New York 11th August 1803

I arrived here after a long & tedious journey & found the yellow fever in the city: I did not stay in it & am in the country two miles from town.

I must confess that I do not see the necessity of writing the intended letter to Duane. Unforeseen circumstances may produce alterations in your present view of the subject, & if you should hereafter think proper to act on a plan somewhat different from that you now consider as the best, a commitment would prove unpleasant. Nor is it probable that abstract reasoning, or even a statement of facts already known to them, will make converts of men under the influence of passions or governed by self interest. Either a schism will take place, in which case the leaders of those men would divide from us, or time and the good sense of the people will of themselves cure the evil. I have reason to believe that the last will happen & that the number of malcontents is not very considerable & will diminish.

Should you however conclude to write, I think Duane greatly preferable to Scott. Clay is his intimate friend & the only man of superior weight & talents who appears to be closely united with Leib & Duane. Clay will during the course of next session become intimately connected with ourselves & the majority of Congress; he will I am confident be perfectly reconciled to us & feel the necessity, when all the important measures shall meet with his approbation, not to divide on account of some slight difference of opinion in points of trifling comparative importance: and it is highly probable that Duane, who may be misled by vanity & by his associates, but whose sincere republicanism I cannot permit myself to doubt, will adhere to us, when his best friend shall have taken a decided part. Although I do not consider a commitment to him eligible, it appears vastly preferable to one to Scott.

If a letter shall be written, I think that, if possible, it should be much shorter than your draft, & have perhaps less the appearance of apology. The irresistible argument, to men disposed to listen to argument, appears to me to be, the perfect approbation given by the republicans to all the leading measures of Government, & the inference that men who are disposed, under those circumstances, to *asperse* administration, seem to avow that the hard struggle of so many years was not for the purpose of securing our republican institutions & of giving a proper direction to the operations of Government, but for the sake of a few paltry offices—offices not of a political & discretionary nature, but mere inferior administrative offices of profit.[+]

The information I have received respecting E. Livingston is still more decisive than what I had at Washington: the enclosed copy of a letter from Mr Osgood will show that he is also a delinquent on suits brought by order of the Supervisor: Mr Gelston informs me that he has not yet paid the whole of the balance which he acknowledges to be due by him; and he adds that he feels a conviction that the return made by Livingston is untrue & of course the balance in his hands much larger than what he acknowledges. It is only by personal application to the persons indebted on bonds put in suit that the true state of his accounts can be ascertained: this will be done & can be done only by a successor in office. I have sent word to DeWitt Clinton who is on Long Island to try to come to me to day or to morrow: at all events the commission to N. Sanford will be delivered in the course of this week.

[+] There is one mistake in your draft. Leonard the store keeper is appointed by the Secy. of war & not by the President

I enclose the answer of Oliver Phelps recommending Robert Lee as collector of Niagara. If you shall approve and are still of opinion that the son of General Irvine is the proper person to be appointed surveyor of the port of Buffaloe Creek which is to be annexed, as a port of delivery to the District of Niagara, the commissions may be issued; but I do not recollect young Irvine's christian name. The denominations of office will be

Collector of the District of Niagara
Surveyor of the port of Buffaloe Creek
and each of them must have another commission vizt.
Inspector of the revenue for the *port* of Niagara
Do do Buffaloe creek.

It is also necessary that you should determine on the application of T. Reddick for the office of Register of the land office at Mobile, being the same for which E. Kirby has a blank commission. Will you be good enough to inform me whenever he (Mr Kirby), Robert Williams, & ______ Nicholas of Kentucky shall have expressed their determination to accept the offices of commissioners, as it is necessary for me to transmit to them some instructions & to make the arrangements for the payment of their salary.

At the request of Doctr. Hunter of Philadelphia I enclose his application which may hereafter deserve attention.

The Bank of the U. States has immediately & chearfully expressed its readiness to lend us the 1,785,000 dollars wanted to complete the intended payment of the american debts assumed by the Treaty with France.

Mr Lyman of Massachusetts is a determined applicant for the Government of Louisiana. As an early, decided, active & persecuted republican he has great claims; but his pretensions are high & he is not accommodating.

I have seen Mr King, but in presence of a third person & could have but a general conversation. In the course of that he incidentally mentioned that the idea of selling Louisiana was, four weeks before the treaty, assimilated at Paris with the sale of Dunkirk by Charles the 2d; and that Mr Livingston had not at that time the least expectation of success. I will return his visit to morrow & may obtain some other information.

With sincere respect & attachment Your obedt. Servt.

ALBERT GALLATIN

RC (DLC); at foot of text: "The President of the United States"; endorsed by TJ as received from the Treasury Department on 17 Aug. and "answr. to ward commees—E. Livingston.—Lee Collectr Niagara Irvin Survr. Buffalo port.—

Riddick register Mobile bank US. lends money—Lyman Govr N. Orleans" and so recorded in SJL. Enclosures: (1) Oliver Phelps to Gallatin, Canandaigua, 23 July 1803, recommending Robert Lee of Niagara as customs collector; he is a man of "Integrity & Capacity" who will "discharge the Duties of that Office to the Satisfaction of the Government" (RC in DNA: RG 59, LAR; endorsed by TJ: "Lee Robert to be Collector Niagara"). (2) Michael Baldwin to Gallatin, 18 July (see note to Thomas F. Riddick to TJ, 15 July). (3) George Hunter to TJ, 2 Aug. 1803. Other enclosures not found. Enclosed in TJ to Madison, 18 Aug.

YELLOW FEVER IN THE CITY: on 11 Aug., the New York *Morning Chronicle* reported that in the preceding three days 47 new cases had been documented by the Committee of Health and eight more deaths confirmed. A mass evacuation took place, especially along the waterfront where the fever was concentrated. Over one-third of the population fled, reducing the number of inhabitants to fewer than 40,000. By the time the epidemic had run its course, 1,639 cases had led to 606 deaths, far fewer than the 2,086 lives lost in 1798. Mayor Edward Livingston was among those who contracted the fever (John Duffy, *A History of Public Health in New York City: 1625-1866* [New York, 1968], 110-11; Sidney I. Pomerantz, *New York, An American City, 1783-1803: A Study of Urban Life* [New York, 1938], 346).

LEONARD THE STORE KEEPER: Dearborn recommended William Linnard, of Philadelphia, as military agent for the middle department, on 9 Apr. 1802. He was nominated by the president and confirmed by the Senate later in the month (see Vol. 37:194-5, 325, 349).

With TJ's approval, Gallatin wrote Republican congressman-elect OLIVER PHELPS seeking a recommendation for collector at Niagara. SON OF GENERAL IRVINE: Callender Irvine. Gallatin had informed the president in June that the organization of the DISTRICT OF NIAGARA, approved by Congress in 1799, could no longer be postponed (first letter at Gallatin to TJ, 21 June, and TJ to Gallatin, 22 June).

For the appointment of Robert C. NICHOLAS OF KENTUCKY, see Memorandum to James Madison, 12 July.

PAYMENT OF AMERICAN DEBTS: as one condition for the acquisition of Louisiana, the United States agreed to pay, during the ensuing year, up to $3,750,000 to American citizens for their claims on France. In his October 1803 report to Congress, Gallatin noted that $2,000,000 had been appropriated and was in the Treasury for "defraying the extraordinary expenses incident to the intercourse with foreign nations." For the rest of the settlement, he recommended that the president be authorized to borrow up to $1,750,000 at an interest rate not to exceed six percent (ASP, *Finance*, 2:48-9).

The application of William LYMAN has not been found, but he wrote Gallatin again on 18 Oct. regarding "the object I so fully communicated to you relative to my self." Lyman requested that the Treasury secretary relieve him from "a continued State of suspense" and inform him as soon as "the sentiments & determination of the President" were known (RC in DNA: RG 59, LAR; endorsed by TJ: "Lyman Wm. to mr Gallatin. for office"). For the administration's efforts to find a position for Lyman, see Vol. 38:51, 52n, 169n; Vol. 39:149, 151.

The SALE OF DUNKIRK to France in 1662 infuriated the British public. Charles II found the port expensive to maintain and difficult to defend, but the general public thought it unpatriotic and mercenary to sell Oliver Cromwell's greatest foreign acquisition. British merchants feared it once again would be used as a base for privateering (Ronald Hutton, *Charles the Second: King of England, Scotland, and Ireland* [Oxford, 1989], 184-5; Madison, *Papers, Sec. of State Ser.*, 5:324-5n).

From Albert Gallatin

SIR Treasury Department 11th Augt. 1803

I have the honor to enclose copies of a letter from the collector of Charleston, and of my letters to him & to the Collector of Beaufort respecting the illegal landing of a number of Africans on the island of Beaufort.

The only step which, besides what has been done, could legally be taken on that subject would be to sell one of the three small cutters employed at Wilmington N.C., Charleston, & Savannah and to substitute one of greater force. Whether that measure be immediately necessary is respectfully submitted to your consideration.

I have the honor to be with great respect Sir Your most obedt. Servt.

ALBERT GALLATIN

RC (DLC); at foot of text: "The President of the United States"; endorsed by TJ as received from the Treasury Department on 17 Aug. and "St. Domingo negroes—buy cutter" and so recorded in SJL. Enclosures: (1) James Simons to Gallatin, 21 July, reports on the seizure of the brig *Vinscal* after it landed 149 African slaves on the island of Beaufort; he is taking action against the armed ship *Nile* for the same violation; proper measures will be taken to recover the penalty of $1,000 "for each Negro *imported*" as provided by law; Simons pledges that with the support of a properly armed vessel, he "will clear the Coast, and put a stop to this traffic"; he advises that the situation of the collector at Beaufort is a "delicate one, as no doubt many Purchasers of Negroes there are his immediate connections"; he requests that Gallatin instruct the Beaufort collector to inform Simons "of the arrival of any Vessel in his neighbourhood with slaves"; a proper force will be required "to seize such vessels and slaves," but "one such seizure brought up to Charleston with the Negroes on board—and this traffic will end!"; without a proper armed vessel, however, he will not be able to prevent the traffic or "preserve the Neutrality" of the port; he requests that the "Commandant of the Troops" at Fort Johnston and Fort Moultrie be instructed to aid him "with as many Men as I may deem necessary to make seizure of any Vessels fitting out" as French or English privateers at Charleston. (2) Gallatin to James Simons, 10 Aug., informing the collector that "no extraordinary armed force" was contemplated by Congress to execute the act of 28 Feb. 1803; he will refer Simons's letter to the president at Monticello. (3) Gallatin to Robert G. Guerard, collector at Beaufort, South Carolina, 11 Aug., informing him of the seizure of the brig *Vinscal* after it landed 149 slaves at Beaufort Island; Gallatin questions how such a "daring violation" of state and federal law was "suffered to pass with impunity" and requests information on "the circumstances of the case and particularly of the causes which enabled the Parties concerned to land those men without your knowledge, and without the fact being afterwards noticed in your District"; Gallatin advises, "it is above all important that you should take the most efficacious measures to detect all those who may have been concerned, in order that the penalties may be recovered, and the Africans taken from those who may have them in possession"; Gallatin orders the Beaufort collector to correspond and exchange information on the subject with the collector at Charleston and with the U.S. attorney for the District of South Carolina (Trs in same; U.S. Statutes at Large, 2:205-6). Enclosed in TJ to Madison, 18 Aug.

ILLEGAL LANDING: the act of 28 Feb. 1803 prohibited the importation of slaves into states that had laws against it under penalty of forfeiture and payment of $1,000 "for each and every negro, mulatto, or other person of colour aforesaid, brought or imported." The collectors and other customs officers were charged with enforcing the law (U.S. Statutes at Large, 2:205-6).

To David Jackson, Jr.

Monticello Aug. 11. 03

Th: Jefferson presents his compliments & thanks to mr Jackson for the pamphlet sent him. the [. . .] [with which] he has been [. . .] monarchists and ecclesiastics on the subject of religion he has ever consid[ered] as the most honourable testimony he could expect from them. they [acknowlege] their apprehension that he would be an obstacle to the alliance between [church] & State which some of them avowedly sought & more of them secretly. [pure] religion, unpolluted by political embraces or political passions will [. . .] most, where it is most free, and if it has experienced any benefit from the present order of things it has proceeded from the encouragement which arises from a consciousness that it is free and safe.

PrC (DLC); faint.

PAMPHLET SENT HIM: see David Jackson to TJ, 6 Aug.

To Étienne Lemaire

DEAR SIR — Monticello Aug. 11. 03.

I recieved yours of the 6th. yesterday and am happy to hear of your recovery. mr Barnes had informed me of your illness. I freely consent to the absence you desire for the reestablishment of your health, & have no doubt you will make such arrangements as will keep every thing safe at the President's house during your absence. I shall not be there myself till the 25th. of September, unless any thing should happen unexpectedly to call me there. I sincerely wish you may by the journey recover your health firmly. be assured of my attachment to you, and accept my best wishes for your health & happiness.

TH: JEFFERSON

PrC (MHi); at foot of text: "Mr. Lemaire"; endorsed by TJ in ink on verso.

To Jacob Wagner

SIR Monticello Aug. 11. 03.

On the 29th. ult. I recieved from mr Madison a petition on behalf of Saml. Miller under sentence of death and a pardon ready drawn, which I signed and returned on the 31st. with a request that before it should be used the recommendation of the judges should be obtained. that I recieved yesterday, & now re-inclose to be filed. I take for granted the pardon got to hand and has been delivered. but lest it should have been detained in Orange expecting mr Madison there, I have thought[1] it safe to address this to you directly, to inform you that such a pardon was signed & forwarded and to desire that, if it has miscarried, this present letter may be considered as evidence of it's existence to the marshal to surcease execution until further orders, and that another may be instantly forwarded to me by post for signature. as the time is short and mr Madison may be on the road, I send this to yourself directly, and it would be better you should send the pardon, if necessary, to me directly, as it would lose a post by passing through mr Madison. Accept my salutations & best wishes.

TH: JEFFERSON

PrC (DLC); at foot of text: "Mr. Wagner." Enclosure: Petition of Samuel Miller, with Recommendation of William Kilty and William Cranch, 28 July 1803.

RECIEVED FROM MR MADISON: Madison to TJ, 26 July 1803.

[1] Word interlined.

To John Breckinridge

DEAR SIR Monticello Aug. 12. 03.

The inclosed letter, tho' directed to you, was intended to me also, was left open with a request that, when perused, I would forward it to you. it gives me occasion to write a word to you on the subject of Louisiana, which being a new one, an interchange of sentiment may produce correct ideas before we are to act on them. our information as to the country is very incompleat: we have taken measures to obtain it full as to the settled part which I hope to recieve in time for Congress. the boundaries which I deem not admitting question are the high lands on the Western side of the Missisipi inclosing all it's waters, the Missouri of course, and terminating in the line drawn from the Northwestern point of the lake of the woods to the nearest source of the Mispi, as lately settled between Gr. Britain & us. we have some claims to extend on the seacoast Westwardly to the Rio Norte or Bravo, and better to go Eastwardly to the Rio Perdido, between Mobile & Pensacola, the antient boundary of Louisiana. these claims will be a subject of negociation with Spain, and if, as soon as she is at war, we push them strongly with one hand, holding out a price in the other, we shall certainly obtain the Floridas, and all in good time. in the mean while, without waiting for permission, we shall enter into the exercise of the natural right we have always insisted on with Spain; to wit that of a nation holding the upper part of streams, having a right of innocent passage thro' them to the ocean. we shall prepare her to see us practise on this, & she will not oppose it by force. objections are raising to the Eastward against this vast extent of our boundaries, and propositions are made to exchange Louisiana or a part of it for the Floridas. but, as I have said, we shall get the Floridas without, and I would not give one inch of the waters of the Mispi to any nation, because I see in a light very important to our peace, the exclusive right to it's navigation, & the admission of no nation into it, but as into the Potomak or Delaware, with our consent & under our police. these Federalists see in this acquisition, the formation of a new confederacy embracing all the waters of the Mispi, on both sides of it, and a separation of it's Eastern waters from us. these combinations depend on so many circumstances which we cannot foresee, that I place little reliance on them. we have seldom seen neighborhood produce affection among[1] nations. the reverse is almost the universal truth. besides if it should become the great interest of those nations to separate from this, if their happiness should depend on it so strongly as to induce them to go through that convulsion, why should the Atlantic states dread it? but especially why should we, their present inhabitants, take side in such a question? when I view the Atlantic states, procuring for those on the Eastern waters of the Mispi, friendly instead of hostile neighbors on it's western waters, I do not view it as an Englishman would the procuring future blessings for the French nation with whom he has no relations of blood or affection. the future[2] inhabitants of the Atlantic & Mispi states will be our sons. we leave them in distinct but bordering establishments. we think we see their happiness in their union, & we wish it. events may prove it otherwise; and if they see their interest in separation, why should we take side with our Atlantic rather than our Mispi descendants? it is the elder & the younger son differing. god bless them both, & keep them in union if it be for their good, but separate them if it be better. the inhabited part of Louisiana, from Point coupeé to the sea will of course be immediately a territorial government & soon a state. but above that, the best use we can make of the country for some time will be to give establishments in it to the Indians on the East side of the Mispi in exchange for their present country, and open land offices in the last, & thus make this acquisition the means of filling up the Eastern side instead of drawing off it's population. when we shall be full on this side, we may lay off a range of states on the Western bank from the head to the mouth, & so range after range, advancing compactly as we multiply. This treaty must of course be laid before both houses, because both have important functions to exercise respecting it. they I presume will see their duty to their country in ratifying & paying for it, so as to secure a good which would otherwise probably be never again in their power. but I suppose they must then appeal to *the nation* for an additional article to the constitution, approving & confirming an act which the nation had not previously authorised. the constitution has made no provision for our holding foreign territory, still less for incorporating foreign nations into our union. the Executive in siesing the fugitive occurrence which so much advanced the good of their country, have done an act beyond the constitution. the legislature in[3] casting behind them Metaphysical subtleties, and risking themselves like faithful servants, must ratify & pay for it, and throw themselves on their country for doing for them unauthorised what we know they would have done for themselves had they been in a situation to do it. it is the case of a guardian, investing the money of his ward in purchasing an important adjacent territory; & saying to him when of age, I did this for your good; I pretend to no right to bind you. you may disavow me, and I must get out of the scrape as I can. I thought it my duty to risk myself for you. but we shall not be disavowed by the nation, and their act of indemnity will confirm & not weaken the constitution, by more strongly marking out it's lines.

We have nothing later from Europe than the public papers give. I hope yourself & all the Western members will make a sacred point of being at the first day of the meeting of Congress; for vestra res agitur. Accept my affectionate salutations & assurances of esteem & respect.

TH: JEFFERSON

RC (MiU-C); at foot of first page: "Mr. Brackenridge." PrC (DLC). Enclosure: Thomas Paine to Breckinridge, 2 Aug., described as Enclosure No. 1 at Paine to TJ, 2 Aug.

LATELY SETTLED: see TJ to the Senate, 24 Oct., below.

VESTRA RES AGITUR: "your interests are involved."

[1] TJ here canceled "neighb."
[2] Word interlined.
[3] TJ here canceled "putti."

From William C. C. Claiborne

Dear Sir, Natchez August 12th, 1803.

I have only time by this days mail, to acknowledge the Receipt of your agreeable favors of the 17th and 18th of July, and to add, that I will with all possible dispatch, give you all the Information I can acquire, in relation to the Province of Louisiana.

I pray you Sir, to receive my sincere congratulations on the success of Mr. Monroe's mission;—The Island of Orleans and the extensive Province of Louisiana, are valuable acquisitions;—the tranquility and security of all the Western Country, are now secured to an incalculable distance of time, and the welfare of the United States greatly promoted.

I shall with great pleasure *postpone my Journey to Tennessee*, and will hold myself in readiness, to embark for Orleans, *immediately* on receiving Orders.

To be appointed on the part of my Government, to receive the Island of Orleans, the Province of Louisiana, & the public property, archives &c, I should esteem the highest honor which could be confer'ed upon me, and I know of no[1] mission which would be so grateful to my feelings.—

I do suppose that three Companies from Fort Adams would be amply sufficient to take care of the Fortifications &c.—

With sentiments the most respectful: I have the honor to subscribe myself—Your faithful friend & Mo: Obt Servt.

William C. C. Claiborne

RC (DLC); at foot of text: "The President of the U. States"; endorsed by TJ as received 7 Sep. and so recorded in SJL.

[1] Claiborne here canceled "other."

From Barthélemy Faujas de Saint-Fond

A paris au Muséum National
d'histoire-naturelle
le 12 aoust 1803.

Monsieur le President

Vos recherches su l'éléphant à dents molaires protuberantes, du voisinage de lhoio, ainsi que Celles sur le *megalonix*, m'ont fourni des objets Comparatifs trés instructifs, sur les restes fossiles des mêmes animaux qu'on trouve sur divers points du globe.

J'ai reuni dans un *essai de geologie*, les materiaux les plus importants a Ce sujet, pour servir de Base a une theorie de la terre; j'ose vous prier de vouloir me faire l'honneur d'accepter le premier volume de Cet ouvrage; le second est sous presse, et lorsquil paroitra je serai trés empressé De le faire parvenir a votre adresse. Je vous prie de reçevoir Ce livre, Comme un foible homage de ma Consideration pour votre gout et pour vos Connoissances dans Cette partie philosophique de l'histoire naturelle. C'est dans ces sentimens que je suis Monsieur le president votre trés humble et trés obeissant Serviteur

FAUJAS-ST FOND

EDITORS' TRANSLATION

National Museum of Natural History
Paris, 12 Aug. 1803

MISTER PRESIDENT,

Your research on the elephant with protuberances on its molar teeth in the vicinity of the Ohio River and on the megalonyx gave me very useful comparisons with the fossil remains of these same animals elsewhere on the globe.

In an essay on geology, I have assembled the most important material on this topic to serve as a basis for a theory of the earth. I take the liberty of sending you the first volume of this work. The second is in press, and I will send it as soon as it appears. Please accept this book as a humble sign of my respect for your interest and expertise in the philosophical aspects of natural history. In this spirit I am, Mister President, your very humble and obedient servant.

FAUJAS-ST FOND

RC (DLC); below signature: "l'un des administrateurs du muséum d'histoire naturelle"; endorsed by TJ as received 24 Dec. and so recorded in SJL.

Barthélemy Faujas de Saint-Fond (1741-1819) practiced law until 1778, when he left the legal profession to become an assistant naturalist under Louis Jean Marie Daubenton at the Muséum d'Histoire Naturelle. Beginning in 1793, Faujas was professor of geology at the museum. He served on a commission of scholars in the mid-1790s that seized the holdings of museums in countries that had fallen under French control, including the significant natural history collections of the former stadtholder of the Netherlands. Faujas became interested in the study of fossils and in theories of evolution and extinction. From the specimens sequestered in the Low Countries, he composed a monograph on fossils that had been found in chalk mines at Maastricht. He studied casts of prehistoric bison bones sent to Paris by Charles Willson Peale. TJ and Faujas never met while TJ was in France, but a few weeks after he received the letter printed above, TJ wrote a long reply in which he confided that "altho' my engagements leave me time to read scarcely any thing, yet I could not resist" the volume Faujas had sent. TJ praised Faujas to Peale, Caspar Wistar, James Monroe, and Thomas Mann Randolph, and in a letter to Peale he gave Faujas "first rate eminence in geological things." TJ purchased a copy of the geologist's published account of a trip he had made through England, Scotland, and the Hebrides Islands. Faujas's interpretations of fossil and geological evidence were often at odds with conclusions reached by Georges Cuvier, who had far more skill as an anatomist and scorned Faujas. Recognizing that Faujas's and Cuvier's classifications of large prehistoric quadrupeds such as the megalonyx conflicted, TJ refused to take sides, declaring that all systems of zoological classification were artificial (DSB; Martin J. S. Rudwick, *Bursting the Limits of Time: The Reconstruction of Geohis-*

tory in the Age of Revolution [Chicago, 2005], 69-70, 325, 360-1, 371-3, 383-4, 402-3, 445, 499, 502, 558, 563; Richard W. Burkhardt, Jr., *The Spirit of System: Lamarck and Evolutionary Biology* [Cambridge, Mass., 1977], 33, 117, 129-30, 136-7, 202, 209-10; Robert E. Schofield, "The Science Education of an Enlightened Entrepreneur," *American Studies*, 30 [1989], 32-3; Richard W. Burkhardt, Jr., "The Leopard in the Garden: Life in Close Quarters in the Muséum d'Histoire Naturelle," *Isis*, 98 [2007], 684; TJ to Monroe, 8 Jan. 1804; to Faujas, 31 Jan. 1804; to Wistar, 27 Mch. 1804, 4 Jan. 1805; to Philippe Reibelt, 24 Dec. 1804; to John Vaughan, 15 Aug. 1805; to Peale, 13 Mch. 1808).

LE PREMIER VOLUME DE CET OUVRAGE: for the book he titled *Essai de géologie*, Faujas drew on his 1802 course of lectures at the Muséum d'Histoire Naturelle. He devoted most of the first volume, which was published in Paris in 1803, to descriptions of fossil remains of animals, some of which he compared to living species. He called the mastodon, which did not yet have that name, an elephant with "dents molaires protubérantes," referring to the animal's molar teeth, which had peaks on the chewing surfaces and were different from the teeth of a mammoth or modern elephant. Faujas knew that Peale had assembled a mastodon skeleton in Philadelphia, but the French scientist associated the animal almost exclusively with Big Bone Lick near the Ohio River and cited TJ's *Notes on the State of Virginia* as a source of information. Faujas devoted a chapter of his book to the megatherium of South America and the megalonyx discovered in Virginia, which he considered to be the same animal. He called it "le *Mégalonix*," using TJ's name for the Virginia specimen, and rejected Cuvier's classification, based on the almost complete South American example, of the megatherium as an animal related to sloths, anteaters, and armadillos. Thinking, as TJ had in assessing the megalonyx fossils in 1797, that the animal's large size and strong claws could mean that it was a fierce beast ("ce fort et terrible animal"), Faujas insisted that it could not yet be affiliated with any living species. Without more information, he thought, it must be treated as its own category—"un grand quadrupède *sui generis*, . . . un type original." The first volume of Faujas's *Essai de géologie* was reprinted six years later when the second volume appeared (Barthelémy Faujas de Saint-Fond, *Essai de géologie, ou Mémoires pour servir a l'histoire naturelle du globe*, 2 vols. in 3 [Paris, 1803, 1809], 1:1, 188-93, 257-66, 273-8, 315-28; Sowerby, No. 640; *Notes*, ed. Peden, 43-4; Vol. 29:292-9, 301n; Vol. 38:97n).

Later, Faujas informed TJ that he was delaying the completion of the SECOND volume of the *Essai de géologie* to incorporate information brought back by the Lewis and Clark expedition. The French scientist apparently thought that the expedition's discoveries might yield new information about geological topics of interest to him. When it appeared in 1809, the second volume of the *Essai* dealt exclusively with minerals, volcanoes, and volcanic rock (Faujas de Saint-Fond, *Essai de géologie*, v. 2, pts. 1-2; TJ to Faujas, 31 Jan. 1804; Faujas to TJ, 15 Oct. 1806, 16 Feb. 1807).

From Joseph Fay

SIR New York 12th. August 1803

This will be handed to you by my Father in Law Mr. Broome, with whom I believe you were some time since acquainted in France, he is on his way to pay his respects to the President of the United States, his object is to solicit the appointment of Collector for the Port of New Haven, which has become Vacant by the Death of Mr. Bishop.

My connection with Mr. Broome by the Mariage of his daughter places me in a delicate situation to solicit in his behalf; I am however induced from Public as well as private motives to State a few facts which will no Doubt be leading principles in your mind in making such appointment, Mr. Broomes known[1] Patriotism & uniform fixed Republican Principles have been long established beyond a doubt. The early part which he took in the American Revolution, and the aid which he afforded by liberal Loans made to the Government in Specie to aid their Sinking Credit are well known to all who are acquainted with him. His character stands unimpeached and pure as an honest man, faithful to his trust, and is a regular bred Merchant. he deserves well of his Country! I believe I may Venture to say that he will give the most General satisfaction of any Gentleman whom you can appoint to fill that office, this last however is a fact which ought to be established by the General Consent of the Merchants & Traders who are more immediately to be Concerned in transacting their business in the Port. This document Mr. Broome was advised not to procure, owing to thinking most of them of different Political sentiments with the Present administration. I shall however lose no time in procuring such Testimony of the most respectable Merchants, & other Public characters as will prove satisfactory on this Point, & forward them for your information, unless they refuse to address you in favr. of any one, as I am told they already have.

I hope my Duty and my anxious desire to Serve my friend, which I hope at the Same time is Marked with an equal desire to Serve my Country, will apologise for giving you this Trouble. I am Sir with the highest respect & Esteem your most obedient & Very Humb. Servant.

JOSEPH FAY

RC (DNA: RG 59, LAR); endorsed by TJ as received 31 Aug. and "Broome Saml. to be Collector New haven" and so recorded in SJL. Enclosed in Fay to TJ, 25 Aug. 1803.

Fay had married Samuel Broome's DAUGHTER Betsey in 1793 (Vol. 33:572n).

[1] MS: "know."

From Joseph Fay

DEAR SIR New York 12th. August 1803

Refering you to my letter of this day to be handed you by Mr. Broome, permit me to add my Congratulations on the most important Events of the Nation; the late fortunate Treaty with France in obtaining the complete Cession of Louisiana goes far towards silencing the opposition to the present Administration. Rely upon it my Dear Sir, that you stand on very high Ground in the hearts of the great Mass of the American Citizens, and the hands of Government are Very much strengthened from the general satisfaction resulting from a wise steady and economical Administration, the People feel themselves releived from oppression, & those overbearing & Tyranical acts of the late Government, which appeared actually to aim at a total destruction of equal rights; they feel as tho' the present Rulers were their friends, and the Great Mass of the People would come forward like a solid Collem in Suport of them! Experience has taught the Public to discredit the Callumnies which have been early so industerously propagated, the many predictions of those who really wished the destruction of the present Administration have failed in *toto*. The People are happy! they feel like prisoners released from the worst of Bondage! all Classes are at their ease & Chearfully pursuing their respective concerns. When I say this permit me to Except a *certain few disappointed undeserving ones*, whose only aim appeared to be to agrandize themselves at the expense of the liberties of the happyest & most enlightened People in the Universe! I hope they may only be remembered as Monuments to Warn others against like *perfidy*! I am sorry also to say that the Present Administration like the *Saviour* are not without their *Judases*, I am at the same time very thankful that in like manner (altho receiving the price of their perfidy) they proceede to hang themselves, or in other words they are on the way to the place chosen for their execution, Permit me here to remind you, that much Watching is Necessary to see that this *monster* with *many heads* is effectually destroyed, I am confident that considerable Influence will Arise out of this faction, & some changes will actually become necessary in order to Destroy this growing evil. We find several Public characters disappointing our highest hopes, or see them Constantly supporting men & Measures dangerous to the present Administration. I refer you to Mr. Broome for a more particular detail, it would not be proper for me to say more. I have been induced to make you this communication from Motives of private friendship, & Public Patriotism, which requires the exertions of every friend to Contribute in strengthening the hands of Government. I shall say more at a future time on this subject, & you are at liberty to communicate it to Mr. Madison *in particular*, and to any others whom you may judge it to be of Public benifit.

I have the honor to be Very respectfully & affectionately your friend & Very Humble Servant JOSEPH FAY

RC (DLC); addressed: "His Excellency Thomas Jefferson Esqr Washington"; endorsed by TJ as received 31 Aug. and so recorded in SJL.

From David Gelston

SIR, New York August 12th. 1803.

The enclosed letter was this day handed to me by Capt. Blagge. I observe by the bill of lading, "no freight to be paid by desire of the captain"— I shall direct the chest to be lodged in the Custom House, and the duties, and charges to be paid—and *presuming* it will be your wish to receive it at the City of Washington, I shall ship it in the first Vessel bound from this Port, to Alexandria or Georgetown,

I also received in our public store a few days since from the Scho. Indiana, Capt. Merrell from Natchez, a cask to your address, said to contain nuts, which will be forwarded with the Wine, unless counter orders are received,

I have the honor to be, very respectfully, Sir, your obedient servant,

DAVID GELSTON

RC (MHi); at foot of text: "Thomas Jefferson President U.S."; endorsed by TJ as received 17 Aug. and so recorded in SJL. Enclosure not identified, but see below.

ENCLOSED LETTER: possibly a copy of Stephen Cathalan, Jr., to TJ, 31 May, which Cathalan also enclosed in a letter to James Madison. TJ recorded in SJL receiving the letter the same day as Gelston's note. The CHEST contained 50 bottles of white Hermitage wine (TJ to Gelston, 19 Aug.).

To George Jefferson

DEAR SIR Monticello Aug. 12. 03

Will you be so good as to send me by the first boat 4. bottles of Hamilton's elixir, which is I presume to be bought in Richmond? the cask of oil was found, as you conjectured, in mr Higginbotham's cellar. all the other articles arrived safe & soon after the date of my letter. I am now expecting to arrive with you, for forwarding, 4. cases of wine, some bar iron, & some boxes of window glass & china, all from Philadelphia from different persons, & probably therefore by different conveyances. Accept my affectionate salutations.

TH: JEFFERSON

PrC (MHi); at foot of text: "Mr. George Jefferson"; endorsed by TJ in ink on verso. Recorded in SJL with notation "Ham's elix."

Advertisements for HAMILTON'S ELIXIR touted it as a "sovereign remedy for Colds, obstinate Coughs, Asthmas, Sore Throats, and approaching Consumptions." The medication might have also found purchasers hoping to treat cases of the whooping cough (New York *Morning Chronicle*, 26 May 1803).

For TJ's IRON order, see TJ to Jones & Howell, 15 July. A response of 19 July from the firm, recorded in SJL as received 25 July with the notation "€7-3-15 bar iron = 45.81," has not been found.

To Henry Dearborn

DEAR GENERAL Monticello Aug. 13. 03.

I inclose you a petition from Aaron Goff of Vermont praying the release of his son under age. the fact of infancy being established, the discharge becomes a matter of right. I have the pleasure to inform you that William Clarke accepts with great glee the office of going with Capt Lewis up the Missouri. in the moment of my departure from Washington mrs Madison informed me you had a thought of travelling with your family as far as their house in Orange. in that case I should hope you would be tempted to come thirty miles further to Monticello, where my daughters and myself would be most happy to recieve yourself & family, and to detain you as long as your affairs would permit. you will find us in the hilliest & healthiest country in the world. I would recommend to you to come & return by different routs. the shortest and levellest is by Fairfax court house, Songster's, Brown's, Slate run church, Elk run church & Orange court house. the best country and entertainment, tho' along a hilly road, is by Fairfax C. H. the Red house Prince Wm. C. H. Fauquier C. H. Culpeper C. H. and Orange C. H. the worst, longest, & most uninteresting road is by Fredericksburg. In hopes that this hope will be realised, I tender you my affectionate salutations & assurances of sincere esteem & respect. TH: JEFFERSON

RC (MHi: Dearborn Papers); signature clipped, supplied from PrC; at foot of text: "The Secretary at War." PrC (DLC). Recorded in SJL with notation "Aaron Goff." Enclosure: Aaron Goff to TJ, 22 July 1803 (recorded in SJL as received 8 Aug. from Berlin, Vermont, with notation "W," but not found).

The RED HOUSE tavern was located in Prince William County at the site of the future town of Haymarket (MB, 1:417).

From Albert Gallatin

DEAR SIR New York 13th August 1803

I have this day received your favour of the 8th instt. My knowledge of the duties required from a neutral on the particular point in question is not sufficient to throw any light on the subject. It is important to confer any thing in the shape of an obligation on the first consul; it is much more important to commit no act which may justly be considered as a breach of neutrality; for, from other nations we want justice much more than favours. Whether the granting a passage to Jerome Bonaparte on board one of the frigates of the United States may be fairly considered by Great Britain as a deviation from the rules of conduct imposed upon us by the law & customs of nations is the point on which I cannot form a precise opinion. Upon a first impression, I would rather incline to the belief that it may be so considered. Private vessels may export contraband articles but are liable to seizure & condemnation. Public vessels ought not, in any instance, to do acts which would expose private vessels to just condemnation. Unless that principle be admitted, the right of the belligerent powers to search & send for adjudication public vessels of the neutrals will be insisted on. Subjects of an enemy & a *fortiori* officers & troops of that enemy are considered as contraband. Is not Jerome Bonaparte an officer in the service of the French republic? If he is, may not the act of transporting him from the neutral country to his own be considered as aiding the enemy of Great Britain?

If you shall be of opinion that the act may be fairly justified, I think it should be done though it may not please Great Britain. If you are of a contrary opinion, it should be refused at the risk of displeasing the first consul. If the act is of a doubtful nature, the effect which granting or refusing a passage may have on both nations may become a proper subject of consideration; and of that also I am unable to judge. If the frigates could be dispatched, before a formal application shall be made; it would be much better.

Samuel Bishop the collector of New Haven is dead. Many applications will be made for the office. I think it my duty to state that if Abraham Bishop can be trusted in money matters & if his appointment should not be judged to produce an unfavorable effect in Connecticut, he has a strong claim on the Treasury Department; having, this summer, completed at my request a digest of all our revenue laws which he understands better than any officer of the United States.

I have the honor to be with perfect respect & sincere attachment Your obedt. Servt. ALBERT GALLATIN

RC (DLC); addressed: "Thomas Jefferson President of the United States at Monticello Milton Virginia"; franked; postmarked 15 Aug.; endorsed by TJ as received 22 Aug. and "Jerome Bonaparte Abram Bishop" and so recorded in SJL.

A FORTIORI: that is, "all the more."

Gallatin made arrangements with ABRAHAM BISHOP to have the DIGEST of the revenue laws delivered to him in New York City. Gallatin planned to produce "a compilation of the decisions" made by the Treasury Department in cases arising under the revenue laws (Gallatin, *Papers*, 8:505, 545, 614). For Bishop's understanding of the collection laws and his call to organize them for the sake of clarity, see Vol. 39:260-4.

To Aaron Goff

SIR Monticello Aug. 13. 03.

I have recieved your petition praying for the discharge of your son Jehiel Goff from military service on the ground[1] of his being under age; and have forwarded it to the Secretary at war to have the fact enquired into, and to order a discharge if found true. I think it proper to inform you also, that the discharge in such a case does not rest on the will of the military alone, but that on your application to a judge of the US. he will issue a Habeas Corpus & the fact of infancy will be enquired into under the civil authority, & the discharge be ordered by the same. as this process may be troublesome to you, you need not resort to it, unless in the enquiry ordered by the military officer, he should decide the fact contrary to what you deem proveable; in which case the Habeas Corpus will furnish you relief. Accept my salutations & best wishes. TH: JEFFERSON

PrC (DLC); at foot of text: "Mr Aaron Goff. Berlin, Vermont."

Aaron Goff was among the organizers of the first Congregational church in Berlin, Vermont (Abby Maria Hemenway, ed., *Vermont Historical Gazetteer*, 4 [Montpelier, 1882], 64).

YOUR PETITION: see TJ to Dearborn, 13 Aug. 1803.

[1] TJ here canceled "that."

To James Madison

DEAR SIR Monticello Aug. 13. 03.

I recieved yesterday the inclosed letter & papers from Governor Mercer, requesting my approbation of the relinquishment of a part of their claim to bank stock in England in order to obtain the residue. this it seems is required by an act of the legislature of Maryland, but with what view, or to what end I am unapprised, never having seen the act. it cannot certainly be with a view to raise any claim against the US. as such an act of mine would be entirely extra-official, it could not affect the US. we have lent the agency of our minister hitherto to obtain their right: but on his departure, mr Pinckney seems to come in as the special agent of the state, and neither deriving nor needing authority from us. perhaps you may be apprised of the act of Maryland alluded to, and may be able to inform me what sort of an approbation it is desired I should give. Accept my affectionate salutations

Th: Jefferson

P.S. will you direct a Commission to Jonathan E. Robinson at Bennington as Commr. of bankruptcy for Vermont?

RC (DLC: Madison Papers); at foot of text: "The Secretary of State." PrC (DLC). Recorded in SJL as a letter to the State Department with notation "Maryland bank stock." Enclosures: see John F. Mercer to TJ, 6 Aug. 1803.

For recommendations in favor of JONATHAN E. ROBINSON, see Enclosures Nos. 4 and 5 listed at Madison to TJ, 26 July 1803.

From James Madison

Dear Sir Aug. 13. 1803

My arrival here was delayed till monday evening last; first by the completion of the business depending at Washington, and then by the breaking down of my carriage just after I had set out which detained me three days. I found at the post office your letter covering the pardon for miller, which was forwarded by the ensuing mail, with the intimation to Wagner which you wished. Yesterday I had your favor of the 8th. with the proceedings of the Indiana Territory under another cover. On the subject of the former I am ready to say that if application were to be made for a frigate in behalf of the brother of Jerome Bonaparte, it ought to be at once rejected, tho' in a manner as little disagreeable as possible. There is however no danger of such an application. Just before I left Washington I had a conversation with Pichon which the excerpt of the letter from Dawson led me into, in which I explained to him the inadmissibility of furnishing a passage in a public ship to a military Citizen of the French Republic. He acquiesced fully in the objection, and told me that he had, by a proper explanation to young Bonaparte stifled such an expectation. I hope therefore that we shall hear nothing more of the matter. Among the papers sent for your perusal are a letter from T. Paine, and another from Duane. I shall communicate to the former what he wishes. To the latter I shall also communicate the fact that no remonstrance such as has been reported, has been made by G.B. but on the contrary that she is satisfied with the acquisition of Louisiana by the U-States. I shall at the same time withold the copy of Lord Hawksburys answer to Mr. King, with a glance at the reasons which make it proper to do so. I am sensible of the advantage on the side of the Adversary prints which mortifies him, but general rules must be observed, and it would be moreover improper to make more than one paper the vehicle of informal or formal communications from the government. In Smith's paper, it was intimated that G. Britain was satisfied with our arrangement with France. On the whole the zeal of Duane is laudable, and the manner of his application strengthens the title to tenderness in the refusal.

The day before I left the City I was obliged to write to Thornton a strong complaint agst. Capt. Douglas of the Boston Frigate, founded on an impressment of 4 seamen two of whom had protections & were known to be native Citizens. The trespass was committed on board the Charles Carter abt. 18 leagues at Sea. She had sailed from Norfolk, the resort of the Boston, which had no doubt made her use of that port subservient to her cruises on our own coast agst. our own trade. Pichon is ripening for a formal protest agst a like use of our ports for seizing French vessels the moment they get beyond our jurisdiction.

Be pleased to return the inclosed papers, as I shall await it, before I give answers to such as require them. With most respectful attachment I am Dr. Sir Yrs.

James Madison

RC (DLC); endorsed by TJ as received from the State Department on 15 Aug. and "Miller's pardon—Jerome Bonaparte—T. Paine—Duane impressmt seamen" and so recorded in SJL, but with notation "Douglass" instead of "impressmt seamen." Enclosures: (1) Thomas Paine to Madison, 6 Aug., stating that after he sent his letter to John Breckinridge under cover to TJ (see Paine to TJ, 2 Aug.), he learned that the president has gone to Monticello; a report has since circulated that the British government warned the United States not to make any payments for Louisiana, for Britain intends to take possession of the province; that Great Britain "is insolent and desperate enough to do this I have no doubt," Paine writes, "but as this does not prove the fact I will be obliged to you to tell me, so far as you find yourself at liberty to do it, whether it be true or not. I can without making use of the fact, make some use of the knowledge" (Madison, *Papers*, *Sec. of State Ser.*, 5:284). (2) William Duane to Madison, 3 Aug., asking, "if you judge it proper," for a copy of Lord Hawkesbury's reply to Rufus King about Louisiana; "I feel very often the extreme want of some leading information, upon which I could rely in rebutting the incessant attacks of the papers adverse to the government," Duane notes; if a way could be found to provide Republican newspaper editors with useful information, "the effect on the public mind I am persuaded would be beneficial, and the mortification and uncertainty in which Editors who are attached to the principles of the Government and its administration would be rendered less painful" (same, 271-2). (3) Tobias Lear to Madison, 3 Aug., acknowledging receipt of his instructions and other papers, including letters from the president to the rulers of Algiers, Tunis, and Tripoli (see TJ to Mustafa Baba, Dey of Algiers, 16

July, and to Hammuda Pasha, Bey of Tunis, 19 July; no letter to Yusuf Qaramanli of Tripoli from around that time has been found or was recorded in SJL, but perhaps Lear received a letter of credence in case he needed to negotiate with Tripoli—see Lear to TJ, 14 July); Lear has also received copies of ciphers for his use and an advance of funds (same, 277-8). (4) Perhaps James Simpson to Madison, 3 June from Tangier, reporting the requisitioning of an American merchant brig by the sultan of Morocco (same, 55). (5) Harry Toulmin to Madison, 25 July, offering his services if Madison and the president need someone to travel into Louisiana to collect information about its inhabitants, laws, land titles, Indian tribes, and other subjects (same, 220-2). (6) William Clark of Massachusetts to Madison, undated, enclosing a copy of a 5 Sep. 1801 memorial by 24 people in Boston, Providence, and Philadelphia recommending Clark for the consulship at Amsterdam; he now suggests that he be appointed consul at Emden, which will become an important port for American shipping if Dutch and Hanseatic ports are blockaded (RC in DNA: RG 59, LAR, enclosure endorsed by TJ; Madison, *Papers*, *Sec. of State Ser.*, 2:87; 5:270-1; 7:393). For additional enclosures, see TJ to Madison, 16 Aug.

ARRIVAL HERE: Madison left Washington for Montpelier on 5 Aug. (Madison, *Papers*, *Sec. of State Ser.*, 5:280). MONDAY was the 8th.

LETTER COVERING THE PARDON: TJ to Madison, 31 July. Madison's communication to Jacob Wagner about the Samuel Miller pardon has not been found (Madison, *Papers*, *Sec. of State Ser.*, 5:320).

For the letter from John DAWSON, see TJ to Madison, 8 Aug., Enclosure No. 1.

Madison drafted replies to PAINE and DUANE on 20 Aug. He advised Paine that the report of a British design to take possession of Louisiana was "utterly destitute of foundation" and the British government "has on the contrary expressed its satisfaction with the cession." To Duane, Madison wrote that "I have long been sensible of the advantage taken of official silence, in propagating false reports for party purposes," but circumstances often prevented "a resort to the remedy which would be most effectual, that of publishing the documents relating to the subject." Madison gave Duane permission to declare, without mentioning "the particular authority for the fact," that the British approved of the transfer of Louisiana to American control (Madison, *Papers*, *Sec. of State Ser.*, 5:327-8, 329).

Rufus KING wrote to Lord Hawkesbury on 15 May, informing him of the treaty between France and the United States for the sale of Louisiana. King noted that the treaty did not infringe on British rights to navigation on the Mississippi. Hawkesbury replied on 19 May to convey "the pleasure with which his Majesty has received this intelligence." The attention to Britain's rights testified, Hawkesbury wrote, to a disposition on the part of the Americans "to promote and improve the harmony and good understanding which so happily subsists between the two countries and which are so conducive to their mutual benefit" (Charles R. King, ed., *The Life and Correspondence of Rufus King: Comprising His Letters, Private and Official, His Public Documents and His Speeches*, 6 vols. [New York, 1894-1900], 4:262-3).

STRONG COMPLAINT: Thomas Newton, Jr., wrote to Madison from Norfolk on 30-31 July, enclosing a newspaper report and other information about the stopping of the merchant ship *Charles Carter* off Cape Henry by the British frigate *Boston.* A boarding party removed three seamen and a carpenter, all of whom were reported to be American citizens, from the *Charles Carter*, which had left Norfolk on 23 July. The British returned two of the men to the merchant ship. The *Boston* entered Hampton Roads soon after the incident, and the third detainee escaped from the frigate by swimming to shore. Although Madison did not know it yet, the British released the fourth individual by 6 Aug. The incident was not the first attempted impressment ordered by the frigate's commander, John Erskine DOUGLAS. In April, Louis André Pichon informed Madison of an attempt to seize an Irish mariner from a French merchant vessel, the *Anne*, in Hampton Roads. During that incident, Douglas detained the *Anne*'s captain and supercargo overnight on the *Boston*. Verbally in late May and in writing on 1 June, Madison lodged a complaint with Edward Thornton about the affair involving the *Anne*. In reply, the British chargé d'affaires said that he would collect information about the incident, but he doubted that Douglas acted with anything but "exemplary correctness." Thornton also suggested that the captain of the *Anne*—who was likely an American, he believed, "or of the British dominions"—had probably encouraged seamen to desert from British warships. Such enticement, Thornton alleged, was "the real cause" of the troubles over impressment around Norfolk. On 5 Aug., before he left Washington for Montpelier, Madison wrote to Thornton about the boarding of the *Charles Carter*. He enclosed a copy of a deposition by the man who swam ashore from the *Boston*. It was unfortunate that any provocation should disrupt the "amity & confidence" between the United States and Great Britain, Madison wrote to Thornton, "and it is the more to be regretted as it awakens apprehensions that effectual steps have not been taken by the British government for suppressing a practice which has heretofore been a source of so much just dissatisfaction." He also protested the use of American ports, "under pretexts which are specious," as sources of supplies and intelligence for cruises off the American coast by British warships. Madison enclosed a copy of a State Department circular of April 1795, which declared it to be against the law of nations for a belligerent nation to use American territorial waters for a hostile purpose. "It is sincerely our desire & our interest to live in friendship and free intercourse with G.B.," Madison confided to Newton, "but it is not less her interest & duty to respect our rights" (Madison, *Papers*, *Sec. of State Ser.*, 4:533-4, 540; 5:48, 64-5, 155, 254-5, 280-3, 290; New York *Daily Advertiser*, 8 Aug.; *Newburyport Herald*, 9 Aug.).

To Daniel D'Oyley

SIR Monticello Aug. 14. 1803

Your favor of July 25. found me at this place, where I habitually pass the two months of August & September, to avoid the bilious diseases then prevailing on the tidewaters. I thank you for the pamphlet it covered, and which breathes the genuine sentiments which separated us from Great Britain. I lament that so many of the worthies of your state, who went well with us through the revolution, have fallen back into the principles they then opposed. I am sure nothing has happened since to give them just reason to apprehend that a government elective at short periods in all it's parts is less practicable than it then appeared to them. on the contrary I consider the crisis of 98. 99 which outraged every feeling & principle dear to a republican as proving by the patience with which the peaceable remedy of election was awaited, the safety which short elective periods give to our government. your state teaches another useful lesson, that neither wealth, nor name, nor ancestry can lead an enlightened nation astray; for many there had all these in their favor when, deflecting from the principles of republican government, they were dropped by their country. it is an honourable thing for the body of your country that they were able to surmount the obstacles opposed to them. the wealth of the particular interests which prevail at Charleston, will be able to make newspaper noise but the dispositions of the state assure us it is "vox et preterea nihil." nobody there or elsewhere is deceived or disturbed by it. I hope the late acquisition of Louisiana will secure to us perpetual peace in that quarter where it was most immanently endangered, and that the dispositions which shall be made of that country will be so wise as to consolidate our population on this side the Missisipi instead of drawing it off to the other. I particularly hope it will be made the means of inducing our Indians to cede their country on this side for an equivalent on the other. Accept my salutations & assurances of great respect & esteem. TH: JEFFERSON

PrC (DLC); at foot of text: "Daniel D'Oyley esquire."

THE PAMPHLET: D'Oyley's *An Oration, Delivered in St. Michael's Church*; see D'Oyley to TJ, 25 July.

VOX ET PRETEREA NIHIL: that is, "a voice and nothing more," or, "an empty threat" (see Vol. 36:392n; Vol. 38:639n; Vol. 39:452).

To Edmund J. Lee, Cuthbert Powell, and Archibald McClean

GENTLEMEN Monticello Aug. 14. 1803.

On my arrival here I recieved from the person I had employed for that purpose, copies of the acts respecting the town of Alexandria, which had been selected from my collection of the printed laws. although I have not had time to examine & compare them myself, the correctness of the transcriber on former occasions gives me entire confidence that these are correct. I now inclose them, & beg leave to assure you of my respect & esteem. TH: JEFFERSON

PrC (MHi); at foot of text: "Messrs. Lee, Powell & Mc.lean"; endorsed by TJ in ink on verso. Enclosures not found, but see TJ to Lee, Powell, and McClean, 15 Apr. 1803, for the list of acts to be transcribed.

PERSON I HAD EMPLOYED: on 3 Sep., TJ paid Thomas C. Fletcher $8.33 "for copyg. acts for Alexandria" (MB, 2:1106). A letter from Fletcher to TJ of 18 July 1803, recorded in SJL as received from Charlottesville four days later, has not been found.

To John Page

Dear Sir Monticello Aug. 14. 1803.

Yours of the 2d. inst. has been duly recieved. I have altogether declined my journey to Bedford, and therefore am in no danger of being absent when yourself & family shall render us the kindness of a visit. as all roads appear bad to the traveller, and he is liable to be ill-advised in the choice of them, I take the liberty, on my own knolege of the routes from Richmond here, as well as on the information of others who have travelled them later than I have done, to recommend to you the Threenotched road through the whole way. it is well known by that name. it begins 3. or 4 miles from Richmond, & keeps generally on the main ridge between the waters of James & York rivers. therefore crosses few streams, & offers few hills. your first stage should be at Leek's, 20 miles from Richmond. the only one afterward's at which you can lodge is Price's about 35. miles from Leek's. the next morning you have 22. miles to breakfast here: the last 9. of which are very hilly. when you get opposite to Milton, 3 miles from hence, do not cross the river there, but come on, along the public road, a mile further, and turn into a gate at a place of mine called Shadwell, through which you pass to the river where I have a smith's shop, the persons in which will set you over in a canoe, & guide your carriage through the ford. this will be more agreeable to you than passing through the ford which, tho' safe, is rough. I trouble you with these details to save you trouble on the way, & especially to prevent your being mis-advised to take the circuitous & worse road round by the Louisa springs. the two houses I have recommended, Leek's & Price's are bad enough, but less bad considerably than any others on the road. in hopes of recieving you here in a few days I tender my best respects to mrs Page, and to yourself unalterable friendship.

Th: Jefferson

RC (Profiles in History, Beverly Hills, California, 1999); at foot of text: "Govr. Page." PrC (DLC); endorsed by TJ in ink on verso.

To John Vaughan

Dear Sir Monticello Aug. 14. 03.

I am much obliged to you for the trouble you have taken in procuring a copy of Dr. Priestley's harmony, yet fear at the same time we may have disfurnished him of the one retained for his own use. I expect that mr John Barnes of George town is at this time at Philadelphia at mr Bissel's 19. South 3d. street. if he is he will take charge of the book and bring it with him to Washington. if not there, if well wrapped up, it will come safely to Georgetown by either the stages, or the vessels plying between Philadelphia & that place. my occupations oblige me to be tardy in acknoleging the reciept of letters which will admit of delay without sufferance. hence your's of July 23. remains unacknoleged till now. Accept my friendly salutations and respects.

TH: JEFFERSON

PrC (DLC); at foot of text: "Mr. John Vaughan"; endorsed by TJ in ink on verso.

From James Bankhead

Broad field Westmoreland County.
August 15th. 1803

DEAR SIR—

This opportunity by Mr. Jos. Monroe, enables me to make a request, so early, that no other can have anticipated me in it; which may secure what I request should there be no other considerations—I have presumed, from report and other circumstances, that Mr. James Monroe will continue in Europe as resident Embassador, and should I be correct in the presumption, it is my ardent wish, to be placed with him as Secretary; which office, I request, from a conviction of the many advantages, I shall derive from it; as well as a desire to be with Mr Monroe, and a belief of my abilities to perform its functions—If I have erred in my conjecture, or have been too precipitate in writing to you on this subject; I hope, Sir, you will excuse me, and attribute the error to the great anxiety I have of being in the office requested—May I flatter my-self with the pleasure of hearing from you on this subject?—

I have the honor to be, Dr. Sir, with great esteem and respect yr Obt. Servt.

JAS. BANKHEAD

RC (DNA: RG 59, LAR); endorsed by TJ as received 31 Aug. and "to be Secy. legn to London" and so recorded in SJL. Enclosed in Joseph Jones Monroe to TJ, 26 Aug. 1803.

Nephew of TJ's friend Dr. John Bankhead, James Bankhead (1783-1856), of Westmoreland County, Virginia, read law in Richmond with another relative, James Monroe. In 1804, Bankhead left for Europe, joined Monroe in Spain, and served as secretary of the legation. When Bankhead returned to the U.S. in 1806, Monroe encouraged the president to consider him for a consular position, noting he was "an intelligent worthy young man." Bankhead began a career in the army in 1808, where he was commissioned as a captain in the Fifth Infantry. He served in the adjutant general's department during the War of 1812. He was promoted to major in 1814 and to lieutenant colonel in 1832. In 1838, he was breveted as a colonel for his meritorious service in the Seminole War and in 1847 to brigadier general for his "conspicuous gallantry" at Veracruz during the war with Mexico. He resided in Baltimore as commander of the U.S. Army's Department of the East at Fort McHenry at the time of his death (JEP, 2:99, 483, 503; Lyon G. Tyler, *Encyclopedia of Virginia Biography*, 5 vols. [New York, 1915], 2:201-2; Madison, *Papers, Sec. of State Ser.*, 6:98, 8:132, 402, 9:406; same, *Pres. Ser.*, 5:254; *Alexandria Gazette*, 17 Nov. 1856; Vol. 36:656n; Monroe to TJ, 15, 20 June 1806).

From Madame de Corny

a paris le 15 aoust 1803.

M. Wilks de new yorck s'est charge en fevrier dune lettre pr vous mon cher monsieur, je vous y comptois une lamentable histoire, celle d une chutte affreuse il y aura un an demain et je ne puis encor ni monter ni descendre lescalier ni croiser ma jambe ni me chausser. chacun de ces mouvements me donne une douleur vive. la marche seul gagne chaque jour et aussi la boiterie qui diminue sensiblement mais me lever, m assoir me fait crier. voila bien des details. j'espere que vous les recvrez avec bonte et que je trouverai quelquinteret aupres de votre Coeur. il est inconcevable que mon *angelique* ne vous ait pas vu depuis son arrivée a new yorck. jay bien du malheur pour les lettres, plus de moitie se pert, je me flatte que M. Short men aportera une de vous. Cest pour moi un vrai plaisir davoir a vous lire. Je ne vis plus que par mes Souvenirs, et celuy que jay [Conserver] de vous tient a une amitie solide et que rien ne peut alterer. vous aurez [ri] de pitie en voyant mes Sollicitudes pour la louisiane qui est devenu un objet de gloire; vous [voyant son union] intime avec la france, certe, personne ne pouvoit deviner une si heureuse fin et vous pardonnerez a ma politique de navoir pu atteindre jusqu'a la votre.

navez Vous donc aucun moyen de repos dans lannèe pour aller a montechillo. je voudrois revoir une lettre datee de ce lieu parceque je croirois que vous ête plus a lamitie quau milieu des grandes affaire qui domine vos pensée. ah que pour un homme detat lamitie est peu de chose! je vous en prie que laccident de M. de la fayette pareil au mien ne prenne pas tout votre interet et donnez men une bonne part. Mde monneroe ma aportee une lettre de vous jesperois quelle restoit avec nous. C'est une femme aimable et que jaurois aimee a voir. M. monneroe ma fait annoncer plusieurs fois sa visitte mais je ne lay point vu.

je vous en prie de ne pas trouver ridicule que je vous aye demandé du the. C'est le dejeuner de toute ma vie et dieu [scait] que mes amis damerique ne sont point oublies dans Cette libation—je suis sur que Cette lettre vous sera remise fidellement *par M. de foncin ancien officier tres distingué au Corps royal du genie*. il aime lamerique. nen est arrive que depuis peu et y retourne avec Son fils. je vous conjure quil trouve près de vous protection. il desire etre employer a la louisianne et je vous prie daccorder une attention particuliere a Sa demande. il vous sera facile de recueillir sur luy des temoignages favorables. adieu mon cher monsieur recevez les sentiments les plus affectueux auxquels je jo[ins] lestime la plus Sincere.

parlez moi de vos filles DE CORNY

EDITORS' TRANSLATION

Paris, 15 Aug. 1803

In February, Mr. Wilkes from New York agreed to bring you a letter. In it, I related the sad story of an awful fall. It was a year ago tomorrow, and I still cannot go up or down stairs, cross my legs, or put on shoes. Every one of these movements causes sharp pain. My only progress is in walking, which I can do better each day, with visibly less limping, but getting up and sitting down make me scream in pain. I hope you will look kindly on all these details and feel some warmth in your heart. It is inconceivable that my Angelica has not seen you since her arrival in New York. I have had so many problems with my mail. More than half of it gets lost. I flatter myself that Mr. Short will bring a letter from you. It is a true pleasure to read something from you. I live only through memories, and my memory of you is of a strong friendship that nothing can alter. You would have laughed with pity if you had seen me worrying about Louisiana, which has become an object of glory. Given its intimate connection to France, no one could have imagined such a happy outcome. Forgive me if my politics did not coincide with yours.

Do you have any possibility of resting in Monticello during the year? I would like to see another letter posted from there, since it would mean that you have time for friendship in place of the weighty matters that dominate your thoughts. Alas, friendship is such a small thing for a statesman. I beg you not to turn all your attention to M. de Lafayette's accident, which is just like mine. Save some for me.

Mrs. Monroe brought me a letter from you. I thought she would stay with us. She is a kind person whom I would have liked to see. Several times Mr. Monroe has announced visits, but I have not seen him.

I beg you not to find it silly that I asked you for tea. I have always had tea for breakfast, and God knows that I do not forget my American friends in this libation.

I am sure this letter will be conveyed faithfully by Mr. de Foncin, a very distinguished former officer in the royal corps of engineers. He loves America. He returned only recently from your country and is about to leave again with his son. I beg you to give him your protection. He wishes to find work in Louisiana and I ask you to look favorably on his request. You will have no difficulty gathering favorable references for him.

Goodbye, my dear sir. Accept my most affectionate sentiments to which I add the most sincere esteem.

Tell me about your daughters. DE CORNY

RC (DLC); endorsed by TJ as received 4 Nov. and so recorded in SJL with notation "by Foncin."

EN FEVRIER: see Madame de Corny to TJ, 15 Feb. 1803. MON ANGELIQUE: Angelica Schuyler Church (Vol. 39:527-8).

For her request for some tea (JE VOUS AYE DEMANDÉ DU THE), see the letter of 15 Feb. and TJ to James Monroe, 5 June.

From Pierre Samuel Du Pont de Nemours

MONSIEUR LE PRÉSIDENT, Paris 15 aoust 1803.

Mr. Foncin retourne dans Votre Pays, et je suis très jaloux de son sort.

Il va vous redemander du service; et j'espere que vous lui en accorderez de nouveau, parcequ'il est très bon homme et très bon Officier, dans un genre qui est une Science et qui par conséquent demande à être cultivé pour sa défense propre, chez la Nation même la plus pacifique.

Il a vu nos mœurs nouvelles et il n'a pu s'y accoutumer. Un homme de bon sens et d'un caractere élevé qui a vécu quelque tems dans les Etats Unis, ne peut se déterminer à mourir en aucune partie de l'Europe.

Je vous remercie d'avance des bontés que vous aurez pour lui.

Je vous remercie de celles que vous témoignez à mes Enfans et à moi même. Vous savez combien mon amour pour votre Patrie est accru par les Sentimens de raison, d'humanité, de liberté, de moderation, de sagesse du Philosophe qui la gouverne.

Salut et respect. DU PONT (DE NEMOURS)

EDITORS' TRANSLATION

MISTER PRESIDENT, Paris, 15 Aug. 1803

Mr. Foncin is returning to your country and I envy his lot.

He is going to ask you for a new assignment and I hope you will grant him another one because he is a very good man and a very good officer, in a scientific domain that should be fostered for national defense, even in the most peaceful nation.

He has observed our new ways of life and could not get used to them. A man of good sense and high character who has lived in the United States for some time cannot bring himself to die in any part of Europe.

Thank you in advance for your kindness toward him.

And thank you for your kindness to my children and me. You know how much my love for your country is enhanced by the spirit of reason, humanity, liberty, moderation, and wisdom of the philosopher who governs it.

Greetings and respect. Du Pont (de Nemours)

RC (DLC); at head of text: "A Son Excellence Thomas Jefferson Président des Etats Unis"; endorsed by TJ as received 4 Nov. and "by Foncin" and so recorded in SJL.

From Albert Gallatin

Dear Sir 15th Augt. 1803.

The above was delivered by Mr Broome the brother of him who was the republican Candidate for member of congress for the city last year. He has resided these twenty years in New Haven & its vicinity & is recommended by Mr Osgood.

With respect & attachment Your obedt. Servt.

Albert Gallatin

RC (DLC); endorsed by TJ as received 22 Aug. from the Treasury Department and "Broome Saml. to be collector New-haven v. S. Bishop decd." and so recorded in SJL.

the above: Gallatin's letter was written at the foot of another solicitation to TJ from Samuel Broome for the office of collector at New Haven. Dated New York, 12 Aug. 1803, Broome's brief letter repeats his desire for the appointment formerly held by the late Samuel Bishop and promises to "furnish such documents for your information as I trust will prove satisfactory" (same; entirely in Broome's hand; at head of text: "The President of the United States").

Broome's brother, John Broome of New York City, lost a bid for a seat in Congress in 1802 but received an appointment from TJ as a commissioner of bankruptcy later that same year (Vol. 37:461n, 516, 698, 708).

Samuel osgood was the naval officer at New York City (Vol. 40:346-7, 717-19).

From Abraham Bishop

District & port of Newhaven

Sir: augst. 16: 1803.

On the 7. instant my respected father, the late Collector of this district, deceased, by which event the duties of his office have devolved on me as his deputy.

Sickness in the family, which has terminated the life of my only brother and threatened that of my only child, has delayed for a few days my giving notice of the Vacancy in this district.

I am desirous of being appointed to succeed my father, provided such appointment shall be consistent with the harmony of the district, the interests of the revenue and the united wishes of the republicans in this State, all which would, I presume, be expressed, were I able to apply for them.

Confidence in the wisdom of the present administration persuades me to repose my own best interests & hopes, where the best interests & hopes of my country have found a faithful deposit.

I have the honor to be, with perfect respect Yr. excellencys. obedient Servant

ABM BISHOP

RC (DNA: RG 59, LAR); at head of text: "To the President of the United States"; endorsed by TJ as received 22 Aug. and "to be Collector New haven v. S. Bishop decd." and so recorded in SJL.

Abraham Bishop (1763-1844), eldest son of New Haven collector Samuel and Mehetabel Bassett Bishop, graduated from Yale in 1778, at the age of 15. Seven years later he was admitted to the bar. He spent much of 1787 and 1788 traveling in Europe. Shortly after returning to New Haven, he delivered an address and a lecture critical of the new U.S. Constitution. Bishop believed in the importance of general education for a republican citizenry. He introduced the graded classroom in New Haven and in 1791 moved to Boston, where he taught, delivered lectures, and frequently wrote articles for the new newspaper, the Boston *Argus*, using the pseudonym "John Paul Martin." He advocated female education and more public funding for schools. By 1794, Bishop had returned to New Haven, where he remained the rest of his life. Through his father's influence, he became clerk of the county court in 1795, the probate court in 1796, and the superior court in 1798. The first two positions he held until 1800, the superior court clerkship until 1801. He worked with leading Connecticut Republicans in the fall of 1800 to develop a campaign strategy. An accomplished speaker, Bishop used an invitation to give the annual Phi Beta Kappa Society address to deliver an attack on the Federalist political and religious establishment in Connecticut. The oration, which, at the last moment, he was barred from delivering at Yale, went through seven editions as *Connecticut Republicanism: An Oration, on the Extent and Power of Political Delusion*, and extracts were printed in newspapers from Vermont to North Carolina. In late November 1800, TJ awaited the arrival of the pamphlet in Washington, noting "it is making wonderful progress, and is said to be the best Anti-republican eye-water which has ever yet appeared." When, at the urging of Connecticut Republicans, TJ appointed Samuel Bishop collector at New Haven in 1801, Federalists considered it a reward for his son's campaign efforts. In 1802, TJ awaited the arrival of another Bishop pamphlet. This one, entitled *Proofs of a Conspiracy, Against Christianity, and the Government of the United States; Exhibited in Several Views of the Union of Church and State in New-England*, again attacked the alliance of church and state. After he succeeded his father as collector in 1803, Bishop continued as a political organizer—writing letters, distributing pamphlets, organizing and publicizing Republican festivals. He remained in office until removed by President Andrew Jackson in 1829 (David Waldstreicher and Stephen R. Grossbart, "Abraham Bishop's Vocation; or, the Mediation of Jeffersonian Politics," *Journal of the Early Republic*, 18 [1998], 617-57; Noble E. Cunningham, Jr., *The Jeffersonian Republicans: The Formation of Party Organization, 1789-1801* [Chapel Hill, 1957], 208-10; ANB; DAB; Franklin Bowditch Dexter, "Abraham Bishop, of Connecticut, and his Writings," *Proceedings of the Massachusetts Historical Society*, 2d ser., 19 [1905], 190-9; Vol. 15:485; Vol. 32:263; Vol. 33:590, 627; Vol. 38:310-11).

MY ONLY BROTHER: in early August, newpapers reported the death of John Bishop at New Haven. He was 36 years old (New Haven *Connecticut Journal*, 4 Aug.; *Newburyport Herald*, 12 Aug. 1803).

MY ONLY CHILD: Mary Ann Bishop, daughter from Abraham Bishop's first marriage to Nancy Dexter of Newburyport, Massachusetts, in 1792, which ended in divorce in 1800. By 1803, Bishop was married to Betsey Law of Cheshire, Connecticut, but their first child was not born until 1804 (Donald Lines Jacobus, comp., *Families of Ancient New Haven*, 3 vols. [Baltimore, 1981], 1:204, 209; Dexter, *Yale*, 4:18-19).

To James Madison

DEAR SIR Monticello Aug. 16. 03.

Your favor of the 13th. came to hand yesterday. I now return Paine's Duane's, Lear's, Simpson's & Toulman's letters, and the two protests on impressment by a British and a French armed vessel. I am glad of the latter, as it will serve as a set-off against French complaints on the British trespasses on us. but the former is an afflicting subject. with every disposition to render them all justifiable services, I fear they will put our patience to the proof. their making our ports also stations for cruising from will require regulation. it seems to me that we shall be obliged to have a battery or two in our principal seaports, and to require armed vessels to lie under them, while they are using our ports for repairs or supplies, the only legitimate purposes of entering them. Toulman's application is at least premature. I presume Congress will enlarge the Indian fund and authorise us to send embassies to the Indian tribes of Louisiana, who may at the same time explore the country and ascertain it's geography. those large Western rivers of the Misipi & Missouri whose heads form the contour of the Louisiana territory ought to be known. I think Duane's zeal merits tenderness and satisfaction, while his precipitancy makes him improper to be considered as speaking the sense of the government. with respect to Clarke's application for a consulship at Embden, I am for holding our hand as to new Consular establishments, and letting a great proportion of those existing drop with the first occasion. their number has obliged us to be very little choice in the characters appointed, and I fear they will degrade our national character. Accept my affectionate salutations and assurances of constant esteem & respect. TH: JEFFERSON

P.S. I inclose for your perusal a letter from Cork on the same subject of the impressment of our seamen.

RC (DLC: Madison Papers); at foot of text: "The Secretary of State." PrC (DLC). Enclosures: (1) See Enclosures Nos. 1-6 listed at Madison to TJ, 13 Aug. (2) Reuben Harvey to TJ, 3 June. For other enclosures, see below.

The first of the TWO PROTESTS was a complaint by Louis André Pichon about the British navy's use of ports in the United States; see Madison to TJ, 13 Aug. The other protest may have been from Edward Thornton about ARMED VESSELS outfitted at Philadelphia. Although the arms were nominally for protection against rebels along the coast of Saint-Domingue, Thornton asserted that one of the vessels was "commanded by a Frenchman capable of any abandoned enterprize." Madison refused to order the detention of the vessels, explaining that the ships were not owned by French citizens or intended for illicit purposes (Madison, *Papers*, *Sec. of State Ser.*, 5:158-60, 215-16).

To Robert Smith

Monticello Aug. 16. 03.

Th: Jefferson salutes mr Smith and incloses him a letter from a mr Nichols of Massachusets desiring to be a midshipman, of whom he knows nothing but what is contained in the letter. health & happiness.

PrC (DLC). Enclosure: John H. Nichols to TJ, 8 Aug. 1803 (recorded in SJL as received from Charlestown on 15 Aug. with notation "to be Midshipman," but not found).

To John Breckinridge

DEAR SIR Monticello Aug. 18. 03.

I wrote you on the 12th. inst. on the subject of Louisiana, and the constitutional provision which might be necessary for it. a letter recieved yesterday shews that nothing must be said on that subject which may give a pretext for retracting; but that we should do sub silentio what shall be found necessary. be so good therefore as to consider that part of my letter as confidential. it strengthens the reasons for desiring the presence of every friend to the treaty on the first day of the session. perhaps you can impress this necessity on the Senators of the Western states by private letter. Accept my friendly salutations & assurances of great respect & esteem. TH: JEFFERSON

RC (DLC: Breckinridge Family Papers); addressed: "The honble John Breckenridge Frankfort Kentucky"; franked; postmarked Charlottesville, 19 Aug. PrC (DLC).

LETTER RECIEVED YESTERDAY: Robert R. Livingston to TJ, 2 June (see TJ to Madison, 18 Aug.).

SUB SILENCIO: in silence; see also TJ's letters of this day to Madison and Paine.

From Stephen Cathalan, Jr.

Dear Sir Marseilles the 18th. August 1803

I had the honor of Paying you my Respects on the 31st. May & 12th. July ulto.—I hope the Provisions I sent you, will now soon reach you;—I will not forgett, before next winter & by the first opportunity, of Sending you an other Invoice for what you are still in want of;

I have now the honor of advising you, that at Lenght, I have duly Received my Exequatur, signed by the First Consul, at Brussels on the 3d. Thermidor (22d. July ulto.) as per Copy of the Same, I am remitting to the Secretary of State;—

Your kind Prophecy Vizt. "what cannot be obtained at one moment, may at a more favorable one" has thus been happily accomplished, and it is with the most Sincere Gratitude, that I acknowledge, that I am indebted to you, Sir, for not only the Commission of Commal. agent of the united States, in this District, but even the Granting of my exequatur;

it is now to me, to Continue to deserve the Special Confidence you have Placed in me, by the strict Performance of my Duties, begging you to rely on my best Exertions in the Execution of the Laws of the united States, in order to meet with your approbation, & to the Satisfaction of both Governments, & the Citizens of the united States;

all my Family & I, we beg Leave to reiterate you, the most Sincere assurances of our Best wishes for you & your worthy family; begging the Allmighty, to Grant you, many ensuing Years, in Good health for the wellfare & Prosperity of the United States, under your Fatherly Presidency.

I have the honor to be with the Greatest Respect Dear Sir Your most obedient humble & Devoted Servant

Stephen Cathalan Junr.

Monseigeur. de Cicé Late archbishop of Bordeaux, Garde des Sceaux & member of the Constituante, now archbishop in this south part, charges me to present you his best Respects.[1]

Mr. Peter Khun Junr. Son of Peter Khun of Philada. with whom I was in Correspondance & Transacted affairs in 1792—has passed with his wife Thro' this Place a few Days ago, on his way to Genoa, intending to stablish him Self in Trade;—he appears to me to be prudent & wise;—I have advised him not to venture in large & foolish speculations, as too many have Done, who ended Poorly! but to Confine him Self in the Good managment of the Cargoes that may be Consigned to him from the United States;

Mr. Fredk. Wollaston Consul of the U.S. has lately failed!—in Some Instances he has compromised the Consular Seal "on the Service of the united States" during the Siege of Genoa for his private affairs, & Since, & he would have compromised me had I complied with his desire;

Should you think proper to appoint a Successor to him; & not have any person in view to fulfill that office; I would take the Liberty of Recomending Mr. Peter Khun Junr. after having Procured better informations on his account than any I could Give you;

I Know he has formed an Stablishment at Gibraltar about Two years ago, under the Firm of Khun & Greene; S. CN. JR.

RC (DLC); at foot of first page: "The honorable Thomas Jefferson Esqr. President of the United States"; endorsed by TJ. Dupl (DNA: RG 59, LAR); in a clerk's hand, signed by Cathalan; at head of text: "(Copy)"; with variations in wording not recorded; endorsed by TJ: "Kuhn, Peter to be Consul Genoa. Cathalan's letter." Recorded in SJL as received 21 Nov.

COPY OF THE SAME: Cathalan also wrote to Madison on 18 Aug., enclosing a copy of his exequatur (Madison, *Papers, Sec. of State Ser.*, 5:325).

YOUR KIND PROPHECY: see TJ to Cathalan, 7 Feb. 1803 (Vol. 39:468).

In the summer of 1789, Jérôme Marie Champion de CICÉ and other political moderates sought to establish a constitutional government in France while leaving the monarchy intact. He was at the time the archbishop of Bordeaux. In July of that year, Champion de Cicé invited TJ to meet with a committee of the National Assembly charged with designing a constitution. TJ received the request less than a week after the fall of the Bastille, and, citing the need to finish dispatches for the United States, declined. Not long after, when the king named new ministers of government, Champion de Cicé became GARDE DES SCEAUX, the keeper of the seals. Falling under suspicion in 1792, the prelate left France, lived in Holland and England, then returned to his native country early in 1802 and became archbishop of Aix (*Dictionnaire*, 8:338-9; François Furet and Mona Ozouf, *A Critical Dictionary of the French Revolution*, trans. Arthur Goldhammer [Cambridge, Mass., 1989], 370-5, 819-21; Jean Egret, *La Révolution des notables: Mounier et les monarchiens, 1789* [Paris, 1950], 52, 74, 82-5, 111-13, 130; Vol. 15:291, 298, 333-4).

TJ had already replaced Frederick Hyde WOLLASTON as consul at Genoa; see Cathalan to TJ, 31 May.

[1]Here, at the foot of his page, Cathalan wrote "P.T.O." for "please turn over."

From Daniel Clark

SIR New Orleans 18 August 1803

I had the Honor of receiving this day your Letter of the 17th. July, to which I shall pay the strictest attention, and without waiting till the whole List of Queries proposed can be answered, shall by each successive Post forward such information as it is possible to procure, in obtaining which I rely greatly on the friendly dispositions of the Officers of the Spanish Government. I have by this Post forwarded to the Secretary of State as exact a Manuscript map as could be procured of this Country, on which the different Posts or Settlements are delineated and numbered, and hope to have a more perfect one compleated in time to be of Service. I have joined to it some Memorandums respecting the Country hastily put together long before the news of the Cession reached us, and am happy to have so far anticipated your Wishes in this particular. As I feel myself honored by your application to me I request you will be pleased to accept the assurance that I shall make every possible endeavor to shew myself worthy of your Confidence, and that if I do not succeed in acquitting myself to your Satisfaction it will not proceed from a want of inclination or exertion. Permit me to offer my sincere congratulations on an Event which must forever insure the safety & prosperity of America.

I have the Honor to remain with Sentiments of the greatest Respect Sir Your most obedient & most humble Servt.

DANIEL CLARK

RC (DLC); at foot of text: "Thomas Jefferson President of the U.S."; endorsed by TJ as received 26 Sep. and so recorded in SJL.

In September, Clark sent his answers to most of TJ's QUERIES about Louisiana to the secretary of state (*Terr. Papers*, 9:28-47; Madison, *Papers*, *Sec. of State Ser.*, 5:389-90).

The MANUSCRIPT MAP that Clark sent to Madison has not been found. It was by Barthélemy Lafon, a French-born surveyor and architect in New Orleans. Clark characterized the map as "the most exact ever made of the Western part of this Country." The MEMORANDUMS included figures from a 1785 census of Louisiana, a census "of the districts or Posts of Louisiana & West Florida," an 1803 census of New Orleans, and demographic data and other information from 1799 for Upper Louisiana. Clark also sent a statement of amounts of customs duties received at New Orleans in 1802. In a letter to Madison, Clark observed that the figures indicated a decline in the number of slaves in Louisiana since 1785, despite importations of slaves through 1792. The decrease, Clark noted, "must be principally attributed to the ravages of the small Pox and a want of a proportionate number of females to keep up the Stock" (same, 317-18). On this or another occasion, TJ acquired an undated set of notes by Clark on what the Spanish called the interior provinces of New Spain. Clark listed the provinces and the population of each as: New Leon (Nuevo León), 26,000; New Santander (Nuevo Santander), 38,000; New Biscay (Nueva Viscaya), 157,970; Sonora, 120,080; Coahuila, 40,000; Texas, 21,000, with Clark's notation "(doubtful)"; and New Mexico, 39,797. The first two provinces in the list were "under the immediate orders of the ViceRoy of Mexico," and the other provinces were part of a captaincy general of the interior provinces administered from Chihuahua, which according to Clark's information was located 260 leagues north-northwest of Mexico City. Clark noted the location, extent, and capital of each of the provinces (MS in DLC: TJ Papers, 236:42268; entirely in Clark's hand; endorsed by TJ: "Mexico. Interior provinces. population by D. Clark").

SHEW MYSELF WORTHY OF YOUR CONFIDENCE: although he was responding to a letter from TJ, Clark was unsure "whether there is or not any impropriety in replying directly to our first Magistrate." He sent the letter printed above unsealed to the secretary of state and asked Madison to pass it along to TJ if appropriate (Madison, *Papers, Sec. of State Ser.*, 5:322-3).

To Albert Gallatin

DEAR SIR Monticello Aug. 18. 03.

My last to you was of the 8th. inst. yesterday I recieved your two favors of the 11th. there ought to be no further hesitation with E. Livingston. the importation of negroes from the French islands ought to be vigorously withstood: but I think we should not tread back our steps as to the reduction of the size of our revenue cutters on bare supposition that they will be resisted. when such a fact happens, we may consider whether it is so great an evil to oblige those smugglers to sheer off to other countries as to induce us to enlarge our vessels to bring them in for punishment, accompanied by the very persons we wish to exclude.

I readily coincide with your opinion as to the answer to the Ward committees. besides that you have formed it on a view of the ground & better knolege of the characters, it was one of those measures which I put into shape merely for an ultimate consideration & decision. I have directed commissions for Robert Lee and Irvine. mr Riddick had before applied to me directly to be Register at Mobile, and through mr Baldwin of Ohio. I know nothing of him myself, so that he stands on the single recommendation of mr B. who mentions him only as qualified as an accountant. I think mr Kirby can make a selection on better information, & that it may have a good effect to name that officer from among the inhabitants, as it is the first instance. mr Kirby accepts. you may take as certain that Rob. C. Nicholas will accept. I have heard nothing from mr Williams. Hunter's application may be worth keeping in view. mr Lyman's measure of himself differs so much from ours that it is not likely we shall agree in a result. I hope you will make every possible occasion of getting information from King as to the views & dispositions of England, & of satisfying him of the perfect friendship of this administration to that country. the impressment of our seamen, & the using our harbours as stations to sally out of & cruize on our own commerce as well as on that of our friends, are points on which he can perhaps give useful advice. Accept my affectionate salutations and assurances of great esteem & respect. TH: JEFFERSON

P.S. I return mr Osgood's letter.

RC (NHi: Gallatin Papers); addressed: "Albert Gallatin Secretary of the Treasury now at New York"; franked; postmarked Charlottesville, 19 Aug. PrC (DLC). Recorded in SJL with notation "E. Livingston. French negroes. revenue cutters. ward commees. Lee. Irvine. Riddick. Kirby. R. C. Nicholas. Hunter. Lyman King. impressmts. cruizing from our ports."

Early in TJ's administration, he and Gallatin adopted a policy to reduce the size of REVENUE CUTTERS (see Vol. 34:356-7; Vol. 35:596n).

TJ DIRECTED COMMISSIONS to be issued in his letter to Madison of this date. The commission appointing ROBERT LEE inspector of the revenue at Niagara is dated 24 Aug. (MS in NBuHi).

RIDDICK HAD BEFORE APPLIED TO ME: see Thomas F. Riddick to TJ, 15 July.

Samuel OSGOOD'S LETTER to Gallatin has not been found.

From Albert Gallatin

DEAR SIR New York 18th August 1803

Messrs. Dickson & Jackson do not agree on the proper person to fill the office of Marshal for West Tenessee. A court will be held on the fourth Monday of November, at which time it is desirable that a new Marshal might act, as Mr Hays has given fresh proofs of unfitness by drawing again on me for one thousand dollars more than was due to him. I do not like, on that account, to remit to him the sum necessary to hold the November court having no doubt that he will mis-apply it & that we shall then be obliged to institute a suit against him. We may not therefore wait longer than the end of October to fix on a successor. The letters of the two gentlemen are enclosed.

I do not perceive any objection to making it a condition of the lease of the Wabash salt springs, that at the end of the lease, the new lessee shall be obliged to pay for the buildings as well as for the kettles at a fair valuation.

Mr Lincoln's letter recommending a second mate is enclosed, and if you shall approve a commission may issue: there is not, however, any necessity to decide before the meeting of Congress. If you shall suspend your determination in that case or in that of the Tenessee marshal, I will thank you to return the letters which serve me instead of memoranda not to forget the subject to which they relate.

Mr King seems to think that he might have renewed the commercial treaty on conditions satisfactory to America. Great Britain has not made any approaches of late on that subject; he thinks that the Govt. has not even thought on the limitation by which it will expire and that Mr Merry will have no instructions on the subject. He is of opinion that in the East Indies the want of a treaty will not place us on a worse footing; that there is no danger to be apprehended on the subject of provisions being considered as contraband; and that the improvement in the West India courts of admiralty will relieve us from many of the embarrassments experienced by our trade during last war. The only ground on which he feels any apprehension is that of impressments; and had he not been on the eve of his departure he might, he thinks, have succeeded in making some arrangement: the greatest obstacle to this resulted from the practical prejudices of Earl St Vincent. Mr King considers the present administration in England as the most favorable that has existed or can exist for the interests of the U. States; but he does not rely much on their permanence: the members who compose it are respected as men of integrity, but have not the perfect confidence of the people particularly of London; their abilities being considered as unequal to the present crisis: Mr K. himself speaking of them, whilst conversing of the British manifesto, called them "little men." He asked me who was to be his successor: I answered that I presumed either Mr Livingston or Mr Munroe: he said that Mr L. would do very well, his deafness excepted which was a strong objection. His Brit. majesty asked him twice who would be sent, & expressed his satisfaction in case Mr L was the man; but when he saw Mr Munroe's name announced in the news-papers for that mission, he enquired particularly of his character, & asked Mr King whether he had not been opposed to him in politics. Upon being answered that their differences of politics had only been shades of opinion, & that Mr Munroe was a man of great probity & integrity; "well, well, if he is an honest man, he will do very well" was the reply; and Mr Hammond assured afterwards Mr K. that Mr M. if appointed would be perfectly well received. Yet Mr K. seems to apprehend that there is still some *prevention* which may render his situation less comfortable & his services less useful than those of another person.

On the subject of Louisiana generally Mr King's opinions, both as relates to N. Orleans & the upper country west of the Mississippi, seem to coincide with yours. He hinted, however, that more advantageous terms might have been obtained, & openly said[1] that if our ministers did not think it safe to risk the object by insisting on a reduction of the price, they had it at least in their power to prescribe the mode of payment; that money might have been raised in England on much more advantageous terms if the mode had been left open to us; that Cazenove who was Taillerand's privy counsel & financier must have suggested the species of stock which was adopted &c. He then asked me what could have been the reason which induced our ministers to agree to make an immediate cash payment for the american debts instead of paying them in stock or more convenient instalments, as the creditors would have been perfectly satisfied to be paid that way, and *that* object at least did not seem to be one on which the French Govt. would insist. I told him that I really could not tell; for I knew that mode or some similar one had been contemplated by the administration, & I had not understood that any explanation on that subject had been received from our ministers. On my mentioning that the French cabinet seemed to have believed that the question of peace or war was in their power & that our ministers being naturally under a similar impression might have been induced to yield to more unfavorable terms than if they had contemplated war as certain, he observed that on the arrival of every messenger from France the correspondence of Lord Whitworth & Mr Taillerand had been communicated to him by the British ministry, and that by the return of every messenger he had communicated its substance to Mr Livingston, as well as his opinion of the certainty of war. We both concluded our conversation on that subject by agreeing that Mr Livingston's precipitancy had been prejudical to the United States; and he observed that Floridas must necessarily fall in our hands and that he hoped too much impatience Would not be evinced on that subject.

I repeated to him verbatim the commercial article of the Treaty, expressed my wish that it had been communicated to him when he made his communication to the British Government & asked whether he thought that the article could possibly create any difficulty. He answered without the least hesitation that it could not, that it was perfectly defensible, must be considered as part of the purchase money, and expressed his full conviction that the Brit. govt. would not cavil at it. He observed that Messrs. Liv. & Munroe had in their letter to him used the word "claim" to which, in his letter to Lord Hawkesbury he had substituted the word "right." I was almost tempted to believe from his conversation that Mr L. had communicated the treaty to him.

On the subject of the boundaries of Louisiana he assures me that they have never been settled by any treaty.

The whole of his conversation was, as I expected, in terms perfectly respectful of the general measures you have adopted in relation to foreign nations, the only subject on which we conversed.

After some preliminary apology, he said he thought it his duty to say that we ought to keep Mr Erving's accountability under strict controul. I told him that he had no accounts with the Treasury, but that finding that he was to receive a large sum in July last in repayment of the advances made by the U.S. for prosecuting the claims, I had written to the Secretary of State requesting that he should direct Mr Erving to lodge the money either in Bank or with the Bankers of the U.S. subject to the drafts of the Treasury department. Mr King said that this was the subject he alluded to, as, without meaning to insinuate any thing against the public agent, he thought it was better he should not have the command of so large a sum; (about 40,000 £ St.) that Mr E.'s father was extravagant & had entered into some silly speculations, by one of which he had lately lost several thousand pounds. I have not been informed of the steps, taken by Mr Madison, on that subject, & will thank you to communicate this to him.

Mr King lent me the rescript of the Emperor of Russia offering his mediation. It is too long to be transcribed: although he says in one place "qu'il avoit deja chargé une fois son ministre de communiquer ses sentimens au Gouvernement François sur la necessité qu'il y aurait de faire cesser diverses causes d'inquiétude, qui agitoient les cabinets de l'Europe," I should think, from the whole tenor of that document, that he will not approve the grounds on which England has placed the renewal of the war.

Amongst the twelve & half millions St. new taxes proposed by Mr Adington, I remark that of one per cent on manufactures exported to Europe & of *three* per cent on those exported to the other parts of the world. On a moderate computation this will be a tax on the United States of six hundred thousand dollars a year; for English manufactures, against which no other can enter into competition, are consumed in the U.S. to the amount of 20 millions of dollars. The blockade[2] shutting up of the port of Hamburg will materially affect us until another channel of communication can be opened with the north of Europe; the prices of American & West India produce being low & unsteady in England.

With sincere respect and attachment Your obedt. Servt.

Albert Gallatin

Mr Sanford received his commission last Monday. I have neither seen nor heard from E. Livingston—

RC (DLC); at foot of text: "Thomas Jefferson President of the United States"; endorsed by TJ as received from the Treasury Department on 24 Aug. and "Marshl. W. Tenessee.—salt springs—2d Mate Boston—King's convstn" and so recorded in SJL; also endorsed by TJ: "British exp. duty—." Enclosures not found. Enclosed in TJ to Madison, 24 Aug.

MARSHAL FOR WEST TENESSEE: for Gallatin's efforts to have Robert Hays removed, see Vol. 40:587-8, 589n, 592-3.

For the terms recommended for the LEASE OF THE WABASH SALT SPRINGS, see Vol. 40:593-4.

COMMERCIAL TREATY: only the first ten articles of the Jay Treaty were permanent. Articles 13 through 27, pertaining to the East and West Indies trade, appointment of consuls, contraband, prizes and privateers, extradition, and other subjects, were to expire 12 years after the exchange of ratifications. WEST INDIA COURTS: in a 16 May letter to the secretary of state, King described his conversation with Earl St. Vincent on 13 May, in which the first lord of the admiralty promised that if war broke out and new American prize courts were established in the West Indies, orders on the subject of captures would be drawn up carefully, so as to be "easily and correctly understood" (Miller, *Treaties*, 2:255-64; Madison, *Papers, Sec. of State Ser.*, 5:2, 4n). For King's attempt to obtain an agreement with the first lord of the admiralty on IMPRESSMENTS, see TJ to Madison, 31 July. PRESENT ADMINISTRATION: Henry

Addington resigned as prime minister in 1804 (Charles John Fedorak, *Henry Addington, Prime Minister, 1801-1804* [Akron, Ohio, 2002], 180-203).

Article 7, the COMMERCIAL ARTICLE OF THE TREATY for the cession of Louisiana, guaranteed ships from France and Spain and their colonies admittance into New Orleans and other ports of entry within the ceded territory on the same terms as ships of the United States for 12 years. The article specified that during that time "no other nation Shall have a right to the Same privileges in the Ports of the ceded territory" (Miller, *Treaties*, 2:502-4). For King's LETTER TO LORD HAWKESBURY on 15 May, see note at Madison to TJ, 13 Aug.

I HAD WRITTEN TO THE SECRETARY OF STATE: Gallatin to Madison, 12 Apr. 1803 (Madison, *Papers, Sec. of State Ser.*, 4:509). Gallatin requested that the agent of the U.S. at London be instructed to keep a distinct account of monies received, the balance to be deposited with Francis Baring & Company, the bankers of the U.S. at London, SUBJECT TO THE DRAFTS OF THE TREASURY DEPARTMENT (same). COMMUNICATE THIS TO HIM: see Madison to TJ, 28 Aug., for the secretary of state's response to King's critique of George W. Erving.

QU'IL AVOIT DEJA CHARGÉ UNE FOIS SON MINISTRE: the French passage reads, "that he had once charged his minister with communicating to the French government his opinions on the necessity of ending various causes of concern that agitated the governments of Europe."

On 16 Aug., the *Aurora* and other newspapers carried a report from London dated 14 June detailing the NEW TAXES PROPOSED by the Addington ministry to finance the war with France, including duties on manufactures exported at the rate of "1 per cent to Europe and 3 per cent to the *other parts of the world*" (*Federal Gazette and Baltimore Daily Advertiser*, 16 Aug.).

[1] Preceding two words interlined.

[2] Word interlined above "shutting up."

From Samuel Henley

SIR Marys Ville August 18th 1803

I am inspired by God; Almighty; I am now at Mr William Burks;—in Marys Ville; I am taking a large quantity of Arsneck daily. it is in your power to releve me from my Situation the United States will be all ruined,[1] if they do not desist—from such wicked practices, it is in your power to Order me to the General Government; when that takes place I am ready to obey your Commands. should you Hang me that will close the scan of my unfortunate life. I shall apply to Esquire McGee: for a Horse Saddle and Saddle and Bridle and he will not refuse me if you give him the directions;

I am Sir your Humble, Servt SAM HENLEY

RC (DLC); at foot of text: "To Thomas Jefferson"; endorsed by TJ as received 31 Aug. from "Mary's ville (Tennissee)" with notation "madman" and so recorded in SJL.

William Burk (BURKS) was sheriff of Blount County, Tennessee, from 1800 to 1802 (*History of Tennessee from the Earliest Time to the Present* [Chicago, 1887; repr. Nashville, 1972], 83).

[1] MS: "runied."

To James Madison

DEAR SIR Monticello Aug. 18. 03.

I inclose you two letters from Rob. R. Livingston. that of the 2d of June is just intelligible enough in the uncyphered parts to create anxieties which perhaps the cypher may remove. I communicate them for your information, & shall be glad to recieve them decyphered. I infer that the less we say about constitutional difficulties respecting Louisiana[1] the better, and that what is necessary for surmounting them must be done sub silentio.

I inclose you also a letter from Derieux, which will explain itself. You will probably have recieved a like one. My ideas as to allowance would be between the limits of what was allowed to Dawson (6. D. a day) or the half of that allowance, as Derieux was coming on his own business. but perhaps it is already sufficiently halved, as we pay his coming only & not his going. decide on this yourself and order him what you think proper without delaying him for further consultation. The inclosed letter from Acton to Barnes was sent me by Mazzei. it shews the government of Naples well disposed: but it shews an impropriety also in Barnes in exciting expectations not within our view. he wishes to become diplomatic, and Mazzei has the same longing. I shall cut up the latter.

Will you be so good as to order the following commissions.

Robert Lee at Niagara, New York, to be Collector of the District of Niagara, & Inspector of the revenue for the port of Niagara.

Irvine at Buffalo creek New York to be Surveyor of the port of Buffalo creek and Inspector of the revenue for the same.

I do not know Irvine's Christian name: but it is known at the War office as he is our Indian agent at Buffalo.

Mr. King said to mr Gallatin that the idea of selling Louisiana was, 4 weeks before the treaty, assimilated at Paris with the sale of Dunkirk by Charles the 2d. and that mr Livingston had not at that time the least expectation of success. Accept my affectionate salutations and assurances

of constant esteem. TH: JEFFERSON

RC (DLC: Madison Papers, Rives Collection); at foot of text: "The Secretary of State." PrC (DLC). Enclosures: (1) Robert R. Livingston to TJ, 2 June. (2) Livingston to TJ, 11 June. (3) J. P. P. Derieux to TJ, 9 Aug. (4) Sir John Francis Edward Acton to Joseph Barnes, 17 Jan., described as enclosure to Barnes to TJ, 4 June. (5) Gallatin to TJ, 11 Aug. (both letters; see Madison to TJ, 28 Aug.). Recorded in SJL with notation "R. Livingston. Derieux. Jos. Barnes. Mazzei. commns to Lee & Irvine. King."

In March 1801, the cabinet agreed to pay John DAWSON six dollars a day to take the ratified Convention of 1800 to Paris (Vol. 33:232, 348-9).

For the letter from Philip MAZZEI that TJ probably CUT UP, see note to Barnes to TJ, 4 June.

[1]Preceding two words interlined.

From James Madison

DEAR SIR Aug. 18. 1803

I have duly recd yours of the 13. covering the papers from Govr. Mercer. The act of Maryland is I believe in the Office of State, having been sent thither by the Govr. after his return to Annapolis. The object of it in requiring the sanction of the President to the measures of the Ex. of the State, was I believe, to prevent an interference with national measures, as well as to be a check in general on the local authority. The letter which I have written to Mr. Pinkney pursues the course hitherto taken as well as I recollect it, and will not probably be either applied or be applicable to any improper pretension agst. the U. States. If it appears in the same light to you, you will be pleased to seal &[1] forward to Mr. Wagner the letter enclosing it. With respectful attacht yrs.

JAMES MADISON

RC (DLC); endorsed by TJ as received from the State Department on 22 Aug. and "Maryland bank stock" and so recorded in SJL. Enclosure: Madison to William Pinkney, 18 Aug. 1803, informing him that in pursuance of Governor John F. Mercer's request to the president, Madison encloses Mercer's instructions to Pinkney regarding the Maryland bank stock and states that it is "the desire of the President that the views of the state of Maryland in this case may be persued, as they are explained by its Executive" (Madison, *Papers, Sec. of State Ser.*, 5:322). For other enclosures, see Mercer to TJ, 6 Aug. 1803.

[1]Word and ampersand interlined.

From François Navoni

Cagliari, Sardinia, 18 Aug. 1803. Navoni tells TJ that he has sent him several letters, the last one dated 3 (i.e. 5) June, asking for a commission as consul general of the United States in Sardinia, but has not received any response. He reminds TJ of his long-standing assistance to the U.S. Navy and his numerous activities with the chamber of commerce. He was overjoyed to hear that Commodore Morris recently distinguished himself by capturing the Tripolitan frigate (see Robert Smith to TJ, 28 Aug.). This augurs well for a glorious and just peace with other warring African kingdoms. Navoni reaffirms his desire to keep rendering useful service to American citizens and commercial interests. He provides an update of the maritime situation. English naval ships and English and French privateers are making navigation dangerous and impeding commerce. It is important to establish a lasting peace and that the king of Sardinia stay on his throne or be indemnified for his states. The grain harvest has been terrible this year but Navoni trusts there will be plenty of salt to attract merchant ships. He will gladly continue to offer his services to Morris and other captains from the great American nation. He has excellent relations with U.S. consuls in other Mediterranean ports. Again he begs TJ to advertise his excellent services in American newspapers, specifying that he is ready to supply merchant ships with all the salt they need and to buy sugar, coffee, and other goods from them. Finally, he implores TJ to respond to his many previous requests for authorization as consul general.

RC (DNA: RG 59, CD, Cagliari); at head of text: "François Navoni Honnoré d'Agent des Etats Generaux des Provinçes Unies de L'Amerique dans ce Royaume de Sardaigne A Monsieur Le Premier Presidant des dits Etats Generaux residant a Wasington"; endorsed by TJ as received 18 Dec. and so recorded in SJL; endorsed by Jacob Wagner as received by the State Department 19 Dec.

To Thomas Paine

Dear Sir Monticello Aug. 18. 1803.

On the 10th. inst. I wrote you on the subject of Louisiana, and mentioned the question of a supplement to the constitution on that account. a letter recieved yesterday renders it prudent to say nothing on that subject, but to do sub silentio what shall be found necessary. that part of my letter therefore be so good as to consider as confidential. Accept my friendly salutations & assurances of great esteem & respect. Th: Jefferson

PrC (DLC); at foot of text: "Mr. Thomas Paine."

letter: Robert R. Livingston to TJ, 2 June.

From Felix Pascalis

Sir, Philadelphia. August. 18—1803.

I Venture with diffidence to offer a few observations on the Subject of Louisiana; and I hope that your Excellency will forgive the liberty I take, on accout of the free access with which our fellow-Citizens may be permitted to adress their first Magistrate.

The territory of Louisiana was never well explored during the Successive dominion of the French and of The Spaniards.—Dupratz, in 1774, and Th. Hutchins Geographer of the United States, in 1784 published very imperfect accounts of the population and of the state of Agriculture of that Province.—Long before The Republican

Governement of the Union can be established there, it may be Supposed that the remote Situation of those Colonists from our organised states, their different language and their rare intercourse with us, will make it difficult to introduce among them all our political tenets and the Sense of our national and Common interest, untill our fellow-Citizens shall have found it profitable to Settle among them and to intermix with their families. But to give encouragement to Such adventurers, a Correct statement of the Territorial and commercial resources of Louisiana and dependencies should be procured and from time to time communicated to all our fellow Citizens. it Would be important to Know what sort of inhabitants are found in its most remote districts, their manners and Customs, what is the produce of their Soil, according to the different degrees of temperature; which places are more exposed to the excursion of indians, and what towns or villages are more resorted to by them or by other adventurers. Such early documents could facilitate whatever measures the Executive might adopt for the internal administration of the Country while they would invite many of our Citizens, and direct their enterprizing industry to the formation of that new State, and to the connection of its inhabitants with every part of the Union. On the[1] other hand, as it is probable that the dominion of the blacks in Some of the West india islands, shall ultimately induce their European planters to Seek for more peaceable shores, it may be a sound policy to explore and describe minutely, that region, its climate, its agricultural pursuits, which are so congenial to their habits.

To procure a perfect description of Louisiana, it would require the enterprizing perseverance of men of prudence and of general information. They should be acquainted with all the branches of public Economy, and especially with the comparative results of Commerce and Agriculture. Natural philosophers and tried friends to the Federal governement they might be like political missionaries, capable of influencing a people perhaps corrupt by Loyalty and priesthood. They should be versed in the French and spanish Languages, and what more, but your Excellency must be the best judge!

The ideas of the best men in private life, are sometimes visionary, when weighed by the wisdom of those who are at the helm of Governement. Therefore, without Surprise, I may hear that my views are premature or that they can be provided for or acomplished, by far better means than those I propose. Thus I Would have miserably failed to recommend myself, having but the merit of expressing in my way, the hommage of admiration and respect to the man of the people.

with these Sentiments, I remain Sir, of your Excellency, The most obedt. & humble Servt. FELIX PASCALIS
one of the Members & Secry. of the Board of Health

RC (DNA: RG 59, LAR); at foot of text: "To The President of the United States."; endorsed by TJ as received 24 Aug. and so recorded in SJL.

Born and educated in southern France, Felix Pascalis Ouvrière (1762-1833) spent several years in the West Indies and arrived in Philadelphia in 1793 shortly before the yellow fever outbreak. He investigated and wrote essays and treatises on yellow fever, including *An Account of the Contagious Epidemic Yellow Fever, which Prevailed in Philadelphia in the Summer and Autumn of 1797*, published in Philadelphia in 1798. He excluded contagion as the means of communicating the disease. As vice president of the Chemical Society of Philadelphia, Pascalis delivered the society's annual oration in January 1801. He concluded with praise for fellow member Joseph Priestley. In 1805, Pascalis traveled to southern Spain, Gibraltar, and South Carolina to study the nature of yellow fever. Upon his return, he settled in New York City, where he remained the rest of his life. He worked closely with Dr. Samuel L. Mitchill. Pascalis published numerous letters and articles in the *Medical Repository*, ranging from his findings on yellow fever to "Peach Trees becoming diseased." In 1812, he became co-editor of the journal with Mitchill and Dr. Samuel Akerly. He also published in the *Philadelphia Medical Museum* and the *American Medical and Philosophical Register*. He was active in the New York state and county medical societies, where he served as a corresponding secretary and as a censor for licensing physicians. Following his interest in botany, he founded and served for a time as president of the New York branch of the Linnaean Society of Paris. In 1823, he wrote an influential pamphlet on the dangers of interments in cities (Pascalis, *Annual Oration, Delivered before the Chemical Society of Philadelphia, January 31st. 1801* [Philadelphia, 1802], 47-8; Pascalis, *Statement of the Occurrences during Malignant Yellow Fever, in the City of New-York, in the Summer and Autumnal Months of 1819* [New York, 1819], vi-vii; *Medical Repository*, 3 [1800], 344-51; 4 [1801], 8-17, 121-30; same, new ser., 2 [1816], 394-5; 5 [1820], 113-14; 6 [1821], 372-6; 7 [1822], 6-14; *Philadelphia Medical Museum*, 1 [1805], 158-62, 410-15; 4 [1808], 235-42; 6 [1809], 197-202; William S. Middleton, "Felix Pascalis-Ouvrière and the Yellow Fever Epidemic of 1797," *Bulletin of the History of Medicine*, 38 [1964], 497-515; DAB; New York *Morning Chronicle*, 10 July 1806; New York *Commercial Advertiser*, 13 Oct. 1810, 21 Nov. 1812, 10 June 1825, 15 Feb. 1826, 27 July 1833; New York *National Advocate*, 13 Feb., 20 July 1813, 4 July 1821, 30 Aug. 1823, 4 Sep. 1824; *New-York Columbian*, 7 Feb. 1820; *Albany Gazette*, 2 Mch. 1821; New York *Evening Post*, 23 Jan. 1828; New York *Spectator*, 28 May 1824, 15 Nov. 1831, 1 Aug. 1833; TJ to Samuel L. Mitchill and Felix Pascalis, 17 May 1824).

DUPRATZ: that is, the account of Louisiana by Antoine-Simon Le Page du Pratz (see TJ to Thomas Paine, 10 Aug.). For *An Historical Narrative and Topographical Description of Louisiana, and West-Florida* by Thomas HUTCHINS, see Vol. 6:535-7, Vol. 17:123n, and Vol. 24:285-6.

[1]MS: "ther."

From Robert Smith

Sir, Balto. Aug. 18. 1803

Upon my return to Balt. last Evening I found your favor of the 8th. and hence it is that I have not had the honor of answering it sooner.

The two schooners equipped at this place have sailed some days since. The frigate Philadelphia left the Capes of Delaware on the 27h. of last month. The other frigate the Constitution, according to the information that has been conveyed to me, ought to have sailed about the 8h. Inst. The Brig Siren built at Philada will weigh anchor probably either this day or tomorrow. And I have reason to believe that the Brig Argus, built at Boston, will sail before this letter can reach you. It hence appears that we shall not have a vessel of any kind that can afford to Jerome Bonaparte the proposed passage. And this, independently of other considerations, will be a sufficient answer to the application in his behalf. I am, however, of opinion that, had we a vessel that could accomodate him, government ought not to grant him a passage in her. It being our disposition to observe sincerely the strictest neutrality, we ought not to do any act whatever respecting either of the belligerent powers, which we could not at the same time avow to the other and justify to all the world. By persuing such a straight course open at all times to the view of both nations, we will probably not have to encounter the suspicions of either. And although we ought to avail ourselves of every occasion to conciliate by friendly offices the good-will of both nations; yet these friendly Offices ought not to extend to any act partaking of the quality of military assistance. Consistently with our neutral character we cannot allow our public vessels to be employed in transporting from place to place the military stores or the military men of either Nation. To afford protection by our flag to such men as well as to such stores would be considered as affording military aid. And it would necessarily tend to bring us eventually into collision with the offended party. The gentleman in question is not a private citizen. Neither is he to be considered merely as the brother of the first Consul. He is a Captain in the French Navy, and, it is said, that, to avoid captivity, he has retreated with others to this Country. It being well known in the U States that he is here, the Brittish cannot but know it. And it is presumable that every exertion will be made to intercept him. To screen him then under such circumstances from their vigilance would in their view manifest a disposition unfriendly to them. It would by them be deemed a military assistance and, perhaps, of more moment than the transporting to France of cannon which had been removed from a French Island that was no longer tenable. Were we to undertake thus to transport *one* military person, what principle would ascertain the number beyond which we would not go?

The rooms, which Jerome Bonaparte has engaged here, have been furnished by him as if he intended remaining here some time. This however may be nothing but a cloak.

From present appearances this war will be of the most vindictive & bloody kind. The takeing of Bremen & Hamburg is a great revolution in the Commercial world. And it is evidently the Object of Bonaparte to preclude Great Britain from all beneficial Commercial intercourse with Europe. Such a system will force Great Brittain to observe a Correct conduct towards us. It will be their interest to favor us by all the means in their power. And it is to be hoped that the first Consul will not think of extending to this Country his schemes of Coercion, and will allow us to enjoy in peace all the advantages of our Neutral character.

Be pleased to accept assurances of the respect & Esteem with which I am, Sir, Your Obed. Servt. RT SMITH

RC (DLC); endorsed by TJ as received 24 Aug. and "sailing of vessels.—Jerome Bonaparte" and so recorded in SJL.

TWO SCHOONERS: *Vixen* and *Nautilus* (NDBW, *Register*, 75, 80; Vol. 40:22-3, 498).

In August 1803, several newspapers circulated inaccurate reports from Europe that French troops had taken possession of the independent German cities of BREMEN and HAMBURG as part of their occupation of the electorate of Hanover. Despite French and British interference with their trade, the two cities retained their neutrality (Boston *Columbian Centinel*, 3 Aug. 1803; Boston *Independent Chronicle*, 4 Aug. 1803; New York *Commercial Advertiser*, 13 Aug. 1803; *Federal Gazette and Baltimore Daily Advertiser*, 15, 17 Aug. 1803; *Alexandria Advertiser*, 18 Aug. 1803; John D. Grainger, *The Amiens Truce: Britain and Bonaparte, 1801-1803* [Rochester, N.Y., 2004], 194-5; Madison, *Papers, Sec. of State Ser.*, 5:93, 197-8, 315-16; Vol. 40:480-4).

From Jean Baptiste Ternant

SIR Paris 18th. of Augt. 1803

Permit me to join some of your old friends, in an earnest recomendation of Col: foncin already known to you by his recent services in America.—Considerations relative to the actual State of things in france, and an enlightened partiality to the constitutions of the united States, having induced him to prefer the latter to the former, for his permanent residence, he is now going back, with a view to Settle in the country, and at the same time, offer his services to Government.—Being confident, from my high opinion of his professional abilities, and of his great worth as a gentleman of honor and delicacy, that he may prove a valuable acquisition to the country, I Sincerely wish that you may find it convenient to employ him Suitably to his talent and dispositions.

with heartfelt congratulations on the success of your Louisiana negotiation, and warm wishes for your health, and very paternal administration I remain

sir your respectfull servant TERNANT

RC (MHi); endorsed by TJ as received 4 Nov. "by Foncin" and so recorded in SJL.

From Alexander Wolcott

SIR Middletown 18. Augt. 1803

The Office of Collector of the district of New Having[1] being, by the death of Mr Bishop, now vacant, I take the liberty of expressing my opinion that the appointment of his son Abraham Bishop to the office, would be as gratifying, I believe more so, to the people of this state, than the appointment of any other man.

I am with perfect respect Sir your Obedt. Servt.

RC (DNA: RG 59, LAR); in Alexander Wolcott's hand; at foot of text: "The President of the United States"; endorsed by TJ as received from "Anon." on 24 Aug. and "Bishop Abram to be Collector N. Haven" and so recorded in SJL with a brace connecting it with two other letters received by TJ on this date (see below).

This unsigned letter is in the hand of Alexander Wolcott, a prominent Connecticut Republican whom TJ appointed customs collector at Middletown in July 1801. TJ received this recommendation on 24 Aug., the same day he received two others from New Haven. Gideon Granger wrote on 16 Aug. and Jesse Atwater wrote two days later. Both are now missing. In SJL, TJ connects these two letters along with "Anon. Middletown" by a brace with the notation "Abram Bishop. to be Collector N.H. vice Saml. Bishop." It is not clear why Wolcott did not sign his letter. Earlier in the year he had written a longer one to the president, with an enclosure seeking the removal of the surveyor at Saybrook and the appointment of his brother, George Wolcott, in his place. In 1805, Wolcott wrote TJ a letter similar to the one above recommending Atwater for a judgeship in Michigan Territory. He signed that letter (Vol. 39:581; Vol. 40:85-7; Wolcott to TJ, 21 Nov. 1805).

[1]Thus in MS.

From William C. C. Claiborne

DEAR SIR, Natchez August 19h, 1803.

My friend Doctor Lattimore, having it in contemplation to pass thro' Albermarle, on his way to the Seat of Government, I have taken the liberty to introduce him to your Acquaintance;—You will find the Doctor a well informed, modest man—his political principles are purely republican, and his firmness may be relied upon.—

I will refer you to Doctor Lattimore for the State of Affairs in this quarter;—*he* is well acquainted with the local Interest of the Territory, and can also give you some general Information concerning the Province of Louisiana.—

I pray you to accept my best wishes for your private & public happiness, and believe me to be—

With great Respect, Your faithful friend & Mos. Obd. hbl Sert.

WILLIAM C. C. CLAIBORNE

RC (DLC); at foot of text: "Thomas Jefferson President of the U. States"; endorsed by TJ as received 15 Oct. and so recorded in SJL.

William LATTIMORE was the new delegate to Congress from the Mississippi Territory, serving from 1803 to 1807 and again from 1813 to 1817 (DAB; *Biog. Dir. Cong.*).

From William Dunbar

DEAR SIR Natchez 19th. Augt. 1803

I have the honor of receiving yours of the 17th & 18th. July. I rejoice exceedingly at the confirmation of the highly important intelligence of the Cession of Louisiana. This Event will form a grand Era in the annals of the U.S: After the attainment of Independence, all other incidents recorded in our history dwindle into nothing, in the presense of an object of such magnitude & so highly interesting to the peace and prosperity of the U.S: It would seem that the Fates themselves (to use a figure) must be foiled in any attempt to disturb the tranquility or retard the growing importance of this great Western Continent. I cannot refrain from adding that the brightest page of our history will record the virtues and talents of those Patriots who have achieved an object of such high interest, and which will become so eminently conducive to the agrandisement of their Country.

Before I received your list of queries, I had set on foot an enquiry on the subject of some part of them, chiefly respecting the geography and population of the Province, the result I have not yet received: a great proportion of your queries can be correctly answered only at New Orleans; the patriotism, ardor & talents of Mr. Clark peculiarly fitted for this research, will procure you the most ample and satisfactory information; In the mean time, knowing that Mr. Clark's detail cannot reach natchez in less time than two or three weeks hence, I have consulted my own scanty stores, & now have the pleasure of conveying to you such imperfect information as they afford; on some few points my knowledge may be sufficiently accurate, but upon other objects, I beg that my answers to your queries may be considered only as aproximations subject to correction by the detail you will receive from Mr. Clark.

I suspect that no tollerable map of the Province can be obtained, but I have some materials, which with information expected from New Orleans, will enable me to prepare a Sketch, that may answer the present purpose, because I do not conceive that extreme accuracy is at all essential at this moment. The two Governments of Spain and france had already begun their preparations for running the line of demarkation between the provinces of Louisiana & Texas, the latter belonging to New[1] Mexico; I was applied to by the Spanish Commission to furnish instruments: I shall probably be able to discover upon what principles this line was intended to be run, for I think it highly probable that the limits were defined in the treaty of Cession by Spain to France in as favorable a manner as possible for the latter, & this I presume is the basis of your treaty.

I shall again have the pleasure of writing you as soon as I may obtain any farther information worth communicating.

With the highest respect I remain Your most Obedient Servant

William Dunbar

RC (DNA: RG 59, TP, Orleans); endorsed by TJ as received 16 Sep. and so recorded in SJL. Dft (Lb in Ms-Ar: William Dunbar Papers).

yours of the 17th. & 18th. july: that is, the letter of 17 July with postscript added the next day. See 9 July for TJ's queries on Louisiana.

[1] Dunbar here canceled "Spain."

To David Gelston

Sir

Monticello Aug. 19. 03.

I have duly recieved your favor of the 12th. and thank you for your attention to the wine & nuts, as well as your purpose of forwarding them on to Washington which is exactly what I wish. being a stranger to the ceremonies requisite from the owner on an importation, I shall be ready to comply with all requisite formalities on your being so good as to inform me what they are, as also to have paiment made of duties & all charges on like information of their amount. it is a French wine called Hermitage, cost at Marseilles 4. francs a bottle (50. bottles). no invoice has come to hand. these circumstances may perhaps enable you to ascertain the duties. Accept my friendly and respectful salutations. TH: JEFFERSON

PrC (MHi); at foot of text: "David Gelston esq."; endorsed by TJ in ink on verso.

In his list of wines purchased during his presidency, TJ recorded paying $4.37½ for customs DUTIES on the Hermitage and $4.75 for freight (MB, 2:1116).

To Benjamin Lincoln

SIR Monticello Aug. 19. 03.

Mr. Cathalan of Marseilles has shipped for me by the ship Fair American of Bath, Capt Spear, bound to Boston, 10. packages, cost there 667. francs, and containing olive oil, olives, capers, dried & preserved fruits & nuts. as I could not foresee to what port of America he might find a conveyance, I desired him to address them to the Collector of the customs of whatever port the ship might be coming to. hence they are addressed to yourself. not being acquainted with the formalities required from the owner on an importation, I inclose you the invoice, and shall be ready to conform to any formalities you will be so good as to advise me are necessary, and to remit to you whatever charges & duties shall be due, on being informed of their amount: and I would ask the favor of you to forward the packages by the first vessel going to Washington. the circumstance which has produced this trouble to you will I hope plead it's excuse, and I pray you to accept my friendly & respectful salutations.

TH: JEFFERSON

RC (Pierce W. Gaines, Fairfield, Connecticut, 1965); signature clipped, supplied from PrC; addressed: "Genl. Lincoln Collector of the Customs Boston"; franked; postmarked Charlottesville. PrC (MHi); endorsed by TJ in ink on verso. Enclosure not found but see Vol. 40:458n.

To James Mease

DEAR SIR Monticello Aug. 19. 03.

I have duly recieved your favor of the 9th. and proceed to answer the two enquiries made in it on the subject of the Mould board. the 1st. indeed as to the modifications of the simpler form of mould board, is answered in the passage of the Philos. transactions[1] where they are mentioned. these modifications are there described, & the reasons are stated which render them necessary. as to the 2d. enquiry respecting the casting them in iron, it was my intention when I wrote that paper to have had it done, but on conversing with judge Peters on the subject, he told me he had tried the mould boards of that material & found them so difficult to fix and[2] liable to be broke that he had given them up, & advised me against the attempt.

I have since thought of an alteration in the form of that mould board which would recommend it more to common opinion, and perhaps improve it. in the one described in the Philosophical transactions the toe of the mould board is at a right angle with the bar and is lodged in a duplication of the hinder edge of the wing like a comb-case. but I would propose to make that duplication parallel with the fore-edge of the fin, and 2. or 3. I. back from it. consequently the mould board would be pointed at the toe, instead of being square. to do this, after the pyramidal block is cut out, the fore-right. corner of the block should be sawed off by a line leading from the fore-left corner parallel with[3] the fore-edge of the wing. this being done, the bevil is to be formed by exactly the same process as in the first description. the principle of this is rigorously the same with the first; it is only one of those accomodations of it to different circumstances & views, which practice may produce. it will probably enter & pass on with less resistance. it will at the same time lose a beautiful & [advanta]geous effect which I observed produced by the first form, which,[4] being fl[at in front] like a wedge, the earth of the furrow rising on it kept it steadi[ly in the ground] without any warbling, and without any effort of the ploughman. [it's motion was] as smooth as that of a ship through the water in a steady wind & [smooth surface.] Accept my respectful & friendly salutations.

TH: JEFFERSON

RC (Profiles in History, Beverly Hills, California, 1998); torn, with text in brackets and part of signature supplied from PrC; at foot of text: "Doctr. Maese." PrC (DLC).

PASSAGE OF THE PHILOS. TRANSACTIONS: APS, *Transactions*, 4 (1799), 313-22.

United States district court judge Richard PETERS was a noted agriculturist and practitioner of scientific farming. He was a founder and president of the Philadelphia Society for Promoting Agriculture (DAB; RS, 1:134n).

[1] Preceding four words interlined.
[2] Preceding four words interlined.
[3] Word interlined in place of "to."
[4] Word and comma interlined.

From David Austin

RESPECTED SIR— New Haven Augt. 20th. 1803.

Your very civil method of receiving former communications induces me to address the President once more: not so much in view of a commission to go abrod, as in view of liberty to serve the public at home.—

But before I open exactly my object, I beg leave to interpret to the President my former views by present events.—I foresaw that another convulsion was to arise in Europe unless the tempest was allayed. In view of assuaging the opening tempest, I asked to succeed Mr. King.—The conflagration is begun, & I feel no impelling principle inviting me to advance.—I shall be happy to withdraw from the storm that arrises, & leave the directing of the storm to him, by whose providence it is excited.

A vacancy in the Collector's Office in this place, falling out, by the death of Esqr Bishop; & finding that various applications are likely to be made for the favor of the appointment; the President will have the goodness to excuse the mention of the undersigned, as a name willing to be remembered, when a decision shall be had.

This Office was held by my hond father, with exactness & precision, until his death. Goodrich wrested it from the expectation of my brother, & eventually it became matter of some question.

The grounds on which I would bottom my claim to attention are, that I have been a steady adherent to the principles of the revolution—have served the public as a Volontier on the North-river—took from the Van of the British army the first man that was taken, at their onset upon N. Haven—afterwards resisted the whole body in a single stand, after every other Man had left the Station—and by sea fought, as a Volontier in my passage to Europe, & aided to carry British prisoners into Hollond—Communicating intelligence to Mr Adams, was in London at the Capture of Cornwallis—was soon with Docr. Franklin at Passy, & made my way home, with intelligence & confidence, in the Count di Grass.—

I perceive a great design to be in the wheel of providence; but do not discern that any thing more will be needful for me, than to eye the motion of revolving events, & to give such light to the political or

Moral World as may be needful to illucidate any dark providence which may arise

In view of such a course I propose to hold my station in this my native place: & as I do not find it needful to employ my week days in the concerns of political, or of moral investigation, I should deem it a singular favor to be invested with the employment wh this Commission would give.—

I have mentioned in public, & that at the late session of the General Assembly at Hartford; of the readiness with which you had subscribed to aid the accommodations of religious worship at Washington; & especially of your bounty to me.—They were silent, & ceased to fear lest Religion should receive a deadly blow from Washington.

I take no pains to ask the names of subscribers, in aid of my application; but believe, that there is not a person of consideration in this place, or in the State, uninterested, who would not readily give the little aid his name might afford.—

The matter is submitted to the President's own good judgment: & shall only add, that on the score of *peace among political parties*, perhaps no appointment would be less exceptionable, & more efficacious, than the one now solicited; & this with all defference, the whole matter, with all respect is most humbly submitted; by your very Obliged friend, & Huml: Servt David Austin

RC (DNA: RG 59, LAR); addressed: "His Excellency Ths. Jefferson Esqr. Pres: U: States. Washington, or Monticello"; franked; postmarked 23 Aug.; endorsed by TJ as received 29 Aug. and "to be Collector of New Haven" and so recorded in SJL.

FORMER COMMUNICATIONS: Austin wrote TJ repeatedly during the first year of his presidency, seeking appointments and offering so much unsolicited advice on foreign and domestic affairs that TJ requested that he cease writing to him. His most recent letter to the president was dated 5 May 1802 (Vol. 36:401-2; Vol. 37:417).

YOUR BOUNTY TO ME: in June 1801, TJ contributed $25 to Austin's chapel in Washington, D.C. (MB, 2:1044; Vol. 34:369n).

From Albert Gallatin

Dear Sir New York 20th August 1803

Since writing my last, I have received the enclosed: although I presume that application supported by proper recommendations has been made to you, I send Mr Granger's letter which was not personally delivered on account of sickness in his family.

Great apprehension is entertained at Philadelphia that John Leib the lawyer should be appointed Clay's successor as one of the board of commissioners of bankruptcy. He is represented as destitute of talents & integrity: that I cannot tell; but certainly he is not respectable. As Dallas, Serjeant, & Dickerson are lawyers, I think that a man in the mercantile line should be appointed: none has been mentioned to me; and first rate merchants we have not. If there is no previous promise, I wish the appointment might be delayed till the time of our meeting.

There is nothing new here; the fever still encreases although more than one half of the inhabitants have left the city. I am told that E. Livingston is much irritated, & that he has given notice to the Governor that whenever the epidemic had subsided, he would resign the mayoralty.

With respect & attachment Your obedt. Servt.

ALBERT GALLATIN

A. Bishop has just left me; he has a very sedate appearance, which from what I had heard of his character I did not expect: before he mentioned his name I mistook him for a clergyman.

RC (DLC); at foot of text: "Thomas Jefferson President U.S."; endorsed by TJ as received 29 Aug. and "Abram Bishop.—J. Leib not be Commr. bkrptcy v. Clay. E. Livingston" and so recorded in SJL. Enclosure not identified.

MY LAST: Gallatin to TJ, 18 Aug.
GOVERNOR: George Clinton.

From James Madison

DEAR SIR Aug. 20. 1803

I have recd. yours of the 16th. with the accompanying papers. The communications &c. recd. since my last are enclosed. The letters from Paris are important, but I do not see in them the Wish of the F. Govt. to retract the bargain with our Ministers, so much as an anxiety to secure its execution agst. the intrusions of G.B. and to feel thro' their pulse, whether we were or were likely to be in any understanding with G.B. on the subject. Thornton's letters &c. are in the spirit, tho' beyond the degree to have been anticipated. I should for that reason have given him no opportunity for his very exceptionable remarks on the subject of impressments, had not his interposition been wanted immediately. I presume it will be best to give no answer, notwithstanding the allegations of some facts which might seem to require notice. Clarke's remarks are judicious, but I think he might have assumed the proper course to be pursued, takg care to foster individual expectations as little as possible. The letters from C. Pinkny[1] will require no particular answer, till we hear from Monroe. What is to be said to Graham? Will it not be best to say nothing to him also, till we hear from the same quarter? You will please to decide on the subject of the Gun Carriages. If good ones can be sent from the Navy in time, I think Simpson's advice ought to be followed. Should this be your opinion, Mr Smith will probably expect it to go to him immediately from yourself. Perhaps you may think it proper to inclose Mr. Gallatin the letters from Paris, which refer to arrangements which touch his Dept.

With respectful attachment yrs always JAMES MADISON

What ought to be the decision of Derieux's claim. With an exception of the gratification for which there is no good pretext, and for which he offers very bad ones, his charge is less objectionable in itself, than as it exceeds the idea of Monroe who could best appreciate the proper extent of it.

RC (DLC); endorsement torn; at foot of text: "The President of the U. States"; endorsed by TJ as received from the State Department on 22 Aug. and

"Liv's & Monr's lres.
Thornton's on impressmts.
cruizing from our ports
Clarke's on indemnificn N. Orleans
troops from Rochambeau
Charles Pinckney's.
Thos. Appleton's. Leghorn
George Davis. Tunis
Graham's resignation
Mitchell. Havre. blockade
Simpson's. gun carriages
Thos. Newton. man restd by B[oston]
Derieux' claim"

and so recorded in SJL. Enclosures: (1) Robert R. Livingston and Monroe to Madison, 7 June, reporting their concern that the French government may be dissatisfied with the Louisiana transaction and will seek ways to change the terms; they also enclose a copy of the Baring firm's contract and warn against any delays on the part of the United States in complying with the conditions of the sale; they consider it "incontrovertible" that West Florida must be included in the Louisiana cession; and they report that they have organized a board of commissioners to process American claims against France as specified by the Louisiana treaty (Madison, *Papers*, *Sec. of State Ser.*, 5:66-72; see also Livingston to TJ, 2 June; enclosed in TJ to Gallatin, 23 Aug.). (2) Monroe to Madison, 7 June, enclosing his examination of the question of the bounds of Louisiana (see Livingston to TJ, 26 May); he reiterates "the propriety of an early decision on and complyance with the stipulations in the treaty & conventions"; he is hesitating about whether to go to Spain or wait in France for word from the United States; he also encloses letters exchanged by Rufus King and Lord Hawkesbury in May about the Louisiana purchase (Madison, *Papers*, *Sec. of State Ser.*, 5:72-7; enclosed in TJ to Gallatin, 23 Aug.). (3) Edward Thornton to Madison, 13 Aug., replying to Madison's complaint about the actions of the British frigate *Boston*; he notes that the impressed seamen are no longer being held by the British and believes that in the correspondence between the collector of customs at Norfolk and the British consul there, one can see "on the part of Captain Douglas some willingness to repair any error, in which the notorious frauds practised by pretended American Seamen cannot fail occasionally to lead him"; Thornton regrets that at a time when Britain is entering a war upon which may hinge "the existence of every independent nation," some newspaper editors in the United States "have seized with an avidity and with a malignity perfectly unaccountable the barely plausible ground of complaint, which His Majesty's Commanders have afforded in a very small number of instances," and so he gives his own views on the subject of impressment; a nation has a right, he asserts, to prevent its subjects from being conveyed to an enemy port; also, in times of war every nation "has an unquestioned claim on the assistance of all its members," and neutrals cannot with justice aid the subjects of another country in avoiding their duty; problems arise with British impressment in America because of the "extreme difficulty" of distinguishing "between persons, whose language, manners and usages are absolutely the same"; few people would deny the right of a French naval commander to remove from a neutral ship "bound directly or by contingency to the country of his enemies, *French* artisans, *French* passengers, *French* sailors, who might eventually contribute to the strength of the enemy, or whose services might be usefully employed for his own country"; it is the "prescribed duty" of a commander of a British ship of war "to demand from every foreign vessel any British Seaman whom it may have on board"; he will not detail the "abuses and frauds" he knows to have occurred to prevent the impressment of British subjects, but surely the U.S. government "will see the necessity of adopting some more effectual regulations" or of cooperating with Britain "in some arrangement, which may tend to place the navigation of the two countries upon a more desirable footing in this particular"; responding to Madison's complaint that British ships use American ports as stations for cruises along the coast, he asserts that without a British squadron on the U.S. coast "these seas would swarm with privateers, either furtively equipped in the ports of the United States, or entering and receiving in them refreshment and asylum"; ships of a nation at peace with the United States "have an undoubted right to an hospitable reception in the country" and a right to obtain information to protect their nation's interests; a "very extensive commerce in articles *contraband of war* is at this moment carrying on from the ports of the Union to the ports of the King's enemies"; the U.S. government, "while it does not prohibit, does not defend or justify this commerce, which to say the best of it in the hands of a neutral individual is a debasing and nefarious traffic"; ships of the U.S. squadron engaged in war with a Barbary state have used the harbors of Britain and of other friendly nations in the Mediterranean, have made use of information obtained in those ports, have blockaded an enemy vessel in the port at Gibraltar, and once entered a port on Minorca in search of a Tripolitan corsair; no one should question the right of the United States to take these actions, and Thornton does not believe that the "justice" and "necessity" of those measures "can be at all weakened by increasing in any assigned ratio the power, the ingenuity, or the civilization of the enemy" (Madison, *Papers*, *Sec. of State Ser.*, 5:304-7; see Madison to TJ, 13 Aug.). (4) Thornton to Madison, 13 Aug., enclosing a copy of a letter from Douglas to John Hamilton, the British consul at Norfolk, regarding Douglas's actions in the incident involving the French vessel *Anne* (see Madison to TJ, 13 Aug.); Thornton is certain "that the sentiments of respect" that Douglas "professes to entertain for the government of the United States are equally genuine and sincere"; Thornton cannot deny the "irregularity of sending a boat to examine a foreign vessel lying within the territorial protection of the United States" but asserts that there was no "intention of offering disrespect either to the American or French Government"; the actions were motivated by a misunderstanding about the instructions to British officers and by the practice of maritime nations "of mutually enquiring after and surrendering deserters from each other's service" (Madison, *Papers*, *Sec. of State Ser.*, 5:308). (5) Daniel Clark to Madison, 20 June from New Orleans, regarding instructions from Madison to keep accounts of "payments exacted from our Citizens" during the suspension of the right of deposit; in addition to payments made by Americans to land their cargoes, there were considerable losses due to "the loss of a market & fall in value of our Commodities which the owners were forced to sell while afloat at any Price offered for them"; if compensation is to be sought from the Spanish crown, "it ought to be on a large Scale, say at least half the Value of the Exports of a Year from the whole of our Western Country," to enable the payment of any claim, "without which it would I think be imprudent to awaken Expectation by calling for an account of Losses from Individuals" who have "generally neglected taking the necessary Precautions to substantiate the damages they have sustained"; Clark will "carefully avoid mentioning the circumstance until I hear again from you," but if anyone applies to him to register a claim he will do so (same, 107-8). (6) Clark to Madison, 1 July, informing him that Spanish colonial authorities believe that the French colonial prefect, Pierre Clément Laussat, has requested troops from Saint-Domingue to help him take possession, and that the troops will soon arrive; the Spanish want Clark to inform the U.S. government of the situation and say that they "will do all in their power" to resist the landing of any force that does not have a royal order from Spain for the transfer of possession; the Vicomte de Rochambeau has informed Laussat that although the situation at Saint-Domingue is "critical," he will send support; the Spanish have asked for sloops of war from Havana; there is obvious "jealousy" between French and Spanish officials in Louisiana, which, Clark notes, "I wish we could turn to our own advantage" (same, 133). (7) Charles Pinckney to Madison, 4 May from Madrid, enclosing a copy of a letter he has received from Pedro Cevallos, the Spanish minister of state, reporting that the king "declines selling the Floridas"; the Spanish government also declares that the 1795 treaty does not provide for indemnification of American losses caused by the closure of the deposit at New Orleans; the Spanish now refer to the right of deposit at New Orleans as a favor granted by the crown, which Pinckney believes reinforces the view that the French want American rights on the Mississippi to be in a doubtful state when France takes possession of Louisiana; he encloses copies of two letters he wrote to Livingston and Monroe; he has not heard from Washington since January and is "entirely in the dark" about actions that Congress may have taken recently; "I am happy I obtained the restoration of the Deposit & hope the Order is arrived before this time"; the Spanish quarantine on ships from America has also been lifted (same, 4:571-2). (8) Pinckney to Madison, 12 May; he hopes that Madison has received the copy he sent of the secret article of the Treaty of San Ildefonso for the retrocession of Louisiana from Spain to France; he sent it also to Monroe and Livingston, who had not been able to obtain it from the French; as war in Europe appears imminent, the United States will be in a strong position as a neutral, for the "spirit shewn by our Country, in the business of New Orleans, has had a very good effect in raising the national Character in Europe, & I hope will prevent agression in future"; he has received Madison's letter informing him that the convention for settlement of American claims will be submitted for further negotiation, and he awaits instructions about whether claims for French captures must be included; it has just been reported in Madrid that France and Britain are at war (same, 595-8; Vol. 38:207-8n). (9) Thomas Appleton to Madison, 23 May from Leghorn; he has not been able to have the quarantine on American ships removed; he reports that Leghorn is "the entrepot of distressed seamen" yet the amount of money allowed by the U.S. government for the support of distressed seamen is too low; having learned that Stephen Cathalan, Jr., has been made naval agent for supplying U.S. ships within his consulate, Appleton hopes that he will receive similar powers; France controls much of Italy, and Bonaparte has troops poised to take the ports of Naples; British forces have left Egypt and strengthened Malta; he encloses letters (not identified) for the president (Madison, *Papers*, *Sec. of State Ser.*, 5:25-6). (10) George Davis to Madison from Tunis, perhaps a letter of 8 Mch. reporting that Richard V. Morris left him at Tunis to act temporarily in the consular post following William Eaton's departure (same, 4:405). (11) John Graham to Madison, 7 May from Aranjuez, Spain, stating that he does not believe the Spanish government will indemnify American claims for damages caused by the revocation of the deposit; the Spanish have shown little disposition to be friendly toward the United States, which, he believes, could successfully seize New Orleans by force; if the army is called into service for this purpose, he "should be happy to join it" and asks in any event to be permitted to retire from his present position as secretary to the U.S. legation in Spain (see Vol. 35:190n), "which from various causes, has long been to me an uncomfortable one" (Madison, *Papers*, *Sec. of State Ser.*, 4:578-81). (12) John Mitchell to Madison, 14 June from Le Havre, forwarding dispatches from Livingston and Monroe and reporting that British ships have prevented several neutral vessels, including two from the United States, from entering this harbor; the British boarded two other American vessels and allowed them to pass after examining their papers; he asks for a permanent appointment as commercial agent (same, 5:98). (13) James Simpson to Madison, 8 June from Tangier, urging that the gun carriages be sent to Morocco, for with the renewal of war it will be impossible to procure gun carriages from Europe, and "it would be hazardous to offer Cash" in place of them; he reports a general belief that Morocco will declare war on the Batavian Republic (same, 5:84-5; enclosed in TJ to Robert Smith, 23 Aug.). (14) Thomas Newton, Jr., to Madison, 8 Aug. from Norfolk, reporting that the British had released the fourth man detained by the *Boston* from the *Charles Carter* (Madison, *Papers*, *Sec. of State Ser.*, 5:290). (15) J. P. P. Derieux, account of expenses, not found, received by Jacob Wagner on 17 Aug. (same, 320).

IDEA OF MONROE: Monroe promised Derieux reimbursement for the time he had to wait in Paris for the preparation of the papers he carried, his passage across the Atlantic, and his expenses to reach Washington, but "it will remain with you," Monroe wrote to Madison, to give Derieux "such compensation as you may think just & reasonable." The total, Monroe thought, would not exceed $200 (same, 5, 24).

[1]Name interlined in place of "Madrid."

To Jacob Wagner

Monticello Aug. 20. 03.

Th: Jefferson presents his compliments to mr Wagner and will be obliged to him to have put into the National Intelligencer an advertisement for the purpose of obtaining the information desired in the inclosed letter. he supposes no names need be mentioned but that of Francis Serraire & his father, and that the request may be to give the information to the department of state.

RC (DNA: RG 59, MLR); endorsed by Wagner as received 25 Aug. and "Francois Serriere." PrC (DLC); endorsed by TJ in ink on verso. Recorded in SJL with notation "Serraire." Enclosure: Joseph Barbier to TJ, 12 Mch. 1803.

An ADVERTISEMENT requesting information on the whereabouts of François (Francis) SERRAIRE appeared in the *National Intelligencer* on 26 Aug. 1803 and was reprinted in newspapers throughout the country (Vol. 40:34).

From James Madison

DEAR SIR Aug. 21.

Yours of the 18. with inclosures has been recd. I must write to Wagner for Livingston's Cypher, before I can return the letter from him. I have with me Monroe's Cypher only. The letters sent you by last mail from those Ministers probably contain the information in cyphered passages of the letter in my hands.

The subject of Duane's letter being somewhat delicate & important, under several aspects, I have thought it not amiss that you should see the answer I propose to give it. If you think it a proper one, you will please to seal & send it to the post-office. If you think it ought to be in a different shape, you will be so good as to return it, with suitable suggestions.

The inclosed newspaper contains what is material to a full view of the paper side of the controversy between G.B. & France. Having seen no republication of it in our Gazettes, I have thought it worth sending you. Yrs. respectfully JAMES MADISON

RC (DLC); endorsed by TJ as received from the State Department at Orange on 26 Aug. and "Duane" and so recorded in SJL. Enclosure: Madison to William Duane, 20 Aug. (see note to Madison to TJ, 13 Aug.). For other enclosure, see below.

PAPER SIDE OF THE CONTROVERSY: Madison may have referred to statements and documents issued by the French government during May following the release by the British ministry of a large set of papers to support the declaration of war (*National Intelligencer*, 19, 22 Aug.; Madison, *Papers*, *Sec. of State Ser.*, 5:80, 331n).

From Richard Willson

SIR Washington Augt. 21. 1803

It is with surprise that I observe the friends of Government destitute of a Coffee House or Hotel to assemble at, on Capitol Hill, at a period when the opposite party are supporting the only House with energy & spirit.

I have formed the plan of opening a National Coffee House and Hotel, on the Hill for the entertainment of the Republican friends, and my finances having continued totally deranged since my application for the appointment of Librarian, on the recommendation of Mr. Wright and Mr. Nicholson, added to the misfortune I experienced a few weeks past of losing my little all in a gale of wind. I am impelled to solicit a small loan from your Excellency & Secretarys and such Gentlemen as may be induced by their benevolence to patronise the undertaking. And as the day on which Congress is to convene is so near at hand as to render promptitude in preparation necessary, that circumstance will I hope excuse me for addressing you on the subject, instead of waiting on you personally to obtain your signature and advance. Any loan from 10 to 50 dollars[1] returnable with Interest in 12 months, will be gratefully received.

I have the honor to be, your Excellencys most Obed. & most Hum Servt

RICHARD WILLSON

RC (CSmH); at head of text: "His Excellency Thomas Jefferson"; endorsed by TJ as received 24 Aug. and so recorded in SJL.

DESTITUTE OF A COFFEE HOUSE: the national capital was not without coffee. Republican supporter William Lovell ran a coffee room in his Union Tavern and Washington Hotel on Pennsylvania Avenue, the "first house east of the President's, and one mile from the Capitol." There he catered to "Members of Congress, Travellers, and those gentlemen whose business calls them to the City of Washington." Lovell built the tavern in 1801 and operated it until 1804 (*Alexandria Advertiser*, 31 Jan. 1803; *National Intelligencer*, 14 Feb. 1803; Wilhelmus B. Bryan, "Hotels of Washington Prior to 1814," RCHS, 7 [1904], 82-3).

Willson continued to worry about his FINANCES. In March 1803, Washington newspapers announced his insolvency. Eight months later he posted a notice about his "limited pecuniary resources" and abrogated any responsibility for payment of articles not received or for contracts not executed by him in person or by his written order. Willson made an unsuccessful bid to become LIBRARIAN of Congress in 1802. He eventually found employment as a clerk in the Treasurer's Office under Thomas Tudor Tucker from 1804 until January 1808, for which he received about $1,000 in annual compensation. Even while he held that post and later resigned to pursue a line of business that fell victim to the embargo, he continued to solicit other lucrative government positions (*National Intelligencer*, 25 Mch., 15 Nov. 1803; Madison, *Papers, Sec. of State Ser.*, 6:505; testimonial of Thomas Tudor Tucker, 13 June 1807, in DNA: RG 59, LAR; Willson to Madison, 16 June 1808, in same; Gallatin, *Papers*, 13:651; 15:394; Vol. 35:451; Vol. 36:436).

[1] Willson here canceled "will."

ENCLOSURE

Proposal for a National Coffee House

The Subscriber observing with surprise the want of a House of entertainment on Capitol Hill, for the reception and deliberation of the friends of administration, at a period when the only House is supported by the Minority with energy and Spirit, he proposes opening the National Coffee House & Hotel on Capitol Hill, to be in readiness on the day Congress Shall convene, and being inadequate to meet the expence necessary to be incurred, he is under the necessity of soliciting a small loan from the friends of Government to enable him to effect his purpose with energy and promptitude, and to conduct his business in that style, regularity and elegance hitherto unknown in the City. And he promises and obliges himself to repay the several sums loaned him with Interest, in twelve months from the date here of.

Richard Willson
Washington Augt. 22. 1803

We whose names are here to annexed to agree to lend to Richard Willson the sums opposite our respective names to enable him to Open a National Coffee House & Hotel in the City of Washington, for the purposes beforementioned.[1]

MS (MoSHi: Jefferson Papers); entirely in Willson's hand.

[1] Preceding sentence on separate sheet.

From Samuel Broome

Greenfield Hill Connecticut
Aug. 22d. 1803

Sir

On the death of the late Collector of the district of New Haven, Samuel Bishop Esquire being Announced, my friends there, advised me to apply for An Appointment to fill the Vacancy, in consequence Whereof, I waited on several of my friends in New York Vizt. Samuel Osgood, DeWitt Clinton, John Broome, Daniel Phœnix, Joseph Fay &C. all of whom knowing my standing in New Haven, recommended it to me, to Address your Excellency, on the Subject, assuring me that great deference, would be had to the Signatures of the Merchants in New Haven, which they assured me I might easily Obtain, this I have found correct. perhaps there is no other person, in whom they would so generally, have united in, those few Gentlemen, who did not add their Signatures, expressed their warmest desire, that I might be Appointed, their reason for not Signing, your Excellency, will find in a letter, enclosed from Timothy Phelps Esquire,—I beg leave to mention a few Circumstances, which leads them in my favour. I am a Native of New York, where I carried on a full Trade, in the Wholesale line, for several years, this I pursued advantageously, Until May 1775. When I removed to New Haven, being convinced the British would invest[1] New York, Since that period, I have spent nearly twenty years, in the City of New Haven, which gave the Citizens full knowledge of my Character and conduct through the whole of the American Revolution, and since, I resided five years of the time in Boston, where I made many Valuable acquaintance, and certain I am that when I removed from thence, in the Autumn of 1783, I left every one my friends. If your Excellency could converse, with Messrs Elbridge Gerry, James Bowdoin Samuel Adams, (late Governour) Dr.

Charles Jarvis, Samuel Brown, and many others, in Boston, John Langdon & Woodbury Langdon, of Portsmouth, Genl James Warren of Plymouth, William Varnum and others of Newport Rhode Island, they would all confirm what I write. At the Commencement of the War I loaned the United States fourteen thousand pounds, so early that I had, John Lawrence of Hartford, Loan office keeper for this State, his private receipt four months, before Continental Certificates came to his hands to Issue, Genl. Gray formed an expedition at New Port, Went to Bedford in Massachusetts and burnt that Town, and Shipping, I had Six Vessels consumed, besides Merchandize. When Arnold destroyed New London, I had an House Burnt there which cost me One thousand pounds, seven Vessels, and much Merchandize, which together with other losses, reduced me from Affluence to Mediocrity.

I would not trouble your Excellency, with a recital of these Circumstances, other than to give information, for your Excellencies Government in selecting a successor, from the many applicants which doubtless will be made, your Excellency will have sufficient evidence, given of all the Characters who may apply for the Office, those who have been uniform, Republicans, and who are not, On this ground I should be willing to rest my application. If your Excellency could converse with his Excellency Governor Clinton, Our Ambassador at Paris, and with many other Characters I could mention, they would I am confident all Unite that the Commission would be placed in Proper hands. The Hon'ble Mr Lowndes, has spent three summers in this City, and has favoured me with a line to the Hon'ble Pierce Butler Esqr. and one directed to myself, which I received with satisfaction,

I have seen Mr Gallatin, who informed me that your Excellency would do no public business, before the 25th of the next month, If I thought further evidence would be necessary to Substantiate my Character, I would be at the City of Washington, in person, at that time, If not I should be glad to dispense with the Journey If your Excellency will be pleased to direct a line to be forwarded to me, on this head—it would Oblige

Your Excellencies Most Assured friend and Obedient Servant.

SAMUEL BROOME

RC (DNA: RG 59, LAR); addressed: "His Excellency The President of the United States Washington"; endorsed by TJ as received 29 Aug. and "to be Collector N. Haven" and so recorded in SJL. Enclosures: (1) Timothy Phelps to Broome, New Haven, 20 Aug. 1803, enclosing a reply from the merchants of New Haven to Broome's request for a letter of recommendation; Phelps notes that while support among the merchants for Broome's appointment was strong, many nevertheless refused to sign, "saying they felt themselves so much hurt at the treatment they received on their former application, they were determined, never to address the President again directly or indirectly"; if Broome's candidacy succeeded, Phelps believed "it would be the means of restoring that harmony so much desired by the Citizens of New Haven" (same). (2) Merchants of New Haven to Broome, 18 Aug. 1803, replying to Broome's 17 Aug. letter requesting a recommendation to the president of his appointment as collector; "We would observe," they state, "that we feel reluctant to address the President again, on the subject of a Collector," but add that if Broome were appointed, "we don't believe there is a republican in the State who would give more general satisfaction to the merchants & all Classes of Citizens, or who would discharge the Duties of the Office with more ability & integrity" (same; signed by Jeremiah Atwater, Joseph Drake, and 39 others).

The reluctance of the MERCHANTS OF NEW HAVEN to write the president again on the subject of their port's collector undoubtedly stemmed from their remonstrance of 18 June 1801 protesting the removal of Elizur Goodrich and TJ's controversial reply of 12 July (Vol. 34:381-4, 554-8).

WILLIAM VARNUM: Broome probably means prominent Newport merchant William Vernon, Sr. (Vol. 35:5-6n).

GENL. GRAY: that is, British general Charles Grey, whose troops captured and burned the town of New Bedford in 1778 (DNB).

OUR AMBASSADOR AT PARIS: Robert R. Livingston.

Congressman Thomas LOWNDES was a Federalist from South Carolina (*Biog. Dir. Cong.*).

[1]MS: "invust."

From Nicholas Fitzhugh

DEAR SIR Ravensworth Augt. 22. 1803

Mr John Thompson Mason informed me that on hearing of Mr Marshals intended resignation as assistant Judge of the District of Columbia he had nominated me by a Letter as a proper Successor—presuming it would be agreable to me to live in Alexandria

The difficulties I have experienced in procuring Teachers for my Children render it proper for me to settle in some Town and I know of none where so many Advantages are combined as in Alexandria—there I can not only educate my Children as elsewhere; but from its vicinity to my Farm, I can live cheaper than in a more remote situation—It would be perhaps indelicate & improper in me to hint my Qualifications, I will only observe that I have been in the practice of the Law from the Year 1786 to this time—

With best wishes for your personal Welfare & a prosperous Administration, I have the Honor to be Your Mo obt. Servt.

N FITZHUGH

RC (DNA: RG 59, LAR); endorsed by TJ as received 24 Aug. and "to be judge Columbia v. Marshall" and so recorded in SJL.

Nicholas Fitzhugh (1764-1814), son of Henry and Sarah Battaile Fitzhugh, resided at Ravensworth in Fairfax County, Virginia. He attended the College of William and Mary and became an attorney. He represented Fairfax County in the House of Delegates from 1790 to 1791 and 1800 to 1803. In 1810, he represented Alexandria on the standing committee of the newly organized Columbian Agricultural Society, designed to collect and distribute information for farmers and domestic manufacturers by offering premiums and publishing the journal *Agricultural Museum*. He also became a trustee of Alexandria Academy. Fitzhugh served as assistant judge of the circuit court of the District of Columbia from late 1803 until his death (Donald Jackson and Dorothy Twohig, eds., *The Diaries of George Washington*, 6 vols. [Charlottesville, 1976-79], 6:255; Leonard, *General Assembly*, 179, 183, 219, 223, 227; Miller, *Alexandria Artisans*, 1:7, 76, 140; *Agricultural Museum*, 1 [1810], 172, 174; *Alexandria Gazette*, 31 Dec. 1814; Vol. 35:569n; John Thomson Mason to TJ, 7 July 1803).

NOMINATED ME BY A LETTER: Mason to TJ, 7 July.

From Albert Gallatin

SIR Treasury Department 22d Aug: 1803

Having heretofore transmitted for your consideration several communications respecting certain infractions of the Act of Congress of last session & of the State laws which forbid the importation of Slaves, I now do myself the honor of enclosing a letter from the collector of Charleston & copies of a correspondence between him & the collector of Beaufort on the same subject.

I have the honor to be with great respect Sir Your obedt. Servt.

ALBERT GALLATIN

RC (DLC); at foot of text: "The President of the United States Virginia Milton"; endorsed by TJ as received from the Treasury Department on 29 Aug. and "importn of negroes into Georgia" and so recorded in SJL. Enclosures not found, but on a separate sheet, dated 22 Aug., Gallatin wrote:
"Enclose in the letter to the President of this date copies of
letter of collector of Charleston to the Secretary
letter of collector of Beaufort to the collector of Charleston
Answer of the collector of Charleston" (same).

HERETOFORE TRANSMITTED: see Gallatin to TJ, 11 Aug. (second letter), and enclosures.

To Albert Gallatin

DEAR SIR Monticello Aug. 23. 03.

Your favors of Aug. 13. and 15. were recieved yesterday. the appointment of a successor to Samuel Bishop must await our re-assembling at Washington. I inclose you the late letters of Livingston & Monroe, for consideration, & to be returned to me when perused. you will find that the French government, dissatisfied perhaps with their late bargain with us, will be glad of a pretext to declare it void. it will be necessary therefore that we execute it with punctuality & without delay. I have desired the Secretary of the Navy so to make his arrangements as that an armed vessel shall be ready to sail on the 31st. of October with the ratification & if possible, with the stock, to France. if the latter can be got through both houses in that time, it will be desireable. would it not be well that you should have a bill ready drawn to be offered on the 1st. or 2d. day of the session? it will be well to say as little as possible on the Constitutional difficulty & that Congress should act on it without talking. I subjoin what I think a better form of amendment than the one I communicated to you before. I have been, with the aid of my books here, investigating the question of the boundaries of Louisiana, & am satisfied our claim to the Perdido is solid, and to the bay of St. Bernard very argumentative. I observe that Monroe & Livingston are clear in our right to the Perdido. how would it do to annex all Louisiana East of the Misipi to the Misipi territory, & all West of that river below the mouth of Arcansa, establish into a separate territorial govmt? Accept my affectionate salutations and assurances of esteem & respect.

TH: JEFFERSON

'Louisiana, as ceded by France to the US. is made a part of the US. it's white inhabitants shall be citizens, and stand, as to their rights & obligations on the same footing with other citizens of the US. in analogous situations.

Save only that as to the portion thereof lying North of the latitude of the mouth of Arcansa river no new state shall be established, nor any grants of land made therein, other than to Indians in exchange for equivalent portions of lands occupied by them, [until an amendment of the Constitution shall be made for these purposes.]

Florida also, whensoever it may be rightfully obtained, shall become a part of the US. it's white inhabitants shall thereupon be citizens, and shall stand, as to their rights & obligations, on the same footing with other citizens of the US. in analogous situations.'

RC (NHi: Gallatin Papers); closing square bracket supplied by Editors; at foot of text: "The Secretary of the Treasury"; endorsed. PrC (DLC). Recorded in SJL with notation "Abram Bishop. Liv's & Monroe's lres. treaty with France. stock. amdmt constn. Louisiana." Enclosures: (1) Robert R. Livingston and James Monroe to Madison, 7 June (see Madison to TJ, 20 Aug. 1803, Enclosure No. 1). (2) Monroe to Madison, 7 June, and enclosure (see same, Enclosure No. 2).

For ARRANGEMENTS to ready a ship, see TJ to Robert Smith of this date.

ONE I COMMUNICATED TO YOU BEFORE: see Constitutional Amendment on Louisiana at 9 July.

To Robert Smith

Dear Sir Monticello Aug. 23. 1803.

I inclose you a letter from mr Simpson to mr Madison shewing very clearly that our plan of having the gun carriages for the Emperor of Marocco made in Europe, cannot take place. to cut short all further delay on this subject, I think we must furnish them from hence. you observe they must be of the very best & fitted for land service. if we have such, really good, tho' wanting for our own service, it will be better to send them, and immediately replace them here by new ones. otherwise they should be made and sent without delay. I think it had been agreed that you would see to the execution of this business.

There is reason to apprehend that the government of France, perhaps not well satisfied with it's late bargain with us, will sieze any pretext which can be laid hold of, to annul the treaty. they have exacted from our ministers a rigorous regard to dates, which will render it necessary for both houses of Congress to perform their respective parts, without a day's delay, & with as little debate as possible: and that we have a public armed ship ready to sail on the 31st. day of October to carry the ratification, & if possible the stock to France. perhaps the last of your small vessels which shall go to the Mediterranean this season, may perform this office. but whether this or any other will be best, you will be so good as to consider & to be in readiness. it is best that as little as possible be said as to the Constitutional difficulty; and that on that Congress do [what] is necessary without any explanation. an investigation of the subject here, among my books, satisfies me that our right to the river Perdido is solid, and to the bay of St. Bernard very susceptible of being insisted on. Livingston & Monroe express a clear opinion as to the Perdido, & advise us to act on it. Accept my affectionate salutations and assurances of great esteem & respect. Th: Jefferson

P.S. when you shall have read Simpson's letter be so good as to return it to me with your conclusion as to the carriages.

PrC (DLC); faint. Recorded in SJL as a letter to the Navy Department with notation "gun-carriages for Marocco. armd vessel for France. Simpson's lre." Enclosure: James Simpson to James Madison, 8 June 1803 (see Madison to TJ, 20 Aug. 1803, Enclosure No. 13).

From Samuel Smith

Sir/ Ballston Springs 23d. Aug. 1803

During the late War between England & France—England levied a Convoy Duty of $\frac{1}{2}$ ℔C: on Goods exported from G.B. to any Port in Europe & One ℔C: to all other Countries—for which difference there was some pretext—Neutrals as well as National Ships were Charged therewith—On the Peace this Convoy Duty was Changed to a Duty on Export, and the U.S. were thus subjected to double the Duty paid by other Nations—this Distinction was particularly levelled against us—If I recollect right, Mr. King protested against this Injustice as being Contrary to the true spirit of the Treaty—The Budget lately presented to Parliament proposes to raise £450,000 Sterlg.—by a duty of One ℔C: on goods exported from G.B. to any port of Europe & *Three* ℔ *Cent* on all Goods exported *Elsewhere*—thus subjecting the U.S. to the payment of three times the Duty paid by all other of her Customers—I think Mr. Madison made the $\frac{1}{2}$ ℔C: difference to amount to £80,000 Sterlg.—I presume their New 3 ℔C: will be a Tax of £350 or £400,000 Sterlg. payable by the U.S. towards the Expences of the New War,—Mr Gallatin can ascertain the Amount precisely—I have taken the liberty to state this subject lest It might escape your Observation—I am at a loss to Concieve how we Shall meet this Grievance, or whether It would be with propriety introduced into the Message.

Those Springs would I am Confident operate an effectual Cure in the case of Mr. Carr—I am Dr Sir/

with Truth Sincerely your Friend and Obedt. Serv

S. Smith

RC (DLC); addressed: "Thomas Jefferson. Esqr President of the US Washington"; franked; postmarked 24 Aug.; endorsed by TJ as received 14 Sep. and so recorded in SJL.

For the BUDGET LATELY PRESENTED TO PARLIAMENT by the Addington ministry, see Gallatin to TJ, 18 Aug. 1803.

For Smith's earlier concerns about the recent poor health of Peter CARR, see Smith to TJ, 1 and 2 June 1803.

From Benjamin Austin, Jr.

Respected Sir Boston August 24 1803

I acknowledge with the greatest pleasure your polite Letter of the 18th July. On a subject so important, intelligence from such a source is greatly satisfactory.—I would not Sir presume to expect a Correspondence too highly flattering, but under existing circumstances, I feel myself under Obligations for your friendly notice.—

The political controversy I expect will increase in its violence till principles are well understood in this Country. As they respect yourself, I have reason to believe the general happiness of the Citizens is the only question contemplated.—

The issue of the present contention in Europe is important in its relations to us, & I hope will terminate in the political & commercial advantage of the United States. But wether in a state of Neutrality, the severe remarks on the first Consul, in *some papers* which are consider'd republican, are prudent, judicious or politic are questions of the highest importance & consideration in my mind.—The peace & prosperity of my country are my only objects, & I should feel myself under the highest obligation to *the person* who could direct me to promote them.—

I hope Sir you will consider my Observations as solely confin'd to the imprudencies of some Editors, & that your candor will apologize for my remarks.—

At the particular request of Nathaniel Fellows Esqr. whose republican character I presume is well Known to you, I am desir'd to mention his Nephew Nathaniel Fellows Junr. as a suitable person to act as Consul in the Havanna—He has lately sail'd from Boston with a valuable Cargo, but unfortunately sprang a leak, & been oblig'd to put into Charles town, South Carolina. As War has commenc'd, he is apprehensive he may meet with some difficulty in case of capture, & is solicitous if any vacancy will admit of his appointment he may be consider'd a Candidate for this Office.—His political sentiments cannot be doubted. He is accompanied with his Wife, grand Daughter to the late patriot the Revd. Docr. Cooper of Boston.[1]

Nothing but the particular request of Mr. Fellows, & the peculiar circumstances of his Nephew could have induc'd me to be thus particular in my application.—

I am respected Sir with the most sincere wishes for your Health & happiness Your most Obedt. Servt Benj. Austin Jr.

RC (DLC); endorsed by TJ as received 5 Sep. and so recorded in SJL.

A Boston merchant and partner of navy agent Samuel Brown, Nathaniel Fellowes (fellows) had tried unsuccessfully in 1801 to secure an appointment for his nephew, Nathaniel Fellowes, Jr., as consul at Havana (Madison, *Papers, Sec. of State Ser.*, 2:225, 232-3, 330-1; 8:558). Writing James Madison on 24 Aug. 1803, he again recommended the young man for the post, stating that his nephew had resided on Cuba for the past six or seven years and was "well acquainted with the Spanish language and commercial relations" (RC in DNA: RG 59, LAR; endorsed by TJ: "Fellowes Nathanl. to mr

Madison. to be Comml. Agent at Havanna"). In May 1803, the younger Fellowes married Julia Hixon, a granddaughter of Dr. Samuel Cooper. Shortly after the wedding, the couple sailed from Boston for Havana, but the young bride became ill on the journey and died at sea on 29 Aug. Fellowes, Jr., did not receive a consular appointment from TJ (Karen Robert, ed., *New Year in Cuba: Mary Gardner Lowell's Travel Diary, 1831-1832* [Boston, 2003], 177; Boston *Gazetteer*, 11 May 1803; Boston *Independent Chronicle*, 26 May, 10, 24 Oct. 1803).

[1]Preceding sentence interlined at end of paragraph.

From William C. C. Claiborne

DEAR SIR, Near Natchez August 24th 1803

My Letter of the 12th Instant, acknowledged the receipt of your agreeable favours of the 17th & 18th of July;—Since which I have turned my attention, to the several subjects embraced in Queries relative to Louisiana, and I now lay before you, the result of my inquiries and reflections—

1st. What are the best Maps general or particular of the whole or parts of the Province? Copies of them if to be had in print?

Ansr. There are I believe, none extant that can be depended upon—I have been told, there are two Maps of the Province by Men of the names of Romane and Gould. That of the former is supposed to be the best and I have been promised a copy of it—I am also informed, that a number of partial, but accurate Geographical sketches of that Country, have been taken by different Spanish officers, but that it has been the Policy of their Government, to prevent the publication of them. A General work of the same nature, is said to have been undertaken by the French, when they were formerly Masters of the Country, but it was never finished. An ingenious Correspondent of mine residing at Nachitoches on the Red River, informs me, that he has nearly completed an accurate Map of the Country between the Mississippi and the River Grand, including the Province of Sta. Fee. I will endeavour to procure a copy of that map, and should I succeed, will forward it to you. And also that of Romane should it be procured for me, according to promise.

2d. What are the Boundaries of Louisiana, and on what Authority does each portion of them rest?

Ansr. On this question, I have not been able to obtain any satisfactory information. It is understood that by the Treaty of 1763 the Island of New Orleans was the only tract of Country east of the Mississippi, included in the Province of Louisiana as then ceded by France to Spain.—It is related to me on the authority of the oldest setlers in this

Territory, that some time previous to that *Treaty* a design was formed of Running a Boundary line on the west of Louisiana, between the French possessions and those of Spain, and that the Mouth of the Sabine River which disembogues itself into the Bay of St Bernard in the Gulf of Mexico, was fixed upon as the Point from which the line should set out. The persons appointed to run the line, accordingly proceeded thence up the Sabine River as part of the Western Boundary of the French Province, to a place where they erected a small fort, and fixed in the ground some small leaden posts; The distance of that Fort from the Mouth of the River, I have not learned—from the fort it appears they left the River, and run the line (in what direction I am ignorant) 'till it intersected a Creek called Bayau Pierre, about five leagues N.W. of Nachitoches. Here the line was discontinued, but for what reason I have no information. It may perhaps be necessary to add, that the Post of Nachitoches is situated on the Red River, about 180 miles from its Mouth, and between 150 & 160 miles from Natchez over land—such is the imperfect knowledge I have been able to acquire on this subject, notwithstanding the utmost diligence of inquiry which I have exerted in this vicinity. Mr Clarke from the local advantages which he may avail himself of in this particular, will no doubt furnish you with an account more accurate and copious.

3d. What is the extent of sea coast from the western mouth of the Mississippi called Peakemenes River?

Ansr. The Bay of St. Bernard has been seldom navigated, and the Coast consequently is but little known—But the distance required by your question is conjectured to be about 200 miles.

4th What is the distance from the same mouth due west to the Western Boundary?

Answer The distance has probably never been measured But an old Inhabitant here, who calculates by days Journey supposes it to be about 160 miles.

5th. "Into what divisions is the Province laid off?"

Answer There are ten Divisions; viz The Island of New Orleans, Point Coupee, Atackapas, Apaulousas, Red River, Ouachetas, Concord, Arkansaws, New Madrid and the Illinois.

6th. "What is the population of the Province distinguishing between White and Black (but excluding Indians on the East side of the Mississippi) of the Settlement on the west side next the Mouth, of each distinct settlement in the other part of the Province, and what the Geographical position, and extent of each of those settlements?"

Answer The information I have as yet been able to collect concerning the population position &c of the several divisions, is not sufficiently authentic, to Justify my hazarding an answer in detail to this question—The population of Louisiana generally, is by some represented to amount to above thirty six thousand whites, and nearly as many Slaves. But how far this estimate may be depended upon, I confess myself wholy unable to say—Mr Clarke will no doubt be able to inform himself upon the subject with some degree of certainty.

7th. "Have they a Militia, and what their numbers—what May be the number of Free Males from 18 to 45 in the different settlements?"

Answer There is a militia in Louisiana; during the administration of General Don Galvez, who was an eminent military character, and an ornament to the service of his Catholic Majesty, the Militia are said to have been well disciplined, and serviceable troops. An old and respectable Inhabitant of this Country, to whom I am indebted for many valuable local communications, states that at the seige of Pensacola, the Spanish Militia (including free mulattoes) amounted to about 10,000 Since the Treaty of 1783, the discipline of the Militia has been considerably relaxed; but they are still enrolled and occasionally called out. A Gentleman who has I should suppose an opportunity of being well acquainted with this subject, computed their present number at between 8 and 9,000—among those enrolled, I have reason to beleive there are many free mulattoes, and possibly some Indians.

8th "As good an Estimate as can be had of the nations of Indians, towit their names, numbers and geographical position?"

Answer I am unable to make an Estimate with the accuracy required. Within a considerable distance of the Mississippi on the Western side, there are but few Indians. In the interior of the Country, and particularly towards the Mexican possessions, the tribes of Indians are said to be numerous. On the west side of the Arkensaw River, there is a nation of Indians called the Ousais, a numerous and warlike people.

9th "What are the foundation of their land titles and what their tenure?"

Answer Many inhabitants claim land under old French patents, more recent titles are derived from Spanish grants issued by the Governor General at New Orleans. The latter, are I believe seldom made, but in favour of actual settlers, and they are usually conditioned for early improvement of the soil, keeping up lev'ees, and such other public services, as local circumstances suggest.

10th "Are there any feudal rights, such as ground rents fines on alienation droit de molines, or any noblesse, as in Canada?"

Answer— To each part of this question I answer from good Authority in the negative. But a correspondent to whom I directed my inquiries on those particulars informs me (perhaps facetiously) that there are in the Province several self created Noblesse.

11th "What is the quantity of granted lands as near as can be Estimated?"

Answer It is impossible for me to make any probable estimate either of the lands already granted, or of those which the United States may find disposed of in that way, by the time we get actual possession of the Province. Between the ratification of the Treaty 1795, and the arrival of the American officers at Natchez, it is confidently asserted that the Spanish Government was generous in the distribution of Lands among the friends they were parting from. How far a similar spirit of Liberality, may be apprehended in Louisiana on the present occasion, I cannot presume to say.

12th "What is the quantity of ungranted in the Island of New Orleans, and in the Settlement adjacent on the West side?"

Answer None of much value

13th "What are the lands appropriated to public use?"

Answer Very little if any.

14th "What Public buildings fortifications barracks or other fixed property belonging to the Public?"

Answer Many of some value, such as the Government house, Custom House, Priests House, and Public Store houses at New Orleans. There are also some barracks and fortifications, both said to be much out of repair. On the River between New Orleans and the sea, there are two or three forts, one called Fort Plackaimine tho' small, commands the River, being Judiciously situated and well built.

15th "What is the quantity and general Limits of the Lands fit for the culture of sugar? What proportion is granted and what ungranted?"

Answer From the Balize to twenty leagues above New Orleans, sugar may be cultivated to advantage. The quantity of vacant Land is uncertain.

16th "Whence is their Code of Laws derived, a copy of it, if in print?"

Answer Louisiana like most other Countries which have undergone a change of Masters, derives Many of its Municipal Customs and regulations from different sources. By what kind of Laws the French formerly governed the province, is unknown to me. After its cession by them to Spain, General OReiley the Governor of the Province, published a collection of Laws (as I am informed) of a general nature, but few in number. But whether that small code was a selection from the previous Laws of the Country, to which hc intended to give new force, or were certain ordinances, then for the first time promulgated by the Authority of the New Government, I have not ascertained. OReily's code is said still to be in print, but I have not been able to procure a copy. Under the Spanish Government at present, the laws are enacted in the Council of State by order of the King. But in cases of small local concern, I understand that the Governor General with the advice of certain other officers of State at New Orleans, has occasionally published some regulations providing for the redress of Grievances in a summary way.

17th "What are the Courts in existence and their Jurisdiction? Are they corrupt? are they popular? are they tedious in their proceedings."

Answer There are in Louisiana, both Civil and Ecclesiastical Courts, the respective Jurisdictions of which are I presume seperated by the usual lines of distinction. Many of the Officers of Government civil and Military, are vested according to circumstances with inferior Judicial Authority. In the several divisions of the Province, the Commandants and other persons commissioned only as alcades or majestrates, hold petty Courts of Limited Jurisdiction. From these petty Courts, an appeal lies to the Governor General, who is invariably assisted with the advice of a Counsellor, called the Auditore. From the decision of the Governor General, an appeal formerly lay to the Governor of Cuba, but now lies to the King and council only. As to the integrity of these Courts, you will perceive from their construction, that this depends upon the honesty of the several Individuals, to whom the charge of administering Justice is entrusted. Fame accuses these courts with corruption, and I fear many notorious facts support the suspicion. It is however, but Justice to add, that some of the Governor's General have been men of honor and principle. But not withstanding that, I believe the Inhabitants of Louisiana, have often had to lament that from the Nature of the Courts, and the unnecessary forms of office, Power was placed into the hands of Men who by various arts of Intrigue, contrived in Many cases to sell Justice, with but little risque of detection. The popularity of these *Courts*, might safely be questioned, were it possible under a despotic Government, to come at the real sentiments of the subject;—Among the Rich and those connected with men in office, *they* may enjoy some favour, but I see nothing to endear *them* to the Poor, but a promptitude in their decisions, and that I suspect must be numbered only among their occasional virtues. For though some trials are speedily disposed of, others again are hung up for years;—Causes appealed are very tedious, but as the influence of the Judge generally travels with the appeal, they are seldom demanded.

18th "What is the number of Lawyers, their fees and standing in society?"

Answer Lawyers so called according to the usage of the United States, and perhaps of Spain and her more important Colonies, are yet unknown in Louisiana. But there are certain Lawyers eminent in their professions, who are employed as officers with salaries from Government, to assist in the administration of Justice: one as I have already stated, counsels the Governor General, and another is I believe allowed the Intendant. The duty of those professional assistants, seems to be to collect and arrange the several pleadings (which are commonly in the forms of petitions) evidences, and other documents for the convenience of the Judges, to prepare themselves in all points of Law likely to occur for the information of the Court, and perhaps occasionally, to assist in the decisions even on facts.

19th "Are the people litigious, what is the nature of most Law Suits, are they for Rights to land, personal contracts, personal quarrels?"

Answer At present the people of Louisiana, are represented to me as being in general mild and submissive; not by any means prone to litigation: But such is generally the Character of Men, under Arbitrary Government—In the "Calm of Despotism," the more violent passions of the vassal, find few opportunities of indulgence,—But when their present shackles are removed, and a Rational system of Free Government shall acknowledge and protect their Rights, the change of disposition, which May accompany so sudden a transition from the condition of subjects to that of Free men, will probably be considerable.—Under the Spanish Government, the Inhabitants of this District, differed little in character, from their Louisianian neighbours, at present the litigation of the Territory, gives Bread to near thirty Lawyers, and I understand the old settlers are considered very good Clients.

20th "What would be the effect of the introduction of the trial by Jury, in Civil and Criminal cases?"

Answer Some of the oldest and most respectable Inhabitants of this Territory, are of opinion, that in Civil causes, the Trial by Jury will at first be unpopular, and I have heard this reason assigned, "that those who have long appealed for Justice to great personages, whom they looked up to as wise and Learned, cannot at first without reluctance, submit to the decrees of Men no better than themselves." And the same Reason is likewise supposed to operate with some of the old settlers in this Territory, even at the present day, to the disrepute of Jury trials. In Criminal cases, on the contrary, the trial by Jury (it is thought) will be extremely acceptable. Indeed it is very observable, that as the people in this District, begin to understand this mode of trial, their attachment to it encreases, and as the people of Louisiana likewise, become enlightened, they will no doubt learn to appreciate fairly, and acknowledge with gratitude, the Superior Excellencies of the System.

21st "What is the nature of Criminal Jurisprudence numbers and nature of crimes and punishments?"

Answer The information which I have been enabled to acquire on this subject, is not by any means satisfactory. To this question therefore, I must at present decline making an answer.

22d. "What public schools and colleges have they? can the Inhabitants generally read and write?"

Answer I understand that there is one public school at New Orleans, supported principally by the King; But it is of little general use, being engrossed chiefly by the Children of the More wealthy Citizens of the Island; there is also a Nunnery at the same place: It was Established early in the 18th century, and still continues to furnish young females with Boarding and tuition; a Majority of the Inhabitants are supposed to be able to read and write; the information of few of them extends beyond those acquirements.

23d "On what footing is the church and clergy, what Land or tythes have they and what other sources of support?"

Answer The Clergy are supported by salaries from the King; they are provided with houses in each parish; they are allowed no lands or tythes, and receive from the people only a few inconsiderable perquisites.

24th "What Officers Civil or Military are appointed to each division of the Province and what to the General Government?"

Answer The Governor General is the highest civil Majistrate, and also commander in chief of the Army and Militia of the Province—The Intendant the second Officer in the Government, has peculiarly in his care all Matters concerning commerce; under both of them, there are several subordinate officers with the duties and powers of whom, I am but little acquainted. To each division of the Province[1] is assigned a military commandant, and alcades, of whom I have already spoken.

25th "By whom are they appointed? are any chosen by the Inhabitants?"

Answer Invariably by the King or his Representative the Governor. Every species of popular election, is yet unknown in Louisiana.

26th "What emoluments have they and from what source derived?"
Answer Nearly all the public officers receive salaries from the King, but (except in a few cases) the value of Office is greatly increased by perquisites.
27th "What are the local taxes paid in each division, for the local expences of such division, such as Roads, poor charity schools, salary of local officers, and by whom are they imposed?"
Answer No direct taxes of any kind, are imposed in Louisiana.
28 "What are the duties on imports and exports respectively; the amount of each, the manner of collecting them, the place where levied, and the time of paying them?"
Answer This question will doubtless be answered with accuracy by Mr Clarke. I do not possess, nor could I readily acquire the information required in detail. This however I can state on good authority, that duties are levied both on imports and some exports; that the amount of the Revenue arising therefrom is considerable, and the whole are collected at New Orleans.
29th "How are the officers paid who are employed in the collection daily or annual salary or by commissions or by Fees?"
Answer They receive annual salaries from the King, but their principal dependence is said to be on certain private resources, which I shall explain better, when I come to speak of the delapedations of the Revenue.
30th "What is the nett amount of those duties paid into the Treasury?"
Answer Of this I have no knowledge.
31st "Are there any other general taxes laid in the Province Whether &c—?"
Answer. I have only to repeat there are no direct taxes levied in the Province.
32d What are the expenses of the Province paid from the Treasury under the following heads: 1. salaries of Governor Intendant Judges and all other Civil officers. 2. Military including fortifications barracks &c. 3. erection and repairs of public Buildings. 4 Colleges and schools. 5. pensions and gratuities. 6 Indians. 7 Clergy. 8. Roads and all other the expenses?"
Answer The Governors Salary is 4000$ per Annum, his Secretary 600$, his Counsellor called the Auditore 2000$. The Intendant 2000$ respecting the salaries of the other officers I am not advised; But all the salaries are I believe moderate, the fees and perquisites attached to most of the officers are high, those of the Governor and some others are said to be considirable. The Civil and Military expenses of

the Province taken together I am informed amount to near 700,000$ annually, and in some years approached nearly to one million. The detail of the expenditures I have not procured.

33 "What are the usual delapedations of the public Treasury before it is collected by smuggling and bribery? 2. In its expenditure, by the unfaithfulness of the agents and contractors thro which it passes?"

Answer It is no easy task to trace with precision, all the ingenious windings of Official peculation under a Spanish Government. That Smuggling to a considerable amount, is carried on at New Orleans by the connivance of the inferior officers of collection, and sometimes by that of their superiors, is understood in this Country, to be a Matter of common notoriety. Merchants calculate on it; every Boat Master on the River, goes down impressed with the Idea, and I never met with any, who have yet returned with the impression removed. To attempt an accurate estimate of What the Revenue looses by these frauds, would be vain, but the losses are certainly great, and in the appropriation &c afterwards, I have been confidently assured, that nearly one half sinks into the coffers of unfaithful Agents. But this as well as the former delapedation can only be conjectured, and may possibly be exagerated.

34 "If the Annual expenditure exceeds the annual Revenue in what manner is the deficiency made up?"

Answer By remittances from the Havannah and Vera Crux.

35 What is the nature amount and depreciation of the paper[2] Currency?"

Answer There is no paper currency.

36 "Exclusively of paper currency are there any other debts incurred by the Spanish Government, their amount, do they bear Interest, are any Evidences of the same in circulation? In what proportion are they due to the Inhabitant of the Province, or of the United States, and to persons not Inhabitants of either?"

Answer There are some Bills of Credit on the Treasury in circulation, for which Government is answerable, they bear no Interest, and are generally in the Hands of the Traders on the Island of New Orleans, their amount is supposed to be several hundred thousand Dollars.

The remaining questions concerning the trade &c. constitute a subject, on which I can make no communications of consequence. I will only add that of the imports by the way of New Orleans, but little is re exported; some to Florida by sea, a little by a contraband trade, into the interior of the Province of Takus, and a small portion to Vera Crux, Havannah, &c. There are a few distilleries on the sugar plantations, where also some sugar is refined. The coasting trade is confined to the Floradas, and small schooners employed in it. The Mississippi is navigated in Batteaux, and other small craft.

Many of the answers which I have returned to your questions, are without certainty. But all the information within my reach, is communicated. We are in this Territory very partially informed of the affairs of our Spanish Neighbours, and even the Individuals under that Government, know but little of their own affairs, beyond the circle, of each Mans peculiar station and duties. Despotic Governments are generally reserved, and corrupt ones are always jealous of inquiry. To inspect the Archives of a Spanish Province, is a priviledge granted but to few, and probably to none, who would not feel an Interest in concealing them; and without an inspection of these archives, it appears to me, that the force of Louisiana, its population &c, or any material part of its political econemy, cannot at this time be ascertained with certainty.

I take this Occasion, to offer you my best[3] wishes for your health and Happiness, and to renew the assurances of my sincere and respectful attachment. WILLIAM C. C. CLAIBORNE

PS I had Just completed this communication, when a letter from a well informed Gentleman now residing in Louisiana, was handed to me, speaking of the Limits of the Province, my correspondent says: "The subject of the Western Boundary of Louisiana, is much talked of here, and various opinions entertained; all I know is, that the *Jurisdiction* of the Government of Louisiana ends, and *that* of the Province of Takus (or as it is spelled Taxas) commences 10 or 12 miles west of the post of Nachitoches on the Red River."

This information corrobarates the statement I have heretofore made on the subject of the Western Boundary.—

WILLIAM C. C. CLAIBORNE

RC (DLC); in a clerk's hand, with signatures, inside address, and several emendations by Claiborne; at foot of text: "His Excellency Thomas Jefferson President of the United States"; endorsed by TJ as received 25 Sep. and so recorded in SJL. Dupl (DNA: RG 59, TP, Orleans); in Claiborne's hand; at head of text: "Duplicate"; endorsed by TJ as received 29 Sep.

The TWO MAPS were by Bernard Romans and George Gauld, both of whom worked as cartographers in the Floridas during the time of British occupation. Romans's map of East and West Florida, which included the Lower Mississippi River and its distributaries and was originally intended for his *A Concise Natural History of East and West-Florida* (New York, 1776; Sowerby, No. 4079), was published in New York in 1781. Romans also executed a map of West Florida in 1772, which extended from the Mississippi River at its junction with the Red River to the Apalachicola River, and as far north as the Yazoo River. That map, however, does not appear to have been published. Gauld conducted surveys along the

Gulf Coast in the 1760s and 1770s and wrote accounts meant to accompany the many maps he executed during the same period, most of which never made it to print. His *Accurate Chart of the Coast of West Florida, and the Coast of Louisiana; from Sawaney River on the West Coast of East Florida to 94° 20′ West Longitude Describing the Entrance of the River Mississippi, Bay of Mobile, Pensacola Harbour &c. Surveyed in the Years 1764, 5, 6, 7, 8, 9, 70 & 71* was published in London in 1803. Romans and Gauld were both elected to membership in the American Philosophical Society (*New-York Journal; or, The General Advertiser*, 3 Feb. 1774; Woodbury Lowery, *The Lowery Collection: A Descriptive List of Maps of the Spanish Possessions within the Present Limits of the United States, 1502-1820*, ed. Philip Lee Phillips [Washington, D.C., 1912], 338-9, 370-1; Phillips, *Notes on the Life and Works of Bernard Romans* [Deland, Fla., 1924], 35-7, 74-5; John D. Ware, *George Gauld: Surveyor and Cartographer of the Gulf Coast*, revised and completed by Robert R. Rea [Gainesville, Fla., 1982], 92 [illus.], 236-9).

INGENIOUS CORRESPONDENT: John Sibley, who settled in Natchitoches in 1803 and later sent Claiborne a map of areas west of the Mississippi (ANB; Claiborne to TJ, 28 Oct.).

The SABINE RIVER empties into Sabine Lake, not ST. BERNARD, or Matagorda, Bay, which lies far west of the Sabine on the Gulf Coast (Ron Tyler, ed., *The New Handbook of Texas*, 6 vols. [Austin, 1996], 5:743-4; TJ to Thomas Paine, 10 Aug.).

OUSAIS: likely the Osage, who in the latter half of the eighteenth century seized control over parts of the Arkansas River valley (William C. Sturtevant, gen. ed., *Handbook of North American Indians*, 15 vols. [Washington, D.C., 1978-], 13, pt. 1:476-8, 494). In answer to the query on Indians, the administration received far more detailed information from Daniel Clark (CLARKE), who, in a letter of 29 Sep. to James Madison, enclosed a long description (in an unknown hand) of Indian groups residing along the river valleys of Louisiana, from the southern bayous to the upper Missouri and Mississippi Rivers. Clark did not indicate how he came by his information, which included population estimates for each tribe as well as characterizations of such qualities as relative temperance, bravery, and peaceableness (DNA: RG 59, CD, Orleans; printed in *Terr. Papers*, 9:61-6; see also Madison, *Papers, Sec. of State Ser.*, 5:472-4).

Clark enclosed answers to the administration's other queries in letters of 26 Aug. and 8 Sep. to James Madison (both in DNA: RG 59, CD, Orleans; printed in *Terr. Papers*, 9:25-6, 28; Madison, *Papers, Sec. of State Ser.*, 5:347-8, 389-90). The first enclosure has not been found, but the second included answers to all but queries 8 and 23. In many cases, Clark's answers were more detailed and expansive than Claiborne's, although the two concurred more often than not. Clark had far better access to figures on DUTIES on imports and exports and other levies in the colony. He incurred personal expenses, for which he requested reimbursement, in copying manuscript surveys and paying clerks in New Orleans for information on the duties of the previous three and a half years, as well as on other financial details (MS in DNA: RG 59, TP, Orleans; printed in *Terr. Papers*, 9:29-47; Madison, *Papers, Sec. of State Ser.*, 5:472-4). Having been in communication with Claiborne, who seems to have received the queries before he did, Clark anticipated some of the information requested by the administration. In a letter of 17 Aug. to Madison, he enclosed several census tables and an account of the monthly customs duties for 1802, the totals of which differed somewhat from the figures he presented in his earlier answers (Clark to Madison, 17 Aug., and one enclosure, in DNA: RG 59, CD, Orleans; three other enclosures in DNA: RG 59, TP, Orleans; Madison, *Papers, Sec. of State Ser.*, 5:317-18; census tables printed in ASP, *Miscellaneous*, 1:382-4). Three days later, Clark sent corrected census data on the Attakapas region (Clark to Madison, 20 Aug. 1803, in DNA: RG 59, CD, Orleans, with enclosure docketed at Clark to Madison, 26 July; *Terr. Papers*, 9:13-14).

Claiborne left out a follow-up query on PAPER CURRENCY, which appeared on the administration's list as No. 36. He instead substituted the 37th query (see Document IV in Queries on Louisiana, at

9 July). Clark's answers to the remaining six queries stressed, as Claiborne's did, the difficulty in getting precise information because of the level of contraband trade and because of the secretive nature of Spanish colonial recordkeeping. Still, he offered specific estimates on the value of exports from Louisiana and predicted that through the encouragement of trade New Orleans "will rival Kingston in Jamaica" and that such trade "will bring an immense Quantity of Silver to our Markets" (*Terr. Papers*, 9:44-7). Clark's last answer, on shipping and the COASTING TRADE, became the basis for the final section of the report that TJ sent to Congress on 14 Nov., published widely as *An Account of Louisiana, Being an Abstract of Documents, in the Offices of the Departments of State, and of the Treasury*. That report also printed Clark's enclosure on Indian groups (*Account of Louisiana* [Washington, D.C., 1803; Shaw-Shoemaker, No. 5196], 21-7, 46-8).

[1] RC: "Provice."

[2] RC: word interlined by Claiborne in place of "Public."

[3] RC: word interlined by Claiborne.

To James Madison

DEAR SIR Monticello Aug. 2[4]. 1803.

Your two favors of the 18th. & 20th. were recieved on the 21st. the letters of Livingston & Monroe are sent to mr Gallatin as you proposed. that of Simpson to mr Smith for the purpose of execution. all of them will be returned. Thornton's, Clarke's, Charles Pinckney's, Graham's, Appleton's, Davis's, Mitchell's, Newton's, & Derieux' letters are now inclosed. with respect to the impressment of our seamen I think we had better propose to Great Britain to act on the stipulations which had been agreed to between that Government & mr King, as if they had been signed. I think they were that they would forbid impressments at sea, and that we should acquiesce in the searches in *their* harbours necessary to prevent concealments of their citizens. mr Thornton's attempt to justify his nation in using our ports as cruising stations on our friends & ourselves renders the matter so serious as to call, I think, for an answer, bien motivé. that we ought in courtesy & friendship to extend to them all the rights of hospitality is certain: that they should not use[1] our hospitality to injure our friends or ourselves is equally enjoined by morality & honor. after the rigorous exertions we made in Genet's time to prevent this abuse on his part, and the indulgences extended by mr Adams to the British cruisers, even after our pacification with France, & by[2] ourselves also, from an unwillingness to change the course of things as the war was near it's close, I did not expect to hear from that quarter, charges of partiality. in the Mediterranean we need ask from no nation but the permission to refresh & repair in their ports. we do not wish our vessels to lounge in their ports. in the case at Gibraltar, if they had disapproved, our vessel ought to have left the port. besides, altho' nations have treated with the pyratical states, they have not, in practice even, been considered as entitled to all the favors of the law of Nations. Thornton says they watch our trade only to prevent contraband. we say it is to plunder under pretext of contraband, for which, tho' so shamefully exercised, they have given us no satisfaction but by confessing the fact in new modifying their courts of Admiralty. certainly the evils we experience from it, & the just complaints which France may urge, render it indispensable that we restrain the English from abusing the rights of hospitality to their prejudice as well as our own.

Graham's letter manifests a degree of imprudence, which I had not expected from him. his pride has probably been hurt at some of the regulations of that court, and has had it's part in inspiring the ill temper he shews. if you understand him as serious in asking leave to return, I see no great objection to it. at the date of your letter you had not recieved mine on the subject of Derieux' claim. I still think the limits therein stated reasonable. I think a guinea a day till he leaves Washington would be as low an allowance as we could justify, and should not be opposed to any thing not exceeding the allowance to Dawson. fix between these as you please. I suppose Monroe will touch on the limits of Louisiana, only incidentally, inasmuch as it's extension to Perdido curtails Florida & renders it of less worth. I have used my spare moments to investigate, by the help of my books here, the subject of the limits of Louisiana. I am satisfied our right to the Perdido is substantial, & can be opposed by a quibble on form only; and that our right Westwardly to the bay of St. Bernard may be strongly maintained. I will use the first leisure to make a statement of the facts & principles on which this depends. further reflection on the amendmt. to the constitution necessary in the case of Louisiana, satisfies me it will be better to give general powers, with specified exceptions, somewhat in the way stated below. mrs Madison promised us a visit about the last of this month. I wish you could have met Govr. Page here, whom with his family I expect in a day or two & will pass a week with us. but in this consult your own convenience, as that will increase the pleasure with which I shall always[3] see you here. accept my affectionate salutations & constant attachment.

TH: JEFFERSON

'Louisiana, as ceded by France to the US. is made a part of the US. it's white inhabitants shall be citizens, and stand, as to their rights and obligations on the same footing with other citizens of the US. in analogous situations.

Save only that, as to the portion thereof lying North of the latitude of the mouth of Arcansa river, no new state shall be established, nor any grants of land made therein, other than to Indians in exchange for equivalent portions of lands occupied by them, until an amendment to the Constitution shall be made for these purposes.

Florida also, whensoever it may be rightfully obtained, shall become a part of the US. it's white inhabitants shall thereupon be citizens, and shall stand as to their rights & obligations on the same footing with other citizens of the US. in analogous circumstances.'

RC (DLC: Madison Papers, Rives Collection); date partially illegible, altered by TJ either from or to "24"; at foot of first page: "The Secretary of State"; endorsed by Madison as a letter of 24 Aug. (see also Madison to TJ, 28 Aug.). PrC (DLC); notation by TJ in ink alongside date: "(shd be 25th.)." Recorded in SJL under 24 Aug. with notation "impressmts. cruizing from our ports. Graham. Derieux. limits Louisiana. amdmt. to constn." Enclosure: Gallatin to TJ, 18 Aug.

For the STIPULATIONS of the convention on impressment that Rufus King had attempted to conclude with the British government, see TJ to Madison, 31 July.

BIEN MOTIVÉ: well justified.

MINE ON THE SUBJECT OF DERIEUX' CLAIM: TJ to Madison, 18 Aug.

See the editorial note and group of documents on boundaries of Louisiana at 7 Sep. for the information that TJ was compiling in his SPARE MOMENTS.

Madison drafted a brief amendment to the Constitution that also began with a reference to Louisiana AS CEDED BY FRANCE. His proposal was: "Louisiana as ceded by France is made part of the U. States. Congress may make part of the U.S. other adjacent territories which shall be justly acquired. Congress may sever from the U.S territory not heretofore within the U. States, with consent of a majority of the free males above 21 years, inhabiting such territory" (MS in DLC: Madison Papers, undated, in Madison's hand, at head of text: "For amendment to the Constitution" and "project of J.M."; Madison, *Papers*, *Sec. of State Ser.*, 5:156).

[1] Word interlined in place of "pervert."

[2] TJ here canceled "mr Adams."

[3] Word interlined.

To John F. Mercer

DEAR SIR Monticello Aug. 24. 03.

On the reciept of your letter of the 6th. inst: I forwarded that to mr Pinckney with the papers accompanying it to the Secretary of state who has, with my sanction, written to mr Pinckney to conform to your wish and forwarded your letter & papers to him. Accept my friendly salutations and assurances of my high consideration & respect.

TH: JEFFERSON

PrC (DLC); at foot of text: "Govr. Mercer."

I FORWARDED: TJ to Madison, 13 Aug. 1803. For the secretary of state's letter to William Pinkney, see Madison to TJ, 18 Aug. 1803.

From John Page

My dear Sir Richmond August 24th. 1803

I received your truely friendly Letter & was determined to set out yesterday, following the directions therein: but Mrs. Page could not be prepared for the Journey 'til to-day; & unfortunately early this morning a Diarhea attacked me so smartly, that I fear I shall not be able to venture out til to-morrow or next day; nor even then, unless it should go off as happily as two similar cases did.

The moment I can venture on the journey I will.

Accept Mrs. Page's & my own best Wishes & assurances of perfect respect & Esteem John Page

RC (DLC); endorsed by TJ as received 26 Aug. and so recorded in SJL.

friendly letter: TJ to Page, 14 Aug.

From Craven Peyton

Dear Sir Stump Island 24th Augt. 1803.

Johnson who tends your lower feald in corn this year, was to see me for the purpose of putting all the feald in wheat & to pay one fourth. the land is much exausted. & on a supposition it woud meet your approbation, I toald him that I expected he might undar certain restrictions, the kind of wheat & the time of seeding woud be requird. Sheckle who occupies your uppar feald I think ought not to continue if any othar tenant can be had. to secure the payment of the present years rent I obtained from him a bill of sale for all the proparty he has, which I am fearfull will be taken for the rent if you wish both or eithar of them put in small grain, you will please let me no by the boy, if I am correct in my calculation of the Interest it amounts to about Sixty Four Pounds. shoud it be intirely convenient to you to let me have about fifty or sixty Dollars of it by the boy you will do me a singular favour

with much Respt Yr. Ob St. C Peyton

RC (ViU); endorsed by TJ as received 25 Aug. and so recorded in SJL.

William johnson, a waterman who transported items to and from Monticello between 1799 and at least 1820, also rented from TJ part of the southern tract of Milton lands purchased from the heirs of Bennett Henderson (mb, 2:1276n; rs, 3:310n). In his account with Craven Peyton of rents and profits from Henderson lands for 1801 to 1811, TJ recorded that Cephus Shekell (sheckle) was delinquent in the amount of £24 for rent "not pd nor extendd" in 1803 (rs, 5:426).

To Craven Peyton

Dear Sir — Monticello Aug. 24. 03.

Your servant finds me just mounting my horse on a call to mr Lilly's. I have only time therefore to say I must leave the renting &c to yourself entirely, only guarding against repetitions of corn planting so as to injure the fields. I am sorry I have not 10. D. by me. I depend on exchanges with the sheriffs, who collect little. Accept my best wishes.

Th: Jefferson

RC (MA). Not recorded in SJL.

From Joseph Fay

Sir — N. York 25th. August 1803

Mr. Broome having defered his Visit to your Excellency until your return to the seat of Government, has requested me to forward the enclosed to aid the other documents which he has already transmitted.

I have the honor to be very respectfully Your Very Humble Servant

Joseph Fay

RC (DNA: RG 59, LAR); endorsed by TJ as received 31 Aug. and "Broome Saml. to be Collector N. Haven" and so recorded in SJL with a brace connecting this letter to enclosures listed below. Enclosures: (1) Fay to TJ, 12 Aug. 1803 (first letter). (2) George Clinton to TJ, 19 Aug. 1803 (recorded in SJL as received 31 Aug. from Albany, but not found). (3) DeWitt Clinton to TJ, 25 Aug. 1803 (recorded in SJL as received 31 Aug. from Newtown, but not found).

From Benjamin Lincoln

Sir — Boston Augt 25th 1803

I just now received your letter of the 19h instant the articles mentioned have been received are now in the public store and will be held there untill an opportunity shall offer of sending them to Washington or Alexandria

I have the honour of being with very great consederatn your most Obedient & most humble servant. B. Lincoln

RC (MHi); at foot of text: "President of the United States"; endorsed by TJ as received 5 Sep. and so recorded in SJL.

From William D. S. Taylor, with Jefferson's Note

Sir — Lexington August 25th 1803:

Presumptuous as an epistle from one entirely unknown to your Excellency may generally be considered, yet conscious that I am addressing our common Father,—The friend and patron of liberty and liberality—I am induced to become a petitioner. Before I state my wish to your Excellency, I will give you as good an account of myself as I possibly can. Being blessed with an indulgent Parent, He gave me as liberal an education as an early emigration to an almost uninhabited Country would admit of; intending me for the profession of the law: but as my Father and most of my relations had been officers during the revolutionary contest, and bore honorable testimony of the confidence their fellow Citizens had in their zeal for the cause of liberty, I imbibed the love of patriotism from my infancy, and impatiently longed for an establishment in the Army or Navy that I might always be in readiness (should ever an occasion offer) to signalize myself against the enemies of my Country.

Nothing but the hopes I had of such an establishment induced me to persue my Studies, always entertaining the opinion that a good education was as requisite in a military Character as in any profession whatever.

As I am acquainted with the present disbanded situation of our military force, I should not have presumed to have troubled you, had I not supposed there would (in all probability) be wanting some more troops to Garrison our newly acquired Teritory of Louisiana.

If Sir you will interest yourself in my favour and procure me a Commission in the Army or Navy that a gentleman need not blush to accept, I will exert myself to make it reflect some small degree of Credit on my patron.

With pleasure I will risk the untried climate of that extensive Teritory or brave the more perulous dangers of the ocean. As grating as a disappointment will be to a young and sanguine mind, should you think proper not to favour me, I shall immediately conclude your reasons sufficient and shall always wish for the health & prosperity of our worthy President, the Father of his Country.

Yrs with much veneration & esteem

William D S Taylor

P. S. If your Excellency should have any doubts respecting who I am: My Father is Colo. Richd. Taylor, who I presume is not unknown to you,—and should you consider letters of recommendation, or further particulars as to my character necessary, they shall immediately be forwarded—upon your condescending to have this answered.

W.D.S.T.

[*Note by TJ*:]

the writer of this is not personally known to me. his father & several of his family were well known. they are of the most respectable families in the county of Orange, highly republican, and I never heard of an indifferent character among them. Th:J.

RC (PHi); with note by TJ on address sheet below endorsement; addressed: "His Excellency Thomas Jefferson Esqr President of the U.S. Washington City" with "Milton Va" later written in another hand in place of "Washington City"; franked; postmarked Lexington 26 Aug.; endorsed by TJ as received 12 Sep. and "for commn. in army" and so recorded in SJL; also endorsed in Dearborn's hand: "enquire of Mr. Brackinridge as to Mr. Taylors private character."

A native of Orange County, Virginia, and a second cousin of James Madison, William Dabney Strother Taylor (1782-1808) was a son of Richard Taylor and Sarah Dabney Strother as well as the older brother of Zachary Taylor, the twelfth president of the United States. The Taylor family moved to frontier Kentucky in 1785 and settled at "Springfield," a farm near Louisville where William Taylor received a classical education from his father and a Connecticut tutor, Elisha Ayers. Taylor pursued a military career and held a commission as a midshipman in the navy from 1806 until February 1807, when he resigned out of "filial obedience" to his parents' concern for his safety, as well as a desire for a higher rank. On 25 Feb. 1807, he received an appointment as second lieutenant in the army artillery, but was killed the following year in a skirmish while serving at Fort Pickering, Tennessee (Christopher McKee, *A Gentlemanly and Honorable Profession: The Creation of the U.S. Naval Officer Corps, 1794-1815* [Annapolis, 1991], 426; Anna Robinson Watson, *Some Notable Families of America* [New York, 1898], 7; Holman Hamilton, *Zachary Taylor, Soldier of the Republic* [Indianapolis, 1941], 25, 33, 261-2, 264; Madison, *Papers, Sec. of State Ser.*, 9:100-1; William D. S. Taylor to Madison, 17 Jan. 1807, in DLC: Madison Papers; Robert Smith to Taylor, 10 Feb. 1807, in DNA: RG 45, LSO).

MY FATHER: Richard Taylor had been a colonel in the Virginia Continental line during the American Revolution and became active in Kentucky state and local affairs thereafter. From 1792 to 1799, he was a member of the Convention of Kentucky and helped frame the state's first and second constitutions (*Baltimore Patriot & Mercantile Advertiser,* 7 Feb. 1829; Kathleen Jennings, *Louisville's First Families* [Louisville, 1920], 129; Heitman, *Register*, 534).

From Stephen Thacher

SIR, Kennebunk August 25, 1803

The subscriber takes the liberty, in the most respectful manner, to solicit the honor of being permitted to present to the President of the United States the oration which he now presumes to enclose to him.

Sir, may a private individual, be allowed, with sentiments of profound veneration to embrace the Father of his country, & be indulged in the freedom of communicating to the President the name of his most obedient and most humble servant STEPHEN THACHER

RC (DLC); at foot of text: "The President of the United States"; endorsed by TJ as received 5 Sep. and so recorded in SJL. Enclosure: Stephen Thacher, *Oration, Pronounced at Kennebunk, District of Maine, on the Anniversary of American Independence, July 4, 1803* (Boston, 1803; Sowerby, Nos. 3298, 4683).

Connecticut native and Yale graduate Stephen Thacher (1774-1859) was a teacher and theology student in Massachusetts before relocating to Kennebunk, Maine, in 1803, where he engaged in trade. An ardent Republican, Thacher went on to hold a number of state and federal offices, including probate judge, postmaster, and collector for the port of Passamaquoddy (Dexter, *Yale*, 5:168-9).

From Jacob Wagner

Depart. State
25 Augt. 1803

J Wagner presents his best respects to the President of the United States and encloses an application for a pardon by Thomas Hutchings and John Hopkins. A blank pardon accompanies the papers, which were put into J.W's hands by direction of the Marshal, with a request that it might be intimated to the President that one of the applicants (*which* is not stated) is labouring under a fit of sickness.

J.W. duly received the President's letter respecting the pardon of Miller, the burglar, and by the same post the pardon itself. The President's letter enclosing one from the Secretary of the Prefecture of the Lower Alps has also been received and its directions executed.

RC (DLC); endorsed by TJ as received from the State Department "from Wagner" on 29 Aug. and "pardon of Thomas Hutchings & John Hopkins" and so recorded in SJL. Enclosures not found, but see below.

In December 1802, the U.S. Circuit Court for the District of Columbia found Thomas HUTCHINGS and John HOPKINS guilty of assaulting and stabbing one John Brown. Each man was fined $50 and sentenced to imprisonment of six months and until the respective fines were paid. TJ granted both a pardon, which was dated 25 Aug. 1803 (FC in Lb in DNA: RG 59, GPR).

J.W. DULY RECEIVED: TJ to Wagner, 11 and 20 Aug. 1803.

From Augustus B. Woodward

Warburton, prince george's county,
maryland; august 25. 1803.

I have the happiness to transmit to the president, by mister digges, a paper entitled "memoir addressed to the president of the united states on the colonization of louisiana," unaccompanied by my signature. Without a comparison of sentiments, the views of different minds are sometimes so dissimilar on the same subject, and so extremely divergent, that it is not without considerable diffidence and apprehension that I make this communication. I have expressed my opinions with frankness, and without reserve, trusting to the habitual condescension of the president for the pardon of any errors. If the president should feel an interest in any thing that is here stated, I should be pleased with being possessed of his present impressions, on the return of mister digges. I shall return them to him, on my enjoying the pleasure of a personal interview. In the mean time, as I have made no person acquainted with these ideas, I submit to the president the expediency of a total reserve on this subject, unless he should be disposed to confer with mister madison on it. In matters of this kind, if any thing is to be done, the judgment of one competent mind is worth a thousand vague opinions; and if nothing is intended, the less that is said or known on the subject[1] is usually the best.

I hope that the president will accept my invariable wishes for his health and felicity. AUGUSTUS B. WOODWARD

RC (DNA: RG 59, LAR); endorsed by TJ as received 7 Sep. and so recorded in SJL. Enclosure not found.

[1] Woodward here canceled "the better."

To Abraham Bradley, Jr.

Monticello Aug. 26. 03.

Having carried most of my maps to Washington I find myself much at a loss here for one of the US. if any more are in hand of those made (by yourself I believe) for the Post Office, I should be thankful to receive one by post.

I should prefer one in simple sheets pasted together but not on linen. Accept my salutations & best wishes. TH: JEFFERSON

PrC (DLC); at foot of text: "Abraham Bradley esq."; endorsed by TJ in ink on verso.

Connecticut native Abraham Bradley (1767-1838) was a lawyer and, briefly, a judge in Pennsylvania. In 1791, he became a postal clerk in Philadelphia under Federalist Timothy Pickering. By 1800, he was assistant postmaster general and supervised the move of the general post office to Washington, D.C. His postal career ended abruptly in 1829 when he was removed from office during the administration of Andrew Jackson. He remained in Washington and served a term as secretary of the Franklin Insurance Company during the last two years of his life (ANB; *Alexandria Gazette*, 10 May 1838).

MAPS: Bradley's attention to detail and knowledge of postal routes around the country contributed to his acclaimed authorship of a detailed map of the United States, in color, which became the official map of the Post Office Department by 1825. The best source of information about the nation's borders, it was among the first maps in the United States to be registered for copyright. The first edition, *Map of the United States, Exhibiting the Post-Roads, the Situations, Connections & Distances of the Post-Offices Stage Roads, Counties, Ports of Entry and Delivery for Foreign Vessels, and the Principal Rivers*, was published in Philadelphia in 1796, printed on four sheets and 36 panels, and could be cloth mounted to make a wall map. A second edition of 1804 reflected the acquisition of the Louisiana Territory and the addition of more post offices (Richard R. John, *Spreading the News: The American Postal System from Franklin to Morse* [Cambridge, Mass., 1995], 69-70; Walter W. Ristow, *American Maps and Mapmakers: Commercial Cartography in the Nineteenth Century* [Detroit, 1985], 70-1).

To Henry Dearborn

DEAR SIR Monticello Aug. 26. 03.

I inclose you a letter from mr Jackson of Tennissee, formerly a Senator from that state on the subject of Colo. Butler. he is a man of great integrity and respectability; carried sometimes beyond strict reason by an overwarm and excellent heart. another from judge Campbell on the subject of Doctr. Vandyke. I also return the one from him[1] to you covering mine. on the subject of the robbery committed by the Cherokee Indian, the judge does not say whether it was on ours, or on the Indian side of the boundary. if on ours, we have jurisdiction without regard to persons or nations: but within their boundary we claim no jurisdiction over them. but the act of Congress of 1802 c.13. §.14. seems to settle accurately what ought to be done. I think it most probable the judge has not a copy of the law, and that he has done right by the coincidence of his own judgment with that of Congress, without knowing they had laid down a rule. if you think so, & will be so good as to signify it to me, I shall say so in the[2] answer which I must write. not having heard from you since mine of the 13th. we live in hopes of seeing yourself & family here. Accept my affectionate salutations & assurances of great esteem & consideration.

TH: JEFFERSON

RC (MHi); signature clipped, supplied from PrC; at foot of text: "The Secretary at War." PrC (DLC). Recorded in SJL as a letter to the War Department with notation "judge Campbell. Butler. Vandyke. Jackson." Enclosures: (1) Andrew

Jackson to TJ, 7 Aug. 1803. (2) David Campbell to TJ, 1 July 1803. Other enclosure not found.

ACT OF CONGRESS: "An Act to regulate trade and intercourse with the Indian tribes, and to preserve peace on the frontiers," passed 30 Mch. 1802. Section 14 of the act specified the means of redress against Indians who committed transgressions against citizens or inhabitants of the United States in the states or territories. Victims were to submit their cases and supporting evidence to the proper U.S. Indian agent, who would make application to the Indian nation or tribe for satisfaction. If the case remained unsettled after a reasonable time, it was to be forwarded to the president for further action. Campbell had referred the above case to Cherokee agent Return Jonathan Meigs (U.S. Statutes at Large, 2:143-4; Campbell to TJ, 1 July 1803).

[1]Preceding two words interlined.
[2]Word written over "my."

From Thomas Kennedy

Williams Port. Maryland
Augt. 26th. 1803

RESPECTED CITIZEN,

Without ceremony, I have made free enough to address you on a subject of a private nature.—

On returning from Cumberland a few days ago, I found (my wife's brother) Francis Thomas considerably alarmed about some reports that he was informed were circulating in George Town respecting his leaving the Naval service, he told me that he had wrote to you stating his case and requesting a pardon; No answer having yet been received is the reason why I have wrote to you now, on the same subject.—

He left the United States Frigate in the month of November 1800.—He was then quite a youth, indeed he is so now, and it is my sincere opinion, that he was not aware of the guilt attached to the action, and further that it was not a voluntary act of his, but done at the request of a female relative, who had considered herself ill used, and ignorant of the danger to which she was exposing him, wished him to come and assist in seeing justice done to her.—The Bounty or money he had received I understand was returned, and a receipt obtained for the same by some friend in Philadelphia

He had been as it were for many years without a guardian, his father William Thomas & his only brother Samuel, went from Frederick County Maryland, about the year 1791 with a cargo of goods to the Western Country, Shortly after Samuel and a Mr Swearingen were killed by the Indians on the Ohio river, on their way to Natchez where his father had settled.—In 1795 or 1796 his father sailed from thence for Baltimore, in order to remove his family to that Country but he—the crew—the vessel and Cargo were lost near the Island of Cuba.—

These facts were never fully ascertained till after Francis had left the Frigate, and gone to Natchez in quest of his father and brother, but—they were—No more. he resided some time there and at New Orleans, Dr. James Speed was one of his most intimate friends there; he went afterwards to Georgia and sailed in a vessel belonging to Mr Wall of Savannah—I wrote to him to come here and live with me; himself and two sisters who are affectionately attached to him are all that remain of his family, we had all promised ourselves much pleasure on his arrival here last June, and we have experienced the pleasures of family friendship, which were heightened by the thoughts—that from a rambling boy, he had become a steady—active young man.—

He is naturally possessed of a brave—a generous disposition, of a hardy Constitution a strong manly form, and should real danger require his assistance, there is none I beleive will sooner fly to the aid of his Country; He has in one respect acted Wrong—he confesses it—is sorry for his misconduct, and were it
now to do, would sooner die.—To
you Sir, he looks as to a father for
Forgiveness.—Grant his request,—
You will thus render him happy and comfort us all—America I trust will not suffer by the act.—

Francis is now under my direction, we shall all be anxious till his fate is known, You will therefore be kind enough to inform us of your determination V. Mail, so soon as matters of more importance will allow.—

Accept the sincere regard of THO. KENNEDY

RC (DLC); addressed: "The Honble. Thomas Jefferson Esq. President of the United States Washington City"; endorsed by Jacob Wagner as received 30 Aug.; endorsed by TJ as received 2 Sep. and so recorded in SJL.

A native of Scotland, Thomas Kennedy (1776-1832) emigrated to the United States in 1796 and eventually settled in Washington County, Maryland, where he engaged in trade and married Rosamond Thomas of Frederick. He also wrote poetry, publishing a book of verse in 1815 that included his piece entitled "Ode to the Mammoth Cheese." A Republican, he entered the Maryland legislature in 1818 and played an active role in passing the so-called Jew Bill in 1826, which allowed Jews in the state to hold public office, serve as militia officers, and practice law. He died in a cholera epidemic in 1832 (*Jewish Quarterly Review*, 19 [1929], 505-6; Thomas J. C. Williams, *A History of Washington County, Maryland, From the Earliest Settlements to the Present Time*, 2 vols. [Hagerstown, Md., 1906; repr. Baltimore, 1968], 1:170-3; Edward Eitches, "Maryland's 'Jew Bill,'" *American Jewish Historical Quarterly*, 60 [1971], 258-79; Vol. 36:xlix-l, 406 [illus.]).

HE HAD WROTE TO YOU: Francis W. Thomas to TJ, 6 Aug. 1803.

From Joseph Jones Monroe

DEAR SIR Orange 26th. Augt: 1803.

The inclosure is a letter from my friend & relation Mr James Bankhead of Westmoreland. Understanding I was on my way to the upper Country & might probably see you before my return he requested me to deliver it to you in person. I regret that owing to forgetfulness I did not comply with his wishes.

I have the honor to be with the highest respect yr: mo: ob: St

JO: JO: MONROE

RC (DNA: RG 59, LAR); addressed: "Thomas Jefferson esqr Prest. of the United States Monticello"; endorsed by TJ as received 31 Aug. and "James Bankhead to be Secy. legn to London" and so recorded in SJL. Enclosure: James Bankhead to TJ, 15 Aug. 1803.

Joseph Jones Monroe was a younger brother of James Monroe (see Vol. 29:198n).

From Alexander White

DEAR SIR Woodville 27th. August 1803

I am inclined to believe that those in power at the close of the former administration, did not attach much merit to the preparing the permanent Seat of Goverment for the reception of Congress; otherwise the man who had promoted that measure by seven years assiduous and successful attention, would not have been entirely overlooked, when the good things which the institution afforded were distributing. But having said this, it may be proper to observe that I then held an Office which Mr. Adams thought ought not to be abolished; and that I never gave the most distant intimation to him or to any of his Council that an appointment would be agreeable. On this occasion I pursued the conduct that I had pursued during life. The few Offices I have held whether by popular election, or Executive appointment, have been spontaneously conferred. Indeed I was not anxious. I doubted whether the salary annexed to any Office in the District of Columbia would compensate for the additional expence of living. Besides, My situation in Washington had not been the most agreeable, and I longed for retirement; but I find (what perhaps all men under similar circumstances find) that what was most pleasing when enjoyed as a relaxation from business, lies heavy on my hands when out of employ. I seem to be prematurely buried, and think that if I were in a situation that would draw my attention to subjects which engaged the study of my Youth, and the practical exertion of my faculties in my riper years, I could yet be useful to society, and at the same time enjoy life with a better relish.

I have taken the liberty of expressing these sentemints in consequence of a report generally believed; that Mr. James Marshall is about to resign his office as a Judge of the[1] Circuit Court of Columbia and to mention that I should, for various reasons, consider an appointment to that Office, under your nomination, as highly honourable—I know not how far I may have already transgress'd the rules of propriety, and therefore shall say nothing with respect to myself; but that I remain with sentiments of the highest respect and regard

Dear Sir Your most Obt Sert ALEX WHITE

RC (DNA: RG 59, LAR); at foot of text: "Thomas Jefferson President of the U: States"; endorsed by TJ as received 15 Sep. and "to be judge of Columbia v. Marshall" and so recorded in SJL.

SEVEN YEARS ASSIDUOUS AND SUCCESSFUL ATTENTION: White served as one of the District of Columbia commissioners from 1795 to 1802 (DAB). He was apparently disappointed about not being offered a place on the district's circuit court when it was created by Congress in February 1801 (U.S. Statutes at Large, 2:103-8).

[1] White here canceled "District."

From John Wilson

Alexandria August 27th 1803

Necessity has so far overcome the delicacy of easier circumstances that I can no longer refrain from taking a liberty, which, I hope, may not be uninteresting—even to a person of your superior station and influence: For it is from a Character so honorable and exalted, that even good men are apt to shrink:—And I must acknowledge the awe that pervades me, on writing to ask your interference: At the same time, I feel a confidence in your disposition to assist any person who has *Conduct*, and desires to acquire competent circumstances, by respectable means—I *did*, not long since, attain to the possession of some little capital to begin with, but lost it all in the misfortunes of mercantile business, in Norfolk, my native place. So unlucky a vississitude, which deprived me of all at once, made me rather wish to leave a place which before gave me pleasure. I form'd the design of settling at Washington City, with a view to seek employment in some of the Offices and procured letters to Mr. Beckley for that purpose. The Salary of his Engrossers and having, as I thought, the principal quality to do the duty, so far as writing a hand most requisite for such business induced me almost to expect a preference. But there were prior applicants and I was somewhat disappointed to hear Mr. B say that an Engrosser ought to know how to draw up reports &c.—I have engrossed for the Legislature of Virginia and thought such a proficiency as I have mentioned, was not indispensable; I still flatter myself other advantages I should manifest, might be deem'd equal to my ignorance in many particulars. In the several visits I paid my friend Mr. B, there was little opportunity, and I did not feel *altogether* free enough, to relate particularly my situation.

Mr. B, I trust, will give some satisfactory account of me: He knew my father Jno. when member of Assembly;—he was also Colo. of Norfolk County and died during the revolution; he requested in his will his Estate shou'd be sold for paper money—so that the whole amo. tho' large, was sank—our family became poor, neglected, and scattered; except however, the eldest Son, who is favoured by a grateful people, in the Clerkship of Norfolk County.

I have a wife and child, we are a young family settled and keeping a Shoe store in the last Brick house on the Avenue E of West market. I went to the City in Jany last, and have some time spent what I had and made many efforts to get in an eligible situation, the small scale of the temporary Business I still continue, seems to repel people from patronizing me—you know the charges of a family there are unproportionably high, and we may add to these, the expense and delay in getting supplies for a small store in the City, which is also much greater than wou'd attend extensive business.

In this situation—in rambling all over the District for employ, I am now, and have been once before, constrained to tare myself from the tenderest connexions, sick and amongst strangers, for employment here; and *here* I must remain, in the charge of an extensive Shoe store, till the owner returns from Boston. Upon this view, where there is a family whose destiny is involved with mine, and a gloomy prospect before me, my Spirits will involuntary fall—my hands feel tied, and I find myself longer and yet longer excluded from a genteel living—a genteel living, I mean, such as may be the reward of services rendered. If I was void of patience and perseverance, capacity or affection—I wou'd ere long drop down under the consciousness of my own inconsistency [but]   You will excuse the pause on this occasion—it wou'd be nothing in favor of a man [on?] many others.

I aspire much to be Book keeper or some sort of writer that will procure me about 1000$ pr ann. but if it does not fall to my lot by the end of the ensuing session shall be unable to support myself longer in the City under the hope of realising my wishes; and must remove to Alexandria or some place where trade or the demands of others business, will better afford means equivalent to Expenses. Even in this case, I shou'd bid adieu to the City with regret—because a stability of opinion urges me to adopt the Seat of Governmt. as a permanent place of residence. Be assured, Sir, your mediation shall always call forth the acknowledgements of a man, who really wishes to do well; and considers it a duty to his family, to make every honest effort to retrieve former circumstances.

Hoping for a proof of your Philantrophy, I beg leave to Subscribe myself with the sincere deference compatible to your Excellency;

Your Excellency's humble servant, JNO. WILSON

NB. I pray you to excuse and not expose the improprieties of my letter it is written in the hurry of business and there was not time to be more particular. I can hardly expect an answer but should be glad to have the liberty of waiting on you. You may remember my father yourself! but be assured I can convince of my own examplary conduct yet I cannot but blush to feel the necessity of saying so myself. As to writing the most peculiar pieces of writing I will venture to say few any where exceed me, and however admirable this qualification I acknowledge myself unacquainted and inexperienced in many points, more essential. How have I dared to trouble you, tis not for my sake—but ah Sir, my family; what tears of joy & gratitude cou'd I tell them of an efficient Benefactor. I rather not accede to any proposition that may be made me here until I can better ascertain my prospects in the City. Respect! J. WILSON

RC (DNA: RG 59, LAR); with postscript written at 90 degrees across the closing two paragraphs, obscuring two words; endorsed by TJ as received 5 Sep. and "for office" and so recorded in SJL.

John Wilson later sought help from James Madison in a letter of 8 Nov. 1804, in which he claimed to have turned down an offer of employment from Joseph Nourse, the register of the Treasury, because of his commitments in Alexandria and because of the small salary, but "at this time such a salary would be very acceptable." During the same month, Thomas Newton, Jr., wrote to an unidentified recipient on Wilson's behalf (Madison, *Papers, Sec. of State Ser.*, 8:268; RC in DNA: RG 59, LAR, 12:468-9).

ELDEST SON: possibly William Wilson, Jr., who in 1806 was identified as clerk of the court in Portsmouth, the principal town in Norfolk County (*The Norfolk Directory, Containing the Names, Occupations, and Places of Abode and Business, of the Inhabitants, Arranged in Alphabetical Order* [Norfolk, 1806], 54).

From Henry Dearborn

SIR Washington August 28th. 1803

I arrived last evening from Bath, where I had been twelve or fourteen days,—on my way home I received a packet from Mr. Wingate inclosing your two letters of the 8th. and 13 Inst.—at Hagerstown, I met with Mr. Pechon with whoom I spent a day, in the course of conversation, I observed to Mr. Pechon that I had been informed by gentlemen from Baltimore that Young Boneparte had announced himself and was making a considerable shew, Mr. Pechon observed that when young Boneparte & Merlen arrived at George Town, the former requested him to apply to our governmt for a Frigate to transport him to France, under a borrowed name, that he, Pechon, informed him that there would be an impropriety in applying for such a favour for an unknown charactor, and that he could not expect the request would be granted, even if his real name should be announced, for it would be compromiting the neutrality of the United States with England, but the young man insisted on having the request made, Mr. Pechon accordingly mentioned the subject to Mr. Madison, who agreed with Mr. Pechon in opinnion, that to grant the request would give just cause of offence to Great Britain, afterwards young Boneparte thought proper to announce himself, and again insisted on another application for a Frigate—he was again told by Pechon that the American Government could not consistantly with its neutral position grant such a request. Mr. Pechon is desidedly of opinnion that the request could not be granted without giving Just cause of offince to England, and he has made arrangements for procuring a French Frigate for the purpose, of conveying Boneparte home—I have been thus perticular in detailing my conversation with Pechon, from a belief that it might be agreable to you to know the circumstances, especially his own opinnion on the subject.—I hope that no further application will be made on the subject, as a denial would be painful; and a compliance (in my opinnion) highly improper.

with sentiments of the most respectfull concideration I am Sir Your Obedt. Huml Servt H. DEARBORN

RC (DLC); at foot of text: "The President of the United States"; endorsed by TJ as received from the War Department on 31 Aug. and "Jerome Buonaparte" and so recorded in SJL.

Joshua WINGATE, Jr., was Dearborn's son-in-law and the chief clerk of the War Department (Vol. 38:296n).

MERLEN: perhaps Pierre Meyronnet.

From Henry Dearborn

SIR, Washington August 28th, 1803

The address from Kaskaskias and the petition of Aaron Goff have been duly received.—Mr. W. Clark, having consented to accompany Capt. Lewis, is highly interesting, it adds very much to the ballance of chances in favour of ultimate success.—

If any considerations whatever would induce my family to make a Journey, it would be that of visiting Monticello, and especially after the friendly & polite invitation of its proprietor, but unfortunately, Mrs. Dearborn & Mrs. Wingate have for ten days past been laid up by intermiting fevers. Mrs. Wingate has nearly recovered, but Mrs. Dearborn is still very low,—when I left home for Bath they were both in such high health, as to decline going into the Country.—

be pleased Sir to present the best respects of myself & family to Mrs. Randolph & Mrs. Epes, and accept for yourself our united esteem & respect. H. DEARBORN

RC (DLC); at foot of text: "The President of the United States"; endorsed by TJ as received from the War Department on 31 Aug. and "Kaskaskia petn. Goff's petn." and so recorded in SJL.

For the ADDRESS from Kaskaskia, see TJ to Dearborn, 8 Aug. 1803. For the AARON GOFF petition and William Clark's acceptance, see TJ to Dearborn, 13 Aug. 1803.

From Gideon Granger

DEAR SIR. Suffield August 28th 1803

I can now speak with confidence on the subject of a Collector at New Haven. I am fully convinced that evry republican in the State who is not himself a Candidate ardently wishes that Abm. Bishop may be appointed—Indeed I should not have beleived that any man for any Office could have united so generally the wishes and feelings of the People—

There are a number who would be fond of the Office. The Marshal, Henry Edwards Esq & O L Phelps Esq are among the most prominent Candidates but all refuse to interfere with Bishop. Either of them are greatly to be preferred to Saml. Broome who I understand by his friends in New York and by a Tory Intrigue at New Haven has been strongly reccommended. If he suceeds either the Office will pass into the hands of his Son in Law a bitter Tory, or a greater evil be experienced. I have seen or heard from most of Our leading friends—They have all wished me to support Bishop and I most cordially (notwithstandg what has heretofore influenced my Opinions) reccommend him for the appointment.

Sir, when conversing on the Subject of a register for the commission of Adams County you mentioned that you had authorized Mr. Kirby to appoint that Officer because you did not know who to select as you tho't the emoluments would not form a sufficient Inducement to persuade any person to undertake the Journey fm. this Country. Upon my return here I found a Young Man who I have heretofore educated to the Law about to remove to that Country & advised Mr. Kirby of the fact & reccommended him for the Office. From him I discovered that he was restricted to appoint a Citizen of that County.

As I supposed this Order originated in the same cause that led to the delegation of the power and as it appeared at least probable that in so infant a Country no person could be found who had not some interest in the Soil, I tho't I might venture to ask whether it would be agreeable to you to have a Citizen appointed who goes into that Country with a view of making it the place of his residence—

The man reccommended is of undoubted integrity and decent acquirements.

The Tories here have at length discovered that Louisiana will ruin us—

I am with great Esteem & respect Yours Sincerely

GIDN GRANGER

RC (DNA: RG 59, LAR); addressed: "Thomas Jefferson Esq President of the UStates Monticello Virginia"; franked; postmarked Hartford, 31 Aug.; endorsed by TJ as received 7 Sep. and "Bishop Abram to be Collector New haven" and so recorded in SJL; also endorsed by TJ: "a register for Mobile."

THE MARSHAL: Joseph Willcox (Vol. 33:590-1n; Vol. 38:575n). TJ appointed HENRY EDWARDS a bankruptcy commissioner at New Haven in July 1802. He was recommended by his father, Pierpont Edwards (Vol. 37:210). O L PHELPS: Granger probably refers to Suffield merchant Oliver Leicester Phelps, a Yale graduate and only son of congressman-elect Oliver Phelps (*Biog. Dir. Cong.*; Dexter, *Yale*, 5:121-2). If Samuel BROOME received the appointment, Granger feared that the New Haven collectorship would PASS INTO THE HANDS of Joseph Fay (Fay to TJ, 12 Aug. 1803).

WHAT HAS HERETOFORE INFLUENCED MY OPINION: in 1801, Connecticut Republicans enthusiastically supported the appointment of Samuel Bishop, but not that of his son (Vol. 33:627; Vol. 34:93).

HE WAS RESTRICTED: see TJ to Ephraim Kirby, 15 July.

From Ephraim Kirby

SIR Litchfield Augt. 28th. 1803

A few days since I had the pleasure of an interview with Mr Granger—He being acquainted with the fact of the Blank Comn. of Register being confided to me, we conversed on that subject. It appears that two young Gentn. of about twenty five or thirty years, both Lawyers, the one from the State of New York, and the other from the State of Connt. are desirous to establish themselves in that part of the country to which I am going.—They are both known to Mr. Granger and myself—We are of opinion that either of them will do ample honor to the office of *Register*.—They are Gentn. of more established integrity and talents than will probably be found in the infant settlements of the Missisippi Territory, and are firmly attached to the present administration of the Genl Government. I laid before Mr Granger your instructions, that the office be confered on "some inhabitant of that part of the country"—He advised me to address you on this subject, as the public interest may probably be better served by confering the office on some person who *will become* an inhabitant of the place in consequence of the appointment. I hope I shall be honored with further instructions in due season, if any are deemed necessary. Letters will reach me in time at Pittsburgh.

I have proposed to myself a rout thro' the western States, not because it will be the most expeditious or agreable, but because it may enable me to render more service to my country. In doing this I shall not limit myself to the more official duties of my commission.

The office of Collector at the port of New Haven has lately become vacant by the decease of Deacn. Bishop. The opposors of the Government have made great exertions to excite a strong competition for the office. As far as my information extends, Abraham Bishop Esqr is the candidate which the friends of the Administration believe the most competent and deserving of the appointment. I have been several weeks confined by ill health, and am unacquainted with all that has passed on this occasion.—

I am Sir, with the highest respect Your Obedt. Servt

EPHM KIRBY

RC (DNA: RG 59, LAR); at foot of text: "The President of the U. States"; endorsed by TJ as received 5 Sep. and "Register of Mobile. Abr. Bishop. Collector N. Haven" and so recorded in SJL.

YOUR INSTRUCTIONS: see TJ to Kirby, 15 July.

From James Madison

Sir Sunday Aug. 28. 1803

I have recd. your two favors, one of the 24th. instant the other covering the letters from Mr. Gallatin, & Barnes now returned.

I had thought it might be best not to answer Thornton's letter because in some parts his manner did not deserve it, because he speaks without the known sentiments of his Govt. and because the Minister of higher grade expected, will be likely to give a more eligible opportunity for these discussions. As I promise the pleasure of being able to take your directions in person in the course of this week probably towards the last of it, I shall do nothing in the case till I can do it with that advantage. The British Govt. I apprehend will not act with us on the subject of seamen, in the manner you hint at. They would sign no convention without reserving to themselves the claim to impress seamen in the narrow seas, and as this was evidently inadmissible, it was no doubt made a condition with a view to prevent any arrangement, and to carry on the impressments as heretofore. In consequence of your letter of I had directed Derieux to be paid his charge of $300 for actual expences, as Hughes was paid his. If any thing further should be thought just in his behalf it can be added. I inclose the communications recd by the last mail from Washington. Pederson I presume may be told that he will have access to the Govt. as the substitute of Olson, who signified his wish to that effect. Will you be so obliging as to have the confidential letter from Monroe to the three Senators put into the hands of Mr. Nicholas. You will see by his public letter that his liberality has been very near seducing him into a very ticklish situation. I have not yet been able to decypher the letter to you from Mr. Livingston, having but just recd the Cypher. I will execute the task for the next mail. I think K's prejudice must have given a sharp coloring to his remarks on E. The caution alluded to in Mr. Gallatin's letter, was if I do not misrecollect, observed in the instructions from the Dept. of State. Yrs. most respectfully

James Madison

RC (DLC); endorsed by TJ as received from the State Department at Orange on 31 Aug. and "our ports made cruising stations.—impresmt seamen. Derieux. Erving" and so recorded in SJL. Enclosures: (1) Peder Pedersen to Madison, 19 Aug., from Frankford, Pennsylvania, stating that he has arrived in the United States and learned that the state of Peder Blicher Olsen's health compelled him to return to Europe already; he asks the secretary of state to inform the president of his arrival so that he may arrange to pay his respects to TJ in person and take up his duties (Madison, *Papers*, *Sec. of State Ser.*, 5:327; see TJ to Christian VII, King of Denmark, 6 June). (2) James Monroe to Madison, 8 June, Paris, marked "private," enclosing a letter of 25 May from Monroe to Stevens Thomson

Mason, Wilson Cary Nicholas, and John Breckinridge (see below). (3) Monroe to Madison, 8 June, official dispatch (see below).

THE OTHER: TJ to Madison, 18 Aug.

MINISTER OF HIGHER GRADE EXPECTED: Anthony Merry.

The British ministry rejected the proposed convention on impressment because it did not give that nation sovereignty over what were called the NARROW SEAS—the waters separating Britain, Wales, and Scotland from Ireland and Europe (Madison, *Papers*, *Sec. of State Ser.*, 5:204; OED; TJ to Madison, 31 July).

YOUR LETTER: 18 Aug.

PEDERSON: from Philadelphia on 30 Aug., Pedersen wrote to Madison again. Madison replied on 10 Sep., stating that the president "proposes to be at the seat of Government about the 25th." Pedersen was in Washington on 30 Sep. and Madison probably presented him to TJ on that day or the next. TJ signed an exequatur on 1 Oct. to recognize Pedersen as consul for Denmark "and declare him free to exercise and enjoy such functions, powers and privileges, as are allowed to Consuls of such friendly powers, between whom and the United States there is no particular agreement for the regulation of the Consular functions" (FC in Lb in DNA: RG 59, Exequaturs; Madison, *Papers*, *Sec. of State Ser.*, 5:363, 400, 478).

Monroe's letter TO THE THREE SENATORS discussed the circumstances that brought about the successful negotiation for Louisiana. "I sincerely wish my colleague to derive all the advantage & credit which his good exertions & intentions entitle him to," Monroe wrote of Livingston in the 8 June cover letter to Madison; "but the transaction ought to rest on its true ground." Concerned that Livingston was distorting the facts to give himself undue credit, Monroe wanted to place the emphasis on actions taken by Congress and the executive branch. Monroe asked Madison to forward the document to the senators or, at his discretion, withhold it from them. "You will readily conceive" the importance of avoiding "every thing like a discussion of the kind referrd to," Monroe confided to Madison. Of Livingston he noted that "I am of opinion that it imports the credit of the admn. to treat him with kindness & attention." In his dispatch to the secretary of state also dated 8 June—which Monroe wrote in code, but Madison called a PUBLIC LETTER to distinguish it from the communication labeled "private"—Monroe recounted a call he had made on Talleyrand and Barbé de Marbois without Livingston. He came to the meeting alone, as he explained to the two officials, to obtain information that Barbé de Marbois had already privately imparted to Livingston (Madison, *Papers*, *Sec. of State Ser.*, 5:81-3; Preston, *Catalogue*, 1:144).

DECYPHER THE LETTER: see TJ to Madison, 18 Aug.

K'S PREJUDICE: that is, Rufus King's comments about George W. Erving (E) in GALLATIN'S LETTER to TJ of 18 Aug.

From Robert Smith

SIR, Baltimore Augt. 28. 1803

Your favor of the 23d enclosing Mr. Simpsons letter to Mr Madison I have received. I am extremely sorry to find that the plan of having made in Europe the gun Carriages for the Emperor of Moracco cannot take effect. I am yet satisfied that the plan was at the time proper. Subsequent events, it seems, have rendered it impracticable. I am also much distressed that Mr Simpson did not deem it expedient to offer the cash. I believe that the Emperor would have been well satisfied with a sum of money much less than will be expended by us in procuring and transporting the carriages. Among the difficulties that have heretofore presented themselves in this business the means of ascertaining the size and the kind of carriages have never been communicated to the Secretary of State. And Mr Simpson in his last letter only informs him that they must be "perfectly complete for land service with iron axle trees" &c &c without specifying the caliber of the gun and without stating whether they are to be for *battery* or *field* service. It is to be presumed from circumstances that they are to be for batteries. Be this, however, as it may, the gun Carriages of the frigates will not answer. They not only do not answer the description in Mr Simpson's letter, but they are not at all fit for either battery or field service. When it was understood that the Navy Department "would see to the execution of this business" it was believed that the Navy gun Carriages would be accepted. But Mr Simpson's last letter informs us explicitly that they are wanted for *Land* service. Possibly the War-Department may be able to supply the demand immediately. We have probably this number of Carriages constructed for embrasures, and as the embrasure construction is now exploded, the Secretary at War may substitute in their place the modern approved plan of carriages. If this should be the case the advantages will compensate for any temporary inconveniences. But at all events I know of no other mode of sending on the Carriages in due season. To build them would require many, perhaps, six, months. And the building of them would call for the careful superintendence of a skilful Artillery Officer. As these Carriages are wanted for *land* service, there is not an Officer nor an agent of the Navy[1] Department competent to the undertaking. They must be constructed upon principles well established and well known to scientifick Artillery Officers, but not professionally to the Officers of the Navy. If the War department cannot immediately supply this demand and new Carriages must be made, I would submit to consideration, whether they could not be made with the least expence under the[2] order of the Secretary at War by his Corps of artificers or at Washington under the superintendence of Col Bearbeck. In case it should be inconvenient to the Secretary at War to have any agency in this business, I will most willingly and without delay undertake it, if he will have the goodness to give me the[3] services of Col Bearbeck or of some other skilful Artillery Officer. Without such a superintending Officer it would be utterly impossible for the Navy Department to accomplish it. But with all the advantages that could be thus afforded me,[4] it must be obvious that Genl Dearborn is much better qualified than I can be. The occasion however is very pressing & our exertions ought to be united to promote dispatch. I have some apprehension that this disappointment to the Emperor connected with the Capture of the Ship by our squadron may provoke a disposition to hostility[5] And therefore I am the more anxious that the War-Department should immediately furnish the number, which may be replaced at leisure.

A copy of the above I will send by this Mail to Genl Dearborn in order that he and I may be progressing in the business and may be the better prepared to act promptly under the instructions which you may be pleased to give either to him or to me.

Measures will be taken to have to a certainty a vessel prepared on the 31st. day of October for the purpose mentioned by you. I have reason to believe from every information I have obtained that the last of the small vessels will have sailed before any orders could reach her Commanding Officer. There would besides be a considerable expence in keeping in port a vessel completely Officered and manned for two months and the appearance would require explanations which could not be given. The frigate that will be equipped for this purpose may also take the gun Carriages, which may be delivered to Simpson after leaving France. This can be done provided the War Department can furnish at once the Carriages. And it is very important to save the expence of a War-freight.

I have the pleasure of informing you that Bonaparte & Rewbell are both well pleased with Baltimore. The former, from the House he has rented, its furniture and the expensive style of his whole establishment, evidently intends to remain among us for some time. The latter has given us a stronger mark of his attachment. He has married last night a very beautiful lady, the daughter of a very honest and respectable *Republican*. Bishop Carroll is assiduously attentive to them. And under his influence certain Feds are visiting them. With the greatest regard & Esteem I am sincerely Your Obedt. Servt.

RT SMITH

RC (DLC); endorsed by TJ as received from the Navy Department on 2 Sep. and "gun carriages. armd vessel for ratifn. Bonaparte. Reubell" and so recorded in SJL. Tr (MB); entirely in Smith's hand; lacks final two paragraphs and signature.

COL. BEARBECK: that is, Colonel Henry Burbeck, commander of the Regiment of Artillerists and one of the most experienced artillery officers in the army (Heitman, *Dictionary*, 1:262; Theodore J. Crackel, *Mr. Jefferson's Army: Political and Social Reform of the Military Establishment, 1801-1809* [New York, 1987], 79).

CAPTURE OF THE SHIP: in August, reports reached the United States of the capture of the *Meshouda*, a former Tripolitan warship that had been blockaded by the American navy at Gibraltar since July 1801. The vessel had finally received a passport from the American consul at Tangier, James Simpson, in September 1802, with the understanding that it now belonged to the emperor of Morocco, Mawlay Sulayman, and that it would not enter blockaded ports. On 12 May 1803, however, the *Meshouda* was captured while attempting to enter the port of Tripoli by the United States frigate *John Adams*, commanded by John Rodgers. Taking his prize to Malta, Rodgers found the *Meshouda* carried not only a contraband cargo of arms and naval stores, but a Tripolitan captain and seamen as well, none of which were permitted under the terms of the American passport. Furthermore, the Tripolitan told Rodgers that ownership of the *Meshouda* had been returned to the pasha of Tripoli. Writing Simpson on 19 May about the capture, Commodore Richard V. Morris exclaimed, "this whole business appears to be a detestable Fraud," but added that he would forgo condemning the *Meshouda* if it could be proven that the ship was not acting under the emperor's orders. Upon receiving Morris's letter, Simpson confronted the governor of Tangier, Abd al-Rahman Ashash, who adamantly disavowed the actions of the *Meshouda*'s commander as "diametrically opposite" to the wishes of the emperor. In his 9 July dispatch to Madison, Simpson expressed his desire to see the *Meshouda* restored to Mawlay Sulayman as an example of America's "Friendly intentions" toward him. In addition, Simpson warned that Morocco was in the process of outfitting cruisers for sea, which "might give trouble" if the *Meshouda* were not returned (*Alexandria Advertiser*, 22 Aug. 1803; *National Intelligencer*, 22 Aug. 1803; Baltimore *Republican, or Anti-Democrat*, 24 Aug. 1803; Christopher McKee, *Edward Preble: A Naval Biography, 1761-1807* [Annapolis, 1972], 91, 115, 143-4; NDBW, 2:283, 379, 385, 408-9, 456-7; Madison, *Papers, Sec. of State Ser.*, 5:157-8; Vol. 35:219; Vol. 38:195n).

Jean Jacques Reubell MARRIED Henriette Pascault, a daughter of Baltimore merchant Lewis (Louis) Pascault. The wedding was presided over by Bishop John Carroll (Charlene M. Boyer Lewis, *Elizabeth Patterson Bonaparte: An American Aristocrat in the Early Republic* [Philadelphia, 2012], 15-16, 100, 182, 233n; Cornelius William Stafford, *The Baltimore Directory, for 1803* [Baltimore, 1803], 101; Thomas O'Brien Hanley, ed., *The John Carroll Papers*, 3 vols. [Notre Dame, Indiana, 1976], 2:422-3).

[1] Word interlined.

[2] Smith here canceled "directions."

[3] Smith here canceled "assistance."

[4] Word interlined.

[5] Preceding six words interlined in place of "will probably provoke his hostility."

From Thomas Appleton

SIR — Leghorn 29th. of August 1803—

I am well aware that in addressing you by letter, I am deviating from the usual mode of Application, but the great distance at which I am placed, and the uncertainty of every other avenue to convey to you my request, will I presume testify, they have been the alone motives for prefering the one I have adopted.—

this being at once Sir my apology and my Reason, suffer me in a few words to state the object of my letter.—I have been informed, and this through a channel which inclines me to believe my intelligence is correct, that Mr. Skipwith intends relinquishing his Office as Commercial Agent in Paris, in the event of his being nominated by you to a place he is desirous of obtaining in the United States.—It is solely in the success of these his wishes, that I should Offer myself to fill the vacancy that would by this means present.—If a Knowledge of the french language, become habitual by a practise of it from my earliest youth, and eleven years residence in france; joined to my having filled the office of Consul at Leghorn for six years, with fidelity I may say, and I hope to the satisfaction of Government, are circumstances which might lead to a preference in your nomination, the gratitude with which I shall be impressed, can only be equalled by my unfeigned respect for your eminent Virtues.—I would in no wise be understood, that I am desirous of relinquishing the Office I at present hold by your bounty, except *only* in the case you should esteem me worthy to be preferred in that of Paris. a circumstance I Confess, I am highly solicitous to obtain.—Accept Sir the Assurances of the unalterable respect with which I have the honor to be Your most devoted Servant TH: APPLETON

RC (DNA: RG 59, LAR); endorsed by TJ as received 2 Dec. and "to be Comml. Agent Paris v. Skipwith" and so recorded in SJL. FC (DNA: RG 84, Consular Records, Leghorn); at foot of text: "given in charge to Mr Smith who sails with Come. Morris & enclosed in the foregoing letter to Mr Madison."

UNCERTAINTY OF EVERY OTHER AVENUE: Appleton's notation on his retained copy of this letter indicates that he enclosed it in a dispatch he wrote to Madison, which was also dated 29 Aug., and put the documents in the care of William Loughton Smith, the former U.S. minister to Portugal. Smith had been in Naples and traveled to Leghorn by way of Malta. Richard Valentine Morris gave him passage on the frigate *Adams* as far as Tangier. From there, Smith hoped to return to the United States aboard one of the navy's frigates (Madison, *Papers*, *Sec. of State Ser.*, 5:84, 354, 360; NDBW, 2:522; 3:127).

From Abraham Bradley, Jr.

SIR Washington August 29. 1803

Your favour of the 26th instant is received & agreeable thereto I have forwarded a map of the United States. The great alterations which have taken place in the U.S. since my map was first published have rendered it of little use & I have for sometime suspended the sale. I intended to have published a new map this summer, but fear it cannot be accomplished as all the good engravers are engaged at book-work.

I have the pleasure to inclose our new List of Post Offices, Previous to the organization of the present government there but 90 post offices & there are now nearly 1300!

I am with great respect your obedient

ABRAHAM BRADLEY JUN

RC (DLC); at foot of text: "His Excellency Thomas Jefferson President of the United States"; endorsed by TJ as received 31 Aug. and so recorded in SJL. Enclosures not found, but see below.

FORWARDED A MAP: probably his *Map of the United States*, published in 1796; see TJ to Bradley, 26 Aug.

On 25 Jan. 1803, Gideon Granger submitted to Congress a statement of the number of POST OFFICES, the length of post roads, and the transportation of the mails. According to these calculations, there were 195 post offices as of 3 Mch. 1793 and an estimated 1,283 as of 24 Jan. 1803 (*Report of the Post Master General* [Washington, D.C., 1803; Shaw-Shoemaker, No. 5475]; ASP, *Post Office Department*, 1:28).

From J. P. P. Derieux

MONSIEUR Washington City 29. aoust 1803.

N'ayant reçu aucune réponse a La Lettre que je pris la Liberté de vous ecrire en arrivant a New-york, j'ai lieu de craindre que la personne a qui je la confiai, ait négligé de la mettre a la poste, car la fievre qui régnoit des-ja dans cette ville m'empecha de quitter le Batiment. Si cependant elle vous etoit parvenue, et que ce fut L'indiscretion de mon importunité qui m'ait privé de L'honneur de votre réponse, je vous Supplie Monsieur de voulloir bien me la pardonner en faveur de mon Empressement a suivre les instructions de Mr. Monroe Lors qu'il me Chargea de ses Dépeches, et vous me rendrés un grand service, Monsieur de voulloir bien ajouter a cette faveur, celle de me renvoyer le Certifficat de Mr. Skipwith, afin que je puisse justiffier a mes creanciers des raisons qui ont donné lieu a mon impossibilité de pouvoir encore les Satisfaire.

J'ai L'honneur d'etre dans Les Sentiments du plus profond respect Monsieur Votre trés humble et trés obeissant Serviteur

P. DERIEUX

EDITORS' TRANSLATION

SIR, Washington City, 29 Aug. 1803

On my arrival in New York, the fever that was already raging there prevented me from leaving the ship, so I took the liberty of writing you a letter. Having received no answer, I fear that the person to whom I entrusted it may have failed to mail it. But if the letter did reach you, and it is the indiscretion of my importunity that has deprived me of the honor of a reply, I beg you, Sir, to forgive me, in view of my zeal in following Mr. Monroe's instructions when he charged me with his messages. You would render me a great service, Sir, if you could add to this favor that of sending back Mr. Skipwith's certificate, so I may document for my creditors the circumstances that have prevented me from satisfying their demands.

With deepest respect, Sir, I have the honor of being your very humble and obedient servant.
P. DeRieux

RC (DLC); at foot of text: "Care of Mr. Wam. O'Neale Washington-City"; endorsed by TJ as received 31 Aug. and so recorded in SJL.

LA LETTRE: Derieux to TJ, 9 Aug.

To James Madison

Dear Sir
Monticello Aug. 29. 1803.

By the last post I recieved & forwarded your letter to Duane, in which there was nothing but what was safe and proper. Duane is honest, & well intentioned, but over zealous. these qualities harmonise with him a great portion of the republican body. he deserves therefore all the just & favorable attentions which can properly be shewn him. by the same post I recieve from the collector of Norfolk the information you desired him to give in the case of capt Cloupet & the contraband negroes.[1] I presume it is by mistake he says he recieved the orders from the Secretary of the Treasury. I now inclose his papers to you with those recieved from you on the same subject. if you think with me that the case is of too doubtful an aspect to justify so early an interposition, it may lie awhile, and with the less inconvenience, as we cannot remit the right of the prosecutor qui tam. should you think otherwise I shall be ready to reconsider it at any time. I return you the letter &c. of Gavino. our two frigates and 4. small vessels have all sailed for Tripoli, and as those in the Mediterranean have at length appeared there, we may hope something will be done this season. I am afraid what has been done as to the Marocco-Tripoline may give us some trouble.

Govr. Page arrived here last night & will stay a week with us. I am not without hopes of seeing you in that time. altho' the post comes from Alexandria here in a day, & every other day, yet I think your letters to me & mine to you are sometimes 5. days old before they are recieved. it is true that I sometimes write on Saturday the letter which goes on Monday, and often write one day before the post. this may account for one & sometimes 2. days of the five. Accept my affectionate salutations for mrs Madison & yourself & assurances of sincere attachment.
Th: Jefferson

RC (DLC: Madison Papers); at foot of text: "The Secretary of State." PrC (DLC). Enclosures: (1) William Davies to TJ, 16 Aug., recorded in SJL as received from Norfolk on 26 Aug. but not found. (2) Louis André Pichon to Madison, 26 July (see TJ to Madison, 8 Aug.). (3) John Gavino to Madison, 18 June from Gibraltar; he encloses a letter to Madison from Richard V. Morris at Malta, 19 May, regarding the *Meshouda*, and reports steps he has taken to forward a letter from Morris to James Simpson; reporting also that a Portuguese warship had engaged in a battle off the coast of Algiers, the British ship *Victory* is at Gibraltar en route to Malta to become Horatio Nelson's flagship, and the last elements of the British army from Egypt are at Gibraltar, some on their way back to Britain; Gavino also encloses information about quarantine charges in the port and forwards a letter just received from Simpson (Madison, *Papers*, *Sec. of State Ser.*, 5:102).

QUI TAM: see Notes on Nathaniel Ingraham's Case, [ca. 9 May 1803].

MAROCCO-TRIPOLINE: see Robert Smith to TJ, 28 Aug.

[1]TJ here canceled "which you directed him."

To Richard Morris

DEAR SIR Monticello Aug. 29. 03.

I recieved two days ago your favor of the 25th. and should have been glad to accommodate your son as desired but that my particular situation has required me to make special provisions of his wood & lumber to ensure a perpetual supply. with this view I have purchased at different times the whole of the mountain adjoining the one I live on, & above the level of the gap uniting them. this circumstance places all it's growth within command as it is to come down hill to the gap, & then only a quarter of a mile up a gentle ascent. on these considerations I have thought myself obliged to decline every application which has been made me for timber of any kind. without that resource I could not have built as I have done, nor could I look forward with any comfort. trusting you will percieve in this only a justifiable attention to futurity, I tender you my friendly salutations & assurances of great esteem & respect. TH: JEFFERSON

PrC (DLC); at foot of text: "Colo. Richard Morris"; endorsed by TJ in ink on verso.

Richard Morris had been commissary of provisions in Virginia during the American Revolution. He owned a plantation in western Louisa County, where he kept a tavern that served travelers to the springs there. TJ likely stayed with Morris while meeting Mary Jefferson Eppes and John Wayles Eppes at the springs during his trip to Monticello in July (Madison, *Papers*, 1:248n; MB, 2:1105; TJ to John Strode, 9 July).

Morris's letter OF THE 25TH. was recorded in SJL as received from Green Springs on 27 Aug. but has not been found. The SON was either William O. Morris, who worked most closely with his father in business matters, or James Maury Morris (*Richmond Enquirer*, 28 Sep. 1819; biographical information in ViU: Morris Family Papers).

Amendment for Annexation of Louisiana and Florida

[30 Aug.-7 Sep. 1803?]

Amendment to the Constitution.

Louisiana, as ceded by France to the US. is made a part of the US. But[1] as to the portion thereof lying North of an East & West line drawn through the mouth of Arkansa river, no new state shall be established, nor any grants of land made, other than to Indians in exchange for equivalent portions of land occupied by them, until authorised by subsequent[2] amendment to the Constitution.[3]

Florida also, whensoever it may be rightfully obtained, shall become a part of the US.[4]

MS (DLC: TJ Papers, 137:23687); undated; entirely in TJ's hand; endorsed by him: "Louisiana."

As originally written (see notes below), this document was a fair copy of the text of the amendment as TJ incorporated it into his letter to Levi Lincoln of 30 Aug.—including an alteration to that letter to refer to an east-west LINE from the mouth of the Arkansas River rather than "latitude," the term used in the amendment as TJ sent it to Gallatin and Madison on the 23d and 24th, respectively. That evidence suggests that TJ did not create this manuscript before the 30th. It is unlikely that he worked on it after 7 Sep., when, in his letter to Wilson Cary Nicholas, he seems to have abandoned his plan for an amendment.

[1]Word interlined in place of canceled "it's white inhabitants shall be citizens, and stand, as to their rights & obligations, on the same footing with other citizens of the US. in analogous situations. Save only that."

[2]Preceding three words interlined in place of "an," with "subsequent" substituted for canceled "further."

[3]TJ here canceled "shall be made for these purposes."

[4]TJ here canceled "it's white inhabitants shall thereupon be citizens, & shall stand, as to their rights & obligations, on the same footing with other citizens of the US. in analogous situations."

To Albert Gallatin

DEAR SIR Monticello Aug. 30. 1803.

Your favors of the 20th. & 22d. came to hand yesterday, and this will go by return of post tomorrow. I now return the letters of Symonds & others on the smugling of negroes into Georgia. his letter to Payne of the revenue cutter will bring to issue the resistance apprehended, and if it be found too great, we must strengthen her. should the Enterprize return here to be refitted, which she needs, we might, in the most suspicious season keep her cruizing off the coast of Georgia & S. Carolina. there is no sentiment I feel stronger than that of a determination to break up this nefarious & dangerous traffic.

I had thought we might let the appointment of the Collector of Newhaven lie till our return to Washington: but the recommendations of Abraham Bishop are already as strong as they can be. Granger, Kirby, Woolcot, Wilcox, Edwards & others concur with earnestness to sollicit it, and I do not suppose we ought to consider any opposition which can be raised, as equal to this in respectability. in fact if we do not rely on those characters, to what others in Connecticut shall we give our confidence? Samuel Broome is recommended by mr Osgood and his own brother of N.Y. and by the Newhaven merchants, signers of the former address against Samuel Bishop. this last[1] has less than no weight. if you think with me that Abram Bishop should be appointed, I will, on recieving your letter, direct a commission, and give no further time for forming combinations of other interests to embarrass us. Accept my affectionate salutations and great esteem & respect.

TH: JEFFERSON

RC (NHi: Gallatin Papers); at foot of text: "The Secretary of the Treasury"; endorsed. PrC (DLC). Recorded in SJL with notation "Smuglg negroes. Abr. Bishop."

The letter from James Simons (SYMONDS) to James PAYNE, master of the revenue cutter at Charleston, has not been found (ASP, *Miscellaneous*, 1:278).

In SJL, TJ recorded receiving two letters from New Haven on 24 Aug. in favor of Abraham Bishop, one from Gideon GRANGER dated 16 Aug., the other from Jesse Atwater dated two days later. Neither has been found. A letter from Pierpont EDWARDS to TJ of 20 Aug., recorded in SJL as received by TJ on the 26th with the notation "Abr. Bishop to be Collectr," is also missing (see Appendix III). TJ did not receive the two strong letters in favor of Bishop from Ephraim Kirby and Granger, both dated 28 Aug., until 5 and 7 Sep., respectively.

BY THE NEWHAVEN MERCHANTS: see enclosures listed at Samuel Broome to TJ, 22 Aug. For the FORMER ADDRESS, see Vol. 34:381-4.

[1] Word interlined.

To Levi Lincoln

DEAR SIR Monticello Aug. 30. 1803.

The inclosed letter came to hand by yesterday's post. you will be sensible of the circumstances which make it improper that I should hazard a formal answer, as well as of the desire it's friendly aspect naturally excites that those concerned in it should understand that the spirit they express is favorably viewed. you can judge also, from your knolege of the ground, whether it may be usefully encouraged. I take the liberty therefore of availing myself of your neighborhood to Boston, and of your friendship to me, to say to the capt. and others, verbally, whatever you think would be proper, as expressive of my sentiments on the subject. with respect to the day on which they wish to fix their anniversary, they may be told that disapproving[1] myself of transferring the honours & veneration for the great birth-day of our republic, to any individual, or of dividing them with individuals, I have declined letting my own birthday be known, & have engaged my family not to communicate it. this has been the uniform answer to every application of the kind.

On further consideration as to the amendment to our constitution respecting Louisiana I have thought it better, instead of enumerating the powers which Congress may exercise, to give them the same powers they have as to other portions of the Union generally, and to enumerate the special exceptions, in some such form as the following.

'Louisiana, as ceded by France to the US. is made a part of the US. it's white inhabitants shall be citizens, and stand, as to their rights & obligations, on the same footing with other citizens of the US. in analogous situations. Save only that as to the portion thereof lying North of an East & West line drawn through[2] the Mouth of Arkansa river, no new state shall be established, nor any grants of land made, other than to Indians in exchange for equivalent portions of land occupied by them, until an amendment of the Constitution shall be made for these purposes.

Florida also, whensoever it may be rightfully obtained, shall become a part of the US. it's white inhabitants shall thereupon be citizens, & shall stand as to their rights & obligations, on the same footing with other citizens of the US. in analogous situations.' I quote this for your consideration, observing that the less is said about any constitutional difficulty, the better: and that it will be desireable for Congress to[3] do what is necessary, *in silence*. I find but one opinion as to the necessity of shutting up the country for some time. we meet in Washington the 25th. proxime, to prepare for Congress. Accept my affectionate salutations, & great esteem & respect. TH: JEFFERSON

RC (MHi: Levi Lincoln Papers); at foot of text: "Levi Lincoln esquire"; endorsed; with unrelated notations by Lincoln on verso. PrC (DLC). Enclosure: Josiah Snelling to TJ, August 1803 (recorded in SJL as received from Boston on 29 Aug. but not found).

For the changes included in this FORM of the constitutional amendment, see Amendment for Annexation of Louisiana and Florida, printed at 30 Aug.

[1] Word interlined in place of "[being?]."

[2] Preceding six words and ampersand interlined in place of "the latitude of."

[3] TJ here canceled "act."

From John Smith

Sir West Florida August 30th 1803

The Cession of the Island of New Orleans, and of Louisiana to the United States, is the most important event that has taken place since the establishment of the Federal Constitution. It will not only give us weight in the Commercial & political scale of European Governments, but, that of national Character and respectability in all the world. It will preserve peace and harmony among ourselves, and secure us from the raging storm, that is now bursting with reiterated terror on the Belligerent powers of Europe. This Cession secures to us the navigation of the Missisippi, and its waters on both sides. It will open to our nation a source of wealth. The Province of Louisiana, being about fifty leagues in breadth from east to west[1] and stretching from the Bay of Mexico on the south, to an unknown Region in the north, will not only afford us a large extent of fertile soil, abounding with navigable streams, admirably calculated both for commerce and agriculture, but if suitable encouragement is given to its population and Culture, we shall soon be effectually secured from invasion in this quarter. It is said that Mr Munroe has gone to Spain, to negociate for Florida. I wish him success in making a fair purchace. But it is with deep regret, that I further hear, that our Minister has gone to Madrid to exchange Louisiana for Florida. This policy would be unwise, and especially at this moment. True, we would by this exchange, have the East side of the Missisippi entire, but in a short time we may have both without feeling the price. Already we have all the navigable waters leading into the Mississippi—Florida is settling with great rapidity by the Americans—All the good land will very soon be entered and settled. His Catholic Majesty must know that this tract of Country will accumulate expence to him, and therefore will in a few years dispose of it for a small consideration—At any rate, Louisiana is of infinitely more value and importance then Florida can possibly be. And permit me to observe that having possession of both sides of the Mississippi (which will be of more[2] value then any other River in north America) we shall form an invincible Bulwark to the western Country, and the epoch of its commercial, manufacturing and political importance.

I think, Sir, it will be indispensible after the exchange of the ratification of the treaty, to take immeadiate possession of such part of this Country as we may have a right to claim.

I shall in a few days leave this for the City Washington.

Be pleased to accept the assurance of the high consideration and respect with which I am Sir your most Obedient And very Humble Servt JOHN SMITH

RC (DLC); at foot of text: "The President of the U. States"; endorsed by TJ as received 2 Oct. and so recorded in SJL.

LEAVE THIS FOR THE CITY WASHINGTON: TJ's papers contain a pass for Smith, in Spanish, granted 8 Sep. 1803 by Carlos de Grand-Pré, the Spanish governor of the Baton Rouge district, allowing Smith to travel through his jurisdiction to Washington. At the foot of this pass was another, in English, from the Spanish alcalde at Bayou Sara, John O'Connor, dated 18 Sep., granting Smith "free permission to pass with his son Mr. Ambrose Smith to the City of Washington" (MS in DLC: TJ Papers, 135:23305; Andrew McMichael, *Atlantic Loyalties: Americans in Spanish West Florida, 1785-1810* [Athens, Ga., 2008], 22-3; William C. Davis, *The Rogue Republic* [Boston, 2011], xi).

[1]Preceding two words interlined.

[2]Smith first wrote "will be of the most" before altering the text to read as above.

From John Vaughan

DEAR SIR Philad. 30 Augt. 1803

Your favor of 14 Augt. I have recieved, & beg leave to repeat what I suggested on a former occasion, that I was so sensible of your important avocations; that I should (except where absolute necessity required it) avoid writing, if I concieved it would[1] always involve you in the trouble of a reply—The Book was forwarded before your letter was received by a regular Washington trader, thro' the medium of Mr Roberts.

I hope you will excuse the liberty I have taken of enclosing a letter for M Livingston, it relates to business of the Society, & will be more likely to go Safe through the public office—

I subjoin an extract of a letter I have received from Mr Dunbar & remain with the greatest respect

Dear Sir Your obedient Servt & friend JN VAUGHAN

RC (DLC); at foot of text: "Thomas Jefferson Esqr"; endorsed by TJ as received 5 Sep. and so recorded in SJL. Enclosure: Extracts of correspondence from William Dunbar, the first one describing "a Curious phenomenon" in the form of a semicircular rainbow of at least three rings observed just after sunset; he surmises that the visual effect is due to horizontal refraction such as has been described in the *Transactions* of the Royal Society as occurring in the English Channel and on the coasts of England and France; in the second extract, Dunbar observes that according to newspaper reports the first week of May was unusually cold in Philadelphia and New York, and his record of meteorological observations indicates that the weather was colder than expected at Natchez that week also; he includes figures comparing temperature, barometric pressure, and weather conditions at Natchez and Philadelphia during part of May (Tr entirely in Vaughan's hand, undated, subjoined to letter beginning on verso of RC); Vaughan conveyed Dunbar's description of the rainbow to the American Philosophical Society in a meeting on 19 Aug. (APS, *Proceedings*, 22, pt. 3 [1884], 340). Other enclosure not found.

[1]MS: "was."

From Samuel Broome

Greenfield Hill, Connecticut,
Augt. 31st. 1803.

SIR

I again take the freedom to address your Excellency, on the Subject of my application for an appointment to the Collectorship for the district of New Haven, Vacant by the Death of Samuel Bishop Esquire. I am confident, your Excellency is desirous to appoint a person, that would give the greatest satisfaction, to the Citizens, I am confident there is not a Merchant of any description there, who does not wish that I might be selected from the applicants, I have resided in that City more than twenty years, having left my native place, at the Commencement of the American War, at its commencement I loaned the United States fourteen thousand pounds, and had John Lawrence Esqr of Hartford's private receipt by me four months, before he received Loan office Certificates to Issue, I had large sums owing, the greatest parts I received in paper Money, and never did in one instance, refuse it. when Genls. Gray, and Arnold burnt Bedford in the Massachusets Bay, and New London, in this State, I had thirteen Vessels destroy'd, besides, other Property to a large Amount, I presume there are many Gentlemen, in the Senate and house of Representatives, who if appealed to would substantiate these facts, I have the happiness of being acquainted with many Worthy Characters in the Eastern States, including New york, I am certain it is the wish of your Excellency to appoint an Unequivocal Character to that and every other office, I am willing mine may be strictly scrutinized, and on that I should be willing to rest my application, I have it in my power to give ample security for the faithful performance of the trust.—I hope I may be excused by this detail, I am with great respect Your Excellencies most Obedt Servant

SAMUEL BROOME

RC (DNA: RG 59, LAR); at foot of text: "His Excellency The President of the United States"; endorsed by TJ as received 7 Sep. and so recorded in SJL with notation "to be Collectr. N. Haven."

From Henry Dearborn

SIR War Department August 31st, 1803

I herewith enclose the proceedings of a Genl. Court Martial which require your approbation, as relates to the sentence respecting Lt. Van Ransselear, and the pardon of Benja. Furgason so far as relates to corporal punishment.

I enclose a letter from Genl. Muhlengburg soliciting the remission of the corporal punishment which Lewis Rush is sentenced to receive—I can discover no reasonable objection to the sentence of the Court against Lt. Van Ransselear, and all circumstances considered it may be proper to remitt the corporal punishment of Benja. Furgason & Lewis Rush.

with sentiments of respect I am Sir Your Huml Sevt

H. DEARBORN

RC (DLC); at foot of text: "The President of the United States"; endorsed by TJ as received from the War Department on 5 Sep. and "Lt. Van Renslaer. Rush. Ferguson" and so recorded in SJL. Enclosures not found, but see below.

LT. VAN RANSSELEAR: at a court-martial held from 8 to 18 Aug. 1803 at Fort Jay, New York, Lieutenant Killian P. Van Rensselaer of the Regiment of Artillerists was tried on two charges exhibited against him by Lieutenant Robert W. Osborn. The first charge accused Van Rensselaer of disobedience of orders and neglect of duty for leaving his recruitment post in Connecticut and going to New York without leave. The second charge accused him of conduct unbecoming an officer and a gentleman for inserting a publication in the New York *Mercantile Advertiser* that "wantonly and maliciously abused" Osborn's character. The court-martial found Van Rensselaer guilty of part of the first charge and the whole of the second and sentenced him to be cashiered. TJ approved the sentence on 7 Sep. (JEP, 1:412; New York *Morning Chronicle*, 1 Oct. 1803; TJ to Dearborn, 7 Sep. 1803).

LETTER FROM GENL. MUHLENGBURG: a letter from J. P. G. Muhlenberg to Dearborn, dated Philadelphia, 24 Aug. 1803, requested that the punishment of Lewis Rush be remitted (recorded in DNA: RG 107, RLRMS as received by the War Department on 28 Aug. 1803, but not found). Rush and Benjamin Ferguson served in Captain James Bruff's company of artillerists. TJ approved the remission of their respective corporal punishments on 7 Sep. (JEP, 1:411; Dearborn to Thomas H. Cushing, 10 Sep. 1803, and Dearborn to James Bruff, 10 Sep. 1803, both in DNA: RG 107, LSMA; TJ to Dearborn, 7 Sep. 1803).

From Henry Dearborn

SIR Washington August 31st, 1803

I have been honoured with your letter of the 26th. inst. enclosing the letters of Judge Campbell & Mr. Jackson,—Judge Campbells opinnion on the subject of thefts, by Indians, is I concieve, in strict conformity with the General principle established by Congress, and peculiarly well[1] calculated for redressing the evils to which it is intended to be applied.

Mr. Jackson[2] seems to have taken for granted, that Col, Butler has been arrested & is to be tried merely on a charge relating to an order for cuting hair, but the fact is, he is to be tried for disobedience of orders & neglect of duty, for not going to Fort Adams in April or May 1802 when ordered from the War Department, and for being absent from his command near twelve months without leave.—on the subject of the Genl. order for cuting the hair of the officers & soldiers of the Army, I have never expressed an opinnion, I have however concidered it as an indiscreet & unnecessary order, and whether it was absolutely binding on the troops or not, may be a question, which the Court Martial will consider and give an opinnion upon.—There has been no directions for moving any part of the Troops from Tennessee except a small detachment on the road between Nashvill & the Chickasaw Country, for the purpose of affording more protection to travelers.—it has not been in contemplation to remove Doctr Van Dike from S.W. point.—

Mr Wagner, principle Clerk in the Secretary of States office, yesterday shew me a letter from Mr. Munro, by which it appears that he was about seting out for London, and in which he has endeavored to establish the fact, that by our Treaty with France, the whole of what has been called West Florida, is fairly included in the Cession of Louisiana and he advises us to take actual possession accordingly.—Mr. Pichon has received instructions for himself & the Prefect at New Orlians. Pichon is authorised to receive & exchange the ratifications of the Treaty, the Prefect is authorised to receive Louisiana from Spain, and deliver it to the U.S. the boundaries which the Prefect & the Spanish Govr. may agree upon, may have a considerable effect on the question stated by Mr. Munroe.—I very well[3] recollect that Mr. Clark, informed me that the Spanish Officers at New Orlians always concidered, what we have called West Florida, as part of Louisiana.—

with respectfull considerations I am Your Huml Servt.

H. Dearborn

RC (DLC); at head of text: "To the President of the United States"; endorsed by TJ as received from the War Department on 5 Sep. and "Campbell. Jackson. Butler. Van dyke" and so recorded in SJL.

LETTER FROM MR. MUNRO: James Monroe to James Madison, dated Paris, 19 June 1803, and received by the State Department on 29 Aug. In it, Monroe explains his determination to go to London, citing the departure of Rufus King, the threat to American commerce posed by the renewal of war between Britain and France, and the completion of the Louisiana negotiations in Paris. In a postscript, Monroe refers to his 7 June letter to Madison detailing his view on whether or not West Florida "is comprized in the cession made us of Louisiana, which I think too clear to admit a doubt." He likewise feels that Spain shares this opinion and if the United States takes possession of West Florida as part of Louisiana, Monroe believes Spain will acquiesce to the measure, "or, at least that it will not be taken ill by it, or impede an amicable and favorable adjustment relative to the territory of Spain eastward of the mississippi." Monroe left Paris on 12 July and arrived in London on 18 July (Madison, *Papers, Sec. of State Ser.*, 5:72-7, 103-5, 201; Vol. 40:229).

For Dearborn's meeting with Louis André PICHON, see Dearborn to TJ, 28 Aug. 1803 (first letter). For the INSTRUCTIONS Pichon received from French foreign minister Talleyrand and minister of marine Denis Decrès regarding the Louisiana treaty, see Robert R. Livingston to TJ, 2 June 1803. Pichon forwarded copies of them to Madison on 30 Aug. (Madison, *Papers, Sec. of State Ser.*, 5:355-7).

PREFECT & THE SPANISH GOVR.: Pierre Clément Laussat and Manuel de Salcedo.

[1] MS: "will."

[2] Name interlined in place of "Judge Campbell."

[3] MS: "will."

From Albert Gallatin

DEAR SIR New York 31st Aug. 1803

Your favour of the 23d and its enclosures were received day before yesterday. A bill shall be prepared for the purpose of carrying the treaty &a. into effect: but neither can you expect that the house will take up the subject before ratification or decide without much debate & opposition; nor is it possible to have the certificates of stock prepared until Baring shall arrive & the form mutually agreed on. I write to Philada. in order to have the proper paper, copper plate engraving & other devices necessary to prevent counterfeits immediately prepared; but the printing cannot be executed until the form shall have been prepared: this must express the nature of the stock, the law by virtue of which issued, and what cannot be done without Baring's consent, the mode of transferring the stock,[1] the place where the interest is payable, the mode of paying it, & the rate of exchange; all which is left indeterminate in the convention, the rate of exchange with Paris only excepted. The moment he or his agent shall arrive, we will agree on a form & have the printing part executed & the blanks filled; but we cannot proceed to signing till after the law shall have passed. For the sake of making the stock negotiable, it must be in certificates of a moderate sum, not certainly more than one thousand dollars each on an average. This will produce 11,250 Certificates to be signed by one person & that person (the register) an officer who has other papers daily to compare & attest. The Certificates must afterwards & before they issue be compared, checked &a: it will be extraordinary dispatch if they can be prepared for delivery within 20 days after the passing of the law. You may, however, rely on my exertions & that every means which may accelerate the completion of the stock shall be adopted.

But, whilst it is proper to be ready to act on the ground you have suggested, there is a strong objection to our *sending* the stock; it is not merely because the Executive will thereby assume a responsibility not contemplated by the convention, the delivery of the stock being, by that instrument, made an act subsequent to the possession of Louisiana; but because we ought to insist that the delivery of the stock here within the three months to the person duly authorized is a good fulfilment of the convention. there is no doubt of its being such both by the letter & the spirit of the instrument; and if we assent to a contrary construction, we become responsible for the delivery in Europe within the three months, render ourselves liable for the accidents of transmission & for those very delays which, if France seeks for a pretence of breaking the contract, may be used by her for that purpose. The condition that the stock shall be transmitted by us to our Minister at Paris is not a part of our agreement, but of the contract between the French Government & Baring to which we are not parties, & was inserted in this for the benefit & security of that Government who did not wish to trust the Baring & Hopes with the whole of the stock at once. We must, as I mentioned before, make every previous preparation in order to be able to adopt in October that mode which, upon due consideration, will appear the safest; but the transmission by us & at our risk does not, in my present view of the subject, appear an eligible measure.

I feel not, however, any apprehension that France intends seriously to raise objections to the execution of the treaty: unless intoxicated by the hope of laying England prostrate, or allured by some offer from Spain to give a better price for Louisiana than we have done, it is impossible that Bonaparte should not consider his bargain as so much obtained for nothing; for, however valuable to us, it must be evident to him that, pending the war, he could not occupy Louisiana, & that the war would place it very soon in other hands. A temporary uneasiness may indeed have existed from various causes: the communication of the substance of the treaty to England & the manner in which it was received may have frustrated the hopes of the first Consul of a misunderstanding or coolness between us & that country; he may have been disappointed on finding that instead of sixty, he would receive only forty five millions for Louisiana; for although I have no doubt of the negotiation with Baring having been part of our own, I am confident that Mr Monroe was not privy to it, & it is very probable that that part of the transaction was not unfolded to Bonaparte till after the signature of the treaty: and it is not impossible that the French Government wants only to guard against the danger of our taking possession immediately after the exchange of ratifications, & of Congress afterwards refusing to comply with our part of the agreement.

I think it, however, more probable that the uneasiness which the letters of our ministers are calculated to create have their origin with Baring or Livingston, or perhaps with both. The anxiety of the first that a convention by which he & his associates will gain near three millions of dollars should not fail in its execution, and the wish of the other that no modifications should be made by Congress in the mode of settling & paying the american claims, as well as a natural desire to persuade us that he has made a most excellent bargain, would lead both to represent every trifling occurrence as a proof that, if we did not hasten the completion of every part of the transaction, we might lose the object.

What persuades me of the desire of France that the treaty should be carried into effect is what they have already done towards it. The treaty is signed as of the 30th April; the powers of Sir Francis Baring are dated London 3d May; the official proposition of Alexr. Baring to the French Government is dated Paris 2d May. These propositions were communicated to our Ministers by Mr Marbois on the 4th of May. On the 10th of the same month Mr Marbois wrote to them the letter in which he states that any extraordinary delay in making the payments stipulated beyond the three months fixed by the Convention would place the contracting parties in the same situation in which they were before treating—Observe here that by Baring's proposition & contract the dates of the payments he is to make to France are determined by that of the delivery & transmission of the stock; the first payment by him at Paris being within thirty days after advice being received there of the delivery of one third part of the stock to his agent in America, & of the transmission of the remainder to our Minister at Paris—On the 22d May Bonaparte ratified the Convention—On the 28th do. our Ministers answered Mr Marbois's letter of the 4th stating that they saw no objection to the contract—On the 2d June they answered his letter of the 10th May—On what day Bonaparte ratified the contract with Baring does not appear. The attestation of Taillerand & that of our ministers that the signature of Maret (the Secy. of State), which as well as that of Marbois & of Bonaparte, is affixed to the instrument, is his own & that the act must be considered as that of the French Governt. bears date the 6th June. The letter of our ministers, to which Mr Livingston adds that it has been agreed to withdraw the letters of 10th May & 2d June is dated 7th June. A comparison of those dates shows that the ratification of the convention & that of the contract were deliberate acts, both done several days after writing that letter of the 10th May which had given the alarm, & followed by the act of withdrawing that very letter. The period which elapsed between the two letters of Marbois of 4th & 10th May & their being answered, is indeed an evidence of a state of some uncertainty arising most probably from the negotiation with Baring not being liked by the Consul; but it is extraordinary that the letters written during that interval by Mr Monroe on the 18th & 23d May show no anxiety on the subject; nay that silence was kept respecting that point by the Ministers in their letter of the 13th which accompanied the treaty; & that Mr Monroe evinces no uneasiness till his short letter of the 2d June. Was he not kept in the dark all the time that any real ground of uneasiness might exist, and informed of it, & his anxiety as well as ours excited, only when there was no longer any[2] reason of alarm?

I write to you as if you had Baring's contract, because the Ministers say it is enclosed in their letter. I have received it from Baring himself accompanied by a letter of the 7th June, brought by Mr Jay, but which went round to Washington, in which he says that he will sail within a month for the United States for the purpose of agreeing on the preliminary arrangements. I am transcribing the contract & some letters relative to it, & will transmit it to you officially, as I think it my duty to leave on record in the office proofs[3] that the low price at which that stock has been sold ($78\frac{1}{2}$ per cent) is not ascribable to the state of public credit nor to any act of your administration & particularly of the Treasury department.

I agree with you that we have a right to claim that part of West Florida which was part of Louisiana: I was of a different opinion; but am now convinced.

With great respect and sincere attachment Your obed. Servt.

ALBERT GALLATIN

P.S. On reading again Mr Livingston's postcriptum, I see that by the instructions to Mr Pichon, the French Govt. agrees that provided that the Stock shall be created within the three months it will be a fair execution of the Treaty. By that instrument it was agreed that the delivery of New Orleans should immediately follow the exchange of ratifications, without any provision being made for the concurrence of Congress which is necessary for the creation of the stock. There can be no objection to agreeing on our part with Mr Pichon that he shall not deliver the order for taking possession of New Orleans, until

Congress shall, by law, have created the Stock; but it seems to me that we ought to insist on not delivering the Stock until the place is in our possession. With expresses & provided that every previous step has been taken to take possession on a day's warning, this will not cause a delay of more than six weeks.

For fear that Baring's contract has not reached you I add its substance.

1. The French Govt. to deliver to the agent of the houses of Hope & Baring an act authorizing the American Govt. to transfer to the sd. houses or to their representatives the 11,250,000 Dollars american stock.

2. The American Govt. may deliver *directement* to the attorney of the sd. houses one third of the sd. stock amounting to 3,750,000 dollars, & shall send the remaining 7,500,000 dollars to their Minister at Paris to be kept by him as a deposit pursuant to the following conditions.

3. Hope & Baring shall pay to the Treasury of France in full for the said Stock, & reserving to themselves the interests & profits accruing from sd. stock, the sum of 52 millions of francs; vizt. six millions within the 30 days following the reception at Paris of an official notice that one third of the Stock has been delivered to the agent of sd. houses, & that the other[4] two thirds have been sent to France; & two millions monthly during each succeeding month untill the payment of the 52 millions shall have been completed.

4. Bills of exchange to the amount of 52 millions of francs drawn by Baring on Hope, accepted by Hope & endorsed by Alexr. Baring, but leaving the dates of payment in blank shall without delay be deposited in the hands of the American minister at Paris, who shall, in concert with the French Minister of finance, fill the blanks in conformity to the preceding article.

5. On receipt of the official notice mentioned in 3d Article, the american minister at Paris shall deliver to the French Govt. seventeen millions, five hundred thousand livres of the said bills & shall keep as a deposit the remainder of said bills & the 7,500,000 dollars[5] american stock sent to him by the American Govt.—Thirty days before the completion of the payment by Hope of the first bills thus delivered to the French Govt., the American Minister shall deliver to the French Govt. 17 millions more of Baring & Hope's bills, and to the agent of Baring & Hope one half of the american stock in his hands vizt. 3,750,000 dollars. The remainder of the bills & stock shall be likewise delivered by him to the parties respectively one month before the completion of the payment of the second set of bills by Hope.

As during the same two years which is fixed for the completion of the payment of 52 millions to France by Hope & Baring, these houses will receive from the United States 7,200,000 francs[6] for interest, they will have to pay in fact no more than 45 millions for the sixty millions stock; which after making the allowance for interest & discount amounts to 78½ per cent for the real price they give for that Stock. At that period our old worthless six per cent stock which is nothing more than a short annuity was in America at 97 & in England at 91; our three was in England at 58; our Dutch 5 ℔% was at Amsterdam at 99 & our Antwerp 4½ ℔% redeemable at will was at this last place at 99½—Add to this that the Barings were bidders for Mr Addington's ten millions St. loan, which they did not get, but for which they offered to take the English three per cent at the then market price with a premium of only 3 per cent; and our threes were in England worth one per cent more at market than the English.

A. G.

RC (DLC); above postscript: "The President of the United States"; endorsed by TJ as received from the Treasury Department on 7 Sep. and "creation of stock" and so recorded in SJL.

UNTIL BARING SHALL ARRIVE: Alexander Baring acted as agent with full powers of attorney for Francis Baring & Company of London and Hope & Company of Amsterdam in drawing up the contract to finance the purchase of Louisiana (J. E. Winston and R. W. Colomb, "How the Louisiana Purchase was Financed," *Louisiana Historical Quarterly*, 12 [1929], 218).

The convention set the RATE OF EXCHANGE WITH PARIS at 5.333 francs or 5.8 livres to the U.S. dollar (Miller, *Treaties*, 2:514).

CONTRACT BETWEEN THE FRENCH GOVERNMENT & BARING: for a printed copy in English of the 12 Floréal (2 May) document signed by Alexander Baring and Barbé de Marbois, the French minister of finance, see Winston and Colomb, "How the Lousiana Purchase was Financed," 215-18.

UNEASINESS WHICH THE LETTERS OF OUR MINISTERS ARE CALCULATED TO CREATE: see Robert R. Livingston to TJ, 2 June, and note. LETTERS WRITTEN DURING THAT INTERVAL: see Monroe to Madison, 18 and 23 May, in Madison, *Papers, Sec. of State Ser.*, 5:12-13, 24-5. For Livingston and Monroe's letter of 13 May that ACCOMPANIED THE TREATY, see same, 4:601-6. Monroe's SHORT LETTER to Madison, in which he urged that it is "highly important" that Congress be called immediately into session to carry the "treaty & conventions" into effect without delay, was dated 3 June (same, 5:55).

Peter Augustus JAY arrived in New York with the treaty and dispatches on 18 Aug. (same, 5:47n).

[1] Preceding six words and comma interlined.

[2] Preceding two words interlined in place of "further ground."

[3] Word interlined.

[4] Preceding three words interlined.

[5] Preceding figures and word interlined in place of "two thirds of the."

[6] Word inserted in margin in place of "dollars."

From Thomas Munroe

Sir, Washington 31t. August 1803

I have the honor of enclosing for your Signature a warrant for $10,000; the balance in my hands, towit about $1000 of the $20,000 heretofore drawn being insufficient to meet the Expenses of the present month which will be demanded in a few days.—

I also enclose Sketches of the Expenditures since the Account last rendered, which was up to the first of July.—

The Expenses on the Streets will I presume cease next week—The two foot ways on the South side of the Pensylvania Avenue are finished, which with the gravelling of the road round the South west side of the Capitol hill, and such repairs as the rains and cutting by Carriages might render necessary on the Avenue, and about the Capitol hill was, I supposed,[1] all you intended to have done on the roads this fall; but on my return from Bath on monday last I found the Labourers engaged in rounding and gravelling A. street south from New[2] Jersey Avenue to Stelles, and in filling up the new road before mentioned, below the South wing of the Capitol, so as to make the descent of it only one foot in ten, as you originally directed it to be done—The latter being a work of ten or twelve days, and of two or three hundred Dollars expense; and being under the impression that altho' the Descent was greater than you intended it should have been, you meant to have dispensed with any alteration at present, I made enquiry of the Overseer about it, who says Mr. Claxton told him in my absence that you wished to have it done as it is now doing, and that you left such directions with him at the time you directed the work which has been done on A. street south—All the other work was done ten days ago.—

I supposed Mr Lenthall had communicated to you from time to time his Operations at the Capitol, as he did while you were here, and had given you a tolerably correct idea of the progress and State of that building, together with the repairs at the Presidents House—He has been indisposed a few days past, but has promised me, if he feels well enough, he will send me a rough report to day to be forwarded herewith to you.—

He is surprised and embarrassed in consequence of not having seen or heard from Mr Latrobe since he was here early in July, and is at a stand for want of instructions in some cases he tells me, and particularly with regard to repairs & alterations at the Presidents house and North wing of the Capitol and for want of some materials which Mr. Latrobe was to procure & send forward.—

The Stair case in the Presidents House is stepped, and the Chamber finished as you directed except the last coat of paint which will be done in a day or two—Mr. Lenox tells me you were more particular in your directions that those two things should be done early, he also says that all the smaller jobs which were committed to him will be done agreeably to your orders by the time you return—All the leaks which have been discovered in the Presidents House & North wing of the Capitol have been stopped Mr. Lenthall says—the sky light has been mended—sundry small jobs of plumbers work, and some little Carpentry work & plaistering has been done, which appeared to be absolutely necessary, but Lenthall says he wants information from Mr Latrobe before he can proceed further in what may have been contemplated to be done by the President or Mr. L.—

I have the honor to be, with the greatest respect Sir, Yr mo Ob Servt

THOMAS MUNROE

RC (DLC); addressed: "President of the United States"; endorsed by TJ as received 2 Sep. and so recorded in SJL. Enclosure printed below. Other enclosure not found.

ACCOUNT LAST RENDERED: see Thomas Munroe's Account of Public Expenditures, 27 June 1803.

[1]Preceding two words and comma interlined.

[2]Word interlined.

ENCLOSURE

Account of Public Expenditures

Expenditures on the Streets in July 1803

Overseers & Labourers wages in June	$763.71
Lumber for trunks &c	53.58
Ironmongery, Blacksmiths work & other small articles	40.94
	$858.23

Expenditures on Streets in August 1803

For	Overseers & Labourers wages	$672.41
	Lumber for bridges & trunks	54.77
	Carpenters work on Do.	109.92
	Bricklayers Do. on Do. and Bricks & Lime for an Arch	64.77
		Ds. 901.87

Expenditures on the Capitol in July 1803

For	Lime & hauling it to the building	$267.66
	Mason, Carpenters & Labourers wages for June	828.59
	Foundation Stone & hauling it (on Acct.)	662.75
	Sand	104.40

Nails	46.55
Lumber	171.40
George Blagdin for freestone work, on acct,	1,500
H. B. Latrobe for Salary & materials to be Accounted for	641.66
Sundry small articles	21.75
	Ds 4,244.76

Expenditures on Capitol in August 1803

Wages of Masons, Carpenters, Labourers &c for month of July—*	$1024.92
George Blagdin on Acct. freestone work	2,000.00
Cordage	81.45
Putlogs	10.50
Oznaburgs	37.27
	$3,154.14
Foundation Stone	240.08
roll Labourers (omitted in the above*)	564.33
	$3,958.55

N.B. the wages of workmen & Labourers for August are not included in the above the rolls not being returned—some small payts. on Acct. have been made

Expenditures on the Presidents house in July & August 1803

For Well	$117.40
reparing pump	16.33
Hardware	102.32
Lead	201.30
Plaistering	80.50
Lumber	156.24
Stone at north front door & Cutting it	5.33
	Ds 679.42

MS (DLC); undated, entirely in Munroe's hand.

From George Wythe

G ' Wythe to T ' Jefferson 31 of august, 1803.

My kinsman James Westwood Wallace proposeth to remove to New-Orleans, invited by the prospect of providing for a numerous and increasing familie there better than he can provide for them here. he professeth medicine. any kind office to him will be grateful to me. adieu.

RC (DNA: RG 59, LAR); endorsed by TJ as received 12 Sep. and "Wallace Dr. James for N. Orleans" and so recorded in SJL.

KINSMAN: Wallace's great-grandmother, Anne Wythe, was Wythe's paternal grandmother. After studying with Dr. Gustavus Brown of Maryland, Wallace attended medical school in Edinburgh, Scotland, where he became a member of the Royal Medical Society. In 1793, he received his medical degree from the University of Pennsylvania and went on to have a successful practice at Fauquier Court House, Virginia. A brother-in-law of Washington, D.C., marshal Daniel Carroll Brent, he died in 1838 (*Daily National Intelligencer*, 5 Sep. 1838; WMQ, 1st ser., 9 [1900-01], 130-1; Madison to TJ, 11 Sep. 1803).

Resolution for Introduction of Constitutional Amendment

[August 1803?]

Resolved by the Senate and House of Repr. of the US. two thirds of both houses concurring, that the following amendment to the constitution of the US. be proposed to the legislatures of the several states; which, when ratified by three fourths of the said legislatures shall be valid to all intents & purposes as a part of the sd constitution.

Louisiana, as ceded by France to the US. is made a part of the US.

MS (DLC: Breckinridge Family Papers); entirely in TJ's hand; undated.

RESOLVED: the location of this manuscript in John Breckinridge's papers suggests that TJ planned to have Breckinridge introduce the amendment on LOUISIANA. When and how TJ conveyed this resolution to the Kentucky senator is unknown. The opening sentence of the amendment, which TJ used to indicate the full text, was from the version he shared with his advisers in August, beginning with his letter to Gallatin of the 23d. His July draft of an amendment began differently (see Constitutional Amendment on Louisiana at 9 July).

From William Bache

DEAR SIR. New Orleans Sepr. 1st. 1803.

You will find William G, Garland, a native of Richmond,[1] Northumberland county in virginia recommended to the attentions of Government for an appointment under the approaching regulations of Louisiana. What his expectations are I know not, but his integrity and industry are unquestionable; and if in the management of accounts, or in any labour of that kind a vacancy may happen he will fill it to the entire satisfaction of his Country. This I say in his behalf from a conviction that, if he is favourably received, he will make a faithful officer. With wishes for your health and a full enjoyment of the gratitude & affection of your Countrymen for your many services I remain your friend

WILLIAM BACHE

RC (DNA: RG 59, LAR); endorsed by TJ as received 3 Nov. and "Garland Wm. G. to be Collector N.O." and so recorded in SJL. Probably enclosed in John Thomas Ricketts to James Madison, 31 Oct. 1803; see Madison, *Papers, Sec. of State Ser.*, 5:597.

WILLIAM G. GARLAND was a highly respected merchant fluent in English, Spanish, and French, who had resided in New Orleans for almost 15 years by November 1803, when Pierre Clément Laussat named him provisional director and general administrator for Louisiana. Laussat also appointed him interim collector at New Orleans, for which Garland expected to be paid five percent of the net customs duties received for the remainder of the French administration (Madison, *Papers, Sec. of State Ser.*, 5:597-8, 6:244; Jon Kukla, ed., *A Guide to the Papers of Pierre Clément Laussat* [New Orleans, 1993], 94-5; Garland to Daniel Delozier, 1 Sep. 1803, in DNA: RG 59, LAR, endorsed by TJ: "Garland Wm. G to be collector of N.O."; John Thomas Ricketts to Madison, 28 Dec. 1803, in same, endorsed by TJ: "Garland to be Collectr. N. Orleans"). For Garland's appointment as surveyor and inspector of the revenue at New Orleans, see Gallatin's list of nominations, printed at 24 Feb. 1804.

[1] Word written in margin keyed for insertion at this point.

From Henry Dearborn

SIR Washington Septr. 1t. 1803

Finding it necessary to remove my family from this place for the recovery of thier health, I have concluded to retire about twenty miles into the country, for two or three weeks, and as billious complaints are becoming prevalent in the City, & will probably increase until Octobr. permitt me to advise you not to return until the first of Octobr; your present situation being a high & healthy one, you will be the more likely to be effected by the change.—

with sentiments of respectfull esteem, I am Sir Yours.

H DEARBORN

RC (DLC); at foot of text: "The President of the United States"; endorsed by TJ as received from the War Department on 5 Sep. and so recorded in SJL.

COMPLAINTS ARE BECOMING PREVALENT: for the public health situation in Washington, Georgetown, and Alexandria, see Robert Smith to TJ, 10 Sep. 1803.

To J. P. P. Derieux

DEAR SIR Monticello Sep. 1. 03.

Immediately on the reciept of your letter from New York, I inclosed it to mr Madison to whom the subject of it belonged, in order that he might be able to answer it without any delay. as I presumed you would immediately [set out] from Washington on reciept of his letter, I thought it unsafe to send your certificate there, & detained it the rather as I hoped you would do us the favor of calling here on your way up the country when I could deliver the certificate into your own hands. I now, however according to your desire, inclose it to you with directions to mr Wagner if you are gone, to return it to myself to be forwarded by post. after congratulating you on your safe return & renewing my hopes of seeing you here on your way, I tender you my salutations & assurances of esteem. TH: JEFFERSON

PrC (DLC); faint; at foot of text: "Mr. Derieux"; endorsed by TJ in ink on verso. Enclosure: Certificate of Fulwar Skipwith, not found (see Derieux to TJ, 9, 29 Aug.).

LETTER: Derieux to TJ, 9 Aug.

From Mary Hazard and Anna Void

HONORED SIR Philadelphia September 1st 1803

I am not much used to write to folks like you, and I must own, that I tremble every joint of me, but since I have begun, I may as well go on. You see sir, we are two poor women, both married, and still young; and as we are too lazy to work, being that we can't get it to do, we thought, as how we might as well tell you, knowing that you are the richest, as allso the greatest Man, in all America. So, Sir, our case is just this, we are too lazy to work, and have a natural repugnance to being wh–es, and as winter will soon be here, we are afraid if you don't allow us 400 dollars a year, that we shall certainly either freeze, or starve to death! They tell me (who am the writer of this) that you are an old batchelor, now as such, I think you can't have much of a family, and see, being that you have no children, and a great income, suppose you would lay by every day one dollar and three sixpenny-bits, I'm sure, I hardly think that in the years run, you could miss such a sorry sum, and only think what a deal of good it would do us. We are sisters by the tie of nature, and sisters in affliction. We are both married to profligate men, and by them abandoned to the mercy of the world. But I forget myself...You see, Sir, writing is my trade; but booksellers are a little knavish, and my poverty is to them a stimulus to imposition. Strange, that, that, which should urge to benevolence, should be the mean of rendering misery still more miserable. But I wish you to answer this, for you see, as how, I shall have no peace day nor night, 'til you drop a line or two in the post office for me. Don't be angry Sir, *You* are the father of our country and *I* am one of your children...The world deals hardly with me...and to whom can a child complain, with more[1] propriety, than to its protector!

Allowing that you only preside over us as gaurdian, to our lawful rights, upon whose protection we have no claims, still, Sir, 'tis nothing derogatory to your honor, to denominate you *father*, and as one of your children, I throw myself, and sister, upon your mercy.—Pray Mr Secratary let the President read this himself. I have read all he has wrote, and sure he will not deem it a trouble to read this trifle!—I cannot flatter, I will not[2] extol, but I can feel, and feeling, know how to appriciate exalted worth.—Good night Sir; I have wrote this with fear and trembling, but I cannot appologise for my rudeness. By habit and education, I am unfit to encounter the evils of life, but by fate or chance, or rather, by the common course of things, I am thrown into the very vortex of misery.

Sighning ourselves

Mary Hazard
and
Anna Void:

I earnestly crave a few lines. directed to Mary Hazard Philadelphia

RC (DLC); in Hazard's hand, including signatures; ellipses in original; addressed: "His Excellency Thomas Jefferson President of the United States"; franked and postmarked; endorsed by TJ as received 7 Sep. and so recorded in SJL; also endorsed by TJ: "a forgery of some federalist."

[1] Word interlined.

[2] Preceding two words interlined in place of "cannot."

From Lafayette

La Grange 14th fruct.
September the 1st 1803

My Dear Sir

This Letter Will Be Delivered By M. de foncin Whose Abilities as an Engeneer, and Whose personal Character Entitle Him to Your particular Notice—our Acquaintance with Him dates from a time Not Unknown to You When an Enterprise Had Been Made at Cayenne for the Gradual Abolition of Slavery—M. de foncin's zeal on the Occasion, and His Actual perseverance in the principles of Humanity and Justice Make me Wish He May be favoured with Your Kind Attention—to Which General Motives I Beg Leave to Add that I am Under Obligations to His friendly interest in My Behalf. My Wife Who Has a Great Regard for Him joins with me in the Recommendation.

I Hope You Have Received My Letters and those to our friend Madisson Respecting the Grant of lands with Which I Have Been Honoured—While I keep the Most Grateful Sense of that Very flattering and Useful favour, and While I Affectionately feel My Obligations to You on the Occasion I took the Liberty to Send a power of Attorney in Blank Requesting You, Madisson, and Mr. Gallating Who Has Been particularly kind to me in this Affair, to Act in My Name for the Location as You think the Best to Be done.

My friends *Cabanis* and *tracy* Have Several Months Ago desired me to present to You Copies of Books Lately published by them—Mr. Livingston, Who took charge of the Envoice Has Not Yet Heard of its Arrival, nor do I know Whether they Have Come to Hand.

To the Correspondance of the American Minister I Refer You for European News—The Cession of Louisiana is to me An inexhaustible Source of Satisfaction—I think the British Government in their Late declaration of War have Misunderstood the Affairs of france, and Mismanaged those of their own Country—to the World I wish Liberty and peace.

The fracture of My thigh is Mended—But I still Walk Upon Crutches—My Wife and family Who are at La Grange Request their Best Respects to be presented to You—We all Join in Affectionate Compliments to Your Amiable daughters—I Had Yesterday a Letter from My dear Cousin tessé who is Well in a Country Seat at Aulnay, where she Has Laid out a Most pleasant Garden.

Adieu, my dear Sir, I am with the Most Affectionate Grateful Regard Your Constant friend LAFAYETTE

RC (DLC). Received 4 Nov. (see TJ to Lafayette of that day).

ENTERPRISE: in the mid-1780s, Lafayette purchased a plantation and slaves in Cayenne, French Guiana, as an experiment in emancipation. He and his family never went there, but undertook to have the plantation's laborers educated and trained in skills to prepare them for their freedom. John Foncin was in Cayenne at the time, and, according to Lafayette, "Shared in my plans." The marquis called the project "My Hobby Horse," but before it could be completed through the liberation of the slaves, the revolutionary government of France seized his properties, including the Cayenne estate. Lafayette had wanted George Washington to join him in the endeavor, but Washington declined to participate (John T. Gillard, "Lafayette, Friend of the Negro," *Journal of Negro History*, 19 [1934], 358-64; Stanley J. Idzerda and others, eds., *Lafayette in the Age of the American Revolution*, 5 vols. [Ithaca, N.Y., 1977-83], 5:91-2, 330; Washington, *Papers*, *Confed. Ser.*, 3:121, 544; Harlow Giles Unger, *Lafayette* [Hoboken, N.J., 2002], 215-16; Madison, *Papers*, *Sec. of State Ser.*, 8:144).

Lafayette discussed his GRANT OF LANDS from Congress in letters to Madison in June and July. Gallatin had given Lafayette options for receiving the grant, and with the July letter Lafayette sent Madison a blank power of attorney "as I did not Know whether it was proper to fill it With names in High public Station." He asked "my dear Friends to do as you think fitt" (same, 5:59, 148-9; Lafayette to TJ, 17 May).

COPIES OF BOOKS: see Vol. 38:615-16.

From William Branch Giles

Warm Springs—
September 2d 1803

Dear Sir

Mr Chevalier, the Gentleman who will probably present you this letter, in passing through your part of the Country, is desirous of making his Respects to you at Monticello.—He is the son in Law of Judge Lions, and formerly had some transactions with you as agent for Beaumarchais, although he is doubtful whither they were of such a nature, as to entitle him to your recollection,—Under these circumstances, I take pleasure in announcing Mr. Chevalier to you; because whilst, I have not the pleasure of an intimate personal acquaintance with him, I have for a long time, had a general acquaintance with his character, which is of a nature, to entitle him to the highest consideration either, as it respects the integrity of his conduct, the correctness of his information, or the amiableness of his manners.—

Be pleased to accept my best wishes for your health, happiness & prosperity &c

Wm B. Giles

RC (DLC); at head of text: "Thomas Jefferson Esquire President of the United States"; endorsed by TJ as received 8 Sep. and so recorded in SJL.

mr chevalier: that is, Jean Auguste Chevallié, who, since emigrating from France to America, had anglicized his name to John Augustus Chevallié. His second wife, Catherine Lyons, was a daughter of Virginia jurist Peter Lyons (Madison, *Papers*, 8:359n; dvb, 3:200; Vol. 11:55). For his activities as agent for Pierre Augustin Caron de Beaumarchais and his heirs, see Chevallié to TJ, 16 Sep. and 14 Oct. 1803.

From Charles Willson Peale

Dear Sir

Museum Sepr. 2d. 1803.

I have just received the enclosed Pamphlet with Letters from my Sons—they closed their Exhibition of the Skeleton of the Mammoth the 18th. of June, and with every exertion have not been able to pay all their expences in London, are gone to Reading, 40 miles distant from London, The Mayor had been so obliging as give them the use of the Common Counsel Hall; prepairing to put up the Skeleton when they wrote, The Inhabitants of Reading are mostly Quakers & Methodists, about 10,000—but being averse to the encouragement of Theatrical entertainments, it is probable, Rembrandt says, that they will be more likely to encourage his exhibition, and he hopes to get a sufficiency to wipe some small debts he left unpaid in London, and transport the Skeleton to Bath. He will also try to make something by his Pensel, as there are no Painters in that Nieghbourhood.

My Son Rubens has sent me 3 Cases of subjects of Natural History—I have not yet got them from the Ship, (Pigou) just arrived at the Warf. every thing he sends me, must be valuable, as filling up the casms of my Museum; making the Collection more complete.

The Inhabitants of Philadelphia are blessed of Health[1] this season. please to accept the profile Bonneparte's brother, taken in the Museum this morning—I am Dear Sir with much esteem your friend

C W PEALE.

RC (DLC); at foot of text: "His Excellency Thos. Jefferson Esqr."; endorsed by TJ as received on 7 Sep. and so recorded in SJL. PoC (PPAmP: Peale-Sellers Papers). Enclosure: Rembrandt Peale, *An Historical Disquisition on the Mammoth, or, Great American Incognitum, an Extinct, Immense, Carnivorous Animal, Whose Fossil Remains Have Been Found in North America* (London, 1803); Peale, *Papers*, v. 2, pt. 1:543-81; Sowerby, No. 1047.

Peale's SONS had both written to him on 14 July from Reading, England. In return for the aid provided by the MAYOR, Lancelot Austwick, Rembrandt Peale undertook to paint a portrait of the mayor's son. Because there were NO PAINTERS in the vicinity, he hoped that the picture of the mayor's son would stimulate "some of the Noblemen & Gentry" of the area to give him commissions (Peale, *Papers*, v. 2, pt. 1:586n, 601).

RUBENS Peale had taken specimens of American birds to England to exchange for natural history objects. He sent home two cases of birds he had obtained and one case holding a collection of insects—"English German, Hungarian and Indian." The ship PIGOU arrived at Philadelphia from London on 1 Sep., stopping at the quarantine station, the Lazaretto, before proceeding to the city's waterfront. The cases, however, were not aboard the vessel and could not be accounted for (same, 486, 529, 530n, 584, 602; Philadelphia *Evening Post*, 3 Sep.).

BONNEPARTE'S BROTHER: the physiognotrace silhouette of Jerome Bonaparte has not been located. Also on his visit to Peale's museum, Bonaparte became interested in the polygraph and decided to obtain one of the writing machines (Peale, *Papers*, v. 2, pt. 1:602).

[1]MS: "Heath."

From Nathaniel Macon

SIR Buck Spring 3 Septr. 1803

It is with real pleasure, that I inform you, that the Republican cause is daily gaining ground with us, not only the late elections but the candid acknowledgment of many that they have been deceived fully confirm the fact; and this gaining is clearly the effect of observation, on the difference between the present & past times by the people, and it is worthy of notice that the district which sends the only federalist from the state to Congress, gave a majority of votes to Republican cadidates, and I must add that it is also worthy of notice, that during the present administration, not a single person has been dismissed from office in this state, although with one exception I believe they were all federal, though not I hope of the same sort, which abound in some other places

The acquisition of Louisianna has given general satisfaction, though the terms are not correctly known; But if it is within the compass of the present revenue, the purchase when the terms are known will be more admired than even now.

If the Floridas can be obtained on tolerable terms, and the belligerent powers only treat us as well as we deserve; we have nothing to make us (the U-S) uneasy, unless it be the party madness of some our dissatisfied citizens

We have tolerable crops in this County though in some degree injured by hard winds

I am Sir With great respect yr. most Obt. Sevt

NATHL MACON

RC (DLC); endorsed by TJ as received on 16 Sep. and so recorded in SJL.

In the LATE ELECTIONS in North Carolina, held in August, Republicans triumphed in eleven of the state's twelve congressional districts. Samuel D. Purviance of Fayetteville was THE ONLY FEDERALIST to win a seat (*National Intelligencer*, 5 Sep. 1803; *Biog. Dir. Cong.*; Delbert Harold Gilpatrick, *Jeffersonian Democracy in North Carolina, 1789-1816* [New York, 1931], 170-1).

From Wilson Cary Nicholas

DEAR SIR Warren. Sept. 3. 1803

I have reflected much upon the conversation that I had with you, when I had last the pleasure of seeing you, about the power of the government of the U.S. to acquire territory, and to admit new States into the union. Upon an examination of the constitution, I find the power as broad as it cou'd well be made, 3d. sec. art. 4th. except that new States cannot be formed out of the old ones without the consent of the *State* to be dismembered; and the exception is a proof, to my mind that it was not intended to confine the congress in the admission of new States to what was then the territory of the U.S. Nor do I see any thing in the constitution, that limits the treaty making power, except the general limitations of the powers given to the government, and the evident objects for which the government was instituted. If it is determined that congress possess exclusively, all the powers that are to be found in the enumeration of powers given to that body, it will be deciding that there does not exist in the U.S. a power competent to make a treaty, for I will venture to assert, that a treaty cannot be formed, without the exercise of one or more of those powers by the President and the Senate, particularly a commercial treaty—nor does it seem to me that the sanction of Congress wou'd cure the defect, & that wou'd be to give them substantially the power of ratification, or rejection. Nor do I believe that we cou'd ever expect any Nation to form a treaty with us under such a construction of our constitution; for I do not see what wou'd prevent subsequent legislatures from repealing the laws upon which the validity of a treaty depended; and indeed making laws in direct violation of such a treaty, if it was admited that it derived all its force from a law. I am aware that this is to us delicate ground, and perhaps my opinions may clash with the opinions given by our friends during the discussion of the British treaty. Upon due consideration, it really appears to me that a different construction of the constitution, from that which I have given it, wou'd be to transfer the treaty making power to congress, or to deprive the govt. of the U.S. of the capacity of making treaties.

I shou'd be wanting in the sincerity and candour with which you have always permited me to give you my opinion if I was to forbear to recommend to you, to avoid giving an opinion as to the competence of the treaty making power, to make such a treaty as that lately entered into with France, by giving an opinion before the Senate act upon it, you wou'd take the whole responsibility of that opinion upon yourself in the public estimation, whereas if the Senate act before your opinion is known they will at least divide the responsibility with you. I shou'd think it very probable if the treaty shou'd be declared by you to exceed the constitutional authority of the treaty making power, that it wou'd be rejected by the Senate, and if that shou'd not happen, that great use wou'd be made with the people, of a wilful breach of the constitution. If you shou'd not think these observations merit the weight that I have given them, I flatter myself you will pardon the liberty that I have taken in suggesting them to you. I have a letter from J Breckinridge, written soon after he received an account of the treaty. he seems to think it will be next to impossible to keep our people from crossing the river, and conjectures (what I think is very probable) that large tracts of land have been granted, perhaps after the cession was contemplated. after stating the danger and inconvenience of spreading our population, he says "Be the consequences what they may, the acquirement of this country is the most Brilliant thing ever atchieved—to double the extent of an empire already large, without the loss of a man, and I confidently believe without the expence of dollar (for the port of Orleans will reimburse the 15 millions in the 15 years) and without for a moment effecting the ordinary operations of the fiscal concerns of the country, is an event which wisdom and good fortune have now for the first time exhibited."

I am Dear Sir with the greatest respect your friend & humble Servant
W. C. NICHOLAS

RC (DLC); endorsed by TJ as received on 5 Sep. and so recorded in SJL.

DELICATE GROUND: in 1796, TJ's and Nicholas's allies in the House of Representatives, unable to prevent the ratification of the Jay Treaty by the Senate, attempted to block the treaty's implementation (Vol. 29:9-10, 42, 45-9, 51, 54-7, 62, 70-1, 93-5).

From Philippe Reibelt

MONSIEUR LE PRESIDENT! Norfolk le 3r. Sept. 1803.

Le devoir, de sauver notre Santè Nous aÿant entre autres principalement et urgement obligè, de quitter la terre Kosciuszko, avec une perte considerable p. E. de doubler fraix de Voyage et cœtera, reduits par çela a tres peu de Moÿens Numeraires; mis par la nouvelle Guerre dans l'impossibilitè, de faire venir des bords du Rhin assez vite des nouvelles remises; donc pour le moment, et qui sait pour Combien de tems encore jettès dans un terrible embaras; sans autre Adresse dans çe paÿs, que çelle du Gen. Kosciuszko à Votre Excellence, parconsequent inconnus à tout le Monde, exceptè heureusement de Vous; sans existence lucrative, et hors d'etat, de Nous en donner une, convenable à Nos facultés—sans autre Aide Superieure—je suis par çes Circonstances—malgrè Moi forcè, de presenter a Votre Excellence l'instance pressante, de vouloir bien me mettre par quels Moyens, que çe sont peut être, par quelques recommandations—à même, de sortir, aussitot que possible, de cette triste situation.

Les parties, dans lesquelles je pouvoir travailler avec Succes, seroient des Speculations de Commerce ou d'Agriculture, aÿant de la practique pour l'un et pour l'autre, particuliérement pour le dernier, et etant pour çelui çi dans toutes ses branches munis d'une Collection Choisie des meill. nouv. auteurs tant Anglais, que francais et Allemands.

J'ai l'honneur d'etre avec le plus profond respect Votre Excellence tr. humble et tr. Obst. Servtr.
PHIL. REIBELT.

EDITORS' TRANSLATION

Mister President, Norfolk, 3 Sep. 1803

I was forced to leave Kosciuszko's land quickly for reasons of health, among others. This entailed a considerable expense by doubling the travel costs, etc., and greatly reduced my cash reserves. Unable to bring new funds across the Rhine with any speed because of the new war, I am plunged in a terrible situation right now and for who knows how much longer. Having no other contact in this country except General Kosciuszko's introduction to Your Excellency, I am unknown to everyone, except, fortunately, to you. With no livelihood nor any means of obtaining one that matches my competence, and with no other eminent patron, I am compelled, against my will, to present this urgent case to Your Excellency and to ask for your help, perhaps through some introductions, to get me out of this sad situation as soon as possible.

I could work successfully in trade of goods or agriculture, since I have experience in both, especially the latter in which I have a fine collection of books by the best new English, French and German authors.

With deepest respect, I have the honor, Your Excellency, of being your very humble and obedient servant. Phil. Reibelt

RC (DNA: RG 59, LAR); endorsed by TJ as received 17 Sep. and so recorded in SJL.

ÇELLE DU GEN. KOSCIUSZKO À VOTRE EXCELLENCE: when Reibelt arrived in the United States to complete the sale of Tadeusz Kosciuszko's military bounty lands to Louise Françoise Felix, he carried correspondence from Kosciuszko, which has not been found, that asked for TJ's special protection (Vol. 39:93-6).

From Robert Smith

Sir, Balt. Sep. 4. 1803

From Genl Dearborns answer to my letter respecting the gun carriages I find that the War department cannot supply them, and that there are not, as I had imagined, any artificers belonging to that department. I also perceive that the Secretary at War cannot possibly by any means have them built. I have however since the receiving of this answer been making such arrangements that I am enabled to assure you that I will have altered One Hundred of the frigate Carriages in such manner as will, I hope, answer and they will be prepared in time to go, if you approve, in the frigate going to France to be delivered on the return-passage. The axle trees would be very costly if made of wrought iron. I shall therefore have them of Cast Iron. Foxall can cast them so as gives them great substance.

Pray, Sir, is there not some ground to apprehend that we shall have occasion to take some strong measures to check the audacious impressments of our Citizens by the Brittish. If we manifest, at the beginning, a becoming resolution the English must yeild to our wishes. Her present circumstances will force her to abjure towards us what is so reasonable.

The Enclosed letter from Com. Morris I have just received.

Be pleased to accept the assurances of my great respect

Rt Smith

RC (DLC); endorsed by TJ as received from the Navy Department on 9 Sep. and so recorded in SJL; also endorsed by TJ: "gun carriages. impressmts." Enclosure not found.

making such arrangements: on 5 Sep., Smith ordered Thomas Tingey at the Washington Navy Yard to prepare 100 naval gun carriages, "in the completest manner and with the utmost dispatch," for the emperor of Morocco. The wooden axle trees were to be replaced with ones of cast iron to be supplied by Georgetown iron manufacturer Henry Foxall, and the carriage wheels were to be enlarged if necessary. If any advice was needed, Tingey was to consult with the secretary of war, "who will Chearfully afford you any Counsel you may need" (FC in Lb in DNA: RG 45, MLS; Vol. 34:46n).

frigate going to france: the *Essex*, which had been in ordinary at the Washington Navy Yard since its return from the Mediterranean in 1802. Smith had issued orders to outfit the warship and to prepare a marine detachment for it, but withdrew them once it was decided instead to send the Louisiana ratification and gun carriages by private vessel (NDBW, *Register*, 71-2; Smith to William W. Burrows, 1 Sep., 11 Oct. 1803, Smith to Thomas Tingey, 15 Sep. 1803, FCs in Lb in DNA: RG 45, MLS; Smith to John Cassin, 12 Oct. 1803, FC in Lb in DNA: RG 45, LSO; Vol. 38:195n; TJ to Smith, 10 Oct. 1803).

To Henry Dearborn

Dear Sir — Monticello Sep. 5. 03.

About a twelvemonth after we came into the administration we learnt by a letter from mr Simpson that our predecessors had promised to the Emperor of Marocco 100. gun carriages. you have known most of the unlucky circumstances which have baffled our execution of it. the last however is but recently known. we had desired mr Simpson to have them made in Europe, or to offer the value to the emperor to have them made himself & in his own way. he writes that it is impracticable for himself to get them made, & advises strongly against offering money. we are therefore now exactly where we were 18. months ago. we had at first proposed to send 100. gun carriages from the Navy stores, and it was therefore referred to the Secy of the navy to do it. but Simpson says they must be for field service, made in the best manner, & equipped with every necessary however minute. in this case mr Smith says he is not in a situation to execute the order, having no such carriages, nor any person skilled in making them. he supposes it possible you might have *good* carriages ready made, & which could be spared & replaced at leisure for ourselves: or that you can command artists who know how to make them. he promised to write to you, and to take on himself any agency which should be inconvenient to you. I have thought it necessary to mention it, because this delay has been so great as to give me serious apprehensions the emperor's patience will not hold out. if we have proper ones, we had better spare them. otherwise I am in hopes it is in your power to have them made expeditiously, and mr Smith will have vessels ready for carrying them. altho' I shall be with you on the 25th. I have thought the case too urgent to defer for consultation with you till that time, and hope you may enable us at length to discharge this engagement of our predecessors. accept my affectionate salutations & assurances of sincere esteem and respect. TH: JEFFERSON

P.S. mr Simpson says nothing of the size of the carriages. I presume they should be of different sizes, & you can best judge of the proportion of each size.—no letter should leave Washington for me after the 17th. inst.

PrC (DLC); at foot of text: "The Secretary at War." Recorded in SJL with notation "gun carriages."

From Albert Gallatin

DEAR SIR N. York 5 Sept. 1803

I receive this moment your favour of 30th ulto.—I am very decidedly of opinion that Abraham Bishop ought to be appointed Collector of New Haven.

I enclose more letters from Simons on the subject of the infractions committed on our neutrality; but am afraid that he took wrong ground in the case of the "Cotton planter," as it seems she was taken within our own limits, in which case she ought to have been claimed whether British or American property. But I really believe that it will be necessary to frame a new circular to the collectors bringing all former instructions into one point of view, with such alterations as either result from a change in our treaties, or may appear eligible on general grounds. It will, however, be well to consider whether it may not be best to give such circular its effect only after the expiration of those articles of the British treaty which cease within two years after the signature of the preliminaries of the late peace.

I enclose an extract of a letter from Mr Marbois received this day, & in which I do not discover any thing more than the desire of obtaining as early a payment as possible.

Permit me to suggest the propriety of having every thing in readiness to take possession of New Orleans, whether the prefect & Spanish officers shall be willing to give it up or not, the moment we shall have received the order to that effect from Mr Pichon: this is recommended by the possible event of our delivering the stock on receiving only the order to take possession & before actual possession shall have been obtained. The *dispensible* regular force at Fort Adams, the militia of the Mississipi territory & the crews of the Kentuckey boats and of American vessels from the Atlantic States then in N. Orleans will be sufficient against any force now in that place, provided that we may arm the boatmen & sailors & provided that the French militia of Louisiana be disposed to be at least neutral. Although I do not share in the alarm of our ministers, I think it wise to be as perfectly prepared as if it had a real ground, & that no time should be lost in having a supply of arms at Natchez; instructions given to Govr. Claiborne; and Clarke, if he can be trusted to that extent, informed by a safe communication of our intentions, with instructions to prepare the way with the inhabitants so as to meet no opposition from them. The establishment of expresses both by Hawkins & Nashville if practicable, and, at all events, by the last route seems also desirable. If there is any apprehension that that force may not ultimately be sufficient, such part of the militia of Kentuckey & Tenessee as may be thought necessary might be ordered under the act of last session to be in a state of readiness to float down the river on the arrival of an express from Claiborne applying for such aid.

If it shall be found necessary to take possession of New Orleans against the will of the possessors, there can be no doubt of the propriety of occupying at the same time that part of W. Florida which we claim. But if N. Orleans & West Louisiana shall be yielded without difficulty, the policy of occupying the rest of what we claim against the will of the Spanish officers is a subject which deserves serious consideration.

With respect & attachment Your obt. Servt.

Albert Gallatin

RC (DLC); at foot of text: "The President of the U.S."; endorsed by TJ as received from the Treasury Department on 12 Sep. and "Abram Bishop to be Collectr. New haven Ship Cotton planter possn of N. Orleans" and so recorded in SJL. Enclosure: probably an extract of François Barbé de Marbois to Gallatin, 7 June, in which he encloses a copy of the articles agreed upon and approved by the

First Consul outlining the financial arrangements for the purchase of Louisiana, noting that this letter will probably reach the Treasury secretary before Alexander Baring arrives in the U.S.; Barbé de Marbois trusts "that the government of the United States will find it convenient to arrange everything in relation to the execution of the Convention, so that after the arrival of Mr. Baring the matter may be consummated within the briefest delay"; he seeks Gallatin's cooperation, appreciates his "immediate and direct attention thereto," and requests a reply (RC in DNA: RG 56, PFLP; J. E. Winston and R. W. Colomb, "How the Louisiana Purchase was Financed," *Louisiana Historical Quarterly*, 12 [1929], 220-1). Other enclosures not found.

On 19 Aug., Charleston newspapers reported that the French frigate *Perseverance* had captured two vessels, one being the American ship COTTON PLANTER as it was coming into Charleston for supplies and then bound for Cowes. It was captured "four leagues from the lighthouse, but within three leagues of the coast." On 23 Aug., the *Charleston Courier* reported that *Cotton Planter* had been "liberated" and was proceeding on its voyage (Charleston *City Gazette and Daily Advertiser*, 19 Aug.; *Charleston Courier*, 19, 23 Aug.).

ACT OF LAST SESSION: earlier in the year, in response to James Ross's attempt to win approval for the use of military force against New Orleans, Congress passed "An Act directing a detachment from the Militia of the United States, and for erecting certain Arsenals." The act, approved on 3 Mch., authorized the president, "whenever he shall judge it expedient, to require of the executives of such of the states as he may deem expedient, and from their local situation shall be most convenient, to take effectual measures to organize, arm and equip, according to law, and hold in readiness to march at a moment's warning a detachment of militia" of up to 80,000 men and officers. The statute allowed the raising of volunteers to fill out the detachment if necessary and appropriated $1,500,000 for pay, subsistence, and "such other expenses as, during the recess of Congress, the President may deem necessary for the security of the territory of the United States" (U.S. Statutes at Large, 2:241; Vol. 39:554n).

To Thomas Munroe

DEAR SIR Monticello Sep. 5. 03.

Your favor of the 31st. came by the last post, and conveyed the first information I had recieved since I left Washington of the progress in the public buildings. I see with extreme concern that we shall not accomplish what was hoped. as nothing is mentioned of the covering of sheet iron being put on either building, I fear it is not done. I am now putting such a cover on my own house, & nothing can be more perfect. possibly the capitol may be patched up for another winter, but that will be a loss of expence, & we may be disappointed in making it effectually tight, which will be mortifying; and nothing can secure the President's house against leaking, but new covering all below the terras. I believe I omitted to ask of mr Lenthall to send me his weekly returns of progress as usual, by post. I wrote to mr Latrobe the morning of my departure & stated to him every thing necessary for the two public buildings. I now inclose you the warrant for 10. ~~M~~. Dollars. will you be so good as to direct in the post office that nothing be forwarded from thence for me after the 17th. instant. Accept my salutations & assurances of esteem. TH: JEFFERSON

PrC (DLC); at foot of text: "Mr. Thomas Munroe"; endorsed by TJ in ink on verso.

A letter from TJ to Benjamin Henry LATROBE was recorded in SJL at 18 July but has not been found.

To Robert Smith

DEAR SIR Monticello Sep. 5. 03.

Your favor of the 28th. came to hand on the 2d. inst. expecting mr Madison daily, I deferred writing till I should confer with him. this is the first post after his arrival, & I write to Genl. Dearborne to contribute his agency with you in such way as may be convenient for both towards carrying into execution the engagement of our predecessors to furnish the hundred gun carriages to the emperor of Marocco. As you think the last of our small armed vessels will be gone before the 30th. of Oct. you propose to prepare a *frigate* for carrying the ratification. not being a judge of comparative expences in naval matters, the object of the present is merely to suggest to your consideration whether there would not be more expence in this, than chartering a small private vessel, slightly arming & putting her into commission as a public vessel of which character she would be divested again on her return. the risking of a frigate on a winter voyage is disagreeable, & an unlucky accident to one of them might occasion great uneasiness, while the loss of a smaller private vessel would never be mentioned twice. I refer this entirely to your own consideration & decision. I hope we shall all be together at Washington on the 25th. inst. Accept my affectionate salutations & assurances of great esteem & respect. TH: JEFFERSON

P.S. no letter should leave Washington for me after the 17th.

PrC (DLC); at foot of text: "The Secretary of the Navy." Recorded in SJL with notation "gun carriages. vessel to carry ratifn."

EXPECTING MR MADISON DAILY: James Madison departed for Monticello on the morning of 3 Sep. (Madison, *Papers, Sec. of State Ser.*, 5:376).

I WRITE TO GENL. DEARBORNE: TJ to Dearborn, 5 Sep. 1803.

The Boundaries of Louisiana

I. CHRONOLOGY OF TERRITORIAL CLAIMS IN LOUISIANA, [ON OR BEFORE 31 AUG. 1803]

II. EXAMINATION OF THE BOUNDARIES OF LOUISIANA, 7 SEP. 1803

EDITORIAL NOTE

The geographic limits of the purchase of Louisiana were ill-defined. Although Jefferson could rightly rejoice that Americans now controlled the entire Mississippi valley, including of course the prize of New Orleans, little else was known about what bounded the acquisition. The purchase treaty merely quoted the vague language of the Treaty of San Ildefonso, which defined Louisiana by "the Same extent that it now has in the hands of Spain, & that it had when France possessed it," and referred to the previous transfer in ceding to the United States "the said territory with all its rights and appurtenances" (Miller, *Treaties*, 2:499-500). In addition to the general ignorance of the unmapped areas of the far west, confusion reigned over how far east and west Louisiana extended along the Gulf Coast. Although Robert R. Livingston and James Monroe insisted in communications about the treaty that the purchase area should include West Florida as far east as the Perdido River, a critical goal of the administration, the boundaries between French and Spanish territory, as Rufus King reported to Albert Gallatin, "have never been settled by any treaty." Spanish claims appeared stronger in Texas, but there too the French had a history of fortification and the Spanish an indifferent effort at settlement (Isaac Joslin Cox, "The Louisiana-Texas Frontier," *Quarterly of the Texas State Historical Society*, 10 [1906], 1-75; Madison, *Papers, Sec. of State Ser.*, 5:72-7; Vol. 40:301-3, 431, 433-4n; Gallatin to TJ, 18 Aug.).

During his summer sojourn at Monticello, Jefferson turned to his library for possible answers to the question of Louisiana's boundaries. He had collected over the years a large number of English, French, and Spanish sources related to the settlement and geography of North America, and he put a portion of this collection to use in developing a historical timeline of Spanish and French efforts to settle and control Louisiana and other areas. He had clearly done much of the research by 23 Aug., when he wrote Albert Gallatin and reported his view that based on his sources, "our claim to the Perdido is solid, and to the bay of St. Bernard very argumentative." The following day, he reported much the same to James Madison. Jefferson's confidence in the legitimacy of American claims to St. Bernard, or Matagorda, Bay represented a shift from the more tentative assessment of the purchase area he had described in letters to John Dickinson on 9 Aug. and to Thomas Paine on the following day, although those letters also reflected his interest in an expansive reading of the purchase area. His historical sources proved to Jefferson that the United States might control not only the Mississippi and Missouri Rivers but also most of Texas and the Red and Arkansas Rivers in their entireties. This confidence reflected in large part his reliance on French sources, which not surprisingly argued in favor of French claims as opposed to Spanish ones, and his neglect of the Spanish sources in his collection. Jefferson finished his chronology by 31 Aug., when Thomas Mann Randolph copied it, perhaps for his own use as an incoming congressman. Randolph's transcription closely followed Jefferson's draft but did not include an extract of an early eighteenth-century French royal charter granting Antoine Crozat proprietorship over Louisiana. Either Randolph was not interested in copying the extract or Jefferson added it at a later time. In addition, Randolph streamlined much of the phrasing of the final section, which Jefferson labeled "Limits," and excluded some quotations drawn from the work of Antoine-Simon Le Page du Pratz, one of Jefferson's most important sources.

The president appears to have used his timeline as an aid in composing a more narrative treatment of the subject, which he entitled "An Examination into the boundaries of Louisiana" and dated 7 September. The many interlineations and long marginal notes indicate that Jefferson drafted the "Examination," like the chronology, over several sittings. The most significant revision was a two-page insertion, the first page of which Jefferson glued on top of the penultimate page of the earlier version, thereby obscuring the original text. In addition, the president added a marginal note based on information the administration received from William C. C. Claiborne and James Wilkinson late in January 1804 (see Document II, note 10 and second authorial note; Madison, *Papers, Sec. of State Ser.*, 6:233, 408). Jefferson may have intended the "Examination" as a general guide for American policy-making and negotiation. In a letter of 8 January 1804 to James Monroe, he reported that Madison would be sending Monroe a copy of the "Memoir" he had written on the limits of Louisiana "last summer while I was among my books at Monticello." Monroe evidently received the document, and another transcript in a clerk's hand ended up in the State Department's records. Jefferson enclosed another copy in a letter of 13 March to William Dunbar, and Madison forwarded one to Livingston in a letter of 31 March (Madison, *Papers, Sec. of State Ser*, 6:643, 648n). Jefferson sent a fair copy in his own hand to the American Philosophical Society in December 1817 (see TJ to Peter S. Du Ponceau, 30 Dec. 1817). In that version, the historical timeline (Document I) takes up five pages of neatly composed text, and after a blank page the "Examination" (Document II) runs for twelve more, each reflecting the many revisions that Jefferson made to his original drafts.

Initially, Jefferson's analysis ignored the question of the purchase area's northern boundary with Canada. In January 1804, however, he turned to this subject and appended two dense pages of text to his original draft of the "Examination." This section also appeared as a postscript in the fair copy that Jefferson sent to the APS and in the State Department transcript. It has not been included here because of the long time between respective compositions and because it dealt with a separate set of diplomatic issues, this time involving Great Britain rather than Spain. Both Jefferson's historical analysis of the east and west boundaries of the purchase area and his later analysis of the northern boundary, nevertheless, reflect his desire to maximize the land area purchased from the French.

I. Chronology of Territorial Claims in Louisiana

[on or before 31 Aug. 1803]

A Chronological series of facts relative to Louisiana.

1673. Spain declares war against France. 4. Russel's Mod. Eur. 68.

Joliet, an inhabitant of Quebec, & the Jesuit Marquette descended from Canada down the Missisipi to the Arkansas in 33.° & returned to Canada. 8. Rayn. 158. Hennepin N.D: 293.

1675. La Salle goes to France to sollicit authority to explore the Misipi. Joutel xvii

1678. The peace of Nimeguen. 4. Russ. 92.

La Salle returned from France to Canada with Tonti to undertake to explore the Misipi. Joutel xviii.

1679. he builds a fort at the mouth of the Miami of the lake. Hennepin Nouv. Decouvertes. 171.

1680. Jan. he builds a fort on the river Illinois. Hennep. N.D. 223. called it Crevecoeur.[1]

Feb. 29. Hennepin with 2. men leave the Illinois to descend the Misipi in a bark canoe. Hennep. N.D. 228. 241. visits the Arcansas 258. the Taensas 263. reaches the sea. 272. returns to the Illinois 294. 349. Nouv. voyage. 96. 1. DuPratz. 4.

1681. La Salle visits fort Crevecoeur & leaves a garrison there of 15. or 16. men. Tonti. 147.[2]

1682. La Salle & Tonti went down the Misipi & named the country Louisiana. he went to the mouths of the Misipi, observed their latitude, & returned to Canada. Joutel xvii.xx. Tonti 153. 1. DuPratz. 5. 2. Dumont 258. says in 1679.

1683. They build a fort, called Prudhomme, in the Chickasaw country 60. leagues below Ohio. Tonti 155. reach the ocean. Apr. 7. 1683. ib. 191. they have 60. persons in their company. set out on their return Apr. 11. 1683. ib. 196.

soon after this some Canadians, enticed by the flattering accounts of the country, went & settled near the mouth of the Misipi, & on the coast. 2. Dum. 260.[3]

1684. Spain declares war against France, but concludes at Ratisbon a truce of 20. years. 4. Rus. 141.

Jul. 24. La Salle sails from Rochelle with 4. vessels to seek the mouth of the Misipi by sea. Joutel 2. Tonti 140. he had with him 100. souldiers & officers, in all 280. persons. Hennepin Nouveau Voyage. 12.

1685. Feb. 18. La Sale landed in the bay of St. Bernard, or St. Louis. Joutel 32. 1. Dupratz 6. Tonti 245. 2. Dum. 259

builds a fort there. Tonti 245. 276. left 100. men there Hen. N.V. 23. 130. persons. Joutel 45.

Apr. 22. he sets out with 20. men to seek a new place. Tonti. 249.[4]

June. he makes a 2d. settlement further up the river. 70. persons go to it. Joutel 49.

1685. July. they abandon the first fort & go to the 2d. Joutel. 51. called it & the neighboring bay St. Louis. Joutel. 54.

Tonti descends the Misipi with 40. men to meet La Sale. Tonti 220. reconnoitres the coast 20. leagues East and West of the mouth. on the jour de Paques (Easter) they set out on their return. 222.

Tonti builds a house on the river Arkansa & leaves 10. Frenchmen there. Tonti 225. Joutel says 6. men, 4 of whom afterwards returned to Canada. Joutel 151.[5] this becomes permanent. 226. 1. Dupr. 6[6] and is afterwards included in Law's grant, who settled it with Germans in 1719. 2. Dum. 68.

1686. Apr. 22. La Sale sets out for Illinois by land. Hennepin N.V. 39. but returns to Fort Louis. ib. 63.

1687. Jan. 7. he sets out again with 20. men. Henn. N.V. 67. is murdered. Joutel 99. Henn. N.V. 77.

La Sale's 2d fort at St. Louis is afterwards abandoned. Tonti 329. Coxe. 39.

after the death of La Sale, Cavelier his brother, with 7. men, set out for Canada. Joutel 132.

July. they find the house on the Arkansa built by Tonti with only 2. men remaining in it. Jout. 151. they leave one of their company there. 157. they strike the Misipi. Joutel 158.

Dec. 3 Tonti sets out from the Illinois, & descends the Misipi a 2d. time. Tonti. 317. finds La Sale's 2d. settlement broke up. 329. finds at the Coroas 2. of the 7. French men who had separated from Cavelier after the death of La Sale. 331. returns to Illinois. 331.

1689. War commenced by Spain against France. 4. Russel. 228.

1696. Spain established a post at Pensacola. 9. Reynal 128.

1697. Sep. 20. Treaty of Ryswick 4. Russell 248.

1698. D'Hiberville discovers the mouth of the Misipi by sea. 2. Dum. 260.

he is made Governor. 2. Dum. 260.

he establishes a colony at Mobile, & Isle Dauphine. 260.

1701. The war of the Spanish succession begins, France & Spain being allies. 4. Rus. 317.

1712. Sep. 14. Louis XIV. grants the exclusive commerce of Louisiana to Crozat. possession & extent described Joutel 196. 2. Dum. 260.

1713. Mar. 31. Treaty of Utrecht establishing the 49th. degree of lat. as the division between Louisiana & the British Northern possessions.

1714. Mar. 6. Treaty of Rastadt.

1715. The French establish Natchitoches on Red river & build a fort 35. leagues above it's mouth. 2. Dum. 65.

1715. The Spaniards make settlements at the Assinais & Adais on one side & at Pensacola on the other. 1. Dupratz 9. 13. 14. (this was 7. or 10. leagues from Natchitoches) to restrict the French limits. 1. Dupratz. 14. 278.

1716. Crozat cedes his charter to the West India company. 2. Dumont. 6. 260.

1717. The company sent inhabitants to Isle Dauphine, where were some settlers before. 2. Dum. 7.

Hubert and Page settle at the Natchez. 2. Dum. 60.

Fort Rosalie is built. 2. Dum. 60.[7]

1718. Two other vessels are sent there. 2. Dum. 8.

France and England declare war against Spain. quadruple alliance. 5. Rus. 6.

1719. The French take Pensacola. 1. Du Pratz 189. 2. Dumont 9. the Spaniards retake it. 191. 12. the French take it again ib. 195. 18.

France and Spain make peace. 5. Rus. 7.

France sends 800. settlers to Louisiana. Du Pratz. xlviii.

Old Biloxi is settled. 2. Dumont 34.

Isle Dauphine is evacuated & every body removed to Old Biloxi, except a Serjeant & guard of 10. men. 2. Dum. 36. 37.

New Biloxi is settled. 2. Dum. 42. 43.
A cargo of Negroes arrives at Old Biloxi. ib.
The grantees now settle, every one on his own grant, to wit, at Old Biloxi, Bayagordas, Point Coupée, Natchez, Yazous, Arkansas, Black river. 2. Dum. 44.
New Orleans is laid off, 30 leagues above the mouth of Misipi, where some settlers from Canada had already settled, & the seat of government is fixed there. 2. Dum. 47.

1720. A fort on the Missouri is built & garrisoned. 2. Dum. 74. called Fort Orleans. Jeffry. 139.
De la Harpe & Dumont, with 22. men, go 300. leagues up the Arkansa. a fine country. salt springs, marble, plaister, slate & gold. 2. Dum. 70.

1722. The Balise is established, & a fort built on piles. 2. Dum. 57.
The Spaniards attempt a settlement among the Missouris, but are all massacred to the number of 1500. 2. Dum. 282.

1733. France, Spain & Sardinia commence war against the Emperor. 5. Rus. 27.

1735. Peace is made. 5. Rus. 29.

1736. The French build a fort at Tombichee. 1. Du Pratz. 85.[8]

1743. The Family compact made.

1748. The Treaty of Aix la Chapelle. 5. Rus. 187.

1762. Spain enters as an ally with France into the war against England.

Nov. 3. France cedes Louisiana West of Iberville to Spain by a secret treaty, and East of Iberville to England. Preliminary treaty. The King of France's order to L'Abbadie.[9]

1763. The Treaty of Paris is made.

1783. Great Britain cedes the two Floridas to Spain.[10]

Limits.

In 1680. the nearest settlements of Spain were on the river Panuco, 100. leagues West of the Misipi. Hennep. N.D. 274. Coxe 115. Coxe's Carolana. 4.

In 1715. they make the settlements at Assinais & Adais, & Pensacola. 1. Du Pratz. 9. 13. 14. 278.

In 1722. they attempt one on the Missouri which is prevented by the Indians. 2. Du Pratz 157. 2. Dumont 282. Jeffry's hist. of the French dominions in America. 139.

Du Pratz sais 'the coast is bounded to the West by St. Bernard's bay, where M. de la Salle landed.' and again 'on the East the coast is bounded by Rio Perdido &c. a little to the East of Mobile &c. 1. Du

Pratz. 216. and 'the Red river bounds the country to the North.' 1. Du Pratz. 272.

2. Du Pratz 301. says 'Canada lies to the North of Ohio, & inclines more to the East than the source of Ohio.' [consequently the Ohio was not in Canada,[11] and must therefore have been in Louisiana, as these two provinces were co-terminous.] and again 'the lands of the Illinois are reputed to be a part of Louisiana.' ib. his book was published in 1758. and the translation in 1763.

The Translator of Du Pratz, in his preface, says 'the mountains of New Mexico run in a chain of continued ridges from North to South, and are reckoned to divide that country from Louisiana, about 900. miles West from the Misipi. pa. xi.

1712. The great document establishing with precision the boundaries of Louisiana, is Louis XIV's grant of this date to Crozat. to be found in the translation of Joutel. 196.[12]

1763. Treaty of Paris Art. VI. France cedes to England the river & port of Mobile & every thing on the left side of the Misipi, which she possesses or ought to possess except the island of N. Orleans:[13] and Art. XIX. Spain cedes to England all she possesses East or S.E. of the Misipi. thus all Louisiana E. of the Misipi is acknoleged to England, and all English claims West of the Misipi acknoleged to Spain.

England divides the country South of Georgia, & East of the Iberville[14] into two provinces, East & West Florida, by the Apalachicola.

1783. England, by Art. V. of the treaty cedes to Spain la Floride Orientale ainsi que la Floride Occidentale.

Spain re-establishes the government of Louisiana as before, & the government of Floridas, that part of what the English had called West Florida being under the Governor of N. Orleans, & the rest under the Governor of Florida. see the Baltimore American Patriot. Vol. 1. No. 97. this is confirmed by M. D'Azara, Spanish Ambassador at Paris who told mr Livingston that Mobile made a part of Louisiana. see Liv's letter to Monroe. Paris. May 23. 1803.

Spain retrocedes to France by the treaty of St. Ildefonso.

1803. France cedes to the US. Louisiana with the same extent that
Apr. 30. it now has, & that it had when France possessed it, and such as it ought to be after treaties passed subsequently between Spain & other powers.[15]

'Objections des Commissaires Anglois sur l'incertitude des limites de l'Acadie &c. 'les limites propres et anciennes de l'Acadie s'etendent depuis l'extremité de la baye Françoise jusq'au cap Canseau. l'objection d'incertitude sur ces limites ne peut donc tomber que sur celles de l'interieur des terres. dans de pareilscas, la regle la plus usitée et la plus convenable est d'etendre les limites dans l'interieur des terres jusque à la source des rivieres qui se dechargent à la cote, c'est à dire que chaque nation a de son coté les eaux pendantes. c'est ainsi qu'on en a usé à la paix des Pyrenèes pour fixer les limites entre la France et l'Espagne' &c. 1. Memoires de l'Amerique. 116.

MS (PPAmP); entirely in TJ's hand, including brackets. PoC (ViU). Dft (DLC: TJ Papers, 137:23690-1); entirely in TJ's hand; lacks final paragraph; includes on last page, "Extract from the Grant to Crozat" (see Document II below). Tr (ViU); in Thomas Mann Randolph's hand, "copied from a sheet in the hand of Th: Jefferson. Aug. 31. 1803." Tr (DLC: Monroe Papers); in a clerk's hand; endorsed by Monroe; also endorsed: "cession of the Commerce of Louisiana by the King of France to Mr Crozat in the year *1712*—limits of the country under that *name*," and "Interesting." Tr (DNA: RG 59, MLR); in a clerk's hand. PrC (NHi: Robert R. Livingston Papers).

TJ compiled his chronology largely from accounts of North America written by French explorers and settlers. Among the works upon which he principally relied were memoirs by three of La Salle's lieutenants: Louis HENNEPIN, Henri JOUTEL, and Henri de TONTI (Sowerby, Nos. 4066, 4067, 4073, and 4072). Two settlers of Louisiana, Antoine-Simon Le Page DU PRATZ and Jean-François Benjamin DUMONT de Montigny, wrote histories of the colony that also shaped TJ's timeline (Sowerby, Nos. 4068, 4069). The choice of these sources elevated La Salle's explorations over those of earlier Spanish parties, and focused attention on the first decades of the eighteenth century, the period when French efforts to settle the lower Mississippi Valley began in earnest (Gordon Sayre, *Les Sauvages Américains: Representations of Native Americans in French and English Colonial Literature* [Chapel Hill, 1997], 326-7, 329; Gordon Sayre, "Plotting the Natchez Massacre: Le Page du Pratz, Dumont de Montigny, Chateaubriand," *Early American Literature*, 37 [2002], 385-6.

An article printed in Baltimore's AMERICAN PATRIOT, appearing originally in the 26 July issue of the Charleston *City Gazette and Daily Advertiser*, claimed as "a pretty well known fact" that Spain had preserved the jurisdictional division of East and West Florida, with the former dependent on the governor general of Cuba, and the latter governed by the colonial administration at New Orleans. It acknowledged also that "we have no regular distinct account of any fixed or ascertained boundaries by Spain, as all the acts of that government are involved in great mystery" (Baltimore *American Patriot*, 11 Aug. 1803).

For Robert Livingston's LETTER TO MONROE, see Livingston to TJ, 26 May.

OBJECTIONS DES COMMISSAIRES ANGLOIS: that is, "The British commissioners' objections concerning the uncertainty of Acadia's borders, etc. The old, established borders of Acadia extend from Bay François (the Bay of Fundy) to Cape Canso. Any claim of uncertainty can refer only to inland boundaries. In such cases, the most common and appropriate rule is to extend the internal borders to the source of the rivers that empty at the coast. In other words, each nation has the flowing waters on its side. This is what was done in the Treaty of the Pyrenees to set the border between France and Spain, etc." The passage replaced an extract of the 1714 French royal grant of Louisiana to Antoine Crozat, which TJ had appended to the draft version. It was drawn from the first volume of *Mémoires des commissaires du roi et de ceux de sa*

Majesté Britannique, sur les possessions & les droits respectifs des deux Couronnes en Amérique, a compendium of documents produced during negotiations over Canada and the West Indies, published in Paris in 1755 (Sowerby, No. 1452). TJ generally referred to the four-volume set as MEMOIRES DE L'AMERIQUE (Vol. 7:288; Vol. 23:298; TJ to Abiel Holmes, 7 Dec. 1804). TJ is quoting from the 12th article of the French response to the British commissioners, dated 4 Oct. 1751. For his own interpretation of the passage, see Document II below.

[1] Preceding two entries interlined in Dft.

[2] Entry interlined in Dft.

[3] Entry interlined in Dft.

[4] Entry interlined in Dft.

[5] Preceding sentence and citation interlined in Dft.

[6] Remainder of entry interlined in Dft.

[7] Preceding two entries interlined in Dft.

[8] Entry interlined in Dft above entry: "1741. Spain joins France in a war. 5. Russ. 85."

[9] Entry interlined in Dft, where it reads: "Secret treaty by which France cedes Louisiana to Spain. the king's order to L'Abbadie. Preliminary articles <*with*> between France Spain & England."

[10] Dft: "1783. Treaty of peace at Paris."

[11] Bracketed passage ends here in Dft.

[12] Entry interlined in Dft.

[13] Here in Dft, TJ canceled "and to Spain the island of N. Orleans, and all Louisiana on the right bank of the Misipi."

[14] Preceding passage beginning with "South" interlined in Dft.

[15] Dft ends here.

II. Examination of the Boundaries of Louisiana

An examination into the boundaries of Louisiana.

The French having for a century and a half been in possession of Canada, and it's inhabitants penetrating to the remote waters communicating with the St. Laurence, they learned of the Indians that, in the neighborhood of those waters, arose a great river, called the Missisipi, running due South to the sea, and through a fine country unpossessed by any white nation. in 1673. the Sieurs[1] Joliet and Marquette, two Canadians, undertook to explore it, descended the Missisipi as far as the river Arkansa, in 33.° & returned to Canada. their account of it inflamed the enterprize of M. de la Salle, who in 1675. went to France to sollicit authority to explore the Missipi. he obtained it, returned to Canada, and in 1680. went as far as the river Illinois, on the lower part of which he built & garrisoned a fort called Crevecoeur, and sent the father Hennepin with 2. men to push his discoveries down the Misipi as far as he could; &, as preparatory to a more formal[2] essay, going himself Northwardly. Hennepin descended the Misipi to the ocean, & returned with the information collected,[3] to the Illinois. in 1682, La Sale & Tonti undertook their expedition: went down the river with 60. men, named the country Louisiana,[4] built a fort in the Chickasaw country, 60 leagues below the Ohio,[5] which they called Prudhomme, reached the ocean, and returned to Canada the ensuing year 1683.

La Sale then went to France, to obtain the means of going thence to the Misipi directly by sea. in the mean time some Canadians descend the river, & settle near it's mouth, & along the coast Eastwardly to the island of Massacre, opposite Mobile. the government of France,[6] entering at once into the view of extending an united possession along the St. Laurence & Misipi, from sea to sea equips la Sale with 4. vessels, on board of which were 280. persons, of whom 100. were officers and soldiers furnished with all necessaries. he sailed in July 1684. from Rochelle, and missing the mouth of the Missisipi, landed Feb. 18. 1685. in the Bay of St. Bernard to the West of it. here he takes possession, makes two successive establishments, building and garrisoning forts at each, the second of which was called St. Louis.

The Chevalier Tonti, about this time, sets out from Canada in quest of La Sale, whom he supposed to be then on the Misipi, descends with 40. men to the mouth of the river, reconnoitres the coast 20. leagues East & West; finding nothing of La Sale, he ascends the river,[7] builds a house on the river Arkansa, and leaves 10. men in it, which becomes a permanent settlement, and he returns to Canada.

In 1686 La Sale attempts to penetrate from fort St. Louis to the Illinois by land, but is obliged to return. in 1687 he makes another attempt with 17. men,[8] and is murdered on the way by some of[9] his own people. Cavelier, brother of La Sale, undertakes the same enterprize with 7. men; they find the house on the Arkansa built by Tonti, with only two men remaining in it; they leave a third, strike the Misipi, and reach Canada. Tonti descends the river a second time, finds two Frenchmen who had separated from Cavelier settled at the Coroas, and returns to the Illinois.[10]

In 1689. a war commenced between France and Spain, which continuing till the treaty of Ryswick in 1697. suspended the aids of France to her colony: but in 1698. D'Iberville was sent as it's governor with recruits.[11] he discovers the mouths of the Misipi, and settles his new recruits at Isle Massacre, which he calls Isle Dauphine, and at Mobile, where they find the Canadians who had settled there in 1683.[12] Spain had, during the war, to wit, in 1696. taken a counter-post at Pensacola.

The result from these facts is that France had formal & actual possession of the coast from Mobile to the bay of St. Bernard, & from the mouth of the Misipi up into the country as far as the river Illinois. the nearest Spanish settlements at this time were on the river Panuco,[13] to the West, 100. leagues from the Misipi, and at Pensacola, to the East leagues distant. there does not appear as yet indeed to have been any formal declaration of the limits of Louisiana: but the practice of nations, on making discoveries in America, has sanctioned a principle that 'when a nation takes possession of any extent of sea-coast, that possession is understood as extending into the interior country to the sources of the rivers emptying within that coast, to all their branches, & the country they cover.' 1. Mem. de l'Amerique 116. it was in support of this principle of virtual and declared possession, that France entered into the war of 1755 against Great Britain, whose settlements began now to reach the Eastern waters of the Misipi, and who opposed the claim of France, not on a denial of this principle, but on a prior possession taken & declared by repeated charters, thro' the space of an hundred years preceding, as extending from sea to sea.[14] France then had possession of the Misipi, and all the waters running into it, and of the sea coast and all it's rivers & territories on them from Mobile to the bay of St. Bernard.[15] the river Perdido, midway between the adversary possessions of Mobile & Pensacola, became afterwards the settled boundary between Spain & France in the East, and the Rio Norte, or Bravo, midway between the bay of St. Bernard and the river Panuco, the then nearest settlement of Spain, was considered by France, if not by Spain, and on the same fair grounds as in the other quarter,[16] as the boundary between them in the West. besides being midway between the actual possessions of the two nations, that river formed a natural and well marked boundary, extending very far into the country Northwardly. and accordingly we find by several* maps, some of them published by authority of the French government, and some Spanish maps,[17] that France claimed to that river. this claim has not been abridged, as far as is known, by any public treaty; and those which are secret, if any such have taken place, cannot bind nations having no notice of them, &[18] succeeding fairly to the rights of France, as publicly avowed & believed to exist.*

But the extent of Louisiana into the interior country is not left merely on the principle of it's[19] dependency on the coast into which it's waters disembogue: nor on the settlements extending up[20] it's great rivers, the Misipi, the Missouri, & the Illinois; but on an authoritative and public document announcing it's extent, and making

*I possess three antient maps which mark the Rio bravo & it's Eastern branch as the dividing boundary between Louisiana & Mexico. 1. Moll's map of the West Indies & adjacent countries. 2. Moll's map of Louisiana &c. published in 1720. in which the South Western parts of Louisiana are said to be copied from a French map published in Paris in 1718. and 3. Homann's Spanish map of Louisiana of about the same date.

*to this may be added the verbal declaration of the French Commr. to those of the US. on the delivery of possession, that his positive instructions from his government were to take possession to the Rio Bravo.

a temporary disposition of it. this is the Letter patent of Sep. 14. 1712. by which Louis XIV. grants to the Sieur Anthony Crozat the exclusive commerce of that country for 15. years. the following extracts from it ascertain the extent of the country.[21]

'Louis by the grace of god, king of France & Navarre to all &c.

'The care we have always had to procure the welfare & advantage of our subjects having induced us &c. to seek for all possible opportunities of enlarging & extending the trade of our American colonies, we did, in the year 1683. give our orders to undertake a discovery of the countries & lands which are situated in the Northern part of America, between New France & New Mexico: & the Sieur de la Sale, to whom we committed that enterprize, having had success enough to confirm a belief that a communication might be settled from *New France to the gulph of Mexico*, by means of large rivers; this obliged us, immediately after the peace of Ryswick, to give orders for the establishing a colony there, & maintaining a garrison, *which has kept and preserved the possession we had taken in the very year 1683.* of the lands, coasts & islands which are situated in the gulph of Mexico, between Carolina on the East, & Old & New Mexico on the West. but a new war having broke out in Europe shortly after, there was no possibility till now, of reaping from that new colony the advantages that might have been expected from thence &c. And whereas upon the information we have recieved, concerning the disposition and situation of the *said countries known at present by the name of the province of Louisiana*, we are of opinion that there may be established therein a considerable commerce &c. we have resolved to grant the commerce of the country of Louisiana to the Sieur Anthony Crozat &c. For these reasons &c. we, by these presents, signed by our hand, have appointed, & do appoint the said Sieur Crozat to carry on a trade in all the lands possessed by us, and bounded by New Mexico, & by the lands of the English of Carolina, all the establishment, ports, havens, rivers, & principally the port & haven of the Isle Dauphine, heretofore called Massacre, the *river of St. Louis, heretofore called Missisipi*, from the edge of the sea as far as the *Illinois; together with *the river St. Philip, heretofore called the Missourys*, and of *St Jerome, heretofore called Ouabache*, with *all the countries, territories, lakes within land, and the rivers which fall directly or indirectly* into that part of the river St. Louis.'

*The French & Spaniards called by the name of *the Illinois*, or Illinois country, the whole country on both sides of the Upper Misipi. that on the Eastern side was called East Illinois, that on the West side West Illinois.

The Articles. I. Our pleasure is that all the aforesaid *lands, countries, streams, rivers & islands* be, and remain *comprised under the name of the government of Louisiana*, which shall be dependant upon the general government of New France, to which it is subordinate: & further that all the lands which we possess from the Illinois be united &c. to the general government of New France, & become part thereof &c.' [here follow 15. other articles relating to commerce only] 'Given at Fontainebleau the 14th. day of Sep. in the year of grace 1712. and of our reign the 70th. Louis. by the King Phelipeaux.'

Here then is a solemn & public declaration sufficiently special to shew that all the waters running directly or indirectly into the Misipi, and the country embraced by them,[22] are held and acted on by France, under the name of the province of Louisiana; and is a full & unequivocal supplement, if any supplement were necessary, to the titles derived, 1. from the actual settlements on the river and it's waters, 2. from the possession of the coast, & 3. from the principle which annexes to it all the depending waters.[23] the treaties of Ryswick, in 1697. where France & Spain were adversary powers, & those of Utrecht in 1713. & Rastadt in 1714. where they were allies,[24] by their silence, as well as by their provisions as to these countries, must be considered as sanctioning the rights of France to this province: to which add the progress made by France, undisturbed & unquestioned,[25] by Spain, in extending her settlements ad libitum within them, till 1763. it is true that in 1715. some Spaniards made small settlements at the Assinais, & Adais, & in 1722. attempted one on the Missouri. the last was prevented by the Indians, and the former were connived at by the Agents of France to favor a smugling commerce with New Mexico, but these contrabrand encroachments[26] cannot weigh as evidence of ownership against the possession taken by France 30. years before, & the solemn establishment of boundary by Louis XIV.

War breaking out between them in 1718. the French took Pensacola; the Spaniards retook it, but the French recovered & retained it till the peace in 1719 when it was restored to Spain; and from this epoch the river Perdido[27] has been the acknoleged and undisturbed boundary between Louisiana and Florida.

The boundaries of Louisiana then, as held by France, were the seacoast & islands from the river Perdido to the Rio Norte or Bravo,[28] then up the Rio Bravo to it's source; thence to the highlands encompassing the waters of the Misipi, and along those highlands round the heads of the Missouri & Misipi & their waters to where those highlands assume the name of the Alleganey or Apalachian mountains, thence along those mountains, and the highlands encompassing the waters of the Mobile, to the source of the Perdido, & down that to the ocean.

In opposition to these claims, both of France and Spain, were those of the then English colonies, now the US. whose charters extended from sea to sea, and consequently covered all Louisiana & Mexico, above the parallel of latitude which formed the Southern boundary of Georgia.[29] these adversary claims were settled by the war of 1755-1763 and the treaty of Paris which closed it, and[30] which made the Misipi & Iberville the Western limit of the English possessions, and thenceforward the Eastern limit of Louisiana.

This war had begun between France & England, Spain being unconcerned in the grounds of it. in the beginning, France had sensibly the advantage, but after awhile it's successes were signally on the side of England. In 1762 Spain entered into it as a volunteer & ally of France. Great Britain immediately attacked & took the town of Havanna, & an important portion of the island of Cuba; which imminently endangering the continental possessions of Spain within the gulf, and her communication with them, negociations for peace were very soon[31] set on foot. Great Britain, in exchange for her conquest in Cuba, required Florida, & that part of Louisiana from the Perdido to the Iberville. besides the[32] just sympathy which France felt for Spain, who had sustained this incalculable loss by friendly endeavors to aid her, she was bound by the family compact, lately renewed, Article XVIII. 'to consider the interests of Spain as her own, & to share in it's losses and advantages.' a considerable change too had taken place in the minds of the government of France, against the possession of distant colonies, which could not be protected but by a great navy. France therefore,[33] by a secret treaty, Nov. 3. 1762. (being the same day on which they publicly signed the preliminary articles with Gr. Britain) consented to cede all Louisiana to Spain, in order to enable her, by the sacrifice of such part of it as she thought proper, to ransom Cuba, and to indemnify her for the loss of Florida, required also by Great Britain to make up the equivalent. the portion of Louisiana from Iberville to Perdido therefore, ceded to Great Britain by the definitive treaty of Feb. 10. 1763.[34] did in substance move from Spain to Gr. Britain, altho' France, as not having publicly conveyed it to Spain, was the formal conveyor[35] to England. yet she acted herein merely as the friend & agent of Spain, who was become in truth the real proprietor of all Louisiana. the importance of seeing this transaction in it's true light will hereafter appear.

England immediately[36] laid off this portion of Louisiana, with so much of Florida as laid West of the Apalachicola, into a separate government, to which she gave the name of West Florida; and the residue of Florida into another government, to which she gave the name of East Florida.[37] and Spain, now proprietor of Louisiana, & of course free to curtail it's future boundary to the Westward, according to her own convenience, extended the limits & jurisdiction of New Mexico to the waters of the river Mexicana inclusively. but this cannot disprove[38] the former extent of Louisiana, as it had been held & ceded by France; but was done in virtue of the right ceded by France.

The war of 1775-1783. began between Great Britain & the US. but France and Spain at length became parties to it. by the treaty of Paris of 1783. which terminated it, Gr. Britain was constrained to restore to Spain Florida, and[39] the territory East of the Iberville, which she had recieved at the close of the former war in exchange for Cuba. if the portion of Louisiana comprised in it had really moved from France, then the restitution of the portion between Iberville & Perdido should have been to France, and that of Florida only to Spain. but as the whole had moved substantially from Spain, the whole was restored to her. on re-entering into possession Aug. 18. 1769. she[40] continued the English annexation of the Eastern portion of Louisiana with a part of Florida, under the name of West Florida, restoring however the whole to the jurisdiction of the Governor of Louisiana, residing at N. Orleans: and in public* instruments, as well as in common parlance that portion has been spoken of under the names of Louisiana, or of West Florida indifferently.

The nation of France had seen with considerable dissatisfaction the separation of Louisiana from the mother country. that province had ever been viewed by it with great partiality. it was inhabited by their relations & fellow citizens: & they considered Spain, in the immensity of her possessions, as not entitled to such a sacrifice from France. besides she had now got back both Florida & Cuba: and there was no justice in her continuing to retain Louisiana, which had been ceded to her only as an indemnification for the loss of one, & the means of getting back the other. as soon therefore as the successful administration of the first Consul of France had raised her into a condition for redemanding from other nations what she deemed her rights, Spain was required to make restitution of Louisiana,[41] under the friendly cover indeed of an exchange, but it's inequality shews it was but a

* one of these was deposited in the office of state.

cover. the real grounds of restitution required that it should not be mutilated, but full and entire as she recieved it. for what had she ever given for it? she was compleatly replaced in her antient possessions. on what just ground then could she propose to retain any portion of the equivalent ceded only as an indemnity for them?[42] accordingly a compleat retro-cession was provided for by the treaty of St. Ildefonso of Oct. 1. 1800. by definitions studiously[43] formed to reach every thing which had been ceded to or for her by France. by that instrument she re-cedes to France the colony or province of Louisiana, with the same extent 1. that it now has in the hands of Spain. 2. that it had when France possessed it, and 3. such as it ought to be after the treaties passed subsequently between Spain and other powers.[44] that is 1. she is to recede the antient country of Louisiana, as it is now recovered back into the hands of Spain & held by her under the name of Louisiana or West Florida, or Mexico, or by whatever other names she or other powers may since have chosen to designate certain parts of it, or to sever it by overlapping Mexico on it's West, and West Florida on it's Eastern quarter: she is to recede the *thing*, as it is in her hands, unaffected by new names. to make it still plainer, she is to retrocede it 2dly. with the same extent that it had when France possessed it. now France never possessed it one day[45] with any less extent than from the Perdido to the Rio Norte, & inland to the sources of all it's rivers. the whole of this extent she transferred on the same day by two treaties of equal date, to wit, all Westward of the Misipi & Iberville to Spain, & all Eastward to Great Britain. but, of the Eastern portion, Spain having since recovered back all below 31.° of latitude, that, with the Western side, composes Louisiana, as now in the hands of Spain, and as it had been possessed by France. but, not to disturb the right of the US. to the portion North of 31.° and to shew that it was only so much of the Louisiana held by France, as *was now in the hands of Spain*, it is expressly limited 3dly. to be such as it ought to be after the treaties passed *subsequently* between Spain & other powers. *subsequently* to what? to the cession of the country by France. when was that cession? Nov. 3. 1762. and Feb. 10. 1763. what are the treaties subsequent to this? those affecting the limits of Louisiana are the treaty of Sep. 3. 1783. with Great Britain, & that of Oct. 27. 1795. with the US. the former was a restitution, by Gr. Britain to Spain, of Florida, & the portion of Louisiana from the Perdido to the Iberville: and consequently, *after this treaty*, the extent of Louisiana *ought to be*, as again consolidated to the Perdido. But inasmuch as by the latter of these two treaties, Spain had confirmed to the US. a degree of latitude [from 32.° to 31.°] which she had long contended to be an unceded[46] part of Louisiana, & consequently not within the limits of the US, therefore by this provision, that right is saved to the US. & the extent of Eastern Louisiana *after this treaty, ought to be* only to the latitude of 31.°

Should it be alledged that this confirmation of the diminutions of Louisiana by treaties subsequent to it's alienation by France, goes to the treaty of 1763. with Gr. Britain also; the answer is that this treaty was *simultaneous* with the alienation, & not subsequent to it, and therefore could not be within the scope of this definition. the confirmation too is in favor of treaties made *by Spain*, with other nations. that with Great Britain is by *France and Spain*. but it might also be justly observed that Louisiana was not lessened in it's dimensions by that treaty; it was only divided, the Eastern portion thereof transferred to Great Britain, the Western to Spain; who might new-name a part of it West Florida, & a part Mexico, for their internal purposes, as they pleased; but when the portion newly called West Florida came back to *the hands of Spain*, it was still a part of antient Louisiana, *as possessed by France, as now in the hands of Spain*, & unalienated by subsequent treaties of Spain with other powers.

On the whole, the intention of the treaty of St. Ildefonso is clearly this. France had in 1763. generously ceded all Louisiana to, or for[47] Spain. Spain consented that the Eastern portion of it, below Georgia, together with her Florida, should go to recover Cuba. afterwards however, in another war, by the arms of France and of the US. (for Spain came in late, & then did little more than waste her resources on the rock of Gibraltar) she recovers back, and has secured to her,[48] her antient Florida, & the Eastern portion of Louisiana, below Georgia. the treaty of St. Ildefonso therefore meant to review this whole transaction, & to restore France & Spain to the Status quo prior to the war of 1755.-63. Spain being now in possession of her original colonies of Florida and Cuba, it was just, & was meant, that France should also be reinstated in Louisiana, so far as Spain, while it was in her hands, had not transferred portions of it by permanent alienations to other powers. she confined her reclamation therefore to the part of her antient possession which was in the hands of Spain, not touching the portions which had been validly transferred to the US.

If Spain then were not to deliver the country from the Iberville & Missipi to the Perdido, this would not be delivering Louisiana with the extent it had when France possessed it, & before it had ever been dismembered: nor with the extent it *now* has in the hands of Spain, since it has been restored to it's antient & integral form: nor such as it ought to be after the treaty subsequently passed with England in

1783. And we trust that these definitions are too exact & unequivocal, & Spain too just, to admit any doubt of what we are entitled to demand, & she bound to deliver.

Whatever Louisiana was, as retroceded by Spain to France, such exactly it is, as ceded by France to the US. by the treaty of Paris of April 30. 1803. Sep. 7. 1803

MS (PPAmP); entirely in TJ's hand, including brackets. PoC (ViU). Dft (DLC: TJ Papers, 135:23267-70); entirely in TJ's hand. Tr (DLC: Monroe Papers); in Lewis Harvie's hand; lacks TJ's authorial notes and two pages, corresponding to the fifth, sixth, and most of the seventh paragraphs; endorsed: "Examination into the Boundaries of *Louisiana*—so named by *La Salle* &ca. discovering [there?] a *party* from *Canada*." Tr (DNA: RG 59, TP, Orleans); in a clerk's hand; lacks TJ's authorial notes.

[1] Preceding two words interlined in Dft.

[2] Preceding two words interlined in Dft in place of "<*more*> better-prepared."

[3] Preceding four words interlined in Dft.

[4] Preceding four words interlined in Dft in place of "went to the mouth of the Misipi."

[5] Preceding four words and numeral interlined in Dft.

[6] In Dft, TJ inserted the passage that follows, through "sea to sea," in margin.

[7] Preceding four words interlined in Dft in place of "sets out on their return."

[8] Preceding two words and numeral interlined in Dft.

[9] Preceding two words interlined in Dft.

[10] In Dft, TJ here added a marginal note: "*to this may be added the verbal declaration of the French Commr. to those of the US. on the delivery of possession, that his positive instructions from his govmt were to take possn to the Rio Bravo."

[11] In Dft, TJ began this paragraph: "In 1698. D'Iberville is sent out by the govmt of France with recruits for the colony" before altering it to read as above.

[12] Remainder of paragraph interlined in Dft.

[13] In Dft, TJ first wrote "100 leagues West of the Misipi" before altering and expanding the remainder of the sentence to read as above.

[14] Preceding sentence interlined in margin in Dft.

[15] Succeeding passage, through "Northwardly," inserted in margin of Dft, in place of "certainly, but in reason & right, to the Midway between that bay & the river Panuco, the then nearest settlement of Spain" and "the Rio Norte or Bravo, which extending very far into the country Northwardly formed a <*convenient*> well marked natural boundary midway between the natural possessions of the two nations."

[16] Dft lacks preceding eleven words.

[17] Preceding four words lacking in Dft.

[18] Preceding five words and ampersand interlined in Dft.

[19] Preceding three words interlined in Dft in place of "ground of the."

[20] The following text to and including ampersand interlined in Dft in place of "to."

[21] Preceding paragraph written on separate scrap of paper in Dft. TJ wrote the extracts of the grant on a separate sheet in Dft and indicated their insertion here.

[22] Preceding six words interlined in Dft.

[23] In Dft, TJ first ended the sentence with "the country whose waters empty <*themselves*> within it," before altering it to read as above.

[24] Preceding four words interlined in Dft.

[25] Remainder of paragraph interlined and inserted from margin in Dft.

[26] Preceding two words interlined in Dft in place of "trifling settlements."

[27] In Dft, TJ continued "between Mobile & Pensacola."

[28] Dft lacks "or Bravo." TJ continues "then up the Rio Norte."

[29] In Dft, TJ first wrote "Northern boundary of Florida" before altering the phrase to read as above.

[30]In Dft, TJ first completed the sentence with "made the Misipi the limit of the English colonies on the East as far down as the parallel & the same river & the Iberville and of Louisiana, on the West" before altering it to read as above.

[31]Preceding two words interlined in Dft in place of "immediately."

[32]In Dft, TJ here canceled "generous &."

[33]In Dft, TJ interlined the passage from this point to the end of the parenthetical phrase.

[34]Preceding five words and date interlined in Dft.

[35]In Dft, TJ here canceled "of that part of it."

[36]In Dft, TJ here canceled "consolidated."

[37]Remainder of paragraph added in margin of Dft, where TJ first wrote "and Spain extended her government of New Mexico over the part of Louisiana from the Eastern waters of the river Mexicana to the Rio Norte."

[38]Word written above "impeach" in Dft, but neither word was canceled.

[39]Preceding two words interlined in Dft.

[40]Remainder of paragraph interlined in Dft in place of "immediately reannexed the Louisiana portion to the province of Louisiana under the governor of that province residing at New Orleans, and reestablished her former province of Florida under the governor of Florida residing at St. Augustine: & so they continued to be governed to this day."

[41]Remainder of sentence interlined in Dft, where TJ at first wrote "appearance" rather than "cover" (both instances).

[42]In Dft, TJ first wrote "with what pretence then could she [absorb?] any portion of what had only been generously conceded as an indemnification" before altering the preceding sentence to read as above.

[43]In Dft, TJ here canceled "calculated."

[44]In Dft, TJ continued with a large body of text that concluded with the final two paragraphs below. The text between this point and the paragraph that begins "If Spain then" is a revision, the first page of which TJ glued on top of a large portion of the first version and the second page of which he produced on an additional sheet of paper. TJ's first version reads, "<*that is,*> with the same extent which it *now* has, as reunited in the hands of Spain, not as it was for a while, when a part was sequestered in the hands of England. and, further to remove doubt, it's extent is expressed in a 2d. form, to wit, that which it had *when France possessed it*. what that was is clear, to wit, from the Perdido to the Rio Norte on the coast, & from thence inland to all the Western waters of the Missisipi; & France never possessed it one moment in any other form but 3ly. (not to violate the rights of other nations) a salvo is added that it is to be re-ceded only such *as it ought to be* after the treaties passed *subsequently* between *Spain* & other powers. *subsequently* to what? to the cession of the country by France. when was that cession? Nov. 3. 1762. and Feb. 10. 1763. the preliminary & Definitive treaties then, of the same dates, with Great Britain, were not *subsequently*, but *simultaneously* <*made*> passed, & consequently are not within the scope of this definition. besides the saving is in favor of treaties made by Spain with other nations. now of these, affecting the limits of Louisiana, there are only two, subsequent to 1763. to wit, that of Sep. 3. 1783. with Great Britain, and of Oct. 27. 1795. with the US. the former was a restitution, by Gr. Britain to Spain, of Florida, & that part of Louisiana which lies between the Perdido & Iberville: and consequently, *after this treaty*, the extent of Louisiana *ought to be*, as again consolidated, to the Perdido. but inasmuch as by the latter of these two treaties, Spain had conceded to the US. a degree of latitude (from 32.° to 31.°) which she had long contended to be a part of Louisiana, & not of the US. as settled in 1783, therefore, by this provision, that right is saved to the US. & the extent of Louisiana, *after this treaty*, *ought to be* only to the latitude <of 31.°> But were we to admit that this saving of *subsequent* treaties by *Spain*, went to the *simultaneous* one of 1762.3. by *France & Spain*, it would furnish but an instance the more of the attentions of friendly nations to our just rights; instances which we always contemplate with satisfaction,

and will faithfully return in kind. France & Spain, according to this construction; solemnly announce that the extent of Louisiana (this retrocession notwithstanding) was still meant to be restricted to what *it ought to be after the treaty of 1762.3.* to wit, to the Missipi, as then settled, and not to the Alleganey, as had been claimed before that time. France & England, before that, had conflicting claims, the former Eastward to the Alleganey, the latter Westward to the South Sea. the treaty of 1762.3. settled these claims, & the boundaries so settled are to be considered, after that, to be the true, antient, & rightful boundaries, divested of false claim. tho' therefore, without supposing this salvo to regard the treaty of 1762.3. no pretence could arise that the rightful boundaries of Louisiana had ever extended to the Alleganey, or that the rightful boundaries of the British colonies had ever extended to the South sea, yet it was an evidence of friendship & good faith to preclude that pretension by an explicit declaration that no extension of Louisiana was contemplated by this act of retrocession beyond *what it ought to be after the treaties of 1762.3.*"

[45] Word interlined in Dft in place of "moment."

[46] Preceding two words interlined in Dft in place of "a."

[47] Dft: "the uses of Spain."

[48] Dft lacks preceding five words and punctuation.

From DeWitt Clinton

Dear Sir Newtown 7 Septr. 1803.

The appointment of Mr Sandford as District Atty. is universally approbated by our friends here: When the Senate ratifies his appointment, (of which I presume there can be no doubt) he intends to resign his office of Commissioner of Bankruptcy—upon the principle that honorary and lucrative offices ought not to be too much confined to a few: In this event, permit me to recommend to your particular attention as his successor Pierre C. Van Wyck—a young lawyer of great worth and respectability—He has attained the degree of Counsellor—This arrangement will be singularly pleasing to his highly respectable connections, particularly to his worthy Uncle Genl. V. Cortlandt.

The removal of E. Livingston excited at first some considerable speculation but the true cause is now well understood—Mr Livingston called upon me the other day—and a free conversation took place to the following effect—He stated that whatever may have been the ground of his removal, the manner in which it had been done had inflicted a stigma upon his character—that he was taken by surprise and that the first notice he had was the annunciation of the fact by Mr. Sandford in person—that the least official hint would have produced a resignation—I informed him that I had communicated to him fully & freely what he had to expect that he had promised to arrange the affair on his arrival at Washington—that instead of complying with his engagement he had observed a profound silence—In reply he admitted the imprudence of his conduct but alledged that when at Washington he had put leading questions to Messrs. Gallatin & Duval that no intimation was given by either of them and that he had even communicated with the latter on the Subject of some official business which he was to transact on his return to New York—He went on to observe that at all events he intended to go to New Orleans with a view to residence even if it was in a private capacity—that in consideration of his past services to the party, he thought the stigma ought to be removed from his character & that this might be done by conferring some office of respectability there upon him—That he should not expect any appointment which would involve any pecuniary responsibility—that he would discharge every cent he owed the Govt—and hush the business with his friends some of whom were dissatisfied. Upon this I promised to represent his wishes to you—You know his talents and past services and you can determine better than myself whether he may not be usefully employed in that Country.

I enclose you a Federal newspaper of New Haven which will throw some light on the proceedings there respecting the appointment of Collector—It is needless to tell you that all that relates to myself is false—I have indeed said what the federalists of Connecticut have said over and over again that A. Bishop is a profligate character—that if he was nominated it would be incumbent on the Connecticut Senators to substantiate the allegations of their friends or to indirectly admit their falsity—that if they should really prove his profligacy, the appointment could not take place.

I am Dr Sir With every Sentiment of the Most respectful attachment Your obedt Servt. DEWITT CLINTON

RC (DNA: RG 59, LAR); at foot of text: "The President of the U.S."; endorsed by TJ as received on 25 Sep. and so recorded in SJL; also endorsed by TJ: "Van Wyck, Pierre C. to Commr. bkrptcy N.Y. vice Sanford who will resign." Enclosure: see below.

RESPECTABLE CONNECTIONS: Pierre C. Van Wyck's mother was Congressman Philip Van Cortlandt's sister Catharine (Jacob Judd, ed., *The Van Cortlandt Family Papers*, 4 vols. [Tarrytown, N.Y., 1976-81], 1:15-16, 24; Vol. 34:164-5).

FEDERAL NEWSPAPER OF NEW HAVEN: the 30 Aug. issue of the *Visitor* included an article reflecting on the candidates for the collectorship at the port. The writer noted that Samuel Bishop had received the appointment in 1801 "to reward the profligate labors of his son Abraham," whose "character was so notoriously abandoned and detestable" that local Republicans requested that the father be appointed instead of the son. It was assumed that Abraham Bishop would succeed his father until he became "suspected of inclining to the vice President." DeWitt Clinton had sworn that "no friend of Mr. Burr, Abraham or other, shall hold the collectorship." Clinton, Samuel Osgood, and John Broome endorsed Samuel Broome, who suddenly appeared in New Haven "with a subscription paper in hand" to obtain signatures of support for his candidacy from local merchants. The writer noted that very few signed, and Clinton's scheme was "entirely defeated." What the New Haven merchants most desired was someone who could manage the business of the office, and Abraham Bishop had proven he could do that as well as "any former collector." Although they abhorred Bishop's moral and political character, New Haven merchants preferred him over other candidates.

Federalists James Hillhouse and Uriah Tracy were the CONNECTICUT SENATORS (*Biog. Dir. Cong.*).

From Benjamin Brown Cooper

Coopers Ferry Gloucester County
N. Jersey Septr 7. 1803

SIR

A Letter has bin forwarded me from Eggharbour, requesting a Solicitation, (to you) for Joseph Whinner to the Office of Collector of the Port of Egg Harbour, in the room of A Freeling that has latterly taken to drink, this change will be highly recommendable in the neighbourhood of Egg Harbour and by the Republicans of the County at Large tho at this critical time in consiquence of the approaching ellection, It will be incumbent on you to dispence with any change til our Election is over, the Republicans of this County has bin divided for two years past, and a union is like to take Place, at the ensuing election—at which time the Republicans of Gloucester Cy. N.J. will triumph over Aristocrasy that has rain'd for five yearse in this Cy. James Sloane and Dr Thomas Henry will write you relative to the above appointment tho highly necessary ought to be dispenced with for the present. the trivial office of a Collector is nothing to republicanising a State being the only one in the Union that Federalm. has regained

from your Obet Servt

BENJAMIN BROWN CO[OPER]

RC (DNA: RG 59, LAR); torn; at foot of text: "Thomas Jefferson [Esqr]"; endorsed by TJ as received on 25 Sep. and so recorded in SJL with notation "Whinner v. Freeling"; also endorsed by TJ: "Whinner Joseph to be Collector Egg harbor vice A. Freeling besotted enquire of Doctr. Condit."

Benjamin Brown Cooper (1779-1835), son of William and Ann Folwell Cooper, was born in Gloucester County, New Jersey. Revenue Supervisor James Linn appointed him excise officer for the county in 1801 and he became the first postmaster when a post office was established at Coopers Ferry (now Camden) in 1802. Established as a reputable farmer, Cooper also speculated in land. In 1805, political opponents claimed that he followed "*no other occupation* than riding about the country, *speculating in land*, and *seeking offices* for himself and associates." He managed the New Jersey estates owned by the Penn and Pemberton families, and, in 1814, he purchased all of the lands still owned by the London-based West New Jersey Society. As an agent for the Holland Land Company, he purchased vast tracts in western Pennsylvania. At the time of his death, he still owned about 170,000 acres in the state. Cooper represented Gloucester County in the New Jersey state assembly in 1824 and 1825 (*Journal of the Rutgers University Library*, 17 [1953], 28-9; Stets, *Postmasters*, 167; George R. Prowell, *The History of Camden County, New Jersey* [Philadelphia, 1886], 188, 738; Elizabethtown *New-Jersey Journal*, 4 Aug. 1801; Trenton *True American*, 26 Dec. 1803; *Trenton Federalist*, 30 Sep. 1805; Bridgeton, N.J., *Washington Whig*, 18 Dec. 1815, 29 Sep. 1817, 23 Oct. 1824).

Joseph Winner (WHINNER) replaced Alexander Freeland (FREELING) as collector at Great Egg Harbor in March 1804. Freeland was appointed by John Adams in 1799 (JEP, 1:326, 466).

TRIUMPH OVER ARISTOCRASY: to promote unity and victory in the fall election, the Democratic Association of Gloucester County was organized in early 1803 with James Sloan as president and Thomas Hendry as vice president. In the fall election, Republicans won all of the state assembly seats in Gloucester County (Walter R. Fee, *The Transition from Aristocracy to Democracy in New Jersey, 1789-1829* [Somerville, N.J., 1933], 133-7; Carl E. Prince, *New Jersey's Jeffersonian Republicans: The Genesis of an Early Party Machine, 1789-1817* [Chapel Hill, 1964], 93-4, 119-23; Trenton *True American*, 4 Apr. 1803).

ONLY ONE IN THE UNION THAT FEDERALM. HAS REGAINED: for Republican losses in New Jersey in the 1802 fall election that led to a stalemate in the state legislature, see Vol. 38:605-6.

To Henry Dearborn

DEAR SIR Monticello Sep. 7. 1803.

I now return you the proceedings of the courtmartial held at Fort Jay with an approbation of the sentence against Lt. Van Renslaer, & a remission of the corporal punishment of Ferguson & Rush as you advised. I am sensible of the risque we run in returning to Washington before the commencement of the [frost?] but the collection & copying of documents & other preparations for the meeting of Congress seem to render three weeks a short enough term before hand. if I should find the place very sickly, I will take quarters in the nearest healthy country and go to Washington occasionaly as may be necessary. will you be so good as to make notes of whatsoever within your department may be proper for communication to Congress? I am sorry to hear that mrs Dearborne's confidence in the air of Washington has cost her so dear: and hope to hear she is reestablished by the country air. the experience of others, & long observation on it, have been a lesson to me never to trust myself in the atmosphere of the tide waters in August & September. Accept my friendly salutations & best wishes for the health & happiness of yourself & family

TH: JEFFERSON

PrC (DLC); blurred; at foot of text: "The Secy. at War." Recorded in SJL as a letter to the War Department with notation "ct. martial. meeting of Congress."

PROCEEDINGS OF THE COURTMARTIAL: see Dearborn to TJ, 31 Aug. 1803 (first letter).

From J. P. P. Derieux

Monsieur Washington Ce 7. Sepbre. 1803.

J'ai reçu de Mr. Wagner La Lettre dont vous avés bien voulu m'honorer le 1er. de ce mois en me remettant le Certificat que j'avois pris la Liberté de vous communiquer. Je suis aussi sensible que reconnaissant aux marques des bontés que vous daignés me donner, en me permettant d'aller vous presenter mon respect; C'est un Empressement que j'aurois craint de satisfaire malgré toutte la contradiction que j'en aurois eprouvé. je n'attends pour quitter Washington que L'arrivée de mes Effets; cela my retient depuis prés d'un mois, n'ayant pu Les prendre avec moi de New-york comme je L'eus fait, sans Les ordres de Mr. Monroe de ne pas perdre un instant pour remettre ses Dépêches. Je ne puis penser d'aller rejoindre ma famille avant de les avoir recus, car les secours que j'ai obtenus de mes parents se reduisant principalement a du Linge et des hardes pour ma femme et mes Enfants, je desire les leur porter avec ce que je pourrai réserver du remboursement qui m'a eté fait ici des Depenses de Voyage. J'avois Esperé pouvoir obtenir quelque compensation pour mes services pendant pres de quatre mois, mais Mr. Madison m'a fait repondre qu'il n'y avoit point d'appropriation faitte pour cet objet.

L'interet que vous paroissés voulloir bien me continuer, me fait esperer, Monsieur que vous apprendrés avec plaisir que mes deux ppaux Creanciérs, Colo. Gamble et L'associé de Mr. Gallego de Richmond, sur L'information que je leur donnai de ma mauvaise reussitte en France, et ma demande d'un prolongation d'indulgence, m'ont respectivement repondus, que loin d'apporter aucun Empêchement a mon Etablissement, qu'ils approuvoient ma résolution a tacher par de nouvelles Exertions de surmonter mes difficultés; ainsi j'ose Esperer, Monsieur que si vous voullés bien me favoriser de la même maniere, que je pourai peut-etre reussir à faire fructifier avec avantage, La petite somme qui pourra me rester a la fin de mon Voyage.

Si mes Effets que J'attends de New york par Mer, peuvent m'arriver avant Le tems que vous quitterés Monticello, j'aurai certainement, Monsieur, L'honneur d'aller vous rendre mes Devoirs, et vous offrir quelques Graines de Jardinage qui m'ont paru Curieuses, C'est principalement Celle d'un Choux dont la tige monte Jusqua Sept Et huit pieds de haut, et qui par sa nature reproductive est d'une grande ressource pour les Bestiaux dans Les pays ou La Secheresse a pu faire manquer les fourages. Il resiste tout L'hiver au froid, qui en rend méme sa verdure plus agreable pour la table, en ce qu'il n'a jamais le gout de musc dont on Se plaint dans les autres Especes. L'autre graine que je crois egalement rare, est un Gros Bled-froment blanc, dont la paille est Solide en dedans, et de plusieurs fois La grosseur ordre. on m'a assuré aussi que la forme de Son Epie différe beaucoup, et est aussi plus productif que dans l'autre espece, et quil doit Se planter a 4. et 6. pouces de distance Suivant la qualité de la terre. Je mestimerai très heureux Si dans mes autres Especes de Graines, il peut S'en trouver qui vous Seroient agreables. Je ne prendrois pas La Liberté de vous importuner d'une pareille offre, Si je ne pensois que vous prenés toujours aux amusements et recreation de La Campagne, Le même plaisir qu'autrefois. J'ai aussi reussi a trouver un peu de graine d'Estragon, plante trés peu connue en amerique et que vous eutes La bonté de chercher a me procurer Lorsque jetois encore a Charlotteville.

Agrées je vous prie, Monsieur, La nouvelle assurance des Sentiments de mon plus respectueux attachement et reconnaissance avec les quels J'ai L'honneur d'être Monsieur Votre trés humble et trés obeissant Serviteur P. DeRieux

EDITORS' TRANSLATION

Sir, Washington, 7 Sep. 1803

I received from Mr. Wagner the letter you did me the honor of sending on the 1st of this month, returning the certificate I had taken the liberty of sending you. I am both touched and grateful for the kindness you showed in allowing me to pay you my respects. I would have hesitated to take you up on this invitation, despite the mixed emotions I would have felt.

I am leaving Washington as soon as my belongings arrive. The wait has kept me here for more than a month. I could not bring them with me from New York, as I would normally have done, because of Mr. Monroe's order not to delay a moment in delivering his messages to you. I cannot return to my family before I retrieve my possessions, since the aid I obtained from my relatives is mostly clothing and linens for my wife and children. I would like to take these things back, along with what I can save from the reimbursement I received for my travel expenses. I had hoped to obtain some compensation for my services during almost four months, but Mr. Madison's office sent a message saying no funds had been allocated for this purpose.

Given your continued interest, Sir, I hope you will be pleased to learn that my two principal creditors, Colonel Gamble and the associate of Mr. Gallego of Richmond, have both responded to the details about my ill fortune in France and to my request for their renewed forbearance. Far from posing any obstacles to my settling here, they approve my decision to redouble my efforts in order to overcome my difficulties. I hope, Sir, that you will favor me in the same way, so I might take whatever the small sum might remain at the end of my trip and make it fructify.

My belongings are coming by sea from New York. If they arrive before you leave Monticello, I will surely have the honor, Sir, fulfilling my duty and giving you some seeds that I found unusual. The first is a cabbage whose stem can grow seven or eight feet tall and whose reproductive nature makes it a great resource in arid regions where animals might lack fodder. Not only does it resist the winter cold, but it becomes even greener and more pleasing to the palate, since it never has the musky taste one complains about in other varieties. The other seed I believe to be equally rare is a large white wheat whose straw is solid inside and several times larger than usual. I have been told that its sheaf is also very different and more productive than other species and that the seeds should be planted four to six inches apart, depending on the quality of the soil. I would consider myself fortunate if you were interested in any of my other seeds. I would not presume to bother you with such an offer if I did not assume that you still enjoy pleasant activities in the countryside as much as you used to. I also succeeded in finding a few seeds of tarragon, a plant that is little known in America and that you kindly tried to obtain for me when I was still in Charlottesville.

Accept Sir, I beg you, the renewed assurance of the most respectful fondness and gratitude with which I have the honor of being your very humble and obedient servant. P. DeRieux

RC (DLC); endorsed by TJ as received 9 Sep. and so recorded in SJL.

d'un choux: in 1810, TJ again received seeds from France of a variety of cabbage with a long stem (RS, 2:271, 272).

un gros bled-froment blanc: TJ later reported to Derieux that the wheat "has failed" (TJ to Derieux, 31 May 1805).

estragon: TJ made a prolonged effort to obtain seeds or roots to cultivate tarragon (RS, 1:481, 600; 5:29-30, 98-9; Vol. 25:306-7, 347; TJ to Philippe Reibelt, 12 Oct. 1805, 22 Dec. 1807, in DLC; Reibelt to TJ, 15 Oct. 1805, 27 Feb., 25 Oct. 1807, 25 Feb. 1808, in same; TJ to Bernard McMahon, 25 Apr. 1806, in same; McMahon to TJ, 30 [Apr.], 12 July 1806, 17 Jan. 1809, in same; John Mason to TJ, 22 Jan. [1809], in MHi; TJ to Ellen Wayles Randolph, 6 Feb. 1809, in same).

To Wilson Cary Nicholas

Dear Sir Monticello Sep. 7. 1803.

Your favor of the 3d was delivered me at court: but we were much disappointed at not seeing you here, mr Madison & the Govr. being here at the time. I inclose you a letter from Monroe on the subject of the late treaty. you will observe a hint in it to do without delay what we are bound to do. there is reason, in the opinion of our ministers, to believe that if the thing were to do over again, it could not be obtained; & that if we give the least opening they will declare the treaty void. a warning amounting to that has been given to them, & an unusual kind of letter written by their minister to our Secretary of state direct. whatever Congress shall think it necessary to do, should be done with as little debate as possible; & particularly so far as respects the constitutional difficulty. I am aware of the force of the observations you make on the power given by the Constn to Congress to admit new states into the Union, without restraining the subject to the territory then constituting the US. but when I consider that the limits of the US. are precisely fixed by the treaty of 1783. that the constitution expressly declares itself to be made for the US. I cannot help believing the intention was to permit Congress to admit into the union new states which should be formed out of the territory for which & under whose authority alone they were then acting. I do not believe it was meant that they might recieve England, Ireland, Holland &c into it, which would be the case on your construction. when an instrument admits two constructions the one safe, the other dangerous, the one precise the other indefinite, I prefer that which is safe & precise. I had rather ask an enlargement of power from the nation where it is found necessary, than to assume it by a construction which would make our powers boundless. our peculiar[1] security is in the possession of a written constitution. let us not make it a blank paper by construction. I say the same as to the opinion of those who consider the grant of the treaty making power as boundless. if it is, then we have no constitution. if it has bounds, they can be no others than the definitions of the powers which that instrument gives. it specifies & delineates the operations permitted to the federal government, and gives all the powers necessary to carry these into execution. whatever of these enumerated objects is proper for a law, Congress may[2] make the law. whatever is proper to be executed by way of a treaty, the President & Senate may enter into the treaty; whatever is to be done by a judicial sentence, the judges may pass the sentence. nothing is more likely than that their enumeration of powers is defective. this is the ordinary case of all human works. let us go on then perfecting it, by adding by way of amendment to the constitution, those powers which time & trial shew are still wanting. but it has been taken too much for granted that by this rigorous construction the treaty power would be[3] reduced to nothing. I had occasion once to examine it's effect on the French treaty made by the old Congress, & found that out of thirty odd articles which that contained there were one, two, or three only which could not now be stipulated under our present constitution. I confess then I think it important in the present case to set an example against broad construction by appealing for new power to the people. if however our friends shall think differently, certainly I shall acquiesce with satisfaction, confiding that the good sense of our country will correct the evil of construction when it shall produce ill effects.—no apologies for writing or speaking to me freely are necessary. on the contrary nothing my friends can do, is so dear to me, & proves to me their friendship so clearly, as the information they give me of their sentiments & those of others on interesting points where I am to act, and where information & warning are so essential to excite in me that due reflection which ought to precede action. I leave this about the 21st. and shall hope the district court will give me an opportunity of seeing you. Accept my affectionate salutations & assurances of cordial esteem & respect. TH: JEFFERSON

RC (CLU-C); at foot of first page: "W. C. Nicholas"; PrC (DLC). Enclosure: James Monroe to Madison, 3 June (see Gallatin to TJ, 31 Aug.).

TO OUR SECRETARY OF STATE DIRECT: a packet of papers that the French government sent to Louis André Pichon in the care of Peter Augustus Jay included a letter from Talleyrand to Madison dated 12 Prairial (1 June). Pichon sent a deciphered copy of the letter to the State Department from Frederick, Maryland, with other papers on 30 Aug. In the communication to the secretary of state, the French foreign minister declared that the efforts of both parties in the Louisiana negotiation had produced a result that was favorable to each of the republics. Talleyrand reported that he had secured the first consul's prompt ratification of the agreements—as desired by the American ministers—to give satisfaction to the United States as well as to allow the transfer of the ceded territory to move forward without delay. Barbé de Marbois had settled the details of the financial transaction with the Hope firm, Bonaparte approved that arrangement, and the French government was making Gallatin acquainted with the details. Talleyrand hoped that Madison would do everything in his power to bring the transaction to completion (Talleyrand to Madison, 12 Prairial Year 11, in DNA: RG 59, NL; Madison, *Papers*, *Sec. of State Ser.*, 5:355-7; Robert R. Livingston to TJ, 2 June).

FRENCH TREATY: the 1778 Treaty of Amity and Commerce between the United States and France (Miller, *Treaties*, 2:3-34).

[1] TJ here canceled "happiness."
[2] Word interlined in place of "is to."
[3] TJ here canceled "abridged."

To Craven Peyton

DEAR SIR Monticello Sep. 7. 03.

I now send you the deed, and a copy of the Virginia law made by D. Carr, which will serve to instruct your agent in Kentucky what is to be done. I think it should be made the interest of Fontrees to stay in Kentucky till a court sets, before which mrs Henderson may appear & acknolege the deed, or the witnesses be summoned & prove it. the deed being proven, he should bring it back to have it recorded here. the deed is full, & sufficient. we have only to have it recorded to secure us in the sole right to a mill. the decision of the question must be put off till the deed is brought back. Accept my friendly salutations.

TH: JEFFERSON

RC (NjP: Andre De Coppet Collection); at foot of text: "Mr. Craven Peyton." PrC (ViU). Enclosure: Elizabeth Henderson Deed for Dower to Craven Peyton, 18 Sep. 1802 (Vol. 38:578). For other enclosure, see below.

VIRGINIA LAW: perhaps the law of October 1748, "An act concerning Water Mills," which detailed the process by which an interested party could petition for the right to land on an opposing side of a water run in order to build a mill. The law also made provision for cases where entailed land had been sold, how it should be created in fee simple, and how recorded by the court. On 2 May 1803, TJ asked Peyton to employ Dabney Carr to petition the county court for permission to build a mill on the site near Milton (William Waller Hening, ed., *The Statutes at Large; Being a Collection of All the Laws of Virginia*, 13 vols. [Richmond, 1809-23], 5:55-60; TJ to Peyton, 2 May 1803).

From Craven Peyton

DEAR SIR Stump Island 7. Sept. 1803

Fantress will set out the last of this week. I have not the smalest doubt but he will have the deed Proven as directed. he will inform the Family of the situation of the present mill, & if I new what you woud be willing to give for the mill House with all the works belonging to it I think he might make the purchase of all the shares of those liveing there. & by that means she might be set to work in about five weeks after a decition of Our Court. I was to day speaking with one of the legatees about his share he appears to think it worth One Hundred Dollars. he says there is One ℘ of stones belonging to the mill—if you shoud wish me to authorise Fantress to make an offer, will thank you to say what each share ought to sell for

with much Respt Yr mst. Obet C PEYTON

RC (ViU); endorsed by TJ as received on 7 Sep. and so recorded in SJL.

For TJ's concern about the Albemarle County mill owned by the Henderson FAMILY heirs living in Kentucky and his desire to purchase all their remaining SHARES in it, see Vol. 40:317-20. Peyton mistakenly thought TJ wanted the value of the mill in working condition. TJ simply wanted to determine the value of the millstones and to keep the mill inactive (Vol. 40:506).

From Isaac Briggs

Washington, near Natchez
Mississippi Territory
MY DEAR FRIEND, 8th. of the 9th. Month 1803.

On the 12th. of the month just past, I arrived at Natchez;—on the day following I waited on Governor Claiborne, who had provided for me an office in this place, and from whom I have experienced the highest proofs of friendship. In a few days after my arrival here, I was attacked with an intermittent fever; a greater prostration of strength, than I ever remember to have felt, was the consequence, yet so perfect has been my recovery, that I believe I never was in better health than at present.

It appears to me probable that not less than thirty millions of acres in the Territory of Louisiana will be hereafter claimed, under fraudulent, antedated Spanish Grants, issued since information has arrived here, of the cession of that Territory to the United States, and under privileges of pre-emption for surveys made since the knowledge of that event. May I propose to the consideration of the President the expediency of sending an Agent to take possession of that Territory, and to stop such unfair practices, without a moments *unnecessary* delay? On the subject of these peculations, I have written fully to the Secretary of the Treasury.

I write to the President, with the freedom, the sincerity, and, let me add, the affection of a real friend—in consideration of my motive, pardon me if I presume too much.

The appointment, of Thomas Rodney and Robert Williams esquires as commissioners, is very popular here, and has given, I believe, universal satisfaction. I cannot say so, of the appointment of Edward Turner esquire. I have not heard any member of the families to which he is allied speak on the subject; but it has been a topic of conversation every where, and in every company in which I have been; and expressions of regret are universal, I believe, without a single exception. I am told he is son-in-law to Colonel Cato West, and nephew to Thomas M. Green esq.—the family-connexions of these two men are said to be very numerous, and very deeply interested in those land-claims, on which the Commissioners are to decide. His moral reputation, I believe, stands fair; but he is represented as young and inexperienced. Republicans and Federalists equally disapprove this appointment: no appointment of a person resident in this Territory would be popular. The Republicans conjecture that the President has been *misinformed* respecting this young man's suitableness for the station. The Federalists surmise, and the leading ones are industrious to fix it as a general belief, that this appointment has been made in consequence of Governor Claiborne's recommendation.

I have no personal dislike to this young man nor to any of his connexions—(I know neither him nor them, except by report)—such a sentiment forms no part of my motive for giving the above information—my sole motive for it is, friendship for the President. As I wish to live in peace with all men, I hope this communication will be considered in confidence. Were I in this young man's precise situation, I would resign: For I imagine, if he continues in it, it will render him an object of almost popular hatred.

I am, with the utmost sincerity thy friend ISAAC BRIGGS

RC (DLC); at foot of text: "Thomas Jefferson Pr. U.S."; endorsed by TJ as received on 2 Oct. and so recorded in SJL.

In a letter to the SECRETARY OF THE TREASURY, also dated 8 Sep. 1803, Briggs reported the prevalence of "practices highly fraudulent and injurious to the United States" in the newly acquired Louisiana Territory. Specifically, "a vast number of Adventurers" were surveying large quantities of land on the west side of the Mississippi River, which Spanish officers were claiming and disposing of at prices as low as ten cents per acre. Even some respectable citizens of Mississippi, Briggs added, "have been invited to a participation in this harvest of iniquity," with offers of valuable land at cheap prices and assurances of good titles, which Briggs implied to mean "*antedated Spanish Grants*." Knowing that similar transactions occurred in the Mississippi Territory in the interim between the signing of the Pinckney Treaty of 1795 and the territory's evacuation by the Spanish, Briggs suggests "an easy solution of the Mystery by which this Peculation will be veiled:—The warrant of survey, the Surveyor's certificate, and the final Grant, will bear concurrent date, prior to the Cession of Louisiana to France." Briggs has been informed that most of the surveyors are Spanish officers and their assistants Spanish soldiers, all of whom will leave Louisiana with the Spanish government. "I therefore apprehend," Briggs wrote, "that for any tribunal hereafter to discriminate between the just and the fraudulent claim, will be difficult, even if Oral testimony be admitted, but if, to its exclusion, the Spanish record be paramount evidence, impossible" (Gallatin, *Papers*, 8:664-5).

EDWARD TURNER had been appointed register of the land office at Natchez after being recommended by Thomas Marston Green and John Breckinridge. TJ removed him in 1804 (Robert V. Haynes, *The Mississippi Territory and the Southwest Frontier, 1795-1817* [Lexington, Ky., 2010], 80-1; Vol. 40:59, 60n).

From Meriwether Lewis

DEAR SIR, Wheeling, September 8th. 1803.

It was not untill 7 O'Clock on the morning of the 31st. Utmo. that my boat was completed, she was instantly loaded, and at 10. A.M. on the same day I left Pittsburgh, where I had been moste shamefully detained by the unpardonable negligence of my boat-builder. On my arrival at Pittsburgh, my calculation was that the boat would be in readiness by the 5th. of August; this term however elapsed and the boat so far from being finished was only partially planked on one side; in this situation I had determined to abandon the boat, and to purchase two or three perogues and descend the river in them, and depend on purchasing a boat as I descended, there being none to be had at Pittsburgh; from this resolution I was dissuaded first by the representations of the best informed merchants at that place who assured me that the chances were much against my being able to procure a boat below; and secondly by the positive assureances given me by the boat-builder that she should be ready on the last of the then ensuing week, (the 13th.): however a few days after, according to his usual custom he got drunk, quarrelled with his workmen, and several of them left him, nor could they be prevailed on to return: I threatened him with the penalty of his contract, and exacted a promise of greater sobriety in future which, he took care to perform with as little good faith, as he had his previous promises with regard to the boat, continuing to be constantly either drunk or sick.

I spent most of my time with the workmen, alternately presuading and threatening, but neither threats, presuasion or any other means which I could devise were sufficient to procure the completion of the work sooner than the 31st. of August; by which time the water was so low that those who pretended to be acquainted with the navigation of the river declared it impracticable to descend it; however in conformity to my previous determineation I set out, having taken the precaution to send a part of my baggage by a waggon to this place, and also to procure a good pilot. my days journey have averaged about 12 miles, but in some instances, with every exertion I could make was unable to exceed 4½ & 5 miles pr. day. This place is one hundred miles distant from Pittsburgh by way of the river and about sixty five by land—

When the Ohio is in it's present state there are many obstructions to it's navigation, formed by bars of small stones, which in some instances are intermixed with, and partially cover large quntities of driftwood; these bars frequently extend themselves entirely across the bed of the river, over many of them I found it impossible to pass even with my emty boat, without geting into the water and lifting her over by hand; over others my force was even inadequate to enable me to pass in this manner, and I found myself compelled to hire horses or oxen from the neighbouring farmers and drag her over them; in this way I have passed as many as five of those bars, (or as they are here called *riffles*) in a day, and to unload as many or more times. The river is lower than it has ever been known by the oldest settler in this country. I shall leave this place tomorrow morning, and loose no time in geting on.

I have been compelled to purchase a perogue at this place in order to transport the baggage which was sent by land from Pittsburgh, and also to lighten the boat as much as possible. On many bars the water in the deepest part dose not exceed six inches.—

I have the honour to be with the most perfect regard and sincere attatchment Your Obt. Servt. MERIWETHER LEWIS.
Capt. 1st. US Regt. Infty.

RC (DLC); addressed: "The President of the United States. Monticello. near Milton Virginia"; franked; postmarked 12 Sep.; endorsed by TJ as received 25 Sep. and so recorded in SJL.

To Craven Peyton

DEAR SIR Monticello Sep. 8. 1803.

I cannot consider the mill as worth either to the proprietors or myself [more?] than the [price] of stone & the [...] because they can never again make [...] and I consider should not. her position, construction & [...] condition makes her unworthy of being [...] set to work for the dam is taken down, which will be [...] from this time. it will [...] till her condition is seen to be. [...] by the [...]. that they will muster [more correction] to sell her [out] than with [...], which I do not consider to [...] worth £100. but to get rid of [...] I would give 500. D. which would be 50. Dollars a share. but I would not give this after I shall have [laid] in my [...] & purchased millstones. if mr Fontrees or yourself can purchase at this [price] I will take [...] such of the shares as can be bought. accept my salutations [&] respects.

TH: JEFFERSON

PrC (ViU); faint and blurred; at foot of text: "Mr. Craven Peyton"; endorsed by TJ in ink on verso.

For TJ's concern over the possibility of inflated WORTH of the mill site, see TJ to Thomas Mann Randolph, 14 June 1803.

From James Iddings

Duck Creek, Kent County—Delaware—
ESTEEMED FRIEND 9th. 9th. mo. 1803—

From a confidence in thy friendly disposition, though personally unknown to each other, I feel no embarrassment in addressing thee, in the language of a friend—and fellow mortal: inasmuch as I owe nothing to the president of the United States and to his administration, but cordial friendship and unaffected love—and which has ever been my inflexible sentiment since thy appointment, although it has been my lot to feel the resentment of persons of a different cast—whom I can freely forgive and hope the eyes of mankind may be more and more opened to truth and conviction, and which I apprehend is gradually effecting in many, if not most places—This being premised shall proceed to the subject more particularly aimed at—

The enclosed proposals—I thought proper to offer to thee, for several reasons—As it is the first attempt of this kind and in this way since thy election,—if not the very first ever since the independence of America—also as it is usual for the inferior to look up to the superior in such cases for a degree of countenance—.

The manuscript has been inspected by several pretty good judges who have given encouragement so far—and which, when publick, will according to the editor's ability and influence, have a tendency to promote, that disposition (and especially among his fellow members in religious society) which is becoming every department—civil and religious, in relation to the government under which we live— The intention is to make it as public as may be throughout the union— I may add had not local situation rendered the thing inconvenient, it would have been my choice thou should'st have seen the work in manuscript. However, this without vanity I think I may say that many sentiments and Ideas therein expressed must very much correspond to thy apprehensions of rectitude, as far as it has any relation to government—to thyself or thy administration—

I shall conclude with observing that if any thing relative thereto one way or another should take thy attention so as to induce a line from thee, either as thy sentiment upon such a work—as any thing that might be proper to insert therein—or in any way as it might strike thee on the occasion—it will be humbly and thankfully received

By thy sincere friend and well wisher JAMES IDDINGS—

N.B. The few proposals herein sent thou wilt be so kind as to put into the hands of persons most suitable—for the purpose of taking subscriptions thereto—in that place— J. I.

RC (ViU); at head of text: "Thomas Jefferson"; endorsed by TJ as received on 16 Sep. and so recorded in SJL. Enclosure: undated prospectus for publishing by subscription *The Monitor's Instructor; or A System of Practical Geography of the United States of America, in Verse*, at one dollar payable on delivery to subscribers, of whom 500 were needed to go to press, and a free copy promised to anyone who obtained 20 subscribers (broadside in DLC); for the publication, see Shaw-Shoemaker, No. 6529.

James Iddings (1755-1811) was an itinerant Quaker minister who, in 1798, had joined the Duck Creek Monthly Meeting, the earliest official meeting of Friends in Kent County, Delaware. His proposed geography text, *The Monitor's Instructor*, was published in Wilmington in January 1804. He served as superintendent of a Friends school, the Southern Boarding School, in what later became Smyrna, Delaware. In 1804, Iddings also advertised opening a school in Easton, Maryland, for "teaching the common branches of an English education," including reading, writing, arithmetic, grammar, mathematics, geography, and bookkeeping. An antislavery advocate, he was a founding member and secretary of Easton's Philanthropic Society "for the relief and protection of free blacks and people of colour unlawfully held in bondage, or otherwise oppressed" and in 1804 helped draft its constitution. His preaching took him throughout Maryland, Virginia, North Carolina, and Pennsylvania. He died in Philadelphia (Easton, Md., *Republican Star*, 28 Feb. 1804, 23 Apr. 1805; J. Thomas Scharf, *History of Delaware,*

1609-1888, 2 vols. [Philadelphia, 1888], 2:1028, 1096, 1104; F. Edward Wright, ed., *Vital Records of Kent and Sussex Counties, Delaware, 1686-1800* [Westminster, Md., 1986], 50; Joanne C. Iddings and others, *Iddings Family Genealogy* [n.p., 1992], 38-9).

From Jacob Wagner

Department of State
4 [i.e. 9] Septr. 1803.

Sir

Lest the annexed may not come to your hands in original, via Orange Ct. house, as soon as by this direct address, I have thought it best to avail myself of it.

With perfect respect I have the honor to be, Sir, Your most humble servt.

Jacob Wagner

(copy)

Por medio del Embaxador del Rey mi amo en Paris ha llegado a su Rl. noticia, que aquel Govierno ha vendido al de los Estados Unidos la provincia de la Luisiana que su magestad habia retrocedido ā la Republica Francesa. Esta noticia ha causado al Rey mi amo no poca sorpresa, a vista de que al Govierno Frances habia contrahido con S.M. el empeño mas solemne de no enagenar *jamas* la citado provincia. Para convencer al Govierno de los Estados Unidos de la naturalesa de estos empeños me tomo la libertad de insertar aqui un parrafo de una nota presentada el 22 Julio de 1802 por Mr. St. Cyr, Embaxador de la Repubca. Francesa en Madrid, al Sr. Secretario de estado de su magestad, y es como sigue:—

"S. Mté. Cathe. a paru desirer que la France s'engage à ne vender et a n'alliener en aucune maniere la proprieté et la jouissance de a Louisiane: son voeu à cet egard est parfaitement conforme aux intentions du Gouvernment Espaniol, et il n'a desiré y entrer, que parce quil tenoit à une possession que avoit fait partie du Territoire François. *Je suis autorisé a vous declarer au nom du Premier Consul que la France ne l'allienera jamais.*"

La simple lectura del parrafo que precede convencera a V.S. como tambien al Sr. Presidente de los Estados Unidos de que la venta de la Luisiana, que ha hecho ultimamente la Francia, es una violacion manifiesta de las obligaciones contrahidas por ella para con S.M. Catca. y que la Francia carece de facultades para enagenar dha Provinicia sin la aprobacion de la España como se vè incontestablimente en la citada oferta del Embaxador St. Cyr autorizado por su govierno.

El Rey mi amo me encarga informe[r][1] quanto antes de esta importante circunstancia a este Govierno, y cumpliendo con su real voluntad me apresuro a ponerlo en noticia de V.S. para que llegue quanto antes a la del Sr. Presidente de los Estados Unidos.

Dios gué a V.S. ms. ans. Philadelphia 4 Septiembre de 1803

BLMo. de V-S su mas ato. y sego. Sr.

El Marques de casa Yrujo

Sr. Dn. Jayme Madison.

RC (DLC); entirely in Wagner's hand; probably misdated and written on 9 Sep., the day on which Wagner saw Carlos Martínez de Irujo's letter to Madison and forwarded it to the secretary of state (see note to translation, below, and Madison to TJ, 12 Sep.); addressed: "The President of the United States Monticello"; franked; postmarked 9 Sep.; endorsed by TJ as received from the State Department on 12 Sep. and "refusal of Spain to cede N. Orleans" and so recorded in SJL with notation "Span. claim to Louisa."

BLMO. DE V-S SU MAS ATO. Y SEGO. SR.: "your obedient servant kisses your excellency's hand."

SR. DN. JAYME MADISON: that is, "Señor Don James Madison."

[1] Wagner's brackets. RC of Irujo's letter to Madison (see below): "informe."

CONTEMPORARY TRANSLATION

Thro' the medium of the Ambassador of the King my master in Paris, it has come to his royal knowledge, that that Government has sold to that of the United States the Province of Louisiana which his Majesty had retroceded to the French Republic. This information has occasioned to the King my master no small surprise, seeing that the French Government had contracted with his Majesty the most solemn engagement never to alienate the said Province. In order to convince the Government of the United States of the nature of these engagements I take the liberty here to insert a paragraph of a note presented on the 22 July 1802 by Mr. de St. Cyr, Embassador of the French Republic at Madrid, to the Secretary of state of his Majesty, as follows:

"His Catholic Majesty has appeared to wish that France should engage not to sell nor alienate in any manner the property and the enjoyment of Louisiana. Its wish in this respect is perfectly conformable with the intentions of the Spanish Government; and its sole motive for entring therein was because it respected a possession which had constituted a part of the French territory. I am authorized to declare to you in the name of the First Consul, that France will never alienate it."

The mere reading of the paragraph which precedes will convince you as well as the President of the United States that the sale of Louisiana, which France has lately made is a manifest violation of the obligations contracted by her with his Catholic Majesty and that France lacks[1] the powers to alienate the said Province without the approbation of Spain, as is seen incontestibly in above recited offer[2] of the Ambassador St. Cyr authorized by his government.

The King my master charges me to inform this Government as soon as possible of this important circumstance and in compliance with his royal will

I hasten to acquaint you therewith in order that it may as soon as possible come to the knowledge of the President of the United States.

God preserve you many years. Philadelphia 4th. Septr. 1803 &c &c.

Tr (DNA: RG 59, NL); translation in Wagner's hand, interlined on RC of Irujo to Madison, 4 Sep., which Wagner endorsed as received 9 Sep. (Madison, *Papers, Sec. of State Ser.*, 5:378-9).

José Nicolás de Azara served as the Spanish minister IN PARIS, Laurent Gouvion Saint-Cyr as minister of France AT MADRID (Vol. 37:501n).

SECRETARY OF STATE OF HIS MAJESTY: Pedro Cevallos.

[1]MS: "wants."

[2]Word supplied by Editors in place of a blank left by Wagner for Irujo's "oferta."

From John Breckinridge

DEAR SIR Lexington (Kentucky) Sepr. 10. 1803

Your favors of the 12. & 18. ulto. came safe to hand three days ago, for which be pleased to accept my best thanks.—Never came any information more welcome. The scanty information I had been able to collect respecting the cession, & of your ultimate views, added to a report in circulation here, that an exhange of Louisa. for the Floridas was projected, had created in me a distressing anxiety. Altho' doubts & apprehensions had in the first moments suggested themselves to me, (the cession being so totally unexpected by me); yet it was not long before I became thoroughly convinced, that it was one of the most important events we have ever witnessed. My principal fear arose from an idea, that many of our Atlantic brethren of *both* parties would be alarmed at so vast an accession of empire in one quarter of the Union, and under the impulse of an improper jealousy would immediately begin to calculate, how long it would be before they would be forced to seperate, or travel to the bank of the Ohio to legislate for the Union. Altho all such calculations are equally vain & visionary, yet they will be made & have their influence. We certainly discharge the duty imposed on us, and have nothing to answer for to our posterity, by seizing every occasion to advance the present prosperity of our Country, & by leaving remote & to us incalculable events, to be governed by those whose immediate duty it becomes to watch & to direct them. Louisea. will, beyond all question, be settled fully at a period not very remote. It is equally certain, that it will be settled by Americans. The single question therefore is, shall we by surrendering it, permit a foreign & perhaps hostile nation to colonize it at our expence & thereby be furnished with the means of annoying us, or shall we hold it ourselves, populate it as events may make necessary, & shut up every avenue of foreign influence. Under these impressions, whatever the future consequences to the confederacy may be, & which I feel totally unable to calculate, I am unwilling to surrender one acre of the territory acquired by the cession.

The magnitude of the acquisition is not less important, than the manner in which it was acquired. To add to our empire more than two hundred Millions of acres of the finest portion of the earth, without a Convulsion, without spilling one drop of blood, without impairing the rights or interest of a single individual, without deranging in the slightest degree the fiscal concerns of the country, & without in short, the expence of a single dollar (for the port of Orleans will of itself reimburse the 15 Millions of dollars in the 15 years) is an atchievement, of which the annals of no country can furnish a parallel.—As to the Floridas, I really consider their acquisition as of no consequence for the present. We can obtain them long before we shall want them, & upon our own terms.

Many of the western people will I suspect turn their views immediately towards Louisa. From the best consideration which my imperfect knowledge of the state of the country enables me to give the subject, I am inclined to think, the country ought to be locked up as closely as possible for the present. This can be pretty easily effected if there are not too many grants made by Spain & secured by the cession. Should this be the case, emigration to the extant of these grants cannot be prevented, and should this Population be considerable a rapid increase will take place; for it will be impossible to prevent our people from stealing across the Mississi. as they can do so with equal ease in every part of it for an extent of upwards of 1000 miles. When they have once crossed it, it will be the Rubicon to them. They have taken their resolution & will hazzard all the consequences.—If the Grants are not extensive the thing will be easy.

Previous to the rect. of your favors, I had written to Colo. Worthington of Ohio & Colo. Cocke of Tennessee requesting that they and their colleagues would meet me in Washington the 15. of Oct, that we might interchange sentiments on the subject, as I feared we would have to encounter a serious opposition. Cockes colleague is not yet elected, & Worthingtons I have lately heard is at Orleans, from whence, it is much to be feared, he will not return in time. The Reps. from this State I have no doubt will attend the first Hour. They have been earnestly requested so to do; & are apprized that the subject of the cession will come immediately before them. Indeed the public anxiety here is so great, that any neglect of duty at this time, would be deemed treasonable.

With the most affecte. regards I am dear sir, Your friend & Sert.

John Breckinridge

RC (DLC); at foot of text: "Mr. Jefferson"; endorsed by TJ as received 27 Sep. and so recorded in SJL. FC (DLC: Breckinridge Family Papers).

Thomas WORTHINGTON and John Smith were to represent Ohio in the U.S. Senate when the Eighth Congress convened. Joseph Anderson, the COLLEAGUE of William Cocke from Tennessee, had been in the Senate in the previous Congress, filling the vacancy created by Andrew Jackson's resignation. Anderson was ELECTED anew for the full term that would span the Eighth through Tenth Congresses (*Biog. Dir. Cong.*).

REPS. FROM THIS STATE: the congressmen from Kentucky for the incoming Congress were George M. Bedinger, John Boyle, John Fowler, Matthew Lyon, Thomas Sandford, and Matthew Walton (same).

From Levi Lincoln

DEAR SIR Worcester Sept. 10th 1803

Your favor of the 30th ulto. was duly recd. I have to reproach myself with a neglect in not having written. My journey from washington to worcester was rather fatiguing. The weather was extreamly hot, & the roads dusty. I was melted with the one, & actually buried by the other. Their joint effects greatly injured my eyes. They have become stronger; It has been with difficulty, that I have endured the rays of the sun, or the blaze of a candle flame[1]—My family were healthy & happy on my arrival. They have experienced a distressing reverse. The disentery has raged in many places, and in some of our towns more mortally, than has the yellow fever in the devoted cities. It prostrated for a time almost my whole family, robbed me of a fine son, but spared others less severely attacked, and my eldest daughter, who, for several days, was but the subject of a feeble hope. I have much to be grateful for, especially, that I was with them a [Sharer] of their troubles, & some support & comfort to them, in their afflictions. The survivors have got about, are recovering their strength, but are as yet feeble & sorrowful—The natural anxiety awakened by my own, & the greater sufferings of others from this cruel disorder, has confined me at home since its first appearance—There have been instances of a mother, and her four, or five children falling victims to it in the course of a few days. An apology is due, for thus troubling you with the gloomy incidents of a private nature. They are stated as reasons for my being less correctly informed of the feelings sentiments & opinions of the people on public affairs in this quarter then I otherwise should have been—

Previous to my being in washington which I will endeavour shall be by the begining of the next month, I shall spend a few days in Boston & will pay particular attention to the subject of the letter you did me the honor of enclosing.

Louisiana has been much the subject of attention & remark with both parties. Republicans are, I beleive, universally pleased with the purchase, indeed, many of them are more than pleased with it. Federalists are vexed, disappointed, mortified, enraged. Some among them however consider its acquistion, as of very great importance to the U.S. giving brilliancy & credit to the administration & have candor enough explicitly to acknowledge it—Mr Granger on his way from Boston has just left me, he thinks one half the federalists approve of the cession. I am satisfied he is mistaken, & greatly overates the number. In the proportion to the wisdom & utility of a republican measure will be their malignity & opposition generally—You have probably seen the mad & vulgar rantings, in many of the federal papers, on this subject—The same, & other stuff, I find the tools of the party are retailing out, and endeavouring to spread among the people; but I beleive without any effect—Our County Court, which are now together & have been in session the whole of this week, has convened here, upwards of thirty lawyers, with many magistrates & other characters of consideration in society, from various parts of the Country—The Uniform Expression of the federal part of them, I am informed, is that the navigation of the Mississippi is important, but that it was ours before the late treaty, That the cession of Louisiana will prove very injurious to U.S. that they are too extensive already, containing more territory than we know what to do with, can dispose of, or Govern, that the [said?] country, is principally a sunken swamp of no value, that the residue will draw from the existing states their useful inhabitants, subject us to expence & trouble & finally become independent &C &C—I understand Stedman, our new Member for the next Congress, Hastings & Foster, whom you know, with many such characters, whom I hope you never will know are labouring to empress these sentiments on the minds of the people. From hence I am satisfied the ratification of the treaty, & a provision for its execution will meet with every obstacle in the power of the opposition. I have not heard from an individual of the party, or seen in their papers one syllable on the constitutionality of the measure, yet I am confident they mean to take that ground, and promise themselves the more success from its being concealed, or held in reserve untill the action shall have progressed. The Govt: and its friends ought to be prepared to establish the right to purchase and possess under the Constitution previous to its amendment—If it can be ascertained That this ground is to be taken, would it not be left for the Executive to preoccupy, & fortify it, in its communication to Congress? This mode may have a tendency to disconnect the enemy in degree, deprive them of the opportunity of originating objections, give direction & weight to the supporters of the measure, & evince that the subject has been viewed by the Executive in all its various aspects & possible bearings—I have not a decided opinion on the subject, But these ideas occuring, I have taken the liberty to submit them. Your proposed mode of amending the constitution appears to me the safest, & the freest from difficulty & exception of any I had contemplated—I have the honor to be most respectfully yours—

LEVI LINCOLN

RC (DLC); words illegible from bleeding of ink; at head of text: "The Presidt of the U States"; endorsed by TJ as received 23 Sep. and so recorded in SJL.

Reports indicated that dysentery RAGED IN MANY PLACES in Massachusetts, Connecticut, Vermont, and New Hampshire. The Boston *Columbian Centinel* noted that many towns experienced, "in proportion to their relative numbers, a mortality much greater than any of our devoted cities, by the fever." It proved "uncommonly fatal, particularly to children." During July, there were 128 reported deaths from the disorder in Rutland County, Vermont, including 41 at Orwell. ROBBED ME OF A FINE SON: three-year-old Waldo Lincoln died during the outbreak. Lincoln's older son Daniel had a less severe case, and his ELDEST DAUGHTER, Martha, was seriously ill but survived (*Newburyport Herald*, 30 Aug.; Boston *Columbian Centinel*, 31 Aug.; Springfield, Mass., *Federal Spy*, 6 Sep.; Northampton, Mass., *Republican Spy*, 13 Sep.; Rebecca M. Dresser, "The Dissolution of a Republican: Daniel Waldo Lincoln, 1784-1815" [Ph.D. diss., City University of New York, 2010], 22, 58-9).

[1]MS: "fame."

From Philippe Reibelt

MONSIEUR LE PRESIDENT! Norfolk le 10xe. Sept. 1803.

J'ai l'honneur, de Vous informer, que je viens de trouver parmi mes livres un Duplicat de la Superbe edition Suisse de l'homme des Champs par l'Abbè delille, 1802 in Gr. 4. avec Notes et 4 Gravures; et qu'elle est à Vos ordres, si elle ne se trouve pas encore dans Votre Bibliotheque.

Je Vous prie d'agreer les Assurances de mon plus profond Respect. Votre Excellence Tr. humble et tr. Obst. Str.

PHIL. REIBELT

EDITORS' TRANSLATION

MISTER PRESIDENT, Norfolk, 10 Sep. 1803

I have the honor of informing you that among my books I have just found a duplicate of the superb Swiss edition of *L'Homme des champs* by the Abbé Delille, 1802, in grand quarto with notes and four engravings. It is at your disposal if you do not already have it in your library.

I beg you to accept the assurance of my deepest respect, Your Excellency. Your very humble and obedient servant.

PHIL. REIBELT

RC (DNA: RG 59, LAR); endorsed by TJ as received 17 Sep. and so recorded in SJL; also endorsed by TJ: "for office."

From Robert Smith

Sir, Balt. Sep. 10. 1803

Your favor of the 23d Ult informed me that the disposition manifested by the French Government had rendered it necessary that we have a public armed ship ready to sail on the 31st. Oct to carry the ratification and if possible the Stock to France and at the same time suggesting the expediency of employing the last of the small vessels in this service. At the time of my receiving these instructions it was impossible to have so employed any of the small vessels as the last of them was then under sailing orders and has actually sailed some time since. I therefore concluded that nothing remained for me but to have one of the small frigates in readiness. I have issued my orders accordingly. In truth there is but little to be done to prepare her for sea. It was my intention not to give her a full complement of men. As to the danger of her being lost I consider that as nothing. So good a Sailer as she is and so well Officered will be perfectly safe. Besides the very apprehension of this danger ought to be to us a caution against employing a common Merchant Vessel as the Non arrival of the ratification of the Treaty might subject us to some difficulties. It appears to me that we ought either to send a frigate or freight or Merchant Vessel in the usual way without undertaking to commission her or to give her any kind of military Character. And the latter would unquestionably be much the Cheapest. But there would not be as much dispatch nor as much Certainty. To Commission such a Vessel would be attended with great additional expence and with many embarrassments. It would not[1] be entirely free of Constitutional Objections. But the sending of a frigate I consider important with respect to the gun Carriages and to the disposition it might produce in the Emperor to receive them. The employing of a Merchant Vessel with or without a Commission would be much cheaper than the sending of a frigate. But if such a Vessel is to be used, I would advise that she go without a Commission. Until I had received your favor of the 23d. Ult I had imagined that this mode of Conveyance would be adopted. The same Merchant Vessel could also take the gun Carriages. Not being possessed of your ideas I am incapable of judging whether a frigate or a Merchant Vessel ought to be employed. But if an armed vessel is necessary, it is my decided Opinion that a frigate ought to be sent. You will be so Obliging as to inform me in your next favor whether I shall have prepared for this business a frigate or a Merchantman.

I am in correspondence with Genl Dearborn respecting the gun Carriages and every thing is, I believe, in good train.

I am very sorry to learn that the Yellow fever is actually at Alexandria and that the City & Geo. Town are both very sickly. Genl Dearborn and his family are much indisposed.

Be pleased to accept my most affectionate regards

RT SMITH

NB. I have not yet ordered any Officers to the frigate, & will wait for your further instructions

RC (DLC); endorsed by TJ as received from the Navy Department on 16 Sep. and "Vessel to carry ratifn & gun carriages" and so recorded in SJL.

ONE OF THE SMALL FRIGATES: the *Essex* (see Smith to TJ, 4 Sep. 1803).

An outbreak of what was generally deemed to be YELLOW FEVER occurred in ALEXANDRIA from late August to late October 1803. The epidemic led thousands of inhabitants to desert the city temporarily and resulted in as many as 200 deaths (James Muir, *Death Abolished: A Sermon* [Alexandria, Va., 1803], appendix; *Medical Repository*, 7 [1804], 190-3; *Alexandria Advertiser and Commercial Intelligencer*, 10, 13 Sep., 1 Nov. 1803). Assertions that Washington and Georgetown were also VERY SICKLY, however, proved erroneous. Earlier in the month, the Baltimore *Federal Gazette* reported that a severe outbreak of dysentery in Georgetown had carried away as many as 500 inhabitants. After receiving several accounts to the contrary, however, the newspaper retracted the assertion, explaining that the story had been reprinted verbatim from a Philadelphia newspaper and that the place in question was not Georgetown on the Potomac River. The *National Intelligencer* soon after asserted that Washington and Georgetown "have been this season more exempt from disease than in ordinary years," except for "a few bilious cases, which, we believe, incident to all warm climates." James Madison and TJ confirmed the prevailing healthiness following their returns to Washington on 24 and 25 Sep., respectively (*Federal Gazette and Baltimore Daily Advertiser*, 3, 8 Sep. 1803; *National Intelligencer*, 12 Sep. 1803; Madison, *Papers, Sec. of State Ser.*, 5:469-70; MB, 2:1109; TJ to Thomas Mann Randolph, 9 Oct. 1803).

[1] Word interlined.

From Philip R. Thompson

SIR Culpeper Sept. 10th. 1803

My friend Doct. James W. Wallace having occasion to go to Charlottesville, I do myself the honor to mention him to you as a gentleman of great private worth and professional ability—I have taken the liberty to advice him to avail himself of this opportunity to make his respects to you at Montecello.—

I have the honor to be with the greatest respect Sir, Yr mo: Obt and most humble Sert PHIL: R: THOMPSON

RC (DNA: RG 59, LAR); endorsed by TJ as received 12 Sep. and "Wallace Dr. James for N. Orleans" and so recorded in SJL.

Philip Rootes Thompson (1766-1837), a graduate of the College of William and Mary and a practicing lawyer, was a member of the Virginia House of Delegates for Culpeper County from 1793 to 1796 and for Kanawha County in 1818. A Republican, he was elected to the Seventh through the Ninth Congresses. On 10 Feb. 1803, he introduced a bill on the governance of the District of Columbia. He was a member of the committee of correspondence for the newly formed American Board of Agriculture (*Biog. Dir. Cong.*; Leonard, *General Assembly*, xxvii, 191, 195, 199, 203, 294; *Albany Register*, 8 Mch. 1803; Vol. 36:33n).

From La Valette

MONSIEUR a Paris ce 11. 7bre 1803

Je ne veux point Laisser echapper L'occasion que me procure Mr. Wheaton negt. de La Nvelle. angleterre, je la saisis avec Empressement pour me rappeller a votre souvenir et vous assurer que les bontés et temoignages d'amitié que vous m'avés donnés pendant Le sejour que vous avés fait a Baltimore et a Paris sont et seront toujours presents dans ma memoire et burinés dans mon coeur.

Jai bien souvent regretté ce tems heureux et particulierement dans ceux orageux que nous avons passé depuis. ils sont heureusement changés et nous sommes heureux: Dieu veuille les prolonger et nous y maintenir.

Je desire de tout mon coeur que quelques circonstances vous ramene dans notre pays pour avoir encore le plaisir de vous voir, je suis trop vieux pour former le projet de retourner sur votre continent, quoique porté toujours de coeur et d'inclination pour cette terre cherie, cest un de mes regrets bien sinceres. J'ai appris dans le tems avec bien du plaisir votre nomination a la place de president du Congres mon interest vous a toujours suivi dans la carriere que vous avés parcouru, personne plus que moy n'a eprouvé une plus vive satisfaction en apprenant que vos concitoyens ont rendu justice a votre merite, vos Lumieres et vos talents. Soyes assuré des voeux bien sinceres que je fais pour votre bonheur.

Recevés L'assurance de tous Les Sentiments que vous mavés inspirés Je suis avec Respect Monsieur Votre tres humble et tres obeissant serviteur DE LAVALETTE

EDITORS' TRANSLATION

SIR, Paris, 11 Sep. 1803

I do not want to miss the opportunity that is provided by Mr. Wheaton, a New England merchant. I seize it eagerly to greet you and assure you that the kindness and friendship you showed me during your stays in Baltimore and Paris are and will always be present in my memory and burnished in my heart.

How many times have I looked back with regret on those happy times, especially during the stormy times we have endured since then. Fortunately, times have changed and we are happy again. May God prolong and preserve this.

I wish with all my heart that circumstances might bring you back to our country so I could have the pleasure of seeing you again. I am too old to envisage returning to your continent. This is one of my very deep regrets, since I remain attached by feeling and disposition to that cherished land. I was very pleased to learn about your nomination to the presidency of Congress. My interest has always followed you in the career you have pursued. No one felt greater satisfaction than I did in learning that your fellow citizens had justly rewarded your merit, enlightened ideas, and talent. Trust in my very sincere wishes for your happiness.

Accept the assurance of all the sentiments you have inspired in me.

I am with respect, Sir, your very humble and obedient servant.

DE LAVALETTE

RC (ViW: Tucker-Coleman Collection); at head of text: "A Son excellence Monsieur Le president du Congres des etats unis d'amerique"; endorsed by TJ as received 28 Oct. and so recorded in SJL.

POUR ME RAPPELLER A VOTRE SOUVENIR: La Valette to TJ, 5 Mch. 1783 (Vol. 6:254-5); TJ to La Valette, 31 Dec. 1786 (Vol. 10:651).

DE RETOURNER SUR VOTRE CONTINENT: the Chevalier de La Valette had been in America as an officer with the Comte de Rochambeau's army during the Revolutionary War (Gilbert Bodinier, *Dictionnaire des officiers de l'armée royale qui ont combattu aux États-Unis pendant la guerre d'Indépendance, 1776-1783* [Versailles, 2005], 99-100).

From Levi Lincoln

DEAR SIR Worester Sept 11. 1803.

The inclosed is a poem spoken by my 2d son on the last commencement at Harvard College—The Presidt of the College objected to the latter part, said it would give offence, and refused to approbate it. The author told him he would not alter it—He was directed to give a copy & consider further of the matter—It was spoken—the circumstance shews the spirit of the governors of that Seminary, altho it has become more moderate—

Accept Sir assurance of my most respectful esteem

LEVI LINCOLN

RC (DLC); at foot of text: "The Presdt of the U States"; endorsed by TJ as received 23 Sep. and so recorded in SJL.

Daniel Waldo Lincoln, the second SON of Levi and Martha Waldo Lincoln, wrote "Benevolence" for his college commencement as a wave of dysentery swept through his family in the summer. Because he was recovering from the illness himself, he had a friend deliver the poem to Joseph Willard, the president of HARVARD, for review. Fearing the poem would offend the largely Federalist audience, Willard rejected it and demanded revision. Lincoln, however, traveled to Cambridge and in defiance read the poem aloud in its original form. An eyewitness to the event on 30 Aug. 1803, described the piece as "worthy a disciple of Voltaire, who in affection for the great whole forgets the parts." Lincoln's other verses in praise of TJ included "Purity of Heart" in April 1803, a Fourth of July oration given at Worcester and published there in 1805, and "New Year" published in Portland, Maine, in 1806. After reading law with his father, Lincoln settled in Portland and received an appointment as county attorney of Cumberland. He practiced law in Boston from 1810 to 1813, but then returned to Portland and resumed his business. A Republican orator described as a "closet cultural Federalist who preferred deference, philosophy and poetry to politics and partisanship," he died in 1815 at the age of 31 (William Lincoln, *History of Worcester, Massachusetts, from its Earliest Settlement to September, 1836: With Various Notices Relating to the History of Worcester* [Worcester, 1837], 271; James Spear Loring, *The Hundred Boston Orators Appointed by the Municipal Authorities and Other Public Bodies, From 1770 to 1852*, 2d ed. [Boston, 1853], 351-2; Charles C. Smith, "Some Notes on the Harvard Commencements, 1803-1848," *Proceedings of the Massachusetts Historical Society*, 2d ser., 5 [1889-90], 169; Rebecca M. Dresser, "The Dissolution of a Republican: Daniel Waldo Lincoln, 1784-1815" [Ph.D. diss., City University of New York, 2010], 39-79, 104, 206-7, 217; Shaw-Shoemaker, Nos. 8788, 13215; RS, 2:504-5, 666).

ENCLOSURE

Poem by Daniel Waldo Lincoln

————"Homo sum.
Nil humani a me alienum puto."

Benevolence

Ere any social intercourse began,
Ere arts subdued, or culture modelled man;
Ere law had learnt his fierceness to restrain;
Ere the rude savage stooped to wear a chain;
He roamed the desart, trod the pathless wild,
And nature catered for her simple child.
With tigers fell he shared the rocky den,
Or chummed with serpents in the gloomy fen;
In constant danger from an host of foes,
Where midnight howlings lulled him to repose.

Man in this state no happiness could know,
Stranger to joys, which from communion flow,
To all the tender charities of life;
Worn by the warfare of continual strife.
A sense of weakness, & a dread of ill,

A gentleness, the desart could not kill,
A native inclination to his kind,
Wakened his dormant faculties of mind.
The charms of beauty made the work complete.
'Twas lovely woman civilized her mate,
Impelled the genial current of his soul,
And taught his wildness to endure control.
All men were equal, equal claims possest,
The weak subserved not, nor the strong opprest.
By equal laws for common profit framed,
The mild were strengthened, & the cruel tamed.
Nature's *great charter* all their rights ensured.
Obedience by their compact was secured.—
Happy condition, from corruption free,
When human kind was one fraternity;
When every peer the sweets of life might prove,
When all was freedom, happiness, & love:
When single wrongs extensively were felt,
And each with others, as his brethren dealt:
When no proud lordling could usurp the state,
Ribbons & garters could not make men great!!
Not yet Bellona climbed her iron car,
Nor crimson slaughter marked the steps of war.
Not yet revenge her baleful touch had waved.
In blood of victims malice had not laved.
Man had not lent to hoary ruin aid;
Nor vice had battened on the spoil he made.
Deceitful grandeur had not learnt the art,
To veil the sordid baseness of the heart.
Ambitious pride not yet had reared a throne.
No ruler but benevolence was known.
Cursed be the policy of modern days,
And all the subtle folly of their ways!
The monstrous vices of the present times
Have swelled the horrid catalogue of crimes.
Disorder, tumult, violence, & rage,
Have deeply stained the annals of the age.
Of earlier, better, happier times the lee:
Accomplished in refined barbarity:
Callous of feeling, pauper too in sense,
Bankrupt declared in moral excellence.
And is this fact? To sad experience trust.
The truth is rigid, but the tale is just.—
Europe distracted her lost heroes mourns,
Like Rachel weeping for her slaughtered sons.
Mark her rent vestments crimsoned o'er[1] with blood!
Lo, camps arise where erst her temples stood!
Hear from her plains the hungry battle's roar!
See, her red fields are overwhelmed with gore!
While the gorged vulture, watchful, poiz'd on high,

Imbibes the purple current with his eye.
From Afric's shores observe the fluttering sail!
Attend the groans, that freight the passing gale!
Behold the captive from his country torn,
His frenzied manner, & his looks forlorn!
He leaps despairing in the briny wave:
No heart to pity, & no hand to save.
The softened monsters of the ebbing flood,
To ease his sufferings round the vessel crowd,
With kind dismission set his spirit free.
E'en ocean blushed for lost humanity.
Pursue the Spaniard's o'er the western main!
Count there the heaps of guiltless natives slain!
Follow the bloodhounds in the furious chase,
Experienced hunters of the human race!
. . . .
. . . .
Seized of their goods, their very lives they crave,
Ruthless as rocks, insatiate as the grave.
Peace they proclaimed, but showed themselves a rod.
They robbed, & murdered in the name of God.
They published truth, but proved the gain a loss,
They made a gibbet of the Christian cross.

Some few there are, a firm, & faithful band,
The lure of gairish splendor, that withstand,
Some, that to Baal have not bowed the knee,
Stedfast, unshook in their integrity:
Some, that on human misery have not preyed;
Some, that from virtue's path have never strayed;
Some, that have watched with care the vestal flame,
Their lives a satire on their neighbors' shame.
They grant to fortune's plaything in their gate
A safe asylum from the wrongs of fate.
The wretched sufferer they will never shun,
Whether he worship "twenty Gods or one:"
The rights of others never will[2] refrain,
Who think with Watson, or agree with Paine.
Tis thus some phenix worthies erst have done.
Thus too has Franklin, thus great Jefferson.
Their noble deeds elude the vulgar ken:
Sages in wisdom, as in feelings men.
Papists had *sainted* those of half their worth,
Applied their maxims as the tests of truth;
Thought them, vicegerents of indulgent heaven,
To alleviate evils by the Godhead given.
When nature gives her precept to remove
Their kindred spirits to the realms of love;
Where he, who *labored in the vineyard's* blest;
Where he, that's slandered, has the wrong redrest.

They'll mount escorted by the widow's prayers,
Be recommended by the orphan's tears. LINCOLN

Cambridge Augt. 31st. 1803.

MS (DLC); probably in the hand of Daniel Waldo Lincoln.

HOMO SUM. NIL HUMANI A ME ALIENUM PUTO: "I am human, so nothing human is alien to me" (Terence, *The Self-Tormenter*, 1.77).

BELLONA: the ancient Roman goddess of war.

For the reference to RACHEL WEEPING for her children because they were no more, see Jeremiah 31:15 and Matthew 2:18.

SOME, THAT TO BAAL HAVE NOT BOWED THE KNEE: in Romans 11:4-5, Paul cited a declaration by God in 1 Kings 19:18—"Yet I have left *me* seven thousand in Israel, all the knees which have not bowed unto Baal"—to assert that there was always a "remnant" of people chosen by "the election of grace."

TWENTY GODS OR ONE: TJ wrote: "It does me no injury for my neighbour to say there are twenty gods, or no god. It neither picks my pocket nor breaks my leg" (*Notes*, ed. Peden, 159).

Richard WATSON, the bishop of Llandaff, wrote *An Apology for the Bible* as a response to Thomas Paine's *Age of Reason* (Vol. 32:193n).

HE, WHO LABORED: Matthew 20:1-16.

[1]MS: "o'er o'er."
[2]MS: "will will."

From James Madison

DEAR SIR Sepr. 11. 1803

I have recd the letters sent me by the last mail under two covers, and return those belonging to your own files. I inclose herewith also the communications last recd from the office of State. I can not without losing the present opportunity make comments on any of them. A few only invite them.

Yours with respectful attacht. JAMES MADISON

Docr. Wallace in whose behalf the letters from Mr. Brent & Mr Thomson were written is with me, and proposes I find to wait on you with a letter from Mr. Wythe, who it seems is his kinsman. I have stated to him the relation of Dr. Bache to the object of his pursuit.

RC (DLC); at foot of text: "The President of the U. States"; endorsed by TJ as received from the State Department at Orange on 12 Sep. and "Wallace" and so recorded in SJL. Enclosures: see below.

For COMMUNICATIONS received from the OFFICE OF STATE, see Jacob Wagner to Madison, 2 and 7 Sep. 1803 (Madison, *Papers, Sec. of State Ser.*, 5:374-5, 385-7).

LETTERS FROM MR. BRENT & MR THOMSON: Virginia congressman Richard Brent of Prince William County wrote to Madison from Fauquier Court House on 11 Aug., informing him of James Wallace's intent to become a citizen of New Orleans. Praising his medical training and noting the physician's desire to apply for any medical position established there, Brent recommended Wallace as a "Man of genious and of knowledge in his profession" with respectable connections who would be deserving of a post at a garrison or hospital (RC in DNA: RG 59, LAR, endorsed by TJ: "Wallace Dr James to superintend hospitl. N. Orleans Richd. Brent to mr Madison"; Vol. 32:460n). See also Philip R. Thompson to TJ, 10 Sep.

WAIT ON YOU: according to SJL, TJ received the 31 Aug. letter from George Wythe on 12 Sep. For William Bache's position, see Vol. 40:461-3.

From John Monroe

SIR. Bath Ct house. Sepr. 11th. 1803.

Unaccustomed as I am to solicit an office, I am almost detered from any application to those who have the power of giving. I have neither the pretensions of exalted talents, or overawing popularity to enforce my request: and be assured, I shd. have remained forever quiet on this Subject, and rejoiced at the success of men better qualified than myself; but for the unhappy state I am at present placed in.

You know me, Sir, and if what I ask is improper to be granted it is your duty to deny it.

The late treaty with France will necessarily increase the number of Offices. At New Orleans, some appointments to office must be made. The Office of collector of the customs at that place, will be both important & profitable. If you think me qualified to fill that office, you will enable me to redeem from poverty and distress, a family of Virtuous and deserving children. But if, on reflection you suppose me better qualified to discharge the duties of an other office, in any other quarter, which may promise some profitable advantages, I shall feel my self Honored by your notice.

I am not, *now*, attached to soil or climate: and death itself is preferable to my present situation. To you alone I have submitted my request. From you alone will I ask; and in full confidence I know you will do me Justice.

Accept my sincere wishes for an increase of that confidence, which you justly deserve from the public

Yours JNO. MONROE

RC (DNA: RG 59, LAR); endorsed by TJ as received on 18 Sep. and "for office" and so recorded in SJL.

To Abraham Bradley, Jr.

Monticello Sep. 12. 03.

Th: Jefferson presents his compliments to mr Bradley and asks the favor of him to let nothing be sent for him to this place after the mail which leaves Washington on Friday the 16th.

PrC (DLC); endorsed by TJ in ink on verso.

From Samuel Broome

Greenfield Hill Connecticut
Sepr. 12. 1803.

Sir

I have to make many Apologies, for addressing your Excellency so often, on my private Concerns, but having a desire to be appointed Collector for the District of New Haven, I think it proper to make my Standing in Society known, on a determination to offer myself as a Candidate for Said office, I wrote to several friends, amongst the number is the Hon'ble Elbridge Gerry Esqr with whom I have been acquainted many years, and lately received many marks of Attention from that Gentleman in Paris. The following is an extract of his reply.

Dear Sir Cambridge 27th Augt 1803.

Nothing will give me greater pleasure than your Attainment of the Object you have in View, because I conceive that your Claim to it is as well established, by your political and Moral principles, and conduct, as that of any One who may offer himself as a Candidate, I remain Dear Sir, with the highest esteem your friend and humble servant

(Copy) E. Gerry

I am with great respect Your Excellency's most Obed Servt

Samuel Broome

RC (DNA: RG 59, LAR); at foot of text: "His Excellency The President"; endorsed by TJ as received 19 Sep. and so recorded in SJL.

From Nicolas Gouin Dufief

Monsieur, Philadelphie, ce 12 de Septembre 1803

Ci-Joint est le Prospectus de l'ouvrage que vous avez si puissament encouragé par vos lettres flatteuses du 9 Janvier 1800 et 15 November, 1803. J'ai taché, du mieux qu'il m'a été possible, de reconnaître devant le Public, les Obligations que je vous ai. J'eusse certainement soumis mon Prospectus a votre Jugement éclairé, avant de le livrer à l'impression, Sans l'idée que je devais respecter les Soins importans dont vous êtes chargé, et que l'année passée J'avais peut-être abusé de votre bonté pour moi, en vous dérobant quelques-uns des momens que vous consacriez à l'administration Publique, ou à vos Méditations particulieres. Quoique je n'eusse sans doute pas besoin d'appuyer mon Prospectus d'aucune autre recommendation, après ce que vous avez eu la bonté de dire de l'ouvrage, j'ai cru cependant qu'il me serait permis de publier aussi l'opinion Du Dr. Smith dont les talens et la libéralité en matière de science sont généralement reconnus. Mr. Girardin dont les connaissances sur la science Grammaticale sont fort etendues, et qui est auteur d'un ouvrage sur l'histoire, qui lui fera beaucoup d'honneur, ayant fort approuvé les principes d'après lesquels l'ouvrage a été composé, il m'est venu à l'idée que sa recommandation pourrait etre de quelque utilité au succès de la Souscription. Il est absolument indispensable d'opposer l'opinion decisive des Gens éclairés aux prejugés des personnes qui voyent toujours d'un œil Jaloux et inquiet, les efforts que l'on fait pour perfectionner les sciences morales, et surtout l'éducation.

Vous verrez par le prospectus que mon ouvrage est plus etendu que je n'avais d'abord imaginé. Vous n'en serez point surpris, car lorsqu'un sujet est profond, une meditation continue y fait découvrir des choses nouvelles et nécessaires qui avaient d'abord échappé.

J'ai appris de Mr. John Vaughan, à mon retour d'un petit Voyage entrepris pour le rétablissement de ma santé, qu'il vous avaint adressé un des ouvrages du Dr. Pristley que je n'avais pu vous procurer. Je l'avais prié d'ecrire à ce sujet au Dr avec qui il a des liaisons d'amitié. Je suis d'autant plus charmé de cette réussite que cet ouvrage est extrêmement rare en Amérique et qu'il ne se trouve que dans quelques bibliothèques publiques. Je n'ai point oublié qu'il vous manque encore deux ouvrages du même auteur, savoir:

disquisitions relating to matter & spirit.

sequel to the disquisitions.

Je continuerai mes recherches à ce Sujet.

J'ai l'honneur d'etre, Monsieur, avec des Sentimens inébranlables d'estime, de respect & de reconnaissance Votre trés dévoué Serviteur.

N. G. Dufief

EDITORS' TRANSLATION

Dear Sir, Philadelphia, 12 Sep. 1803

Attached is the prospectus for the book you so strongly encouraged in your flattering letters of 9 Jan. 1800 and 15 Nov. 1803. I have made every effort to acknowledge in public my debt to you. I would surely have submitted the prospectus for your judicious comments before sending it to the printer if I had not been mindful of your important responsibilities and the fact that I might have imposed upon your generosity last year by taking time away from your governmental tasks or your own reflections. While the prospectus undoubtedly needed no other recommendation than your own kind words, I thought it would be fitting to include the review by Dr. Smith, whose talents and broad-mindedness in scientific matters are widely recognized. Since Mr. Girardin approved the founding principles of the work, it occurred to me that his recommendation, as a grammarian and author of a historical work that is destined to receive acclaim, could be useful to the success of the subscription. It is essential for the informed views of enlightened people to counteract the prejudices of those who look with fear and jealousy on all efforts to perfect the moral sciences, especially education.

You will see from the prospectus that my work is broader in scope than I had originally conceived. This will not surprise you, for when a subject is profound, prolonged reflection leads us to discover vital new things we had not previously noticed.

On my return from a short trip to restore my health, I learned from Mr. John Vaughan that he had sent you one of Dr. Priestley's books that I had not been able to find for you. I had asked him to write to the doctor whom he knows personally. I am all the more delighted by this success because the work is rare in America and belongs to only a few public libraries. I have not forgotten that you still seek two books by the same author:

Disquisitions Relating to Matter and Spirit

Sequel to the *Disquisitions*

I will continue to look for them.

With unwavering feelings of esteem, respect, and gratitude, I have the honor, Sir, of being, your very devoted servant. N. G. Dufief

RC (DLC); endorsed by TJ as received 16 Sep. and so recorded in SJL. Enclosure not found, but see below.

The prospectus for the publication by subscription of Dufief's book, *Nature Displayed*, appeared in newspapers in October. In it, Dufief quoted TJ's letters to him of 9 Jan. 1801 (which TJ misdated 1800) and 15 Nov. 1802. The prospectus also included the full text of letters from Samuel Stanhope smith of the College of New Jersey at Princeton and Louis H. girardin, who taught modern languages at the College of William and Mary. Girardin, who also taught history and geography at the college, translated a manuscript account of recent events in France and later completed John Daly Burk's *History of Virginia*. According to Dufief's announcement, *Nature Displayed* would require "two handsome octavo volumes, of about five hundred pages each," with a price for subscribers of $2.50 per volume (*National Intelligencer*, 14 Oct.; Jean Henry De Croisoeuil, *Revolutionary Annals, or History of the French Revolution, from the Convocation of the States-General to the Treaty of Amiens, in 1802. Part V. Buonaparte, During the First Three Years of his Consulate*, trans. L. H. Girardin [Norfolk, 1805]; rs, 1:633-4n; Vol. 32:415; Vol. 39:9-10).

From James Madison

Dear Sir Monday Sepr. 12. 1803

I recd. last night the inclosed letter from Yrujo. Mr. Wagner informs me that a copy was sent directly to you by the same mail, but as a further security for your receivg the communication without delay, I take advantage of the present oppy. for forwarding the original. It is a curious circumstance that near three months after the sale of Louisiana, the French Ambasr. should have given the assurance stated. Still it was not to be expected that Spain would have undertaken to enter such a caveat. If it could be supposed the result of a secret understanding with France or even with G.B. the incident would take a very serious aspect; but as collusion on the subject with either is highly improbable, the step seems most readily explained, by supposing it the offspring of a wish in Spain to make a merit or obtain a price for her consent, and to contest with more advantage the extension of Louisiana[1] to the limits she must be aware that we have in view. As Mr. Pinckney will doubtless have recd. the notice now communicated here, and have transmitted it to Paris, we may presume that our Minister there will have called on the French Govt. to prevent any obstruction to the fulfillment of the Treaty on its part. It will notwithstanding be proper to transmit the communication of Yrujo to both. It is to be considered also whether any, & what reply to Yrujo, and what intimations to Pichon, may be proper in the mean time. Perhaps, as the return to Washington is drawing so nigh it may be as well to wait for that oppy. of communicating with the latter; and for the same reason as well as in expectation of soon learning more on the subject, to postpone the observations due to the note of the former. Your instructions will decide those points. Whatever may be the views of Spain, there will be no difficulty, if she stands alone, and above all if she opposes the views of France, in going thro' with our own purposes.

I inclose also a letter & papers from Forbes, increasing the file of wrongs to be brought into our remonstrance to the British Govt. on the subject of impressments.

Yrs. with respectful attachment James Madison

RC (DLC); at foot of text: "The President of the U. States"; endorsed by TJ as received from the State Department at Orange on 12 Sep. and "Spanish claim to Louisiana" and so recorded in SJL. Enclosures: (1) Carlos Martínez de Irujo to Madison, 4 Sep.; see Jacob Wagner to TJ, [9] Sep. (2) John Murray Forbes to Madison, 13 June (see below).

Wagner had informed Madison on 9 Sep. that he sent a copy of Irujo's letter directly to TJ "lest the President might not receive it with the greatest celerity"

(Madison, *Papers*, *Sec. of State Ser.*, 5:390-1).

NEAR THREE MONTHS AFTER THE SALE: Madison apparently misread the date 22 July 1802 in Irujo's letter as 22 July 1803 (same, 403n).

Writing from Hamburg and enclosing copies of several documents, FORBES reported the seizure of an American sailor by a British press gang. After complaints to the British chargé d'affaires failed to bring the man's release, Forbes determined to make a formal protest to the government of Hamburg. He refused to alter his course of action even though a British consular official informed him that the British government would bring pressure to bear against him in the United States if he issued the protest (same, 5:96-8).

[1] Abbreviated in MS.

From Frank Nash

DEAR SIR September the 12 D 1803

I have take my pen in hand to inform you of what a situation thaiam I that I amin and I will likwise inform you of the situation that I have been In sence I left america I lef Norfolk the twelf of november and after twenty days days passage arrived at berbadous and from there I went to merte neceke and in mertenecake as I was awalking the strete I got taken and put in prison and then sent abord of a slope of war and then put abord abord of a merchant ship and sent to bordax and I then went a shore to mister leas the american consul's and they gave me a pretection wrote in french and after wards one wrote in english but I dont find much releaf from your consuls nor yet much imploy [...] from the french marchince nor yet have I found much relief from my riting to bonepart or not at least so much as fifty dollars but if you and your has all allik benn such friends to me as I exect they I dont se as I shall have enny peace in enny part of the world without it is amongxt th engins in the western world but Dear sir I hear of your telling of this I shall think of noless than being in public but a public prince is not allways presed from day to day as I am carred away from the wise dom of the north america but Dear sir I shall want to have your wits forgive mne my Dear what is this that I have wrote to you hear for it is come and se or send to me for I am not so far from free but that I expect once mour america to sea and like wise your family without a tree or eaven going from sea to sea lord what a time Lord what atim it is for me al this world to sea to sea and not a single happence to spend nor yet a friend I hope I hope I hope hope came when help was gown but I hope it will be not long before I shall be able hold help by the hand O dear sir I am affraid that you will not ker for me as much as you du for her If you du I shall expect to come back to new London sir Dea sir you may nede this with and welcome sir but

Sir I ask your pardon sir for what you habe red before sir my god I will forgive you for what I have or for what you will read mour Sir wit wand wonder FRANK NASH

DEAR SIR

I take my pen in hand to inform you that I am well and in dublin the twelf day of september and that I am a bord of an american ship Waldin Maste of her she is a ship of about thre hundred tones it is the ship venus of new york The mates name [of the ship][1] Saltison of new york and that I shipt a bord of her in bordax I then expected that she was bound to america but sence the the ship has arribed at dublin and I expect that I shall gow to london or liveripool and if I dont git apasage from there to america I expect that I shall gow to the westinges and from there to america but If you please you can keep your wits as I did mine and like wise your riches whilst I am Ninty and nine but sence I should like to say that I have been a fool from mind to mind but as long as I have been as well forgot as lost I will not think that I might have been saved as weas lost but I am affraid th I shall be again overtaken by the frost untill my time is lost but yet I have such time as I due not wish to see but your mind It would be agree able for me to hear though you ar so far from hear though yough your mind I but little fear but pleas god I hope I shal get to america to hear that I may but little fear the gold silver that is hear but I am inhopes that it will shine by daylight and not by night but I ame affraid that my shining will be out of your site for my enimys finds mour friends than I due by God my God dont think of what you have got becasue If you talk I will give you ten times mour than you have had before but my god dont think of my being not a fool untill I have been where I have not yet been before but dont think of my not thinking you my friend but my god dond think your works and your ways and not of your friends these these days as well as nights and like wise money to bar with our fights. Dear sir dont a better friend to shew this tew than you your self but I [bet?] as you have been welcom ever sence you first be gun you can say what you please to some but I expect that I shall come home [or at least][2] some time this winter or Next spring if I dont git prest abord of a man of war or at least If I can get a dis charge from the american ship that I am abord of

FRANK NASH

Dear sir as I write this letter What can I say or du anny better than to say that I beleave that I wrote you this letter dear sir can you pay me avisit anny better or will you please to send me a litter for I am in hopes to make you welcome of mour than this letter

Dear Sir I am the yong mand that pearhaps you migh hear of liveing in the county of farfield and nigh the river housatonoc [lelet?] perhaps if if and wil Dear sir I hav past away manny a long gand troublesom long day and have roved fare away Dear sir if I should get abord of a man of war I Should [. . .] perhaps want to have some of your friends take me out

Dear sir if you please forgive me of my egnorance perhaps I may gow to london and stay there long enough for you to get this letter and then have time enough to send to london and give me apassage home to america if that would beagreable to you but I think that I shall gow to the westinges this winter but however I expect nowthing but that I shall come to ammerica next spring or before and I cant tel Nothing but that I shall like to Searve your country as perhaps they may like to Serve me but If you please you may Se what is to be given as well as taken as you may be mistaken untill that you sea how the fool is forsaken—time cuts downall both great and small and so perhaps if you call me a fool I shalnot have enny thing to say to you at all unless I be cald by you with apleasant call but [If] you please you can for git what has gown and [hast?] and that I may see your friends at last friends and as they will have [nuse] for no one [. . .] friends [until?]

RC (MHi); evidently written in several sittings, with the date appearing at the head of the third and final page of text; with ink smudges; frayed at margin; addressed: "To the President of the united States of america"; franked; endorsed by TJ as received 30 Oct. and so recorded in SJL.

In March 1804, a report circulated that the ship *Monticello* out of London had "shipped a sea" off of Sicily and that a man named Frank Nash of Stamford, Connecticut, had been washed overboard. Stamford is in Fairfield (FARFIELD) County, through which the Housatonic River flows (*New-York Commercial Advertiser*, 20 March 1804).

[1] Nash's brackets.

[2] Nash's brackets.

From John Page

MY DEAR SIR Richmond Sepr. 12th. 1803

Having this Moment heard that Mr. Harvey intends to set out tomorrow morning to Monticello,[1] I sent to request he would call on me & take charge of a Letter to you. I thought he would be a proper Conveyance of the Letter which you had permitted me to copy. I now inclose it with thanks for this fresh proof of your friendship, & for your Confidence in me. Mrs. Page joins in presenting our Compliments & best Wishes to you & your charming Family

I am with the highest respect & Esteem your most obedient Servt.

JOHN PAGE

P.S.

As Mr. Harvey did not call for this Letter I have taken out yours to Dr. Rush & will keep it for a safer Conveyance than a Post. I have been so engaged ever since my return here that I can only add that I am

sincerely yours. J.P.

RC (DLC); endorsed by TJ as received 16 Sep. and so recorded in SJL.

MR. HARVEY: possibly TJ's secretary Lewis Harvie.

Likely during Page's recent visit to Monticello, TJ shared his letter of 21 Apr. to Benjamin RUSH and probably his comparative view of the doctrines of Jesus that the letter enclosed (see TJ to James Madison, 29 Aug.).

[1]MS: "Montiello."

From Thomas Rodney

DR SIR Wheeling Monday Septr. 12th. 1803.

In Compliance with your appointments in the Misisipi Territory I left Dover on the 14th. and Wilmington in Delaware the 21st. of August and arrived at this Place on the 5th. of this Instant—Mr. Wm. Shields whom I mentioned to you in a former Letter, comes with me, and Major Richard Claybourn of Virginia, who was recommended to me by several respectable Gentlemen and who Says he is known to you, arrived the next day—both of them are going With me to the Natchez—Not being able to procure a suitable Boat here ready made to decend the River we are obliged to wait the building a light Batteau which is to be ready in three days from this time so that in the Course of this Week we Shall leave this Place on our Voiage down the Rivers—What time it may take us to reach Natchez Seems uncertain and will depend on Circumstances—Some of those who are used to the business of decending these Rivers Say we may go down in a light boat in four weeks others Say five and others Six weeks—It is Said by those who reside here that they Never saw less water in the Ohio—many Riffs or shoals have not more than 15 or 18 Inches water over them, but as our Batteau will not draw more than 8 or 10 Inches water none of them will Stop us.

Captn. Lewis left here on Fryday last—he had some trouble in Coming from Pittsburg down here by having to unload and to have his Barge drawn by Oxen over several riffs or Shoals—before he left here he made his boat as light as possible by putting his lading in several Canoes—we heard of him after he had passed 16 miles below this, when he had passed Several of the worst riffs or Shoals below this place without their stoping him and probably he will Soon reach better waters—yet as Our Boat is much Lighter than his we Expect to Overtake him before he gits out of the Ohio. With Sentiments of the highest respect and Esteem I remain

Your Most Obedient THOMAS RODNEY

RC (DLC); endorsed by TJ as received 25 Sep. and so recorded in SJL.

FORMER LETTER: Thomas Rodney to TJ, 1 July.

Richard Claiborne (CLAYBOURN), cousin of William C. C. Claiborne, began corresponding with TJ in 1781, when he became deputy quartermaster of Virginia. He applied to TJ for an appointment in the public service in August 1802 (Dwight L. Smith and Ray Swick, eds., *A Journey through the West: Thomas Rodney's 1803 Journal from Delaware to the Mississippi Territory* [Athens, Ohio, 1997], 46-7, 213n; Vol. 38:271-2).

For Rodney's visit with Meriwether LEWIS, who left Wheeling on 9 Sep., see Smith and Swick, eds., *Journey through the West*, 47, 50-3.

From Juste Chanlatte

MONSIEUR LE PRÉSIDENT Baltimore 13 Septembre 1803.

Pardonnés si ma foible voix s'élance jusques vers votre personne importante, pour lui témoigner, en quittant ce païs heureux & où l'hospitalité s'éxerce aussi humainement, mon regret de ne pouvoir pas l'habiter; mais je conserverai éternéllement en ma mémoire le souvenir de la bonté de ce climat et de ses habitants. il me reste, Monsieur Le président, à vous donner l'assurance que j'adresserai des vœux à la providence pour la conservation de vos précieux jours, nécessaires à une nation qui les îdolatres à de si justes tîtres!

Excusé aussi, Monsieur Le président, de la liberté que je prends de vous distraire de vos éminants, penibles et Salutaires traveaux, pour uniquement vous offrir ce gage de mon admiration, pour vôtre intégrité, vos vertus comme mon inaltérable & profond respect.

CHANLATTE aîné

EDITORS' TRANSLATION

MISTER PRESIDENT, Baltimore, 13 Sep. 1803

As I leave this happy country where hospitality is so humanely offered, forgive my feeble voice reaching out to your important person, to express regret that I cannot live here. I shall forever remember the goodness of this country and its inhabitants. All that remains, Mister President, is to assure you that I will pray to Providence to preserve your precious days which are necessary to a nation that rightly idolizes them.

Please forgive as well, Mister President, my taking the liberty of distracting you from your worthwhile, painful, and salutary tasks, simply to offer you this sign of my admiration for your integrity and character along with my deep, unwavering respect.

CHANLATTE the elder

RC (DLC); endorsed by TJ, who misread the name as Charlotte Amé, as received 16 Sep. and so recorded in SJL.

Juste Chanlatte (1766-1828) was a native of Saint-Domingue of mixed European and African ancestry. He received an excellent education in Paris, then became involved in the movements in Saint-Domingue for emancipation and independence. He sat on the "intermediate commission" that Léger Félicité Sonthonax established in the fall of 1792 to replace the colonial assembly. Political changes forced Chanlatte, with the assistance of merchants at Port-au-Prince, to seek refuge in the United States in 1797. A list of letters to be picked up at the post office in Baltimore in 1801 and the "aîné" he attached to his signature in the letter printed above suggest that his younger brother, François Desrivières Chanlatte, who was also well educated and later became a government official and writer, accompanied him. TJ's mistaking of Chanlatte's name in the endorsement and in his epistolary register may indicate that the two had never met. After returning to Saint-Domingue, Chanlatte became secretary general of the government under Jean Jacques Dessalines. In that capacity, which he continued under Dessalines's successor, Henri Christophe, Chanlatte played a key role in drafting the Haitian declaration of independence in 1804 and constitution of 1805. From Christophe he received a title of nobility, becoming the Comte des Rosiers. Chanlatte composed plays and verse, edited the Haitian government's official gazette, and wrote tracts on Haiti and race, including *Le Cri de la nature* (Cap-Haitien, 1810), which he called, in its subtitle, an *hommage haytien* to Henri Grégoire (Ertha Pascal Trouillot and Ernst Trouillot, *Encyclopédie Biographique d'Haïti*, 1 vol. to date [Montreal, 2001], 1:211-13; Joseph Saint-Rémy, *Pétion et Haïti: Étude monographique et historique*, 2d ed., 5 vols. in one [Paris, 1956], 4:11, 19-21; David Nicholls, "Race, couleur et indépendance en Haiti [1804-1825]," *Revue d'histoire moderne et contemporaine [1954-]*, 25 [1978], 185-6, 189, 201; Doris Y. Kadish, "Haiti and Abolitionism in 1825: The Example of Sophie Doin," *Yale French Studies*, 107 [2005], 111, 121-4; Albert Valdman, "Haitian Creole at the Dawn of Independence," same, 151-3, 156-7; Thomas O. Ott, *The Haitian Revolution, 1789-1804* [Knoxville, Tenn., 1973], 66; Baltimore *Federal Gazette*, 16 June 1801).

From Meriwether Lewis

On board my boat opposite Marietta.
September 13th. 1803.

DEAR SIR,

I arrived here at 7. P.M. and shall pursue my journey early tomorrow. This place is one hundred miles distant from Wheeling, from whence in descending the water is reather more abundant than it is between that place and Pittsburgh, insomuch that I have been enabled to get on without the necessity of employing oxen or horses to drag my boat over the ripples except in two instances; tho' I was obliged to cut a passage through four or five bars, and by that means past them: this last operation is much more readily performed than you would imagin; the gravel of which many of these bars are formed, being small and lying in a loose state is readily removed with a spade, or even with a wooden shovel and when set in motion the current drives it a considerable distance before it subsides or again settles at the bottom; in this manner I have cut a passage for my boat of 50 yards in length in the course of an hour; this method however is impracticable when driftwood or clay in any quantity is intermixed with the gravel; in such cases Horses or oxen are the last resort: I find them the most efficient sailors in the present state of the navigation of this river, altho' they may be considered somewhat clumsey.—

I have the honour to be with much respect Your Obt. Servt.

MERIWETHER LEWIS.
Capt. 1st. US. Regt. Infty.

RC (DLC); at foot of text: "Thomas Jefferson President of the UStates"; endorsed by TJ as received 30 Sep. and so recorded in SJL.

From Benjamin Lincoln

SIR Boston Sept 13 1803

Yesterday your ten packages were Shipped on Board the Schooner Alert Azariah Smith Master enclosed you will find his receipt I hope they will arrive safely

I am sir with the highest consideration your most Obedient servant

B LINCOLN

RC (MHi); at foot of text: "Thomas Jefferson President of the United States"; endorsed by TJ as received 25 Sep. and so recorded in SJL. Enclosure not found.

For the TEN PACKAGES, see TJ to Lincoln, 19 Aug.

From George Jefferson

DEAR SIR Richmond 14th. Septr. 1803

A waggoner has called with your memorandum. I expect to day to forward by him 32 bars of Iron, & *nine* boxes; instead of 6 as you expected. The window glass & sheet-iron have not arrived; nor has a box of screws which Mr. Barnes informed me about a week ago he had forwarded by the preceding stage. I have informed him of their miscarriage, but fear he may not be able to replace them in Geo. Town, as he mentioned it had been with difficulty he had procured the quantity. It really seems as if you are never to get any.

I am Dear Sir Yr. Very humble servt. GEO. JEFFERSON

RC (MHi); at foot of text: "Thos. Jefferson esqr."; endorsed by TJ as received 16 Sep. and so recorded in SJL.

To James Madison

Dear Sir Monticello Sep. 14. 03.

I now return you the several papers recieved by the last post, except those sollicting office, which as usual, are put into my bundle of like papers. I think it possible that Spain, recollecting our former eagerness for the island of N. Orleans, may imagine she can, by a free delivery of that, redeem the residue of Louisiana: and that she may withold the peaceable cession of it. in that case no doubt force must be used. however the importance of this measure, the time & the means, will be for discussion at our meeting on the 25th. in the mean time I think Clarke might be trusted with a general hint of the possibility of opposition from Spain, & an instruction to sound in every direction, but with so much caution as to avoid suspicion, & to inform us whether he discovers any symptoms of doubt as to the delivery, to let us know the force Spain has there, where posted, how the inhabitants are likely to act, if we march a force there, and what numbers of them could be armed & brought to act in opposition to us. we have time to recieve this information before the day of ratification, and it would guide us in our provision of force for the object. Accept my affectionate salutations & respects. Th: Jefferson

RC (DLC: Madison Papers); at foot of text: "The Secy. of State." PrC (DLC). Recorded in SJL with notation "Spanish protest."

general hint: in a letter of 16 Sep., Madison informed Daniel Clark that "the President wishes you to watch every symtom which may shew itself, and to sound in every direction where discoveries may be most practicable." Clark must, however, proceed "with all the caution necessary to avoid suspicion." Madison closely followed TJ's instructions, asking Clark to get information about the military force of Spain, where the military was posted and "what are its dispositions," how inhabitants might respond to the arrival of troops from the United States, and the numbers of inhabitants the Spanish might be able to use against an incursion by the U.S. "You will be sensible that the value of information on those points may depend much on the dispatch with which it is forwarded," Madison advised Clark. The letter did not reach Clark until 20 Oct., although by that time he had already sent some of the requested information in his responses to TJ's queries on Louisiana (Madison, *Papers*, *Sec. of State Ser.*, 5:429, 551-6; *Terr. Papers*, 9:32-3, 35).

To Jacob Wagner

Sir Monticello Sep. 14. 03.

Be pleased to fill up a commission for Abraham Bishop of Connecticut to be Collector of Newhaven. the stile of the commission to Samuel Bishop, his father, now dead, will be a guide in the present case. I believe it will be best for you to send it to mr Madison direct for his signature, & to be returned by him to you instead of forwarding it to me, as I shall then probably be on the road to Washington where I can sign it on my arrival. Accept my salutations [& respects]

TH: JEFFERSON

PrC (DLC); faint; at foot of text: "Mr. Wagner." Recorded in SJL with notation "commn Abr. Bishop."

The State Department recorded the appointment of ABRAHAM BISHOP at 16 Sep. (see Memorandum from State Department, printed at 11 Nov. 1803).

From Edwin B. Smith

DR. SIR, Warm Springs Spr. 15th. 1803

I will acknowledge it as a particular favour if you will lend me 200$ if it suits your convenence. I shall save 500 by it & will return it in 6 months or if it will be inconvenent to prolong the payment untill that date I will do it in any time you shall mention after 3 months. If you will favour me Sir with this request, it will for ever oblige

Yr. Humble. Sert. EDWIN BN SMITH

RC (MHi); endorsed by TJ as received 25 Sep. and so recorded in SJL.

Edwin B. Smith may have been the same individual who advertised as a merchant in Staunton, Virginia, which is in a county neighboring that of Warm Springs, in August 1801. Someone of the same name advertised as a portrait painter in Lexington, Kentucky, in 1807 (Staunton *Political Mirror*, 11 Aug. 1801; Lexington *Kentucky Gazette*, 29 Dec. 1807).

From James Jones Wilmer

SIR, Baltimore, Septr. 15th. 1803.

Permit me to present you with a Copy of a recent Publication, entitled "Man as he is" &c.—Its favorable reception by virtuous and intelligent minds will be very pleasing to

Sir, Your most respl. and obt. Servant JS. JS. WILMER

RC (DLC); at foot of text: "The President of the United States"; endorsed by TJ as received 25 Sep. and so recorded in SJL. Enclosure: *Man as He Is, and the World as It Goes*, addressed to the citizens of the United States (Baltimore, 1803; Sowerby, No. 1676).

James Jones Wilmer (ca. 1749-1814), a native of Maryland, received his education in London and in Oxford at Christ Church. In 1773, he was ordained in England as an Anglican minister and subsequently returned to Maryland, where he had difficulty securing a church. After 1779, he held a succession of posts in Kent and Harford Counties. He was a prominent advocate of Swedenborgian theology and preached the doctrines of the New Jerusalem Church in Baltimore in

1792. His 1804 Wilmington, Delaware, publication, *Wisdom, which "Cometh Down from Above"; and As Communicated through Mediums*, was dedicated to TJ as "the first distinguished literary character; as well as the ablest statesman in America" (Shaw-Shoemaker, No. 7778). In *Men and Measures, from 1774 to 1809*, printed in Washington in 1809, he acknowledged that TJ had "laid the foundation of much benefit to posterity," but also had been "more calumniated and persecuted" than either of his presidential predecessors (Sowerby, No. 3386). Wilmer advertised plans to establish an academy in Havre de Grace, and he became chaplain to the U.S. Congress from 1809 to 1813 and to the Northwestern army during the War of 1812 (Wilmer, *Memoirs* [Baltimore, 1792]; Washington, *Papers, Rev. War Ser.*, 20:179n; J. Thomas Scharf, *History of Baltimore City and County from the Earliest Period to the Present Day* [Philadelphia, 1881], 588; Baltimore *Republican, or Anti-Democrat*, 16 Sep. 1803; Baltimore *Federal Gazette*, 24 Sep. 1803; Baltimore *American and Commercial Daily Advertiser*, 24 July 1810; Vol. 33:162-4).

From John A. Chevallié

SIR Richmond September 16th. 1803.

I have the honor to send to your Excellency, a letter from General Lafayette which I found at my house at my return from Monticello; a copy of a letter from General Mathieu Dumas to Messrs. Livingston & Monroe; a Note on the actual Situation of the affairs Belonging to Beaumarchais's Estate in America & a Printed Mémorial Which was to have been presented to Congres, if The Executive had raported The said Claim & if it had been Brought to discussion. I flatter myself that The perusal of These papers will be able to Destroy the prepossessions Which have been formed By the the officers of Government against the claims of Beaumarchais & that Justice will soon be granted to his unfortunate family without The intervention of an Ambassador from france.

having been Charged during more than Sixteen years, With These Business, Messrs. hamilton & harrison have often acknowledged my Great Exertions; how hard would be my fate, if others upon mere applications, were to reap the advantages which I have deserved.

I Beg of your Excellency to honor me with an answer & to accept the assurance of the Great regard & Respect With whom I am

Your most obedient humble servant J. A. CHEVALLIÉ

in Case of a Probability of Success, I will be Very happy to Go to the City of Washington & to present myself before the Secretary of The Threasury.

RC (DLC: Gallatin Papers); at foot of first page: "Thomas Jefferson Esquire President of the United States"; endorsed by TJ as received 25 Sep. and so recorded in SJL. Enclosures: (1) Lafayette to TJ, 22 May 1803. (2) Mathieu Dumas to Robert R. Livingston and James Monroe, 1 Prairial Year 11 (21

May 1803), a copy attested by Chevallié, 16 Sep.; Dumas explains that he is the brother-in-law of Louis André Toussaint Delarue, who is married to Pierre Augustin Caron de Beaumarchais's daughter; he outlines the history of transactions between Beaumarchais and Congress during the American Revolutionary War; the U.S. Treasury, repeatedly refusing the Beaumarchais claim, has argued that the matter was settled by a payment of 1,000,000 livres to Beaumarchais by Louis XVI; great nations, Dumas declares, have a moral obligation to honor their debts, and the United States should feel a particular obligation to repay those who supported the American Revolution; reminding the envoys that he fought on the American side in that war, Dumas states his readiness to write to TJ to seek justice for his unfortunate family (DLC: Gallatin Papers). (3) "Nottes Sur la Situation Actuelle des affaires de la Succession Beaumarchais en Amérique," signed by Chevallié in Richmond on 16 Sep.; he states that Delarue and Dumas, who have interests in the Beaumarchais family's claim, received a request from Gallatin for more information from the French government about the million livres received by Beaumarchais from the king on 10 June 1776; that money, Chevallié avers, was for secret intelligence services by Beaumarchais on behalf of France, not for matériel for the United States; Monroe has examined the details and finds no legal evidence against the family's claim, only conjecture and insinuation; given the friendly relations between France and the United States, it would be a political advantage if the two governments could resolve the matter honorably and expeditiously (same). (4) *The Memorial and Claim of Amélie Eugénie Caron de Beaumarchais, Wife of André Toussaint de La Rue, Heir and Representative of Caron de Beaumarchais by Her Agent John Augustus Chevallié* (Richmond, 1801), outlining the arrangement made between Beaumarchais and Silas Deane in 1776; Beaumarchais expended, for cargoes of arms, ammunition, and clothing, plus freight, insurance, and other charges, more than 5,000,000 livres, of which only about 3,000,000 livres was reimbursed; with interest, the unpaid balance amounts to more than 3,300,000 livres; Beaumarchais repeatedly solicited Congress for payment, but the Treasury rejected some parts of the claim, and Beaumarchais's enemies used evidence of the payment of the million livres in France to give the impression that Beaumarchais had received all that was due to him; the memorial presents arguments and evidence to refute the deductions and the crediting of that payment against the claim (Shaw-Shoemaker, No. 1429).

MORE THAN SIXTEEN YEARS: Chevallié first traveled to the United States from France in the mid-1780s to pursue a claim of his father, who had been associated with Beaumarchais in the venture to supply arms during the Revolutionary War. Chevallié became a partner in a New York City mercantile firm and acted as Beaumarchais's agent in the United States (Syrett, *Hamilton*, 20:355-61; Brian N. Morton and Donald C. Spinelli, *Beaumarchais and the American Revolution* [Lanham, Md., 2003], 290, 293; Vol. 11:55).

From Albert Gallatin

DEAR SIR New York 16th Septer. 1803

I have not heard from you for a long while, not since I returned the letters of our Ministers at Paris & forwarded the copy of Mr Marbois's letter & some letters from Simons. I trust that this is not owing to want of health, but feel somewhat uneasy, as I have not even received any indirect account of you. I had waited for your opinion of the proper answer to Mr Marbois, but have in the meanwhile sketched a very general answer which I enclose for your consideration. Finding difficulties in copper engraving which might have created delay, I have concluded to have all the certificates merely printed at Washington, and have directed the Register to take all the necessary measures to have the whole printed within ten days after notice given to the printers; so that the moment Mr Baring arrives and the form of the certificates shall have been agreed on, the whole may be executed at once. You may, therefore, rely that the whole will be ready for delivery the day that a law shall have been passed to carry the convention into effect.

I enclose a letter from John Pintard who resided some time at New Orleans, on the subject of Louisiana. He is certainly mistaken as to the population of the province, but some of his hints may be of service.

Being disappointed in horses, having lost one on the road, & the fever here & in Philada. having deranged the usual travelling resources, I do not think that I will be able to leave this before the 22d inst., or arrive in the city before the 30th. So far as relates to my own office, this short delay will not be attended with any inconvenience, as I have received here & am arranging the documents necessary for Congress.

With sincere respect & attachment Your obdt. Servt.

Albert Gallatin

RC (DLC); at foot of text: "Thomas Jefferson President of the United States"; endorsed by TJ as received from the Treasury Department on 25 Sep. and "Marbois answ. new stock. Pintard" and so recorded in SJL. Enclosure: John Pintard to Albert Gallatin, New Rochelle, New York, 14 Sep. 1803, enclosing observations on New Orleans recollected from his visit there in 1801; he notes that revenues under the Spanish administration included a six percent duty on imports, an unknown duty on exports, and an internal tax of $.50 per barrel of flour that was used principally for lighting the streets of New Orleans; the other revenues were used primarily to support the civil and military departments, the estimated costs being $900,000 in times of peace and $1,500,000 in periods of war; Spain covered the costs of the Louisiana colony with proceeds from mines in Mexico; the salaries of civil officers were moderate, the governor's salary not exceeding $5,000, but all government officers "were open to bribery & corruption & to peculation"; using "the Bishops returns of marriageable females, within his diocese," Pintard estimates the population of the province, including Mobile and Pensacola, at 156,000, excluding "Blacks," and, according to 1801 census returns, New Orleans had a population of 12,000; Pintard notes that the choice of governor will be very important in establishing the new government; he should speak French and must be provided with an adequate salary, because "the reciprocation of hospitalities, in a very hospitable country, will be expensive"; a house and steward must be provided at government expense; the secretary should also be bilingual; noting that the colony was accustomed to a military regimen, Pintard recommends that the choice of a commanding officer be given as much consideration as that of governor, for he must be firm and decisive "to support, in case of necessity, the civil arm"; Pintard recommends introducing some of the respected city officials from the 12-member town council of New Orleans into the new American system of jurisprudence to give it credibility and energy to contend with "riots of untractable sailors, drunken Indians, and Kentuckey boatmen, more vicious & savage then either"; the practice of having the military, "which guards the city by night," support the police ought to be continued; Pintard notes that the Spanish government maintains the clergy and a bishopric at New Orleans and recommends that if the U.S. "Government could devise some expedient to continue the existing salaries, during the lives of the present incumbents, it would attach the priests to the new order of things, and their influence would be serviceable," the expense being not more than $3,000 per year; as to the custom house and collection of revenues, Pintard recommends an "entire new set of officers, from the Collector to the Inspector" because "None of the present race can be trusted—they are all hacknied in the practices of bribery & cheating the revenue," and he contemplates the establishment of a custom house at the English Turn, about 18 miles below New Orleans (Gallatin, *Papers*, 8:678-9; *Terr. Papers*, 9:49-54; Jedidiah Morse, *The American Gazetteer*, 2d ed. [Charlestown, Mass., 1804]). Other enclosure not found.

For the correspondence RETURNED and FORWARDED, see Gallatin's letter to the president of 5 Sep.

Gallatin met with New York City merchant JOHN PINTARD on 13 Sep. and evidently discussed the Queries on Louisiana, printed at 9 July (*Terr. Papers*, 9:49; Vol. 17:352-3n; enclosure described above). For other estimates on the POPULATION OF THE PROVINCE and New Orleans, see ASP, *Miscellaneous*, 1:348, 381-4; Daniel Clark to TJ, 18 Aug.; and William C. C. Claiborne to TJ, 24 Aug.

From George III, King of Great Britain

George The Third, By the Grace of God, of the United Kingdom of Great Britain and Ireland King, Defender of the Faith, Duke of Brunswick and Lunenburgh, Arch-Treasurer and Prince Elector of the Holy Roman Empire &ca.—To The United States of America sendeth Greeting.—Our Good Friends. Having Nothing more at Heart than to cultivate and improve the Friendship and good Understanding which so happily subsist between Us, and having the fullest Confidence in the Fidelity, Prudence and other good Qualities of Our Trusty and Well-beloved Anthony Merry Esquire, We have thought proper to appoint him Our Envoy Extraordinary and Minister Plenipotentiary to reside with You, not doubting from the Experience We have had of his good Conduct on other Occasions but that he will continue to merit Our Approbation, and at the same Time conciliate Our Friendship and Good Will, by a strict Observance of the Instructions he has received from Us to evince to You our constant Friendship and sincere Desire to cement and improve the Union and good Correspondence between Us: We therefore desire that you will give a favorable Reception to Our said Envoy Extraordinary and Minister Plenipotentiary, and that you will give entire Credence to whatever he may represent to You in Our Name, especially when, in Obedience to Our Orders, he assures you of Our Esteem and Regard, and of Our hearty Wishes for your Prosperity. And so We recommend You to the Protection of The Almighty.—Given at Our Court at St. James' the 16th. Day of September 1803 in the Forty Third Year of Our Reign.

Your very good Friend GEORGE R.

Dupl (DNA: RG 59, Communications from Heads of State); entirely in a clerk's hand; at head of text: "Copy"; at foot of text: "Hawkesbury," representing a countersignature; endorsed by Jacob Wagner as received 28 Nov. and "Copy of Mr. Merry's credence."

ANTHONY MERRY sailed from England on 25 Sep. and landed at Norfolk on the evening of 4 Nov. He arrived in Georgetown on the 26th of that month and presented his credentials to Madison on the 28th. The following day, Madison took him to meet TJ at the President's House. Merry reported to his government that by accident his first encounter with the president was an awkward meeting in a narrow passageway and that TJ was dressed in his "usual morning attire." In 1806, Josiah Quincy preserved an account of the meeting from Merry that has become famous: "I, in my official costume, found myself, at the hour of reception he had himself appointed, introduced to a man as the President of the United States, not merely in an undress, but actually standing in slippers down at the heels, and both pantaloons, coat, and underclothes indicative of utter slovenliness and indifference to apperances, and in a state of negligence actually studied." This was the first permanent appointment as minister plenipotentiary for the 47-year-old Briton, a career diplomat who had spent much of his career in consular positions or as chargé d'affaires. Lord Hawkesbury had used him, however, as an unofficial envoy in preliminary overtures to France in 1801, and the following year Merry acted as his country's interim minister to France. Rufus King, who described him as "a plain, unassuming and amiable man," had lobbied the British Foreign Office to send Merry to the United States rather than Francis James Jackson. William Cobbett, railing against the appointment of "mere stop-gaps of the corps diplomatique" to represent Britain in the United States, expected puzzled Americans to ask, "*Who* is Mr. Merry?" (Madison, *Papers*, *Sec. of State Ser.*, 3:118-19; 6:xxvii, 17, 103; Edmund Quincy, *Life of Josiah Quincy of Massachusetts* [Boston, 1867], 92-3; William H. Masterson, *Tories and Democrats: British Diplomats in Pre-Jacksonian America* [College Station, Tex., 1985], 74-7; Lucia Stanton, "Looking for Liberty: Thomas Jefferson and the British Lions," *Eighteenth-Century Studies*, 26 [1993], 650; DNB; Vol. 35:295, 297n; Vol. 38:584, 588n).

From Thomas Martin

MY DEAR SIR Lexington Kentucky Sept. 16. 1803

I have thought proper to make my present situation known to some of the Senators in Congress, and as I have always experienced your friendship, must once more beg your Attention to my Claims, as it might be a means of releiveing me and my little family from poverty.

It seems that an Arsenal is to be fixd at the Mouth of Licking I do not know Whether it will be an Object or not: Should it be, and you should think me Adequate for the task, do beg the favor

I am with great Esteem Your Obt. Huml Servt.

THO. MARTIN

RC (PHi); at head of text: "To the President of the U. States"; endorsed by TJ as received 21 Dec. and "for emploiment at Arsenel" and so recorded in SJL with notation "W."

In another letter dated 16 Sep., Martin made his PRESENT SITUATION KNOWN to Senator John Breckinridge, noting in it that he had also written Senator James Jackson of Georgia and "my good friend Mr. Brown," probably Senator John Brown of Kentucky. Martin asks Breckinridge to present his letter to the president, as well as a certificate from the senator's brother, Robert Breckinridge, regarding his rank during the American Revolution. Martin hopes Breckinridge can help him secure an appointment relating to the proposed arsenal in Kentucky. "If my nation forgets me," he lamented, his family "must infalliably Starve as I have had no other trade but War" (RC in DLC: Breckinridge Family Papers).

ONCE MORE BEG YOUR ATTENTION: for Martin's earlier request for an appointment, see Vol. 37:313.

In April 1803, TJ and Henry Dearborn determined to establish an ARSENAL, magazine, and barracks near the mouth of the LICKING River at Newport, Kentucky. The site was located and acquired by Charles Scott, and James Taylor of Newport supervised the erection of the works (John E. Kleber, ed., *The Kentucky Encyclopedia* [Lexington, Ky., 1992], 680; Madison, *Papers, Sec. of State Ser.*, 5:459; Dearborn to Charles Scott, 12 Apr., 11 June, 23 Sep. 1803, Dearborn to James Taylor, 12 Apr., 15 June, 13 July 1803, all in DNA: RG 107, MLS). Martin was appointed military storekeeper of the post the following year (Vol. 37:313n).

From Thomas Munroe

SIR, Washington 16th September 1803

The Post of last night brought a Letter from you to Mr. Latrobe, which I will forward to him immediately I can ascertain where it will probably find him—. He came to the City on the evening of the 9th. Instant, and, I am informed, went off in the Stage yesterday morning—I saw him once only, and then had but a few minutes conversation with him—I do not know when he is to be here again, or what he expects to have done before the meeting of Congress—the enclosed Letter, however, I presume, contains a full account of the progress & State of the public buildings, and of all matters committed to him by the President, as he told me he should write such a Letter before he left the City.—

The Carters and most of the Labourers on the Streets were discharged four or five days ago—A few hands have since been employed in making some repairs which were deemed absolutely necessary about the Capitol, the bridge at the presidents gate &c—Several other jobs were pointed out by different inhabitants on Pennsya. avenue elsewhere which they importuned me much to have done but I have declined doing any thing, until your return, that was not absolutely necessary & directed by you.—I enclose a Memdm of disbursements since 31t. ulto. (the date of my last sketch) which, with prior Expenditures, Amt. to about $22,000 leaving about $28,000 of the $50,000 unexpended.—I have lately recd $1200 more of Genl Forrests debt; about $400 still remains due from him—I have also recd a few hundred Dollars from other Debtors against whom suits have been brought—. The receipts for the year 1803 will be very small indeed I fear—I have not been able to sell a single Lot since the last Session of Congress—The effects of the public sales at $10. 20 & 30 ℔ lot, last year will long be felt I'm afraid—the few offers I have recd this year have been so very low as to forbid the thought of accepting them, conceiving it would have been unwarrantably sacraficing the property.—

I have the honor to be with the greatest respect, Sir Yr mo Ob Servt.

THOMAS MUNROE

RC (DLC); at foot of text: "President of United States"; endorsed by TJ as received 19 Sep. and so recorded in SJL. Enclosure: Benjamin H. Latrobe to TJ, 14 Sep. (recorded in SJL as received 19 Sep. but not found). Other enclosure printed below.

TJ's LETTER to Benjamin Henry Latrobe, recorded in SJL at 14 Sep., has not been found.

For the DEBT that Uriah Forrest owed to the City of Washington and information on the PUBLIC SALES of lots in the city, see Vol. 37:604n and Vol. 38:174-5n, 404-5.

ENCLOSURE

Account of Public Expenditures

Expenditures from 1 to 16 Sep 1803		
on Capitol		
for Lumber	117.10	
B H Latrobes Salary	283.33	
workmen &. Labrs.	760.35	
Stone (foundation)	200.	
Cordage	14.02	
sundry small articles	10.37	1385.17
on Streets		
for Labourers & Carters wages	938.41	
Lumber for Bridges	61.79	
Blacksmiths work to Labourers tools	15.96	1016.16

Presidents House		
for Casting lead for sash weights	19.52	
Ironmongery & Blacksmiths work	24.75	44.27
		$2,445.60

MS (DLC); entirely in Munroe's hand.

From James Wilson

SIR [on or before 16 Sep. 1803]

It is with considrable embarassment I attempt to address you, conscious that I have no Claim to your Patronage either from recommendation or services done the states, my dependance is entirely upon your Known Benevolence towards the necessitous it is this that induces me in this manner earnestly to solicit your Favour that you would be pleas'd in your Goodness to have me promot'd to some inferior place in the Revenue or any other department that shall seem most agreeable to, Sir, your generous intentions, I take the liberty to observe that my Idea's dont lead me to expect any respectable situation I will be well satisfied with any small place that will barely procure a subsistance for my Familey in any part of the union that you shall in your Pleasure think proper, should you think me an Object of your Bounty I hope, Sir, by my deligence and care to shew my thankfullness for such unmerretid favour JAMES WILSON

RC (DNA: RG 59, LAR); undated; at head of text: "To Thomas Jefferson President of the United States"; endorsed by TJ as received 16 Sep. and so recorded in SJL with notation "for office. he is from Baltimore"; also endorsed by TJ: "for a small office. Baltimore."

To James Lyle

DEAR SIR Monticello Sep. 17. 03.

According to request I have examined here my papers respecting the bond to R. Harvie, and a memorandum in writing given me by him during the interval of his visit to this neighborhood preceding his death, enables me to add the following facts & observations to those contained in my note of July 22 1795, furnished to you. the difficulties in R. Harvie's account respect those sums of £25, of £19 and of £70.

1. The £25 was charged to me Aug. 31. 1768 by Kippen & co. as [allowed] R. Harvie on my acct. & no credit was given me for it by him. in the memm abovementioned he says that 'William Hickman has a credit of £25. in Aug. 1768. by Neill Campbell by an order of Colo. Jefferson.' all my papers to 1768. having been lost in my mother's house, which was burnt that year, I have no means of examining the state of things between Wm. Hickman & myself. but he was my overseer a little before that, & it is possible & not unlikely that this was a paiment to him for me, & that I recieved credit for it in his account. I acquiesce therefore in this explanation by mr Harvie & give up this article.

2. The £19. was part of a sum of £42–15–11½ of which R. Harvie was the bearer to me, and as he charged the delivery, he ought to have credited the reciept of it. mr Harvie says in his memm 'he can recollect nothing of the cash transaction in Williamsburg, (the £42–15–11½) but he sees I am charged 'to cash £19.' in his own handwriting, which he is sure is just.' this is true: the objection being that he omitted to credit it as recd on my acct. from N. Campbell. my notes of July 22. 1795. & the exact coincidence of fractional sums there observable, place this article as I concieve beyond the possibility of doubt. it was an error of mr Harvie, who was as honest a man as lived, but not a clear-headed one. the bond then ought to be corrected as follows.

1775. Apr. 18.	Bond to R. Harvie given for		£198–12–7.½
1772. Apr. 24.	By credit omitted for cash		
	from N. Campbell	£19– 0–0	
	Int. on do. to Apr. 18. 1775	2–16–8	21–16–8
	gives what should have been the amount of the bond		176–16–

3. What is observed as to the £70[1] in my notes of July 22. 1795. is just, and on a settlement of that day, had it taken place, even had the Donalds been bankrupt, it would have been the loss of mr Harvie for not using due diligence in demanding paiment, or notifying me of the non-paiment; & the rather as the stores of the two concerns were not an hundred yards apart. but as I had some accounts to settle with the different firms of the Donalds, I pressed on them the allowance of Anderson's whole assumpsit of £170. of which this £70. was part: and in a settlement with mr Strange in 1799. I obtained an allowance of it; as that that article is now redeemed from difficulty, and the responsibility for that sum has returned upon me. an endorsement therefore of the £21–16–8 on the bond reducing it to £176–16 currency equal to £132–12 sterl. that sum, with interest from Apr. 19. 1783. is what I

am now justly liable for to you on that bond. Accept my affectionate salutations and assurances of constant esteem & respect.

Th: Jefferson

PrC (MHi); blurred; at foot of first page: "James Lyle esq."; endorsed by TJ in ink on verso. Enclosed in TJ to Lyle, 15 Oct.

according to request: see Vol. 40:602-3.

An undated memorandum, entitled "A memo of Entrys on Richd Harvie & Co Books" and presumably in Harvie's hand, attempted to untangle several transactions from the 1760s and 1770s that also involved neill campbell, a factor for Kippen & Co., the predecessor of Lyle's firm Henderson, McCaul & Co. Campbell managed the firm's Albemarle County store until the end of 1768 and afterward its store in Richmond. TJ apparently did not have this memorandum at hand while attempting to modify his bond to Harvie in July 1795, when he claimed a deduction of £25 from the bond's total (MS in MHi, undated, endorsed by TJ: "Notes on the bond to R. Harvie but see my letter of Sep. 17. 1803. to James Lyle, settling this bond at £176–16 currcy. = £132–12 sterl. & int. from Apr. 19. 1783"; mb, 1:26n; Vol. 28:413).

For TJ's payment to the firms of the donalds, James and Robert Donald & Co. and Donald, Scott & Co., see Vol. 30:609. As part of this payment, TJ reassumed responsibility for a portion of a bond that had previously shifted from him to Richard Anderson, the Donalds' Albemarle representative (mb, 1:751, 2:996; Vol. 16:196n; Vol. 22:203-4; Vol. 28:416).

[1]Preceding three words and financial figure interlined.

From James Brown

Dear Sir, Lexington Septr. 18th. 1803

The sentiments of the Inhabitants of the western Country, respecting the purchase of Louisiana must have been fully conveyed thro' the public prints to those who are Constitutionally authorized to ratify or reject the Cession. Considering the future peace and prosperity of our State as depending upon the decision of the next Congress, we await their determination with a degree of sollicitude which can be more easily conceived than described. Our late elections have terminated in favor of the republican interest, and we are happy in being represented by men from whom the real sense of the people can be fairly collected. On this interesting question we shall expect an exertion of all their Zeal, talent, and influence. If they shall be so fortunate as to meet with support from the republican representatives of the other States we may anticipate a favorable issue to the most important measure which has occurred in the history of our Government.

Should our hopes and wishes be reallized in the ratification of the purchase, I presume New Orleans will become a Port of Entry. Having a disposition to remove to that place, I take the liberty of expressing my wish to fill the Office of Collector of the Revenue. Of my character and qualifications to discharge the duties of the Office you can easily be correctly informed; And should you honor me with the appointment, I shall be ready to remove so soon as you may direct.

I am well aware that this application may appear premature, but when I reflect that the whole of your time will be usefully employed during the Session, I consider it better to apprize you of my wishes at a moment when you may have more leisure to attend to them

With every sentiment of respect and esteem I am Sir Your Most obt Hble Servant—

JAMES BROWN

RC (DNA: RG 59, LAR); addressed: "The President of the United States Washington-City"; franked; postmarked 20 Sep.; endorsed by TJ as received 4 Oct. and "to be Collector N. Orleans" and so recorded in SJL.

James Brown (1766-1835) was a native of Virginia and brother of Kentucky senator John Brown. A law student of George Wythe, Brown moved to Lexington, Kentucky, in 1789, where he put his legal acumen to use as an attorney and a professor of law and politics at Transylvania University. TJ appointed him secretary of the Orleans Territory in 1804, and he relocated to New Orleans that same year. He declined TJ's offer of a federal judgeship, but accepted an appointment as U.S. attorney for Orleans in 1805. His legal skills were also utilized in creating a civil code for the territory in 1806 and framing Louisiana's first state constitution. He represented Louisiana in the U.S. Senate from 1813 to 1817 and again from 1819 to 1823, when he was appointed minister to France. Returning to America in 1829, he settled in Philadelphia, where he died (ANB).

Republicans swept the LATE ELECTIONS to Congress in Kentucky. Reporting the returns on 4 Aug., the Frankfort *Palladium* assured its distant friends that the state would send "an *unanimous republican representation*" to Washington (Frankfort *Palladium*, 4, 11 Aug. 1803; New York *American Citizen*, 22 Aug. 1803).

To David Campbell

DEAR SIR Monticello Sep. 19. 03.

On the reciept of your favor of July 1.[1] I communicated with the Secretary at war on the subject of the robbery committed by the Cherokee Indian, and we both concur in the opinion that your proceedings were strictly proper, and conformable to the provisions of the act of Congress of 1802. c. 13. in cases of violence committed by Indians on our citizens within their territory. where within our own, they are bound by our laws as other aliens & citizens are. the acquisition of Louisiana promises us future tranquility with our Indian neighbors. it removes, in the first instance, all foreign nations to a distance from which their intrigues cannot reach these ignorant people to our disturbance. and ultimately it opens an asylum for them, where we can offer them a country better suited to their manner of

THE

HISTORY

OF

LOUISIANA,

OR OF

THE WESTERN PARTS

OF

VIRGINIA AND CAROLINA:

Containing a DESCRIPTION of the

Countries that lie on both Sides of the River MISSISIPPI:

With an ACCOUNT of the

SETTLEMENTS, INHABITANTS, SOIL,
CLIMATE, AND PRODUCTS.

Tranflated from the FRENCH

Of M. LE PAGE DU PRATZ;

With fome Notes and Obfervations relating to our Colonies.

A NEW EDITION.

LONDON,
Printed for T. BECKET, Corner of the Adelphi, in the Strand.
MDCCLXXIV.

History of Louisiana by Le Page du Pratz

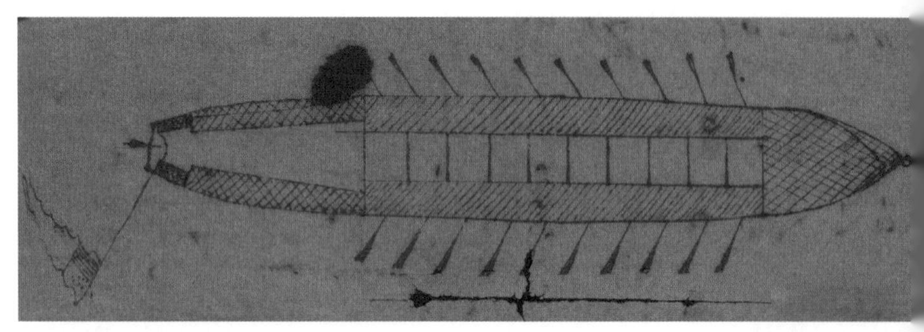

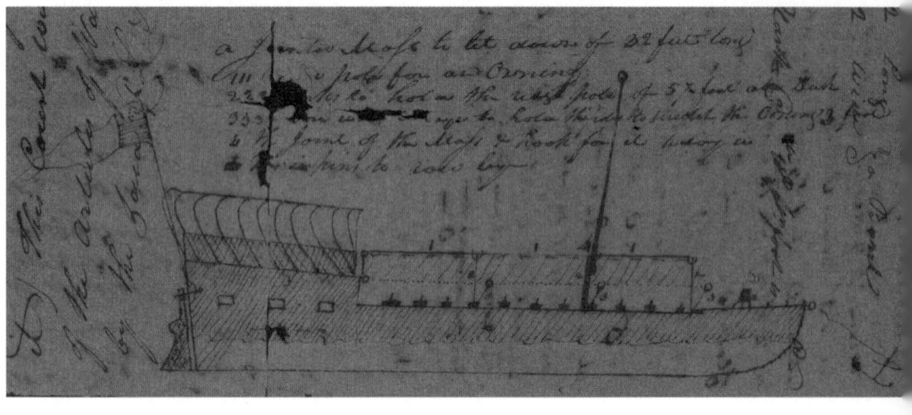

Boat for the Western Expedition

William Clark

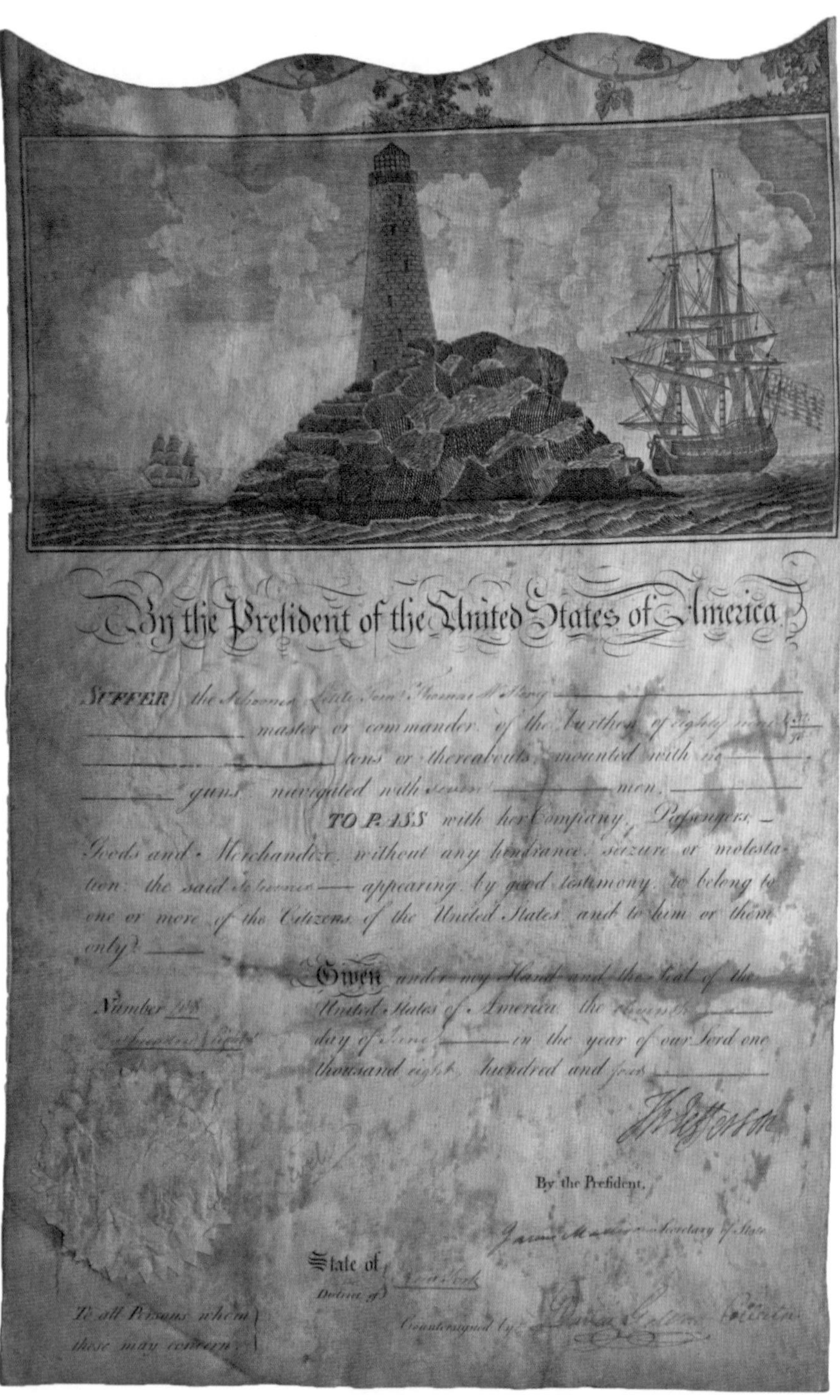

By the President of the United States of America.

SUFFER the Schooner Little Tom Thomas M. Story master or commander of the burthen of eighty nine tons or thereabouts, mounted with no guns navigated with seven men,

TO PASS with her Company, Passengers, Goods and Merchandize, without any hindrance, seizure or molestation: the said Schooner appearing by good testimony to belong to one or more of the Citizens of the United States and to him or them only.

Number 198

Given under my Hand and the Seal of the United States of America the eleventh day of June in the year of our Lord one thousand eight hundred and four

Th: Jefferson

By the President.

James Madison Secretary of State

State of New York

District of

To all Persons whom these may concern.

Countersigned by

Sea Letter

Monticello by Robert Mills

William Charles Coles Claiborne

View of New Orleans

Washington Jockey Club Races.

WILL commence on the Second Tueſday in November next over an excellent Courſe well prepared, and encloſed with a poſt and rail fence.

1ſt day. A Sweepſtake of 1600 dollars.

2d. do. A purſe of 400 dollars—4 mile heats,

3d. do. A do. of 200 dollars—3 mile heats.

4th. A 50 guinea ſilver cup——10 horſes.

5th. A handſome City and Town purſe. 2 mile heats.

All Horſes, Mares and Geldings to be entered and run agreeaby to the Rules of the Club, and to carry the following weights.

An aged horſe 126, a ſix years old 120, a five years old 112, a four years old 100 and a three years old 90 pounds.—Three pounds being allowed to Fillies, Mares, and Geldings.

The following tolls to be paid at the gate to the Clerk of the Courſe Mr. C. Baily, or any perſon authoriſed by him to receive the ſame.

Four wheel Carriages,	1 Dollar each.
Two ditto ditto,	50 Cents Ditto.
Every man and horſe,	25 Cents.

Booths will be let on application to the ſubſcriber,

It is probable that the 2d, and 3d days purſes will be encreaſed, as the ſurplus of the tolls after defraying the expences &c. will be added to them.

CH's M'LAUGHLIN,

Sept. 10, 1803. Secr'y & Treaſurer.

N. B. The CLUB will meet at the Union Tavern on the evening preceding the firſt day's race.

Notice of Washington Jockey Club Races

living in exchange for theirs, holding out the hand of friendship, patronage & commerce there as well as here; & thus making this acquisition the means of consolidating instead of diluting our settlements. I am just in the hurry of departure for Washington & therefore must here offer you my friendly salutations, & assurances of great respect & esteem. TH: JEFFERSON

P.S. the Secretary at war informs me that it has not been in contemplation to remove Doctr. Vandyke from S.W. point.

PrC (DLC); at foot of text: "Judge Campbell."

COMMUNICATED WITH THE SECRETARY AT WAR: TJ to Dearborn, 26 Aug.

[1]Date interlined in place of "Aug. [1.]."

To Andrew Jackson

DEAR SIR Monticello Sep. 19. 1803.

On reciept of your favor of Aug. 7. I made it the subject of some communication with the Secretary at War. he informs me that the charge against Colo. Butler on which stress is laid is for disobedience of orders & neglect of duty for not going to fort Adams when ordered, & for an absence from his command of near twelve months without leave. on this he will have the benefit of a trial by his peers, who no doubt will do him justice.

The acquisition of Louisiana is of immense importance to our future tranquility insomuch as it removes the intrigues of foreign nations to a distance from which they can no longer produce disturbance between the Indians & us. it will also open an asylum for these unhappy people, in a country which may suit their habits of life better than what they now occupy, which perhaps they will be willing to exchange with us: and to our posterity it opens a noble prospect of provision for ages. the world will here see such an extent of country under a free and moderate government as it has never yet seen. being in the hurry of departure for Washington I must here offer you my friendly salutations & assurances of great respect & esteem.

TH: JEFFERSON

PrC (DLC); at foot of text: "Andrew Jackson esq."

COMMUNICATION WITH THE SECRETARY: see TJ to Dearborn, 26 Aug. and Dearborn to TJ, 31 Aug. 1803 (second letter).

To Stephen Thacher

Monticello Sep. 19. 1803.

Th: Jefferson presents his respectful salutations to mr Thatcher, and his thanks for the excellent oration of which he was pleased to send him a copy. while such sentiments as are therein expressed animate the breasts of our citizens, we have every thing to hope for their happiness & freedom. he owes mr Thatcher his particular thanks for the friendly terms of his letter.

RC (MeHi); addressed: "Stephen Thatcher esquire Kennebunk"; franked; postmarked Charlottesville. PrC (DLC); endorsed by TJ in ink on verso.

HIS LETTER: Thacher to TJ, 25 Aug. 1803.

Agreement with John H. Craven

Articles of agreement made & concluded between Th: Jefferson and John H. Craven, both of the county of Albemarle.

It is agreed between these parties that the lease of lands & other property of the sd Thomas at Monticello, originally made by the sd Thomas to the sd John H. for five years, & now existing, shall be renewed and continued from the end of the sd five years for the term of four years more in addition to the said five, & shall be considered as if it had been an original lease for nine years, all the covenants & conditions therein provided for the course of five years being hereby extended to the additional four years: that the rent during the four additional years shall be uniformly the same as provided for the 2d. 3d. 4th. & 5th. years of the preceding term, and the rotation of crops through which each field was to go in the first five years, shall be continued for it uniformly in the same course through the four additional years.

In consideration of the young labourers grown & growing up, it is agreed that after the 1st. day of August 1804. the girl called Fanny, daughter of Ned, shall be withdrawn from the lease, and return into the possession & service of the said Thomas: that he may also withdraw any other young female now under the age of titheable when he shall think proper, delivering the girl called Ursula, not now in the lease, in exchange for her: and that after the 31st. day of Dec. 1808. he may withdraw the man called Ned, the elder, delivering in lieu of him a labourer of equal value.

The said Thomas agrees also to underpin & plaister the house inhabited by the sd John H. to wall up the cellar under the same which shall be dug by the sd John H. & to build a shed round the barn in the course of this & the next year.

The division fence between the two parties shall be maintained at their joint & equal expence: and each party covenants at the desire of the other to execute a formal lease of the purport of the above agreement: Witness our hands this 20th. day of September 1803.

TH: JEFFERSON
JOHN H. CRAVEN

MS (MHi); in TJ's hand, signed by TJ and Craven; endorsed by TJ: "renewed agreement for 4. additional years."

For TJ's August 1800 agreement with Craven, NOW EXISTING and to be RENEWED, see Vol. 32:108-9. ROTATION OF CROPS: see Vol. 32:110. TJ added four years to the rotation plan, making it nine years in all (same).

FANNY, DAUGHTER of Edward (NED) and Jane (Jenny) Gillette, was born in 1788. TJ brought her to Washington in 1806 to be trained in French cookery by TJ's chef Honoré Julien. She was married to David Hern, who remained at Monticello (Stanton, *Free Some Day*, 62-4, 87-8, 129, Gillette and Hern Family Trees).

Born in 1787, URSULA, daughter of Bagwell and Minerva Granger, was the only family member not leased to Craven in the 1800 agreement. Instead she went to Washington to be trained as a pastry chef in the President's House. She returned to Monticello in 1802, after giving birth to her first child. She was married to Wormley Hughes (same, 45, 129, 135, George & Ursula Family Tree; Betts, *Farm Book*, pt. 1, 57, 60; Annette Gordon-Reed, *The Hemingses of Monticello: An American Family* [New York, 2008], 568-9; Vol. 36:671).

From Barthélemy Faujas de Saint-Fond

au muséum national
d'histoire naturelle a paris,
le 20 Septembre 1803

MONSIEUR LE PRESIDENT

J'ose prendre la liberté de recommander à vos Bontés un libraire qui va etablir un Commerce de librairie dans les etats unis de l'amerique; il a demeuré plusieurs annés a paris ches messieurs Levrault qui m'ont dit Beaucoup de Bien de lui, et qui lui feront parvenir les meilleur ouvrages, particulierement dans la classe des Sciences; il porte dailleurs avec lui un fond assés Considerable de Bons livres.

J'eu l'honneur, il y a environ un mois de vous envoyer par un jeune americain qui frequentoit Beaucoup le jardin des plantes de paris, le premiere tome, d'un ouvrage de Geologie que je viens de publier, dans lequel já fait figurer plusieur animaux fossiles, parmi lesquels le *megalonix* du paragaÿ, qui est dans le Cabinet d'histoire naturelle de Madrid et dont vous avés trouvé des restes dans l'amerique Septentrionale; aussitot que le Second tome qu'on imprime, verra le jour, j'aurai l'honneur de vous le faire parvenir, en vous priant de vouloir

le recevoir avec Bonté et Comme un homage de mon respect pour vos Connoissances dans les hautes parties de l'histoire de la nature.
Je suis avec un profond respect Monsieur le president votre trés humble et trés obeissant Serviteur FAUJAS-ST FOND

EDITORS' TRANSLATION

National Museum of Natural History
MISTER PRESIDENT, Paris, 20 Sep. 1803

I dare take the liberty of recommending to you a bookseller who is going to found a business in the United States of America. He lived in Paris for several years, working for the Levraults, who praise him highly. They will furnish him with the best works, especially in the sciences. He is already bringing a large stock of good books with him.

About a month ago, I had the honor of sending you, through a young American who has spent considerable time in the Paris botanical garden, the first volume of a work of geology that I just published. In the book I depict several animal fossils, including the megalonyx from Paraguay, now at the natural history collection in Madrid. Remains of the megalonyx have also been found in North America. The second volume is in press. As soon as it is published, I shall have the honor of sending it to you. Please accept it with kindness and as a homage to your knowledge of the deepest realms of natural history.

With deep respect, Mister President, I am your very humble and obedient servant. FAUJAS-ST FOND

RC (DLC); below signature: "l'un des administrateurs du jardin des plantes et du muséum national d'histoire naturelle"; endorsed by TJ as received 11 Oct. 1804 and "by Fleischer. bookseller"; so recorded in SJL, but as received 10 Oct. Enclosed in William Fleischer to TJ, 8 Oct. 1804.

MESSIEURS LEVRAULT: a few years earlier, the Strasbourg publishing, type manufacturing, and bookselling firm of the Levrault family had opened a branch in Paris. The company formed relationships with businesses in various countries (Frédéric Barbier, *Trois cents ans de librairie et d'imprimerie: Berger-Levrault, 1676-1830* [Geneva, 1979], 203-11).

ENVIRON UN MOIS: see Faujas to TJ, 12 Aug.

The botanical garden known as the JARDIN DES PLANTES was the foundation for the creation of the Muséum d'Histoire Naturelle in 1793 (Tulard, *Dictionnaire Napoléon*, 1212).

From James Monroe

DEAR SIR London Sepr. 20. 1803.

I send you by Mr. Law a book from a Mr. Williams of this place who was presented to me by Mr. Barlow, as an old friend of Dr. Franklin. He appears to be a well enformed worthy man. If you chuse to answer it I will present the answer. He stood ill with his govt. some years since, but is on tolerable footing with it now. Your answer if you send one will certainly be spoken of, tho' I presume not published, as he is a prudent man. If you chuse to give thro me a verbal one I shall be careful to deliver it in a suitable manner; I see no impropriety in either course, and well know that he wod. be gratified to receive a line from you.

I had doubts on my arrival in France whether yr. correspondence with certain characters there produc'd a good or ill effect; and hinted the same to you. I had no doubt before I came away that on the whole it was useful. I am also persuaded that the continuance of it on literary subjects only will be useful. The national institute is perhaps the strongest body in France, the Executive excepted. You stand well with that body, and it appears to me important that you preserve your footing with it. Under its present organization it is less independent than by its first institution; yet it has an influence in France which is powerful. Lacepede, Dupont-Nemours, Volney, who are yr. principal correspondents, have characters wh. secure any one with whom they correspond from compromitment. They have the highest respect & attachment for you and are delighted with your attention. I am convinc'd that the French gentlemen who have been in America, who retain in general a strong affection for the country, have and do promote by their opinions & exertions, the common interest & good understanding wh. subsists between them.

I saw Genls. La Fayette & Kusciusko often. They are the men you always knew them to be. La Fayette has the same ardor that he had when he began the French revolution while you were in France. He had unfortunately dislocated his thigh in its junction with the hip, & experienced unexampled sufferings by the application of a new invented machine, wh. the surgeons thot. necessary to his cure. The prospect, tho' doubtful when I came away, was in favor of his perfect recovery. I have not heard from him since. Kusciusko lives near the barrier St Andre not far from St. Antoine, where he cultivates his own garden. Col: Mercer & myself on our first visit found him returning from it with his water pots. He thinks seriously of returning to the UStates.

I have declined writing you, as I shod. have done frequently, had I not thought it better to continue the communication uninterrupted, publick and private, thro Mr. Madison. It was of the same advantage to you as if I had written to you, without the inconvenience of hasarding a compromitment of you. My communications to him by Mr. Law are so full as to leave nothing for me to add here. Mr. Law will give you the state of the war and his forebodings of distress to this country, wh. seem to be not altogether visionary.

We are very anxious to hear what has become of our friends in Albemarle. Major Randolph I see is in the H. of Reps., as is Mr. Eppes. How are Mrs. Trist & family & where are they? Col: Lewis Mr Divers & families? Peter & Dabney Carr & families, and how are other friends?

I have had as you have seen a laborious and in some respects very difficult service since my arrival in Europe. My health has not been at all times good; indeed I have had a severe shock or two of short continuance: from wh. I appear at present to be perfectly recovered; tho' I have learned to respect the council you gave me a year or two past, & to be more on my guard. I have exerted my best energies in the cause in which I came, and shall continue to do so, till I get back. If I contribute in any degree to aid yr. administration in the confirmation of the just principles on which it rests, and promotion of the liberty & happiness of my country, it will prove in more than one view a delightful mission to me. My family unite in their affectionate regards to you and yours. With my best wishes for your health and welfare I am very sincerely your friend & servt JAS. MONROE

RC (DLC); endorsed by TJ as received 1 Nov. and so recorded in SJL.

BOOK: David Williams, *Claims of Literature* (see Jefferson's Letters to David Williams, 14 Nov.).

From Craven Peyton

DEAR SIR Stump Island Sept. 20th. 1803

If you can with any possible degree of convenience give me a draft on Gibson & Jefferson in Richmd for One Hundred & fifty Dollars, payable as short a time as your convenience will permit, you will singularly Oblige me, it gives me a singular pleasure to inform you I have every reason to suppose J. Henderson was not able to do any thing with the mill seat in Kentuckey. I am fearfull the proportions in the Oald Mill cant be bought at present for there real value as John will try to impress on there minds that she will still continue to grind by makeing the race deeper, which he is now about therefore it Will take some time to effect the purchase in full I am afraid

with great Respt. Yr. Mst. Ob st. C PEYTON

RC (ViU); with note by TJ at foot of text: "64=213.33" and "£64.=213.33 D Sep. 20. gave ord. on Gibson & Jefferson"; endorsed by TJ as received 20 Sep. and so recorded in SJL.

To Craven Peyton

Dear Sir Monticello Sep. 20. 03.

According to the settlement of interest made by you, and mentioned in your last letter to be sixty four pounds, I now inclose you an order on Gibson & Jefferson for that sum, to wit two hundred & thirteen & a third dollars, which closes the paiments principal & interest for all the lands & interests of the Henderson family hitherto bought. it is payable in 30. days which is as early as I could make it, having to remit the funds after I get to Washington. Accept my friendly salutations Th: Jefferson

RC (Mrs. Charles W. Biggs, Lewisburg, West Virginia, 1950); at foot of text: "Mr. Craven Peyton." PrC (ViU); with enclosure pressed below signature; endorsed by TJ in ink on verso. Enclosure: Order on Gibson & Jefferson, 20 Sep., for payment of $213.33 to Craven Peyton (PrC in same; pressed on same sheet as PrC above; at foot of text: "Messrs. Gibson & Jefferson"; endorsed by TJ in ink on verso).

settlement of interest: in his financial accounts for this day, TJ recorded the order on Gibson and Jefferson and noted "the interest settled by him on the paiments to the Hendersons which closes all sums due on that account, paiable at 30. days" (MB, 2:1107).

your last: TJ refers to Peyton's letter of 24 Aug. 1803.

Petition of Puckshunubbee and Others

To the President of the United States through Silas Dinsmoor his Agent 20th September 1803

The Petition of the undersigned Chiefs and Warriors of the Choctaw Nation of Indians Humbly Sheweth

That Whereas considering the situation of our Country & the large and many failures on the part of our Nation in making due and regular payments to our Merchants and Traders for supplies furnished our Said Nation from time to time by them, and the Game having so decreased that we find it impossible to discharge the arrearages due by us, unless we do it by disposing of so much Land as will pay the same.

We therefore Humbly Pray Our Father the President to take our case into his serious consideration, and relieve us from the heavy debts which we now justly owe and are desirous to pay, if our Father will accept of so much land, as he may deem adequate and sufficient to pay the same; and should he receive the Land, we Pray that he will pay to our Merchants & Traders whatever may appear to be justly due them.

The Land we wish to dispose of lies bounding on the Mississippi, the Yazo, and the line run by General Wilkinson near the latter river. And your Petitioners will ever pray

Signed

PUCKSHUNNUBBEE	his × mark	Head Chief	of Oak, tuck, foliah
OAK CHUMMA	his × mark	Ditto	of The Town
TUSKA MIUBBA	his × mark	Ditto	of Coffetroy
TISH SHA HULUTTO	his × mark	Ditto	of Shu, Nock, Koha
PONSHABA WELA	his × mark	Warrior	of Ditto
BAUKATUBBA	his × mark	Warrior	of Oak, Tuck, foliah

Tr (DNA: RG 11, Ratified Indian Treaties). Tr (DNA: RG 75, Ratified Treaties).

Puckshunubbee (ca. 1739-1824), in a conference with commissioners Benjamin Hawkins, James Wilkinson, and Andrew Pickens at Fort Adams in December 1801, spoke for the Choctaws' Upper Towns. On that occasion he asked for a blacksmith, tools, and spinning wheels, but, describing himself as a factor for a merchant, he said that the Choctaws were satisfied with their ties to firms that traded through Mobile and had no wish to establish new commercial connections. He also urged, without success, that the United States compensate the Choctaws for lands conveyed in an earlier era. By the autumn of 1805, he was the leader of the westernmost of three divisions of the Choctaw nation. Federal commissioners, using the Choctaw term for a chief, recognized the three division chiefs as "medal mingoes." Puckshunubbee used annuity payments from an 1816 land cession to establish a school run by Protestant missionaries. In 1820, he resisted a major cession of lands negotiated by Andrew Jackson but, along with the other medal mingoes, acceded to the final agreement. Puckshunubbee was the son or nephew of one of Franchimastabé's leading advisers. A non-Indian settler described him late in his life as "a large man, tall and bony," who "had a down look and was of the religious or superstitious cast of mind." He was considered to be "a good man, and it was said that he was a man of deep thought and that he was quite intellectual." He died from an accident while traveling to Washington with a Choctaw delegation. His name appears sometimes with an *A*—"Apukshinubi," for example—and sometimes with a *B*, as in "Buc-shun-abbe" and "Buckshun Nubby." Oak Chummy, the nephew of a deceased primary chief of the Choctaws, also addressed the commissioners at Fort Adams in December 1801. He granted permission for a road, but declared that it was "not our wish that there should be any houses built" along the route. He also asked for a marking of the boundary of the Choctaws' territory and in 1802 was one of the signers of a convention for running the boundary. He attended the 1820 conference with Jackson. Tuskamiubbee also signed the 1802 convention. He, Puckshunubbee, and Oak Chummy were signers of a November 1805 treaty that was intended to complete the offer made in this petition to give up land for payment of Choctaws' debts to merchants. Tuskamiubbee may have been the person described in 1822 as "an aged chief" who visited the school established by Puckshunubbee. In 1830, Tish Sha Hulutto was perhaps one of the signers of the treaty that provided for the exchange of the Choctaws' remaining lands east of the Mississippi River for territory in the west. Ponshaba Wela may have participated in at least one of the treaty conferences, but his name is difficult to relate with authority to any of the signers. Baukatubba may have signed the 1801 Fort Adams treaty (ASP, *Indian Affairs*, 1:661-2; Charles J. Kappler, comp. and ed., *Indian Affairs: Laws and Treaties*, 5 vols. [Washington, D.C., 1975], 2:57, 64, 88, 137, 194, 316; Gideon Lincecum, *Pushmataha: A Choctaw Leader and His People* [Tuscaloosa, Ala., 2004], 26, 29, 86; Clara Sue Kidwell, *Choctaws and Mis-*

sionaries in Mississippi, 1818-1918 [Norman, Okla., 1995], 17, 37, 42, 46-7, 66, 93-4; Greg O'Brien, *Choctaws in a Revolutionary Age* [Lincoln, Neb., 2002], 34-5, 102, 104, 105, 110-11; Richard White, *The Roots of Dependency: Subsistence, Environment, and Social Change among the Choctaws, Pawnees, and Navajos* [Lincoln, Nebr., 1983], 104, 114-16, 125; *Missionary Herald*, 18 [1822], 181).

TAKE OUR CASE INTO HIS SERIOUS CONSIDERATION: Silas Dinsmoor, the U.S. agent for the Choctaws, probably sent this petition to Washington with a letter of 2 Oct. in which the agent informed the secretary of war that the Choctaws were ready to offer land to clear their debts. In a letter dated a few days earlier, Dinsmoor also reported that a Choctaw delegation would be traveling to the capital. Earlier in the year, TJ and Dearborn had instructed Dinsmoor and Wilkinson to push the Choctaws to give up land, particularly between the Yazoo River and the Mississippi, and to use payment of the debts to trading firms as an incentive. The president referred to the petition printed above in remarks to the visiting delegation, which included Puckshunubbee, in Washington on 17 Dec. (Dinsmoor to Dearborn, 30 Sep., 2 Oct., recorded in DNA: RG 107, RLRMS; Vol. 39:494n, 529-30).

To James Walker

SIR Monticello Sep. 20. 03.

The walls of my tollmill will be finished in a fortnight, and the mason mr Hope wishes immediately to begin the manufacturing mill, as he thinks he can raise the walls to the lowest floor this season. I must therefore ask the favor of you to come over in the course of a fortnight & lay off the foundation & give him a plan to proceed on. you know we agreed to make it 10. f. longer than mr Cocke's, and to arrange the space for the milltail so that we might hereafter turn her into a geered mill if it should become desireable. the toll mill will be going in a month. a person has undertaken to have the sawmill built himself & pay me rent for her. there remains therefore for you to have every thing ready for the manufacturing mill to be going by this time twelvemonth. by laying the foundation story this fall, we shall have such a start in the spring as will ensure the walls & house being compleated within the next summer. I hope therefore you will be able to occupy yourself entirely with your part of the work so as to keep pace with the other parts. the compleating her for grinding the next crop will make a year's rent (1000. D.) [odds] to me. Accept my best wishes.

TH: JEFFERSON

P.S. I go to Washington the day after tomorrow.

PrC (MHi); blurred; at foot of text: "Mr. Walker"; endorsed by TJ in ink on verso. Recorded in SJL with notation "millwright."

TJ contracted with Michael HOPE to build mill houses for the large and small mills. In March, TJ had requested that Hope begin work on his smaller mill "immediately" (Vol. 40:110).

WE AGREED: see Vol. 38:429-30.

To William Dunbar

Dear Sir Monticello Sep. 21. 03.

Your favor in answer to my queries came to hand a few days ago, and I thank you for the matter it contains & the promptness with which it has been furnished. just on my departure from this place, where I habitually pass the sickly months of Aug. & Sep. I have time only to ask information on a particular point. it has been affirmed by respectable authority, that Spain on recieving the East & West Florida of the English, did not continue that distinction, but restored Louisiana to it's antient boundary the Perdido. and that the country from the Perdido to the Iberville has been ever since considered as a part of Louisiana, & governed by the Governor of Louisiana residing at New Orleans: while the country from the Perdido Eastwardly to the Atlantic has been called, as antiently, by the simple name of Florida, & governed by the governor of Florida residing at St. Augustine. the terms of the treaty render this fact very interesting if true, inasmuch as it fills up the measure of reasoning which fixes the extent of the cession Eastwardly to the Perdido. I write the present to ask of you to ascertain this fact & to give me the information as quickly as possible, as it may yet be recieved in time to determine our proceedings. Accept my friendly salutations & assurances of great esteem & respect.

Th: Jefferson

PrC (DLC); at foot of text: "William Dunbar esq."

your favor: Dunbar to TJ, 19 Aug.

From David Gelston

Sir, New York Septr. 21st. 1803.

I have received your letter of the 19th August, and have this day shipped on board the Scho. Friendship, John Quandrill Master, bound to Alexandria, (being the first opportunity) *the box of wine* and *cask of Nuts*, bill of lading enclosed, an account of the duties & charges attending, will be forwarded when ascertained—

I have the honor to be, very respectfully, Sir, your obedt. Servt.

David Gelston

RC (MHi); at foot of text: "Thomas Jefferson President U.S."; endorsed by TJ as received 25 Sep. and so recorded in SJL. Enclosure not found.

To George Jefferson

Dear Sir Monticello Sep. 21. 03.

Tomorrow I leave this for Washington. on the 6th. instant I drew on you for 600 D. paiable to Dabney Carr, and this day I have drawn on you in favor of Joel Yancey for 375 D. & of Thos. Carr for 408 D. 55 c. these two [last] will probably be presented towards the close of the month & are paiable at sight. yesterday I drew on you in favor of Craven Peyton for 213 D. 33 c paiable at 30 days [...]. in the first week of the ensuing month I shall remit a sum to you sufficient with what will remain in your hands to authorise a draught then to be made of [500. D]

Mr. Fitz, who is going [out?] a surveyor to Natchez, [will] send to your care a box containing his instruments, books &c. addressed to Isaac Briggs at the Natchez, which you will oblige me by putting into the best channel of conveyence you can adopt. Mr. John H. Craven, who rents my farms here & my negroes, is [setting] up a boat for the carriage of his own produce to Richmond. as this will be conducted by my own negroes, I would hereafter give him a preference in bringing whatever may be in your hands for me when his boat is down. at other times mr Higginbotham's boat to be preferred as heretofore. Accept my affectionate salutations.

Th: Jefferson

P.S. the articles mentd in yours of the 14th. to be [...] [taking?] by a waggon are not yet heard of.

PrC (MHi); blurred and faint; at foot of text: "Mr. Jefferson"; endorsed by TJ in ink on verso.

TJ departed for WASHINGTON the following day, traveling his most common route and arriving there on 25 Sep. (MB, 2:1108-9).

In his financial memoranda, TJ recorded the payment to DABNEY CARR "on account of Craven Peyton for Henderson's land." The payments to JOEL YANCEY and Thomas Carr were for settling Albemarle County taxes and court fees, as well as loans of cash that each had made to TJ (MB, 2:1107-8).

From George Jefferson

Dear Sir Richmond 21st. Septr. 1803

You will before this, have found that I was disappointed in forwarding the articles mentioned in my last.

The Waggoner who brought your note having failed to call again, although he promised positively to do so; and altho' we supposed he had engaged as positively with you to carry them. I conclude he must have got an extra price for taking some other loading.

If the River continues low be pleased to get some one in Milton to engage a Waggoner who is known to call on me; I do not know any, and should not like to trust a stranger.

The screws have at length arrived. they were not forwarded I expect until my letter reached Mr. Barnes informing him they had not come to hand.

Yr. Mt. humble servt. GEO. JEFFERSON

RC (MHi); at foot of text: "Thos. Jefferson esqr."; endorsed by TJ as received 25 Sep. and so recorded in SJL.

MY LAST: George Jefferson to TJ, 14 Sep.

To Robert R. Livingston

DEAR SIR Monticello Sep. 21. 03

The bearer hereof is mr Robert Carter, one of the sons of Colo. Charles Carter of Shirley in this state, our first citizen in point of wealth, and head of one of the oldest & most distinguished families in it. the son having past some time in the study of medicine & surgery in Philadelphia, now goes to London, Edinburgh, & Paris to pursue the same studies. apprehensive that in the present contentious state of Europe it may be necessary that a stranger should be known, & especially an American in France who may be so readily suspected of being an Englishman, he has been desirous that I should make known to you his true character & objects, as the person whose patronage in such a case would be most efficacious. I undertake therefore to assure you that you will be safe in any declarations it may be necessary to make as to the correctness of his character, and the innocence[1] of his objects in visiting Europe, & particularly that he is not an Englishman, nor Anglo-man, but a native citizen of Virginia with whose family I have been intimate all my life, and whose person I have known from his infancy. I would also ask from yourself for him those attentions & counsels which may be useful to him & not troublesome to you. Accept my affectionate salutations & assurances of constant esteem & respect. TH: JEFFERSON

RC (NNMus); addressed: "His Excellency Robert R. Livingston esquire Minister Plenipotentiary of the US. of America at Paris by mr Carter"; endorsed by Livingston; in a different hand: "A.O. 1st. July 1804 J. Walsh." PrC (DLC); endorsed by TJ in ink on verso. Recorded in SJL with notation "by Robt. Carter."

Recently widowed and dissatisfied with plantation life, ROBERT CARTER sailed for Europe in October and returned to Virginia in 1805. He died in November of that year. His father died the following year, leaving an estate that included about 13,000 acres and over 700 slaves (Robert Carter to Hill, Anne, Lucy, and Thomas Carter, 12 Oct. 1803, in ViWC: Shirley Plantation Collection; *New-York Gazette & General Advertiser*, 3 Dec. 1805; DVB, 3:57-9).

[1]MS: "innoncence."

To James Monroe

DEAR SIR Monticello Sep. 21. 03.

The bearer hereof is mr Robert Carter, one of the sons of Colo. Charles Carter of Shirley, whose person & character are so well known to you that nothing on that subject need be said. the son is a character of great respectability, has passed some time at Philadelphia in the study of medicine & surgery, & now goes to London, Edinburgh & Paris to pursue the same studies. apprehensive that in the present contentious state of things in Europe it might be necessary that his true character & objects should be known, he has been desirous that I should make him known to you, as the person whose patronage in such a case would be most efficacious. I therefore state these things to you & assure you you will be safe in declaring on any occasion the regularity of his character and the real object of his visit to Europe. your own knolege of the family will of course procure for him those personal attentions & counsels which may be useful to him. Accept my affectionate salutations & assurances of constant esteem & respect. TH: JEFFERSON

PrC (DLC); in ink at foot of text: "James Monroe"; endorsed by TJ in ink on verso. Recorded in SJL with notation "by Robt. Carter."

From Gurdon Bachus

SIR, Trinidad Port Spain Sepr. 22d. 1803

Its now about one year & a half Since this port has been Open for the Vessells of the United States & most likely will Continue so as long as Great Brittain & America remain on friendly terms. the great demand in this Island for all kinds of Lumber and provisions from the United States induces many of my Countrymen to adventure to this port, at Same time the produce of this Island they find of a Superior quality & to Answer the Markets, the duties inwards & outwards are 3½ ℔Ct. on Valuation which Amt. to about 2 ℔Ct. or Say One dollr. ℔ Hhd for Sugar and other produce in proportion! there is nothing prohibited[1] that is the growth & produce of the United States, meaning provisions, also the article of Tobo. is admissable, and the Consumpsion great, as great quantities find its way to the Main—Our Vessells May take in in[2] return the full Amt. of their Cargoes in Sugars, Rum, Cocoa, Coffee and Molasses, or any One of those articles as may Suit them best, Dye Woods, Indigo, Cotton & Hides are prohibited—

Since the renewal of hostilities between England & France, Some impresments of Americans has taken place here besides other abuses on the American Commerce, which induces me to Come forward at this time to offer my Services as Consul for this Island, by the Solicitation of all the Americans who have Visited this port for Some months past—Before my residence in the W. Indies I resided eight years in Petersburg Virga where I have many very Valuable freinds & Acquaintances! I refer you to those who may be most Convenient for your enquirey, from Virga. & Connecticut, Viz, W. B. Giles, John Randolph, & T. Newton Esquires and Roger Griswold Esqr. from Connecticut—I was unfortunately formerly Connected with Fullar Skipwith Esqr. now Consul in France in Shipts. to Martinique & other places—

Should you think fit to honr. me with the Appt. of Consul at this place, you may direct any papers for me to my Father Ebr. Bachus Esq Mercht. New York, with Such Instructions as may be necessary for my goverment—I Can only add that I am a true American, particularly attached to Virga. & now tender my Services in any way that I may be usefull to the United States

I am With Great Esteem & high respect your Obt. Servt.

Gurdon Bachus

P.S. My Brother who resided in France a long time, was, well acquainted with Mr. Paine, but more particularly Mr. Barlow who he lived with nearly two years—

RC (DNA: RG 59, LAR); addressed: "Thomas Jefferson Esquire President of the United States &C. &C. &C—City of Washington"; endorsed by TJ as received 27 Feb. 1804 and "to be Consul there" and so recorded in SJL.

A native of Windham, Connecticut, Gurdon Bachus (1762-1810) was a son of New York City merchant Ebenezer Bachus. By the early 1790s, he had established himself in business at Petersburg, Virginia, trading primarily with the West Indies. Petersburg collector William Heth believed Bachus also conducted illicit dealings and deemed him "capable of any thing in that way." In addition to the individuals named in the above letter, Bachus also claimed an acquaintance with James Madison, whom he wrote in late 1804 seeking a West Indies post and asking Madison to recommend him to the president. He did not receive an appointment from TJ (William L. Weaver, *History of Ancient Windham, Ct. Genealogy…Part I, A.-Bil.* [Willimantic, Conn.,

1864], 61-2; Syrett, *Hamilton*, 15:581-3; *American Historical Review*, 3 [1898], 697-8; WMQ, 1st ser., 13 [1904], 59; Bachus to Madison, 7 Nov. 1804, RC in DNA: RG 59, LAR; New York *Columbian*, 15 Dec. 1810; Richmond *Virginia Patriot*, 25 Dec. 1810; Vol. 25:487n).

Spain ceded TRINIDAD to Great Britain under the terms of the Amiens treaty (Vol. 38:585, 588n).

MY BROTHER: probably DeLucena Bachus, a younger brother of Gurdon, who traveled to France in 1793 to restore his health, but died of yellow fever on his return voyage the following year (Weaver, *History of Ancient Windham*, 62; Dexter, *Yale*, 5:3-4).

[1]MS: "prohibtuted."

[2]Word interlined.

From J. P. G. Muhlenberg

SIR Philadelphia Septr. 22d. 1803—

Mr. Philips, a young Gentleman of this City, intends to wait on The President, & to solicit the appointment of Comissioner of Bankruptcy—Mr. Philips is a stranger in the Foederal City, & his friends request me, to give him a line of introduction—In compliance with Their request, I beg leave to state To The President, that I have been acquainted with Mr. Philips for some years past—That he is a Young Gentleman whose Character is without reproach, & that he is considered as a Man of abilities—

I have the Honor to be with Perfect Respect Sir Your Most Obedt Servt. P MUHLENBERG

RC (DNA: RG 59, LAR); at foot of text: "The President of The United States"; endorsed by TJ as received 3 Oct. and "Phillips to be Commr bkrptcy" and so recorded in SJL; also endorsed by TJ: "v. Clay or Vancleve."

WAIT ON THE PRESIDENT: see Zalegman Phillips to TJ, 1 Oct.

From William Kirkpatrick

SIR Malaga 23 Sept 1803

A Vessel offering from hence for Alexandria, at the Opening of our Fruit Season, for the first time, I have taken the Liberty of shipping on board of her, a few of what the Vineyards of my Family produce, to the Care of James Madison Esqr with a request to present them to your Excellency, in my name, as also a qr Cask cased of the very best Old Mountain or Malaga Wine (being of the Vintage 1747) that my Stores can boast of.

I sincerely hope these trifling Objects may arrive in safety, and be delivered in good Condition to your Excellency, who I flatter myself will do me the Honor to admit of them, as a rarity not to be met with in America.

I profit with much pleasure of this Occasion, to assure your Excellency of the high Esteem with Which I have the Honor to be,

Your Excellency's, most obedt & huml Servt

WILLM. KIRKPATRICK

RC (MoSHi: Jefferson Papers); at foot of text: "His Excellency Thomas Jefferson Esqr President of the U. S of America"; endorsed by TJ as received 10 Dec. and so recorded in SJL.

A native of Scotland, William Kirkpatrick established himself as a successful merchant in Malaga, Spain. Recommended to George Washington to become the American consul in that port, he was eventually named to the position in 1800. He diligently filed reports to the administration, often about affairs in the Barbary states, and in 1807, Robert Smith appointed him U.S. naval agent in Malaga. In addition to his mercantile business, Kirkpatrick owned a vineyard and a cotton plantation. Mixing easily with the Spanish landed class, he successfully married his daughters to nobles, and one of his granddaughters became Empress Eugénie of France (Desmond Seward, *Eugénie: The Empress and Her Empire* [Stroud, Eng., 2004], 1-2; John S. Doskey, ed., *The European Journals of William Maclure* [Philadelphia, 1988], 155; JEP, 1:332-3; NDBW, 6:514; Washington, *Papers, Pres. Ser.*, 7:455n; Madison, *Papers, Sec. of State Ser.*, 5:42, 127, 370-1, 457-8, 502; Vol. 25:309n; Vol. 36:383n).

From Thomas Paine

Stonnington, Connecticut,
Sepr. 23. [1803]

DEAR SIR

Your two favours of the 10. & 18 Ult. reached me at this place on the 14 Inst, also one from Mr. Madison. I do not suppose that the framers of the Constitution thought anything about the acquisition of new territory, and even if they did it was prudent to say nothing about it, as it might have suggested to foreign Nations the Idea that we contemplated foreign Conquest. It appears to me to be one of those cases with which the Constitution had nothing to do, and which can be judged of only by the circumstances of the times when such a case shall occur. The Constitution could not foresee that Spain would cede Louisania to France or to England, and therefore it could not determine what our conduct should be in consequence of such an event. The cession makes no alteration in the Constitution; it only extends the principles of it over a larger territory, and this certainly is within the Morality of the Constitution, and not contrary to, nor beyond, the expression or intention of any of its Articles. That the Idea of extending the territory of the United States was always contemplated, whenever the opportunity offered itself, is, I think, evident from the opinion that has existed from the Commencement of the Revolution that Canada would, at some time or other, become a part of the United States; and there is an Article either in the treaty with france (I have not the treaty by me) or in some Correspondance with that Government, that in case of a Conquest of Canada by the assistance [of] france, Canada should become a part of the United States, and therefore the cession of Louisania says no more than what was said before with respect to Canada. The only difference between the two cases, for with respect to the Constitution there is none, is, that the first, that of Canada, was generous; and the stipulation, that *the Louisanians shall come into our Union* was politic. It precludes us from selling the territory to another power that might become the enemy of france or Spain or both. It was like saying I will sell the territory to you for so much *on Condition* that it is for yourselves, but not as land-jobbers to sell it again. It is an Item in the purchase with which the Constitution has nothing to do, and it would only confuse and puzzle the people to know why it was questioned. I was very glad to see by your second letter that the Idea was given up, and I hope that my remarks upon it will be acceptable.

Were a question to arise it would apply, not to the Cession; because it violates no Article of the Constitution, but to Ross and Morris's Motion. The Constitution empowers Congress to *declare* War, but to make war with out declaring it is anti-constitutional. It is like attacking an unarmed Man in the dark.

There is also another reason why no such question should arise. The english Government is but in a tottering condition, and if Bonaparte succeeds that Government will break up. In that case it is not improbable we may obtain Canada, and I think that Burmuda ought to belong to the United States. In its present condition it is a Nest for piratical privateers. This is not a subject to be spoken of, but it may be proper to have it in mind.

The latest News we have from Europe in this place is the insurrection in Dublin. It is a disheartening Circumstance to the english Governt. as they are now putting arms into the hands of people who but a few weeks before they would have hung had they found a pike in their possession. I think the probability is in favour of the descent, and I form this opinion from a knowlege of all the Circumstances combined with it. I know that Bonaparte puts the whole upon making good his landing, and as he can chuse the time of setting off, a dark night and a calm, and also chuse his place of landing, for the english coast on the North Sea is an open flat sandy beach for more than 200 Miles, to wit, the counties of Essex, Suffolk, Norfolk and Lincolnshire, and as about 36 hours will carry them over by rowing the probability is that he will arrive. If this should take place it will throw a temptation in my way to make another passage cross the Atlantic to assist in forming a Constitution for England.

I shall be employed the ensuing Winter in cutting two or three thousand Cords of wood on my farm at New Rochelle for the New York Market distant twenty Miles by water. The wood is worth 3½ dollars per load as it stands. This will furnish me with ready money, and I shall then be ready for whatever may present itself of most importance next spring. I had intended to build myself an house to my own taste, and a workshop for my mechanical operations and make a collection, as authors say, of my works, which, with what I have in manuscrip will make four, or five octavo Volumes and publish them by subscription, but the prospects that are now opening with respect to England hold me in suspence.

It has been customary in a President's discourse to say something about religion. I offer you a thought on this subject. The word, *Religion*, used as a word [*en*] *masse* has no application in a Country like America. In catholic Countries it would mean exclusively the Religion of the Romish Church; with the Jews the Jewish Religion; in England the protestant Religion, or in the sense of the english Church, the established Religion; with the Deists it would mean Deism, with the Turks Mahohetism &c &c. As well as I recollect it is *Lego*, *Religo*, *Religio*, *Religion*, that is, to be tied or bound by an oath or obligation. The french use the word properly; when a woman enters a Convent, she is called a Novisiate, when she takes the oath she is a *Religieuse*, that is, she is bound by an oath.—Now all that we have to do, as a Government,[1] with the word, *religion*, in this Country, is with the civil rights of it, and not at all with its *creeds*. Instead therefore of using the word Religion as a word en Masse as if it meant a Creed, it would be better to speak only of its civil Rights, *that all denominations of Religion are equally protected, that none are dominante, none inferior, that the rights of conscience are equal to every denomination and to every individual, and that it is the duty of Government to preserve this equality of consciencious rights*. A man cannot be called a hypocrite for defending the civil rights of religion, but he may be suspected of sincerity in defending its creeds.

I suppose you will find it proper to take notice of the impressment of American [sea]men by the Captains of british Vessels, and procure a list of such Captains and report them to their Government. This pretence of searching for british Seamen is a new pretence for visiting and searching American Vessels.

I think it probable that Bonaparte will attempt a descent in November. All the preparation he wants is the boats and he must by this time have more than a 1000 besides the cut down vessels and small craft he will get from Holland. Accounts say that 500 have been built up the Rhine and floated down to flushing and the waters of the Schelt. I believe the war has taken a turn very different to what the english[2] Government expected. It is however a subject, and in such a State of Crisis that it is best for us to say nothing about it. Mr Washington gave a great deal of Offence by lugging the Affairs of Europe into his discources. I wish that Bonaparte may overthrow the english Government as a necessary step towards putting an end to Navies, and if he does one I hope he will do the other, but in the present state of things it would not be prudent to say it.

I am passing some time at this place at the house of a friend till the wood cutting time comes on and I shall engage some Cutters here and then return to N. Rochelle. I wrote to Mr. Madison concerning the report that the british Govert. had cautioned ours not to pay the purchase money for Louisania as they intended to take it for themselves. I have received his answer, and I pray you make him my compliments.

The british Government appears to have two alarms on their hands at once. The alarm of an invasion[3] caused them to arm the Nation *en Masse*, and they are now alarmed at the consequence of that measure. A London paragraph says—Government have come to a resolution by no means to arm the lower Classes of people at present, at least in the Metropolis.

We are still afflicted with the yellow fever, and the Doctors are disputing whether it is an imported or a domestic disease. Would it not be a good Measure to prohibit the arrival of all Vessels from the West Indies from the last of June to the Middle of October. If this was done this Session of Congress and we escaped the fever next summer we should always know how to escape it. I question if performing quarantine is a sufficient Guard. The disease may be in the Cargo, especially that part which is barreled up, and not in the persons on board, and when that Cargo is opened on our Wharfs the hot steaming Air in contact with the Ground imbibes the infection. I can conceive that infected air can be barrelled up, not in a hogshead of rum, nor perhaps sucre, but in a barrell of Coffee. I am badly off in this place for pen and Ink and short of paper.

Accept my best wishes THOMAS PAINE

Sepr. 26.

I heard yesterday from Boston that our old friend S. Adams is at the point of death.

RC (DLC); partially dated; torn; endorsed by TJ as received 30 Sep. and so recorded in SJL.

For the letter from MADISON, see below.

ROSS AND MORRIS'S MOTION: for the resolutions introduced in the Senate by James Ross in February and supported by Gouverneur Morris, see Vol. 39:552-4.

An uprising in DUBLIN on 23 July, intended by its leaders to be the opening act of a rebellion throughout Ireland, failed to coalesce and collapsed after army units mobilized against the rebels (Ruán O'Donnell, *Robert Emmet and the Rising of 1803* [Dublin, 2003], 56-146).

PUTTING ARMS INTO THE HANDS: fearing a French invasion of the British Isles, the British government reconstituted the militia in Ireland, strengthened other local military units known as the yeomanry, and expected to include several thousand Irish in a large, newly formed defensive army (Sir Henry McAnally, *The Irish Militia, 1793-1816: A Social and Military Study* [Dublin, 1949], 71, 92-3, 172-83; J. E. Cookson, *The British Armed Nation, 1793-1815* [Oxford, 1997], 42-4, 166-7; *Aurora*, 20 Aug.).

CARRY THEM OVER BY ROWING: since 1800, Paine had urged the French government to use oar-powered boats to invade England (Vol. 32:188, 191n; Vol. 34:282; Vol. 35:192).

In 1784, the state of New York gave Paine a 300-acre tract of land at NEW ROCHELLE that had been confiscated from a Loyalist (John Keane, *Tom Paine: A Political Life* [London, 1995], 251-2).

Paine's FRIEND in Stonington, Connecticut, was Nathan Haley. Paine visited Haley there for part of 1803 (Vol. 32:202-4).

WROTE TO MR. MADISON: Paine wrote to Madison on 6 Aug. and Madison, after conferring with TJ, replied with a letter dated the 20th of that month. See Madison to TJ, 13 Aug.

SUCRE: sugar.

[1] Preceding three words interlined.
[2] Word interlined.
[3] MS: "invason."

From William Buckner, Jr.

DEAR SIR/ Kentucky Scott Cty Septr 24th 1803

If Congress ratifise the Treaty with France respecting the Louisiany Country it will I suppose be necessary to appoint Surveyors to lay the Country off in such a manner as Congress in their wisdom shall think proper my acquaintance with the members of Congress is not sufficient to expect a recommendation I therefore solisit the appointment of Surveyor in this new Country and if you have not confidence enough in me to appoint me Surveyor Gen'l I woud accept that of a deputy in either case I woud endeavour not to disgrase the appointment I am Sir with much esteem your Friend & Hb'l Serv't

WM BUCKNER JUNR

formerly of Orange Cty Virginia now of Scott Cty Kentucky

RC (DNA: RG 59, LAR); endorsed by TJ as received 13 Oct. and "to be a surveyor of Louisiana" and so recorded in SJL.

From M. A. F. P. Engrand

Monsieur, philadelphie [before 25 Sep. 1803]

En apprenant que Votre génie avoit conçu, Et que Vous alliez mettre a exécution une Expédition de recherches sur les bords de L'océan pacifique, jai saisi une Lueur d'espérance de rentrer dans une carrière ou La passion des voyages Et Le Désir d'acquérir de L'instruction m'avoient Engagé, Et D'ou Les revers les plus déplorables m'ont arraché pour me plonger dans une inaction qui m'est Encore plus insupportable que L'infortune qui L'accompagne. J'avois, il y a bientot deux ans, Entrepris une incursion dans plusieurs contrées des deux mondes avec Le projet de m'occuper Spécialement de L'histoire Naturelle de L'homme, de L'influence du climat Et des autres agents aux quels il Est soumis sur Les modifications de son physique Et de son moral; Et de noter, dans L'etat Le moins avancé de sa civilisation, Les idées qu'il a Lui même de son organisation, des désordres qui Laffectent, Et des moyens de Le prévenir ou d'y remédier; apeine avois je perdû de Vuë ma patrie que Les Eléments conspirerent pour traverser mes desseins, Et me jetterent dans une Isle ou des orages plus affreux devoient m'envelopper dans un Labyrinthe de perils auxquels je n'ai Echappé qu'en perdant le fruit De plusieurs années d'Epargne et de sacrifises que j'avois consacré à Laccomplissement de mon Entreprise. Je ne m'etois pourtant point decouragé: je m'acheminois vers la France pour Exprimer de mon patrimoine de nouveaux moyens de suivre mon plan; Et Voila que La guerre me ferme Le passage! Ma Liberté Est menacée; mes dernières ressources sont consumées; Et il ne me reste d'autre consolation que m'être réfugié au sein d'une nation hospitalière que de grands Souvenirs Et un interrêt reciproque rendent L'amie de mon pays. Quelle félicité pour moi Si, quoique Etranger, quoique vous étant inconnu, Monsieur, Et ne M'étayant d'aucune recommandation j'étois jugé digne d'Être compté au nombre de ceux qui concourront a L'execution de Vos Vuës sublimes Et patriotiques. Il ne m'importe quel rôle j'y remplirois; quel titre j'y obtiendrois: que je voyage, Et que j'aye occasion de m'instruire d'Être utile, peut Être! ... mon ambition sera satisfaite; mes vœux seront remplis. Le philosophe de genève disoit que, s'il Eut Vécû Du temps de Fénélon, il auroit aspiré a Être son Valet de chambre, Espérant devenir son sécrétaire, Et voir de près une si grande Lumière. Ah! Je suis prêt à açcepter un poste bien plus humble au service de La sçience pour Être Le confident de quelques uns de ses sécrèts! Je n'ai point Le génie de Votre illustre compatriote Mr. Ledyard; mais je me sens capable de son Extraordinaire résolution, Et de son opiniâtre dévouêment. Je m'adresse a un ami des Français, a une âme genereuse, à un Sçavant: je suis français, infortuné, Et je Veux m'immoler aux progrès des sçiences … que de motifs pour me flatter de n'être pas défavorablement accueilli! …

agréez, je Vous prie, Monsieur, L'hommage de ma haute admiration pour Vos talents, Et de mon respêct profond pour Votre personne.

M. A. F. P. ENGRAND

EDITORS' TRANSLATION

SIR, Philadelphia [before 25 Sep. 1803]

When I learned that your engineers had charted a research expedition along the Pacific coast, and that you are authorizing the project, I seized a glimmer of hope of returning to a career that I pursued out of a passion for travel and a thirst for knowledge. The most deplorable reversals have torn me from that career and plunged me into an unemployment that I find even more unbearable than the poverty that comes with it. Almost two years ago I began an expedition to several regions of the two worlds with the goal of studying the natural history of human beings, the influence of climate and other agents to which they are subjected, and the changes to their bodies and characters. I sought to observe, in the least advanced state of civilization, how human beings organize themselves, what disorders affect them, and how to accommodate or remedy them. I had barely left my country when the elements conspired to thwart my plans. They tossed me upon an island where the most awful storms enveloped me in a labyrinth of dangers from which I escaped only by losing the fruit of several years of savings and sacrifices that I had used to undertake my mission. I was not discouraged, however. I made my way back to France to tap my patrimony for new funds to continue my project. Then I was blocked by war! My freedom is threatened; my last resources are spent. And I have no other consolation than having taken refuge in the bosom of a welcoming nation whose noble memories and reciprocal interests make it friendly to my country. How happy I would be, Sir, if, even though a foreigner whom you do not know, and without any recommendation, I could be judged worthy of helping carry out your sublime and patriotic vision. I do not care what role I perform or what title I have. If I can travel and learn, perhaps even be useful.… My ambition will be satisfied and my wishes fulfilled. The Geneva philosopher said that if he had lived in Fénelon's time, he would have aspired to be his valet, with hopes of becoming his secretary and seeing all that brilliance at close range. Ah! I am ready to accept the humblest job in the service of science, in order to be privy to some of its secrets. I do not have the genius of your illustrious compatriot Mr. Ledyard, but I can match his extraordinary resolution and indomitable devotion. I appeal to a friend of the French, a generous soul, a scholar.… All these are reasons to flatter myself that I will not be welcomed with disfavor.

Accept, Sir, I beg you, the tribute of my high admiration for your talents and my profound respect for you. M. A. F. P. ENGRAND

RC (DLC); undated; ellipses in original; below signature: "Médeçin de paris, membre correspondant de la société des observateurs de L'homme &c."; at foot of text: "philadelphie south-fourth street number 5"; endorsed by TJ as received 25 Sep. and so recorded in SJL.

L'HISTOIRE NATURELLE DE L'HOMME: below his signature Engrand identified himself as a corresponding member of the Société des Observateurs de l'Homme, an association formed by a group of French physicians, naturalists, political economists, linguists, and other scholars in 1799. Volney and Georges Cuvier were members. The organization sought to collect information about humankind in all regions of the globe. Its most notable achievement was the preparation of instructions for a French expedition to Australia. Engrand's name does not appear in lists of the society's members and corresponding members (Jean Copans and Jean Jamin, eds., *Aux Origenes de l'anthropologie française: Les Mémoires de la Société des Observateurs de l'Homme en l'an VIII* [Paris, 1978], 73-8, 222-3; Joseph-Marie de Gérando, *The Observation of Savage Peoples*, trans. F. C. T. Moore [Berkeley, Calif., 1969], 17-20; Jean-Luc Chappey, *La Société des Observateurs de l'Homme [1799-1804]: Des anthropologues au temps de Bonaparte* [Paris, 2002], 240, 485-6).

PHILOSOPHE DE GENÈVE: Rousseau.

When TJ was minister to France, he assisted John LEDYARD, a native of Connecticut who had been on Captain James Cook's final voyage in the Pacific, in an unsuccessful effort to obtain permission from the Russian government for Ledyard to travel through Siberia, across to Alaska, and then overland to the United States. Ledyard attempted the journey, but Russian officials stopped him in Siberia. He died in Egypt in 1789 as he was about to embark on a trip into the interior of Africa. TJ deemed him to have "ingenuity" but "too much imagination" (ANB; Vol. 10:170-1, 258; Vol. 12:159-60).

From "A Frien to Jefferson"

[before 25 Sep. 1803]

Information wanted to the following queries.

First. has Gabrail Lilley given mr. Jefferson credt. for corn and poark which he suppyd. John perry with in 1801. and in 1803.
30 Gallons peach Brandy for self taken from the ... cellar. Do. Puench. 5 gallons. Do. 15 bottles. of wine. exlusive of two dys drunk.= || at the mountain on wine.
the winter of 1803. 25 hogs fattend waying from 150 to 200 Lbs.
Time of negroes working Tobacco and clearing of land for Do.
corn to Jams. Olhm. 1803.

A FRIEN TO JEFFERSON

before the workmen had the furnishing of them-selves with provisions, perry and his hands ware supplyd. by Lilley. and are still with corn.

= || 1803.

RC (MHi); undated; ellipses in original; addressed: "The President. monticello"; endorsed by TJ as received from "Anon." on 25 Sep. and "G. Lilly."

From Nicholas King

Surveyor's Office, Washington, 25 Sep. 1803. King sends a report on the work of the district's surveying department and on some of the problems confronted in the execution of the plan of the City of Washington. A "recurrence to many of the early transactions of the city" will be necessary as "most of the present difficulties may be traced to that period." He offers brief descriptions of the congressional acts of 16 July 1790 and 3 Mch. 1791 that fixed the permanent seat of the government and alludes to the president's responsibilities. He explains President Washington's role in locating the public buildings and in forging an agreement between the original proprietors and the government. By that agreement, the proprietors conveyed their lands to be laid out subject to the president's approval. Half of the land was to belong to the proprietors and the other half to the government, with proceeds of sales of the government's moiety assigned to the president as a grant of money to be used for construction of the public buildings. King next discusses the act of 19 Dec. 1791 by which Maryland's legislature ceded authority over the part of the district east of the Potomac River, particularly as it related to the licensing of wharves on the Potomac and Anacostia Rivers. The acts of Congress and of the Maryland legislature "are the sources of authority" for the actions of the president and his appointed commissioners for the district. King turns to the early surveying of the district and of the plan developed by Pierre L'Enfant, quoting from a letter of 16 Mch. 1798 by commissioners Gustavus Scott and William Thornton to Alexander White, the third commissioner, in which they allude to the preliminary plan that President Washington presented to the proprietors and in which they hint at the difficulties that might arise from alterations to the arrangement of land appropriated for public buildings. He discusses the early actions of the first commissioners of the district and quotes from an advertisement for the initial public sale of lots. At that time, Andrew Ellicott, acting surveyor under L'Enfant, urged the commissioners in a letter of 8 Sep. 1791 not to sell plots adjacent to the locations of the President's House and Capitol, and to focus on other areas more immediately eligible for profitable development. That same day, the commissioners and TJ, acting as secretary of state, reached agreement on several queries, prompting the commissioners to request that L'Enfant prepare 10,000 maps of his city plan. King now provides details of the initial public sale, held on 17 Oct. 1791, and quotes from communications that President Washington made to Congress indicating the emergence of an official city plan. He discusses the dispute that led to L'Enfant's dismissal in 1792 and Ellicott's drafting of a revised plan for engraving. This plan, which appeared in slightly different form in engravings published in Boston and Philadelphia, included a number of alterations to L'Enfant's plan. President Washington rejected additional changes suggested by the commissioners. The public sales held in October 1791 underscored the differences between the new engraved plan and that of L'Enfant. Most notably, Samuel Davidson, largest proprietor of the lots adjacent to the public appropriation for the President's House, deemed the changes injurious to his interests. Davidson has consistently sought the restoration of L'Enfant's plan as it related to the public square touching his land. King annexes a settlement of account executed in 1794 between Davidson and the commissioners that grew out of the division of squares between the two parties. Davidson's claim remains in limbo, thereby retarding "the improvement of one of the most eligible parts of the city." He encloses four plats to help illustrate the dispute: copy of part of a plan "supposed to be that sent to Congress"; copy of a plan shown at the initial sale of lots; part of a plan, "said to be taken from Mr. L'Enfant's plan as executed on the ground"; and a "plan of the President's square, agreeably to Mr. Davidson's claim." King now indicates the extent to which appropriations of public land deriving from L'Enfant's plan but not included in Ellicott's engraved plan have nevertheless been used as inducements to purchasers of lots. He adds that subsequent to the publication of the engraved plan, many alterations have been made, most notably the introduction of building squares in places previously allocated for open space. These alterations have diminished the health and beauty of the plan, while depriving adjoining lots of the advantages that the open spaces would have provided. As for the development of waterfront areas, it is essential that "this part of the plan be established before many wharves are built, or much property involved in the decision." King urges that any plan include a Water Street "beyond which no house or building which may impede the access of air, or be the cause of a nuisance, will be allowed." Unfortunately, the enclosed regulations on wharfing, which the commissioners issued on 20 July 1795, allow purchasers to wharf and build as far as they choose, as long as they do not impede the river channels. Not only do these regulations risk "the evils of docks, slips, and receptacles of filth," they violate the spirit of the engraved plan, which established the "principle of a Water street, beyond which wharfs only, but no buildings can be erected." Furthermore, no channel line has been fixed, and the regulations related to land claimed from the water introduce additional sources of confusion. The commissioners have inconsistently upheld these regulations, granting permission to wharf to James Barry in October 1795 while denying permission to Thomas Law a month later. King encloses these responses. In 1798, the commissioners denied any capacity to rule on questions of wharfing and water privileges, arguing that such decisions should be left to the courts. "It is unnecessary," King remarks, "to comment on sentiments like these, or state their effect on the minds of persons wishing to improve, yet cautious as to title, and the rights they acquire." He urges a speedy settlement of the plan, "so as to leave nothing for conjecture, litigation, or doubt," and offers a few observations that he hopes will serve the "permanent interest of the city." He puts particular stress on the role of poorly designed wharves in the spread of the diseases that afflict eastern seaboard cities. A proper water plan will help Washington avoid such calamities. The principle of a Water Street, such as exists in the engraved plan, combined with proper regulations will "preserve the purity of the air." He details some of the regulations he has in mind. He encloses four additional plats: the plan as it appeared in the Boston plate; the plan as it appeared in the Philadelphia plate; an additional Philadelphia engraving, which exhibits alterations made to the plan since its original inception; and a map sent by the proprietors to the executive, illustrating the need for new regulations for the Anacostia shoreline. King acknowledges that many of the alterations to the plan, while injurious, will have to be preserved, but he hopes that all remaining open areas and public spaces contemplated in the plan will "be forever secured to the city." The surveying of the city is now at a stage where the sanctioning of a definitive plan is both possible and desirable as a bar to litigation and doubt. Even now, it will be difficult to devise a "system which shall combine justice with convenience." Further delay in sanctioning a definitive plan will create more "serious disadvantages."

Tr (printed in Saul K. Padover, ed., *Thomas Jefferson and the National Capital* [Washington, D.C., 1946], 302-20); at head of text: "To the President of the United States." Enclosures: (1) Agreement between commissioners of the District of Columbia and Samuel Davidson, 24 to 31 Jan. 1794, noting "final adjustment of Samuel Davidson's account," which the commissioners acknowledge as a grant to Davidson of 22 acres for his part of the square reserved for the president; that a certificate in fee simple is delivered to Davidson for lot 2 in square 254, lot 13 in square 489, all of square 221, and lot 1 in square 487; that the commissioners further agree that should any portion of Davidson's remaining part of the president's square be appropriated, except for public use, then Davidson is entitled to "his dividends of such square or squares & other appropriations agreeably to his Deed in Trust" (DNA: RG 42, Proceedings of the Board of Commissioners for the District of Columbia). (2) District of Columbia Board of Commissioners, regulations concerning buildings and wharves, 20 July 1795, decreeing that proprietors of water lots be permitted to build as far out into the Potomac and Anacostia Rivers "as they think convenient" without impeding the channels and navigations of those rivers; that they should leave space for streets noted in the general plan and that in locations where streets do not intersect the wharf, they must "leave a space of Sixty feet for a street at the termination of every three hundred feet of made ground" (same). (3) Commissioners to James Barry, 5 Oct. 1795, acknowledging Barry's letter of 3 Oct. and agreeing with Barry that "an imaginary continuation of Georgia avenue thro' a considerable depth of tide water thereby cutting off the water privilege of square 771 to wharf to the Chanell too absurd to form a part of the plan of the City of Washington" and that Barry's purchase of that square entitles him to construct a wharf (DNA: RG 42, LRDLS). (4) Commissioners to Thomas Law, 30 Nov. 1795, responding to Law's letter of 19 Nov.; the board recognizes "the advantages resulting from the measures you propose" but insists that it has "no power to stop or appropriate for any other purposes the streets as laid down in the Original plan of the City" (same). (5) *Plan of the City of Washington in the Territory of Columbia, ceded by the States of Virginia and Maryland to the United States of America, and by them established as the Seat of their Government, after the Year MDCCC* (Boston, 1792). (6) *Plan of the City of Washington in the Territory of Columbia, ceded by the States of Virginia and Maryland to the United States of America, and by them established as the Seat of their Government, after the Year MDCCC* (Philadelphia, 1792); see Vol. 23:xxxv, illus. Other enclosures not found, but see below.

Nicholas King, former and current surveyor for the city of Washington, had long sought a more definitive plan for the city, particularly with regard to the waterfront. He was most unhappy with changes introduced in what was called the "Appropriation Map" of James Dermott. That map, which both George Washington and John Adams had approved, reflected alterations made since release of the L'Enfant-Ellicott engraved map, provided much richer data on the soundings of the river channels, and conformed to the natural shoreline, not to the imagined, built waterfront illustrated in the earlier map. In 1797, King chided the commissioners, who had requested that he prepare a series of plats intended to display a Water Street, wharfs, and water lots, for their neglect in determining a water line. A memorial sent by several proprietors in 1798 to John Adams, which criticized the many alterations introduced to the original plan and which has been attributed to King, included many of the same points as King's letter above (Ralph E. Ehrenberg, "Mapping the Nation's Capital: The Surveyor's Office, 1791-1818," *Quar-*

terly Journal of the Library of Congress, 36 [1979], 296, 302-4; Bob Arnebeck, *Through a Fiery Trial: Building Washington, 1790-1800* [Lanham, Md., 1991], 489-90, 500; ASP, *Miscellaneous*, 1:331-3; Vol. 39:498n).

The Editors cannot be certain of most of the maps and plats that King enclosed. By his own description, most appear to have been documents generated in the surveying office for internal use. From the first four maps King identified, the fourth, a plat of the president's square, bears some resemblance to one of the series of maps constituting an informal plan of the city executed by King, his father Robert King, Sr., and his brother Robert King, Jr., and known collectively as the King plats. From the second group of maps, number 8 likely accompanied the proprietors' memorial to President Adams (Ehrenberg, "Mapping the Nation's Capital," 306-8; ASP, *Miscellaneous*, 1:332).

From Calvin Chaddock

MAY IT PLEASE YOUR EXCELLENCY, Rochester Sept. 26, 1803

permit a Stranger to address you on a subject, though disagreeable in itself yet necessary for the public good. You very well know that Edward Pope Esqr. of Newbedford in the County of Bristol and Commonwealth of Massachusetts now holds the office of the customhouse for that District. This is to inform your Excellency, that he is a Sworn enemy to the present administration of the federal Government; That he is negligent with respect to the laws of the United States, and inattentive to the duties of his office. The truth of which the following circumstance will evince. Samuel Rodman of Newbedford fitted out a ship a few days since for Europe, sent his Captain to Mr Pope for a role *de* equipage, Mr Pope told the Capt. it was totally unnecessary[1] as no existing treaties between this and foreign nations requird it, and refused to give one. The same day a vessel from South-Carolina enterd at Newbedford the Capt. of which repaird to the Custom house office and among his other papers presented his Role de equipage, after seeing this Mr Pope went on to examine the laws of the Unitd States and among them found one of the last Cession of Congress which requird such a paper. Tho he had been in possession of the law thus long, Yet he was so inattentive to the laws of his Country, that he knew nothing of it, and has cleared a number of vessels for Europe without, and thereby exposd the property to capture. The above I had from Mr Rodman the owner and a decided Federalist, and one of the most respectable characters in Newbedford. Besides a number of other pieces of misconduct which might be brought forward if necessary. This is therefore to pray your Excellency to remove the said Edward Pope from the office of the customs and supply his place with a better man. That your Excellency, may obtain some information of the character who now presumes to address you, please to enquire of Mr Lincoln The Atorney General, who knows my character and that of my family. My Father resides in the Town of Oakhem in the same county with the Atorney General. Besides Mr. Lemuel Williams of Newbedford a member of the house of representives of the national Government, likewise of Mr Bishop of Rehoboth another member, who I beleive is acquainted with my character tho not with my person.—

And as Mr Pope and myself are on good terms as Neighbours, tho opposite in politics therefore I wish your Excellency, to make use of my name no farther than necessary on this business. I will only add that I will be responsable for what I have here said with respect to Mr Pope.

I am with every Sentiment of esteem Your Excellencys sincere friend & very humble Servt. CALVIN CHADDOCK A:M:

RC (DNA: RG 59, LAR); addressed: "To Thomas Jefferson President of the United States Washington City" and "By the Politeness of the Hon. Phanuel Bishop"; endorsed by TJ as received 13 Oct. and "Pope Edwd. Collector of New Bedford to be removd" and so recorded in SJL; also noted by TJ "enquire of mr Lincoln & mr Bishop" and, in pencil, "do nothing unless further [application] be [made?]."

Son of Captain Joseph and Sara Bruce Chaddock of Oakham, Massachusetts, Calvin Chaddock (1765-1823) graduated from Dartmouth in 1791 and three years later earned a Master of Arts degree from the college. In 1792, he married Meletiah Nye of Oakham. He became pastor of a Congregational parish in Rochester, Massachusetts, the next year, and in 1798 he opened an academy for the instruction of youth of both sexes. By 1804, he had "a respectable number of Students from different parts of the United States." A firm and active Republican, Chaddock represented Rochester in the state house of representatives in 1806. That year, he became pastor of a congregation in Hanover, Massachusetts. He founded and served as the principal teacher at Hanover Academy from 1808 until he was dismissed from his parish in 1818. He spent a short time in Marietta, Ohio, before settling in Charleston, now in West Virginia (*Medley or Newbedford Marine Journal*, 22 Dec. 1792, 18 Oct. 1793, 7 Sep. 1798; Boston *American Apollo*, 11 Sep. 1794; *Massachusetts Spy, or Worcester Gazette*, 26 Dec. 1798; New Bedford *Columbian Courier*, 9 Oct. 1799, 28 Sep. 1804; *Pittsfield Sun; or, Republican Monitor*, 21 June 1806; *New-Bedford Mercury*, 4 July 1823; David B. Ford, *History of Hanover Academy* [Boston, 1899], 9-14; Nathan Willis and others to Gallatin, 3 June, and Samuel Sprague to Gallatin, 22 June 1804, both in DNA: RG 59, LAR).

Heeding the recommendation of Massachusetts congressman George Leonard, Washington appointed EDWARD POPE collector at New Bedford when the customs service was organized in August 1789. After his appointment, Pope continued to operate his general store on the waterfront and to serve as a county court judge. Active in local politics, he appointed only Federalists to office in his district (Washington, *Papers, Pres. Ser.*, 3:300-1; JEP, 9, 13; Carl E. Prince, *The Federalists and the Origins of the U.S. Civil Service*, [New York, 1977], 24-5, 40).

ROLE DE EQUIPAGE: according to the first section of the 28 Feb. 1803 act for the "further protection of American seamen," masters of ships bound for foreign ports were to provide collectors with a list and description of the persons who composed the "ship's company." The collector then certified and returned the list.

According to instructions sent by the Treasury secretary in July 1803, the collectors were to provide the captain with a separate, certified list of seamen on board who were citizens of the United States. The law also called for masters of U.S. vessels to carry a ship's register, sea letter, and Mediterranean passport to be deposited with the U.S. consul or other official on arrival at a foreign port (U.S. Statutes at Large, 2:203; Gallatin to TJ, 6 July 1803).

[1] MS: "unnessary."

Report from George Blagden

The mode stone cutters practice for the valuation of columns, in stone similar to that got at Aquia.

1st. The stone in a quarried state per foot cube

Add workmanship $

Base if the Attic 1/40 per foot superficial

if tuscan 1/ do

Capital 1/40 do

Shaft suppose in three pieces, first block including cincture and third the astragal at $/50 per foot Super

For the circumferance of bare girt the upper toras and capital the upper part of Ovolo.

Girt the shaft at bottom and that multiplied into the height including cincture and astragal.

The above prices is for a column of two feet diameter, setting will be an extra expence.

GEO BLAGDEN

Washington 27 Septr. 1803

MS (DLC); in Blagden's hand, with calculations added by TJ in pencil in the margin, partially obscured by tape, for a total of $101.80; endorsed by TJ: "Prices. Stone cutting of columns."

On 9 July, Blagden sent John Lenthall an estimate for the cost of a Corinthian column for the Capitol (RC in DLC; endorsed by TJ: "Capitol. Blagden's cost of a column. 736.62
the Middle block of the Capitol is 100 f.
each recess 30. f. the two 60
each wing 90. f. the two 180
340").

From William Jarvis

SIR Lisbon 27th Septr. 1803

I have had the honor to receive your letter of the 10th May, & immediately set about executing the Commission you favoured me with; but found it more difficult to get pure Termo Wine than I was aware of: for although this name is indiscriminately given to all the White

Wines made in the vicinity of this City, yet amongst all the foreign Houses, who are the principal Wine Merchants, I could not find a single Cask that was unadulterated. I then applied to the only considerable Portug'u Merchant in this line; he had just received 160 pipes of the last Vintage that had remained since at the Estates on which it was made: out of the several parcels I chose two pipes from different Estates, that I hope will meet your approbation. I was desirous to get that which had more age, but I presumed you would rather have pure Wine of the last Vintage, than the older which had gone through a manufactory operation. For the greater certainty Sir of serving you to your entire satisfaction, I coul'd have wished that I had been on such terms with Mr Bulkeley as to have got some of the same he sent you, or a sample of it, the produce of almost every Estate differing somewhat in point of flavour; but he, with that liberality which so wonderfully distinguishes the Chosen ones, whose unfeigned piety is equalled by nothing but their political sagacity, having in a little underhand manner attempted to injure me, occasioned such a difference as not to allow of my making an application of this nature, & for this reason for the first time, I feel very sorry for it. Supposing that two pipes would be more agreeable than one, if they suited your taste, I have taken the liberty to engage two & should either of them prove to your liking a constant supply can be had of the same: the Estates from whence they came are designated with chalk on the head. Had the cases been ready they would have gone by this Vessel, none being here from Norfolk. A very old pipe of Oeyras Wine was offered me by a gentleman going to England, but it was almost as sweet as that I sent—Putting Brandy into the Wines is generally practised in Portugal; the quantity for each pipe is from $1\frac{1}{2}$ to $2\frac{1}{2}$ gallons half-yearly; another custom more injurious & pretty generally prevailing, is the adding sugar to it when new as they say, to assist fermentation, and of boiling down to the consistence of Syrop Wine from the press, & mixing, with a view to make it richer; the Wine shipped under the name of Lisbon being naturally dry. These probably are the causes why the wine of this Province is not in higher estimation, for when old & pure, it certainly is very pleasant. I am highly gratified to learn that my poor endeavours should have been of any sirvice to my Country; but had I not been informed of it by a person of such eminent abilities & thorough knowledge of the interest & sentiments of my fellow Citizens I should have doubted whether the admission of flour was generally deemed advantageous, or gave much satisfaction, as few of our Countrymen that come here, seem disposed to acknowledge either.

With the most profound Veneration & Respect—I have the honor to be Sir Your most obedient and most devoted Servt.

WILLIAM JARVIS

RC (DLC); at foot of text: "Thomas Jefferson Esquire"; endorsed by TJ as received 9 Nov. and so recorded in SJL.

Thomas BULKELEY, who in 1803 inherited the prominent Lisbon firm John Bulkeley & Son, preceded Jarvis as American consul in the city (Madison, *Papers, Sec. of State Ser.*, 4:318n, 458; Vol. 37:674n).

From John Bird

SIR, New Castle 28th. Sepr. 1803

With extreme concern I have beheld the inclosed publication; and have read it with those emotions, which will actuate the honest heart of every genuine democratic Republican of the State.

The piece is vile and slanderous beyond measure. It is a collection of falshood from beginning to end; and the authors and abettors thereof, ought to be put down. Those who are within your reach, ought, in my humble opinion, to feel the full force of their own wicked machinations. By continuing them, they are furnished by yourself, with the very means of traducing the present administration.

Their envy, their diabolic enmity to republican men and measures will not permit them to remain quiet: But like Lucifer himself, they would, were it in their power, excite rebellion even in *heaven*!

It is needless for me to say more, than I think it my duty to inform your Excellency of those things—so that those persons may be placed before you in their proper colours.

I have the Honor to be, with the most perfect consideration Your obt. Hb Servant JNO; BIRD

Since writing the above, I have been informed, that Senator S White is supposed to be the author of the inclosed.

RC (DLC); endorsed by TJ as received 2 Oct. and so recorded in SJL. Enclosure: see below.

INCLOSED PUBLICATION: perhaps the undated broadside entitled "Address of the Federal Republican Committee of Kent County, To the Electors of the same," submitted by John Clarke, chairman of the Kent County Committee of Correspondence. The address also appeared in full on the first and second pages of the 24 Sep. issue of the *Federal Ark*. It criticized the $15 million expenditure for the purchase of Lousiana. Delaware's share of this debt would be more than $200,000. The writer warned: "Our population is already too much diffused, and by still enlarging our bounds we actually weaken the nation." The writer criticized the expenditures for the repair of the *Berceau*, a French vessel; Gallatin's sale of the Bank of the United States stock; and Congress's grant of $2,000,000 to the president for foreign intercourse without specifying how or when it would be accounted for. The accumulation of debt would lead to "new taxes upon our houses, lands and upon the necessaries of life." The elimination of taxes on "pleasurable carriages" and loaf sugar did not help the ordinary people as long as taxes remained on coffee, molasses, brown sugar, and salt. Finally, the writer pointed to TJ's patronage policy. People were no longer appointed because they were honest, diligent, and capable, but because of their political affiliation. The writer feared the "principles and measures of Mr. Jefferson and *his friends*" would be applied in Delaware. To check this outcome, it was important to elect Federalists in the coming election (see Shaw-Shoemaker, No. 4192).

THOSE WHO ARE WITHIN YOUR REACH: Bird and other Delaware Democratic Republicans especially sought the removal of Wilmington collector Allen McLane. Bird was an applicant for the collectorship in place of McLane (Vol. 37:116-18, 542-4; Vol. 38:24-5, 159-60, 362-3; Vol. 39:640).

From James Monroe

DEAR SIR London Sepr. 28. 1803.

Mr. Halsey a respectable citizen of R Island who has been some years in Europe, will have the pleasure to present you this. He has been introduc'd to me as a young man of merit, of the best connections at home, and expressing a desire of being known to you, I take the liberty of giving him this letter stating his pretentions in the light, they have appear'd to me, and to add that what I have known of his character at Paris & here, justifies the introduction given of him by his friend there. I am happy in the occasion of renewing to you the assurance of my great respect and esteem. JAS. MONROE

RC (DLC); endorsed by TJ as received 8 Dec. and so recorded in SJL with notation "by mr Halsey."

Thomas L. Halsey's FRIEND in Paris was Fulwar Skipwith (see Skipwith to TJ, 6 Apr.).

From Hore Browse Trist

SIR, Fort Adams 28 Sept. 1803

On forming my returns for the Treasury, I was led to discover, that in the Abstract of Exports I had the honor to transmit you on the 16th, under the head *Cordage*, the value thro mistake was expressed 63, instead of 6275 dolls. This error I beg leave to correct, which will make the true sum Total 323,205 dollars for that month.

Presuming that some Missisippi water might be acceptable as a Curiosity, I have in readiness two Barrels, which I shall give myself the pleasure of putting on board the first Boat that passes to your Address, desiring the Vice Consul to forward them by the first opportunity. That it might on its arrival be a correct sample, I have caused one of the Barrels to be bottled & sealed—the river however being very low, the Water is more clear than it generally is. I have understood that its quality is somewhat different from below the confluence of Red river, whose waters are strongly impregnated with Salt.—With perfect respect and esteem I am Sir your Obedt. Servt.

HORE BROWSE TRIST

RC (DLC); at foot of text: "President of the United States"; endorsed by TJ as received 23 Oct. and so recorded in SJL.

RETURNS FOR THE TREASURY: as inspector of the revenue for the port of Fort Adams and collector for the Mississippi Territory, Trist was required to submit regular returns to Gallatin (Vol. 40:10-11).

TRANSMIT YOU ON THE 16TH: Trist's letter to TJ of 16 Sep., recorded in SJL as received from Fort Adams on 16 Oct., has not been found but was enclosed in TJ to Gallatin, 17 Oct.

From William C. C. Claiborne

Near Natchez
September the 29th 1803

DEAR SIR,

I persuade myself that my letters of the 12th and 24th of August, have reached you in safety. I have not yet been enabled to procure Romane's map of Louisiana, and I fear the Geographical sketches which were promised me, by a *Gentleman* residing at Nachitoches on the Red River will not be forwarded. This *Gentleman* is a Doctor Sibly, formerly of North Carolina, and a man of good general information. A Captain of militia, by the name of *Vidal* who is the commandant of a small spanish settlement, immediately opposite to Natchez, has discovered that Doctor Sibly had addressed to me several letters, and this circumstance (I am informed) has excited the jealousy of *this very little Spanish Tyrant*, in so great a degree, as to induce him to report Sibly to the Governor General of Louisiana as a dangerous subject; And the probability is, that for the present, I shall be deprived of the benefit of the Doctors correspondence.

By a late publication in the National Intelligencer, I discover that west Florida is supposed to be included in the Cession from *Spain to France*, and *if so* is now ceded to the United States.—The *Treaty* between France and Spain, I have never seen; but it was reported here that by this *Instrument*, Spain had ceded *Louisiana* with the same extent she *had acquired it from France*;—And that in consequence thereof, the Marquis de Cassa Calvo and Governor Salcedo, the Spanish commissioners had said, that the Island of New Orleans was the only tract of Country, east of the Mississippi which was ceded to France: From this opinion the Prefect dissented, but upon what grounds, I was not informed;—but if the tenor of the Treaty, be as Mr Smith represents, and *Spain has ceded Louisiana to France as the same was previously possessed by France*, there can be no doubt, but the greater part of what is now termed west Florida is included.—It is a fact I believe, universally admitted, that Louisiana when possessed by the French, was considered as extending to the River Perdedo. This River is east of the Mobile, and falls into the Ocean about 12 miles west of the Bay of Pensacola.

I do suppose that three or four companies of regular Troops, will be sufficient to take care of the *fortifications &c* at New Orleans and *between* that City and the mouth of the Mississippi. But permit me to suggest that it would also be advisable, to transport to New Orleans, *four or five thousand* stand of Arms, and a suitable proportion of ammunition. The negroes in the Island of Orleans are very numerous, and the number of free mulattoes is also considerable;—on the change of Government, it is not impossible, but these people may be disposed to be riotous, and the organising and arming the white Inhabitants, (which the American Commissioners might immediately do), would not only discourage any disorderly spirit, but give entire safety to the Province.

In my letter of the 24th ultimo, I stated that a majority of the Citizens of Louisiana could read and write: on further inquiry, I beleive this information to be incorrect. Our new fellow Citizens are indeed involved in great ignorance, a Gentleman on whose veracity I can depend, assures me, that in the settlement of Point Coupee where the society is esteemed wealthy and polished, that not a third of the free Inhabitants can write their names, and among the illeterate, are *those*, whose annual income exceeds $6000: my informant adds, that mental Ignorance pervades the other parts of the Province in an equal, and he beleives in a greater degree.—

The form of Government which may be prescribed for our new Territory, excites great anxiety in this quarter. The present Government of Louisian'a is a Despotism, partly Civil, partly military, and in some degree ecclesiastical. The regeneration of a system thus compounded of ingredients, the most abhorrent to those principles, which we would wish to cultivate in the same district, seems to be an arduous task. Sudden and total reformation is best calculated for enlightened minds; the experiment may prove hazardous with Creole ignorance;—I believe however, that our newly acquired fellow Citizens may be trusted very far, even at first—but I am inclined to an opinion, that until a *knowledge* of the American Constitutions, Laws, Language and customs, *is* more generally diffused, a state Government in Louisiana, would not be managed with descretion.

The Surveyor General Mr Briggs has established his office in the Town of Washington, and added greatly to the happiness of our little society; I hold him in high estimation, and discover with pleasure, that he is acquiring very fast the esteem and confidence of the people. Mr Rodney and Mr Williams have not yet arrived; their appointments as commissioners are very popular, and they are themselves great acquisitions to the Territory.

I have not seen Mr Trist the collector at Fort Adams for some time, but I understand he enjoys good health, and I know he is attentive to his duties; he is indeed a faithful officer, and Justly merits the confidence reposed in him by the Government.

I pray you to accept my best wishes for your individual, domestic, and public happiness

I am Dear Sir With great respect your faithful friend

William C. C. Claiborne

RC (DLC); in a clerk's hand, with signature and inside address by Claiborne; at foot of text: "Thomas Jefferson President of the U. States"; endorsed by TJ as received 23 Oct. and so recorded in SJL.

The Marqués de Casa calvo, former Spanish military commander of Louisiana, served with Manuel de Salcedo on the commission that handed over the colony to the French prefect Pierre Laussat (Ron Tyler, ed., *The New Handbook of Texas*, 6 vols. [Austin, Tex., 1996], 1:1007-8; Madison, *Papers, Sec. of State Ser.*, 4:424, 472).

mr smith represents: that is, Samuel Harrison Smith, editor of the *National Intelligencer*. Claiborne was likely referring to an editorial of 26 Aug. in which the newspaper disputed a claim by another sheet that a separate treaty had ceded West Florida to the United States. Information on such a treaty had not come to light, and in any event "a fair construction of the convention with France" ceding Louisiana left "no doubt that West-Florida is included in the territory ceded."

To Samuel Snowden

Sir — Washington Sep. 29. 03.

I pray you to recieve & apply the within sum of one hundred dollars to the use of those among you afflicted with the present sickness, who may be in need of it. I further request that no acknolegement may be made of it in the public papers, nor otherwise in any manner. I offer my best wishes for the reestablishment of the health of Alexandria, & to yourself my respectful salutations.

Th: Jefferson

PrC (MoSHi: Jefferson Papers); at foot of text: "Mr. S. Snowden"; endorsed by TJ in ink on verso. Recorded in SJL with notation "100. D. Alexa."

Samuel Snowden (1776-1831) was printer and publisher of several Alexandria newspapers over the course of his life, including the *Alexandria Daily Advertiser* in 1803. In his financial memorandum for this day, TJ recorded $100 given to Snowden, as secretary for the Alexandria Committee of Health, "in charity for the sick of Alexandria." Honoring TJ's request for anonymity, Snowden printed in his newspaper the committee chairman's acknowledgment "with gratitude, the receipt of 100 dollars from a gentleman, who has requested that his name may not be published." Yet in the appendix of the local Presbyterian pastor's published sermon on the yellow fever, James Muir listed the "cheerful and voluntary contributions of citizens and of neighbours both in their collective and individual capacities" as of 16 Nov. 1803, and recorded a donation of $100 "supposed to be the President" (James Muir, *Death Abolished: A Sermon* [Alexandria, 1803; Shaw-Shoemaker, No. 4690]; Brigham, *American Newspapers*, 2:1105; MB, 2:1109; Miller, *Alexandria Artisans*, 2:142; *Alexandria Advertiser*, 13 and 30 Sep. 1803; Vol. 36:272n).

From John Wheatcroft, Sr.

Ardennes près Caen
6 Vendemaire An XII.
[i.e. 29 Sep. 1803]

Sr.

Being convinced that a Virtuous, & good Republican, and an amiable & friendly man is approachable at all times; I take the liberty of addressing you in your present elevated situation; knowing that you are an excellent naturalist, & a friend to the Sciences, I conceived an authentic account of a very curious & interesting phenomenon which has lately presented itself in this neighbourhood could not be dissagreeable to you.—a phenomenon that will scarcely be credited, out of the country where it happened, & where exists in this moment several thousands eye witnesses of the fact. The Institute National, were doubtfull themselves, of it's reality, & sent one of their members M. Biot an excellent naturalist, on the Spot, to collect the testimonies of the people resident there, & now they as well as all France are perfectly convinced of its verity. The inclosed is a copious extract of M. Biot's report, which I have faithfully translated; to which I have added, the opinnions of the French Astronomers, and chimists, & communicated to me by M. La Lande the Astronomer, in a conversation I had with him on the Subject. I have also added another hypothesis, of my own, which has I believe the advantage of novelty, if it has no other merit.

If this communication should afford you a moments entertainment, I shall be exceedingly happy, and if you think it merits communicating to your American Philos. Society, you will do me great honour, in being the means of presenting it, or of procuring it's publication in any way you think proper.

In respect to myself, I have since the violence of the revolution has subsided, sat me down quietly on a little Farm, near Caen, where I have been employed in Agricultural, Philosophical, & Literary pursuits, but still hope I shall be able some day, to realize my long wished project, of visiting the United States; among others, one of my strongest inducements, is that of paying you my respects in person.

I am Sr. with constant wishes for the prosperity of yourself, and the United States. Your most Devoted Hmble. Servant

J. WHEATCROFT père

RC (DLC); English date supplied; addressed: "His Excellency Thomas Jefferson President of the United States of America"; endorsed by TJ as received 25 Feb. 1804 and so recorded in SJL. Enclosure: "An Account of a Meteor which passed over Normandy, and let fall a Shower of Stones, in the environs of Laigle. Apr. 26th. 1803. at 1 OClock in the afternoon. with some conjectures on the cause of this phenomenon"; in two parts, the first part consisting of Wheatcroft's translation of an extract from a letter written to the minister of the interior by Jean Baptiste Biot, who reports that he has spoken to a number of people in 20 hamlets in the region around L'Aigle and examined several of the stones that reportedly fell from the sky; the rocks are unlike anything previously collected in that region; they were hot when they hit the ground, and the larger ones still have a sulfurous smell; the many witnesses' accounts are all consistent, and from them Biot concludes that a fireball was seen over an area 30 leagues in diameter and that explosive noises in the sky lasted four or five minutes; the stones fell in an elliptically shaped area two and a half leagues long and one league wide; in the second part of the manuscript, titled "Conjectures on the Origin of the Meteor of L'aigle," Wheatcroft takes issue with French scientists who suggest that the rocks came from a volcanic eruption on the moon or formed in the earth's atmosphere; his own theory is that the meteoric stones could be pieces of a comet; Wheatcroft signs himself as "Associate of the Academy of Sciences, Arts, & Belles Lettres of Caen" (MS in same; entirely in Wheatcroft's hand).

BIOT'S REPORT: Biot, who at the time was a professor of mathematical physics, had been a corresponding member of the National Institute since 1800 and became a full member in April 1803. That month, the minister of the interior—the chemist Jean Antoine Chaptal—sent Biot to investigate the meteorites at L'Aigle. Biot presented his report to the National Institute in July (DSB, 2:133-4; Tulard, *Dictionnaire Napoléon*, 219, 401).

ON A LITTLE FARM: Wheatcroft previously lived at Le Havre, where TJ became acquainted with him in 1784, upon TJ's arrival in France. In the fall of 1789, as TJ and his daughters were leaving Europe, Wheatcroft with his wife and daughter entertained them in Le Havre, and Wheatcroft took charge of some shipments of wine and personal items for them. Prior to the letter printed above, the last correspondence between Wheatcroft and TJ consisted of several letters from Wheatcroft in 1793, including two written at Le Havre that have not been found, one of them of 29 Aug., recorded in SJL as received on 11 Nov., the other dated 28 Oct. and received on 14 Feb. 1794. In 1794 and 1795, Wheatcroft's son, also named John, manufactured soap at Le Havre and was the landlord and friend of Mary Wollstonecraft and Gilbert Imlay (Claire Tomalin, *The Life and Death of Mary Wollstonecraft* [London, 1974; repr. 1992], 213, 218-19; Janet Todd, ed., *The Collected Letters of Mary Wollstonecraft* [New York, 2003], 245n, 252n, 285n,

288; Vol. 7:395; Vol. 15:491-2, 494-6, 498-9, 518-19; Vol. 25:548-9; Vol. 26:443).

Wheatcroft's intellectual PURSUITS included studying the aurora borealis, magnetic variation, water vapor, and the effects of sunlight on colors (*Monthly Magazine; or, British Register*, 18 [1804], 32; Royal Society, *Catalogue of Scientific Papers [1800-1863]*, 6 [1872], 343).

From William Dunbar

DEAR SIR Natchez 30th. September 1803

I had the pleasure of writing you the 19th. of last month, inclosing such imperfect information on the subject of your queries, as I at that time possessed; since which I have been favored with the perusal of the result of Mr. Clark's researches, which are, as I expected, ample, leaving nothing more to be desired respecting most of the points of enquiry; He informs me also that he procured a chart of the Western province to be sketched and sent to you: this notice supercedes the necessity of my furnishing you with any thing at the present moment on the same subject. I shall shortly receive a Copy of the same Chart, & should I find room for improvement, which it may be in my power to bring forward, I shall new model the whole and forward it to you: I perceive a difference of our statements respecting militia, but this is to be reconciled by taking Mr. Clark's as the roll of the militia contained in the Government Registers and mine as the number of men from 18 to 45 years able to bear arms, to which Mr. Clark assents. It is probable that Mr. Clark's information is better than mine respecting the extent of Louisiana along the Sea coast; but I have had reason to suppose that the waters of the inundation extended upon the Coast 3° of longitude & that from thence to the river Sabine was considerably less.

The Gentleman who was to have been entrusted with the scientific part of the Spanish Commission for running the boundary line between Louisiana and the Spanish territory, writes in answer to my inquiries as follows. 'You have devined the real cause of our commissioners remaining inactive; the news of the cession of the province (tho' not official) shackles them in their operations, and will not allow them to adopt any decisive measures, and for this reason they have not yet determined on any thing concerning the instruments that may be wanted, should it be necessary to run a line, which it is generally expected will not be the case; for it is presumed that the two Floridas will be given to the United States by Spain in exchange for the west side of the Missisippi. The Spanish Commissioners had not, nor have they as yet come to any determination, as to the method and principles, on which the line of demarkation ought to be run, neither has any point of the line been defined except one, which is two leagues from Nachitoches W.S.W. on the road to Nacokdoches, the most eastern post of the province of Texas; formerly the Spaniards had a fort at the Adaïs, five leagues west (nearly) from the bayu de Laurier, which is the place where the line crosses the road from Natchitoches to Nakogdoches. It is generally understood here, that the limits of Louisiana are not defined in the treaty of cession by Spain to France, and this conjecture is warranted by the instructions transmitted by our Court to the Commissioners, wherein among a variety of Objects relative to the cession, they are ordered to *determine* and run the boundary line, and no data given them by which they can be guided in the Operation.'

I possess a sketch taken from a chart in the possession of the Spanish government, where the boundary line is represented quitting the Sabine river in a direction nearly E.N.E. to a point distant about 2 leagues from the red river, thence making a right angle with the last course in the direction of nearly W.N.W. (including the post of Adaïs within the angle) was drawn an indefinite line, which appears to have been intended as a parallel to the general course of the red river at that place. Hence it is fair to conclude that this parallel to the red river ought to be continued to the northern Andes, from which chain of mountains the Red river and Messouri derive their Sources; the western boundary consequently will be along this natural division of the middle from the western waters to the Latitude (perhaps) of the Lake of the Woods.[1]

I am with the highest respect Your Obedient & devoted Servant

WILLIAM DUNBAR

RC (DNA: RG 59, TP, Orleans); endorsed by TJ as received 23 Oct. and so recorded in SJL; also endorsed by a clerk. FC (Lb in Ms-Ar: William Dunbar Papers); dated 29 Sep.; printed in Eron Opha Moore Rowland (Mrs. Dunbar Rowland), ed., *The Life, Letters and Papers of William Dunbar* (Jackson, Miss., 1930), 124-5.

MR. CLARK'S RESEARCHES: most of the information that Daniel Clark compiled in response to TJ's queries on Louisiana he directed to Madison, sending letters and detailed enclosures to the secretary of state on 8 and 29 Sep. (*Terr. Papers*, 9:28-47, 61-6).

CHART OF THE WESTERN PROVINCE: see Daniel Clark to TJ, 18 Aug.

Answering TJ's query number 7, Clark copied an official Spanish return of MILITIA units in Louisiana that came to a total of 5,440 men. Dunbar, in his retained copy of the letter printed above, estimated that 10,000 men met the criteria for militia service (*Terr. Papers*, 9:33-4; Rowland, *William Dunbar*, 124).

ALONG THE SEA COAST: responding to the president's third and fourth queries, which supposed that the Piakemines River (Bayou Plaquemine) formed the "western mouth" of the Mississippi, Clark stated that the westernmost mouth of the Mississippi was the Atchafalaya River, into which the Plaquemine flowed. Clark stated that the distance along the coast from the mouth of the Atchafalaya to the bay into which the Sabine River emptied was about three degrees of longitude and that the direct distance west from the Plaquemine to the Sabine, which was "the supposed Western Boundary of Louisiana," was also about three degrees of longitude (*Terr. Papers*, 9:31).

The GENTLEMAN of Dunbar's acquaintance who was to have been part of the SPANISH COMMISSION to mark the boundary between Spanish and French possessions was Stephen Minor. He had been the leading commissioner for Spain in Andrew Ellicott's survey of the southern border of the United States. Originally from the area that became western Pennsylvania, Minor served as an officer in the Spanish army during the American Revolution and remained in the service of Spain after he settled at Natchez (Arthur H. DeRosier, Jr., *William Dunbar: Scientific Pioneer of the Old Southwest* [Lexington, Ky., 2007], 126; Jack D. L. Holmes, *Gayoso: The Life of a Spanish Governor in the Mississippi Valley, 1789-1799* [Baton Rouge, La., 1965], 147n, 198-9, 232-4; Rowland, *William Dunbar*, 132-3).

NORTHERN ANDES: the Rocky Mountains.

[1]In FC Dunbar continued: "Should it be found necessary to run a line of demarcation I would suggest the impropriety of sending white laborers with the commission from the Seat of Govt. as in the Case of Mr Ellicot—negroes hired here will be more tractable & will execute much more labor—a proof which we had upon the line of 31°."

From John Mandeville

SIR Alexandria 30th. Septr. 1803

The Committe of Health with thanks acknowledge the receipt of your humane donation of one hundred Dollars transmitted to us through the medium of our Secretary who is now indisposed—

By Order of the Committe JOHN MANDEVILLE
Sectry. Pro tem.

RC (MHi); at foot of text: "Thomas Jefferson Esqr."; endorsed by TJ as received 1 Oct. and so recorded in SJL with notation "recd 100. d."

Virginia merchant John Mandeville was part of the nine-member Committee of Health, organized by the Alexandria council on 10 Sep. and chaired by Andrew Jamieson. Any three committee members were empowered to use all necessary measures to "arrest the progress of disease and to support and relieve those who may be afflicted" and occasionally publish an accurate statement of the health of the town (James Muir, *Death Abolished: A Sermon* [Alexandria, 1803], appendix; Miller, *Alexandria Artisans*, 1:314-15; *Alexandria Advertiser and Commercial Intelligencer*, 10 Sep. 1803).

OUR SECRETARY: Samuel Snowden.

From Philippe Reibelt

MONSIEUR LE PRESIDENT! Norfolk le 30e Sept. 1803.

Dans la Supposition, que ma lettre de 3 Sept. par la quelle j'ai pris la libertè de Vous informer de ma Situation, et d'implorer Vos secours, Vous soit parvenüe, et que Vous Soÿez disposé, de m'y soulager en quelque Sorte, j'ose Vous representer de plus, que Vous me pouvriez faire la Graçe-pêut etre-de me conferer une place à la Nouvelle Orleans p. E. çelle de Maitre de poste aux Lettres.

Si çela ne seroit pas possible, et que Vous n'aÿez d'autres Vües pour Moi, je pourois aussi m'etablir a la Nouv. Orleans avec un Magazin de Drogues, si j'avois encore la Somme de 500 Gourdes, qui me manque. j'oserois donc, dans çe Cas Vous prier de me l'avançer pour 1 ou 2 ans, en Vous observant, que je serois en etat, de Vous les rendre plustot, si Vous Vouliez les accepter en tableaux et gravures Suisses et en Livres anglais et français qui restent a Bordeaux pour Moi, et que j'attend au plus tard pour le printems prochain.

Je repete les excuses exprimèes dans ma derniere, et suis avec le plus profond Respect Votre Excellence Tr. humble et tr. Obeiss. Str.

REIBELT

EDITORS' TRANSLATION

MISTER PRESIDENT, Norfolk, 30 Sep. 1803

Assuming that you received my letter of September 3 in which I took the liberty of informing you about my situation and imploring your help, and that you are inclined to help me in some way, I dare add that you might perhaps favor me with a position in New Orleans, as postmaster, for instance.

If that is not possible, and you do not have other plans for me, I could nevertheless settle in New Orleans and, with 500 additional dollars, open a pharmacy. In that case, I would be so bold as to ask you for a loan for one or two years, while pointing out that I would be in a position to reimburse you earlier if you would accept payment in the form of Swiss paintings and prints and French and English books, which await me in Bordeaux and should arrive by next spring at the latest.

Echoing the apologies expressed in my last letter, I am, your excellency, with the deepest respect, your very humble and obedient servant.

REIBELT

RC (MHi); below signature: "français de la rive gauche du Rhin" (French, of the left bank of the Rhine); endorsed by TJ as received 4 Oct. and so recorded in SJL.

To Robert Smith

DEAR SIR Washington Sep. 30. 03.

Having understood that you have been unwell, & that your family is still so, I have not asked your attendance here, lest these circumstances should stand in the way. Mr. Madison, Dearborne & Gallatin are here & mr Lincoln expected tomorrow. we have not only to decide on the matters to be communicated to Congress, but as early a decision of the administration as possible is requisite on one of the Louisiana questions, which requires immediate & important orders. should your own health or that of your family not render it inconvenient we should be very happy to see you on Monday & to recieve your aid at a meeting which I propose for Tuesday next. but this is not meant to be pressed against considerations of health or of family distress. Accept my affectionate salutations & assurances of esteem & respect.

TH: JEFFERSON

PrC (DLC); at foot of text: "The Secretary of the Navy"; endorsed by TJ in ink on verso. Recorded in SJL as a letter to the Navy Department with notation "possn of N. Orleans."

MEETING WHICH I PROPOSE FOR TUESDAY NEXT: see Notes on a Cabinet Meeting, 4 Oct. 1803.

From James Wilson

SIR/ [on or before 30 Sep. 1803]

I beg leave to inform you I am the person that made application to you at Monticillo for a small employment under Goverment you were pleas'd to refer me to Mr. Gallatan and I have waited in Town untill I am destitute of the means to stop longer unless it is your pleasure the little money when I set out from Baltimore to Montcillo was only Eight dollars which was the whole sum I was possess'd in the world and it is entirely exaust'd I likewise beg leave to inform you that I have left a wife and three helpless Children in Baltimore in very poor circumstances waiting with Anxious impatience for my return it is unnecessary for me to attempt to describe my distress'd situation further it is obvious to your Benevolent Mind my humble request of you Sir, is that you will pleas'd in your Goodness to give me a little releif to help me home to my Familey I inform'd you at Monticillo that I am a Mechanic but my Trade being Insignificant I cannot get work but in large Towns and very uncertain Sir, if I had a small sum to purchase a few raw matterials I have got Tools by me, I should be Able by my Industry to support and raise my Familey which beleive Sir, would be me greatest pride

JAMES WILSON

RC (DLC); undated; at head of text: "To the President of the United States"; endorsed by TJ as received 30 Sep. 1803 and so recorded in SJL.

For Wilson's previous APPLICATION, see Wilson to TJ, [on or before 16 Sep. 1803].

From Henry Dearborn

[September 1803?]

to be proposed to Congress—

The several Indian Treaties.

progress made in the introduction of the arts of civilization among the Indians, highly flattering.

the several trading houses established in different parts of the Indian Country appear from the best Information, to have had a very usefull effect, and without any diminution of the Capital, imployed.

an attempt to procure an additional cession of lands from the Creek Nation of Indians has failed.

ought we not without delay to take measures for runng the lines as agreed on by the Treaty last year, with the Creeks[1]

RC (DLC: TJ Papers, 136:23477); undated; endorsed by TJ "Departmt. War. Oct. 03. matter for Congress."

TO BE PROPOSED TO CONGRESS: it is likely that Dearborn gave this memorandum to TJ on the president's arrival in Washington on 25 Sep. or soon after. By the beginning of October, the draft of TJ's annual message to Congress included a reference to the treaty with the Kaskaskia Indians (see Madison's remarks, Document II of Drafting the Annual Message to Congress, below at 1 Oct.).

TJ did not use the phrase ARTS OF CIVILIZATION in the annual message, choosing instead to mention "improvements in agriculture & houshold manufacture." He did echo the language of the memorandum printed above when he stated that the government's TRADING HOUSES had "the most conciliatory & useful effect" (Annual Message to Congress, 17 Oct.).

In an 1802 agreement with the state of Georgia, the United States pledged to obtain from the CREEK NATION the land between the Oconee and Ocmulgee Rivers. Negotiating with leaders of some Creek towns in June of that year, however, U.S. commissioners Benjamin Hawkins, James Wilkinson, and Andrew Pickens could get only a portion of that tract. TJ and Dearborn thought that the Creeks would be willing to give up more land and might be persuaded that the Ocmulgee River would be a more effective boundary between their territory and Georgia settlers than a surveyed line could provide. In February 1803, when TJ expected France to take possession of Louisiana and become a dominant influence on American frontiers, he gave high priority to securing the "residue" of the area between the Oconee and the Ocmulgee before the French could "entirely stiffen the Indians against the sale of lands." Early in May, Dearborn sent commissions and instructions to Hawkins, Wilkinson, and Robert Anderson (who, like Pickens, was from South Carolina). Dearborn also arranged for the deposit of $12,000 in the Bank of Georgia and for $2,000 in specie and $3,000 in goods to be available at Fort Wilkinson. Yet in mid-August, in a letter received by the War Department on 19 Sep., Hawkins and Anderson reported their inability to get the Creeks to negotiate for the land (Dearborn to Hawkins, to Anderson, and to Wilkinson, Hawkins, and Anderson together, 5 May, in DNA: RG 75, LSIA; Hawkins and Anderson to the secretary of war, 17 Aug., recorded in DNA: RG 107, RLRMS; Vol. 34:7; Vol. 39:223-4, 355, 529, 530n).

TAKE MEASURES FOR RUNNG THE LINES: on 6 Oct., Dearborn wrote to

Thomas Freeman, who had surveyed the limits of some other cessions of land by Native Americans. Dearborn instructed Freeman to mark the boundary of the tract the Creeks had ceded in June 1802. Dearborn also notified John Milledge of the survey and asked Hawkins to make preparations (Dearborn to Freeman, 16 June 1802, Dearborn to Freeman, to Hawkins, and to Milledge, 6 Oct. 1803, in DNA: RG 75, LSIA; Vol. 40:365).

[1]Dearborn added this note in smaller handwriting at the foot of the page.

Drafting the Annual Message to Congress

I. NOTES FOR A DRAFT, [BEFORE 1 OCT. 1803]

II. JAMES MADISON'S REMARKS ON THE DRAFT, [1 OCT. 1803]

III. REFERRAL OF THE DRAFT TO ALBERT GALLATIN, 3 OCT. 1803

IV. GALLATIN'S NOTES ON THE DRAFT, [3-4 OCT. 1803]

V. GALLATIN'S REMARKS ON THE DRAFT, [4 OCT. 1803]

VI. HENRY DEARBORN'S REMARKS ON THE DRAFT, [6 OCT. 1803]

VII. LEVI LINCOLN'S REMARKS ON THE DRAFT, 10 OCT. 1803

VIII. GALLATIN'S REMARKS ON THE FINANCIAL SECTION, [11 OCT. 1803]

EDITORIAL NOTE

Jefferson's summoning of the new Congress to convene on 17 Oct. and his desire that the legislators be ready to take up the acquisition of Louisiana without delay meant that he would have to prepare his annual message earlier than had been the case in 1801 or 1802. He could, however, rely on the procedures for building the message that he had honed in the previous years. As he had done in crafting those earlier annual messages, in 1803 he prepared a draft that he asked the heads of the executive departments and the attorney general to review in succession. This time he omitted Robert Smith, who had been detained in Baltimore as severe illness afflicted members of his family.

Although the draft that the president began to circulate by 1 Oct. has not been found, one can infer something about it from a set of notes that he apparently made in the early stages of forming the message (Document I below) and from the cabinet members' comments (Documents II, V-VII). A set of notes that Gallatin made for his own use (Document IV) provides additional information. The text that Jefferson sent around was incomplete, lacking the section on finance, and he dubbed it a "projet," or prospectus (see Document III). Madison's comments imply that it consisted of half a dozen substantive paragraphs, plus an introduction and a closing. Judging from Gallatin's first set of comments (Document V), the text was in sections labeled by topics, such as "Louisiana," "Indians," and "War in Europe & Neutrality." As he had done in 1801 and 1802, Jefferson dropped those headings by the time the message went to Congress (Vol. 39:15, 168-9n).

Jefferson, as before, drew on his confidants' advice but did not follow all of their recommendations. He acted on Gallatin's suggestion to remove a section that the secretary of the Treasury referred to as "the Missouri paragraph," which involved the president's desire, embodied in his draft amendment to the Constitution in July, to reserve the upper portion of Louisiana for Native Americans (Document v; see the annual message at 17 Oct.). He also, following Gallatin, removed a reference to roads through Indians' lands. In the third paragraph of the finished message he included a forecast from Madison that "in due season" and with good management, Louisiana would provide "important aids to our Treasury" (Document ii).

Madison's and Gallatin's responses show that when the president wrote the draft, he expected to send the treaty and conventions for the purchase of Louisiana to both houses of Congress with the annual message. Rapid legislative action to comply with the terms of the deal and to enable an immediate assertion of possession would, after all, deny the French government any opportunity to force a reconsideration of the transaction. Jefferson, however, submitting to arguments made by Madison and Gallatin, revised the text to state that he would send the purchase instruments to the House of Representatives only after the Senate had ratified them. He followed Madison's advice to use a "separate & subsequent communication" to convey the treaty and conventions to the Senate.

The long final paragraph of the finished message, which dealt with effects on the United States of the renewed war between Great Britain and France, incorporated contributions from all of them. It included phrasings that Jefferson had in his preliminary notes for the draft (Document i), such as "flames of war," "every act of justice, & of innocent kindness," "merit the character of a just nation," "redress of wrongs not our own," "preferring every consequence to insult & habitual wrong," "calamitous scenes" (recast from "calamities"), "all evil" (from "serious evils"), and something borrowed from James Monroe: "to cultivate the friendship of the belligerent nations." Yet the finished paragraph also contained modifications put forward by Madison, Gallatin, Dearborn, and Lincoln. In his revisions, Jefferson backed away from a threat to cut off trade—to levy some form of embargo. His sketchy first notes contain no explicit reference to that. Madison, remarking on the conclusion of the draft, used the phrase "suspensions of intercourse," but did not make clear if he was introducing a new idea or altering one that he saw in the president's manuscript (Document i). The concept was there by the time Gallatin, who referred to "a menace of interdicting all intercourse," and Lincoln, who used the phrase "non intercourse," saw the text. Gallatin warned that the declaration was "much too strong for the present time," and the attorney general thought that it would arouse sharply divided opinions (Documents iv, v, and vii). Yielding to their objections, Jefferson removed the threat from the message.

In November 1802, Jefferson had not completed the section about finances when he began circulating the draft annual message. Only Madison saw it in that state, however, for within a day, by the time the draft went to Gallatin, the part relating to the Treasury was in place (Vol. 39:15). In October 1803, the text was further along in the review process before Jefferson could fill that hole. Gallatin's notes and remarks show that the initial draft only indicated where "the intended Finance paragraph" would go. Gallatin provided information that he anticipated the president would need to fill in that "blank" part of the message. Jefferson may not have had a draft of the section on finances ready until 10 or 11 Oct. He received Gallatin's comments about it on the 11th. At some point in the process Madison also saw Gallatin's remarks on the financial section and altered some of Gallatin's suggested phrasing (Document VIII and notes). In the finished message, the paragraphs on finances incorporated several of the Treasury secretary's suggestions about wording, deletions, and reordering of material. The early date for the opening of Congress hampered Gallatin and Jefferson, for they needed data from the just-ended fiscal year both for the annual message and for the secretary's own report to Congress. Only on 17 Oct., the day the annual message went to Congress, was Gallatin able to give the president a last piece of information to be inserted into the text (see the annual message and the correspondence between them on that day).

Jefferson made his notes for the draft message on the reverse side of a sheet that contains, on its front, three paragraphs of undated notes in his hand. Those paragraphs are not included here. In structure, tone, and ideas, the first of them resembles the opening passages of his first annual message, although using different words. The second paragraph also probably relates to the 1801 annual message. The third paragraph represents an early stage of work, subsequently transformed, on a portion of his second inaugural address. Together, his jottings on the two faces of the sheet encompass pieces of the compositional history of two annual messages and one inaugural address. He first used the paper in the fall of 1801 as he roughed out ideas for his first annual message. Probably late in September 1803, he returned to the sheet to fill much of the back side with notes for the third annual message (Document I below). Still he retained the leaf, coming back to it yet again, likely in February or early March 1805, to find space on the front side for some thoughts and expressions as he framed his second inaugural address. Afterward, although only limited space remained on the page and he had put most of what he had written on it to use, he kept it in his papers.

I. Notes for a Draft

[before 1 Oct. 1803]

Congress witnessed,[1] & themselves participated in the uneasiness produced at the close of the last year, by the violation of treaty committed by the Intendant of the govmt of N. Orleans, in the suspension of our right of deposit at that place before any other had been assigned. we then believed on good grounds that this was unauthorised by his govmt, and having made proper representns to that we recieved[2] the strongest assurances[3]

British export duty of 1. p. cent to Europe 3. pr cent elsewhere

'to cultivate frdship of both powers by fair & honble means while it pays a scrupulous attention & maintains with firmness the respect which is due to our national character rights & interests.' Monroe[4]

We have seen with sincere concern the flames of war lighted up again in Europe. it's heaviest[5] calamities will be on those immediately engaged in it, but serious evils must also be expected by nations pursuing peace. let it be our endeavor, as it is our interest & desire[6] to cultivate the frdshp of both belligerent[7] parties by every act of justice & of innocent kindness;[8] to receive their armed vessels with hospitality from the distresses of the sea but not to increase[9] their means of annoyance;[10] to establish in our harbors [such] a police as may maintain law & order; to restrain our citizens from embarking individually in a war in which their country takes no part; to punish severely those persons, citizen or alien, who shall usurp the cover of our flag for property not entitled to it, who infect thereby with suspicion the ships & goods of the real[11] American, & commit us to the risk of war to[12] redress wrongs not our own: to expect from every nation the observance towards our vessels & citizens of those principles[13] & practices of which all civilized nations acknolege the obligation; to merit the character of a just nation in all things, & maintain that of an independt one, [preferg][14] every consequence to insult & wrong.[15]

The small vessels sent to the Mediterranean will enable us to confine the Tripoline corsairs more rigorously in port and thereby save[16] the necessity of convoy to our commerce[17] in that sea.

by opening from thence a way thro' the Indn territory[18] to such roads in the intervening states as lead by the shortest & most direct course to the seat of govmt

---

as it's inhabitants could descend with rapidity to support the lower country

RC (DLC: TJ Papers, 128:22128); undated; entirely in TJ's hand; portions obscured by tape.

CONGRESS WITNESSED: this paragraph formed the basis for the second paragraph of the annual message (Annual Message to Congress, 17 Oct.).

See Gallatin to TJ, 18 Aug., for the proposed BRITISH EXPORT DUTY, a topic that TJ omitted from the message.

TO CULTIVATE FRDSHIP: TJ quoted a letter of 19 June from James MONROE to Madison. Monroe indicated that he did not think the French would be offended by his going to Great Britain. The government in Paris, he wrote, "seems to have a just view of the policy of our government in regard to both powers, which is to cultivate their friendship by fair & honorable means while it pays a scrupulous attention & maintains with firmness the respect which is due to our national character rights & interests." TJ used the phrase in the final paragraph of the message (Madison, *Papers*, *Sec. of State Ser.*, 5:104).

WE HAVE SEEN WITH SINCERE CONCERN THE FLAMES OF WAR: TJ retained this clause through the drafting process. It opens the last paragraph of the finished message.

In the seventh paragraph of the message TJ discussed the SMALL VESSELS for the Mediterranean squadron.

The draft seen by the cabinet had a paragraph on ROADS through Native American lands, but TJ excised it from the message, apparently on Gallatin's suggestion (Documents IV and V below).

DESCEND WITH RAPIDITY TO SUPPORT THE LOWER COUNTRY: TJ incorporated this phrasing in the fifth paragraph of the message.

[1]TJ first wrote: "Congress were witnesses" before altering the phrase to read as above.

[2]TJ here canceled "unequivocal."

[3]TJ canceled this paragraph with a diagonal stroke.

[4]TJ canceled this paragraph with a diagonal stroke.

[5]Word interlined in place of "greatest."

[6]Ampersand and word interlined.

[7]TJ here canceled "powers by fair & honble means, to extend to them in our harbours & waters those equal accomodns which the rights of hospitality require, maintaining."

[8]TJ probably broke off writing here or at the end of the next clause, left a gap, wrote the paragraph that follows, and then after an interval returned to resume this paragraph.

[9]Word interlined in place of "aliment."

[10]Preceding eight words interlined.

[11]TJ here canceled "& fair-dealing."

[12]TJ here canceled "avenge."

[13]Word interlined in place of "rules."

[14]TJ here canceled "to meet with firmness."

[15]TJ here canceled "be these the laws of our [. . .] and this the line in which every nation will meet us." Following the cancellation he wrote a block letter "A," probably as a key to another manuscript.

[16]MS: "safe."

[17]Word interlined in place of "vessels." TJ canceled this paragraph with a diagonal stroke and also drew a long stroke through this paragraph and the one above it.

[18]Word interlined in place of "country."

II. James Madison's Remarks on the Draft

[1 Oct. 1803]

✓ (0) for "before" is suggested "without" The former seeming to imply that after the suspension, an assigmt. had been made.

✓ (1) after or for "friendly" insert "proper"
omit "without difficulty or delay" There was perhaps somewhat of both, and it may become expedient to say so to Spain.

(2.) "The enlightened mind of the first Consul of France saw in its true point of view the importance of an arrangement on this subject[1] which might contribute most towards perpetuating the peace & friendship, and promoting the interest of both nations; and the property & sovereignty of all Louisiana, (as it had been ceded to France by Spain,) was conveyed to the U. States by instruments bearing date on the 30th. day of April last. (These stipulations[2] will be immediately laid before the Senate, and if sanctioned by its concurrence, will, without delay be communicated to the House of Reps. for the exercise of its constitutional functions thereon.)"[3]

Such a modification of the paragraph is meant to avoid the implication that the transfer made by France, was covered by the terms "territory adjacent to ours" which describe our proposition. It will also avoid, what the Theory of our constitution does not seem to admit, the influence of deliberations & anticipations of the H. of Reps. on a Treaty depending in the Senate. It is not conceived that the course here suggested can produce much delay, since the tenor of the Treaty being sufficiently known, the mind of the House can be preparing itself for the requisite provisions. Delay would be more likely to arise from the novelty & doubtfulness of a communication in the first instance, of a Treaty negociated by the Executive, to both Houses for their respective deliberations.

✓ (3). after "assure"—are proposed "in due season, and under prudent arrangements, important aids to our Treasury, as well as," an ample &c

Quere: if the two or three succeeding ¶s. be not more adapted to the separate & subsequent communication, if adopted as above suggested.

✓ (4). For the first sentence, may be substituted, "In the territory between the Mississippi & the Ohio, another valuable acquisition has been made by a treaty &c." As it stands, it does not sufficiently distinguish the nature of the one acquisition from that of the other, and seems to imply that the acquisition from France was wholly on the other side of the Mississippi.

✓ May it not be as well to omit the detail of the stipulated considerations, and particularly, that of the Roman Catholic Pastor. The jealousy of some may see in it a principle, not according with the exemption of Religion from Civil power &c. In the Indian Treaty it will be less noticed than in a Presidents Speech.

"Tho' not so indispensable since the acquisition of the other bank" conveys an idea that an immediate settlement of the other bank is in view, & may thence strengthen objections in certain quarters, to the Treaty with France.

✓ With a tacit allusion to profit, "is yet well" may be struck out and "may be the more worthy" inserted.

The last sentence in this ¶ may be omitted, if the reason applied to a former one be thought good.

(5). "must also be expected" better perhaps "are also to be apprehended"

for "both"—"all" or "the" belligerent &c. Holland already makes more than two

After "cover of our flag" substitute for "vessels" not entitled to it, "infecting thereby with suspicion the property of the real

American & committing us to the risk of war[4] to redress wrongs not our own";

———

✓ instead of "to expect from every nation," which does not follow well the antecedent "endeavor" may be inserted "to exact"—"to draw,"—This member of the sentence may indeed be dispensed with, being comprehended in the ensuing member viz. "maintain the character of an independent one &c." "Maintain" being repeated several times within a small compass—"pursue this course," may be preferable.

(6). For this conclusion, is offered for consideration, the following "for the possibility of failure in these reasonable expectations, it will rest with the wisdom[5] Congress to consider how far and in what form, provision may properly be made, for suspensions of intercourse where it cannot be maintained on principles of justice & self respect." or

✓ "and therewith prevented, the necessity of remedial provisions on the part of the U. States"

(7). for "unconcerned in"—"and from"

RC (DLC); undated; in Madison's hand with TJ's checkmarks; endorsed by TJ as received from the State Department on 1 Oct. and "Message of Oct. 1803."

ENLIGHTENED MIND OF THE FIRST CONSUL: whether this phrase originated here with Madison or was in TJ's first draft is not known. See also Gallatin's notes (Document IV below) and his suggestions for revision (Document V).

SEPARATE & SUBSEQUENT COMMUNICATION: see TJ to the Senate, 17 Oct.

A treaty concluded by William Henry Harrison in August required the United States to pay $100 annually for seven years to support a ROMAN CATHOLIC priest for the Kaskaskia Indians (Charles J. Kappler, comp. and ed., *Indian Affairs: Laws and Treaties*, 5 vols. [Washington, D.C., 1975], 2:67-8; TJ to the Senate, 31 Oct.).

MAY BE INSERTED "TO EXACT": following Madison's suggestion, TJ changed "to expect from every nation the observance" (Document I) to: "to exact from every nation the observance" (Annual Message to Congress, 17 Oct.).

[1] Opening quotation mark supplied by Editors. Madison first wrote "The enlightened mind of the first Consul in France saw in a true point of view an arrangement on this subject" before altering the clause to read as above.

[2] Madison interlined "instruments" above this word but did not cancel either word.

[3] Closing parenthesis supplied by Editors.

[4] Madison enclosed the preceding five words in brackets and interlined "into controversies," enclosing that phrase in brackets also to mark it as an alternative to "to the risk of war." In revising what became the 14th paragraph of the finished message, TJ used the interlined alternative.

[5] Preceding two words interlined (and Madison apparently neglected to add "of").

III. Referral of the Draft to Albert Gallatin

Oct. 3. 03.

Th: Jefferson asks the favor of mr Gallatin to examine with rigour the inclosed projet of the message to Congress, and to note on a separate paper the alterations he thinks advantageous. as it is to go thro' the hands of the other gentlemen of the Cabinet, his immediate attention to it is desireable. he also asks the favor of mr Gallatin to meet the heads of department here tomorrow at 10. aclock.

RC (NHi: Gallatin Papers); addressed: "Mr. Gallatin"; notes by Gallatin on verso (see the next document). Not recorded in SJL.

TOMORROW AT 10: see Notes on a Cabinet Meeting, 4 Oct.

IV. Gallatin's Notes on the Draft

[3-4 Oct. 1803]

Period—What? of representations or of restoration of deposit?

propositions had been authorized—When? prior to that period? *Quere*

subsequent appropriation—to what? to the authorizan. of proposition by executive?

enlightened mind of first Consul—

Treaties *now* laid before both houses—

Introduce idea of possession of N. Orleans being a bond of Union and, if possible, of prevention of early settlements beyond Mississippi

---

Authorization from legislature to take possession
Is it necessary? Will it not delay?

Omit road as not of equal importance
& perhaps Missouri

Then add after paragraph "for confirming to Indians their right" there "to establish friendly relations with them"[1]

Omit 3 parag. commencing "authority from the Legislature" & ending "diligence & fidelity" & incorporate their substance with the preceding

—

Recommendation to open for settlement the Kaskakia Country doubtful unless connected with that of preference to settlements on this side of Mississippi

—

Laying treaty before ratification before Congress doubtful

—

Tripoli—small vessels will be able &a. add "with less expence"

European war—May not the idea of our having so happily escaped, by the success of the late negotiation, becoming parties to it, be mentioned?

—

Menace of interdicting intercourse too early & unprovoked—Add that treaties of commerce oppose it.

—

Conventions for limits with Gr. Britain
why not mentioned?

—

Neutral passions

—

Finance to proceed "War in Europe" and perhaps some parts of the two paragraphs of War & Neutrality blended as similar

MS (NHi: Gallatin Papers); undated; in Gallatin's hand, written on verso of Document III above; with checkmarks by Gallatin alongside all entries except those beginning with "Tripoli" and "Menace."

PERIOD: Gallatin probably began some entries in these notes, which he did not transmit to TJ, with words or phrases from the draft.

[1]Closing quotation mark supplied by Editors.

V. Gallatin's Remarks on the Draft

[4 Oct. 1803]

Remarks on President's message

—

Louisiana– 1. It seems to me that the treaty ought not to be laid before both houses of Congress until after ratification by Senate. The rights of Congress in its legislative capacity, do not extend to making treaties, but only to giving or refusing their sanction to those conditions which come within the powers granted by the Constitn. to Congress. The house of Rep. neither can nor ought to act on the treaty until after it is a treaty; and if that be true, no time will be gained by an earlier communication to that body. In asserting the rights of the house, great care should be taken to do nothing which might be represented as countenancing any idea of encroachment of the constitutional rights of the Senate. If in order to be enabled to carry on a negotiation, the Executive wants a previous grant of money or other legislative act, as in the Algerine treaty, some Indian treaties, & last session 2 millions appropriation, an application may be necessary before the negotiation is opened or the treaty held; but when, as in the present case, the negotiation has been already closed & the treaty signed, no necessity exists to consult or communicate to the house until the instrument shall have been completed by the Senate & President's ratification: in this instance, there is no apparent object for the communication but a supposition that they may act, or, in other words, express their opinion & give their advice, on the inchoate instrument which is, at that very time, constitutionally before the Senate.

2. There is some ambiguity in that paragraph about the *period* previous to which propositions for obtaining New Orleans had been authorized. I presume that by that period is meant, not the time when representations were made to Spain respecting the deposit, but that when the deposit was restored. Quere, also, whether the appropriation of two millions was *subsequent* to the time when those propositions, for obtaining New Orleans & adjacent territories, were authorized?

3. Although the personal compliment to the first Consul may be pleasing to him &, on that account, consistent with policy, yet it is doubtful whether it should not be omitted, because it will produce an opposite effect in Great Britain, because he is certainly very unpopular with all parties & descriptions of men in the United States, and because, if my memory serves me right, personal compliments to foreign sovereigns are not usual anywhere in communications from the Executive

to the Nation except under very particular circumstances. Perhaps something more general might be substituted showing still our sense of the motives which have actuated or which it may be proper to ascribe to France, and applying what we may say to the French Government rather than to the Consul himself.

4. In enumerating the advantages resulting from the acquisition of Louisiana, the most obvious, that of securing the advantages of navigation & outlet to the[1] Western States, which is the subject of the preceding part of the paragraph, might perhaps without inconvenience, be repeated, next to or preceding that of securing us from collision with foreign nations. But there is another which, if it does really proceed from that event, ought not to be omitted, vizt. that the acquisition of New Orleans is a most solid bond of the Union. Another delicate & difficult subject to introduce, but which, if it could be touched, would tend to remove the only objection which, so far as I know, the eastern federalists have been able to press with any success, is that our object should at present be to restrain the population & settlements on this side of the Mississippi, and that the acquisition of the country west of it enables us in fact better to regulate & controul the progress of our settlements. Perhaps that idea might be introduced in connection with what is said in a subsequent part of the message of the settlement of the country lately obtained from the Kaskakias.

5. If the authorization to take military possession is not strictly necessary, it will be much more convenient to order its being done immediately after ratification; otherwise, a delay equal to the whole time employed in Congress in debating the general question whether the treaty shall be carried into effect, will take place. Situated as we are as respects both France and Spain every day may be precious. Observe that Mr Baring informs me that his house have advanced already ten millions of livres to France on the guarantee of Mss. Munroe & Livingston grounded on the authority they had to dispose of 2 millions of dollars. Should we, through any accident, miss the opportunity of taking possession, both the treaty & the money may be lost.

It must be observed generally that not even Congress can prevent some constitutional irregularity in the proceedings relative to occupying & governing that Country before an amendt. to the Constitn. shall take place. I think that, at all events, it will be better not to ask in direct terms for that authorization; but some general terms may be introduced in the immediately preceding article which will cover the object such as "for the occupying & temporarily[2] governing the country, and for its ultimate incorporation in the Union"

6. The paragraph in relation to the road may be omitted as of not sufficient relative importance when compared to the other objects recommended to the consideration of Congress. I should be also inclined to strike out, for the same reason, the Missouri paragraph, especially because the result of the mission contemplated by last year's appropriation is not yet known & cannot therefore be communicated, & because so far as relates to what Congress should do on that subject, the substance of the paragraph might also be introduced by adding a few words to that in which the attention of Congress is called to the measures rendered necessary or expedient on account of the acquisition of Louisiana. Thus after the words "for confirming to the Indians &a" might be added "& for establishing commercial & friendly relations with them" and also "for ascertaining the geography of the territory acquired." Upon that idea the three paragraphs commencing with the words "Authority from" & ending with the words "diligence & fidelity" might be omitted; and the substance of the first & last incorporated with the preceding paragraph commencing with the words "With the wisdom" and now ending the with the words "to impair."

Indians— 1. If the idea of laying the Louisiana treaty before the house only after its ratification, shall be adopted, a similar modification of expression would of course be adopted in the expressions communicating the substance of the treaty with the Kaskaskia tribe

2. Unless the idea of controuling settlements beyond the Mississippi can, as before hinted, be connected with that of opening for settlement the Kaskaskia cession,

I think that, under present circumstances, it would be best for the Executive to omit the expression of an opinion in favor of extending settlements on the Mississippi within that cession, as it will be misrepresented in the Eastern parts of the Union as a proof of partiality toward that western quarter and as a wish to promote migration & to weaken rapidly the eastern interest. The subject will, without being further recommended than merely stating the cession, be taken up by the Kentuckey members who ardently wish to see a frontier settled north of them.

Great Britain is not mentioned in the message except by an allusion to her aggressions, which cannot well be omitted, but which contrasted with what must be said of the French Govt. respecting Louisiana, may be more displeasing to her than is necessary & may also be misrepresented as giving on the whole an aspect of partiality to the message. For the purpose of removing any such impression or insinuation, and also, in order to complete the *tableau* of our happy situation in every respect might not the two conventions made with that power, by which our eastern & north western limits are fixed and every territorial subject of dispute with them is removed, be mentioned? If a paragraph to this effect was introduced, it might immediately precede that of the Kaskaskias.

War in Europe & Neutrality

1. Those two subjects are so nearly the same that I think they should not be divided by the intended Finance paragraph. This might follow then Tripoli, & in connecting the two others, some modifications in their arrangement; on account of the similarity of some of the ideas contained in them might be introduced.
2. Without expressing any thing like self-applause, but referring every thing to the moderate & wise policy adopted by last Congress and on great provocations, and with a due acknowledgment of gratitude to Providence, I think it but fair to introduce the idea of our having, by the late successful negotiation, so happily escaped becoming parties to the war, & to contrast our situation with that of the bellig. powers or rather with what would have been ours, had a different course been pursued. In the view presented by the message, the

serious evils to be apprehended by us as neutrals are alone stated.

3. It may be proper in a general enumeration to mention the propriety of restraining our citizens from embarking individually in the war. The laws on that subject are, however, as complete as possible.
4. The sentence which conveys a menace of interdicting all intercourse appears to me much too strong for the present time. The aggressions & provocations are not yet sufficient to justify the idea; it does not seem consistent with our general policy to throw out such menace before negotiation has been tried & exhausted; and the anticipation of such state of things darkens the pleasing impression resulting from the general aspect of the message.
5. *arena* this expression is rather strong as applied to the parties in the war—*neutral passions* is ambiguous as instead of conveying the idea that passions should be neutralized or rendered neuter, (for the observance of a neutral conduct) it seems to mean that there is a certain class of passions which are called *neutral*

Finance— I will not be able to give to the President the precise amount of the receipts in the Treasury during the last year (ending 30th Septer) nor of the balance in the Treasury on that day, as the Savannah & Charleston returns to that date will not reach me in time; but I will, within next week give the amount of both within 100,000 dollars so as to enable the President to say that the receipts have exceeded ____ millions ____ hundred thousand dollars & that the balance amounted to near ____ millions ____ hundred thd. dollars. I will also either this week or early next, be able to give the precise amount applied during that year to the paymt. of principal & interest of the public debt, distinguishing the paymts. on acct. of principal from those on acct. of interest. As to the revenue *accrued* during the year, on which our estimates of receipts hereafter must be grounded, it will be impossible to speak with any degree of precision before 1st of Nover. I can only say that it has exceeded the estimate heretofore made by the Secy. of the Treasy., and on which our present arrangements have been made. As to the necessity of additional taxes my present impression drawn from an exact review of the revenue accrued during the year 1802 & a tolerably correct one of that accrued during the two first quarters of this year, and from the Louisiana resources is that we want about 300,000 dollars. This is grounded on the following sketch

The revenue estimated by last year's report was equal or nearly so to the estimated expenditures of the year. The revenue accrued during the year ending 30th June last exceeds the estimate by say—

300,000 dollars

The imports of Louisiana in foreign articles do not exceed 2,500,000 dollars, which at our rate of duties will produce a revenue of about 350,000 dollars from which deducting vizt.

duties on 4 millions ℔ sugar the annual exports of Louisiana & which coming in the U.S. duty free will be consumed there at $2\frac{1}{2}$ cents pr. ℔	100,000	150,000
do. on 100,000 ℔ indigo do. a 25 cents	25,000	
expences of the province	25,000	
nett revenue		200,000

Which two items make a revenue of 500,000 dollars applicable to new objects

Of the 15 millions purchase money of Louisiana, we may pay two millions in specie; the interest on the remaining 13 millions is 780,000 dollars, of which 675,000 payable in Europe which on that acct. will cost at least 3 p% more or 20,000 dollars. The interest to be provided is not certainly less therefore than	800,000
deficiency	300,000

I am afraid of a further deduction in the revenue on account of the slow sale of lands this year & of the slower payments; this, however may be considered as temporary. If on account of the small vessels now employed for Tripoli, the navy estimates can be reduced from 900, to 600 thd. dollars, I think that we may venture without additional taxes; but at all events, it will be best that the subject if mentioned by the President, should be stated in doubtful terms, as rather a hope than a certainty & as a subject to be investigated by Congress when they shall have received the usual estimates. The paragraph may in the mean while remain blank till the middle of next week, as that will enable me to obtain more precise results.

RC (DLC); undated; in Gallatin's hand, including endorsement "Remarks on the President's message—AG"; endorsed by TJ as received from the Treasury Department on 4 Oct. and "Message of Oct. 1803."

AS IN THE ALGERINE TREATY: in 1792, at the request of President Washington acting on advice from TJ as secretary of state, Congress approved an appropriation of $50,000 that would let the United States, in TJ's words, "go to Algiers with the cash in our hands" to redeem American captives and secure a treaty (Vol. 23:256-7).

LAST SESSION 2 MILLIONS APPROPRIATION: the authorization by Congress in February 1803 of $2,000,000 to enable Monroe and Livingston to bargain for New Orleans (Vol. 39:584).

ABOUT THE PERIOD PREVIOUS TO WHICH: see the third paragraph of the annual message at 17 Oct.

For the PERSONAL COMPLIMENT TO THE FIRST CONSUL, see Documents II and IV above. In the finished message (see the third paragraph), TJ called the French government, rather than its head, "enlightened."

TJ referred to the INCORPORATION of Louisiana into the union in the fourth paragraph of the completed annual message.

For the TREATY WITH THE KASKASKIA TRIBE, see TJ to the Senate, 31 Oct.

EASTERN & NORTH WESTERN LIMITS ARE FIXED: see the eighth paragraph of the finished message.

DIVIDED BY THE INTENDED FINANCE PARAGRAPH: in the final version of the message, TJ dealt with the renewed war in Europe and issues of American neutrality together in the final paragraph, following a series of paragraphs on financial affairs.

[1] Gallatin here canceled "present."
[2] Word interlined.

VI. Henry Dearborn's Remarks on the Draft

[6 Oct. 1803]

+ they must have been sensible, that alth'o the right of deposit was of little value to the U.S. when compaired with the actual & peaceable possession of New Orleans and the adjacent country on both sides the river, the continuance of the privation must have produced an important effect on the peace & tranquility of our Country.

‡ but from the assurances of the respective Beligerant powers we have reason to[1] expect, as well from their sense of Justice as from their wisest policy, the most fair & friendly treatment from each, that our neutral rights will be scrupelously regarded, and of course, that the irregularities which have been practized by any Commanders of armed Ships or vessels, upon any of our Citizans and our neutral or

sovereign rights, will not only be disapproved but punished, as soon as proper representations of the cases shall have been made.

extending along the Mississippi from the mouth of the Illinois to the mouth of the Ohio about 150 miles, and on the Ohio from its mouth to within[2] twelve miles of the mouth of the Wabash.

RC (DLC); undated; in Dearborn's hand; endorsed by TJ as received from the War Department on 6 Oct. and "Message."

THEY MUST HAVE BEEN SENSIBLE: Dearborn used symbols to connect his remarks to three places in TJ's draft. It appears that in each case Dearborn was proposing new or revised wording. His first suggestion relates to the second paragraph of the annual message as TJ sent it to Congress, his second suggestion to the long final paragraph, and his third suggestion to the fifth paragraph of the message (Annual Message to Congress, 17 Oct.)

[1] Dearborn here canceled "believe."
[2] Dearborn here canceled "ten or."

VII. Levi Lincoln's Remarks on the Draft

SIR — Washington Octo 10—1803

I have perused, and reperused with increased satisffaction the proposed message which you did me the honor of submitting to my inspection. Was I obliged to maintain an exception to any part of it, I should select for that purpose, the close of the last paragraph but one. Would not the sentiment present itself more formidable to foreign nations, & less exceptionable to many of our citizens, if expressed in terms more general? Altho non intercourse, &, if possible, non consumption is, and always has been, my favorite system of defence against maritime aggressions, especially British; yet as it is a measure both in principle & practice, about which our citizens & even republicans, are zealously divided in their interest, feelings & opinions, I doubt the policy of awakening their sensibility pointedly on the subject, unless it should become necessary—or of even holding out to the aggressing nations, that non intercourse, is all they have to fear, should they continue their outrages—To leave such nations to fear the worst as the effects of their wrongs, and our citizens to hope for the best according to their several, but variant conceptions of what would be best, under possible oppressions, would not the closing sentence stand better if expressed in some such manner as the following? viz—"*And supercede the necessity of considering how far*" *on principles of justice & self-respect, recourse ought to be had to one or more of those efficient measures obviously placed within our power—*

Under such a general expression, non intercourse with, or without other measures, might or might not be adopted in future as should be judged expedient, and in the mean time no particular claim would be given to a certain portion of our community, who above all things dreading such a measure, would endeavour by exaggerating its evils, to produce groundless fears &[1] Jealousies in the minds of the people—My mind is but freely[2] impressed with the ideas above expressed, yet as they occurred, I thought it my duty to submit them—

I am Sir most respectfully your most obedt Sert

LEVI LINCOLN

RC (DLC); at foot of text: "The President of the U.S."; endorsed by TJ as received 10 Oct. and "Message" and so recorded in SJL.

LAST PARAGRAPH BUT ONE: in the finished message presented to Congress on 17 Oct., the passages to which Lincoln referred are in the final paragraph.

[1] Lincoln interlined "fears &."

[2] MS: "feely."

VIII. Gallatin's Remarks on the Financial Section

[11 Oct. 1803]

a. instead of the words "those of the first three quarters &a" to the end of the paragraph; insert. It is already ascertained that the receipts on account of duties on tonnage & merchandize have exceeded dollars; and that the revenue accrued on the same objects during that period[1] has exceeded the sum at which our peace revenue had been established.

b Omit whatever relates to interest & say only. The amount of public debt paid for the same year is estimated at nearly 3,200,000 dollars, making with the paiment of the preceding year, dollars applied towards the discharge of the principal of the debt: and there remain &a.

c. instead of the words "pledged in" substitute "still applicable towards the payment"

omit altogether the words "the residue" to the end of the paragraph it being matter of course

d the word "then" might be added between "will" and "be," in order to connect this with the preceding paragraph

e instead of the words "we have supposed" &a to the word "discharged" say "the present existing debts[2] will be discharged by the ordinary operation of the sinking fund"

f. I would wish to see all the words from "and such economies" to "injury" altogether omitted; but if the President shall think it proper to retain the idea, the words "and the economies which may still be introduced in our public expences." This will be more general & embrace the reduction which may result from peace with Tripoli & all other executive savings.

g omit altogether the paragraph "I trust in it" to "counted on"

h instead of the words "I have not used the power" say "it was not thought expedient to use the power" and after the words "domestic debt" add "although proposals to that effect had been received from Holland

Note. That paragraph would be better in order if connected with that which states the payment made during the year of principal of the debt

i This paragraph may be omitted or connected with the first saying that the Estimates & account of receipts & expenditures will be laid before Congress by the Secrey. of the Treasy.

RC (DLC); undated; in Gallatin's hand; with emendations by Madison (see note 1 below); endorsed by Gallatin: "Remarks on the financial paragraph respectfully submitted—A.G."; endorsed by TJ as received from the Treasury Department on 11 Oct. and "Financl branch of message."

A: in the finished message TJ made no reference to revenues from customs DUTIES.

B: TJ discussed the amount paid on the PUBLIC DEBT in the tenth paragraph of the message.

C: also in the tenth paragraph, TJ noted the $2,000,000 appropriated by Congress for the acquisition of New Orleans and STILL APPLICABLE to the purchase of Louisiana.

TJ incorporated the changes that Gallatin suggested in sections D, E, and F into the eleventh paragraph of the revised text.

OMIT ALTOGETHER THE PARAGRAPH: the phrase "counted on," perhaps a remnant of the paragraph to which Gallatin referred, is in the ninth paragraph of the message.

NOT THOUGHT EXPEDIENT TO USE THE POWER: for TJ's incorporation of this change and for the reference to DOMESTIC DEBT, see the twelfth paragraph of the message.

LAID BEFORE CONGRESS: see the ninth paragraph of the message.

[1]Madison altered the preceding text to read "on the importations during the same period."

[2]Gallatin first continued "must necessarily be discharged by the operation of the provisions alread" before altering the text to read as above.

To John Condit

DEAR SIR Washington Oct. 1. 1803.

Your kindness on a former occasion in procuring me the cyder of Newark, encourages me to trouble you again in the same way. I should be very glad to get eight barrels of the first quality, to be forwarded here as soon as it is in a proper state to move. your engaging this for me will be thankfully acknoleged.

I hope we shall see you on the first day of the session, as the unavoidable absence of two Western members of the Senate will leave us nothing to spare. Accept my friendly salutations and assurances of respect & esteem. TH: JEFFERSON

PrC (DLC); at foot of text: "Doctr. Condit"; endorsed by TJ in ink on verso.

FORMER OCCASION: see Condit to TJ, 30 Dec. 1802.

UNAVOIDABLE ABSENCE: John Smith of Ohio did not take his seat until 25 Oct., but Thomas Worthington, Ohio's other senator, and the senators from Tennessee and Kentucky attended the opening session on 17 Oct., as did Condit (*Biog. Dir. Cong.*; JS, 3:295-6, 302).

From David Gelston

SIR— New York Octo. 1st. 1803

I had the honor to write to you the 21st. ultimo, and enclosed bill of lading of one box of wine, and one cask of nuts—I have this day received from Messrs. Perrot & Lee (Bordeaux) bill of lading & Invoice, of five cases red, and five cases white wine, ℔ the Thetis, capt Adams—Invoice enclosed—presuming as before, it will be your wish to have it forwarded to the City of Washington, I shall have it entered here, and then forwarded by the first vessel bound to alexandria, or Georgetown—unless, counter orders are received—

Very respectfully, I am, Sir, your obedient servant

DAVID GELSTON

RC (MHi); at foot of text: "Thomas Jefferson President U.S."; endorsed by TJ as received 4 Oct. and so recorded in SJL. Enclosure: Invoice, 22 Aug., from Perrot & Lee of Bordeaux, for five cases of red wine of the 1798 vintage of "Mde. Rozan Margau," worth 675 shillings, and five cases of white wine of the 1798 vintage of "Dufiethe Sauterne," worth 525 shillings, for a total of 1,200 shillings (MS in MHi; in a clerk's hand except for signature of firm; endorsed by TJ: "Lee William. invoice of 1803").

For TJ's order of wine of Bordeaux from William LEE, see Vol. 40:539-40 and Lee to TJ, 8 Aug. In his financial memoranda, TJ recorded paying on 23 Oct. about $124 for 150 bottles of "Rozan Margau," the RED vintage, and about $96 for 150 bottles of sauterne, not including customs and freight charges (MB, 2:1116).

From John Langdon

Sr. Portsmouth 1st. Octob 1803

I am informed that the time for which the Marshal for the Destrict of Maine was chosen will soon expire, and that the probability is, he will not be reappointed; I would therefore beg leave to name, Major Joseph C. Boyd of Portland in sd. Destrict for that office. this gentleman is perfectly correct in his Politics, and in every way well qualified for the Business.

The Honbl. Mr. Cutts can give any further information relative to this Gentlemans Charecter that may be tho't necessary.

I am very respectfully Sr. Your Obliged Hbl. Servt

John Langdon

RC (DNA: RG 59, LAR); at foot of text: "President of the United States"; endorsed by TJ as received 12 Oct. and so recorded in SJL with notation "Joseph C. Boyd to be Marshl. of Maine"; also endorsed by TJ: "Boyd Joseph C. to be Marshl. of Maine v. ."

The marshal for maine was Isaac Parker, a Federalist, whose term of office was to expire in December 1803. Writing William Eustis on 10 Nov. 1803, Parker asked that his desire to be reappointed be made known to the president. "If, being a federalist," Parker wrote, "but never a reviler of the present administration or its measures, I can be re-appointed to Office; I shall exercise it, as heretofore, with impartiality, & never to the prejudice of those who bestow it" (RC in DNA: RG 59, LAR, endorsed by TJ: "Parker Isaac. to Dr. Eustis"; Vol. 38:613n). TJ, however, had marked Parker for removal early in his administration, deeming him "a very violent & influential & industrious fed." (Vol. 33:219).

TJ had appointed joseph c. boyd a bankruptcy commissioner for Maine in 1802, but he failed to qualify due to his absence from the country (Vol. 38:28; Vol. 39:154n, 612). Writing James Madison on 25 Aug. 1803, shortly after his return from France, Boyd explained his awkward position after learning that his commission was not valid and that John Mussey had been appointed in his place. Acting on Langdon's advice, Boyd asked Madison to inform him of "the will of the President, and your Orders for my future government" (RC in DNA: RG 59, LAR; endorsed by TJ: "Boyd Joseph C. to mr Madison. for renewal of commn of bankruptcy"). Boyd was not reinstated as a bankruptcy commissioner, nor did he receive the marshal's appointment despite additional recommendations in his favor. In a 20 Nov. letter to Madison, Boyd's brother, John P. Boyd, touted his sibling's qualifications for the Maine marshalcy and referred Madison to Congressman Richard Cutts for information as to his brother's "capacity, integrity, attachment to the constitution and his zeal in favor of the present Administration" (same; endorsed by TJ: "Boyd Joseph C. to be Marshal of Maine. John P. Boyd to mr Madison"). On 26 Nov., U.S. Attorney George Blake of Massachusetts wrote Gideon Granger on behalf of Boyd, stating with confidence that he was a "worthy respectable man, & has been & is a uniform zealous Republican" (same; endorsed by TJ: "Boyd Joseph C. to be Marshal of Maine. Blake's lre to Granger").

From Zalegman Phillips

Rhodes Hotel Washington
October 1st 1803

Respected Sir,

I take the liberty to solicit the appointment of Commissioner of Bankrupts for the District of Pennsylvania, in the place of John W Vancleve Esquire deceased or of Mr Joseph Clay, who will resign his Commission in the course of a few Days, I enclose a certificate from some Gentlemen of known respectability, which I trust will be sufficient to establish my Character and Principles. I have a letter of Introduction from General Muhlenberg of Philadelphia, with which I shall have the honour of presenting myself to you on Monday next,

I am with Respect Your most obedient very humble Servant.

Zalegman Phillips

RC (DNA: RG 59, LAR); at head of text: "To his Excellency Thomas Jefferson President of the United States"; endorsed by TJ as received 1 Oct. and "to be Commr. bkrptcy Pensva v. Clay or Vancleve" and so recorded in SJL. Enclosure: Certificate, dated at Philadelphia, 5 Sep. 1803, recommending Zalegman Phillips, attorney, to the president as a suitable person to fill the position of bankruptcy commissioner for the District of Pennsylvania; signed by Moses Levy, Israel Israel, John Purdon, Mathew Carey, James Gamble, Lewis Rush, George Bartram, William Duane, David Jackson, James Ker, Thomas Procter, William P. Gardner, and six others, all "very well acquainted, with the Character & Principles" of the candidate (MS in same; in Phillips's hand, signed by all).

A Philadelphia native, Zalegman Phillips (1779-1839) entered the University of Pennsylvania in 1795 and four years later was admitted to the Philadelphia bar. He established a thriving practice in criminal law. In 1805, he married Arabella Solomon of a prominent Jewish family in Baltimore. A Jeffersonian Republican noted for his support of democratic causes, Phillips became an ardent advocate of Andrew Jackson as early as 1822. He wrote an address "To the Electors of the Second Congressional District," published in Philadelphia in 1828, when he ran unsuccessfully for Congress as a Jacksonian Democrat. A leader in the Jewish community, he served as president of the Mickvéh Israel Congregation from 1822 to 1834 and of the United Hebrew Beneficent Society of Philadelphia, founded in 1822 (Henry Samuel Morais, *The Jews of Philadelphia: Their History from the Earliest Settlements to the Present Time* [Philadelphia, 1894], 45, 49, 143, 431; Edwin Wolf II and Maxwell Whiteman, *The History of the Jews of Philadelphia from Colonial Times to the Age of Jackson* [Philadelphia, 1957], 219, 296-8, 350-1, 471; Harold D. Moser and others, eds., *The Papers of Andrew Jackson*, 9 vols. [Knoxville, 1980-], 7:53-5; *Jewish Quarterly Review*, new ser., 45 [1955], 620; *Daily National Intelligencer*, 14 Nov. 1823, 24 Aug. 1839; *Philadelphia Inquirer*, 7 Oct. 1829).

letter of introduction: see J. P. G. Muhlenberg to TJ, 22 Sep., which Phillips presented to the president on Monday, 3 Oct.

From James Walker

Buckingham October 1st. 1803—

I am sorry to inform you that it will be quite out of my power to fulfill my engagement to you so early as you wish, it seems as if it will be impossible with me to get Mr. Scotts Mill in opperation sooner than some time next faul—as the walls of the house will not be began untill spring I shall be very busyly employed all next summer in puting up the mechinery in his Mill, I do not suppose that either yourself or Mr. Scott would consent for me to carry on both Mills at the same time nor do I think that I can do it to any advantage, as both jobs consists chiefly in Mechinery. it will require the greatest attention to be paid by the master workman, if you cannot pospoan puting up the works next summer I must loose the job but if you can I will as soon as possible draw a plan of the house and direct Mr. Hope how to procede on his part, likewise draw bills of scantling plank &c. for the wood work in order that it may be got in due time to be well seasoned, you will please to send me an answer as soon as convenient—

I am with great esteem Sir, Your Mo. Obt. H. Servt.

James Walker

RC (MHi); addressed: "Mr. Thomas Jefferson Washington City." Recorded in SJL as received 16 Oct.

fulfill my engagement to you: see TJ to Walker, 20 Sep.

From Benjamin H. Latrobe

Dear Sir, Newcastle, Octr. 2d. 1803

I have delayed to answer your favor of the 14h.[1] September for a few days, untill I had compleatly ascertained whether by any exertion it would be possible to procure sheet Iron sufficient to cover the public buildings & to make up the deficiency for Monticello this Autumn, and I have now the satisfaction to inform you, that all your Iron is rolled & will be sent off by the first opportunity, & that two or three Tons intended for the President's house at Washington are also ready & will be dispatched by the earliest Vessel.—The fever at present raging both at Philadelphia & Alexandria renders it however doubtful when an opportunity directly to George town may occur. It is my intention, that should it appear probable that considerable delay will be occasioned by waiting for a vessel, the Iron shall be sent to Baltimore, & from thence by Land, as the Iron will be sufficient to load two or three Waggons, and the expence of Transportation will not, I find on enquiry, be encreased more than 8 or 10 Dollars ℔ Ton,—or about 5 ℔Cent on the value of the Iron.—

By a letter written to you from Washington I endeavored to inform you of the exact state of the work at the Capitol, and of the difficulty of procuring stone; which has from the commencement most materially retarded the work. As I shall have the honor of seeing you at Washington in the course of next Week, I will not take up your time at present further than to say that the stoves & flues for heating the Senate Chamber will be forwarded from Philadelphia in the course of this month, and that the fever having driven away our best Coppersmith, I have ordered the pipes for the Water closet at the President's house, at Baltimore, where, by this time, they must be ready to be sent on.

The universal drought of this summer has silenced many of the best Pensylvanian forges, at least during many hours out of twenty four., I must beg that you will admit this apology for the delay in forwarding the Sheet iron, to procure which, at last, has required no small degree of exertion.

I write this letter with Mr Peale's polygraph,—a machine the most useful that has, I believe, as yet been invented for the purpose of copying letters. I am not yet entirely Master of its motion so as to write exactly the same hand, which a single pen produces; but in an hour's practice I learned to write with the same ease & rapidity as with the common pen. I doubt not but that you have heard of the machine, & perhaps you possess one of them. What I have written on the other side is a specimen of the truth with which the copy is made.—The young Gentleman whom you did me the favor to recommend to me has now been in my office upwards of two months. He possesses that valuable substitute for Genius,—laborious precision, in a very high degree; and is therefore very useful to me, though his professional education has been hitherto much misdirected.—His personal character and habits are very singular. He is an enthusiastic methodist, devoting many hours of the evening & morning to prayer & singing of psalms,—and though a temper violently choleric appears through the viel of religious mildness, he has himself so perfectly under command, as never to have exhibited any visible anger, though the provocations to it by the motley crew of my people have been sometimes beyond the common bounds of human patience. I think he will become a very useful citizen, though never a very amiable Man.

Believe me with the truest respect and attachment Your faithful hble Servt B Henry Latrobe

RC (DLC); endorsed by TJ as received 6 Oct. and so recorded in SJL. PoC (same); fourth page only, that is, the last paragraph and closing.

YOUR FAVOR: TJ's letter to Latrobe, recorded in SJL at 14 Sep., has not been found. It was likely that mentioned by Thomas Munroe in a letter of 16 Sep.

TJ first learned of the POLYGRAPH in January, but it would be several more months before he experimented with one (Vol. 39:306-7; TJ to Latrobe, 26 Feb. 1804).

YOUNG GENTLEMAN: Robert Mills, who had formerly studied architecture under TJ (Latrobe, *Correspondence*, 1:331n; Vol. 38:4n).

[1] Date altered from "24."

From J. D. Rittener

[Vev]ey 2e 8bre. 1803
en Suisse

Des longtems J'ai le Projet de M'aller fixer dans Votre Patrie, & di conduire Quelques—bons laboureur. si Jusqu'ici je ne l'ai Executé c'est le Manque de Moyen, Car pour Se procurer des laboureur il faut pouvoir leurs payer les fraix de Voyage, qui sont assé Conséquand. J'ai donc crus Monsieur le Président devoir M'adresser directement a vous pour Vous demander si le Gouvernement, (Qui Paroit S'interresser a ce qu'il s'introduise des Collomb Agriculteur) ne payeroit pas les fraix de Voyage a ceux qui iroit. tant pour l'agriculture que des Gens De Professions, dans ce Cas il faudroit Qu'une Maison a Bordeaux féut chargèr de Payer les fraix, a l'arrivée audit Bordeaux & une au lieux du Debarquement Jusqu'a la Destination, Quand aux terres Qu'elle Sonts les Conditions Sous les Qu'elles ont Les delivres & la Quantité a châque famille, Je prend la Liberté de vous adresser la Presente Sous Envelope de notre Consul de Comerce a Bordeaux: dans l'attente d'une réponse, recevez Monsieur le Pres. les Salutations bien Sincerres de Votre devoue Serviteur

J. D. RITTENER

EDITORS' TRANSLATION

[Vevey], Switzerland
2 Oct. 1803

It has been my longtime intention to settle in your country and bring workers there. I have not yet accomplished that goal because I lack the means to do so. To hire workers one must pay their travel costs, which are considerable. I thus feel obliged, Mister President, to address you directly to ask if your administration (which seems to be interested in having farmers immigrate) could pay the travel expenses of those who go there for farming or other professions. In that case, a company in Bordeaux would need to be entrusted with paying the costs upon arrival in Bordeaux and again from there to the destination. As for land, under what terms is it distributed? And how much for each family? I take the liberty of including this letter in the pouch of our commercial consul in Bordeaux. In hopes of your reply, please accept, Mister President, the very sincere greetings of your devoted servant.

J. D. Rittener

RC (DLC); torn; addressed: "a Monsieur le President des Etats Unis a Vasencton en Amerique"; addressed at head of text to president of the United States at Boston ("a Bostond"); franked; postmarked (blurred) New York, [30] Jan.; endorsed by TJ as received 3 Feb. 1804 and so recorded in SJL.

In 1810, Rittener obtained a concession to mine coal at a location not far from Vevey in the canton of Vaud, but the operation closed after a few years when he was unable to make an arrangement to supply fuel for a salt works (Michel Maignan, "L'Histoire des exploitations houilleres Vaudoises," *Minaria Helvetica*, 7 [1987], 25; Marcel Godet and others, eds., *Dictionnaire historique & biographique de la Suisse*, 7 vols. [Neuchatel, 1920-33], 2:159).

From Meriwether Lewis

Dear Sir, Cincinnati, October 3rd. 1803.

I reached this place on the 28th. Ult.; it being necessary to take in a further supply of provisions here, and finding my men much fatiegued with the labour to which they have been subjected in descending the river, I determined to recruit them by giving them a short respite of a few days; having now obtained the distance of five hundred miles: on the evening of the 1st. inst. I again dispatched my boat with orders to meet me at the Big Bone lick, to which place I shall pass by land, it being distant from hence only seventeen miles while by water it is fifty three, a distance that will require my boat in the present state of the water near three days to attain.—

The late reserches of Dr. William Goforth of this plase at that Lick has made it a place of more interesting enquiry than formerly, I shall therefore seize the present moment to visit it, and set out early tomorrow morning for that purpose.

Dr. Goforth in the begining of May last with a view to obtain a complete skeleton of the Mammoth, sunk a pitt 30 feet square and eleven feet in debth in a moist part of the Big Bone Lick, from which he obtained a large number of specimens of the bones of this anamal, tho' generally in a very imperfect and mutilated state; he also obtained from the same pitt several grinders of the anamal generally supposed to be an Elephant from their affinity to the teeth of that anamal; these last are very perfect: a part of this collection of bones the Dr. has in his possession at this place and has been so obliging as to favour me with an examinetion of them; the other part of the Dr's collection is yet at the Lick, these he informs me are much more perfect than those he shewed me, particularly the *upper portion of a head*, and some other specimens which had been obtained from a small pitt, sunk in a dryer part of the Lick by a young man to whom, in his absence he had confided the prosecution of his researches; among these specimens the Dr. also mentioned a tusk of an immence size, the dementions of which he could not furnish me with, not having yet seen it, but from the information of his assistant, states it's weight at 180 lbs.; this tusk is said to be in a good state of preservation. The Dr. informed me that he had been interdicted by the Agent of Mr. David Ross of Virginia, (the proprietor of the Lick) from removing these bones, as he was also from the further prosecution of his researches; he is much chagrined at this occurrence, and seems very anxious that some measures should be taken by which to induce Mr. Ross to suffer him to prosecute his enquiries. The Doctr. presented me with two handsome specimens, the one a grinder of the Elaphant, the other, that of the Mammoth, the former weighs ten and ½ pounds, the latter I have not weighed, from the circumstance of it's roots being attatched to a lump of clay, without seperating from which, it's weight could not be accurately asscertained; I concluded it would be better to forward it in it's present state, as the clay will not only guard this part of the tooth from injury in transporting it, but will at the same time furnish a good specimen of the earth of which the lick is formed. Dr. Goforth was so good as to grant me his permission to take from those bones now at the Lick the large tusk before noticed, and any other bones that are to be found among his collection at that place: Capt. Findley who accompanys me to the Lick says he is well acquainted with the Agent of Mr. Ross, and thinks that he can obtain his permission also for the same purpose; should I succeed you may expect to recieve through Mr. Trist, this large tusk together with the two grinders before mentioned, and such other specimines as I may be enabled to procure, and which, I may think worthy your acceptance.

All the bones, which I observed in the possession of Dr. Goforth appear to be those of the Mammoth, accept only the Elephant-like grinders;[1] the most remarkable among them was a portion of the lower or larger part of a tusk; measuring one foot ten inches in circumpherence and five feet eight inches in length, the Dr. informed me when he first obtained it, it was upwards of six feet in length and weighed one hundred pounds; the greatest[2] circumpherence of the tusks of Mr. Peale's skeleton I believe is not more than one foot six ½ inches. As the anatomy of the Mammoth has already been so well asscertained by the skeleton in the possession of Mr. Peal (the upper portion of the head excepted) I confined my enquiries mearly to a search for this part of the skeleton, and for such specimens of the tusks as would enable me to deside a question which appears not yet fully to have been satisfyed (viz) Whether the flat or sythe-shaped tusks so frequently found in the same bed with the acknowledged tusks of the Mammoth, are the tusks of that anamal, or a different one?—

With regard to the first[3] of these enquiries I was unsuccessfull, finding only one mutilated specimen of the upper portion of the head, the frontal bone of which had entirely decayed; I was therefore unable to form any just idea of it's shape; as to the second, I was more fortunate, obtaining many specimens of both the acknowledged Mammoth tusks, as well as those of the flat tusks, both in a sound and an imperfect state; these I compared with attention; but before I proceed to express an opinion with respect to the homogeniallogy of these tusks I will give a short description of these specimens, in order Sir, that you may from thence draw your own inferences, and make your own deduction.—

The tusks of the Mammoth were conical, much Curved, and also spiral or twisted; the fragments of whatever portion of the tusk were homologus to the same part of a complete tusk; when by decay the end of a section of any large part of the tusk was observed, the ends of the broken lateral stratas of the lamina, formed a number of circular rings, each imbracing and inclosing the other from the center to the circumpherence of the tusk, these rings however, were of unequal thicknesses; when perfect[4] the lamina assumes a yellowish white or creem colour, in it's decayed state it resembles white chalk, both in colour and consistance (see No. 2. specn. inclosed); the surface of the tusk sometimes assumes partially a black colour, which from it's resembleance to the Buffaloe horn might on a slite examineation betaken for a similar substance, but on a more minute investigation it appears to be ivory, or the common lamina of the tusk, which, has acquired that colour from some cause, most probably, from the properties of the clay in which they had been so long deposited; this black Ivory (No. 2) is rarely more than two lines in thickness, gradually loossing it's hue inwards, untill it becomes the common colour of the tusk.—

The flat or sythe-like tusks assumed a great variety of figures, tho' uniformly curved; one was flat on both sides near the large end of the tusk, where it was connected with the head; this was rendered conspicuous from the conic concavity common to this part as well of the Mammoth, as these tusks, at the larger end; and so much was it flatened, that this end of the tusk was left in a forked shape, while the smaller end assumed the curved, and connic shape, and was also spiral, as is that of the Mammoth: several were flated unequally on both sides near the small extremity of the tusk, the larger end being conical, curved, and spiral; while others were flat on one side only, throughout the whole extent of the tusk: the lamina of these tusks whether perfect, decayed, or assuming the horn-like appearance, is the same substance precisely of the Mammoth tusk: in every instance where the tusk is flatened, the circular rings of lamina are perfect when the diameter of those rings do not exceed the thickness of the tusk, which last I found unequal in the different specimens; and when the rings of lamina exceed the thickness of the tusk they are broken, but still we find the corresponding parts of these broken rings, attatched to either side of the perfect one, and succeeding each other throughout the whole width of the tusk; thus presenting the exact figure of the Mammoth's tusk reduced to a flat surface on both sides by being grownd down.—

I also observed that several bones that were in a good state of preservation, appeared to have been woarn away in the same manner, or from the same cause which had flattened the tusks, particularly a large grinder of the Mammoth which struck my attention, it was unconnected with the jaw bone; one third of the volume of this tooth seemed to have been woarn away, as if reduced on one side by being grown down to a plane surface; the enamal of the fractured edge appeared to have given way equally with the bone of the tooth and presented a smooth surface; no part of this tooth shewed any sharp fracture which, might[5] induce a belief that it was reduced to it's present[6] shape by a violent or sudden stroke.—

Finding that the upper part of a tusk was flattened, which shape it could not have acquired during the existence of the living anamal, it being that part of the tusk which by bone or cartilage must have been united with the head; that in every case where the same specimen united both the character of the Mammoth and flat tusk, that portion resembleing the Mammoth tusk was in all respects it's prototipe; that the tusk of the Mammoth is well defined, and that it's characteristics strongly mark it; that the lamina of both the flat and the conic tusks, are invariably the same in similar states of preservation; and that in all instances where the tusk is flattened the lateral lamina shews evedent marks of violence; I can therefore have no remaining doubt of these flat or *sythe-like tusks* being *the tusks of the Mammoth*; and from the appearance of the flattened grinder of the Mammoth before noticed, I am strongly disposed to believe that these flat tusks of the

Mammoth have acquired that shape in consequence of the sand and gravel passing over them for a great length of time caused by a running stream or agitated water.—

The Elephants teeth which I saw in the possession of Dr. Goforth weigh from four to eleven pounds, and appear to me precisely to resemble a specimen of these teeth which, I saw in the possession of Dr. Wister of Philadelphia; and which if my recollection serves me, Dr. Wister informed me was found in S. Carolina: the Dr. has since assured me, that from a comparison of this specimen with the plates representing the teeth of the Asiatic Elephant[7] contained in the late Vols. of the British philosophical transactions, that he is perfectly convinced that it is the tooth of the Asiatic Elephant or an anamal very much resembleing it. Relative to these teeth it may not be unworthy of remark, that so far as I have been able to inform myself, they are never found adjacent to the bones of any anamal of their comparitive size, except those of the Mammoth; or such as from their affinity to the anatomy of that anamal, have always been admitted to be the bones of the Mammoth. These teeth are never found attatched to the bones of the jaw; and notwithstanding the high state of preservation in which those Elephant's teeth are found, that no other part[8] of it's fraim should yet have been discovered in America. From the shape and termination of both extremities of these grinders they each appear to have completely filled it's respective jaw bone.—

Not any of the bones or tusks which I saw were petrifyed, either preserving their primitive states of bone or ivory; or when decayed, the former desolving into earth intermixed with scales of the header or more indissoluble parts of the bone, while the latter assumed the appearance of pure white chalk.—

I would thank you to forward me some of the Vaxcine matter, as I have reason to believe from several experiments made with what I have, that it has lost it's virtue.—

Conner, the interpretter I had calculated on engaging, has declined; however I do not feel much disappointment at this occurrence, being well assured that a suitable person of that discription can be procured at St. Louis.—

So soon Sir, as you deem it expedient to promulge the late treaty, between the United States and France I would be much obliged by your directing an official copy of it to be furnished me, as I think it probable that the present inhabitants of Louisiana, from such an evidence of their having become the Citizens of the United States, would feel it their interest and would more readily yeald any information of which, they may be possessed relative to the country than they would be disposed to do, while there is any doubt remaining on that subject.

As this Session of Congress has commenced earlyer than usual, and as from a variety of incidental circumstances my progress has been unexpectedly delayed, and feeling as I do in the most anxious manner a wish to keep them in a good humour on the subject of the expedicion in which I am engaged, I have concluded to make a tour this winter on horseback of some hundred miles through the most interesting portion of the country adjoining my winter establishment; perhaps it may be up the Canceze River and towards Santafee, at all events it will bee on the South side of the Missouri. Should I find that Mr. Clark can with propiety also leave the party, I will prevail on him also to undertake a similar excurtion through some other portion of the country: by this means I hope and am pursuaded that by the middle of February or 1st. of March I shall be enabled to procure and forward to you such information relative to that Country, which, if it dose not produce a conviction of the utility of this project, will at least procure the further toleration of the expedition.

It will be better to forward all letters and papers for me in future to *Cahokia.*—

The water still continues lower in the Ohio than it was ever known.—

I am with every sentiment of gratitude and respect.—Your Obt. Servt.

MERIWETHER LEWIS Capt.
1st. U.S. Regt. Infty.

RC (DLC); at foot of text: "The President of the United States"; endorsed by TJ as received 26 Oct. and so recorded in SJL.

Among the specimens in the possession of William Goforth, Jr., Lewis saw fossils from both mammoths and mastodons. In this letter, Lewis used the word MAMMOTH to mean what is now called the mastodon. The fossil teeth that appeared to be like those of an ELEPHANT were from mammoths (Robert Silverberg, *Mammoths, Mastodons and Man* [New York, 1970], 90-1; Vol. 38:97n).

At Big Bone Lick in Kentucky, DAVID ROSS owned salt works and 2,000 acres of property (Stanley Hedeen, *Big Bone Lick: The Cradle of American Paleontology* [Lexington, Ky., 2008], 11, 13).

CAPT. FINDLEY: James Findlay of Cincinnati (Lewis to TJ, 20 Apr. 1803).

WORTHY YOUR ACCEPTANCE: Lewis sent several fossils down the Mississippi for shipment to TJ, but the boat that carried them had an accident at Natchez and the specimens never reached New Orleans (Jackson, *Lewis and Clark*, 1:132n; Thomas Rodney to TJ, 23 Apr. 1804).

PLATES illustrating teeth of the Asian elephant accompanied a paper by Everard Home, "Some Observations on the Structure of the Teeth of Graminivorous Quadrupeds; Particularly Those of the Elephant and *Sus Æthiopicus*," Royal Society of London, *Philosophical Transactions*, 89 (1799), 237-58.

For the prospect that John CONNER might serve as interpreter for Lewis's expedition, see Lewis to TJ, 20 Apr.

CANCEZE RIVER: that is, the Kansas River.

[1] MS: "griners."
[2] MS: "greates."
[3] MS: "fist."
[4] MS: "perfet."

[5]MS: "mighht."
[6]MS: "pesent."
[7]MS: "Elephat."
[8]MS: "pat."

From Méry

Monsieur Frankford 3 octobre 1803.

la persuasion ou Je suis que c'est avec plaisir que vous saisisez l'occasion d'obliger, m'a seule enhardi à implorer vôtre protection. Je me trouve ici dans une facheuse position; les lettres dont J'etois porteur et avec lesquelles Je devois me procurer des fonds pour me rendre a St Domgue ma destination, m'ayant été enlevées pas les Anglois, une seule a eté preservée du malheur general l'ayant cachée plus soigneusement, comme m'ayant eté recommandée par Mr. de la Fayette vous devez, Monsieur, l'avoir reçu depuis quelque temps. veuillez bien avoir la bonté de m'adresser a quelque maison qui puisse m'avancer une modique somme Jusqu'a ce que J'aye touché des fonds de chez moi ce qui ne peut être long. Mon intention etant de me fixer dans ce pays, J'espere avoir un Jour l'occasion Monsieur, de vous témoigner ma reconnoisance.

Votre très humble Serviteur Méry
a frankford près philadelphie
chez Jossua Sullivan

Ps. n'ayant pas l'honneur d'etre connu de vous Monsieur, Je prends la liberte de m'appuyer d'une lettre de Mr. de la Fayette, que Je viens de trouver dans mes papiers.

EDITORS' TRANSLATION

Dear Sir, Frankford, 3 Oct. 1803

The only thing that emboldens me to seek your protection is my conviction that you welcome opportunities to oblige. I find myself in an awkward position here. The British have confiscated the letters I was carrying and with which I was to have procured the funds to reach my destination in Saint-Domingue. Only one letter escaped this misfortune because I had hidden it carefully, as Mr. Lafayette recommended. You should have received it some time ago, Sir. Please could you introduce me to some company that could lend me a modest sum until I have received funds from home? It would not be for very long. Since I plan to settle in this country, Sir, I hope some day to have the opportunity to express my gratitude to you.

Your very humble servant Méry
Frankford, near Philadelphia,
care of Joshua Sullivan

P.S. Since I do not have the honor of being known by you, I am taking the liberty of relying on a letter from Mr. de la Fayette that I just found among my papers.

RC (ViW: Tucker-Coleman Collection); endorsed by TJ as received 5 Oct. Enclosure: Lafayette to Elisbeth Marie de Grassin d'Astorg, not found (see TJ to Méry, 6 Oct.).

Joshua SULLIVAN owned a weaving mill on Pennypack Creek about ten miles from Philadelphia (Clark Hunter, ed., *The Life and Letters of Alexander Wilson* [Philadelphia, 1983], 64-6, 220-1, 251-2).

From John Page

MY DEAR SIR Richmond Octr. 3d. 1803

I left Wmsburg the first day that the weather & my little Son's state of health would permit, & had he not relapsed into a dangerous Illness, I should have pushed on alone, to spend if it were only a day with you at Monticello, even though Mr. Harvey informed me that you were on the point of setting out to Washington. My dear little boys illness, which 'till today scarcely gave us any hopes of his recovery, must be my Apology for delaying so long an explanation of our breach of promise, & a renewall of our promise to endeavour to make amends for it next year.

Accept our thanks for your very friendly invitation, & our best Wishes for your health & Happiness, & the strongest assureances of the highest respect & Esteem of your sincere

Friend JOHN PAGE

RC (DLC); endorsed by TJ as received 7 Oct.

Notes on a Cabinet Meeting

Oct. 4. Present Secretaries of State, Treasury, War.

will it be adviseable for forcible possn of N. Orleans to be taken, if refused. unanimous it will.

should we now prepare force, so as to have it ready the moment Congress authorises it? unan. it will.

what force? 400. regulars from F. Adams, 100. do. from Chickasaw bluffs & Massac, 500. militia of Mis. tery. boatmen & sailors.

MS (DLC: TJ Papers, 131:22677); entirely in TJ's hand; follows, on same sheet, Notes on a Cabinet Meeting of 16 July.

PRESENT: TJ notified Gallatin of this meeting on 3 Oct., when he referred the draft annual message to the secretary of the Treasury. See Document III of Drafting the Annual Message to Congress, above at [before 1 Oct.].

To Benjamin Rush

DEAR SIR Washington Oct. 4. 03.

No one would more willingly than myself pay the just tribute due to the services of Capt Barry, by writing a letter of condolance to his widow as you suggest. but when one undertakes to administer justice it must be with an even hand, & by rule, what is done for one, must be done for every one in equal degree. to what a train of attentions would this draw a President? how difficult would it be to draw the line between that degree of merit entitled to such a testimonial of it, & that not so entitled? if drawn in a particular case differently from what the friends of the deceased would judge right, what offence would it give, & of the most tender kind? how much offence would be given by accidental inattentions, or want of information? the first step into such an undertaking ought to be well weighed. on the death of Dr. Franklin the king & convention of France went into mourning. so did the House of Repr. of the US. the Senate refused. I proposed to Genl. Washington that the Executive department should wear mourning. he declined it, because he said he should not know where to draw the line, if he once began that ceremony. mr Adams was then Vice-President, & I thought Genl. W. had his eye on him, whom he certainly did not love. I told him the world had drawn so broad a line between himself & Dr. Franklin on the one side, and the residue of mankind on the other, that we might wear mourning for them, and the question still remain new & undecided as to all others. he thought it best however to avoid it. on these considerations alone, however well affected to the merit of Commodore Barry, I think it prudent not to engage myself in a practice which may become embarrassing.

Tremendous times in Europe! how mighty this battle of lions & tygers with what sensations should the common herd of cattle look on it? with no partialities certainly. if they can so far worry one another as to destroy their power of tyrannising the one over the earth, the other the waters, the world may perhaps enjoy peace, till they recruit again. affectionate & respectful salutations. TH: JEFFERSON

RC (CtY); addressed: "Doctr. Benjamin Rush Philadelphia"; franked and postmarked; endorsed by Rush. PrC (DLC).

A letter of 19 Sep. from Rush, recorded in SJL as received 1 Oct., has not been found. In it, Rush evidently requested that TJ express condolences to the widow of John BARRY, senior officer in the U.S. Navy, who died in Philadelphia on 13 Sep. (ANB).

From Robert Smith

SIR, Balt. Oct. 4. 1803—

The sickness of my Children continues and appearances are at this moment very afflicting. Mrs. Smiths extreme anxiety has for several days made her consider it necessary to watch over them day & night. It was my intention to have been at Washn. last Sunday. The painful fear of never again seeing my youngest Daughter has prevented me. I have brought my family to the House of Mrs. Smiths good father in order that their situation may be more Comfortable during my absence. And I will avail myself of the first appearance of recovery to go to Washn. With the most affectionate & respectful regard I am Sir,

Your Obed Ser— RT SMITH

RC (DLC); endorsed by TJ as received from the Navy Department on 5 Oct.

Smith's YOUNGEST DAUGHTER, Mary Williams Smith, died shortly after this letter was written. Smith suffered the tragic loss of several children during his tenure as TJ's secretary of the navy, including sons Robert and William Carvil in 1801 and his eldest daughter, Elizabeth Louisa, and youngest son, Robert, in 1806. Of Robert and Margaret Smith's eight children, only one, Samuel William, reached maturity (table of Robert Smith's children, in MdHi: Dielman-Hayward Biographical File; Vol. 35:219, 269, 273, 325, 723; Vol. 36:3n; TJ to Robert Smith, 10 Oct. 1803; Samuel Smith to TJ, 10 Feb. 1806; TJ to William Branch Giles, 23 Feb. 1806).

MRS. SMITHS GOOD FATHER: William Smith, a Baltimore merchant and former member of Congress (*Biog. Dir. Cong.*; Syrett, *Hamilton*, 12:213, 214n).

From Thomas T. Davis

Kaskaskie. Indiana Territory
DR SIR October 5th 1803.

Since the Date of my Letter to you at Saint Vincennes I have been employed in visiting the Spanish settlements on the other side the Mississippi. The People are wealthy & the Land rich. most of them are averse to the Cession of Louisiana to the U.S. but I think by a little attention & moderation they may be easily won over. They are affraid of the Liberation of their Slaves (of which they have great numbers). I advised them to petition Congress on the subject they have done so. Tomorrow I set out for Saint Louis: to see a French man named Shoto who it is said has Just returned from Santofee &

Reports that he has found a Salt Rock of immense size on the Dividing Ridge that seperates the Head Waters of the Arkinsaw River from the head waters of the Missouri Shoto & his party have brought some Considerable quantity. I shall be at great pains to ascertain this fact. Those who live on the River Arkinsaw affirm that when that River is high the water is salt.

In the upper Louisiana there is about ten thousand Souls. The americans are setling fast on the Spanish side. It will be most agreeable to the people on the Spanish side to form a seperate Territory. But if that side is added to Indiana Territory an increase of Judges must be necessary.

I am respectfully your Obt Sevt.

THO. T DAVIS

RC (DLC); endorsed by TJ as received 10 Nov. and so recorded in SJL.

MY LETTER TO YOU: Davis to TJ, 26 Sep. 1803, recorded in SJL as received 18 Oct. from Vincennes, but not found.

SHOTO: either Auguste Chouteau or his half-brother Pierre Chouteau, who were partners and dominant players in the western fur and Indian trades. Auguste conducted most of his business from St. Louis, while Pierre had resided for many years among the Osage Indians in western Missouri. In early 1804, TJ received a number of mineral samples from the Chouteaus, including salt from "the great Saline of the Osage Nation" located on a southern branch of the Arkansas River about 600 miles from St. Louis (ANB, s.v. "Chouteau, René Auguste" and "Chouteau, Jean Pierre"; Davis to TJ, 28 Jan. 1804; Meriwether Lewis to TJ, 18 May 1804).

SALT ROCK OF IMMENSE SIZE: see John Bradford to TJ, 29 Nov. 1803.

If UPPER LOUISIANA was formed into a separate territory, Davis hoped to be named its governor. Writing to James Madison on 18 Oct. 1803, Davis asked to have his wish made known to the president, adding that "My standing in the Estimation of the people in the Western Country will render such an Appointment very popular" (RC in DNA: RG 59, LAR; endorsed by TJ: "Davis Thos. T. to be a Governr. Louisa. lre to mr Madison").

To David Gelston

SIR

Washington Oct. 5. 03.

I recieved last night your favor of the 1st. inst. as I had before done that of the 21st. Ult. informing me of the forwarding the box of wine & cask of nuts, by a vessel bound to Alexandria & which doubtless may be now hourly expected. I will thank you to forward in like manner the ten cases of wine mentioned in your last by the first conveyance to Alexandria or Georgetown. the meeting of Congress renders their early reciept desireable; but at the same time the epidemic at N. York may perhaps subject us to the delay of quarantine, if the vessel touches at any intermediate place before arriving within the territory of Columbia, where no quarantine is established. I must pray you to inform me of the duties & other expences on both parcels which shall be immediately remitted you, & of any formality necessary on my part for their regular entry which shall be complied with. Accept my friendly & respectful salutations. TH: JEFFERSON

PrC (MHi); at foot of text: "David Gelston esq."; endorsed by TJ in ink on verso.

From George Logan

DEAR SIR Stenton Octbr: 5th 1803

I am informed that several Persons are applying for the Office of Mr: Clay which will become vacant on his taking his seat in Congress Mr: Walter Franklin a young Gentleman of the Law in Philadelphia, spoke to me some time since on this subject; he wished me to mention to you, that should you honor him with the appointment, he would do the duties of the office with care & fidelity. The Father of Mr Franklin was an eminent Merchant in New York, previous to the American revolution. On the British taking possession of that City, he retired to Philadelphia, making a great sacrifise of his property. Mr: Walter Franklin was educated to the Bar, has considerable Professional abilities & is universally esteemed. Some time ago he married the Grand Daughter of Saml Howell an old revolutionary Patriot. Of this character and of Mr: Franklins Father, General Washington in his official Letters speaks with great respect. Mrs. Logan has copied the enclosed extract on this subject for your information; she desires her best respects to be remembered to you—and is of opinion with me that the cause of Republicanism will be served by giving the office to Mr: Franklin in preference to some whose names have been mentioned to us as applying for it—

I shall leave Stenton on the 12th and expect to be at Washington on the 16th—The Marquis Yuries with his Family dine with me to day. They will leave this in two or three days, for the Seat of Government.

With sentiments of great Respect I am your Friend

GEO LOGAN

RC (DNA: RG 59, LAR); endorsed by TJ as received 8 Oct. and "Franklin Walter. to be Commr. bkrptcy v. Clay" and so recorded in SJL. Enclosure: Extract from General George Washington's "official Letters" requesting Congress to appoint "two Person's to purchase stores and clothing for the use of the Army after the evacuation of Philadelphia"; Washington writes, "Some gentlemen have mentioned Messieurs Samuel Howell and Thomas Franklin as well qualified both on account of their integrity and attachment to our cause, and from their knowledge of the city" (MS in same, in Deborah Logan's hand, being a partial extract of Washington to Henry Laurens, Valley Forge, 31 May 1778, in *Official Letters to the Honourable American Congress, Written, During the War Between the United Colo-*

nies and Great-Britain, By his Excellency George Washington, Commander in Chief of the Continental Forces, Now President of the United States, 2 vols. [Boston, Mass., 1795], 2:263; see Washington, *Papers, Rev. War Ser.*, 15:283-4).

In 1797, Walter Franklin MARRIED Sarah Howell, daughter of Captain Samuel Howell, at the Friends Meeting House on Market Street in Philadelphia. She died two years later. In 1802, he married Anne Emlen, whose father was a prominent Quaker preacher. In 1809, Franklin became attorney general of Pennsylvania (*Claypoole's American Daily Advertiser*, 15 Apr. 1797; *Porcupine's Gazette*, 26 June 1799; Franklin Ellis and Samuel Evans, *The History of Lancaster County, Pennsylvania, with Biographical Sketches of Many of Its Pioneers and Prominent Men* [Philadelphia, 1883], 235; Josiah Granville Leach, *Genealogical and Biographical Memorials of the Reading, Howell, Yerkes, Watts, Latham, and Elkins Families* [Philadelphia, 1898], 159, 171-2; Vol. 29:89n).

MARQUIS YURIES WITH HIS FAMILY: that is, Carlos Martínez de Irujo, the Spanish minister to the United States who had recently become marqués of Casa-Irujo, and his wife, Sally, daughter of Governor Thomas McKean (Vol. 30:194n; Vol. 39:293).

From John Thomson Mason

DEAR SIR George Town 5th October 1803

I have this moment received the inclosed letter from a Gentleman I beleive personally known to you. The letter I think might have been properly addressed to you and therefore it is that I take the liberty of thus sending it. The great respect and attachment which I formed for the author of this letter in early life, and which the lapse of seventeen years has ripened into a sincere friendship, authorized him to ask and expect that I should make his wishes known to you. The mode which I have adopted is the best that has suggested itself to my mind

I have the honor to be with great respect and regard Your Obedt. Servt.

JOHN. T. MASON

RC (DNA: RG 59, LAR); endorsed by TJ as received 6 Oct. and "Brown James. to be Collector of N. Orleans" and so recorded in SJL. Enclosure: James Brown to Mason, Lexington, 20 Sep. 1803, writes that the "general sentiment of joy" in Kentucky caused by the purchase of Louisiana is being replaced with "the gloomy apprehension" that the Senate may block the acquisition; Federalists will feel no restraint in opposing the measure, and only unanimity among the Republicans will ensure success; Brown worries, however, that "Eastern jealousy" may divide the Republicans; the middle and southern states will partially sacrifice the value of their property as inhabitants migrate to Louisiana, and Brown is convinced that, except for residents along the lower Mississippi River, no part of the country will gain more from the purchase than the eastern states, which will undoubtedly come to dominate the western carrying trade; in addition, western dependence on eastern warships will help to "cement the Union"; concerns over declining real estate values caused by removals to Louisiana are well founded, but Brown observes that this migration would take place even if Louisiana remained in foreign hands; "The population of Louisiana is at all events to flow from the United States," opines Brown, so it is only good policy for the United States to possess the country; Brown has decided to become an inhabitant of New Orleans for reasons "partly personal and partly political"; the warmer climate will improve his health and he has long wished to "convert my property into Cash and live upon the interest"; as an opponent of the Federalists and an admirer of the present administration, Brown wishes to "aid in implanting the same correct opinions and political principles" in Louisiana; to support himself, Brown has solicited the office of collector at New Orleans, but admits that his acquaintance with TJ is limited to "one or two visits" and his "ties of consanguinity" with both Kentucky senators "renders it indelicate" to use them as references; Brown feels that no one has known him longer or better than Mason, and he hopes that Mason "can find an opportunity of conversing with Mr. Jefferson on the subject and of promoting my views"; if the collectorship is unobtainable, then any equivalent office would be acceptable and Brown asks Mason to inform him of his prospects for an appointment soon (same).

From Thomas Munroe

Wednesday 5 Octo 1803

T Munroe with his most respectful Compliments sends to the President a Letter from the Treasurer of Maryland concerning which he respectfully solicits the Presidents directions

The Amt. of Interest due 1t. Instant will be forwarded by the next mail (friday) at which time T.M. will answer the Treasurers Letter if it should be convenient for the President to honor him with his sentiments in the mean time.

Mr. Claxton has recommended a man by the name of Aaron Bunton to be employed on the roads in the manner mentioned by the President the other day—T.M. supposing this man will probably be as good an one as we shall meet with thinks of employing him today at about $20 ℔ month (a little more than Labourers wages) and setting him to work tomorrow instead of monday that he may have a little more time to do what is necessary before the members of Congress & others get to the City.

RC (DLC); endorsed by TJ as received 5 Oct. Enclosure not found, but see Thomas Munroe to TJ, 6 Oct.

To Robert Smith

DEAR SIR — Washington Oct. 5. 9. P.M. [1803]

Your favor of yesterday is this moment recieved. mine of Sep. 30. [was] written without any accurate information of the state of your family. the question hinted in that was decided on Tuesday & is gone into action. there is therefore now no cause for separating you from your family, and I shall be sorry if it should take place before you recieve this. I am sure you will approve what we have done, & that will be sufficient. let me pray you therefore not to leave your family while there remains any cause of apprehension or uneasiness. altho' we should be the better of your revising what we propose to lay before Congress, yet there is no subject of difficulty enough to require a distressful attendance from you. I again therefore beseech you not to leave a scene so interesting to you, till such a change take place as may permit it without any uneasiness to yourself. that this may soon be the case I sincerely wish from higher motives th[an] the desire I always feel of your assistance here. present me respectfully to mrs Smith & accept yourself my affectionate salutations & anxious sympathies.

TH: JEFFERSON

PrC (DLC); partially dated; torn; at foot of text: "Robert Smith esq." Recorded in SJL as a letter to the Navy Department.

DECIDED ON TUESDAY: see Notes on a Cabinet Meeting, 4 Oct. 1803.

From Albert Gallatin

DEAR SIR Thursday afternoon [6 Oct. 1803]

The navy estimates have not yet been sent to Mr Smith for approbation & the substance will be communicated to me to morrow morning. I will call with it on you so that you may write by to morrow's mail.

I find that the establishment now consists of

The Constitution } each 44
The Philadelphia }

& five small vessels all of which are now out & intended to stay the whole year as the crew is enlisted for two years. In my opinion one half of the force vizt. one frigate & two or three small vessels were amply sufficient. The large item of repairs for vessels may be postponed till next year

With respect Your obt. Servt. ALBERT GALLATIN

RC (DLC); partially dated; endorsed by TJ as received from the Treasury Department on 7 Oct. and "Navy approprn" and so recorded in SJL.

SUBSTANCE WILL BE COMMUNICATED: the estimates the Navy Department sent to Gallatin have not been found, but see TJ to Robert Smith, 10 Oct.

To Méry

Oct. 6. 1803. Washington

Th: Jefferson has recieved the letter of mr Mery dated the 3d inst. and regrets that, having no acquaintance in the mercantile line, at Philadelphia, there is not a single house there of whom he is authorised to ask the favor desired by mr Mery, & that his entire unacquaintance with every person & thing connected with money-matters disables him from indicating any other resource for the advance of money mr Mery may have occasion for. he returns him the note from the Marquis de la Fayette to Madame Astorg & presents him his salutations.

PrC (ViW: Tucker-Coleman Collection); endorsed by TJ in ink on verso. Enclosure: see Méry to TJ, 3 Oct.

MADAME ASTORG was likely Élisabeth Marie de Grassin d'Astorg, whose husband had been a naval officer with the French fleet that supported the American and French armies during the American Revolution and a member of the National Guards formed in 1789 on Lafayette's initiative (*Dictionnaire*, 3:1373-4; John H. Stewart, *A Documentary Survey of the French Revolution* [New York, 1951], 110).

To Thomas Munroe

Oct. 6. 03.

Th: Jefferson presents his salutations to mr Munroe: he does not recollect whether any act of Congress authorises the paiment of the instalments to Maryland, & he has not had an opportunity of consulting mr Gallatin. under this state of uncertainty it would be improper to say any thing to mr Harwood which should be any thing like a promise or assurance on the part of the Executive. he thinks it best to say that 'mr Munroe is unapprised whether any & what provisions have been made by the legislature for the paiment of these instalments: that altho' nothing within his knolege has indicated a want of either the will or the means of paying with punctuality every just demand, yet that it is not within mr Munroe's province to say what they will do specifically.'

PrC (DLC); endorsed by TJ in ink on verso.

From Thomas Munroe

Octo. 6. 1803

T Munroe has had the honor of recieving the Presidents note of this morning and will conform strictly to the directions therein given—To save the president the trouble of examining the Acts of Congress when he takes the subject into consideration T. M. begs leave to refer to the Act of 1t. May 1802 Abolishing the Board of Comrs. Section 5, page 126. as the president says in his note he does not at present recollect the Act of Congress on the subject—

RC (DLC); addressed: "President"; endorsed by TJ as received 6 Oct. and so recorded in SJL.

In conformity with directions suggested by TJ in his NOTE OF THIS MORNING, Munroe wrote Maryland treasurer Thomas Harwood on 7 Oct., enclosing a $3,000 quarterly interest payment due the state on its $200,000 loan to the District of Columbia. Regarding payments on the loan's principal in 1804, Munroe stated that "altho' nothing within my knowledge has indicated a want of either the will or the means of the Government to pay with punctuality every just demand of the State of Maryland yet it is not within my province to say what they will do specifically" (FC in DNA: RG 42, LRDLS).

In SECTION 5 of the 1 May 1802 act abolishing the Washington board of commissioners, the superintendent was authorized, under the president's direction, to sell as many city lots as necessary to make interest payments on the Maryland loan. However, if the president was of the opinion that a sufficient number of lots could not be sold "without an unwarrantable sacrifice of the property," then any deficiency was to be taken from money in the Treasury not otherwise appropriated (U.S. Statutes at Large, 2:176).

From Caspar Wistar

DEAR SIR Philada. Oct. 6. 1803—

Since my last, which inclosed a letter to Major Lewis, I have been informed that Monsieur Pieroux, while Commandant near the mouth of the Missouri, had sent a party of Indians up the river on a voyage of discovery, & that they returned after an absence of two years—this was communicated to me by Col: OHara of Pittsburgh who saw Pieroux at Kaskaskias during the Revolution War—I believe that Pieroux is still in Louisiana, & that he is Proprietor of a Saline near St. Genevieve—I avail myself of this opportunity to state to the Major as a subject for enquiry, the trees on the Bark of which the Indians on the West Coast are said to subsist in times of scarcity. I have heard from persons who have been on that coast, that the natives are frequently forced to subsist in this way during winter—perhaps this information may be useful to the first settlers of that Country.—Here perhaps I ought to conclude, but I cannot refrain from mentioning to you a subject which has frequently occurred to me when thinking on the happy course of the events which relate to Louisiana—The Seaport at the Mouth of the Missisippi will probably be a town of immense size & importance, but the situation of New Orleans seems every way unfit for such a town—If a place communicating more directly with the Sea & near the River, could be found, (resembling the situation of Alexandria with respect to the Nile) would it not be proper to form a town there—if such a thing is proper & practicable, ought it not to be attempted soon before N. Orleans increases so much as to prevent such a measure—I am not without apprehension that you will laugh at the scheme as impracticable, but I feel confident that your good nature will forgive the liberty I am taking—

Mr Patterson has lately been informed by his Son that Major Lewis wished him to join the expedition as assistant Surgeon, & in consequence requested me to inform you what I knew of his qualifications—I therefore beg leave to say that he attended two courses of the Anatomical Lectures with diligence & assiduity, & appeared to devote himself with great industry to the study of Medicine, under the care of Dr Church a very respectable young Physician of this City, whose practice being very extensive among the poor, must have afforded him a great opportunity of improvement—He also appeared very correct & proper in his habits of Life—

To this miscellaneous letter I will only add the assurance of the sincere & affectionate regard of your friend & Servant

C. WISTAR JUNR.

My Sister Mrs. Bache is near the City, & in good health—having lately exhibited to us a second Daughter—

RC (DLC); endorsed by TJ as received 9 Oct. and so recorded in SJL.

MY LAST: 18 July.

SAW PIEROUX AT KASKASKIAS: in 1778, James O'Hara was a captain in a Virginia regiment during George Rogers Clark's campaign into the Illinois region (ANB).

When Meriwether Lewis passed through Wheeling in September, he met a son of Robert PATTERSON, William Ewing Patterson, who had gone there to practice medicine but "expressed a great desire" to join Lewis's expedition. Lewis could give him little time to prepare, however, and when Patterson could not meet the deadline Lewis went on without him (Moulton, *Journals of the Lewis & Clark Expedition*, 2:75-6).

Catharine Wistar BACHE, the wife of William Bache, had given birth to Emma Mary, their third child (Richard Wistar Davids, *The Wistar Family: A Genealogy of the Descendants of Caspar Wistar, Emigrant in 1717* [Philadelphia, 1896], 9).

From Thomas Dill

fort Enquiry
where monongehela & Alegainey meets[1]
October the 7th 1803

DEAR SIR,

Your honourable office place & station your weighty Important Charge & Care & Inspection over & for the welfare health & preservation protection & prosperity and Support & Defence of the Common wealth of the American states; O that the lord of heaven may give you wisdom a penetrating sound well Informed Judgment in all Matters & Cases Intricate and precarious; An Eagles Eye you Need from him who is Eyes to the blind & feet to the lame & the help of the helpless; a husband to the widow & a father to the father to the fatherless the strangers shield & orphans stay; who can heal the sick, Raise the Dead open the Eyes of the blind & lead them by a way they know Not; kings and governors & presidents & princes should be very watchful Careful Just honest Affectionate tender Nursing fathers to the poor & Needy widows & orphans & the lords poor pilgrims such as god calls Strangers in his holy word on Earth; the sea ports & outline Coasts well watched & Guarded from the Evil Intentions & Undermineing Schemes & devices & Evil Counsels of Evil Spies & Evil Designing Enemies; the Invisible powers of hell has no good will nor good wishes nor good desires for the welfare of the Americans souls; & bodys; O how much need Every Individual high & low bond & free Noble & Ignoble Rich & poor stands in of the lord god of heaven for a portion & Inheritance in Christ Jesus to make them Eternally happy in the enjoyment of God; beyond the grave O who can tell how precious Christ & gods free grace in him is to all that believe in Jesus O how precious is the blood of Jesus that Cleanses from all sin O how precious is the time that god lengthens out & prolongs to the children of men to prepare for Death to Escape hell & fly to heaven on the wings of faith & love; but without saving faith in christ & true sincere unfeigned love to god who is love & Repentance unto life that great salvation the lord Christ has purchased by his Death & sufferings cannot be obtained & enjoyed Alas Alas how Ignorant & blind and Dead and wild proud & foolish Self willed; this is case & state & Condition & situation & circumstance of the Children of men their moral taste depraved and all the Intellectuals & faculties & powers of the souls of men all out of tune because of Original & Actual sin; & the Dreadful fatal Ruinous effects & Consequences of our killing fall in & with the first Adam; O how much all the souls in America and England & Ireland & Scotland and wales & france &

germany & Spain; doth Need the lord Christ; O how happy they might all be in the enjoyment of the lord in heaven forever if they Did or could or would but believe in Christ the second Adam O when god and Christ & heaven is lost forever lost; then Eternal misery Ensues; Jesus Christ According to your faith so be it unto you, he that believes has the witness in himself & out of his belly flows rivers of living water; while m,r[2] love money would Rather have a thousand Ships loaded with money and a thousand Guineas Coming in every day & let it lie & Rust on hands rather than Clothe the Naked or give good Education to poor orphan Children O Read & See the words of Eternal truth in the 58th of Isaiah & 6th verse & 7th; also in Deuteronomy 15th & 7th & 8th 9th 10th & 11th Verses we must be good & do good we must be merciful to the poor and Charitable to the poor because God is merciful to us Sinners we must Relieve the Distressed because god has often Relieved us when we were in Distress; when we have been sick god has made us well again; god gives us the fleece of his sheep to Clothe us; & the milk to sup & drink of his when we are hungry & thirsty the lord feeds us & gives us the produce of the Earth to Nourish and strengthen us; the gold & silver is the lords as you may see where he says so in haggi 2d & 8, but he lends the money to the Children of men all the Cattle on a thousand hills are his but he gives and lends to worthy & unworthy the good & bad the righteous & wicked; but lest I weary your patience I subscribe my self poor Tom love honey; & Need a Deep blue broad Cloth Neat Setout Coat for winter A New Shirt & a New Strait Coat for winter; for I am sick & sore & wounded & unable to help myself

THOS. DILL

I have been Robbed & spoiled by thieves & Robbers cruel & unjust

RC (MHi); addressed: "To President Jefferson of the United States these with Care"; franked; postmarked Pittsburgh; endorsed by TJ as received 13 Oct. and so recorded in SJL.

For Dill's previous letter to TJ, see Vol. 34:9-11.

[1]Address written perpendicular to text in left margin.

[2]Thus in MS.

From Gabriel Duvall

DEAR SIR, Washington, 7 Oct. 1803.

It is with pleasure that I inform you that, according to the returns which are published in the Intelligencer of this morning, & I take it for granted they are correct, there will be at least forty six Republican

Members in the next House of Delegates of Maryland; of course there can be no more than 34 federal—.

With great respect & esteem I am, your obedt. Srvt.

G. DUVALL

RC (DLC); at foot of text: "The President, U.S."; endorsed by TJ as received 7 Oct. and so recorded in SJL.

Partial RETURNS of the 3 Oct. Maryland election published in the 7 Oct. *National Intelligencer* indicated that 35 Republicans and 7 Federalists had been elected to the 80-member assembly. On 10, 12, and 14 Oct., the *Intelligencer* printed more returns and pointed out where the Republicans were doing better than in the previous election. In Washington County, for instance, the Republican ticket prevailed in 1803 by a majority of 700 votes, in 1802 by less than 400. By the final count 47 Republicans and 33 Federalists were elected to the House of Delegates, the same party distribution as in 1802 (Michael J. Dubin, *Party Affiliations in the State Legislatures: A Year by Year Summary, 1796-2006* [Jefferson, N.C., 2007], 84-5).

From Richard O'Brien

MOST ESTEEMED SIR Algiers The 8th. of October 1803.

By The return of The american Ship Betsy Walk Captain Riddick from Algiers for Norfolk I take The liberty to send your Excellency an Antelope a few Algerine Pigions & doves, a bottle of otto of roses, & a Burnuce or Moorish Ladies Cloak allso a few of the large breed of Constantine fowls and 2 Measures of Algerine wheat which I hope your Excellency will please to accept of—

from Sir Your most Obt Servt. RICHD. OBRIEN

RC (MHi); at foot of text: "Excellency Thomas Jefferson President of The United States"; endorsed by TJ as received 20 Dec. and so recorded in SJL.

The ship BETSY WALK of Norfolk, commanded by Mills (Miles) RIDDICK, had been chartered by the Navy Department to carry naval stores to Algiers and provisions to the Mediterranean squadron (NDBW, 2:395, 432, 437, 448, 452; 3:142, 496; Madison, *Papers, Sec. of State Ser.*, 5:486, 502, 548).

OTTO OF ROSES: or attar of roses, "A very fragrant, volatile, essential oil obtained from the petals of the rose" (OED).

BURNUCE: that is, a burnous, "A mantle or cloak with a hood, an upper garment extensively worn by Arabs and Moors" (OED).

To Samuel Harrison Smith

[8 Oct. 1803]

Th: Jefferson salutes mr Smith & having copied the inclosed, returns it with some queries & supplements for his use.

RC (DLC: J. Henley Smith Papers); undated; addressed: "Mr. Samuel H. Smith"; endorsed by Smith: "From Th. Jefferson Oct. 8. 1803." Not recorded in SJL. Enclosure not identified.

From William J. Stone

SIR Columbia (Va) Octo 8th. 1803

I suppose that Louisiana will be laid off in States, and it will be necessary to have Registers of Land Offices appointed in each; when the arrangement is made I have no doubt but what you wou'd as soon give me such an appointment as any other person by your having sufficient recommendation and assurances of my capability of fulfilling the duties of the Office. You will please give me an answer on the subject and consider me as if I was satisfactorily recommended to you—your humble Servant W. J. STONE

RC (DNA: RG 59, LAR); at head of text: "Mr Thomas Jefferson"; endorsed by TJ as received 12 Oct. and "to be Register ld off. Louisiana" and so recorded in SJL.

William J. Stone (d. 1822) resided in Fluvanna County and served as an infantry lieutenant and clerk during the War of 1812. He did not receive a Louisiana appointment from TJ and unsuccessfully sought his assistance in 1810 and 1812 in settling a land dispute (RS, 3:179, 211; 5:15-16, 97).

From Joshua Fry

DEAR SIR Danville 9h. Octbr. 1803

Mr. Benjamin Shackleford has been my neighbour for the last twelve or fifteen months, during which period his sobriety & general exemplary deportment have procured him my esteem & regard. I consider him as a young man of decent aquirements (bred to the law) respectable understanding & sound political sentiments. I presume to recommend or sollicit public appointments for no one, with a few to which I immagine this gentleman is forwarding testemonials of his character to the Executive, but what I have said in his favr. I consider as an act of justice which I could not properly withhold, but which had I been acquainted with the secretary of state should have been addressed to him—Having trespassed thus far on your time permit me to add my sincere felicetations on the complete success of your late well timed & judicious negotiations, & as a citizen of the western country my cordial thanks for your particular attention to our interest—You have long merited & uniformly possessed for your private happiness & welfare the best wishes of your friend & respectful Srvt.

JOSHUA FRY

RC (DNA: RG 59, LAR); endorsed by TJ "Shackleford Benj. office in Louisiana" and so recorded in SJL at 27 Oct.

Like Fry, Benjamin Shackelford (SHACKLEFORD) was a native of Virginia. He moved to Kentucky in 1802 and practiced law. He did not receive an appointment from TJ, but went on to enjoy a lengthy career as a state jurist (William Henry Perrin, ed., *Counties of Christian and Trigg, Kentucky. Historical and Biographical* [Chicago and Louisville, 1884], pt. 1:87-9).

CITIZEN OF THE WESTERN COUNTRY: after emigrating from Virginia to Kentucky, Fry established a prestigious private academy and became a well-regarded classics instructor. He joined the faculty of Centre College in Danville in 1823, specializing in Latin grammar (Philip Slaughter, *Memoir of Col. Joshua Fry* [Richmond, 1880], 42; Woods, *Albemarle*, 197-8; James J. Holmberg, ed., *Dear Brother: Letters of William Clark to Jonathan Clark* [New Haven, 2002], 176-7; *Frankfort Argus*, 1 Oct. 1823; Vol. 28:302n).

To Thomas Mann Randolph

DEAR SIR Washington Oct. 9. 03.

I have been so closely engaged since I came here that I have not had time to write any letter which could be postponed. this place is unusually healthy. some persons from Alexandria have been taken with the fever here & died, without communicating it: so that we consider our rural situation as perfectly exempt from the danger. it seems to get worse in Alexandria, Philadelphia & New York, & so will continue probably till a frost which infallibly & instantly arrests it. we have no news from Europe but what the newspapers contain. I left at Orange C.H. one of my Turkish pistols, in it's holster, locked. I shall be glad if either yourself or mr Eppes can let a servant take it on to this place. it will either bind up in a portmanteau flap, or sling over the back of the servant conveniently. a systematic opposition to the Louisiana purchase is said to be intended. the party divisions will be 39 & 103. and 9 & 25. but it is apprehended some Eastern republicans may oppose it. we shall expect you here in the evening of the 16th. or morning of the 17th. at farthest. do not make too long rides. they do you a lasting injury, altho' not sensible of it at the time. you would not give as much for a horse which has had rides of excessive severity, altho they have not done him a visible injury. kiss my dear Martha & the little ones for me & assure them of my tender love. the same to Maria who I presume is with you. mr Eppes I suppose is below. affectionate salutations to yourself.

Th: Jefferson

RC (DLC); at foot of text: "T M Randolph"; endorsed by Randolph as received 14 Oct. PrC (MHi); endorsed by TJ in ink on verso.

To Paul Verdier

Sir Washington Oct. 9. 03.

I left at your house, the morning after I lodged there, a pistol in a locked case, which no doubt was found in your bar after my departure. I have written to desire either mr Randolph or mr Eppes to call on you for it, as they come on to Congress, to either of whom therefore be so good as to deliver it. Accept my salutations

Th: Jefferson

PrC (DLC); at foot of text: "Mr. Verdier"; endorsed by TJ in ink on verso.

Paul Verdier (d. 1848) moved from Berkeley County, Virginia, to Orange County near the end of the 1790s. There, he purchased a large plot of land that included a tavern and became the leading figure in the establishment of the town of Orange (*Richmond Enquirer*, 11 Aug. 1848; Madison, *Papers, Pres. Ser.*, 1:78-9).

To Robert Bailey

Dear Sir Washington Oct. 10. 03.

I recieved lately from France a few grains of a wheat with a solid stem. as from this circumstance it will probably be proof against the Hessian fly I am dividing it among those who I think will take care of it. I send you a few grains, as also some seed of a cabbage said to grow 7. feet high, to put on several heads & reproduce them when cut off. this seems wonderful, but is worth seeing into. I also send seeds of the Alpine strawberry which in this country would yield about 8. months in the year. I hope you have been mindful of my commission of the last year, and that the seeds & plants then desired will all be prepared. about the 1st. day of the ensuing month we shall dispatch a ship to France, and I shall be very happy to send them by that opportunity without fail, as an opportunity from here at the exact season might never again happen. Accept my best wishes

Th: Jefferson

PrC (MHi); at foot of text: "Mr. Bailey"; endorsed by TJ in ink on verso.

For TJ's receipt of grains of WHEAT and cabbage seeds, see J. P. P. Derieux to TJ, 7 Sep. TJ had enlisted Bailey's help in his COMMISSION to supply seeds to Madame de Tessé (Vol. 39:125-6).

From Joseph Barnes

Leghorn Octr. 10th. 1803

When I had last the honor of addressing Mr Jefferson from Paris june the 29th. last, I expected before this to have been at my Post in Sicily, but having order'd my letters from Sicily to meet me here, and expecting the pleasure of a few lines from Mr Jefferson, or from the secretary of state relative to the Neapolitan affair &c &c I have remain'd in Leghorn some time, not wishing to Embark for Sicily, and to return again by Sea to Naples, Should Mr Jefferson have thought any part of my communication worthy of attention. Having observed so much in my former letters respecting what may be effect'd with the Neapolitan Government, I should think it intrusion were I to trouble Mr Jefferson further on the subject.—I am at present in correspondence with the heads of the Neapolitan Govt. who, I shall only observe are anxiously waiting any powers I may receive; and, I am well convinced with very little expence to the United States we may be as much dreaded by all the Barbary Powers & respected in the Mediterranean as the British.—From my advice from Sicily I am well assured that my absence as yet has been of but little importance, but very few Vessels having touched at Sicily, tho' it has caused me much anxiety. I shall wait about fifteen days more, and then depart for Sicily—& be assured that no person shall Act as deputy consul in any of the Ports who shall not be worthy of his Post.—On my arrival here I had a short interview with Commodore Morris, in which he inform'd me he was, and his successor would be *Charge des affaires* for the States of Barbary, and that he should make arrangements, but not having power to interfere in commercial affairs, he suggested to me the necessity of some commercial arrangements with the Neapolitan Government, especially in regard to the heavy quarantine laid on all Vessels from the United States; I observed I had anticipated him in this, having, from a representation of the Mutual advantages which would result, obtain'd overtures from the Court of Naples relative to a Treaty of commercial relations between the U.S. and His Sicilian Majesty; a copy of which I had forwarded to the President of the U.S. And, in consequence expected some person or persons well qualified would be immediately Appointed for this purpose.—I was however Sorry to find Commodore Morris hand in hand, & from the first Authority coincident in sentiments with Mr W. Smith of S.C. whose principles are so *contrary* to those of true Republicans. Consequently *opposed* to the present Administration, a *friend* to *War* & *a public debt*: in demonstration of which, I am told by good Authority that he has repeatedly expressed his *disapprobation* of the Conduct of the President of the U.S. in having purchased Louisiana at so *great* an expence, while, as he said, it might have been *taken for nothing*!! in terms of the severest censure—In confidence, 'tis said he saluted at Gibraltar on the birthday of the Queen of England, & *not* on the 4th. of july!!! but this I do not vouch for.—The respect & esteem I have ever had for Mr Jefferson in private life would not permit me to *hear silently* nor *pass unnoticed* these Matters.—

As to the *Quarantine*, which is laid indiscriminately on all our Vessels—20 days! permit me to suggest, in order to enable the respective consuls to *obviate* it as far as possible, it ought to be made *obligatory* in the clearance of every Vessel, that the Master should obtain a *certificate* from the *Board of health*, properly Authenticated, of the *state* of the health of the port, *its situation* & the *season* of the *year* in which he *takes his departure*; it being well known that the Malignant yellow Fever only prevails at certain periods & in but few ports; for, without such a certificate *no relief* or alteration can be obtain'd.—I Shall take Naples in my way for Sicily, altho' it will be a considerable expence; as I could Embark from Leghorn directly, instead of going by Land to Naples, more than 400 Miles; but, as I expect to be able to render services to my fellow Citizens, I do not mind the expence, especially as I think I can put the Quarantine business in a plan of arrangement—well knowing that Genl. Acton is more than the King, I must of necessity go to Naples to effect any good; I sincerely wish I could have met him with powers & orders from the United States.—

As to the Overtures made by the court of Naples, I hope by Commodore Pribble, who we are informed is coming out, that the requisite powers, or some person Authorized to meet them will arrive; & I need not assure Mr Jefferson, whether I should or should not be Authorized with my friends as suggested in my former letters, that *every* effort in my power shall be made to *effect* the *object in question*—I am persuaded no man living can have a higher esteem for Mr Jefferson than Mr Mazzei, and tho' seventy odd his Talents are by no means impair'd, & his political interest thro' good management great—even with those Governments which he would wish to destroy.

The information from which I suggested in my letter from Paris, that the English were in Sicily & the French in Naples, was premature—as the French did not enter nor take possession of the *City* of Naples, but only of the Ports on the south East coast which they[1] Occupied last War, the English could not entre Sicily, which however they intended had the first taken place.—

As to the *Event* of *this War*, 'tis yet *incalculable*—Spain 'tis said has certainly declared War against England, & the French are marching towards Portugal—another report which is credit'd, is, that a Treaty is made between Russia & Portugal—'tis certain the Russians have demand'd permission to pass the Dardanelles with a Fleet—as yet the Northern powers remain Neutral—Between England & France 'tis a *War of destruction*; one or the other must *triumph* in order to bring it to an end—'tis said there are a Million under Arms disciplin'd and disciplining! and the greatest Patriotism exert'd thro' out England. And, in France the *spirit* of the *invasion* of England is *excited* generally, especially in the North, from whence *no* communication whatever is permitted with England.—A secret expedition they report has sail'd from England on the 16th Ult—

While I hope from all circumstances that our Flag will *enjoy* the *rights of Neutrality*, I am well persuaded should either of the contending powers take any undue liberties with it, that prompt tho' prudent measures will be adopt'd under the Administration of Mr Jefferson.—The despotic commercial arrangements of France made with the view of injuring England, will however *injure* all the Neutrals severely, but especially the Americans—they *enforce* the *same Laws* in Tuscany as in France!! Notwithstanding they apparently made it an independent Govt.—consequently, no Vessel can enter with Colonial produce without the clearest Certificates, from the French Consul at the port from it cleard out, that 'tis not the produce of British Colonies, nor any Merchandize of British Manufactory—! This measure, tyrannical as it is, & contrary to the treaty existing between the U.S. & France, will, in my opinion, Ultimately *distress France herself*, & all countries over which the French have any power; by Augmenting the price of Colonial produce particularly, which has become from habit almost as necessary as Bread.—

From the *propensity* in *Nature* to *enjoy* whatever is *prohibited*, the People will have these Articles cost what they may—And, instead of England receiving many Articles from this Country, they are sending their *hard Cash* to Malta to purchase.—Leghorn comparitively is like a desert'd Village—Genoa is the same—And, the Govt. Bills of Tuscany, which have from 12 to 24 Munths to run, have been offer'd to me at from 4 to 5 pr cent pr Month discount!!—Commodore Morris, Mr Smith of S.C. went with Mr Appleton to Florence to endeavor to obtain a revocation of the Decree of France or *order* of the First Consul from Leghorn, but the only answer they reced. from the Ministers was *regret*—that the country would be ruin'd, that the Queen would however write to the First Consul, which she did—but no answer—

The Emperor of Germany has laid the extraordinary duty of about 50 pr cent on Sugar, Coffee, Cocoa &c &c to recruit his Coffers—There is no doubt of his disposition towards France, fearful of the consequences.—Advice from Spain purports, that Capn. Rogers of the John Adams having taken one Tripolian Vessel & driven another on shore, but I am fearful it will turn out to be the Morrocco Vessel with her prize, Captur'd by Captain Bainbridge of the Philadelphia—a copy of the letter specifying the particulars, I take the liberty of annexing.—

In my former letters, I have troubled Mr Jefferson with my sentiments fully as to the Necessity of my residence being at the seat of Government at Naples, if I am to render my country service—and, tho' Sicily would be more advantageous, as far as pecuniary interest, having three or four Ports, & Naples but one, I would prefer Naples not only for the above reasons, but for the advantage of Society &c &c &c—the *pecuniary* interest of the consulate *not* being the object, but the *Utility* I can be of to my *country* & *countrymen*—should Mr Jefferson not think proper, from the variety of applications, to invest me with both, being but one Kingdom, & generally but one consulate—thus I have taken the liberty of suggesting my wishes, my only ambition being the good of my Country—having means sufficient to procure all the comforts of life—luxuries I wish *not*—hoping, indeed not doubting, Mr Jefferson will be continued in the Presidency as long as he wishes for the good of our common Country—I remain

with the highest consideration & respect Mr Jefferson's Obedt. Servt.

J: BARNES

P.S. Before I conclude I am induced to state some circumstances, which have come within my own knowledge, that will stagger the independent & honorable Mind of Mr Jefferson—Viz—The French Genl. here receives a paolo pr head pr day from all the unfortunate women of the Town, whose distress compel them to seek their bread by prostitution! these are about 3000 in number—

All Vessels, Americans &c &c arrested here on the most frivolous pretext, when cleard out, under Idea of their being destined for England, Malta &c &c merely to *extort* money! An American Vessel cleard out for Spain, tho' destined for England, the knowledge of which was acquired by secretly opening letters at the Post office, which is common in these Countries, was *arrested* for some days, but on the French Genl. having reced. near £1000 sterg. was suffer'd to depart as a special favor!! Such are the inequitous proceeds in fact in every department of Govt. that it cannot continue long—I could recite numberless instances, but it would be taking up too much of the invaluable time of Mr Jefferson, on subjects which would cause, *not* pleasure, but *pain*. The *slavery* of near 40 Millions of People—

News is arrived here which is credited, & which I hope is true that Lord Nelson has compell'd the Dey of Algiers to pay Six Million of Dollars, & release all the slaves, except those of Genoa—this will do more credit to the British name amongst men of real information, than the destruction of Toulon with all its Arsenal—I had the pleasure of seeing Mr Mazzei the other day who is very well, & means soon to send Mr Jefferson a variety of Vines, shrubs &c &c &c tho' complains he has not reced. a letter since near two years!

RC (DLC); with letter of William Kirkpatrick copied between signature and postscript (see below); addressed: "H.E. Thomas Jefferson President of the United States Washington" with notations by Barnes: "Leghorn Octr. 8th. 1803" (probably meaning 18 Oct.) and "Fvr. of Capn. Bounds—Brig Nancy—deliverd. Octr. 18th 1803"; franked; postmarked Baltimore, 9 Dec.; endorsed by TJ as received 10 Dec. and so recorded in SJL.

By February 1804, the QUARANTINE at Naples banned all ships from the southern United States and required vessels from northern U.S. ports to undergo a waiting period (Madison, *Papers*, *Sec. of State Ser.*, 6:473-4).

For the OVERTURES FROM THE COURT OF NAPLES RELATIVE TO A TREATY, see Barnes to TJ, 4 June, and TJ to Madison, 18 Aug.

SUGGESTED IN MY LETTER FROM PARIS: Barnes to TJ, 29 June (Barnes was also in Paris when he wrote his letter to TJ of 4 June).

'TIS YET INCALCULABLE: Barnes's information about Spain, Portugal, and Russia was faulty, but reflected the uncertainty of international relations in Europe at the time (Madison, *Papers*, *Sec. of State Ser.*, 6:9, 60-1, 162).

The kingdom of Etruria, created by France in exchange for the cession of Louisiana by Spain, included TUSCANY. The QUEEN of Etruria—María Luisa, a daughter of the monarchs of Spain—ruled as regent following the death of her husband in May 1803 (Desmond Gregory, *Napoleon's Italy* [Madison, N.J., 2001], 50, 114-15; Vol. 28:518n; Vol. 38:588n).

TRIPOLIAN VESSEL: the *Meshouda* (see Robert Smith to TJ, 28 Aug.).

TAKE THE LIBERTY OF ANNEXING: Barnes subjoined a copy of a letter he had received from William Kirkpatrick at Malaga, Spain. In the letter dated 7 Sep., Kirkpatrick advised other consuls that the frigate *Philadelphia* had seized the 22-gun Moroccan cruiser *Mirboka* (also written as *Mirboha*) and liberated the American brig *Celia*, which the *Mirboka* had captured. The captain of the *Mirboka* had a passport from James Simpson, and "'tis natural to Suppose," Kirkpatrick wrote, that the sultan of Morocco was seeking to protect his cruisers with American passes but "intends to declare War against the United States." Kirkpatrick warned that American merchant ships should not ply the Mediterranean except in the safety of convoys, and commanders of U.S. naval vessels should be advised of the situation. He wrote to Madison about the *Mirboka* incident on 31 Aug. (Tr in Barnes's hand, on same sheets as the letter printed above, with "Copy" at head of text; Madison, *Papers*, *Sec. of State Ser.*, 5:370-1).

Horatio NELSON had taken command of the British fleet in the Mediterranean a few months earlier, but his attention was on the French squadron at TOULON, not on Algiers (DNB).

[1]MS: "the."

From Elijah Clarke

SIR— Wooburn. October. the 10. 1803.

I have taken the liberty of writing you on a subject highly interesting to the Citizens of our state, and perhaps not more so, than to those of Tennesee & Kentucky—An attempt will probably be made at our next legislature, to improve the navigation of the Savanah river, between the towns of Augusta & Petersburg—The intelligent & enterpriseing part of our Citizens, are turning their attention to this great source of wealth—Indeed political economy is daily becomeing more, & more, the topic both of individual & publick discussion—The opening of a road from Knoxville in Tennesee, to the town of Petersburg, is a measure inseperably connected with the navigation of the River. The people here have been lead to expect, that the federal government, *apprized* of the vast & extensive field of improvement, which this road would open, alike to the Western & Atlantic states, would *ere* this, have effected it. This expectation though somewhat weakened, is not lost sight of,—But the business still remains in an unimproved, or infant state, and we are as yet uninformed of the real intentions of the federal government in relation to it—a knowledge of their views, would naturally aid us in our legislative deliberations, at the succeeding session—The interest Sir, which you have uniformly taken in the political prosperity of the remotest parts of the union, is a sure pledge that no request which has for its object the "publick good," will ever be heard of by you either reluctantly, or with none effect—A conviction of this truth, together with the magnitude of the object, must be my apology for troubling you at this time—Our Legislature meets on the first Monday in November, where I shall be in a legislative capacity.

I have the honour to be with Sentiments of the highest respect & Esteem, Your Excellenceys Friend & obedient Servent

ELIJAH CLARKE

RC (DLC); addressed: "His Excellency Thomas Jefferson President of the United States Washington City"; franked; postmarked "Wash. Ga.," 16 Oct.; endorsed by TJ as received 8 Nov. and so recorded in SJL.

Elijah Clarke, Jr. (1781-1830), a twin, was born in Georgia to Hannah Arrington Clarke and the Revolutionary War militia general and frontiersman Elijah Clarke, Sr. Graduating from Yale in 1801, he hoped to practice law in Washington, D.C. He was recommended in 1802 to TJ as a candidate for secretary of legation in London because of his "correct morals, soundness in the Principles of the administration and a Classical education." Although he did not receive that appointment, he served in the Georgia state legislature representing Richmond County from 1803 to 1804, and became commissioner of Wilkes County Academy in 1805. He was solicitor general of the Ocmulgee circuit court from 1807 to 1810, before moving in about 1815 to Louisiana, where he was a circuit judge until his death in New Orleans (Kenneth Coleman and Charles Stephen Gurr, eds., *Dictionary of Georgia Biography*, 2 vols. [Athens, 1983], 1:190-2; Louise Frederick Hays, *Hero of Hornet's Nest, A Biography of Elijah Clark, 1733 to 1799* [New York, 1946], 142, 293, 295, 301-2, 366n; *Charleston Courier*, 14 Mch. 1830; Vol. 35:144; Vol. 39:69-70).

WOOBURN: Woodburn, in Lincoln County, Georgia, was a family plantation and the burial site of Elijah Clarke, Sr. (Hays, *Hero of Hornet's Nest*, 295).

From James Dickinson

MAY IT PLEASE YOUR EXCELLENCY,

Charles Township Chester County Pennsylvania 10th October 1803

The Session of Louisania to the United States is an Acquisition of such magnitude, that it surpasses the Idea of most Citizens; the wisdom pursued to obtain it astonishes all; and is greatly ascribed to a supreme Power, willing a further Blessing to the american People; and in affording a safe Retreat where Peace and Plenty dwells in a much more happy Clime and Government than is presently found in distressed Europe.

That this so favourable Blessing may be improved is my earnest wish, & that of many more; and think it can in no way more effectually & expeditiously be done than by sending to explore the Country—

Louisania if I am not greatly mistaken is bounded on the west with the Pasific Ocean, and if like other american Countries must abound in Rivers flowing from some middle high Ground dividing its eastern & western Waters: now if a Serch was diligently pursued along this middle ground & began at its most southerly boundaries a discovery would be made of the approach of those Rivers, their quantities of Water, Navigableness and distance of Porterage between them.

It is likely too, several Tribes of Natives would be found in this Rout with whome a Friendship would be established & cultivated by a civil deportment in our Travelers and a few small Presents. I have mentioned to begin on the southermost bounds because probable there are spanish Settlements near those Bounds where possibly Interpreters might more conveniently be got which would much facilitate: moreover Necessaries for our Travelers if they should stand in need.

But in order for a thoroughdoing Serch, I could wish a small Sea Vessel fitted & sent round the Cape, to fall in with the American Shore on the West Side of Louisania at its most southerly Point; thence to visit every Inlet & River worth the noting northerly as far as Nootka Sound, or the Rivers of the West, at the same time to take their Latitude & Soundings at least as far into the Land as their tidewater reaches, often making little excursions on shore to view the Soil, its aptness to cultivation and suitableness for a Town & Settlement, especially where a fine & capacious harbour is found! Probable by this time our inland Travelers may have hit upon some water determining them to pass down it & meet the others.

To send such an expedition and make a purchace too of the Natives would be attended with much Expense. This objection is answered by bringing into View the Utility such a Settlement, Town and good Harbour would be to the United States on a future Day. Here will be the Repository, of the Siberian and Northwest american Firs, the rich merchantdize of India; the Fish of the Pasific, the precious Metals & Merchantdize of all the west Side of south America and the Productions of all the newly discovered Islands in that great Sea; and if the eastern & western Rivers should be found to interlock or lay near each other & to afford a pretty easy communication with each other, then it would presently become the deposit of every manufactory & Produce of the United States suitable for the south Sea Trade: and in return transmit the States all those valuable Articles abovesaid; and perhaps on so reasonable terms as to admit their Transportation to Europe across the Atlantic.

In short such Settlement [woul]d open a Commerce to more than half the richest part of the World, give security to our shiping from tyrany so common in the Atlantic, and soon become a Depository the whole power of Europe could never dislodge.

Under this view, the Expense of such an undertaking vanishes. Moreover the present peacable Situation of the States, the readiness of the present Government to concur in every thing of Utility to the Happiness of Man, the favourable situation of the fiscal Department, the probability of a satisfactory Discovery, the Prospect of so valuable a Commerce opening a peaceble & secure Trade with all the Inhabitants of the Pasific all conspire to fan a hope that Government will adopt & patronize the investigation of this invaluable Territory.

I am confident none of these remarks have escaped your Excellencys Notice; yet an earnest desire to have them put in motion under so favourable Auspicies as is the present Government, and a fear the promising Prospect would sink into Oblivion if now neglected, hath although with the greatest reluctance drawn from me these Observations which I pray you to Pardon, and not look upon the request of granting me a Share in the enterprise as arising from any self Intrested view or sinister Motive—But declare from my Heart, they have wholey arisen from a desire soley to apply my Mite to the Benefit of fellow Man; and wish a speculation in Land and monopoly in Trade so detrimental to Individuals be fully Quashed by provision made to that effect.

Be pleased good Sir to grant me permission to wish you long Life & Happiness and to subscribe myself your sincere Friend & Humble Servant JAMES DICKINSON

RC (DNA: RG 59, LAR); torn; addressed: "Thomas Jefferson President of the United States of America"; at foot of text: "Favoured by Isaac Anderson Esqr. Member of Congress"; endorsed by TJ as received 19 Oct. and so recorded in SJL with notation "Louisiana"; also endorsed by TJ: "to explore Louisiana."

To Levi Lincoln

Th: Jefferson requests the favour of *mr Lincoln* to dine with him *tomorrow (11th.)* at half after three.

Oct. 10. 03.

The favour of an answer is asked.

RC (MWA); printed form, with blanks filled by TJ reproduced in italics; addressed: "Levi Lincoln esq. Atty Genl US."; with unrelated notations added later by Lincoln perpendicular to text and on verso relating to land sales and financial transactions extending from 23 Dec. 1808 to 21 Jan. 1818.

Lincoln received another invitation, dated 24 Oct., to dine with the president on the 26th (RC in same; printed form, with blanks filled by TJ; Lincoln later wrote notes relating to land sales and payments on recto and verso of the folded invitation).

From Blair McClenachan

SIR, Philadelphia 10th Octr: 1803

The discharge of sums of Money, for the payment of which, my name had been engaged in behalf of another, has brought before me the dreadful prospect of want, or dependance during the remainder of my days; notwithstanding this, only for the sense I entertain of your goodness, I should not be induced by my circumstances, however adverse, to give you this trouble.

By Mr: Clay's occupancy of his seat in Congress, his Office as a Commissioner of Bankruptcy will become vacant, were you Sir, to deem me worthy of that place, I would endeavour to shew my gratitude, in the manner most acceptable to you, by a faithful discharge of my duty.

I Pray you to accept the assurence of my most profound respect

BLAIR MCLENACHAN

RC (DNA: RG 59, LAR); in a clerk's hand, signed by McClenachan; at foot of text: "His Excellency Thomas Jefferson President of the United States"; endorsed by TJ as received 13 Oct. and "to be Commr. bkrptcy. Phila" and so recorded in SJL. Enclosed in Pierce Butler to TJ, 11 Oct. 1803.

Notes on Reducing Navy Expenses

[ca. 10 Oct. 1803]

Navy estimate Oct. 1803.

		D	
In actual service.	2. frigates	209,807.36	
	5. small vessels	185,158.19	394,965.55
In ordinary.	11. frigates	180,845.17	
Pay of officers on shore		27,500.	208,345.17
Contingencies			40,000.
Ordnance & stores			15,000.
Marine corps			90,780.43
Navy yards			30,908.85
			780,000.
from which a reduction is needed of			180,000.
			600,000.

Six months of half the force is $\frac{1}{4}$ of the whole		98,740.
Repairs & contingencies		
last year's report	182,000	
this year's do.	257,000	75,000.
Ordnance & stores		5,000.
Navy yards		10,000.
		188,740
Deduct $\frac{1}{4}$ repairg actl. force		24,625.
		164,115

tual service.	Proposed estimate						
			Provisions	Pay	Medical	Contingencies including repairs	
	1. frigate	44. guns 6. mo.	17,247	25,483	625	18,000.	
	1. do.	36. 12. do.	29,806	44,293	1125	12,800	
	1. brig	16. 6. mo.	5,267	9,086	325	3,500	
	1. do.	16. 12.	10,534.	18,172	650.	7,600	
	1. Schooner	14. 6. mo.	3,961	5,310	250	2,500	
	2. do.	12.	17,844	21,240	1000.	10,000.	
dinary.	6. frigates	44. &. 36.	13,792.	20,616	300	54,000.	
	5. do.	32.	10,597.	15,740	250	45,000	
neral contingencies						30,000.	
lf pay				20,000			
	Provisions		109,016				109,016
	Pay			179,940			179,940
	Medical				4,525		4,525
	Contingencies & repairs					172,800	172,800
	Ordnance						10,000.
	Navy yards						21,000.
	Ordinary of 1. frigate & 2 small vessels 6. months						12,000.
	Marine corps						90,760
							599,061

MS (DLC: TJ Papers, 136:23476); undated; entirely in TJ's hand.

LAST YEAR'S REPORT: for navy estimates for 1803, see Vol. 39:344-7, 348-50, 376-9. The navy appropriation act for 1804, passed by Congress on 31 Jan. 1804, contained a total appropriation of $650,000 (U.S. Statutes at Large, 2:249).

Notes on Treasury Estimates for 1804

[ca. 10 Oct. 1803]

Resources	
Balance in the treasury Oct. 1. 1803. say	5,888,000.
Revenue of 5. quarters to Dec. 31. 1804 @ 10,400,000.	13,000,000
Arrears of direct taxes & other sources	150,000
Louisiana	200,000.
	19,238,000

Demands in last			
In last quarter of 1803			
Balance due to 7,300,000 D. approprn.		2,350,000	
¼ of last years estimate for other objects		650,000.	
British paiment		888,000	3,888,000
		3,888,000	
In 1804			
Annual approprn for debt		7,300,000	
2d. British paiment		888,000	
Civil estimate	700,000.		
Foreign do.	200,000.		
Army	875,000		
Navy	800,000	2,575,000	
British awards & treaty expenses		150,000.	
1. year's int. on Louisiana loan		1,025,000.	
6. months on 1,750,000. Bank		98,000.	12,036,000.
Paiment of American claims			2,000,000
		17,924,000	
Arrears of direct tax and internal revenue		500,000.[1]	<*500,000*>
Balance in Treasury Dec. 31. 1804.		1,314,000	1,314,000
		1,814,000	
			19,238,000.

Balance in the Treasury		5,888,000
Arrears of direct tax & internal revenue		800,000
do. adv. pros claims &c.		150,000
		6,838,000

American claims		2,000,000
British paiments		2,664,000
Do. awards & treaty exp.		150,000
Maryland loan		200,000
	5,014,000.	
remain in treasury		1,824,000
		6,838,000

Annual revenue.	
Impost	10,070,000.
Louisiana	200,000.
Postage	30,000
Land	300,000
	10,600,000

Annual expenses		
Sinking fund		8,100.000.
Civil	750,000.	
Foreign	200,000	
Army	875,000	
Navy	675,000	2,500,000
		10,600,000

MS (DLC: TJ Papers, 136:23475); undated, but see below; entirely in TJ's hand; arranged by TJ with the "Resources" and "revenue" column to the left of the "Demands" and "expenses" column; in three distinct sections as indicated by horizontal rules, with totals of $19,238,000 in the first section, $6,838,000 in the second, and $10,600,000 in the third; probably made in several sittings; endorsed by TJ: "Oct. 1803."

RESOURCES: on 17 Oct., Gallatin informed TJ that the Treasury balance as of 30 Sep. was $5,860,000. In his 1802 report to Congress on the state of the finances, Gallatin estimated the ongoing revenues for 1803 at $10,000,000, with all but $500,000 coming from duties on imports and tonnage (ASP, *Finance*, 2:5). In early October, Gallatin calculated that the LOUISIANA revenues collected at New Orleans would amount to $200,000 (see Document v of Drafting the Annual Message to Congress, printed at 1 Oct.).

DEMANDS IN LAST: the 1803 estimate of permanent expenses for government offices, the military, and other objects was $2,660,000, bringing the total, with the $7,300,000 for the retirement of public debt, to $9,960,000 (ASP, *Finance*, 2:5-6; Vol. 39:25-7). BRITISH PAIMENT: under the convention signed on 8 Jan. 1802, the U.S. agreed to pay $2,664,000, in three annual installments of $888,000, to settle British prewar debt claims (Vol. 33:277n; Vol. 34:323-7). TJ probably based the CIVIL ESTIMATE and other estimates for 1804 expenditures on documents submitted by the departments, which have not been found. His entry of $800,000 for the initial navy estimate seemingly was based on the report by the Navy Department that Gallatin promised in his letter to TJ of 6 Oct. and that TJ used as the basis of his Notes on Reducing Navy Expenses of this date and his letter to Robert Smith of 10 Oct. The convention under the Louisiana Purchase, which called for the payment of $3,750,000 in claims of U.S. citizens against France, would partially be paid for with a $1,750,000 BANK loan. The remainder of the payment for AMERICAN CLAIMS would come from the $2,000,000 appropriated earlier in the year for the acquisition of New Orleans (ASP, *Finance*, 2:48-9; Gallatin to TJ, 11 Aug.; Document v of Drafting the Annual Message, printed at 1 Oct.; Annual Message to Congress, 17 Oct. 1803).

ADV. PROS CLAIMS: that is, the advances made in England for the prosecution of claims, which would be repaid to the U.S. It appears in the expense column as "British awards & treaty expenses." TJ's entry of $150,000 is the same amount entered by Gallatin in his report to Congress (ASP, *Finance*, 2:48).

ANNUAL REVENUE: in his late October report to Congress, Gallatin estimated $10,000,000 in revenue from imports after deducting expenses for collection and drawbacks. He added nothing for postage, noting that the "extension of post roads, and the acceleration of the mail, whilst diffusing and increasing the benefits of the institution, have, as an object of revenue, rendered it less productive" and negligible. He entered $400,000 in revenues from the sale of lands, giving a total in estimated revenues for 1804 of $10,400,000 (same, 47-8; *Report of the Secretary of the Treasury, Containing the Present State of the Finances of the United States, and the Estimates of Receipts and Expenditures for the Ensuing Year* [Washington, D.C., 1803; Shaw-Shoemaker, No. 5477], 3-5).

ANNUAL EXPENSES: TJ's entry for the sinking fund is based on the $7,300,000 appropriated annually for the retirement of the public debt, plus an additional

$800,000 to cover the interest on the new Louisiana stock, for a total of $8,100,000. In the Treasury report received by Congress on 25 Oct., Gallatin allowed $700,000 for interest on the new stock for a total sinking fund payment of $8,000,000. Gallatin also informed Congress that he would seek appropriations of $791,000 for the civil department; $184,000 for permanent expenses "attending the intercourse with foreign nations"; $875,000 for the "Military and Indian departments"; and $650,000 for the navy, for a total of $2,500,000 (same, 6, 8; ASP, *Finance*, 2:48-9).

[1]This entry was interlined by TJ and then added to give the total of "1,814,000" but TJ erased the "500,000" from the column with totals and did not include the amount in the "19,238,000" balance.

From William Pryce

VERY DEAR SIR, Wilmington (Del) Octr. 10th. 1803.

I have Just Issued proposals for publishing by subscription, the History of our Blessed Lord and Saviour Jesus Christ, with the Lives of the Apostles, and their Successors for 300 years after the Crucifixion, by Ebenezer Thomson D.D. and William Charles Price L.L.D.

Your high Station in Life, and Literary character naturally Pointed you out to me, as most likely to patronise so interesting a work.

The History of great and Good Men, in all ages, has been Justly considered, as highly worthy the attention of Mankind; and surely none so much so, as the divine Character, here set forth, and his first followers, who thro' much difficulty paved, the way for the Glorious Gospel, to Shine with its' benign influence on our guilty Globe.

The work is to be printed in a handsome Quarto volume, with a general index, on a fine paper, Embellished, with an elegant copper plate, frontispiece, neatly bound and lettered, and subscribers names added, and delivered at $4-50 per Copy.

Should I be so fortunate as to have permission to add your Name to the list, I am well aware the great advantage I shall derive from the patronage of so Illustrious a Character, and I flatter myself you will never have cause to regret, the promotion of the work proposed; of which I should think it my duty to say more, if I did not believe, the Compilers, and the work, both familiar to you.

I hope Sir, you will pardon this Intrusion; as well as the liberty I take of mentioning myself to be, a Minister of Christ, (tho' perhaps among the unworthyest who bear the sacred name) in the protestant Episcopal Church in this place; who will not cease to address God's Throne of Grace, "that the high and mighty Ruler of the Universe may continue to behold and bless you: and so replenish you with the Grace of his holy Spirit, that you may always incline to his *will* and walk in his ways: that he may crown you with health and happiness here below: and finally after this life, bring you to everlasting Joy and Felicity, thro' Jesus Christ our Lord."

Your's Sincerely WILLIAM PRYCE

RC (ViW: Tucker-Coleman Collection); at foot of text: "Thomas Jefferson Esqr."; endorsed by TJ as received 13 Oct. and so recorded in SJL.

William Pryce (1771-1818) was rector of several Episcopal churches in Delaware, including Christ Church in Kent County from 1795 to 1800, Trinity Church in Wilmington from 1800 to 1812, and St. James Church in Newport. About 1817, he returned to Wilmington, where he had been a bookseller and stationer on Market Street, previously reprinting eighteenth-century literary and religious materials. A member of the Delaware Bible Society, he was also vice president of the Union Harmonic Society of Wilmington, president of the Abolition Society of Delaware, and a trustee of Wilmington College, to which he gave $5,000 in lottery winnings in 1811 (J. Thomas Scharf, *History of Delaware, 1609-1888*, 2 vols. [Philadelphia, 1888], 2:828, 1196; Arthur Lowndes, ed., *Archives of the General Convention*, 6 vols. [New York, 1912], 3:24; Wilmington *Mirror of the Times and General Advertiser*, 22 Jan. 1806; *The Town and Country Almanac for the Year of Our Lord, 1806* [Wilmington, 1805; Shaw-Shoemaker, No. 9492]; Wilmington *Delaware Gazette*, 29 Nov. 1809; Wilmington *American Watchman; and, Delaware Republican*, 10 Nov. 1810; Raleigh, N.C., *The Star*, 12 Apr. 1811; Salem, Mass., *Essex Register*, 4 Apr. 1818).

PROPOSALS FOR PUBLISHING the work were issued by Pryce and William Black of Wilmington in the fall of 1803. Black, printer of the laws of Delaware and of a Federalist newspaper, the *Federal Ark*, was not listed on the title page of the work as published in 1805 and printed by Bonsal and Niles (Brigham, *American Newspapers*, 1:77; Easton, Md., *Herald and Eastern Shore Intelligencer*, 8 Nov. 1803; Ebenezer Thompson and William C. Price, *The History of Our Blessed Lord and Saviour Jesus Christ: With the Lives of the Holy Apostles*, 2 vols. [Wilmington, 1805; Shaw-Shoemaker, No. 9473]). Pryce recorded TJ as "President of the United States" at the top of his list of subscribers in the second volume (Sowerby, No. 1493).

Described by a London reviewer as "two learned doctors," authors EBENEZER Thompson (THOMSON) and WILLIAM CHARLES PRICE had previously collaborated on a translation from the Greek of *The Works of Flavius Josephus*, published in London in 1777 (*London Review of English and Foreign Literature*, 5 [1777], 154).

From Philippe Reibelt

MONSIEUR LE PRESIDENT! Baltimore le 10e. Oct. 1803

L'embarras de notre Situation augmente de jour en jour; inconnû à tout le Monde je ne puis nul part reusir.

Je dois donc prier Votre Excellence, de vouloir bien me faire parvenir une reponse favorable à mes lettres *ici*.

Plein de respect Votre Excellence Tr. humble et tr. Obst. Str.

REIBELT

EDITORS' TRANSLATION

MISTER PRESIDENT, Baltimore, 10 Oct. 1803

My situation grows worse every day. Since no one knows me, I cannot succeed anywhere.

I must therefore beg Your Excellency to send me a favorable response, addressed *here*.

With deep respect, Your Excellency, I am your very humble and obedient servant.

REIBELT

RC (MHi); endorsed by TJ as received 11 Oct. and so recorded in SJL.

To Robert Smith

DEAR SIR Washington Oct. 10. 03.

I have heard of your misfortune and lament it, but will say nothing, ha[ving] learnt from experience that time, silence, & occupation are the only medicines [...] such case. I should have regretted the necessity of writing to you on a subject of business, did I not believe it useful to withdraw the mind from what it is too apt to brood over, to other objects.

You know the importance of our being enabled to announce in the message that the interest of the Louisiana purchase (800,000. D) can be paid without a new tax, and what advantage the necessity of a new tax would give the opposition to the ratification of the treaty, where two or three desertions would reject it. to avoid a new tax we had a deficiency (on the estimates as given in) of about 400,000. D. our colleagues have set their shoulders heartily to the work: mr Madison has struck us off 100,000. D. Genl. Dearborn something upwards of that, & we still want 180,000. D. to be quite secure. the estimate recieved from your office, which I inclose you, amounts probably to 770, or 780. & were it possible to reduce it to 600. it would place us at ease. I am not sufficiently acquainted with the details to specify particulars: of this you are the best judge, & feeling with us the importance of the operation, will I am sure do what can be done in it: speaking only in general, I should conjecture there might be some reduction of operat[ions] in Navy yards; that if the Contingent column & repairs[1] were reduced to what they were the last year, it would give us about 75. ~~M~~. and that probably an equal sum can be saved by estimating only for the force which will probably be employed in the Mediterranean,[2] which according to my idea would be for the next year (if peace be not made this) 1. frigate & about 3. of the largest of the small vessels. I suppose that 1. of the 2. frigates last sent, when the season for retiring into winter quarters arrives, might as well retire hither, & 1. or 2. of the small ones. I repeat however that I leave these details to yourself. you are sensible that we must recieve them finally this week, that I may be able to say in the message whether there must be a new tax or not. the embarrasment is only for the first year; for after that we shall be full handed, & can go liberally into *repairs* &c.—we are all of opinion it would be better to send a private vessel, rather than a frigate, with the ratification & gun carriages. both houses will be full on the 1st. day, & the message may go in on that day. Accept affectte. salutations

TH: JEFFERSON

PrC (DLC); torn and blurred; at foot of text: "The Secretary of the Navy." Enclosure not found, but see Notes on Reducing Navy Expences, [ca. 10 Oct. 1803].

YOUR MISFORTUNE: the death of Smith's youngest daughter, Mary Williams Smith (Smith to TJ, 4 Oct. 1803).

SEND A PRIVATE VESSEL: on 12 Oct., Smith directed Thomas Tingey at the Washington Navy Yard to charter immediately, "if practicable," a vessel in Washington or Alexandria large enough to carry 100 gun carriages to Morocco. Tingey chartered the schooner *Citizen* of Georgetown, which left Washington on 13 Nov. (NDBW, 3:129, 221; TJ to Aaron Vail, 4 Nov. 1803).

[1] Word and ampersand interlined.
[2] Preceding three words interlined.

From Robert Young

Tennessee State Hawkins County
Octobr. 10th 1803

SIR

After My Compliments To You With My Greatest Respect I Make free to Write to You Although I am but a Common Citizen. We Were formerly Country Men in Virginia and I once Paid You a fee in Stanton And You Did My Bussiness in Williamsburg Without further trouble to Me. I Now must Congratulate With You on the Great Esteem the People of the United States have for You in puting You into the Greatest Place of Honour and Trust belonging To the United States and I Can inform You With the Greatest Satisfection that Since You Were put in President the People heare are Much Pleased With Goverment and they have Great Reason to be Satisfyed for You and the Good Members of Congress have taken off all the Direct or Goverment taxes off the United States and the People Can Now boast and Say They are the free People of the United States of America; People Injoy Great Priviledges Under the Present Goverment if they Would Only Consider it; they are Not Bound Down Under the Slavery of Church Goverment—Which is one Great Freedom—

There is a Great Talk Amongst the People here About the Purchas of the Louisiana Which Pleases the People Well If it Could be Settled On Such Terms that Every Poor Man that Would Gow to Live there Could Gett a Right to a Small Part of it; What Would it be to Give Encouragement by Letting it be Without Taxing it a few Years; how Would be to Settle it by head Rites Or Makeing the Survays Very Small Oblidging Every Man that holds Land to Clear So Much for Every hundred Acres in Such a Term of time and to keep Every Man from Monopolizeing that Land Somthing Like this Would Make it Quickly[1] Settled: Perhaps I have Gone too farr in Giveing Directions for You and the Good Members have Proved Yourselves friends to the Poor People and We have No Reason to Make a Doubt but You Will Continue So—

The People of this State Seem Somewhat Dissatisfyed Allowing they have Not the Same Priviledges that Other States heave Land hear is Survayed by the Athority of this State and Pattened by the State of North Carolina. People Allow we have been Long Enough To have the Governing of our Own Internal Policy although the Land Was Entered in the State of No Carolina before We became a State but when We became a State Doth not the Constitution allow Us the Governing of our Internal Policy We have No Athority to Make a Right to one foot of Land and all the Vacant Land that Lies in this State Out of the Indian boundary Can be but of Very Little Value to the United States for it Must be Hills and Ragged Mountains but bad as It is If this State Could have a Right to it It would put them on an Equal footing With Other States These Greavances Might have a Small Consideration Perhaps the Might be Removed And I Make Not the Least Doubt but You and the Good Members Will Do all You Can for the Good and benefitt of these People in Genral Whilst I Remain Your Old friend With the Greatest Respect—

Robert Young

P:S People here Would Wish to hear of the two floradas being Purchased too and that Would Joyn Louisiana to the United States

RC (DLC); addressed: "To the Honorable Thos. Jefferson Presedent of the United States In the City of Washington—Virginia"; franked; postmarked Rossville, 15 Oct.; endorsed by TJ as received 23 Oct. and so recorded in SJL.

In 1768, Robert Young had engaged TJ's legal services to protect his property in Augusta County, Virginia, against a caveat entered by William Waterson. The following year, Waterson and several partners hired TJ to file dozens of petitions and caveats in order to gain control over thousands of acres of lapsed and unpatented land in the same county. The scheme failed and TJ received little in compensation from its prosecutors to offset his considerable effort on their behalf (Case Book, No. 121, "Young v. Waterson," 14,

18 June 1768, in CSmH; MB, 1:32, 54, 56, 59, 65; Frank L. Dewey, *Thomas Jefferson: Lawyer* [Charlottesville, 1986], 35-44).

Prior to ceding its western lands to the federal government in 1789, the STATE OF NORTH CAROLINA exercised jurisdiction over the territory that became the state of Tennessee and established seven counties there from 1777 to 1788, including Hawkins County in 1787 (William S. Powell, ed., *Encyclopedia of North Carolina* [Chapel Hill, 2006], 1109).

[1]MS: "Qqickly."

From Pierce Butler

DEAR SIR Philada. October 11. 1803—

The inclosed letter was put into my hand to deliver in person, which I intended doing; but learning that an application wou'd be made to You by a second person for the same post; sooner than I may reach the Federal City, I have preferd sending by Post—

I have been so unsuccessful in two or three recommendations I offerd to Yourself and the Secretay of State, that I shall limit myself on the present occasion, to observing, that if the place was such as to require the approbation of Senate, Mr. McClennigan woud have my Vote. I have cause to believe he wou'd have the Votes of the two Senators from Pennsylvania—

I have the honor to be with great consideration Yr Most Obedient

P. BUTLER

RC (DNA: RG 59, LAR); endorsed by TJ as received 13 Oct. and "Mc.lanahan Blair to be Commr. bkrptcy" and so recorded in SJL. Enclosure: Blair McClenachan to TJ, 10 Oct.

DELIVER IN PERSON: the South Carolina legislature appointed Butler to the U.S. Senate seat vacated by John Ewing Colhoun. Butler produced his credentials and was sworn in on 18 Oct. (JS, 3:299). Butler's recent RECOMMENDATIONS included support for John M. Pintard and Thomas Fitzpatrick (Madison, *Papers, Sec. of State Ser.*, 4:176; Vol. 39:438n; Vol. 40:250)

TWO SENATORS FROM PENNSYLVANIA: George Logan and Samuel Maclay (*Biog. Dir. Cong.*).

From Benjamin Galloway

SIR. Hagers Town Octr. 11th. 1803—

Your favour of July last in answer to my Letter of 19th same Month, I had the pleasure of receiving, for which be pleased to accept my warmest acknowledgments—I have been lately visited by a severe attack of a complaint, which has confined me to my House for some weeks—I am just so far recovered, as to enable me to set off tomorrow to Annapolis; at which place I must be on Saturday morning next to attend to a Law argument before the general court on a motion made by my friend J T Mason in arrest of Judgment, and for a new trial—L Martin is the *adverse* Counsel, and I expect, he will on that occasion act the *black-guard* in like manner as he did at same place in June last—With Intention of gratifying a malevolent disposition, he introduced your name in his address to the Jury; and you will not be surprized to learn that his representation of your conduct was not calculated to impress on the public Mind a *very favourable* opinion—his expectations however were completely disappointed, so far as they respected you—his Behaviour was highly censured by men whose political opinions are in opposition to your administration; and I have the best ground to *beleive*; that if he should misbehave on Saturday next, as *he did in June*, Mr Attorney General will be put in *durance vile*—He offered me, a *personal* apology, in the presence of Mr Richard Lowndes, and Mr B Ogle junior, for (as he said) *one* expression which he had used in his *Philippic* against me—I asked him, whether he intended to *confine* his *apology* to *one* expression *only*—his reply was—*Yes*—I rejoined; that I wished to have no further Conversation, or Communication with *Luther Martin* at that time, except to *tell him*, that he was a *dirty fellow*—he *speedily* took his departure; and being more than *half Seas over reeled* into the *general court*—Martin was informed, that I was at that time bound in a recognizance to keep the peace in consequence of an *abusive* attack made on me last August twelvemonth in Hagers Town, by a *Friend to Order*, who had published a Libel against Mr Gallatin, and which I had the disorganizing effrontery to contradict in the News Paper—when so attacked, I called on two Gentlemen who were present; (I was most shamefully abused and threatened to be *Cow-skinned* If I would indemnify my adversary)—I declared, that I had a loaded Pistol in my pocket; that I would not use it, to offend *any one*: but that if my *Adversary* after the *threat*, he had thrown out (he is a *powerfull* Man) did make an *attack* on my *person*; I would blow a brace of Balls *through* him. The *Chief Justice* of the District *was* present, and heard all that passed—bound over my *adversary*; and to my astonishment *did so also as to my self*—

L Martin by telling me, that he meant to *confine his apology* to *one* expression *only*; *intended to irritate* and *provoke me*, to a *breach of the Peace*; which would have been a forfeiture of my Recognizance—such was the conduct of L.M Atty Genl of Maryld. The Recognizance was £500. In the course of his address to the Jury, he declared me to be a most *outrageous* Character, and as a proof that I was such a Character, He had the Effrontery to tell the Jury, that after I came from England in 1775. I resided twenty Years in Anne Arundel County: that scarce a Court met, that an Action of Asst & Batty. or Slander was not brought agst. me: that I had lived eight Yrs in Washington Cy; and the Docquets of that County would prove on search that my Conduct had been equally *exceptionable* and *outrageous there also*—As Acts of Asst & Batty, or Slander never was brought against me either in A A County, or Washn. in verification of which declaration, I shall give publicity to two certificates from the Cy Clks of A A and Washn, which must satisfy every man of candour that *LM* is a *dirty fellow*.

I shall be *extremely* obliged to you Sir; if you will cause to be inclosed to me at Annapolis by *next* Mail; an *authenticated* Copy of the Letter I requested a favour of you to supply me with, in my address to you dated July 19th last—

On the Subject of Politicks, I can assure you, that in this County, the approvers of yr Admn encrease *daily*. The Louisiana purchase has *paralized opposition here*! If in my power, I will do myself the pleasure of paying my personal respects to you on my Return from Annapolis.

I am Sir With Consideration and great personal Regard Yrs &c

BEN: GALLOWAY

RC (DLC); endorsed by TJ as received 13 Oct. and so recorded in SJL.

YOUR FAVOUR OF JULY LAST: see TJ to Galloway, 28 July.

DURANCE VILE: restraint.

HALF SEAS OVER: that is, intoxicated. Galloway used this same expression in an article attacking Luther Martin captioned "A Dialogue." He questioned: "Is it not scandalous? is it not highly disgraceful to the State of Maryland that its Attorney General, should day by day *almost* as *often* as he appears *in court*, be *half seas over*?" Galloway contended that Martin should be removed from office (Fredricktown, Md., *Republican Advocate*, 22 July 1803). For Galloway's petition to the Maryland General Assembly calling for Martin's removal, see *Aurora General Advertiser*, 23 Dec. 1803, and Galloway to TJ, 5 Jan. 1804.

William Clagett was CHIEF JUSTICE OF THE DISTRICT that included Washington County (*Bartgis's Republican Gazette*, 20 Aug. 1802).

From George Jefferson

DEAR SIR Richmond 11th. Octr. 1803

You will receive inclosed your last quarterly account, from which you will find there is a balance due you of £224–7–7.

The things for which the Waggoner omitted to call, I am sorry to inform you, are not yet forwarded.

I am Dear Sir Yr. Very humble servt. GEO. JEFFERSON

RC (MHi); addressed: "Thomas Jefferson esquire Washington"; franked and postmarked; endorsed by TJ as received 13 Oct. and so recorded in SJL; also endorsed by TJ: "1803. July. Aug. Sep." Enclosure not found.

From Mawlay Sulayman, Sultan of Morocco

Translation.—

In the name of the Clement and Most Merciful God.—
In him we have put our trust and he is our best Protector.

There is no Power or Strength but in the Great God.—

From the Servant of God. Prince of the Believers.

He who has put his trust in the Lord of all the Creation, Soliman Ben Mohamet—Ben Abd Allah—Ben Ismail,—decended from the Prophet from Hassan and from Alli.—

May God magnify his charge and may his Sun and Full Moon shine in the highest Heaven with Splendour.—

Impression.—Soliman Ben Mohamet—Ben Abd Allah—
May God be merciful to him.—
In six Angles.—God—Mohamet—Abubeker—Omar—
Ottoman—Alli—
Around the Seal—God alone directs me, in him I trust and to him
I turn.—

To the President of the Americans—a Prince and to all the Senate*—Health.—

Know ye that between some of our Vessels rendered Victorious by God and some of yours some enmity has happened at Sea, and the affair became so serrious as that some Vessels of each party were taken.—

So soon as we heard of this we felt concern at it, as we were still in Peace and Friendship and we desired that all the Vessels might be brought to Tangier which is under the protection of God.—When we had seen what had happened between the Nations we found it was a matter of little consequence and such as demanded no great attention, we sought to accommodate it and we have succeeded.—And we make

*The Arabic word is Divan.

known to you what has happened that you may know we continue upon that Peace and Friendship you settled with our Lord and Master and Father (to whom God be Merciful) in the Year 1200, and the same which you settled with us (exalted by God) when we renewed that Treaty in the year 1210.—

And know ye that all the Treaties entered into between the two Nations remain as they were and that they shall not be altered or changed—This you are all to understand, and be assured of with all certainty and you are to hold to this.—This has been written to you at the Port of Tangier (which God surround) on the 24h. Chemadi the second in the year 1218 which corresponds to the European date the last of September in the year of the Messiah 1803.—

Memorandum.—

As the Moors reckon by the old style, the date corresponds to the 11h. October 1803.—

Tr (DNA: RG 59, CD, Tangier); in James Simpson's hand; at foot of text above memorandum: "I hereby Certify that the original of the foregoing Letter from His Imperial Majesty Muley Soliman was translated from the Arabic to Spanish by Dn Manuel de Baccas and in my presence Revised, and that the translation from Spanish to English was done by me according to the best of my skill in those Languages.—James Simpson Tangier 15h. October 1803"; endorsed by Jacob Wagner as enclosed in dispatch no. 67 from Simpson to Madison, which was dated 15 Oct. (Madison, *Papers*, *Sec. of State Ser.*, 5:533-4). Tr (same); in Simpson's hand; attestation: "The foregoing translation was done from the Arabic (and in my presence revised) by Dn Manuel de Baccas to Spanish, and from Spanish to English (Mr Baccas also assisting) by—James Simpson Tangier 12h. October 1803"; endorsed by a clerk. Tr (DLC: Edward Preble Papers); a copy in an unidentified hand of the preceding Tr, including Simpson's attestation. Enclosed in Edward Preble to Madison, 15 Oct. (Madison, *Papers*, *Sec. of State Ser.*, 5:532-3).

SOUGHT TO ACCOMMODATE IT: Simpson also sent copies of a decree that Mawlay Sulayman issued at Tangier on 21 Jumada al-Thani 1218 (9 Oct. 1803). The order informed regional governors, sea captains, and other officers that Americans were at peace with Morocco, their ships were to have safe passage, and anyone who molested them would be severely punished. The order also affirmed the treaty of peace of the year 1200 (i.e. 1786) between the United States and Morocco. One copy of the decree that Simpson sent was in Arabic, which on its arrival in Washington was mistaken for the sultan's letter printed above (Tr in DNA: RG 59, CD, Tangier, in Arabic, endorsed by Wagner: "Letter from the Emperor of Morocco to the President 30 Septr. 1803"; Tr in same, in English, in Simpson's hand, attested by him to be his translation of a Spanish translation of the original; Tr in same, also in English by Simpson; Tr in DLC: Preble Papers, printed in NDBW, 3:118; enclosed in Simpson to Madison, 15 Oct., which is summarized in Madison, *Papers*, *Sec. of State Ser.*, 5:533-4).

Edward Preble and Simpson, with Tobias Lear observing, met with the sultan at Tangier on 10 Oct. On Simpson's suggestion, the American commodore, with the schooner *Nautilus* and the frigates *Constitution*, *New York*, and *John Adams* anchored in the harbor, offered to release the *Mirboka* and its crew in return for confirmation of the treaty between Morocco and the United States. Sulayman expressed a desire for peace, sent a present of livestock to the U.S. ships, and ordered the release of an American brig and its cargo that the Moroccans had seized at Mogador. He agreed to insert an acknowledgment of the treaty into the order of 9 Oct. and to write the letter to the president printed above. Receiving the letter for transmittal on 12 Oct., Preble, "agreeable to my promise," as he reported to the Navy Department, turned over the *Mirboka* (same, 421, 461-2, 503, 532-4, 536-9, 541-7; NDBW, 3:119-20, 141; Mohamed El Mansour, *Morocco in the Reign of Mawlay Sulayman* [Wisbech, Eng., 1990], 110).

RENEWED THAT TREATY IN THE YEAR 1210: the United States and Morocco agreed to the treaty of peace and friendship in 1786, during the reign of Mawlay Sulayman's father, Sidi Muhammad ibn Abd Allah. In 1795, Sulayman received money and presents from the United States in exchange for writing a letter to George Washington that acknowledged the peaceful relationship between the two countries (Miller, *Treaties*, 2:227; ASP, *Foreign Relations*, 1:525-7; Madison, *Papers*, *Sec. of State Ser.*, 5:533; Vol. 38:117n).

From Samuel Broome

SIR Greenfield Hill Connecticut Octr. 12th. 1803.

I find by a New Haven paper of the 6th Instant, that Abraham Bishop, is appointed Collector for the Port of New Haven, in this State, no doubt your Excellency has good reasons for giving him the preference, which I conclude will not be permanent,[1] and that another will be Selected more agreeable to the wishes of the Merchants, and all classes of the Citizens of New Haven, I think I know the person, and in that Gentleman, I beleive they would be suited, I took the liberty to apply for the office, and wrote to several of Our first revolutionary Characters, to mention what they knew of Mine, since the year One thousand Seven hundred and Seventy five, and I flattered myself, they would have some weight, and I still flatter myself they have. If there is any Vacancy to be filled, in New York, my Native state, or in any Other of importance I should be happy to fill it, according to the best of my Abilities, having ample Security to offer, for the faithful performance of any trust reposed in me, I was in affluence at the commencement of our late Cruel War, we were forced into, or give up all which is dear to freemen, *Liberty*, I had thirteen Vessels, with other Valuable property destroyed, by Genls. Gray and Arnold, at Bedford in the Massachusetts Bay and New London in this State, I gave a Currency as far as was in my power to the Continental paper, by which I Suffered greatly, but as it was a means of our Success I am happy, at the same time my finances are so far circumscribed that an office under Government would be convenient and agreeable to me. I am fixed on this Hill four Miles from fairfield and half a Mile from the Post Road. If Circumstances should lead to a Journey in Connecticut, I hope you will honor me with a Visit. The Hon'ble Mr Baldwin can inform you that I can Accommodate a *republican* President, and to that Gentleman please to be referd, I am with sincere regard, Your Excellencies most

Obedient Servant SAMUEL BROOME

RC (DNA: RG 59, LAR); addressed: "The President of the United States Washington"; endorsed by TJ as received 15 Oct. and "for office" and so recorded in SJL.

A NEW HAVEN PAPER: the 6 Oct. edition of the *Connecticut Journal* reported the appointment of Abraham Bishop as collector for New Haven.

MR BALDWIN: probably Simeon Baldwin of New Haven, a newly elected congressman from Connecticut (*Biog. Dir. Cong.*; Vol. 24:692n).

[1]MS: "pemanent."

From David Gelston

SIR, New York Octo. 12th 1803

I have received your letter of the 5th instant, and this day shipped on board the Schooner Harmony, Capt. Levering, for Alexandria (who sails immediately) the ten cases of wine, bill of lading enclosed, the account of duties, and other expenses attending, shall be forwarded. Capt. L. goes direct for Alexa.

I have the honor to be, with great regard, Sir, your obedient servt.

DAVID GELSTON

RC (MHi); at foot of text: "Thomas Jefferson President U.S."; endorsed by TJ as received 15 Oct. and so recorded in SJL.

From John Langdon, with Jefferson's Note

SR. Portsmouth Octobr 12h. 1803

I have this day received a letter from Mark L. Hill Esq of Georgetown Kennebec, a very respectable Gentleman, and another from, Samuel Davis Esq. of Bath, one of the first Merchants of that place, desireing me to Name to the President, Andrew Greenwood Esq. of Bath for Collector at that port, in the place of William Webb Esq who resigns. from the recommendation of Those Gentlemen, who I am personally aquainted and Connected with, and who may be depended on; Mr. Greenwood may be considerd as suitable a person for the Collectors Office as any in The Destrict. you'll please accept my best wishes for your Happiness and beleive me with the highest respect,

Sr. your Oblig'd Hbl. Servt JOHN LANGDON

Mr. Cutts has the letters mentioned

[*Note by TJ*:]

Hill & Davis are connections of J.L. but both tories
Greenwood is a tory also.
Bath is entirely a tory place of rising importance.

RC (DNA: RG 59, LAR); at foot of text: "President of the United States"; TJ's notes written on verso below endorsement, probably after consulting with Dearborn (see below); endorsed by TJ as received 19 Oct. and "Greenwood Andrew to be Collectr. Bath v. Webb resd" and so recorded in SJL.

The letters of recommendation from Mark Langdon HILL and SAMUEL DAVIS have not been found but were probably enclosed in TJ's letter to Dearborn of 20 Oct. In 1803, Hill ran for the Massachusetts state senate as a "firm federalist," but he later served in Congress as a Republican. In 1824, he was appointed collector at Bath. Both Davis and ANDREW GREENWOOD, a prominent attorney in Bath, were Federalist leaders (*Boston Gazette*, 28 Mch. 1803; *Portland Gazette and Maine Advertiser*, 10 Mch. 1806; *American Advocate, and Kennebec Advertiser*, 3 Apr. 1819; *Biog. Dir. Cong.*; William Willis, *A History of the Law, the Courts, and the Lawyers of Maine, From Its First Colonization to the Early Part of the Present Century* [Portland, Me., 1863], 318-23, 501).

IN THE PLACE OF WILLIAM WEBB: on 30 Sep., the collector at Bath wrote the Treasury secretary of his decision to resign "on acct. of my health." He proposed to remain in office until 31 Dec. "to close the business of the year if possible" (RC in DNA: RG 59, RD; endorsed by TJ: "Webb Wm. to mr Gallatin resigns as Collector of Bath"). Webb wrote Madison of his decision on 29 Sep. (Madison, *Papers, Sec. of State Ser.*, 5:475).

Congressman Richard CUTTS arrived in Washington and took his seat on 17 Oct., the opening day of Congress (JHR, 4:401, 403).

On 17 Oct., David Trufant and others wrote James Madison from Bath, also recommending Greenwood for the collectorship. They noted that his "public education, moral character & standing in society" placed him "in the most favorable point of light" with those who knew him, including several gentlemen at the seat of government who were personally acquainted with him and could answer any queries the president "may be pleased to make on this subject" (RC in DNA: RG 59, LAR; in Trufant's hand, and signed by him and eight others; endorsed by TJ: "Greenwood Andrew. to be collector of Bath").

From John S. Lillie

SIR Boston Octor: 12th. 1803

When I was Editor of the News Paper called the *Constitutional Telegraphe*, I sent it on to you, as did Docr. Parker, who was the original Editor of that Paper. I should not at this late period have thought of forwarding my Bill to You, which I have inclosed in this Letter, but for my misfortunes. I have suffered, Sir, very much in consequence of my too ardent zeal in the Republican cause, & am willing, if it should be necessary, still to suffer more, neither the neglect of my Republican friends, nor the contumely or contempt of my federal enimies; will, I trust, ever induce me to alter my political creed. Perhaps my zeal in the Republican cause when I edited the *Telegraphe*, made me rather imprudent, I certainly meant well, & my concience does not reproach me with an intention, to injure, either directly, or indirectly, the private character of any man. The distress of my family was great during my unfortunate imprisonment for a supposed libel on *Judge Dana*; at that time, two of my Childreen lay at the point of Death, particurlarly, the Youngest, who has the honor to bear your name,*= both these childreen by the goodness of Providence, who blessed the means used by my worthy & much esteemed friend, *Doctor Jarvis*, (whose kindness & attention to my sick family during my imprisonment, has made an indellible impression on my mind,) by his exertions, under God, they were restored to the arms of their unfortunate father.

You no doubt will recollect Sir, that the *Constitl. Telegraphe*, was, at one time, the only decided Republican Paper in this State. and if I know my own heart, when I became its Editor, I had no other view, than the good of my native Country, in the promotion of Republicanism in your Election to the Cheif magistracy of the nation, and to this single point I exerted with pleasure all the abilities which I possessed, & had the inexpresible satisfaction to find the cause triumphant. My earnest prayer to Heaven, now is, that Your Excellencey may long live to enjoy the confidence & esteem of a large majority of your fellow citizens, as the chief Magistrate of the freest, & happiest, nation in the world; & when your days on earth are finished, receive the plaudits from the Judge of quick & dead, of "*well done good, & faithful Servant.*"

With the highest sentiments of respect & veneration for your distinguished character, I beg leave to subscribe myself, Your Excellency, Obednt, Humble Servant, JOHN S. LILLIE

=* This Child has been often to see, the late venerable *Govr. Adams* who used to say, that his countenance bore a striking resemblance to yours.

RC (DLC); at foot of text: "His Excellencey, Thomas Jefferson Esqr. President of the United States"; endorsed by TJ as received 22 Oct. and so recorded in SJL. Enclosure: Invoice in Lillie's hand and signed by him, dated Boston, 12 Oct. 1803, requesting TJ's payment of $4.50 for a subscription to the *Constitutional Telegraphe* from 1 Oct. 1801 to 1 Apr. 1802 at $3 per year (MS in same, also in

Lillie's hand: "Recvd payment"; see William Eustis to TJ, 27 Nov. 1803).

I SENT IT ON TO YOU: for TJ's subscription to the *Constitutional Telegraphe*, see Vol. 37:312.

For Lillie's three-month IMPRISONMENT FOR A SUPPOSED LIBEL involving Francis DANA, see Vol. 37:188-9.

WELL DONE GOOD, & FAITHFUL SERVANT: Matt. 25:21.

Notes on the Plan of the City of Washington

Note. for many of the facts & documents here stated reference must be had to State papers. Dec. 17. 1800. Jan. 30. 1801. Apr. 8. 1802.

Questions arising from time to time What is the plan of the city of Washington? have not unauthoritative alterations been made in it? how do these alterations affect the rights of individuals? it becomes necessary to review the facts on which they depend, to deduce principles from these, & to apply them to individual cases.

Act of Congr. 1790. c. 28. prescribes to Commissioners, under the direction of the Pres. of the US. to survey, & by metes & bounds define & limit the territory &c to purchase or accept land, as the Pr. US. shall deem proper, for the use of the US. and to provide suitable buildings for the accomodation of Congress, & of the President, & for the public offices of the govmt of the US. according to such plans as the Pr. shall approve. the Pr. is authorised to accept grants of money for defraying the expence of such purchases & buildings.

1791 Apr. The proprietors of the lands on which the city is laid, convey to trustees as follows. the lands to be laid out, with such streets, squares, parcels & lots as the Pr. US. for the time being shall approve. the trustees to convey to the Commrs. for the time being, for the use of the US. all the streets, & such squares, parcels & lots, as the Pr. shall deem proper for the use of the US. the residue of the lots to be divided one half to the proprietor, the other half to be sold on such terms & conditions &c. as the Pr. US. shall direct the trustees to convey to the purchasers, & the proceeds of the sales to be applied, 1st. to pay the proprietors for the lots, squares & parcels appropriated to the use of the US. at £25. per acre, the balance to the President as a grant of money, & to be applied for the purposes & according to the act of Congr. the conveyor to possess & occupy, until the same shall be occupied under the said appropriations for the use of the US. or by purchasers: & to cut & take the trees, timber & wood, except such of the trees & wood growing as the Pr. or Commrs. may judge proper & give notice shall be left for ornament; for which a just value to be paid. the trustees, at the request of the Pr. US. for the time being, to convey all the lands hereby conveyed to such person as he shall appoint subject to the trusts.

Oct. 17. The first sale of lots took place. squares 77. 78. 79. 105. 106. 107. 127. 128. were divided, &[1] were sold. it is to be observed that none of these touch the Pr's square, either as then projected, or afterwards established.

1791. Oct. 25. President Washington informs Congress of the state in which the business then was, to wit. that the district was located, & a city laid out on a plan which he should[2] place before them. and Dec. 13. he communicated to them L'Enfant's projet, & after time given for inspection, he withdrew it.

Dec: 19. The legislature of Maryland pass an act. by §.5. all the squares, lots, pieces, & parcels of land within the city, which have been or shall be appropriated for the use of US. & also the streets, shall remain & be for the use of the US. and all the lots sold shall be to the purchasers according to the conditions of purchase. the Commrs. for the time being, shall from time to time, until Congress shall exercise the jurisdiction, have power to license the building of wharves adjoining the city, in the manner, & of the extent they may judge[3] convenient, and agreeing with general order; but no wharf to be built before the land of another, nor without licence. they may direct as to ballast, materials for building, earth from cellars &c the thickness of walls, under penalties not exceeding £10. grant licences for retailing spirits.

1792. Mar. 14. Pr. Washington having employed Ellicot to prepare the plan of the city for engraving,[4] the groundwork of which was L'Enfant's projet with several alterations approved by him, and particularly with an omission of the specific appropriations of the public squares, proposed in the projet, which, except those of the Capitol & President's square were struck out and left for future determination as the uses should occur. Ellicot now compleated it: and it was put into the hands of engravers at Philadelphia & Boston to be engraved.

Apr. 20. The commissioners having proposed to the President some further alterations, the Secretary of state informs the Commrs. that the Pr. declines making any alterations in the city, in consideration of the expediency of fixing the public opinion on the thing as stable & unalterable, the loss of work done if altered, the changing all the avenues which point to the Capitol, removing the two houses to a still greater distance, change in the engraving &c. [it may be conjectured that one of their proposed alterations was the removal of the Capitol Eastwardly to the highest part of the ground to save digging down that.]

Oct. [5] A sale of lots takes place, at which the Boston engraved plan was exhibited. in this the lines next to the water are omitted.

At this sale a division took place between the Commrs. & Davidson, squares 167. & 186. are assigned to Davidson, & 200. 221. to the US. Davidson becomes the purchaser of 221. and 200 is sold to others,[6] and he recieves payment at the rate of £25. per acre for every foot of the residue of the Pr's square, & consequently for the very ground he since reclaims. on this occasion the Commrs. & Davidson enter into a written agreement that if any squares or buildings or other appropriations, except as a public square, are hereafter made on Davidson's part of the Pr's square, bounded on the W. by 17th. street, N. by H. street, E. by 15th. S by Dav. Burnes's line (except the two squares 167. & 221. already established & laid off),[7] the sd Saml. Davidson should be entitled to his dividend thereof.

1795. July 20. The Commrs. published regulations respecting wharves (expressing it to be under the authority given them by the act of Maryland.) they permit the proprietors of water lots to wharf as far out as they think proper, not injuring or interrupting the channel, leaving space where the plan of the streets requires it, and 60. f. at every 300. f. for a street where the plan indicates none.

1795. Oct. 5. they permit mr Barry to wharf across the Georgia avenue.

at various times they sell lots on the bank *with a water privilege*, viz. Nos. 1. 2. 3. 4. 5. 6. 7. 17. 18. square no. 8. sold to mr Templeman.

1797. Mar. 2. Genl. Washington executes an instrument of directions to the Trustees to convey to the Commrs. all the streets as delineated in a plan said to be annexed, and 17. spaces of ground, as therein specially designated, for public reservations. by accident the plan was not annexed, but this annexation was supplied by President Adams July 23. 1798.

Other appropriations[8] of the reserved squares have been inferred from President Washington's letters of Oct. 21. & Dec. 1. 1796. to wit of the 4th. reservation for an University, and of the 13th. for a Marine hospital. but the uncertain language of those letters is decided negatively by his subsequent omission of these appropriations in the Plan & Declaration of 1797.[9] The 7th. reservn & the angular space between 78. and 101. have been regularly appropriated for a market.

1799. Apr. President Adams designated[10] the 14th. reservation to a Navy yard, & it has been assumed for that purpose: but the appropriation has not yet been formally made.

1801. Feb. 27. Congress assume the jurisdiction of the territory.

1802. May 3. Congress establish a corporation, giving them powers which in various instances abridge or supersede those of the Commissioners.

From these facts the following legal deductions may be drawn.

The power of the President to establish the plan of the city is derived solely from that part of the deeds of the proprietors which requires the trustees to convey to the Commissioners *such streets and squares as the Presidt. should deem proper*, for the use of the US. these having left him free as to the time & form of executing this power, we are to seek for those acts, words, or instruments proceeding from him which did amount in law to a full execution of his power, or a compleat declaration of all the streets and squares reserved, premising that it was not requisite that he should execute his power all at once, but by successive acts as he should find best.

1. The sales and divisions of squares & lots made by his authority, were an execution of his power as to so much of the plan as limited them, & their limits would thenceforward be established & unalterable. but these did not determine his power as to other parts not conveyed or divided.

2. His message to Congress of 1791. and communication of a first projet of the city by Lenfant, was merely a matter of information of the progress of the business, and not a determination of it. his letter of Feb. 20. 1797. to the Commrs. explicitly declares this, his subsequent alterations shew it, and the solemnity of his instrument of directions to the trustees for a more extensive execution of his powers when he thought the business ripe for it, are a conclusive proof of his intentions.

3. This direction of 1797. Mar. 2. to the trustees to convey streets & squares according to the plan annexed, was plainly intended as a solemn execution of his powers, and conclusive on him & his successors, as far as it went: and the plan therein referred to, the annexation of which was supplied by President Adams, taken in conjunction with the explanatory instrument of directions, may be considered to be the established plan of the city so far as it went.[11] it appears indeed to have been made on a survey not accurate in every part, so that certain designations in it could not be applied to the ground, & were liable either to correction from that, or to nullity. such portions of the power as were not executed by this instrument, remained of course in the President. such were the future appropriations of the areas reserved except the Capitol & President's squares: and the destination of many angular points formed between the intersections of streets, and the building squares delineated in the plan. these being left vacant in the plan, & not disposed of in the act of Mar. 2. 97. were left to be acted on thereafter. some of them have since been reserved & paid for, others divided as building squares; others still remain to be divided or reserved & paid for.

This plan of Pr. Washington's is controuled by another circumstance. by the common law of England, presumed to be unaltered in Maryland in this particular, the property, tam aquae quam solé, of every river, susceptible of any navigation probably, but certainly of every one having flux & reflux, is in the king, who cannot grant it to a subject because it is a highway[12] except for purposes which will increase the convenience of navigation. the ordinary low water mark is the limit of what is grantable by the crown to an individual. accordingly the grants from the crown, on such rivers, are ordinarily limited by the river: and so probably were the grants to the proprietors on the Potomak & Eastern branch. in the only deed I can recur to, that of Abraham Young, I observe he bounds his conveyance *by & with the waters of the Eastern branch & Potomak river*; and if the other proprietors have not done the same, the law has done it for them. the bed of the river vested, on the revolution in the states of Maryland & Virginia, & by their cessions was transferred to the US. but no act of the US. authorised the Pr. to lay out or establish the plan of a city. he recieved that authority only from the proprietors, & consequently it could extend no farther than their right extended, to the water edge. whatever parts of the plan therefore went beyond the water edge, were null for want of authority to lay them there.

Let us now proceed to examine the alterations which have been made and the effect they have on the rights of individuals.

1. The alteration pretended by mr Davidson, is no alteration at all. the building squares he claims were never established as such. they appeared indeed in the first project of Lenfant, but never were authorised by any act of the President's. this is proved by mr Davidson's own agreement with the Commrs. in which the provision, that 'if any building squares other than 167. & 221.[13] should afterwards be established on his part of the Pr's square the limits of which are there distinctly specified,[14] he should have his dividend of them' admits there were none then,[15] and he recieves paiment at £25. an acre for the residue on the footing of a public square. it is proved by the authentic plan established in 97. and the written directions, reserving the ground expressly for the public use. it is explicitly declared by President Washington in his letter of Feb. 20. 97. and is said to have been also declared by Pr. Adams. it is impossible for any thing to be more definitively decided, and I will venture to affirm that there exists no where a power to alter[16] it, not even in Congress. for as the Proprietors were masters of their property, to give, or not to give, so were they of the conditions and limitations on which they would give. having more confidence in the cordiality of the then President, than in that of Congress, towards their new city, they preferred placing under his discretion even what they should give for the use of the US. they trusted that all the material powers would be executed in his time, as

in fact they were, & by himself. as to trusts thus submitted to the President, Congress cannot legislate. e.g. they cannot change the location, direction or dimensions of streets or squares or otherwise alter the plan of the city, appropriate squares or building lots, alter the conditions of conveyance, as by authorising wooden houses* &c. on the other hand they have the right to legislate over every thing ceded to them by Maryland. but that cession contained an express reservation of all individual rights. they have the legislation over the bed of the river, may regulate wharves, bridges &c. built into or over it &c

2. the conversion into building lots[17] of the angular spaces left vacant in the plan and declaration of 97. have been called alterations. but they are not: they are only successive & supplementory executions of the power, the location of the bed of the canal in 1795. and the establishment of more building lots on Nottley Young's ground, than appear in the engraved plan, was previous to the plan and declaration of 1797. and expressly established by them. the actual location of squares 728. 729. being different from what they appear to be in the engraved plan, have been deemed alterations. so also the establishment of building squares in a space in Hamburg South of 104. which appears vacant in the engraved plan. but these are errors of the engraved plan; all of them having been laid off before it was engraved, altho' it escaped Ellicot's notice.

3. when the Plan & Declaration of 1797. were established, the whole of the delineations had not been actually made on the ground. hence it happened that when they came to be made, they were found impossible & inconsistent with the ground. thus the 15th. & 16th. reservations were intended for a market with a canal leading to it from the river. the actual ground was found too far withdrawn from the river, & that a canal could not be drawn to it. they were therefore corrected by being converted into building squares 852. & 881. and the reservation was located between them & the river.[18] [it is now said that these alterations were before the authentic plan, and make a part of that plan.]

4. The plan & Declaration of 97. were void as to so much of them as projected beyond the water edge, beyond which the President's power did not extend.

5. The bed of the river being vested in the state of Maryland, & by them ceded to the US. with a reservation of the right of legislation until it should be assumed by Congress, the alienations of the right of

* —qu: whether some of the provisions in the act of 1802. ch. 41. respecting the canal, do not rest merely on the assent of the President given to that act, & how far they could be revoked?

wharfing so far as they were actually made by the Commissioners before Feb. 27. 1801. consistently with the act of Maryland, were valid. but their regulations of July 20. 1795. did not convey a *general* right to all purchasers of Water lots. it was no more than an advertisement which they were free to depart from at any time before actual sale. the deed of conveyance is the only thing which could convey the right actually. the Commissioners possessed, as to wharves, not a mere naked power, but a power coupled with an interest: and could therefore vary their terms as a private individual may at any time before an actual contract.

On the whole the Question now recurs. What is the Plan of the city of Washington.

It is, as to it's main part, the Plan and Declaration of 1797.

1st. emarginated as to so much as projected beyond the water edge.

2. with such wharves added as the Commrs. validly authorised before 1801.

[3. with the alterations of the 15th. & 16th. reservations & of squares 852. & 881.] qu?

4. with the insertion of such angular spaces as have been reserved or[19] converted into building lots.

5. the insertion of the appropriation for a market &[20] of the 14th. reservation to a Navy Yard.

Th: Jefferson
Oct. 12. 1803.

Oct. 18. 1803. Since writing the above I have seen the opinion of mr Charles Lee, while Attorney Genl. on the subject above considered, and I concur in most of it's contents. in the following particulars however, I do not.

1. he supposes the Pr.'s sanction will be necessary for such streets as shall be reclaimed from the water. I think that power rests with Congress.

2. he quotes these words of the constitution to wit, 'Congress shall have power to dispose of and make all needful rules & regulations respecting the territory or other property belonging to the US.' and supposes they give Congress a power over the squares reserved for the US. but they can have no power over them further than the proprietors have granted. the US. are the cestuy que trust, the President (not Congress) is the trustee. the only question in the case of the Queen of Portugal is whether a lot appropriated for the residence of her minister, is appropriated to a public use?

3. he thinks the angular spaces are public ways. I do not think any act of the President's has made them so.

4. he thinks the Pr. could sell a public square, & lay out the money in other grounds for the same purpose. I think that having declared it reserved for public use, he has so far executed his power, & cannot afterwards alien it for private use.

Dft (DLC); in TJ's hand, including brackets. FC (same); in Lewis Harvie's hand, with "Note" at head of text and signature by TJ.

Although TJ did not record receiving Nicholas King's letter of 25 Sep., that letter clearly prompted the president to compile the above notes. The question of a new, definitive plan for the city had also been raised in Congress the preceding year and in a letter of 13 Apr. 1802 from Alexander White, a former commissioner for the district (Vol. 37:224-5). For some of the FACTS and DOCUMENTS from which TJ was drawing, see ASP, *Miscellaneous*, 1:219-31, 330-6, and U.S. Statutes at Large, 1:130; 2:103-8, 195-7.

TJ condensed but did not alter the meaning of the original agreement ceding control of land within the federal district from the current PROPRIETORS to the public. Under the agreement, the president enjoyed "the sole power of directing the Federal City to be laid off in what manner he pleases" (Washington, *Papers, Pres. Ser.*, 8:24-6).

Because Pierre L'Enfant failed to make available a map of his plan suitable for engraving, President Washington and TJ had Andrew Ellicott (ELLICOT), who was surveying the district, prepare one. Ellicott's map included changes, many of them initiated by TJ, to the original plan (Bob Arnebeck, *Through a Fiery Trial: Building Washington, 1790-1800* [Lanham, Md., 1991], 94-6; Vol. 20:60-3).

For the dispute between Samuel DAVIDSON and the district's commissioners, see Vol. 34:647-8 and Vol. 35:47-8.

James BARRY planned to build a wharf on the Eastern Branch in 1795 at the end of New Jersey Avenue. The revised city plan left a large section of public space at about the same spot for GEORGIA AVENUE, which was roughly to run along the right side of the Eastern Branch. Fearing that his improvements would be later claimed as public space, Barry argued that as planned, Georgia Avenue would run through water and that he should therefore be granted formal acknowledgment of his right to wharf that part of his property. Two of the commissioners concurred (James Barry to the Board of Commissioners, 3 Oct. 1795, and Commissioners to Barry, 5 Oct. 1795, Lb in DNA: RG 42, LRDLS; Arnebeck, *Through a Fiery Trial*, 322).

TAM AQUAE QUAM SOLÉ: that is, "as well of the water as of the soil."

For the act of Congress respecting the CANAL running between the Potomac and the Eastern Branch, see U.S. Statutes at Large, 2:176-8.

Distressed by the many alterations allowed by the commissioners to the engraved plan, a number of the federal district's original proprietors petitioned President Adams on 10 Nov. 1798 to fix a permanent plan from which the commissioners would not be allowed to deviate. In an opinion of 7 Jan. 1799, CHARLES LEE ruled against the proprietors' memorial, arguing that an authenticated plan of the city already existed (essentially the same claim that TJ makes above on what constituted the plan of the city), that adjustments based on new surveys could easily be applied to this plan, and that a new plan was therefore "unnecessary and moreover highly improper." Lee also argued that determining uniform regulations for water lots was impracticable and that commissioners should not be required to expend public monies on redeeming land from the water to form a water street (one of the principal objectives of the proprietors). Lee agreed with the memorialists that the commissioners did not have the authority to dispose of lands in the district allocated in the city plan to public use. Such deviations from the plan would, Lee argued, require congressional assent. TJ's view was more rigid on this point, and his disagreement may have encouraged him to add a large body of text to the analysis (see note 16 below). The United States through the president (and his commissioners) acted as beneficiary, or CESTUY

QUE TRUST, for the proprietors. Congress had no authority to dispose of public spaces, as the United States could not go beyond the proprietors' acknowledged intent. In the case highlighted in the proprietors' memorial, the commissioners had conveyed a part of the president's square for the residence of the minister of PORTUGAL. Although TJ agreed that the president could not ALIEN public spaces for private use, he nevertheless viewed the conveyance as potentially legitimate because a foreign minister's residence might be deemed an acceptable use of public space (ASP, *Miscellaneous*, 1:331-3; Charles Lee to John Adams, 7 Jan. 1799, in DNA: RG 42, LRDLS; Arnebeck, *Through a Fiery Trial*, 500-1).

[1] Preceding numerals, two words, and ampersand interlined in place of "78. 101. 105. 107. 126. & 127."

[2] TJ here canceled "communicate."

[3] TJ here canceled "proper."

[4] TJ first continued the sentence, "towards which L'Enfant's projet was taken as the ground work, but several alterations made with his approbation and particularly the specific appropriations of the public squares, proposed in the projet being struck out and left for future determination as the uses should occur, except those of the Capitol & President's square," before altering it to read as above.

[5] Here, a clerk added "8th."

[6] Remainder of sentence interlined.

[7] Closing parenthesis added by Editors.

[8] Word interlined in place of "reservations."

[9] Remainder of paragraph added at later time but included in FC.

[10] Word interlined in place of "appropriated."

[11] TJ here canceled, "[some?] designations in it, inconsistent."

[12] Remainder of sentence interlined.

[13] Preceding two words, numerals, and ampersand interlined.

[14] Preceding eight words interlined.

[15] Remainder of sentence interlined.

[16] TJ first ended the paragraph just after this point. He then canceled one or two illegible words and added the remainder of the paragraph, most of which he wrote in the margin.

[17] Preceding three words interlined.

[18] Remainder of paragraph added at later time.

[19] Preceding two words interlined.

[20] Preceding three words and ampersand interlined.

From Benjamin Stoddert

SIR Geo town 12 Octo 1803.

The attention the City of Washington has constantly experienced at your hands, leads me to hope, that any honest plan which promises advantage to the City, and which can injure nobody, will have your countenance.

Washington suffers more than any other place, for want of active capital. Men of money, have not shewn a disposition to move to Washington with their money; nor is it probable they will, until they see that capital can be had without them. The City never can flourish, until active capital, without which, there can be no enterprize, shall by some means, be introduced.

It was from considerations like these, that an effort was made last session of Congress, to get an insurance Company incorporated, on a plan similar to the one, I have now the honor to enclose. After passing the house of Reps. by a large majority, it failed in the Senate, by one or two votes. I think it failed because some members did not understand it—and perhaps it was taken up at too late a period of the Session.

The remarks that accompany the bill, were made for the People of the City & Town—I enclose them, not under the impression, that the subject is not already well understood by you.—Nor have I taken the liberty thus to obtrude upon your time, from an expectation, or even a wish, that you should make this thing of sufficient importance to notice it to Congress.

I have the honor to be With high respect Sir Yr. Mo Obed. Serv.

BEN STODDERT

RC (DLC); endorsed by TJ as received 18 Oct. and so recorded in SJL. Enclosures not found, but see below.

EFFORT WAS MADE LAST SESSION OF CONGRESS: on 31 Dec. 1802, the House of Representatives received a petition from the citizens of Washington and Georgetown asking Congress to incorporate the Columbia General Insurance Company. The company was to have a capital stock of $300,000, with one-sixth paid in money and the remaining five-sixths paid in Washington city lots. At least five percent of these lots were to be sold annually until the entire amount was disposed of, with the money arising from the sales added to the capital stock of the company. Although the House approved the petition, the Senate failed to do so by a vote of 10 in favor and 12 against (*An Act for Incorporating an Insurance Company in the City of Washington* [Washington, 1803; Shaw-Shoemaker, No. 5201]; JHR, 4:263, 285, 296; JS, 3:255, 262, 265, 278).

From Jeremiah Van Rensselaer, with Jefferson's Note

SIR — Albany 12th. October 1803.

There being a vacancy in the commission of Bankruptcy for this City and as I Presume there is a necessity for filling it as soon as possible, permit me to recommend to your notice as a very proper person to fill the same Sebastian Visscher Esquire of this place in whom the trust and confidence may be placed.

I am Dr. Sir with respect your obt. Servt.

JER V RENSSELAER

[*Note by TJ*:]

Lansing
Ten Wyck
Merchant } are now commrs. & sufft.

RC (DNA: RG 59, LAR); at foot of text: "Thomas Jefferson President of the United States of America"; with TJ's note written on verso below endorsement; endorsed by TJ as received 19 Oct. and "Visscher Sebastn. to be Commr. bkrptcy Albany" and so recorded in SJL.

For the commissioners OF BANKRUPTCY at Albany, see Vol. 37:709 and Nicholas N. Quackenbush to TJ, 8 June 1803.

SEBASTIAN VISSCHER regularly served as secretary at Republican meetings in Albany, while George Merchant served as chairman. In 1803, both were elected aldermen of the First Ward. In 1808, Visscher was appointed clerk to the state senate (*Albany Gazette*, 21 Apr. 1803; 8 Mch. 1804; 1 Oct. 1807; *New-York Herald*, 5 Oct. 1803; *Albany Register*, 11 May 1804; 2 Apr. 1807; 16 Feb., 19 Apr. 1808).

TEN WYCK: that is, Abraham Ten Eyck (Vol. 40:505n).

To Archibald McCall

SIR Washington Oct. 13 03.

Your letter of Aug. 23 has been lately recieved, & on the same paper that of Nov. 19 preceding, which had not before come to my hands. my letter formerly written to you on the subject of the bond to Flood, from Reuben Skelton[1] whose administrator mr Wayles was, and of the paiment of it to Colo. Peachy, being at Monticello, I cannot now turn to it. but I placed the subject in that on what I thought proper grounds, and see no new reason for changing it. Colo. Peachy may have sworn, & with truth, that I sent him the money by mr Carter: but not that he did not apply for it. on the contrary I never saw a more persevering course of dunning than he used to obtain it: & I think it probable the acting[2] executor possesses written proofs of it. the money was made up by equal contributions, and passed through me, [...] Colo. Peachy would be also, but not being there it was sent by mr Carter. the actual paiment to him, & the full administration of Reuben Skelton's estate by mr Wayles, which will be pleaded & proved will be a just as well as legal bar to any demand you may think proper to institute. I have before informed you that Francis Eppes esq. in the vicinity of Richmond was the acting exr & in possession of all the books & papers of mr Wayles, and that I have not meddled in the administration. a service of process on him will be good as to the whole: but still if you desire it should be on me also, that my absence from the state may occasion no delay, I will acknolege a service on mr Eppes as a personal service on me, and consent that the officer shall return it as served on me. or if you will inform me when you shall have taken out process, I will have my appearance entered immediately in any court at Richmond to which it is returnable. I tender you my respects. TH: JEFFERSON

PrC (ViW: Tucker-Coleman Collection); torn and blurred; at foot of text: "Mr. Archibald Mc.Call"; endorsed by TJ in ink on verso.

McCall's LETTER of 23 Aug., recorded in SJL as received 5 Sep., has not been found. For McCall's efforts to collect money on behalf of the estate of his father-in-law Nicholas FLOOD, see Vol. 39:35-6.

[1] Preceding three words interlined.
[2] Word interlined.

From John A. Chevallié

MONSIEUR LE PRESIDENT Richmond le 14 Octobre 1803.

J'ay eu l'honneur de vous Ecrire le 16 du mois passé & de vous envoyer une lettre du Gl. La fayette, un mémoire imprimé des héritiers Beaumarchais, Copie d'une lettre du Gl. Mathieu Dumas à Messrs. Munroe & Livingston, & une Note de la situation actuelle de la Succession Beaumarchais. J'ay reçu, depuis, une lettre du Genl. Dumas mantionnant que L'Ambassadeur des Etats unis à Paris a dû Vous envoyer Copie des Instructions du Gouvernement français au Gl. Bernadotte au sujet de cette même affaire.

ce Seroit pour moi une Satisfaction bien douce après 16 ans d'un travail penible & Sans recompense, de Voir terminer ces réclamations en faveur de mes Comettants. Je compte Sur la Justice du Gouvernement des Etats unis & Je supplie, Votre Excellence, de Pardonner la Priere que Je luy fais, d'accuser la réception des Papiers contenûs dans ma lettre du 16 septembre.

Je suis avec Respect Monsieur Le President Votre très humble & très obéissant Serviteur J. A. CHEVALLIÉ

EDITORS' TRANSLATION

MR. PRESIDENT, Richmond, 14 Oct. 1803

I had the honor of writing to you on the 16th of last month and sending you a letter from General Lafayette, a printed memo from the Beaumarchais heirs, a copy of a letter from General Mathieu Dumas to Messrs Monroe and Livingston, and a note on the current situation of the Beaumarchais estate. Since then, I have received a letter from General Dumas mentioning that you should have received from the American ambassador to Paris a copy of the French government's instructions to General Bernadotte concerning this same matter.

After sixteen years of hard work, with no compensation, it would give me sweet satisfaction to see these requests met in favor of my clients. I count on the justice of the United States government, and I beg Your Excellency to forgive my asking you to confirm that you received the papers enclosed in my September 16th letter.

With respect, Mr. President, I am your very humble and obedient servant.

J. A. CHEVALLIÉ

RC (DLC: Gallatin Papers); endorsed by TJ as received 16 Oct. and so recorded in SJL.

To Benjamin Galloway

Dear Sir Washington Oct. 14. 03.

I recieved yesterday your favor of the 11th. and immediately proceeded to search for the letter of Nov. 30th. 1800. which you suppose to have been delivered to me. I found on reiterated examination that I possess no such letter. as every letter I recieve is filed away alphabetically, the search is short & easily practicable. I then turned to my letter list, for I note in a particular list the name & date of letters as I recieve them daily. I examined it from Nov. 1797. (the time when I recieved from you the note formerly mentioned) to the spring of 1801. and find no letter from you within that period, & think therefore I may safely say I recieved none within that period. I should have concluded the note receivd Nov. 1797 to be the one mr Smiley supposes he delivered me; but I observe that is endorsed 'to the care of mr Archibald Stuart Staunton.' I inclose you a copy of it, & am sorry I have nothing else to offer in compliance with your desire. Accept my salutations & assurances of great respect.

Th: Jefferson

PrC (MHi); at foot of text: "Benjamin Galloway esq."; endorsed by TJ in ink on verso. Enclosure: see Vol. 29:566-7 for the undated missive from Galloway endorsed by TJ as a letter of October 1797 received 6 Nov.

From Mary Hazard and Anna Void

Philadelphia, Octr 14, 1803

Gottes gnade und seegen zum gruß; du lieber *President*

Ich habe dir schon einmal in Englisch meine iämerliche noth geklagt, aber es scheint mir als wen du dich nicht sehr viel darum bekümmern thätest, dan du last aus, uns über kopf und ohren in schülden rennen ehe du uns unser gelt schickst. Was meinst du dabeÿ? Du lieber *President*; hast du keine gefühlung in deinem herzen? schlägt dich dein gewisen nicht an? uns arme weiber so aus unsern gelt zu betrugen! dan ich will dir sagen wie ich meÿne, sehr du hast viel überflüsig gelt, und wir haben keines, nun denke ich, das ein wenig von deinem uberfluss uns angehöret, weil du es nicht vermissen thätest, und uns thäte es, aus aller unserer armuth und noth helfen. Ach du lieber Gott! wan es nur so einmal in der welt thät zugehen das die Presidente über 16 staten wissen mögten, wie es einem anstehet, mit einem hungerigen magen uber den schank zu gehen, und da nicht einmal eine drukenen Kruste zu finden den appetit zu besättigen; ach! ach! was wäre das nicht zu beiamern! aber, unser lieber *President* der kan uns klagen hören, wie wir nichts zu thun können bekommen, weil das fieber hier ist und das man doch essen will; er hört uns sagen, das wir keine schue an den füsen haben das unser holtz schier verbrennt ist; und das der kalte winter heran eilt, uns vieleicht zu tote zu verfrieren, und doch schließt er seine ohren, und sein herz zu und will uns nicht ein wenig von seinem uberflusse mitheilen!! ach! ach! was ist das doch nicht eine schande! .... da schaffe ich, und meine Schwester für einen schneider. dreÿ dage aus den sieben bekommen wir arbeit, und wen wir aus schon krank arbeiten, so können wir beiten nicht mehr als acht schilling verdienen, die acht schillinge müssen uns dan eine ganze woche ernähren! und kan sich ietzt der liebe *President* einbilden, wie das möglich seÿn kan? nein; nein; es ist nicht möglich; es kostet uns iust einen Thaler das stück, des woches;[1] und da kanst du sehen wie unser schulden aufgeloffen sint; ach! schike uns doch balt unser gelt, sonst vergehen wir in unserm iamer! Zweÿ woche will ich noch gedult mit dir haben, und wan du uns dan nicht schreibst, und uns zwanzig oder dreissig thaler shiken thuß, so schreib ich dir einen französchisen brief, und der soll dir ein wenig von meiner meunung sagen!–Ich habe alles gelernnt, nur nicht wie man gelt verdienen kan, wan man nichts zu thun krigen kan.–Ich will dir sagen, lieber *President*, alle dein nähen, für dich, und deine ganze haushaltung, will ich und meine schwester dir thun, wan du uns es anvertrauen wilst; und so wohlfeil, als es uns möglich zu thun ist. Lass uns nun bald wisen was du im sinn hast, währender zeit verbleiben wir wie Zuvor–

MARY HAZARD
&
ANN VOID

EDITORS' TRANSLATION

Philadelphia, 14 Oct. 1803

Greetings and God's blessing to you, dear *President*

I have already complained to you once in English about my wretched state of need, but it seems to me as if you are not troubling yourself much over that, for you are letting us run into debt over our head and ears before you send us our money. What do you mean by this? You dear *President*; have you no feeling in your heart? Doesn't your conscience bother you? To be cheating us poor women out of our money in such a way!

For I want to tell you what I mean, Sir, you have money in great abundance, and we have none. Now I am thinking that a little of your abundance belongs to us because you will not miss it, and it will serve to help us out of all our poverty and want. Oh, dear God! If only once in the world it would happen that the President in charge of 16 states might know what it is like for a person with a hungry belly to go to the public house and there not even once find a dry crust of bread to satisfy the appetite. Oh! Oh! What reason might there be not to complain!

But, our dear *President* can hear us complaining, how we are not able to get work, because there is fever here and still a person has to eat. He hears us saying that we have no shoes on our feet, that all our firewood has been burned, and that the cold winter is hurrying on, perhaps to freeze us to death. And still he shuts tight his ears and his heart and is not willing to share with us a little of his abundance!! Oh! Oh! What is this then if not a disgrace!

Here I and my sister work for a tailor. Three out of seven days we have work. And even if we work when we are sick, we are able to earn no more than eight shillings. The eight shillings must then sustain us for one entire week! And now can the dear *President* imagine how that can be possible? No, no. It is not possible. It means for us just one dollar per piece per week. And then you can see how our debts continue to mount up. Oh! So send us our money soon, lest we perish in our misery!

For two weeks more I will have patience with you. And if you then do not write to us and arrange to send us twenty or thirty dollars, then I am writing you a letter in French. And that letter ought to give you a piece of my mind! I have learned everything except how a person can earn money if that person can get no work. I want to tell you, dear *President*, that I and my sister will do all your sewing for you and your entire household if you will entrust this to us; and do the work as cheaply as is possible for us. Now let us know soon what you have in mind. In the meantime we remain as before—

Mary Hazard
&
Ann Void

RC (DLC); in Hazard's hand, including signatures; ellipses in original; addressed: "His Excellency Thomas Jefferson President of the U.S. Washington"; franked and postmarked; endorsed by TJ as received 16 Oct. and so recorded in SJL.

EINMAL IN ENGLISCH: Mary Hazard and Anna Void to TJ, 1 Sep. 1803.

[1]Preceding two words and semicolon interlined.

From Mustafa Baba, Dey of Algiers

If you are my friends and wish to remain so and wish to preserve your treaty with me you will send to me 10 Guns Brass 24 pounders with Cariages &c. and allso 5 Brass Guns 18 pounders with Cariages &c. Guns long for Batteries. I request you will not forget our friendship. I have spoken to your Consul on the subject and he is not inclineable to write although I consider him as Equal to one of your divan—and therefore request for our friendship and our treaty That you will not write me Evasive to my demand, as any favour demanded on your part I shall comply therewith whether your demand is great or small—

this letter by order of Mustapha Pascha dey of Algiers & with his great seal The 26th. of The moon of Giumad Alahar 1218—Corresponding with The 14th. of October 1803—

NB The dey further requires 60 Thsd. Bricks for furnaces

Tr (DNA: RG 59, CD, Algiers); in hand of Richard O'Brien; at head of text: "Copy by Translation—This letter of Mustapha Pascha dey of Algiers to The Great of The Govt. of The divan of America"; at foot of text: "Certified to be The substance or translation of The deys letter wrote in Moorish—OBrien"; endorsed by TJ as received 6 Feb. 1804 and so recorded in SJL. Tr (same); in O'Brien's hand; endorsed and notations by Jacob Wagner. Tr (same); in O'Brien's hand. Tr (DLC: Edward Preble Papers); in O'Brien's hand. RC (DNA: RG 59, CD, Algiers); in Arabic; with Mustafa's seal at head of text; editors' translation: "This letter is by order of our master Mustafa Pasha, God grant him victory, to the senior official of America and their head of the chancellery. If you are friends with us and faithful to the ancient pact that exists between us, send us ten brass cannons, 25-pounders, and the carriages with them. Send also five brass cannons with their carriages, 18-pounders. It is imperative that you fill this need of ours. I have spoken with all the (foreign) representatives who are present among us in Algiers, and they have duly supplied us with cannons. You are one of them, and it is unacceptable that you should refuse us a response. You say you have nothing to give, but this is impossible. It is imperative that you fill our need. We are friends, and if you require anything from us, we shall supply it. Written with the permission of our venerated master, Mustafa Pasha, God grant him victory"; added obliquely in margin (ink smeared): "And also send us baked bricks in the amount of [sixty] thousand that we may use as beds for the cannons. In Arabic these bear the name *ajur*"; endorsed by Wagner: "The Dey of Algiers to the President. 14 Octr. 1803 request to be supplied with Battery guns." Enclosed in O'Brien to Madison, undated but probably 15 Oct. (Madison, *Papers*, *Sec. of State Ser.*, 5:531-2).

I HAVE SPOKEN TO YOUR CONSUL: on 13 Oct., Mustafa sent word to O'Brien that he wanted 40 guns, half of them 24-pounders and half of them 18-pounders. The consul pointed out that the United States government had responded to a similar request five years earlier by stating that it possessed no brass cannons and did not manufacture them. In an audience at the palace on 14 Oct., however, Mustafa insisted that O'Brien write to his government. O'Brien reported the conversation in a dispatch to Madison. "I will," the dey told him, "have none of yr. excuses. You must acquise." O'Brien advised the dey to request iron artillery pieces instead of brass ones, but Mustafa declined, saying "I have plenty of Iron guns." Mustafa finally declared that he would write to the U.S. government himself "and make the demand of yr. Govt. and let me see if They refuse me." O'Brien informed Madison that the dey had requested cannons from several other foreign consuls also (same, 5:517-19).

EVASIVE TO MY DEMAND: in his exchanges with the consul, Mustafa more than once reduced the number of guns in his request, and according to O'Brien, the ruler offered to pay the costs of obtaining them. The consul suggested to the secretary of state that the United States might be able to order the cannons and bricks from England and send them to Algiers in place of one year's annuity. However, O'Brien also "presumed to Sketch" a reply that the president might make to the dey's letter. That draft response took the form of a proposed reply from TJ to "The Meditteranian Don Quixotte." It opened by informing Mustafa that the United States had no guns to send him, then went on to detail instances in which he had made demands beyond what was due to him under the treaty. O'Brien's suggested reply to the dey also noted actions by Mustafa in support of Tripoli and complained of his haggling over the value of stores and money used for the annuity. The United States wished to maintain the treaty on "terms of equity & Justice," the consul's draft concluded, "but we have too great a Regard to our Honor & dignity Then to Condescend and acquise to all The unjust and Extra demands of your Highness." O'Brien acknowledged that such an answer could provoke Mustafa to war. The consul suggested to Madison that the U.S. government prepare three different answers to the dey's letter and let the consul in Algiers decide which one to give Mustafa based on the circumstances at hand when the documents arrived. He also urged the construction of more warships. "We shall have it to do at last if Some great Event of Europe does not Curb The pride avarice & System of Barbary," he wrote (same, 518, 531-2; proposed "Ansr. to the deys letter" by O'Brien in DNA: RG 59, CD, Algiers; NDBW, 3:135-6).

O'Brien reported that after he and the dey discussed the request for artillery pieces on 14 Oct., they "Parted Cooly." Mustafa summoned him back to the audience chamber, however, to talk about the BRICKS, which he apparently wanted for a cannon foundry. "I answered I shall write," O'Brien indicated to Madison, "and Cannot Say if Bricks used in an iron furnace would resist the heat of a Brass furnace." To that Mustafa replied, O'Brien reported: "Bring them sayes he and I shall write on the business of The Guns" (Madison, *Papers*, *Sec. of State Ser.*, 5:518).

To George Jefferson

DEAR SIR Washington Oct. 15. 03.

I have this day drawn on you in favor of James Lyle for 500. D. the only articles in your possession for me which are much wanted at Monticello are the bar-iron & the screws. the latter are distressingly wanted, because the cover of sheet iron laid on a part of the house is only tacked on with nails, & in danger of being blown off were a strong wind to happen. will you be so good as to inform me whether vessels from Philadelphia can unload at Richmond without quarantine? we are nearly out of nail rod at Monticello & I would order some immediately if I did not doubt whether it could be recieved. a line by return of post on this subject will oblige me. I must get the favor of you to engage Colo. Macon's hams again this year as usual. about 100. will suffice for me. Accept my affectionate salutations.

TH: JEFFERSON

PrC (MHi); at foot of text: "Mr. George Jefferson"; endorsed by TJ in ink on verso.

To James Lyle

DEAR SIR Washington Oct. 15. 03.

It was not till a day or two before I left home that I was able to look into the papers respecting Richd. Harvie's account, and committed the result to a letter which accompanies this, but which the accumulation of business I found here has prevented my forwarding sooner. I now inclose you also an order on Messrs. Gibson & Jefferson for 500. Dollars, and must take some time to provide another of equal amount which shall be done as early as I can, as well as such successive paiments as I shall be able to accomplish. Accept assurances of my constant & affectionate respect. TH: JEFFERSON

PrC (MHi); at foot of text: "Mr. James Lyle"; endorsed by TJ in ink on verso. Recorded in SJL with notation "500. D." Enclosure: TJ to Lyle, 17 Sep. Other enclosure not found.

To William Pryce

SIR Washington Oct. 15. 03.

Your favor of the 10th. is duly recieved, and I subscribe with great pleasure to the work you propose. it comprehends exactly the most interesting period of Christian history, and it will be the more interesting if, as I presume it does, the plan embraces the object of giving the primitive & earlier opinions entertained: being persuaded that nothing would place Christianity on so firm a base as the reducing it simply to it's first & original principles. I am thankful for the kind sentiments you are pleased to express towards myself. I reciprocate them with sincerity, and pray you to accept my respectful salutations

TH: JEFFERSON

PrC (DLC); at foot of text: "The revd. William Pryce."

From William Goforth, Jr.

Cincinnati Hamilton County State of Ohio
October the 16th: 1803

SIR,

From your known liberality and philanthrophy I feel myself emboldened to address you. I have been a resident in the western country for fifteen years, and always behold with indignation the artifices used by the men in power, in the late Territory, to prolong the period of our colonial humiliation. Whenever I found that our population entitled us to be ranked among the sister states, in conjunction with some of the citizens of this neighbourhood we established Republican Corresponding societies throughout the country for the purpose of ascertaining the general will; and I had the honor of presiding at the first meeting ever held for that purpose in this place. How far our efforts have been successful is unnecessary for me to relate as the circumstances must be still fresh in your recollection. Previous to this period, from the wealthier class of citizens, who were those who had enriched themselves by the posession of the publick offices, I experienced in my practice as a physician, most of my support; but the moment I began to be active in obtaining the honourable rank this country now holds in the union, they withdrew from me all their interest, and have left no mode untried by which they might totally ruin me. They have but too well succeeded in their plans, and I am left with a numerous family a victim to their nefarious designs. My prospects for some time have been rather gloomy, but since the cession of Louisiana I have fancied I saw a new scene opening. Some of my friends have advised me to apply for an office in that country; and as I have a complete knowledge of surveying they have held out the office of Surveyor General as one I could fill with justice to my country and honour to myself. Since I turned my thoughts this way I have been favoured with a visit from Mr: Lewis, who called upon me to see part of the bones of the mamoth which I have collected in this country. I took the liberty of mentioning my views to him & he obligingly promised me his patronage. Several of the Kentucky members, the members of this State, and some of Pensylvania have profered their assistance, and I now presume with the utmost respect to solicit yours. I wish to settle myself in Louisiana but so cramped are my circumstances that without an appointment I shall be unable either to leave this place with honour, or to transport my family thither. I have mentioned the office of Surveyor General conceiving myself qualified for it; but any other office you may think me capable of enjoying with reputation I shall gladly accept. If it is not intruding too far on your goodness I beg leave earnestly to entreat a few lines from you as soon as possible.

I am Sir very respectfully your most Obdt: Humble Servt:

W: Goforth jr:

RC (DNA: RG 59, LAR); at head of text: "Thomas Jefferson Esqr."; endorsed by TJ as received 1 Nov. and "to be Survr. Genl. Louisiana" and so recorded in SJL; also endorsed by TJ: "a warm republican, but entirely drunken."

William Goforth, Jr. (1766-1817), a son of Ohio jurist and Republican William Goforth, studied medicine in New York before migrating west in 1788, practicing first in Kentucky, then relocating to Ohio in 1799. His Republican proclivities, however, caused his practice to suffer. Although he did not receive an office from TJ, Goforth nevertheless moved to Louisiana in 1807, where he secured an appointment as a parish judge and later served as a member of the state constitutional convention. He died shortly after his return to Cincinnati in early 1817 (ANB; Daniel Drake, *Discourses: Delivered by Appointment, Before the Cincinnati Medical Library Association, January 9th and 10th; 1852* [Cincinnati, 1852], 38-44).

On 15 Oct., Goforth sent Albert Gallatin a nearly identical application for THE OFFICE OF SURVEYOR GENERAL for

Louisiana, which Gallatin forwarded to TJ with a note "William Goforth applies for an appointment in Louisiana" (RC in DNA: RG 59, LAR; endorsed by TJ: "Goforth Doctr. W. to mr Gallatin—to be Survr. Genl. Louisiana").

BONES OF THE MAMOTH: see Meriwether Lewis to TJ, 3 Oct. 1803.

Annual Message to Congress

To the Senate and
House of representatives of the United States.

In calling you together, fellow citizens, at an earlier day than was contemplated by the act of the last session of Congress, I have not been insensible to the personal inconveniencies necessarily resulting from an unexpected change in your arrangements. but matters of great public concernment have rendered this call necessary; and the interest you feel in these will supercede in your minds all private considerations.

Congress witnessed, at their late session, the extraordinary agitation produced in the public mind by the suspension of our right of deposit, at the port of New Orleans, no assignment of another place having been made according to treaty. they were sensible that the continuance of that privation would be more injurious to our nation, than any consequences which could flow from any mode of redress. but reposing just confidence in the good faith of the government whose officer had committed the wrong, friendly & reasonable representations were resorted to, and the right of deposit was restored.

Previous however to this period, we had not been unaware of the danger to which our peace would be perpetually exposed, whilst so important a key to the commerce of the Western country remained under foreign power. difficulties too were presenting themselves as to the navigation of other streams, which, arising within our territories, pass through those adjacent. propositions had therefore been authorised for obtaining, on fair conditions, the sovereignty of New Orleans, & of other possessions in that quarter interesting to our quiet, to such extent as was deemed practicable: and the provisional appropriation of two millions of dollars, to be applied & accounted for by the President of the US. intended as part of the price, was considered as conveying the sanction of Congress to the acquisition proposed. the enlightened government of France saw, with just discernment, the importance to both nations of such liberal arrangements as might best and permanently promote the peace, friendship & interests of both: and the property & sovereignty of all Louisiana, which had been restored to them, has, on certain conditions, been transferred to the US. by instruments bearing date the 30th. of April last. when these shall have recieved the constitutional sanction of the Senate, they will, without delay, be communicated to the Representatives also, for the exercise of their functions as to those conditions which are within the powers vested by the constitution in Congress. whilst the property & sovereignty of the Missisipi and it's waters secure an independant outlet for the produce of the Western states, & an uncontrouled navigation through their whole course, free from collision with other powers, & the dangers to our peace from that source, the fertility of the country, it's climate & extent, promise, in due season, important aids to our treasury, an ample provision for our posterity, & a wide spread for the blessings of freedom and equal laws.[1]

With the wisdom of Congress it will rest to take those ulterior measures which may be necessary for the immediate occupation, & temporary government of the country; for it's incorporation into our union; for rendering the change of government a blessing to our newly adopted brethren; for securing to them the rights of conscience & of property; for confirming to the Indian inhabitants their occupancy & self-government, establishing friendly & commercial relations with them, & for ascertaining the geography of the country acquired. such materials for your information, relative to it's affairs in general, as the short space of time has permitted me to collect, will be laid before you when the subject shall be in a state for your consideration.

Another important acquisition of territory has also been made, since the last session of Congress. the friendly tribe of Kaskaskia Indians, with which we have never had a difference, reduced, by the wars & wants of savage life, to a few individuals unable to defend themselves against the neighboring tribes, has transferred it's country to the US. reserving only for it's members what is sufficient to maintain them, in an agricultural way. the considerations stipulated are, that we shall extend to them our patronage & protection, & give them certain annual aids, in money, in implements of agriculture, & other articles of their choice. this country, among the most fertile within our limits extending along the Missisipi from the mouth of the Illinois, to, and up, the Ohio,[2] tho' not so necessary as a barrier, since the acquisition of the other bank, may yet be well worthy of being laid open to immediate settlement, as it's inhabitants may descend with rapidity, in support of the lower country, should future circumstances expose that to foreign enterprise. As the stipulations, in this treaty also, involve matters within the competence of both houses only, it will be laid before Congress so soon as the Senate shall have advised it's ratification.

With many of the other Indian tribes, improvements in agriculture & houshold manufacture, are advancing; and, with all, our peace & friendship are established on grounds much firmer than heretofore. the measure adopted of establishing trading houses among them, & of furnishing them necessaries in exchange for their commodities, at such moderate prices as leave no gain, but cover us from loss, has the most conciliatory & useful effect on them, & is that which will best secure their peace and good will.

The small vessels authorised by Congress, with a view to the Mediterranean service, have been sent into that sea; and will be able more effectually to confine the Tripoline cruisers within their harbours, & supercede the necessity of convoy to our commerce in that quarter. they will sensibly lessen the expences of that service the ensuing year.[3]

A further knowledge of the ground in the North Eastern, & North Western angles of the US. has evinced that the boundaries, established by the treaty of Paris, between the British territories & ours in those parts, were too imperfectly described to be susceptible of execution. it has therefore been thought worthy of attention, for preserving & cherishing the harmony & useful intercourse subsisting between the two nations, to remove by timely arrangements what unfavorable incidents might otherwise render a ground of future misunderstanding. a Convention has therefore been entered into, which provides for a practicable demarcation of those limits, to the satisfaction of both parties.

An account of the reciepts & expenditures of the year ending the 30th. of September last, with the [estimates] for the service of the ensuing year, will be laid before you by the Secretary of the Treasury, so soon as the reciepts of the last quarter shall be returned from the more distant states. it is already ascertained that the amount paid into the treasury, for that year, will exceed [4] and that the revenue, accrued during the same term, exceeds the sum counted on, as sufficient for our current expences, & to extinguish the public debt, within the period heretofore proposed.

The amount of debt paid, for the same year, is about 3,100,000. Dollars, exclusive of interest, & making, with the paiment of the preceding year, a discharge of more than eight millions & an half of Dollars of the principal of that debt, besides the accruing interest: and there remain in the treasury nearly six millions of dollars. of these, 880,000. have been reserved for paiment of the first instalment due, under the British convention of Jan. 8. 1802. and two millions are, what have been beforementioned, as placed by Congress under the power & accountability of the President, towards the price of New

Orleans & other territories acquired, which, remaining untouched, are still applicable to that object, and go in diminution of the sum to be funded for it.

Should the acquisition of Louisiana be constitutionally confirmed & carried into effect, a sum of nearly thirteen millions of Dollars will then be added to our public debt, most of which is paiable after fifteen years; before which term the present existing debts will all be discharged, by the established operation of the sinking fund. when we contemplate the ordinary, annual, augmentation of impost, from increasing population & wealth, the augmentation of the same revenue, by it's extension to the new acquisition, & the economies which may still be introduced into our public expenditures, I cannot but hope that Congress, in reviewing their resources, will find means to meet the intermediate interest of this additional debt, without recurring to new taxes. and applying to this object only the ordinary progression of our revenue, it's extraordinary increase, in times of foreign war, will be the proper and sufficient fund for any measures of safety or precaution, which that state of things may render necessary in our neutral position.

Remittances for the instalments of our foreign debt having been found practicable without loss, it has not been thought expedient to use the power, given by a former act of Congress, of continuing them by reloans, & of redeeming, instead thereof, equal sums of Domestic debt, although no difficulty was found in obtaining that accomodation.

The sum of fifty thousand Dollars, appropriated by Congress for providing gunboats, remains unexpended. the favorable & peaceable turn of affairs, on the Missisipi, rendered an immediate execution of that law unnecessary; & time was desireable, in order that the institution of that branch of our force might begin on models the most approved by experience. The same issue of events dispensed with a resort to the appropriation of a million & a half of dollars, contemplated for purposes which were effected by happier means.

We have seen with sincere concern the flames of war lighted up again in Europe, & nations with which we have the most friendly & useful relations, engaged in mutual destruction. while we regret the miseries in which we see others involved, let us bow with gratitude to that kind providence, which, inspiring with wisdom & moderation our late legislative councils, while placed under the urgency of the greatest wrongs, guarded us from hastily entering into the sanguinary contest, & left us only to look on, & to pity it's ravages. these will be heaviest on those immediately engaged. yet the nations pursuing peace will not be exempt from all evil. in the course of this conflict, let it be our endeavor, as it is our interest & desire, to cultivate the friendship of the belligerent nations by every act of justice, & of innocent kindness; to recieve their armed vessels, with hospitality, from the distresses of the sea, but to administer the means of annoyance to none; to establish in our harbours such a police as may maintain law & order; to restrain our citizens from embarking individually in a war in which their country takes no part; to punish severely those persons, citizen or alien, who shall usurp the cover of our flag, for vessels not entitled to it, infecting thereby with suspicion those of real Americans, & committing us into controversies for the redress of wrongs not our own; to exact from every nation the observance, towards our vessels & citizens, of those principles & practices which all civilized people acknowledge; to merit the character of a just nation, & maintain that of an independant one, preferring every consequence to insult & habitual wrong. Congress will consider whether the existing laws enable us efficaciously to maintain this course, with our citizens in all places, & with others while within the limits of our jurisdiction; & will give them the new modifications necessary for these objects. Some contraventions of right have already taken place, both within our jurisdictional limits, & on the high seas. the friendly disposition of the governments from whose agents they have proceeded, as well as their wisdom & regard for justice, leave us in reasonable expectation, that they will be rectified & prevented in future: & that no act will be countenanced by them which threatens to disturb our friendly intercourse. separated by a wide ocean from the nations of Europe, & from the political interests which entangle them together, with productions & wants which render our commerce & friendship useful to them, & theirs to us, it cannot be the interest of any to assail us, nor ours to disturb them. we should be most unwise indeed, were we to cast away the singular blessings of the position in which nature has placed us, the opportunity she has endowed us with, of pursuing, at a distance from foreign contentions, the paths of industry, peace, & happiness, of cultivating general friendship, and of bringing collisions of interest to the umpirage of reason, rather than of force. how desirable then must it be, in a government like ours, to see it's citizens adopt individually the views, the interests, & the conduct which their country should pursue, divesting themselves of those passions & partialities, which tend to lessen useful friendships, & to embarras & embroil us in the calamitous scenes of Europe. Confident, fellow-citizens, that you will duly estimate the importance of neutral dispositions, towards the observance of neutral conduct, that you will be sensible how much it is our duty to look on the bloody Arena spread before us, with commiseration indeed, but with no other wish than to see it closed, I am persuaded you will cordially cherish these dispositions, in all discussions among yourselves, & in all communications with your constituents. and I anticipate with satisfaction the measures of wisdom, which the great interests, now committed to you, will give *you* an opportunity of providing, & *myself* that of approving, and of carrying into execution, with the fidelity I owe to my country.

TH: JEFFERSON
Oct. 17. 1803.

MS (DLC: TJ Papers, 135:23402-3); entirely in TJ's hand; torn, text in brackets supplied from MS in RG 46. MS (DNA: RG 46, LPPM, 8th Cong., 1st sess.); in Lewis Harvie's hand with emendations by TJ (see note 4 below); signed and dated by TJ; endorsed by a Senate clerk. MS (DNA: RG 233, PM, 8th Cong., 1st sess.); in Lewis Harvie's hand; signed, dated, and insertion by TJ (note 4); endorsed by a House clerk. Recorded in SJL with notation "Genl. message."

CALLING YOU TOGETHER: most members of the Senate and the House of Representatives were present on the morning of Monday, 17 Oct., and each chamber began organizing for the first session of the Eighth Congress. Aaron Burr was absent, but the Senate by a large majority on the first ballot made John Brown president pro tempore. The House reelected Nathaniel Macon as speaker. A joint committee, consisting of DeWitt Clinton and John Breckinridge of the Senate and John Randolph, Roger Griswold, and Joseph H. Nicholson of the House, called on TJ to report that the two houses had assembled and were "ready to receive any communications he may be pleased to make to them." TJ had only that morning received information from Gallatin that allowed him to fill a blank in the message with an estimate of revenue received in the recently completed fiscal year (see the correspondence between TJ and Gallatin on 17 Oct.). Immediately following the committee members' return to the Capitol, Lewis Harvie delivered a signed copy of the document to each chamber. After the reading of the message, the House referred it to the Committee of the Whole House on the State of the Union. The Senate ordered the printing of 500 copies, and the House also had the text printed (JHR, 4:401-8; JS, 3:295-9; Shaw-Shoemaker, Nos. 5363, 5364).

ENLIGHTENED GOVERNMENT OF FRANCE: an early state of the text referred to the "enlightened mind" of Napoleon Bonaparte; see, at 1 Oct., Drafting the Annual Message to Congress, Documents II, IV, and V.

ANOTHER IMPORTANT ACQUISITION: see TJ to the Senate, 31 Oct.

DEMARCATION OF THOSE LIMITS: see TJ to the Senate, 24 Oct. He added this paragraph to the message following a suggestion by Gallatin (Drafting the Annual Message to Congress, Document V).

Congress made the $50,000 appropriation for GUNBOATS within the act of 28 Feb. 1803 that authorized funds for adding four small vessels to the Mediterranean squadron (Vol. 39:367n).

APPROPRIATION OF A MILLION & A HALF: see Gallatin to TJ, 5 Sep.

ENABLE US EFFICACIOUSLY TO MAINTAIN THIS COURSE: Madison, noting that the word "maintain" appeared several times in the paragraph, suggested the substitution of "pursue." TJ perhaps made such a change later in the paragraph, where he referred to "the conduct which their country should pursue" (Drafting the Annual Message, Document II).

DIVESTING THEMSELVES OF THOSE PASSIONS: according to Gallatin's notes and remarks on the draft, TJ first used the phrase "neutral passions" (Documents IV and V at 1 Oct.). Gallatin advised against referring to the conflict in Europe as an ARENA (Document V).

[1]MS in RG 233 continues without a paragraph break.

[2]TJ interlined the passage that begins "extending along the Missisipi."

[3]TJ here canceled "should it not sooner be terminated." The clause was erased from the MS in RG 46. TJ probably removed the clause from the text before Harvie made the MS in RG 233.

[4]In MS in RG 46 and MS in RG 233, TJ canceled the preceding two words and in the blank inserted "has been between eleven & twelve millions of Dollars."

From Simon Didama

Oldenbarnevelt, Town of Trenton,
County of Oneida, State of New-York.
October 17 1803.

Dear Sir!

being a Stranger to your Person but not with your Merits, I hope you will excuse the liberty I do take by sending this letter on your address. I beg leave in requesting you to be so kind to deliver the inclosed to the Person to whom I have[1] addressed, on account I am unacquinted with the residence of Thomas Paine, Esqr. Otherwise if this had not been the case, I should not have been so free in doing so.

to relieve the distressed, the Children of Sorrow and adversity from Tyranny and Oppression, and in doing good to my Fellow-Citizens, is the only object I mean to pursue. the love, obligations and intrest I have to this Country, besides the publicq good and well-being I have at heart, I hope will answer the expectations that may arise from the Plan I have laid open to that Honorable Gentleman, from whom I do expect He will do all in His power to support it, and (if possible) it might once be brought in moving, I have no doubt but what it will turn out to an happy event for hundreds, if not thousands; besides the profit and Publicq Intrest for this Free, Happy, and independent Country.*

It is in your Power Dear Sir! to support it, and Humanity requires your assistance with all the zeal and ambition due to your estimable Character, and High Station you hold in these Republicq. and We Humbly beseech Thou to pay your attention on the Subject, and to assist us in Our undertaking, in order you might for ever be the Object and love of all those who are willing to devote their life time in praying for your Happiness, and those Gentlemen, who always have been and still are, the Friends of Humanity, and Liberty.

*in regard to that Plan I do Send to Thomas Paine esqr.; it is nothing less then to settle Louisiana with hundreds of Industrious Families from Europe. and to make that colony into a Few years a flourishing one. and also to restore a great part of the money what it cost to the republicq of France in to the Thesaury of the United States of North *America*.

That your Person and Government may be blessed by Him! who rules the Universe, in Order you may be for many and many years the proper Instrument into his hands in regard to relieve all those who are suffering, and bending under the heavy burdens of Tyranny and Oppression. that you for ever may be the Friend of the forlorn, and helpless, in the different parts upon this Globe.

that your name may last for ever and ever, and always be remembered with blessings of Gratitude by a thank full Nation, Worthy to be Free, and independent amongst the Nations upon Earth.

With all the Sentiments of High esteem due to your Worthy character, and High Station you hold in this Happy and blessed Country,

and after recommending myself into your Friendschip and esteem.

I remain Dear Sir! your most Humble, and Obedient Servant

SIMON DIDAMA

NB: I hope you will excuse my Stile and spelling if you do find fault with it. because I am a Dutchman who did come from Holland as a Physician, a little more then six years ago, and never did learn the english language, but what I did my self, in this Happy Country.

RC (DLC); addressed: "Thomas Jefferson, Esqr President of the United States of North America"; endorsed by TJ as received 31 Oct. and so recorded in SJL. Enclosure not found.

Simon Didama (d. 1805), a surgeon from the Netherlands, emigrated to America with his family in 1798 and settled in central New York (Pieter J. Van Winter, *American Finance and Dutch Investment, 1780-1805, With an Epilogue to 1840*, 2 vols. [New York, 1977], 2:699, 778; Didama to TJ, 17 Feb. 1804).

[1]MS: "havt."

From Albert Gallatin

DEAR SIR Monday morning 17 Oct. 03

As far as I can ascertain, the balance in Treasury on 30th Septer. last was only 5,850,000 instead of six millions we had estimated it. The receipts in the Treasury during the year ending 30th Septer. last (which is left blank in your message) have certainly exceeded 11,300,000 dollars.

Respectfully yours ALBERT GALLATIN

RC (DLC); addressed: "The President of the United States."

BALANCE IN TREASURY: TJ retained the original estimate of "nearly six millions of dollars" in his annual message at this date (see the tenth paragraph). LEFT BLANK IN YOUR MESSAGE: see the ninth paragraph.

To Albert Gallatin

TH:J. TO MR GALLATIN Oct. 17. 03.

Will you be so good as to enable me this morning to fill up the blank in the following passage of the Message. 'An account of the reciepts & expenditures of the year ending the 30th. of Sep. last, with the estimates for the ensuing year, will be laid before you by the Secy. of the Treasy. so soon as the reciepts of the last quarter shall be returned from the more distant states. it is already ascertained that the amount paid into the treasury for that year will exceed & that the revenue accrued during the same term, exceeds the sum counted on as sufficient for our current expences, & to extinguish the public debt within the period heretofore proposed.'

I inclose you a letter &c from mr Trist at Fort Adams. I think he will be found to be a very exact & attentive officer. I recieved some time ago a letter from Chevallié agent of Beaumarchais, & referred it either to yourself or mr Madison, I do not recollect which; nor do I certainly know to which the business belongs: but I presume to the Treasury, unless Pichon has applied formally to the Secy. of State. I inclose another recd last night. Affectionate salutations.

RC (NHi: Gallatin Papers); addressed: "The Secretary of the Treasury." PrC (DLC). Recorded in SJL with notation "Message." Enclosures: (1) Hore Browse Trist to TJ, 16 Sep. (not found; see Trist to TJ, 28 Sep.). (2) John A. Chevallié to TJ, 14 Oct.

FILL UP THE BLANK: see the preceding letter.

I RECEIVED SOME TIME AGO: see Chevallié to TJ, 16 Sep.

From Albert Gallatin

DEAR SIR Oct. 17. 1803

I wrote you this morning that the receipts in the treasury have exceeded for the year ending 30th Septer. last 11,300,000 dollars. That was the sum left blank in the message—The balance in the treasury which you state at near six millions was only 5,850,000 dollars—

Respectfully yours ALBERT GALLATIN

RC (DLC); endorsed by TJ as received from the Treasury Department on 17 Oct. and "Treasury rects. for Message" and recorded in SJL as a single entry for the letters from the department at this date with notation "Beaumarchaise. Message."

From Albert Gallatin

Treasury Department
SIR, October 17h. 1803.

I have the honor of returning the letters respecting the late Mr: Beaumarchais claim. They throw no further light on the subject; and cannot alter the opinion formed by this Department, and communicated at large to the Secretary of State in a letter of the 20th: November ulto. We still conceive it just that the French Government should communicate to us the name of the person to whom the *million* was paid, if, contrary to the official information received from that Government, by Mr. Morris then our minister at Paris, it was not paid to Mr: Beaumarchais: and until that communication shall be made, we must consider the payment as having been made to him.

I have the honor to be, very respectfully, Sir, Your obedient Servant

ALBERT GALLATIN

RC (DLC: Gallatin Papers); in a clerk's hand, signed by Gallatin; at foot of text: "The President of the United States"; endorsed by TJ as received from the Treasury Department on 17 Oct. and "Beaumarchais" and recorded in SJL as a single entry for the letters from the department at this date with notation "Beaumarchais. Message." Enclosures: (1) probably John A. Chevallié to TJ, 16 Sep., and enclosures. (2) Chevallié to TJ, 14 Oct.

OPINION FORMED BY THIS DEPARTMENT: in a 20 Nov. 1802 letter to Madison, the Treasury Department reviewed the Beaumarchais claim and enclosed documents that supported the decision against the claimant. The evidence included a 21 June 1794 letter from Gouverneur MORRIS to Philibert Buchot, the French minister of foreign affairs, and Buchot's reply of 7 July 1794, enclosing a copy of Beaumarchais's receipt for one million livres dated 10 June 1776. On 2 Dec., Madison forwarded the opinion to Louis André Pichon, who had requested the review (Madison, *Papers, Sec. of State Ser.*, 4:127, 173-4; Syrett, *Hamilton*, 11:209; ASP, *Claims*, 1:314-15, 580-1; Vol. 26:277).

From Andrew Jackson

SIR South West Point October 17th. 1803

Least misrepresentations and unfavourable reports should be made you, respecting Doctor Vandyke of South West Point relative to a meeting I had with John Sevier esqr present Governor of this State on the morning of the 16th. Instant—That Justice may be done to the Doctor, it becomes my duty to declare and I pledge myself for the truth of the declaration that the Doctor did no one act, but what was consistant with the strictest principles of propriety and consistant with the true principles of a man of honour and that of a gentleman—and from these rules the Doctor is incapable of departing—

The object of this letter, is, in case a communication is made by Governor Sevier, or at his instance thro Major McCray unfavourable to Doctor Vandyke, that impression, founded thereon may be suspended untill a full and compleat statement may be made you on the subject, which when made, I pledge myself that the propriety of the Doctors conduct will be made manifest—It will be found that all the Doctor did do, was at my request, to hand the Governor a note from me which he refused to accept in a rude and ungentlemanly[1] manner—and his low abuse induced me in the presence of Doctor Vandyke his son & Two other Gentlemen to treat him cavalierly, and when a pistol was drew upon me by his son, the Doctor drew also to protect me. It is so congenial with the mind of the Governor to do little and dishonourable things, that I suspect him to be mean enough to misrepresent things to injure the Doctor because he is my friend, and was so on that day.

Health & Respect— ANDREW JACKSON

RC (PHi: Daniel Parker Papers); addressed: "Thomas Jefferson President of the United States of America City of Washington"; endorsed by TJ as received 8 Nov. and so recorded in SJL.

Thomas J. VANDYKE, a U.S. army surgeon's mate at Southwest Point, had been accompanying Jackson on the road to Knoxville when they encountered the party of Governor JOHN SEVIER on 16 Oct. Although insults were made and many weapons drawn, no violence ensued. The awkward confrontation was the culmination of a bitter political and personal feud between Jackson and Sevier (Andrew Burstein, *The Passions of Andrew Jackson* [New York, 2003], 41-8; Carl S. Driver, *John Sevier: Pioneer of the Old Southwest* [Chapel Hill, 1932], 182-4; Harold D. Moser and others, eds., *The Papers of Andrew Jackson*, 9 vols. [Knoxville, 1980-], 1:389-90, 489-505).

MAJOR MCCRAY: William MacRea, the commander at Southwest Point (Vol. 40:426, 445). HIS SON & TWO OTHER GENTLEMEN: Washington Sevier, Andrew Greer, and John Hunter (Driver, *John Sevier*, 182-4).

[1] MS: "ungentlemany."

List of Members of the Eighth Congress

[ca. 17 Oct. 1803]

N. Hampsh. 5.
✓ – Betton, Silas
✓ – Claggett. Clifton.
✓ – Hough David
✓ – Hunt Samuel
✓ – Tenney Saml.

——

Massach. 17.
✓ Bishop Phanuel
– Bruce Phineas
✓ Crowninshield Jacob
✓ – Cutler Manasseh
✓ Cutts Richd.
✓ – Dwight Thos.
✓ Eustis Wm.
✓ – Hastings Seth
✓ – Mitchell Nahum
✓ Seaver Ebenezer
✓ Skinner Tomson J.
✓ – Steadman Wm.
✓ – Thatcher Saml.
✓ Varnum Joseph B.
✓ – Wadsworth Peleg
✓ – Williams Lemuel
✓ – Taggart Saml.

——

R. Island. 2.
✓ Knight Nehemiah
✓ Stanton Joseph—

——

Connect. 7.
✓ – Baldwin Simeon
– Dana Saml W.
✓ – Davenport John
– Goddard Calvin
– Griswold Roger
✓ – Smith John Cotton
✓ – Talmage Benj.

——

Verm. 4.
✓ – Chamberlain
✓ – Chittenden Martin
✓ Elliott James
✓ Olin Gideon

——

N. York. 17.
\ Hasbrouck[1]
✓ – Griswold Gaylord
\ – Livingston Henry W.
✓ Mc.Cord Andrew
✓ Mitchel Saml. L.
\\ Palmer Beriah
\\ Patterson John
\ Phelps Oliver
✓ Root Erastus
✓ Salmons Jacob, or Thos.
– Sands Joshua
✓ Smith John
✓ Thomas David
– Tibbets Benj. or George
✓ Van Cortlandt Philip
\ Rensselaer Kilian K
✓ Verplank Danl. C.

——

N. Jersey. 6.
\ Mott James
\ Southard Henry
\ Elmer Ebenezer
\ Helms Wm.
\ Boyd Adam
\ Sloane James.

——

Pensva. 18,

✓ Anderson Isaac
✓ Bard David
✓ Brown Robert
✓ Clay Joseph
✓ Conrad Frederick
✓ Findley Wm.
✓ Gregg Andrew
✓ Hanna John A.
✓ Heister Joseph Gen
✓ Hoge Wm.
✓ Leib Michael
✓ Lucas John B. C.
✓ Rhea John
✓ Richards Jacob.
✓ Smilie John
✓ Stewart John.
✓ Vanhorne Isaac
✓ Whitehill John.

———

Delaware 1.

✓ Rodney Caesar A.

———

Maryland. 9.

✓ Archer John
Bowie Walter
✓ — Campbell
\ — Dennis John
\ Heister Daniel Colo.
✓ Mc.Creery Wm.
✓ Moore N. R.
✓ Nicholson Joseph H
— Plater Thos.

———

Virginia. 22.

✓ Claiborne Thos.
✓ Clay Matthew
✓ Clopton John.
✓ Dawson John
✓ Eppes John W.
✓ Goodwyn Peterson
✓ Gray Edwyn
✓ — Griffin Thomas
✓ Holmes David
✓ Jackson John G.
✓ Jones Walter.
✓ — Lewis Joseph jr.
— Lewis Thos.
✓ New Anthony
✓ Newton Thos. jr.
✓ Randolph John jr.
✓ Randolph Thos. M.
✓ Smith John
✓ — Stephenson James
✓ Thompson Philip R.
\ Trigg Abram.
✓ Trigg John.

———

N. Carolina. 12.

✓ Alexander Nathl.
✓ Allston Willis.
✓ Blackledge Wm.
\ Gillespie James
✓ Holland James
✓ Kennedy Wm.
✓ Macon Nathanl.
— Purviance Saml. D.
✓ Stanford Richd.
✓ Williams Marmaduke
✓ Winston Joseph
✓ Wynns Thos.

———

S. Carolina 8.
✓ Butler Wm.
✓ Casey Levi
✓ Earle John
✓ Hampton Wade
✓ – Huger Benj.
\ – Lowndes Thos.
✓ Moore Thos.
✓ Winn Richd.

———

Georgia. 4.
✓ Early Peter
\ Hammond Saml.
✓ Meriwether David.
\ Bryan.

———

Missisipi.
✓ Lattimore Wm.?

———

Tennissee 3.
✓ Campbell Geo. Washingtn.
✓ Dickson Wm.
✓ Rhea John.

———

Kentucky 6.
✓ Bedinger G. M.
✓ Boyle John
✓ Fowler John
✓ Lyon Matthew
Sandford Thos.
✓ Walton Matthew

———

Ohio. 1.
✓ Morrow Jeremiah

———

<Indiana.>
<✓> *< Parke>*

Senate.

N. Hamp.
– Olcott Simeon.
\\ – Plumer Wm.

———

Mass.
✓ – Adams John Q.
✓ – Pickering Timothy

———

R. Island
✓ Ellery Christopher
✓ Potter Saml. J.

———

Connect.
✓ – Hillhouse Jas.
– Tracey Uriah.

———

Vermont.
✓ Bradley Steph. R.
✓ Smith Israel

———

N. York
✓ Bailey Theodorus
✓ Clinton Dewitt

———

N. Jersey.
✓ Condit John
✓ – Dayton Jonathan

———

Pensva
✓ Logan George
✓ Mc.lay Saml.

———

Delaware.
✓ – Wells Wm. H.
✓ – White Saml.

———

Maryland.
✓ Smith Saml.
✓ Wright Rob.

———

Virginia.
✓ Nicholas Wilson C.
✓ Taylor John.

———

N. Carolina.
✓ Franklin Jesse
✓ Stone David

———

S. Carolina.
✓ Butler Pierce
Sumter Thos.

———

Georgia.
✓ Baldwin Abram.
✓ Jackson James.

———

Tennissee
✓ Cocke Wm
✓ Anderson

———

Kentucky
✓ Breckenridge John
✓ Brown John

———

Ohio.
✓ Smith John
✓ Worthington Thos.

✓ Otis
<*Missisipi.*>
< *Lattimore*>

MS (MHi); undated; entirely in TJ's hand.

The above document appears to have been based, at least initially, on a list of the members of the Eighth Congress printed in the *National Intelligencer* on 10 Oct. 1803, which TJ apparently copied and subsequently modified and updated at least through December 1803. The *Intelligencer* printed Federalist members in italics, whereas TJ identifies them on his list here with a dash to the left of the name. Like the *Intelligencer*, TJ did not include the first name of Vermont representative William Chamberlain. Nor did the *Intelligencer* initially include the names of Representatives Samuel Taggart of Massachusetts and Joseph Bryan of Georgia or Senator Joseph Anderson of Tennessee, but supplied the missing names in its 12 and 19 Oct. editions; TJ added these names at the bottom of their respective delegations out of alphabetical sequence. TJ also corrected the *Intelligencer*'s 10 Oct. list by replacing New York representative John Cantine with Josiah Hasbrouck, who won a special election in April 1803 to fill a vacancy in the delegation caused by Cantine's resignation (*Biog. Dir. Cong.*; Vol. 37:461n). The entire House delegation from New Jersey was also absent from the *Intelligencer*'s 10 Oct. list, since they were not elected until mid-December 1803 (Hudson, N.Y., *Bee*, 6 Dec. 1803; Newark, N.J., *Centinel of Freedom*, 20 Dec. 1803; *National Intelligencer*, 28 Dec. 1803). TJ added their names in the order in which they appeared in the 28 Dec. edition of the *Intelligencer*, which reported the election results. With the exception of the New Jersey delegation, however, TJ does not appear to have revised his list to reflect changes in membership that took place after Congress convened on 17 Oct. For example, TJ's list makes no note of the resignation of DeWitt Clinton from the Senate on 11 Nov. or the arrival of his successor, John Armstrong, on 7 Dec. Nor does TJ record the replacement of Senator John Taylor of Virginia with Abraham B. Venable on 13 Dec. (JS, 3:310, 321, 324).

The purpose of the check marks and slashes on TJ's list is uncertain. They do not appear to correspond to attendance or to record any particular vote in Congress. They may, however, relate to the dinners TJ hosted at the President's House for members of Congress, and the above list may have been a precursor to the more detailed dinner records that TJ began keeping at the start of the second session of the Eighth Congress in November 1804 and continued to the end of his presidency. In these records, at the start of each session TJ created lists of all Senate and House members, arranging the latter by state and party affiliation—Republicans in one column and Federalists in the other—then alphabetically by last name. Senators were listed in a single column, with Republicans listed first and Federalists second, but not alphabetized. When a congressman accepted an invitation to dine with the president, TJ placed a check mark to the left of the name to record his attendance. Those declining an invitation received a dash next to their names. TJ occasionally included slashes or other symbols in his records, but their meaning is unclear (TJ's dinner records of 5 Nov. 1804 to 6 Mch. 1809 are located at MHi). For analyses of TJ's presidential dinners and his recordkeeping system for them, see Charles T. Cullen, "Jefferson's White House Dinner Guests," *White House History*, 17 (2006), 24-43; Merry Ellen Scofield, "The Fatigues of His Table: The Politics of Presidential Dining During the Jefferson Administration," *Journal of the Early Republic*, 26 (2006), 449-69; and Vol. 36:xlvi-xlvii. Images of the dinner records from MHi are reproduced in Cullen, "Dinner Guests," 30-7.

A 14 Feb. 1807 letter from TJ to Rhode Island senator James Fenner provides additional information as to how the president's lists of congressional dinner guests were compiled. Apologizing to Fenner for not sending him an invitation to dine sooner, TJ explained that he "always makes out himself, a list of the gentlemen who are so kind as to call on him." By "some accident which he does not recollect," TJ omitted Fenner's name from his list, and "his invitations being taken from that list, that omission has produced the effect now apologised for." This letter suggests that TJ's dinner lists were used to record not only dinner invitations and guests, but also congressmen who paid calls on the president (RC in NjP: Andre De Coppet Collection). In accord with this letter, TJ's dinner guest list for the 1806-7 session of Congress does not include Fenner under his list of senators (Cullen, "Dinner Guests," 34).

The arrangement of the names and symbols on the list above closely resembles the method of recording dinner guests that TJ commenced in November 1804, with check marks presumably for those who attended a dinner and slashes possibly used to note those who called on the president or declined his invitations, or perhaps both. As explained previously, TJ uses dashes here to identify Federalists. Members lacking either check mark or slash on the list above—that is, those who apparently neither paid a call on TJ or received an invitation from him—were primarily Federalists, those whose attendance in Congress was limited, or both. Federalist senators Simeon Olcott of New

Hampshire and Uriah Tracy of Connecticut, as well as Representatives Samuel W. Dana, Calvin Goddard, and Roger Griswold of Connecticut, Joshua Sands of New York, and Samuel D. Purviance of North Carolina, apparently did not receive invitations during the first session of the Eighth Congress, nor did they receive one during the following session (Scofield, "Fatigues," 466n; Cullen, "Dinner Guests," 30). The election of Federalist Thomas Lewis of Virginia to Congress was contested early in the session by Republican Andrew Moore, and the House awarded Lewis's seat to Moore on 5 Mch. 1804 (Vol. 40:407-8). Illness prevented Federalist Phineas Bruce of Massachusetts from attending either session of the Eighth Congress. George Tibbits of New York did not arrive until 15 Nov. 1803 and was granted a leave of absence from the House on 19 Jan. 1804. Calvin Goddard left Congress on 26 Dec. (*Biog. Dir. Cong.*; JHR, 4:443, 500, 542). Most of the Republicans lacking either a check mark or a slash were late in taking their seats; William Helms of New Jersey arrived 9 Jan. 1804, Walter Bowie of Maryland arrived 23 Jan., and Senator Thomas Sumter, Sr., of South Carolina did not arrive until 6 Feb. (JHR, 4:523, 546; JS, 3:350).

TJ commenced his dinner gatherings at the President's House during the Seventh Congress, and the practice continued into the succeeding sessions. Writing his wife on 27 Oct. 1803, Samuel L. Mitchill reported his recent attendance at a "very agreable" dinner with the president, along with Senators James Jackson, Abraham Baldwin, George Logan, and Stephen R. Bradley, and Representatives Caesar A. Rodney, Isaac Anderson, William MacCreery, Joseph H. Nicholson, Thomas Mann Randolph, and John Wayles Eppes. TJ's new private secretary, Lewis Harvie, was also present. Mitchill dined again at the President's House on 21 Jan. 1804, this time with Joseph B. Varnum, Joseph Stanton, Marmaduke Williams, and Andrew McCord, and again with Randolph and Harvie. Mitchill attended his final dinner of the session on 17 Mch. 1804, sharing TJ's hospitality again with Jackson, Baldwin, and Nicholson as well as with Nathaniel Macon, Wilson Cary Nicholas, Abraham B. Venable, Jacob Crowninshield, William Eustis, Samuel Smith, Joseph Clay, and Captain John Rodgers of the navy (Mitchill to Catharine Mitchill, 27 Oct. 1803, 22 Jan., 19 Mch. 1804, RCs in NNMus: Samuel Latham Mitchill Papers). The diary of freshman senator John Quincy Adams records that he and his wife, Louisa Catherine Adams, dined with TJ on 7 Nov. and 23 Dec. 1803. Adams noted 17 persons attended the November gathering, including James and Dolley Madison and Dolley's sister Anna Payne; Senator Robert Wright, his two daughters, and a Miss Gray; Senator Pierce Butler and General William McPherson; and Thomas Mann Randolph and John Wayles Eppes. Senator Venable and Representatives Macon and John Randolph arrived after dinner. At the December occasion, Adams recorded the attendance of Secretary of the Navy Robert Smith and his wife, Senator Wright and his daughters, Representative MacCreery and his wife and daughter, and Representative Henry W. Livingston and his wife (John Quincy Adams, diary 27 [1 Jan. 1803-4 Aug. 1809], 52, 58, in MHi: Adams Family Papers). In her own diary, however, Mrs. Adams recorded that this dinner took place on 24 Dec. and without the presence of Congressman Livingston (Judith S. Graham and others, eds., *Diary and Autobiographical Writings of Louisa Catherine Adams*, 2 vols. [Cambridge, Mass., 2013], 1:207).

[1] Name written over "Cantine John."

To the Senate

GENTLEMEN OF THE SENATE

In my message of this day to both houses of Congress, I explained the circumstances which had led to the conclusion of conventions with France, for the cession of the province of Louisiana to the United States. those Conventions are now laid before you, with such communications relating to them as may assist in deciding whether you will advise and consent to their ratification.

The Ratification of the First Consul of France is in the hands of his Chargé des affaires here, to be exchanged for that of the United States, whensoever, before the 30th. instant, it shall be in readiness.

TH: JEFFERSON
Oct. 17. 1803.

RC (DNA: RG 46, EPFR, 8th Cong., 1st sess.); endorsed by a Senate clerk. PrC (DLC). Recorded in SJL with notation "Message. Conventns. Louisiana." Enclosures (all in DNA: RG 46, EPFR, 8th Cong., 1st sess., Trs in clerks' hands except as noted): (1) Treaty between the United States and the French Republic for the cession of Louisiana, 30 Apr.; endorsed by Jacob Wagner as received 2 Sep. (2) Convention for payment for Louisiana, 30 Apr.; endorsed by Wagner as received 2 Sep. (3) Convention for payment of debts to U.S. citizens, 30 Apr. (4) Madison to Robert R. Livingston and James Monroe, 2 Mch., instructions for negotiation to acquire New Orleans and East and West Florida; no. 1 in John Quincy Adams's notes (see below); Madison, *Papers*, *Sec. of State Ser.*, 4:364-79; ASP, *Foreign Relations*, 2:540-4. (5) Madison to Livingston and Monroe, 18 Apr. (see Preparations to Negotiate an Alliance with Great Britain, Vol. 40:227-33); with one paragraph that explains contingencies for the use of blank commissions and letters of credence heavily canceled; no. 2 in Adams's notes; Madison, *Papers*, *Sec. of State Ser.*, 4:527-32; ASP, *Foreign Relations*, 2:555-6. (6) Madison to Livingston and Monroe, 18 Apr., second letter, giving them the president's authorization to conduct confidential communications with ministers of the British government if circumstances should warrant; no. 3 in Adams's notes; Madison, *Papers*, *Sec. of State Ser.*, 4:533; ASP, *Foreign Relations*, 2:556. (7) Rufus King to Madison, 28 Apr., an extract stating that when King informed Lord Hawkesbury of the purpose of Monroe's mission to France, Hawkesbury "received the communication in good part, suggested no doubt of our right to pursue separately and alone the objects we aim at, and appeared to be satisfied with the Presidents views on this important subject"; no. 13 in Adams's notes; Madison, *Papers*, *Sec. of State Ser.*, 4:557; ASP, *Foreign Relations*, 2:557. (8) Pedro Cevallos to Charles Pinckney, 4 May (see Enclosure No. 7 listed at Madison to TJ, 20 Aug.); extract stating that the king of Spain declines to sell any of his possessions to the United States, adding however that as Spain has retroceded Louisiana to France, the United States "can address themselves to the French Government to negotiate the acquisition of Territories which may suit their interest"; no. 19 in Adams's notes; ASP, *Foreign Relations*, 2:557. (9) King to Livingston and Monroe, 7 May, informing them that in the event of war between Britain and France, the British intend to send an expedition to occupy Louisiana; no. 14 in Adams's notes; ASP, *Foreign Relations*, 2:557. (10) Livingston and Monroe to King, May 1803, notifying him of the conclusion of a treaty for the acquisition of Louisiana and that it does not infringe on rights of Great Britain in navigation of the Mississippi; no. 15 in Adams's notes; ASP, *Foreign*

Relations, 2:557. (11) François Barbé de Marbois to Livingston and Monroe, 20 Floréal Year 11 (10 May 1803), an English translation incorrectly dated 9 Apr.; he reiterates that according to the terms of the convention regarding payment, the cession of Louisiana to the United States will become void if the stock is not turned over to the government of France or its agent within three months after ratification and the transfer of possession of the province; no. 9 in Adams's notes; ASP, *Foreign Relations*, 2:565. (12) Livingston and Monroe to Madison, 13 May, transmitting the treaty and explaining their negotiation of the terms (Dupl in a clerk's hand, signed by Livingston and Monroe; endorsed by Wagner as received 2 Sep.); no. 6 in Adams's notes; Madison, *Papers, Sec. of State Ser.*, 4:601-6; ASP, *Foreign Relations*, 2:558-60. (13) King to Hawkesbury, 15 May, informing him of the treaty between France and the United States for the cession of Louisiana; no. 16 in Adams's notes; ASP, *Foreign Relations*, 2:560. (14) Livingston and Monroe to Madison, 16 May, regarding the claims to be covered by the second convention and reporting that Bonaparte will ratify the agreements immediately; no. 7 in Adams's notes; Madison, *Papers, Sec. of State Ser.*, 5:4-5; ASP, *Foreign Relations*, 2:560. (15) Hawkesbury to King, 19 May, replying to King's letter of the 15th and informing him that King George III is pleased at the news of the cession of Louisiana to the United States (see Madison to TJ, 13 Aug.); no. 17 in Adams's notes; ASP, *Foreign Relations*, 2:560. (16) Madison to Livingston and Monroe, 28 May, probably an extract consisting of the first two paragraphs of the letter (ASP prints the full text); relaying information from King that in the event of war between Britain and France, the British will probably occupy New Orleans, but with no intention of keeping it permanently; no. 4 in Adams's notes; Madison, *Papers, Sec. of State Ser.*, 5:38-41; ASP, *Foreign Relations*, 2:562. (17) Livingston and Monroe to Barbé de Marbois, 2 June, acknowledging the responsibility of the United States to comply with the terms of the Louisiana agreements; no. 10 in Adams's notes; ASP, *Foreign Relations*, 2:565. (18) Livingston and Monroe to Madison, 7 June, forwarding the French ratification of the treaty and conventions and warning that the French government might seek a way to get out of the bargain (see Livingston to TJ, 2 June, and notes); no. 8 in Adams's notes; Madison, *Papers, Sec. of State Ser.*, 5:66-72; ASP, *Foreign Relations*, 2:563-5. (19) Madison to Livingston and Monroe, 29 July, acknowledging receipt of the treaty and conventions and conveying the president's approval of the results of the negotiation; no. 5 in Adams's notes; Madison, *Papers, Sec. of State Ser.*, 5:238-40; ASP, *Foreign Relations*, 2:566-7. (20) Monroe to Madison, 15 Aug., a brief extract identifying enclosure: Joseph Fenwick to Monroe, 5 Aug. from Paris, extract, reporting "from a faithful source" that the Spanish government is protesting the sale of Louisiana by France and will attempt to stop the transaction; warning also that "it is now well understood" that the French government will nullify the transaction if the U.S. Senate introduces "any conditional clause" to the ratification; nos. 11 and 12 in Adams's notes; see Madison, *Papers, Sec. of State Ser.*, 5:310, 312n; ASP, *Foreign Relations*, 2:567. (21) Carlos Martínez de Irujo to Madison, 4 Sep., English translation; see Wagner to TJ, 4 Sep.; no. 20 in Adams's notes; ASP, *Foreign Relations*, 2:569. (22) Irujo to Madison, 27 Sep., English translation, protesting that under the terms of the retrocession of Louisiana, France cannot transfer the province to another nation, and declaring that France has failed to comply with the terms of the agreement for the retrocession; no. 21 in Adams's notes; Madison, *Papers, Sec. of State Ser.*, 5:464; ASP, *Foreign Relations*, 2:569. (23) Madison to Irujo, 4 Oct., stating that the "United States have given unquestionable proofs to the Spanish Government and Nation of their justice, their friendship, and their desire to maintain the best neighbourhood; and the President confides too much in the reciprocity of these sentiments so repeatedly and so recently declared on the part of his Catholic Majesty to have supposed that he would see with dissatisfaction a convenient acquisition to the United States of territories which were no longer to remain with Spain"; Madison also cites and quotes (in Spanish, here with an English translation) Cevallos's statement of 4 May, Enclosure No. 8 above; no. 22 in Adams's notes; Madison, *Papers*, *Sec. of State Ser.*, 5:488-9; ASP, *Foreign Relations*, 2:569-70. (24) Madison to Livingston, 6 Oct., discussing among other subjects Spain's opposition to the cession of Louisiana to the United States; with postscript of 14 Oct.; no. 18 in Adams's notes; Madison, *Papers*, *Sec. of State Ser.*, 5:491-6; ASP, *Foreign Relations*, 2:567-9. (25) Irujo to Madison, 12 Oct., arguing that Cevallos's letter to Pinckney of 4 May is not a declaration that the United States is free to acquire Louisiana from France; no. 23 in Adams's notes; Madison, *Papers*, *Sec. of State Ser.*, 5:513-15; ASP, *Foreign Relations*, 2:570. (26) Madison to Pinckney, 12 Oct., suggesting arguments to counter Spain's opposition; "What is it that Spain dreads?" he writes; "She dreads, it is presumed, the growing power of this country, and the direction of it against her possessions within its reach. Can she annihitate this power? No. Can she sensibly retard its growth? No"; it is possible, Madison concludes, that the Spanish are resisting only in order to obtain "concessions of some sort or the other" from France or the United States; no. 24 in Adams's notes; Madison, *Papers*, *Sec. of State Ser.*, 5:511-13; ASP, *Foreign Relations*, 2:570-1. (27) Louis André Pichon to Madison, 14 Oct., English translation; the Treaty of San Ildefonso, Pichon states, contains no stipulation to prevent France from disposing of Louisiana; he argues also that France has complied with the terms of that treaty, as acknowledged by the Spanish crown when it ordered the transfer of Louisiana to French possession; no. 25 in Adams's notes; Madison, *Papers*, *Sec. of State Ser.*, 5:528-31; ASP, *Foreign Relations*, 2:571-2.

NOW LAID BEFORE YOU: the Senate took up this message in executive session on 17 Oct. and ordered the printing of the message, the treaty, and the conventions for senators' confidential use. The Senate devoted most of its time on the 18th and all of its time on the 19th and 20th to the topic. On the 20th, a motion by William H. Wells, who wanted to ask the president to turn over the American envoys' journal of the negotiations and papers establishing France's title to Louisiana, failed. The Senate approved ratification on that day by a vote of 24 to 7. Pierce Butler then offered a resolution to request the executive to renegotiate the third article of the treaty, which stated that the inhabitants of Louisiana would become U.S. citizens, so that the United States might sell Louisiana or trade it to Spain for East and West Florida. The Senate considered Butler's motion on the 21st and 22d, but voted on the 24th to end the discussion (JEP, 1:449-51; JS, 3:299-300; Everett Somerville Brown, ed., *William Plumer's Memorandum of Proceedings in the United States Senate, 1803-1807* [London, 1923], 3, 14).

WITH SUCH COMMUNICATIONS: with this message in the Senate's records is a large collection of documents that range in date from March 1801 to May 1804. They could not all have accompanied TJ's message of 17 Oct. 1803, although the entire body of material is printed with the message in ASP, *Foreign Relations*, 2:506-83. A detailed set of notes made by John Quincy Adams in one of his diaries provides a definitive list of the papers included with the message. Adams, beginning his term as a senator from Massachusetts, did not arrive in Washington until late in the day on 20 Oct. On 5 Nov., a rainy Saturday when the Senate did not meet, he "employed the principal part of this day, in reading the Correspondence and papers sent by the President to the Senate with the Louisiana Treaty." Adams identified 25 documents in addition to the treaty and conventions and called each one by a number that apparently reflected the arrangement of the set when he saw it. At the end of his notes he wrote: "Such is the analysis of the papers communicated by the President to the Senate with the Louisiana cession Treaty, and conventions. I have made it at such length, considering the transactions in itself and in its consequences, as the most important which as occurred since the adoption of our National Constitution." Another list, hastily written at the foot of the RC of the message in an unidentified hand and printed in ASP, *Foreign Relations*, 2:506, is less complete and probably of later date (John Quincy Adams, diary 51 [3 Feb. to 14 Nov. 1803], 2, 6-12; diary 27 [1 Jan. 1803 to 4 Aug. 1809], 27, 51; both in MHi: Adams Family Papers).

Just before dusk on 20 Oct., Samuel A. Otis took a carriage from the Capitol to the President's House to deliver the Senate's resolution approving the treaty and conventions. Madison and Pichon EXCHANGED ratifications the following day, but only after they resolved questions about the addition of conditional clauses. Talleyrand had directed Pichon to attach a clause to the French ratification declaring that a failure by the United States to fulfill the terms of payment would void the treaty. On 21 Oct., Madison informed Pichon that if France added conditions to the ratifications, so too would the United States, in the form of a statement that the treaty would have force only if France fulfilled its obligations "relative to the delivery of Louisiana to the United States." Pichon could not refer the matter to his government for instructions without causing a long delay in the completion of the sale, so he yielded to Madison's urging that they exchange ratifications immediately without the proposed conditions (Adams, diary 27, p. 27; Madison, *Papers*, *Sec. of State Ser.*, 5:357n, 558, 561-2; Livingston to TJ, 2 June).

From Hore Browse Trist

DEAR SIR/ Fort Adams 17 Oct. 1803

The period rapidly approaching when we are to take possession of New Orleans, & feeling anxious that the revenue Department should have every thing prepared for immediate operation, I take the liberty to enclose you a rough sketch of a Seal I designed for the Custom House. Should it meet your approbation, Mr Harvey will please to deliver it to Mr Henry Brown, to whom I have given particular directions to have it properly executed in Philadelphia.—The Collectors, using their discretionary powers, have generally adopted the Arms of the States in which their Offices were situated. But this Country not having yet been admitted as a State, induced me to trouble you thus early, wishing to be certain of the propriety of the Device, & apprehending if longer delayed, inconvenience might ensue from the length of time requisite to procure that indespensible article, not to be obtained nearer than at some of the Northern Cities. For my present Office, I have been necessitated to use the Seal & Screw belonging to the former Supreme Court. With sentiments of the most profound respect I beg you to accept my sincerest wishes

HORE BROWSE TRIST

RC (DLC); at foot of text: "President of the United States"; with note by TJ at foot of text: "non rapui, sed redemi. redemi, non rapui," loosely translated as "I did not steal it, but I bought it back. I bought it back, but I did not steal it," which was the motto of William III, who assumed the English throne after the Glorious Revolution; endorsed by TJ as received 13 Nov. and so recorded in SJL. Enclosure not found.

SKETCH OF A SEAL: the Treasury Department did not establish an official seal for all custom houses until 1869. INCONVENIENCE MIGHT ENSUE: the collector used the seal as a stamp on documents to indicate the payment of import duties (W. V. Combs, *Third Federal Issue, 1814-1817 and Other Embossed Revenue Stamped Paper 1791-1869* [Rockford, Iowa, 1993], 103, 113).

While collector at Fort Adams, Trist used the SEAL & SCREW of the SUPREME COURT. This seal, commissioned in 1790, derived from the Great Seal of the United States and featured a bald eagle holding a striped shield and clutching an olive branch and arrows in its talons. Beneath the eagle's claw, a single star symbolized the Constitution's creation of one Supreme Court (Kenneth Jost, "Seal of the Supreme Court," *The Supreme Court A to Z*, 4th ed. [Washington, D.C., 2007], 426).

To John Barnes

Oct. 18.[1] 03.

Th: Jefferson having been obliged to send what pocket money he had to Monticello will thank mr Barnes for 25. or 30. D. in small bills.[2]

RC (ViU: Edgehill-Randolph Papers); addressed: "Mr. Barnes"; endorsed by Barnes. Not recorded in SJL.

TJ's financial memoranda records that he received $25 from Barnes the same day (MB, 2:1110).

[1] Date altered from "17" to "18."

[2] Preceding three words and period interlined.

From John Crawford

SIR! Baltimore 18th. Octr. 1803

It is an advantage peculiar to the inhabitants of this country, that they may address their first Magistrate on a subject of adequate importance, without incurring the imputation of being presumptuous. In other countries they are restrained by a fear of having their suggestions with-held from his view by minions who dread an interference with their power, or a disclosure of their own improper conduct.

The dearest interests of a large portion of the community are connected with the object of this communication, and I trust this will be deemed a sufficient apology for the intrusion and bespeak for it that attention which circumstances of such extensive moment may appear to merit.

My first thoughts were to have conveyed what I have to offer to the public, through the medium of a news-paper; but on more mature reflection, I was apprehensive that more injury than good might be the consequence. I therefore determined to make my application to the fountain head of power, as in your hands, revered Sir! all the advantages would be secured, without a risk of doing any mischief.

It may be safely asserted that there is no country in any part of the Globe, the inhabitants of which enjoy so extensively the blessings of life as that which belongs to the people of the united States. There perhaps never was any portion of the Earth, at any prior period, so highly distinguished by the favour of Heaven, if we except the Land of Indea while the government of it was avowedly a Theocracy.[1]

Whilst other nations of the world are either laid waste by or threatened with the most devastating wars, we not only enjoy peace, but are in the possession of the most perfect tranquility, and this too, we may almost say, without a soldier, or a strong police to guardent us against the turbulent, who are so numerous in every other country, and whose frequent invasion of the rights of others require the most coercive restraint.

These are benefits we can not be too anxious to perpetuate; but we are not to suppose it will be possible for us to preserve them, if we are not continually on the watch, and vigilant in observing all the avenues by which dangers may assail us, through which we may be attacked by all the evils that are harrassing so many other countries. Although so far removed from the excesses we deplore, our fate may be involved in theirs to an extent many may think impossible.

France and England appear to have brought their national existence to issue, or rather their respective governments have subjected their continuance to one great effort. Let us suppose that, contrary to every reasonable expectation, the former should be successful, and the power of the latter should be destroyed. In what way, it may be asked, can this expose us to a calamity so solemnly prefaced, or how can our connection with that country implicate us in their fate?

I hope to make it appear that our fate most intimately depends upon that of England, unless we adopt measures that will effectually secure us against every influence connected with European politics. Unless we are governed by the only wisdom that can avert such dreadful calamities, our sufferings must be equal to any the English may be destined to endure.

The French, when under the influence of phrenzy, declared their slaves free. When the delirium abated, they endeavoured to recal the boon, and to reduce the cultivators of their coffee, their sugar, cotton &ca. to the condition from which they had been emancipated; but they found the task more arduous than they were capable of performing.

The climate destroyed the Troops employed in a service more pregnant with embarrassments than any they had before experienced. The war breaking out with England frustrated all the plans that had been formed for the reduction of St. Domingo, and if not already relinquished, the French Nation must in a very short time, abandon the wanton enterprise. They must be now satisfied that it is impossible again to reduce to a state of slavery, those they had made equal to themselves. It might indeed have been foreseen, that no exertions, under such circumstances would renew[2] the states of bondage from which they had been liberated.[3] Their endeavurs proved vain. The taste of freedom had been permitted; it was too sweet to be relinquished, but with life—The whole of the sanguinary struggle to reduce the Negroes again to the obedience from which they had been emancipated evidences as much the interposition of supreme will as any human events are capable of manifesting. The contest is nearly terminated in the compleat triumph of the slaves over their masters. After exhibiting such scenes of savage barbarity on both sides, for the civilised have no preeminence to boast of, except in ferocity, as perhaps have never been exceeded.

If it can be supposed that the emancipation of the slaves in question were the result of a supreme feat, can it be imagined that he has no favour of a like nature in view for those who are similarly situated? The author of our divine religion has declared that it shall prevail universally. From the nature of it—there is every reason to believe it will neither be correctly inculcated, nor efficiently embraced by slaves. As soon as christianity began to influence the minds of men generally, and the greatest government then upon the Earth found the adoption of it necessary to its existence, slavery was soon after abolished over the widely spreading Roman Empire. Abolition may be safely employed to express the termination of slavery in the Dominions of ancient Rome. Freedom being given to all who abjured Idolatry had an effect similar to what abolition could have produced. If the adoption of christianity extinguished slavery in the old world, and if christianity must equally obtain every where, it plainly follows that the Author of it will not permit slavery to continue as an obstacle to its universal propagation. If he has began to occasion a removal of it in one spot, is it reasonable to believe that he will not equally remove it from every other?

This language may have some influence over the minds of believers, but as sir, we know many whose opinions may have much weight in the decision to be made on this momentous occasion who may not be disposed to give any credence to a divine ascendancy over the minds of men, it may be proper to take such a view of the question as naturally arises in the ordinary course of human affairs.

The Negroes of St. Domingo have established their freedom by force of Arms. Is it possible that their success will not create a similar desire in those who, in their vicinity, are similarly situated? The Negroes in the servitude of the English are their nearest Neighbours; and the wise policy, and well directed power of their sagacious masters apparently provides against a revolution in their favour at present. But suppose the power of these masters to be extinguished, what then will be the condition of the slaves over whom they have held dominion? In such a case there would not be an individual in the whole of the west Indies that would not be perfectly free in the course of one year. The same thing would quickly after follow in every part of south america. The power of the Spaniards and of the Portugeese over the blacks and the Indians would be anihilated in a shorter space of time than a traveler would require in visiting their several possessions.

If the emancipation of the slaves in the west Indies and South America should happen, to what are we to look forward here? It would be a dereliction of the simplest suggestion of common sense, not to feel a conviction that we also must relinquish the bondage in which we hold our fellow creatures in this part of the world, and the question is whether we shall sacrifice it willingly, or whether we shall engage with our slaves in a war which may exterminate, but can not retain them in their present state.

If the sword is once appealed to, the southern states will experience every thing the most direful that imagination can conceive, and more bloody scenes perhaps never disgraced humanity than will be there exhibited. The assistance of the Eastern parts of the Union would perhaps be absolutely necessary, to the complete subjection of these relentless foes; but it is probable these would never be induced to heartily engage in such a war. They have abolished slavery in their own country, and it must be with a very bad grace they would make exertions to maintain it elsewhere. The obligations of the general compact might prevail upon them to yield assistance; but the individuals ordered on such a service would take no interest in, they would probably be opposed to it. The Eastern States then, if their aid should be necessary, can not be relied on, with any security, for the preservation of our authority over our slaves in this and the southeren parts of the union. If our success in the struggle depends upon our own exertions, it must clearly appear that it will be very doubtful; and this is rendered more so, because the dread of such an alternative seems to be so very alarming,[4] that we do not appear to dare even to make the smallest preparations for it.

What then, much respected sir, have we before us, for preserving our country from the desolations of insatiable revenge, or the horrors of unbridled rage? The People of this country fought gloriously for their liberty, and by their manly courage, established it on the firmest basis. The Glory they acquired on that brilliant occasion would be wholly eclipsed, by their refusing to grant to those who are under their authority what they have a right to claim under circumstances infinitely more impressive. From what has been urged, there can not a colour of doubt remain that the slaves of this country will, at no distant period, establish their freedom on as firm a basis, as that on which our own was erected. This can be accomplished only in one of two ways. It must either be wrested from us by violence, or we must relinquish our pretensions by a compact made with those who have hitherto submitted to our uncontrouled authority.

In the prosecution of the first, havoc and desolation are inevitable; and the final result must be, that those who have much to lose must lose all that they have, and that those who have nothing to lose must gain all that they contend for. The only alternative as to the issue of a contest with the Negroes, will be either that they must conquer, or they must be exterminated. Let the example of St. Domingo teach which of these may be expected. If the war should be carried on in the low marshy parts of the country which approximate the sea shore, they will prove as unhealthy to white soldiers, as they did to white labourers, and the cause which urged our resorting to Negroes for cultivating the Earth will enable them to become the possessors of the country, they alone were capable of reclaiming from a state of nature: Here the robust sons of the mountains will soon be weary of following them, and after a bloody struggle and a massacre *of all the Proprietors and their Families*, they will I am confident[5] be left in quiet possession of Lands they have themselves fertilised. In the adoption of the last measure, there will be extensive occasion for self-denial, and an abatement of that pride, and those notions of superiority which now render every kind of arangement concerning the Negroes so extremely difficult.

You sir, with many others have advocated an opinion that the Negroes are an inferior order of the human species. In your discussion of the question, it must not be forgotten that you only suggest doubts, and that it is with hesitation you admit the probability of your own conjectures.

For my own part, I firmly believe that they are as capable of being influenced by the moral principle as any other description of men whatsoever. To have felt more of the moral influence than was compatible with their servile condition would have been a cruel distinction. It may be safely adopted as an axiom, that every thing in nature is a type of every other thing, although no two things are alike. The seeds of plants, with due care, have been preserved for more than a century, and afterwards, when placed in a situation favourable for their developement, have become productive. The higher degrees of moral influence have been ever distributed partially. Nations formerly eminently distinguished by them are now sunk into the most disqualifying barbarity, when those from whom we sprung were then savages, although they now claim the appellation of *Homo sapiens Europeus*. I am unacquainted with any proof that the aborigines of the People we now so much depreciate were not as enlightened in former ages as we are at present, so much pride ourselves in being. Ægypt, Carthage, Æthiopia were in their day the seats of illumination, it should therefore seem no strain upon the belief, that Affrica once was, what Europe now is, nor is it impossible that the favour should be restored of which they were deprived, probably because they[6] made a bad use of it. Whether we resort to negotiation or to war, we shall probably discover, in the people with whom we are to adjust our differences, a strength of intellect we at present deem them incapable of. Occasion has often produced characters that would have remained unnoticed, had this never offered.

If these momentous concerns should become a subject of deliberation, and the suggestions of reason should predominate over passion, great and solid advantages may be obtained. The mode of Government established in this country, so fruitful of blessings superior to what has been heretofore experienced, clearly points out the way by which we ought to proceed. The influence of habit is powerful on the minds of men. The effect of this will facilitate the arangements necessary to be made with our slaves. If their feelings are consulted, and they are applied to for a disclosure of the terms on which they may obtain their freedom, they will be found ready to secure a provision for those who, in case of an appeal to arms, they would immolate with the most unrelenting barbarity.

An anecdote recurs to my memory, which may not be unworthy of attention on the present occasion. Mr. Steel, a gentleman who possessed large Estates, and many slaves in the Island of Barbadoes felt much repugnance to the mode in which authority was exerted over the Negroes. He resolved to try whether a mode might not be adopted, by which equal advantages should be secured, and the sufferings of his slaves mitigated, or at least that such punishment as their delinquencies might require infflicted[7] in a way less offensive to their feelings. He divided his people into different classes, according to their strength and capacity. He appointed certain daily wages for the individuals of the several classes. He allotted a certain portion of ground for the use of every family, and he gave them saturday, sunday was their own, to work their gardens. He authorised them to chuse a certain number who were to be the judges of the manner in which the duty assigned to the several classes was performed, and who were to determine what punishment should be inflicted on those whose conduct required correction, and also to carry their determination into effect. Fines alone were to be exacted of those who failed to perform their appointed tasks. Other crimes were to be restrained by imprisonment, or means of more severity, as the case might demand. The White servants were prohibited from every kind of interference with those chosen Judges, or indeed the slightest chastisement of any offender. Mr. Steel reserved to himself the right of mitigating every sentence, but in no other respect, made use of his authority. In this arrangement, the Negroes were to furnish their own food and cloathing; but a store was provided on the Plantation, in which was to be purchased every article the People could have occasion for on terms as moderate as they could be procured for in the public stores. Mr. Steel had the happyness to experience, by these wise regulations, an improvement of his fortune, and to be satisfied that his Slaves enjoyed a degree of felicity they had never known before, nor was elsewhere to be met with.

Were application made to the reason of the Negroes, and their degraded situation no longer considered as an adequate cause for treating them as an inferior class of beings, they would, I am persuaded, chearfully consent to make provision for those they have been hitherto bound unconditionally to serve. The great mass of mankind can procure no more for themselves, by their utmost labour, than food, cloathing, and shelter, and if the mode of procuring these can be more reconciled to justice, and divested of tyranic controul, they Negroes[8] may, in every probability be modeled into an orderly and well regulated society. If they were to be hereafter employed as hirelings, and no longer to be treated as slaves; if they were to have tribunals appointed among themselves, for the punishment of delinquents, and they were to be subjected to Judges of their own description; if farther, they were rendered capable of holding property, and secured in the enjoyment of their honest earnings, a sense of morality would be gradually introduced among them, to which they are at present strangers, and a pride of character would be acquired, which is incompatible with their present state of debasement.

There is a wonderful propensity in mankind to hold in high estimation things that are very distant, and attainable by great difficulty, while objects of infinitely higher value, of much more real importance, are at their door, and soliciting their daily attention. This is remarkably examplifyed by the Institutions both of the old and the new world, for propagating the Gospel. They send Missionaries to remote countries, often not to be visited without imminent danger, and who are generally useless from their ignorance of the language, and of the manners of those they are expected to convert, whilst those who live in their vicinity are wholly neglected, and their impiety, and disregard for every thing sacred is viewed with indifference. Instead of expending considerable sums in the employment of Missionaries amongst the Indians, were the instruction of our Negroes in the concerns of Religion made a national object, and a due reverence for the Deity, and the Revelations of his divine will assiduously inculcated, a new order of things would quickly arise, and the happyness of society be provided for in a way far superior to that which has been hitherto pursued.

I have, highly respected Sir! long trespassed on your patience, and perhaps detained you much longer than was necessary for conveying to your mind every thing important contained in these sheets. But if there is any thing found really important, it must plead for such parts as may be deemed irrelevant. In your hands Sir! the measure proposed may be matured, and woes unutterable averted which are evidently pressing on to assail us, and which can alone be obviated by the wisdom and by the influence of the President.

I have the honor to be, with all possible respect, revered sir! Your most faithful and most devoted humble servant

John Crawford, M:D.

RC (DLC); endorsed by TJ as received 20 Oct. and so recorded in SJL.

A native of Ireland, John Crawford (1746-1813) was one of four sons of a prominent Presbyterian minister, all of whom would go on to distinguished careers in medicine, science, or the clergy. After some study in Dublin, Crawford served as a surgeon with the East India Company and later held surgical posts at Barbados and Demerara. He subsequently received medical degrees from the University of St. Andrews and Leiden University. In 1796, Crawford moved to Baltimore, where he quickly established himself as both a physician and a civic leader. He was an early promoter of smallpox vaccination and led successful efforts to establish a dispensary in Baltimore as well as a state penitentiary. Crawford is best remembered, however, for his ideas on the role of insects and other "animalculae" in spreading disease and that specific infectious agents caused specific diseases, both of which posed radical challenges to the medical orthodoxy of his day. TJ read Crawford's medical theories with interest, but deemed them "too new & unrecieved" to have an immediate impact on public health (ANB; James McGuire and James Quinn, eds., *Dictionary of Irish Biography: From the Earliest Times to the Year 2002*, 9 vols. [Cambridge, 2009], 2:965-6, 968-9, 974; RS, 4:336-8, 394-5; Crawford to TJ, 18 Aug. 1807; TJ to Crawford, 8 Sep. 1807).

NEGROES ARE AN INFERIOR ORDER: in his *Notes on the State of Virginia*, TJ speculated at length on what he perceived to be the inferiority of blacks in comparison with whites, especially in reason and imagination. "I advance it therefore as a suspicion only, that the blacks, whether originally a distinct race, or made distinct by time and circumstances, are inferior to the whites in the endowments both of body and mind" (*Notes*, ed. Peden, 138-43).

[1] MS: "Thocracy."

[2] Word interlined in place of "bring."

[3] Preceding six words and period interlined.

[4] Word interlined in place of "dreadful."

[5] Preceding three words interlined.

[6] MS: "the."

[7] Crawford first wrote "afflicted" before altering text to read as above.

[8] Word interlined.

From James L. Henderson

October 18th. 1803.
Shelby County Kentucky

D SIR

About Novembr 1801 being Sensible that my Mothr togethr with the Infant Heirs of my Father was sertin to loose the most staple property Wee then possesd Which was the Milton Mills & Knowing when that was the case that wee Showld be oblidged to abandon our former way of living which was but moderate & by some more frugal wey which was sertingly painfull to me not on my own account so much but on the account My Mother & the four Infant females Heirs then & now with her altho I am only twenty four years of age I had accumilated[1] by my Industry a sum sufficient to purchase a small plantation in Kentucky & determind to pursuade my mother to find an assilum in this state & when shee come to trav her life which was once flurishing & Knowinng her then Indigence she determind to Risk her fortune to try a new World which she was pleasd with but had not the means to Rescue her from those toils which the hours of poverty drives her to this is truly painfull to Me when I recollect her once opulent Situation & by the wheel of fortune she is thrown into the Current of poverty to gether with her four Infant Daughters lands in this Country being hard to get without the means to purchase & not having A Knough for both families my mothers & my own I have some time since detirmend to give her my possessions in this Country & by It I Cant find a better World some Wherre on the Mississippi & as I espect that Country will be put on a footing to settle or at least the Island of

New orleans will become american property & as the government will want officers & a great many at your own disposal therefore Sir let me beg[2] leave to become one of your humble petitioners for any office the functions of which may be discharged by a man of common understanding the office of Collector of the port of New orleans will I espect be a task which a man of common mind will be competent to however I am not Choice what ever work you may think proper to assign me the small energies[3] which I possess shall be devoted to as much for my own honour as a barriour against esceative sensure It is common for petitioners I believe to draw up amamorial In form together with their Character certifide by Respectable men this I as to my own part think use less Intill I hear from you I know Wheather there be a Vacancy as I believe I have the Confidence of My freinds & those of My acquaintance I shall not hesitate to Say that shall not be lacking when Calld on your answr to the foregoing Sir shall be greatfully Receivd & what ever shall be your dissission shall be an object with Me of the highest Veneration & believe Me Sir to be your most faithfull fellow citizen as well as your Obt Humb Servt

J L Henderson

RC (DNA: RG 59, LAR); endorsed by TJ as received 26 Oct. and "office in Louisiana" and so recorded in SJL.

MILTON MILLS: in a deed executed on 29 Nov. 1801, Henderson conveyed to Craven Peyton, acting on TJ's behalf, his lands and the property of his late father with the exception of the family mill and James Henderson's portion of the house and lot in Milton. In the partition of his father's estate, James Henderson's parcel of the divided lands below the town of Milton included an undeveloped mill seat (Vol. 35:413, 743-4).

MY MOTHER & THE FOUR INFANT FEMALES HEIRS: Elizabeth Henderson and her four youngest daughters, Eliza, Frances, Lucy, and Nancy Crawford (Vol. 28:520).

[1] Henderson here canceled: "out of the small [...] of my Fathers estate."

[2] MS: "geg."

[3] MS: "enigies."

From George Jefferson

Dear Sir — Lunenburg 18th. Octr. 1803

It was not my intention ever more, to have taken the liberty of recommending any one to you for an office; but on the present occasion, I cannot forbear.

My old neighbour, and school-mate, and friend, Mr. Waller Taylor, who will hand you this—having determined to remove to New Orleans, wishes to get some office under Government.—I do not precisely know what office he would prefer, or what he would decline accepting.

I can only say, that from my knowledge of him from his child-hood, I have the most unbounded confidence in his *integrity*—and that I feel equally confident he will fill any Office for which you may think him competent, with honor to himself, and advantage to his Country. Perhaps it may be some aid to you, in deciding for what he is best fitted, to be informed, that in his more early Youth, he occasionally assisted in the Office of his Father, who is Clerk of this County—he has since for several years been a practitioner of the law, but which he lately declined, on determining to remove to the western country.

I shall feel much gratified, if I shall in the smallest degree, contribute to the promotion of so worthy a character, as I conceive Mr. Taylor to be; and particularly, as there are but too few of my old neighbours, whom, with the same pleasure and confidence, I can recommend.

I am Dear Sir Your Very humble servt. GEO. JEFFERSON

RC (DNA: RG 59, LAR); at foot of text: "Thos. Jefferson esqr."; endorsed by TJ as received 29 Oct. and "Taylor, Waller. office in N. Orleans" and so recorded in SJL.

WALLER TAYLOR had previously represented Lunenburg County in the Virginia House of Delegates for two terms. He ended up settling in Indiana (Leonard, *General Assembly*, 220, 224; Waller Taylor to TJ, 14 May 1806).

From Robert Leslie

SIR Philadelphia October 18th 1803

I should have taken the liberty of writeing you sooner, but wished to have got some farther information conserning the mint, and waited for that purpose till I could with safcty go into the City, which was not the case till a few days ago on account of the Fever, I find myself disappointed however in that respect, as I cannot with properiety make inquirey of any of the persons imploy'd in the business, and nothing seems to be known to any one else, all that I have been [able] to obtain is the inclosed, which I found [in] a newspaper, by which it appears that the profit on coining Cents, is five thousand dollars pr annum. if this is true, I am confident that all the machanical operations of the mint may be done without any expence to the U.S.s, as that sum is quite sufficent.

I have since my return considered the subject in every point of vew, and should be willing to enter into the following engagment Viz

If I should be alowed all the Buildings and machinery now in use, free from rent and other expences, and to be furnished with Copper in the manner the mint now receives it, I would engage to deliver free from all expences to government, in the first year the useual quantity of Cents, and the amount of ten thousend dollars in small silver, and the second year I think by practice &c, I should be able to do considerably more, either in small Silver, Gold, or dollars, as you might think proper to direct.

I am informed that a Mr Scott, the present engraver to the mint, proposed at the last Session of Congress, to Coin Cents without any expence to the government, if so, his having been already imploy'd in the mint, may[1] in the opinion of some, give him a preference, on this, I shall only observe that the machinery I shall make use of, is I am confident vastly superior to that of Mr Bolton or any that has ever been used in any part of the world, and if I should be alowed to introduce it here, it will on my death or removel, be left in the posesion of the U.S.s, which cannot be the case if any other person is imploy'd.

Since my return home my health has been gradually improving, and I am confident that my recovery, is in a great measure owing to your kindness, for which I feel myself under an obligation far beyond what will ever be in my power to repay, as I can at present only send you my most sincear thanks for your goodness.

I am at present able to attend to any business that may offer, but shall engage in nothing till I hear from you, if you should want any thing from this place for the finishing your house, or any other purpose, I hope you will let me have the pleasure of procureing and sending it to you.

please give my best respects to Mr Randolph and the famely.

I am with respect your much obliged and Humbl Servt

ROBERT LESLIE

RC (DLC); torn at seal; addressed: "The President of the United States Washington"; franked; postmarked 20 Oct.; endorsed by TJ as received 22 Oct. and so recorded in SJL. Enclosure not found, but see below.

For Leslie's earlier proposals for improving operations at the MINT, see Vol. 33:521-2; Vol. 34:236-9, 352-3; Vol. 35:15-16.

PROFIT ON COINING CENTS: in his 1 Jan. 1803 annual report, Director of the Mint Elias Boudinot reported the profit on all copper coinage for the previous year amounted to $5,644.33 (Vol. 39:319, 320n).

Robert Scot (SCOTT), engraver of the Mint, sent a proposal to Albert Gallatin on 4 Mch. 1802, offering to coin cents for the United States "free of all expense to Government, excepting that of receiving them when coined, and paying the nominal amount." The proposal was made while a bill to abolish the Mint was under consideration by Congress (ASP, *Finance*, 1:744-5).

MR BOLTON: English coin manufacturer Matthew Boulton (Vol. 33:522n).

MY RETURN HOME: Leslie had visited TJ at Monticello in September 1803. While there, TJ gave him an order on John Barnes, dated 8 Sep., for $50 in payment for a watch (MS in ViU: Edgehill-Randolph Papers, in TJ's hand and signed by him, signed by Leslie acknowledging payment, endorsed by Barnes as paid 14 Sep.; MB, 2:1107).

[1]MS: "my."

From Oliver Pollock

SIR Philada. 18th. Octr. 1803

Having had the honor of being employed in the Service of the United States, as agent to the spanish Goverment in Loussiana, during the revolution that established our Independance, and having during my residence there in that capacity, discharged my trust as well to the satisfaction of my fellow citizens, as to that of the Goverment near which I resided, acquiring at the same time a perfect local knowledge of the Country, and an acquaintance with its inhabitants, which the possession of both the french and spanish language permitted me to cultivate intimately, I have vanity[1] enough to presume that an offer of my services at this period, when that country is on the eve of forming part of the union, will not be deemed, by its first Magistrate, too presumptuous, especially when the facts I have just mentioned will no doubt be coroborated by his own memory.

I should not presume to address you, Sir, on the present subject if I yet labour'd under any embarassments, which might be considered as impediments, rendering me unfit to discharge the duties of a public servant, but having happily and honorably obtained an award of the Commissioners named under the 7th. article of the convention with Great Briton, and thereby secured a considerable claim I had against said Goverment, as a priviledged creditor of John Swanwick Esqr. & having actually recoverd one third thereof, I find myself once more independent and in a situation to act as a person free from every incumbrance whatever. I would have waited on you in person, sir, with this application, if the confinement of my youngest daughter whose dangerous situation demands the presence of an only parent, permitted me, but I am persuaded this apology will sufficiently plead with you in my behalf, as will also my friend the Honorable Pierce Butler, who does me the favour, & has the honor of presenting you this letter.

In consequence of having transacted mercantile bussiness upon a verry extensive Scale for several eminent houses in this country—as well as in Europe during my residence in New Orleans, I have been able to acquire a complete knowledge of the commerce of that City & its dependencies; this circumstance induces me to think that I could not better offer my services to my Country than in the Capacity of Collector of the Revenue[2] at the Port of New Orleans; assuring you, Sir, that should you deem me worthy & capable of filling this important post, I shall accept it with gratitude, and give such securities as the law of my Country requires in similar cases, endeavouring at the same time, by a faithfull discharge of my duties, to merit a continuation of your protection & the approbation of my fellow Citizens. It is perhaps needless to Observe, that as proprietor of some lands directly on the Banks of the Mississippi, the prosperity of its Navigation & commerce is an object to me, even as a private Citizen, of the greatest concern. However, although I presume to sollicit from you the Collectorship of the Port of New Orleans, permit me to observe that in whatever other situation you may deem my services most usefull to my Country I shall with unremitting zeal endeavour to discharge the duties thereof as becomes a faithfull Citizen, and, Sir,

Your most Obedient humble. Servant OLR. POLLOCK

RC (DNA: RG 59, LAR); at foot of text: "Thomas Jefferson President of the U.S."; endorsed by TJ as received 21 Oct. and "to be Collectr N. Orleans" and so recorded in SJL.

OFFER OF MY SERVICES: in 1801, Pollock applied for office, first in Philadelphia and then as consul at New Orleans. He cited his service as commercial agent at New Orleans during the Revolution, where he obtained supplies for the Continental Congress and Virginia, for which he still sought compensation (Vol. 33:537-8; Vol. 35:326-8).

For Pollock's entanglements as a CREDITOR OF JOHN SWANWICK, see Vol. 33:537-8. On this date, Pollock wrote Gallatin that the Swanwick estate was awarded £5,445.13.11 sterling by the commissioners under Article 7 of the British Convention. He also noted that he was applying for the collectorship (RC in DNA: RG 59, LAR; endorsed by TJ: "Pollock Oliver to mr Gallatin. to be Collectr. N. Orleans").

Pollock's DAUGHTER Lucetta died on 26 Mch. 1804 after a "tedious and distressing illness." She was 21 years old. ONLY PARENT: Pollock's first wife, Margaret O'Brien, with whom he had eight children, died in 1799. Pollock remarried in 1805 (*Aurora General Advertiser*, 28 Mch. 1804; ANB).

Pollock's LANDS along the MISSISSIPPI River included the Old Tunica Plantation at Tunica Bend, north of Baton Rouge (Light T. Cummins, "Oliver Pollock's Plantations: An Early Anglo Landowner on the Lower Mississippi, 1769-1824," *Louisiana History*, 29 [1988], 35-48).

[1] MS: "vaniety."

[2] MS: "Revnue."

From Elkanah Watson

SIR Albany. 18th Oct 1803

As few Americans have tho't proper to Submit their observations & travels in other Countries to the press; my Short Tour in Holland was on that account Considered Interesting, & I Submitted to its publication Several years ago, without however being at that time Known as the Author.

But Since the fact has become Notorious, will you Sir, do me the honer to accept, the Inclosed little essay as a Small token of my profound Respect & Veneration ELKANAH WATSON

RC (DLC); at foot of text: "The President of the United States"; endorsed by TJ as received 17 Mch. 1804 and so recorded in SJL. Enclosure: *A Tour in Holland, in MDCCLXXXIV* (Worcester, Mass., 1790), by "An American," consisting of eight letters to various correspondents from 24 May to 23 June 1784 and an appendix on the Dutch East Indies; the eighth letter identifies Haarlem resident Laurens Janszoon Coster, not Johann Gutenberg of Mainz, as the inventor of movable type (see Sowerby, No. 3872; Vol. 8:447, 448n).

To Robert Bailey

DEAR SIR Washington Oct. 19. 1803.

A gentleman here has given me 40. Balsam poplars to send to Monticello, and mr Randolph's servant, who was to have returned tomorrow, will be detained till the next day, to carry them. as I set much store by these trees which I have been a long time trying to get to Monticello, I wish them to be carefully taken up & packed in bundles for safe transportation. if it would suit you to come tomorrow morning & take them up & bundle them properly for the journey, it would oblige me, besides satisfactory compensation. I shall also be glad to recieve the box for France, as the vessel will sail in a week. Accept my best wishes & salutations. TH: JEFFERSON

PrC (MHi); in ink at foot of text: "Mr. Bailey"; endorsed by TJ in ink on verso.

MR RANDOLPH'S SERVANT: TJ recorded in his financial memoranda giving Davy Bowles two dollars "to take care of trees" on 21 Oct. (MB, 2:1110).

For the BOX FOR FRANCE, see TJ to Bailey, 10 Oct.

From Thomas Claxton

HOND. SIR [19 Oct. 1803]

Through delicacy, I have always, in making drafts on the Treasury for public money, made it a point to draw no more than I had a prospect of spending in a short period—It now appears that I have been unfortunate in the method I have pursued—I have this day been informed by one of the Clerks in the Treasury, that the little balance of the furnishing fund is likely to be swallowed by the sinking fund—I called on you Sir this morning, but found you were engaged

I have the Honor to be Sir Your most Hble Servt

THOS. CLAXTON

RC (MHi); undated; endorsed by TJ as received 19 Oct. and so recorded in SJL.

BALANCE OF THE FURNISHING FUND: Claxton, in his capacity as purchasing agent, received warrant payments from the Treasury of $200 for procuring furniture for the President's House between 1 July and 30 Sep. (Gallatin, *Papers*, 8:884; *Letter from the Treasurer of the United States, Accompanying His General Accounts of the Receipts and Expenditures of Public Monies, From the First of October, 1802, to the 30th of September, 1803, Inclusive* [Washington, D.C., 1803; Shaw-Shoemaker, No. 5345], 84; Vol. 33:153n).

SINKING FUND: the amount of $145.17 for furniture for the President's House was appropriated by Congress in 1804, "being the balance of a former appropriation, carried to the credit of the surplus fund" (U.S. Statutes at Large, 2:269).

From Joseph Clay

SIR October 19th. 1803.

I formerly took the liberty of recommending to your notice Mr. John Harrison of the City of Philadelphia, as a person suitable to succeed the late Mr. VanCleve as a General Commissioner of Bankruptcy. As no person was at that time appointed I presume that a successor was thought unnecessary. Another vacancy has been since occasioned by my own resignation. The remaining Commissioners have authorised me to suggest the propriety of making an appointment in my room. Should it be your intention to comply with their wish, permit me to offer once more to your attention the name of Mr. Harrison, assuring you that no Gentleman could be nominated to the office who would be more acceptable to the present board.

I am Sir with sentiments of the highest Respect Your most obedt. Servt.

JOSEPH CLAY

RC (DNA: RG 59, LAR); at foot of text: "The President"; endorsed by TJ as received 20 Oct. and so recorded in SJL; also endorsed by TJ: "John Harrison to be Commr. bkrptcy Penva."

FORMERLY TOOK THE LIBERTY: see Clay to TJ, 29 Mch.

REMAINING COMMISSIONERS: Alexander J. Dallas, Mahlon Dickerson, John Sergeant, and Thomas Cumpston (same).

From David Stone, Willis Alston, and Thomas Wynns

TO HIS EXCELLENCY THE PRESIDENT OF THE UNITED STATES.

City of Washington 19th. Octr. 1803.

A case of Bankruptcy having occurred in the North Eastern part of the State of North Carolina where no Commissioners of Bankruptcy have hitherto been appointed—We take the liberty to name as persons proper to discharge the duties of that office—Nathaniel Allen of Edenton, Goodorcen Davis and John Eaton of Halifax and William Cherry the younger of Bertie County.

We have the honor to be with the highest Respect Your Excellency's Humble Servants

DAVID STONE
WILLIS ALSTON JUR
THOS. WYNNS

RC (DNA: RG 59, LAR); in Stone's hand, signed by all; endorsed by TJ as received 20 Oct. and

"Allen, Nathanl. of Edenton } to be
Davis, Goodorcen } of } Commrs.
Eaton John } Halifax } bkrptcy
Cherry Wm. junr. of Bertie } N.C."

and so recorded in SJL.

Born at the family plantation on Fishing Creek in Halifax County, North Carolina, Willis Alston (1769-1837), nephew of Nathaniel Macon, entered state politics in 1790, serving first in the house of commons and then one term in the state senate. In 1798, he was elected to Congress, defeating Republican congressman Thomas Blount. He served in the House from 1799 to 1815. Perhaps under the influence of Macon, Alston soon became a Jeffersonian Republican. Federalist William R. Davie unsuccessfully ran against him in 1803. Alston continued to support TJ after Macon and John Randolph broke with the administration. He was noted for his altercations with Randolph. He supported the War of 1812 and did not stand for reelection in 1815. Alston returned to state politics, serving in the house of commons from 1820 to 1824. He was again elected to Congress, this time as a Jacksonian Democrat, and served three more terms, from 1825 to 1831, after which he retired to his plantation (*Biog. Dir. Cong.*; William S. Powell, ed., *Dictionary of North Carolina Biography*, 6 vols. [Chapel Hill, 1979-96], 1:30; ANB, s.v. "Davie, William Richardson"; Manning J. Dauer, *The Adams Federalists* [Baltimore, 1953], 313, 319, 324; RS, 3:330).

Born at Barfields, the family plantation on the Chowan River, Thomas Wynns (1760-1825) represented Hertford County briefly in the house of commons and in the state senate in 1786 and from 1790 to 1800. He advocated the founding of the state university at Chapel Hill and became one of its first trustees. As a presidential elector, Wynns voted for TJ in 1800. He served as a Republican congressman from 1802 to 1807. After he returned to North Carolina, he again represented Hertford County in the state senate and received a commission as major general in the state militia (*Biog. Dir. Cong.*; Powell, *Dictionary of North Carolina Biography*, 6:285; Raleigh *Star*, 23 Aug. 1810). For the election of Wynns to Congress, see Vol. 39:410n.

TAKE THE LIBERTY TO NAME: TJ appointed all four nominees with commissions dated 14 Nov. 1803 (list of commissions in Lb in DNA: RG 59, MPTPC; Vol. 37:710).

To Henry Dearborn, with Jefferson's Note

Oct. 20. 03.

Will General Dearborne be so good as to recommend some person? or will it be better for him to retain the papers & consult the republican members from Maine?

[*Note by TJ*:]

Dudley Broadstreet Hobart of Gardener recommended by Genl. Dearborne, who candidly states that he is his son in law, but the applicn is from many respectable persons of the neighborhood, & the only competiton is a young man at college, son of a federalist.

RC (DNA: RG 59, LAR); addressed: "The Secretary at War"; entirely in TJ's hand, written in two sittings. Not recorded in SJL. Enclosures not found, but see John Langdon to TJ, 12 Oct. 1803.

Gallatin received a petition from Bath, MAINE, dated 6 Oct., recommending Joshua Shaw "as a person well qualified to discharge the duties" of the Bath collectorship. He had a knowledge of the mercantile business and had served as deputy collector for five years, frequently officiating in the collector's absence. John Dunlap and Richard Tappan of Brunswick, along with 11 others, signed the petition (RC in DNA: RG 59, LAR; endorsed by TJ: "Shaw Joshua to be Collectr. of Bath vice Webb resigned").

On 21 Oct., Levi Lincoln received an application for the collectorship from John Winslow, a former student in his law office, dated 12 Oct. Winslow considered retiring from the practice of law for health reasons and noted that the duties of collector were "far from being severe" and the pay was "at least a competence." He described four others who were seeking the office. Andrew Greenwood, a young, unmarried attorney, who came to Bath from South Carolina, could discharge the duties, but in politics he was "a firm advocate of the measures of the former administration." Joshua Shaw, a respectable merchant, probably wanted the position for his son, who was attending Harvard. Shaw called himself a Federalist but "never engages with zeal in any political debates." James Davidson, the third candidate, was a native of Scotland who led "a life of complete idleness." He favored the British system of government. Samuel E. Duncan, the last named by Winslow, would doubtless receive strong recommendations from his father-in-law William Webb, the former collector, but he possessed no qualifications for the office and voted with the Federalists (RC in same; endorsed by Lincoln; endorsed by TJ: "Winslow John to mr Lincoln. to be collector of Bath, vice Webb resigned"; endorsed by Gallatin: "*Bath* To be attended to").

An additional recommendation in favor of appointing Dudley B. HOBART collector at Bath was received by Gallatin from Barzillai Gannett, who wrote the Treasury secretary on 21 Nov. 1803 and enclosed an undated memorial from Seth Gay and 11 others, who stated that no one possessed the "*essential* and *peculiar* qualifications for that office more fully than Mr. Hobart" (RC in same; endorsed by TJ: "Hobart Dudley Broadstreet. to be Collector of Bath vice Webb. resigned"). TJ would send Hobart's nomination for the Bath collectorship to the Senate on 9 Dec.

From John Thomson Mason

DEAR SIR Annapolis 20th Octo. 1803

I some time ago took the liberty to mention to you my friend N. Fitzhugh as a person willing to fill the vacancy about to be made by the resignation of James Marshall. Why or wherefore I know not, I have this day received two letters from thorough going Feds. To you I take the liberty of inclosing them, not because I think them recommendations but merely because they relate to a subject upon which it belongs exclusively to you to judge.

Did I not from an intimacy of upwards of twenty years know Fitzhugh to be a man entirely to be relied on, I should I confess feel my suspicions excited by such letters from such men

Wishing you health and happiness I have the honor to be with great respect Your friend & Servt JOHN T. MASON

RC (DNA: RG 59, LAR); endorsed by TJ as a letter from "Geo. T." received 25 Oct. and "Fitzhugh Nichs. to be judge" and so recorded in SJL. Enclosures: (1) Thomas Swann to Mason, Fairfax Court House, 20 Sep. 1803, recommending the appointment of Nicholas Fitzhugh as associate judge of the District of Columbia upon the resignation of James Marshall; 12 years as a practicing attorney in Fairfax County has given Fitzhugh a knowledge of the rules and proceedings of the Virginia courts, and "his character as a Citizen and neighbour is respected and esteemed." (2) Charles Simms to Mason, Fairfax Court House, 20 Sep.; as the president will probably consult Mason when deciding upon a replacement for Marshall, Simms recommends Nicholas Fitzhugh, noting the appointment would be "pleasing to the people of the County of Alexandria, his competency and integrity being well known to them from his long practice as an attorney in Fairfax Court and his character as a Citizen and a neighbour respected and esteemed" (both RCs in same).

Mason's letter to TJ recommending Nicholas FITZHUGH is dated 7 July.

THOROUGH GOING FEDS.: during his last days in office, John Adams nominated Alexandria attorney Thomas Swann as U.S. attorney for the District of Columbia, but he did not take office; TJ nominated Mason in his place. Charles Simms, appointed collector at Alexandria in 1799, continued to carry on his law practice while he served as collector. An ardent Federalist, he actively campaigned against TJ in the 1796 presidential race (Carl E. Prince, *The Federalists and the Origins of the U.S. Civil Service* [New York, 1977], 113-14; Washington, *Papers, Ret. Ser.*, 1:399n; RS, 4:221n; Vol. 29:193-6; Vol. 33:123-4, 172-3, 203n, 238, 333).

From Robert Ware Peacock

SIR, City of Washington October 20. 1803.

It seems to be a defect in the present system of public Education, that a proper course of Studies is not provided for Gentlemen designed to fill the principal stations of active Life, distinct from those of the Learned professions.

The objects of human attention are multiplied; the connexion of the United States much extended; a reflection upon our present advantages, and the steps by which we have arrived to the degree of happiness we now enjoy, has shewn the true sources of them; and so thoroughly convinced are the people of the United States to a sense of their true interests, that they are convinced the same inattention which formerly prevailed is no longer safe—and that without a continuation of the superior degrees of wisdom and vigour in our political measures, which have marked the course of the present administration, their happiness will be destroyed.

In this posture of affairs, more lights and superior industry, are requisite to all persons who have any influence in schemes of public and national advantage, and consequently a different and a better furniture of mind is requisite to be brought into the business of Life.

This produces a call for the examination of the State of Education in this Country—And it will readily be admitted that an Education in our own, is preferable to an Education in a foreign Country. For passing by the advantages to the Community which result from the early attachment of Youth to the Laws and Constitution of their Country, I will only remark, that Young men who have trodden the pathes of Science together, or have joined in the same sports, generally feel through Life, such ties to each other as add greatly to the obligations of mutual benevolence.

Therefore it becomes the duty of every one to render their aid to the establishment of such plans as will contribute to the desired end—Warmed by a zeal to be useful, I am prompted to undertake the task—and submit the inclosed plan to the Lovers of Literature and Science, for their patronage and support, in this its infantine state—

I shall endeavour to make such observations as will lead those who attend the Lectures to the perfect understanding the means of promoting national prosperity and independence—Knowing the consequence, in a Republic, of the youth being taught to think justly upon the great subjects of Liberty and government.

I hope I shall be pardoned the Liberty I take in soliciting your sanction to the inclosed—For I am well convinced, that no reasonable proposal for the honor, or the advantage of the United States however foreign to your more immediate office, was ever neglected by you.

I remain, with due respect, yr. obed. Sev

Robert Ware Peacock

RC (ViW: Tucker-Coleman Collection); addressed: "His Excellency Thomas Jefferson Esquire President of the U. States"; endorsed by TJ as received 20 Oct. and so recorded in SJL. Enclosure not found, but see below.

Robert Ware Peacock was born about 1770, probably in Virginia. He was admitted to the Albemarle County bar in 1791, practiced law in nearby counties as late as 1800, and may also have worked in Maryland. About that year, he settled in the federal district, where he kept a lodging house and was admitted to practice at the Supreme Court. He advertised his services as an attorney and conveyancer but in December 1804 was convicted of forgery. After his failure to gain a pardon, Peacock escaped from the Washington jail. A notice announcing a $100 reward for his capture described him as a "stout man" of 34 or 35 years of age, "much inclined to corpulency." He was not heard from again (*Gazette of the United States*, 11 Feb. 1801; *National Intelligencer*, 1 May 1805; William P. Palmer and others, eds., *Calendar of Virginia*

State Papers ... Preserved in the Capitol at Richmond, 11 vols. [Richmond, 1875-93], 9:130; Woods, *Albemarle*, 380; Allen C. Clark, "The Mayoralty of Robert Brent," RCHS, 33-34 [1932], 275-8; Washington, *Papers, Pres. Ser.*, 14:286; TJ to John P. Van Ness, 12 Mch. 1805).

In 1802 Peacock began soliciting subscribers to a proposed work, "A Direction, or, Preparative to the Study of Law," a series of LECTURES intended to make legal studies "less intricate." He later also advertised a course of study in history and the law, for which he charged one dollar per lecture (Georgetown *Olio*, 7 Oct. 1802; *National Intelligencer*, 14 Dec. 1803).

From Stephen Sayre

SIR Point Breeze 20th octor 1803.

I have received a letter dated 8th of sepr. of Mr Lewis le Coutould, who is now at Detroit, & is, I presume, well known by all the principal officers of government.

He informs me, that the inhabitants were then about petitioning the President to appoint a Governor over that part of our Territory; and he requests me to make immediate application, for the appointment, because, he supposes I should be well received by the people, for many reasons; but especially, for the proofs I can give of my attachment to the french nation the services I have render'd, & my knowledge of their language.

Will you Sir, do me the justice, to look back, & call to your memory the period which tried mens souls. Do I offend your Secretary of State because all my past applications have been made on the ground of past services? My opinion of his good sense, & integrity, forbid flattery, or mean sollicitation thro' others; and if he can find any citizen of the union, who has done half the services, or who has suffered a tythe of what I have done—or who is capable of doing more honor to the Administration in the above named territory, let him be sent there, & I will not complain

I shall be at Washington some few days hence, when I shall produce the above letter. Inclosed I take the liberty to send you my printed case, so long before Congress, that you may see how ungratefully I have been treated, both by the old & new Congress

My Claims here stated do not reach the most important of my services, which respect the armed neutrality I am very respectfully yours &c &c

STEPHEN SAYRE

RC (DNA: RG 59, LAR); at foot of text: "President of the United States"; endorsed by TJ as received 27 Oct. and "to be Govr. Detroit" and so recorded in SJL. Enclosure: *The Case of Stephen Sayre* (Philadelphia, 1803; Shaw-Shoemaker, No. 5022).

Lewis Le Couteulx (COUTOULD), a French native who became an American citizen in 1789 and settled in New York, had been arrested in Niagara on his way to Detroit in 1798. Unjustly imprisoned in Quebec as an enemy alien and natural-born subject of a nation at war with Great Britain, Le Couteulx was eventually released and received Madison's assistance in obtaining British compensation for losses due to imprisonment (Madison, *Papers, Sec. of State Ser.*, 2:213; 5:1-2, 11).

A memorial of 20 Mch. 1803, signed by certain inhabitants of Detroit, supporting the creation of an independent Michigan TERRITORY separate from Indiana was introduced in the Senate on 21 Oct. 1803. Detroit petitioners also submitted a similar request to Congress dated 1 Sep. 1803. The act for division of the territory, which would mandate the appointment of a governor, was not approved until early 1805 (*Terr. Papers*, 7:99-106, 118-23).

For Sayre's PAST APPLICATIONS for government patronage and claims for compensation for Revolutionary War services, see Madison, *Papers, Sec. of State Ser.*, 1:186-7, 226, 284-7; 2:190-1. Sayre's petition came before the Senate again on 2 Feb. 1803. He had the PRINTED CASE, along with accompanying papers, issued as a 21-page pamphlet later that year (ASP, *Claims*, 1:81-3, 123-4, 223-6; *Annals*, 12:51; Vol. 35:416-17).

To Benjamin Stoddert

SIR Washington Oct. 20. 03.

The pressure of business & of ceremony at the commencement of a session rendered it impossible for me to peruse the inclosed till yesterday evening. I sincerely wish well to whatever may contribute to give growth to the city, under which term I include Georgetown also: for I consider that & Washington as standing in the same relation to the general government, & as constituting on[ly] different wards of the same city, & seat of government. altho' conversant with the general theory of the subject of the within, I am not so familiar with the details as to consider myself competent to decide on it. of these, yourself, [& those with] whom you have [probably] consulted, are much better judges, and I [rea]dily therefore suppose the plan to be useful. in fact it appears to be a [sure] method of converting land into a circulating medium, by a paper representative [...] divided into smaller & more convenient transfers. the fact you mention of the Baltimore company, which deposited only $\frac{1}{5}$ of it's capital in money, the remaining $\frac{4}{5}$ resting on their personal responsibility, is a leading one. a sing[le] experiment is worth a great deal of theory: I consider the remaining $\frac{4}{5}$ when bottomed on land, as far preferable to that resting on personal security. I do not know that I can be useful in promoting this object, but certainly will if I can, as I would in every other way which could prosper this place. there seems to be a general conviction in Congress that they cannot legislate for the distr[ict.] perhaps they may determine to give it a legislature. a society without a legislative power is a novelty which ought not to be hazarded. Accept my salutations & assurances of respect. TH: JEFFERSON

PrC (ViW: Tucker-Coleman Collection); torn and faint; at foot of text: "Benjamin Stoddert esq."; endorsed by TJ in ink on verso. Enclosure not found, but see Stoddert to TJ, 12 Oct. 1803.

From Augustus B. Woodward

Washington, october 20. 1803.

In the volume of the encyclopédie, which the president was so kind as to lend me, I find a reference to a figure which is not contained in the same volume. I conclude therefore the plates are in a separate volume. The reference is (fig. Astron. 171.). If the president can conveniently turn to this figure I will be obliged to him to permit the bearer to bring the volume containing it.

I transmit a work which contains at the end an account of a singular pecuniary institution in spain, called a bank, and which the president may be inclined to look at.

The work which the president enquired for, entitled I think "usages et coutûmes de paris" is not the same with a work I have seen, and which I shall shortly procure from alexandria; but I have reason to believe the work I allude to contains a great deal of information on the domestic jurisprudence of france. I hope to have the pleasure to send it next week.

A. B. Woodward.

RC (DLC); endorsed by TJ as received 20 Oct. and so recorded in SJL.

PECUNIARY INSTITUTION IN SPAIN: the original purpose of the Banco de San Carlos, chartered in 1782, was to provide a means for the redemption of promissory notes issued by the crown against Spain's war-related expenditures (Gabriel Tortella, "Spanish Banking History, 1782 to the Present," in European Association for Banking History, *Handbook on the History of European Banks*, ed. Manfred Pohl and Sabine Freitag [Aldershot, Hants, Eng., 1994], 865-6, 886-7).

USAGES ET COUTÛMES DE PARIS: prior to the national codification of law under Bonaparte, French legal usage varied widely among regions and from locale to locale. The *Coutume de Paris*, compiled by the *Parlement* of Paris and published in the 16th century, recorded the practices of courts there regarding property, seigneurial rights, wills and inheritance, sales, servitude, and other aspects of civil law. The French crown applied the *Coutume de Paris* to Canada in 1663 and to Louisiana in 1712. Daniel Clark, in his reply to the 16th of TJ's queries on Louisiana, stated that the province's laws were derived from Spanish legal codes and from "les uses & Coutumes de Paris for what respects usages & Customs." Clark, writing in New Orleans, added: "the French uses & Coutumes may I presume be easily found among the Booksellers in the United States, they are not to be had here" (*Terr. Papers*, 9:35; Jerah Johnson, "La Coutume de Paris: Louisiana's First Law," *Louisiana History*, 30 [1989], 145-55).

To John Barnes, with Barnes's Note

Oct. 21. 03.

Mr. John Barnes, of Georgetown will always answer my subscription to the Columbian Repository TH: JEFFERSON

[*Note by Barnes:*]
Bradford & Burgess
paid ℔ JB. 1st Nov 1803
$2.50 Entd. 193—

RC (MHi); endorsed by Barnes. Not recorded in SJL.

The COLUMBIAN REPOSITORY was a weekly newspaper published in Georgetown by Thomas G. BRADFORD and B. BURGESS from 30 Sep. 1803 until early 1804. Proposals for the paper, originally to be entitled the *Mercury* and published in Alexandria, stated that it would be dedicated to the impartial dissemination of useful knowledge "to enlighten the understanding" and "to aid the cause of virtue and *religion*" (Brigham, *American Newspapers*, 1:89; *Alexandria Advertiser*, 27 June 1803; *Washington Federalist*, 13 July 1803). An undated, printed receipt for TJ's subscription to the *Columbian Repository* is in MHi.

From William Dunbar

DEAR SIR Natchez 21st. October 1803

I have been honored with your letter of the 21st. Ulto. and now make haste to reply to its contents. The information you have received relative to the re-annexation (by the Spanish Govt.) of that part of W. Florida lying between the Missisippi and river Perdido is perhaps incorrect: The stile and title of the Spanish Govr. (up to the present time) has been Governor General of the two provinces of Louisiana and W. Florida; the Govr. of Pensacola has always been subordinate to, and under the immediate orders of the Govr. genl. of the two provinces. I have every reason to believe that the distinction of East and West Florida has continued to subsist under the Spanish Govt. as it was received from the British, and that the Jurisdiction of the Govr. of St. Augustin did never extend beyond the limits of british East Florida; it certainly never comprehended Pensacola which was a part of ancient Spanish Florida: one or two Circumstances nevertheless occur to my mind which might induce an idea that a portion of W. Florida had been consolidated with Louisiana. The command of the opposite banks of the Missisippi within or rather on the Western boundary of british W. Florida has ever been united (since the cession by the british) in the person of the same Commandant as if belonging to the same province; this is however by no means conclusive: a stronger Circumstance is the following—Before the conquest of W. Florida by the Spanish arms, a Surveyor General of Louisiana was in Commission; and when warrants were afterwards issued by Government for the Survey of lands on the east side of the Missisippi, they were directed to the Surveyor general of Louisiana; no mention has ever been made of W. Florida in those warrants of survey, the lands being states to be situated in the Districts of Baton rouge or Natchez. No surveyor was ever appointed expressly for W. Florida. The subordinate surveyors were all deputies of the Surveyor General of Louisiana, and as it was often impossible to procure such as were qualified, concessions of land have very often remained without survey or been badly done by Commandants or their servants. You have probably been furnished with a Copy of the orders of the Spanish Court, to the Govr. and Intendant of Louisiana, to deliver up the province to the french Commissioner. Being uncertain, I enclose you a Copy thereof taken from a faithful copy drawn from the original by the Writer; from which it will be seen, that what was properly Louisiana under the Spanish Govt. was to have been delivered up to the french *republic*: the explanation given by the Spanish Officers at New Orleans has been, that Spain was to deliver no more to France than what She had received from her, & that consequently the whole of british W. Florida was to be retained; upon this point the french Prefect differed widely from them, claiming ancient Louisiana as it formerly existed under the french dominion, so far as it now continues in the possession of Spain; and writ to his government on the Subject; declaring with french confidence that an application from the chief Consul to the Court of Spain would speedily rectify the errors of its officers.

In my account of indian nations within the province of Louisiana, I have stated that they are few in number and harmless; this is to be understood only of such divisions of the province as are partially inhabited by the Whites; but if my conjectures are well founded, that its barriers extend to the Northern Andes, we remain completely in the dark as to the Aboriginal Tribes which are scattered over that immense region; a few only are imperfectly known to us; they inhabit the banks of the Missouri and some of its (almost) innumerable branches. Those I observe are detailed by Mr. Clark in his letter by last mail to Mr. Madison.

I remark with satisfaction that by the same occasion Mr. Clark has communicated many useful hints to the Secretary of State respecting the people of Louisiana, their characters, their ignorance and their prejudices, which will furnish them with very false ideas of the nature of the government & courts of Justices which they are to expect from us. I have reflected upon this subject, but have always been disinclined to obtrude any opinions not pointedly called for, much less to amuse you with speculative ideas, which perhaps are false in theory and might lead (in practise) to evils of greater magnitude than those which they were erroniously calculated to obviate: I have furnished our Delegate Mr. Lattimore with some reflections on Courts and on men of the law; which reflections I know to be very crude, but will convey the idea of an evil which is rapidly growing up in this Country to an enormous magnitude; fortunate will be the lot of the new province if by any means She may escape so great a Scourge: to me it is evident that the period is fast approaching when the men of the Law will be the Lords & nobility of this Country and the Planters will be their Vassals; they will then govern us with despotic sway. The Governor of our territory deeply impressed with the importance of this subject, proposes, I believe, to second those ideas in his future Communications with Government. I have written to Mr. Clark on the same topic, proposing that the Louisianians should send an intelligent Agent to Congress in order to state the situation and Circumstances of the new Province and its Inhabitants before the sage Legislators of our Nation; but he informs me, the Spanish Govt. will not permit any such measure to be publickly taken while the reins of Govt. remain in their hands.

I am with the highest respect Your Obedient & devoted Servant

William Dunbar

RC (DLC); endorsed by TJ as received 13 Nov. and so recorded in SJL. Enclosure: Miguel Caytano Soler to Juan Ventura Morales, 30 July 1802 (see Vol. 40:27n).

The letter by last mail from Daniel Clark to Madison was dated 29 Sep. and enclosed Clark's answer to TJ's query about American Indian tribes (*Terr. Papers*, 9:61-6).

many useful hints: also on 29 Sep., Clark sent Madison "some Memorandums" that contained his "reflections" on unidentified subjects. It is possible that those papers furnished some of the material for a compilation of information that TJ sent to Congress in November (Madison, *Papers*, *Sec. of State Ser.*, 5:472; TJ to the Senate and the House of Representatives, 14 Nov.).

From Gibson & Jefferson

SIR — Richmond 21st. October 1803—

We have your favor of the 15th. advising a draft for $500 in favor of Mr James Lyle, which is paid—We yesterday sent the Iron, screws &c by Mr. Craven Peyton's waggon—

We find upon enquiry that Mr. Richards schooner the Sally has been performing quarentine upwards of a fortnight—but we are in hopes that a continuance of the present cool weather, will hereafter render it unnecessary—We shall engage Coll. Macon's hams as you direct—With respect we are

Your obt Servts.

GIBSON & JEFFERSON

RC (MHi); in a clerk's hand; endorsed by TJ as received 23 Oct. and so recorded in SJL.

Since August, ports of entry in Virginia had been subject to a quarantine of any vessels arriving from areas suffering from "an infectious and malignant disease" (Richmond *Virginia Argus*, 15 Oct. 1803).

From "Horatio"

GREAT AND GOOD SIR/ — [on or before 21 Oct. 1803]

The inclosed are precious morsels—Read them with attention—They will do you good—Fearing you might not read the honest papers from whence I have taken them, I have, like a "d—d good natured friend"—cut them out as you see.—Consider this, my Gracious President—*thou lover of justice and toleration*—as the *Signal* of the commencement, and continuation of my attentions, (which shall be manifested in various ways) to raise and perpetuate thy great fame, and to promote thy tranquility of mind.—This shall be done—untill—we meet at Philippi—Yes—*Thou "shalt see me at Philippi. Ay, at Philippi."*

Accept the "*homage of my respects*"—Your loving fellow Citizen

HORATIO.

RC (DLC); undated. Recorded in SJL as received from "Anon." on 21 Oct. with notation "scurrilities." Enclosures not identified.

The writer of this letter uses the pseudonym "Horatio," the trusted friend of the Prince of Denmark in *Hamlet*.

A D—D GOOD NATURED FRIEND: a line by Sir Fretful Plagiary in Richard Brinsley Sheridan, *The Critic; or, A Tragedy Rehearsed*, 1.1.

THOU SHALT SEE ME AT PHILIPPI: Shakespeare, *Julius Cæsar*, 4.3.

Proclamation on Ratification of the Louisiana Purchase Treaty and Conventions

[21 Oct. 1803]

Whereas a certain Treaty and two several Conventions between the United States of America and the French Republic were concluded and signed by the Plenipotentiaries of the United States and the French Republic, duly and respectively authorised for that purpose, which Treaty and Conventions are, word for word, as follows: viz:

[*Text omitted.*][1]

And whereas the said Treaty and Conventions have been duly ratified and confirmed by me, on the one part, with the [advice] and consent of the Senate, and by the First Consul of the French Republic, on the other, and the said ratifications were duly exchanged at the City of Washington on the Twenty first day of this present month of October:

Now therefore to the end, that the said Treaty and Conventions may be observed and performed with good faith on the part of the United States, I have ordered the premises to be made public, and I do hereby enjoin and require all persons bearing office, civil or military, within the United States, and all others, Citizens or Inhabitants thereof, or being within the same, faithfully to observe and fulfil the same Treaty and Conventions and every Clause and Article thereof.

In testimony whereof, I have caused the seal of the United States to be affixed to these presents and signed the same with my hand.

Given at the City of Washington in the year of our Lord one thousand eight hundred and three, and of the Sovereignty and Independence of the United States, the Twenty eighth.

TH: JEFFERSON

MS (Christie's, New York City, 1996); undated, but probably 21 Oct. (Miller, *Treaties*, 2:507); torn; in Daniel Brent's hand, signed by TJ; at head of text: "By the President of the United States of America, A Proclamation"; at foot of text: "By the President," signed by Madison; with seal; endorsed by Jacob Wagner.

TO BE MADE PUBLIC: the *National Intelligencer* published the texts of the treaty and conventions on 21 Oct. and printed this proclamation, including the texts of the diplomatic instruments, on 2 Nov.

[1]Not printed here are the texts in English of the treaty for the cession of Louisiana, the convention covering payment, and the convention for the assumption by the United States of debts from France to citizens of the U.S. Each document, dated 30 Apr. 1803, included the names and facsimile seals of Robert R. Livingston, James Monroe, and François Barbé de Marbois as signers. For the texts, see Miller, *Treaties*, 2:498-528.

To the Senate and the House of Representatives

TO THE SENATE & HOUSE OF REPRESENTATIVES
OF THE UNITED STATES.

In my communication to you, of the 17th. instant, I informed you that conventions had been entered into, with the government of France, for the cession of Louisiana to the United States. these, with the advice & consent of the Senate, having now been ratified, & my ratification exchanged for that of the First Consul of France in due form, they are communicated to you for consideration in your legislative capacity. you will observe that some important conditions cannot be carried into execution, but with the aid of the legislature; and that time presses a decision on them without delay.

The ulterior provisions also suggested in the same communication, for the occupation & government of the country, will call for early attention. such information, relative to it's government, as time & distance have permitted me to obtain, will be ready to be laid before you within a few days. but as permanent arrangements for this object may require time & deliberation, it is for your consideration whether you will not forthwith, make such temporary provisions for the preservation, in the mean while, of order & tranquility in the country, as the case may require.

TH: JEFFERSON
Oct. 21. 1803.

RC (DNA: RG 233, PM, 8th Cong., 1st sess.). PrC (DLC). RC (DNA: RG 46, EPFR, 8th Cong., 1st sess.); endorsed by Senate clerks. Recorded in SJL with notation "Message. Louisiana Conventions." Enclosures: Louisiana treaty and conventions (printed for the House of Representatives as *Message from the President of the United States, Inclosing a Treaty and Conventions, Entered Into and Ratified by the United States of America and the French Republic, Relative to the Cession of Louisiana* [Washington, D.C., 1803], Shaw-Shoemaker, No. 5361).

MY COMMUNICATION TO YOU: Annual Message to Congress, 17 Oct.

CONSIDERATION IN YOUR LEGISLATIVE CAPACITY: Lewis Harvie delivered this message to the House and the Senate on Saturday, 22 Oct. In each chamber, an administration ally was ready to act. The day before, John Breckinridge had given notice in the Senate that he would "bring in a bill to enable the President of the United States to take possession of the territories ceded by France to the United States, by the treaty concluded at Paris on the 30th of April last, and for other purposes." He introduced his bill immediately after TJ's message arrived on the 22d. In the House, a motion by John Randolph referred the message to the Committee of the Whole, and Randolph then offered a resolution "That provision ought to be made for carrying into effect the Treaty and Conventions." Breckinridge's bill had been furnished to him by Gallatin, probably two days earlier. In a brief letter to the senator dated "Thursday evening," Gallatin wrote: "I send in the shape of a bill, the substance of what the President seems to think necessary in order to authorize him to occupy & temporarily govern Louisiana. Will you consult with your friends & decide whether the authority be necesary, and if so, what form should be given to it" (in DLC: Breckinridge Family Papers, enclosing text of bill also in Gallatin's hand). With a slight modification of one phrase, changing "necessary & expedient" to simply "necessary," the bill as the senator introduced it was identical to what Gallatin sent him. The Senate approved it with no changes on 26 Oct. by a vote of 26 to 6. It had two parts. The first section authorized the president to "take possession of and occupy" the territories ceded by the treaty, and to draw on the military forces of the United States and the funds appropriated by the March act for raising a detachment of militia (see Gallatin to TJ, 5 Sep.). The second section would allow the president to name individuals to maintain existing civil, military, and judicial offices "until Congress shall have made provision for the temporary government of the said territories." The latter provision met resistance in the House—from Randolph. Stating that "he could conceive no cause for giving a latitude, as to time, so extensive," Randolph offered an amendment to prevent the ad hoc administration of Louisiana from extending beyond the end of the current session of Congress. A second motion by the Virginian resulted in an addition stating that the temporary exercise of powers under the president's direction would be "for maintaining and protecting the inhabitants of Louisiana in the free enjoyment of their liberty, property and religion." The bill passed the House, 89-23, with Randolph's amendments on 28 Oct. The Senate accepted the alterations the following day. TJ signed the bill into law on the 31st (JS, 3:301-4; JHR, 4:412; *Annals*, 13:18, 382, 497-515; U.S. Statutes at Large, 2:245).

The House assumed the lead role in creating legislation for the EXECUTION of the two conventions. The representatives referred those subjects to Randolph's Committee of Ways and Means on 25 Oct. Randolph, for the committee, presented bills that became "An Act authorizing the creation of a stock, to the amount of eleven millions two hundred and fifty thousand dollars" and "An Act making provision for the payment of claims of citizens of the United States on the government of France." The House passed the measures on 29 Oct., the Senate agreed to them a few days later, and TJ signed them on 10 Nov. (JHR, 4:415, 417, 420, 425-7, 438; JS, 3:307, 309; U.S. Statutes at Large, 245-8).

On 25 Oct., the House of Representatives handed the matter of TEMPORARY PROVISIONS for governing Louisiana to a select committee consisting of Randolph, John Rhea, William Hoge, Gaylord Griswold, and George M. Bedinger. Breckinridge's bill superseded that initiative, but on 27 Oct. the House named the same members as a select committee on "permanent arrangements for the government of Louisiana" (JHR, 4:417, 422).

From Elizabeth House Trist

DEAR SIR Pen Park October 21st 1803

You were so kind as to offer to forward my letters to Mr Monroe I avail my self of your always friendly disposition to oblige and inclose one for that purpose. I hope you continue to enjoy your health. the family at Edge Hill I had the pleasure to hear yesterday were well

The expectation that we entertaind of being on the Mississippi this winter begins to subside Browses last letter 14th Sept was not at all satisfactory on that subject. he seems to take it for granted that the Custom House wou'd be removed to Orleans and that it wou'd be incumbent on him to be there at the time, he expresses great satisfaction at the prospect of so advantageous a change as well on acct of its being much more healthy and better situated for business the vessels he says have been this season frequently Six weeks warping up to the Natchez. Wm Brown had not arrived, his Brother rec'd a letter from him dated 2d Sept Havanah where they had put in in distress. the Vessel almost a wreck had been in a violent Storm lost their Bowsprit and all most all the Sails and without water for eight days we are all extremely anxious on his account, when I reflect on their situation and how much depends on him for their happiness and comfort I tremble with apprehension for his safety. The Idea too that we ere long will have to encounter these wrangling elements is not replete with much pleasure

The family Unite with me in Wishing you every felicity and believe me truly Your sincere and Much obliged Freind

E. TRIST

RC (NcU: Nicholas Philip Trist Papers); endorsed by TJ as received 23 Oct. and so recorded in SJL. Enclosure not found.

BEING ON THE MISSISSIPPI THIS WINTER: Trist did not move to New Orleans until spring 1804 to be with her son Hore BROWSE upon his appointment as customs collector at New Orleans. William BROWN, the brother of Elizabeth Trist's daughter-in-law Mary, became port collector after Hore Browse Trist's death from yellow fever in August 1804 (Madison, *Papers, Pres. Ser.*, 2:424-6; RS, 1:73-4n; Elizabeth House Trist to TJ, 10 Feb. 1804; William C. C. Claiborne to TJ, 29 Aug. 1804).

To Caleb Bickham

SIR Washington Oct. 22. 03.

I recieved yesterday your letter on the subject of the tides. my partiality for subjects of that kind in preference to all others, endangering a neglect of duties of a higher order, and which occupy me without intermission, I have been obliged to lay it down as a law for myself to decline corresponding on philosophical subjects generally. the generality of this rule must be my apology in any special case. I am under great obligations to you however for the very friendly dispositions towards me which you are pleased to express. if a steady pursuit of the public good according to the best of my understanding, and without regard to private interests or passions, will preserve to me the good will of my fellow citizens, I feel a consciousness that I shall continue to have claim on it. I pray you to accept my salutations & respects TH: JEFFERSON

PrC (DLC); at foot of text: "Mr. Caleb Bickham"; endorsed by TJ in ink on verso.

YOUR LETTER: Bickham to TJ, 12 July 1803.

To John Crawford

SIR Washington Oct. 22. 03.

Your favor of the 18th. has been duly recieved, and it's contents perused with deep interest, as every thing is by me on a subject so pregnant of future events as that. but that subject is not within the constitutional powers of the General government. it exclusively belongs to each state to take it's own measures of justice or precaution relative to it[1]: and it would contravene the duties which my station imposes on me towards them were I to intermeddle in it directly or indirectly. I have only therefore to express my wishes that it may some day terminate in such a way as that the principles of justice & safety of the whole may be preserved. accept my acknolegements for the expressions of your esteem, and assurances of my respect & consideration towards yourself. TH: JEFFERSON

PrC (DLC); at foot of text: "Doctr. John Crawford."

[1] Preceding three words interlined.

From Jonathan Faw

SIR/ Washington Jail Oct 22nd: 1803

When I tell you that among other authors, I have read with much attention the political writings of Godwin, and of Edmund Burke, that I have seperated the sound parts from the absurd, (for they contain both abundantly) and formed a System of my own, you will not expect from me the language of adulation. Unaccustomed to the etiquette of Courts, I am an enemy to ceremony and form, and acknowledge no superiority except such as flows from superiour intellectual endowments. For the President of the United States, *merely as such* I entertain no very remarkable degree of respect. For *Thomas Jefferson* the firm, enlightened, liberal, Scientific, *consistent Republican*, I entertain such sentiments of respect mingled with admiration as cannot easily be expressed. By the term *Republican*, I mean what the word conveyed, when you were Secretary of State; and not what those profligate politicians who have attempted, to bewilder all political science, in the mazes of metaphysical Jargon for their own nefarious purposes, intend it shall *now* signify. I have attended to, & examined, with a scrutinizing eye, *all* even the most minute of your political actions, for the last twelve or fourteen years, and the sentiments I have just stated have by me been uniformly held, and on all *proper* occasions unequivocally expressed.—

I know the imperfection of human nature, and if in this opinion, I am the victim of delusion, it is a delusion, which I shall be much mortified to see destroyed. I also know, that my opinion must be altogether unimportant to *you*, upon any other principle, than as it tends to shew, the degree of estimation, in which you are held by a human being who can have no possible motive but the love of Truth for expressing it, of one upon whom misfortune has expended all her arrows, who is equally removed from the terrors of further evil, or the blandishments of hope, and who may safely say to Fate I despise thy utmost malice.—

Your Enemies say you are cold blooded, phlegmatick, *too calmly philosophic*, to be sensible to the social affections. This I cannot conceive, for there never yet existed a *very enlightened* mind, a genius of the highest order, and an insensate, ungenerous, callous heart, in the same person. That fire, that animated, sensible, delicate texture of mind, which constitutes true genius, invariably gives existence, to the tender, sympathetic, charities of our nature.—I should not have addressed an Adams at all upon this subject, but among my other apologies for taking up your time *is this*, I consider you the confirmed votary of *Principle*, one upon whose mind, *pride, passion, caprice* and prejudice, have as little influence as they have on that of any of the sons of Adam.—Besides Sir, I have been much flattered (and who would not be flattered) by observing a complete coincidence of *Political Opinion*, between yourself and him who now has the temerity to address you.—

The Basis of my system *is*, that the People is the only legitimate source of power, that every possessor of such power, will abuse it in a greater or less degree; from whence follows the corollary, that they only ought to be entrusted with it, who will abuse it *least* &c &c &c. You may perhaps be displeased to find, that the inhabitant of a Jail dares to hold the same political tenets with yourself. But suppose you choose to hold "that all the parts are equal, & no more than equal to the whole"; "that parallel lines will never meet &c, if my mind is fashioned in a certain way, what power on Earth can prevent my perceiving the truth of the Axioms? If this is so in Mathematicks why not in the science of political Justice? Am I to be accused of vanity and persumption, because I cannot marshal my thoughts with all the adjutancy of tactical science? Is the fault mine, or is it the fault of Nature? Does my being placed in *Jail*, without any earthly cause, alter the constituent Qualities of my mind? Can I arrest its progress, mould it at pleasure, and *say* thus far shalt thou go and no farther, thus shalt thou conceive and not otherwise? The Body may be shackled, but who ever heard of fetters being imposed on thought? Beleive me sir it is no puerile vanity, no petulant itch for scribbling, that propels me to trouble you with the crude offspring of my brain. I well know the value of your time, the momentous affairs that are committed to your charge, the high claim the Community has to your Talents, and every moment that you can devote to its concerns. But I consider you *individually*, as well as the first officer of a free people, *to be*, opposed to tyranny & oppression in every form. You will then rejoice at any opportunity of discountenancing a flagrant invasion of civil right. Nor is this obligation on your part[1] at all weakened, when such Act of oppression is committed within your own immediate & peculiar jurisdiction the Territory of Columbia. *There* sir as you well know, the Citizens are deprived of their most important *constitutional priviledges*; and consequently possess scarcely any Rights, except such as are secured by their system of *Jurisprudence*. Now am I right in the position, when I assert, that it is the duty of every citizen not rendered infamous by crime, or misconduct, to afford to the President of the united States correct information with respect to the violation of one of the most important rights of the Citizen, and its correlative the *maladministration of office*, by those who are appointed *by*, and responsible to *him*, as well as to the Community? If I am correct in this assertion, is the obligation imposed by this principle, at all lessened, when I myself am the victim, upon whom Oppression under the semblance and habiliments of Justice, has laid her iron fangs? As you are not possessed of omniscience, your situation in some particulars resembles that of a Monarch; as you must in a great[2] measure with respect to things not of the *first magnitude, hear* and *see*, as those in whom you place confidence desire. And I beg you will have the goodness to consider, my being impressed with this idea, among the other apologies for my boldness in soliciting your attention.—

I am not the only person over whom petty despotism & illegality, have extended their rule, for (be assured) I have witnessed such flagrant violations of the most sacred rights of the citizen, as have made *me* shudder for the consequences, if the public mind should have acquired that degree of debasement *generally*,[3] which exists in that part of this district which was formerly Virginia.—And I am the only one it would seem, who has had the temerity to remonstrate[4] to the source of all inferior executive authority. The situation of this district, does indeed present a phenomenon, in the politics of a free Country. The assumption of its exclusive Jurisdiction by the Congress, *at the particular* time in which it took place, originated in views the most profligate & abandoned; and like a stream descending from a polluted source, every thing attached to it is degrading and loathsome. If it should continue to exist for any length of time, it will become as *petty, pitiful*, oppressive an Aristocracy, as the annals of the world[5] do exhibit. Indeed the men in office, (with a few exceptions) appear to me, to merit the observation, which Montesquieu applies to the standing army of England, "like the Eunuchs in an Eastern seraglio they take a malignant pleasure in destroying, what they themselves are incapacitated from participating."[6] The civil liberty of the subjects of Great Britain, Monarchical & imperfect as their Constitution is (if they have one) does not deserve to be named, on the same day with the rights which we possess. Nay sir *pure, unmixed, defecated,* dephlegmated slavery, is preferable to such a state as ours: for if I resided within the Jurisdiction of a Hyder Ali Khan, or a Sultan Tippoo his son, I should make my conduct correspond with my situation; and my mind being reduced to the level of Slavery, I might perhaps escape personal injury. *At all events*, I should not be tantalized with the Shadow of Liberty, whilst the substance was withheld, having her constantly within reach, but perpetually eluding my grasp. Excuse my warmth, for liberty like health is seldom properly appreciated, until by a depravation, we are taught her value. Ever since I commenced this Letter, I have been endeavouring to avoid prolixity, and you see how unsuccessfully; and as I despair of my own efforts to procure a pardon for my rashness, I must summon the eloquence of a *Sterne* as my advocate. The truth of the fact *is*, having mounted my hobby, I could not dismount at pleasure; and why a man may not be permitted to ride a little even in a jail, I know not; for you may rest assured, the horse ambles as finely, and the rider is as much delighted, as if he dwelt in a Palace.—But least you should apply to me the same observation, that the Critics have directed to the author of the "Pursuits of Literature" when they tell him, that the body of his work, is like a peg to hang his Notes upon, I shall proceed to relate those circumstances, which have occasioned the writing of this Letter.—As I wish to be treated precisely according to my merits, I will first give you a sketch of my own character, this I can do best, as I best know myself, and I pledge myself to you, that it shall be done with the pen of Truth and of candour, "I will nothing extenuate" and I suppose I need not add "or set down ought in malice." For the Truth of what may be stated in this particular I refer you to Danl C Brent, Judge Cranch and John T Mason.—

I am a man aged 30 years, & brought up to the science of the Law, under L Martin whom you very well know.—Possessed of a mind active, ardent, and a sensibility almost[7] morbid, I have been nursed in the lap of prosperity; and until within the last year of my life[8] have never exerted the powers of mind which I possess. Want of Fortitude, (not active courage) has hitherto been the great defect in my character, and the prime cause of my misfortunes. Ardent & restless as I before observed, never in a medium, I have alternately experienced the solid pleasures of severe study, and the miseries of excessive dissipation. The sensibility of my mind, aided by a very vivid imagination, magnified[9] unexpected inconveniences, & a failure of prospects, into evils incurable; and despair & drinking was the consequence, which was quickly succeeded by a fit of intense study, for 3 or 4 months by way of atonement.—I speak of the last two years of my Life; the seven immediately preceeding, were spent in professional pursuits, the acquistion of science, and the deceitful[10] pleasures of dissipation.—A stranger to apathy, I have lived in a continued storm, & have been very happy and very miserable.—I have lived for a number of years upon very uneasy terms, with Abraham Faw, one of the Justices of the peace appointed by yourself, and who says he is my Father. About seven weeks ago, he desired me for ever, to quit his roof and protection which I cheerfully complied with; As lately I have found his protection *to be* precisely that sort of protection, which the British East India Company afforded, to the Indian princes who applied for it, "*that is they protected them*"[11] according to the Account of Edmund Burke "*to their utter extirpation.*" Thus situated my state[12] corresponded exactly with that of Richard Savage according to the account of Docr Johnson. In order to procure what I think an honourable subsistence,[13] I intended to have had recourse to the labours of my pen. As I am no very great favourite of the *Nine* the Field of Politics, though much beaten, presented to my mind a flattering prospect. For I entertain no very exalted opinion, of the newspaper and pamphlet writers in America, *federal or* democratic, either with respect to their style or their matter.—I remained in this state for the space of a Week when Mr Faw requisted me to become again[14] a resident in his House, which I refused: upon which, as a Justice of the peace, he wrote the following commitment viz,

Alexandria County St}

Whereas Jonathan Faw is going at large about the Town, insulting and abusing the Citizens contrary to Law & he being adjudged to find security for his good behaviour which he has failed to do You are therefore required to receive him into your Custody & jail and him keep until such security be given, or otherwise discharged according to Law. Given under my hand & seal this 15th September 1803.

signed
A: FAW (seal)

Capt. James Campbell

Now sir this commitment & the proceedings thereon, *are* I will venture to pronounce, *unprecedented* in the Annals of Tyranny under the form of Law.—The Commt is the first notification I had of the kind intentions of Mr. Faw; there never was a complaint to my knowledge, made to him, there was not a human being in Alexandria who could have made any[15] complaint, as I had given just cause of offence to none. The Commitment itself does not state any complaint, made against me, of my having[16] violated, or that there was just ground to suspect I would violate, any even the most minute Law of my Country. It stated indeed some nonsense about *insults* &c, which even if true, (*as it is*[17] *the reverse*), he as a Justice of the Peace had nothing to do with: for insults offered by one *free white* individual to another, I have always understood to be cognizable in a Court of honour, *injuries or the reasonable probability of their commission* before the civil Magistrate.—But to proceed. There never was a warrant either issued or served upon me, I was never, brought before him, or any other Magistrate,[18] I was never adjudged to give any security, (because he very well knew that I could easily have procured the most respectable characters in Alexa. to have bound themselves for me.)[19] *The trial, the judgt the failure to comply with it on my* part, I solemnly declare, never existed any where except in the prolific fancy of Mr Faw; and the commitment aforesaid, the first the only proceeding on his part, was at once put into the hands of a Constable, with directions to apprehend me wherever I might be found, and carry me to Prison. In pursuance of which, on the Day mentioned therein, about four OClock pm, as I was peceably and orderly conversing with some Gentlemen at the upper end of King Street, I was accosted by the officer and desired to walk to jail. As much astonished, as if I had been requested to walk to Circassia, I demanded to know, to what authority I was indebted for his polite attention, when he produced the Commitment. Enraged at the villainy, as well as the illegality of the proceedure, I told him nothing but the exertion of superiour physical power, could procure a compliance on my part. Consequently he summoned the *Posse Comitatus.* The Gentlemen who were present refused to participate in the infamous transaction; and I should have escaped the clutches of petty despotism, had it not been for the interference of a poor wretch, one of the lowest among the very dregs of Society.—With his assistance, I was forcibly dragged through the streets like the vilest malefactor, and confined in a prison for the space of three weeks, in which under existing circumstances, I declared I should have thought myself a monster of inhumanity, to have shut up the most excerable villain, that ever disgraced[20] the world. For you will be pleased to observe, that the Jail I speak of, *is the very same,* in which, on account of the prevailing epidemick, Docr. Dick the health officer of Alexandria, had previously declared, that it was impossible for any human being to exist for any length of time; and from *which*, the humane interference of the Judge, *had* (to the knowledge of Mr Faw,) before my confinement, *removed* every Prisoner, even the poor wretch, who owes his existence, to a late just & merciful exercise of your constitutional Prerogative.

With respect to the illegality of this whole procedure, I declare I shudder at the bare idea, of painting it in the true colours of all its native deformity. When I consider its author, the certain knowledge he had, that the Laws of this Country did not permit even a *Murderer* to be confined without a previous hearing, and when I consider[21] the Crime involved in it, the ideas it excites in my mind, are *too horrid, too vilely loathsome*, for a moments contemplation. Let a veil be thrown over it for ever. But such a man is not a proper person, indeed he is not, to be entrusted with powers, which were designed to protect the *weak, the poor*, and the *defenceless*, from the attacks of the *strong*, the *rich*, and the *lawless*. Here the Community is interested, and it is treason against it, to continue *such* powers in *such* hands any longer than absolute necessity requires.—

However strange it may seem, yet it is a melancholy fact, that dreadful as the picture is, when we view this Man acting as a Justice of the peace, it is notwithstanding the most favorable point of view for *him*, in which it[22] can be placed. For admitting the legality of his proceedings, when I consider, that in consequence of a misunderstanding between us of a private & domestic nature, *he, the author of my existence, knowingly, & willingly*, placed me in a situation, from which according to all human probability, it was fifty chances to one, that I did not escape with life, great God what conclusion am I to form? And how much is the dye of this transaction deepened, when I consider, that the very day after he had thus placed me in the center of contagion, he removed himself with his family, from the most healthy part of Alexandria to Fredk Town, in order to escape the prevailing disease? That Family consists of one brother, & two sisters by my Fathers side, & their mother his *present* wife. With respect to this part of the subject, I shall only observe, that during the late war between Great Britain & her then Colonies, the celebrated Docr Samuel Johnson wrote a Pamphlet in favour of the british Ministry, to which he affixed the title of "*Taxation no Tyranny*"; which was completely refuted, by another Pamphlet written in vindication of the Americans, by a Gentleman who entitled it "*Killing no Murder.*" When I was a very young man, and read these works, I little thought that an attempt would ever be made, to realize the ironical title of this last writing in my own person.

After remaining as I before observed, three weeks in the Jail of Alexandria, I was on the eighth Day of this month, in consequence of an order from Judge Cranch, *removed* to the jail of this City, where altho the humanity of the Marshal sometimes permits me to walk about on my *parol*, I am still in Law a prisoner. I do not know that you have any constitutional power to interfere in my case, the best method of obtaining a release *is*, to be discharged by a Judge on a *Habeas Corpus*; and with respect to obtaining a Redress for the injury I have sustained, the Laws of my Country afford me the Action of *False Imprisonment*. But when I bring my suit in Alexa., the Jury empannalled to try it will be a Jury of Merchants, who may if they please give me only *nominal* Damages. For what is a Merchant, and what conception has he of the consequence of a persons being permitted, to violate a *fundamental principle of Civil Liberty* with impunity? Perhaps the Idea entertained of him by Edmund Burke may not be altogether erroneous.

Talk not to me (says he in his own emphatick language) of a Merchant, his *counting house* is his *Church*, his Desk is his *Altar*, his Ledger is his *Bible*, Gain is *God*. But it is high time to put an end to this Letter, already I have trespassed much too long on your patience. If I take up much of that time, which *is*, and ought to be, devoted to weightier concerns than the Case of any individual whatever, then am I guilty of palpable injustice. I must however here be permitted to tell you, that I expect an answer, but as I am not vain enough to hope for a correspondence with Mr Jefferson, not absolutely a candidate for contempt, and as I do not wish (however gratifying it might be to my own vanity) to give your Enemies an opportunity, of depicting the President of the United States as corresponding with the Inhabitant of a Jail; a simple acknowledgement of the receipt of this Letter is all I request.

I am well aware of the delicacy of your situation, and the great noise your political opponents made about the trifling notice you took of that wretch Callendar, and with what avidity they seize every opportunity, of misconstruing your intentions as well as your Actions. But after all, upon whom but *themselves*, did their charge on that score reflect disgrace? They reminded every enlig[htened] impartial Person, of the fool in the fable, who scattered dust against the Sun. But did that diminish his Splendor or tarnish the lustre of his Rays?—

I rely for my justification for the whole of this letter on your liberality and nobleness of mind, which will not permit Truth to depend upon time, place, or accident; and upon the maxim *"Homo sum et nihil humanum alienum a me puto,"* by which I believe you to have been always actuated, and which you must have read before I was born.—

Accept my poor wishes for your health and prosperity, and permit me to subscribe myself, with sentiments of very great respect Yr Obedt Servt.

JONA. FAW

RC (DLC); word obscured by tape; at foot of text: "His Excellency Thos Jefferson Esqr"; endorsed by TJ as received 24 Oct. and so recorded in SJL.

Jonathan Faw (ca. 1773-1807) was admitted to practice law in Alexandria in 1801. TJ had appointed his father, Abraham Faw, a justice of the peace for Alexandria in 1801 (*Alexandria Advertiser*, 14 Apr. 1801, 7 Feb. 1807; Vol. 33:674).

LIKE THE EUNUCHS IN AN EASTERN SERAGLIO: rather than Montesquieu, Faw appears to be quoting Josiah Quincy, Jr.'s, comments on the soldiers of Great Britain: "Excluded, therefore, from the enjoyments which others possess, like Eunuchs of an Eastern seraglio, they envy and hate the rest of the community, and indulge a malignant pleasure in destroying those privileges to which they can never be admitted. How eminently does modern observation verify that sentiment of Baron Montesquieu—a slave living among freemen will soon become a beast" (Quincy, *Observations on the Act of Parliament, Commonly Called the Boston Port-Bill; with Thoughts on Civil Society and Standing Armies* [Boston, 1774], 33).

Haidar Ali (HYDER ALI KHAN) and his son, Tipu Sultan (SULTAN TIPPOO), ruled the kingdom of Mysore in southern India successively from 1761 to 1799 (Lewin B. Bowring, *Haidar Alí and Tipú Sultán and the Struggle with the Musalman Powers of the South* [Oxford, 1899], 10).

English satirist Thomas James Mathias published PURSUITS OF LITERATURE anonymously in four parts from 1794 to 1797. The work drew considerable commentary, both positive and negative, with English literary scholar George Steevens opining that its poetry was "merely a peg to hang the notes on." TJ acquired a subsequent edition of the work, published in 1798 in Dublin (DNB, s.v. "Mathias, Thomas James," "Steevens, George"; Sowerby, No. 4513).

NOTHING EXTENUATE . . . OR SET DOWN OUGHT IN MALICE: Shakespeare, *Othello*, 5.2.

RICHARD SAVAGE ACCORDING TO THE ACCOUNT OF DOCR JOHNSON: Samuel Johnson, *An Account of the Life of Mr Richard Savage, Son of the Earl Rivers* (London, 1744).

JAMES CAMPBELL was keeper of the Alexandria jail (*Alexandria Advertiser*, 12 Jan. 1803; *Alexandria Expositor*, 16 Feb. 1804).

LATE JUST & MERCIFUL EXERCISE OF YOUR CONSTITUTIONAL PREROGATIVE:

possibly a reference to TJ's recent pardon of Samuel Miller; see William Kilty and William Cranch to TJ, 28 July 1803.

HOMO SUM ET NIHIL HUMANUM: for this quotation from Terence, see the enclosure to Levi Lincoln to TJ, 11 Sep.

[1] Preceding three words interlined.

[2] Preceding two words interlined in place of "some."

[3] Preceding word and comma interlined.

[4] Preceding two words interlined.

[5] Preceding three words interlined.

[6] Closing parenthesis supplied by Editors.

[7] Word interlined.

[8] Preceding three words interlined.

[9] Word interlined.

[10] Word interlined.

[11] Closing quotation mark supplied by Editors.

[12] Word interlined in place of "situation."

[13] Word interlined in place of "existence."

[14] Word interlined.

[15] Word interlined in place of "such a."

[16] Preceding six words and comma interlined in place of "that I had."

[17] Preceding two words interlined in place of "they are."

[18] Preceding four words and comma interlined.

[19] Closing parenthesis supplied by Editors.

[20] Faw here canceled "humanity."

[21] Preceding three words interlined.

[22] Word interlined in place of "his conduct."

From David Gelston

SIR, New York Oct: 22. 1803

Enclosed is my account of duties &ca paid on wine & nuts—I shall be happy to hear of the safe arrival of the whole—

I have the honor to be, with great regard, Sir, your obedient servant

DAVID GELSTON

RC (MHi); at foot of text: "Thomas Jefferson President U.S."; endorsed by TJ as received 26 Oct. and so recorded in SJL.

In addition to the ACCOUNT below, Gelston likely also enclosed an invoice for freight charges, dated 10 Oct., from a representative of the *Thetis*, the brig that had transported TJ's wine from Bordeaux (MS in ViU; in J. Speyer's hand and endorsed by him for receipt of payment of $25.55 on 14 Oct.).

ENCLOSURE

Statement of Account with David Gelston

Thomas Jefferson President U.S.

To David Gelston Dr

1803		
Augt. 29th	for cash pd. duties on one case of wine	3.75
	permits carting & storing	1
	carting & storing nuts	62
Oct: 8.	pd. duties on 10 cases wine	23.80

permits & carting	90
pd. freight from Bordeaux	25.55
dollars—	55.62

New York Octo. 22d. 1803—

David Gelston

[*Note by John Barnes*:]
paid ℔ draft on B B Ny.
& inclosed in J B. Letter.
to Mr Gelston 27 Oct 1803 } Entd 189—

MS (ViU); in Gelston's hand, with note in Barnes's hand; endorsed on verso by Barnes: "David Gelston Esqr: Collector N York for Duties & freight &ca on Wine & Nuts from Bordeaux 27 Oct. 1803 $55.62."

To Robert Ware Peacock

Sir Washington Oct. 22. 03.

My business not permitting me to participate in the benefit of the course of lectures proposed in the inclosed paper, and having been obliged moreover to lay it down as a law to myself not to put my name to any subscription paper; I can but return it to you with my wishes for it's success, both as it regards yourself, and for those whose situations may enable them to attend. certainly the position in this city has the advantages you point out and invites youth to give it a preference to any other. Accept my salutations & respects.

Th: Jefferson

PrC (ViW: Tucker-Coleman Collection); at foot of text: "Robert Ware Peacock esq."; endorsed by TJ in ink on verso. Enclosure not found, but see Peacock to TJ, 20 Oct.

From Joseph Yznardi, Sr.

Honoured Sir. 22d. October 1803.

I had the honour of writing your Excellency the 19th. July last whereof the above is a fourth Copy.

T,F, I have now that of inclosing your Excellency Bill Lading of One Butt of Sherry Wine which I have Shipped on board the American Ship Eliza Capt. N. C. Bissel bound to Philadelphia and Consigned to the Collector of said Port subject to your Excelly. orders—I also remit the Invoice from the House at Sherry from whom I have had the Liquor amounting to \$194, $\frac{85}{100}$ which your Excellency will remit me whenever it is agreable.

I have made no Insurance on said Wine as your Excellency had given no orders respecting it.

The advices I have from Madrid are that our Governt. is doing all in its power to remain perfect Neutral in the actual differences between France & England—

This is the very first oppertunity that has offered since I had the honour of receiving your Excellencys order—

I have the honour to be with the most profound respect Honoured Sir. Your most obt. hble Servt.

Josef Yznardy

RC (DLC); in a clerk's hand, signed by Yznardi; follows, on same page, quadruplicate of Yznardi to TJ, 19 July; at foot of text: "To His Excellency Thomas Jefferson President of the United States of America at the City of Washington"; endorsed by TJ as received 22 Dec. and so recorded in SJL. Dupl (same); at head of text: "Copy"; in a clerk's hand, signed by Yznardi; endorsed by TJ as received 20 Jan. 1804 and so recorded in SJL. Enclosures: (1) Bill of lading, Cadiz, 22 Oct. 1803, being a printed form, with blanks filled by a clerk and signed by N. C. Bissell, master of the ship *Eliza*, describing a shipment consisting of "One Doubled Cased Butt of Sherry Wine," with freight costs of "Ten Mexican Round Dollars," and addressed to the collector in Philadelphia or Norfolk (MS in same: TJ Papers, 136:23437; Dupl in same, 136:23438). (2) Invoice, dated 18 Oct. 1803, for a cased butt of "superior Sherry Wine" sold by Gordon & Co. of Jerez, Spain, to Yznardi for a total cost of $194.85 (MS in same, 135:23415). Enclosed in Anthony Terry to the collectors of "any of the Ports of the United States," 22 Oct. (same, 136:23435).

From Horatio Gates

Dear Sir Rose Hill 23d. Octr: 1803.

Wednesday Noon Our Whigg Printer sent me your Message to Congress; he delivered it to The public in a seperate publication; I read it Greedily; It has fix'd your Fame upon an everlasting Foundation.—I am not surprized I did not receive an Answer to my two last Letters; for however you might be disposed to listen to my Recomendations, you could say nothing conclusive until the Louisiana business had received the Approbation of Congress;—I confess myself anxious for Success to General Armstrong, but that is full as much for your sake, as His; Conscious how much he is attached to You, & convinced of his Abilities to Grace the appointment.—The other Gentleman has a good Lucrative Office to Vacate, which another Man might think better than the one Solicited; but this Candidate, I gave you my Reasons for taking the Liberty to Recommend; Your Decision will prefectly satisfy me.—Inclosed is a Letter I received the first Instant from Marquiss La Fayette; together with what passd between me, & Consul Arcambal, upon the Subject.—I hope Citizen Laussat is arrived at Washington, and that every Sanction that can be obtain'd from an Ambassdor will Grace your Message to Congress;—when Mr: Gallatin was here, I lent Him Le page Du Pratz History of Louisiana; I am inclined to think it a very scarce Book in America; if you have not already perused it, nor have it not in your Library, I am willing to send it you by any conveyance you shall direct, it is in one Vol: in Octavo. there is much information in it—at this time I have only earnestly to recommend it to you to take care of your Health, & your Person, for I veryly believe the future porsperty of the Union depends much upon the preservation of both.—believe me ever

Your Faithfull & Obedient Servant HORATIO GATES

RC (DNA: RG 59, LAR); endorsed by TJ as received 30 Oct. and "Armstrong to be Govr. Louisiana" and so recorded in SJL. Enclosures not found.

WEDNESDAY NOON: that is, 19 Oct. OUR WHIGG PRINTER: James Cheetham, editor of the daily New York *American Citizen* (MB, 2:1123n).

Gates's TWO LAST LETTERS to TJ are dated 7 and 18 July. OTHER GENTLEMAN: William Stephens Smith, surveyor and inspector of customs for the port of New York (see Gates to TJ, 7 July).

LETTER I RECEIVED: Lafayette may have written Gates, as he did TJ, regarding the Beaumarchais claim (Lafayette to TJ, 22 May).

Louis ARCAMBAL was the French commissary of commercial relations for the city of New York in 1803 (New York *Mercantile Advertiser*, 16 Sep. 1803, 18 May 1804; Vol. 38:311, 312n).

TJ regularly cited the history by Antoine-Simon LE PAGE DU PRATZ in his notes on territorial claims in Louisiana (see Editorial Note and Document I at The Boundaries of Louisiana, 7 Sep.).

From DeWitt Clinton

[24 Oct. 1803]

Mr Clinton's compliments to the President and sends him at the request of the owner of the Quarry a specimen of black marble a large quarry of which has been discovered at Marbletown Ulster County about 100 miles North of New York and 10 west of the Hudson River

RC (MHi); undated; endorsed by TJ as received 24 Oct. 1803.

Located about ten miles southwest of Kingston, New York, MARBLETOWN was noted for its abundance of "a superior quality, finely clouded" marble, which quarried well and received a high polish. In 1805, a stone cutter in New York City advertised "real Black Marble, beautifully variegated" from New York State, which was superior to that imported (Horatio Gates Spafford, *A Gazetteer of the State of New-York* [Albany, 1813], 109-10, 230-1; New York *Daily Advertiser*, 28 Aug. 1805).

From John Dickinson

MY DEAR FRIEND, Wilmington the 24th of the tenth Month 1803

Accept my heartiest Thanks for thy late Message to Congress, carrying in it Communications of the highest Moment to the fortunes of[1] our beloved Country.

I hope, that the great outline drawn by thee with so steady a Hand, will in due Time be filled with establishments dictated by wisdom and Virtue, all contributing to the advancement of human Happiness.

May thy Life be continued long enough to recieve the grateful Acknowledgements of Millions for the Blessings of thy administration, and to enjoy a clear Prospect of those which it promises[2] to realize to Ages unborn.

At a season peculiarly engaging thy Attention to these arduous Affairs,

"in commoda publica peccem si longo sermone tandem tua tempora"

After all I could say, the Expressions would but faintly convey the mingled sensations of public and personal Considerations, with which I am thy obliged and affectionate Friend

JOHN DICKINSON

RC (DLC); at foot of text: "The President"; endorsed by TJ as received 28 Oct. and so recorded in SJL. Dft (PHi); written on cover sheet addressed to "John Dickinson" in unknown hand.

THY LATE MESSAGE TO CONGRESS: TJ's Annual Message to Congress, 17 Oct.

IN COMMODA: a variation of "in publica commoda peccem si longo sermone morer tua tempora," that is, "I would sin against the public good if I wasted your time with tedious chatter" (Horace, *Epistles*, 2.1.3-4).

[1] In Dft preceding five words interlined in place of "Importance to."

[2] In Dft Dickinson interlined "in future" before altering the passage to read as above.

From Samuel D. Purviance

SIR, Washington City, Octo. 24th. 1803.

I have the honor of laying before you certain papers which were enclosed to me in a letter from Joseph Pickett Esquire, of Anson County, in the District of Fayetteville, respecting the case of John Campbell and Farquhar Campbell, insolvent debtors. Mr. Pickett informs me that the former of these Gentlemen has been, for some time past, and still is, confined within the bounds of the Prison of that county. Mr. Howard, one of the Commissioners mentioned in the letter of Mr. Tillinghast, is since dead; Mr.[1] Hay or Mr.[2] Cochran, of Fayetteville, or the above named Mr. Pickett, would perhaps be deemed proper by the Executive to succeed him. Either of these gentlemen, is, in the opinion of the writer of this Note, perfectly qualified.

I am, very respectfully, your most obt. servt.

SAML. D. PURVIANCE

RC (DNA: RG 59, LAR); in TJ's hand, at foot of text: "Robert Troy"; TJ probably entered the emendations, including the interlineations (see notes below), after receiving Nathaniel Macon's letter of 17 Nov.; endorsed by TJ as received 24 Oct. and "Commrs. of bkrptcy for N. Cara." and so recorded in SJL. Enclosure: perhaps William Johnson and Others to TJ, 24 July 1803. Other enclosures not found.

Of Huguenot descent, Samuel Densmore Purviance (1774-1806) was born at Castle Fin House near Wilmington, North Carolina. In 1795, he began to practice law at Fayetteville, where he also owned a plantation on the Cape Fear River. He served several terms as a state legislator before being elected as a Federalist to the Eighth Congress. His election was unsuccessfully contested by Republican Duncan McFarland. Purviance did not stand for reelection in 1804. In that year, North Carolina elected a full Republican contingent of 12 representatives to the House. Purviance died while on a western expedition along the Red River (Delbert Harold Gilpatrick, *Jeffersonian Democracy in North Carolina, 1789–1816* [New York, 1931], 169-71; William S. Powell, ed., *Dictionary of North Carolina Biography*, 6 vols. (Chapel Hill, 1979-96), 4:146-7; 5:159; *Biog. Dir. Cong.*; ASP, *Miscellaneous*, 1:389).

Both JOSEPH PICKETT and John HAY ran unsuccessfully for Congress from North Carolina's Seventh District in 1804. McFarland won the election (Gilpatrick, *Jeffersonian Democracy in North Carolina*, 242-3; Michael J. Dubin, *United States Congressional Elections, 1788-1997: The Official Results of the Elections of the 1st through 105th Congresses* [Jefferson, N.C., 1998], 27-8, 32).

[1] TJ here interlined "John."

[2] TJ here interlined "Robert."

To the Senate

TO THE SENATE OF THE UNITED STATES.

I lay before you the Convention signed on the 12th. day of May last, between the United States and Great Britain, for settling their boundaries in the North Eastern & North Western parts of the United States, which was mentioned in my general message of the 17th. instant; together with such papers relating thereto as may enable you to determine whether you will advise & consent to it's ratification.

TH: JEFFERSON
Oct. 24. 1803.

RC (DNA: RG 46, EPFR, 8th Cong., 1st sess.); endorsed by Senate clerks. PrC (DLC). Recorded in SJL with notation "Conventn. with Gr. Br." Enclosures: (1) Convention between the United States and Great Britain, 12 May, signed by Rufus King and Lord Hawkesbury, consisting of five articles relating to running the boundaries specified in the 1783 treaty of peace; the first article defines the course of the boundary between various islands from the mouth of the Saint Croix River to the Bay of Fundy; the convention also requires the appointment of three commissioners to determine the northwest angle of Nova Scotia and have the boundary between it and the source of the Saint Croix marked; the commissioners will then determine the northwesternmost head of the Connecticut River and have the boundary between that point and the northwest angle of Nova Scotia marked; the fifth article notes that it is now uncertain that the Mississippi River extends far enough to the north to be intersected by a line drawn due west from the northwesternmost point of Lake of the Woods, as specified for the course of the boundary by the 1783 treaty; that boundary is now declared to be the shortest line between the northwest point of the Lake of the Woods and the nearest source of the Mississippi River, and on the demand of either government, commissioners will be appointed to ascertain those geographical points and have that segment of the boundary run (Tr in DNA: RG 46, EPFR, in multiple clerks' hands; ASP, *Foreign Relations*, 2:584-5). (2) Madison to King, 28 July 1801, extract, recommending that the boundary through Passamaquoddy Bay from the mouth of the Saint Croix to the Bay of Fundy be defined in a way that allows both nations access to the navigable channel, which appears to be the intent of the 1783 treaty (Tr in DNA: RG 46, EPFR, in a clerk's hand; Madison, *Papers*, *Sec. of State Ser.*, 1:484). (3) Madison to King, 8 June 1802, providing instructions for settling "whatever remains to be decided in relation to the boundaries between the two nations"; he reports that it is "now well understood" that the most northern source of the Mississippi River is south of the Lake of the Woods; as a remedy, King may agree to "a line running from that source of the Mississippi which is nearest to the Lake of the Woods, and striking it Westwardly as a tangent and from the point touched along the Watermark of the Lake to its most Northwestern point at which it will meet the line running thro' the Lake"; Madison refers King to the map in Alexander Mackenzie's *Voyages* (Tr in DNA: RG 46, EPFR, in a clerk's hand; Madison, *Papers*, *Sec. of State Ser.*, 3:287-9); enclosing James Sullivan to Madison, 20 May 1802 from Boston; Sullivan, the agent of the United States for the commission on the Saint Croix boundary in 1798, sends detailed information about the channels and provides his interpretation of the requirements of the treaty (RC in DNA: RG 46, EPFR, in a clerk's hand, with closing and signature by Sullivan, endorsed for the State Department as received 28 May; Madison, *Papers*, *Sec. of State Ser.*, 3:237-42, 289n). (4) Christopher Gore to Madison, 6 Oct. 1802 from London, reporting his discussions with the British government on the boundary issue in King's absence; he encloses his notes to Hawkesbury of 24 Aug., 22 Sep., and 28 Sep., "Minutes &c." of some of the points of discussion, and a reply from Hawkesbury dated 4 Oct. (Trs in DNA: RG 46, EPFR, in a clerk's hand; Madison, *Papers*, *Sec. of State Ser.*, 3:611-13; ASP, *Foreign Relations*, 2:587-9). (5) Madison to King, 16 Dec. 1802, extract, reporting that the president is disappointed that the British are not satisfied with the propositions of the United States for resolving the boundary between Lake of the Woods and the Mississippi River, inasmuch as the propositions were favorable to Britain; the U.S. will not press that matter at this time but hopes to have the other boundary questions resolved, and meanwhile both nations can gather more information about the headwaters of the Mississippi, "it being understood that the United States will be as free to be guided by the result of such enquiries in any future negociation, as if the proposition above referred to had never been made by them" (Tr in DNA: RG 46, EPFR, in a clerk's hand; Madison, *Papers*, *Sec. of State Ser.*, 4:193). (6) King to Madison, 28 Feb. 1803, extract, reporting his progress in discussions on some of the boundary issues (Tr in DNA: RG 46, EPFR, in a clerk's hand; summarized in Madison, *Papers*, *Sec. of State Ser.*, 4:359-60). (7) King to Madison, 13 May, enclosing the convention; according to Mackenzie's report, the Lake of the Woods is "nearly circular" and the source of the Mississippi River nearest to the lake is about 20 miles away, which means that the course of the line contained in the convention is "equally advantageous with the Lines we had proposed" (Dupl in DNA: RG 46,

EPFR, endorsed for the State Department as received 8 July; also Tr in same; Madison, *Papers*, *Sec. of State Ser.*, 4:607).

WHETHER YOU WILL ADVISE & CONSENT: Lewis Harvie delivered the message to the Senate on the 24th. After some consideration of the convention during executive sessions, the Senate on 15 Nov. handed the matter over to a committee consisting of John Quincy Adams, Wilson Cary Nicholas, and Robert Wright (several weeks later, Abraham Venable replaced Nicholas, who was absent). Adams wrote to Madison on 3 Dec. to say that a question had come up about whether the fifth article of the convention "may by a possible future construction, be pretended to operate as a limitation to the claims of Territory" that the United States acquired through the purchase of Louisiana. Adams asked if the negotiators had known of the Louisiana transaction when they framed that article. On 16 Dec., Madison passed along an answer from King in New York, who stated that the terms of the convention had been worked out and agreed to before news of the Louisiana deal reached London. The committee reported to the Senate late in December, declaring that without "means of ascertaining the precise northern limits of Louisiana, as ceded to the United States," it was not possible to say where the boundary projected by the convention would fall relative to the limits of Louisiana. When ratification of the convention finally came to a vote on 9 Feb. 1804, only nine senators, including Adams but not the other members of the committee, favored keeping the article that related to the boundary between the Lake of the Woods and the Mississippi River. Unable to win approval of the convention in its entirety, they joined the majority to give unanimous approval of ratification "with the exception of the 5th article." The British government declined to accept the conditional approval of the agreement by the United States, and the convention did not take effect (JEP, 1:451-2, 454, 461-4; Madison, *Papers*, *Sec. of State Ser.*, 6:134, 141, 152-3, 180; *Annals*, 14:1253; Bradford Perkins, *The First Rapprochement: England and the United States, 1795-1805* [Berkeley, Calif., 1967], 143-9).

From George Taylor, Jr.

DEAR SIR, Philadelphia, Octr: 24th: 1803.

Permit me, on the present occasion to incroach upon your time for a few moments merely by bringing to your view that a vacancy has taken place in the Post office Department by the death of Colonel Bauman at N. York and that if consistent with the arrangements you have made I should be much gratified by the appointment and am with the most perfect respect

Sir, Your most obt. Servant

GEO: TAYLOR JR:

RC (DNA: RG 59, LAR); at foot of text: "The President of the United States"; endorsed by TJ as received 27 Oct. and "to be postmaster N.Y." and so recorded in SJL.

Taylor succeeded Henry Remsen as chief clerk in the State Department in April 1792, a position he retained for the remainder of TJ's tenure as secretary of state. He was dismissed by Timothy Pickering in 1798 (Vol. 17:358n; Vol. 27:635-6). For his subsequent career as a broker in Philadelphia, see Vol. 36:114-15.

New York City postmaster Sebastian BAUMAN died on 19 Oct. "after an illness of several weeks." In January 1804, Theodorus Bailey submitted his resignation as senator of New York to accept the appointment (New York *Morning Chroni-*

cle, 20 Oct. 1803; *Biog. Dir. Cong.*; Stets, *Postmasters*, 184; Vol. 29:403-4; Vol. 37:399n).

On 23 Oct., Francis Bailey, a former Pennsylvania newspaper editor and state printer, wrote Madison recommending Philip Freneau for the position. He noted: "I know of no man in the United-States, who would fill that office, with more ability, or greater integrity" (RC in DNA: RG 59, LAR, endorsed by TJ: "Freneau Philip to be P.M. N. York"; Madison, *Papers, Sec. of State Ser.*, 5:570; Brigham, *American Newspapers*, 2:1372).

From Jerome Bonaparte

George town 25 octobre. 1803.

Mr. Bonaparte aura l'honneur de diner avec le President des Etats-Unis demain 26. Octobre.

EDITORS' TRANSLATION

Georgetown, 25 Oct. 1803

Mr. Bonaparte will have the honor of dining with the president of the United States tomorrow, 26 Oct.

RC (DLC); addressed (torn): "[...]onsieur. Jefferson [. . .] Etats Unis. Washington."

Jerome Bonaparte (1784-1860), the youngest of Napoleon Bonaparte's brothers and sisters, was born on the island of Corsica. He was quite young when their father died, and as Jerome matured, Napoleon took over the management of his education. The elder brother was frustrated in his efforts to make Jerome apply himself to his studies. In 1800, Napoleon put him in the navy as a midshipman. Jerome's connections to the first consul brought him rapid promotion, and by the end of 1802, when he was barely 18 years old, he was a *lieutenant de vaisseau* with command of a brig. After his arrival in the United States in July 1803, he met Elizabeth Patterson of Baltimore, and they married in December of that year (see TJ to Robert R. Livingston, 4 Nov.). Napoleon refused to recognize the union and summoned his brother home to France. Jerome embarked from the United States in March 1805. Against his brother's wishes he took Elizabeth with him, but when they arrived at Lisbon, Napoleon's orders prohibited her from going ashore with Jerome or landing in any port controlled by the French. She went to England, where she gave birth to a son in July 1805. Unable to reunite with her husband, she returned to the United States. An ecclesiastical court in France nullified the marriage. Napoleon made the now-compliant Jerome an imperial prince, gave him the rank of rear admiral, and named him to the *Légion d'honneur*. In 1807, Jerome became king of Westphalia and married Catherine, daughter of the elector of Württemberg (Tulard, *Dictionnaire Napoléon*, 969-71; Glenn J. Lamar, *Jérôme Bonaparte: The War Years, 1800-1815* [Westport, Conn., 2000], 2-20; ANB, "Elizabeth Patterson Bonaparte"; Edouard Dentu, ed., *Mémoires et correspondance du roi Jérôme et de la reine Catherine*, 7 vols. [Paris, 1861-66], 1:293-8).

L'HONNEUR DE DINER AVEC LE PRESIDENT: Louis André Pichon had urged young Bonaparte to make a visit to Washington to call on the president. The young man arrived from Baltimore with Joshua Barney on 23 Oct. The next day, the chargé d'affaires presented him to TJ, who invited them to return for dinner on the afternoon of the 26th. Pichon also introduced Bonaparte to the heads of departments (the "secrétaires d'État") then in the capital—probably Madison, Gallatin,

Dearborn, and perhaps Lincoln. On the 26th, Pichon brought along two officers from a French frigate that was in the harbor at Baltimore. Bonaparte left Washington to return to Baltimore following the dinner. Pichon reported to his government that "le citoyen Bonaparte" conducted himself well on the visits to the President's House (same, 140, 232, 239-41).

From B. Delaferre

SIR Newrochelle N.y: october 25th 1803

If I was to address any other person of Your Excelencys exalted situation and charactur I should be at a loss for an appology for the liberty of this intrusion but my perfect Knoledge of your philantropy and benevolent disposition make me certain of finding a rady excuse in your heart when I mention that I am unfortuate & Sick for redress from the comun father the wretched before I come to the objet of my request I must trespass on Your Excellency's patience that you may Judge of the propriety of granting or refusing it

I am Sir one of the french officiers who under General Rochambeau had the honor to serve the american Cause my part in the Ever memorable and Glorious Campaign of 1781 was not a passive one and a sever wound which I recived at the siege of york has for Ever incapaciated for any laborious Exercise, soon after the peace prefering the blessing of an Enlightened liberty to the allurements & flatering prospect of court favour I left my native land and become a Citizen of thos states and remained Ever since in america wher I injoyed for many years the blessing of a large fortune and the Estim and respect of my fellow Cityzens but helas! a series of misfortunes (which I am sorry but candid Enough to confess ware the fruit of my own folly and misconduct) have striped me of all and left me penny and freind less in a word no wrechedness can surpass mine! nex to my wish of Been usefull to my self, to My adopted country, and to society my most ardent desir is to remouve from the stage of my folly and humiliation to a spote where I may hope to concel the Estem of the respectable part of society By application to my duty and the propriety of my conduct. after that candid confession I hope your Excelency will forgive me if I Bessige you to Employ me in some capacity in one of the offices to be fellet in the new settlement of Louisiana; I flater my self that the Knoledge of the french and English languages my Education and my former habit of life will Enable me to be usefull and to Give satisfaction and Your Excelency may Depend on the Exactitude and fidility of a person on whom you should have confered such a favour

I am with the greatest respect Sir Your Excellency's Most humble & obedient Servant
B. DELAFERRE

RC (DNA: RG 59, LAR); addressed: "His Excellency Thomas Jefferson Esq. President of the united States Federal City"; franked; postmarked 26 Oct.; endorsed by TJ as received 29 Oct. and "emploimt. Louisiana" and so recorded in SJL, but at 30 Oct.

In November 1804, B. Delaferre advertised the opening of his school in New York City for instruction in the French language and also offered his services as a French and English translator (New York *Daily Advertiser*, 8 Nov. 1804).

To Jonathan Faw

SIR
Washington Oct. 25. 03.

The case, which is the subject of the letter you handed me yesterday, s[eems] so perfectly understood by yourself, what the law is, & what the remedy, and that that remedy, the Habeas corpus, is always within your own reach, that no information respecting it seems necessary from me, or to be required. indeed it appears altogether a family misunderstanding, in which the exercise of paternal & legal authorities have perhaps been improperly blended, & that the submission on your part is voluntary and respectful. it is impossible for a stranger to judge between parties whose relations & whose feelings constitute the whole difficulty of the case. and altho' I should certainly interpose in any case of illegal & involuntary confinement communicated to me, yet it would not be till a Habeas corpus had been refused, or an inability to apply for it made known to me. in the present case I suppose neither of these alternatives to exist, and I persuade myself that the parties will find in their affections a remedy & reconciliation. Accept my wishes that this may soon take place.

TH: JEFFERSON

PrC (DLC); frayed at margin; at foot of text: "Mr. Jona. Faw."

THE LETTER: Faw to TJ, 22 Oct. 1803.

From James Gamble

SIR
Philadelphia Octr. 25th. 1803

In taking the liberty of transmitting a private letter to the President of the United States, I wished that I had nothing of my personal interest to mention, and that it were dictated only to discharge the duty of my private homage to the best friend to our Country, This we all cherish by native inclination and to the other, every one of us must at last feel much indebted, with confidence however I thought I might humbly request from your Excellency, the favour of being considered as a Candidate for the office of Surveyor or Naval Officer of the Port of Philadelphia, My long residence in this port, a long Experiance in Navigation, and my numerous Mercantile Connections, together with the approbation of my fellow Citizens in all our political Contests, all these Circumstances have Suggested to me that your favour of such appointment would not perhaps be much imbittered for me by the stings of envy, Those Offices, I know were long ago filled up, nor do I presume to Suggest Changes, or wish for any beyound What can be in the eventual rotation of the Public servants or accidental events in life, and what is thought proper by the Wisdom of the Executive. but in Justice to myself and to my family it is perhaps a duty to Aspire to distant or future advantages, as much as I was happy in the discharge of the duties of a good Citizen. Still happier do I feel at present, in having the Oppertunity of Subscribing my w[ish] and my prayer for the prolongation of your life and the Glory of your Administration, with

Profound respect I am your Excellency's Most Obt. Servt

James Gamble

RC (DNA: RG 59, LAR); frayed at margin; at head of text: "Thomas Jefferson Esqr. Prest. of the U. States"; endorsement partially torn away but recorded in SJL as received 29 Oct. and "to be Survr. or Navl. Off. Phila."

James Gamble (d. 1813), a Philadelphia merchant at 200 Spruce Street, began his career as a ship captain. On 20 Nov. 1800, Gamble was elected chairman and William Duane secretary of a Republican meeting at the state house, where resolutions were passed advocating a joint rather than concurrent vote in the general assembly to give the Republican-dominated house power to select the state's 15 presidential electors. In 1801, Gamble won election to the Pennsylvania House of Representatives and in 1802 to the senate. In the growing Republican factionalism in Philadelphia, Gamble alienated Duane and Michael Leib, the radical or Democratic Republicans, and sided with Thomas McKean and Alexander J. Dallas, the more conservative Constitutional Republicans or Quids. As a state senator in 1805, he voted against the Republican-led impeachment and trial of the Pennsylvania Supreme Court justices. When McKean appointed Gamble an auctioneer for the city of Philadelphia later in the year, Duane charged it was because he "voted for the acquittal of the judges." Gamble's business partners included Caspar Rehn, an active Republican, and John McIlhenney. McKean appointed Gamble to a vacancy on the Board of Health in 1808 (Philadelphia *Aurora*, 19, 22 Nov. 1800, 1 Oct. 1804, 9, 16 Nov. 1805; *Philadelphia Gazette & Daily Advertiser*, 14 Oct. 1801, 16 Nov. 1802; *Poulson's American Daily Advertiser*, 15 Oct. 1801, 21 Aug., 18 Sep. 1805, 20 Sep. 1813, 27 Apr. 1814; *Philadelphia Evening Post*, 19 May 1804; Philadelphia *United States Gazette*, 18 Sep. 1805, 26 Aug. 1807; James Robinson, *The Philadelphia Directory for 1806* [Philadelphia, n.d.], s.v. "Gamble, James," "Gamble and Rehn," "Gamble and M'Ilhenney"; Andrew Shankman, *Crucible of American Democracy: The Struggle to Fuse Egalitarianism & Capitalism in Jeffersonian Pennsylvania* [Lawrence, Kan., 2004],

96-103, 131-5; Sanford W. Higginbotham, *The Keystone in the Democratic Arch: Pennsylvania Politics 1800–1816* [Harrisburg, 1952], 77-105; Harry Marlin Tinkcom, *The Republicans and Federalists in Pennsylvania 1790-1801: A Study in National Stimulus and Local Response* [Harrisburg, 1950], 250; Vol. 32:307-10).

For an earlier recommendation in favor of Gamble as naval officer at Philadelphia, see Vol. 35:57n.

From Philip Mazzei

[25 Oct. 1803]

La ragione per cui preferisco le barbatelle che si attaccheranno tutte, e presto Ma siccome l'uva seralamanna, pessima per farne vino, è la meglio per mangiarsi in natura che io abbia gustato [?] in qualsiasi parte del mondo [...] per Asia Minore, Le ne ò destinate 6 piante che ànno già[...] onde spero che le mangierà a Monticello nel prossimo 7bre.

Quando Le parlai della situazion di cose in questo paese, non mi pareva che si potesse peggiorare. Il tempo mi à dimostrato il contrario, e me lo dimostra ogni giorno più. Il Lusso reale cresce, mentre e imposizioni sono eccedenti e la maggior parte dei tassabili non può [...] a pagarle. Si vendono le future rendite dello Stato e i capitali, e non si perviene a poter supplire che le spese giornaliere. La gente che ne soffre è numerosissima. La sola Teocrazia gode e trionfa. Si aspetta in [...] il ristabilimento [...]. Chi rendesse conto in dettaglio di tutto ciò che s'[...] in ogni ramo d'amministrazione, rischierebbe di passar per uno esageratissimo maldicente.

Ella sentirà tanto dalla Francia che dall'Inghilterra, un'infinità d'istorielle relativamente alle disposizioni della Russia. Io fui pregato d'insinuare ciò che può tendere a far diffidare del gabbinetto inglese per favorire la parte opposta. Quel che risposi le potrà servire per darle un'idea del vero, e distruggere la faragine di novellette che si propagano, per ignoranza o per ingannare. Le ne trascrivo.

"Certo è che le precauzioni contro quel sempre inquieto politico – mercantile gabbinetto non possono essere mai troppe. Ma bisognerebbe essere ben ciechi per gettersi dall'altra parte. La condotta di quel despota non può inspirare la minima confidenza a chi non à perduto affatto l'odorato. Si conoscono bastantemente in Russia le vedute dei 2 rivali, che si disputano se non la privativa, almeno il primato, nella nobile professione di Cartuccio. L'imperatore Alessandro brama ardentemente la pace, tanto per principj d'umanità, che per il bene de' suoi sudditi. La sua intervenzione per impedire che si diano sulle corna tra loro procede principalmente dal vedere l'impossibilità, che gli altri ancora non risentano, chi più chi meno, le ripercussioni del terremoto. Io credo dunque, che si farà tutto per non entrare in ballo; e che, se le circostanza l'obbligheranno a tirar la spada, si volterà la punta contro quello, che si dimostrerà più ostinato in voler la guerra. Non è più il tempo della della cabala degl'intrighi, e della corruttela. Quelle armi, altre volte potentissime, non ànno adesso più forza d'un fil di paglia."

Termino con pregarla di ricordarsi, che non ò ricevuto direttamente le sue nuove dopo la sua dei 17 marzo 1801, e di credere, che la sua prosperità, tanto per il bene dei presenti e futuri miei concittadini, che individualmente per Lei, è uno dei più fervidi voti del mio cuore.

Dev.mo e Aff.mo Servo e Amico, F. M.

EDITORS' TRANSLATION

[25 Oct. 1803]

The reason why I prefer the vine shoots that will all successfully grow and soon.

However, since the seralamanna grape, really bad for making wine, is the best table grape available in nature, the best I have ever tasted in any part of the world, [...] through Asia Minor, I have set aside 6 plants to be sent to you, and I hope that [...] next September.

When I spoke to you about the state of affairs in this country, I thought it could not get worse. What happened next proved me wrong, and keeps proving me wrong more and more every day. The royal luxury grows, while taxes are excessive, and the greatest part of those subject to them cannot pay. The future income and the capital of the state are being sold, and yet we manage only to cover the daily expenses. The people who are affected are really many. Only theocracy rejoices and triumphs. People expect [...] the return [...]. Anyone giving a detailed account of what happens in every branch of the administration would be taken for an exaggerating slanderer.

You may be hearing both from France and England an endless strain of fantasies regarding the intentions of Russia. I have been asked to insinuate what may help create distrust in the English cabinet and favor the opposite side. What I answered may help you get a sense of how things stand and dispel the great number of stories that are being circulated, either on account of ignorance or in order to deceive. Here is a passage:

"It is certain that one cannot be too careful when it comes to that ever-restless political and mercantile cabinet. But one would be really blind to side with the opposite front. The behavior of that despot cannot inspire any kind of confidence in anyone who has not lost all his sense of smell. In Russia, the points of view of both contenders are sufficiently well known: they are fighting over the primacy in, if not the exclusive control of, the noble profession of Cartuccio. Emperor Alexander craves peace, both because of his humane principles and for the sake of his subjects. His intervention to stop them from clashing horns with one another stems essentially from his knowledge that everyone else will suffer from the aftershocks of the earthquake though in different degrees. I believe, thus, one will try as much as possible not to be involved, and that, if he will be forced by circumstances to draw his sword, he will point its tip toward the one who will prove himself more obstinate in wanting the war. The time for schemes, intrigues, and corruption has passed now. Those weapons, most powerful in other circumstances, have now the strength of a straw."

I stop here, asking that you please bear in mind that no news about you has reached me directly since your letter of March 17 1801. Be assured that one of the most fervent wishes in my heart is always your prosperity, both for the sake of my current and future fellow citizens and for you individually.

Your most devoted and affectionate servant and friend, F. M.

Dft (Archivio Filippo Mazzei, Pisa, Italy); part of a conjoined series of Mazzei's drafts of letters to TJ, where it precedes Mazzei's letter of 28 Dec. 1803 (see Margherita Marchione and Barbara B. Oberg, eds., *Philip Mazzei: The Comprehensive Microform Edition of his Papers*, 9 reels [Millwood, N.Y., 1981], 5:425); several illegible words. RC recorded in SJL as received from Pisa on 13 Apr. 1804, but not found.

TJ grew six plants and eleven cuttings from the SERALAMANNA grape or muscat of Alexandria in his northeast vineyard at Monticello according to a plan of 25 Mch. 1807, which he noted in his Weather Memorandum Book (Betts, *Garden Book*, 333; Peter J. Hatch, *The Fruits and Fruit Trees of Monticello* [Charlottesville, 1998], 135, 155).

QUEL DESPOTA: Napoleon Bonaparte.

CARTUCCIO: the Parisian-born Louis-Dominique Cartouche was a legendary leader of a band of robbers. The son of a wine merchant, he was reputedly stolen by gypsies as a child and gained notoriety for his skill and daring before being broken on the wheel in 1721 (Sir Paul Harvey and Janet E. Heseltine, eds., *The Oxford Companion to French Literature* [Oxford, 1969], 105).

TJ's letter of 17 MARZO 1801 did not reach Mazzei until 1 Apr. 1802 (Vol. 33:328-9).

To John Randolph

Oct. 25. 03.

Th: Jefferson being informed of the question which occupied the H. of R. yesterday, and of the argument founded on the English expression 'engages to cede.' altho' he knows it has been decided, yet for mr Randolph's satisfaction incloses him the following extracts from the French originals on the paper herein sent. the 2d. treaty, which was in all our newspapers, tho' never authentically published, shews they considered the 1st. as an actual conveyance, that no other was ever contemplated, & that nothing more remained to be done but to *redeliver* the country, for which the king signed an order, which is in possession of the French Chargé here, and will be forwarded by our messenger as soon as we are authorised to recieve the possession. affectionate & respectful salutations.

PrC (DLC); at foot of text: "Jno. Randolph."

The previous day, Connecticut congressman Roger Griswold argued that available information suggested merely a promise by Spain to CEDE Louisiana to France, thereby calling into question the existence of an actual cession. He proposed a resolution that the House of Representatives call on the president to present a copy of the Treaty of San Ildefonso, a copy of the deed of cession (if one existed), and any communications between the executive branch and the government of Spain that might indicate Spain's views on the retrocession. Randolph led opposition to the motion, asserting that the legitimacy of the transfer was indisputable. After accepting a couple of amendments that softened the resolution's language, the House narrowly rejected the motion, 59 to 57 (*Annals*, 13:385-420).

On 21 Mch. 1801, the French and Spanish signed the TREATY of Aranjuez, which guaranteed the ruling Bourbon family of Spain control over the kingdom of Tuscany, or Etruria, thereby fulfilling one of the conditions stipulated in the Treaty of San Ildefonso (THE 1ST) for the retrocession of Louisiana to France. A report from Robert R. Livingston, received in February 1803, cast some doubt about whether the duke of Parma and his son, who was to become king of Etruria, had renounced rule over Parma, also one of the conditions of the treaty. Subsequent reports indicated that France, which had seized control of Parma, might exchange it with Spain for Florida (Parry, *Consolidated Treaty Series*, 55:375-8; 56:45-7; Madison, *Papers, Sec. of State Ser.*, 4:110-11n, 115, 121, 204, 302, 311; Vol. 38:584, 588n).

ENCLOSURE

Memorandum on the Cession of Louisiana from Spain to France

The treaty of St. Ildefonso, dated Oct. 1. 1800. between Spain & France, Article 3d. is in these words, in French, the language in which it was written.

"Sa Majesté catholique promet et s'engage de son coté a *retroceder* a la republique Française, six mois aprés l'execution pleine et entiere, les conditions et stipulations cy-dessus, relatives a son Altesse Royale le Duc de Parme, la Colonie ou province de la Louisiane, avec la meme etendue qu'elle a actuellement entre les mains de l'Espagne, et qu'elle avait lorsque la France la possedoit, et telle qu'elle doit etre d'aprés les traités passés subsequemment entre l'Espagne et d'autres etats."

The word *ceder* in French means to convey[1] to abandon, to deliver &c. the above is an engagement to *redeliver* Louisiana to France within 6. months after France shall have performed certain conditions. what those were, the world knows not, because nothing of that treaty was ever communicated but the preceding sentence. certainly neither power ever contemplated any other written instrument as necessary to convey the title to France, or any thing more than an act of redelivery. In a treaty executed 6. months after, towit, Mar. 1. 1801. at Madrid which has appeared in all our newspapers[2] they shew that they consider the former one as having conveyed the title or right to France: for the 5th. article is in these words: "Ce traité etant en consequence de celui deja conclu entre le premier Consul et sa majesté Catholique par lequel le roi *cede* à la France la possession de la Louisiane, les parties contractantes conviennent d'effectuer le dit traité, et de s'arranger a l'egard de leurs droits respectifs."

this 2d. treaty was only a modification of the conditions of the 1st. which were to flow from France. it was not an actual execution of a conveyance promised in the 1st. but an express affirmation that the 1st. *had conveyed* Louisiana to France, and that the new modifications of the 2d. were satisfactory to Spain, & that they were "conviennent d'effectuer le dit traité" to carry the treaty into effect. from that moment Spain was ready to *redeliver* to France, whenever the latter should be ready to recieve: and the king has actually signed the order for delivery, which is now in the hands of mr Pichon here, and will be carried by our express. Oct. 25. 03.

PrC (DLC: TJ Papers, 136:23450); entirely in TJ's hand.

ARTICLE 3D: that is, "His Catholic Majesty promises and undertakes on his part to retrocede to the Republic of France, six months after the full and entire execution of the conditions and stipulations relative to His Royal Highness the Duke of Parma, the colony or province of Louisiana with the same extent that it has in the hands of Spain, and that it had when France possessed it, and such that it must have after treaties subsequently passed between Spain and other states."

A translation of the Treaty of Aranjuez was printed in many NEWSPAPERS, with the article TJ singled out reading "As this treaty derives its origin from that which has been concluded by the First Consul with his Catholic Majesty, by which the King cedes to France the possession of Louisiana, the contracting parties agree to execute the articles of the anterior treaty; and to employ their respective power in the adjustment of the differences therein mentioned." The text TJ used for the article was identical to that found in a version that the administration received from Rufus King in February 1802. The official French text of the treaty differed somewhat and also made the section in question the sixth, not the fifth, article (Rufus King to James Madison, 20 Nov. 1801, and enclosure, DNA: RG 59, DD; *National Intelligencer*, 24 Mch. 1802; Baltimore *Republican; or, Anti-Democrat*, 29 Mch. 1802; New York *American Citizen*, 30 Mch. 1802; Parry, *Consolidated Treaty Series*, 56:47; Madison, *Papers, Sec. of State Ser.*, 2:254-5).

[1] Preceding two words interlined.

[2] Preceding seven words interlined.

From John Randolph

Tuesday 25 Oct. 1803.

John Randolph junr. thanks mr Jefferson for his communication—for which, however, he expects there will be no immediate occasion. The *constitutionality* is the theme of opposition. J.R. reciprocates mr J's sentiments of esteem & regard.

RC (DLC); endorsed by TJ as received 25 Oct. and so recorded in SJL.

From William Short

Prestwould—Oct. 25. [1803]

Jeffn.—as to Catlett—& my land to be rented &c.—& to write to me at Richd. if not too inconvenient—if not dissuaded by him shall rent—as to the report of Strobels failure

FC (DLC: Short Papers); partially dated; entirely in Short's hand, consisting of an entry in his epistolary record. Recorded in SJL as received from "Prestwood" on 5 Nov.

On his return from Kentucky, Short stopped off at PRESTWOULD, the estate in Mecklenburg County, Virginia, owned by his uncle Peyton Skipwith (George Green Shackelford, *Jefferson's Adoptive Son: The Life of William Short, 1759-1848* [Lexington, Ky., 1993], 140-1).

From Fulwar Skipwith

Dear Sir Paris 25th. Octor. 1803

For some time past, I have been waiting to obtain from Havre & Rouen, a note of the expences paid by Mr. Mitchell & Mr. White on the ten hampers of Wine shipped from Havre for your account, in order to furnish you with a general account of their cost & charges, which are as follows

		fs. C.	fs.
for	400 Bottles non-mosseux Wine	a 3.75[1]	1500.—.
	101 do Chambertin do.	3.25[2]	353.50.
	Expences paid by Mr. White at Rouen for transportation of 8 hampers Wine from Epernay		136.50.
	Paid by Mr. Mitchell at Havre for portage of 2 Hampers from Paris & on shipping the ten Hampers.		104.50
		francs	2,094.50
	Balance due Mr. Jefferson		5.50
			2,100.—

The bills of Loading for the above mentioned Wine Mr. Mitchell has forwarded, for the two hampers of Chambertin, to the Collector at Norfolk, and for the Champagne, to the Collector at Philadelphia. The Champagne non-mosseux I think will please you

With every sentiment of attatchment & respect, I have the honor to remain, Dear Sir, Your Mo Ob Servant Fulwar Skipwith

RC (DLC); with two emendations by TJ (see notes below); at foot of text: "Mr. Jefferson"; endorsed by TJ as received 3 Feb. 1804 and so recorded in SJL.

[1] TJ here entered "(60$\frac{3}{4}$."

[2] TJ here entered "(.59$\frac{1}{2}$."

From William Jarvis

SIR Lisbon 26th Octr. 1803

I had the honor to address you the 27th. Septr. by the Bark Elisabeth, Captn Larson via New York. The two pipes wine therein mentioned goes by the ship Edward, Captn Craig & are cased. Agreeable to your instructions I have address'd them to the Collector of Philada or N York, the vessel being bound to the former port, but if the delaware is frozen, will put into & unload in the latter. Had the Wine more age I think Sir it would please you; at least it has the merit of being pure & of a good Vintage; but should it be found not full enough, probably mixing some out of the two hogsheads, would improve it in this respect. The two pipes cost on board one hundred & seventy Milrus; but the two hogsheads Sir I never meant to draw for, and which I must beg you will oblige me so far, as to do me the honor to accept. The pipe mark'd KAR with chalk on the head, was made on an estate called Carrasqueira, the other mark AR on one called Arruda.

With the most profound Veneration I am Sir Your Most obedient & most devoted Servt. WILLIAM JARVIS

RC (DLC); at foot of text: "Thomas Jefferson Esquire"; endorsed by TJ as received 29 Dec. and so recorded in SJL.

To John Barnes

Oct. 27. 03.

Th: Jefferson asks the favor of mr Barnes to have the inclosed paid to mr Gelston. he will thank him also for 20. D. in 5 dollar bills.

RC (MHi); endorsed by Barnes. Not recorded in SJL. Enclosure: see enclosure printed at David Gelston to TJ, 22 Oct. 1803.

In his financial memoranda at 27 Oct. 1803, TJ recorded his request that Barnes pay David GELSTON $55.62 "for freight & duty of 300. bottles of wine from Bordeaux" (MB, 2:1111).

From John Barnes

SIR Geo: Town 27 Oct 1803

I have sent to the B. at W. for the Cashiers draft in favr. of D. Gelston Esqr: on B. B. NYork for $55.62 and shall write him of the Wines safe arrival—the depy: Collector of Alexa also advises of their being forwarded to Washingn. have wrote him for his a/c of expences,

by Mr Dougherty you will $25 in 5 dolr notes,
I am most Respectfully Sir Your Obed H St

JOHN BARNES

RC (MHi); at foot of text: "The President U States."

TJ's financial memoranda records the receipt of $20 from Barnes on 27 Oct. (MB, 2:1111).

B. AT W.: Bank at Washington.

B. B.: Branch Bank at New York.

From David Campbell

Campbella State of Tennessee
Octr 27th. 1803

DEAR SIR,

The acquisition of Louisiana will be of great and lasting importance to the United States. In its magnitude it approaches to a second Declaration of Independance. We may now form, on the surest foundations, a general System of politics, on principles and rules, which the circumstances of different conjunctures may appropriate to the eternal advantage of the Western Country, and consequently of the United States in general.

I might descend into a much greater detail; but I shall limit myself, only, to a few particulars. But before I proceed, permit me to express my gratitude to Heaven, for permiting me to see, under your wise Administration, the most perfect theory in politics, reduced to genuine practice. By you, Sir, excesses have been asswaged, abuses and misapplications, in some degree, diverted or checked; and like a skilful pilot, though you could not lay the storm for a while, yet you have carried the Ship of the Commonwealth, by your art, better through it, and prevented the wreck that would have happened, without your wise and prudent Administration. You have secured to us the free navigation of the Mississipi. You have procured an immense and fertile Country: And all these great blessings are obtained without war or bloodshed.

Your Ideas of exchanging Countries with our Indian neighbors, will be both pleasing and benificial to the Citizens of the Western Country: but there will be som delay, and no little difficulty in effecting the thing.

There are a great many white persons of flimsy characters settled in the Cherokee Country; they live an idle life, supported principally by the females, whom they marry, and who are much more industrious than the men. Many of them are settled on farms; begin to raise

Cotton, and manufactor it in their own Country. They have also small stocks of Cattle, horses, and hogs. They have plenty of cane to support their stock in Winter. The climate is very mild, seldom covered with snow. Thus are they enabled to live with ease, and thus are many of them attached to their beautiful & fertile Country. There are, however many of the young fellows who prefer hunting, and a wandering life. A certain John Taylor, a half breed, who was educated at William & Mary College in the State of Virginia, an aspiring fellow, has emigrated to some part of white River in the Mississipi Country, and has formed a settlement. I do not know the number that accompanied Taylor: but there are several families. With proper management, I think in time, the whole nation may be induced to follow Taylor. But who is the man capable to perform this great work? The knowledge of naked facts, without being able to penetrate into the causes that will produce them, and the circumstances that may accompany them, will not be sufficient to characterise the actions or counsels of the negociator. He must be careful in developing the secret motives of the actions of this subtile people, and not to lay the causes of events too deep, or deduce them through a series of progression too complicated and too artistly wrought. I mean, the same kind of knowledge, that would make an able negociator in a civilized and polite nation, will not succeed with uncivilized nations. The man you employ ought to be somewhat acquainted with the manners of the people. My neighbourhood with the Indians for several years, has furnished me with this knowledge. I am willing to undertake the business, if you think proper to appoint me. Col. John McKee is well quallified also. I write to you without reserve, I have known you long and esteem you as the father of my Country. Farewell. DAVID CAMPBELL

RC (DLC); addressed: "His Excellency Thomas Jefferson President of the United States City of Washington"; endorsed by TJ as received 14 Nov. and so recorded in SJL.

Bands of Cherokees began to settle west of the Mississippi by 1796. Some groups, such as the 150 individuals led by JOHN TAYLOR in 1797, took up residence on the St. Francis River. Others established themselves on the WHITE RIVER. Although the commandant at New Madrid gave permission to settle, in 1798 the then-governor of Louisiana, Manuel Gayoso de Lemos, ordered the Cherokees to leave the province and return to United States territory. Some complied, but Cherokees still lived in the Arkansas region in the first years of the 19th century (Robert A. Myers, "Cherokee Pioneers in Arkansas: The St. Francis Years, 1785-1813," *Arkansas Historical Quarterly*, 56 [1997], 127-57; *Terr. Papers*, 13:228-9; S. Charles Bolton, "Jeffersonian Indian Removal and the Emergence of Arkansas Territory," in Patrick G. Williams, S. Charles Bolton, and Jeannie M. Whayne, eds., *A Whole Country in Commotion: The Louisiana Purchase and the American Southwest* [Fayetteville, Ark., 2005], 85).

JOHN MCKEE had served at various times as a commissioner in negotiations and as an agent with the Cherokees, the Chickasaws, and the Choctaws (ANB).

From Elbridge Gerry

Dear Sir, Cambridge 27th Octr 1803

The message, which You did me the honor to transmit, I have read with great pleasure. it exhibits to my mind, respectful, friendly, firm, & vigilant conduct towards foreign powers—acquisitions of territory, by purchase & cession, inestimable, as they respect the wealth, security, & happiness of our western sister states, the fiscal resources of the nation, and the excision of a fertile source of foreign & domestic wars & discord—great wisdom, & œconomy on the management of our finances—pleasing prospects of the extinguishment of the national debt—easy, judicious, & unexpected arrangements, for paying, without additional taxes, the Louisiana purchase—just, generous, & politic propositions, for attaching to us the inhabitants of that territory—effectual measures for preventing foreign territorial disputes—& in general, pacific, salutary & profound principles of policy, for the promotion of national peace, power, & prosperity.

This is, in a disinterested veiw of the subject, a just tribute; free from those servile practices, which are equally disgraceful to the addresser, & addressed.

Three of the eastern states are still anterepublican; they had great merit in establishing their independence, but owe the preservation of it to the southern states.

Pursue Sir your just system of politics, it must be sanctioned by the Sovereign of the Universe, and infallibly raise the US to the acmè of national wealth, security, & honor. this is my candid opinion, & with few exceptions, I beleive the opinion of the impartial part of the community.

Congress, I hope, will make effectual provision for preventing those elective contentions, which had nearly involved us in a civil conflict.

I have the honor to remain, dear Sir, with unfeigned esteem & respect, yours sincerely E Gerry

RC (DLC); at foot of text: "His Excellency President Jefferson"; endorsed by TJ as received 6 Nov.

three of the eastern states: Connecticut, Massachusetts, and New Hampshire (*Biog. Dir. Cong.*; Vol. 40:366, 405-7, 414-15).

From Thomas Mann Randolph

SIR, October 27, 1803.

Mr Rawlings who hands you this having a desire to render service to the U.S. upon the Mississippi in some civil capacity has applied to me among others to certify to the proper authority what we know of his fitness and pretentions to be so employed. So long an interval has happened in my acquaintance & intercourse with Mr Rawlings that it is not proper for me to pronounce as decisively with respect to him as I should incline, to do where I consented to speak at all. Indeed the youth of Mr. R. when I was in the way of intercourse with him would forbid my vouching in any positive way; as by the distance of his residence from mine since, I have not ever heard very frequently of him. I can say however that he has very respectable connexions in Virginia, and that they are not only anxious for his advancement from personal attachment to himself but that they feel an honest conviction of his fitness from morals, understanding and habits, for some civil employment of confidence and exertion under the U.S.

With the highest respect. TH: M. RANDOLPH

[...] Representative of Virginia

RC (DNA: RG 59, LAR); torn; at foot of text: "The President of the U.S."; endorsed by TJ as received 15 Nov. and "Rawlins. appmt Louisiana" and so recorded in SJL. Enclosed in Benjamin Rawlings to TJ, 14 Nov.

From John Shee

[before 28 Oct. 1803]

This copy of a memorial to the Senate of the Union, is, with the utmost respect laid before the President of the United States.

RC (DLC); undated, unsigned; written on verso of final page of first enclosure; endorsed by TJ as received from John Shee on 28 Oct. 1803 and so recorded in SJL with notation "a memorial to Congress on the Kaskaskia purchase." Enclosures: (1) Copy of a Memorial and Petition of the Illinois and Wabash ("Ouabache") Land Company to the Senate, dated Philadelphia, 17 Oct. 1803, stating they have learned that their memorial presented at the last session of Congress had been dismissed by the Senate on the grounds that a decision regarding its merits had already been made; the memorialists are unaware of any such decision and again address Congress on the subject with even greater urgency upon learning that the United States has recently acquired a considerable tract of land from the Kaskaskia Indians; the memorialists have repeatedly informed Congress that they made a similar purchase many years ago not only from the Kaskaskias, but also from the Illinois and other Indian tribes possessing lands on and near the Wabash River; should the land purchase recently undertaken by the United States interfere with the previous purchases by the memorialists, "they must ascribe it to a benevolent and liberal policy extended towards an indigent and helpless Race, rather than to any doubts entertained of the aforementioned Indians having alienated the therein described property; or of the validity of the title of your memorialists"; the memorialists are still willing to cede their land to the United States under the terms of an earlier proposal, which the House of Representatives recommended accepting since it deemed the memorialists' title to the land valid; therefore the memorialists pray the Senate will reconsider their petition from the last session of Congress (Tr in same; signed "John Shee; sole survivor of the Committee appointed and authorised to solicit and negociate the affairs of the Company with Congress"). (2) Copy of a Memorial and Petition of the Illinois and Wabash Land Company to the House of Representatives, dated Philadelphia, 17 Oct. 1803, similar in wording and content to the memorial and petition sent to the Senate, and likewise asking that the House of Representatives reconsider the memorial and accompanying papers presented at the last session of Congress (Tr in same; signed "John Shee, sole survivor of the Committee appointed and Authorised to Solicit and negociate the affairs of the Company with Congress").

John Shee (d. 1808) was born in Ireland and emigrated to America with his family in the 1740s. A veteran of the American Revolution and an influential Republican in Philadelphia, Shee was commandant of the Philadelphia Militia Legion and a major general in the state militia. TJ appointed him collector of Philadelphia in 1807 (PMHB, 49 [1925], 184-6; JEP, 2:56; Vol. 33:246n; Vol. 37:6n).

Shee's MEMORIAL was the most recent attempt by the Illinois and Wabash Land Company to secure legal ownership of western lands it claimed to have acquired from various Indian nations in 1773 and 1775. These efforts, which commenced in the late 1770s, had recently taken on greater urgency since much of the land in question had just been acquired by the United States through treaties with the Kaskaskias and other western Indians. The Senate and House of Representatives received Shee's memorials on 27 Oct. The Senate took no action, but on 14 Feb. 1804 a House committee reported that legal title to the land had not been established by the petitioners, and therefore their prayer should not be granted (Lindsay G. Robertson, *Conquest by Law: How the Discovery of America Dispossessed Indigenous Peoples of Their Lands* [New York, 2005], 3-27; JS, 3:303; JHR, 4:421, 465, 577; ASP, *Public Lands*, 1:27, 72-3, 74-5, 160-1, 189; TJ to the Senate, 31 Oct. 1803).

From William C. C. Claiborne

DEAR SIR, Natchez October 28th. 1803.

About 20 minutes since, I received a Letter from my friend Docter Sibley, enclosing me a Map of the Country West of the Mississippi, which I hasten to forward to you:—The Doctor's Letter contains much useful Information, & therefore I have taken the liberty to transmit it for your perusal & must beg you to receive it in confidence.—

The Northern Mail is now closing, and the Post-Master allows me but two Minutes to close my *Communication*, which I hope will be received as an apology for *its brevity*:—

Accept my best wishes.— I have the honor to subscribe myself Your faithful friend & mo: Obt. Servt.

WILLIAM C. C. CLAIBORNE

RC (DLC); at foot of text: "The President of the U. States"; endorsed by TJ as received 20 Nov. and so recorded in SJL; also endorsed by TJ: "Sibley's lre." Enclosures: (1) John Sibley to Claiborne, Natchitoches, 10 Oct., responding to Claiborne's letter of 30 Sep., Sibley expresses his exhilaration at the news of the coming cession of Louisiana and the possibility of West Florida's cession; even without Florida, the acquisition will secure free passage to the Tombigbee settlement, control of both banks of the Mississippi, and possession of Baton Rouge, "the Best Situation for a large Town between the Balize & Chickasaw Bluff"; he holds high hopes for Natchitoches, which has access to the "Great Road towards Mexico" and which could easily be connected by road to Natchez; he apologizes for not being able to obtain a map of the interior country, but he has learned the names of the rivers between the Mississippi and Rio Grande; west of the Red River is first the "*Quelqueshoe*" (Calcasieu), which is "not of much Account for its Navigation" but "affords some beautifull Bodies of Pararie Land" and some land for sugar cultivation and is under Louisiana's jurisdiction; next comes the Sabine, which appears navigable in high water, has much good land, particularly for livestock, and is said to have formed the ancient limit of Louisiana; next is the Angelina River, which flows by Nacogdoches and which, along with the Sabine, bounds an "Excessively Rich" area of land; then come the Trinity, Brazos, Colorado, San Antonio, Guadalupe, Nueces, and Rio Grande; from Nacogdoches to the settlement of San Antonio is a fine country, with only about 100 families at the former town and more than twice as many at the latter; there is also a small settlement of Christianized Indians along the San Antonio River, and throughout the area are "numerous tribes of Indians"; beyond the Rio Grande the country has many towns and mines, and high up the river is New Mexico, with Santa Fe sitting on the east side of the river amid mountains and towns; the head of the Red River is understood to be in Louisiana and in the same mountains as the Rio Grande; its length is unknown, but it is navigable 600 miles to the lands of the Pawnees and is said to be navigable for 1,000 miles more, flowing always through fine country; he acknowledges the article printed in the *City Gazette* of Charleston, which he attributes to Judge Elihu Hall Bay, with whom he is well acquainted; the judge has stated the limits of Louisiana and Florida correctly but has grossly mischaracterized the area along the Red River between its mouth and Natchitoches, and Sibley suspects that the judge has been trying to prop up his "famous Walnut Hill Tract" in the Natchez area; Sibley adds that the lands along the Red River already have about 25 cotton gins that produced 3,000 bales of cotton last year and an equal amount of tobacco and peltries, and an estimated 7,300 horses also passed through Natchitoches; he adds that the area between the Red and Calcasieu Rivers could support some 1,000 sugar plantations and produce more tobacco of a superior quality than is presently made in all of the United States; he describes the method of growing tobacco near Natchitoches; a leader of the Caddos has been visiting Natchitoches and has inquired about the prospects of American control of the region; Sibley has been circumspect but has assured him of Americans' good intentions and believes that though dwindling in numbers, the Caddos might make useful allies; there is talk of the Spanish reoccupying their presidio at Los Adaes, which, lying 40 miles east of the Sabine, is uncontestedly part of Louisiana, and Sibley urges that the Americans occupy this area before the Spanish; he describes the lands between the headwaters of the Calcasieu River and the Sabine River, as well as the land northwest of Natchitoches; he encloses a map he sketched out the previous evening; he discusses the prospects for shipbuilding on the Red River and the Great Raft, a logjam 30 miles above Natchitoches that forms a not insurmountable barrier between the lower and upper parts of the river; he thanks Claiborne for writing on his behalf to Daniel Clark and believes that he no longer faces any trouble from Trudeau, the commandant at Natchitoches; he does not hold a high opinion of the local residents' capacity for self-government or for conducting trials by jury; he advises the safekeeping of "Nearly a Cart Load of Old Records"; as to public property, he notes only the jail but adds that there exists a large church and a fine parsonage house (RC in same: TJ Papers, 135:23369-74; endorsed by TJ: "Sibley John to Govr. Claiborne." Printed in *Terr. Papers*, 9:72-8). (2) Map not found.

From Thomas Digges

SIR, Book store Capitol Hill 28. Octo [1803]

The Bearer is Mr Wm Byrne an ornamental stucco worker & Plasterer whose good Conduct, sobriety, and rectitude I think I can answer for, having known Him as a respectable Tradesman in Ireland as well as in the City. If you have not engagd one for Monticello, I make no doubt but He will ansr. your purpose and be full as reasonable in Charges, & perhaps moreso, than others of His trade hereabouts.

I am in some hopes Mr. Latrobe may employ him at the Capitol; But this will be a job after what you have in contemplation at Monticello

I am with very great esteem & attachment Sir yr obt Serv

THOS DIGGES

RC (MHi); partially dated; endorsed by TJ as received 2 Nov. and "by Wm. Byrne. plaisterer" and so recorded in SJL.

From Albert Gallatin

DEAR SIR Octr 28 1803

I have conversed with most of the Western members of Congress respecting the possibility of raising volunteers to assist the force already prepared for occupying New Orleans; I think that I have seen thirteen out of the seventeen who compose the delegation of the three western States; and I believe that they have all conferred on the subject. Not only do[1] they Appear to be strongly impressed with the importance of the subject; but some amongst them were more alarmed than I had expected, as it had been reported that the effective regular force at Fort Adams which may be spared did not exceed[2] 300 men. How that fact is I do not remember, but had believed that the regulars there would amount to double that number. The result of the conversation with those Gentlemen and which they requested might be communicated to you is; that, if the Executive shall think it necessary to call any militia or volunteers, in that part of the Country, it[3] may be confidently relied on that within a fortnight after the reception of the orders by the Executives of Tenessee & Kentuckey fifteen hundred horsemen, all of them volunteers & well selected shall be at Nashville, and then proceed immediately to Natchez which they may reach within 20 days afterwards[4] at most. About one third of that number might meet at Nashville a few days earlier & march across the wilderness[5] within a fortnight; the rest to follow in divisions of two or three hundred as they met from the more distant parts; which will also be more convenient on account of forage for the horses. Every man shall carry his own provisions across & will be completely accoutred and armed, unless, as there are muskets at Fort Adams, it should be thought more eligible to induce[6] a number of the volunteers not to take their rifles and to take muskets on their arrival. The idea of going by water must be abandoned so far as relates to an immediate expedition, because the water is too low and there are not on the spot any immediate means of transportation. All the Gentlemen agree that as to the number of men, considering that all the crops are in, the season the most favourable in point of health of the whole year, and the general Zeal of the country, five thousand men could be raised at once without any difficulty, and that the only struggle will be for having permission to go. The proportion agreed on is that Tenessee should send one third & Kentucky the other two thirds.

In order to judge of the benefits which may be derived from the adoption of the measure, it is necessary to compare dates, and this will show that they are less than if the measure had been adopted a fortnight ago.

Supposing that on Monday next 31 Octer. the mail should carry the order of the French Govt. to deliver the province to our officers, & your instructions to Gen. Wilkinson & Govr. Claiborne, they shall be received at Natchez on the 12th or 14th of November; and if all the arrangements have been made according to orders, the militia which may be spared in the Mississippi territory may be collected within a week at farthest & the whole regular & militia force there, depart for New Orleans on the 20th. This I presume may be considered as the greatest possible expedition

Supposing that the same mail should carry the requisition to the Governor of Tenessee, it will reach Knoxville on the 5th Nover. If he shall issue his orders on the 7th, they will reach Nashville about the 10th, and as the population of that district is pretty compact, (and the gentlemen here will write preparatory letters to the principal men there which by the mail will have reached Nashville the 7th or 8th) one half of the 500 men may be ready to set off the 12th or 14th & the other half the 17th. Supposing them also to cross the wilderness in a fortnight the whole body would reach Natchez from the 27th Nover to the 3d Decer. This may also be[7] considered as the greatest possible dispatch. As to the men from Kentucky, the mail takes 12 days to go there, & it cannot be expected that their volunteers Would be able to leave Nashville before 25th Nover. to 1st Decer. or to arrive at Natchez before 15th Decer.

It results from thence that no part of the Tenessee & Kentuckey volunteers can, on any possible supposition reach Natchez until ten or twelve days after the time when, if the orders to Govr. Claiborne go Monday next, the regular force & militia there shall have left it for New Orleans; and that the main body will arrive two weeks still later.

The advantages, therefore, to result from adopting the measure are confined to the following two points.

1st. Govr. Claiborne being informed at the same time that he shall receive his instructions of the expected reinforcement and of the time when they shall arrive, may, if he shall have been informed that the Spanish officers have refused to give possession to Laussat, wait until the first corps or the whole body (according to the degree of resistance which he may expect) shall have arrived. If Laussat shall have received possession, Govr. Claiborne may proceed immediately with his own force writing by mail a counter-order to such part of the militia as shall not have yet left Nashville.

2dly. He may, at all events, march a much greater part of the Mississippi territory militia, who will be relieved from any uneasiness respecting the Choctaws by the march of the volunteers from Tenessee & Kentuckey. Thus it is possible that the regular & militia of the territory would in his & Gen. Wilkison's opinion be sufficient to overcome the resistance of any existing Spanish force at New Orleans & that dispatch was essentially necessary for fear of any reinforcement from Havannah or other unforeseen causes. In that case, the knowledge of the march & expected arrival of the volunteers would enable him to draw the whole active militia of the territory & go on without losing an instant.

For these reasons, and also because I think that the expedition itself, which at a distance will certainly be magnified, will add to the opinion entertained abroad of our forces, resources & energy particularly as applicable to the future defence of the acquired country, and also to that which the newly acquired inhabitants ought to have of our Govt., I think that the measure, even at this late hour, is eligible. Be pleased to excuse the freedom with which I give an opinion & perhaps interfere on a question so foreign to my proper business. But to lose the object at this time, to fail in an attempt to take forcible possession, would in every point of view, be evils of such magnitude, that I cannot help feeling much anxiety for fear that in that event we should have to reproach ourselves with the omission of any practicable measure which might have prevented the misfortune. As to the expence it is but a trifle compared with the object. 2000 volunteers at one dollar a day for seventy days are 140,000 dollars.

It is understood that if 1,500 effective volunteers are wanted to arrive at Natchez the requisition should be for 2,250. vizt. 750 from Tenessee & 1500 from Kentuckey. As a measure which will cost nothing, will, in respect to Spain, add to their opinion of us, and may under certain circumstances be ultimately serviceable, to this force might be added ten thousand nominal men from the same States & Ohio, to be only enrolled or drafted & considered as ready to march whenever called upon. There has been something said of the want of gallies which would have been useful against those of Spain. Is not there one at Bayou Pierre?

Little reliance can be placed on the regular force at Massac, Kaskakia & Chickasaw bluff, unless they have already received orders to proceed. Otherwise, on account of the low water, they will arrive too late. Yet there would be no harm in pursuing by immediate orders their departure.

Respectfully Your obet. Servt. ALBERT GALLATIN

RC (DLC); addressed: "The President of the United States"; endorsed by TJ as received from the Treasury Department on 28 Oct. and "New Orleans" and so recorded in SJL.

Sixteen members made up the DELEGATION from the THREE WESTERN STATES, that is, Kentucky, Tennessee, and Ohio (see John Breckinridge to TJ, 10 Sep., and List of Members of the Eighth Congress, printed at 17 Oct).

EXECUTIVES OF TENESSEE & KENTUCKEY: that is, governors John Sevier and James Garrard, respectively (Notes on Preparations to Occupy Louisiana, printed at 30 Oct.).

[1] Word supplied by Editors.
[2] MS: "exceeded."
[3] Word interlined in place of "they."
[4] Word interlined.
[5] Preceding two words interlined.
[6] Word interlined in place of "suffer."
[7] Word supplied by Editors.

To Henry Dearborn

DEAR SIR Washington Oct. 22. [i.e. 29.] 03.

I am very much pleased to find that the Choctaws agree to sell us their country on the Missisipi, and think we ought to accept it to any extent they will agree to, only taking care the price be not too high. they are poor; and will probably sell beyond what will pay their debts, so as to be entitled to an annual pension, which is one of the best holds we can have on them. their strength & the weakness of our settlements adjacent to them, renders it prudent to take them into our friendship. after this purchase, nothing breaks the continuity of our possessions on the hither bank of the Missipi, from the mouth to the Illinois but the Chickasaw possessions.

I think Govr. Harrison's proposition to treat with the Poutewatimas, Sacs & Kickapoos is proper not only for settling the limits we are entitled to under the Kaskaskia purchase but for extending them up the Missisipi from the mouth of the Illinois. if the Iawas[1] whom he represents as so poor, hold lands on the hither bank perhaps they will sell. if from the others he could obtain all within a line uniting the N.W. angle of the Vincennes square with the N.E. angle of the Kaskaskia purchase, it would be well; or to make what advances he can towards it. I make no doubt you attend to what Govr. Harrison observes as to the high prices of goods, & refusal of credit, by Genl. Irving. both of these measures thwart our views in extending this trade.

I shall hope to see you at twelve tomorrow to decide with the other gentlemen definitively on our measures to be dispatched Westwardly the next day; and that we shall all dine together. Accept my affectionate salutations Th: Jefferson

P.S. if you have not seen mr Smith the Ohio Senator lately from N. Orleans, it will be well worth while for you to see him before our meeting as he gives very important information as to the force, the dispositions, and the topography of the country.

RC (PHi: Daniel Parker Papers); at foot of text: "The Secy. at War"; endorsed by Dearborn as received 28 Oct. PrC (DLC); date overwritten in ink by TJ to 29 Oct. Recorded in SJL at 29 Oct. with notation "Choctaw purchase."

For the land cession proposed by the CHOCTAWS, see Petition of Puckshunubbee and Others, 20 Sep. 1803.

William Henry HARRISON'S PROPOSITION has not been found, but was probably contained in letters he wrote to Dearborn from Vincennes dated 15 and 23 Aug. Dearborn acknowledged their receipt on 23 Sep. (DNA: RG 75, LSIA). Neither letter from Harrison has been found, but War Department registers note that both related to Indian treaties, with the 23 Aug. letter adding that "the indians continue to be constantly intoxicated" (DNA: RG 107, RLRMS). For Harrison's recent negotiations and treaties with Indians in the Indiana Territory, including the KASKASKIA PURCHASE, see Harrison to TJ, 29 Oct. 1803, and TJ to the Senate, 31 Oct. 1803.

GENL. IRVING: William Irvine, superintendent of military stores (Vol. 38:93n).

[1]MS: "Tawas." TJ probably misread Harrison's handwriting.

To Albert Gallatin

TH: JEFFERSON TO MR GALLATIN Sat. Oct. 29. 03.

I must ask the favor of you to meet the heads of departments here tomorrow at 12. aclock & afterwards to dine with us. the object is to decide definitively on the arrangements which are to be dispatched Westwardly the next day. Genl. Dearborne & myself[1] had concluded to submit to the meeting a plan little different from that suggested in your letter of yesterday. towit. to send orders to Claiborne & Wilkinson to march instantly 500. regulars (which are prepared) from Fort Adams, & 1000. militia from the Missipi territory (if the information from Laussat to them shall indicate refusal from Spain). to send hence on the same day a call on the Govr. of Tennissee for 2000. volunteers, & of Kentucky for 4000. to be officered, organised, accoutred & mustered on a day to be named, such as that Claiborne & Wilkinson might by that day send them information whether they would be wanted, & to march or do otherwise accordingly. I had since thought myself to propose that on recieving information that there would be resistance, they should send sufficient parties[2] of regulars & militia across the Missisipi to take by surprise New Madrid, Ste. Genevieve, St. Louis & all the other small posts: & that all this should be made as much as possible the act of France, by inducing Laussat with the aid of Clarke to raise an insurrectionary force of the inhabitants, to which ours might be only auxiliary. but all this with much more is to be considered tomorrow. affectionate salutations.

RC (NHi: Gallatin Papers); addressed: "The Secretary of the Treasury"; endorsed. PrC (DLC). Recorded in SJL with notation "arrangemts for possn. of Louisiana."

[1]Preceding word and ampersand interlined.

[2]TJ first wrote "a sufficient party" before altering the text to read as above.

From William Henry Harrison

DEAR SIR Vincennes 29th Octbr. 1803.

In the month of May last I received the letter you did me the honour to write by Mr. Parke and at that time I also received from the Department of State a renewal of my Commission as Governor of the Indiana Territory For this mark of your Confidence permit me to make you my most grateful acknowledgements—It has indeed ever been & shall Continue to be my Chief Aim to Conduct the Administration of this Government in such a manner as to merit your approbation.

I transmitted some time ago to the Secretary of War two Treaties & a Convention which were the results of my negotiations with the Indians—Nothing remains of your plan to be executed but the Settlement of our boundaries in the Illinois Country with the Sacs, Putawatemies & Kickapoos, I expected to have completed this the present fall but I have not yet received the necessary instructions for the purpose.

I wish I could inform you that the benevolent intentions of the Government in their indeavours to prevent the use of ardent spirits amongst the Indians had been successful—It is my opinion that more Whisky has been Consumed by the Indians & more fatal Consequences ensued from the use of it since the traders have been prohibitted from taking it into the Indian Country than there ever was before—To remedy the evil effectually the law ought to be so amended as to prevent any person whatever from selling ardent spirits to the Indians or even trading with them at all without a license—On this subject I have expressed my sentiments fully in my official letters to the Secretary of War—

The plan which has been adopted for the management of the salt springs below the Wabash & the prospect of their being enabled to procure salt at the reduced price of 50 Cents per bushel has diffused a general joy amongst the Citizens of this Territory & the neighbouring states of Kentucky & Tennasse—I have taken the liberty to enclose herewith a small sample of the salt from those springs, at one of which a furnace of 20 or 25 Kettles has been in operation for a twelvemonth past—the salt is I think superior to any that is made in the Western Country & you may rest assured that there is no want of water—I have not been able to ascertain the existence of any considerable quantity of Coal adjacent to the springs. there is a small shew of it in the bank of the Saline Creek between the lower spring & the Ohio & a larger quantity in the bed of the Ohio a few miles above the mouth of the Saline.

General Gibsons Commission as Secretary of this Territory will expire in May next & I presume that an appointment will be made during the present Session of Congress—Permit me to recommend him to you as an honest man & one who discharges the duties of his office to the best of his abilities—he is now far advanced in life & from the emoluments of his office himself & family derive their whole support

If the appointment of an other Commissioner to treat with the Indians should be necessary I beleive it would be very acceptable to Judge Davis—

I took the liberty last spring to send to you a small barrel of Peccans which I hope has been received—it was put into the hands of the

Public[1] Factor at Detroit with a request that he would send it to the Military Agent at Albany. We have in this Country an abundance of these Nuts, & I shall make use of every opportunity to send you some—but these very seldom occur—I have Collected a few Indian & natural[2] Curiosities designed also for your Cabinet—& the Lieut. Governor of Upper Louisiana was so obliging as to give me one of two bears that were brought from a great distance up the Missouri & is of a kind not hitherto described that I know of—this shall be sent with the other articles as soon as I get some one to take them—

The streets of the town of Jeffersonville are made to pass diagonally through the squares & not parrallel with them as I knew to be your intention—but the proprietor was so parsimonious that he would not suffer it to be laid out in that manner—

I am my Dr. Sir with the Sincerest attachment your Hum Servt.

WILLM H HARRISON

Enclosed herewith—a sample of salt from the springs below the Wabash, a sample of Rock salt from the Missouri—Also of plaister of Paris from the same River

RC (DLC); at foot of text: "Thomas Jefferson President of the United States"; endorsed by TJ as received 22 Nov. and so recorded in SJL.

LETTER YOU DID ME THE HONOUR TO WRITE BY MR PARKE: TJ to Harrison, 27 Feb. 1803.

TWO TREATIES & A CONVENTION: see TJ to the Senate, 31 Oct. 1803.

For the plan of the town of JEFFERSONVILLE, see Vol. 38:165-7; Vol. 39:589-90.

[1] Word interlined.

[2] Word and ampersand interlined.

From John Langdon

SR. Portsmouth Octobr. 29th. 1803

You'll please accept my Acknowledgements for the Message, and permit me in the most sincere manner to Congratulate you on the unparalled prosperity and Happiness of the United States, which surpasses any thing that has ever been seen or heard of, under any other government on earth. You Sr. can much better concieve then I can possably describe the feelings of all true friends to our Country on the glorious prospects before us.—

John Goddard Esq who is one of the Commissioners of Bankruptcy for this District informed me few day since, that he should resign his office; should this be the case, I would Ask leave to mention the Name of Richard Cutts Shannon Esq of this Town (who has been for many years in The practice of the Law), as a suitable person to take his place—

I have the hono'r to be very respectfully Sr. Your Oblig'd Hbl. Servt JOHN LANGDON

RC (DNA: RG 59, LAR); at foot of text: "President of the United States"; endorsed by TJ as received 11 Nov. and "Shannon, Richd Cutts, to be Commr. bkrptcy Portsmth. v. Goddard" and so recorded in SJL.

In a letter to the secretary of state on 3 Nov., JOHN GODDARD submitted his resignation as bankruptcy commissioner "with much Regret." He noted that "a concurrence of unforeseen events" made it difficult to attend to the duties of the office and requested that Madison inform the president of his decision (RC in DNA: RG 59, LAR; endorsed by TJ: "Goddard John to mr Madison. resigns as Commr bkrptcy"). On 16 Nov., the State Department issued a commission to Richard Cutts SHANNON (list of commissions in Lb in same; see also Appendix I: List of Appointments).

To Levi Lincoln

Sat. Oct. 29. 03.

Th: Jefferson asks the favor of the Attorney General to meet the heads of departments here tomorrow at 12. aclock & to dine with him on the same day.

RC (MWA); addressed: "Levi Lincoln esq. Atty Genl US"; Lincoln later wrote notes relating to land sales and payments on verso.

From William Marshall

Christ Church Parish, So. Carolina
Octr. 29th. 1803.

SIR,

I do myself the honor of presenting you, with an accurate Chart of the Coast of West Florida and Louisiana, including a survey and soundings of the Mississippi river, extending, considerably above New Orleans. It was sent to me, a few days ago, by a gentleman who married the widow of Mr. Gauld, by whom the Chart, was made. I hasten to send It to you, as, If there be none such in possession of the administration It may be of some service, to the navigation of The new world, wh. you have lately obtained for us;—and tend to appreciate, the advantages of an acquisition, in every View so immensely valuable to the United States. Wishing, that It may prove in any respect, beneficial to the Governmt. and acceptable to you, I remain,

With the Highest resp Yr. most Obdt. St. W. MARSHALL

RC (DLC); at foot of text: "The President of The United States"; endorsed by TJ as received 18 Nov. and so recorded in SJL. Enclosure: probably George Gauld's *Accurate Chart of the Coast of West Florida, and the Coast of Louisiana* (see William C. C. Claiborne to TJ, 24 Aug. 1803).

Charleston attorney William Marshall (ca. 1770-1805) served in the South Carolina legislature for most of the 1790s before being elected a chancellor of the state court of equity in 1799. He also owned a plantation in Christ Church Parish (*S.C. Biographical Directory, Senate*, 2:1060; Vol. 37:574n).

From Wilson Cary Nicholas

Dear Sir Washington Oct. 29. 1803

Mr. Rawlins the Gentn. who will deliver you this letter, is anxious to obtain an appointment in the Custom house at New Orleans. This Gentn. formerly lived in Virginia in a mercantile house engaged in extensive business, I have not had such an acquaintance with Mr. Rawlins as woud justify me in asking an office for him, I can only speak of him, as to his having been regularly brought up to the business I have mentioned, and as to an impression that was, and is, upon my mind, that he is a respectable man. I am much strengthened in this opinion by an intimate acquaintance with the friends of Mr. Rawlins, who are much esteemed. I have no doubt that it is in the power of Mr. Rawlins, to give you such testimonials from Baltimore, of his character and qualifications, (from persons who have known him more recently, and more intimately than I have) as will shew that he is worthy of your confidence

I am with the greatest respect Your humble Servant

W. C. Nicholas

RC (DNA: RG 59, LAR); endorsed by TJ as received 15 Nov. and "Rawlins for appmt Louisiana" and so recorded in SJL. Enclosed in Benjamin Rawlings to TJ, 14 Nov.

From Mary Hazard

Mon Cher President Philadelphia October 30. 1803

Je vois bien, que vous n'avez pas envie d'entre en correspondence avec moi, mais, je vous dis, que je ne cesserai pas de vous ecrire, jusque les temps que je serai repondue. Vous pensez, peutetre, que je suis homme, qui n'ecrivet que pour s'en faire quelquechose de plaisenterie, mais, en verité, ce n'est pas ausi; je suis femme; et pauvre femme; et si vous ne le croyez pas, venez et voir; et alors vous serez persuadé que tout ce que je vous ai dis de ma pauvrté est vrai....A le temps de vottre inauguration, vous avez promis, de garder, fiddelement, les droits, et les libertés du peuple, souvenez vous de cella, mon Ami, et permettez moi de vous prier, de ne nous laisez pas aller au prison; car vous savez bien, que person n'a pas la, la moindre de la liberté; vingte ou trente gourds nous mettrons hors de tous nos miséres est nos grands troubles: ayez donc la bonté, mon cher Ami, de nous envoyez ce vingte ou trente gourds, et si vous ne pouvez pas nous les donner, et bien donc, appretez les moi, est quant je serai rich, je vous en payerai avec mille de graces; c'est un mauvais chose d'etre pauvre et que dieu vous en garderai est le plus fiddele wish de vottre correspondent.

M R

Jetz Sehest du, lieber President, das ich dir mein wort gehalten habe; mein französchiser brief ist kurz; die ursache ist, weil ich keine zeit habe mich in diesen zweÿ sprachen genug zu swactiziren. Ach es ist die armuth die mir die hände bindet und auch das gehirn zuschlisen will, aber mein thränendes herz nichts, nichts kan das bezwingen. da denke nur, du lieber President, ich und meine schwester arbeiten für einen schneider, und, las uns auch schaffen bis uns die augen übergehen, so können wir doch nicht mehr als zweÿ schillinge des tags verdienen; nun denke nur, gestern schickte er uns ein stück zu machen da fingen wir an zu singen, wir waren so froh und, hoften, unsern schilling balt verdient zu haben aber! iamer! rathe nur was er uns dafür erlaubte? ach nur leütige 8 pence $\frac{1}{2}$ peny!......Wir schafen fröh und spät für den schneider, und mit all unserer arbeit können wir uns nicht brott genug anschaffen; sag, was sollen wir anfangen?–Kanst du uns kei -nen rath mitheilen? dan ich sehe wohl, das du nicht für uns schiken wilst nach Monticello zu kommen deine haupt näthern zu werden!–Schreib nun bald, und rathe uns was zu thun, dan die armuth ist schlimer als der Toth.– M.R.

Pray, Honored Sir, what may be your oppinion of me! If reason suggests to me, that I must appear to you an artful, desighning creature, why should not the same voice check the daring assumption I am guilty of in forcing my nonsense into your presence; but the consciousness of being totaly unknown to you, and the certainty of remaining so in person, supported me hitherto in my wild vagaries, and these have served to make me laugh away several hours, which would otherwise have been sacrificed to mellancholy.......I am poor! and would be contented with my lot, could I, with all my exertions of industry, earn enough to discharge those debts, wich are incured toward sustaining my life. Twenty or thirty dollors would put me out of the power of several creditors, and change the aspect of my days to something more cheering, and prove consolotory to my feelings; to this end, I addressed several of those who style themselves my friends, but complaints of great losses &c—soon silenced my requests; and by one I was advised, to tell my troubles to *my friend* the President; the idea was new and laughable, and to check the turbulency of my disappointed heart, I persued their advice—Pray Sir pardon me, it is the last time you ever hear from M—HAZARD

EDITORS' TRANSLATION

[*From French:*]

MY DEAR PRESIDENT, Philadelphia, 30 Oct. 1803

I can see that you do not wish to correspond with me, but I assure you that I will not stop writing until you reply. You think, perhaps, that I am a man, who is writing merely for amusement, but that is not the case. I am a woman, a poor woman, and if you do not believe me, come and see. Then you will be convinced that everything I have said about my poverty is true.…At the time of your inauguration, you promised faithfully to preserve the rights and liberties of the people. Keep that in mind, my friend, and allow me to beg you not to let us go to prison, for you know very well that no one has the slightest liberty there. Twenty or thirty dollars would preserve us from all our distress and tribulations. Be good enough, my dear friend, to send us those twenty or thirty dollars. If you cannot give them to us, lend them to me and when I am rich I will pay you back with a thousand thanks. It is a terrible thing to be poor. The most faithful wish of your correspondent is that God spare you from poverty. M R

[*From German:*]

Now you see, dear President, that I have kept my word to you; my letter in French is brief. The reason is because in these two letters I do not have enough time to chatter and gossip. Oh! It is poverty that ties my hands and also would put a lock on my brain; but my tear-filled heart, nothing, nothing can conquer. Now just think, dear President, I and my sister work for a tailor, and he keeps us busy even until we are bug-eyed. And still we cannot earn more than two shillings a day. Now just picture this. Yesterday he sent us a piece to make. Then and there we started to sing we were so happy, and we hoped soon to have our well-earned shilling. But, misery! What did he allow us for that, do you think? Oh! Only a measly eight pence and half a penny! . . . labor early and late for the tailor, and with all our work we cannot buy bread enough for us. Tell me, what are we to do? How to begin? Can you share any advice with us? For I see full well that you are not willing to send for us to come to Monticello to become your head seamstresses! – Write soon, and advise us what to do, for poverty is worse than death. M.R.

[*Letter concluded in English.*]

RC (DLC); ellipses in original; addressed: "To His Excellency Thomas Jefferson—President of the U.S—Washington"; franked; postmarked 1 Nov.; endorsed by TJ as received from "Hazard. Anon." on 4 Nov. and so recorded in SJL.

Notes on Preparations to Occupy Louisiana

[ca. 30 Oct. 1803]

Ord. to Claib. & Wilk.

write to Laussat & Clarke force or no force.

1. if no force proceed with regulars, & militia at their discretion.
   treat inhabitants & officers particularly with courtesy
   take nothing without paying
   arrange with Laussat manner of delivery.
   issue proclamation[1]
   suffer the Govr. &c. to remain in his house
   get orders from Laussat &c. for delivery of all the posts.
   take possessn of those within their reach.
   send orders up the river for all others.
   be particularly civil & accomodating in all these acts of possession
   public archives &c[2]—money in treasury theirs.
   dispatch procès verbal & informn to us.

2. if force regulars
   Missipi militia ad libitum of the Governor[3] & other volunteers from any quarter
   order Govr. Tennissee to send instantly 500. mountd militia to Natchez[4]
   notify Govrs. of Ten. & Kent. *<to march the force 1st. ordered>*
      1000. from Ohio. 1500. from Ten. 4000. from Kentucky to be organised & mustered.[5]
      provisions to be procured & forwarded with them.
      to be in the field on the 10th. of Dec.
      embodied[6] into companies & to remain together till orders.
      upper posts. regulars or militia
      Mobile. Kirby
   proceed in all things according to their own discretion
   <take possn of Baton rouge, & garrison as a precautionary measure of safety>
   treat the inhabitants as fellow citizens
   produce a cooperating insurrectionary movemt by Laussat & Clarke on their appearg.
      have arms for them.

if successful, send the officers & souldiers, blacks as well as whites to Hava undr convenn
issue proclamation
secure every military store, gallies &c.[7]
dispatch us informn.

<*money*> Claiborne may draw for expences after delivery, not
<*a frigate.*> exceeding 400. D. a month.

Write to Govr. Kentucky
Tennissee
<*Kirby.*>
Clarke
Laussat.
<*officers at upper posns to be ready to obey ord. of Wilkinson.*>

MS (DLC: TJ Papers, 136:23462a); entirely in TJ's hand; undated, but see below.

ORD. TO CLAIB. & WILK.: in letters dated 31 Oct., Madison and Dearborn instructed William C. C. Claiborne and James Wilkinson, respectively, regarding the steps for taking possession of Louisiana. Both sets of instructions followed the same structure as these notes by TJ, first covering the procedures to be followed if the transfer was routine, then outlining measures in case Spanish officials refused to cede the territory. Madison and Dearborn also covered many of the details, and echoed some of the phrasing, found in the memorandum printed above. TJ perhaps made his notes in preparation for the cabinet's discussion on 30 Oct. or as a record of what he and his advisers decided in that meeting (Madison, *Papers, Sec. of State Ser.*, 5:589-92; *Terr. Papers*, 9:96-8; TJ to Gallatin, 29 Oct.).

WRITE TO LAUSSAT & CLARKE: Madison sent Claiborne a copy of the ratified treaty for the transfer of Louisiana, a commission for Claiborne and Wilkinson as agents of the United States to receive possession, a commission enabling Claiborne to govern Louisiana temporarily, and copies of the just-enacted "Act to enable the President of the United States to take possession of the territories ceded by France to the United States." "The intention of the President," Madison wrote, "is that the moment these documents arrive, you take the most expeditious measures for learning, if not previously known to you," whether Pierre Clément Laussat had, or expected to obtain, possession of Louisiana and could "transfer it peaceably to the United States." The instructions to Claiborne anticipated that he and Wilkinson would communicate with Laussat and Daniel Clark at New Orleans. Madison enclosed a copy of a dispatch from Louis André Pichon to the prefect "which apprizes Mr. Laussat of the views of the American Government, and prepares him for a correspondence with you," and Dearborn informed Wilkinson that Laussat "has received the most positive instructions on the subject." In a letter to Laussat dated 31 Oct., Pichon, who had dined at the President's House on the 29th, reviewed the positions of the governments of France, the United States, Spain, and Great Britain on the Louisiana issue and noted the renewal of armed conflict between Britain and France. Noting that the United States was prepared to enforce the transfer of Louisiana, Pichon wanted Laussat to warn Spanish officials that a delay in ceding the province might cost Spain the Floridas. Madison wrote to Clark on 31 Oct., urging him to form a good relationship with Laussat (Madison, *Papers, Sec. of State Ser.*, 5:589-93; *Terr. Papers*, 9:94-5, 97; Jon Kukla, ed., *A Guide to the Papers of Pierre Clément Laussat* [New Orleans, 1993], 86-7; Edouard Dentu, ed., *Mémoires et correspondance du roi Jérôme et de la reine Catherine*, 7 vols. [Paris, 1861-66], 1:238; TJ to the Senate and the House of Representatives, 21 Oct.).

IF NO FORCE: if Claiborne and Wilkinson expected a peaceful transfer of power, they were to go to New Orleans as quickly as possible to establish Claiborne's authority. Wilkinson was to take along six companies of REGULARS and 100 volunteers from the MILITIA of Mississippi Territory. TREAT INHABITANTS ... WITH COURTESY: "You will be led by your own judgment and your correct principles and dispositions to a prudent moderation and a conciliating deportment," Madison advised Claiborne. "Policy and justice towards the inhabitants equally require both." To Wilkinson, Dearborn wrote: "I need not mention to you the propriety of treating all the Officers and Inhabitants of the Territory with the most polite and soothing attentions." Madison enclosed a "form" of a PROCLAMATION for Claiborne's use (see Draft of a Proclamation for the Temporary Government of Louisiana, at 31 Oct.). SUFFER THE GOVR. &C. TO REMAIN IN HIS HOUSE: because Governor Manuel de Salcedo "is understood to have given proofs of just dispositions and an amicable character," he should be treated with respect and "allowed to remain in his House, and to retain any other personal accommodations of a like kind." Using the language of TJ's notes printed above, Madison indicated that Laussat would as a matter of course issue orders for the DELIVERY OF ALL THE POSTS to the United States and that Wilkinson should use his troops to occupy Spanish military stations within REACH—specifically the garrisons at New Orleans and downriver. The general was then to SEND ORDERS UP THE RIVER to let U.S. detachments know that they should replace Spanish soldiers at St. Louis, New Madrid, and elsewhere in upper Louisiana. MONEY IN TREASURY THEIRS: "money paid into the Spanish Treasury before the delivery of possession," Madison informed Claiborne, "and whatever may be due thereto at that date, is to be considered as the property of Spain" (*Terr. Papers*, 9:96; Madison, *Papers*, *Sec. of State Ser.*, 5:590).

DISPATCH PROCÈS VERBAL & INFORMN: Madison instructed that upon the transfer of Louisiana to the United States, Claiborne and Wilkinson were to exchange with Laussat "certificates of the time and the transaction"—a "procès verbal," or official record of proceedings. Madison advised Claiborne "that the earliest information will be expected by the President of every important stage of the business committed to you" (same, 590, 592; OED).

IF FORCE: if the governor and the general had reason to think that Spanish officials would refuse to turn over the province, Madison wrote to Claiborne, "it is determined to give effect to our title which is clear and just, by employing force for the purpose. The act of Congress authorizes it, and the President will exert the authority." Claiborne and Wilkinson would have to decide if rapid action using troops immediately at hand—300 to 400 regulars from Fort Adams and an estimated 600 to 900 militiamen from Mississippi Territory—would be likely to succeed in taking control of Louisiana before the Spanish government could send reinforcements. If Wilkinson and Claiborne did not think that a quick use of the available forces would be sufficient, as a final contingency the general could expect 6,000 men from the western states. Letting it be known that an armed body "sufficient to overwhelm all possible resistance" was gathering would "add the effect of terror to the force of arms," Madison advised Claiborne, and might help bring about the collapse of any opposition by the Spanish. The successful outcome of a rapid strike without waiting for the additional troops would, Dearborn suggested to Wilkinson, "add much to your Military fame." Dearborn did not give Wilkinson the authority to use the large force of western militia at his own discretion. Should "such formidable opposition be made on the part of the Spanish Government, as to render an Army of considerable force necessary," Dearborn ordered, Wilkinson must "send the earliest notice with a minute detail of the business, to the Seat of Government, where the subject will be considered and the ultimate measures determined on" (Madison, *Papers*, *Sec. of State Ser.*, 5:591-2; *Terr. Papers*, 9:97-8).

TO SEND INSTANTLY 500. MOUNTD MILITIA: on 31 Oct., Dearborn wrote to John Sevier at the president's direction, requesting the organization of a regiment of 500 mounted Tennessee militiamen "with the least possible delay." The regiment should be assembled within six days of the governor's receipt of Dearborn's letter and sent to Natchez. Dearborn advised Wilkinson that the men would be on the way, but if the general "can take possession without waiting for them, which I presume will be the case," he was to proceed to New Orleans without them. Dearborn also conveyed to Sevier the president's request that Tennessee raise a brigade of 1,500 men. Letters from Dearborn, also dated 31 Oct., asked Governor Edward Tiffin for 500 men from OHIO and James Garrard for 4,000 from KENTUCKY. In all cases the term of service would be up to four months, the men were to be organized into COMPANIES and regiments, they must be ready to march no later than 20 Dec. (rather than the 10th as in TJ's notes above), and if the men were put into actual service, each would receive the same pay as a soldier in the regular army. The secretary of war also took steps to have boats ready to carry each state's troops (Dearborn to Sevier, Tiffin, and Garrard, in DNA: RG 107, LSMA; Dearborn to James Morrison and Nathaniel Armstrong, both 31 Oct., in DNA, RG 107, MLS; *Terr. Papers*, 9:97; Harold D. Moser and others, eds., *The Papers of Andrew Jackson*, 9 vols. [Knoxville, 1980-], 1:392).

If Wilkinson had to seize Louisiana by force, Dearborn's orders gave him the option of either taking control of the post at BATON ROUGE on his way down the Mississippi or not, depending on whether "the conduct of the Commandant" was "hostile or otherwise" (*Terr. Papers*, 9:98).

COOPERATING INSURRECTIONARY MOVEMT: Madison and Dearborn advised Claiborne and Wilkinson that if the Spanish refused to turn over the province, many inhabitants of Louisiana could be expected to support the United States. This support—neither Madison nor Dearborn referred to it as an insurrection—would be of "considerable aid," Dearborn anticipated, and Madison deemed it "a critical advantage." Madison's communication to Clark on 31 Oct. was to advise the consul that such a "co-operating movement" might be needed and to emphasize the important roles that Clark and Laussat would need to play in bringing it about (same, 97; Madison, *Papers*, *Sec. of State Ser.*, 5:591-3).

IF SUCCESSFUL: "And in the event of taking forcible possession of New Orleans," Dearborn wrote to Wilkinson, "you will cause the Officers and Garrison to enter into such convention as may be practicable, permitting them to depart for the Havannah, taking care however to secure all the Arms and Military Stores Gallies &ca." He added that "all private property should be held sacred." DISPATCH US INFORMN.: Dearborn instructed Wilkinson "to inform me by every mail of your movements" (*Terr. Papers*, 9:98).

CLAIBORNE MAY DRAW FOR EXPENCES: observing that there was no provision yet with regard to "compensation for the new service in which you are to be employed," Madison authorized Claiborne "to draw on the Department of War, at a rate not exceeding four hundred dollars a month" (Madison, *Papers*, *Sec. of State Ser.*, 5:590-1).

READY TO OBEY ORD. OF WILKINSON: Dearborn wrote to officers at the army's western posts to prepare them to occupy Spanish garrisons across the Mississippi once they heard from the general, but those orders, dated 7 Nov., were not part of the communications sent from Washington on 31 Oct. (Dearborn to Daniel Bissell, George Washington Carmichael, and Amos Stoddard, 7 Nov., in DNA: RG 107, LSMA).

[1] TJ interlined this entry in the list.

[2] Preceding two words interlined in place of "property moveable."

[3] Remainder of entry interlined.

[4] Entry interlined.

[5] TJ interlined this entry and the next three entries.

[6] TJ here canceled "formed."

[7] Entry written in place of canceled "public property. gallies &c."

From Thomas Jefferson Randolph

DEAR GRAND PAPA Edghill Oct. 30 1803

I was at Monticello yesterday and Mr. Dinsmore had almost finished the cornice in the hall and was to set off[1] for Philadelphia to day. they have almost done the canal and the mill house also.

I have read Goldsmith's grecian history Thucidides & I am now reading Goldsmith's Roman hitory. give my love to Papa and uncle Eppes. adieu Grand Papa your most afectionate Grand son

THOMAS JEFFERSON RANDOLPH

RC (Mrs. Edwin Page Kirk, Charlottesville, Virginia, 1956, on deposit at ViU); dateline probably in Martha Jefferson Randolph's hand; endorsed by TJ as received 7 Nov. and so recorded in SJL.

TJ had been employing a gang of enslaved workers to dig a canal for his long-planned millworks at the Shadwell estate. The smaller toll MILL, which was used mostly for grinding grain for his own household, began operation in December, although the canal required several adjustments (MB, 2:1099n; Thomas Mann Randolph to TJ, 24 Dec.; TJ to James Walker, 28 Jan. 1804).

[1] MS: "of."

From Horatio G. Spafford

SIR, Canaan, (N. York) Oct. 30th. 1803.

A plain man, wishes to lay before you in a plain way, some observations. He chooses to offer to you, Sir, from the consideration of respect which is due to the rank you enjoy, & the fame of your Philosophy. I am also proud of the sentiment, that a respectful duty to the first man of our nation, prompts me to offer to your patronage, an invention, which I am led to believe may be of general utility. Respectfully wishing to invite your attention to a description of the

Close Fire Place; it follows.—

The Jambs & back forming an equal mitre, the Mantel high, [...]; the back from the bottom swelling forward toward the top at [...] [out?] of the chimney;—The Jambs projecting beyond the Mantel an half inch; containing a groove on the inside, in which is to play up & down behind the caseing of the breastwork, a sheet of Iron, Copper, or Tin; the whole size of the front of the fire place: suspended by weights by means of a cord at each end, so as to form an exact equillibrium.

Also a lid, hung by hinges to the inside of the Mantel of such size as to fill completely the throat of the chimney when let down; but suspended by weights, as the other; so that it may be varied to fill the half, or the whole of the throat at pleasure.

The various uses of these improvements will probably be seen by you so readily as to render a description of them superfluous—but I will mention a few that are experienced.

When wood is laid on the fire, by sliding the plate close to the hearth, & opening a small door at the bottom of the same, the air which is rushing in to supply the place of the rarified air which has escaped through the Funnel of the chimney, will be so concentrated as to press forcibly on the fire, & occasion it to kindle immediately.

When the fire burns clearly, raise the Plate as high as may be, & yet confine the Smoak: by this, all the benefits of a moveable Mantel are enjoyed.

It cannot have escaped your notice, that [with?] air heat in rooms by fire places of the common construction, more than 7 eighths passes off through the chimney. By lessening the throat of the chimney to a size which will but just carry off the smoak, that evil is remedied in a very considerable degree.

When the air is clear & light, & the smoak rises freely, it is found that the great Plate may be raised considerably higher than Mantels commonly are; which gives additional heat from the blaze, (being commonly hidden behind the Mantel piece.)

In summer, the disagreeable blackness of the fire place is entirely hidden by the great Plate; which may be painted conformably to the room, & be extremely ornamental.

It is obvious that the smoak may at all times be confined to the chimney by lowering this Plate sufficiently.

When wood is completely in a state of ignition, by lowering the Plate, & lid, so as to prevent the action of air on the coals, fire may be retained sufficient through the night, to do considerable toward keeping the room comfortably warm.

I could have treated this subject more Philosophically, but it were needless—to you, Sir, I submit it, wishing that you would do me the favour to transmit me your opinion of the premises.

I earnestly beg of you, Sir, to excuse the liberty I have taken, & the best wishes of a citizen attend you.

I have the honour to be Sir, with perfect respect your Obt. Servt.

HORATIO G. SPAFFORD

RC (MoSHi: Jefferson Papers); torn; addressed: "His Excellency Thomas Jefferson Esq. President of the United States of America"; postmarked Hudson, N.Y., 22 Nov.; endorsed by TJ as received 28 Nov. and so recorded in SJL.

Horatio G. Spafford (1778-1832) was an inventor and writer who corresponded frequently with TJ during the latter's retirement. He received several patents for his inventions, but his most ambitious schemes foundered, including a process for producing steel that anticipated the Bessemer process and plans for a progressive agricultural community in northwestern Pennsylvania, which he abandoned about 1819 after two years. Spending most of his career in the capital region of New York, he published in 1809 in Hudson *General Geography, and Rudiments of Useful Knowledge* and four years later in Albany *A Gazeteer of the State of New York* (Sowerby, Nos. 3828, 4172). His plan to publish gazetteers for the other states never came to fruition, and his *American Magazine*, to which TJ subscribed, was short-lived. After his return from Pennsylvania, he edited for a time the *Montgomery Monitor* in Johnstown and established the *Saratoga Farmer*, a short-lived sheet devoted to scientific topics and opposition to the "deep despotism that reigns supreme in Tammany-Hall." He died of cholera a few months after Congress narrowly approved a bill granting him an unusual permission to maintain secrecy over a patented invention intended to augment the power of steam engines (Julian P. Boyd, *Horatio Gates Spafford: Inventor, Author, Promoter of Democracy* [Worcester, Mass., 1942]; *List of Patents*, 53, 243; Philadelphia *Franklin Gazette*, 11 Nov. 1818; Bennington *Vermont Gazette*, 1 June 1819; *New-York Columbian*, 27 Oct. 1820; *Brattleboro Messenger*, 25 Aug. 1832; *Register of Debates in Congress*, 22d Cong., 1st sess., 8:1091, 2199-2200; Brigham, *American Newspapers*, 1:591; RS, 1:106n; 9:339-40).

Spafford began advertising his CLOSE FIRE PLACE shortly after receiving a patent in 1805 (*Rutland Herald*, 8 June 1805; *List of Patents*, 53).

From Thomas Tew

HONORIED SIR — Newport October 30th 1803

you will Please to Excuse my Boldness in Addressing you on this Ocasion but by being Assured of the goodness of your hart I am Imbolden to Address you on a Subgect that Much Consarnes me I find a Law was passed the Last Session of Congress that any Person haveing a Clame for Lands are to put in their Clames Some Whare and at a Certain time not Only the Clames they may have on this Goverment but all British Grants formyly made and as I think I have a Just Clame for Some Land in this Cuntry for Servises Done in my youth in the old French War the King of Grate Briton Issued a Proclimation for the Incouragement of Officers and Soldiers to Enter and Continue in the Kings Servis Untill Canaday was Reduced to his Majistes Obedience that Every grade Should be intitiled to Certain Quantityes of Lands and at that time I had the Honnour to Command a Company and was Entitiled to 3000 Acers of Land as I Continued Untill the war was at an End in this Cuntrey and I have all the proof necesary Except the Proclimation it is not to be found in this State I have my Commiscion and the pay Masters Books to proove that I Did Duty all the time Now Sir what I wish to be Informed by you is weather the act of Congress Contemplates Such grants as these. I am groing Old and that Land may be Somet[hing?] to Suport me in my Old Age—the Reason I make bold to Address you is because you have had Consarnes with Publick Life all Most your Days and would be able to give me the Information on the Subgect and would be willing to Answair a friend and True Republickan for the truth of this Assertion Pease to Enquire of the Gentilman Repersenting this State Either in Senite or Repersentives—

and If you Could be Pleased to Give me your answear to this Request you will Grately Oblige your Exelances Most Obedient and Very Humble Servent THOS TEW

RC (DLC); torn; at foot of text: "His Excelencey Thomas Jufferson—City of Washington"; endorsed by TJ as received 12 Nov. and so recorded in SJL; also endorsed by TJ: "mr Ellery promises to answer."

At the time of his death, Thomas Tew (ca. 1737-1821) had been keeper of the jail at Newport, Rhode Island, for thirty-five years. He briefly served as a captain of infantry during the American Revolution (*Newport Mercury*, 15 Dec. 1821; *Rhode-Island Republican*, 19 Dec. 1821; Heitman, *Register*, 537).

Draft of a Proclamation for the Temporary Government of Louisiana

[on or before 31 Oct. 1803]

By H.E.[1] W.C. Commandant & Intendant of the Province of Louisiana

A Proclamation

Whereas by treaties entered into between the governments of France and Spain on the 1st. day of Oct. 1800. at St. Ildefonso & on the 1st. day of March 1801. at Madrid the latter ceded to the former the colony & province of Louisiana, with the same extent which it had at the date of the first mentd treaty in the hands of Spain, & that it had when France possessed it, and such as it ought to be after the treaties subsequently entered into between Spain & other states; and the govmt of France hath ceded the same to the US. by a treaty duly ratifed[2] which is in the following words, to wit. [here enter the treaty] and possession of the said colony & province is now in[3] the US. according to the tenor of the sd treaty: and Whereas the Congress of the US. by an act passed on the 31st. day of October in this present year did enact that until the expirn of the session of Congress then sitting, unless[4] provision for the temporary govmt of the said territories be sooner made by Congress[5] all the military, civil, & judicial powers, exercised by the officers of the existing govmt. of the same shall be vested in such person & persons, & shall be exercised in such manner as the Pr. of the US. shall direct,[6] for maintaining and protecting the inhabitants of Louisiana in the free enjoimt of their liberty, property & religion & the President of the US. has by his commission bearing date the same 31st day of Oct. invested me with all the powers & charged me with the several duties heretofore held and exercised by the Commandant & Intendant of the province, I have therefore thought fit to issue this my Proclamation making known the premise, and to declare that the government heretofore exercised over the sd province of Louisiana[7] has ceased, and that that of the US. of A. is henceforth[8] established over the same: that the inhabitants thereof will be incorporated in the union of the US & admitted as soon as possible, accordg to the principles of the federal constn, to the enjoyment of all the rights, advantages & immunities of citizens of the US. that in the meantime they shall be maintained & protected in the free enjoiment of their liberty, property, & the religion which they profess: that all laws which were in existence at the cessation of the former government remain[9] in full force, & all civil[10] officers charged with their execution, other than those whose powers have been specially vested in me, are continued in their functions until provision shall otherwise be made. And I do hereby exhort and enjoin all the inhabitants & other persons within the said province to be faithful & true in their allegiance to the US. and obedient to the laws and authorities of the same, under full assurance that their just rights will[11] be under the guardianship of the US. and will[12] be maintained & protected from all force & violence from without or within.

In testimony whereof &c.

Given at the city of New Orleans the day of 1803 &c.

Dft (DLC: TJ Papers, 137:23709); undated; in TJ's hand, except for closing bracket supplied by Editors.

A form of the above PROCLAMATION was forwarded to William C. C. Claiborne by James Madison with instructions dated 31 Oct. 1803 (see Notes on Preparations to Occupy Louisiana, printed at 30 Oct. above). Madison directed Claiborne to issue the proclamation immediately after the transfer of the territory, "making however any unessential variations or additions which may be necessary" to adapt it to local circumstances. Claiborne formally issued the proclamation, with minor changes, at New Orleans on 20 Dec. 1803, a copy of which was forwarded to Congress by TJ on 16 Jan. 1804 and appeared in the *National Intelligencer* on the same date (Madison, *Papers, Sec. of State Ser.*, 5:589-90; ASP, *Foreign Relations*, 2:582).

HERE ENTER THE TREATY: as issued by Claiborne, the proclamation did not include the text of the Louisiana treaty. Instead, it merely stated that the territory had been ceded by France to the United States by a "treaty duly ratified, and bearing date the 30th of April, in the present year." In a 27 Dec. letter to Madison, Claiborne explained that the full text of the treaty had already appeared in New Orleans newspapers, in both English and French, and was therefore in "general circulation." Inserting the treaty into his proclamation would have "considerably retarded" its publication, Claiborne added, "and the lively anxiety of the people at that interesting Crisis forbad the delay of my proclamation" (Madison, *Papers, Sec. of State Ser.*, 6:230-1).

ACT PASSED ON THE 31ST. DAY OF OCTOBER: see TJ to the Senate and the House of Representatives, 21 Oct. TJ's draft above includes the text of section two of the act in its entirety and nearly verbatim (U.S. Statutes at Large, 2:245).

Claiborne's COMMISSION from the president, dated 31 Oct. 1803, authorized him to assume in Louisiana "all the powers and authorities" formerly exercised by the governor and intendant of the territory until the end of the present session of Congress "unless provision be sooner made" for its temporary government. It also specifically forbade Claiborne from collecting any new or additional taxes or to grant or confirm land titles within the territory. A separate commission by TJ of the same date authorized Claiborne and James Wilkinson to take possession of Louisiana (FCs in DNA: RG 59, MPTPC; *Terr. Papers*, 9:94-5, 143-4).

ALL CIVIL OFFICERS ... ARE CONTINUED: Claiborne's formal proclamation of 20 Dec. here deviated from TJ's draft by excepting "such officers as have been entrusted with the collection of the revenue" from the civil officers to be continued by the new government (ASP, *Foreign Relations*, 2:582; *National Intelligencer*, 16 Jan. 1804).

[1] Preceding two initials interlined.

[2] Preceding two words interlined.

[3] Preceding three words interlined in place of "hath been actually delivered to."

[4] Preceding ten words and comma interlined in place of "they should have made."

[5] Preceding five words interlined.

[6] TJ interlined the text from this point to "& religion."

[7] TJ first wrote "the province," then altered the text to read as above.

[8] Word interlined.

[9] Word interlined in place of "are continued."

[10] Word interlined.

[11] Word interlined in place of "shall."

[12] Word interlined in place of "shall for ever."

From Philippe Reibelt

MONSIEUR LE PRESIDENT! Le 31e. Oct. 1803.

Tout près de l'abime de la misére—dans un paÿs etranger—sans autre recomandation, qu'a Vous—J'ose iterativement implorer Votre protection, de quelque manière, qu'il Vous plaira, de me l'accorder: Ou par la place de maitre de poste, de Chef du bureau de la Vente de terres, ou autre a la Nouvelle Orleans, ou par la recomandation a un grand Proprietaire, au quel je pourrois je pourrois etre util en Qualité d'Administrateur de defrichement, ou de plantation—ou par la recomandation a un grand Negociant, au quel je pourois rendre des services par la Direction de quelque entreprise p. E. d'une Construction des batimens de Mer sur l'Ohio, d'une fabrique de porcelaine, de terre Anglaise, faÿence &c—ou enfin par l'avance de quelques cent Gourdes, jusqu'a ce que j'aurois obtenu des Nouv. Moÿens de l'Europe.

Dans le Cas, ou on pourroit, comme je le Soupçonne, Vous avoir referè du Mal contre Moi, je Vous prierai, de ne pas en juger sans m'avoir entendû, bien persuadé, que je pourrois repondre a tout, a votre parfaite Satisfaction.

J'ai l'honneur d'etre avec le plus profond respect Votre Excellençe Tr. Hble, et tr. Obst. Sert. REIBELT francais

EDITORS' TRANSLATION

MISTER PRESIDENT! 31 Oct. 1803

Nearing the abyss of misery, in desperation, in a foreign country, with no other recommendation than yours, I dare once again implore your protection in whatever way you are willing to give it: whether by appointing me director of a post office, head of the land office, or any other position in New Orleans; or by recommending me to a large landowner to whom I could be useful overseeing lot clearing or managing a plantation; or by recommending me to a major merchant to whom I could render service by directing a company, such as the construction of boats on the Ohio River, a porcelain factory from British clay, faience, etc.; or, alternatively, by lending me about 100 dollars until I receive new funds from Europe.

If, as I suspect, someone has given you a negative report about me, I beg you not to make a judgment without having heard me, for I am confident I can answer any critique to your full satisfaction.

With the deepest respect, your excellency, I have the honor of being your very humble and obedient servant. REIBELT, the Frenchman

RC (MHi); below signature: "poste restante a Baltimore" (general delivery, Baltimore); endorsed by TJ as received 2 Nov. and so recorded in SJL.

To the Senate

TO THE SENATE OF THE US. OF AMERICA.

I now lay before you the treaty mentioned in my general message at the opening of the session, as having been concluded with the Kaskaskia Indians, for the transfer of their country to us, under certain reservations & conditions.

Progress having been made in the demarcation of Indian boundaries, I am now able to communicate to you a Treaty with the Delawares, Shawanese, Poutewatamies, Miamis, Eel-rivers, Weeaws, Kickapoos, Piankashaws, & Kaskaskias, establishing the boundaries of the territory around St. Vincennes:

Also a supplementary treaty with the Eel rivers, Wyandots, Piankeshaws, Kaskaskias & Kickapoos, in confirmation of the 4th. article of the preceeding treaty:

Also a treaty with the Choctaws, describing & establishing our demarcation of boundaries with them.

Which several treaties are accompanied by the papers relating to them, and are now submitted to the Senate for consideration whether they will advise & consent to their ratification.

TH: JEFFERSON
October 31. 1803.

RC (DNA: RG 46, EPIR, 8th Cong., 1st sess.); endorsed by Senate clerks. PrC (DLC). Recorded in SJL with notation "treaties Kaskaskias &c. & Choctaws." Enclosures: (1) Treaty between the United States and the Kaskaskia tribe, "so called, but which Tribe is the remains, and rightfully represent, all the Tribes of the Illinois Indians"; signed at Vincennes on 13 Aug. by William Henry Harrison for the United States and by Jean Baptiste Ducoigne and five others for the Kaskaskias; the Kaskaskias cede all their lands in the Illinois country except for a tract of about 350 acres near the town of Kaskaskia that was secured to them by treaty in 1791 and another tract of 1,280 acres; the United States will take the Kaskaskias "under their immediate care and patronage" and "afford them a protection, as effectual, against the other Indian tribes, and against all other persons whatever, as is enjoyed by their own Citizens"; the annuity for the tribe will be increased to $1,000 payable in money, merchandise, provisions, or domestic animals at the Kaskaskias' option; the U.S. will have a house built for the chief of the tribe and enclose a field; the U.S. will also give $100 annually for seven years for the support of a Catholic priest who in addition to performing "the Duties of his Office" will "Instruct as many of their Children as possible, in the Rudiments of Literature"; the U.S. will grant $300 for the construction of a church and $580 to allow the tribe to clear debts and buy necessary articles (Tr in DNA: RG 46, EPIR, certified as a true copy by Joshua Wingate, Jr., 15 Oct.; printed copy in same). (2) Treaty between the United States, represented by Harrison; the Delawares, Shawnees, Potawatomis, Miamis, and Kickapoos, represented by chiefs and head warriors; and the Eel River Indians, Weas, Piankashaws, and Kaskaskias, represented by the Miamis and Potawatomis; signed at Fort Wayne, 7 June, by 15 members of the tribes, including Little Turtle of the Miamis and Buckongahelas of the Delawares; Hendrick Aupaumut of the Stockbridge Mohicans also present as one of the witnesses (see John Sergeant of New Stockbridge to TJ, 25 June 1803); the treaty specifies the bounds of the tract around Vincennes that is reserved to the U.S. and provides for the cession of the Wabash saline and a plot around it four miles square, in return for which the U.S. will provide 150 bushels of salt each year for distribution among the tribes; the U.S. will have the right to set aside four locations on roads for accommodations for travelers (printed copy in DNA: RG 46, EPIR). (3) Treaty signed at Vincennes on 7 Aug. by Harrison and ten leaders of the Eel River, Wyandot, Piankashaw, and Kaskaskia nations, with Eel River chiefs also representing the Kickapoos; confirming the right of the United States to locate the four tracts for travelers' accommodations and specifying that each of the tracts will be one mile square (printed copy in same). (4) Treaty signed 31 Aug. between James Wilkinson as commissioner for the United States and Mingo Pouscouche and Alatala Houma as commissioners for the Choctaws; specifying the course of the boundary of the land ceded by the Choctaws between the Tombigbee, Mobile, and Pascagoula Rivers; in return for their confirmation of the cession, the Choctaw commissioners and six chiefs residing on the Tombigbee receive personal articles and quantities of blankets, powder, and lead (printed copy in same). Other enclosures not identified. Message and enclosures printed in ASP, *Indian Affairs*, 1:687-9.

NOW LAY BEFORE YOU: after Lewis Harvie delivered the message and papers on 31 Oct., the Senate ordered that the treaties be printed for use by its members. The body took up consideration of the treaties on 15 Nov. and approved the four of them unanimously on the 16th (JEP, 1:451-2, 454-6). TJ signed proclamations announcing the treaty with the Kaskaskias and the treaty with the Eel River and affiliated nations on 23 Dec. On 26 Dec., he issued proclamations for the treaty with the Delawares, Shawnees, and associated groups and the treaty with the Choctaws (*National Intelligencer*, 28, 30 Dec. 1803, 2 Jan. 1804).

To Madame de Tessé

Dear Madam Washington Oct. 31. 1803.

In my letter of Jan. 30. I informed you that the person whom I had employed in this neighborhood had provided such seeds of the list therein stated to you, as the lateness of the season had permitted. I had the mortification to see them remain here till summer without any opportunity occurring to forward them. our only commercial port is Alexandria, five miles distant. by casting your eye on a map you will percieve that to send a package from thence to Baltimore, Philadelphia, or New York to be reshipped to France, is as difficult as to send one from Havre to Marseilles for America. it would add much to the risk of miscarriage & more to the delay, which in the case of plants is fatal. it remains therefore that we depend solely on Alexandria, which has not a great intercourse with France. it happens fortunately at this moment that we are sending a ship on public account to the Mediterranean, but to touch at Lorient on her way. I have therefore required the gardener employed, to make up his box of plants and seeds, which he has accordingly done; & delivered them to me. they will be put on board tomorrow, addressed to the care of mr Aaron Vale, Consul of the US. at Lorient, with directions to find the cheapest mode of conveying them to you; the box being very heavy. it's bulk is of about 13. cubical feet. perhaps you can advise him the best method of sending it. I did not open it to see how it was packed, but the following is the list furnished by the gardener.

Plants No. 1. Magnolia glauca.
2. Laurus Sassafras
3. Cornus florida.
} about 1½ dozen of plants of each of these

Seeds. No. 1. Wild roses of various kinds.
2. Quercus alba.
3. Quercus prinus, 2 kinds, castaneae foliis, called Chesnut oak.
4. Quercus Hispanica, a variety of the Rubra.
5. Quercus Rubra
No. 6. acorns of the Box-oak. I do not know this.
7. Lyriodendron
8. Juglans nigra.
Magnolia glauca
Laurus Sassafras
Cornus florida.
Juniperus Virginiana
} the names of these are written on the bags.

I am sorry to find he has not put up any acorns of the Quercus Phellos (live-oak) which abound here more than anywhere, nor seeds of the Catalpa, which I presume is to be found in the gardens here. as the ship is not yet gone, perhaps I may be able to get them still. I will take care to renew this supply annually till you are sufficiently furnished with the articles composing it. I undertake it with the more satisfaction because it is within the limits of those attentions I may justifiably spare for it. they will sometimes fail, for want of a conveyance from Alexandria to Havre, the only port I would have ventured to send to, had not the advantages of the present conveyance overbalanced the inconvenient distance of Lorient from Paris. perhaps mr Vale will be able to send the box round to Havre & up the Seine, for which he will have plenty of time.

Altho' the times are big with political events, yet I shall say nothing on that or any subject but the innocent ones of botany & friendship. I shall be much gratified if I am able to contribute any thing to your botanical pleasures & emploiments. I feel their importance to you the more, as they are congenial to my own mind. permit me to place here my friendly respects to M. de Tessé, and M. & Mde. de la Fayette: and to assure yourself of my constant & affectionate esteem and respect.

TH: JEFFERSON

PrC (MoSHi: Jefferson Papers); at foot of first page: "Mde. de Tessé"; endorsed by TJ in ink on verso. Enclosed in TJ to Robert R. Livingston, 4 Nov.

PERSON WHOM I HAD EMPLOYED IN THIS NEIGHBORHOOD: Robert Bailey.

MAGNOLIA GLAUCA: for the plants and seeds that TJ was sending, see Vol. 39:125-6, 416-17. Species of oaks are in the genus QUERCUS.

To Madame de Corny

Washington Nov. 1. 03.

Your two favors, my dear friend, of Feb. 15. & June 15. have been duly recieved. the latter was forwarded to me by mr Ledet, who remained himself in London, & whom I should have recieved with great pleasure on your recommendation, had he come here. I learn with joy from yourself that you have good hopes of improvement in your health. my prayers for it are sincere, as the recollections of your friendship are very dear to me. having understood that you were become a great tea-drinker I procured the last year a cannister of very fine tea, & kept it by me a twelvemonth seeking an opportunity of conveying it to you. but none occurred. a vessel happens now to be sailing from this place on public account for Lorient, of which I avail myself, to send you a small box of Imperial, of the freshest & best quality, consigned to the care of mr Aaron Vale our Consul at Lorient, under the address of mr Livingston at Paris, from whom you will recieve it. I wish it may be to your taste, & sometimes remind you of a friend. our Congress is now in session, & fills us with business; to which much is added by our being now in the act of taking possession, & of organising the government of Louisiana, which has been so happily disposed of for the peace and friendship of our two countries. in the midst of hurry therefore, & of closing dispatches for the vessel, I can only repeat my prayers for your health and happiness, & assurances of my affectionate & respectful attachment.

TH: JEFFERSON

PrC (DLC); at foot of text: "Mde. de Corny"; endorsed by TJ in ink on verso. Enclosed in TJ to Robert R. Livingston, 4 Nov.

From James Doughty, Jr.

SIR

Philada. November 1st. 1803

With all diffidence do I approach the Chief Magistrate of my country; sensible that in averting his attention, but for a moment, from the interest He takes in the general welfare; I set by far too high an estimate on my own particular concerns.

But, altho' under these impressions, I make bold, Knowing the affability of Your Excellency, simply to prefer my suit, and leave the result to your wise discretion.—

In the arrangements about to be made for a provisional or temporary government of the lately acquired territories, there will, no doubt, be wanting persons of trust and confidence, to fill and occupy certain stations, and discharge certain functions, under the appointment of the President of the United States;—to present myself to your Excellency as a person qualified for the discharge of any duties whatever—I am convinced would not be recommending myself in a manner, agreeable to your just sense of genuine modesty, and therefore will only state that my acquaintance with the Spanish and French Languages, (Especially with the Latter—that with the former being chiefly grammatical and without much practice) is such as would be very useful in that country; my education has been mercantile and my family and connexions are such, that I could present your Excellency, on being demanded, ample recommendations and a suitable guarantee—

Having, perhaps, said more than is necessary on such an occasion, I must now beg your Excellency's pardon for having thus obtruded my name into your presence: Should any notice be taken of this application, I shall feel myself obliged to strain every nerve for the Honor of my country—But, if otherwise, I shall console myself with reflecting, that your Excellency has chosen persons more worthy of your confidence and the confidence of their country.

With such sentiments I shall still continue to be With Humble Esteem and most profound respect Your Excellency's most faithful & most obedt: Servant JAMES DOUGHTY JUNR

RC (DNA: RG 59, LAR); at foot of text: "His Excellency the President of the United States"; endorsed by TJ as received 3 Nov. and "office Louisiana" and so recorded in SJL.

James Doughty, Jr., was probably the son of Southwark shipwright James Doughty, who died in 1805 (Philadelphia *United States Gazette*, 30 Oct. 1805; *Poulson's American Daily Advertiser*, 9 Nov. 1805).

To Pierre Samuel Du Pont de Nemours

MY DEAR SIR Washington Nov. 1. 03.

Your favors of Apr. 6. & June 27. were duly recieved, & with the welcome which every thing brings from you. the treaty which has so happily sealed the friendship of our two countries has been recieved here with general acclamation. some inflexible federalists have still ventured to brave the public opinion. it will fix their character with the world & with posterity, who not descending to the other points of difference between us, will judge them by this fact, so palpable as to speak for itself in all times & places. for myself & my country I thank you for the aids you have given in it: & I congratulate you on having lived to give those aids in a transaction replete with blessings to unborn millions of men, & which will mark the face of a portion on the globe so extensive as that which now composes the United States of America. it is true that at this moment a little cloud hovers in the horizon. the government of Spain has protested against the right of France to transfer; & it is possible she may refuse possession, & that this may bring on acts of force. but against such neighbors as France there, & the United States here what she can expect from so gross a compound of folly and false faith, is not to be sought in the book of wisdom. she is afraid of her mines in Mexico. but not more than we are. our policy will be to form New Orleans, & the country on both sides of it on the gulf of Mexico, into a state; &, as to all above that, to transplant our Indians into it, constituting them a Marechaussée to prevent emigrants crossing the river, until we shall have filled up all the vacant country on this side. this will secure both Spain & us as to the mines of Mexico for half a century, and we may safely trust the provisions for that time to the men who shall live in it.

I have communicated with mr Gallatin on the subject of using your house in any matters of consequence we may have to do at Paris. he is impressed with the same desire I feel to give this mark of our confidence in you, & the sense we entertain of your friendship & fidelity. mr Behring informs him that none of the money which will be due from us to him as the assignee of France will be wanting at Paris. be assured that our dispositions are such as to let no occasion pass, unimproved, of serving you, where occurrences will permit it. present my respects to Mde. Dupont, and accept yourself assurances of my constant and warm friendship. TH: JEFFERSON

PrC (DLC); at foot of text: "M. Dupont de Nemours." Enclosed in TJ to Robert R. Livingston, 4 Nov.

MARECHAUSSÉE: marshalcy.
MR BEHRING: Alexander Baring.

From Christopher Ellery

Novr. 1st. 1803

C. Ellery has the honor to offer his highest respects to the President, and to request his permission to present a little pamphlet, on a subject to be brought before Congress, extremely interesting to the merchants of R. Island, and worthy of attention in a political point of view—

RC (DLC); endorsed by TJ as received 1 Nov. and so recorded in SJL. Enclosure: William Hunter, *Observations on the Petitions from Various Merchants of Rhode-Island, to the Congress of the United States, Praying to be Relieved from the Penalties of Certain Exportation Bonds* (Newport, R.I., 1803; Sowerby, No. 3308).

On 1 Nov. 1803, Rhode Island MERCHANTS Charles D'Wolf, Constant Taber, William Gardner, Simon Davis, and Samuel Martin presented petitions to the House of Representatives praying to be relieved from bonds they entered into as principal and sureties "for the delivery of a quantity of domestic distilled spirits without the limits of the United States." Certificates to cancel the bonds had been rejected for what the petitioners called "technical difficulties." After consideration by the Committee of Commerce and Manufactures, the House referred the petitions to the comptroller of the Treasury on 20 Jan. 1804 (JHR, 4:428-9, 459, 460, 463, 471, 485, 545; Hunter, *Observations*, 4).

From Albert Gallatin

[1 Nov. 1803]

The pressure of business & interruption prevents my doing justice to the subject of Louisiana. I have returned his to Mr Wagner; Mr Madison will correct it, that part which relates to revenue & expenditures excepted which I will revise—

Respectfully Your obt. Servt

ALBERT GALLATIN

RC (DLC); undated; addressed: "The President of the United States"; endorsed by TJ as received from the Treasury Department on 1 Nov. and "Documents Louisa" and so recorded in SJL.

For the compilation of documents on the SUBJECT OF LOUISIANA for publication, see Madison to TJ, [5 Nov. 1803].

From Jesse Hawley

SIR

Freehold 2 Novr 1803

An obscure Citizen, young in age, in experience, who conceits he possesses a small share of observation & of feeling for the civil & political interests of his Country, so far presumes on your wisdom as to take the liberty of suggesting some ideas which occurred to him on the perusal of your Excellency's late message to Congress, which has just came to hand—

The previous possession of large tracts of unoccupied Land, together with the recent acquisition of the Louisiana Territory opens a vast field for the extension of the American Empire, within the term of 50 or an 100 Years, if we can presume on the perpetuation of our Confederated system of Government—

The prosperity of infantile settlements depend greatly on either the fostering aid of the Government they are under, or of that of individual Capitalists—The former, if judicious, will perform the part of an affectionate parent[1] for the better—The latter, almost universally, are governed by motives of private interest, which too frequently, & almost unpardonably partake of a selfish monopolizing disposition—The government is as often still more unpardonable in abandoning the inhabitants of new-settlements to the disposition of these land-jobbers—This has notoriously been the case with Virginia & this state (N York)—Not only abandon the land-settler to the extortionate price of the[2] land-holder; but to the numerous cases of disputed, & frequently defeated Titles of their land—

The considerable part of the land in the township of Freehold has been paid for twice, by the present proprietors, in consequence of its having different claimants as Patentees—I have not been sufficiently early acquainted with the polity of this state to assign an able cause for this defectibility in their legislation, other than an[3] incomplete system of Recording Grants & Conveyances of Land—In this state, at present, they have only County offices for the Record of Land Conveyancing—In Connecticut, they have Town offices for that purpose—

The defective, "bad titles" of land in this state has greatly retarded emigration from the New England states—They are jealous of Titles—

The establishment of Recording Offices—the extention of these with the progression of Population & rendered of frequent & easy of access—Admitting no conveyance to be valid untill entered on public Records—The price of Land put as low as policy will admit of to actual settlers with deferred payments for 5, 7, or 10 Years—& the prohibition to large monopolies of land, will, I conceive, be a course of policy which will greatly contribute to the settlement of the Territory with free & independent Farmers—also lead to the personal industry of the proprietor, perhaps mostly to the extention of slaves—

There are other subjects which the Government might use as means to promote the settlement of the Country some of which are not readily within the reach of individual enterprize—At the Confluence of all principal Rivers—at the head of all Navigable Waters—at every considerable enlargement of Navigation of the Rivers—& many other situations which from their peculiar localities may become, in time, places of considerable settlement & business; let them be laid out in town Lots (which will be particularly necessary in the warmer & more healthy parts of the Territory)[4]—Also impose a legislative restriction on the size & draft of town plots laid out by individuals—Let the Government lay out the principal Roads leading to & thro' all the principal settlements as fast as they take place, & in the out-set to lay them in the most direct & on the most advantageous ground the Country will admit & improved as well as circumstances will afford—It is often that new, & more particularly older settlements suffer very considerably (by injury done individuals) from an inattention to this particular—Many more subjects of improvement[5] would suggest themselves on making the experiment of settlements—But I have protracted my first intentions—The chief inducement to offer these remarks was, not that I conceived any want of a disposition in the Chief Magistrate to attend to them; but from the multifarious business of the whole Administration they might escape attention—They are most respectfully submitted by,

Sir, Yours with sincere sentiments of Esteem

JESSE HAWLEY

RC (DLC); addressed: "His Excellency Thomas Jefferson Esqr. Prest. of U.S. Washington"; franked; postmarked Albany, 7 Nov.; endorsed by TJ as received 14 Nov. and so recorded in SJL.

Jesse Hawley (d. 1842) was a native of Connecticut and a recent immigrant to upstate New York. Shortly after writing the above letter to TJ, he established himself as a flour merchant in Geneva, a business that soon succumbed to an embezzling partner and unreliable transportation to eastern markets. In 1807 and 1808, while fleeing creditors and serving time in prison for debt, Hawley published a series of newspaper articles under the pseudonym "Hercules" that promoted the idea of a canal between Lake Erie and the Mohawk River. Years later, after his authorship of the essays became public, Hawley gained recognition as one of the founding fathers of the Erie Canal. He later served in the New York legislature and as collector for the district of Genesee (Gerard Koeppel, *Bond of Union: Building the Erie Canal and the American Empire* [Cambridge, Mass., 2009], 7, 13-14, 33-40, 44-5, 333-4, 365-7; JEP, 3:132; *Albany Evening Journal*, 12 Jan. 1842).

[1] MS: "paret."

[2] Hawley here canceled "land-jobber."

[3] Hawley here canceled "incompatible."

[4] Closing parenthesis supplied by Editors.

[5] Preceding two words interlined.

From Jean Baptiste Say

MONSIEUR [before 3 Nov. 1803]

Daignez recevoir l'hommage que je vous fais de mon Traité d'Economie politique, comme une marque de la haute considération que j'ai pour vos qualités personnelles et pour les principes que vous professez. Puissiez-vous y reconnaître quelques traces de cet amour eclairé de l'humanité et de la liberté qui vous rend si recommandable aux yeux des hommes qui pensent bien.

Le bonheur dont jouit votre patrie et qui s'est fort accru sous votre administration, est fait pour exciter l'envie des nations d'Europe; et cependant votre prosperité sera peut-etre la source de la leur. Elles verront le degré de bonheur auquel peut prétendre une societé humaine qui consulte le bon sens dans sa legislation, l'économie dans ses dépenses, la morale dans sa politique; et les conseils de la Sagesse ne pourront plus etre representés comme de pures théories non-susceptibles d'application.

Il vous appartient également de montrer aux amis de la liberté repandus en Europe, quelle étendue de liberté personnelle est compatible avec le maintien du corps social. On ne pourra plus alors souiller par des excès la plus belle des causes; et l'on s'apercevra peut-être enfin que la liberté civile est le veritable but de l'organisation sociale, et qu'il ne faut considerer la liberté politique que comme un moyen de parvenir à ce but.

Les Etats-unis sont enfans de l'Europe; mais les enfans valent mieux que leurs pères. Nous sommes de vieux parens, elevés dans de sots prejugés, garottés par beaucoup d'anciennes entraves et soumis à une foule de considerations pueriles. Vous n/ous montrerez les veritables moyens de nous en affranchir; car vous avez fait plus que conquérir votre liberté. Vous l'avez affermie.

Agréez, Monsieur, les assurances de mon devouement sincere et de mon profond Respect. J. B. Say

EDITORS' TRANSLATION

Dear Sir, [before 3 Nov. 1803]

Please accept my *Treatise on Political Economy* in homage, as a sign of my high esteem for your personal qualities and the principles you profess. May you find herein some traces of the enlightened love of humanity and liberty for which right-minded people so admire you.

The happiness your country enjoys, and which has so greatly increased under your administration, is justly envied by European nations. Yet, your prosperity may well be the source of theirs. They will see the level of happiness to which a human society can aspire when it brings reason to its legislation, economy to its spending, and morality to its politics. It is no longer possible to depict the path of wisdom as a purely theoretical construct that cannot be implemented.

You also demonstrate to the friends of liberty throughout Europe the breadth of personal liberty that is compatible with maintaining community. People can no longer sully noble causes with excesses. Perhaps they will come to realize that civil liberty is the true goal of society and that political liberty is only a means to that end.

The United States are the offspring of Europe, but the children have more merit than their fathers. We are elderly parents, raised with stupid prejudices, bound by ancient impediments, and subject to puerile ideas. You will show us the right way to free ourselves, for you did more than just conquer your freedom: you affirmed it.

Accept, Sir, the assurance of my sincere devotion and deep respect.

J. B. Say

RC (DLC); undated; addressed: "A Monsieur Jefferson President des Etats-Unis d'Amérique"; endorsed by TJ as received 3 Nov. and so recorded in SJL.

Jean Baptiste Say (1767-1832) grew up in Nantes in a Huguenot family with strong connections to Geneva. He became a bank clerk at the age of 15 and three years later went to England, where he worked for a mercantile firm. Returning to France in 1787, he became secretary to Etienne Clavière, who co-wrote *De la France et des États-Unis* with Jacques Pierre Brissot de Warville and corresponded with TJ about aspects of political economy. During his association with Clavière, Say began to write pamphlets and for periodicals. In 1794, he became managing editor of *La Décade philosophique, littéraire et politique*, a new serial associated with the *idéologistes* (or *idéologues*) such as Pierre Jean Georges Cabanis and Antoine Louis Claude Destutt de Tracy. At Bonaparte's request, Say put together a collection of books to serve as a traveling library for Bonaparte's Egyptian campaign. In 1800, Say published *Olbie, ou Essai sur les moyens de réformer les mœurs d'une nation*, which expressed his ideas about improvement of society. Courting the political economists affiliated with *La Décade*, Bonaparte put Say on the Tribunate, the body that nominally reviewed legislation, but Say realized that the first consul expected him to give sanction to the government's policies. Say's two-volume *Traité d'économie politique, ou Simple exposition de la manière dont se forment, se distribuent, et se consomment les richesses* was published in Paris in 1803. Disapproving of the coronation of Bonaparte as emperor, Say in 1804 lost his seat on the Tribunate, refused a proffered tax collectorship, and devoted his attention to developing a cotton-spinning factory. Only after Napoleon's fall would Say's writings on economics begin to be published again. In 1830, he became a professor of political economy (Evert Schoorl, *Jean-Baptiste Say: Revolutionary, Entrepreneur, Economist* [London, 2013], 3-14, 23-37; Tulard, *Dictionnaire Napoléon*, 577-8, 902-4, 1544; Sowerby, No. 3547; Vol. 10:261-4, 384-5; Vol. 11:9; Vol. 13:281, 319-23, 600-1; Vol. 25:62; Vol. 38:525n).

DAIGNEZ RECEVOIR L'HOMMAGE: TJ replied to Say on 1 Feb. 1804. Ten years later, Say revived the correspondence (RS, 7:416-21, 598-600; 8:303-8).

To John Barnes

DEAR SIR Nov. 3. 03.

Mr. Dinsmore is arrived here from Monticello on his way to see his brother at Baltimore, and asks for 40. Dollars in Philadelphia bills if to be had, which I must pray you to accomodate him with. he will call on you to-day. affectionate salutations. TH: JEFFERSON

RC (MHi); endorsed by Barnes: "Mr Dinsmore 3d Nov 1803 $40." Not recorded in SJL.

TJ noted in his financial records that on this day he gave James DINSMORE an order on Barnes for $40 (MB, 2:1111).

From Isaac Darneille

St. Louis, in Upper Louisiana.
SIR, 3d. of November 1803.

A knowledge of your patriotism and zeal manifested on many occasions; and the great and important services you have rendered to your Country, in the long course of your public services, in supporting with manly firmness, measures calculated to promote the welfare of the Republic, as well as in opposing, in the same manner, measures tending in their consequences to tyranny oppression and Slavery; and a firm reliance that such will be the rule and guide of your conduct in discharge of the present important duties which have devolved upon you as President of the United States; An anxious solicitude for the welfare of the Republic in general, and that part in particular in which I have made a residence; Are objects sufficient with me to solicite your attention to the present critical situation of that part of the Indiana Territory which bears the name of the Illinois Country upon the Mississippi and upper Louisiana.—

This country (I mean the western part of the Indiana Territory together with upper Louisiana) is an object which requires the utmost attention at the present moment. Considered as to population, this country is respectable; the citizens of which have never yet felt the mild operation of a republican form of Government. They have always been taught to obey the voice of a Commandant. They have not yet learned that they have rights and privileges of their own, which are equal to the rights and privileges of their Commandants and other great men. They have always heretofore been taught, and yet believe themselves bound to obey whatever has been or shall be commanded them by their superiors. It is for this reason that there are so few signers to a petition which has been sent forward to Congress praying a division of the Indiana Territory and for annexing the western part thereof to Upper Louisiana; which would connect the settlements on both sides of the Mississippi under one and the same government. Which is an object of the utmost importance to the people on both sides of the Mississippi river; As their common interest, their commercial connection and daily intercourse with each other furnish at once a demonstrative proof. And the division cannot by any means injure the Government of the Indiana Territory, nor any part of the citizens thereof, as it is well known that there is a tract of country of two hundred miles, between the settlements in the Illinois Country and those in the County of Knox on the Wabash river, at Vincennes where the seat of Government for the Indiana Territory is now fixed. Although this is a measure which would be productive of the greatest good to the Inhabitants on both sides of the Mississippi, yet many have refused to sign the petition on the eastern bank of the Mississippi, fearing that the measure would be detrimental to the Governor of the Indiana Territory!—And however rediculous such reasonings may be in the contemplation of well informed men, yet I assure you it is the reasoning made use of there by the Creatures of the Governor of the Indiana Territory.—The people here in Louisiana are not permitted by Government to sign any petition to Congress untill the province shall be given up to the United States. But

To shew the arrogance of that party in the Indiana Territory; They propose using their influence in Congress to Join the whole of upper Louisiana to the Indiana Territory. A measure the most arrogant, absurd, rediculous and injurious to the people of upper Louisiana that could possibly be imagined!—I should be sorry, indeed, should Governor Harrison be active in this measure, for it will render him odious to the people of upper Louisiana; notwithstanding his present good understanding with the Lieutenant Governor of this place. To force and oblige the people of upper Louisiana to go to Vincennes the seat of Government in the Indiana Territory when ever it might be necessary to make a communication to the Government, or to obtain a final adjudication of any Suit at Law, at all seasons of the year, across the Mississippi, and through a Desert of two hundred miles, which is rendered uninhabitable for want of wood and water—would be a grievance insupportable; And which has already been spoken of in this place with *deep regret and concern*. The apprehension of the people of Upper Louisiana of their being put under the Laws and Government which now exist in the Indiana Territory is matter of the greatest inquietude, and has filled the minds of those who reflect, with *great alarm and anxiety*. And notwithstanding how desirable soever the measure might be of dividing the Indiana Territory by a line drawn from the bank of the Wabash and St. Vincennes to run due north to Lake Michigan and the Territorial line between the United States and Canada, and of annexing the western part thereof to upper Louisiana, and of putting the whole under one and the same Government for the mutual advantages of both parties;—Yet if this cannot be done without subjecting the Citizens of Louisiana to the Grievances innumerable, of being subject to the Government and Laws of the Indiana Territory, it will be much better for upper Louisiana to be made a seperate and distinct Government from the Indiana Territory *And every part thereof.*—

In consequence of the want of information among the Citizens of this country (which I have already observed) it is probable that petitions will be signed and sent forward to the President and Senate, for the appointment of some designing men in the Illinois Country, East of the Mississippi (who now occupy places sufficient to give them influence over the ignorant and uninformed part of the people, who are, by the by, a great majority) to places of the utmost importance in the Government of Upper Louisiana. We are informed that petitions have been circulated on the Eastern Shore of the Mississippi, in the name of the people of Upper Louisiana, And signed by many and addressed to the President and Senate, praying that John Edgar of Kaskaskias may be appointed Governor of Upper Louisiana. And we are further informed that he is causing letters to be written in his name (for he is incapable of writing them himself) to several members of the Senate, soliciting their Interest in his favour. We are further informed that one John Rice Jones, who is at present Attorney General of the Indiana Territory, and who is a kind of instrument for Governor Harrison, and therefore one of his favorites, has made pretensions, and is supported by Harrison and his influence, for the Commission of one of the Judges of the Province of Louisiana. John Edgar and John Rice Jones have both lived at Kaskaskias for many years past; perhaps, for fifteen or twenty years both the one and the other; And are both well known to the people of Upper Louisiana, And are both hated and detested by them—As having been the cause of the almost entire depopulation of the Town of Kaskaskias and its environs. As for Edgar, as I hinted before, he is a man of no information at all, nor can he be placed in any higher than the most common rank as to natural abilities; And as to education or acquired abilities, he is as perfectly devoid as any country clown you ever saw. In the time of the American Revolution, Edgar lived in Upper Canada under the British Government; he there acted the traitor, and was seised or arrested and sent down to Montreal where he lay in Jail in Irons for a long time untill at last he found means to escape into the United States; otherwise he would have been hanged. Since he has been in this country he has been and is a sort of land Speculator, having brought some merchandise to the Country with him, he was enabled to carry on in some manner his Speculations—by the Assistance of Jones, who formerly wrote for him.—But now there is a young man who serves him in that capacity of a different turn of mind, and who without understanding the English language or any other, produces nothing but bombast; as you will see by his letters as I make no doubt but that you have seen, or will shortly see some of them. Jones is a *cunning fellow* and capable both from natural and acquired abilities of overshooting the greater part of the people—He is a man of a bad character, for which reason he was not suffered by Governor St. Clair to set at the same table with him, while the Governor was at Kaskaskias.—In fact, should both, or either of these persons be appointed to any of the General Offices in the Government of Louisiana, it will be directly contrary, to the wishes of the people of this Country (I mean both sides of the Mississippi, notwithstanding, the petitions may be signed through fear and ignorance) for they are both hated and detested by the people on both sides of the Mississippi. It is thought very strange by many people, that Governor Harrison has taken Jones into favour.—But, it is not strange to those who reflect, for *Jones is a convenient fellow enough*, and is ready *at all times to serve the Governor in any thing he pleases*. In fact *Jones is the very humble servant of the Governor, which is a sufficient reason.*

I have very little time as I only consented last evening to write, and am obliged to send this letter off immediately to the post office in Cahokia for the mail will be closed there this evening. In consequence of which, I shall be obliged to solicite the favour of you to request of

Mr. John Breckinridge who is a Senator from the State of Kentucky to whom I have made a communication some time ago and to whom I have enclosed some remarks that I made on the System of Government and it's operations in the Indiana Territory, the first of January last; which contains a good deal of information on facts which did then and do yet exist in that unhappy Government.—I wish you to be possessed of all the information that I can give you, for which reason, I hope you will pardon the trouble which I propose giving you, by referring you to Mr Breckinridge of Kentuckey—You will be so good as to pardon also any impropriety which you may observe in the style or diction, as I have not been accustomed for many years past to write in English; and this the rather because the *facts are true*.—

Believe me, Sir, that nothing could have induced me to have made the present intrusion, nor to have presumed to approach the first Magistrate of the United States, with this letter and reference but a *feeling sense* of the grievances of the people in this Country, and a full reliance on your Urbanity and benevolence.

The important affairs in which you are engaged will not admit of a leisure moment to drop a line in answer to this, to say only if it has come to hand. But should time permit, and such should be your pleasure a line addressed to the care of the post Master in Cahokia will be forwarded on to me.

I have the honour to be with every sentiment of Respect and Esteem Sir, Your Most Obedient and very humble Servant

I: DARNEILLE

RC (DNA: RG 59, LAR, 4:0460-4); at head of text: "Mr. Jefferson"; endorsed by TJ as received 6 Dec. and so recorded in SJL; also endorsed by TJ:
"Edgar John of Kaskaskia / Jones John Rice } not to be appointed in Louisiana"
and "the writer of this letter is an unprincipled dissipated swindler."

Isaac Darneille (d. 1830) was a former U.S. attorney for the Northwest Territory at Cincinnati. He subsequently settled at Cahokia in the Illinois country and later at St. Louis. A letter from Darneille to TJ dated Cahokia, 27 July 1802, has not been found, but apparently sought increased military protection for settlers in the Illinois country from the Potawatomis. In 1805, writing under the pseudonym "Decius," Darneille composed a series of letters highly critical of William Henry Harrison and his associates in the Indiana Territory, which were soon after published in pamphlet form. Little is known of his subsequent activities. An 1818 petition from members of the Kentucky bar recommending Darneille for a judicial appointment described him as "a practising lawyer, and the Editor of a republican print" (*Indiana Magazine of History*, 43 [1947], 263-4; *Terr. Papers*, 3:430; 14:98-9; 17:604-5; *Letters of Decius* [Louisville, 1805; Sowerby, No. 3342]; Robert M. Owens, *Mr. Jefferson's Hammer: William Henry Harrison and the Origins of American Indian Policy* [Norman, Okla., 2007], 114-16; Vol. 38:314, 315n, 343n, 686).

PETITION WHICH HAS BEEN SENT FORWARD TO CONGRESS: on 26 Oct. and 8 Nov. 1803, the House of Representatives received memorials from the two western counties of the Indiana Territory, St. Clair and Randolph, describing the inconvenience and embarrassment they suffered under their current connection with the eastern counties of the territory and praying that they may instead be united under a single government with upper Louisiana. On 24 Nov., a House committee report denied the memorialists' request, stating that the inconveniences caused by their remote situation were common to all new settlements and would eventually be remedied by the rapid settlement of the area between the eastern and western portions of the territory, especially if the Indian claim to the region was extinguished. The report added further that there was no evidence that the eastern counties were exercising an uncommon or unjust power, or that the situation of the western counties would be improved by a connection with upper Louisiana (JHR, 4:419-20, 439, 457; *Terr. Papers*, 7:140-5, 157-8).

LIEUTENANT GOVERNOR OF THIS PLACE: Charles Dehault Delassus (Vol. 40:654n).

Darneille had sent Senator JOHN BRECKINRIDGE a COMMUNICATION dated 22 Oct. 1803 that was nearly identical in style and content to his letter above to TJ. It also enclosed some REMARKS by Darneille ON THE SYSTEM OF GOVERNMENT entitled "A New year's Gift to those who may be interested in the affairs of the Indiana Territory," dated 1 Jan. 1803 and signed "A Citizen of the World." Darneille explained to Breckinridge that he had intended to publish the essay in Washington but that the "inclemency of the season" delayed his plan and made the information outdated. His remarks denounced the tyrannical authority wielded by the governor and judges of the territory and lamented the "servile attachment" of the inhabitants. The Illinois country suffered in particular, due to its great distance from the territorial courts at Vincennes, which made the pursuit of justice prohibitively expensive and inconvenient. In addition, Darneille criticized Governor Harrison for thwarting efforts to advance the territory to the second stage of government and accused him of forcing residents to sign petitions for his reappointment in exchange for confirming their land titles. Darneille also argued that Harrison was too slow in settling Indian boundaries in the Illinois country (*Terr. Papers*, 7:129-40). Breckinridge apparently showed Darneille's letter and its enclosure to TJ, who returned them with a note addressed to "The honble John Breckinridge" that stated "with compliments & thanks for the perusal" (RC in DLC: Breckinridge Family Papers).

To Albert Gallatin

Thursday morn. Nov. 3. 03.

Th: Jefferson asks the favor of mr Gallatin, on his arrival at his office, to call & accompany him to the Secretary of State's office, where a matter of moment & urgency is to be considered.

RC (NHi: Gallatin Papers); addressed: "Mr. Gallatin." Not recorded in SJL.

MATTER OF MOMENT & URGENCY: on this day the State Department learned that on 17 Aug. a Moroccan cruiser had captured the brig *Celia*, a U.S. merchant vessel (see TJ to the Senate and the House of Representatives, 4 Nov.).

From "The Unfortunate Debtors in Washington County Goal"

Sir Novr. 3rd. 1803

This Address is made to You as the common Father of Us all—the Unfortunate claim I am sensible in your bosom an equality of protection with the fortunate—

We know not immediately the propriety of what We are doing, Whether our Application should come to the Head of the Executive or to some other branch of Authority—

We shall subscribe Ourselves the unfortunate Debtors in Washington County Goal & our present claim on Your Humanity & Philantrophy is Fuel

Several fruitless applications have been made to the Marshall, who informs Us, He has contracted for Coal & We must await its arrival—

May it please Your Excellency—Water is a fluctuating Element & the Wind blows from different points of the Compass: the Young & old immured within the cold & dreary Walls of a Prison would wish for more immediate Advantages of Comfort than what rests upon the Marshall's Contract

with every Hope for relief in Your power & every possible sentiment for Your political & domestick Happiness We write Ourselves

The Unfortunate Debtors in Washington County Goal

RC (DLC); at head of text: "To His Excellency Thomas Jefferson Esqr. President of the United States"; endorsed by TJ as received 3 Nov. and so recorded in SJL.

From Joseph Yznardi, Sr.

Exmo Señor Cadiz y Noviembre 3. de 1803.

Mi mas venerado Señor: desde mi llegada á esta hé cumplido como devy dandole cuenta de la gratitud de mi reconocimiento a sus distinciones y parece hé tenido la desgracia de que no hayan llegado a sus manos segun el contenido de su ultima apreciable.

Bajo fha 22. del Corriente hallará V.E. mi carta remitiendole la Bota de Vino que há costado á mi ver mui caro, sin embargo de ser su calidad excelente por la mucha escasez de esta clase de vinos en España, pero si me autoriza para que le mande una Bota cada 6. meses de vino de igual calidad pero poca Edad, me parece que con la variacion de Clima y dexarla reposar algun tiempo podria estar provisto con mayor Equidad: el importe de dhos Vinos lo Libraré en primera ocasion que se presente para que no sufra descuentos ni cambios que lo harian subir mucho mas.

En algunas de mis dhas cartas signifiqué á V.E. el justo sentimiento q. me havia causado los malos informes q. el Caballero Yrujo dió á esta Corte respecto mi conducta en esa, y de los perjuicios tan considerables q. se me hán causado por no querer yo rebatirlos desconceptuandolo como bien podria, dejando al Silencio toda venganza contentandome con despreciar recompensas de mis meritos y desvelos en servir á este gobierno como consta á V.E. á quien suplico por el cordial afecto con que se há servido distinguirme haga lo posible para que se me pague lo que justamente se me deve hace tantos años cuyas cuentas mandaré al Secretario de Estado pronto, q. no hé podido verificar por mis males y aucencias hasta el dia.

Tambien me es del mayor interes el que se me liberte justamente de la falza calumnia de Josef Israel, por cuya causa se me detiene en esa algunos fondos de consideracion, por la Fianza de un Pleyto q. se me há originado indevidamente, por haber desempeñado con fidelidad los deveres de my Empleo servido con imponderable desinteres y considerables gastos mios sin haver tenido valor para emprender negociaciones de comercio hasta no vindicarme de las supuestas calumnias—todo lo qual represento á la Alta consideracion de V.E.

Asi mismo en una de dhas mis cartas propuse á V.E. el Interes que podria resultar en favor de los comerciantes de ese Pays si se me nombrare por uno de los comisarios para la liquidacion de Presas en la guerra ultima con el justo fin de manifestar mis conocimientos gratitud y desinterez como por reembolzarme yo de los varios Suplementos que hice en dha guerra en las defensas de los Pleytos de Presas en los Puertos de mi distrito y que como Consul el mas Antiguo restableceria los Privilegios establecidos por my, como que los Consules que se nombrasen fueren condecorados por meritos personales y conocidos por hombres de Probidad, y no jovenes llenos de Ambicion afanados por sus particulares intereses en descredito de la nacion que representan, acarreando á esta controversia y no logrando los beneficios generales á favor de su Comercio.

Quando V.E. se dignó nombrarme Consul de esta Ciudad y su distrito fué bajo el Seguro supuesto de la notoriedad de mi conducta y de que lo serviria durante su feliz Administracion con el fin de realizar mis asuntos en dho intermedio y a pezar de no haber logrado esto ultimo, continuaré hasta verificarlo sin embargo de ser Publico de Sumo Trabajo y ningun beneficio que me resulta y comunes desazones q. acarrea el oficio; pero la ultima q. me hé franqeado, manifiesta el Inclusio Parrafo Original que se me acaba de dar por parte de su Autor por haverle negado prestarle mas Dinero quando le hé Subministrado 400.$. y me es bien sensible en que tal Sujeto Tenga valor de Publicar deberle yo lo que el dice ni que meresca ser uno de los Consules de los Ests. Unidos.

Espero en esta á Mr. Pikney y Mr. Graham, segun hé llegado á Saber el primero desea restituirse á ese Continente y si por la cierta experiencia que V.E. tiene de los Sinceros deseos que siempre me hán animado á favor de ese Pays y por el conocimiento personal, Amabilidad y talento como buena reputacion que se há Adquirido en la Corte Mr. Graham me parece seria la unica persona á proposito en quien podria recaer con acierto el Ministerior de Madrid, á donde precirandome pasar á terminar varios asuntos mios propios si se me autorizase con el nombramiento del Consulado Gral ally con retencion de este y dexando aqui competente vice consul desempeñaria aquel unido á dho Mr. Graham con solo el pago de mis gastos y entonces no dudará V.E. que los asuntos de la nacion serán defendidos con completo conocimiento y tal vez con ventajas no esperadas.

Hace tres dias llegó á este Puerto Comodore Preble en su Fragata Constitucion y Schooner Interprice, á proveerse de Aguada y Cables q. necesita, el que dentro de tres o quatro dias Saldrá despachado del todo.

Puedo decir á V.E. que dho comandte. llena verdaderamente el hueco de su Empleo, por Prudencia, Afabilidad y Espiritu el que sin duda debe dar honor á su nacion como lo há principiado con la valerosa resolucion de Tanger que me há llenado de contento porque V.E. Sabe fué uno de mis Planes de ser el unico modo de tratar á los Despotas Gobiernos Berberiscos; pues en una Palabra há hecho mas en pocos dias que otros Soberanos en Años, y no dudaré azote á Tripoly cortando el Yugo conque Solicitan entorpecer el comercio en estos Mares.

La maligna enfermedad de Malaga sigue en aumento segun las ultimas cartas y para q. ese gobierno no formalize queja en tiempo alguno; es de corazon la falta de Policia ni contra el derecho de gentes el rigor con que este trata á los que aprehende infestados, que varios Buques procedentes de Malaga que hán llegado á este Puerto ultimamente, los hán hechados á la mar sin ser admitidos baxo ningun pretexto ni consideracion de naturales, en cuyo caso toda queja de Forasteros es Ilusoria, cerrando la Puerta á todo reclamo en casos semejantes con lo que concluyo teniendo el honor de repetir á V.E. mis consideraciones y respectos.

Exmo. Señor BLM á VE su mas Obte. Servr

JOSEF YZNARDY

EDITORS' TRANSLATION

Most Excellent Sir, Cadiz, 3 Nov. 1803

My most revered Sir: since my arrival here I have fulfilled my duty, as I should have, by sending you an account of my gratitude in recognition of your distinctions toward me, and it seems that I have had the misfortune that this has not reached your hands, according to the contents of your last letter.

Under the date of the 22d of the current month, Your Excellency will find my letter sending a butt of wine of very expensive cost, to my view; however, its quality is excellent given the great scarcity of wines of this kind in Spain. Yet if you authorize me to send you every six months a butt of wine of equal quality but younger age, it seems to me that with the variation of the weather and by letting it rest for some time, you could be provided with greater consistency. The importation of these wines I will put in the books on the first occasion that presents itself so that it does not suffer discounts or changes that would make it go up much more.

In some of my other letters I expressed to Your Excellency the just feelings that the bad reports that the Chevalier Irujo gave to this court caused me, with respect to my behavior in it, and the considerable prejudices that have befallen me for not wanting to refute them and discredit them as I could well do—leaving in silence all vengeance and contenting myself with rejecting the rewards of my merits and cares in serving this government, as Your Excellency can attest, and to whom I beg, for the cordial affection with which you have distinguished me, to do whatever is possible so that what is justly owed to me from so many years is repaid. I will send the accounts, which I have not been able to verify because of my troubles and absences until this day, to the secretary of state soon.

It is also of greatest interest to me to have myself justly freed from the false lies of Joseph Israel, for whose cause some considerable funds of mine are retained for the bail of a lawsuit that wrongly originated from fulfilling with fidelity the duties of my employment served with imponderable disinterest and considerable expense to myself, not having the valor to engage in commercial negotiations until I am vindicated from these alleged lies—all of which I present to the high consideration of Your Excellency.

In this same manner, in one of my other letters I proposed to Your Excellency the interest that might result in the merchants of that country if I were named as one of the commissioners for the liquidation of prizes of the last war with the just end of expressing my knowledge, gratitude, and disinterest, so as to reimburse myself of the various supplements that I made in that war in the defense of lawsuits of prizes in the ports of my district; and that as oldest consul I would reestablish the privileges established by me, such as that the consuls who were named would be rewarded for their personal merits and known as men of probity, and not young men full of ambition, driven by their particular interests to the detriment of the nation that they represent, adding to this controversy and not accomplishing general benefits in favor of your commerce.

When Your Excellency named me consul of this city and its district, you did so under the sure assumption of the reputation of my conduct and how useful I would be during your happy administration, with the end of taking care of my business matters in the interim time. Even though I have not accomplished this last, I will continue until I have carried it out; however, being in a public position of utmost work, no benefits result for me along with the common disappointments that the job brings. The last one that I have overcome, the enclosed original paragraph expresses, which I have just received from its author for having denied to lend him more money when I have given him 400 dollars. It is lamentable to me that this individual has the courage to publish that I owe him what he claims and that I do not deserve to be one of the consuls of the United States.

I expect Mr. Pinckney and Mr. Graham soon, as I have learned that the former desires to return to that continent. For the true experience that Your Excellency has of the sincere wishes that have always animated me in favor of your country and for personal knowledge, kindness, and talent, as well as the good reputation that he has acquired in the court, Mr. Graham seems to me the only person to whom the ministry at Madrid should rightly fall. Having to take care of some of my own matters in that place, if I am authorized with the title of consul general there while retaining this title and leaving here a competent vice consul, I would undertake this new post together with Mr. Graham with only the payment of my expenses. Then Your Excellency will not doubt that the matters of the nation will be defended with great knowledge and unexpected rewards.

Three days ago Commodore Preble arrived at this port with his frigate *Constitution* and the schooner *Enterprize*, to supply himself with water and cables that he needs, and in three or four days he will set sail.

I can say to Your Excellency that the said commander truly fulfills his job, given his prudence, affability, and spirit that no doubt give honor to your nation, as he has shown in the resolution at Tangier, which has filled me with joy because as Your Excellency knows, it was one of my plans that it was the only way of dealing with the despotic Berber governments; for in a few words, he has done more in a few days than other sovereigns in years, and I do not doubt lashes Tripoli, cutting the shackles with which they wish to make the trade in these seas difficult.

The evil disease of Malaga is on the rise according to the last letters, and so that government does not formalize the complaint in due time. It is at heart the fault of policing, even against the law of nations, and so rigorously are those who are thought to be infected treated, that several ships coming from Malaga that have arrived in this port ultimately have been returned to sea without being admitted under any pretext or consideration for local people. In all cases the complaints of foreigners are illusory, the door being closed to all claims in similar cases; with which I conclude, having the honor of repeating to Your Excellency my considerations and respect.

Most Excellent Sir, your obedient servant kisses Your Excellency's hand.

JOSEF YZNARDY

RC (DLC); in a clerk's hand, closing and signature by Yznardi; at foot of text: "Exmo Sor. Dn. Tomas Jefferson"; endorsed by TJ as a letter of October 1804 received 20 Jan. 1804 and so recorded in SJL. Enclosure: extract in Yznardi's hand, undated, reading in its entirety (with two letters supplied in brackets): "I[n]form Mr. Yznardy from G. W. M. El Roy he o[w]es, *his Life* his Consularship and his Reputation to G. W. Mc.ElRoy" (Tr in same).

SI SE ME NOMBRARE POR UNO DE LOS COMISARIOS: in August 1802, Yznardi suggested that he be appointed to the bilateral commission that was anticipated for the settlement of American claims against Spain (Vol. 38:205-8).

SU AUTOR: Yznardi's dispute with George Washington McElroy centered on what Yznardi deemed to be false statements by McElroy about Yznardi's actions as consul. Earlier they had been on better terms, McElroy using a certificate from Yznardi in his successful application in 1802 to become the U.S. consul at Tenerife (Madison, *Papers*, *Sec. of State Ser.*, 3:83; 7:458; Vol. 36:371-2).

In response to increasing mortality from epidemics of yellow fever and typhus at MALAGA, officials closed the port there for a few days in October, then reopened it, then on 21 Oct. ordered ships that had had any illness aboard to leave and seek other harbors to undergo quarantine. That order, like the original closure of the port, was reversed after a few days. Early in November, on instructions from the royal government, authorities decreed that no vessel could leave Malaga even if there was no evidence of disease aboard (Madison, *Papers*, *Sec. of State Ser.*, 5:502, 546, 584; 6:123-4).

From Albert Gallatin

DEAR SIR Friday [4 Nov. 1803]

I enclose the proposals for leasing the salt springs together with some observations of Messrs. Breckenridge & Worthington.

Will it be proper to authorize Govr. Harrison to make a contract with Mr Bell on his giving proper security at $\frac{66\frac{2}{3}}{100}$ or, if he shall think that Bell cannot be depended upon, with any of the other persons (Beiler excepted) on the same terms? For fear that the whole plan should be defeated by the incapacity of the undertaker, some discretion should be given to Harrison, but under what limitations? is the question.

Respectfully Your obt. Servt. ALBERT GALLATIN

RC (DLC); partially dated; endorsed by TJ as received from the Treasury Department on 4 Nov. and "Saltsprings" and so recorded in SJL. Enclosures not found.

For the call for PROPOSALS and the conditions to be met by the leaseholder of the SALT SPRINGS, see Gallatin to TJ, 22 June 1803. William Bell won the three-year contract (Lexington *Kentucky Gazette*, 17 Jan. 1807; Gallatin to TJ, 10 Nov. 1806).

From James Garrard

SIR Frankfort Novr. 4th. 1803

I have taken the liberty to address you on a subject, in which I feel no Other interest, than what is connected with a wish to see real merit rewarded. Report, and your last message to congress, induces a belief, that one, or more governments, will be erected this Session of Congress in the western & southern countries. Should that be the case, I will take the liberty to recommend to your notice Mr. Harry Toulmin, as a gentleman of talents and integrity, to fill the office of secretary of state; or a Judge of a superior court. The former of these offices he has filled in this state for somthing more than seven years, with credit to himself, and the approbation of all ranks of our citizens. His acknowledged abilities in the knowledge of the Laws, will enable him to discharge the duties of a Judge with approbation. I have no hesitation to say he has been a faithful servant to the people of Kentucky. He has discharged the duties of his Office with wisdom, promptness and fidelity. And I have no doubt, but he will discharge the duties of any Office to which he may be appointed, that requires talents and integrity, in the same manner. The Senators and representatives in congress for this state are intimately acquainted with Mr. Toulmin, and I doubt not, but they will second this recommendation with their cordial approbation, to whom (if necessary) I beg leave to refer you for information, and at the same time beg you will not ascribe this application to any other motive, than what is connected with a sincere wish to see government honorably, and profitably administered, and men of real merit promoted.

I have the Honour to be Your Excellency's Most Obt Servt.

JAMES GARRARD

RC (DNA: RG 59, LAR); endorsed by TJ as received 17 Nov. and so recorded in SJL with notation "Toulmin judge or Secy."; also endorsed by TJ: "Toulmin Harry to be Secretary of Judge in Louisiana."

A letter from HARRY TOULMIN to TJ, dated 30 Sep. 1803 and recorded in SJL as received from Frankfort on 18 Oct., has not been found. Toulmin was first recommended to TJ in 1793, shortly after his arrival in Virginia as a Unitarian minister from England. TJ appointed him a judge of the Mississippi Territory in 1804 (ANB; Vol. 27:270-1)

To Lafayette

Washington Nov. 4. 03.

I have recieved several letters from you, my dear friend, since I last wrote to you. that by mr Foncin is delivered this morning. you know my situation too well not to be sensible that I cannot be a punctual correspondent, and you will ascribe the rarity of my letters to it's probable cause, & not to the impossible one of a want of friendship for you. in the affair of your lands be assured we shall do for the best. we are not without hopes of getting a permission by Congress to locate them in any part where they shall have lands to dispose of, which might render them more agreeable & more valuable. I sincerely wish you were here on the spot, that we might avail ourselves of your service as Governor of Louisiana, the seat of which government, New Orleans, is now among the most interesting spots of our country, and constitutes the most important charge we can confer. I believe too you would have found it a pleasant residence. but the circumstances of the country require that officer to be on the spot, & to enter instantly on his charge. I am happy to hear of Madame de Tessé's health, & of the continuance of her taste as an arborist. I know the delight it affords & her enthusiasm for it. I send her by this vessel a box of plants & seeds. I have recieved from mr Cabanis, his book, and wrote him on the 13th. of July, which I hope he has recieved. nothing from mr Tracy has come to my hands, or I should certainly have acknoleged it with pleasure. Spain has protested against the right of France to transfer Louisiana to us: but we have ordered troops to New Orleans to *recieve* or to *take* possession, under the authority of France. we shall know in one month whether force is opposed to us. I am happy to learn you are likely to recover from your unfortunate accident, after so much suffering. I pray you to present my affectionate respects to Mde. de la Fayette & to assure her of my continual attachment. you know my sincere friendship for you, & that no time will affect it. Cordial salutations.

TH: JEFFERSON

RC (NIC: Dean Lafayette Collection); at foot of text: "M. de la Fayette." PrC (DLC). Enclosed in TJ to Robert R. Livingston, 4 Nov.

THAT BY MR FONCIN: Lafayette to TJ, 1 Sep.

For the book sent by Antoine Louis Claude Destutt de TRACY, see Vol. 38:615-16.

To Robert R. Livingston

DEAR SIR

Washington Nov. 4. 1803.

A report reaches us this day from Baltimore (on probable, but not certain grounds) that Mr. Jerome Bonaparte, brother of the first Consul, was yesterday married to miss Patterson of that city.* the effect of this measure on the mind of the first Consul, is not for me to suppose: but as it might occur to him, primâ facie, that the Executive of the US. ought to have prevented it, I have thought it adviseable to mention the subject to you, that, if necessary, you may by explanations set that idea to rights. you know that by our laws, all persons

*Nov. 8. It is now said that it did not take place on the 3d. but will this day.

are free to enter into marriage if of 21. years of age, no one having a power to restrain it, not even their parents: and that, under that age, no one can prevent it but the parent or guardian. the lady is under age, and the parents, placed between her affections which were strongly fixed, and the considerations opposing the measure, yielded with pain & anxiety to the former. mr Patterson is the President of the bank of Baltimore, the wealthiest man in Maryland, perhaps in the US. except mr Carroll, a man of great virtue & respectability: the mother is the sister of the lady of Genl. Saml. Smith;[1] and consequently the station of the family in society is with the first of the US. these circumstances fix rank in a country where there are no hereditary titles.[2]

Your treaty has obtained nearly a general[3] approbation. the Federalists spoke & voted against it, but they are now so reduced in their numbers as to be nothing. the question on it's ratification in the Senate was decided by 24. against 7. which was 10. more than enough. the vote in the H. of R. for making provision for it's execution was carried by 89. against 23. which was a majority of 66. and the necessary bills are going through the houses by greater majorities. Mr. Pichon, according to instructions from his government, proposed to have added to the ratificn a protestation against any failure in time or other circumstance of execution on our part. he was told that in that case we should annex a counter-protestation, which would leave the thing exactly where it was. that this transaction had been conducted from the commencement of the negotiation to this stage of it with a frankness & sincerity honorable to both nations, & comfortable to the heart of an honest man to review: that to annex to this last chapter of the transaction such an evidence of mutual distrust, was to change it's aspect dishonorably for us both, and contrary to truth as to us; for that we had not the smallest doubt that France would punctually execute it's part; & I assured mr Pichon that I had more confidence in the word of the First Consul, than in all the parchment we could sign. he saw that we had ratified the treaty, that both branches had past by great majorities one of the bills for execution, & would soon pass the other two; that no circumstance remained that could leave a doubt of our punctual performance, & like an able & an honest minister (which he is in the highest degree) he undertook to do, what he knew his employers would do themselves were they here spectators of all the existing circumstances, and exchanged the ratifications purely and simply: so that this instrument goes to the world as an evidence of the candor & confidence of the nations in each other, which will have the best effects. this was the more justifiable as mr Pichon knew that Spain had entered with us a protestation against our ratification of the treaty grounded 1st. on the assertion that the First Consul had not executed the conditions of the treaties of cession:[4] & 2ly. that he had broken a solemn promise not to alienate the country to any nation. we answered that these were private questions between France & Spain, which they must settle together; that we derived our title from the First Consul & did not doubt his guarantee of it: and we, four days ago, sent off orders to the Governor of the Missisipi territory & General Wilkinson to move down with the troops at hand to New Orleans to recieve the possession from mr Laussat. if he is heartily disposed to carry the order of the Consul into execution, he can probably command a voluntary force at New Orleans, and will have the aid of[5] ours also if he desires it[6] to take the possession & deliver it to us. if he is not so disposed, *we* shall take the possession, & it will rest with the government of France, by adopting the act as their own, & obtaining the confirmation of Spain, to supply the non-execution of their stipulation to deliver, & to entitle themselves to the compleat execution of our part of the agreements. in the mean time the legislature is passing the bills, and we are preparing every thing to be done on our part towards execution, and we shall not avail ourselves of the three months delay after possession of the province allowed by the treaty for the delivery of the stock, but shall deliver it the moment that possession is known here, which will be on the 18th. day after it has taken place.

I take the liberty of putting under this cover, some letters to my friends who are known to you. that to Mde. de Corny has a small box accompanying it (of about 8. or 9. I. cube) containing a complement of tea to her. the address on the top is to you; but there is nothing in it but the tea. the whole are sent to the care of mr Vale at Lorient, and will probably be taken on by the French gentleman who is the bearer, from mr Pichon, of the ratification of the treaty. Accept my affectionate salutations & assurances of my constant esteem & respect.[7]

TH: JEFFERSON

RC (NNMus); author's note written perpendicularly in margin of first page; addressed: "His Excellency Robert R. Livingston M.P. of the US. Paris"; endorsed by Livingston. PrC (DLC). Dupl (NNMus); at head of text: "Duplicate"; consisting only of first paragraph with some additional text (see notes 2 and 7 below); endorsed by Livingston. Enclosures: (1) TJ to Madame de Tessé, 31 Oct. (2) TJ to Madame de Corny, 1 Nov. (3) TJ to Pierre Samuel Du Pont de Nemours, 1 Nov. (4) TJ to Lafayette, 4 Nov. Enclosed in TJ to Aaron Vail, 4 Nov.

MARRIED TO MISS PATTERSON: on 25 Oct., during his brief visit to Washington, Jerome Bonaparte surprised Louis André Pichon by announcing his intention to marry 18-year-old Elizabeth Patterson. Madison was aware of the pending marriage by 28 Oct., writing on that day to advise Livingston about it, and Pichon dined at the President's House on the 29th.

Jerome invited Pichon to attend the wedding in Baltimore on 3 Nov., but after consulting his copies of French laws and paging through issues of the *Moniteur* for recent information, the diplomat concluded that the young man was not of legal age and the union would not be valid in France. Pichon refused to take any part in the ceremony. Carlos Martínez Irujo, however, and his wife, the former Sally McKean of Philadelphia, encouraged the couple to go ahead with their plans. Pichon shared his information about French matrimonial law with the prospective bride's family, including her father, William Patterson, and her uncle by marriage, Samuel Smith. Although Jerome, who turned 19 in mid-November, claimed that his commission as a *lieutenant de vaisseau* in the French navy proved him to be at least 21 years of age, Pichon advised Patterson that under current law in France, a person must be at least 25 to marry without parental consent. In addition, the bride's family received information about liaisons between Jerome and several women. Patterson put an end to the wedding plans and sent his daughter away to visit relatives. Jerome, too, left Baltimore, making an excursion to New York. Yet Elizabeth, supported by some members of her family, wanted the marriage. In December, she and Jerome were both back in Baltimore and she prevailed on her parents to sanction the wedding. Her father hired Alexander J. Dallas to review the legal issues and craft a prenuptial agreement that Patterson hoped would protect his daughter's interests. The couple wed in a Catholic ceremony in Baltimore on 24 Dec. (Edouard Dentu, ed., *Mémoires et correspondance du roi Jérôme et de la reine Catherine*, 7 vols. [Paris, 1861-66], 1:233-59; Helen Jean Burn, *Betsy Bonaparte* [Baltimore, 2010], 48-53; Charlene M. Boyer Lewis, *Elizabeth Patterson Bonaparte: An American Aristocrat in the Early Republic* [Philadelphia, 2012], 24-8; Madison, *Papers*, *Sec. of State Ser.*, 5:586-7; 6:317).

Elizabeth Patterson's MOTHER was Dorcas Spear Patterson, the sister of Samuel Smith's wife, Margaret Spear Smith (Lewis, *Elizabeth Patterson Bonaparte*, 13).

WE ANSWERED: Madison to Irujo, 4 Oct., noted as Enclosure No. 23 to TJ to the Senate, 17 Oct.

The FRENCH GENTLEMAN whom Pichon chose to be the courier was perhaps M. A. F. P. Engrand; see his undated letter to TJ at [before 25 Sep.]. Late in October, the secretary of the navy informed Thomas Tingey that "Mr. Ingran" would sail to France on the vessel chartered to carry the ratification documents to Europe (Robert Smith to Tingey, 29 Oct., in DNA: RG 45, MLS).

[1] Dupl: "the mother of the young lady is the sister of mrs Smith, wife of Genl. Sam. Smith."

[2] Dupl here continues and concludes: "in fact the grade of members in society among us is precisely what it now is in France, attached to the individual, not to his family. the scale of honours is always the same, but it is liable to mutations among those who occupy it's different parts. Accept my friendly salutations and assurances of constant esteem & respect."

[3] TJ here canceled "ratification."

[4] Word interlined in place of "St. Ildefonso."

[5] TJ first wrote "he can command a voluntary force at New Orleans, and is authorised to [act]" before altering the passage to read as above.

[6] Preceding four words interlined.

[7] TJ added two postscripts to the Dupl, the first reading "P.S. Nov. 8. it is now said the marriage did not take place on the 3d. but will this day" and the second reading "P.P.S. Dec. 31. immediately after the preceding date, mr Patterson refused his consent peremptorily to the marriage, which was believed then to be broken off. M. Bonaparte went to N.Y. and miss Patterson was sent to mr Nicholas's on James river, in Virginia. it happened that she found his family just setting out on a visit to their friends in Baltimore, she returned with them. M. Bonaparte was quickly back, & their wishes were at length yielded to."

From Thomas Munroe

Friday [4 Nov. 1803]

T. Munroe presents his most respectful Compliments to the President.—Drafts of the Surveyor of the public buildings for freestone & workmanship, & for foundation stone to the Amt. of between two & three thousand Dollars having been presented today & TM not having so much money in his hands has the Honor of inclosing a requisition for the Presidents signature if approved.

RC (DLC); partially dated; addressed: "President"; endorsed by TJ as a letter of 4 Nov. received that day and "Warrt. 10. ~~M~~. D." and so recorded in SJL. Enclosure not found.

From Simon Nathan

Sir [New York] 4 November 1803

Having had the Honor of your personal acquaintance during our Revolution in 1777. 1778. & 1779. at the time you presided as chief Magistrate for the State of Virginia, you no doubt Sir, will recollect that I was not inactive in rendering the assistance to Government at that time in my power, which the minutes of the then presiding Council will shew.—that I gave also my Services with money, and my own credit to the State of South Carolina in 1780 & 1781. after the British had taken possession of Charleston &c. that I procured cloathing &c &c for Governor John Rutledge for the Carolinia Troops. Since that period I have acted with the Same uniformity in my Political Sentiments. These circumstances are well known to many Gentlemen of note in virginia, Baltimore, Philadelphia, & New York.

I have since 1783 been engaged in Mercantile business and Navigation in which I have met with many heavy losses, so that I have been under the necessity of closing my affairs in 1800.—Since which Adversity has prest hard upon me—and all my industry has but merely been sufficient to give bread to my Family. thus unfortunately Situated, I am led respected Sir, to make my application to you, in the hope that If any Post should offer wherein my services might be deemed competent, that you would esteem me worthy, from the statement I have drawn of my conduct to bestow it on me

I will no longer presume to wrest your attention to my hard necessities, but in the full confidence that you will take my earnest appeal into due consideration, I beg leave to Subscribe myself, Sir with the highest Sentiments of Respect & Esteem, your mo. obedt. Humble Servant

SIMON NATHAN

RC (DNA: RG 59, LAR); dateline torn; addressed: "Thomas Jefferson Esqr. President of the United States Washington"; postmarked; endorsed by TJ as received from New York on 7 Nov. and "for office" and so recorded in SJL.

Simon Nathan, a merchant, engaged in a lengthy dispute with the state of Virginia, beginning during TJ's governorship, over the rate at which certain bills of exchange were to be discharged in paper money. In 1803, Nathan was residing in New York (*Longworth's American Almanac, New-York Register and City Directory, for the Twenty-Eighth Year of American Independence* [New York, 1803; Shaw-Shoemaker, No. 4535], 224; Vol. 3:315-16, 428; Vol. 5:152-3; Vol. 6:200, 270, 321-4n).

From Beriah Palmer, Thomas Sammons, and David Thomas, with Jefferson's Query

SIR Washington Novr. 4th. 1803

Although three Commissioners of Bankruptcy has been heretofore appointed in the city of Albany, state of New York; only one of those acts in that capacity, the others haveing accepted appointments under the state government incompatible with the duties of this office—Permit us therefore to recommend Sebastian Visscher and Elisha Dorr as suitable persons to fill these vacancies—

As we reside in the vicinity of Albany we are enabled to Judge of the propriety of these appointments, and do hope they will meet with your Excellencys approbation—

BERIAH PALMER
TH. SAMMONS
DAVID THOMAS

[*Query by TJ:*]

Who are those who have disqualified?

RC (DNA: RG 59, LAR, 11:0388-9); in Thomas's hand, signed by all; at head of text: "To His Excellency The President of the United States"; endorsed by TJ as received 5 Nov. and "Visscher & Dorr to be Commrs. bkrptcy" and so recorded in SJL.

Born in Massachusetts, Beriah Palmer (1740-1812), a practicing attorney, settled in Ballston Spa, Saratoga County, New York, in 1774. In 1791, he was appointed judge of the court of common pleas. He served several terms in the state assembly before his election to the Eighth Congress. Thomas Sammons (1762-1838), a farmer, lived on his homestead near Johnstown in Montgomery County, New York. Elected for the first time to the Eighth Congress, he served three more terms. Both congressmen were Revolutionary War veterans and both were delegates to the state constitutional convention in 1801. During the 1804 gubernatorial campaign, Palmer and Sammons questioned the assertion of Burrite Republicans that TJ "had expressed himself equally favorable" to the election of Burr or Morgan Lewis. The two New York congressmen met with TJ, who recalled that during the earlier meeting he had expressed regret at division "AMONG REAL REPUBLICANS" and noted that in that case the administration would remain neutral. TJ had clarified, however, that he did not consider the "Little Band," that is, the friends of Burr, "AS MAKING ANY PART OF THE REAL REPUBLICAN INTEREST" (New York *American Citizen*, 10 Apr. 1804; Mary-Jo Kline, ed., *Political Correspondence and Public Papers of Aaron Burr*, 2 vols. [Princeton, 1983], 2:852-3; *Biog. Dir. Cong.*; *Albany Centinel*, 15 Sep. 1801; New York *Republican Watch-Tower*, 7 Apr. 1802). For Thomas's position in the 1804 New York election and his previous recommendations for bankruptcy commissioners, see Vol. 39:629n. Upon their election to the Eighth Congress, DeWitt Clinton described Palmer, Sammons, and Thomas as "members of the Old republican party—In whom every reliance may be placed" (Vol. 37:516-7).

APPOINTMENTS UNDER THE STATE GOVERNMENT: in early 1803, Abraham G. Lansing was appointed Treasurer of New York State. Nicholas Quackenbush resigned as bankruptcy commissioner after the New York Council of Appointment named him "First Judge" for the county of Albany. In April, the council appointed Abraham Ten Eyck, Quackenbush's replacement, a judge of the court of common pleas, and George Merchant, the third bankruptcy commissioner, an assistant judge. In the fall election, Ten Eyck, Merchant, and Sebastian Visscher were elected aldermen in Albany, but that would not effect their eligibility (New York *American Citizen*, 17 Feb.; New York *Chronicle Express*, 14 Apr.; *Albany Gazette*, 25 Apr.; *New-York Herald*, 5 Oct. 1803; Nicholas N. Quackenbush to TJ, 8 June; Jeremiah Van Rensselaer to TJ, with Jefferson's Note, 12 Oct.).

ELISHA DORR made and sold hats "as cheap as can be purchased" in New York City or Albany. They were "not inferior in colour to any imported, and more durable." Dorr was an officer in Albany's society of mechanics. He was a member of the Republican corresponding committee in 1803, and in 1804 he served on the general committee, led by Merchant and Visscher, in support of Lewis as the Republican candidate for governor (*Albany Centinel*, 12 Oct. 1802; *Albany Gazette*, 3 Feb., 25 Apr. 1803, 1 Mch. 1804).

TJ appointed no new bankruptcy commissioners at Albany (list of commissions in Lb in DNA: RG 59, MPTPC; Vol. 37:704, 707-11).

To the Senate and the House of Representatives

TO THE SENATE AND HOUSE OF REPRESENTATIVES OF THE UNITED STATES.

By the copy, now communicated, of a letter from Capt Bainbridge, of the Philadelphia frigate, to our consul at Gibraltar, you will learn that an act of hostility has been committed, on a merchant vessel of the United States, by an armed ship of the Emperor of Morocco. This conduct on the part of that power is without cause, and without explanation. It is fortunate that Capt Bainbridge fell in with, and took, the capturing vessel, and her prize; and I have the satisfaction to inform you that, about the date of this transaction, such a force would be arriving in the neighborhood of Gibraltar, both from the East, and from the West, as leaves less to be feared for our commerce, from the suddenness of the aggression.

On the fourth of September, the Constitution[1] frigate Capt. Preble, with Mr Lear on board, was within two days sail of Gibraltar, where the Philadelphia would then be arrived with her prize, and such explanations would probably be instituted as the state of things required, and as might perhaps arrest the progress of hostilities.

In the mean while, it is for Congress to consider the provisional authorities which may be necessary to restrain the depredations of this power, should they be continued. TH: JEFFERSON

Nov. 4. 1803.

RC (DNA: RG 46, LPPM, 8th Cong., 1st sess.); in Lewis Harvie's hand, signed and dated by TJ; endorsed by a Senate clerk. PrC (DLC); in TJ's hand. Recorded in SJL with notation "Marocco." Enclosure: William Bainbridge to James Simpson, dated 29 Aug. 1803 on board the frigate *Philadelphia* near Malaga, reporting his capture of the Moroccan cruiser *Mirboka* and liberation of the American brig *Celia*, which the Moroccans had taken on 17 Aug. near Barcelona; Bainbridge took possession of both vessels and confined the Moroccan officers on the *Philadelphia*, who subsequently confessed that their cruiser went to sea "for the sole purpose of Capturing Americans" and with the authority of the governor of Tangier, Abd al-Rahman Ashash; Bainbridge and his prisoners blame Ashash for the affair, and Bainbridge hopes that his capture of the *Mirboka* will convince the emperor of Morocco "that if he injustly goes to Warr with the U.S. he will loose every large Cruiser he has"; Bainbridge has treated his prisoners with leniency and civility in order to "impress on their mind a favourable Opinion of the American Character"; Bainbridge is anxious to receive Simpson's reply as well as instructions from Commodore Preble regarding the captured ship (Tr in DNA: RG 59, CD, Gibraltar, at head of text: "Copy"; Tr in DNA: RG 233, PM, in a clerk's hand, incomplete; PrC in DNA: RG 46, LPPM, incomplete; ASP, *Foreign Affairs*, 2:591-2; Vol. 38:176n).

Bainbridge's dispatch was forwarded by the American CONSUL AT GIBRALTAR, John Gavino, in a brief letter to James Madison dated 1 Sep. 1803, which was received by the State Department on 3 Nov. (RC in DNA: RG 59, CD, Gibraltar; Madison, *Papers, Sec. of State Ser.*, 5:373-4).

A brief dispatch dated THE FOURTH OF SEPTEMBER from Edward PREBLE to the secretary of the navy stated that the *Constitution* was near Cape St. Vincent, Portugal, and would anchor at Gibraltar "the day after tomorrow" (NDBW, 3:18).

FOR CONGRESS TO CONSIDER: the Senate took no immediate action on TJ's message, but the House of Representatives referred it to a special committee for consideration. On 15 Nov., the committee reported a bill "for the further protection of the seamen and commerce of the United States," which authorized the president to permit public and private armed vessels of the United States to seize all vessels, goods, and effects of the emperor of Morocco or his subjects. The House passed the bill unanimously on 17 Nov. and sent it to the Senate, where an amended version passed on 28 Nov. A second House committee reported on 1 Dec., but further consideration of the bill ceased after TJ's message of 5 Dec. announced the reaffirmation of peace with Morocco (JHR, 4:436-7, 444, 446-7, 461, 465, 467; JS, 3:308, 312-13, 316; *A Bill For the further protection of the Seamen and Commerce of the United States*, 15 Nov. 1803 [Washington, D.C., 1803; Shaw-Shoemaker, No. 5223]; *Mr. Samuel Smith, from the committee appointed on "the bill for the further protection of the seamen and commerce of the United States," reported the following amendments*, 23 Nov. 1803 [Washington, D.C., 1803; Shaw-Shoemaker, No. 5309]; TJ to the Senate and the House of Representatives, 5 Dec. 1803).

[1] Word interlined in TJ's hand in place of "Boston"; also corrected by TJ in PrC.

To Aaron Vail

SIR Washington Nov. 4. 03.

The schooner Citizen, capt Lawson, being employed by our government to carry some gun carriages to the Emperor of Marocco, and to touch at Lorient, in going, in order to deliver there the ratification of our late treaty with France, I take the benefit of your cover for a letter to mr Livingston, our Minister Plenipotentiary, accompanied by a small box of about 8. or 9. inches cube addressed to him; which I will pray you to put into the care of the French gentleman, whom mr Pichon has entrusted with the ratification, if he can conveniently take charge of it, or otherwise to send it by the Diligence or such other conveyance as will be safe and not too costly for the value of the box which is but small. I avail myself of the same occasion to send a box of plants to my friend Madame de Tessé (aunt of the Marquis de la Fayette) at Paris. this is about three quarters of a ton in bulk (say 15. cubic feet) and is heavy; consequently requires the cheapest transportation possible to avoid it's becoming a very burthensome present. if the state of the war will permit it's going round by sea to Havre, & up the Seine to Paris, that is the best conveyance. but if Havre is blockaded, I must leave to you to chuse the cheapest mode of conveyance to be depended on. if you could take the trouble to drop a line to Madame de Tessé (to the care of mr Livingston) suggesting to her the practicable modes of conveyance, she would probably say which she would prefer. but if they can go by Havre, that is so obviously the best, that she need only be informed you have sent them by that route. I pray you to excuse the trouble I give you, which is occasioned by the accident of the ship's touching at your port; & to accept my salutations & good wishes.

TH: JEFFERSON

PrC (MoSHi: Jefferson Papers); at foot of text: "Mr. Aaron Vale"; endorsed by TJ in ink on verso. Enclosure: TJ to Robert R. Livingston, 4 Nov., and enclosures.

FRENCH GENTLEMAN: see TJ to Livingston, 4 Nov.

To Albert Gallatin

TH:J. TO MR GALLATIN Nov. 5. 03.

Bell being the lowest bidder for the saltsprings has on that ground the first claim for preference. his character moreover, & the moderation of his views recommend him: but there seems just reason to apprehend he is too moderate, and that he has erred against himself in his calculations, being perhaps too sanguine. it is never the interest of a landlord to break his tenant. in this case it would be peculiarly unfortunate, as it would furnish ground to the next undertaker to fix a higher price than is proper, & this would be permanent, & consequently lastingly injurious to that country. I think therefore we should not hold him to his bid of .49 cents, but allow him what he can live by. I wish Govr. Harrison had informed us what was his first bid, as that was probably made on sounder views. as the next lowest bid is 80. cents, I think we might recieve Bell at $\frac{2}{3}$ of a dollar: & if his first bid was more than that & under 80. cents I should think it best for the country to allow him that: for it is their interest to give a living price. his security should be solid for the money advanced; but if sufficient for that, I should not be for losing the bargain for want of security equal to a larger sum. if he cannot give security I think we should leave the whole to Govr. Harrison's discretion, with a single exception against any person interested or concerned directly or indirectly in any other saltwork. Affectionate salutations.

PrC (DLC). Recorded in SJL with notation "Salines."

LOWEST BIDDER: on 20 Nov., Tennessee congressman William Dickson wrote Andrew Jackson that "a Mr. Bell of Kentucke has offered to make in the year 120.000 Bushl. of Salt at 49 Cents. Some other propositions have been made as low as from 70 to 80 cents. I believe orders have been issued to close the contracts" (Harold D. Moser and others, eds., *The Papers of Andrew Jackson*, 9 vols. [Knoxville, 1980-], 1:259n, 398-9).

From James Madison

[5 Nov. 1803]

The Louisiana documents did not come from Mr. Gallatin till a day or two ago. I have this morning delivered 38 revised pages, which will go to the press, a few of which have been some time in the types. There will be abt. $\frac{1}{3}$ or $\frac{1}{2}$ as many more. No time will be lost. The bulk of the work will apologize to the House for the delay

RC (DLC); undated; address clipped: "The Presid"; endorsed by TJ as received from the State Department on 5 Nov. and "Louisiana documents" and so recorded in SJL.

The LOUISIANA DOCUMENTS were compiled from letters sent by Daniel Clark in answer to queries composed by TJ and Albert Gallatin and also from information Gallatin and Madison obtained from other sources. Madison dispatched Jacob Wagner to draft a report that TJ submitted to Congress on 14 Nov. and that was widely published as *An Account of Louisiana, Being an Abstract of Documents, in the Offices of the Departments of State, and of the Treasury* (DNA: RG 59, TP, Orleans; *Terr. Papers*, 9:49-54; Queries on Louisiana, at 9 July; William C. C. Claiborne to TJ, 24 Aug.; Gallatin to TJ, 8 Nov.).

From Jared Mansfield

SIR, Marietta Novemb 5th 1803

Agreeably to instructions received from the Secretary of the Treasury, I set out from New Haven About the end of September & arrived in this place the 26th ultimo. Some troubles & inconveniences experienced on my journey, have prevented me from addressing you on a subject which I intended should have been understood previous to my entering on the duties of Surveyor General. It was my intention to have requested the favour of a reservation of my commission of Captain in the Corps of Engineers, in case of any unauspicious circumstance which might occur to me in this country. The reasons for this request are more immediately these—1st. The weak state of my nerves, & badness of my health in general, which prevent me from any certain calculation of what I may be able to perform. I recollect to have stated this, when I had the honor of conversing with you at the city of Washington—2d The particular esteem & attachment,[1] which I had acquired from the whole corps of Engineers, & the improvements which I was about to advance, rendered the situation extremely pleasant, though not profitable. It would be above all things a most desirable object, when through bodily debility, or indeed any circumstances, the public interest might be more promoted by my removal, that I might be reinstated in the Corps of Engineers. I have no doubt, that the same Goodness & Attention which have thus far advanced me, would be extended to the provision of some suitable place, if it were possible that I could be of any Utility. To me it appears, that a man of science, with habits of sobriety, though advanced in years, or in a state of debility arising from disease, or naturally weak nerves, would not be, by any means, unfit for the instruction & education of youth. This would more particularly be the case, when by long habit & experience the person had acquired talents for the business.

I do not know how far the granting of this request may be consistent with the rules established by Government. I think I have been informed that, it is not a novel procedure—

At any rate I conceive that a reappointment might take place, & I must in conformity to my wishes, humbly beg the favour in such case, as I have suggested, that you would regard one who is with the most sincere Attachment

Your devoted Humbe. Servt, JARED MANSFIELD
Surveyer General

RC (DLC); endorsed by TJ as received 18 Nov. and so recorded in SJL.

RESERVATION OF MY COMMISSION: on 28 Nov. 1803, TJ received an undated letter from Henry Dearborn that stated "I presume Sir that Capt. Mansfield may be continued as an officer of the Corps of Engineers, agreably to his request" (RC in DLC; undated; addressed "The President of the United States"; endorsed by TJ as received from the War Department on 28 Nov. 1803 and "Capt Mannsfield" and so recorded in SJL).

[1]MS: "attachmen."

To Jones & Howell

GENTLEMEN Washington Nov. 6. 03.

Be pleased to send two tons of nailrod assorted from 6 d. to 20 d. sizes to Richmond addressed to messrs. Gibson & Jefferson for me, & with as little delay as possible. the suspension of intercourse by the fever has occasioned my nailery to be nearly out & it will be quite so before this supply arrives. mr Barnes will remit you immediately 45 D. 81 c the amount of the last bill now due. Accept my salutations & good wishes. TH: JEFFERSON

PrC (MHi); endorsed by TJ in ink on verso. Recorded in SJL with notation "2. tons rod."

LAST BILL: see TJ to George Jefferson, 12 Aug. In a letter of 8 Nov. to Jones & Howell, TJ reminded the firm of his intention to have John Barnes remit the sum: "he yesterday sent me the enclosed check on the bank of the US. which I now forward to you with my salutations & respects" (PrC in MHi; at foot of text: "Messrs. Jones & Howell"; endorsed by TJ in ink on verso; recorded in SJL with notation "45.80"). See also MB, 2:1111.

To William Short

DEAR SIR Washington Nov. 6. 03.

Your's of Oct. 25. from Prestwood came to my hands last night. it is the first knolege of your motions I have had since you set out for Kentucky: and having long expected you were on the road back, I knew not how to write to you. this has been the cause of my keeping a letter recieved for you from France a considerable time ago: & I do not send it now lest you should have left Richmond, where you say you should arrive the 1st. inst. on your way here. that land is the best form in which one can have property in this country is my fixed opinion. there is a reasonable chance by renting it, to get an active interest of 5. or 6. per cent; and there is a silent rise of value of two or three times that amount; which serves to cover the depreciation of the money in which it is nominally valued, & leave still a large increase of capital. money in the funds or banks, offers but it's annual interest, while it depreciates fully as much. no body can doubt that the value of money compared with the necessaries of life is lessened here one third or one half, within the last 10. years. this has two causes; the inordinate increase of paper circulation from banks, which must be 3, 4, or 5 times of the whole circulation existing at the commencement of the present government: & 2dly a similar depreciation in England, with whose affairs we are so intimately united, that they produce a common effect. there is this difference in our favor, that *as yet* an individual[1] can get *dollars* for his paper, & therefore has it in his power to replace his depreciation, which cannot be done in England; as a guinea is now never seen there. the evil here will I trust cure itself. the annual increase of banks will render the evil visible to every eye, & they will be spunged by a legislative stroke, & a scale of depreciation. I cannot say I am satisfied you can rent all your lands advantageously, because my farm at Lego has laid idle 7. years for want of tenants, & Shadwell as good as idle, having been in the hands of little tenants from whom nothing can be got, & who cannot be kept within any rules of culture. yet I confidently expect that the facility of obtaining tenants will increase daily. in the leasing your lands you must not expect to lease every hundred acres. a considerable proportion of it is on the mountain side, a noble appendage to the residence of a proprietor, if kept in wood & inclosed & laid down in grass. but nobody would rent it for these purposes. and if it were cleared, a great deal of it is of inferior quality & would infallibly run off in gullies in a very few years. I think you could not do better than to continue Durret's lease. the rent is sufficient, & the course of culture very advantageous for the land. in whatever you determine however, have nothing to do with Catlett. his character is in three words, a sharper, bankrupt & besotted. he has a neat industrious & valuable wife; but she has not been able to save him. I say this to you in confidence of course, because I do not wish to quarrel even with an indifferent neighbor; but every person in that neighborhood would in confidence tell you the same. I think you had better put every thing respecting your land into the hands of Price. he is illiterate, & slow, but very steady, honest & punctual. he would be equal to the two objects of seeing that the tenants observed the rules of culture, & of remitting your rents to Richmond where your affairs will of course require you to have a resident agent. after taking a view of the neighborhood, I cannot see any one who can so effectually take care of your land as Price. these loose & hasty ideas may give you some views which, matured by your own reflections, may enable you to settle things to your mind.

On your arrival here I shall expect you to be of our daily mess as usual. mr Barnes has removed his dwelling in Georgetown. whether he has room for a lodger in his new situation I know not. we have a vessel sailing immediately on public account to Lorient. she was to have gone yesterday: but the Marocco news has made the owner desirous to get off of his bargain.[2] if he goes it will be in a day or two. if not, another will be procured to go as immediately as practicable. I mention this as you might wish to write. Accept my salutations and assurances of constant affection & esteem. TH: JEFFERSON

RC (DLC: Short Papers); at foot of first page: "Mr. Short"; endorsed by Short as received 10 Nov.

For the NEWS from Morocco, see TJ to the Senate and the House of Representatives, 4 Nov.

[1] Preceding two words interlined in place of "we."

[2] Preceding three words interlined.

From Joseph H. Nicholson

SIR Novr. 7. 1803

I do myself the Honor to enclose you a Letter from Major Thomas Smyth; requesting that he be named to you, as an Applicant for Office in Louisiana—Knowing the number of Applications which are now before the Executive for Office in this Country, I would not have added another to the List, but under an Impression of Duty—I beg

Leave to add that this Gentleman is a Man of Business, with a good Character, and that I believe he served in the American Army, during the greater part of the Revolutionary War—

I am Sir with the highest Consideration Yr. Ob. Servt.

JOSEPH H. NICHOLSON

RC (DNA: RG 59, LAR); endorsed by TJ as received 7 Nov. and "Smyth Thos. for office N.O." and so recorded in SJL. Enclosure: Thomas Smyth, Jr., to Nicholson, Baltimore, 4 Nov. 1803, noting that he plans to move to the newly acquired territory with his family "as soon as it is deliver'd to our Government"; he requests that Nicholson, a long-time acquaintance, apply to the president on his behalf for an appointment "in the Revenue" at New Orleans (RC in same).

Believing that his earlier application had not received the "earnest solicitation, or particular recommendation" he desired, Smyth, a merchant of Chestertown, Kent County, Maryland, wrote Madison later in November and applied specifically for the position of naval officer at New Orleans. For information respecting his "Capacity and principles," Smyth referred the secretary of state to Maryland senators Samuel Smith and Robert Wright and Senator John Taylor. In the House, he used Samuel Hammond of Georgia and Walter Bowie "and the Representatives of Maryland generally" as references. Smyth noted that he would have secured "independence and comfort" as a merchant during the Revolutionary War if he had not taken up arms for the American cause (Smyth to Madison, 25 Nov., RC in same, endorsed by TJ: "to be Navl officer N.O."; Madison, *Papers, Sec. of State Ser.*, 6:100).

To Martha Jefferson Randolph

Washington Nov. 7. 03.

So constant, my dear daughter, have been my occupations here since Congress met, that it has never been in my power to write any thing which could admit of delay at all: and our post now passing but once a week, lessens the opportunities, tho the rapidity is increased to 24. hours between this place & Charlottesville. I recieved by mr Randolph the frills & a pair of stockings. it will be impossible to judge as to the proportion of fur until the season comes for wearing them. I think that with the stock I now have, a supply of 2. pair every winter will keep me furnished. I judge from your letter that you are approaching an interesting term, & consequently we shall be anxious to hear from you or of you by every post. I hope you have mrs Suddarth with you, & that on the first alarm you will require the attendance of a physician, because being on the spot, a word of advice often saves a case from being serious which a little delay would render so. never fail therefore to use this precaution. we are all well here, but immersed in the usual bickerings of a political campaign. the feds are few, with little talent on their side, but as much gall at least as those who are wicked & impotent usually have. how much happier you in the midst of your family, with no body approaching you but in love and good will. it is a most desireable situation, & in exchanging it for the scenes of this place we certainly do not calculate well for our happiness. Jerome Bonaparte is to be married tomorrow to a miss Patterson of Baltimore.—give my warm affections to my Maria & tell her my next letter shall be to her. kiss all the fireside, and be assured yourself of my never-ceasing love. TH: JEFFERSON

RC (NNPM); at foot of text: "Mrs. Randolph." PrC (MHi); endorsed by TJ in ink on verso.

A LETTER of 22 Oct. from Randolph, recorded in SJL as received 30 Oct., has not been found.

Martha SUDDARTH was a midwife and nurse in Albemarle County (Vol. 35:511n).

From James Jones Wilmer

SIR, Annapolis, Novr. 7th. 1803.

I did myself the honor some time ago to transmit you a copy of the publication entitled "Man as he is &c." I am about printing a second edition with the 3d part added, which will make the work compleat, and meet with, I trust, your entire approbation. Having in my time contributed to the stock of knowledge in the republic of Letters, I think I have some small claim on my Countrys protection. The Church has nothing to give. I must therefore solicit your Excellencys benevolence to procure me some appointment, immaterial where, if I can be useful and have a support. Perhaps in the arrangement of matters to the southward you can nominate me to an office. Living a life of temperance in all things, my health and intellects are sound and active. I have three Sons, the eldest in the navy of the United States. The other two are yet to be brought forward as Providence may direct.

I have the honor to be, with Sentiments of respectful attachment, Your most obt. JS. JS. WILMER

RC (DLC); endorsed by TJ as received 8 Nov. and so recorded in SJL.

TRANSMIT YOU A COPY: see Wilmer to TJ, 15 Sep. 1803.

From John Alexander

SIR November 8th. 1803.

I have taken the liberty of writing to you, on a subject which I deem will be of use to the Citizens of America in general, and to the American youth in particular.

Having been for many years employed in the Study & instruction of the Mathematics, I have found great inconvenience, as well as expense, arising to Students, in procuring books on the different branches in which they have been educated. I have long thought that this inconvenience might be remidied, by the publication of a book on Theoretical and practical Mathematics; having the rules and Suitable examples laid down in a clear & comprehensive manner. For Some time past I have had it in view to Compose a work of this kind, in which I propose to insert every thing useful in the different branches, with accurate calculations, and (when necessary) concise demonstrations rendering the whole So plain, as to be acquired by a tolerable genius, without the assistance of a teacher. It may be said by Some, that there are a sufficient number of books written on the Subject of Mathematics, and to publish more would be useless: to Such I would only remark, that tho' many learned and ingenious men have written on this Subject, yet their productions are generally large Volumes and couched in Such abstruse terms, that young beginners are really afraid of looking into them; and I have taken notice, that such books instead of encouraging often prevent youth from ever entering upon Such Studies. Therefore my design in publishing a book of the above description, is not so much to extend the limits of Science; as it is to clear away the rubbish which Stands in the way to what is already known; and to open a path, by which the youth of the united States, may have an easy access to whatever is curious and useful in that Kind of Knowledge. This work may be comprised in one quarto Volume containing about 500 pages, the contents, and arrangement of which, will be nearly as follows. viz.

1 Useful Geometrical problems & Theorems demonstrated.
2 Plane Trigonometry
3 Mensuration of Superfines & Solids
4 Gauging
5 Surveying—by Calculation
6 Navigation
7 Dialing
8 Conic Sections—applied in Gunnery
9 The projection of the Sphere
10 The construction of Maps
11 The Use of the Globes
12 Mechanics
13 Spherical Trigonometry
14 Astronomy &c.

Now the object I have in view in addressing you on this Subject, is, to obtain your opinion respecting the utility of a work of this kind? the manner in which it ought to be executed? and (if you think it will meet with encouragement) the plan I must pursue in order to get it published? Your answer directed to the care of Mr. Overton Carr, Hinson Branch, will oblige

Sir, your most Hble. Servant JOHN ALEXANDER

RC (DLC); endorsed by TJ as received 8 Nov. and so recorded in SJL.

The Alexander family of Rockbridge County had been prominent in educational institutions and academies in western Virginia. In April 1801, TJ had considered a young man named John Alexander from Rockbridge County and his brother Andrew as possible candidates for marshal of the western district of Virginia (Madison, *Papers, Sec. of State Ser.*, 8:540; Vol. 32:359-60; Vol. 33:643; Vol. 34:258, 494).

From Albert Gallatin

DEAR SIR 8 Nov. 03

By conversation with Doctr. Jones, I find that the Bentleys who apply for the office at Yeocomico are tories: why Mr Taliafero, recommended one of them I cannot understand; but Doctr. Jones lives within three or four miles from the spot, & his information is certainly to be preferred. Major Tapscott is the republican candidate; as there is no surveyor or other officer in the district, it will, notwithstanding the unimportance of the office, be eligible to fill it early, as a vessel might land there a cargo without a single individual opposing it.

I enclose the rough draft of the answer to Govr. Harrison; if the discretion given to him be too great, please to correct it. I have modified the express prohibition against those concerned in any lick, as I believe that almost every applicant was concerned in some small spring or another—Mr Bell, I know, was so engaged. Mr Bedinger of Congress has given me a letter from a Mr Morgan who he says may be depended upon as to veracity, although he may be mistaken in the quantity of water, and which I enclose on account of his information respecting Mr Bell.

Several of the memoranda enclosed by Mr Clarke to Mr Madison deserve notice; and I have noted such as relate there particularly to the Treasury department. It is necessary to observe that none of the general officers of the Spanish province of Louisiana can be appointed & perhaps very few can be removed by the Governor or Intendant;

and that great many of those offices ought immediately to cease or to be exercised by other persons. I think therefore

1st. that the Collector of Natchez (Mr. Triest) should by next mail receive a commission Vesting in him the powers heretofore exercised by the *Administrator Treasurer* & *Contador* of the custom house, which will enable him to collect the revenue

2d. that the Governor (Claiborne) should be specially authorized & directed to suppress all useless offices & to suspend all officers as he shall think fit. In order to throw light on this subject I enclose two papers which I have extracted from the several documents sent by Clarke & which are much more correct than his own results as, from having neglected to analyse the treasurer's accounts of which he had obtained a copy, he had supposed the expence of the Province more than 200 thd. dollars greater than they really are

The first paper or "Receipts & Expenditures for 1802" is authentick, being the real account for that year. the other paper is the estimate of the annual expence drawn in 1785, but corrected for 1803 by the Contador of the army, and arranged by me for the purpose of classifying the several species of officers; it will, though only an estimate give more information for the intended object than the account. I have preserved copies of neither & will occasionally want them again. I think that they ought not to be printed with the other papers as they bear evident marks of official documents & would injure the person from whom obtained who is the same whom Clarke recommends for Spanish Consul at New Orleans.

Respectfully Yr. obt. servt. ALBERT GALLATIN

RC (DLC); addressed: "The President of the United States"; endorsed by TJ as received from the Treasury Department on 8 Nov. and "Bailey & Tapscott. Salines. New Orleans" and so recorded in SJL. Enclosures not found, but see below.

The BENTLEYS who applied for office have not been identified. TJ clearly wrote "Bailey" in his endorsement and in SJL.

REPUBLICAN CANDIDATE: according to SJL, Joseph Jones Monroe wrote TJ from Westmoreland County, Virginia, on 3 Nov. and recommended "Tapscott" as collector at Yeocomico in place of James A. Thompson, but the letter has not been found. Monroe probably informed TJ of Thompson's death. Martin Tapscott received the appointment (TJ to the Senate, 9 Dec.).

The MEMORANDA ENCLOSED by Daniel Clark to the secretary of state with a letter of 8 Sep. included Clark's responses to TJ's set of queries on Louisiana and additional information, some of which the president sent to Congress and was printed as the *Account of Louisiana* (*Terr. Papers*, 9:28-47; Madison to TJ, [5 Nov.]; Notes on Spanish Expenditures for Louisiana, printed at 8 Nov.; TJ to the Senate and the House of Representatives, 14 Nov.).

A commission dated 14 Nov. authorized Hore Browse Trist (TRIEST) "to exercise all the powers and authority heretofore exercised by" the ADMINISTRATOR (*administrador*) of the custom house; the TREASURER, who according to the information seen by TJ and Gallatin was essentially "a cashier"; and the CONTADOR, sometimes referred to in English as a comptroller general, who "keeps all accounts and documents respecting the receipt and expenditure of the revenue." The commission also gave Trist "generally all the powers and authorities respecting the Collection of such public Revenues which were or might be exercised by any other officer of the said Province" (FC in Lb in DNA: RG 59, MPTPC; *An Account of Louisiana, Being an Abstract of Documents, in the Offices of the Departments of State, and of the Treasury* [Washington, D.C., 1803; Shaw-Shoemaker, No. 5196], 39-40; *Terr. Papers*, 9:39-40).

FOR SPANISH CONSUL: Clark recommended Gilberto de Leonard, that is, Gilbert Leonard, an Irishman who was the acting *contador* and treasurer at New Orleans (Madison, *Papers, Sec. of State Ser.*, 5:497-8; 7:94).

Notes on Governing Louisiana

[on or after 8 Nov. 1803]

Hospital provision for
administration of justice to be prompt.
shipping to be naturalised.

Slaves, importation of
religion support of it to be explained.
Ursuline Nuns. their landed property secured.
debts from Spain to the inhabitants. 500,000. D

the powers of the Administrator, Treasurer & Contador
to be exercised by Collector of Natchez.
power to suppress useless offices,
to suspend all officers
to appoint necessary officers.

MS (DLC: TJ Papers, 137:23684); undated, but see below; entirely in TJ's hand.

TJ wrote these notes after seeing Gallatin's letter of 8 Nov. and the materials from Daniel Clark. For the first four items in TJ's list—from the notation about the HOSPITAL through the one on importation of SLAVES—see his reply to Gallatin on 9 Nov.

SUPPORT OF IT TO BE EXPLAINED: according to Clark's answers to TJ's queries on Louisiana and other information that the administration probably received through Clark, the province's bishop, canons, and parish priests received salaries from the government and allowances for chapel expenses (*Terr. Papers*, 9:41; *An Account of Louisiana, Being an Abstract of Documents, in the Offices of the Departments of State, and of the Treasury* [Washington, D.C., 1803; Shaw-Shoemaker, No. 5196], 36).

About 10 or 12 URSULINE NUNS, described as "all French," lived in the order's convent at New Orleans. Previously, about the same number of "Spanish ladies belonging to the order" had resided there also, but they had all gone to Havana when they thought that Louisiana would be coming under the control of France. The nuns ran a boarding school for young women and received rental income on about a thousand acres of land attached to the convent (same, 36-7).

DEBTS FROM SPAIN TO THE INHABITANTS: Clark reported that inhabitants of

Louisiana and U.S. merchants in the province held certificates totaling about 450,000 Spanish dollars for government salaries, payments owed to workers, and purchases of supplies. The provincial treasury did not have the cash to pay those obligations, but Clark understood that the money might be obtained from Veracruz (*Terr. Papers*, 9:44).

Notes on Spanish Expenditures for Louisiana

[on or after 8 Nov. 1803]

Louisiana.	
Executive	8996.
Judiciary.	3600.
Revenue officers	16,600.
Custom house	10,430.
navigation	9,600
hospitals	30,546
Posts	9,810
miscellaneous	9,234
Clergy	11,484
Education	2,350
Civil list	112,600[1]
Army	372,988.
Indians	61,814.
Presidarios	25,000.
Gallies	100,000
Mobile	13,917
Pensacola	57854
	744,173[2]

MS (DLC: TJ Papers, 137:23682); entirely in TJ's hand; undated, but see below.

TJ probably made these notes from data on LOUISIANA from Daniel Clark. One of TJ's queries asked about expenses of maintaining the province. With his response to that question, Clark included statements, now unlocated, of expenses of the colony in 1785 (totaling 537,869 Spanish dollars); of offices and categories of expenditures created since that time; of receipts and cash outlays in 1802; and of additional sums paid in certificates. TJ may have compiled the list printed above from those statements. For his reply to that query, William C. C. Claiborne lacked the detailed information available to Clark, but gave a total close to the one above—approximately 700,000 Spanish dollars for annual civil and military expenses of Louisiana (*Terr. Papers*, 9:28, 42-3; Queries on Louisiana, 9 July; Claiborne to TJ, 24 Aug.).

[1]The sum is actually $112,650.

[2]That is, 744,223, with the corrected total above (see note 1).

From the Tennessee General Assembly

SIR.

The Representatives of the people of Tennessee concieve it to be their duty to express their entire approbation of the Measures pursued by the Federal Government since the commencement of your administration and a full and complete confidence that such measures will be adopted as will maintain the respectability of the United States abroad—and promote the interest and harmony of our fellow citizens

It is with peculiar pleasure we have felt the fostering hand of the National Government extended towards our remote and infant State. Altho our chartered limits occupy a small spot within the United States and altho we are permitted to inhabit only a small part of our territory, yet we have the gratification of experiencing every aid the General Government can bestow in procuring the friendship of the Indian tribes and obtaining convenient passages through their territory We enjoy a pleasing hope that the utmost exertions will be made by the General Government to extend the Indian boundary line: which would be all important, as well to those who enjoy their rights in the inhabited part of the State as to that part of our citizens who have labored under a deprivation of their property for twenty years—under the confidence that Government would procure an extinguishment of the Indian claim

this subject we are confidant will attract the attention of the Federal Government and recieve the friendly aid of the Executive

The negociation for Louisiana has been as highly appreciated by the citizens of Tennessee as by any others in the United States and we feel ourselves authorised to express an unbounded satisfaction at the event and acknowledge it to be the utmost effort of human wisdom. Sorry are we to suppose there can be any inconvenience in obtaining possession of that desirable country. We feel a confidence from the measures now adopted that the freemen of Tennessee will be foremost in lending their aid to remove any difficulty that may occur from an opposition to the United States taking possession of New Orleans—

Should the measures adopted by the government of the United States be succeeded by the establishment of a Republican Government on the west of the Mississippi, it will remain an existing proof to future generations of the zeal of our government in dethroning ignorance and superstition and establishing in room thereof liberty and right—

In Senate read and unanimously concured with & sent to the House of Representatives—
Attest
James Trimble C.S.

James White
Speaker of the Senate

House of representatives
November 8th 1803
read and unanimously adopted
Edw Scott C H R

James Stuart
Speaker of the
house of representatives

RC (DLC); in Trimble's hand, signed by White, Stuart, Trimble, and Scott; at head of text: "An address from the Legislature of the State of Tennessee to the President of the United States"; endorsed by TJ as received 20 Nov. and so recorded in SJL.

James White (1747-1821) was a pioneer settler in Tennessee and founder of the town of Knoxville. He served in the state senate from 1796 to 1797 and from 1801 to 1805. Surveyor and tavern keeper James Stuart (1751-before 1816) represented Washington County in the house of representatives from 1796 to 1799 and from 1803 to 1805, serving as speaker during each of his three terms (Robert M. McBride and Dan M. Robison, *Biographical Directory of the Tennessee General Assembly*, 2 vols. [Nashville, 1975-79], 1:704, 779-80).

To James Jones Wilmer

Washington Nov. 8. 03.

Th: Jefferson presents his compliments to mr Wilmer & his thanks for the pamphlet he was so kind as to send him, which he shall read with pleasure the first moment of leisure he has: his present situation rarely presenting him that enjoiment, & especially during the session of the legislature.

PrC (DLC); endorsed by TJ in ink on verso.

PAMPHLET: see Wilmer to TJ of 15 Sep.

From Henry Dearborn

War Department
9th. Nov. 1803.

Sir,

I have the honor to transmit you a list of the promotions and appointments which have taken place in the Army of the United States, during the last recess of Congress.—

Accept, Sir, assurances of my high respect and consideration

H. Dearborn

RC (DLC); in a clerk's hand, signed by Dearborn; at foot of text: "The President of the United States"; endorsed by TJ as received from the War Department on 17 Nov. and "Military appointments" and so recorded in SJL. FC (Lb in DNA: RG 107, LSP). Enclosure: "List of Promotions and Appointments in the Army of the United States, during the last recess of Congress" (MS in DLC: TJ Papers, 136:23478, undated, in a clerk's hand; FC in Lb in DNA: RG 107, LSP). See TJ to the Senate, 18 Nov. 1803.

To Albert Gallatin

Th:J. to mr Gallatin Nov. 9. 1803.

The memoranda you inclosed me from mr Clarke deserve great attention. such articles of them as depend on the executive shall be arranged for the next post. the following articles belong to the legislature.

the administration of justice to be prompt. perhaps the judges should be obliged to hold their courts weekly, at least for some time to come.

the ships of resident owners to be naturalized, & in general the laws of the US. respecting navigation, importation, exportation &c to be extended to the ports of the ceded territory.

the hospital to be provided for.

slaves not to be imported, except from such of the US. as prohibit importation.

Without looking at the old Territorial ordinance I had imagined it best to found a government for the territory or territories of *lower* Louisiana on that basis. but on examining it, I find it will not do at all; that it would turn all their laws topsy-turvy. still I believe it best to appoint a governor & three judges, with legislative powers; only providing that the judges shall form the laws, & the Governor have a negative only, subject further to the negative of the National legislature. the existing laws of the country being now in force, the new legislature will of course introduce the trial by jury in *criminal* cases, first; the habeas corpus, the freedom of the press, freedom of religion &c as soon as can be, and in general draw their laws & organisation to the mould of ours by degrees as they find practicable without exciting too much discontent. in proportion as we find the people there ripen for recieving these first principles of freedom, Congress may from session to session confirm their enjoiment of them.

As you have so many more opportunities than I have of free conference with individual members, perhaps you may be able to give them these hints, to make what use of them they please. affectionate salutations. TH: JEFFERSON

P.S. my idea is that upper Louisiana should be continued under it's present form of government, only making it subordinate to the National government, and independant of Lower Louisiana. no other government can protect it from intruders

RC (NHi: Gallatin Papers); addressed: "The Secretary of the Treasury"; endorsed. PrC (DLC). Recorded in SJL with notation "Louisiana."

MEMORANDA YOU INCLOSED: see Gallatin to TJ, 8 Nov.

OLD TERRITORIAL ORDINANCE: Northwest Ordinance of 1787 (*Terr. Papers*, 2:39-50). On 26 Mch. 1804, the president signed "An Act erecting Louisiana into two territories, and providing for the temporary government thereof." The law provided that LEGISLATIVE POWERS in Orleans Territory be shared by the governor and a legislative council made up of 13 "of the most fit and discreet persons of the territory" appointed annually by the president. For the legislation, see U.S. Statutes at Large, 2:283-9.

UPPER LOUISIANA: see TJ to William Henry Harrison, 31 Mch. 1804.

To Robert R. Livingston

DEAR SIR Washington Nov. 9. 1803.

My letter of the 4th. with a P.S. of the 8th. being delivered to the Captain of the vessel, the object of the present is to inform you that the reports of both those days prove to be unfounded, and that it is questionable whether the marriage spoken of is to take place. you will therefore depend on future evidence as to the fact, & only use the apology if the issue should render it necessary. our last news from New Orleans state such a degree of tranquility there as indicates that no forcible opposition to our possession is meditated. affectionate salutations & good wishes TH: JEFFERSON

RC (NNMus); addressed: "Robert R. Livingston esquire Minister Plenipotentiary of the US. of America at Paris" and "to the care of mr Vail Commercl. Agent of the US. at Lorient"; endorsed by Livingston. PrC (DLC).

From James Low

November 9 1803
New Jersey state
somerset County Near Princeton

Worthy Sir

you will prhaps be surprised at recieving this leter from a person whome you have never as mutch as heard of before, but I hope you will exuse my freedom as I had no other way to introduce my[1] self to your notice. and being encouraged by the Charecter that I have heard you represented under that is a benovelent frind to mankind and one who Did not pay attention to fortune, but to abilities and principal. I had no person to make application for me I therfor Concluded to make application to you my self in this maner and leave it to your Honour whether you thought me worthy of your attention or not—if you think me worthy of your notice I Can produce Recomendations from some of the Princaple Repubcan Citizens of the state of my good Conduct and fidelity

I am now in my twnty sixth year a Pennsylvania by Birth: I lost my father three months before I seen the light. he fell at Brandywine fighting for his Countrys rights which you are now maintaining to the satisfaction of a great majority of the american Citizens: I am the only Child and had the misfortune to loose my surviving parent at five years of age I was put to a trade but not being able to folow it after I had learned it un act of my health: I was then without Learning or any way to maintain my self but by perticular attention I learned to write a tolarable hand and got acquaind with figures and was soon Capable of teatching a small school which I now folow for a Living I have from my earliest Days been fond of acquiring Knowledg. and wishing if it was posable to attain to something greater than a Country schoolmaster I Did not know to whome I Could apply with more hopes of sucess than to you Sir who has so mutch in[2] your power and who I belive from every information to be a friend to the unfortunate and virtious I have nothing to recomend me to you or any other person but my Character and behaviour and I am proud to say that I have ever suported a good Charecter

By the Late traty with france I supose there will be a Number of [young?] men who may to get into impoy[ment In?] the Louisana Country or in the indian Department as I find by your speech to Congress that you intend establishing trading houses among them. perhaps Sir I might be Capable of acting in some of them places to the advantage of Country If you Sir would see fit to put me into some small post or office whare I might make a living and acquire knoledg and Reputation. I Should indevour as far as my abilities would permit to gain the aprobation of my patron by my fedility and applications to business If it is possable for you to Do anything for me in that way I shall try to express my gratitud beter by my actions than by my words

If you think me worthy your attention a line will be attended to as soon as recieved. In Hopes of your approbation I Remain your Humble Servant

James Low

RC (DNA: RG 59, LAR); torn; addressed: "To His Excellency Thomas Jefferson President of the united States Washington City"; franked; postmarked Princeton, 8 Nov.; endorsed by TJ as received 11 Nov. and "for emploiment in Louisiana" and so recorded in SJL.

James Low was born in late 1777, three months after his father became a casualty in the battle of Brandywine on 11 Sep. On an undated list of candidates for employment or office in the Louisiana Territory, TJ wrote next to his name "illiterate. 26. y. old. schoolmaster" (list of candidates for office in Louisiana, undated MS in DLC: TJ Papers, 119:20570-1, printed in Vol. 43: Appendix II).

[1]MS: "my my."
[2]MS: "in in."

To James Madison

Th:J. to Mr Madison. Nov. 9. 1803.

I inclose you Clarke's memoranda. the following articles seem proper for Executive attention.

an instrument vesting in the Collector of Natchez the powers of the administrator, Treasurer & Contador.

Instructions to Claiborne to suppress useless offices
to remove any existing officers.
to appoint others

it would be well these could go by next post.

would it not be well to send in what documents we have, and furnish what is not yet prepared, as well as what may come hereafter in a supplementary way from time to time as recieved.

PrC (DLC). Recorded in SJL as a letter to the State Department with notation "powers to Claiborne." Enclosures: see Madison to TJ, [5 Nov. 1803], and Gallatin to TJ, 8 Nov. 1803.

INSTRUCTIONS TO CLAIBORNE: in a 14 Nov. 1803 letter to William C. C. Claiborne, Madison enclosed a "supplimental commission" from the president, also dated 14 Nov., which expanded the authority granted in his previous commission of 31 Oct. The additional document gave Claiborne the power "to remove such officers and to appoint to such offices which are or may become vacant, and to suppress such other offices," in Louisiana, "as the public good may seem to you to require" (FC in Lb in DNA: RG 59, MPTPC; Madison, *Papers, Sec. of State Ser.*, 6:36-7).

From James Stevens

HOND. SIR— Stamford Novr. 9th A 1803

Without the happiness of being personally known to you I take the liberty to solicit of you a favor; which I have no doubt will be granted provided it be Consistent with the publick good:—I say without being[1] personally known to you, for the presentment to you which, I had the honor to procure through the agency of Mr *John Griffiths* in January 1799 at Philedelphia must long Since have given place in your mind to more important objects—

The late cession by France to the United States of the Territory of *Louissiana* togather with the proceedings of Congress theron, has left the Executive of the United States the temporary government of that Territory togather with the appointment of proper officers to Execute it:—I have entertained an inclination to see that part of the world, and if any Subordinate office Should remain vacant which I might be capacitated to fill it would be highly gratifying to me to be appointed thereto—

I confess prudence has much to do in the Solicitation, perhaps more than ambition; Still I have so much ambition that I Should dread no punishment worse than filling an office with Small dignity—Should any office remain unfilled I do not Solicit[2] an appointment thereto untill I shall forward my Charracter by some freind in whom you may repose confidence, I am only giving you this early trouble because Mr. Edwards through whom I intend to Solicit is [not at] hand; and I wish not to fail for want of favourable application—

Should your weightier concerns leave time to inform me whether any such vacancy exists it would much oblige Sir your most Obedt. Huml. Servt. JAMES STEVENS

Note I have not specified any office by name as it may depend on what one may remain unfilled and also[3] on the nature of my recommendation

RC (DNA: RG 59, LAR); torn; at head of text: "Thomas Jefferson Esquire President of the U.S."; endorsed by TJ as received 14 Nov. and "for employment in Louisiana" and so recorded in SJL.

James Stevens (1768-1835) of Stamford, Connecticut, studied law and served in the state legislature for several terms beginning in 1804. On his list of candidates for employment in Louisiana, TJ recorded his name with the adjacent comment "illiterate." Stevens received a recess commission as principal assessor for the second collection district of Connecticut in 1816 and became a probate district judge in 1819. He was elected that year as a Republican to the Sixteenth Congress, serving a single term in the United States House of Representatives (*Biog. Dir. Cong.*; JEP, 3:26, 31; list of candidates for office in Louisiana, undated MS in DLC: TJ Papers, 119:20570-1, printed in Vol. 43: Appendix II).

MR. EDWARDS: possibly Pierpont Edwards of New Haven.

[1]MS: "being being."
[2]Preceding four words interlined.
[3]MS: "als."

From Joseph Anderson and William Cocke

SIR Nov 10th [1803]

In Compliance with the request express'd in your note of the 5th Instant—we Recommend James Trimble Esqr Atty at Law—as a Commissioner of Bankruptcy—in the room of Edward Scott resign'd—Mr. Trimble resides at Dandridge in the County of Jefferson—

with Sentiments of Very high Consideration—we are most Respectfully

JOS: ANDERSON
WM. COCKE

RC (DNA: RG 59, LAR); partially dated; in Anderson's hand, signed by him and Cocke; endorsed by TJ as received 11 Nov. and "Trimble James to be Commr. bkrptcy. Ten. v. Edwd Scott" and so recorded in SJL.

TJ's NOTE of 5 Nov. to the Tennessee senators is not recorded in SJL and has not been found.

The State Department issued a commission for JAMES TRIMBLE as bankruptcy commissioner for the District of East Tennessee on 12 Nov. and TJ entered the change on his list of nominations for bankruptcy commissioners (list of commissions in Lb in DNA: RG 59, MPTPC; Vol. 37:711).

Writing from Knoxville, EDWARD SCOTT notified Madison on 22 Aug. that he found "it inconvenient to discharge the duties of Commissioner of Bankruptcy" and was returning his commission (RC in DNA: RG 59, LAR; endorsed by TJ: "resigns as Commr. bkrptcy Tennissee"). For Scott's appointment, see Vol. 38:469-70 and Vol. 39:272-3.

From J. P. G. Muhlenberg

Custom House Philadelphia
SIR Novr. 10th. 1803.

I have the Honor to inform You, That by the Ship Mary Ann, just arrivd from Havre, I have receiv'd Eight Boxes of Wine, for The President of the U. States directed to my care—I have had the Wine landed, & as soon as the Duties, & the freight can be ascertained I will do myself the Honor to transmit the information To The President—The Sloop Harmony, Capt. Ellwood, sails from this Port, on Saturday next, for George Town and as so good an Opportunity may not offer, for some time to come, I shall forward the Wine in her, hoping it will meet The Presidents approbation.

I have the Honor to be with unfeign'd Respect Sir Your Most Obedt P MUHLENBERG

RC (MHi); at foot of text: "The President of the U States"; endorsed by TJ as received 13 Nov. and so recorded in SJL.

The EIGHT BOXES contained still champagne (Fulwar Skipwith to TJ, 25 Oct.).

From William Short

Richmond Nov. 10 [1803]

Jeffn.—ansr. his of 6.—as to land—Catlett &c.—shall employ Price & consult with Mr G. Jeffn.—hope he will also give his directions when at Monti.—as to [Britony]—Durrets lease—Mr Barnes I shall stop at Semmes's—letter to be still kept for me—shall leave this in a few days & only stop at [Mt. Vernon]—anxious to get into winter quarters before the cold sets in—as to the vessel going to France, I have just written via Norfolk, & my letter wd. not probably be in time—but thank him for his attention

FC (DLC: Short Papers); blurred; partially dated; entirely in Short's hand, consisting of an entry in his epistolary record. Recorded in SJL as received 13 Nov.

From Albert Gallatin

DEAR SIR 11 Nover. 1803

The law having authorized the President to lease the salt springs, it is found necessary that there should be a positive authorization from you to Govr. Harrison. A form is enclosed which, if you shall approve, may be signed & returned to this office by the bearer.

Respectfully Your obt. Servt ALBERT GALLATIN

RC (DLC); at foot of text: "The President of the U. States"; endorsed by TJ as received from the Treasury Department on 11 Nov. and "power to Govr. Harrison to lease Saltsprings" and so recorded in SJL. Enclosure not found.

For the law of 3 Mch. 1803 authorizing the PRESIDENT TO LEASE THE SALT SPRINGS, see Vol. 39:354-5.

List of Interim Appointments from the State Department, with Jefferson's Queries

[on or before 11 Nov. 1803]

Appointments by the President during the recess of the Senate.

1803.			
15	March 4.	Hore Browse Trist,	*of the Missipi territory* Collector for the District of Mississippi. *vice Carmichael removd.*
	9	Same,	Inspector of the Revenue for the post of Fort Adams, in the Mississippi District.
14		Joseph Turner,	*of Georgia* Inspector of the Revenue for the post of Brunswick, in Georgia. *v. Claud Thompson become incapable*
		Same—	Collector of the Customs for the District of Brunswick.
1		Henry Warren—	*of Mass.* Inspector of the Revenue for the port of Plymouth, in Massachusetts. *v. Wm. Watson removd.*
		Same—	Collector of the Customs for the District of Plymouth.
12	15.	Thomas Dudley—	*of N. Carola, now Surveyor of Swansboro' to be* Inspector of the Revenue for the *same* port of Swansborough, in North Carolina. *v. Alexr Carmalt dead.*
2	April 20.	Isaac Ilsley—	*of Mass.* Collector for the District of Portland and Falmouth, in Massachusetts *instead of Daniel Ilsley jr. which was a misnomer*
10	May 10.	Jeremiah Bennet junr—	*of N.J.* Collector for the District of Bridge Town, in New Jersey. *v. Eli Elmer removd. for delinquency*
		Same—	Inspector of the Revenue for the several ports within the District of Bridge Town.
7		Samuel Osgood—	*of N.Y.* Naval Officer for the District of New York, in the State of New York. *v. Richd Rogers removd.*

3		Samuel Ward—	*of Mass.* Naval Officer for the District of Salem and Beverly, in Massachusetts. *v. Joseph Story declined.*
13	June 16.	Brian Hellen—	*of N.C.* Collector for the District of Beaufort, in North Carolina. *a new district*
		Same—	Inspector of the Revenue for the port of Beaufort.
4		Thomas Durfee—	*of R.I.* Inspector of the Revenue for the port of Tiverton, in Rhode Island. *new.*
11		Charles Gibson—	*of Maryld* Inspector of the Revenue for the port of Easton, in Maryland. *new.*
	16. June 1803.		
		Charles Gibson—	Surveyor of the port of Easton, in Maryland.
5		Thomas Durfee—	Surveyor for the port of Tiverton, in Rhode Island.
8	Augt 24.	Callender Irvine—	*of N.Y.* Inspector of the Revenue for the port of Buffaloe Creek. *new*
		Same—	Surveyor of the port of Buffaloe Creek.
9		Robert Lee—	*of N.Y.* Collector for the District of Niagara. *new?*
		Same—	Inspector of the Revenue for the port of Niagara.
6	Sep: 16.	Abraham Bishop—	*of Conn.* Collector for the District of New Haven, in Connecticut. *v. Saml. Bishop dead.*
A		*James Monroe*[1]	
e.		Edward Turner,	of the Mississippi Territory Register of the Land office within the same, for the Lands lying west of Pearl River, in the County of Adams.*
d.		Isaac Briggs,	of Maryland, Surveyor of the Lands of the US. South of the State of Tennessee,

* A similar Commission was issued blank for the County of Washington, and since, we have not been informed, with whose name it was filled.

f.	Charles Jones Jenkins	of South Carolina—a Commissioner of the US. under the act of Congress of the 9th July 1798 providing for the valuation of Lands & dwelling houses & the enumeration of slaves—for the 5th. Division of said State *v. Saml Hay resd.*
	James Wilkinson,	Benjamin Hawkins and Robert Anderson—Commissioners for the purposes of treating with the Creek nation of Indians for a cession of their lands.[2]
a.	Thomas Rodney	of Delaware. a Judge of the Mississippi Territory.
g	Tench Coxe	of Pennsa. Purveyor of Public Supplies of the US. *v. Israel Wheelen resd.*
b	Nathan Sanford	*of N.Y.* Attorney of the US for the District of New York—*v. Edwd. Livingston*
c	Jared Mansfield	of Connecticut Surveyor General of the[3] *lands of the US. N.W. of the Ohio v. Rufus Putnam removd for incompet.*[4]
		Consuls
E	John Leonard—	*of New Jersey* Vice Consul of the US for the Port of Barcelona *v. Wm. Willis*[5] *resigned*
F	Isaac Cox Barnet	*N.J.*[6] Commercial Agent for the port of Havre de Grace in France *v. Peter Dobell resd.*
G	Levitt Harris of Pennsa.	Consul for St. Petersburg in Russia
C	James L. Cathcart	Consul of the US for the City and Kingdom of Tunis *v. Wm. Eaton resd.*
D	John M Goetschius of *N.York*[7]—	Consul for the port of Genoa *v. Fred. H. Walloston superseded.*
B	Tobias Lear of Virginia—	Consul Genl. for the City and Kingdom of Algiers; also a Commissioner to treat of peace with the Bashaw of Tripoli. *v. James Leander Cathcart translated to Tunis.*

[*Queries by TJ*:]

1803. Supplement.

Mar. 1.	Zachariah Stevens Survr. & Inspectr. Gloster Mass. Wm Patterson N.Y. Coml. Agt. Nantz John Martin Baker N.Y. Consul Minorca	these were nominated to the Senate Feb. 2. and commissions were signed Mar. 1. qu. whether they had been approved by the Senate?

Isaac Ilsley jr. Collector of Portland. in the nominaton to the Senate he was, by misinformation called *Danl.* Ilsley jr. by what name was he approved by Senate?

Mr. Wagner's list has enabled me to supply some omissions in my own, & particularly the blanks filled up in my absence: but if my list is not erroneous, the following are omitted in his: & if so I must ask the precise *designation* of their office, mine being entered shortly.

Apr. 18. James Monroe. M. P. to London.

May 4. Commercial Agent at Antwerp v. Barnet. with whose name is the blank filled?

MS (DLC); undated; in the hands of Daniel Brent and two other clerks, with TJ's emendations rendered in italics; numerals and letters in left margin added by TJ in pencil as he arranged the nominations for his letter to the Senate of 11 Nov.; TJ later drew two diagonal strokes through his queries; endorsed by TJ: "Renominations, Nov. 11. 1803."

Daniel Brent and two other clerks, under the direction of Jacob Wagner, worked on this list of temporary commissions issued by the State Department after the 3 Mch. adjournment of Congress. Brent wrote the caption and entered, in chronological order, custom house officers, that is, collectors, surveyors, and naval officers, appointed between 4 Mch. and 16 Sep. A second clerk entered the territorial, land office, and other appointments, from Edward Turner to Jared Mansfield. A third person entered the consular appointments. Upon receipt of this list, TJ added information—rendered in italics in the document above—including the names of those removed or replaced and the reason for the change. TJ also added the numerals and the lowercase and capital letters to the left of the entries as he rearranged the appointments for submission to the Senate. In his message to the Senate of this date, he began with the diplomatic appointments, the first entry being James Monroe, whom TJ had added to the list above (see note 1, below) and noted with an "A" in the margin. He continued with the consular nominations, ending with Levitt Harris, "G." TJ next listed the territorial, land office, and other entries, next to which he placed lowercase letters, from Thomas Rodney, "a," to Tench Coxe, "g." Finally TJ entered the names of the custom house officers, which he rearranged, as indicated by the numerals placed in the left margin, from chronological to geographical order, beginning with the Massachusetts nominees and ending with those from Georgia and Mississippi Territory (see TJ to the Senate, 11 Nov.).

INSTEAD OF DANIEL ILSLEY JR. WHICH WAS A MISNOMER: in January 1803, Republicans recommended Isaac Ilsley to replace Nathaniel F. Fosdick as collector. In the nominations he sent to the Senate on 2 Feb., however, TJ wrote "Daniel Illsley junr." In the letter to the Senate, a clerk interlined "Isaac" in place of "Daniel," but TJ's retained copy remained unaltered. On his personal chronological list, TJ entered "Isaac Illsley jnr." at 1 Mch., the person confirmed by the Senate. On 20 Apr., when TJ became aware of the mistake, he entered "Isaac Illsley" on his personal list in place of "Isaac Illsley, junr. by misnomer" (Vol. 39:415n, 437, 438n, 634; Vol. 40:243n, 717).

Robert Lee was the first collector appointed FOR THE DISTRICT OF NIAGARA, although Congress had authorized its organization in 1799 (Vol. 40:585-6, 592).

REGISTER OF THE LAND OFFICE: on 15 July, TJ instructed Ephraim Kirby to select Edward Turner's counterpart for lands lying east of Pearl River. On 16 Dec., Kirby informed TJ that he had filled the blank commission entrusted to him with the name of Joseph Chambers.

TREATING WITH THE CREEK NATION: for the appointment of the commissioners and their failure, in the summer of 1803, to procure "an additional cession of lands," see Dearborn to TJ, printed at September 1803. There was no longer any need to have the nominations confirmed by the Senate. TJ canceled the entry and did not include the commissioners on his list to the Senate of this date.

On 3 Mch., Senator Thomas Sumter of South Carolina informed the secretary of state that JOHN LEONARD would readily accept the position of vice consul at Barcelona and would leave immediately (RC in DNA: RG 59, LAR; endorsed by TJ: "Sumter Genl. to mr Madison. Leonard to be Consul at Barcelona"). The State Department issued his temporary commission on 7 Mch. (MS in DNA: RG 59, PTCC). For the resignation of William WILLIS, see Madison, *Papers, Sec. of State Ser.*, 4:357, 358n).

The 2 Feb. nominations of Stevens, Patterson, and Baker were among those referred to a Senate committee on 8 Feb. The committee reported on 1 Mch. and on the same day the nominees were APPROVED BY THE SENATE (Vol. 39:436-7, 438n).

OMISSIONS IN MY OWN: see Appendix I.

On 5 May, Madison sent Robert R. Livingston a blank commission for the appointment of a COMMERCIAL AGENT AT ANTWERP, with instructions to name either Daniel Strobel or Jacob Ridgway to the position. Ridgway accepted the appointment. His was among the nominations TJ sent to the Senate on 9 Dec. (Vol. 40:719n; TJ to the Senate, 9 Dec. 1803).

[1] Entry interlined by TJ in pencil.

[2] Preceding entry canceled with a diagonal stroke.

[3] As he emended this entry, TJ canceled "U. States," written in a clerk's hand.

[4] MS: "inompet."

[5] TJ here canceled "removd."

[6] Interlined by TJ in place of "Pensva," an emendation also in his hand.

[7] MS: "*N. York* of."

From George Maxwell

SIR, Flemington, [11] November 1803.

Having had the honor to receive the enclosed Commission appointing me District Attorney of the United States for the District of New-Jersey, I have endeavoured as far as was in my power to merit the Confidence thus reposed in me. And I assure you Sir, that from the high opinion I entertain of the present Administration I would chearfully retain the Commission, was it not that my private affairs are such that I must attend to them, and that by being absent for some time from this State. Having considerable concerns in the western Country

I must go there and attend to them or else lose very considerably. You will therefore please to accept my resignation of the appointment, and will I hope be of opinion that I would not resign it, could I attend to the Duties thereof.

I am informed and I beleive that the Republican Interest in this State will be promoted by the appointment of William S. Pennington to the office. I am of Opinion that he is fully capable of fulfilling the Duties of the Office, and I know that he is firmly attached to the present Administration.

I remain with Sentiments of the highest esteem and respect for you, Sir, Your obedient Servant, GEORGE C. MAXWELL

RC (DNA: RG 59, RD); torn at dateline; at foot of text: "Thomas Jefferson Esquire"; endorsed by TJ as a letter of 11 Nov. received the 17th and so recorded in SJL with notation "resigns as distr. Atty." Enclosure: Commission dated 26 Jan. 1802 appointing George C. Maxwell "Attorney of the United States in and for the District of New Jersey"; signed by TJ and countersigned by Madison (FC in DNA: RG 59, MPTPC).

A New Jersey native, George Clifford Maxwell (1774-1816) graduated from the College of New Jersey at Princeton, studied law under James Kinsey, chief justice of the state supreme court, and was admitted to the bar in 1797. He resided in Flemington and practiced law in the Hunterdon County courts. At the urging of James Linn and other New Jersey Republicans, the president designated Maxwell U.S. attorney for New Jersey in place of Frederick Frelinghuysen, whose "midnight" appointment the president "considered as null." TJ recorded the interim appointment at 26 June 1801; the Senate confirmed him on 26 Jan. 1802. Maxwell again held a federal office when he was elected as a Republican to the Twelfth Congress. He served a single term and then returned to his New Jersey law practice (*Biog. Dir. Cong.*; J. Jefferson Looney and Ruth L. Woodward, *Princetonians, 1791-1794: A Biographical Dictionary* [Princeton, 1991], 194-6; Vol. 33:183, 184n, 671, 676; Vol. 36:331, 333, 336n).

To the Senate

TO THE SENATE OF THE US.

During the last recess of the Senate, I have granted commissions for the offices, and to the persons following: which commissions will expire at the end of the present session of the Senate. I therefore nominate the same persons to the same offices for reappointment, to wit.

James Monroe of Virginia, Minister Plenipotentiary of the US. to the government of Great Britain, vice Rufus King resigned.

Tobias Lear Consul General of the US. for the city & kingdom of Algiers, & a Commissioner to treat of peace with the Bashaw of Tripoli, vice James Leander Cathcart appointed to another place.

James Leander Cathcart to be Consul of the US. for the city & kingdom of Tunis, vice William Eaton resigned.

John M. Goetschius of New York, to be Consul of the US. for the port of Genoa: vice Fred. H. Wolloston superseded.

John Leonard of New Jersey, Vice-Consul of the US. for the port of Barcelona, vice William Willis resigned.

Isaac Coxe Barnet of New Jersey Commercial agent of the US. for the port of Havre de Grace in France, vice Peter Dobell resigned.

Levitt Harris of Pensva Consul of the US. for St. Petersburg in Russia.

Thomas Rodney of Delaware, a judge of the Missisipi territory vice Seth Lewis resigned.

Nathan Sandford of New York Attorney of the US. for the district of N. York; vice Edward Livingston

Jared Mansfield of Connecticut, Surveyor General of the lands of the US. North West of the Ohio, vice Rufus Putnam removed.

Isaac Briggs of Maryland, Surveyor of the lands of the US. South of the state of Tennissee.

Edward Turner of the Missisipi territory, Register of the land office within the same, for the lands lying West of Pearl river in the county of Adams.

Charles Jones Jenkins of S. Carolina, a Commissioner of the US. under the act of Congress providing for the valuation of lands & dwelling houses, & the enumeration of slaves, for the 5th. division of South Carolina, vice Samuel Hay resigned.

Tenche Coxe of Pensylva Purveyor of public supplies of US. vice Israel Wheelen resigned.

Henry Warren of Massachusets Collector of the customs for the district of Plymouth in Massachusets and Inspector of revenue for the port of Plymouth, vice William Watson removed.

Isaac Ilsley[1] of Massachusets, Collector for the district of Portland & Falmouth in Massachusets, being the same person intended, but misnamed, in a former nomination for the same post to the Senate.

Samuel Ward of Massachusets Naval officer for the district of Salem & Beverley in Massachusets vice Joseph Story declined.

Thomas Durfee of Rhode island Inspector of revenue, & Surveyor for the port of Tiverton in Rhode island.

Abraham Bishop of Connecticut, Collector for the district of New Haven in Connecticut vice Samuel Bishop deceased.

Samuel Osgood of New York, Naval officer for the district of New York in the state of New York vice Richard Rogers removed.

Callender Irvine of New York, Inspector of the revenue & Surveyor of the port of Buffalo creek in New York.

Robert Lee of New York, Collector for the district of Niagara in New York, & Inspector of revenue for the port of Niagara.

Jeremiah Bennet junr. of New Jersey Collector for the district of Bridge town in New Jersey & Inspector of revenue for the several ports within the same district vice Eli Elmer removed.

Charles Gibson of Maryland Inspector of the revenue & Surveyor for the port of Easton in Maryland.

Thomas Dudley of N. Carolina, now Surveyor of Swansboro' in North Carolina, to be Inspector of the revenue for the same, vice Alexander Carmalt deceased.

Brian Hellen of N. Carolina, Collector for the district of Beaufort in N. Carolina, and Inspector of revenue for the port of Beaufort.

Joseph Turner of Georgia, Collector for the district of Brunswick in Georgia, & Inspector of the revenue for the port of Brunswick.

Hore Browse Trist, of the Missisipi territory, Collector for the district of Missisipi in the said territory, & Inspector of revenue for the port of Fort Adams, vice J. F. Carmichael removed.

TH: JEFFERSON
Nov. 11. 1803.

RC (DNA: RG 46, EPEN, 8th Cong., 1st sess.); endorsed by Senate clerks, who also added a check mark at each entry. PrC (DLC); TJ added "approvd" in ink in left margin at head of entries and then added a check mark at each entry. Recorded in SJL with notation "re-nominations."

Lewis Harvie delivered this message to the Senate on 11 Nov., where it was read and ordered to lie for consideration. Four days later, the Senate defeated a motion to refer the nominations to a committee and approved the appointments of Monroe and 17 others. The remaining nominees were approved on 18 Nov., but not without discussion. John Quincy Adams reported that the Senate spent the whole day in debate over the appointment of ABRAHAM BISHOP as collector at New Haven. Senator William Plumer recorded that objections were made "on the ground of his *immoral character*," to which Senator Robert Wright of Maryland replied that "'honesty & capacity were not *yet* requisite qualifications for office—That the great object that we ought now to keep in our constant view is to place *Democrats* in office.'" Plumer observed that all present, except the Federalists, voted for Bishop's confirmation (JEP, 1:452-4, 455, 456; Everett Somerville Brown, ed., *William Plumer's Memorandum of Proceedings in the United States Senate, 1803-1807* [London, 1923], 33-4; John Quincy Adams, diary 27 [1 Jan. 1803 to 4 Aug. 1809], 53, in MHi: Adams Family Papers).

[1]TJ here interlined and then partially erased "junr."

From Samuel Carr

Dear Sir Dunlora Novr. 12th. 1803

Your favor of 24th. October came this day to hand, and I hasten to answer it immediately, but am afraid it will not come in time to answer any purpose. In the course of my conversations with Dr Baker upon the subject of your letter, I inferred from what passed that he would not dispose of him for life, but if he did, not less than four hundred dollars would be his price. The family at this place are all well, as they are also at Carrs brook & Edgehill. My mother and Nelly join me in wishing you welfare and happiness. With sentiments of esteem & affection

I remain Yr friend & sert Samuel Carr

RC (ViU: Carr-Cary Papers); endorsed by TJ as received 20 Nov. and so recorded in SJL.

TJ did not record sending a favor to Carr on 24 Oct., and the letter has not been found. Presumably, TJ inquired about the possibility of purchasing John Freeman, an enslaved servant at the President's House, from William baker. Carr and Baker were friends (Vol. 38:108n).

From Edmund Custis

Sir/ Baltimore 12th Novemr. 1803—

I hope you will pardon the liberty of Soliciting a favor, which I flatter myself my general Character may justify,—finding the Cession of Lousiana ratified, & having been much afflicted with the rumatizm, to which a Warm Climate is favourable, has induced me to think of settling in that Country & as there will probably be many Vacancies, to request the favor of some appointment,—the Collectorship of N. Orleans wou'd be particularly desirable, Or any other that you please,—I have been confined to my House upwards of a Month with the rumatizm, am now on the recovery & hope in a few days to be well enough to do myself the Honor of Waiting on you, with such Credentials as I have no doubt will be Satisfactory—I am with due respect, Sir your Obt. Servt. Edmund Custis

RC (DNA: RG 59, LAR); endorsed by TJ as received 14 Nov. and "to be Collector of N. Orleans" and so recorded in SJL.

For Custis's earlier applications for some appointment, see Vol. 33:301 and Vol. 38:203.

From Nicoll Fosdick

SIR New London Novr. 12th. 1803

I feal it a duty incumbent on me, more perticularly as I am requested by several Respectable Republicans, to state to you some facts respecting Mr. Thomas Paine, which we think you ought to be acquainted with—I presume to do it with less reluctance from the Information I have had of your Character, perticular from my Deceased Friend and near Relation Jonathan Nicoll Havens. I feal confident you will excuse me when I declare my only object in writing is the good of our Cause, and the Respect I owe you—Mr. Paine has been two or three months in Stonington about Eight miles from this, with a Capt. Hayly, an acquaintance of his in France. Sensible of the good Services Mr. Paine had done our Country by his Common Sense, Crisis, Rights of Man &c. I thought with several other old Seventy Six men, that notwithstanding the unfavorable impression his age of Reason had made against him (even among the Republicans) we ought to make him a visit, which we did and found him sociable & civil in Conversation, untill he had made too free with ardent spirits, which we ware very sorry to see, as it made him very vain, and we thought Imprudent, in repeating sentences from his Letters to you, and from yours to him, and in Reading part of one of your Letters to him that gave a description of Louisiana, which tho very pleasing to us we thought improper to be read in a circle, though composed of Republicans, and I think most likely that has been the case whenever he has read that account, which has been several times in different companies—I have not heard of his reading any thing more from your Letters (which he observed was two that he had Received since he had been in this quarter) we have seen Mr. Paine several times, and have in the Course of Conversation observed to him that the Circulation of his age of Reason in this Country had been rather unfortunate, as it had hurt our cause more than benifited it, He was very sanguine we ware mistaken, and that a large majority of the Republicans in the union ware of a Different opinion, and that he was about to give the public a nother part on the same subject, (which some of us had heard before) and which is so far true that he has absolutely wrote a third part, and we have reason to belive it is much more severe and disgusting then any of his former writings on that subject, and therefore we are very anxious some plan should be taken to prevent its publication,—We did not contend with Mr. Paine as to the authenticity of the Scriptures, and I am not certain but half the Company ware of Mr. Paines Opinion when the conversation was had; But we ware all agreed as to any further publications on that subject—We think from Mr. Paines age, and manner of Living that there ought not to be that Confidence placed in him as formerly. Notwithstanding what has been said we feal Tender towards the old Gentleman, and wish not to hurt his Fealings, therefore request this to be Confidential—

Mr. Pain is now in the vicinity of this place, some distance from the Post Rode, and observed to me a few days ago (since the Conversation aluded to) his wish to get to the mail Stage that went to the westward as he was bound to his Farm, which is not far to the eastward of New York, where he went to spend the winter, I told him he must come to New London by water, and call on me, so that I expect to have a short visit from him, which may be rather unpopular; for even by treating him with common hospitality we are Charged with approving of all his writings and all his Conduct, and was I to Justify his age of Reason I should loose most of my Influance among the Republicans in this part of the state—

We have apologized for Mr. Pains age of Reason, by saying he wrote it in France, more perticularly for the French Nation, when they ware rather inclining to Atheism, and on that account was the more excuseable. But if he persists in his plan and publishes the same principals to us in this Country, it will injure our cause very much here, & we shall hardly know what to say—As I am frequently writing the Post Master General, I think it most proper to send this under cover to him, without, however hinting a word to him as to its contents; But refer you to him for any information you may wish respecting myself—Under the pleasing Idea that the apology already made for writing this will be accepted—I am Sir with Sentiments of the highest Esteem & Respect your very

Huml. sevt NICOLL FOSDICK

RC (DLC); at foot of text: "His Excellency Thomas Jefferson"; endorsed by TJ as received 24 Nov. and so recorded in SJL.

Nicoll Fosdick (1750-1820) served during the American Revolution as master of at least two Connecticut-based privateers. While in charge of the *Randolph*, he took 16 prizes. After the war, he became a merchant in New London, where he emerged as a leader of the local Republican organization. He was commissioned by the Treasury Department to help survey Long Island Sound, served as a bankruptcy commissioner under the revised Judiciary Act, and became a collector of internal revenue during the Madison administration (Louis F. Middlebrook, *Maritime Connecticut during the American Revolution*, 2 vols. [Salem, Mass., 1925], 2:7, 68, 180-6; New London *Connecticut Gazette*, 14 May 1784, 3 Jan. 1821; New London *Bee*, 11 April 1798, 26 June 1799; Hartford *American Mercury*, 23 Mch. 1809; JEP, 2:455, 460; Vol. 37:704; Vol. 38:491n).

THOMAS PAINE apparently read from TJ's letter to him of 10 Aug., as well as his response of 23 Sep. In a letter of 18 Aug., TJ advised Paine to keep some aspects of the previous letter confidential.

Paine arrived in NEW YORK within the following week (*New-York Gazette & General Advertiser*, 21 Nov. 1803).

From Albert Gallatin

DEAR SIR Saturday [12 Nov. 1803]

I enclose the sketch of a letter to Mr Triest which requires consideration. If the 5th Article is proper, and I think the principle correct, Mr Claiborne must receive instructions to the same effect from the Dept. of State. The Intendant had the general superintendence of the revenue & the power of directing payment. The first of those powers will be exclusively vested in the collector by that 5th. Art.; and as to the power of paying, I have by the 9th art. directed the collector to advance, on their bills, such money as he may have to officers of the U.S. authorized to draw by either the Dept. of State, or of war. I would wish something more precise & to be informed of the authority given to either Govr. Claiborne or Gen. Wilkinson to draw on the departments.

Respectfully your ob. Sevt. ALBERT GALLATIN

RC (DLC); partially dated; endorsed by TJ as received from the Treasury Department on 12 Nov. and "collection of customs at N.O." and so recorded in SJL. Enclosure: see below.

The SKETCH of Gallatin's letter to Hore Browse Trist has not been found, but the points can be followed in the 14 Nov. letter sent to the Natchez collector, which was enclosed in Madison's of the same date to William C. C. Claiborne (*Terr. Papers*, 9:106-7; Madison, *Papers, Sec. of State Ser.*, 6:36-7). The commission granting Trist power to exercise his new duties as collector at New Orleans was sent by the same post (see Gallatin to TJ, 8 Nov.). Gallatin directed Trist to proceed immediately to New Orleans and leave a deputy in charge of the Mississippi District, or he could remain at Fort Adams and appoint a deputy at New Orleans. Gallatin confided in Trist that it was "impossible to prescribe from this department any precise rules of conduct" and that much depended on his "zeal & judgement," in which Gallatin had complete confidence (*Terr. Papers*, 9:106).

Gallatin arranged his directive to Trist as ten articles that outlined his powers and responsibilities. 5TH ARTICLE: unlike the collectorship under Spanish rule, Trist would be "perfectly independent" from the intendant or governor, "it being the contention of the President that you should be alone responsible for whatever relates to the collection of the Revenue," the same as "regularly appointed" collectors at other U.S. ports. The ninth article DIRECTED THE COLLECTOR TO ADVANCE to the governor, as authorized by the State Department, up to $10,000. This article was evidently modified from Gallatin's draft, because the 14 Nov. letter says nothing about advances under the authority of the War Department (same, 106-7).

Petition of Jacob Hoffman and Others, with Jefferson's Order

Alexandria 12th. November 1803

The Petition of the undersigned, Magistrates of the County of Alexandria respectfully represents—

That William Galloway was convicted in the Court of this County, at their November[1] Session in the year 1802, of receiving stolen goods, knowing them to be stolen, and was by the Court in consequence thereof, sentenced to Corporal punishment, and the payment of fines amounting to 870$[2] and the costs of prosecution, and to stand committed until the said fines and costs was paid—Your petitioners state that the said Galloway hath received the Corporal punishment to which he was sentenced, and now remains in confinement in consequence of not being able to pay his fine & costs & from the best information your petitioners have been able to obtain respecting the circumstances of the said Galloway, they are satisfied he hath no means of paying his said fines and costs, and that a continuation of confinement will only be a continuation of expences to the United States—Your petitioners state that during the confinement of said Galloway, some attempts to escape was contemplated by the other prisoners, and their plan so far executed as to leave no doubt of it's success, had not Galloway communicated to the Jailor (by a note from the window) the plot then in execution, by which means a number of criminals, convicted of very high offences against society was secured from a repetition of their crimes;—and that he has frequently informed the Jailer of other attempts, contemplated by the prisoners for their escape, but as no effort was made to carry them into effect, no means was afforded to ascertain the truth of the information—and they beg leave further to state that a few days after the pardon of Miller (who was to have been executed for burglary) Galloway informed the Mayor of Alexandria that during their confinement together he learnt that Miller's right name was *Smith* that he had been convicted of Burglary in the State of New York, and sentenced to the State prison for life, and that he had escaped from that place The Mayor took immediate measures to ascertain the truth of said information and from a correspondence with the proper officer of New York on the subject, the said information has been corroborated even to the most trivial circumstance, and the description from the keeper of State prison leaves no doubt as to the identity of the person—These circumstances together with the general conduct of said Galloway during his confinement have impressed your petitioners with favourable sentiments towards him, and have induced them to solicit a remission of his fine, and a discharge from his confinement—

JACOB HOFFMAN
JOHN. C. HERBERT
CUTHBERT POWELL
PETER WISE JR
GEORGE TAYLOR
ELISHA C. DICK
GEORGE SLACUM
GEORGE GILPIN
CHARLES ALEXANDER
ALEXR SMITH
A FAW
CHS. ALEXANDER JR.

We the Subscribers, Judges of the Circuit Court of the district of Columbia are induced by the reasons above stated, respectfully to recommend to the President of the United States a Compliance with the above Petition

W KILTY
W. CRANCH.
Novr. 19th. 1803.

[*Order by TJ*:]
let a pardon issue

TH: JEFFERSON
Nov. 25. 1803.

MS (DNA: RG 59, GPR); petition in an unidentified hand, signed by all; recommendation in Kilty's hand, signed by Kilty and Cranch; at head of text: "To the President of the United States."

Alexandria merchant Jacob Hoffman was mayor of the city. TJ appointed him a justice of the peace in 1801, but mistakenly rendered his name "Houghman." The remaining signers had likewise been appointed justices of the peace for Alexandria County by TJ, except for Charles Alexander, Jr., who was among the late-term appointees of John Adams for the office that TJ did not renominate (Miller, *Alexandria Artisans*, 1:209-10; JEP, 1:388, 404, 423; Vol. 33:674; Vol. 36:335-6; Vol. 37:154, 181).

The above PETITION and related papers were enclosed in a brief cover letter to TJ from Daniel Carroll Brent, dated 23 Nov. 1803, in which Brent added his opinion that the conduct of WILLIAM GALLOWAY "has been such since his confinement that I think him an object to whom your mercy can properly be extended" (RC in DLC; addressed: "The President of the United States"; endorsed by TJ as received 23 Nov. and so recorded in SJL with notation "Wm. Galloway's case").

For TJ's pardon of convicted burglar Samuel MILLER, see William Kilty and William Cranch to TJ, 28 July.

TJ issued a pardon and remission to Galloway on 28 Nov. 1803 (FC in Lb in DNA: RG 59, GPR).

[1]Word inserted in a different hand.
[2]Figure inserted in a different hand.

From J. P. G. Muhlenberg

Custom House, Philadelphia
Sir Novr. 12th. 1803.

Enclos'd I have the Honor to transmit the Bill of Freight, paid Abm. Piesch, for eight Cases of Wine, imported in the Brig Mary Ann, from Havre—Also, the Bill of Lading, for said Wine, Shipp'd on Board the Sloop Harmony, Captn. Ellwood for Georgetown—The Duty on the Wine amounts to $29-66—

I have the Honor to be with Perfect Respect Sir Your Most Obed servt.

P Muhlenberg

RC (MHi); at foot of text: "The President of The U. States"; endorsed by TJ as received 16 Nov. and so recorded in SJL. Enclosures not found.

In his financial memoranda, TJ recorded at 17 Nov. requesting John Barnes to pay Muhlenberg $40.26 for freight, in addition to the $29.66 for duties on the wine (MB, 2:1112).

From the Portsmouth, Virginia, Baptist Society

Honoured Sir Portsmouth 12 November 1803

Your Third Session as president of the United States with the members of congress has commenced—

The news of the purchase of Louisiana together with the Indian Land,—which we observed in Your inaugurate Speech, is truly gratifying especially as they are purchased with money and not with human blood! Though the aristocratical party has been billowing forth their War Whoop along time,—We believe their sanguinary dispositions are such that they would willingly, help to push the present administration, into a State of war, and rapine, if they could.—but they are minor, and are forced to Submit. and as the Scripture says "render unto all Their due custom to whom custom."—We the Baptist society of the Town of Portsmouth, and Norfolk, feel grateful sensations of the Worth of the character now who fills the Seat of a chief Magistrate, over this great and enlightened people.—We would not say like of old "O King live forever." but in our own simple language, We will say Lord let Jefferson live as long as he should be useful to the Nation, his own family and connections.—While We have such pilots as Jefferson, Madison, and Galatin, together with a Large majority of both Houses of Congress, who are truly Republicans what have we to fear from Steering the Ship constitution alltho the former administration had bored several holes through her bottom and sides, yet—The present administration has stopt them all again, so that we may set under our own Whim and there is nothing to make us affraid.—

The large sums which have been paid out of the Treasury toward the National Debt together with the other necessary disbursements which have been made—The Internal Tax which has been removed,—And yet the funds in the Treasurys charge must prove to every unprejudiced informant, that We have a good economist at the Helm of our national affairs.—

May the Lord bless you in life and Death and to all Eternity is the fervent prayers of

Your Very humble Servant
In behalf of the whole[1]

DAVIS BIGGS
JOHN FOSTER

RC (DLC); in a clerk's hand, signed by Biggs and Foster; at head of text: "Thomas Jefferson"; endorsed by TJ as received 6 Dec. and so recorded in SJL; also endorsed by TJ: "Address Baptist society of Portsmouth."

The Virginia Portsmouth Baptist Association was formed in May 1791. In 1797, Davis Biggs (1763-1845), a native of Camden County, North Carolina, received a call to the pastorate in the Portsmouth Baptist Church and moved to the Norfolk area, where he preached for the next thirteen years. Biggs migrated west in 1810 to Bourbon County, Kentucky, and served as a pastor and itinerant preacher. In 1820, he settled permanently in Pike County, Missouri, and became one of the founders of the Salt River Baptist Association (R. S. Duncan, *A History of the Baptists in Missouri* [St. Louis, 1882], 216-18; Robert B. Semple, *A History of the Rise and Progress of the Baptists in Virginia* [Richmond, 1894], 453, 457-8; *Poughkeepsie Journal*, 30 Aug. 1845).

YOUR INAUGURATE SPEECH: that is, TJ's annual message to Congress, 17 Oct. 1803.

RENDER UNTO ALL THEIR DUE CUSTOM TO WHOM CUSTOM: Romans 13:7.

O KING LIVE FOREVER: Daniel 6:21.

[1]Preceding five words probably in Biggs's hand.

From Caspar Wistar

SIR, Philada. Novr. 12. 1803.

I beg leave to inform you that Mr Hulings of New Orleans formerly lived in this City & appeared to be a very promising young gentleman—

He has resided a long time on the Missisippi I have often heard him mentioned & allways with respect as a man of business and a good citizen—

With the highest esteem I have the honour to be your friend & servant CASPAR WISTAR JUNR

RC (DNA: RG 59, LAR); at head of text: "To his Excellency the President of the United States"; endorsed by TJ as received 20 Nov. and "Hulings for emploimt in N.O." and so recorded in SJL.

William E. HULINGS sought the position of naval officer in the custom house at New Orleans and had written to Gallatin and Madison about it. The appointment went to Benjamin Morgan. He declined, but by the time he did so, Hulings was already making plans to leave New Orleans for Philadelphia (Benjamin Morgan to Chandler Price, 7 Aug., extract in DNA: RG 59, LAR, endorsed by TJ; Hulings to Gallatin, 26 Sep., RC and Dupl in same, both endorsed by TJ; Madison, *Papers*, *Sec. of State Ser.*, 5:461; *Terr. Papers*, 9:193, 218).

From George Wythe

G' WYTHE TO TH' JEFFERSON Novembr', 12, 1803.

In the list of successfull candidates for office, in the territorie latelie ceded by the government of France to the united states, his friends will rejoice to find the name of Humphrey Brooke. He is reported by those best acquainted with him to be a man of capacitie, diligence, benevolence, urbanitie, blameless manners. The object of his contemplated migration from his present residence in the county of Essex, is to provide for a numerous progenie better than in his scantie circumstances he can do here. Farewell.

RC (DNA: RG 59, LAR); endorsed by TJ as received 16 Dec. and "Brooke Humphrey for Louisiana" and so recorded in SJL.

Humphrey B. BROOKE served as a delegate from Essex County in the Virginia General Assembly for 1796. In 1805, a friend recommended him to TJ as "one of the best Surveyors in our state" (Leonard, *General Assembly*, 203; Thomas Lomax to TJ, 16 Mch. 1805).

From Joseph Bloomfield

SIR, Trenton 14: November 1803.

George C. Maxwell the Attorney of the United States, for the district of New-Jersey, with difficulty has been prevailed upon, not to resign, untill Willm. S. Pennington, representative in Council for Essex, could be Spared from the Legislature of this State. This time having arrived, Mr. Maxwell by the Mail that takes this letter, Sends his resignation.

The Republican Members of the Legislature of New-Jersey, have desired me to request the appointment for Mr. Pennington, who was the leader of the twenty-six Republican Members of the Legislature of New-Jersey last Autumn, and who has done & indeed sufferred much on account of his activity and time devoted in support of the present National administration.

Although Mr. Pennington is not at the head of the profession, Yet for talents, indefatigable industry and integrity, is not inferior to any of the Bar of New-Jersey, and a man, who will advocate the interest, and I am confident, do as much justice to the office of District Attorney as Mr. Maxwell: it is therefore with great satisfaction that I have the honor to recommend and solicit this appointment for Mr. Pennington.

The day of the reception of the Commission, Mr. Pennington will accept and qualify, in order, that an election may be held on 13 & 14 Decembr. (time of election of Members to the present Congress) to Supply the Vacancy, which will thereby be occasioned in Council and prevent the expense of an extraordinary election to the County of Essex.

I cannot add to the great respect and esteem, with which I am, Your most obedient Very Humble Servt.

JOSEPH BLOOMFIELD

RC (DNA: RG 59, LAR); at foot of text: "The President of the United States"; endorsed by TJ as received 17 Nov. and "Pennington Wm. S. to be District Atty" and so recorded in SJL.

GEORGE C. MAXWELL: see his letter to TJ of 11 Nov.

Essex County's earliest Republican organizer and with his brothers an editor of the *Centinel of Freedom*, William S. PENNINGTON did not study law until around 1800, when he was in his forties. He was still serving a clerkship when he was elected to the state's council, which, along with other duties, acted with the governor as a final court of appeals and court of pardons. In 1802, he became a member of the bar and the next year he was appointed county clerk of Essex County. For Pennington's nomination as U.S. attorney, see TJ to the Senate, 21 Nov. His commission is dated 25 Nov. Pennington served only a few months before the legislature elected him a justice of the New Jersey Supreme Court. He accepted the appointment and submitted his resignation to the secretary of state in March 1804 (commission in DNA: RG 59, MPTPC; DAB; Madison, *Papers, Sec. of State Ser.*, 6:73n; Donald H. Stewart, *The Opposition Press of the Federalist Period* [Albany, 1969], 11, 619; Carl E. Prince, *New Jersey's Jeffersonian Republicans: The Genesis of an Early Party Machine, 1789-1817* [Chapel Hill, 1967], 79-80; Newark *Centinel of Freedom*, 31 May, 7 June, 8 Nov. 1803; Philadelphia *United States Gazette*, 7 Mch. 1804).

The ELECTION to fill the seat vacated by Pennington, who had recently been reelected to the legislative council, did not take place until 17 and 18 Jan. 1804. John Dodd, the Republican candidate from Newark, won the election (Trenton *True American*, 24 Oct. 1803, 9, 30 Jan. 1804; *Centinel of Freedom*, 27 Dec. 1803; Prince, *New Jersey's Jeffersonian Republicans*, 79).

Madison received correspondence from leading New Jersey Republicans recommending Pennington. On 18 Nov., New Jersey senator John Condit wrote from Washington and encouraged the secretary of state to inform the president that Pennington's recommendations were good but "not better than his Character deserved" and that it was important that the vacancy be filled as soon as possible. Condit enclosed a letter addressed to him by John Lambert, vice president of the state, and New Jersey congressman James Mott. Lambert noted that Pennington was not only the "most Suitable person to supply" the vacancy, but was "the only Republican Lawyer of any Standing in N Jersey at the Bar, & who does not fear to oppose the whole federal clan of Lawyers in opposition." The president could be assured that Pennington's appointment would "be more Satisfactory to the Republicans of New-Jersey, than any other person" (RCs in DNA: RG 59, LAR; endorsed by TJ: "Pennington Wm. S. to be Distr. atty v. Maxwell resigned" and "Condit's lre to mr Madison").

From William P. Gardner

No. 6 of the Seven Buildings
City of Washington
14th. November 1803.

SIR

I trust you will excuse the Liberty which I take in addressing this Letter to you at a time when your Attention is naturally occupied by Concerns important and interesting to our Nation. In the first place I would wish to convey to you my thanks for the honor which you conferred upon me in the Appointment as Consul of the United States for Demerary and Essequibo and tho' not accepted as such by the Government of those Colonies I shall ever hold it as a mark of your Confidence in my Abilities and integrity, which, while it is flattering to my feelings, claims the Tribute of my unfeign'd Gratitude.—On my Arrival at these Colonies I immediately waited upon Mr. Rousselet, our late Consul, to whom I was handsomely recommended by Mr. Gallatin. Mr. Rousselet informed me that he had never been accepted by the Government as Consul, nor had his predecessor Mr. Brush of New York, and as there appear'd to be no probability that the Government wou'd accept a Consul from this Country he had some time since transmitted to America his Resignation, which was accepted by the President of the United States. I wrote several Letters while in those Colonies to the Secretary of State informing him of these things and stating to him the Nature of the Trade between the Dutch Colonies on the Coast of Guiana and the United States of America. Tho' not acting officially, yet in my individual Capacity I was the means of rescuing several Americans from an Impressment on Board English and Dutch Ships and considering the mortality which raged on Board those vessels in all probability was likewise the means of saving some of their Lives.

My Expenses in going to Demerary, residing there and returning to America were much more than my pecuniary Resourses could well support and have reduced my Circumstances to a low Ebb.—I believe that I have before mentioned to you that I have been in the Public

Employment near Eight Years as a Clerk, two Years of which were with Joseph Nourse Esqr. Register of the Treasury in his own Room and as his Confidential Clerk. To that Gentleman, I with Confidence beg leave to refer you for information respecting me. I left the Treasury Department to accept an appointment in the Bank of Pennsylvania of 200 Dollars ℔. Annum more than I received in the Treasury. A short time after I Entered the Bank of Pennsylvania I resign'd that situation and went to Europe. On my Return from Europe I again received an Appointment in the Treasury Department, where I continued untill that Event took place of which I have already informed you, as likewise the motives which led thereto. I wrote to Richard Harrison Esqr: Auditor of the Treasury to return me the Recommendations which I deposited with him; in Reply, he informed me, that they were all consumed by Fire in the Treasury Department. I have others, however, equally strong from public Bodies and public Characters in Philadelphia. My Exertions, however feeble, have always been used in support of the Principles of Republicanism and I can safely declare that those Exertions and the open Avowal of my political principles have been the Cause of considerable personal Loss and Embarrasment to me. I beg leave to observe to you, that it was never my intention to have made another application for Employment, but my necessities at this Time strongly urge me to the Measure and I indulge the hope that you will excuse the Liberty I have taken. I cou'd wish Sir, in case there are any Vacancies in that Line, a pursership on Board one of the Frigates, or some place in New Orleans which would yield me a Livlihood. The best Recommendation shall be furnish'd and so far as regards myself no personal Exertion and Attention shall be wanting in discharge of the Duties.

I beg leave to enclose a Copy of my Letter to Mr. Rousselet, late Consul at Demerary, together with his Answer, by which you will find that he mentions his having sent his Resignation to the Executive and that it was accepted. He told me further, that he informd the Secretary of State, that no Consul wou'd be received in Demerary, a Circumstance which I was not informed of previous to my leaving America.—Mr: Rousselet strove all in his power to injure me in the Estimation of the Governor of those Colonies and not only myself but the present Administration of the United States, by sending to the Governor those News papers which contain'd the most infamous Abuse agt Republicans. When call'd upon for explanation he denied it was with that intent. Mr. Rousselet is not a Citizen of the United States and in other Respects I assure you Sir, is but ill calculated to watch over the interests of our Citizens. The Duty I owe to my Country induces me to mention these things in Regard to Mr. Rousselet, as I understand he has made application for a Consulship in some one of the ports of France.—With the highest Respect and Esteem,

I have the Honor to be Sir, Your most obedt: & most hb: Sert:

WM. P. GARDNER

RC (DNA: RG 59, LAR); at foot of text: "To His Excellency Thomas Jefferson President of the United States of America"; endorsed by TJ as received 15 Nov. and "emploiment" and so recorded in SJL. Enclosures not found.

When Gardner was appointed consul in March 1802, the colonies of Demerara (DEMERARY) and ESSQUIBO on the coast of Guiana were under British control. The Treaty of Amiens restored the South American colonies to the Dutch. The British were making plans to evacuate when Gardner arrived at Demerara in September (Madison, *Papers, Sec. of State Ser.*, 2:167; 3:589-90; Vol. 37:52, 53n).

I WAS HANDSOMELY RECOMMENDED: for Gallatin's 24 June 1801 letter to Nicholas Rousselet introducing Gardner, see Vol. 35:75n. TJ was secretary of state when Ebenezer Brush was appointed consul to Surinam in 1790. TJ noted in 1792 that he had not heard from Brush and did not know whether he was admitted by the government and exercising his functions as consul "or whether objections were made" to his admission. In 1793, TJ indicated that Brush had "abandoned" his post (Vol. 17:247, 423-4; Vol. 23:619; Vol. 25:203). TRANSMITTED TO AMERICA HIS RESIGNATION: according to SJL, on 5 Mch. 1802, TJ received a letter from Rousselet dated 21 Dec. 1801, but it has not been found. In his nomination of Gardner, TJ noted that he was being appointed in place of Rousselet, who was "not recieved" by the government (Vol. 36:682; Vol. 37:52).

I WROTE SEVERAL LETTERS: on 18 Sep. 1802, Gardner informed Madison of his arrival at Demerara and his meeting with Rousselet, who informed him that the British governor Anthony Beaujon had refused to recognize him as a U.S. consul because the Jay Treaty "made no provision for the Residence of American Consuls in their foreign possessions." Gardner also noted that the new governor, Anthony Meertens, appointed by the Batavian government, was expected to arrive shortly. In a letter dated 13 Jan. 1803, Gardner discussed the cases of three impressed seamen. He noted that 200 of the Dutch troops had died and as many more were sick and hospitalized. He also reported that the regulation of American trade remained unchanged but there was some movement to permit the exportation of sugar in U.S. vessels. Governor Meertens wrote to the Netherlands inquiring about the residence of a U.S. consul, but Gardner believed that even if accepted, the consular duties would be very limited. On 22 June, Gardner wrote Madison from Philadelphia, having left the Dutch colonies after Governor Meertens refused his exequatur. Gardner informed the secretary of state that he was officially resigning his commission (Madison, *Papers, Sec. of State Ser.*, 3:589; 4:253; 5:114-15, 143).

For a previous account of Gardner's career, including PUBLIC EMPLOYMENT in the Treasury Department, see Vol. 35:699-706. EVENT TOOK PLACE: see same. The FIRE IN THE TREASURY DEPARTMENT occurred on 20 Jan. 1801 (Vol. 32:435-6).

HE HAS MADE APPLICATION: on 16 Sep., Rousselet wrote Gallatin requesting his intercession with the president for a consular appointment in the south of France. Born in Holland, Rousselet was educated in the French language. He settled in Portsmouth, New Hampshire, and was related to John Langdon by marriage. For health reasons, Rousselet could not return to the "cold Region" of New Hampshire; his delicate constitution required a warm climate. He wished to "flee from the Sultry Atmosphere" of Demerara to France or Italy (RC in DNA: RG 59, LAR; endorsed by TJ: "to be Consul in the South of France").

To J. P. G. Muhlenberg

DEAR SIR Washington Nov. 14. 1803.

I recieved last night your favor of the 10th. and am thankful to you for the prompt dispatch of the wine, every day's delay counting during a session of Congress. the wines are Champagne & Burgandy. so soon as you will be so good as to let me know the amount of the duties & charges, they shall be immediately remitted to you. accept my friendly salutations & assurances of respect. TH: JEFFERSON

P.S. I have no invoice of the wines, nor any notice of the prices or quantity. I wrote for 500. bottles. you can perhaps judge by the size of the boxes, or by opening one, whether they contain that quantity.

PrC (MHi); at foot of text: "Genl. Muhlenberg"; endorsed by TJ in ink on verso.

Muhlenberg did not handle the burgundy (BURGANDY), which had been shipped from Le Havre to Norfolk (Fulwar Skipwith to TJ, 25 Oct.; Edward Johnston to TJ, 23 Nov.).

From William Prentis

SIR, Virginia—Petersburg, Nov. 14, 1803.

I have long had it in contemplation to promote a work, so interesting to the State of Virginia, and indeed to the present as well as future generations, that I cannot refrain, on viewing its magnitude, from addressing a letter to you on the subject of it.

Mr. Burke has informed me, that he communicated to you, his intention to write a History of Virginia. A work of this kind I have long wished to see published—For several years I have endeavored to press the subject, in order to induce some gentleman, competent to the undertaking, to come forward—but the insurmountable difficulties which it is said are in the way of procuring the necessary materials, hath been the principal obstacle. I wrote to Mr. Madison, of Williamsburg, upwards of three years ago, and solicited him to engage in the compilation, but he declined it principally from the embarrassments in the way. These embarrassments, however, if they do exist, will forever remain, and the longer we are without a History, the difficulties will necessarily increase. I therefore suggested it to Mr. Burke, who readily saw the importance and necessity of such a publication, and immediately proceeded to collect every information in his power to effect the object.—He has, he informs me, made some progress, so far as to be ready to publish the First Volume—but altho' I have confidence in the abilities of Mr. Burke, I feel a conviction in my mind, that his residence in this country has been so short, as to render it impracticable for him to be so fully acquainted with the occurrences here, as those whose lives have been devoted to public service, and who have passed through so many years study and application, in order to acquaint themselves with the rise and progress of their country—And, Sir, it is an object too interesting, too important, to be suffered to pass through the press without undergoing a previous examination. A publication of such magnitude, correctly and faithfully compiled, would be a work of inestimable value, and would amply compensate, as well as do honor to, the compiler:—but if hurried over without a proper regard to its importance and dignity, may prove injurious to our literary and moral character, and be a subject of severe animadversion and reproach. Posterity too would still be as much in the dark as ever—and indeed had better remain so, that to have a compilation in which they could not implicitly rely.

Mr. Burke, since he has prepared his first volume, has applied to me to print it for him. In a conversation I had with him, I have suggested to him a plan which it appeared to me, as well as other friends of the work, he ought to pursue, to give credit and stability to the History—informing him that I was sensible every literary gentleman of Virginia felt himself interested in a correct and faithful History, and that I would not undertake it unless it bore that character; and that some gentlemen I could name, I believed would readily afford their aid in revising the work before it was printed. I therefore took the liberty of naming yourself, Mr. Page, (our Governor), and Mr. Madison, (of Wmsburg)—In doing so, Sir, I have been actuated by motives which I feel a conviction prevail in your mind—a wish that such a publication should go forth as would be both useful and honorable to our national character. In this proposition Mr. Burke readily and chearfully acquiesed; and altho' I have no other interest in the publication, than that of every other citizen of Virginia, I have at heart so much a correct work of the kind, that, if time and opportunity will enable you, I flatter myself you will chearfully afford your aid in effecting so desirable an object, by perusing the volumes respectively before they are printed.

You will no doubt surmise that I am interested—it is true, as a printer, if I undertake the work I should expect to be paid for it—but Mr. Burke is at liberty to have the History printed where he pleases.—All the concern that I feel about it is, that having first mentioned it to

Mr. Burke, I should regret extremely ever having done so, if the History should not be faithfully and correctly executed.

When at leisure I would thank you to honor me with an answer—as it is Mr. Burke's wish and mine also, that he should commence the publication as early as possible, and go through with it in the course of the ensuing year.

Accept, Sir, the assurances of my profound respect and veneration.

WILLIAM PRENTIS.

RC (ViW: Tucker-Coleman Collection); addressed: "Thomas Jefferson, Esqr City of Washington"; franked; postmarked 15 Nov.; endorsed by TJ as received 18 Nov. and so recorded in SJL.

William Prentis (ca. 1740-ca. 1824), probably the son of Williamsburg merchant William Prentis, who died in 1765, was a Virginia printer who worked on the Richmond *Virginia Gazette and Weekly Advertiser* from 1781 to 1785, the *Norfolk and Portsmouth Chronicle* from 1789 to 1792, and the Petersburg *Virginia Gazette* from 1786, continuing its publication as the *Petersburg Intelligencer* until 1804. He also produced almanacs and served several terms as mayor of Petersburg from 1793 to 1806 (Brigham, *American Newspapers*, 2:1123, 1131, 1149; Madison, *Papers*, 4:48n).

TJ and John Daly Burk had COMMUNICATED with one another in February 1803. In March, Burk delivered an oration in Petersburg commemorating the anniversary of TJ's inauguration (*An Oration, Delivered on the Fourth of March, 1803, at the Court-House, in Petersburg: to Celebrate the Election of Thomas Jefferson, and the Triumph of Republicanism* [Petersburg, 1803; Sowerby, No. 3297]; Vol. 34:388-9n; Vol. 39:434, 559).

While not specified here, the EMBARRASSMENTS IN THE WAY for Bishop James Madison may have related to the popular perception of his British allegiance and ties to the Church of England. He left Virginia for Great Britain in 1775 to be ordained an Anglican priest. In 1777, Madison became president of the College of William and Mary, which had a royal charter and close ties to the Anglican Church. Because of the likelihood of a British occupation during the Revolution, Madison declared the college closed on 1 June 1781, and Cornwallis soon took over the vacated president's house. All of Madison's papers, books, and instruments were destroyed in a fire when his home was occupied by French troops (ANB, s.v. "Madison, James [1749-1812]"; Susan H. Godson and others, *The College of William and Mary: A History*, 2 vols. [Williamsburg, 1993], 1:122, 128, 137, 139).

From Benjamin Rawlings

SIR, Washington Novr 14th, 1803.

Being desirous of an employment under the present Administration of my Country, induced me to obtain the enclosed letters, from your respected Son in Law Thos M, Randolph and Wilson C, Nicholas Esqrs.—These letters although they speak of my connexions as respectable, could mention myself only when a minor; and therefore in your opinion, I fear, may not be deemed sufficient to prove, that either my character or Politic's deserves your confidence.—Since that period, (say for about ten years) my pursuits in life have obliged me to travel over many parts of America, the West Indies and to Europe, and therefore, has given me but little opportunity of making Political friends, who have the pleasure of your personal acquaintance: although I have always been *truely* a Republican, as can be vouched for by many now in this City, who have known me for some years.—

If Certificates from Merchants of respectability in Baltimore (I having resided principally there since my return from Europe,) will suffice to shew my respectability or Politic's, they shall be laid before you without [...]—

I do not know that my informing you, I am step Son to Mr Nathaniel Anderson of Albemarle County Virginia, who has the pleasure of a personal acquaintance with you, will avail me much, yet, I hope, it may induce a further confidence.—

The Office I have contemplated requesting of you, the honor of being appointed to, is, either Naval Officer, or, Inspector of the Port at New Orleans:—one of these I should prefer, yet shall feel myself much honored by any other there, or elsewhere, which you may be pleased to confer.—

After beging pardon for taking up so much of your useful time, I am, With the highest respect, Yr Mt Obt Sert

BENJ: L, RAWLINGS

RC (DNA: RG 59, LAR); torn; endorsed by TJ as received 15 Nov. and "for Naval officer or Inspector. N. Orleans" and so recorded in SJL. Enclosures: (1) Thomas Mann Randolph to TJ, 27 Oct. 1803. (2) Wilson Cary Nicholas to TJ, 29 Oct. 1803.

A native of Virginia, Benjamin Rawlings had written TJ in 1801 seeking a consular appointment, preferably to the island of Guadeloupe. His stepfather, Nathaniel Anderson, had also written on his behalf. He did not receive an appointment from TJ (William B. Magruder, *An Answer to Mr. John Bannatyne's Defence of the Conduct of Messrs. Findlay, Bannatyne, and Company, of the City of London, in their Commercial Transactions with William B. Magruder of the City of Baltimore* [Baltimore, 1802], 31; *Baltimore Evening Post*, 28 Nov. 1792; Vol. 33:266-7).

To the Senate and the House of Representatives

To the Senate & House of Representatives of the United States.

I now communicate a digest of the information I have recieved relative to Louisiana, which may be useful to the legislature in providing for the government of the country. a translation of the most important laws in force in that province, now in the press, shall be the subject of a supplementory communication, with such further and material information as may yet come to hand.

Th: Jefferson
Nov. 14. 1803.

RC (DNA: RG 46, LPPM, 8th Cong., 1st sess.); endorsed by a Senate clerk. PrC (DLC). RC (DNA: RG 233, PM, 8th Cong., 1st sess.). Recorded in SJL with notation "Louisiana documents." Enclosure: see below. Message and enclosure printed in ASP, *Miscellaneous*, 1:344-56.

Lewis Harvie delivered TJ's message and DIGEST of information to the Senate on 14 Nov. and to the House of Representatives the following day. The Senate ordered the message and digest to lie for consideration, while the House referred them to the committee appointed on 27 Oct. to arrange the governance of Louisiana (JS, 3:311; JHR, 4:443).

Congress likely received a printed version of the digest, although the original enclosure was not preserved in congressional records. The work, compiled from information the administration received from Daniel Clark and other informants and possibly from published accounts as well, was published widely as *An Account of Louisiana, Being an Abstract of Documents, in the Offices of the Departments of State, and of the Treasury* (Shaw-Shoemaker, Nos. 3615, 3617-21, and 5196; Washington *Universal Gazette*, 17 Nov. 1803; James Madison to TJ, 5 Nov.; John Bradford to TJ, 29 Nov.). On 29 Nov., TJ sent Congress the TRANSLATION of laws in Louisiana, and at least two subsequent printings of the *Account* included it as an appendix (Shaw-Shoemaker, Nos. 5197, 5199).

From Abel Spencer

Sir. Westminster Novr. 14th. 1803

In pursuance of the directions given me by a Resolution of the Genel. Assembley of the State of Vermont I hearewith Transmit you an Address of Said Assembley—passed Novr. 11th. *1803*. I am Sir. with Grate Respect your Obediant Humble Servt. Abel Spencer

RC (MHi); at foot of text: "the President of the United States"; endorsed by TJ as received 23 Nov. and so recorded in SJL with notation "coverg. address of legislat."

Abel Spencer, who had served in the Vermont militia during the Revolutionary War, joined British forces on the approach of John Burgoyne's army in 1777 and was later fined for treason. He represented

Clarendon in the Vermont legislature from 1791 to 1797, with the exception of 1794, and served as a state attorney from 1796 to 1803. He ran as a Federalist for the Senate in October 1802, but was defeated by Israel Smith. Continuing to serve in the legislature, representing Rutland in 1802, 1803, 1806, and 1807, he was also speaker of the house in 1797, 1802, and 1803. By unanimous vote of the house, he was expelled from his seat in November 1807 for stealing bank bills from several other legislators (Lafayette Wilbur, *Early History of Vermont* [Jericho, Vt., 1899], 153, 350-1; John J. Duffy and others, eds., *Ethan Allen and His Kin: Correspondence, 1772-1819,* 2 vols. [Hanover, N.H., 1998], 2:470n).

On 9 Nov. 1803, the Vermont General Assembly voted in favor of Udney Hay's RESOLUTION to present the president a "respectful address," largely in response to TJ's annual message. Hay, James Fisk, and Amos Marsh formed a committee to draft the address, which the General Assembly approved on 11 Nov. (*Journals of the General Assembly of the State of Vermont, at Their Session, Begun and Holden at Westminster, in the County of Windham, on Thursday, the Thirteenth Day of October, A.D. One Thousand Eight Hundred and Three* [Windsor, Vt., 1804; Shaw-Shoemaker, No. 7660], 241-3, 264-7).

ENCLOSURE

From Vermont General Assembly

SIR, [11 Nov. 1803]

Though opposed to frequent addresses to those who fill important stations in our Government, yet there are times, when it would be improper to refrain from expressing our grateful acknowledgments to the Ruler of the universe, for the prosperous situation of our common Country; and our approbation of those, who guide the helm of State. While we view the United States, individually and collectively, rapidly increasing, in wealth and population; secured in the uninterupted enjoyment of life, liberty, and property; and almost without contention with any foreign Nation,—we cannot forbear congratulating you, Sir, on the happy effects of those principles, put in operation, which have so frequently appeared in your official communications. The late suspension of our right of deposit at New Orleans, excited a universal spirit of indignation; a spirit, which must convince the World, that, while we earnestly desire to maintain peace, with the whole family of Mankind, we will not tamely submit to injury or insult, from any nation on Earth. While we contemplate the acquisition of an extensive and fertile territory, with the free navigation of the river Missisippi, we cannot but venerate that spirit of moderation, and firmness, which, among divided Councils, finally enriched our Country, without the effusion of blood. And, it is with much satisfaction we learn, from the highest authority, that no new taxes will be requisite, for the completion of the payment for this valuable acquisition. Permit us, then, to tender to you, Sir, our warmest thanks, for the conspicuous part you have taken, in this important arrangement. We gratefully contemplate those humane and benevolent measures, which civilize our savage neighbors, and learn them to exchange their hostile weapons, for the Implements of Agriculture, and houshold manufacture. We recognize, with sentiments of esteem, that vigilance and parental care, which have enlarged our territory, by a negociation with one of the friendly tribes of Indians. From knowing that our maritime force is diminished, and that our trade is still protected, we obtain imposing proof, that vigilance and economy go hand in hand, in the management of our governmental affairs. The flourishing state of our Treasury, demonstrates our growing greatness; and must convince every good Citizen, that the indecent and vilifying expressions, too frequently uttered through the medium of the press, against the administrators of our Government, must, finally, with equal certainty as justice, revert on the authors. Your advice to the House of Representatives, respecting our conduct towards the contending powers of Europe, meets our highest approbation. From our own feelings, as well as from the general knowledge we possess of the sentiments of our Constituents, you may be assured, that the hardy sons of Vermont, though earnestly engaged in their peaceable pursuits, will be ready to fly, on the call of their Country, at the risk of their lives, their fortunes and domestic felicity, to maintain their rights as an independent nation; prefering every consequence, to insult and habitual wrong. Permit us to assure you of our most earnest wish, that every possible happiness may attend you, through life; and that you may, finally, receive the plaudit of the *Great Judge of All.*

Abel Spencer Speaker

RC (DLC); undated; in engrossing clerk's hand, signed by Spencer; at head of text: "To the President of the United States"; attested by Anthony Haswell as clerk, as being an address of the Vermont General Assembly on 11 Nov., "Read, Accepted, and directed to be engrossed, and signed by the Speaker, and by him, transmitted to the President." Recorded in SJL as received 23 Nov.

From Lawrence Wartmann

Dear and most beloved
Father of our Country! Reading the 14 Novr. 1803.

I take the Liberty to write your Excelency, I pray Your will pardon me, I hope your Excelency will believe me, that this few lines come from one of your true Subject. Dear Sir, your Excelency in this present moment the only person which can save a very poor and distressfull Family, I trust in God and in your Excelency, as a Father of our Country, that your Excelency will open your pityfull arms, and will look down upon a distressfull Family, like my, which consist out four persons, viz. my dear and beloved wife, two innocent Children, the age of two years and a half, and the other of 5 months and me, Heaven may protect your Excelency, and may send me so soon as your Excelency please some relief.

Dear and most beloved Sir, There is not one Family that had to undergo so much Misfortune as myself, in less than two years I have lost better than 300 Dollars by my Employers, which I serve all with honesty, this Six Months I was out work, and took the Resolution to depart from my dearstet family and went to the City of Philadelphia, there I was oblige to leave the City because the Sickness, and took the Resolution to go to Reading where I got employ, but my Dear Sir, the wages are so little here, that it is out my power to suport my dear family, upon such Condition, my family in Lancaster and I in Reading, the Lost I had is to great for me, by the present moment, the Winter is near, and I am in want of every things, my House Rente is due, and if I could only make up, so much money to pay my House Rente I would think me save with my family. the amount of 18 Dollars, or if it would be only a part of it, although I trust in Providence, Your Excelency will be so pityfull and remember, my dearest and beloved family and me, by receive of this, your Excelency may depend upon that I shall be always ready to let my Blood for your Excelency and your Excelency family and beloved Country.

I beg your Excelency pardon once more for the Liberty I took to write to your, and Heaven may protect your Excelency for ever.

I am with a true and pityfull Heart. Your humble Petioner.

Lawrence Wartmann
Journymen Printer

P.S. I beg your Excelence pardon because my bad spelling I am only 7 years in this Happy Country, and I was born in Switzerland, in St Gall.

RC (DLC); at head of text: "His Excelency Thomas Jefferson, President of the United States"; endorsed by TJ as received 17 Nov. and so recorded in SJL.

Lawrence Wartmann (1774-1840), a Swiss native who lived briefly in Pennsylvania, became the superintendent of the German-language Henkels press in New Market before settling in Harrisonburg, Virginia, where he became a prominent printer. In 1822, he established a weekly newspaper there, the *Rockingham Register*, which remained in his family for almost a century (John Walter Wayland, *Men of Mark and Representative Citizens of Harrisonburg and Rockingham County, Virginia: Portraits and Biographies of Men and Women* [Staunton, Va., 1943], 434; WMQ, 2d ser., 16 [1936], 414).

Jefferson's Letters to David Williams

I. TO DAVID WILLIAMS, 14 NOV. 1803

II. TO DAVID WILLIAMS, 14 NOV. 1803

EDITORIAL NOTE

Joel Barlow introduced David Williams to James Monroe "as an old friend of Dr. Franklin." On 20 Sep., Monroe informed the president that he was forwarding Williams's 1802 London publication, *Claims of Literature: The Origin, Motives, Objects, and Transactions of the Society for the Establishment of A Literary Fund.* Monroe agreed to present any response Jefferson wished to make to the author. Monroe continued: "Your answer if you send one will certainly be spoken of, tho' I presume not published, as he is a prudent man. If you chuse to give thro me a verbal one I shall be careful to deliver it in a suitable manner."

In response, the president wrote the two letters, below. On 8 Jan., he enclosed them in a letter to Monroe and requested that, based on his knowledge of persons and circumstances, he use his discretion and "deliver whichever you think best, suppressing the other." It is not clear which letter Monroe presented to Williams.

I. To David Williams

SIR Washington Nov. 14. 1803.

I have duly recieved the volume on the Claims of literature which you did me the favor to send me through mr Monroe, & have read with satisfaction the many judicious reflections it contains on the condition of the respectable class of literary men. the efforts for their relief made by a society of private citizens are truly laudable. but they are, as you justly observe, but a palliation of an evil, the cure of which calls for all the wisdom & the means of the nation. it is an evil which springs from the vicious distribution of the members of society among the occupations called for, while your institution, by it's benevolent aids, will lessen for the present the sum of suffering occasioned by this, it will also draw the attention of those endowed with wisdom & power to look to the means of radical cure. I pray you to accept my thanks for this mark of your attention, with the expressions of the sense I entertain of the merit of your endeavors, & assurances of my high consideration & respect. TH: JEFFERSON

PrC (DLC); at foot of text: "David Williams esquire." Enclosed in TJ to James Monroe, 8 Jan. 1804.

David Williams (1738-1816) was a Welsh-born educator, dissenting clergyman, and author. Williams wrote several works on a reformed Christian liturgy. In 1782, he published *Letters on Political Liberty*, a defense of the American colonists and an argument for parliamentary reform and expansion of the franchise. In 1790, after several unsuccessful attempts, Williams created the Literary Fund to assist authors in distress. In its first 12 years, it aided 105 people, with a total disbursement of £1,680. In 1800, members of the fund selected Williams to prepare its history, *Claims of Literature: The Origin, Motives, Objects, and Transactions, of the Society for the Establishment of A Literary Fund*. A prolific writer, Williams published *Egreria: Elementary Studies in the Progress of National Political Economy, Legislation and Government* in 1803. In the last six years of his life, he suffered from paralysis and lost his usual source of income. In 1815, the Literary Fund voted support for its founder and authorized grants of £50 at six-month intervals (DNB; Whitney R. D. Jones, *David Williams: The Anvil and the Hammer* [Tuscaloosa, Ala., 1986], 33-4, 176-7; H. P. Richards, *David Williams (1738-1816): Author, Philosopher, Educationist, Politician and Founder of the Royal Literary Fund* [Cowbridge, Wales, 1980]; *Claims of Literature* [London, 1802; Sowerby, No. 3553], 10, 105-6, 139, 147; RS, 3:207; James Bowdoin to TJ, 17 Feb. 1808).

II. To David Williams

SIR Washington Nov. 14. 1803.

I have duly recieved the volume on the Claims of literature which you did me the favor to send me through mr Monroe; & have read with satisfaction the many judicious reflections it contains on the condition of the respectable class of literary men. the efforts for their relief, made by a society of private citizens, are truly laudable: but they are, as you justly observe, but a palliation of an evil, the cure of which calls for all the wisdom & the means of the nation. the greatest evils of populous society have ever appeared to me to spring from the vicious distribution of it's members among the occupations called for. I have no doubt that those nations are essentially right, which leave this to individual choice, as a better guide to an advantageous distribution than any other which could be devised. but when by a blind concourse, particular occupations are ruinously overcharged, & others left in want of hands, the national authorities can do much towards restoring the equilibrium. on the revival of letters, learning became the universal favorite. and with reason: because there was not enough of it existing to manage the affairs of a nation to the best advantage, nor to advance its individuals to the happiness of which they were susceptible, by improvements in their minds, their morals, their health, & in those conveniencies which contribute to the comfort & embellishment of life. all the efforts of the society therefore were directed to the increase of learning, & the inducements of respect, ease & profit were held up for it's encouragement. even the charities of the nation forgot that misery was their object, and spent themselves in founding schools to transfer to science the hardy sons of the plough. to these incitements were added the powerful fascinations of great cities. these circumstances have long since produced an overcharge in the class of competitors for learned occupation, & great distress among the supernumerary candidates; & the more, as their habits of life have disqualified them for reentering into the laborious class. the evil cannot be suddenly, nor perhaps ever entirely cured: nor should I presume to say by what means it may be cured. doubtless there are many engines which the nation might bring to bear on this object. public opinion, & public encouragement are among these. the class principally defective is that of agriculture. it is the first in utility, & ought to be the first in respect. the same artifical means which have been used to produce a competition to learning, may be equally succesful in restoring agriculture to it's primary dignity in the eyes of men. it is a science of the very first order. it counts, among it's handmaids, the most respectable sciences, such as, chemistry, natural philosophy, mechanics, mathematics generally, natural history, botany. in every college & university a professorship of Agriculture, & the class of it's students might be honored as the first. young men, closing their academical education with this as the crown of all other sciences, fascinated with it's solid charms, & at a time when they are to chuse an occupation, instead of crowding the other classes, would return to the farms of their fathers, their own, or those of others, & replenish & reinvigorate a calling now languishing under contempt & oppression. the charitable schools, instead of storing their pupils with a lore which the present state of society does not call for, converted into schools of agriculture, might restore them to that branch, qualified to enrich & honor themselves, & to increase the productions of the nation instead of consuming them. a gradual abolition of the useless offices, so much accumulated in all governments, might close this drain also from the labors of the field, and lessen the burthens imposed on them. by these, & the better means which will occur to others, the surcharge of the learned, might in time be drawn off to recruit the laboring class of citizens, the sum of industry be increased, & that of misery diminished.

Among the antients the redundance of population was sometimes checked by exposing infants. to the moderns, America has offered a more humane resource. many, who cannot find employment in Europe, accordingly, come here. those, who can labour, do well for the most part. of the learned class of emigrants, a small portion find employment analagous to their talents. but many fail, & return to compleat their course of misery in the [scenes] where it began. even here we find too strong a current from the country to the towns; & instances beginning to appear of that species of misery which you are so humanely endeavoring to relieve with you. altho' we have, in the old countries of Europe, the lesson of their experience, to warn us, yet I am not satisfied we shall have the firmness & wisdom to profit by it. the general desire of men to live by their heads rather than their hands, & the strong allurements of great cities to those who have any turn for dissipation, threaten to make them here, as in Europe, the sinks of voluntary misery.—I percieve however that I have suffered my pen to run into a disquisition, when I had taken it up only to thank you for the volume you had been so kind as to send me, & to express my approbation of it. after apologising therefore for having touched on a subject so much more familiar to you, & better understood, I beg leave to assure you of my high consideration and respect.

TH: JEFFERSON

PrC (DLC); blurred; at foot of first page: "David Williams esquire." Enclosed in TJ to James Monroe, 8 Jan. 1804.

From Joseph Crockett

State of Kentucky
Frankfort Novr 15th 1803

SIR

The cession of Louisiana to the united States, I expect will make it Necessary for a collector of the revenue to be appointed at the port of New Orleans: If so I would beg leave to inform you Sir, Mr. George Madison of Frankfort, wishes to be considered a candidate for that Office.

I have been well acquainted with Mr Madison ever since a small boy his character is equal to any for honesty and industry, he is a good accomptant, and in full practice in transacting public business in this State. I expect he will be mentioned to you sir by some of our representitaves.

I have the honor Sir to be your Most Obedt Servt.

JOSEPH CROCKETT

RC (DNA: RG 59, LAR); endorsed by TJ as received 1 Dec. and "Madison George to be Collector N.O." and so recorded in SJL.

A native of Virginia and auditor of public accounts in Kentucky, GEORGE MADISON was the brother of Bishop James Madison and a second cousin of James

Madison. He became governor of Kentucky in 1816, but died shortly after taking office (John E. Kleber, ed., *The Kentucky Encyclopedia* [Lexington, Ky., 1992], 601-2). Writing to the secretary of state on 15 Nov. 1803, Madison made known his interest in the New Orleans collectorship, stating that the appointment "is a kind of business which not only suits my Genius and inclination, but is one the duties of which I feel myself more competent to discharge than any other." As references, he named John Breckinridge, John Brown, "and the rest of the Representatives from Kentucky," and hoped that the secretary would recommend him to the president. Madison did not receive an appointment from TJ (RC in DNA: RG 59, LAR; endorsed by TJ: "Madison George to be Collector of N. Orleans. his lre to mr Madison").

From William Polk

Somerset County Maryland
Novbr. the. 15 1803

Sir/

The warm Attachment[1] I feel to your Person and Principles, as displayed in your Administration I hope will be Accepted as my excuse for troubling you with this Address—

I have lately seen an Address signed by a Number of Gentlemen Residing in Worcester County Maryland directed to the Secretary of the Treasury, Soliciting the Removal of William Selby the present Collector of the district of Snow hill from Office, and Recommending John Cutler Esqr to fill his place.—I beg leave to State to you Sir, That I am intimately acquainted with all the Gentlemen who have signed that address, and know them to be of Unblemished Reputation, warmly attached to the present Administration and the measures persued by them, And I firmly believe the facts Stated by them are true.—I beg leave further to State that I am well acquainted with Mr. Selby, and know him to be as implacable, and Riveted an Enemy, to the present Administration, as any in the United States, Agreeably to his Abilities, which indeed must be Confest are Very Small, but are Nevertheless Constantly employed when he thinks he Can have the least influence in Rendering Odious every Salutory Public measure—

Should you think it proper to displace him, I have no hesitation in Recommending Mr. Cutler to fill the place, I believe him to be a man of Integrity well furnished to fill the office with advantage to the Public, and Honor to himself—

May you Continue long And be amply Supported in pursuing measures such as hath hitherto blest your Country and endeared you to every true american

I am my Good Sir with sentiments of the greatest esteem for and Veneration of your Talents and Virtues

WILLIAM POLK Chief Justice of The 4th. Maryland district—

RC (DNA: RG 59, LAR); endorsed by TJ as received 29 Nov. and "Cutler John to be Collectr. distr. of Snohill v. Willm Selby for active federalism &c" and so recorded in SJL, where it is connected by a brace with that from Joseph H. Nicholson of 29 Nov.

Son of Elizabeth Gillis and David Polk, a planter in Somerset County, Maryland, William Polk (1752-1812) became an attorney. He represented Somerset County in the state's lower house in 1777 and again in 1797. In 1801, John F. Mercer introduced Polk to the president as a steadfast Republican in a Federalist stronghold on the Eastern Shore. Polk was appointed chief justice of Maryland's Fourth Judicial District in 1802, a position he held until his death. In 1806, he also began serving as judge of the court of appeals (Edward C. Papenfuse, Alan F. Day, David W. Jordan, and Gregory A. Stiverson, eds., *A Biographical Dictionary of the Maryland Legislature, 1635-1789*, 2 vols. [Baltimore, 1979-85], 1:76; 2:654-5; Baltimore *Republican; or, Anti-Democrat*, 6 Feb. 1802; Baltimore *Federal Gazette*, 11 Dec. 1812; Vol. 36:225-6).

I HAVE LATELY SEEN AN ADDRESS: 13 residents of the port of Snow Hill, including Joshua Pudeaux, Samuel A. Harper, Matthew Hopkins, Edward Robins, and James B. Robins, signed an undated address to Gallatin. They noted that according to law, the collector for the district was to reside at Snow Hill, but William Selby, the present collector, lived five or six miles away. Calling first at Snow Hill and then at his residence, masters and owners of vessels were "either altogether disappointed, or met with considerable Delay in transacting their Business." Selby always hired deputies who were opposed to the administration, and the person he frequently appointed lived at least 12 miles from the inlet where vessels usually received their cargo. The subscribers recommended John Cutler as a man of integrity and character who resided at Snow Hill, served as a justice of the peace, and was "fully qualified to the Discharge of the Duties." Republicans in the district would welcome his appointment (RC in DNA: RG 59, LAR).

On 8 Nov., Polk wrote the Treasury secretary, endorsing the call from Snow Hill residents for Selby's removal. Polk asserted, "I have no question but the man ought to be Removed upon every Principle." He endorsed Cutler as "a man of Integrity and abilities far superior to the present Collector And friendly to the present administration" (RC in same; endorsed by TJ: "Cutler John to be Collector of Snowhill. Polk to mr Gallatin").

[1]MS: "Attachmen."

From John Tarver

HONBLE SIR, Charleston, 15th November 1803

To attempt an apology for the Liberty I t[ake] in addressing you, or to say what gave birth in my mind [...] the idea of the application is out of my power, but hope that my boldness will find excuse in that exalted goodness which I have, with thousands of others been some Year's an humble admirer off.

My Prayer Honble Sir, is to find employment, in our new acquired and much admired acquisition of Louisiana my being equally acquainted with the French & Spanish Languages as with my own, leads me to offer my services to Government in any Capacity whatever.

I am by birth Honble Sir an English-man but some Years since a Resident of Charleston, and a Citizen of the United States.

Aware Honble Sir of the Multiplicity of your Occupations I shall not waste more of your time, but to assure you, that your Goodness in my favor is daily included in the hu[mble] prayers of (and family)

Honble Sir Your obedient humble Servant JOHN TARVER

RC (DNA: RG 59, LAR); torn; at foot of text: "The Honble Thos. Jefferson." Recorded in SJL as received 27 Nov. with notation "emploimt. Louisa."

John Tarver was born in London and resided in Paris before emigrating to Charleston, South Carolina, where he taught French, English, and other subjects as a private instructor and, for three years, as a member of the faculty at the College of Charleston. In 1802, he was an assistant assessor of the Direct Tax in Charleston. He did not receive an appointment from TJ (Charleston *City Gazette and Daily Advertiser*, 9, 14 June, 27 Sep. 1794; 2 Sep. 1796; 27, 30 Mch. 1798; 18 June 1802).

Appendix I

EDITORIAL NOTE

Jefferson kept an ongoing list of appointments and removals that extended throughout his two terms as president, with entries from 5 Mch. 1801 to 23 Feb. 1809. For the first installment of this list, from 5 Mch. 1801 to 14 May 1802, see Vol. 33, Appendix I, List 4. Subsequent installments have appeared as Appendix I in Volumes 37, 38, 39, and 40. This segment continues at 12 July 1803, with the president's recording of Thomas Rodney's appointment as judge in Mississippi Territory. It includes the entries for the period covered by this volume. This was a working list, which Jefferson updated as he received information. Several of the appointments entered below, excluding those for bankruptcy and land commissioners and those for taking possession and overseeing the immediate governance of Louisiana, were interim and required Senate confirmation (see TJ to the Senate, 11 Nov. 1803).

List of Appointments

[11 July-15 Nov. 1803]

July 12. Thomas Rodney of Delaw. to be a judge of Missipi. v. Seth Lewis resd.

12. Thomas Rodney of Delaware } Commrs. West of
Robt. Williams of N. Carola } Pearl river
Ephraim Kerby of Connecticut } Commrs. East of
Rob. Carter Nicholas of Kentucky } Pearl river

12. Joseph Chambers. Misipi. Register East of Pearl river

Aug. 1. Tenche Coxe of Pensva. Purveyor v. Israel Wheelen resd.

26. Callender Irvine of Pensva. to be Survr & Inspectr. of the rev. for the port of Buffalo creek. new.

Robert Lee of   to be Collector for the district & Inspector for the port of Niagara.

30. Jonathan E. Robinson of Vermont. Commr. bkrptcy Vermont vice Richd Skinner resigned.

Sep. 16. Nathan Sandford. Atty of the US. for N.Y. v. Edwd Livingston removed. [. . .]

Jared Mansfield of Conn. Surveyor Genl. of the lands of the US. N.W. of the Ohio v. Rufus Putnam removd for incompetence

John Leonard of N.J. Vice Consul Barcelona

John M. Goetschius of N.Y. Consul Genoa[1]

Sep. 27. pro 16. Abraham Bishop. Collectr. New Haven v. Saml Bishop. district of New Haven. Connecticut

Oct. 13. Wm. O. Sprigg. Commr. bkrptcy for Columbia.

14. 19. Blair Mc.lanachan. Comr. bkrptcy for Pensva

31. Wm. C. C. Claiborne to exercise powers of the Govr. & Intendt. of Louisiana

Wm. C. C. Claiborne & James Wilkinson, jointly or severally to take possn of Louisiana.

1803.

Nov. 14. James Trimble Commr. bkrptcy East Tennissee

<table>
<tr><td colspan="2">Nathanl. Allen of Edenton.</td><td rowspan="4">Commrs. bkrptcy N.C.</td></tr>
<tr><td>John Eaton</td><td rowspan="2">of Halifx</td></tr>
<tr><td>Goodoreen Davis</td></tr>
<tr><td colspan="2">Wm. Cherry junr. of Bertie county</td></tr>
</table>

Wm. C. C. Claiborne to remove, appoint & suppress offices in Louisiana.

MS (DLC: TJ Papers, 186:33097-8); entirely in TJ's hand; being the continuation of a list that extends from 5 Mch. 1801 to 23 Feb. 1809; for the installment immediately preceding this one, see Vol. 40: Appendix I; one word obscured by tape.

JOSEPH CHAMBERS: TJ probably left a space at this date and filled it in after 1 Jan. 1804, when he received Ephraim Kirby's letter of 16 Dec., notifying the president that he had decided to enter Chambers's name in the blank commission for land office register east of Pearl River (TJ to Kirby, 15 July 1803).

[1]Preceding entries for 16 Sep. entered by TJ in right margin with a brace to mark insertion at this point.

Appendix II

Letters Not Printed in Full

EDITORIAL NOTE

In keeping with the editorial method established for this edition, the chronological series includes "in one form or another every available letter known to have been written by or to Thomas Jefferson" (Vol. 1:xv). Most letters are printed in full. In some cases, the letter is not printed but a detailed summary appears at the document's date (for an example, see Nicholas King to TJ, 25 Sep. 1803). Other letters have been described in annotation, which, for the period covered by this volume, are listed in this appendix. Arranged in chronological order, this list includes for each letter the correspondent, date, and location in the volumes where it is described. Among the letters included here are brief letters of transmittal, multiple testimonials recommending a particular candidate for office, repetitive letters from a candidate seeking a post, and official correspondence that the president saw in only a cursory way. In other instances, documents are described in annotation due to the near illegibility of the surviving text. Using the list in this appendix, the table of contents, and Appendix III (correspondence not found but recorded in Jefferson's Summary Journal of Letters), readers will be able to reconstruct Jefferson's chronological epistolary record from 11 July to 15 Nov. 1803.

To George Jefferson, 23 July. Noted at Notes on Shipment, 23 July 1803.
From Louis de Vergennes, 23 July. Noted at Charles Tierlin to TJ, 4 Mch. 1808.
From Joseph M. Ledet, 25 Aug. Noted at Madame de Corny to TJ, 15 June 1803.
From John Broadbent, 23 Sep. Noted at Broadbent to TJ, 15 Apr. 1801.
From Benjamin Vaughan, received 7 Oct. Noted at Vaughan to TJ, 24 Mch. 1803.
From De Chanlas, 1 Nov. Noted at De Chanlas to TJ, 20 Sep. 1801.
To Jones & Howell, 8 Nov. Noted at TJ to Jones & Howell, 6 Nov. 1803.

Appendix III

Letters Not Found

EDITORIAL NOTE

This appendix lists chronologically letters written by and to Jefferson during the period covered by this volume for which no text is known to survive. Jefferson's Summary Journal of Letters provides a record of the missing documents. For incoming letters, Jefferson typically recorded in SJL the date that the letter was sent and the date on which he received it. He sometimes included the location from which it was dispatched and an abbreviated notation indicating the government department to which it pertained: "N" for Navy, "S" for State, "T" for Treasury, and "W" for War.

From James Dinsmore, 11 July; received 14 July from Monticello.
From William Stewart, 11 July; received 14 July from Monticello.
From the Treasury Department; received 12 July; notation: "House's 2d. and 3d. mates."
To Thomas Appleton, 13 July.
To Gabriel Lilly, 15 July.
From Thomas C. Fletcher, 18 July; received 22 July from Charlottesville.
From Sofia Hartman, 18 July; received 25 Sep. from Brunswick (duplicate received 21 Mch. 1804 from Brunswick).
To Benjamin H. Latrobe, 18 July.
From Benjamin H. Latrobe, 18 July; received 12 Sep. from Philadelphia.
From Caspar Wistar, 18 July; received 22 July from Philadelphia.
From Jones & Howell, 19 July; received 25 July from Philadelphia; notation: "€7-3-15 bar iron=45.81."
From Aaron Goff, 22 July; received 8 Aug. from Berlin, Vt.; notation: "W."
From Caesar A. Rodney, 22 July; received 27 July from Wilmington.
To John Barnes, 23 July.
From Gideon Granger, 23 July; received 27 July from Washington.
To Henry Sheaff, 23 July.
From John Mitchell, 24 July; received 25 Sep. from Le Havre.
From Thomas McKean, 25 July; received 1 Aug. from Philadelphia; notation: "John Mitchell Coml. Agt. Havre."
To Joseph Moran, 26 July.
From John Barnes, 28 July; received 3 Aug. from Georgetown.
From the Citizens of Randolph County, Indiana Territory; received 29 July from Kaskaskia.
From the State Department, 29 July; received 1 Aug. from Washington; notation: "Pichon on importn negroes."
From the State Department, 31 July; received 3 Aug. from Washington; notation: "Pichon's for."
From Gideon Granger; received 1 Aug.; notation: "Thos. F. Riddick Register E. of Pearl riv."
From John Barnes, 2 Aug.; received 6 Aug. from Georgetown.
From John Barnes, 4 Aug.; received 8 Aug. from Georgetown.

From Henry Sheaff, 4 Aug.; received 10 Aug. from Philadelphia; notation: "July for Aug. 4."
To John Barnes, 5 Aug.
From William Maddox, 6 Aug. 1803; received 12 Aug. from Columbia, Va.
From John H. Nichols, 8 Aug.; received 15 Aug. from Charlestown; notation: "to be Midshipman."
To John Barnes, 9 Aug.
From John Barnes, 9 Aug.; received 12 Aug. from Georgetown.
From John Barnes, 12 Aug.; received 15 Aug. from Georgetown.
From John Barnes, 13 Aug.; received 3 Sep.
From William Davies, 16 Aug.; received 26 Aug. from Norfolk.
From Gideon Granger, 16 Aug.; received 24 Aug. from New Haven; connected by a brace with entry for letter received the same day from Jesse Atwater of 18 Aug. with notation: "Abram Bishop to be Collector N.H. vice Saml. Bishop."
From Jesse Atwater, 18 Aug.; received 24 Aug. from New Haven; connected by a brace with entry for letter received the same day from Gideon Granger of 16 Aug. with notation: "Abram Bishop to be Collector N.H. vice Saml. Bishop."
From DeWitt Clinton, 19 Aug.; received 24 Aug. from Newtown, N.Y.; notation: "S. Broome to be Collector Newhaven."
From George Clinton, 19 Aug.; received 31 Aug. from Albany; connected by a brace with entries for letters received the same day from DeWitt Clinton of 25 Aug. and from Joseph Fay of 12 and 25 Aug. with notation: "Saml. Broome to be Collector N. Haven."
From Larkin Smith, 19 Aug.; received 26 Aug. from King and Queen County; notation: "to be loan officer Virga."
From George Watson, 19 Aug.; received 30 Aug. from Richmond; notation: "to be keepr. lighthouse O.P. Comfort v. Eddins [decd.]."
From Pierpont Edwards, 20 Aug.; received 26 Aug. from New Haven; notation: "Abr. Bishop to be Collectr."
From Archibald McCall, 23 Aug.; received 5 Sep. from Tappahannock; notation: "Aug. 23 & Nov. 19."
From John Barnes, 24 Aug.; received 29 Aug. from Philadelphia.
From DeWitt Clinton, 25 Aug.; received 31 Aug. from Newtown; connected by a brace with entries for letters received the same day from George Clinton of 19 Aug. and from Joseph Fay of 12 and 25 Aug. with notation: "Saml. Broome to be Collector N. Haven."
From Richard Morris, 25 Aug.; received 27 Aug. from Green Springs.
To John Barnes, 26 Aug.; notation: "wood screws."
From Lafayette, 26 Aug.; received 13 Nov. from La Grange; notation: "Coffyn Consul Dunkirk."
From Josiah Snelling, August; received 29 Aug. from Boston.
From John Barnes, 2 Sep.; received 5 Sep. from Georgetown; notation: "two lres."
From Samuel Coleman, 3 Sep.; received 5 Sep. from Richmond.
From John Barnes, 5 Sep.; received 9 Sep. from Georgetown.
From Benjamin H. Latrobe, 5 Sep.; received 12 Sep. from New Castle.
From Burgess Griffin, 6 Sep.; received 19 Sep. from Poplar Forest.

From M. J. Stewart; received 6 Sep.
From John Brown, 7 Sep.; received 25 Sep. from Frankfort.
From Hammuda Pasha, Bey of Tunis, 7 Sep.; received 16 Nov.
From John Barnes, 8 Sep.; received 12 Sep. from Georgetown.
From Gideon Fitz, 9 Sep.; received 8 Sep. from Monticello.
From Benjamin H. Latrobe, 11 Sep.; received 14 Sep. from Washington.
To John Barnes, 12 Sep.
From Hammuda Pasha, Bey of Tunis, 14 Sep.; received 11 Dec.
From John Barnes, 12 Sep.; received 19 Sep. from Georgetown.
From John Langdon, 14 Sep.; received 25 Sep. from Portsmouth; notation: "Broome v. Bishop."
To Benjamin H. Latrobe, 14 Sep.
From Benjamin H. Latrobe, 14 Sep.; received 19 Sep. from Washington.
From John Barnes, 16 Sep.; received 19 Sep. from Georgetown.
To George Divers, 16 Sep.
From Hore Browse Trist, 16 Sep.; received 16 Oct. from Fort Adams.
From John Barnes, 18 Sep.; received 25 Sep. from Georgetown.
From William Tunstall, 18 Sep.; received 25 Sep. from Bristol, Pa.
From Benjamin Rush, 19 Sep.; received 1 Oct. from Philadelphia.
To Burgess Griffin, 20 Sep.
From George Divers, 21 Sep.; received 21 Sep.
From James Paterson, 21 Sep.; received 20 Jan. 1804 from Maghera, Ireland; notation: "W."
From John Barnes, 24 Sep.; received 25 Sep. from Georgetown.
From Thomas T. Davis, 26 Sep.; received 18 Oct. from Vincennes.
From Harry Toulmin, 30 Sep.; received 18 Oct. from Frankfort.
From William Henry; received 1 Oct.; notation: "his case."
From Christopher Tillinghast, 1 Oct.; received 8 Dec. from Cork; notation: "S."
From Martin Dawson, 7 Oct.; received 13 Oct. from Milton.
From Andrew Buchanan, 8 Oct.; received 9 Oct. from Baltimore.
To Martin Dawson, 9 Oct.
To George Divers, 9 Oct.
To Gabriel Lilly, 9 Oct.
From James Oldham, 9 Oct.; received 13 Oct. from Monticello.
From Gabriel Lilly, 12 Oct.; received 16 Oct. from Monticello.
From Samuel Hanson, 14 Oct.; received 14 Oct.
From William Stewart, 14 Oct.; received 16 Oct. from Monticello.
To Martin Dawson, 15 Oct.; notation: "120. D."
To James Oldham, 15 Oct.
From Alexander Smyth, 15 Oct.; received 7 Nov. from Wythe County; notation: "for office."
From William Mahy, 18 Oct.; received 4 Dec. from Gibraltar; notation: "N."
To John H. Craven, 19 Oct.
To George Divers, 19 Oct.
To Gabriel Lilly, 20 Oct.
From Robert Phillips, 20 Oct.; received 7 Nov. from "Stanton."
From Martha Jefferson Randolph, 22 Oct.; received 30 Oct. from Edgehill.
From Mary Jefferson Eppes, 23 Oct.; received 30 Oct. from Edgehill.
From Gabriel Lilly, 23 Oct.; received 30 Oct.
From William Stewart, 23 Oct.; received 30 Oct. from Monticello.

From William Tunstall, 24 Oct.; received 27 Oct. from Bristol, Pa.
From David Valenzin, 24 Oct.; received 26 Oct. from "Fed. city"; notation: "N."
To James Dinsmore, 26 Oct.
From John Randolph, 27 Oct.; received 27 Oct.; notation: "David Walker to be Chief Survr. or Commr. Louisiana."
From John Foncin, 28 Oct.; received 30 Oct. from New York; notation: "emploimt Louisa."
From Michael Hope, 28 Oct.; received 3 Nov. from Milton; notation: "352.75."
From LeRoy, Bayard & McEvers, 29 Oct.; received 3 Nov. from New York.
From Pierce Butler, 1 Nov.; received 31 Oct.; notation: "George Cross to be Consul at Havana."
From Henry Sheaff, 2 Nov.; received 5 Nov. from Philadelphia; notation: "155.40."
From Joseph Jones Monroe, 3 Nov.; received 7 Nov. from Westmoreland; notation: "Tapscot to be Collectr. Yeocomico v. Thompson."
From Gamaliel Thatcher, 3 Nov.; received 26 Nov. from Ballston.
From Gabriel Lilly, 4 Nov.; received 7 Nov. from Monticello.
From Michael Hope, 4 Nov.; received 13 Nov.
From Samuel A. Otis, 4 Nov.; received 4 Nov.; notation: "returns Tuscan treaty. W."
From Mary Jefferson Eppes, 5 Nov.; received 7 Nov. from Edgehill.
From Caesar A. Rodney, 9 Nov.; received 10 Nov.; notation: "Lewis. Hulings. Morgan."
From John Wayles Eppes, 12 Nov.; received 12 Nov.; notation: "Wm. Robertson office in Louisiana."
From James Oldham, 12 Nov.; received 20 Nov. from Monticello.
From John Bracken, 13 Nov.; received 22 Nov. from Williamsburg; notation: "Mann Page to be distr. atty."
From Samuel Morse, 13 Nov.; received 30 Nov. from Savannah.
To Michael Hope, 14 Nov.
To Robert Phillips, 14 Nov.
To Henry Sheaff, 14 Nov.
From William Cocke, 15 Nov.; received 15 Nov.; notation: "Sharks to open road."
From William Stewart, 15 Nov.; received 20 Nov. from Philadelphia.

Appendix IV

Financial Documents

EDITORIAL NOTE

This appendix briefly describes, in chronological order, the orders and invoices pertaining to Jefferson's finances during the period covered by this volume that are not printed in full or accounted for elsewhere in this volume. The orders for payments to Étienne Lemaire and Joseph Dougherty pertain, for the most part, to expenses associated with running the President's House. The *Memorandum Books* are cited when they are relevant to a specific document and provide additional information.

Order on John Barnes for payment of $24.46½ to Elisha Lanham, agent for James Oldham, Washington, 18 July 1803 (MS in MHi; in TJ's hand and signed by him; signed by Lanham acknowledging payment; endorsed by Barnes as paid on 18 July).

Order on John Barnes for payment of $55.47 to Étienne Lemaire, Washington, 18 July (MS in MHi; in TJ's hand and signed by him; signed by Lemaire acknowledging payment; endorsed by Barnes as paid on 21 July). TJ recorded this transaction as payment of Lemaire's accounts from 10 to 16 July for provisions and President's House furniture (MB, 2:1105).

Order on John Barnes for payment of $81.94 to Joseph Dougherty, Washington, 19 July (MS in MHi; in TJ's hand and signed by him; signed by Dougherty acknowledging payment; endorsed by Barnes as paid on 21 July). TJ recorded this transaction as payment of Dougherty's accounts for saddlery, farriers, President's House furniture, servants, and contingencies (MB, 2:1105).

Order on John Barnes for payment of $5.50 to Edward Frethy, Washington, 19 July (MS in MHi; in TJ's hand and signed by him; signed by Charles McLaughlin acknowledging payment; endorsed by Barnes as paid on 29 July; notation on verso: "Pay the Within to Chs McLaughlin July 19 1803 for Mr Frithy," signed Peter [Ra]llet).

Invoice submitted by Joseph Dougherty to TJ for $26.31½ for the purchase of 1,250 pounds of hay at $8.37½ from Mr. Lurgan on 23 July 1803, 8 bushels of corn at $5.44 from A. Kaldenbach on 7 Aug., and 1,562 pounds of hay at $12.50 from Mr. Shuber on 5 Sep. (MS in CSmH; entirely in Dougherty's hand and signed by him acknowledging payment; endorsed by Barnes as paid on 10 Sep.).

Invoice submitted by Henry Ingle to TJ for $6.00 for the purchase of six gross of screws at $3.90 and three gross at $2.10, Washington, 10 Sep. 1803 (MS in CSmH; in Ingle's hand and signed by him acknowledging payment; additional charges of $2.45 for a gross of screws at 95 cents to Mr. Maffet and two gross of screws at $1.50 to Mr. Patterson recorded at foot of text by Barnes).

Order on John Barnes for payment of $739.11 to Étienne Lemaire, Washington, 29 Sep. (MS in MHi; in TJ's hand and signed by him; signed by

Lemaire acknowledging payment; endorsed by Barnes as paid 18 Nov.). TJ recorded this transaction as payment of Lemaire's accounts from 17 to 19 July and from 20 July to 25 Sep. for provisions, wood, servants' wages, and contingencies (MB, 2:1109).

Order on John Barnes for payment of $10 to Edward Frethy, Washington, 1 Oct. (MS in MHi; in TJ's hand and signed by him; signed by Joseph [. . .] acknowledging payment; endorsed by Barnes as paid 1 Oct.). TJ recorded this transaction as a payment "in advance" to Frethy (MB, 2:1109).

Order on John Barnes for payment of $207.98 to Étienne Lemaire, Washington, 2 Oct. (MS in MHi; in TJ's hand and signed by him; signed by Lemaire acknowledging payment; endorsed by Barnes as paid 22 Oct.). TJ recorded this transaction as payment of Lemaire's accounts from 26 Sep. to 1 Oct. for provisions, President's House furniture, servants, and contingencies and for payment of servants' wages to 4 Oct. (MB, 2:1109).

Order on John Barnes for payment of $42.41 to Joseph Dougherty, Washington, 9 Oct. (MS in ViU; in TJ's hand and signed by him; signed by Dougherty acknowledging payment; endorsed by Barnes as paid 10 Oct.). TJ recorded this transaction as payment of Dougherty's accounts for forage, smiths, and contingencies (MB, 2:1110).

Order on John Barnes for payment of $71.68 to Étienne Lemaire, Washington, 10 Oct. (MS in MHi; in TJ's hand and signed by him; signed by Lemaire acknowledging payment; endorsed by Barnes as paid 22 Oct.). TJ recorded this transaction as payment of Lemaire's accounts from 2 to 8 Oct. for provisions, President's House furniture, and contingencies (MB, 2:1110).

Order on John Barnes for payment of $88.30 to Étienne Lemaire, Washington, 18 Oct. (MS in MHi; in TJ's hand and signed by him; signed by Lemaire acknowledging payment; endorsed by Barnes as paid 22 Oct.). TJ recorded this transaction as payment of Lemaire's accounts from 9 to 15 Oct. for provisions and contingencies (MB, 2:1110).

Order on John Barnes for payment of $48.64½ to Joseph Dougherty, Washington, 24 Oct. (MS in MHi; in TJ's hand and signed by him; signed by Dougherty acknowledging payment; endorsed by Barnes as paid 24 Oct.). TJ recorded this transaction as payment of Dougherty's accounts for forage, farriers, utensils, contingencies, carriages, and freight (MB, 2:1111).

Order on John Barnes for payment of $74 to Étienne Lemaire, 24 Oct. (MS in MHi; in TJ's hand and signed by him; signed by Lemaire acknowledging payment; endorsed by Barnes as paid 27 Oct.). TJ recorded this transaction as payment of Lemaire's accounts from 16 to 22 Oct. for provisions and contingencies (MB, 2:1110).

Order on John Barnes for payment of $43.98½ to Joseph Dougherty, Washington, 31 Oct. (MS in MHi; in TJ's hand and signed by him; signed by Dougherty acknowledging payment; endorsed by Barnes as paid 31 Oct.). TJ recorded this transaction as payment of Dougherty's accounts for forage, smiths, and contingencies (MB, 2:1111).

Order on John Barnes for payment of $108.57 to Étienne Lemaire, Washington, 31 Oct. (MS in MHi; in TJ's hand and signed by him; signed by

Lemaire acknowledging payment; endorsed by Barnes as paid 18 Nov.). TJ recorded this transaction as payment of Lemaire's accounts from 23 to 29 Oct. for provisions and contingencies (MB, 2:1111).

Order on John Barnes for payment of $10 to the Reverend Jacob Eÿermann, Washington, 5 Nov. (MS in MHi; in TJ's hand and signed by him; signed by Eÿermann acknowledging payment; endorsed by Barnes as paid 5 Nov.). TJ recorded this transaction as charity (MB, 2:1111).

Order on John Barnes for payment of $26.80½ to Joseph Dougherty, Washington, 7 Nov. (MS in MHi; in TJ's hand and signed by him; signed by Dougherty acknowledging payment; endorsed by Barnes as paid 8 Nov.). TJ recorded this transaction as payment of Dougherty's accounts for forage, smiths, and contingencies (MB, 2:1111).

Order on John Barnes for payment of $230 to Étienne Lemaire, Washington, 7 Nov. (MS in MHi; in TJ's hand and signed by him; signed by Lemaire acknowledging payment; endorsed by Barnes as paid 22 Nov.). TJ recorded this transaction as payment of Lemaire's accounts from 30 Oct. to 5 Nov. for provisions, furniture, and contingencies and for payment of servants' wages to 4 Nov. (MB, 2:1111).

Order on John Barnes for payment of $142.91 to Étienne Lemaire, Washington, 14 Nov. (MS in MHi; in TJ's hand and signed by him; signed by Lemaire acknowledging payment; endorsed by Barnes as paid 14 Nov.). TJ recorded this transaction as payment of Lemaire's accounts from 6 to 12 Nov. for provisions, charcoal, and contingencies (MB, 2:1112).

INDEX

A comprehensive index of Volumes 1-20 of the First Series has been issued as Volume 21. Each subsequent volume has its own index, as does each volume or set of volumes in the Second Series.

THE PAPERS OF THOMAS JEFFERSON are composed in Monticello, a font based on the "Pica No. 1" created in the early 1800s by Binny & Ronaldson, the first successful typefounding company in America. The face is considered historically appropriate for The Papers of Thomas Jefferson because it was used extensively in American printing during the last quarter-century of Jefferson's life, and because Jefferson himself expressed cordial approval of Binny & Ronaldson types. It was revived and rechristened Monticello in the late 1940s by the Mergenthaler Linotype Company, under the direction of C. H. Griffith and in close consultation with P. J. Conkwright, specifically for the publication of the Jefferson Papers. The font suffered some losses in its first translation to digital format in the 1980s to accommodate computerized typesetting. Matthew Carter's reinterpretation in 2002 restores the spirit and style of Binny & Ronaldson's original design of two centuries earlier.

✧